The Cash Constituents of Congress

PROPERTY OF
PUBLIC INTEREST
INSTITUTE

The Cash Constituents of Congress

Larry Makinson
Joshua Goldstein
Center for Responsive Politics

Congressional Quarterly Inc.
1414 22nd Street N.W.
Washington, D.C. 20037

Copyright © 1994 Center for Responsive Politics

All rights reserved. No part of this publication may be reproduced or transmitted in any form or by any means, electronic or mechanical, including photocopy, recording, or any information storage and retrieval system, without permission in writing from the publisher.

Printed and bound in the United States of America.

Library of Congress Cataloging-in-Publication Data

Makinson, Larry.
    The cash constituents of Congress / Larry Makinson,
Joshua Goldstein.
      p.   cm.
    Drawn from the latest edition of Open secrets.
    Includes index.
    ISBN 1-56802-010-4
    1. United States. Congress--Elections, 1992. 2. Campaign funds-
-United States. 3. Political action committees-United States.
I. Goldstein, Joshua, 1966-   II. Makinson, Larry. Open secrets.
III. Title.
JK1991.M257   1994
324.7'8'0973--dc20
                                                                      94-31799
                                                                        CIP

Editorial, Research & Production Staff

Author/Editors:	Larry Makinson & Joshua Goldstein
Assistant Editor:	Sheila Krumholz
Research Assistants:	Amy Taylor
	Kristen Hubbard
Intern Assistants:	Marc Ricks
	Michael Baranek
	Marni Ezra
	Trista Gaiotti
	Sherri Stevens

Acknowledgments

More than 18 months of painstaking research and production went into the publication of this reference work and dozens of people and organizations were extremely helpful in the process. *Cash Constituents* is an outgrowth of the Open Secrets project of the Center for Responsive Politics. The information contained in this book would never have emerged in this form or any other without the untiring efforts of the Center's director, Ellen Miller, to win the enthusiasm and support of the foundations whose grants made it possible. The staff of the Federal Election Commission provided invaluable assistance, as usual. Kent Cooper, the FEC's Assistant Staff Director for Public Disclosure has offered advice, assistance and encouragement at every step of this project from its earliest days to its completion. Michael Dickerson, chief of the Public Records Office, has graciously and expertly assisted several generations of Center staffers in finding the buried treasures within the FEC's filing cabinets and microfilm readers. Bob Biersack, the FEC's Supervisory Statistician and chief computer guru, provided critical assistance at many points in the project — and deserves special thanks for making major improvements to the FEC's on-line database. Particular thanks also goes to Jacqueline R. Duobinis of the Center's National Library on Money & Politics for her invaluable assistance at many stages of this project, and for her blessed predilection for never throwing away a scrap of paper that has anything to do with money and politics. Finally, the authors extend their appreciation to the small but amazingly hard-working staff of the Center for Responsive Politics, who endured many trying moments during the months and years of research that have gone into successive editions of this book.

The funding that made this book possible came from major grants from the Joyce Foundation, the Florence & John Schumann Foundation, the Carnegie Corporation of America and the Rockefeller Family Associates.

The Center for Responsive Politics

The Center for Responsive Politics is a non-profit, non-partisan research group in Washington, D.C. Founded in 1983 by former Senators Frank Church (D-Idaho) and Hugh Scott (R-Pa), it specializes in the study of Congress, and particularly the role that money plays in its elections and actions. The Center's National Library on Money & Politics provides custom research for news organizations and others, using a computerized database that combines contributor classifications with current and historical federal campaign records. The Center's funding comes from a variety of foundations. It serves as a non-partisan resource for the public, the academic community and the news media. Interested readers can contact the Center at 202-857-0044 or by writing to Center for Responsive Politics, 1320 19th St. NW, Suite 700, Washington, DC 20036.

Board of Directors

Paul M. Thomas, Chair	Peter Kovler
Martha Angle	John Murphy
Thomas R. Asher	David Stern
The Hon. Dick Clark	Robert A. Weinberger
Paul S. Hoff	Ellen S. Miller, Executive Director
Sonia Jarvis	

Contents

Introduction viii
Scope, Limitations & Methodology ix

1. The Big Picture 1
The Price of Admission 2
The Dollars & Cents of Incumbency 4
Rules of the Game 10
Independent Expenditures 15
Soft Money 16
The Role of PACs 18
The Patterns in PAC Contributions 20
Serious Money: The Top 100 Contributors 24
Individual Givers: A Counterpoint to the PACs 26
Targeting the Committees 36

2. Industry Profiles 41
Industry Profiles in Brief 42
Business Contributors 44
Agriculture 46
Communications & Electronics 50
Construction 54
Defense 58
Energy & Natural Resources 60
Finance, Insurance & Real Estate 64
Health 68
Lawyers & Lobbyists 74
Miscellaneous Business 76
Transportation 80
Labor 84
Ideological/Single-Issue 88
A Potpourri of Issue PACs 92

3. Committee Profiles 94
Introduction to Committee Profiles 95

Senate Committees
    Senate Agriculture, Nutrition and Forestry Committee 96
    Senate Appropriations Committee 98
    Senate Armed Services Committee 100
    Senate Banking, Housing & Urban Affairs Committee 102
    Senate Budget Committee 104
    Senate Commerce, Science and Transportation Committee 106
    Senate Energy and Natural Resources Committee 108
    Senate Environment and Public Works Committee 110
    Senate Finance Committee 112
    Senate Foreign Relations Committee 114
    Senate Governmental Affairs Committee 116
    Senate Judiciary Committee 118
    Senate Labor and Human Resources Committee 120
    Senate Rules and Administration Committee 122
    Senate Small Business Committee 124
    Senate Veterans' Affairs Committee 126

House Committees
- House Administration Committee 128
- House Agriculture Committee 130
- House Appropriations Committee 132
- House Armed Services Committee 134
- House Banking, Finance & Urban Affairs Committee 136
- House Budget Committee 138
- House District of Columbia Committee 140
- House Education and Labor Committee 142
- House Energy and Commerce Committee 144
- House Foreign Affairs Committee 146
- House Government Operations Committee 148
- House Interior and Insular Affairs Committee 150
- House Judiciary Committee 152
- House Merchant Marine and Fisheries Committee 154
- House Post Office and Civil Service Committee 156
- House Public Works and Transportation Committee 158
- House Rules Committee 160
- House Science, Space and Technology Committee 162
- House Small Business Committee 164
- House Veterans' Affairs Committee 166
- House Ways and Means Committee 168

4. Member Profiles 171
Introduction to the Member Profiles 172

State Delegations

Alabama 174	Louisiana 220	Ohio 263
Alaska 176	Maine 222	Oklahoma 268
Arizona 177	Maryland 223	Oregon 270
Arkansas 179	Massachusetts 226	Pennsylvania 272
California 181	Michigan 229	Rhode Island 277
Colorado 191	Minnesota 233	South Carolina 278
Connecticut 193	Mississippi 236	South Dakota 280
Delaware 195	Missouri 238	Tennessee 281
Florida 196	Montana 241	Texas 284
Georgia 201	Nebraska 242	Utah 290
Hawaii 204	Nevada 244	Vermont 292
Idaho 205	New Hampshire 245	Virginia 293
Illinois 206	New Jersey 246	Washington 296
Indiana 211	New Mexico 250	West Virginia 299
Iowa 214	New York 252	Wisconsin 301
Kansas 216	North Carolina 259	Wyoming 304
Kentucky 218	North Dakota 262	

5. PAC Profiles 305
Introduction to the PAC Profiles 307
PAC Profiles 308

Appendix A: Classification Categories 346

Appendix B: Members' Totals by Sector 356

Index 367

Introduction

While American voters are all too familiar with the hype and hoopla of election-year politics, there's another side to modern electioneering that takes place off-camera and well out of earshot of most voters. It's what might be called the "phantom" campaign — the race not for votes, but for the money it takes to win them. The costs of winning election to Congress have become so high — over half a million dollars for the average U.S. House seat in 1992 — that virtually no serious candidate is immune from the money chase, and that includes incumbents as well as newcomers.

Where do the dollars come from? The answers are as diverse as the candidates, and this book gives a glimpse of each member's leading "cash constituents" on the Member Profile pages that begin on page 174. Though each campaign is unique, there are a number of important patterns in the funding of modern elections that readers may find particularly revealing:

- Incumbents often rely on the industries they regulate to provide an important source of money for their campaigns. Members of the Agriculture committees, for example, often get a substantial part of their campaign cash from PACs and individuals that represent agribusiness interests. Members of the Armed Services committees routinely get thousands of dollars from defense contractors. Members on key committees rewriting the nation's health care policy are the top recipients of contributions from doctors, insurance companies and others connected with the health care industry. *(Committee Profiles, listing the top contributors to each committee, are on pages 96-169.)*

- Democrats get a big assist from labor unions (primarily labor PACs), but most Democratic incumbents are relying less on labor and more on business contributors than in years past. Organized labor has always been a big supporter of the Democratic Party, and Democratic newcomers to Congress typically get a majority of their campaign funds from labor PACs. But once they're in office, the Democrats' labor dollars are often surpassed by contributions from business groups. *(See pages 7-9.)*

- Most industries split their dollars fairly evenly between Democrats and Republicans. In contrast to ideological and single-issue groups, which usually tilt heavily toward one party or the other, business groups are careful to give to both sides. This reflects the philosophically Republican tilt of many business groups, as well as the political reality that Democrats have a edge in political power in Washington, since they hold solid majorities in both the House and Senate. *(See the Industry profiles on pages 42-93.)*

- While political action committees, or PACs, get most of the media attention, large contributions from individuals make up an important part of the funding pie, especially in Senate campaigns. The mix of PAC and individual money is shown in each member's profile and in the Industry Profile section. It's also discussed in detail in the Big Picture section on pages 18-30.

While candidates seem never to be at a loss for words during election season, the funding of their campaigns is not a subject many candidates prefer to talk about. This book aims to fill the vacuum by giving voters a wealth of information on where the campaign cash comes from — both for their own representatives and for Congress as a whole. Our aim is to shed some light on the "cash constituents" of Congress, a constituency whose role in American elections — and in the drafting of the nation's laws — becomes more important with each passing year, as campaigns become ever more expensive.

The narrative in this book is sparse. The data is presented as directly, and graphically, as possible. The authors present no grand unifying theories, but rather leave readers to draw their own conclusions about the role of money in our American political system.

Larry Makinson/Joshua Goldstein
Center for Responsive Politics
June 1994

Scope, Limitations & Methodology

Cash Constituents is a paperback distillation of *Open Secrets: The Encyclopedia of Congressional Money & Politics*. The larger book is over 1300 pages long and includes detailed two-page campaign finance profiles for every member of Congress. The Big Picture section, Industry Profiles and Committee Profiles are identical in both books. The PAC Profile section uses the same format in both books, though in *Open Secrets* the list includes all PACs that gave $20,000 or more in the 1992 elections. In *Cash Constituents*, the PAC Profiles include only those PACs that gave $50,000 or more.

The biggest difference is in the Member Profiles, which have been abbreviated here and arranged state-by-state. Given that the information provided here had to be greatly abbreviated from the larger book, every effort was made to provide the most important information about each member's financial supporters and present it in a clear and useful format. So that readers can understand the procedures that were used, and the limitations that apply, the following section explains how the data which forms the basis of both books was collected and analyzed.

The starting point for this book was the official record of campaign contributions made to congressional and presidential candidates in the 1992 elections. That data was provided both by candidates and by political action committees, and was collected and computerized by the Federal Election Commission in Washington, D.C. Using those computer tapes, the authors, assistant editor and several additional staffers undertook the laborious task of identifying the contributors — both PACs and individuals — by industry and interest group.

What's Included in this Study

The primary focus of this book is on the 535 members of the U.S. Congress. Each member has a capsule contribution profile that details the leading industries and interest groups that contributed to his or her campaign. Those profiles are arranged by state and district and begin on page 174.

Profiles of each of the 37 standing committees of the House and Senate are also presented, showing which industries and interest groups contributed most heavily to members of that committee. Those listings begin on page 96.

An industry-by-industry breakdown of contributor groups (beginning on page 42) examines in detail which segments of the business, labor and ideological communities give the biggest share of dollars to members of Congress. The top contributors within each sector are listed, as are the top recipients in the House and Senate.

At the end of the book, a directory of political action committees is included. This brief statistical overview shows the general patterns by which each PAC that gave $50,000 or more distributed its money. The PAC profiles begin on page 306.

What's Missing

Small individual contributors — those giving $200 or less — are not itemized on federal campaign reports, so no analysis was done of the origin of that money in this book. The proportion of campaign revenues received from small individual contributors is listed, however, in each member's mini-profile.

Unknown contributors. Federal law requires that candidates identify all contributors who gave $200 or more to their campaign. Individual contributors are supposed to be identified by name, address, occupation and employer. In many cases, however, they are not. In researching the federal records, the authors found many thousands of cases of unidentified (or under-identified) contributors. In almost every case, names and addresses were provided, but quite often information on employer and occupation was left blank, incomplete, or so generic as to be useless in identifying the contributor's financial interest.

In all, of the approximately $298 million in individual contributions of $200 or more that went to federal candidates in the 1992 elections, the authors were able to classify 71 percent. Among elected members of Congress whose profiles appear in this book, the rate was over 75 percent. The breakdown of the unidentified dollars is as follows:

- **No employer listed or found:** ....$33.5 million

By far the worst offenders in identifying their contributors' economic affiliations were the presidential candidates — Bill Clinton, George Bush and Ross Perot, in particular. Most candidates for Congress identified the occupations and employers of all but a small portion of their contributors. Those members of the House and Senate who left the most blanks in their disclosure reports are identified on page 35.

- **Employer listed but category unknown:** ....$34.4 million

    With over 70,000 individual companies to identify, the task of finding them all and filling in their classifications was simply impossible, given our limitations of staff and time. As the Center refines and updates its database, we hope to reduce this figure in future editions of *Cash Constituents*.

- **Homemakers, students and other non-income earners:** .... $13.6 million

    Where contributors' occupations were listed as "homemaker," "housewife," or some equivalent, the Center tried to match them with an income-earning spouse. In many, many cases this was possible. It is a common practice for wealthy contributors to double their effective limit by giving both personally and with their spouse. In some cases this even extends to children, who are often identified by occupation as "student." Whenever the source of the family's income could not be determined, the contribution was put into this category — with one exception. Persons with no income who contributed both to candidates and to political action committees — whether corporate or ideological — were assigned the classification of the PAC they contributed to.

- **Generic occupation/impossible to assign category:** ....$3.0 million

    When a candidate identifies a contributor as "businessman" or "entrepreneur," classifying them in the right category becomes a hopeless task. Fortunately, many of these generic contributors gave to more than one candidate, sometimes enabling us to discover their employer or occupation.

Contributions from individuals who gave before 1989. Members of the U.S. Senate run for reelection every six years. Classifying their PAC contributions from previous election cycles was a difficult, but possible task. Identifying their *individual* contributors in those previous cycles, however, was beyond the capability of our limited time and staff. Consequently, contribution profiles of senators in this book include only PACs for the years prior to 1989.

How this Book Was Prepared

The first step in this project — and one that began in 1989 with the original edition of *Open Secrets* — was creating a classification system for the industries and interest groups that make political contributions. Since a majority of PACs and individual contributors come from the business world, the starting point was the system of Standard Industrial Codes (SIC codes) developed by the U.S. government's Office of Management and Budget. The SIC codes are used widely by reference organizations, such as Standard & Poors, that publish business directories. The codes were then streamlined to eliminate fine lines of distinction between industries and to make them more relevant to the political realities of congressional committee jurisdictions.

No similar codes cover non-business groups, so the Center developed its own, both for labor unions and for ideological and single-issue PACs. During the course of the project the classification system underwent a continual evolution, as the real world patterns of political giving gradually became apparent. A complete list of the categories — with the totals each contributed — is included in Appendix A, beginning on page 346.

Classifying the Contributions

The contemporary American business world does not lend itself to simple classification. Modern corporations are often extremely diversified in their lines of business — and in their political interests — and in recent years many have been buying and selling subsidiaries almost routinely. To allow for this, the Center developed a multi-level system for classifying corporate PACs and other diversified contributors. A primary code was assigned, based on the company's primary business or profit center. Secondary codes were then added to account for subsidiary interests contributing more than 10 percent of the company's revenues or profits.

These multiple codes were then matched against the committee assignments of the candidates who received contributions. If the committee's jurisdiction did not relate to the PAC's main category, but did relate to a secondary code, that secondary code was used to classify the contribution. For example, a contribution from the Boeing PAC to a member of the Armed Services Committee was classified as a defense contribution. A similar contribution to a non-incumbent, or to someone sitting on a non-defense committee, would be classified under Boeing's primary category as an aircraft manufacturer. This system was used to determine unique codes for each contribution made to congressional candidates during the 1991-92 election cycle.

Classifying contributions from individuals presented a new level of complexity. While it is generally safe to assume that a PAC is giving to further its economic interests, it is quite another matter to try to divine the motivations behind an individual's contribution to a politician. The Center's approach was not even to try. Rather, *the classifications in this book are based on the economic interests of the contributor's employer or line of business.* The only exception to this rule is in the case of individuals who have contributed to ideological or single-interest PACs. In that case, the contributor was generally assigned the same category as the PAC *if* they contributed to a candidate who received money from the PAC as well.

The following example illustrates the methodology: If a real estate developer contributes both to a pro-Israel PAC and to a candidate who received direct contributions from one or more pro-Israel PACs, the contribution would be classified under "pro-Israel." If the donor gave to someone who got no money from pro-Israel PACs, it would be classified under "real estate."

"Homemakers" and Other Non-Income Earners

If one to were take at face value the occupations and employers listed on federal campaign finance reports, one would quickly come to the conclusion that the biggest political interest group in the nation is made up of "homemakers" and "housewives." In fact, the use of contributions by spouses and other family members is common practice among wealthy contributors. Whenever a connection could be found between students, homemakers, or other non-income earners and a member of the household who did earn an income, the breadwinner's classification was used for all family members. Thus, a bank president, his wife and children would all be classified under "commercial banking" unless the wife listed a different occupation or employer, in which case she would be classified separately.

The only exception to this rule was in the case of ideological contributors. Non-income earning family members are not classified as ideological givers unless they themselves have contributed to an ideological PAC.

Compilation and Publication

Once all the data was collected and categorized, the final step was to arrange it in some order that would make it comprehensible — both for our own analysis and for readers of this book. Viewing the mountains of data that this book covers from only one angle would be limiting at best, so the information is presented here from a number of perspectives. Profiles cover not only the finances of individual members of Congress, but of PACs, congressional committees and specific industries as well. Wherever possible, the data is presented graphically, so readers can view not just the detail in the numbers, but also the patterns.

Technical Notes

This entire project, from the first drafts of foundation proposals to the compiling of the databases, the charting and final desktop publishing, was done using Apple Macintosh™ computers. A large ensemble of software was used to gather and report the data. The workhorses included: FoxBase+/Mac™ and Panorama II™ for database work, DeltaGraph Professional™ for the charts and graphs, Microsoft Word™ for word processing, and Aldus PageMaker™ for final page layout.

The research to identify the thousands of PACs and individual contributors was done in libraries (primarily the Library of Congress), over the telephone, and in the Center's own growing library of reference materials. Standard & Poor's *Register of Corporations, Directors and Executives* was an invaluable reference work in identifying companies and matching the names of corporate officials and directors. *Washington Representatives*, published by Columbia Books, is the definitive guide to Washington lobbyists and was a constantly-appreciated reference tool. Also immensely useful was the *Yellow Book* series of business and congressional directories published by Monitor Publishing of Washington, DC.

Even with the vast resources of the Library of Congress and the dozens of business directories the Center consulted, the classification of the thousands of small businesses whose owners and officials gave money would not have been possible without the newly emerging medium of electronic reference works. Three CD-ROMs in particular proved to be worth more than their weight in gold: *Dun's Business Locator*, published by Dun & Bradstreet Information Services, was indispensable. On a single disk it classifies more than 10 million American businesses. Standard & Poors *Corporations CD-ROM* provides extremely valuable details on the business activities of the same public and privately-held corporations listed in their hardcover volume. Finally, the *Martindale-Hubbell Law Directory on CD-ROM* made it possible to identify an unprecedented number of law firms and individual attorneys — a particularly valuable resource considering that 86 percent of lawyers' contributions in the 1992 elections came from individuals, not PACs. Without those CD-ROMs, tens of thousands of small businesses and professionals identified on these pages would have been impossible to classify.

1.
The Big Picture

Cash Constitutents of Congress

The Price of Admission

...to the House of Representatives

Even when adjusted for inflation, the cost of a seat in the U.S. House of Representatives took a big leap forward in 1992. Just two years earlier, the cost of the average winning House campaign was $407,000. In 1992, the average House seat cost $543,000. Another telling statistic: in 1990, 11 House candidates waged campaigns costing $1 million or more. In 1992, the number of million-dollar campaigns soared to 46.

Several factors combined to boost the cost of a campaign, but the overriding factor was an increase in serious competition in districts all across the nation. Incumbents spent more to counteract widespread public anger with Congress, and to raise their profile among new constituents, as district lines were reapportioned. Reapportionment, combined with a surge in congressional retirements, opened many more seats than usual, creating open-seat races that traditionally cost more to win than incumbents spend to defend themselves. In 1992, however, that tradition fell, as incumbents spent more on average than open seat winners.

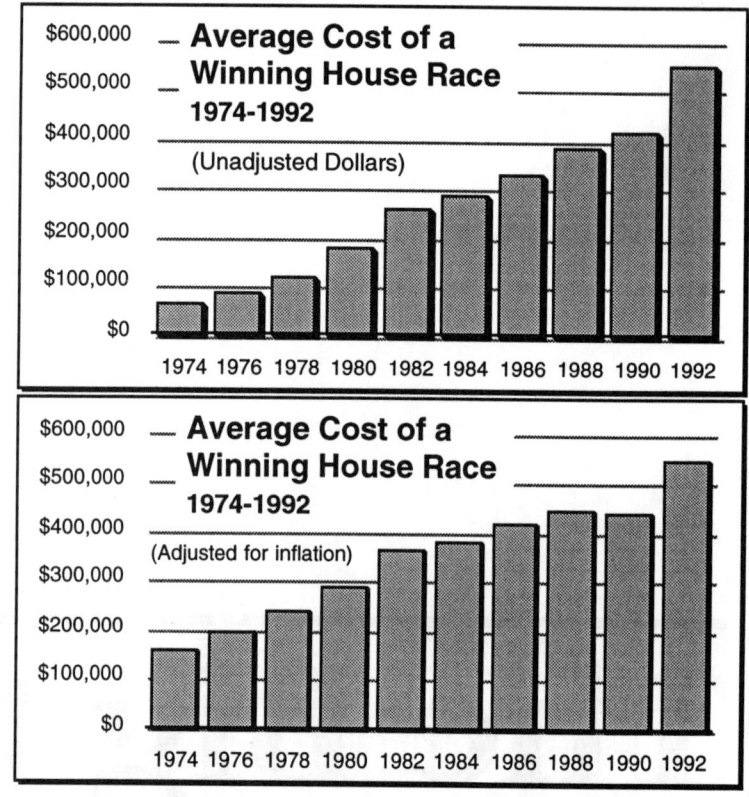

Source: Federal Election Commission and Center for Responsive Politics

...to the Senate

While average spending figures offer good yardsticks for measuring the rising cost of seats in the U.S. House of Representatives — where all 435 seats are up for election every two years — they are more problematic in the Senate. For one thing, only one-third of the 100 Senate seats are up for election in a given year, and a sample of 33 or 34 races is less reliable when measuring averages. For another thing, the costs of Senate races in a particular year can vary dramatically depending on which states are holding elections that year. In years when the largest states — such as New York and California — have races, average costs tend to be higher.

Over the past three elections, the cost of a winning Senate campaign has remained steady at around $4 million, but variations in spending have been wide. The chart below gives a sense of those variations in recent years, by highlighting the most and least expensive successful Senate campaigns in each of the last four elections.

Year	Most Expensive	State	Least Expensive	State
1986	$11,571,587	Calif	$883,977	Utah
1988	$14,656,367	Calif	$790,710	Hawaii
1990	$17,761,579	NC	$533,632	Kansas
1992	$14,958,095	NY	$1,095,154	NH

The most expensive Senate campaign ever waged was Jesse Helms' $17.8 million reelection race in 1990. The costliest race in 1992 was that of New York Republican Alfonse D'Amato, which totalled just under $15 million.

The Spending Gap Between Incumbents and Challengers

For years there has been a large — and widening — gap in the financial resources available to U.S. House incumbents versus those of candidates running to unseat them. In the 1992 elections, the spending gap between challengers and incumbents widened farther than ever. The average incumbent spent $578,475 in 1992. The average challenger (counting unopposed races as $0) spent $148,127. That left a gap of more than $430,000 between the ins and outs.

The chart at right gives a graphic perspective to the differences. Spending for both groups increased in 1992, but even though challengers spent more than ever, the rise in incumbent spending far outstripped the increase for challengers.

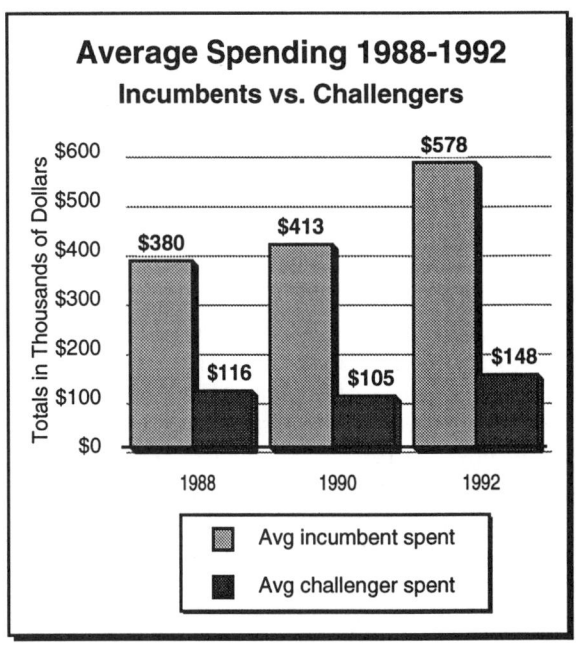

Fewer Incumbents Skating to Easy Victories

For the first time in years, there actually *was* competition in races for the U.S. House of Representatives. The great majority of incumbents won, as they usually do, but there were far fewer runaways than in previous years. The comparative pie charts below show the story. In 1988 most incumbents breezed to victory with little difficulty. In 1990, the number of close and marginal races nearly doubled. In 1992, barely half the winners captured more than 60 percent of the vote. The large number of open seat contests was the biggest reason, but incumbents also found their vote totals squeezed by better-funded challengers than in years past, and a rising restlessness among voters who were more willing than ever to give new candidates the benefit of the doubt.

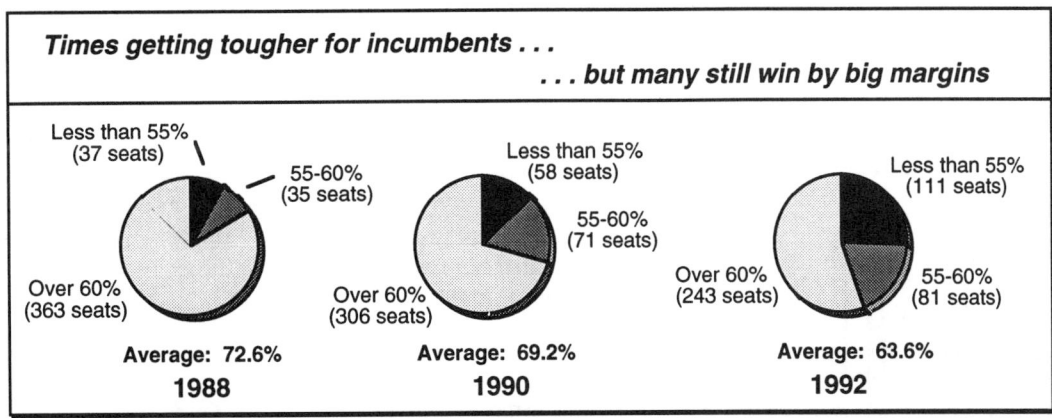

The Dollars and Cents of Incumbency

Incumbents, for any office at any level of government, have always enjoyed a natural advantage at election time. Their names are already well known, they have established a record of service for all to see, and if they have served their constituents well, the voters are likely to be reminded of it time and again come election time. Congressional incumbents also have the benefit of regular news coverage during their term in office — coverage which often gives them credit for federal grants and projects in their districts. And they have the congressional franking privilege, enabling them to send correspondence and periodic newsletters to their constituents postage free.

Members of Congress also have the inside lock on contributions from political action committees. In 1992 PACs accounted for 43 percent of all the dollars received by House incumbents and more than one-quarter of total contributions to Senators. More than three-quarters of the dollars contributed by PACs in 1992 went to incumbents.

What all this adds up to is an overwhelming advantage by incumbents over challengers, particularly in races for the House of Representatives. Yet for each of the last two elections, the cost of beating an incumbent has declined. In 1992, 19 challengers beat incumbents in November. On average, they spent less than $435,000 against incumbents who averaged $840,000 defending their seats. Of the 19, only one spent more than the incumbent they defeated, indicating once again that beating incumbents doesn't require outspending them, but rather raising enough money to be visible. (Five other incumbents in November lost to fellow incumbents; another 19 incumbents lost their seats in the primaries).

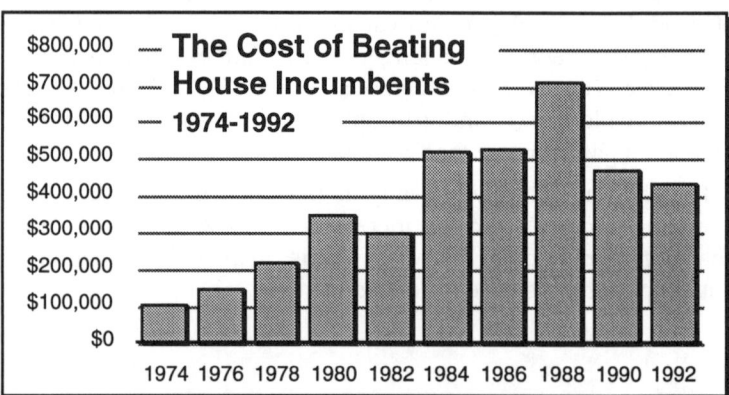

The Cost of Beating House Incumbents 1974-1992

NOTE: Does not include races between two incumbents

Year	Average Challenger	Average Incumbent	No.
1974	$100,435	$101,102	40
1976	$144,720	$154,774	12
1978	$217,083	$200,607	19
1980	$343,093	$286,559	31
1982	$296,273	$453,459	23
1984	$518,781	$463,070	17
1986	$523,308	$562,139	6
1988	$703,740	$876,678	7
1990	$462,546	$631,025	16
1992	$435,829	$840,922	19

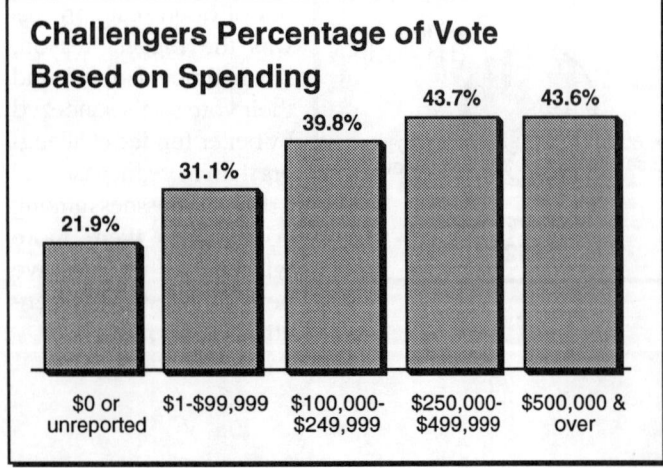

Challengers Percentage of Vote Based on Spending

- $0 or unreported: 21.9%
- $1-$99,999: 31.1%
- $100,000-$249,999: 39.8%
- $250,000-$499,999: 43.7%
- $500,000 & over: 43.6%

Even though adding extra money to a campaign was no guarantee of winning, there was a clear correlation between the amount of money spent by challengers and their share of the total votes on election day — up to a point. The correlation also held when comparing the chances of winning, as seen in the chart below.

Amount Spent by Challenger	Odds of Winning
$0 or unreported	0
$1-$99,999	0
$100,000-$249,999	13:1
$250,000-$499,999	4:1
$500,000 & over	2:1

Reelection Rates through the Years

Reelection rates for incumbents in both the House and Senate dipped below the 90 percent mark in 1992, to 88.3 percent in the House and 82.8 percent in the Senate.

What the figures don't show— particularly in the House of Representatives — is that a number of congressional incumbents who might have faced difficult races in 1992 decided not to seek reelection, and retired instead. But what the charts do show is that even in one of the most turbulent elections in recent decades, the great majority of incumbents were still able to hold onto their seats — regardless of the voters' low opinion of Congress in general.

The charts also show a contrast in reelection patterns between the House and Senate. Senate races tend to be more competitive than House races, as both parties usually attract (and support) credible candidates. They are also more subject to major swings in the political temperament, as in 1980 when the Reagan landslide swept nine Senate Democrats out of office, shifting control of that body to the Republicans.

Reelection rates in the House have proved much more stable over the years. The last time the reelection rate for House members dropped below 80 percent was in 1948.

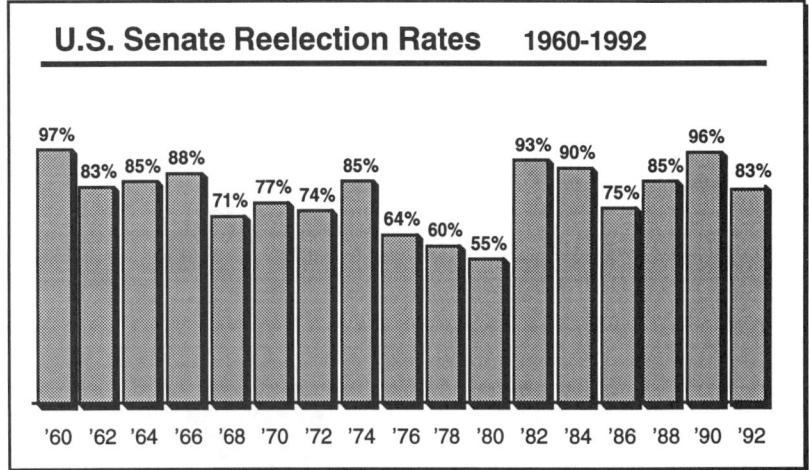

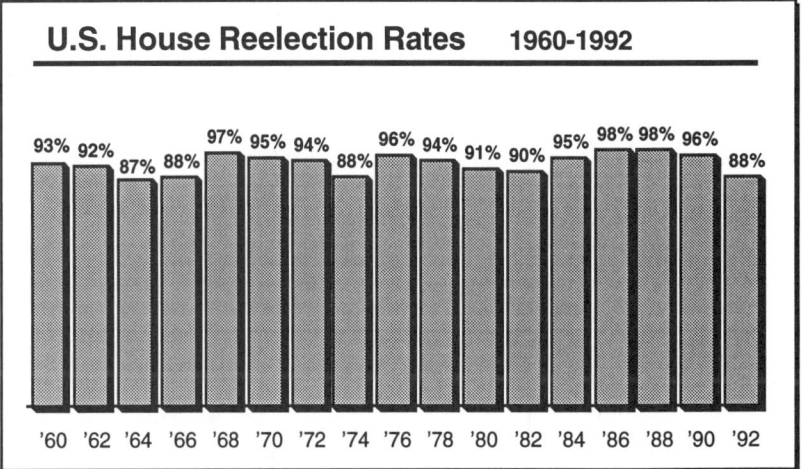

The 10 Top-Spending Challengers in House Races

Challenger	Party	District	Spent	Vote Pct	Outcome
Michael Huffington	Rep	Calif 22	$5,435,177	52.5%	Won
Dick Chrysler	Rep	Mich 8	$1,761,841	46.3%	Lost
Linda Bean	Rep	Maine 1	$1,441,720	35.0%	Lost
Gwen Margolis	Dem	Fla 22	$936,960	37.1%	Lost
Mark Neumann	Rep	Wis 1	$920,174	40.7%	Lost
James M. Talent	Rep	Mo 2	$916,868	50.4%	Won
H.L. "Bill" Richardson	Rep	Calif 3	$841,530	40.3%	Lost
Martin T. Meehan	Dem	Mass 5	$811,459	52.2%	Won
James C. Greenwood	Rep	Pa 8	$726,702	51.9%	Won
Martin R. Hoke	Rep	Ohio 10	$681,166	56.8%	Won

The High Cost of Losing

As Ross Perot could readily testify after his experience in the 1992 elections, an abundance of money doesn't always bring victory on election day. Like Perot, half of the 10 biggest-spending challengers in races for the U.S. House were defeated at the polls in November. But that ratio was a big improvement over previous elections. In 1990, seven of the 10 top-spending challengers lost; in 1988 nine of the 10 lost. More than $5 million from his personal bank account did help California Republican Michael Huffington win a seat in Congress, but runners-up Dick Chrysler and Linda Bean both suffered expensive losses despite their personal fortunes.

Where the Money Came From

The dollars that drove winning campaigns in 1992 came from different mixes of sources depending on the office and the status of the candidate. These pie charts highlight the differences.

Political action committees were most important to incumbent House members, who collected 43 percent of their revenues from that source. PACs were less important — but still a sizeable slice of the overall funding pie — to Senate incumbents and to new House winners. They were least important to Senate newcomers.

Large contributions from individuals were important to all groups — particularly Senate incumbents, who drew 39 percent of their dollars from individual donors giving $200 or more. Small individual contributions were most important to freshman senators — a possible reflection of the

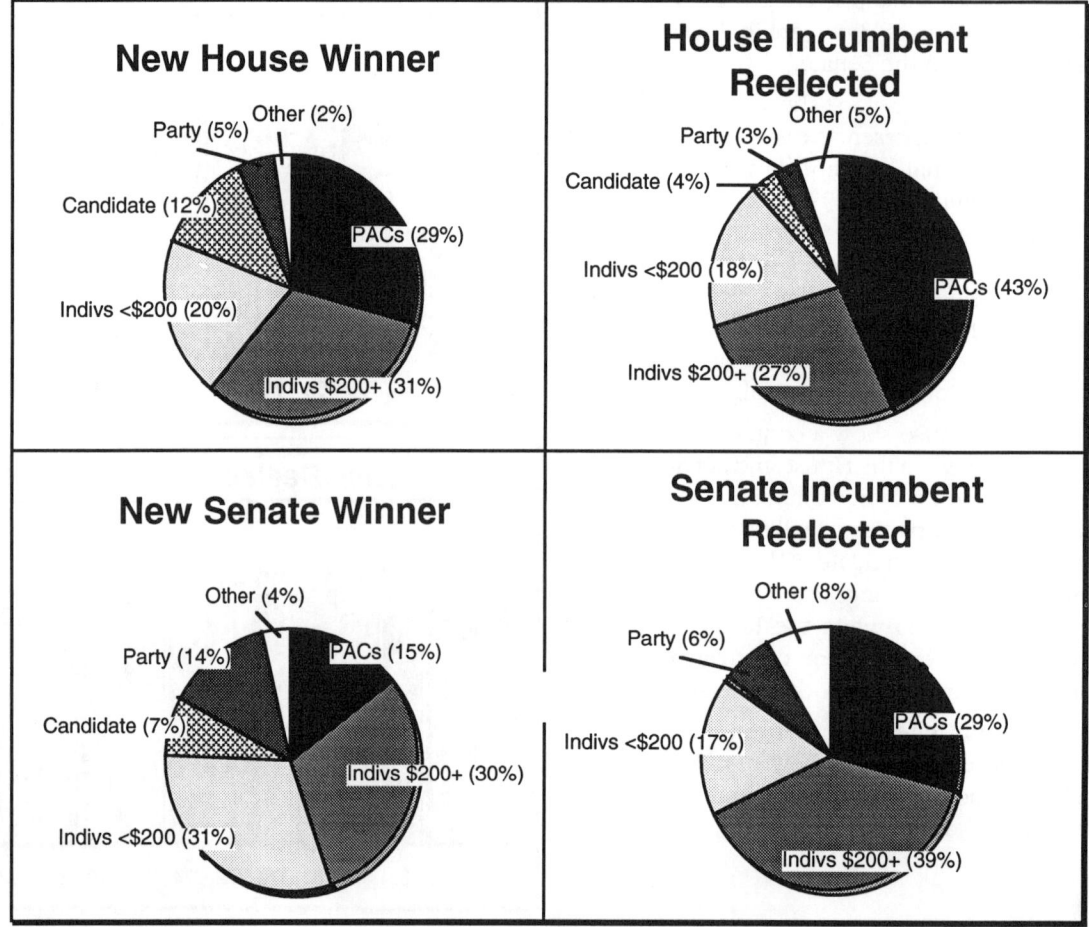

grass roots financial support that helped elect four women candidates to the U.S. Senate. Only one senator drew a majority of campaign dollars from small donations in 1992: Democrat Carol Moseley-Braun of Illinois. California's Barbara Boxer drew the largest dollar amount in that category — just over $5 million from contributions under $200.

Another fact of political financing that is clear from these charts is the relatively minor role that candidates' personal funds play in most campaigns — particularly among incumbents.

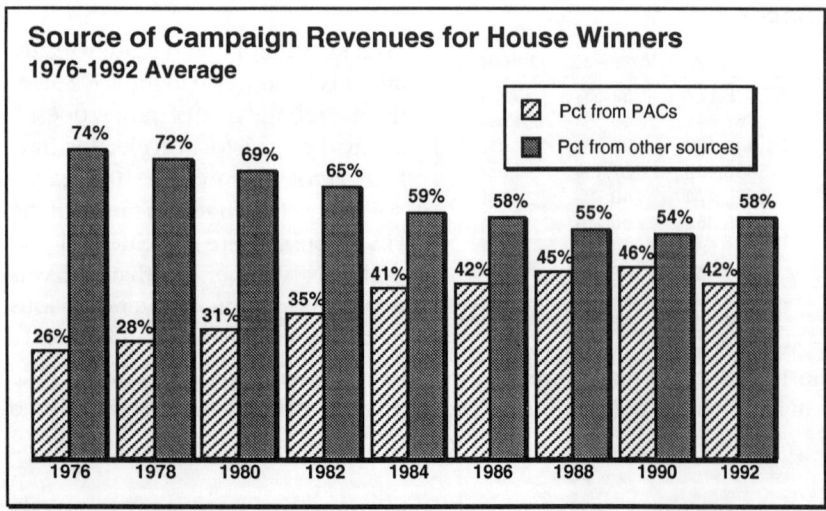

Sources: Federal Election Commission and Center for Responsive Politics

A Small Decline in PAC Dependency

The long-term trend toward greater PAC dependency among U.S. House winners reversed itself in 1992, albeit modestly. Though it may have been the beginnings of a new anti-PAC trend among incumbents feeling the heat from voters, the dip was more likely due to the unusually large number of non-incumbents who won office in 1992. As the charts on the following page indicate clearly, PACs give far more heavily to incumbents than to newcomers.

Source of PAC Funds — House Freshmen vs. Incumbents

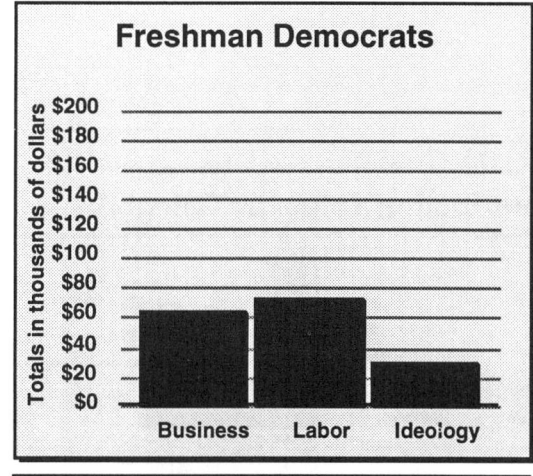
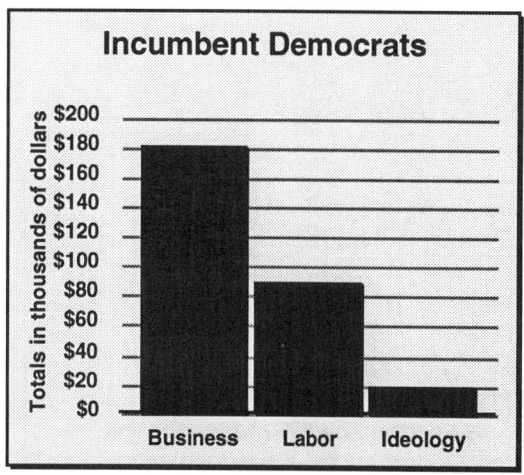
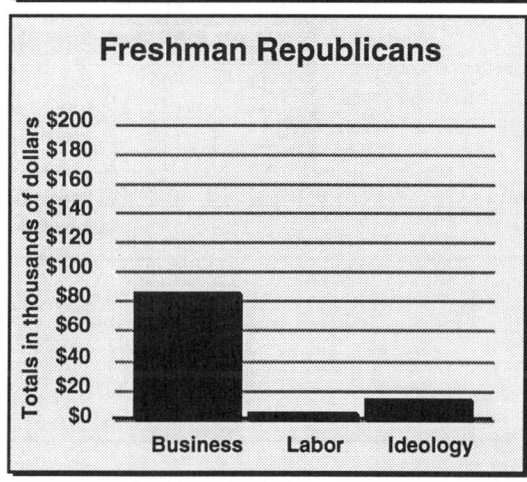
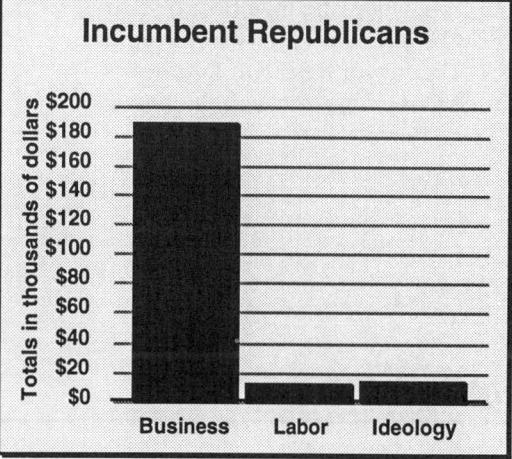

When PAC receipts are clustered into three distinct groups — business, labor and ideological — significant contrasts in the source of PAC funds can be seen between Democrats and Republicans, and between freshman members of Congress versus incumbents. The biggest source of funds for newly-elected Democrats comes from Labor PACs, which gave an average of more than $71,000 per Democratic winner in the 1992 elections. That is slightly more than the freshman Democrats got from all business PACs combined. Ideological and single-issue PACs are also an important source of funds for newly-elected Democrats.

Once the House Democrats have served one or more terms in Congress, the complexion of their PAC contributions shifts significantly. Labor dollars are still an important source of campaign revenues, but they are swamped by the combined dollars collected from business PACs. Ideological PACs, meanwhile, play only a minor part in the reelection war chests collected by Democratic House incumbents.

Republicans — whether freshmen or incumbents — collect the great preponderance of their PAC dollars from business interests. Labor PACs are almost non-existent for newly-elected Republicans, and ideological PACs provide less than half the dollars for freshman Republicans than they do for Democrats. As Republicans take office and seek reelection, their proportion of business dollars continues to vastly outweigh their combined contributions from labor and ideological groups. Labor and ideological PACs also come closer into balance.

Among both Democrats and Republicans, one trend is consistent. Incumbents — whatever the mix of business, labor and ideological PACs that give to their campaigns — routinely draw far more total PAC dollars than candidates who have not yet won election to Congress.

Where Newcomers Found the Money . . .

Freshman Democrats

PAC contributions from organized labor were the single biggest source of campaign funds for most freshman Democrats who broke into the House of Representatives in 1992. On average, the new Democratic members received just over $71,000 from labor PACs. Ideological PACs were another important source of funds for this group. Many of the most promising challengers and open seat candidates drew contributions from "leadership PACs" operated by Democratic members of Congress. Financial interests and lawyers were the other leading sources of funds for freshman Democrats. Most of those dollars came through individual contributions.

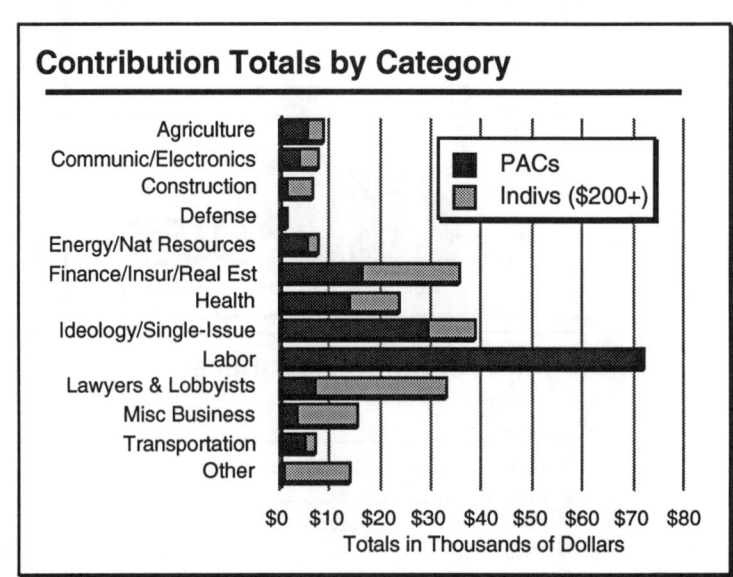

Freshman Republicans

Newly-elected Republicans had a markedly different contribution profile from their Democratic colleagues. Financial interests and miscellaneous business contributors were the two leading sources of campaign cash for the GOP freshman. Both those groups gave about half their money through PACs and half through large contributions from individuals. Health industry contributors — primarily doctors and other health professionals — were another important source of funds, providing about $25,000 to the average new Republican member of Congress. The remainder of the Republicans' dollars came from a wide cross-section of business groups.

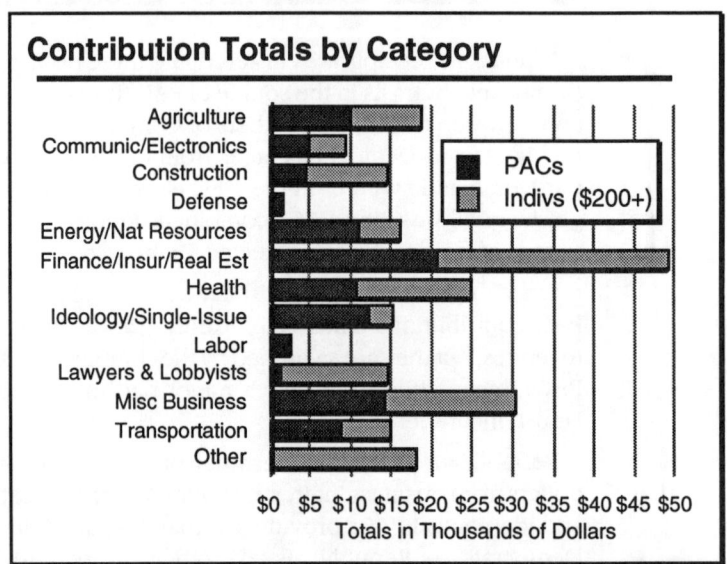

Where Incumbents Found the Money . . .

Incumbent Democrats

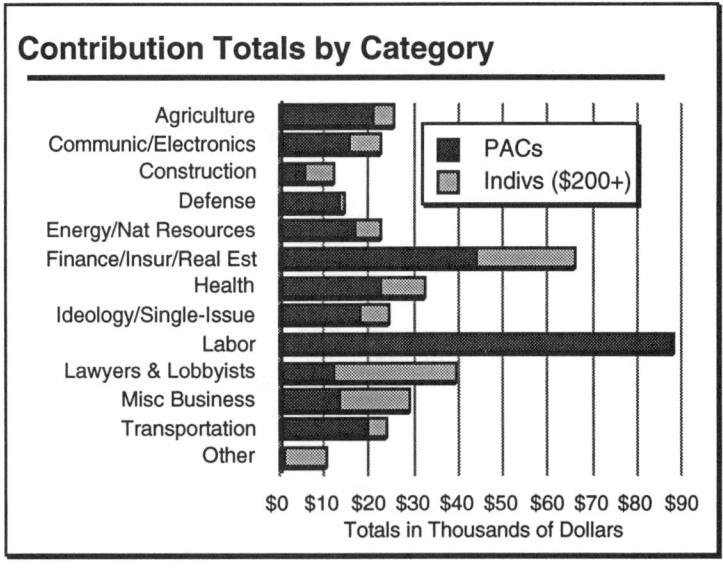

Once they've been elected to Congress — and received their committee assignments — Democrats begin to receive contributions from many business groups that rarely give to non-incumbents. Organized labor continues to be an important source of campaign funds, but not nearly as important as it is to freshman Democrats. The finance/insurance/real estate sector is by far the most important source among business groups for incumbent Democrats. The "second tier" of business contributors is led by lawyers & lobbyists, but there is wide variation among members in the mix of different industries. The industry patterns to individual members tend to parallel their committee assignments as well as the economic profile of their home district.

Incumbent Republicans

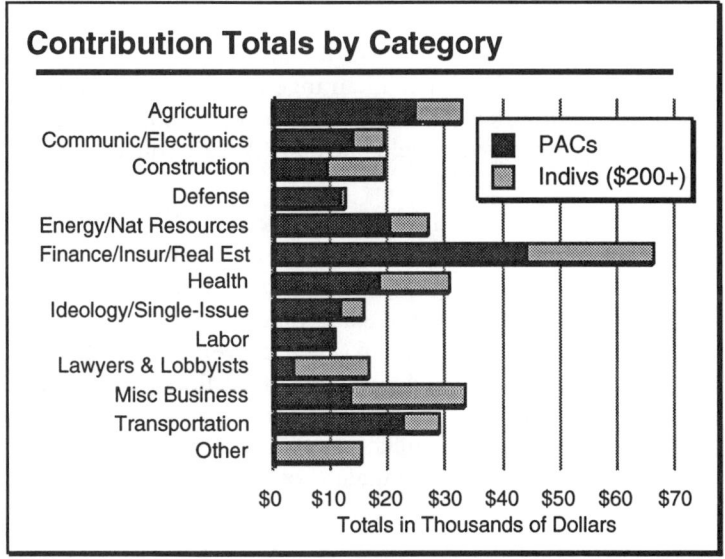

By a wide margin, the finance/insurance/real estate sector is the leading source of campaign funds to incumbent House Republicans. Other important sectors include agriculture, energy, health, transportation, and miscellaneous business — though Republican incumbents drew significant funds from all other business sectors as well. Like their Democratic colleagues, most Republican incumbents get only a small proportion of their funds from ideological groups. Their share of labor PAC dollars, while still small in comparison to Democrats, is significantly higher than that received by Republican freshmen.

Rules of the Game

The rules that govern the financing of elections can be complicated enough to keep a small army of Washington lawyers perpetually employed. But federal election laws are not so complicated that the average voter can't figure out the basics. Outlined below is an overview of the rules. Significant changes in these laws were under consideration by the 103rd Congress, but any new rules are not likely to take effect before the 1996 elections.

Who Can Contribute and Who Cannot

Any American citizen can contribute funds to candidates for federal office or to political parties. There is only one exception to this broad rule: individuals and owners of sole proprietorships that have contracts with the federal government. (That prohibition does not extend to employees, partners, officers or shareholders of larger businesses with federal contracts — many of whom are active contributors).

Foreign nationals who do not have permanent residence in the United States are prohibited from contributing to *any* political candidates in the U.S. — at the federal, state, or local level.

Cash contributions exceeding an aggregate of $100 are also prohibited, no matter where they come from. And no candidate can accept an anonymous donation of more than $50.

Corporations, labor unions, national banks and federally chartered corporations are also prohibited from contributing to federal campaigns or parties — though they may make unlimited contributions to the parties' "soft money" accounts (see page 16). They may also organize political action committees (or "PACs") that enable the employees of the company, or members of the union, to pool their resources and deliver their funds as a bloc. The prohibition against direct corporate giving has been a part of federal law since the passage of the Tillman Act in 1907. The ban was extended to labor unions in 1943.

In recent years, the issue of political action committees operated by foreign-owned corporations has become contentious — particularly since a growing number of American companies have been acquired by Japanese and European investors. The Federal Election Commission has ruled that such companies *may* operate political action committees as long as American citizens are the only contributors to the PAC.

The Birth of PACs

When Congress acted in 1943 to ban direct contributions from labor unions to federal candidates, organized labor was quick to react. That same year, the first modern "political action committee" was formed by the Congress of Industrial Organization (which later merged with the American Federation of Labor to form the AFL-CIO). The dollars the PAC distributed came not from the union treasury, but from voluntary contributions by its members. While such an arrangement was not explicitly sanctioned by federal law, neither was it prohibited. Over the next 30 years the idea gradually caught on as other labor unions, then corporations and business groups, formed PACs of their own. But many groups held back. PACs were still a loophole in federal election laws — tolerated, but not officially sanctioned.

In 1974, amid the post-Watergate climate of political reform, Congress gave PACs the green light. In its 1974 amendments to the Federal Election Campaign Act, Congress specifically sanctioned the formation of "political committees" to enable employees of corporations, members of labor unions, or members of professional groups, trade associations or any other political group to pool their dollars and give to the candidates of their choice. At the same time, it gave PACs higher contribution limits than individual contributors, and set up the Federal Election Commission (FEC) to oversee elections and to collect and monitor campaign finance reports filed by PACs and candidates. It was an opening of the floodgates. By the end of 1974, 608 political action committees were officially recognized by the FEC. By 1992 that number had grown to more than 4,700. The dollars they pumped into federal elections mushroomed from $12.5 million in 1976 to nearly $189 million in 1992. The great majority of those dollars — then and now — went to finance the campaigns of incumbent members of Congress.

Contribution Limits

Candidates for Congress can spend as much money as they can raise, whether from their own pockets or from those of contributors. No spending limits apply. Contributors to federal campaigns, on the other hand, do face limits in what they can give to a federal candidate or a national political party. The limits were set as part of the 1974 Federal Election Campaign Act, and they are summarized in the chart below:

Federal Campaign Spending Limits

	To any candidate or candidate committee	To any national party committee	To any PAC or other political committee	Total
Time period	per election*	per calendar year	per calendar year	per calendar year
Individual can give...	$1,000	$20,000	$5,000	$25,000
Multicandidate Committee† can give...	$5,000	$15,000	$5,000	No limit
Other Political Committee can give...	$1,000	$20,000	$5,000	No limit

SOURCE: Federal Election Commission

* Primary and general elections count as two separate elections; so this contribution can be effectively doubled during a normal election year in states with primaries.

† Multicandidate committees are those with more than 50 contributors, that have been registered for at least six months, and (with the exception of state party committees) have made contributions to five or more federal candidates.

Enforcement of the Campaign Laws

Enforcement of the federal campaign laws lies in the hands of the six-member Federal Election Commission in Washington, D.C. Appointed by the president to serve staggered six-year terms, commission members are traditionally split 3-3 between Republicans and Democrats.

The 3-3 split is also common in many of the commission's votes on rulings that would likely benefit one party over the other. Many analysts and commentators have contended that the institutional paralysis which sometimes results was exactly what the drafters of the Federal Election Campaign Act had in mind — namely, to keep the commission from being too vigilant or activist in its enforcement.

Over the years, the commission has come under considerable attack by critics on both sides of the political fence for its lack of direction in enforcing and interpreting the campaign finance law. While the commissioners have fairly regularly cited candidates and fined their campaigns for relatively minor offenses (and occasionally for serious ones), they have been unable to reach consensus on many larger issues affecting the conduct of federal elections.

One area for which the FEC has received well-deserved praise, however, is in its role as a provider of campaign finance information to the public. The FEC has collected millions of pages of detailed records since 1975 on the financing of federal elections, and citizens curious about the identity of their representatives' financial backers can find a wealth of information in the FEC's files.

Public Disclosure

By law, every candidate for federal office must file periodic reports with the Federal Election Commission in Washington, D.C., detailing both the income and expenditures of their campaign. Copies of these reports, which are timed to coincide with various high points in the two-year election cycle, must also be filed in the candidate's home state with the state election commission or equivalent agency.

Individual contributors who give an aggregate of $200 or more must be identified by name, address, occupation and employer. All PAC and party contributions, no matter how large or small, must also be itemized.

In addition, PACs themselves must file reports four times a year with the FEC in Washington, detailing both the contributions received by the PAC and the names of candidates and other groups that received the PAC's donations. While PACs are required to file at least quarterly, they may choose to file monthly if they wish — and many of the larger PACs do.

When it compiles the official records of PAC contributions, and records them on its computers, the FEC uses the reports filed by the PACs — *not* those filed by the candidates. Because of this, occasional discrepancies are inevitable between the contributions reported by the candidates and those recorded in the FEC's official records. In itemizing those contributions, this book relies on the official FEC data.

Filing Deadlines

Members of Congress and candidates for Congress must file their FEC reports according to the schedules shown in the following charts. Each report must list the candidate's contributions and expenditures during the reporting period. As the charts show, the schedules vary during election years and off years. In the course of a typical election year, a candidate for Congress may file as many as seven reports. In other years, only two reports are required.

Election Year Reporting Deadlines

Reports	Deadline	Period covered
Pre-election reports	12 days before primary election	Up to 20 days before the election
	12 days before general election	Up to 20 days before the election
Post-general report	30 days after general election	Up to 20 days after the election
Quarterly reports	Apr 15	Jan 1 - Mar 31
	Jul 15	Apr 1 - Jun 30
	Oct 15	Jul 1 - Sep 30
	Jan 31	Oct 1 - Dec 31 of previous year

NOTE: If two of the above deadlines closely coincide, a single report may be sufficient.

Non-election Year Reporting Deadlines

Reports	Deadline	Period covered
Semi-annual reports	Jul 31	Jan 1 - Jun 30
	Jan 31	Jul 1 - Dec 31 of previous year

Where to Find a Candidate's Reports

Any member of the public can view current and past campaign spending reports filed by their own representatives in Congress, or those of any other candidate for federal office. The central repository for these reports is the Public Records office of the Federal Election Commission at 999 E Street NW, Washington, D.C. 20463. The FEC's toll-free phone number is 1-800-424-9530. In the Washington area, the number is 202-219-4140.

The FEC also maintains a number of remote computer terminals around the country, generally in the offices of the secretary of state or the state election commission. As of April 1994, some 28 states were equipped with FEC terminals. Computer printouts of candidate or PAC reports can be ordered either from the FEC in Washington or from these state offices with terminals. A nominal charge is made for the materials, generally calculated on the cost of reproducing each page. One caveat: itemized contribution reports for major campaigns, such as those for the U.S. Senate, can be quite lengthy, even when reduced to computer printouts. Browsing through them (and in some cases even picking them up and carrying them out the door) can be quite an effort.

Federal campaign records are also available on-line to anyone with a computer, a modem, and an interest in obtaining the information. The on-line fee is $20 an hour and new subscribers must first request the service in writing and include a deposit before receiving their password. Among the reports available on-line are full contribution reports for any candidate or group of candidates (such as the congressional delegation from a particular state) and any PAC or groups of PACs. Recent FEC news releases are also available on line.

Copies of the candidates' FEC filings are also available in the candidate's home state. The reports are filed with the secretary of state's office or the state election commission, or whichever other agency in the state monitors elections.

In addition to campaign reports, the FEC also publishes pre-election and post-election reports listing summary statistics on campaign spending and fundraising by federal candidates, as well as a number of informative brochures outlining federal campaign laws and how they apply to candidates, PACs and contributors.

National Library on Money & Politics

The Federal Election Commission is no longer the only source for campaign finance data. The non-profit, non-partisan National Library on Money & Politics (a project of the Center for Responsive Politics) maintains a computer database that takes the raw FEC data and classifies each contribution by the same system of industry and interest group categories used throughout this book.

The Library was established primarily to work with news organizations, academic researchers and others who want to follow the trends and specifics of who's funding federal elections. It can prepare custom reports analyzing the contributions of any member of Congress or other federal candidate. Reports can also be compiled on the spending patterns of a particular company, industry, or interest group.

The Library's computerized databases include FEC data going back several election cycles. It also has access to congressional voting records, so reports can be compiled comparing a member of Congress' voting pattern with his or her contributions.

Standard reports are priced from $10 to $25, depending on their complexity. Custom reports can be done on an hourly fee schedule.

For more information or to place an order for a report, the Library can be reached at 202-857-0318.

Deciphering the Candidates' FEC Reports

Sifting through a candidate's FEC reports is not always an enlightening experience. Many candidates, instead of entering the full name of a PAC, often enter the PAC's informal acronym. Even if you knew, for example, that the Association of Trial Lawyers of America was the nation's largest PAC representing lawyers, you might not be able to decode the PAC's shorthand name — ATLA — when it appears on a candidate's report.

Making matters worse, there are no conventions to PAC acronyms and no FEC guidelines to ensure that each PAC uses a unique name. In fact, there are many duplications of shortened PAC names. "APAC," for example, is the informal acronym of at least three PACs: The Alltel Corporation PAC, the American Society of Association Executives PAC, and the Armco Employees PAC. Many other duplicates can also be found among the more than 4,700 currently-registered political action committees.

Aside from the acronyms, most PAC names are fairly self-explanatory — at least in naming the organization that sponsors them. There is nothing mysterious, for example, about the Boeing Company PAC or the Mid-America Dairymen PAC. Identification becomes more difficult when the PAC sponsor is less well known and the company's name offers no hint of its line of business. Without consulting a corporate directory on the shelves of the nearest library, for example, one might not know that Malone & Hyde is a major food wholesaler, that the Kaman Corporation is a defense contractor, or that the Summa Corporation runs a Las Vegas hotel and casino.

Many other PACs, particularly ideological or single-issue PACs, have names that can be maddeningly obscure. Few casual observers would guess, for example, that the "Fund for Southern Progress" is actually the leadership PAC of South Carolina Governor Carroll Campbell, or that the "Committee for a Level Playing Field" represents banks that want Congress to allow them to begin offering stock brokerage services.

To assist those wanting to decipher the mysteries of PAC names that appear on candidates' FEC filings, the final section of this book (beginning on page 1251) identifies the primary interests of each PAC that gave $20,000 or more in the 1992 election cycle. But new PACs do spring up each election year, so the job of classifying the more obscure ones is a never-ending task.

Individual contributors present a different set of problems. Though candidates are required by law to list the name, address, occupation and employer of each contributor who gives $200 or more, this information is often incomplete. In the process of analyzing individual contributions undertaken for this book, these shortcomings stood out in stark relief. Some typical problems:

- **Missing information.** Federal election law requires that candidates for federal office make their "best effort" to obtain full information on employers and occupations of their contributors, and to report this information on their campaign filings for all contributors giving $200 or more. In 1993 the FEC finally served notice that it will begin to enforce the rule, which has long been ignored by some candidates since penalties have rarely been imposed for non-compliance. Most candidates are conscientious and do list the information for the great majority of their contributors. A few do not. A list of the leading offenders in the 1992 election can be found on page 35.

- **Incomplete information.** Sometimes the information listed by candidates is so generic that it is impossible to trace the economic interest of the contributor. "Businessman" or "Executive" is one example. "Self-employed" is another. Another commonly used euphemism is to identify contributors only by the term "consultant." The Center's analysis has found that many of these "consultants" — particular those from the Washington, DC area — turn out to be lobbyists.

- **Unemployed spouses and children.** If one were to take at face value the reports filed by candidates, one might come to the conclusion that the single most powerful constituency in America today is that of "homemakers" and "housewives." According to the reports filed by federal candidates for Congress in the 1992 elections, "housewives, homemakers, home managers, *executive* home managers" and various other variations on the theme contributed some $22.4 million — higher than any other listed occupation. In reality, the money that supplied these donations came overwhelmingly not from the "homemaker" but from her (or his) spouse. The same can be said of contributors identified as "students." In the research that went into this book, the Center took great pains to try to identify the spouses (or parents) of unemployed contributors. In many cases this was possible by comparing addresses, dates of contributions, etc. Where the connection with the income-earner was found, the contribution was classified as having the same economic interest as that of the person earning the family income.

Independent Expenditures

Direct contributions to candidates are not the only outlet for political action committees wishing to influence elections. "Independent expenditures" — funds spent independently by PACs to either support or oppose a candidate — offer another potentially powerful option. Unlike regular PAC gifts to campaigns, which cannot exceed $10,000 for the typical election cycle, independent expenditures can total any amount at all. They may directly attack or support a candidate by name, but the expenditures (or the advertising they support) cannot be made in conjunction or coordination with the campaign or staff of any candidate. In all, some 222 PACs and individuals spent more than $11.1 million on independent expenditures during the 1992 elections. About $4.4 million of that was directed at the presidential race, the rest was spent trying to influence congressional campaigns.

A total of 72 groups spent $10,000 or more on independent campaigns. Of those, 17 ran campaigns exceeding $100,000. The chart below lists the chief contributors of independent expenditures in 1992 and the top beneficiaries and targets of their funds.

Top PACs Making Independent Expenditures in 1992

PAC Name	Total	Top Beneficiaries/Targets	Amount	For/Agn	Office
Presidential Victory Committee	$2,057,757	George Bush	$2,057,757	For	Pres
National Right to Life PAC	$1,614,440	George Bush	$795,290	For	Pres
		Mike DeWine (R-Ohio)	$27,644	For	Senate
		Don Davis (R-NC)	$27,419	For	House
American Medical Assn	$1,024,210	Vic Fazio (D-Calif)	$255,085	For	House
		Bob Packwood (R-Ore)	$227,808	For	Senate
		Scott McInnis (R-Colo)	$184,910	For	House
		Michael A. Andrews (D-Texas)	$118,985	For	House
		Gary Franks (R-Conn)	$81,254	For	House
		Scott L. Klug (R-Wis)	$80,968	For	House
		Tony Meeker (R-Ore)	$75,200	For	House
National Assn of Realtors	$999,016	Les AuCoin (D-Ore)	$329,289	For	Senate
		Rod Chandler (R-Wash)	$169,950	For	Senate
		E. Clay Shaw Jr. (R-Fla)	$125,209	For	House
		Beryl Anthony Jr (D-Ark)	$100,000	For	House
		Ben Nighthorse Campbell (D-Colo)	$98,953	For	Senate
		Newt Gingrich (R-Ga)	$60,000	For	House
		Tom McMillen (D-Md)	$49,300	For	House
		Ronald K. Machtley (R-RI)	$45,100	For	House
National Rifle Assn	$957,666	Gene Green (D-Texas)	$139,468	For	House
		Mike Synar (D-Okla)	$137,574	Against	House
		Beryl Anthony Jr (D-Ark)	$86,412	Against	House
		W.A. Drew Edmondson (D-Okla)	$76,930	For	House
		Paul Coverdell (R-Ga)	$61,844	For	Senate
		Tom Coleman (R-Ga)	$61,209	Against	House
		Dan Glickman (D-Kan)	$52,080	Against	House
		Harris Wofford (D-Pa)	$40,292	Against	Senate
		Bill McCuen (D-Ark)	$30,137	For	House
		Pat Danner (D-Mo)	$25,890	For	House
National Abortion Rights Action League	$718,756	Russell Feingold (D-Wis)	$148,426	For	Senate
		Steven D. Pierce (R-Mass)	$144,091	Against	House
		Ben Nighthorse Campbell (D-Colo)	$137,487	For	
		Pat Williams (D-Mont)	$77,885	For	House
		Judith M. Ryan (R-Calif)	$59,827	For	House
		Robert Abrams (D-NY)	$47,930	For	Senate
		Alfonse M. D'Amato (R-NY)	$44,583	Against	Senate
		Dick Thornburgh (R-Pa)	$30,869	Against	Senate
Freedom Leadership PAC	$191,584	Bill Clinton	$190,597	Against	Pres

"Soft Money" — The Sky's the Limit

In the eyes of many observers — and many political practitioners who make use of it — the principal loophole in the federal campaign spending law is something that has come to be called "soft money." In the broadest sense, soft money encompasses any contributions not regulated by federal election laws. The exemption was made to encourage "party-building" activities which benefit the political parties in general, but not specific candidates. In reality, though, the loophole has emerged as the parties' primary means of raising tens of millions of dollars from wealthy contributors during the fall presidential campaigns, when direct contributions to candidates are prohibited. They are also used to support congressional candidates in key battleground states during off-year elections.

Technically, soft money contributions are supposed to be used only for state and local political activities — such as voter registration, get-out-the-vote drives and bumper stickers — and for such generic party-building activities as TV ads supporting the Democratic and Republican platforms, but not naming specific candidates. Typically, however, the funds pay for much more — including office overhead, the purchase of expensive computer equipment, and other behind-the-scenes expenses — thus freeing up other contributions to the party to be used directly to support candidates.

During the 1992 presidential campaign, the Democratic and Republican parties raised an estimated $34 million and $48 million respectively in soft money contributions on the national level alone. The exact figures will never be known (except to the parties), however, because much of the soft money was contributed directly to state and local political committees. Under new rules which took effect Jan. 1, 1991, soft money contributions to the national parties must now be reported to the Federal Election Commission. Even so, soft money can still be given with virtually no strings attached. This offers four main benefits to soft money contributors and recipients:

- **Soft money is not subject to any contribution limits.** Contributions to candidates or federal party committees are subject to specific limits (outlined in the chart on page 11). Soft money contributions can be made for any amount at all. The list on the facing page shows just how high the biggest contributions were in the 1991-92 election cycle.

- **Soft money contributions can be made by anyone — including groups prohibited from making contributions to federal candidates or parties.** In federal campaigns, corporations and labor unions are explicitly prohibited from making direct contributions to federal candidates, federal parties, or federal PACs. Their soft money contributions are subject only to the restrictions passed by the legislatures in the individual states where the contributions are made. Many states currently allow corporate and labor union contributions.

- **Soft money offers an extra means of political giving for individuals who've already given the maximum to candidates and federal parties.** Under the federal election laws, individual contributors are limited to an annual maximum of $25,000 in contributions to all candidates, PACs and national parties. Once they've "maxed out" they can give no more — except in soft money. Using this device, wealthy contributors, often with the encouragement of the national parties, have been able to give substantially more than the nominal limit.

- **Soft money offers a way for corporations, unions and wealthy contributors to directly support presidential candidates in the fall elections.** Since 1974, when Congress authorized the $1 checkoff on federal income tax returns (Since raised to $3), presidential elections have been publicly financed. While presidential candidates can (and do) raise millions during the primary election battles for the nomination, once the parties have officially nominated their candidate at their party conventions, no more private contributions are allowed. Because of the soft money loophole, however, the period during the fall campaign has turned into the most intensive period of political fundraising in American politics. In 1988 the Republicans even organized an exclusive club — called "Team 100" — made up of soft money contributors who gave $100,000 or more. Several Team 100 members were later appointed ambassadors to foreign nations after the Bush administration took office. In 1992, Team 100 was back, giving more than ever. Not to be outdone, the Democrats created a new circle of elite givers called the "Managing Trustees." Admission to this blue-chip group requires giving or raising at least $200,000 in soft money.

Top Soft Money Contributors in 1991-92

Contributor	Amount	To Repubs	To Dems	Industry
Archer-Daniels-Midland*	$1,374,500	$1,107,000	$267,500	Agricultural Svcs & Prod/Transport
RJR Nabisco*	$875,305	$529,305	$346,000	Tobacco/Food Products
Atlantic Richfield Co*	$857,958	$579,641	$278,317	Oil & Gas/Chemicals/Coal
Philip Morris*	$816,580	$589,080	$227,500	Tobacco/Beer
Joseph E Seagram & Sons*	$731,637	$524,727	$206,910	Beer, Wine & Liquor
American Financial Corp	$715,000	$715,000	$0	Insurance
US Tobacco	$652,768	$525,004	$127,764	Tobacco
International Marketing Bureau	$633,770	$633,770	$0	Business Services
Merrill Lynch*	$594,900	$485,100	$109,800	Securities & Investment
New Jersey Gala '92	$566,286	$0	$566,286	Democratic/Liberal
National Education Assn	$423,752	$7,750	$416,002	Public Sector Unions
United Steelworkers*	$404,876	$0	$404,876	Bldg Trades/Industrial Unions
Time Warner*	$398,573	$100,240	$298,333	TV & Movies/Publishing
Chevron Corp	$361,760	$256,372	$105,388	Oil & Gas
Occidental Petroleum	$336,030	$224,080	$111,950	Oil & Gas/Chemicals
Sony Corp of America	$332,650	$100,000	$232,650	TV & Movies/Electronics
American Intertrade Group*	$322,800	$322,800	$0	Business Services
Tobacco Institute	$317,202	$164,927	$152,275	Tobacco
Alida Rockefeller Messinger	$300,650	$0	$300,650	Philanthropist
Goldman, Sachs & Co*	$293,520	$248,520	$45,000	Securities & Investment
Limited Inc	$288,600	$247,100	$41,500	Retail Sales
Revlon Group Inc	$286,700	$140,000	$146,700	Cosmetics
Anheuser-Busch*	$279,280	$108,080	$171,200	Beer, Wine & Liquor
Lawrence Kadish	$276,200	$276,200	$0	Real Estate
Communications Workers of America	$275,680	$0	$275,680	Bldg Trades/Industrial Unions
Swanee Hunt	$262,200	$0	$262,200	Philanthropist
Bechtel Group*	$259,797	$124,347	$135,450	General Contractors
MCA Inc*	$257,730	$20,000	$237,730	TV & Movie Prod/Distribution
American Fedn of State/County/Munic Employees*	$256,574	$0	$256,574	Public Sector Unions
United States Surgical Corp	$255,200	$232,400	$22,800	Pharmaceuticals/Health Prod
Bell Atlantic*	$252,325	$159,700	$92,625	Telephone Utilities
International Assn of Firefighters	$250,869	$10,450	$240,419	Public Sector Unions
Brown-Foreman Corp*	$250,449	$250,449	$0	Beer, Wine & Liquor
Henley Group Inc*	$250,000	$200,000	$50,000	Pharmaceuticals/Health Prod
Forstmann, Little & Co*	$245,000	$245,000	$0	Securities & Investment
Kohlberg, Kravis & Roberts*	$240,000	$200,000	$40,000	Securities & Investment
Morgan Stanley & Co*	$238,827	$130,977	$107,850	Securities & Investment
United Auto Workers	$236,965	$0	$236,965	Bldg Trades/Industrial Unions
Lazard Freres & Co*	$236,500	$20,000	$216,500	Securities & Investment
Sheet Metal Workers Union*	$234,500	$0	$234,500	Bldg Trades/Industrial Unions
Thomas J. Watson	$234,000	$84,000	$150,000	Computer Equipment & Svcs
Peter B. Lewis	$231,300	$0	$231,300	Insurance
Connell Co	$225,100	$0	$225,100	Crop Prod & Basic Processing
Pacific Telesis Group	$223,927	$142,627	$81,300	Telephone Utilities
Mesa Limited Partnership	$221,100	$219,600	$1,500	Oil & Gas
Coca-Cola Co*	$218,830	$160,127	$58,703	Food & Beverage
Waste Management Inc*	$213,057	$155,327	$57,730	Waste Management
Merle C. Chambers	$210,200	$0	$210,200	Oil & Gas
Agenda for the 90's	$210,000	$0	$210,000	Democratic/Liberal
Peter & Eileen Norton	$210,000	$0	$210,000	Computer Software

* Total came from more than one affiliate or subsidiary.

The above list includes contributions made to the Democratic and Republican National Committees, as well as the National Republican Senatorial Committee, the Democratic Senatorial Campaign Committee, the National Republican Congressional Committee, the Democratic Congressional Campaign Committee, the President's Dinner Committee and the Democratic Congressional Dinner Committee.

The Role of PACs

Political action committees were born in the 1940s out of a perceived political necessity. When labor unions were prohibited from spending union treasury funds to contribute to federal candidates, they invented the idea of pooling donations from their members and presenting *that* money to the candidates instead. The idea appealed not only to labor unions, but to business and ideological groups as well, though the lack of a formal federal sanction for PACs kept many groups from setting up their own committees. When Congress passed the 1974 amendments to the Federal Election Campaign Act, officially sanctioning the concept of "political committees," the great PAC rush began. In recent years, the number of political action committees has stabilized, and even begun to decline. Total PAC dollars, however, continue to rise — particularly to House and Senate incumbents.

More than 4,700 political action committees were officially registered at the close of the 1992 election year. Of those, just over 3,100 actually contributed funds to federal candidates. Many of those PACs were small-scale operations, sponsored by small businesses, political clubs, or labor union locals, and contributed only to candidates in their own state or region. Only one out of four of the registered PACs gave $20,000 or more to federal candidates, but those that did accounted for over 94 percent of all PAC giving. The chart below shows the relative distribution of small, medium and large PACs, and their respective spending power in the 1992 elections.

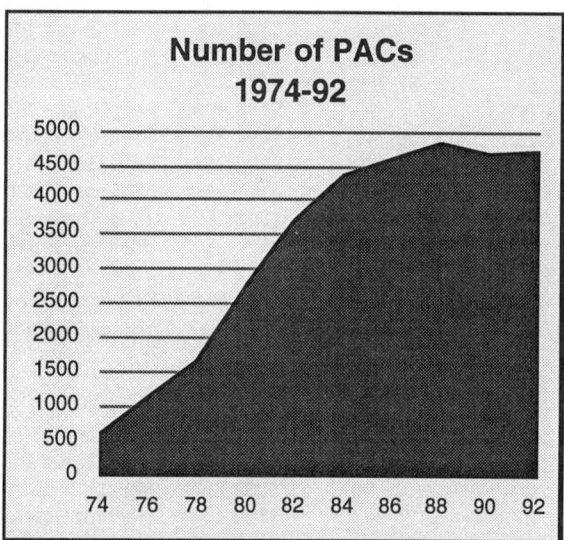

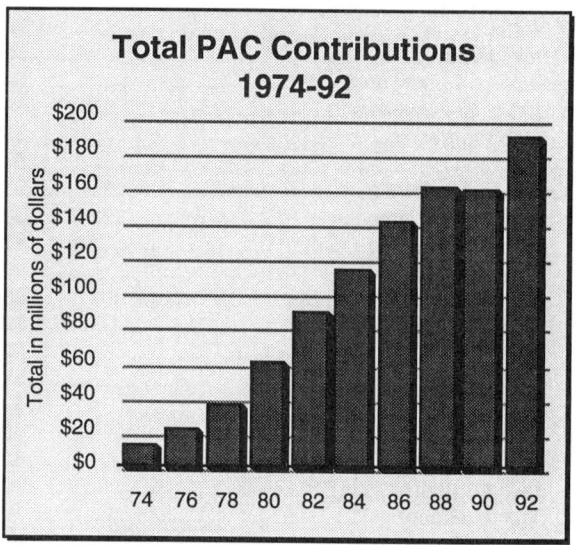

Biggest PACs Deliver the Biggest Punch

This many PACs...	Gave this much money...	for this total impact...
1637	$0	
1496	Less than $10,000	
407	$10,000-$19,999	
499	$20,000-$49,999	
294	$50,000-$99,999	
398	$100,000 or more	

As is evident from this chart, the real power of PACs lies not in their numbers, but in the dollars they can deliver. In 1992, as in every year since PACs emerged as an important force in federal elections, a comparatively small number of large PACs delivered the biggest share of the money. Less than one-tenth of the total PAC community provided nearly three-fourths of all the dollars in the 1991-92 election cycle. On the other side of the spectrum, over 1,600 PACs — more than a third of all registered political action committees — made no contributions at all to congressional candidates.

With Outstretched Hands...

The financial clout of PACs is not something that has been forced upon members of Congress over their objections. Modern campaign techniques, centered around 30-second TV spots and highly targeted direct mail appeals, have prompted many incumbents to hire campaign consultants, pollsters, media advisors, fund-raisers and a retinue of specialists who are the behind-the-scenes operatives of today's high-tech campaigns. The pressures of raising the money it takes to pay for them all have forced nearly every incumbent to spend an increasing amount of time appealing to PACs and other large contributors for funds. Because of their higher contribution limits ($5,000 per election, versus $1,000 per election for individuals), PACs offer the most convenient means of raising large sums of campaign cash quickly.

In contrast to the pro-forma reelection races that many incumbents have enjoyed in recent years, the 1992 elections were worrisome for nearly every member of Congress. Those shown in the tables below relied the most heavily on PACs to provide the funds that helped them weather the political storm. (Dan Coats, the Senate leader, ran in both 1990 and 1992).

Top Recipients of PAC Contributions

House Members (1991-92)

Name	PAC Rcpts	Total Rcpts
Richard A. Gephardt (D-Mo)	$1,240,597	$3,238,479
Vic Fazio (D-Calif)	$1,147,938	$1,993,452
Dan Rostenkowski (D-Ill)	$961,937	$1,587,234
David E. Bonior (D-Mich)	$934,589	$1,295,553
John D. Dingell (D-Mich)	$767,931	$1,112,141
Newt Gingrich (R-Ga)	$756,347	$2,507,668
Steny H. Hoyer (D-Md)	$705,642	$1,304,867
Martin Frost (D-Texas)	$666,804	$1,241,725
Al Swift (D-Wash)	$649,844	$914,905
Charles Wilson (D-Texas)	$638,825	$1,188,912

Senate Members (1987-92)

Name	PAC Rcpts	Total Rcpts
Daniel R. Coats (R-Ind)	$2,349,342	$7,727,256
Lloyd Bentsen (D-Texas)	$2,349,054	$9,614,793
Arlen Specter (R-Pa)	$2,011,791	$10,463,911
Frank R. Lautenberg (D-NJ)	$1,884,342	$9,033,987
Phil Gramm (R-Texas)	$1,848,480	$18,457,261
Tom Harkin (D-Iowa)	$1,834,857	$5,867,588
Tom Daschle (D-SD)	$1,832,046	$4,122,119
Dave Durenberger (R-Minn)	$1,723,548	$6,388,791
Christopher S. Bond (R-Mo)	$1,717,017	$5,087,184
Richard C. Shelby (D-Ala)	$1,690,444	$3,778,582

...And 26 Members Who "Just Said No" to PACs

In an era when more and more voters are equating PAC contributions with "special interests," a growing number of House and Senate candidates are making an issue of running without the support of PACs. Twelve House incumbents turned down PAC contributions in the 1992 elections. So did nine newly-elected members. In the Senate, four incumbents have either refused PAC funds in the past or vowed not to accept any in the future. Here's the list of those who took the No-PAC Pledge.

1992 House Incumbents Who Took No PAC Funds

Name	Party	District	'92 Vote Pct
Bill Archer	Rep	Texas 7	100.0%
Anthony C. Beilenson	Dem	Calif 24	55.5%
Jim Cooper	Dem	Tenn 5	64.1%
Philip M. Crane	Rep	Ill 8	55.7%
Bill Goodling	Rep	Pa 19	45.3%
Bill Gradison	Rep	Ohio 2	70.1%
Andrew Jacobs Jr.	Dem	Ind 10	64.0%
Jim Leach	Rep	Iowa 1	68.1%
Edward J. Markey	Dem	Mass 7	62.1%
Romano L. Mazzoli	Dem	Ky 3	52.7%
William H. Natcher	Dem	Ky 2	61.4%
Glenn Poshard	Dem	Ill 19	69.1%
Ralph Regula	Rep	Ohio 16	63.7%
Mike Synar	Dem	Okla 2	55.5%

Senate Incumbents Elected Without PAC Funds

Name	Party	State
David Boren	Dem	Okla
Herb Kohl	Dem	Wis
John Kerry	Dem	Mass

1992 House Freshmen Who Took No PAC Funds

Name	Party	District	'92 Vote Pct
Scotty Baesler	Dem	Ky 6	60.7%
Terry Everett	Rep	Ala 2	49.5%
Peter Hoekstra	Rep	Mich 2	63.0%
Martin R. Hoke	Rep	Ohio 10	56.8%
Steve Horn	Rep	Calif 38	48.6%
Michael Huffington	Rep	Calif 22	52.5%
Martin T. Meehan	Dem	Mass 5	52.2%
Nick Smith	Rep	Mich 7	87.6%
Peter Torkildsen	Rep	Mass 6	54.8%

As the anti-PAC sentiment grows around the country, other members are likely to join the list. One prominent incumbent who announced early he would take no PAC funds in his 1994 reelection bid was Massachusetts Democrat Ted Kennedy. At least one of the candidates, however, had second thoughts. Freshman Republican Congressman Terry Everett of Alabama took no PAC funds until he was elected, but accepted them in 1993 after he took office.

The Patterns in PAC Contributions

Pragmatism — not partisanship and not political philosophy — appears to be the guiding principle behind many PAC contributions to congressional candidates, at least in the world of business PACs. Of the nearly 1,600 PACs that gave $10,000 or more in the 1992 elections, 92 percent gave to members of both parties. About one-third of those top-spending PACs — nearly all of them within the business community — split their dollars fairly evenly between Democrats and Republicans, giving no more than 60 percent of their money to either side. Ideological and labor PACs were far more likely to concentrate their funds with candidates of a single political party, as seen in the chart below.

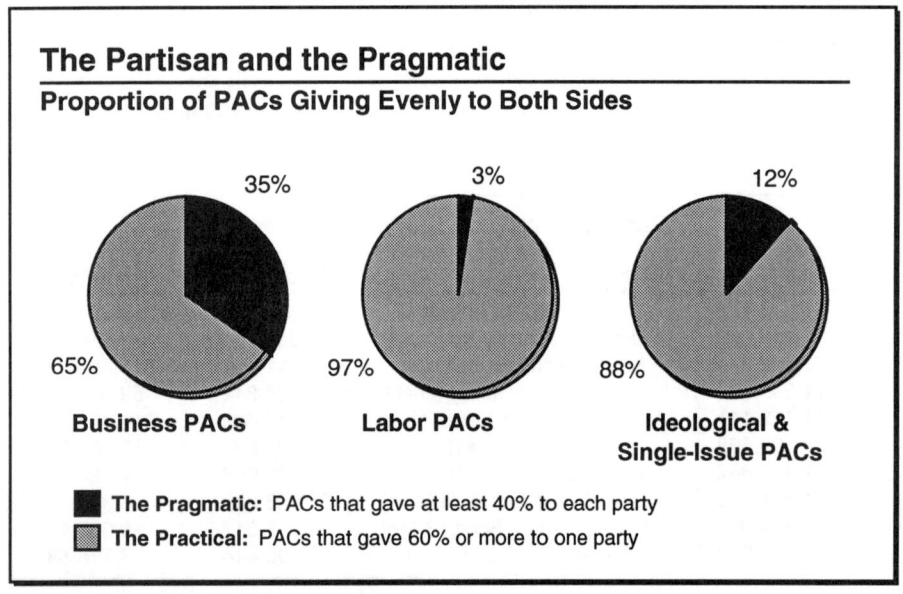

The Big Three Sectors:
Business, Labor & Ideological/Single-Issue

While it is certainly possible to learn something about PAC behavior by looking at the overall patterns of PACs, it can be far more revealing to examine the many different segments of the PAC community one by one. It quickly becomes apparent that different groups of PACs behave differently. Labor and ideological PACs, for instance, distribute their money in a quite a different pattern from business PACs — as the charts on this page show.

Business PACs gave almost exactly the same amount to Democrats as Republicans. Ideological PACs favored Democrats two-to-one. And labor PACs, long the stalwarts of the Democratic Party, favored the party's candidates by a ratio of 16-to-one when handing out their contributions.

The overwhelming proportion of labor contributions to Democratic candidates tips the scale in favor of that party in overall PAC contributions, even though business PACs as a group gave nearly three times as much as labor PACs, and nearly twice as much as labor and ideological PACs combined. (See the chart on the facing page.)

Within these three main categories of PACs many other patterns can be found. The rest of the book explores their differences and similarities in detail.

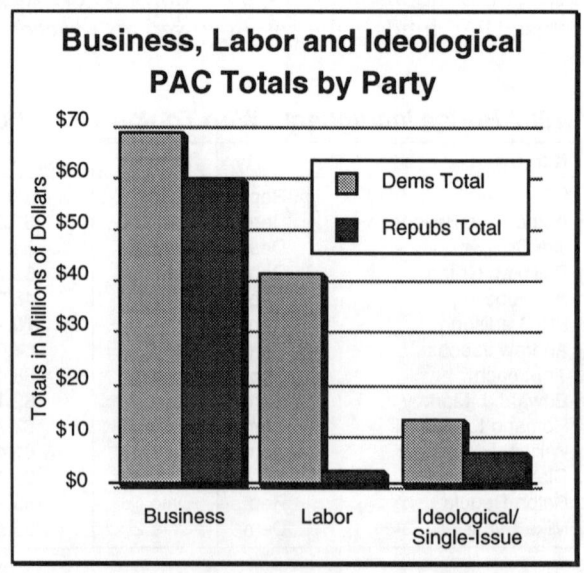

The World of PACs from Three Different Angles

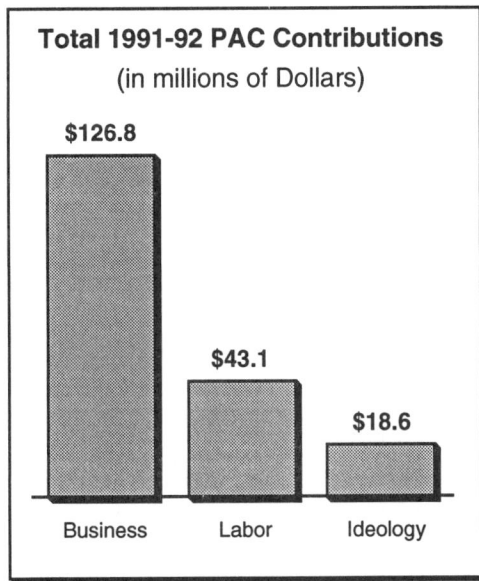

The dollar power of business PACs can be clearly seen in the chart at left. With nearly $127 million in contributions to federal candidates in the 1992 election cycle, PACs representing every industry from car dealers to morticians sought to help their political friends and win their favor. Compared to labor and ideological/single-issue PACs, their dollar power was overwhelming.

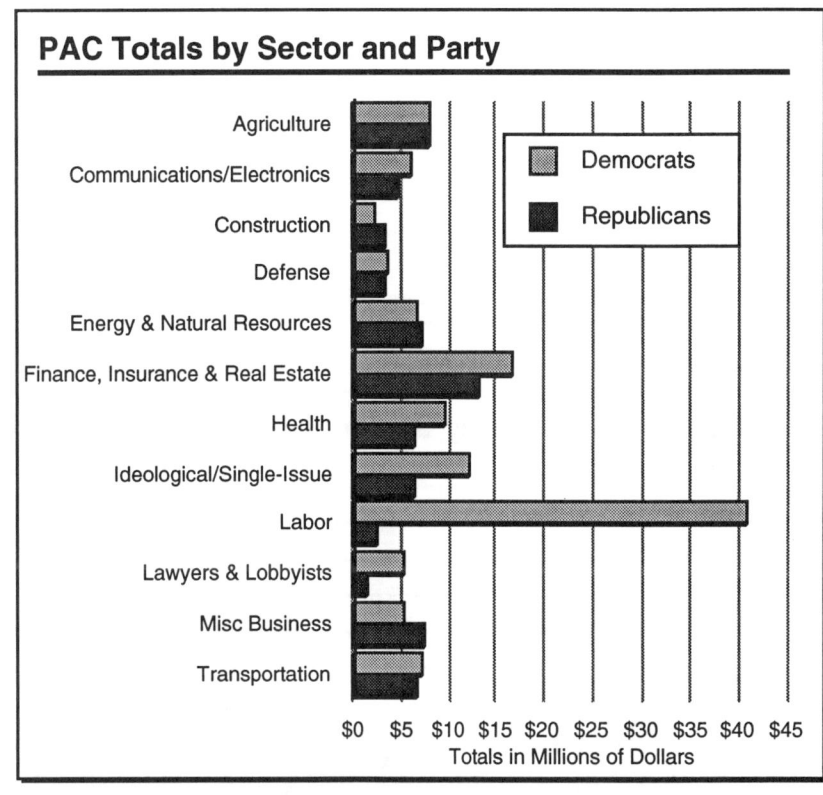

A different story emerges when you turn the chart on its ear and break apart the business PACs into their individual sectors. No business sector comes close to offering either party the dollars that labor PACs produce for Democrats. While business PACs were giving relatively equal amounts to members of both parties, labor put 94 percent of its PAC dollars into Democratic campaigns. Even ideological and single-issue PACs rank high compared with the many diverse components of business PACs.

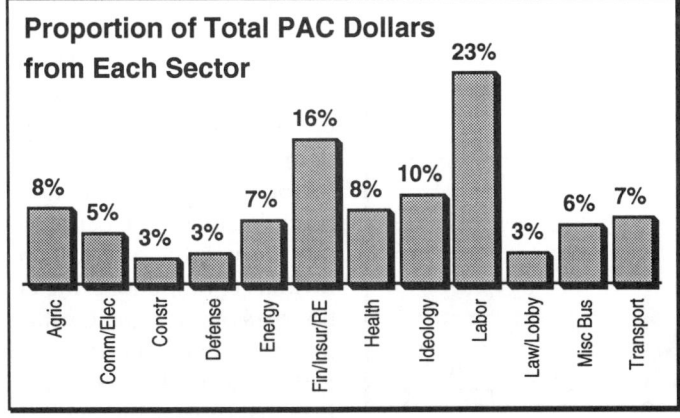

After labor, the financial sector was the biggest PAC contributor to congressional campaigns, supplying 16 percent of all PAC dollars given in the 1992 elections. Banks, investment firms, insurance companies and real estate agents and developers combined to make it the biggest segment by far within the community of business PACs. What the charts on these pages don't show (but what can be seen in the pages that follow) is that PACs are only one source of campaign cash for members of Congress. When large individual contributions are added in, the picture changes again. Financial interests move to the top, lawyers rise to financial prominence from almost nowhere, and the dollars from organized labor are buried under an avalanche of dollars from business interests.

PACs and Individual Contributions Compared

The charts below illustrate the similarities and contrasts in spending patterns between individual contributors and PACs. Two sectors in particular are strikingly different — organized labor and lawyers and lobbyists. Nearly all the Labor dollars are delivered through political action committees. Looking only at PAC contributions therefore strongly overstates the political punch of labor unions. The charts at the bottom of the page underline this even more.

Lawyers and lobbyists, on the other hand, are dramatically undercounted when looking only at PACs. Some 86 percent of the legal community's contributions come from individuals, not PACs.

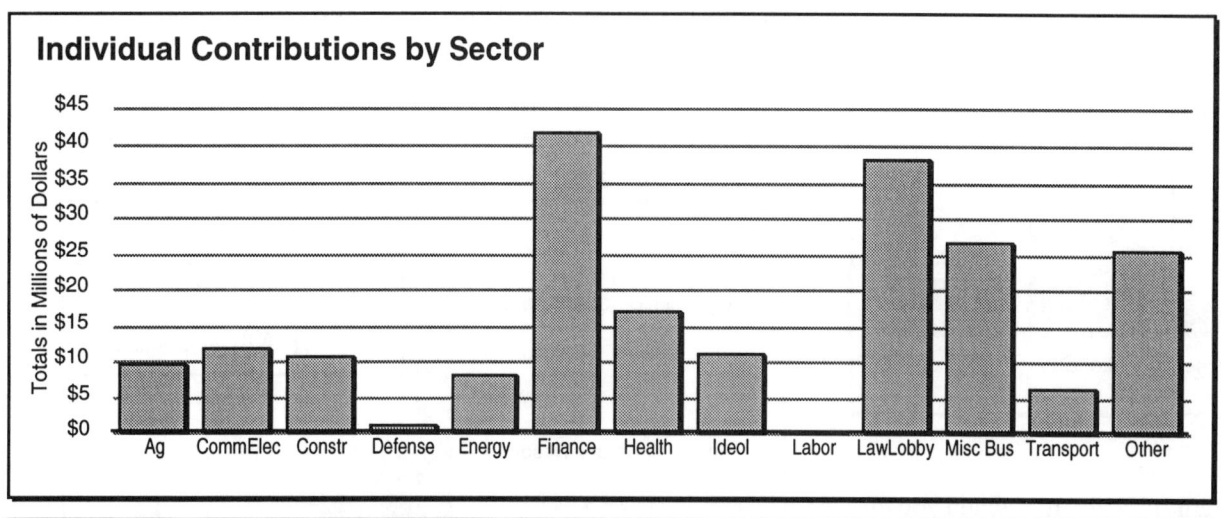

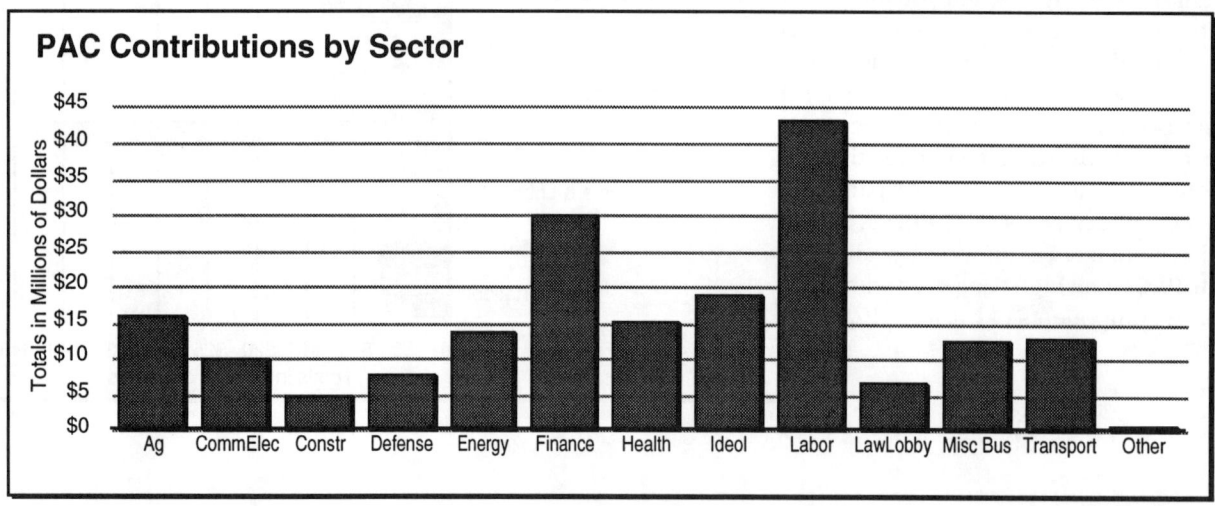

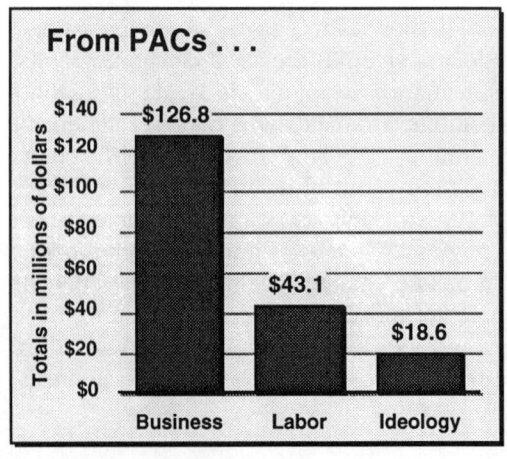

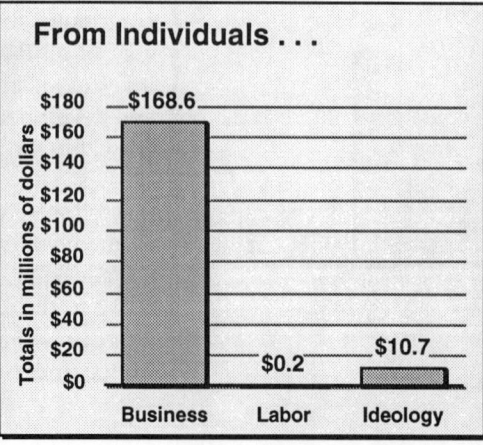

Comparing the individual dollars versus PAC dollars in the three large sectors of business, labor and ideological groups, shows the overall dominance of the business sector. Among PAC contributions, business outspends labor about three-to-one. In individual contributions, the ratio soars out of sight. Overall, business contributors gave $295 million in 1991-92. Organized labor gave $43 million. Ideological groups' combined total was $29 million.

Where the Individual Dollars* Came From: Top Metro Areas

Totals in Millions of Dollars

New York	$23.8
Los Angeles	$21.9
Washington	$17.4
Chicago	$8.8
Boston	$8.3
Philadelphia	$8.1
San Francisco	$7.5
Houston	$5.4
Atlanta	$4.8
Nassau County, NY	$4.6
Dallas	$4.2
Anaheim	$4.1
Miami	$3.7
St. Louis	$3.5
Bridgeport/Fairfield, Conn	$3.5
Newark, NJ	$3.3
San Diego	$3.2
Pittsburgh	$3.1
Cleveland	$3.0
Detroit	$3.0

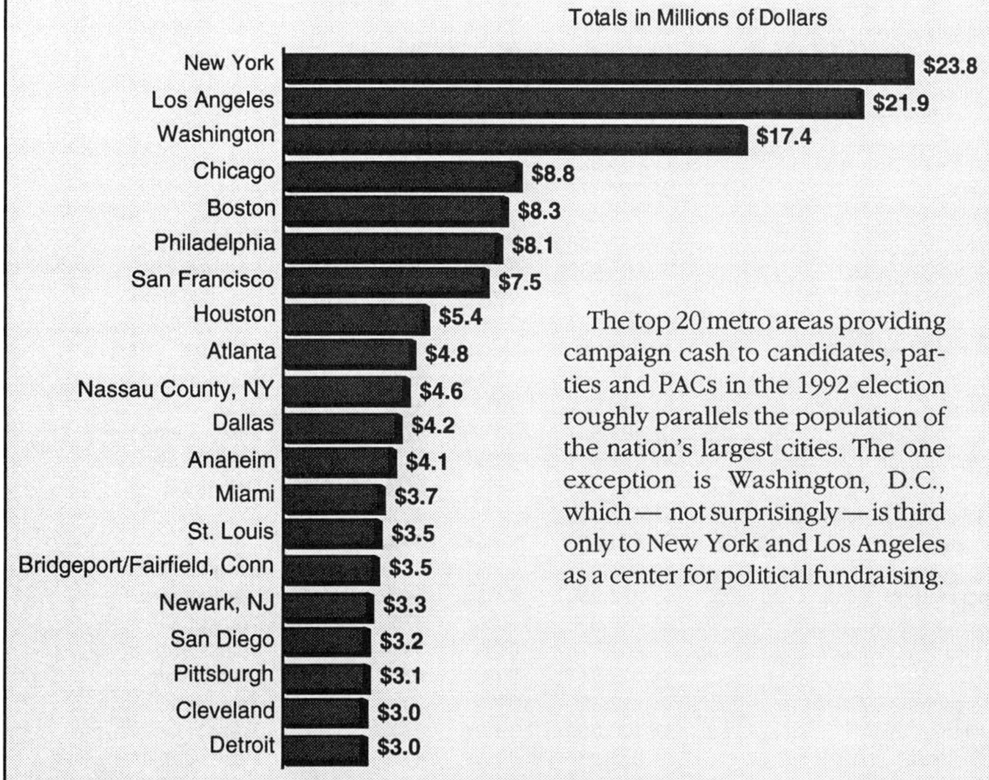

The top 20 metro areas providing campaign cash to candidates, parties and PACs in the 1992 election roughly parallels the population of the nation's largest cities. The one exception is Washington, D.C., which — not surprisingly — is third only to New York and Los Angeles as a center for political fundraising.

* Contributions of $200 and above

Where the PAC Dollars Came From: Top Metro Areas

Totals in Millions of Dollars

Washington	$91.4
New York	$12.9
Chicago	$9.6
San Francisco	$4.9
Los Angeles	$4.5
Detroit	$3.8
Bridgeport/Fairfield, Conn	$2.9
Houston	$2.9
Cleveland	$2.8
Pittsburgh	$2.5
St. Louis	$2.3
Dallas	$2.2
Atlanta	$1.8
Philadelphia	$1.8
Newark, NJ	$1.6
Birmingham, Ala	$1.6
Kansas City	$1.5
Boston	$1.5
Minneapolis	$1.4
Greensboro, NC	$1.2

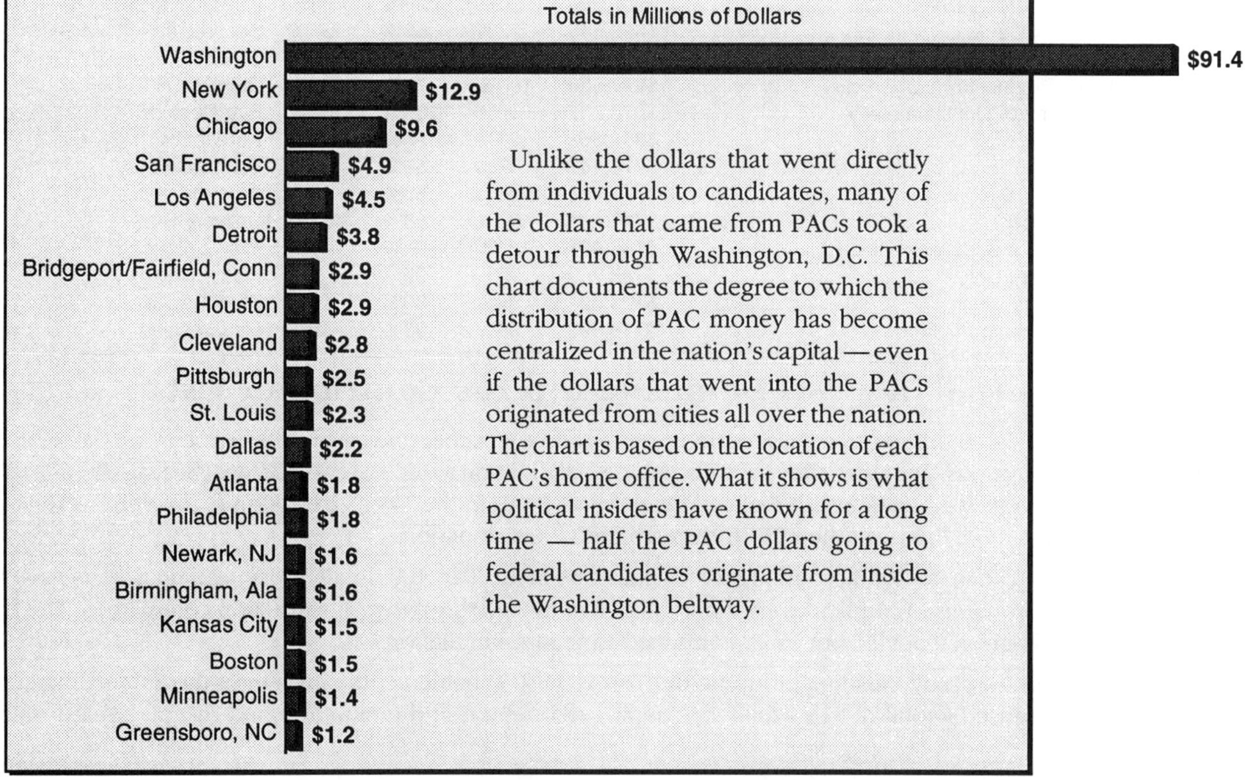

Unlike the dollars that went directly from individuals to candidates, many of the dollars that came from PACs took a detour through Washington, D.C. This chart documents the degree to which the distribution of PAC money has become centralized in the nation's capital — even if the dollars that went into the PACs originated from cities all over the nation. The chart is based on the location of each PAC's home office. What it shows is what political insiders have known for a long time — half the PAC dollars going to federal candidates originate from inside the Washington beltway.

Serious Money: The Top 100 Contributors

Rank	Contributor	Total	PAC Pct	Dem Pct	Rep Pct	Principal Category
1	American Medical Assn*	$3,245,544	99%+	49%	51%	Doctors
2	National Assn of Realtors	$2,954,973	99%+	55%	45%	Real Estate
3	Teamsters Union*	$2,532,956	99%+	94%	5%	Transpt Unions
4	Assn of Trial Lawyers of America	$2,361,135	100%	92%	8%	Trial Lawyers
5	National Education Assn*	$2,360,017	99%+	95%	3%	Teachers
6	United Auto Workers*	$2,251,489	99%+	98%	1%	Manuf Unions
7	American Fedn of St/Cnty/Munic Employees*	$1,954,063	99%+	97%	2%	Govt Unions
8	National Auto Dealers Assn	$1,784,375	100%	39%	61%	Auto Dealers
9	National Rifle Assn	$1,736,446	99%+	36%	63%	Pro-Guns
10	American Bankers Assn*	$1,692,508	99%+	50%	49%	Comml Banks
11	National Assn of Letter Carriers*	$1,661,880	100%	90%	10%	Postal Workers
12	Machinists/Aerospace Workers Union*	$1,641,746	99%+	97%	1%	Indust Unions
13	Marine Engineers Union*	$1,605,574	99%+	73%	27%	Transpt Unions
14	Intl Brotherhood of Electrical Workers*	$1,575,999	99%+	96%	3%	Electrical Wrkrs
15	American Institute of CPA's	$1,544,701	99%+	56%	44%	Accountants
16	Carpenters & Joiners Union*	$1,493,572	98%	94%	5%	Bldg Trades
17	Food & Commercial Workers Union	$1,488,961	100%	97%	2%	Misc Unions
18	Laborers Union*	$1,472,681	99%+	94%	5%	Bldg Trades
19	United Parcel Service	$1,472,357	99%	54%	46%	Delivery Svcs
20	National Assn of Retired Federal Employees	$1,437,250	100%	80%	19%	Govt Unions
21	American Dental Assn*	$1,434,408	99%+	60%	40%	Dentists
22	AT&T*	$1,397,883	93%	61%	39%	Long Distance
23	National Assn of Life Underwriters	$1,373,955	99%+	54%	46%	Life Insurance
24	Air Line Pilots Assn	$1,279,093	100%	87%	13%	Transpt Unions
25	United Steelworkers	$1,267,774	99%	99%	1%	Indust Unions
26	AFL-CIO*	$1,118,214	99%+	97%	2%	Misc Unions
27	American Federation of Teachers	$1,112,350	100%	99%	2%	Teachers
28	United Transportation Union	$1,100,050	99%+	97%	3%	Transpt Unions
29	National Assn of Home Builders*	$1,074,827	99%+	44%	56%	Resid Constr
30	Communications Workers of America*	$1,012,468	99%+	98%	1%	Indust Unions
31	RJR Nabisco*	$1,004,848	95%	55%	45%	Tobacco/Food
32	Emily's List	$999,755	37%	98%	0%	Women's Issues
33	Plumbers/Pipefitters Union*	$992,638	99%+	95%	4%	Bldg Trades
34	National Beer Wholesalers Assn	$977,081	100%	38%	62%	Beer Distrib
35	Seafarers International Union*	$970,476	99%+	92%	8%	Transpt Unions
36	BellSouth Corp*	$963,353	92%	59%	41%	Phone Utilities
37	National Cmte to Preserve Social Security	$941,650	99%+	88%	12%	Sr Citizens
38	American Postal Workers Union*	$900,390	100%	96%	3%	Postal Workers
39	Goldman, Sachs & Co	$898,545	22%	67%	33%	Securities
40	American Express*	$881,820	38%	69%	30%	Stocks/Credit
41	Associated Milk Producers	$877,550	100%	79%	21%	Dairy
42	American Academy of Ophthalmology	$870,227	99%+	63%	37%	Eye Doctors
43	General Electric*	$851,852	84%	58%	42%	Aerospace
44	Philip Morris*	$775,147	87%	59%	41%	Tobacco/Food
45	General Motors*	$771,474	88%	53%	46%	Auto Manuf
46	Federal Express Corp	$747,445	99%+	68%	32%	Delivery Svcs
47	Service Employees International Union	$745,931	99%+	98%	1%	Misc Unions
48	Sheet Metal Workers Union*	$745,749	99%+	95%	3%	Indust Unions
49	Operating Engineers Union*	$723,524	98%	89%	11%	Bldg Trades
50	Human Rights Campaign Fund	$718,590	99%+	92%	6%	Gay/Lesbian

Labor PACs, Financial Interests Dominate Top 100 Contributor List

These 100 corporations, labor unions, trade associations, professional societies and assorted interest groups were the top contributors in the 1992 elections. Together, they gave a combined $95 million to federal candidates. The total includes some $89 million in PAC contributions — nearly half the total given by all PACs in the 1991-92 election cycle. Only seven of the top 100 contributors gave more than half their funds through individual donations.

Labor unions were the leading sector, accounting for 29 positions in the Top 100. In all, those leading unions gave over $36 million in direct contributions to candidates — almost all of it delivered through political action committees. The figure is particularly remarkable given that all labor PACs combined gave just $43 million.

Financial interests were the second leading group on the Top 100 list. Nineteen companies from the Finance, Insurance & Real Estate sector dispensed a total of $13.4 million. Topping that sector, and ranking second overall behind only the

Rank	Contributor	Total	PAC Pct	Dem Pct	Rep Pct	Principal Category
51	Union Pacific Corp*	$713,390	96%	33%	67%	Railroads
52	National PAC	$684,000	100%	65%	35%	Pro-Israel
53	Waste Management Inc*	$683,558	78%	62%	38%	Waste Mgmt
54	Associated General Contractors*	$677,899	99%	24%	76%	Genl Contract
55	American Chiropractic Assn*	$658,596	99%+	73%	27%	Chiropractors
56	National Cmte for an Effective Congress	$651,250	99%+	100%	0%	Dem/Liberal
57	National Cable Television Assn	$644,249	99%	54%	46%	Cable TV
58	Prudential Insurance*	$640,040	63%	59%	41%	Insurance
59	US Tobacco*	$636,120	69%	34%	66%	Tobacco
60	GTE Corp*	$631,869	97%	52%	48%	Phone Utilities
61	Merrill Lynch*	$627,864	30%	51%	48%	Securities
62	ACRE (Action Cmte for Rural Electric)*	$627,155	100%	74%	26%	Rural Electric
63	American Hospital Assn*	$617,102	95%	69%	31%	Hospitals
64	Sierra Club	$612,130	99%+	96%	3%	Environment
65	Independent Insurance Agents of America	$589,798	100%	60%	40%	Insurance
66	Time Warner*	$583,089	24%	76%	24%	Movies/Publish
67	American Council of Life Insurance	$581,880	99%+	59%	40%	Life Insurance
68	Credit Union National Assn*	$581,830	99%+	67%	33%	Credit Unions
69	National Restaurant Assn*	$571,197	99%+	23%	77%	Restaurants
70	International Assn of Firefighters*	$565,353	100%	94%	6%	Firefighters
71	Ameritech Corp*	$562,342	92%	55%	45%	Phone Utilities
72	Ironworkers Union*	$551,480	99%+	92%	7%	Bldg Trades
73	American Family Corp	$550,000	91%	61%	39%	Health Insur
74	Chicago Mercantile Exchange	$549,500	90%	74%	26%	Commodities
75	Auto Dealers & Drivers for Free Trade	$538,550	100%	38%	62%	Import Auto Dlrs
76	Akin, Gump et al	$538,228	57%	79%	21%	Law/Lobby
77	Martin Marietta Corp	$536,335	95%	51%	49%	Air Defense
78	Food Marketing Institute	$531,778	100%	35%	65%	Food Stores
79	National Rural Letter Carriers Assn	$526,528	100%	86%	14%	Postal Workers
80	Dow Chemical*	$525,569	82%	22%	78%	Chemicals
81	National Assn of Broadcasters	$522,400	95%	55%	45%	Entertainment
82	National Abortion Rights Action League*	$517,705	100%	94%	8%	Pro-Choice
83	Women's Campaign Fund	$513,067	100%	76%	22%	Womens Issues
84	Rubber Cork Linoleum & Plastic Workers	$505,730	100%	100%	0%	Indust Unions
85	Atlantic Richfield	$493,092	66%	25%	74%	Oil & Gas
86	Aircraft Owners & Pilots Assn	$482,695	100%	56%	44%	Air Transport
87	Americans for Free International Trade	$475,150	100%	20%	80%	Import Auto Dlrs
88	JP Morgan & Co	$473,175	89%	56%	44%	Comml Banks
89	Morgan Stanley & Co	$470,781	47%	54%	46%	Securities
90	General Dynamics	$464,055	94%	61%	39%	Air Defense
91	United Mine Workers	$459,600	100%	98%	2%	Mining Unions
92	CSX Corp*	$453,750	93%	53%	47%	RR/Sea Trans
93	Metropolitan Life Insurance*	$453,564	81%	57%	43%	Insur/Real Est
94	Blue Cross & Blue Shield Assn*	$453,134	75%	59%	41%	Health Insur
95	Pepsico*	$452,363	66%	26%	63%	Soft Drinks/Rest
96	Textron Inc	$446,570	89%	64%	36%	Air Defense
97	League of Conservation Voters*	$443,062	97%	93%	7%	Environment
98	KidsPAC	$440,600	100%	95%	4%	Child Rights
99	Arthur Andersen & Co	$440,377	48%	56%	44%	Accountants
100	C&S/Sovran Corp*	$436,867	99%+	61%	38%	Comml Banks

* Contributions came from more than one affiliate or subsidiary.
NOTE: Contributors with PAC percents of "99%+" gave more than 99.5% but less than 100% of their contributions through PACs.

American Medical Association, was the National Association of Realtors, whose PAC contributed nearly $3 million to some 540 federal candidates.

Ideological and single-interest groups, led by the National Rifle Association, held 11 of the Top 100 slots. The Transportation and Communications/Electronics sectors ranked next, with eight contributors each.

A total of 31 contributors gave $1 million or more in the 1992 elections. Just outside that select circle was Emily's List, the leading women's rights group, whose PAC and individual supporters gave $999,755 that could be traced by the Center. The group claims to have bundled up to $6 million in contributions in the last election — the great bulk of it directed by the PAC toward a roster of favored candidates, but paid directly by individuals. That figure is impossible to verify, since much of it came in contributions under $200 that need not be itemized by candidates.

Individual Givers: A Counterpoint to the PACs

While much of the attention by the public and the news media is concentrated on contributions from political action committees, an entirely different community of contributors has quietly been filling the campaign coffers of candidates. Individual contributors giving $200 or more accounted for more than $289 million in contributions to congressional and presidential candidates in the 1992 elections. The Center's research, which eventually resulted in the identification and classification of approximately 71 percent of that $289 million, shows that many of the same industries and interest groups that have come to dominate the PAC world also give heavily through individual contributions.

The biggest contributors of all were lawyers and lobbyists, who delivered $37.7 million in individual contributions to federal candidates — six times as much as they gave through PACs. The Finance, Insurance & Real Estate sector ranked second, accounting for nearly $30 million in individual donations. In contrast to its high profile in the world of PACs, organized labor was scarcely in evidence among individual donors; nearly all of labor's dollars were delivered through PACs. Defense contractors were also very small players compared with other industries. A chart comparing each sector's PAC and individual contributions can be found on page 22.

Who Gives Individually

One notable pattern that emerges from a study of individual versus PAC giving is that, by and large, PACs are an instrument of large organizations, while individual givers tend to be connected with smaller companies. A clear example of this can be seen in the oil industry, where a discernible split can be found in the spending patterns of large oil companies versus small ones. Nearly all the dollars delivered by major oil companies — such as Exxon, Atlantic Richfield, or Mobil — are funneled through PACs. Few oil executives from these companies make substantial contributions directly to candidates. Among smaller companies — known in the trade as "independents" — PACs are rare and most of the dollars are given as individual contributions.

That trend is consistent among a cross-section of American industries. Firms that are big enough to form PACs tend to use them as their primary means of delivering campaign dollars. Firms that are smaller tend to rely on individual donations. The one exception to the rule is in the case of small businesses connected with nationwide organizations — such as doctors, Realtors, or trial lawyers. Those groups often give both ways — directly through individual contributions, and again through the PAC of their national affiliate.

Wall Street and Washington Lawyers Lead Individual Givers

Another pattern that emerges from examining individual contributions is that certain industries, whether large or small, tend to prefer individual contributions to PACs. Most noteworthy among these are the securities industry based on Wall Street and the influential community of lobbyists and lawyers concentrated in Washington, DC.

Some of the biggest contributors (seen in the chart on the facing page) give both through PACs and individually. Some of them also tend to deliver large bundles of contributions to selected candidates. The "bundling" of individual contributions from a group of executives within a particular company has become a popular means of supporting favored candidates. PACs alone are limited to a maximum $10,000 contribution during a normal election cycle. But a group of, say, a dozen vice presidents or partners in a law firm, can easily give much more than that, particularly if their spouses (and sometimes children) add contributions of their own. A list of the biggest "bundled" contributions to candidates in the 1992 elections can be found on pages 28 and 29.

The chart on the opposite page shows the biggest individual contributors in 1991-92. Goldman, Sachs & Co., the Wall Street investment firm, was the biggest of all, giving more than $700,000 in individual donations. The biggest recipient of that money was Bill Clinton — in fact, Goldman, Sachs was the number one contributor to his campaign. (The firm also gave substantial sums to George Bush.) Emily's List, the women's rights PAC that used bundling as its primary tool for directing tens of thousands of dollars to favored women candidates, was second. The total shown here is very conservative. It includes only "earmarked" individual funds coordinated by the PAC and funds from major Emily's List donors who also gave large individual donations directly to candidates the PAC supported.

American Express ranked third. The bulk of their funds were delivered through the company's chief securities subsidiary, Shearson Lehman Brothers. In all, 12 securities firms ranked among the top 30 individual contributors.

But the biggest cluster of contributors on the top 50 list were law firms. Thirteen of them show up on the list, and though their home offices are based in cities around the nation, 11 of the 13 (all but Milberg, Weiss and Wachtell, Lipton) also maintain offices in the nation's capital. The line between legal work and lobbying is often a thin one in Washington, and nearly all

Top 50 Individual Contributors

Rank	Contributor	Individual Total	Grand Total	Category
1	Goldman, Sachs & Co	$704,237	$898,545	Securities
2	Emily's List	$634,437	$999,755	Womens Issues
3	American Express*	$546,545	$881,820	Stocks/Credit
4	Time Warner*	$445,089	$583,089	Movies/Publish
5	Merrill Lynch*	$436,600	$627,864	Securities
6	Cassidy & Associates	$372,666	$372,666	Lobbyists
7	Walt Disney Co*	$304,384	$401,834	Movies/Resorts
8	Skadden, Arps et al	$254,849	$350,566	Law/Lobby
9	Forest City Enterprises Inc	$252,833	$252,833	Real Est Devel
10	Morgan Stanley & Co	$250,585	$470,781	Securities
11	Prudential Insurance*	$239,205	$640,040	Insurance
12	US House of Representatives	$239,171	$239,171	Govt
13	Bear Stearns & Co	$233,885	$233,885	Securities
14	Akin, Gump et al	$233,572	$538,228	Law/Lobby
15	PaineWebber*	$233,372	$318,847	Securities
16	Arthur Andersen & Co	$230,504	$440,377	Accountants
17	Salomon Brothers	$230,035	$285,885	Securities
18	Smith Barney	$219,846	$234,702	Securities
19	First Boston Corp	$219,121	$315,621	Securities
20	Gallo Winery	$217,984	$217,984	Wine
21	Lazard Freres & Co	$214,450	$214,450	Securities
22	University of California*	$206,915	$206,915	Universities
23	US Tobacco*	$197,870	$636,120	Tobacco
24	Ernst & Young	$183,357	$419,653	Accountants
25	Latham & Watkins	$180,389	$180,389	Law/Lobby
26	Williams & Jensen	$178,795	$269,264	Law/Lobby
27	Bear, Stearns & Co	$178,145	$267,095	Securities
28	Okeelanta Corp	$170,800	$170,800	Sugar
29	Atlantic Richfield	$169,558	$493,092	Oil & Gas
30	Equitable Life*	$169,182	$308,857	Insur/Securities
31	Jones, Day et al	$168,529	$344,611	Law/Lobby
32	Hospice Care Inc	$163,150	$163,150	Nursing Homes
33	Patton, Boggs & Blow	$160,937	$160,937	Law/Lobby
34	O'Melveny & Myers	$160,509	$160,509	Law/Lobby
35	Deloitte & Touche	$158,026	$282,530	Accountants
36	Waste Management Inc*	$153,069	$683,558	Waste Mgmt
37	MacAndrews & Forbes Group	$147,750	$147,750	Personal Prod Mfg
38	Milberg, Weiss et al	$146,700	$146,700	Law/Lobby
39	Gibson, Dunn & Crutcher	$145,595	$145,595	Law/Lobby
40	Wachtell, Lipton et al	$144,300	$144,300	Law/Lobby
41	KPMG Peat Marwick	$141,930	$141,930	Accountants
42	Sony Corp*	$141,635	$141,635	Movies
43	General Electric*	$140,136	$823,486	Aerospace
44	Mintz, Levin et al	$136,171	$136,171	Law/Lobby
45	US Senate	$135,875	$135,875	Government
46	MCA Inc*	$134,543	$317,193	Movies/TV
47	Amway Corp	$133,271	$149,121	Direct Sales
48	Wunder, Diefenderfer et al	$132,416	$132,416	Law/Lobby
49	Republic National Bank of New York	$125,550	$125,550	Comml Banks
50	Willkie, Farr & Gallagher	$124,550	$124,550	Law/Lobby

* Contributions came from more than one affiliate or subsidiary.

the firms maintain a high-profile presence on Capitol Hill. So does Cassidy & Associates, the Washington lobbying firm that ranked sixth on the top 50 list. One of Cassidy's partners early in the election cycle was Bob Farmer, chief fundraiser for Michael Dukakis in the 1988 presidential election and later for Bill Clinton in the 1992 campaign.

Four firms that operate major Hollywood movie studios also appeared on the top 50 list — Time Warner, Disney, Sony and MCA. They too share the stockbrokers' and lawyers' penchant for relying more heavily on individual donations than on corporate PACs.

Bundles of Money: Biggest Contributions in the 1992 Elections

In the Senate...

Despite the fact that political action committees are limited to a maximum of $10,000 in one election cycle and individuals are limited to $2,000, a total of 21 Senators received contributions of $20,000 or more from a single company or interest group in the 1992 elections. Most of the dollars were given through individual contributions from company executives and their families, supplemented in many cases by PAC funds. But the biggest bundling operation at all in 1992 was not a corporation, but an ideological PAC — Emily's List, the women's rights group that raised money for female Democrats and helped elect four of them to the U.S. Senate.

The Center was able to identify just under $1 million in contributions from Emily's List. The money came from three sources — the PAC itself, which handed out $365,318 directly; "earmarked" contributions forwarded by the PAC but counted as individual donations; and direct contributions to women candidates made by donors to the PAC. Nearly all those individual contributions were coordinated (at least informally) by Emily's List, but they do not count against the PAC's $10,000 limit. The total the Center found was almost certainly only the tip of the iceberg. Individual contributions under $200 are not itemized under federal rules, and many of the donations the group coordinated were undoubtedly in that range. The PAC itself claimed to have raised $6 million for women candidates in the 1992 elections. Nearly all of it went to Democrats.

Barbara Boxer was by far the biggest recipient of Emily's List money. The $130,000 the Center tracked to her campaign was the biggest bundle of the year by any group. Carol Moseley-Braun ranked second, with $83,000. The year's two other female Senate winners — Dianne Feinstein of California and Patty Murray of Washington state — also got help from Emily's List, but their totals were much lower. The only other ideological group on the top bundler list was the Council for a Livable World, a pro-peace group that also used earmarks and bundled individual gifts to give Barbara Boxer nearly $34,000.

The bulk of the biggest bundle list at left did come primarily from business executives and their families. Securities firms, which traditionally have been the most active bundlers, accounted for nine of the top contributions shown here. Three law firms also made the list.

These were not the only top bundles of the 1992 election. The list includes only those to candidates who were actually elected.

Biggest Contributions to Senators

Contributor	Total	Type	Recipient
Emily's List	$130,405	PAC/Ind	Barbara Boxer (D-Calif)
Emily's List	$83,190	PAC/Ind	Carol Moseley-Braun (D-Ill)
Bear, Stearns & Co	$62,051	Indiv	Alfonse M. D'Amato (R-NY)
Eli Lilly & Co	$44,650	PAC/Ind	Daniel R. Coats (R-Ind)
Time Warner*	$38,000	PAC/Ind	Bob Packwood (R-Ore)
Council for a Livable World	$33,894	PAC/Ind	Barbara Boxer (D-Calif)
Goldman, Sachs & Co	$32,600	Indiv	Alfonse M. D'Amato (R-NY)
Disney Channel*	$32,250	Indiv	Patrick J. Leahy (D-Vt)
Anheuser-Busch	$31,250	PAC/Ind	Christopher S. Bond (R-Mo)
Salomon Brothers	$31,000	PAC/Ind	Bob Dole (R-Kan)
McDonnell Douglas	$30,735	PAC/Ind	Christopher S. Bond (R-Mo)
Greenwich Capital Markets	$29,250	Indiv	Christopher J. Dodd (D-Conn)
Flowers Industries	$28,750	PAC/Ind	Paul Coverdell (R-Ga)
Morgan Stanley & Co	$28,450	PAC/Ind	Alfonse M. D'Amato (R-NY)
Time Warner*	$27,500	PAC/Ind	Christopher J. Dodd (D-Conn)
Seafarers International Union*	$26,000	PAC	Dianne Feinstein (D-Calif)
Republic National Bank of New York	$26,000	Indiv	Daniel K. Inouye (D-Hawaii)
US Tobacco Co	$25,200	PAC/Ind	Christopher J. Dodd (D-Conn)
Merrill Lynch	$24,605	PAC/Ind	Alfonse M. D'Amato (R-NY)
University of California System*	$24,445	Indiv	Barbara Boxer (D-Calif)
Arkla Inc	$24,300	PAC/Ind	Dale Bumpers (D-Ark)
Waste Management Inc	$24,187	PAC/Ind	Bob Dole (R-Kan)
Mitchell, Williams et al	$23,750	Indiv	Dale Bumpers (D-Ark)
Smith Barney	$23,600	PAC/Ind	Alfonse M. D'Amato (R-NY)
BellSouth Corp	$23,550	Indiv	Ernest F. Hollings (D-SC)
Merrill Lynch	$23,500	PAC/Ind	Christopher J. Dodd (D-Conn)
Barrack, Rodos & Bacine	$23,500	PAC/Ind	Harris Wofford (D-Pa)
Coopers & Lybrand	$22,990	PAC/Ind	Alfonse M. D'Amato (R-NY)
National Assn of Broadcasters	$22,886	PAC/Ind	Ernest F. Hollings (D-SC)
Jones, Day et al	$22,850	PAC/Ind	Paul Coverdell (R-Ga)
Warner-Lambert	$22,750	PAC/Ind	Frank R. Lautenberg (D-NJ)
Albertson's Inc	$22,700	Indiv	Dirk Kempthorne (R-Idaho)
Monsanto Co	$22,700	PAC/Ind	Christopher S. Bond (R-Mo)
Tyson Foods	$22,500	PAC/Ind	Dale Bumpers (D-Ark)
BankAmerica Corp	$22,300	PAC/Ind	Dianne Feinstein (D-Calif)
Goldman, Sachs & Co	$22,000	PAC/Ind	Christopher J. Dodd (D-Conn)
Conseco Inc	$22,000	Indiv	Daniel R. Coats (R-Ind)

* Contributions came from more than one affiliate or subsidiary.

In the House . . .

The biggest bundle of cash delivered to any House member in the 1992 election went to freshman Republican Michael Castle of Delaware. Castle's top benefactor was MBNA Corp., a Delaware-based bank holding company. Castle was hardly an unknown political figure in his home state. He was its governor before his election to Congress.

Dow Chemical executives and their families bestowed over $55,000 on Republican Dave Camp, whose district includes the corporation's home office in Midland, Mich. Camp got an additional $9,500 from Dow Corning. Those two companies combined in the 1992 election to give Camp just over $100,000 in contributions.

Emily's List, the group which boosted the campaigns of Democratic women in both the House and Senate, bundled big donations to congressional newcomers Anna Eshoo of California, Elizabeth Furse of Oregon, and Karen Shepherd of Utah. As with their contributions to Senate candidates, these totals are undoubtedly low as they do not include individual contribution under $200.

Emily's List was the only ideological group represented in the list below. All the others were business groups, with the notable exception of the top contributors to freshman Democrat Robert Menendez of New Jersey. Menendez, who served as mayor of Union City, N.J. before winning election to Congress, got more than $28,000 in large contributions from employees of its municipal government. He got an additional $30,150 from the Union City School Board.

In all, some 29 House members drew contributions of $20,000 or more from a single source in the 1992 elections. The biggest recipient of all was House Majority Leader Dick Gephardt, who collected large donations from five different contributors — $43,350 from Anheuser-Busch; $22,185 from the Wall Street investment firm of Salomon Brothers; $21,500 from the law firm of Sills, Cummis et al; $21,000 from the Gallo Winery and $20,000 from the St. Louis Law firm of Thompson & Mitchell.

Biggest Contributions to House Members

Contributor	Total	Type	Recipient
MBNA Corp	$61,300	PAC/Ind	Michael N. Castle (R-Del)
Dow Chemical	$55,319	PAC/Ind	Dave Camp (R-Mich)
Emily's List	$43,839	PAC/Ind	Anna G. Eshoo (D-Calif)
Anheuser-Busch	$43,350	PAC/Ind	Richard A. Gephardt (D-Mo)
Stephens Inc	$40,500	Indiv	Ray Thornton (D-Ark)
Anesthesia Professional Assn Inc	$38,000	Indiv	E. Clay Shaw Jr. (R-Fla)
Hospice Care Inc	$36,000	Indiv	Carrie Meek (D-Fla)
Schnitzer Steel Industries	$32,328	Indiv	Dick Swett (D-NH)
Jones, Day et al	$31,400	PAC/Ind	Jane Harman (D-Calif)
Union City Board of Education	$30,150	Indiv	Robert Menendez (D-NJ)
Corning Inc	$30,050	Indiv	Amo Houghton (R-NY)
Kirkpatrick & Lockhart	$29,975	PAC/Ind	Rick Santorum (R-Pa)
Emily's List	$29,105	PAC/Ind	Elizabeth Furse (D-Ore)
Cabletron Systems Inc	$28,940	Indiv	Bill Zeliff (R-NH)
Union City (NJ) Municipal Govt	$28,350	Indiv	Robert Menendez (D-NJ)
Veco International Inc	$27,790	Indiv	Don Young (R-Alaska)
Forest City Enterprises Inc	$25,350	Indiv	Eric D. Fingerhut (D-Ohio)
Chrysler Corp	$25,200	PAC/Ind	John D. Dingell (D-Mich)
Emily's List	$25,005	PAC/Ind	Karen Shepherd (D-Utah)
Latham & Watkins	$23,500	Indiv	C. Christopher Cox (R-Calif)
Ford Motor Co	$23,000	PAC/Ind	John D. Dingell (D-Mich)
Forest City Enterprises Inc	$23,000	Indiv	Louis Stokes (D-Ohio)
Beneficial Management Corp	$22,850	PAC/Ind	Dick Zimmer (R-NJ)
United Steelworkers	$22,500	PAC	Gene Green (D-Texas)
Archer-Daniels-Midland Corp	$22,300	PAC/Ind	Robert H. Michel (R-Ill)
Salomon Brothers	$22,185	Indiv	Richard A. Gephardt (D-Mo)
Guardsmark Inc	$21,750	Indiv	Don Sundquist (R-Tenn)
Sills, Cummis et al	$21,500	Indiv	Richard A. Gephardt (D-Mo)
Gallo Winery	$21,000	Indiv	Richard A. Gephardt (D-Mo)
Golden Rule Insurance Co	$20,565	PAC/Ind	Newt Gingrich (R-Ga)
Chicago Mercantile Exchange	$20,250	PAC/Ind	Dan Rostenkowski (D-Ill)

* Contributions came from more than one affiliate or subsidiary.

Leading Categories of Individual Contributions

Contributions from lawyers towered over all other industries and interest groups among individual contributions made to congressional candidates in the 1992 elections. In all, attorneys gave over $32 million of their personal funds — twice as much as the second leading category, retirees. Securities dealers and investment firms were next, followed by doctors, real estate agents, insurance agents and executives, lobbyists and real estate developers.

Pro-Israel contributors ranked ninth on the list, with nearly $3.4 million in contributions. This total was compiled by counting individuals who had contributed $200 or more both to a pro-Israel PAC and to a candidate who was supported by pro-Israel PACs. Because of that conservative criteria for counting ideological contributors, the actual total of pro-Israel givers can be safely assumed to be considerably higher.

Retirees, whose total contributions put them in second place behind only lawyers, includes all individuals who described themselves as "retired," except those who were classified as ideological contributors because of contributions to ideological or single-issue PACs.

Category	Total from Individuals	Grand Total
Attorneys & law firms	$32,182,674	$38,233,716
Retired	$15,930,210	$15,930,210
Security brokers & investment companies	$8,607,241	$10,383,262
Physicians	$8,174,796	$11,939,475
Real estate agents & managers	$4,556,362	$7,626,300
Insurance companies, brokers & agents, diversified	$4,191,395	$9,109,055
Lobbyists & public relations	$4,084,934	$4,353,571
Real estate developers & subdividers	$3,484,524	$3,797,455
Pro-Israel	$3,378,436	$7,401,113
Commercial banks & bank holding companies	$2,999,119	$10,349,223
Civil servant/public employee	$2,995,085	$2,995,085
Construction, unclassified	$2,634,132	$2,634,132
Investment banking	$2,496,011	$3,149,515
Business services	$2,447,213	$2,520,185
Accountants	$2,395,128	$4,877,052
Schools & colleges	$2,355,025	$2,355,025
Motion picture/TV production & distribution	$2,261,460	$2,596,760
Investors	$2,163,731	$2,163,731
Women's issues	$2,159,244	$3,725,735
Public works, industrial & commercial construction	$2,111,875	$3,623,909
Real estate	$1,936,926	$1,937,926
Building operators and managers	$1,876,581	$1,903,331
Finance, insurance & real estate, diversified or unclassified	$1,757,658	$1,757,658
Management consultants & services	$1,694,609	$1,697,109
Conservative/Republican	$1,685,903	$2,479,934
Restaurants & drinking establishments	$1,639,522	$2,994,793
Crop production & basic processing	$1,637,380	$1,748,430
Independent oil & gas producers	$1,525,308	$2,048,958
Registered foreign agents	$1,467,682	$1,467,682
Book, newspaper & periodical publishing	$1,463,934	$1,674,934
Auto dealers, new & used	$1,426,894	$3,211,769
Oil & gas	$1,280,446	$1,645,123
Liberal/Democrat	$1,268,347	$2,658,027
Advertising & public relations services	$1,233,583	$1,256,983
Misc physician specialists	$1,214,166	$2,182,598
Hospitals	$1,205,446	$2,369,306
Industrial/commercial equipment & materials	$1,170,428	$1,651,109
Liquor wholesalers	$1,091,909	$2,273,554
Health, unclassified & diversified	$1,088,045	$1,088,045
Cable & satellite TV production & distribution	$1,013,955	$2,226,214

The $8.6 million from securities executives, plus the $2.5 million from individuals involved in investment banking, illustrates the tendency of those in the securities and investment industry to favor individual contributions over PACs. Many of the larger Wall Street firms bundled contributions from partners, brokers and their families to deliver sizable contributions to particularly favored candidates. Those donations were often supplemented by PAC contributions from the parent firm.

Real estate brokers, developers and investors were also very much in evidence with individual contributions. Developers in particular were far more likely to give individually than through political action committees. Bankers and insurance executives were also high on the list of individual contributors, but those industries did tend to give large sums through PACs as well.

Industry Support of Democrats & Republicans

The widespread assumption that labor unions support Democrats while business groups support Republicans is only partially true — and in many cases is downright wrong. Organized labor is indeed heavily Democratic in its politics and its campaign contributions, though Republicans on committees important to labor often receive substantial financial support from unions. But the world of business is much more diverse in its political orientation than most casual observers realize. Overall, business groups split their dollars nearly evenly between Democrats and Republicans in Congress. It is common even for individual companies to support both parties — sometimes even in the same race.

Even among industries and individual businesses that are Republican in their politics, there is a tendency — presumably born of hard-headed pragmatism — to ensure a favorable reception on Capitol Hill by giving to members on both sides of the aisle. That inclination is strengthened by the fact that Democrats hold solid majorities in both the House and Senate. In that environment, virtually no bill becomes law without wide support among Democratic members — a fact that business groups must take into account, whatever their political orientation.

A glance at the charts at right illustrates several noteworthy patterns in the sectors' contributions during 1992. Most obvious is the contrast in Labor dollars between Republicans and Democrats. Also clear, both from the charts and the bottom line below is that Democrats received considerably more money overall than Republicans in the 1992 elections.

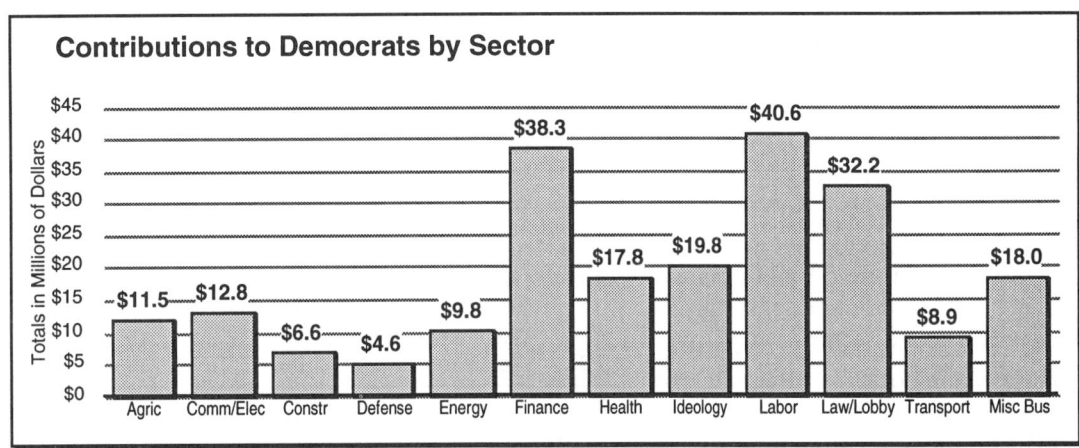

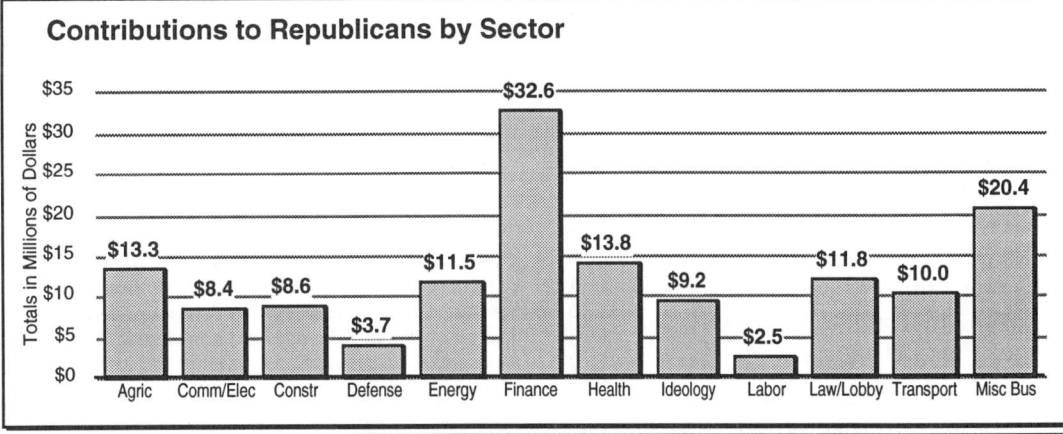

Other interesting findings can be seen by looking more closely. The finance, insurance and real estate sector, for example, is the heaviest business contributor to both parties. Moreover, the bankers, Realtors, insurance agents and others that make up that sector gave more to Democrats than to Republicans. Lawyers and lobbyists were even more strongly Democratic in their contributions, as were ideological and single-issue contributors.

A more detailed examination of the spending patterns in each of these sectors can be found in the Industry Profiles section beginning on page 41. A closer look at the individual categories most important to members of each party can be found on the following two pages.

Sector	To Democrats	To Republicans
Agriculture	$11,533,853	$13,315,969
Communic/Electronics	$12,758,180	$8,391,147
Construction	$6,584,436	$8,617,049
Defense	$4,609,451	$3,714,903
Energy/Natural Resources	$9,794,836	$11,518,607
Finance/Insur/Real Estate	$38,321,025	$32,574,212
Health	$17,774,140	$13,780,085
Ideological/Single-Issue	$19,790,462	$9,161,539
Labor	$40,610,113	$2,471,102
Lawyers & Lobbyists	$32,160,897	$11,827,725
Transportation	$8,940,802	$10,020,890
Misc Business	$17,962,336	$20,354,469
GRAND TOTAL	**$160,439,956**	**$134,115,056**

Top-Dollar Categories to Each Party

Listed below are the industry and interest group categories that gave the most money to congressional Democrats and Republicans in the 1992 elections. A complete listing of categories used throughout this book, and the totals they provided in contributions, can be found in Appendix A, which begins on page 1314.

To Democrats...

Lawyers and labor unions provided the biggest financial assistance to Democratic candidates in the 1992 elections. Attorneys and law firms were by far the leading single category giving to Democrats, though taken as a whole, unions contributed more heavily than any other sector.

Of the top 20 categories contributing to Democrats, five came from the Labor community, three (Pro-Israel, women's issues and Liberal/Democrat) were ideological, and 11 were from the world of business. Among the business categories, six were from the finance, insurance & real estate sector.

The category totals in this list include contributions both from PACs and individuals. In this list, and throughout the book, PAC classifications are based on the industry or interests of the sponsoring organization or company. Contributions from individuals are classified based on the occupation or employer of the contributor. Individuals are classified as ideological givers only if they made contributions to an ideological/single-issue PAC.

Rank	Category	To Democrats	Dem Pct
1	Attorneys & law firms	$27,990,120	73.2%
2	Retired	$7,150,286	44.9%
3	Manufacturing unions	$6,767,277	98.0%
4	Building trades unions	$6,466,973	93.7%
5	Security brokers & investment companies	$6,083,313	58.6%
6	Physicians	$5,978,992	50.1%
7	Commercial banks & bank holding companies	$5,422,745	52.4%
8	Pro-Israel	$5,289,881	71.5%
9	Insurance companies, brokers & agents, diversified	$4,280,150	47.0%
10	Real estate agents & managers	$4,040,672	53.0%
11	US Postal Service unions & associations	$3,419,083	89.5%
12	Teachers unions	$3,340,592	96.1%
13	Lobbyists & public relations	$3,164,061	72.7%
14	Women's issues	$3,138,406	84.2%
15	Accountants	$2,680,609	55.0%
16	Defense aerospace contractors	$2,635,229	55.5%
17	Liberal/Democrat	$2,612,692	98.3%
18	Mechant marine & longshoremen unions	$2,572,292	82.3%
19	Telephone utilities	$2,504,997	55.4%
20	Life insurance	$2,441,220	57.0%

To Republicans...

Attorneys and law firms also topped the Republicans' Top 20 list of leading categories, though lawyers gave only about one-third as much to Republicans as they did to Democrats.

Seventeen of the top 20 categories were business related. The two ideological categories were Pro-Israel and Conservative/Republican. Retirees ranked second on the list both for Republicans and Democrats.

The finance, insurance & real estate sector accounted for seven of the Republicans' top 20 categories — more than any other sector.

Rank	Category	To Republicans	Repub Pct
1	Attorneys & law firms	$10,175,425	26.6%
2	Retired	$8,556,245	53.7%
3	Physicians	$5,869,848	49.2%
4	Commercial banks & bank holding companies	$4,915,548	47.5%
5	Insurance companies, brokers & agents, diversified	$4,817,610	52.9%
6	Security brokers & investment companies	$4,268,926	41.1%
7	Real estate agents & managers	$3,537,494	46.4%
8	Conservative/Republican	$2,406,051	97.0%
9	Public works, industrial & commercial construction	$2,227,578	61.5%
10	Accountants	$2,183,101	44.8%
11	Pro-Israel	$2,110,670	28.5%
12	Defense areospace contractors	$2,110,299	44.4%
13	Auto dealers, new & used	$2,047,417	63.8%
14	Telephone utilities	$2,009,499	44.5%
15	Major (multinational) oil & gas producers	$1,998,225	74.0%
16	Restaurants & drinking establishments	$1,929,286	64.4%
17	Life insurance	$1,839,779	43.0%
18	Pharmaceutical manufacturing	$1,662,422	52.8%
19	Real estate developers & subdividers	$1,619,235	42.6%
20	Chemicals	$1,495,770	68.5%

The Most Heavily Partisan Categories

These were the categories that gave most heavily to one party or the other during the 1991-92 election cycle. The categories have been pared to include only those that accounted for $50,000 or more in contributions to one party.

To Democrats...

Labor unions dominate the list of most-partisan categories giving to Democrats. As a group, organized labor delivered 94 percent of its campaign dollars to Democratic candidates, making it by far the most important sector for Democrats. In fact, the strong partisanship of labor unions accounts for much of the overall edge in fundraising that congressional Democrats enjoyed over their Republican opponents.

In all, 15 of the 20 most partisan categories on the Democrats' list were from the Labor sector. The remaining five were from ideological & single-issue groups.

Rank	Category	To Democrats	Dem Pct
1	Other unions	$164,063	100.0%
2	Democratic leadership PAC	$1,341,037	99.9%
3	Human rights	$74,057	99.4%
4	Labor unions	$858,015	98.7%
5	Liberal/Democrat	$2,612,692	98.3%
6	Communications & hi-tech unions	$1,401,740	98.3%
7	Other commercial unions	$730,799	98.1%
8	Manufacturing unions	$6,767,277	98.0%
9	Mining unions	$448,100	97.5%
10	State & local govt employee unions	$1,902,863	97.3%
11	Retail trade unions	$1,476,986	97.2%
12	Other transportation unions	$1,238,150	97.1%
13	Railroad unions	$1,571,421	96.8%
14	Energy-related unions (non-mining)	$132,840	96.4%
15	Teachers unions	$3,340,592	96.1%
16	IBEW (Intl Brotherhood of Electrical Workers)	$1,512,817	96.0%
17	Children's rights	$433,800	95.6%
18	Food service & related unions	$539,950	94.7%
19	Teamsters union	$2,392,539	94.5%
20	Environmental policy	$1,536,840	94.1%

To Republicans...

Ideological and single-issue contributors accounted for four of the five most heavily partisan categories giving to Republicans, and six of the top 20. But a number of business categories were also heavily Republican in their giving.

Note that the partisan percentages of the Republicans' top supporters drop off quickly after the ideological categories at the top. Even the most conservative business groups tend to give at least a token share of their campaign dollars to candidates of both parties. The Republicans have no ideological stronghold comparable to the Democrats' rock-solid union money.

Rank	Category	To Republicans	Repub Pct
1	Republican leadership PAC	$845,393	99.2%
2	Labor, anti-union	$367,406	98.2%
3	Conservative/Republican	$2,406,051	97.0%
4	Fiscal & tax policy	$107,154	96.2%
5	Builders associations	$178,828	92.8%
6	Pro-business organizations	$130,501	91.1%
7	Abortion policy, Pro-Life	$432,460	88.9%
8	Direct sales	$176,112	83.9%
9	Paper packaging materials	$407,700	81.2%
10	Farm machinery & equipment	$256,947	80.2%
11	Animal feed & health products	$102,112	79.6%
12	Small business organizations	$293,146	79.4%
13	Air freight	$39,950	78.3%
14	Construction equipment	$247,150	77.6%
15	Hardware & tools	$62,265	77.2%
16	Truck & trailer manufacturers	$66,900	77.1%
17	Plastics & rubber processing & products	$400,543	75.9%
18	Forestry & forest products	$947,396	75.6%
19	Defense policy, pro-military	$144,385	75.2%
20	Truck/automotive parts & accessories	$628,661	74.8%

In-State vs. Out-of-State Contributions

Highest Percent of Out-of-State Contributions: US House*

Rank	Name	Out-of-state Pct	Out-of-state Total
1	David R. Obey (D-Wis)	93.8%	$76,470
2	Earl Pomeroy (D-ND)	89.0%	$55,077
3	Lee H. Hamilton (D-Ind)	87.6%	$132,800
4	Nick J. Rahall II (D-WVa)	85.5%	$71,500
5	Dick Swett (D-NH)	85.3%	$317,718
6	Sidney R. Yates (D-Ill)	83.6%	$131,350
7	Pete Stark (D-Calif)	83.4%	$91,550
8	Bruce F. Vento (D-Minn)	80.5%	$16,750
9	Les Aspin (D-Wis)	79.5%	$405,850
10	Bernard Sanders (I-Vt)	78.9%	$49,825
11	Charlie Rose (D-NC)	76.9%	$46,700
12	Patricia Schroeder (D-Colo)	76.5%	$110,503
13	Richard A. Gephardt (D-Mo)	75.9%	$1,230,248
14	William D. Ford (D-Mich)	74.3%	$55,700
15	William L. Clay (D-Mo)	72.4%	$18,818
16	Joseph M. McDade (R-Pa)	68.9%	$63,150
17	John T. Myers (R-Ind)	64.6%	$18,350
18	Jack Brooks (D-Texas)	63.3%	$58,276
19	Mike Espy (D-Miss)	62.5%	$26,500
20	Timothy J. Penny (D-Minn)	61.1%	$7,000

* Among members with $10,000 or more in individual contributions.

Most House members drew the bulk of their large individual contributions (76 percent on average) from within their own state. Many collected less than 10 percent of their cash from out-of-state contributors. Of the 435 members of the House of Representatives, only 47 drew the majority of their large individual contributions from outside their home states. The 20 members in the chart at left had the highest proportion of out-of-state contributions from large individual contributors.

All the totals on this page include only large individual contributions ($200 and above). Smaller contributions are not itemized, so it is not possible to check where they came from. PAC contributions are not counted, since many PACs with local affiliates maintain their headquarters in Washington, D.C. or other major cities.

Highest Percent of Out-of-State Contributions: US Senate

Rank	Name	Out-of-state Pct	Out-of-state Total
1	Byron L. Dorgan (D-ND)	100.0%	$146,200
2	Kent Conrad (D-ND)	93.8%	$673,334
3	Patrick J. Leahy (D-Vt)	90.0%	$812,156
4	Orrin G. Hatch (R-Utah)	89.0%	$1,982,816
5	Joseph R. Biden Jr. (D-Del)	87.7%	$1,375,960
6	Larry Pressler (R-SD)	86.7%	$1,447,824
7	Tom Daschle (D-SD)	84.3%	$1,836,522
8	Bob Dole (R-Kan)	79.2%	$1,468,458
9	Bob Packwood (R-Ore)	78.0%	$3,513,276
10	Claiborne Pell (D-RI)	77.7%	$1,445,166

Senators were much more likely than House members to draw substantial support from out-of-state contributors — particularly those senators from small states. The more prominent senators have developed national constituencies that help out with campaign cash at election time. Even those less well known can often corral dollars from party loyalists in major financial and political centers such as New York, Los Angeles, Washington and Chicago.

Two senators with high out-of-state percentages who were not included on this list were Tom Harkin and Bob Kerrey. Most of the money they raised in the 1991-92 was not for their Senate reelections, but for their presidential campaigns, where in-state/out-of-state ratios do not apply.

The 10 senators on the list at right got the highest proportion of large individual contributions from within the borders of their own states. The list includes four members — Lauch Faircloth, Dianne Feinstein, Barbara Boxer and Paul Coverdell — who won election to the Senate for the first time in 1992.

Highest Percent of In-State Contributions: US Senate

Rank	Name	In-state Pct	In-state Total
1	Lauch Faircloth (R-NC)	85.0%	$1,711,318
2	Connie Mack (R-Fla)	84.6%	$5,090,194
3	Phil Gramm (R-Texas)	83.8%	$15,081,604
4	Dianne Feinstein (D-Calif)	83.4%	$6,621,980
5	Barbara Boxer (D-Calif)	82.9%	$5,907,594
6	Nancy Kassebaum (R-Kan)	82.5%	$254,398
7	Slade Gorton (R-Wash)	81.4%	$1,706,514
8	Alfonse M. D'Amato (R-NY)	81.3%	$10,514,058
9	Daniel R. Coats (R-Ind)	81.0%	$4,870,192
10	Paul Coverdell (R-Ga)	79.8%	$3,103,796

Unidentified Contributors

While nearly every political action committee was identified and categorized by the Center, many thousands of *individual* contributors remain unclassified. Of the $289 million in large individual contributions that went to candidates for Congress and the presidency in the 1991-92 election cycle, the Center was able to identify and classify 71 percent. Of the remaining $85 million which was not identified . . .

- $34.4 million was given by contributors who did list their employers. The Center, however, was unable to identify the types of business these companies were engaged in — mainly due to limitations of staff and time.

- $13.6 million came from homemakers, students and other non-income earners whose income-earning spouses or parents were not found.

- $3.0 million came from individuals whose listed occupations were so generic they could not be classified. Examples are "businessman," "entrepreneur" and "self-employed."

- $33.5 million came from people whose occupation and employer was not listed at all. In many cases, the Center was able to discover the missing information by searching for other contributions by the same individuals. But a large portion of these contributors remain unclassified.

Federal law requires candidates to disclose the name, address, occupation and employer of each contributor giving $200 or more to their campaign. Most members of Congress complied with that requirement, providing information on all but a tiny fraction of their contributors. Some members, however, were less forthcoming. The following lists show the members of Congress with the biggest information gaps in their 1991-92 disclosure reports.

Senators Who Disclosed the Least in 1991-92

Rank	Name	Pct with No Employer Listed	Total No Employer Listed	Total Identified by Center	Final Total with No Employer Known	Final Pct with No Employer Known
1	Carol Moseley-Braun (D-Ill)	65.5%	$1,206,553	$601,758	$604,795	32.8%
2	Robert F. Bennett (R-Utah)	61.9%	$122,741	$61,000	$61,741	31.1%
3	Bob Kerrey (D-Neb)*	58.4%	$1,710,105	$750,968	$959,137	32.8%
4	Tom Harkin (D-Iowa)*	57.3%	$920,334	$416,794	$503,540	31.3%
5	Bob Packwood (R-Ore)	47.4%	$944,304	$649,291	$295,013	14.8%
6	Charles E. Grassley (R-Iowa)	38.8%	$211,856	$123,850	$88,006	16.1%
7	Daniel K. Inouye (D-Hawaii)	35.3%	$562,620	$259,102	$303,518	19.1%
8	Dennis DeConcini (D-Ariz)	29.2%	$50,950	$26,000	$24,950	14.3%
9	Ben Nighthorse Campbell (D-Colo)	29.0%	$163,401	$95,551	$67,850	12.0%
10	Alfonse M. D'Amato (R-NY)	24.6%	$896,040	$290,010	$606,030	16.7%

* Includes contributions to his 1992 presidential campaign.

House Members Who Disclosed the Least in 1991-92

Rank	Name	Pct with No Employer Listed	Total No Employer Listed	Total Identified by Center	Final Total with No Employer Known	Final Pct with No Employer Known
1	Eddie Bernice Johnson (D-Texas)	94.1%	$79,210	$37,630	$41,580	49.4%
2	Bobby L. Rush (D-Ill)	72.7%	$69,000	$28,950	$40,050	42.2%
3	Walter R. Tucker (D-Calif)	72.3%	$95,192	$23,525	$71,667	54.5%
4	Earl F. Hilliard (D-Ala)	60.0%	$69,800	$49,175	$20,625	17.7%
5	Melvin Watt (D-NC)	57.9%	$78,540	$35,750	$42,790	31.6%
6	Albert R. Wynn (D-Md)	56.5%	$69,386	$25,700	$43,686	35.6%
7	Fred Grandy (R-Iowa)	53.2%	$29,750	$15,250	$14,500	25.9%
8	Ron Klink (D-Pa)	52.3%	$18,940	$7,340	$11,600	32.0%
9	Philip M. Crane (R-Ill)	52.2%	$73,032	$30,306	$42,726	30.5%
10	Alcee L. Hastings (D-Fla)	49.4%	$71,650	$30,250	$41,400	28.5%
11	John T. Doolittle (R-Calif)	46.2%	$92,980	$48,225	$44,755	22.3%
12	Calvin Dooley (D-Calif)	45.9%	$66,879	$38,204	$28,675	19.7%
13	Edolphus Towns (D-NY)	45.6%	$76,935	$30,250	$46,685	27.7%
14	Nydia M. Velazquez (D-NY)	44.7%	$49,050	$14,900	$34,150	31.1%
15	Ed Pastor (D-Ariz)	44.2%	$150,172	$82,825	$67,347	19.8%
16	Major R. Owens (D-NY)	43.9%	$8,575	$0	$8,575	43.9%
17	Jay C. Kim (R-Calif)	39.8%	$127,960	$21,850	$106,110	33.0%
18	Eva Clayton (D-NC)	39.8%	$25,502	$16,300	$9,202	14.4%
19	Jim Clyburn (D-SC)	37.7%	$35,384	$18,850	$16,534	17.6%
20	Richard E. Neal (D-Mass)	36.5%	$28,000	$9,550	$18,450	24.0%

Targeting the Committees

One of the first patterns that becomes apparent when reviewing the political contributions to incumbents in Congress is that the member's profile of contributors tends to parallel his or her committee assignments. Members of the Banking Committees of the House or Senate, for example, typically receive substantial contributions from commercial banks, savings & loans, as well as related (and sometimes competing) industries, like securities firms and insurance companies. Members sitting on industry-specific committees (like the House Merchant Marine and Fisheries Committee) often receive funds both from business interests involved in the industry and from Labor PACs whose members provide the industry's work force. The consistency of these patterns can be seen on the member profile pages (beginning on page 171) and in the committee profiles that begin on page 94.

It can also be seen in the following charts that show the average contributions given by selected industry groups to members of various committees in the House of Representatives. The charts focus on House committees because industry contribution patterns are clearer there than in the Senate. House members generally have only one or two major committee assignments, while most senators must split their attention among three or four different committees. In addition, because senators face the voters only once every six years, the volume of dollars flowing to specific Senate committees tends to have more to do with the number of committee members seeking reelection than with the overall agenda of either the committee or the contributors.

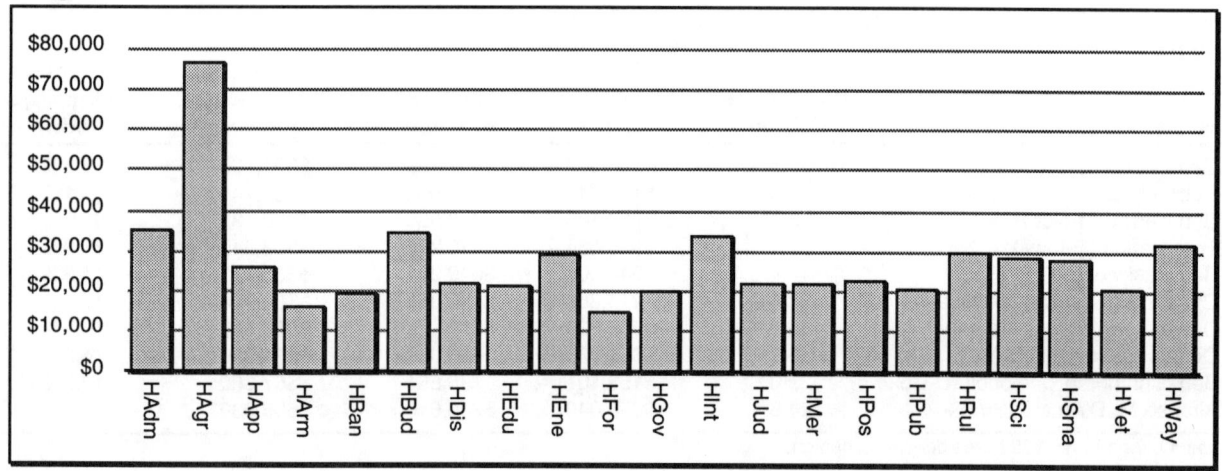

Agriculture

House Committee Key	
HAdm	House Administration
HAgr	House Agriculture
HApp	House Appropriations
HArm	House Armed Services
HBan	House Banking, Finance & Urban Affairs
HBud	House Budget
HDis	House District of Columbia
HEdu	House Education & Labor
HEne	House Energy & Commerce
HFor	House Foreign Affairs
HGov	House Government Operations
HInt	House Interior & Insular Affairs
HJud	House Judiciary
HMer	House Merchant Marine & Fisheries
HPos	House Post Office & Civil Service
HPub	House Public Works & Transportation
HRul	House Rules
HSci	House Science, Space & Technology
HSma	House Small Business
HVet	House Veterans' Affairs
HWay	House Ways and Means

The chart above illustrates the correlation between industry spending and members' committee assignments. Agricultural industry contributors concentrated the biggest portion of their campaign dollars on the committee that most affects their business. Members of the House Agriculture Committee received an average of $76,000 from farmers, ranchers, pesticide manufacturers, and other agricultural interests during the 1991-92 election cycle.

Communications/Electronics

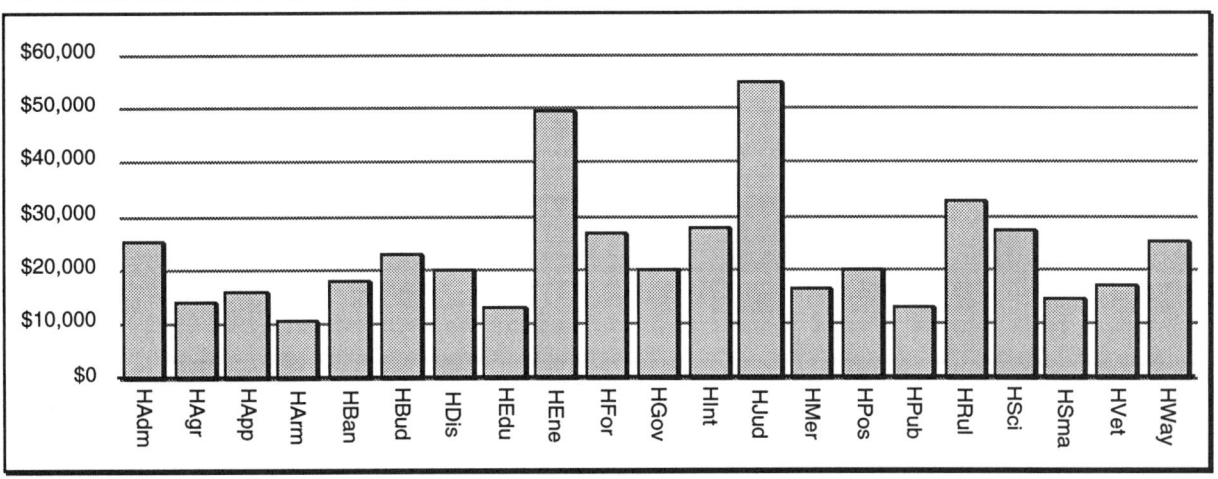

The Judiciary and Energy & Commerce committees attracted the biggest share of contributions from the communications and electronics sector. The Telecommunications and Finance subcommittee of Energy & Commerce is particularly important to telephone utilities and to TV and radio broadcasters. Both groups were major contributors to that committee. Hollywood film studios and TV broadcasters also gave heavily to the Judiciary Committee, which rules on such matters as copyright laws affecting the motion picture industry.

Defense

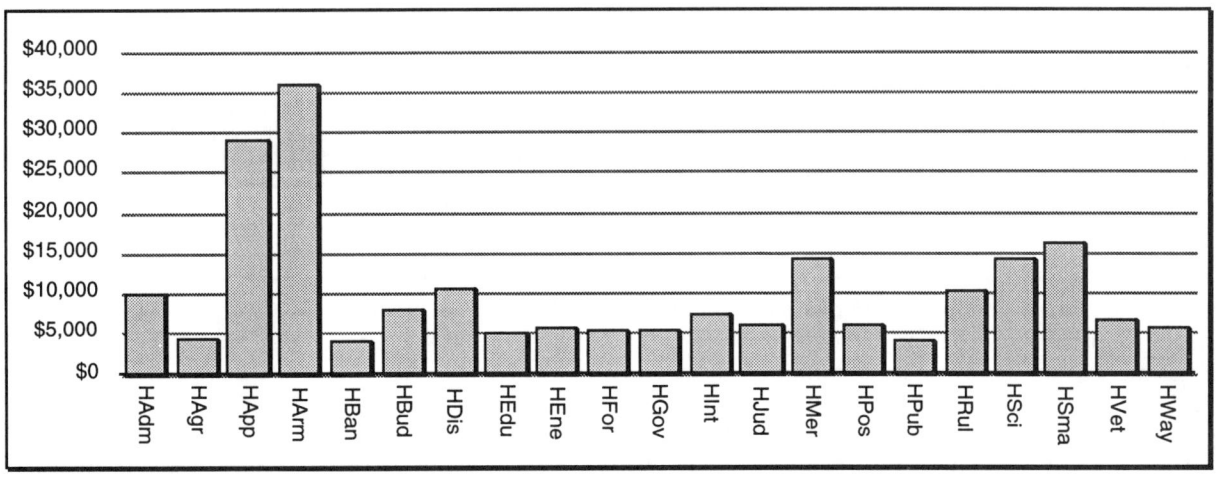

Defense contractors took careful aim at the Appropriations and Armed Services Committees when dispensing their dollars in the 1992 election. Armed Services makes crucial decisions on weapons systems and overall military budget priorities. Appropriations allocates the money to pay for it all. Both are crucial to the defense industry, particularly as defense spending winds down after the close of the Cold War and the dissolution of the former Soviet Union.

Energy & Natural Resources

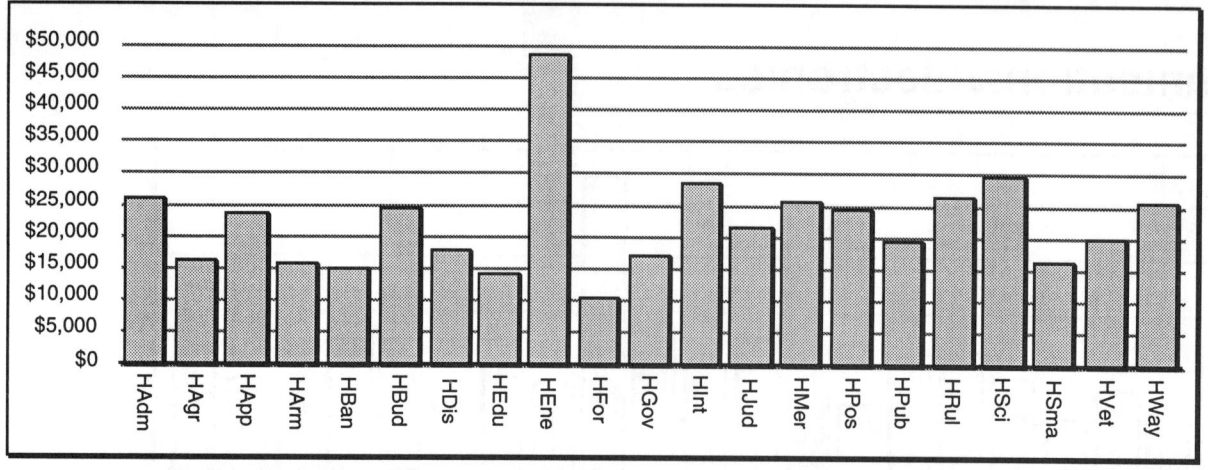

The Energy and Commerce Committee, with direct responsibility for the nation's energy policy, was the biggest beneficiary of campaign funds from the oil and gas industry. The committee's energy money was also boosted by large contributions from electric utilities.

Finance, Insurance & Real Estate

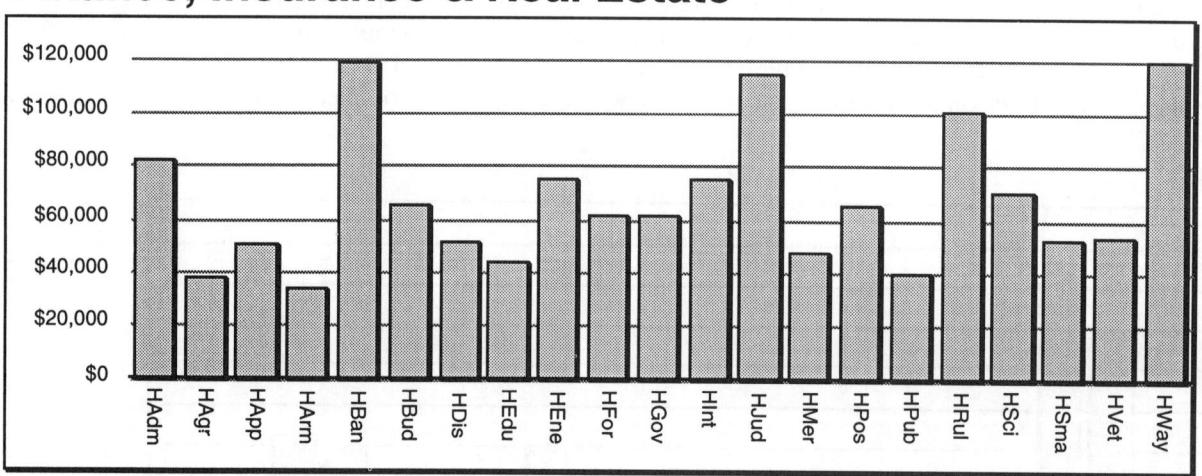

Within the financial sector, commercial banks gave an average of $36,000 to members of the Banking Committee. Insurance interests gave nearly $48,000 on average to members of the Ways & Means Committee. Securities & investment interests gave heavily both to Judiciary and to Ways & Means.

Health

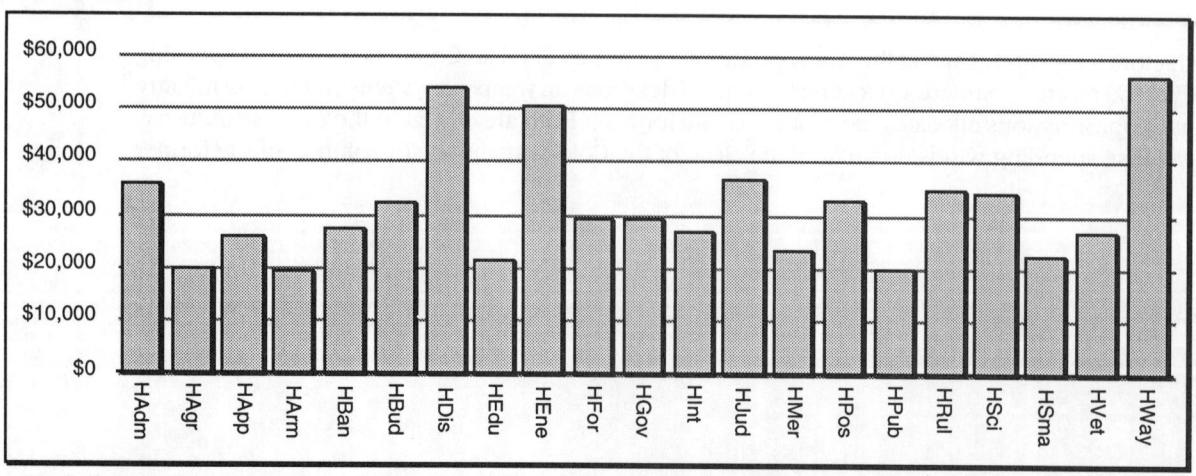

Both Energy & Commerce and Ways & Means have subcommittees dealing with Health matters. Both panels got generous funding from doctors, hospitals, pharmaceutical companies and other health care interests.

Labor

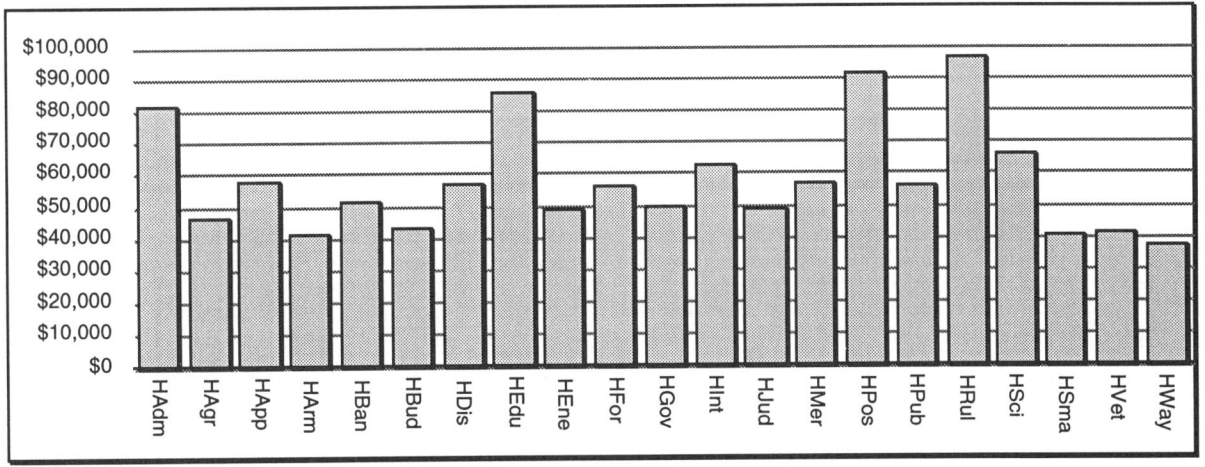

With 94 percent of its campaign dollars going to Democrats, organized Labor for the most part gave its dollars to Democratic members without regard to their committee assignments. But the Energy & Labor Committee and Post Office & Civil Service Committee — both particularly important to public sector unions — got extra, as did members of the Rules Committee.

Lawyer & Lobbyists

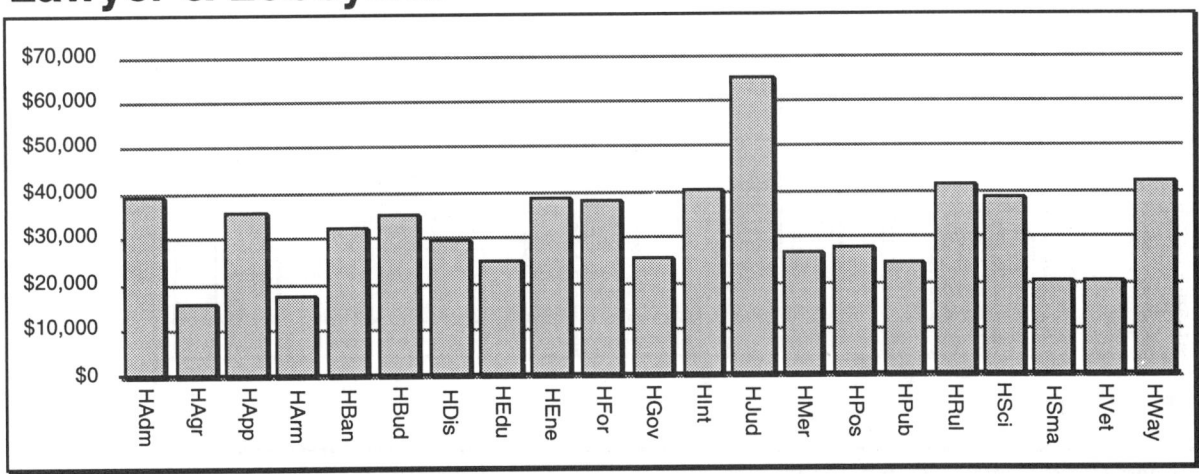

The House Judiciary Committee stood above all others in contributions from lawyers and lobbyists. Trial lawyers are most interested in combatting any movement toward tort reform. Lobbyists, perhaps the most pragmatic group of any contributors, give to all committees, largely to ensure access on behalf of their clients.

Transportation

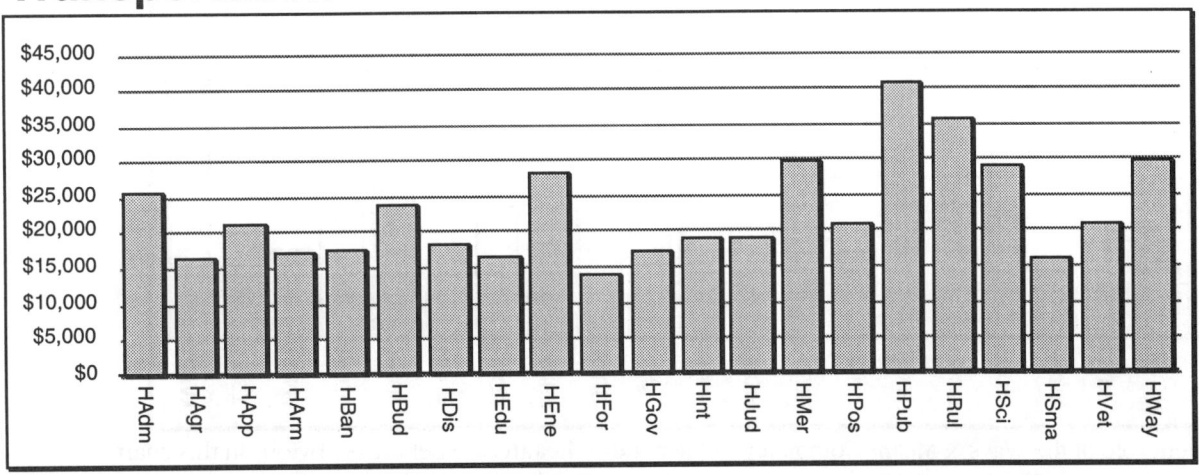

Not surprisingly, the Public Works and Transportation Committee was the biggest recipient of transport industry dollars. The Merchant Marine & Fisheries Committee got the most from shipping interests.

Construction

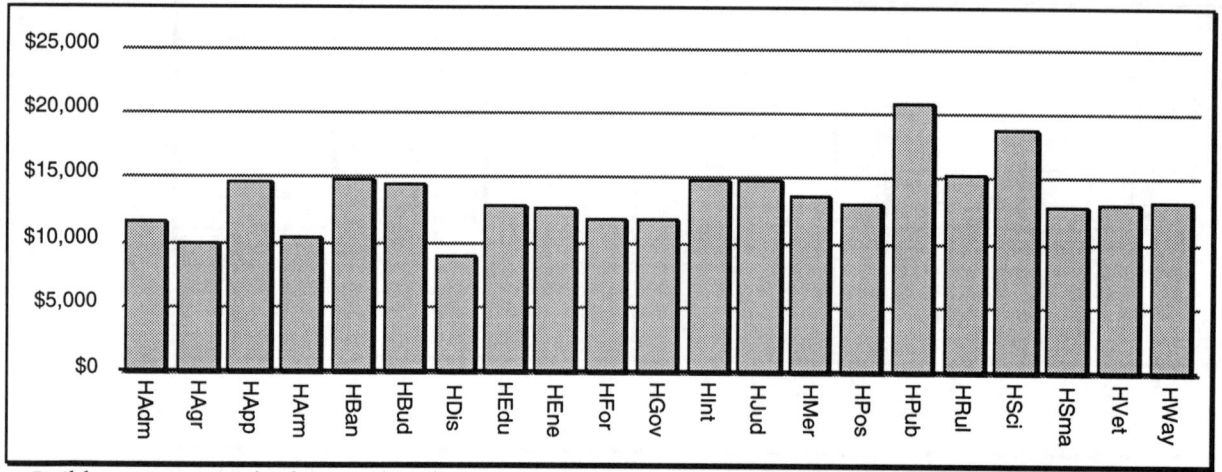

Builders groups and others within the construction sector spread their dollars to candidates in all committees. Public Works and Transportation Committee members, whose jurisdiction includes major federal building projects, got the most.

Ideological/Single-Issue

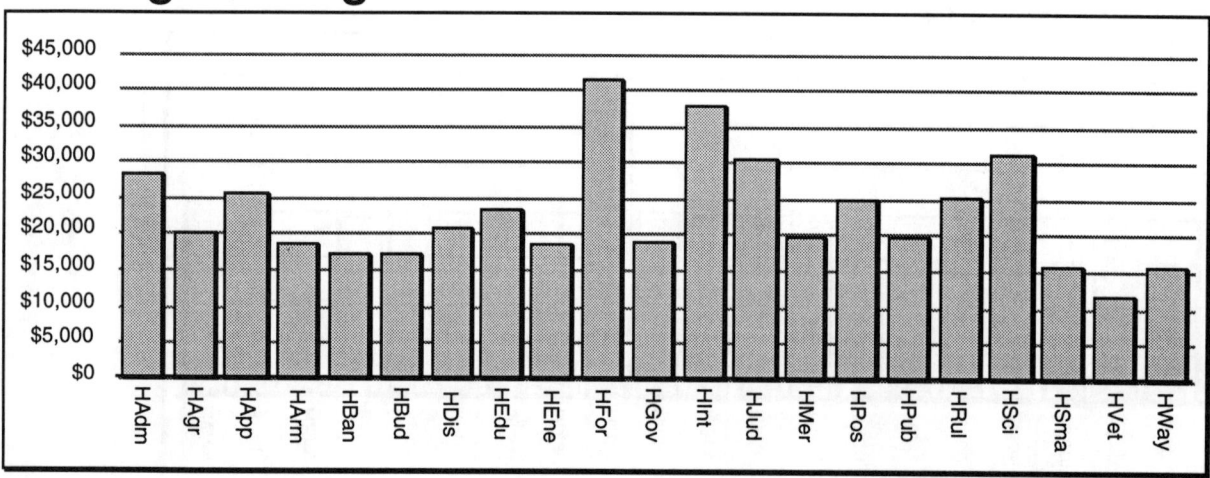

The House Foreign Affairs Committee drew the most in contributions from ideological contributors. The leader there was pro-Israel groups, which gave more than $18,000 per member. Environmental groups favored the Interior Committee; the Sierra Club was the committee's biggest single contributor.

Health & Insurance

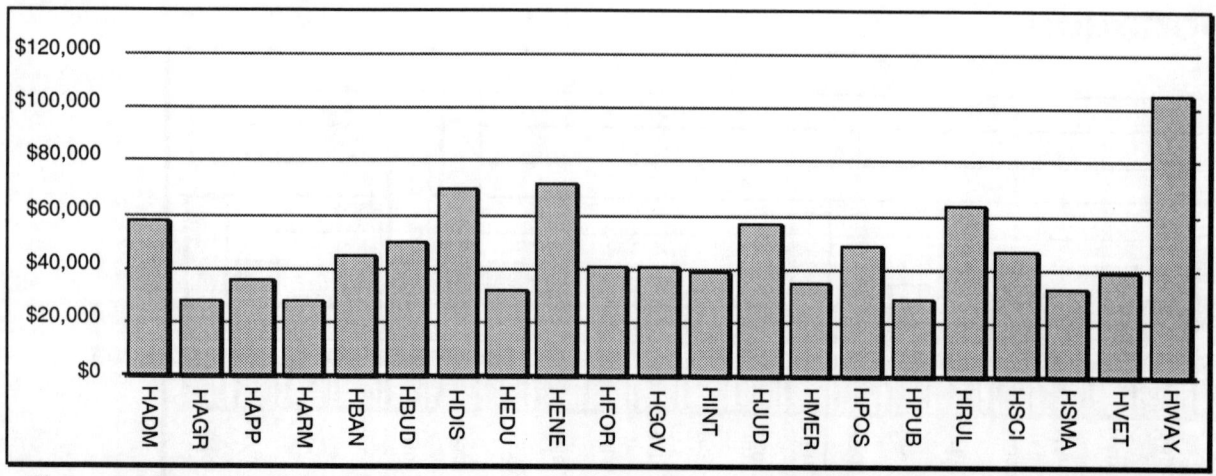

The preeminent role of the Ways & Means Committee in the nation's health care debate is obvious in this chart, which combines dollars given by insurance companies with those given by the health care sector.

ant
2.
Industry Profiles

Cash Constituents of Congress

Industry Profiles in Brief

With today's expensive election campaigns, and the almost infinite spectrum of legislation considered on Capitol Hill, members of Congress draw their campaign funds from dozens of different industries and interests. The industry profiles on the following pages provide the details on which industries are the biggest givers and which members are the biggest recipients of their funds. The profiles have two sections: one shows graphically where the money comes from and where it goes. The other gives more detail about the smaller categories within each industry. Following is a thumbnail sketch of each of the 12 main industry and interest group sectors:

Agriculture ....$24.9 million

An important player in Washington that has maintained its longtime influence despite the decline of the family farm, agricultural contributors gave nearly $25 million in contributions to congressional and presidential candidates in 1991-92. Crop production and processing was the sector's leading source of campaign funds, but it accounted for only one-quarter of the sector's total dollars. The rest came from a wide range of affiliated industries, from food processors and supermarkets to pesticide and fertilizer manufacturers, tobacco companies, dairy farmers, poultry and livestock producers, and the forest products industry.

Communications/Electronics ....$21.2 million

The big money here comes from two main sources: the telecommunications industry (primarily local and long distance telephone companies) and the entertainment industry, made up mainly of the TV and motion picture industries. The phone company money comes predominantly from AT&T and the regional Bell systems. Nearly nine-tenths of that money was delivered through political action committees. The broadcasting and movie money — which tilted heavily toward Democratic candidates — came mostly through individual donors rather than PACs.

Construction..$15.2 million

General contractors engaged in commercial, industrial, utility and highway construction were the biggest single source of campaign funds within the construction sector. Overall they outspent home builders by nearly three-to-one. Other notable sources of contributions were more specialized subcontractors, engineering and architectural firms, and building materials suppliers. A close partner of the construction industry, often weathering the same economic ups and downs, is the real estate industry, which is included separately in the Finance, Insurance & Real Estate sector, described below.

Defense ....$8.3 million

While every one of the 12 main industry and interest group sectors increased their giving in 1992, the Defense sector grew the least. That reflects the industry's continuing post-Cold War economic slump. Within the sector, defense aerospace contractors gave about twice as much as defense electronics firms. Overall, nearly 90 percent of the Defense industry's contributions came from PACs.

Energy & Natural Resources ....$21.3 million

Oil and gas producers supplied the biggest share of campaign dollars from this sector, as they have consistently over the years. In 1991-92 they gave $9.2 million to congressional and presidential candidates. Natural gas pipeline companies added another $2.4 million. The other big givers here were the nation's electric utilities, which doled out nearly $4.6 million — nearly 90 percent of it through PACs.

Finance, Insurance & Real Estate ....$71.1 million

This is the giant of all the contributor sectors, providing more than $71 million to federal candidates in the 1992 elections. Within the sector, four heavyweight industries provided most of the money — real estate interests gave $16.5 million, the securities & investment industry gave $15.9 million, insurance companies and agents gave $14.9 million, and commercial banks passed out $11.2 million to candidates for Congress and the presidency. Two-thirds of the banking and insurance contributions came from political action committees, while three-quarters of the real estate and securities money came from individuals.

Health ....*$31.7 million*

With a complete overhaul of the nation's health care system looming at the top of the agenda of both Congress and the White House, the nation's health providers dramatically boosted their political contributions in the 1992 elections. Physicians and other health professionals led the way, providing more than $21 million in campaign cash to federal candidates. Pharmaceutical companies and health products manufacturers added another $4.4 million, and hospital and nursing homes gave $3.6 million. The insurance industry, included in the financial category above, added nearly $15 million of its own, bringing the combined health & insurance outlay to more than $46 million in the 1992 elections.

Lawyers & Lobbyists ....*$44.1 million*

When looking at PAC contributions alone, lawyers and lobbyists appear to be a second-tier player among business sectors, but a closer examination of their contributions finds that that is due more to the way they give than to how much they give. Fully 86 percent of the contributions from lawyers and lobbyists came through individual donations, and when added to the PAC dollars, their overall total during 1991-92 rose to more than $44 million — second only to the Finance, Insurance & Real Estate sector. Democrats were the main beneficiaries, capturing nearly three-quarters of the total contributions.

Miscellaneous Business ....*$38.5 million*

This catchall category includes everything from steelmakers to beer distributors, restaurants to casinos, chemical companies to advertising agencies. Major contributor groups within the sector include the food & beverage industries ($4 million), the alcohol industry ($4 million), chemical manufacturers ($3 million), and a wide collection of business services and manufacturing companies.

Transportation ....*$19.0 million*

The automotive and air transport industries were the biggest givers within the transportation sector during 1991-92, though within those groups much of the money came not from airlines and automakers, but from auto dealers and from the nation's two giant delivery services, UPS and Federal Express. The air transport sector was also boosted by the presence of the widely-diversified General Electric. Though known by consumers mostly for its light bulbs and home appliances, GE's biggest revenue source is from its aerospace division, which makes jet engines for both commercial airliners and the military.

Labor ....*$43.3 million*

Though the number of union members continues to dwindle nationwide, and the political impact of organized labor has been in a long decline — witness their inability to derail the NAFTA agreement — labor unions remain a financial stalwart of the Democratic Party. Union PACs, which account for 99 percent of the labor contributions, delivered $40.6 million to Democratic candidates in the 1992 election. Republicans got $2.5 million.

Ideological/Single-Issue ....*$29.3 million*

While the most highly-publicized ideological groups tend to be the National Rifle Association and abortion groups, the biggest source of campaign funds among ideological and single-issue groups continues to be the large nationwide network of pro-Israel PACs. The biggest growth in 1992, however, came from Women's Groups — led by Emily's List. Though the Center was able to track more than $3.7 million from women's issue PACs and individual contributors, that number is undoubtedly much lower than the actual figure, since only contributions of $200 and above are itemized under federal law and many of the women's group donations were for smaller amounts.

Business Contributors

Where the money came from . . .

By far the largest source of campaign contributions — for both congressional and presidential candidates — are the corporations, trade associations and professional groups that are loosely classified under the label of "business" contributors. The PACs and individual contributors in this group come from every sector of American industry — sectors which are explored in greater detail on the pages that follow. Together, giving both through PACs and individuals, business groups delivered nearly $300 million to federal candidates in the 1992 elections.

The Finance, Insurance & Real Estate sector was far and away the largest, providing more than $71 million in contributions. Lawyers and lobbyists — one of the smallest business sectors if one looks at PAC contributions alone — ranked second overall in their giving. Eighty-six percent of their campaign dollars came not from PACs but from individuals.

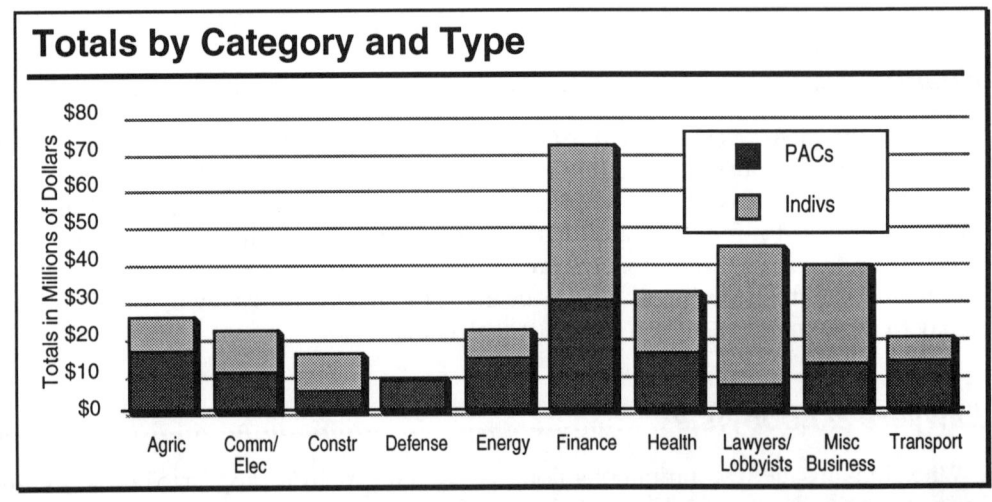

Category	Total	From PACs	PAC Pct	From Indivs	Indiv Pct
Agriculture	$24,892,124	$15,556,854	62%	$9,335,270	38%
Communic/Electronics	$21,232,464	$9,712,904	46%	$11,519,560	54%
Construction	$15,246,489	$4,730,644	31%	$10,515,845	69%
Defense	$8,328,760	$7,398,411	89%	$930,349	11%
Energy/Natural Resources	$21,341,235	$13,532,584	63%	$7,808,651	37%
Finance/Insur/Real Estate	$71,091,876	$29,617,353	42%	$41,474,523	58%
Health	$31,710,239	$14,932,301	47%	$16,777,938	53%
Lawyers & Lobbyists	$44,058,744	$6,319,679	14%	$37,739,065	86%
Misc Business	$38,478,007	$12,234,888	32%	$26,243,119	68%
Transportation	$18,989,690	$12,767,017	67%	$6,222,673	33%
Total	**$295,369,628**	**$126,802,635**	**43%**	**$168,566,993**	**57%**

Top 20 Business Contributors

Rank	Total	Contributor	Category	PAC Pct	Dem Pct	Repub Pct
1	$3,245,544	American Medical Assn*	Doctors	100%	49%	51%
2	$2,954,973	National Assn of Realtors	Real Estate	100%	55%	45%
3	$2,361,135	Assn of Trial Lawyers of America	Trial Lawyers	100%	92%	8%
4	$1,784,375	National Auto Dealers Assn	Auto Dealers	100%	39%	61%
5	$1,692,508	American Bankers Assn*	Comml Banks	99%	50%	49%
6	$1,544,701	American Institute of CPA's	Accountants	100%	56%	44%
7	$1,472,357	United Parcel Service	Delivery Svcs	99%	54%	46%
8	$1,434,408	American Dental Assn*	Dentists	100%	60%	40%
9	$1,397,883	AT&T*	Long Distance	93%	61%	39%
10	$1,373,955	National Assn of Life Underwriters	Life Insurance	100%	54%	46%
11	$1,074,827	National Assn of Home Builders*	Resid Constr	100%	44%	56%
12	$1,004,848	RJR Nabisco*	Tobacco/Food	95%	55%	45%
13	$977,081	National Beer Wholesalers Assn	Beer Distrib	100%	38%	62%
14	$963,353	BellSouth Corp*	Phone Utilities	92%	59%	41%
15	$898,545	Goldman, Sachs & Co	Securities	22%	67%	33%
16	$881,820	American Express*	Stocks/Credit	38%	69%	30%
17	$877,550	Associated Milk Producers	Dairy	100%	79%	21%
18	$870,227	American Academy of Ophthalmology	Eye Doctors	100%	63%	37%
19	$823,486	General Electric*	Aerospace	86%	60%	43%
20	$775,147	Philip Morris*	Tobacco/Food	87%	59%	41%

* Contributions came from more than one affiliate or subsidiary.

Where the money went . . .

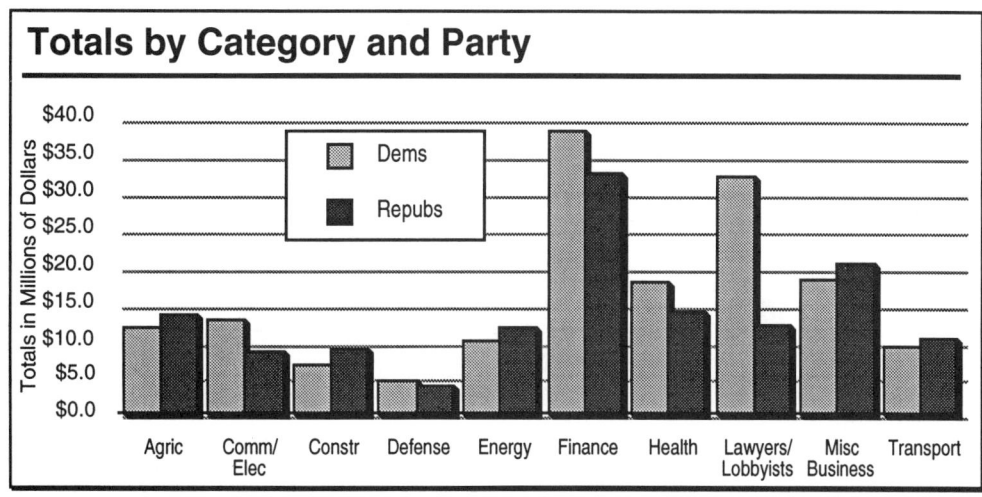

Totals by Category and Party

Category	Total	To Dems	Dem Pct	To Repubs	Repub Pct
Agriculture	$24,892,124	$11,533,853	46%	$13,315,969	53%
Communic/Electronics	$21,232,464	$12,758,180	60%	$8,391,147	40%
Construction	$15,246,489	$6,584,436	43%	$8,617,049	57%
Defense	$8,328,760	$4,609,451	55%	$3,714,903	45%
Energy/Natural Resources	$21,341,235	$9,794,836	46%	$11,518,607	54%
Finance/Insur/Real Estate	$71,091,876	$38,321,025	54%	$32,574,212	46%
Health	$31,710,239	$17,774,140	56%	$13,780,085	43%
Lawyers & Lobbyists	$44,058,744	$32,160,897	73%	$11,827,725	27%
Misc Business	$38,478,007	$17,962,336	47%	$20,354,469	53%
Transportation	$18,989,690	$8,940,802	47%	$10,020,890	53%
Total	**$295,369,628**	**$160,439,956**	**54%**	**$134,115,056**	**45%**

Overall, Democrats attracted a slight majority of the dollars from within the business community — a fact that many might find surprising, since most business groups tend to be more Republican in their political outlook. Whatever their personal preferences, however, the one quality that marks nearly all business groups is their pragmatism. Bluntly speaking, the Democrats control both houses of Congress with sizable majorities. Since the 1992 election, they also control the White House. Business leaders know well that if legislation is to succeed, the majority party is going to have to go along with it.

Most sectors within the business community split their dollars fairly evenly between Republicans and Democrats. The most notable exception was the legal community, which gave nearly three-quarters of its dollars to Democrats. The communications & electronics sector also favored Democrats by a fairly wide margin — primarily because of the heavily Democratic-leaning entertainment industry based in Hollywood and New York. The most heavily Republican sector was the construction industry, which gave 57 percent of its dollars to GOP candidates.

The Top 20 contributor chart on the opposite page illustrates an important point about contributions in American politics: the biggest overall contributors tend to be political action committees that represent large nationwide organizations or Fortune 500 companies. But behind those headline-grabbing leaders are tens of thousands of smaller organizations — law firms, doctors' offices, insurance agents, and every other kind of business from beer wholesalers to casinos. Individually they are small enough not to attract attention. Together, however, their donations amount to tens of millions of dollars. To fully reveal the patterns by which industries and interest groups make their opinions heard in Washington, one must aggregate *all* the contributors — large and small — into specific categories. That is the approach taken throughout this book and it will reveal many surprising (and not so surprising) patterns on these pages, and in the committee and member profiles that follow.

The totals on these pages, and in all others in the Industry Profile section of this book, reflect contributions both to congressional and presidential candidates. They do not include small contributions, however, as federal law does not require any itemization of individual donations under $200. What these pages do show are the patterns in giving from major contributors — political action committees, and those individuals giving $200 or more. Those two groups together provide the great majority of dollars that fuel the ever more expensive machinery of modern American elections.

Agriculture

Where the money came from . . .

The agriculture sector encompasses thousands of independent farmers, ranchers and dairy producers from Maine to California, but that's just the half of it. Also included in this widely diversified category are commodities brokers, lumber companies, grocery wholesalers, pesticide manufacturers and giant food industry conglomerates making everything from cigarettes to frozen pizzas. In all, the industry contributed nearly $25 million to federal campaigns in the 1992 elections. About 62 percent came from political action committees and just over half went to Republican candidates.

Within the farming community, the heaviest crop of dollars came from sugar growers and dairy producers, though detailed classifications were not always possible since many contributors described themselves simply as "farmers." More than 80 percent of the tobacco and dairy money was delivered through PACs, while cattle ranchers and poultry producers were the groups most likely to give through individual contributions.

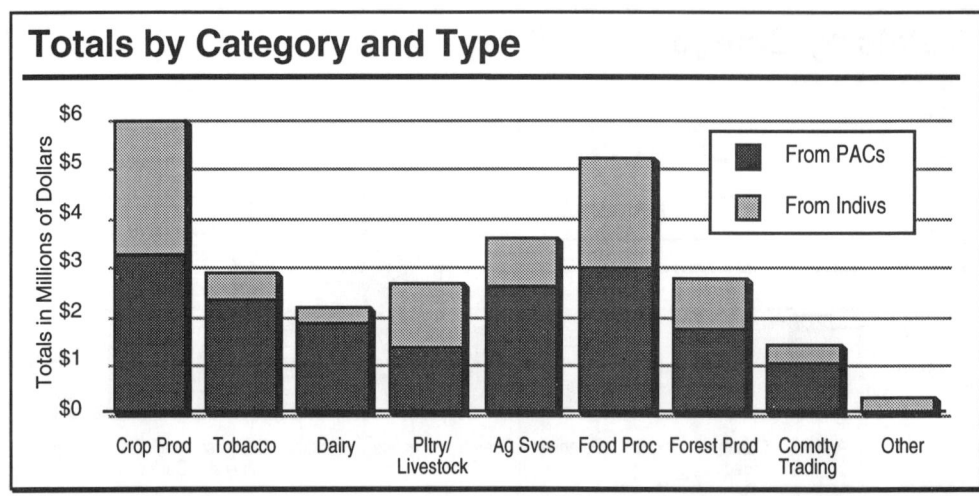

Category	Total	From PACs	PAC Pct	From Indivs	Indiv Pct
Crop Production/Processing	$5,868,649	$3,197,726	54%	$2,670,923	46%
Tobacco	$2,818,861	$2,280,012	81%	$538,849	19%
Dairy	$2,107,911	$1,753,112	83%	$354,799	17%
Poultry & Livestock	$2,551,679	$1,266,751	50%	$1,284,928	50%
Agricultural Services/Products	$3,470,020	$2,522,628	73%	$947,392	27%
Food Processing & Sales	$5,108,064	$2,886,974	57%	$2,221,090	43%
Forest Products	$2,709,343	$1,649,651	61%	$1,059,692	39%
Commodity Trading*	$1,325,102	$959,300	72%	$365,802	28%
Other & Unclassified	$257,597	$0	0%	$257,597	100%
TOTAL	**$24,892,124**	**$15,556,854**	**62%**	**$9,335,270**	**38%**

* Listed for information only. Total is included under Finance/Insurance/Real Estate.

Top 20 Agriculture Contributors

Rank	Total	Contributor	Category	PAC Pct	Dem Pct	Repub Pct
1	$1,004,848	RJR Nabisco*	Tobacco/Food	95%	55%	45%
2	$877,550	Associated Milk Producers	Dairy	100%	79%	21%
3	$775,147	Philip Morris*	Tobacco/Food	87%	59%	41%
4	$636,120	US Tobacco*	Tobacco	69%	34%	66%
5	$531,778	Food Marketing Institute	Food Stores	100%	35%	65%
6	$427,470	National Cattlemen's Assn*	Livestock	99%	44%	55%
7	$345,650	Archer-Daniels-Midland Corp	Grain Traders	82%	51%	49%
8	$345,071	Mid-America Dairymen	Dairy	100%	74%	26%
9	$313,588	ConAgra Inc	Food Products	96%	30%	69%
10	$311,707	American Sugarbeet Growers Assn	Sugar	100%	68%	32%
11	$301,000	American Veterinary Medical Assn	Veterinarians	100%	59%	41%
12	$297,015	American Crystal Sugar Corp	Sugar	100%	71%	29%
13	$266,010	Tyson Foods	Poultry	65%	86%	14%
14	$252,850	Winn-Dixie Stores	Food Stores	90%	37%	63%
15	$248,650	Westvaco Corp	Paper/Pulp	99%	21%	79%
16	$237,980	Anheuser-Busch	Beer	53%	54%	46%
17	$221,860	International Paper Co	Paper/Pulp	99%	10%	90%
18	$199,000	Freeport-McMoRan Inc	Ag Chemicals	67%	58%	42%
19	$197,925	American Sugar Cane League	Sugar	100%	76%	24%
20	$189,200	Tobacco Institute	Tobacco	97%	51%	49%

* Contributions came from more than one affiliate or subsidiary.

Where the money went . . .

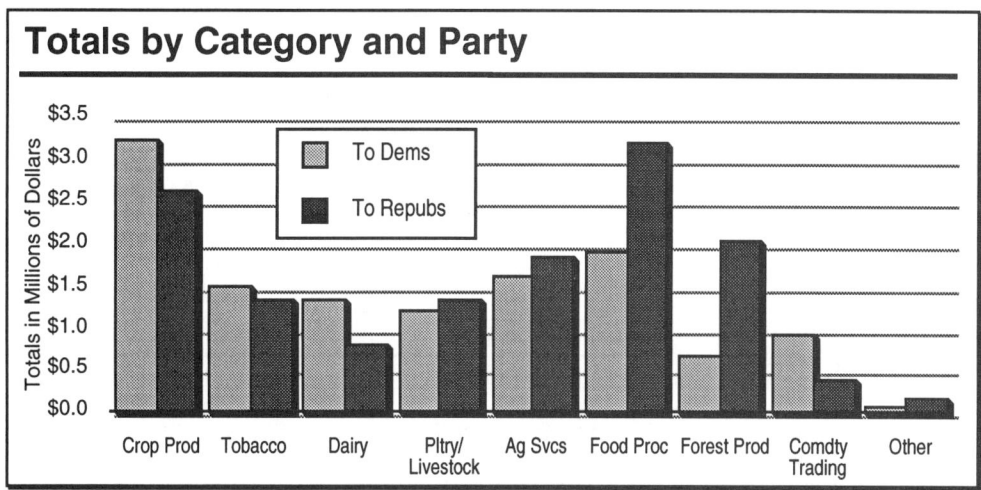

Totals by Category and Party

Overall, the agriculture sector gave a slight majority of its campaign dollars to Republicans, though there were wide variations within the sector. Most partisan was the forest products industry, which gave three-quarters of its money to Republicans. Dairy farmers, however, preferred Democrats nearly two-to-one.

Category	Total	To Dems	Dem Pct	To Repubs	Repub Pct
Crop Production/Processing	$5,868,649	$3,229,687	55%	$2,629,576	45%
Tobacco	$2,818,861	$1,494,566	53%	$1,322,876	47%
Dairy	$2,107,911	$1,324,596	63%	$783,315	37%
Poultry & Livestock	$2,551,679	$1,201,531	47%	$1,346,698	53%
Agricultural Services/Products	$3,470,020	$1,619,109	47%	$1,844,911	53%
Food Processing & Sales	$5,108,064	$1,900,655	37%	$3,187,590	62%
Forest Products	$2,709,343	$678,905	25%	$2,028,438	75%
Commodity Trading*	$1,325,102	$936,452	71%	$387,150	29%
Other & Unclassified	$257,597	$84,804	33%	$172,565	67%
TOTAL	**$24,892,124**	**$11,533,853**	**46%**	**$13,315,969**	**53%**

* Listed for information only. Total is included under Finance/Insurance/Real Estate.

California Republican John Seymour tapped successfully into the huge agribusiness industry of his home state, collecting more than half a million dollars in the 1992 election. The voters, however, preferred Dianne Feinstein. Only two of the remaining top recipients in the Senate held seats on the Agriculture Committee, though all came from states where farming is an important part of the economy.

In the House, farm-state incumbents drew the heaviest support from the agriculture sector. Five of the top 10 also sat on the House Agriculture Committee. Texas Democrat Kika de la Garza, who ranked seventh, is the committee's chairman. Ron Marlenee, the top-ranking recipient, lost his seat in a showdown with fellow incumbent Pat Williams, after Montana lost one of its two seats in Congress due to reapportionment. Marlenee, a conservative Republican, got most of the business support, but Williams, a liberal Democrat, was the winner in a close, bitterly-fought race.

Top 10 Senate Recipients

Rank	Name	Amount	Status	W/L
1	John F. Seymour (R-Calif)	$553,503	Incumb	L
2	Wyche Fowler Jr. (D-Ga)	$381,699	Incumb	L
3	Christopher S. Bond (R-Mo)	$293,303	Incumb	W
4	Bob Kasten (R-Wis)	$285,235	Incumb	L
5	Dale Bumpers (D-Ark)	$262,420	Incumb	W
6	Rod Chandler (R-Wash)	$251,707	Open	L
7	Paul Coverdell (R-Ga)	$230,707	Chall	W
8	Bob Dole (R-Kan)	$225,881	Incumb	W
9	Dirk Kempthorne (R-Idaho)	$222,886	Open	W
10	Don Nickles (R-Okla)	$217,228	Incumb	W

Top 10 House Recipients

Rank	Name	Amount	Status	W/L
1	Ron Marlenee (R-Mont)	$187,305	Incumb	L
2	Jerry Huckaby (D-La)	$186,374	Incumb	L
3	Charles Hatcher (D-Ga)	$176,621	Incumb	L
4	Vic Fazio (D-Calif)	$160,739	Incumb	W
5	Wally Herger (R-Calif)	$155,748	Incumb	W
6	Calvin Dooley (D-Calif)	$145,723	Incumb	W
7	E. "Kika" de la Garza (D-Texas)	$145,099	Incumb	W
8	Charles W. Stenholm (D-Texas)	$144,303	Incumb	W
9	Bill Emerson (R-Mo)	$143,925	Incumb	W
10	Tom Coleman (R-Mo)	$136,225	Incumb	L

Closeup on Agriculture

Crop Production & Basic Processing .... $5.9 million

Though this category includes farmers raising every crop under the sun, six of the top 10 contributors (and five of the top six) were sugar growers. California's preeminence as the nation's leading agricultural producer is reflected by the presence of five Californians on the list of top recipients among House and Senate candidates.

Top Contributors	
1 American Sugarbeet Growers Assn	$311,707
2 American Crystal Sugar Corp	$297,015
3 American Sugar Cane League	$197,925
4 National Cotton Council	$184,989
5 Okeelanta Corp	$170,800
6 Florida Sugar Cane League	$167,075
7 Ocean Spray Cranberries	$145,945
8 Sunkist Growers	$134,360
9 Southern Minn Beet Sugar Co-op	$120,400
10 Sun-Diamond Growers*	$106,685

* Contributions came from more than one affiliate or subsidiary.

Top Senate Recipients			
1 John F. Seymour (R-Calif)	$226,537	Incumb	L
2 Wyche Fowler Jr. (D-Ga)	$137,651	Incumb	L
3 Dale Bumpers (D-Ark)	$78,720	Incumb	W
4 Kent Conrad (D-ND)	$72,890	Incumb	W
5 Tom Campbell (R-Calif)	$60,078	Open	L

Top House Recipients			
1 Jerry Huckaby (D-La)	$131,424	Incumb	L
2 Vic Fazio (D-Calif)	$95,774	Incumb	W
3 Charles Hatcher (D-Ga)	$91,121	Incumb	L
4 Calvin Dooley (D-Calif)	$82,122	Incumb	W
5 Wally Herger (R-Calif)	$76,165	Incumb	W

Tobacco .... $2.8 million

The nation's most controversial agricultural related industry, still supported by federal subsidies, delivered $2.8 million to federal candidates in the 1992 election. A number of tobacco state lawmakers appear on the list of biggest recipients, as expected. The only non-incumbent on the list was Oklahoma Democrat Drew Edmondson, who opposed Mike Synar, a longtime tobacco industry foe. Edmondson lost in the primary, and Synar was reelected despite the tobacco industry's efforts to unseat him.

Top Contributors	
1 RJR Nabisco*	$1,004,848
2 Philip Morris*	$775,147
3 US Tobacco*	$636,120
4 Tobacco Institute	$189,200
5 Pinkerton Tobacco	$66,475

* Contributions came from more than one affiliate or subsidiary.

Top Senate Recipients			
1 Wendell H. Ford (D-Ky)	$68,148	Incumb	W
2 Bob Kasten (R-Wis)	$62,502	Incumb	L
3 Wyche Fowler Jr. (D-Ga)	$43,000	Incumb	L
4 Christopher J. Dodd (D-Conn)	$35,700	Incumb	W
5 Terry Sanford (D-NC)	$34,250	Incumb	L

Top House Recipients			
1 Drew Edmondson (D-Okla)	$53,830	Chall	L
2 Thomas J. Bliley Jr. (R-Va)	$38,991	Incumb	W
3 Sam M. Gibbons (D-Fla)	$25,250	Incumb	W
4 Charles Hatcher (D-Ga)	$24,950	Incumb	L
5 Richard A. Gephardt (D-Mo)	$22,848	Incumb	W

Dairy .... $2.1 million

Price supports to the dairy industry have long been a staple of federal agricultural policy. In return, the industry has been generous to Capitol Hill lawmakers seeking reelection. Overall, Democrats got 63 percent of their campaign dollars in 1991-92.

Top Contributors	
1 Associated Milk Producers	$877,550
2 Mid-America Dairymen	$345,071
3 Dairymen Inc*	$173,874
4 Milk Industry Foundation	$132,600
5 Milk Marketing Inc	$84,700

* Contributions came from more than one affiliate or subsidiary.

Top Senate Recipients			
1 Bob Kasten (R-Wis)	$36,035	Incumb	L
2 Ben Nighthorse Campbell (D-Colo)	$26,600	Open	W
3 Arlen Specter (R-Pa)	$26,250	Incumb	W
4 John F. Seymour (R-Calif)	$25,600	Incumb	L
5 Charles E. Grassley (R-Iowa)	$22,950	Incumb	W

Top House Recipients			
1 Jill L. Long (D-Ind)	$23,500	Incumb	W
2 Wayne Allard (R-Colo)	$21,100	Incumb	W
3 Harold L. Volkmer (D-Mo)	$20,500	Incumb	W
4 Jim Jontz (D-Ind)	$18,250	Incumb	L
5 Charles W. Stenholm (D-Texas)	$18,000	Incumb	W

Agricultural Services & Products ....$3.5 million

The support industries that provide everything from fertilizers and pesticides to crop insurance form a major segment of the agriculture sector's contributions to Congress. The top contributor in this category, Archer-Daniels-Midland, a giant agribusiness firm that is the nation's largest supplier of ethanol, was also the biggest contributor of "soft money" in the 1992 elections. ADM gave over $1.3 million in soft money — most of it to the Republican National Committee in support of President Bush's reelection.

Top Contributors	
1 Archer-Daniels-Midland Corp	$345,650
2 American Veterinary Medical Assn	$301,000
3 Freeport-McMoRan Inc	$199,000
4 Farm Credit Council	$170,023
5 American Assn of Crop Insurers	$152,726
6 Deere & Co*	$140,710
7 Cargill Inc	$134,850
8 Alabama Farm Bureau Federation	$131,231
9 National Council of Farmer Co-ops	$128,000
10 Land O'Lakes Inc	$80,525

* Contributions came from more than one affiliate or subsidiary.

Top Senate Recipients			
1 John F. Seymour (R-Calif)	$92,299	Incumb	L
2 Bob Dole (R-Kan)	$65,500	Incumb	W
3 Christopher S. Bond (R-Mo)	$64,134	Incumb	W
4 Charles E. Grassley (R-Iowa)	$60,429	Incumb	W
5 Wyche Fowler Jr. (D-Ga)	$57,848	Incumb	L

Top House Recipients			
1 Tom Coleman (R-Mo)	$40,850	Incumb	L
2 E. "Kika" de la Garza (D-Texas)	$37,670	Incumb	W
3 Charles W. Stenholm (D-Texas)	$29,000	Incumb	W
4 Pat Roberts (R-Kan)	$27,500	Incumb	W
5 Robert H. Michel (R-Ill)	$26,982	Incumb	W

Food Processing & Sales ....$5.1 million

This category encompasses the companies that provide most of the groceries we find on supermarket shelves, as well as the supermarkets themselves and grocery wholesalers. The industry favored Republican candidates by a wide margin.

Top Contributors	
1 Food Marketing Institute	$531,778
2 ConAgra Inc	$313,588
3 Winn-Dixie Stores	$252,850
4 General Mills*	$205,683
5 Flowers Industries	$187,200
6 Fleming Companies Inc	$181,650
7 American Meat Institute	$107,129
8 Connell Rice & Sugar Co	$92,638
9 Nestle Enterprises Inc	$83,867
10 National Wholesale Grocers Assn	$83,839

* Contributions came from more than one affiliate or subsidiary.

Top Senate Recipients			
1 John F. Seymour (R-Calif)	$89,560	Incumb	L
2 Christopher S. Bond (R-Mo)	$86,875	Incumb	W
3 Dirk Kempthorne (R-Idaho)	$79,982	Open	W
4 Arlen Specter (R-Pa)	$70,700	Incumb	W
5 Paul Coverdell (R-Ga)	$70,150	Chall	W

Top House Recipients			
1 Michael D. Crapo (R-Idaho)	$38,750	Open	W
2 Tom Coleman (R-Mo)	$30,250	Incumb	L
3 Pete von Reichbauer (R-Wash)	$28,870	Open	L
4 H. Martin Lancaster (D-NC)	$28,550	Incumb	W
5 Charles W. Stenholm (D-Texas)	$28,528	Incumb	W

Forest Products ....$2.7 million

Candidates from the Pacific Northwest were the biggest recipients of dollars from the forest products industry. This was the most Republican-leaning industry within the agriculture sector. Only one dollar in every four went to Democrats.

Top Contributors	
1 Westvaco Corp	$248,400
2 International Paper Co	$221,860
3 Weyerhaeuser Co*	$180,423
4 Georgia-Pacific Corp	$137,442
5 Champion International Corp	$127,612
6 Simpson Investment Co	$112,575
7 Scott Paper Co	$84,148
8 Union Camp Corp	$82,810
9 Boise Cascade	$82,507
10 Potlatch Corp	$78,828

* Contributions came from more than one affiliate or subsidiary.

Top Senate Recipients			
1 Rod Chandler (R-Wash)	$132,193	Open	L
2 Bob Packwood (R-Ore)	$107,400	Incumb	W
3 Dirk Kempthorne (R-Idaho)	$83,554	Open	W
4 Paul Coverdell (R-Ga)	$71,995	Chall	W
5 Bob Kasten (R-Wis)	$64,200	Incumb	L

Top House Recipients			
1 Tony Meeker (R-Ore)	$63,975	Open	L
2 Bob Smith (R-Ore)	$43,762	Incumb	W
3 Pat Fiske (R-Wash)	$40,300	Chall	L
4 Steve Buyer (R-Ind)	$39,698	Chall	W
5 Jennifer Dunn (R-Wash)	$28,868	Open	W

Communications & Electronics

Where the money came from . . .

Increasingly, the thread that ties the American nation together is an electronic one. We plug into television for the day's news, weather, football games and soap operas. We flash faxes by the millions across the continent each business day. Our telephones are never far from reach, whether we're in the backyard, the interstate, or 30,000 feet in the air. And our computers — desktop, laptop, or palm-of-the-hand varieties — are becoming more ubiquitous and more necessary every day. We are a nation plugged in, and our unceasing appetite for instant news, communications and entertainment have spawned industries that have become an increasingly important sector of the American economy.

Since much of the telecommunications industry comes under federal regulation, decisions made in Washington can mean billions to the industry. Both sides know it, and the flow of dollars to federal campaigns reflects that fact. In the 1992 elections this sector contributed more than $21 million to congressional and presidential campaigns.

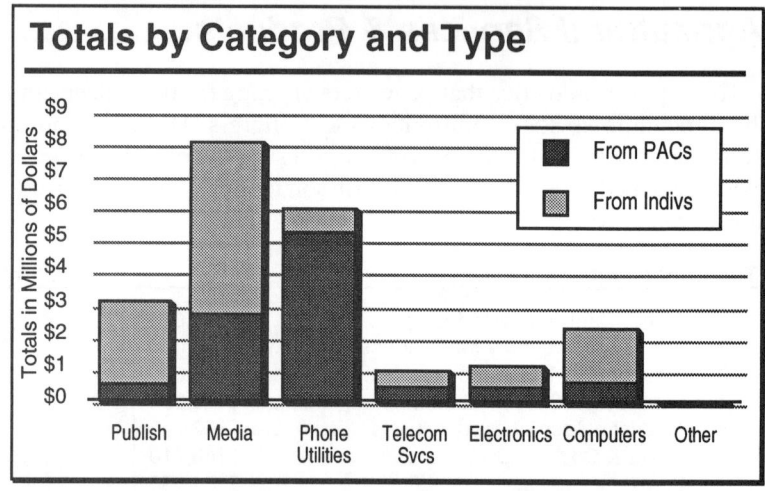

Category	Total	From PACs	PAC Pct	From Indivs	Indiv Pct
Publishing	$3,059,581	$465,102	15%	$2,594,479	85%
Media/Entertainment	$8,018,782	$2,598,430	32%	$5,420,352	68%
Telephone Utilities	$5,904,399	$5,167,442	88%	$736,957	12%
Telecom Equipment & Svcs	$909,340	$449,199	49%	$460,141	51%
Electronics Mfg & Services	$1,088,233	$455,250	42%	$632,983	58%
Computer Equipment & Svcs	$2,212,954	$576,981	26%	$1,635,973	74%
Other & Unclassified	$39,175	$500	1%	$38,675	99%
TOTAL	**$21,232,464**	**$9,712,904**	**46%**	**$11,519,560**	**54%**

The two most generous segments of the communications/electronics sector were the Media & Entertainment industries — which includes TV and motion picture production as well as the Cable TV and recorded music industries — and the nation's network of local and long distance telephone utilities. Most of the media dollars came through individual contributions, while the phone companies gave most of their money through political action committees.

Top 20 Communications & Electronics Contributors

Rank	Total	Contributor	Category	PAC Pct	Dem Pct	Repub Pct
1	$1,397,883	AT&T*	Long Distance	93%	61%	39%
2	$963,353	BellSouth Corp*	Phone Utilities	92%	59%	41%
3	$644,249	National Cable Television Assn	Cable TV	99%	54%	46%
4	$631,869	GTE Corp*	Phone Utilities	97%	52%	48%
5	$583,089	Time Warner*	Movies/Publish	24%	76%	24%
6	$562,342	Ameritech Corp*	Phone Utilities	92%	55%	45%
7	$522,400	National Assn of Broadcasters	Entertainment	95%	55%	45%
8	$432,910	United Telecommunications*	Phone Utilities	98%	33%	67%
9	$401,834	Walt Disney Co*	Movies/Resorts	24%	77%	23%
10	$331,512	Pacific Telesis Group	Phone Utilities	94%	63%	37%
11	$325,113	US West*	Phone Utilities	82%	54%	46%
12	$317,193	MCA Inc*	Movies/TV	58%	84%	16%
13	$311,690	Southwestern Bell	Phone Utilities	80%	59%	41%
14	$270,011	Bell Atlantic*	Phone Utilities	87%	56%	43%
15	$258,377	Westinghouse Electric*	Electronics	83%	56%	43%
16	$242,750	Corning Glass Works	Telecom Equip	100%	39%	61%
17	$237,745	NYNEX Corp*	Phone Utilities	86%	50%	50%
18	$220,680	Harris Corp	Electronics	94%	3%	96%
19	$194,661	Hallmark Cards	Publishing	74%	22%	78%
20	$179,210	ASCAP	Music Prod	97%	87%	13%

* Contributions came from more than one affiliate or subsidiary.

Where the money went . . .

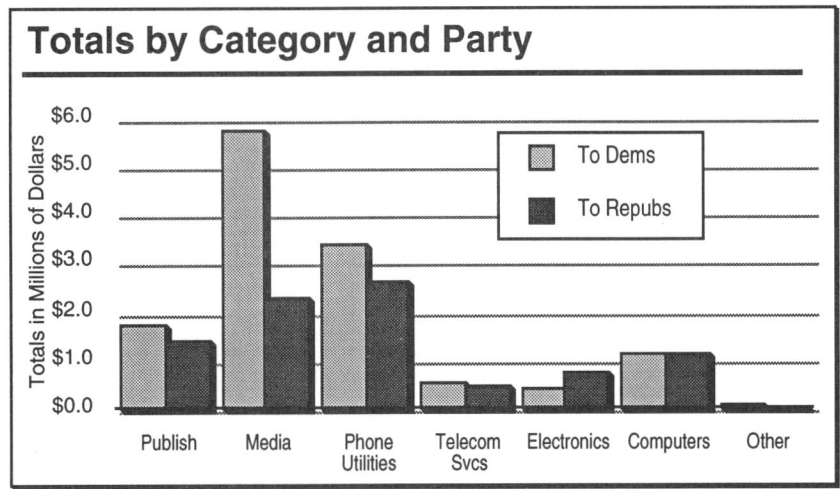

Totals by Category and Party

The Hollywood film community — both the studios and the stars — have always shown a strong preference for Democrats, a fact clearly reflected in the chart on the left. Telephone utilities were more even handed, though they too gave a majority of their dollars to Democratic candidates. Overall, the sector's 60-40 split in favor of Democrats was the second biggest of any business sector. Only lawyers and lobbyists were more supportive of the Democratic party.

Category	Total	To Dems	Dem Pct	To Repubs	Repub Pct
Publishing	$3,059,581	$1,678,693	55%	$1,354,284	44%
Media/Entertainment	$8,018,782	$5,746,780	72%	$2,252,427	28%
Telephone Utilities	$5,904,399	$3,333,625	56%	$2,565,484	43%
Telecom Equipment & Svcs	$909,340	$473,469	52%	$434,669	48%
Electronics Mfg & Services	$1,088,233	$401,368	37%	$683,515	63%
Computer Equipment & Svcs	$2,212,954	$1,099,595	50%	$1,086,243	49%
Other & Unclassified	$39,175	$24,650	63%	$14,525	37%
TOTAL	**$21,232,464**	**$12,758,180**	**60%**	**$8,391,147**	**40%**

Californians were the prime recipients of communications/electronics money in the 1992 elections in U.S. Senate races — a reflection of the fact that both Hollywood and Silicon Valley lie within the Golden State. The fact that both of California's Senate seats were up for election in 1992 was also a major factor. Oregon's Bob Packwood, ranking Republican on the Senate Commerce Committee's Communications subcommittee, was the top beneficiary of telephone and telecommunications industry money.

In the House, Majority Leader Dick Gephardt led all other members in donations from the sector. Five of the top 10 House recipients held seats on the influential Energy & Commerce Committee, which regulates telecommunications policy. John Dingell is the committee's chairman. Mike Synar, Don Ritter and Tom McMillen all sat on the panel's Telecommunications and Finance Subcommittee in 1992.

Top 10 Senate Recipients

Rank	Name	Amount	Status	W/L
1	Mel Levine (D-Calif)	$499,165	Open	L
2	Barbara Boxer (D-Calif)	$489,034	Open	W
3	Dianne Feinstein (D-Calif)	$382,515	Chall	W
4	Bob Packwood (R-Ore)	$331,850	Incumb	W
5	Arlen Specter (R-Pa)	$248,875	Incumb	W
6	Tom Campbell (R-Calif)	$234,488	Open	L
7	Robert Abrams (D-NY)	$231,370	Chall	L
8	John F. Seymour (R-Calif)	$223,658	Incumb	L
9	Ernest F. Hollings (D-SC)	$210,612	Incumb	W
10	Christopher J. Dodd (D-Conn)	$206,268	Incumb	W

Top 10 House Recipients

Rank	Name	Amount	Status	W/L
1	Richard A. Gephardt (D-Mo)	$191,855	Incumb	W
2	Mike Synar (D-Okla)	$130,354	Incumb	W
3	John D. Dingell (D-Mich)	$126,350	Incumb	W
4	Don Ritter (R-Pa)	$111,074	Incumb	L
5	Howard L. Berman (D-Calif)	$102,350	Incumb	W
6	Al Swift (D-Wash)	$99,000	Incumb	W
7	Vic Fazio (D-Calif)	$91,200	Incumb	W
8	David E. Bonior (D-Mich)	$88,150	Incumb	W
9	Tom McMillen (D-Md)	$86,200	Incumb	L
10	Jack Brooks (D-Texas)	$83,900	Incumb	W

Closeup on Communications & Electronics

Printing & Publishing .... $3.1 million

The list of leading publishing industry contributors may seem surprising, but that's largely because many of the nation's best known publishing houses have been bought up by media conglomerates like Time Warner. The two leading companies in the list below have long been politically active. Hallmark is the nation's largest greeting card publisher. West Publishing is the leading supplier of legal texts.

Top Contributors		
1	Hallmark Cards	$194,661
2	West Publishing	$140,400
3	Printing Industries of America	$118,002
4	RR Donnelley & Sons	$77,700
5	Forbes Inc	$41,700

Top Senate Recipients				
1	Robert Abrams (D-NY)	$97,270	Chall	L
2	Barbara Boxer (D-Calif)	$55,526	Open	W
3	Christopher S. Bond (R-Mo)	$48,288	Incumb	W
4	Mel Levine (D-Calif)	$44,800	Open	L
5	Dianne Feinstein (D-Calif)	$44,015	Chall	W

Top House Recipients				
1	Richard A. Gephardt (D-Mo)	$18,850	Incumb	W
2	Gerry Sikorski (D-Minn)	$15,500	Incumb	L
3	Tom Coleman (R-Mo)	$14,300	Incumb	L
4	Patricia Schroeder (D-Colo)	$14,281	Incumb	W
5	Mike Synar (D-Okla)	$12,950	Incumb	W

TV & Movies Production/Distribution .... $5.8 million

Two distinct categories of contributors make up this group — the Hollywood-based TV and motion picture industry that produces much of the nation's mass-market entertainment, and the nationwide network of TV and radio broadcasters, represented primarily by the National Association of Broadcasters. While the broadcasters delivered most of their dollars through the NAB's political action committee, a major share of the movie money came from individuals. Time Warner and Disney both ranked among the 10 largest sources of individual contributions in the 1992 elections.

Top Contributors		
1	Time Warner*	$583,089
2	National Assn of Broadcasters	$522,400
3	Walt Disney Co*	$399,834
4	MCA Inc*	$317,193
5	Paramount Communications*	$174,005
6	Sony Corp*	$141,635
7	Creative Artists Agency Inc	$66,702
8	CBS Inc	$64,483
9	Interscope Group	$62,800
10	Fox Inc	$62,650

* Contributions came from more than one affiliate or subsidiary.

Plenty of Hollywood stars donated money to presidential and congressional candidates, but their dollars were small compared to those of the studio chiefs, producers, agents and other behind-the-scenes figures in the film community. One thing they all shared was a strong inclination to direct their dollars to Democrats.

Broadcasters too gave most of their dollars to Democratic candidates, but their distribution of funds was much more evenly balanced. Overall, commercial radio and TV operators gave 57 percent of their money to Democrats, while the TV and motion picture industries gave Democrats well over 80 percent of their dollars.

The biggest recipients of the entertainment industry's generosity were Californians. Democratic Congressman Mel Levine of Los Angeles made a run for the U.S. Senate, but never made it past the primary. Even so, he captured more media money than successful candidates Barbara Boxer and Dianne Feinstein.

In the House, two LA-area incumbents — Howard Berman and Anthony Beilenson — collected respectable sums from the TV and movie industry. So did House Majority Leader Dick Gephardt, who was one of Hollywood's favorites when he ran for president in 1988.

Top Senate Recipients				
1	Mel Levine (D-Calif)	$370,925	Open	L
2	Barbara Boxer (D-Calif)	$361,944	Open	W
3	Dianne Feinstein (D-Calif)	$251,956	Chall	W
4	Christopher J. Dodd (D-Conn)	$126,000	Incumb	W
5	Gray Davis (D-Calif)	$112,500	Chall	L

Top House Recipients				
1	Howard L. Berman (D-Calif)	$66,750	Incumb	W
2	Richard A. Gephardt (D-Mo)	$64,755	Incumb	W
3	Anthony C. Beilenson (D-Calif)	$48,150	Incumb	W
4	John D. Dingell (D-Mich)	$39,550	Incumb	W
5	Mike Synar (D-Okla)	$39,374	Incumb	W

Cable TV ....$2.2 million

One segment of the TV and entertainment industry politically sensitive enough to merit special attention is the cable TV industry. Its spending patterns were similar to that of over-the-air broadcasters — 55 percent of their money went to Democrats — but their issues were unique. Unlike broadcasters, most cable companies operate regulated monopolies. Besides facing occasional conflicts with broadcast stations and the major networks, they also come under fire from time to time from disgruntled customers who complain about bad service, high subscription rates and no alternatives. Under pressure, Congress finally acted in 1993 to beef up regulation and lower rates, but many cable operators used the opportunity to raise their rates, or to pare down the list of channels in their "basic" cable package.

	Top Contributors	
1	National Cable Television Assn	$644,249
2	Tele-Communications Inc*	$162,400
3	Comcast Corp	$154,740
4	Viacom International*	$150,825
5	Turner Broadcasting System	$89,270
6	Adelphia Communications	$56,400
7	Cablevision Systems Corp	$53,000
8	Jones International	$42,950
9	Cox Cable Communications	$35,000
10	Home Shopping Network Inc	$32,830

	Top Senate Recipients			
1	Bob Packwood (R-Ore)	$120,650	Incumb	W
2	Arlen Specter (R-Pa)	$57,600	Incumb	W
3	Wyche Fowler Jr. (D-Ga)	$54,649	Incumb	L
4	Alfonse M. D'Amato (R-NY)	$53,025	Incumb	W
5	Richard C. Shelby (D-Ala)	$52,000	Incumb	W

	Top House Recipients			
1	Peter H. Kostmayer (D-Pa)	$31,999	Incumb	L
2	Mike Synar (D-Okla)	$31,380	Incumb	W
3	Bill Richardson (D-NM)	$29,000	Incumb	W
4	Tom McMillen (D-Md)	$27,650	Incumb	L
5	Richard A. Gephardt (D-Mo)	$25,600	Incumb	W

* Contributions came from more than one affiliate or subsidiary.

Telephone Utilities ....$5.9 million

As the phrase "information superhighway" has emerged as the buzzword of the 90s, telephone utilities have begun moving quickly to take advantage of new opportunities to wire the nation's homes and offices with the next generation of telecommunications and entertainment services. The plans on their drawing boards have often put them at odds with the cable TV industry, though a few of the regional "Baby Bells" have begun acquiring cable companies themselves, so that no matter what the "superhighway's" eventual mix of cable and telephone services, they'll be covered.

The dollars they have steadily pumped into federal campaigns have helped guarantee that Congress listens when the phone utilities talk. They spent nearly $6 million in the 1992 elections, splitting it fairly evenly between Democrats (56 percent) and Republicans (44 percent).

	Top Contributors	
1	AT&T*	$1,397,883
2	BellSouth Corp*	$963,153
3	GTE Corp*	$631,869
4	Ameritech Corp*	$562,342
5	United Telecommunications*	$432,910
6	Pacific Telesis Group	$331,512
7	US West*	$325,113
8	Southwestern Bell	$311,690
9	Bell Atlantic*	$270,011
10	NYNEX Corp*	$237,295

	Top Senate Recipients			
1	Bob Packwood (R-Ore)	$83,750	Incumb	W
2	Ernest F. Hollings (D-SC)	$76,551	Incumb	W
3	Wendell H. Ford (D-Ky)	$54,000	Incumb	W
4	Charles E. Grassley (R-Iowa)	$47,066	Incumb	W
5	Rod Chandler (R-Wash)	$46,850	Open	L

	Top House Recipients			
1	David E. Bonior (D-Mich)	$49,250	Incumb	W
2	Richard A. Gephardt (D-Mo)	$46,250	Incumb	W
3	Jim Slattery (D-Kan)	$46,050	Incumb	W
4	Al Swift (D-Wash)	$43,850	Incumb	W
5	Don Ritter (R-Pa)	$43,300	Incumb	L

On Capitol Hill, the primary centers for debate on telecommunications policy are the House Energy and Commerce Committee and the Senate Commerce, Science and Transportation Committee. Oregon Republican Bob Packwood, the ranking Republican on the Commerce Committee's Communications Subcommittee, led all other recipients of phone company money in 1992. The number two recipient, Ernest Hollings of South Carolina, chairs the full committee.

* Contributions came from more than one affiliate or subsidiary.

Construction

Where the money came from...

Home builders, public works contractors, project management firms, architects, engineers and a host of assorted contractors supplying everything from plumbing to air conditioning to cement make up this sector of American business — the nation's construction industry.

Many construction firms — particularly the largest ones — are dependent for major portions of their work on decisions made in Washington. Government contracts to build new highways, bridges, dams and other public works projects can bring substantial amounts of business to a host of construction-related contractors and suppliers as well.

Home builders have a different perspective on federal policies. Instead of keeping an eye on the public works committees of Congress, they're more affected by the Banking committees, which set policies that can deeply affect the housing market.

The pattern of construction industry contributions reflects the nature of the industry. Unlike some industries that are dominated by large corporations, many contractors and subcontractors are relatively small shops that operate independently. Because of this, more than two-thirds of the sector's campaign dollars came from individual donors rather than political action committees. Even the two PACs that dominated the top contributors list — the National Association of Home Builders and Associated General Contractors — are nationwide trade associations that represent thousands of independent builders and suppliers.

Differentiating between home builders and public works contractors is not always easy, when analyzing campaign finance reports. Many contributors simply put "builder" as their occupation, giving no clue whether they concentrate on commercial, residential or industrial construction. Many other construction firms are diversified and do it all. In dealing with such contributors this book classifies them under the "general contractors" category.

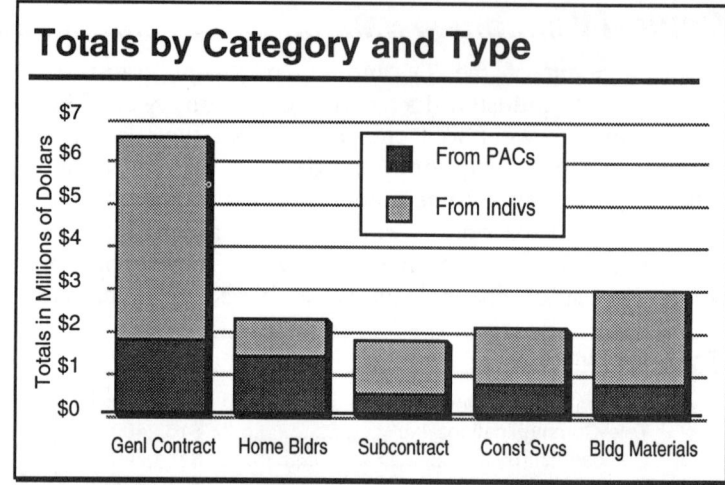

Category	Total	From PACs	PAC Pct	From Indivs	Indiv Pct
General Contractors	$6,500,194	$1,696,184	26%	$4,804,010	74%
Home Builders	$2,216,175	$1,318,292	59%	$897,883	41%
Special Trade Contractors	$1,686,428	$401,601	24%	$1,284,827	76%
Construction Services	$1,974,020	$656,253	33%	$1,317,767	67%
Building Materials	$2,869,672	$658,314	23%	$2,211,358	77%
TOTAL	$15,246,489	$4,730,644	31%	$10,515,845	69%

Top 20 Construction Contributors

Rank	Total	Contributor	Category	PAC Pct	Dem Pct	Repub Pct
1	$1,074,827	National Assn of Home Builders*	Resid Constr	100%	44%	56%
2	$677,899	Associated General Contractors*	Genl Contract	99%	24%	76%
3	$353,558	Fluor Corp*	Heavy Constr	95%	44%	56%
4	$203,580	National Utility Contractors Assn	Utility Constr	100%	38%	62%
5	$191,877	Bechtel Corp	Heavy Constr	74%	53%	47%
6	$184,150	Associated Builders & Contractors	Builders Assn	100%	8%	92%
7	$163,500	National Electrical Contractors Assn	Subcontractors	100%	15%	85%
8	$161,901	Sheet Metal/Air Conditioning Contractors	Subcontractors	100%	5%	94%
9	$128,703	CH2M Hill	Engineers	95%	47%	53%
10	$116,375	Morrison-Knudsen	General Contractors	93%	63%	37%
11	$97,930	Caterpillar Tractor	Constr Equip	94%	12%	88%
12	$95,500	American Consulting Engineers Council	Engineers	100%	47%	53%
13	$87,770	Walter Industries*	Building Materials	87%	82%	18%
14	$84,307	Brown & Root	Heavy Constr	96%	27%	73%
15	$82,340	Manufactured Housing Institute	Mobile Homes	99%	49%	50%
16	$82,050	National Soc of Professional Engineers	Engineers	100%	39%	61%
17	$76,607	Jacobs Engineering Group	Engineers	83%	65%	35%
18	$69,034	Owens-Corning Fiberglas	Bldg Materials	92%	34%	66%
19	$63,300	Edward C Levy Co	Bldg Materials	0%	35%	65%
20	$58,100	Vulcan Materials Co	Bldg Materials	76%	53%	47%

* Contributions came from more than one affiliate or subsidiary.

Where the money went . . .

Totals by Category and Party

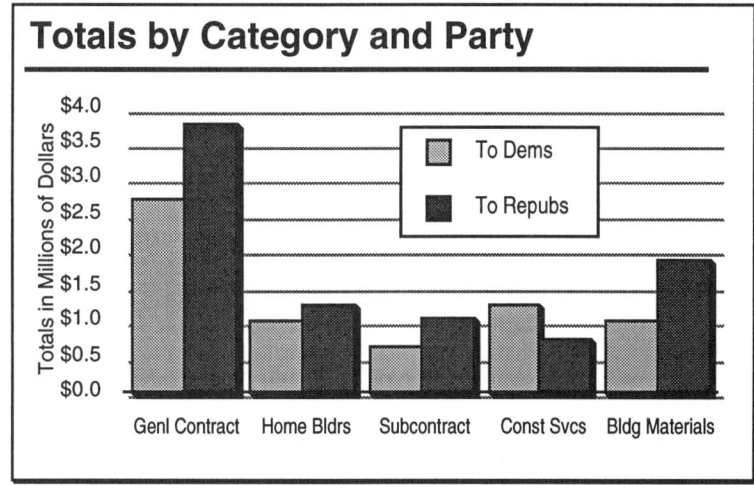

By and large, builders prefer Republicans. Some 57 percent of the sector's contributions went to Republican candidates — the most heavily Republican tilt of any sector. Only the construction services industry — engineers, architects and the like — gave a majority of its dollars to Democrats.

Category	Total	To Dems	Dem Pct	To Repubs	Repub Pct
General Contractors	$6,500,194	$2,717,136	42%	$3,767,141	58%
Home Builders	$2,216,175	$991,851	45%	$1,222,374	55%
Special Trade Contractors	$1,686,428	$645,098	38%	$1,031,913	61%
Construction Services	$1,974,020	$1,223,955	62%	$746,390	38%
Building Materials	$2,869,672	$1,006,396	35%	$1,849,231	64%
TOTAL	**$15,246,489**	**$6,584,436**	**43%**	**$8,617,049**	**57%**

New York Republican Alfonse D'Amato was the leading congressional recipient of construction industry money in the 1992 elections. The top 10 list of Senate candidates was dominated by Republicans. Among House members, the party split was even. The leading House recipient, Bud Shuster of Pennsylvania, is ranking Republican on the Public Works and Transportation Committee's Surface Transportation Subcommittee — the panel that oversees highway construction. Democrat Norman Mineta, who ranked third, chairs that subcommittee. Fifth-ranking Robert Roe, who retired after the 1992 elections, chaired the full committee.

Top 10 Senate Recipients

Rank	Name	Amount	Status	W/L
1	Alfonse M. D'Amato (R-NY)	$224,990	Incumb	W
2	John F. Seymour (R-Calif)	$212,584	Incumb	L
3	Arlen Specter (R-Pa)	$196,820	Incumb	W
4	Dick Thornburgh (R-Pa)	$190,550	Chall	L
5	Daniel R. Coats (R-Ind)	$189,735	Incumb	W
6	Christopher S. Bond (R-Mo)	$149,418	Incumb	W
7	Bob Kasten (R-Wis)	$137,820	Incumb	L
8	Dianne Feinstein (D-Calif)	$129,220	Chall	W
9	Bob Graham (D-Fla)	$122,335	Incumb	W
10	Tom Campbell (R-Calif)	$115,762	Open	L

Top 10 House Recipients

Rank	Name	Amount	Status	W/L
1	Bud Shuster (R-Pa)	$105,500	Incumb	W
2	Richard A. Gephardt (D-Mo)	$81,297	Incumb	W
3	Norman Y. Mineta (D-Calif)	$66,500	Incumb	W
4	Ron Marlenee (R-Mont)	$63,672	Incumb	L
5	Robert A. Roe (D-NJ)	$63,650	Incumb	Ret
6	Bill Paxon (R-NY)	$63,185	Incumb	W
7	Bob Carr (D-Mich)	$52,300	Incumb	W
8	Joe Moakley (D-Mass)	$50,600	Incumb	W
9	Spencer Bachus (R-Ala)	$48,425	Chall	W
10	Newt Gingrich (R-Ga)	$47,400	Incumb	W

Closeup on Construction

General Contractors ....$6.5 million

The leading contributor in this category, the Associated General Contractors, is the nation's largest organization of builders concentrating mainly on commercial, industrial and public works construction. Though the Top 10 list includes a number of large nationwide construction firms — like Fluor, Bechtel and Brown & Root — most of the industry is made up of smaller local contractors. Their dollars tend to come primarily through individual contributions, since their companies are generally too small to operate political action committees of their own.

Overall, general contractors and related builders' groups gave 58 percent of their campaign dollars to Republicans. This contrasts with many other industries that may be Republican in philosophy but pragmatically Democratic in their campaign contributions. The Democrats currently hold solid majorities in both houses of Congress and thereby control all committee and subcommittee chairmanships as well as the general flow of legislation.

Top Contributors

1	Associated General Contractors*	$677,899
2	Fluor Corp*	$353,558
3	National Utility Contractors Assn	$203,580
4	Halliburton Co*	$196,319
5	Bechtel Corp	$191,877
6	Associated Builders & Contractors	$184,150
7	Morrison-Knudsen	$116,375
8	Brown & Root	$79,807
9	Suffolk Construction Co	$45,300
10	HB Zachry Co	$36,299

* Contributions came from more than one affiliate or subsidiary.

Top Senate Recipients

#	Recipient	Amount	Status	Result
1	John F. Seymour (R-Calif)	$97,038	Incumb	L
2	Alfonse M. D'Amato (R-NY)	$96,590	Incumb	W
3	Dick Thornburgh (R-Pa)	$82,950	Chall	L
4	Arlen Specter (R-Pa)	$74,100	Incumb	W
5	Dianne Feinstein (D-Calif)	$65,220	Chall	W

Top House Recipients

#	Recipient	Amount	Status	Result
1	Bud Shuster (R-Pa)	$57,750	Incumb	W
2	Ron Marlenee (R-Mont)	$49,322	Incumb	L
3	Richard A. Gephardt (D-Mo)	$34,985	Incumb	W
4	Bill Paxon (R-NY)	$31,950	Incumb	W
5	Joe Moakley (D-Mass)	$31,600	Incumb	W

Home Builders ....$2.2 million

This segment of the construction industry closely follows the ups and downs of interest rates and federal housing policies, as opposed to the level of funding for major public works projects. In that sense, home builders' legislative interests are similar to those of the real estate industry — particularly real estate developers. In many cases, the line between real estate and construction is a thin one; many companies engage in both. This book distinguishes between the two, however, as does the federal government's Standard Industrial Classification Index. The real estate industry deals primarily in the financial end of the business and is classified under finance in this book. Builders deal more in hammers, nails and road graders, and are classified in construction.

The National Association of Home Builders is the industry's main trade association, and by far its leading contributor. Both the PAC and individual contributors split their dollars fairly evenly between the parties. Republicans collected 55 percent in all.

Top Contributors

1	National Assn of Home Builders*	$1,074,827
2	Manufactured Housing Institute	$82,340
3	Perry-Houston Interests	$53,000
4	Toll Brothers Inc	$49,550
5	Rural Builders of America PAC	$40,750

* Contributions came from more than one affiliate or subsidiary.

Top Senate Recipients

#	Recipient	Amount	Status	Result
1	Daniel R. Coats (R-Ind)	$70,300	Incumb	W
2	John F. Seymour (R-Calif)	$36,646	Incumb	L
3	Les AuCoin (D-Ore)	$26,100	Chall	L
4	Gray Davis (D-Calif)	$24,750	Chall	L
5	Paul Coverdell (R-Ga)	$24,550	Chall	W

Top House Recipients

#	Recipient	Amount	Status	Result
1	William J. Hughes (D-NJ)	$35,850	Incumb	W
2	Robert H. Michel (R-Ill)	$21,500	Incumb	W
3	Thomas J. Bliley Jr. (R-Va)	$20,450	Incumb	W
4	Leonard R. Sendelsky (D-NJ)	$18,800	Chall	L
5	Dennis Hastert (R-Ill)	$17,400	Incumb	W

Construction Services ....$2.0 million

Architects, engineers and construction management specialists are an important (and politically active) segment of the construction industry. Big engineering firms are often competing for federal contracts. They are also clearly affected by upturns and downturns in construction cycles. The leading contributor in this category, the engineering firm of CH2M Hill is involved not only in construction engineering, but in environmental services as well. The company is a major federal contractor for hazardous waste cleanup projects.

One practical problem in classifying donors from this category is the lack of specificity in contributors' declared occupations. Contributors who put down "engineer" as their occupation could be involved in any number of industries. For that reason, only "structural engineers," "civil engineers," or others clearly identified with the construction industry were classified in this category. The overall total for this category, therefore, is almost certainly understated.

Top Contributors

1	CH2M Hill	$128,703
2	American Consulting Engineers Council	$95,500
3	National Soc of Professional Engineers	$82,050
4	Jacobs Engineering Group	$76,607
5	Parsons Brinckerhoff Inc	$52,750
6	Kaiser Engineers Inc	$49,896
7	Stone & Webster	$48,406
8	Sverdrup Corp	$37,950
9	American Institute of Architects	$36,125
10	Parsons Corp*	$31,750

* Contributions came from more than one affiliate or subsidiary.

Top Senate Recipients

1	Daniel K. Inouye (D-Hawaii)	$24,400	Incumb	W
2	Christopher S. Bond (R-Mo)	$24,300	Incumb	W
3	John F. Seymour (R-Calif)	$23,950	Incumb	L
4	Wyche Fowler Jr. (D-Ga)	$22,900	Incumb	L
5	John B. Breaux (D-La)	$22,258	Incumb	W

Top House Recipients

1	Norman Y. Mineta (D-Calif)	$29,850	Incumb	W
2	Robert A. Roe (D-NJ)	$21,300	Incumb	†
3	Richard A. Gephardt (D-Mo)	$21,262	Incumb	W
4	Robert E. Andrews (D-NJ)	$20,225	Incumb	W
5	Bob Carr (D-Mich)	$19,250	Incumb	W

† Did not seek reelection in 1992

Building Materials & Equipment ....$2.9 million

These are the companies that supply everything from gravel to earth movers to high-speed elevators in skyscrapers. Those involved in road building projects are particularly affected by federal decisions, especially those on the public works committees.

Top Contributors

1	Caterpillar Tractor	$97,930
2	Walter Industries*	$87,770
3	Owens-Corning Fiberglas	$69,034
4	Edward C Levy Co	$63,300
5	Vulcan Materials Co*	$58,100
6	American Supply Assn	$55,525
7	National Crushed Stone Assn	$50,875
8	Dravo Corp	$48,800
9	Cubic Corp	$47,797
10	National Concrete Masonry Assn	$45,509

* Contributions came from more than one affiliate or subsidiary.

Top Senate Recipients

1	Daniel R. Coats (R-Ind)	$57,150	Incumb	W
2	Dick Thornburgh (R-Pa)	$55,750	Chall	L
3	Paul Coverdell (R-Ga)	$49,341	Chall	W
4	Arlen Specter (R-Pa)	$47,200	Incumb	W
5	Christopher S. Bond (R-Mo)	$46,751	Incumb	W

Top House Recipients

1	Bud Shuster (R-Pa)	$31,500	Incumb	W
2	Don Ritter (R-Pa)	$17,910	Incumb	L
3	Harris W. Fawell (R-Ill)	$16,674	Incumb	W
4	Steve Buyer (R-Ind)	$15,240	Chall	W
5	Sam M. Gibbons (D-Fla)	$14,300	Incumb	W

Defense

Where the money came from...

Defense contractors have always been influential players in congressional politics, though the dollars they dispensed in the 1992 elections were fairly modest by contemporary standards. In all, the defense sector gave $8.3 million to federal candidates. Nearly nine-tenths of it was delivered through political action committees sponsored by corporations.

That figure can be considered to be quite conservative, however. Few U.S. corporations rely on defense work for the majority of their income, but many firms do some defense work or have defense-related subsidiaries. Under the system used to compile this book, contributions from PACs or employees of those firms were counted as defense related only if they were given to a member sitting on the Armed Services or Appropriations committees — panels that deal specifically with defense policy and defense spending. Most contributions from Boeing, for example, are classified under air transport, since Boeing makes most of its money from the sale of commercial, not military, aircraft. Many other major defense contractors — from General Motors to General Electric to AT&T — fall in the same category

If one were to include *all* contributions from those big corporations as defense related (effectively double-counting the dollars since they serve more than one purpose) the sector's total would be much higher.

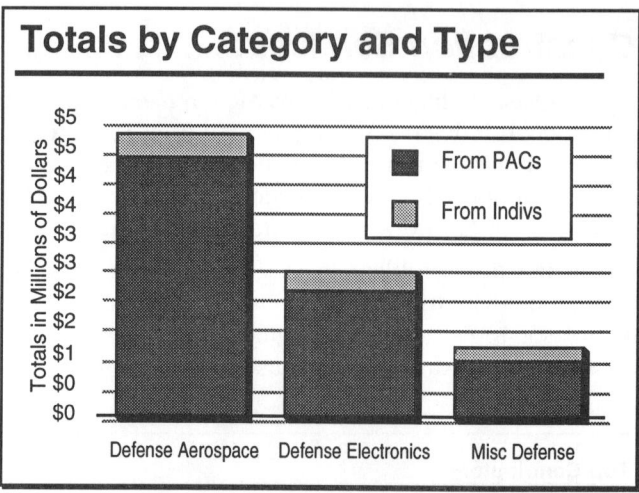

Totals by Category and Type

Category	Total	From PACs	PAC Pct	From Indivs	Indiv Pct
Defense Aerospace	$4,748,928	$4,359,923	92%	$389,005	8%
Defense Electronics	$2,433,503	$2,088,860	86%	$344,643	14%
Misc Defense	$1,146,329	$949,628	83%	$196,701	17%
TOTAL	**$8,328,760**	**$7,398,411**	**89%**	**$930,349**	**11%**

Top 20 Defense Contributors

Rank	Total	Contributor	Category	PAC Pct	Dem Pct	Repub Pct
1	$536,335	Martin Marietta Corp	Air Defense	95%	51%	49%
2	$464,055	General Dynamics	Air Defense	94%	61%	39%
3	$446,570	Textron Inc	Air Defense	89%	64%	36%
4	$377,515	Northrop Corp	Air Defense	95%	46%	53%
5	$376,383	Rockwell International	Air Defense	90%	46%	54%
6	$371,643	McDonnell Douglas*	Air Defense	81%	53%	47%
7	$366,537	Lockheed Corp	Air Defense	92%	54%	46%
8	$312,300	General Atomics	Misc Defense	98%	65%	35%
9	$311,531	Chrysler Corp*	Air Defense	82%	71%	29%
10	$307,100	Raytheon*	Air Defense	93%	64%	36%
11	$300,040	United Technologies	Air Defense	95%	56%	44%
12	$297,145	General Motors*†	Def Electronics	92%	55%	45%
13	$256,526	Grumman Corp	Air Defense	98%	66%	34%
14	$226,965	Loral Corp	Def Electronics	65%	77%	23%
15	$221,084	Allied-Signal	Air Defense	89%	51%	49%
16	$198,700	Tenneco Inc	Naval Ships	86%	55%	45%
17	$197,425	AT&T†	Def Electronics	100%	70%	30%
18	$194,575	General Electric†	Air Defense	98%	64%	36%
19	$186,374	E-Systems Inc*	Def Electronics	89%	53%	46%
20	$166,325	TRW Inc	Def Electronics	92%	51%	49%

* Contributions came from more than one affiliate or subsidiary.   † Includes defense operations only.

Where the money went...

Totals by Category and Party

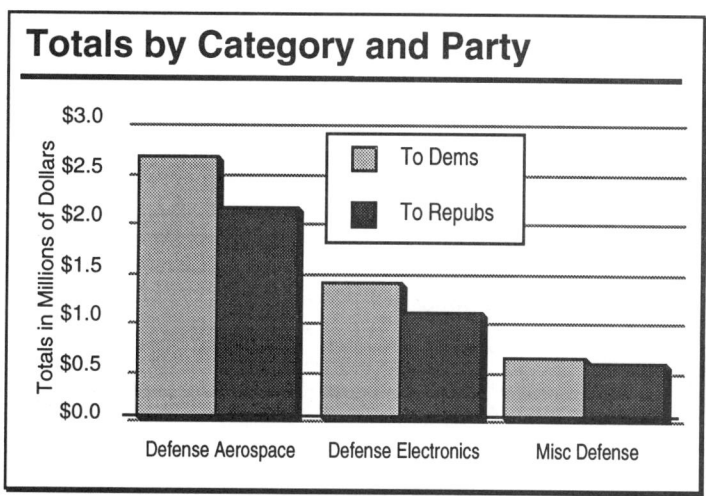

Considering the traditionally conservative slant to the defense industry and the military services, it is somewhat surprising that the industry delivered 55 percent of its campaign dollars to Democrats in the 1992 elections. This is a classic example of political pragmatism at work. Democrats control both houses of Congress (and the Pentagon and White House too, after Bill Clinton's election). They therefore hold the power of the purse over the defense industry. Whatever their personal political preferences, defense contractors have learned to accommodate both sides of the aisle when pulling out their checkbooks.

Category	Total	To Dems	Dem Pct	To Repubs	Repub Pct
Defense Aerospace	$4,748,928	$2,635,229	55%	$2,110,299	44%
Defense Electronics	$2,433,503	$1,371,777	56%	$1,061,220	44%
Misc Defense	$1,146,329	$602,445	53%	$543,384	47%
TOTAL	**$8,328,760**	**$4,609,451**	**55%**	**$3,714,903**	**45%**

Though the federal government's annual defense budget is voted on by the entire House and Senate, defense industry lobbyists spend most of their time concentrating on the Armed Services and Appropriations committees in each house. Armed Services sets the military policy, but the Appropriations panels — particularly the Defense Appropriations subcommittees — actually allocate the hundreds of billions of dollars the federal government spends annually on defense. Consequently, members of those committees receive by far the biggest proportion of defense industry contributions. Of the top 20 House and Senate recipients of defense dollars in 1992, eight served in the Armed Services committees and 12 sat on Appropriations.

John Murtha, the top defense contributor in Congress, is chairman of the House Defense Appropriations Subcommittee. Les Aspin, the number two recipient, was head of the House Armed Services Committee until he resigned his seat in early 1993 to become Secretary of Defense in the Clinton administration.

Top 10 Senate Recipients

Rank	Name	Amount	Status	W/L
1	Daniel R. Coats (R-Ind)	$175,350	Incumb	W
2	Arlen Specter (R-Pa)	$147,849	Incumb	W
3	John Glenn (D-Ohio)	$145,595	Incumb	W
4	Don Nickles (R-Okla)	$139,700	Incumb	W
5	Richard C. Shelby (D-Ala)	$139,675	Incumb	W
6	John McCain (R-Ariz)	$130,900	Incumb	W
7	Barbara A. Mikulski (D-Md)	$129,287	Incumb	W
8	Bob Kasten (R-Wis)	$126,450	Incumb	L
9	Alfonse M. D'Amato (R-NY)	$104,030	Incumb	W
10	Daniel K. Inouye (D-Hawaii)	$101,500	Incumb	W

Top 10 House Recipients

Rank	Name	Amount	Status	W/L
1	John P. Murtha (D-Pa)	$230,200	Incumb	W
2	Les Aspin (D-Wis)	$220,875	Incumb	W
3	Charles Wilson (D-Texas)	$210,650	Incumb	W
4	Dave McCurdy (D-Okla)	$129,450	Incumb	W
5	Herbert H. Bateman (R-Va)	$103,750	Incumb	W
6	Norm Dicks (D-Wash)	$98,963	Incumb	W
7	Richard Ray (D-Ga)	$92,050	Incumb	L
8	Vic Fazio (D-Calif)	$92,025	Incumb	W
9	Joseph M. McDade (R-Pa)	$91,350	Incumb	W
10	C. W. Bill Young (R-Fla)	$91,250	Incumb	W

Energy & Natural Resources

Where the money came from . . .

In a nation that grew to world prominence by exploiting its abundant natural resources, then building new industries on the strength of its home-grown oil, gas, minerals and electricity, it is not surprising that energy producers pack a powerful political punch on Capitol Hill.

The oil & gas industry was by far the biggest contributor within the sector, sending more than $9.2 million to congressional and presidential candidates in the 1992 elections. About half that money came from political action committees — mainly from large multinational oil companies. Another $2.4 million came from operators of natural gas pipelines that connect the southwestern oil and gas fields with consumers around the country.

The electric utilities lent power to their political arguments with over $4.5 million in contributions, most of it from PACs. Mining interests gave $1.8 million; half of that came from coal mine operators. Overall, the energy & natural resources sector gave $21.3 million to federal candidates in the 1992 elections.

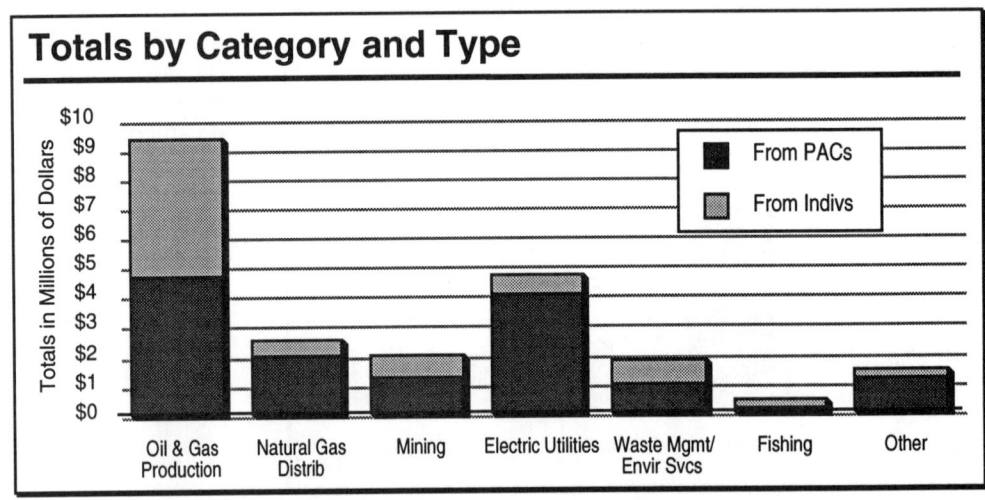

Totals by Category and Type

Category	Total	From PACs	PAC Pct	From Indivs	Indiv Pct
Oil & Gas Prod/Marketing	$9,234,077	$4,579,941	50%	$4,654,136	50%
Natural Gas Distribution	$2,393,866	$1,827,800	76%	$566,066	24%
Mining	$1,844,760	$1,118,704	61%	$726,056	39%
Electric Utilities	$4,555,470	$3,975,798	87%	$579,672	13%
Waste Mgmt/Environ Svcs	$1,717,181	$903,363	53%	$813,818	47%
Commercial Fishing	$314,209	$108,909	35%	$205,300	65%
Other & Unclassified	$1,281,672	$1,018,069	79%	$263,603	21%
TOTAL	**$21,341,235**	**$13,532,584**	**63%**	**$7,808,651**	**37%**

Top 20 Energy & Natural Resource Contributors

Rank	Total	Contributor	Category	PAC Pct	Dem Pct	Repub Pct
1	$683,558	Waste Management Inc*	Waste Mgmt	78%	62%	38%
2	$627,155	ACRE (Action Cmte for Rural Electric)*	Rural Electric	100%	74%	26%
3	$493,092	Atlantic Richfield	Oil & Gas	66%	25%	74%
4	$420,581	Chevron Corp	Oil & Gas	92%	28%	72%
5	$397,825	Coastal Corp*	Natural Gas	84%	72%	28%
6	$364,541	Southern Co*	Electric Utilities	87%	58%	42%
7	$358,060	Exxon Corp	Oil & Gas	92%	19%	81%
8	$348,250	Cooper Industries	Power Plant Constr	99%	2%	97%
9	$306,450	Occidental Petroleum*†	Oil & Gas	83%	52%	48%
10	$298,650	Southern California Edison	Electric Utilities	89%	76%	24%
11	$293,200	Amoco Corp	Oil & Gas	90%	24%	75%
12	$267,123	Petroleum Marketers Assn*	Oil & Gas	100%	37%	63%
13	$245,398	Mobil Oil	Oil & Gas	80%	11%	88%
14	$245,277	USX Corp*	Oil & Gas	76%	53%	47%
15	$244,648	National Coal Assn	Coal Mining	98%	25%	75%
16	$237,752	Columbia Gas System*	Natural Gas	100%	51%	54%
17	$237,000	Texas Utilities Co*	Electric Utilities	97%	61%	39%
18	$217,748	Ashland Oil*	Oil & Gas	86%	39%	61%
19	$204,291	Phillips Petroleum	Oil & Gas	84%	27%	73%
20	$195,330	Texaco	Oil & Gas	90%	30%	70%

* Contributions came from more than one affiliate or subsidiary.

† Does not include Occidental's non-oil operations.

Where the money went . . .

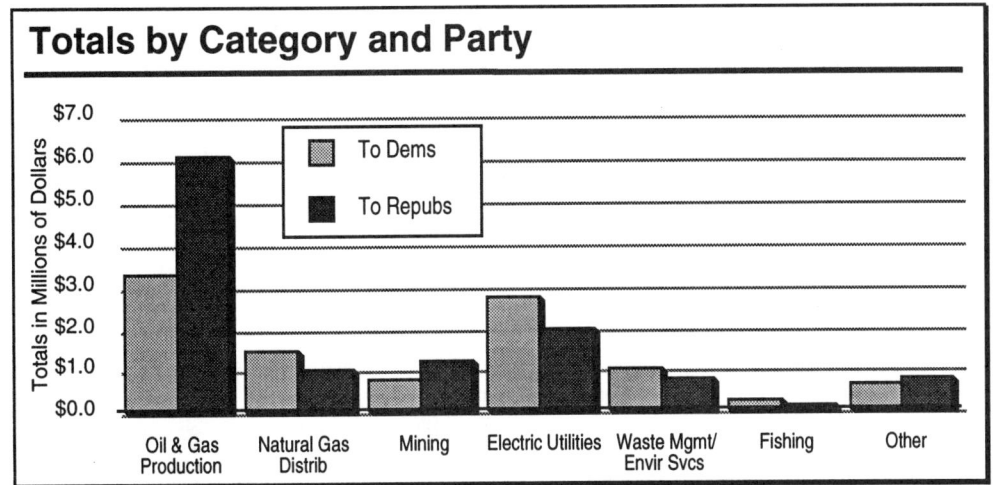

The oil & gas industry distinctly prefers Republican candidates, as seen clearly in the chart on the left. It favored them by a nearly two-to-one margin over Democrats — a ratio that has been consistent over the years. Natural gas distributors, electric utilities and waste management firms slightly favored Democrats. Miners mostly backed the GOP. In all, 54 percent of the energy sector's campaign dollars wound up in the hands of Republicans.

Category	Total	To Dems	Dem Pct	To Repubs	Repub Pct
Oil & Gas Prod/Marketing	$9,234,077	$3,209,243	35%	$6,006,774	65%
Natural Gas Distribution	$2,393,866	$1,408,863	59%	$981,771	41%
Mining	$1,844,760	$709,468	38%	$1,135,092	62%
Electric Utilities	$4,555,470	$2,655,368	58%	$1,897,952	42%
Waste Mgmt/Environ Svcs	$1,717,181	$994,557	58%	$719,424	42%
Commercial Fishing	$314,209	$227,892	73%	$85,817	27%
Other & Unclassified	$1,281,672	$589,445	46%	$691,777	54%
TOTAL	**$21,341,235**	**$9,794,836**	**46%**	**$11,518,607**	**54%**

Republican Don Nickles of Oklahoma received more than twice as much from the energy sector as anyone else in Congress in 1992. Four other colleagues of his on the Senate Energy and Natural Resources Committee also appear on the Senate's top 10 recipient list—John Seymour, Wendell Ford, Richard Shelby and Frank Murkowski.

Oil-state congressmen dominated the Top 10 list in the House, led by Don Young of Alaska, who is ranking minority member of the House Interior Committee. Mike Synar of Oklahoma ranked second overall. Behind him were four Texans and Montana Republican Ron Marlenee, whose 1992 race against fellow incumbent Pat Williams was a flashpoint between energy versus environmental interests. The only representatives on the list from non-energy-rich states were House Majority Leader Dick Gephardt and Indiana Democrat Phil Sharp, who chairs the Energy and Power Subcommittee of the powerful House Energy and Commerce Committee.

Top 10 Senate Recipients

Rank	Name	Amount	Status	W/L
1	Don Nickles (R-Okla)	$572,766	Incumb	W
2	John B. Breaux (D-La)	$281,125	Incumb	W
3	John F. Seymour (R-Calif)	$271,125	Incumb	L
4	Wendell H. Ford (D-Ky)	$259,950	Incumb	W
5	Arlen Specter (R-Pa)	$242,316	Incumb	W
6	Richard C. Shelby (D-Ala)	$240,889	Incumb	W
7	Christopher S. Bond (R-Mo)	$218,789	Incumb	W
8	Bob Dole (R-Kan)	$217,437	Incumb	W
9	Frank H. Murkowski (R-Alaska)	$213,827	Incumb	W
10	Daniel R. Coats (R-Ind)	$210,795	Incumb	W

Top 10 House Recipients

Rank	Name	Amount	Status	W/L
1	Don Young (R-Alaska)	$181,497	Incumb	W
2	Mike Synar (D-Okla)	$146,474	Incumb	W
3	Richard A. Gephardt (D-Mo)	$144,800	Incumb	W
4	Joe L. Barton (R-Texas)	$137,282	Incumb	W
5	Jack Fields (R-Texas)	$126,605	Incumb	W
6	Philip R. Sharp (D-Ind)	$116,791	Incumb	W
7	Michael A. Andrews (D-Texas)	$116,050	Incumb	W
8	Harold Rogers (R-Ky)	$112,475	Incumb	W
9	Martin Frost (D-Texas)	$109,850	Incumb	W
10	Ron Marlenee (R-Mont)	$104,669	Incumb	L

Closeup on Energy & Natural Resources

Oil & Gas Production & Marketing ......$9.2 million

The oil industry looks at itself as having two main divisions: the "major" multinational oil companies—like Exxon and Mobil—and the smaller operators called "independents." Both groups tend to give to the same candidates, for the most part preferring Republicans to Democrats, but they deliver their dollars by different methods. The major oil companies give almost all their donations through corporate PACs, while the independents give mainly as individuals.

All of the top recipients of oil money in both the House and Senate come from major oil-producing states. Don Nickles of Oklahoma led them all, with over $405,000 in contributions. Republican Phil Gramm of Texas ranked third on the Senate list even though he didn't run in 1992. Gramm has his eye on the 1996 presidential nomination, and has continued his fund-raising even though it's an off-year for his Senate seat. A longtime favorite of the oil industry, Gramm raised over $600,000 from the industry during his 1990 reelection race.

Top Contributors

1	Atlantic Richfield	$472,142
2	Chevron Corp	$420,581
3	Exxon Corp	$358,060
4	Occidental Petroleum*†	$306,450
5	Amoco Corp	$293,200
6	Petroleum Marketers Assn*	$267,123
7	Mobil Oil	$245,398
8	USX Corp*	$243,277
9	Ashland Oil*	$215,798
10	Phillips Petroleum	$204,291

* Contributions came from more than one affiliate or subsidiary.
† Does not include Occidental's non-oil operations

Top Senate Recipients

1	Don Nickles (R-Okla)	$405,371	Incumb	W
2	John Seymour (R-Calif)	$152,250	Incumb	L
3	Phil Gramm (R-Texas)	$146,275	Incumb	†
4	Frank H. Murkowski (R-Alaska)	$143,827	Incumb	W
5	John B. Breaux (D-La)	$129,750	Incumb	W

Top House Recipients

1	Mike Synar (D-Okla)	$112,348	Incumb	W
2	Don Young (R-Alaska)	$108,095	Incumb	W
3	Jack Fields (R-Texas)	$76,705	Incumb	W
4	Pete Geren (D-Texas)	$73,105	Incumb	W
5	Sam Johnson (R-Texas)	$72,925	Incumb	W

† Did not run for election in 1992

Natural Gas Distribution ......$2.4 million

Quite apart from drilling for oil, refining it and marketing it in gas stations, there is another distinct industry involved in interstate transportation of natural gas. Gas pipelines criss-cross the nation, connecting the energy-rich oil patch states with the energy-hungry Northeast, Midwest and Southeast. Because of the interstate nature of the business, pipeline carriers are heavily regulated by the federal government. In contrast to the strongly Republican tilt of oil producers, the natural gas industry gives the majority of its dollars to Democrats.

Top Contributors

1	Coastal Corp*	$397,825
2	Columbia Gas System*	$241,852
3	Enron Corp	$187,850
4	Enserch Corp	$151,785
5	Arkla Inc*	$121,505
6	Panhandle Eastern Corp*	$116,350
7	Pacific Enterprises	$104,230
8	Interstate Natural Gas Assn	$96,443
9	Michigan Consolidated Gas	$86,900
10	Williams Companies	$69,236

* Contributions came from more than one affiliate or subsidiary.

Top Senate Recipients

1	Don Nickles (R-Okla)	$68,350	Incumb	W
2	Bob Dole (R-Kan)	$63,750	Incumb	W
3	John B. Breaux (D-La)	$46,175	Incumb	W
4	Dale Bumpers (D-Ark)	$46,150	Incumb	W
5	Wendell H. Ford (D-Ky)	$45,250	Incumb	W

Top House Recipients

1	Michael A. Andrews (D-Texas)	$32,400	Incumb	W
2	Charles Wilson (D-Texas)	$30,900	Incumb	W
3	Philip R. Sharp (D-Ind)	$26,716	Incumb	W
4	Jack Fields (R-Texas)	$24,800	Incumb	W
5	Greg Laughlin (D-Texas)	$24,550	Incumb	W

Mining ....$1.8 million

Two distinct branches of the mining industry provide the bulk of its campaign dollars. Coal miners gave $918,000 in the last election, while companies dealing with metal mining and processing gave $685,000. Diversified interests, non-metal miners and mining services and equipment manufacturers gave the rest.

Kentuckians Wendell Ford in the Senate and Harold Rogers in the House led all other recipients of mining dollars. Both got the bulk of that money from coal mine operators in their home state and in nearby West Virginia.

Not included in these totals—but important in areas dealing with federal regulation of mine safety and other issues—are contributions from the United Mine Workers Union, classified under Labor. The UMW's political action committee gave $459,600 during the 1991-92 election cycle. Ninety-eight percent of it went to Democrats, in sharp contrast with their employers, the mining industry, which gave 62 percent of its dollars to Republicans.

	Top Contributors	
1	National Coal Assn	$244,648
2	Phelps Dodge Corp	$96,049
3	Cyprus Minerals Co	$86,323
4	Reynolds Metals	$86,248
5	Drummond Co	$78,350
6	Peabody Coal	$78,213
7	Pittston Co	$60,350
8	Alcoa	$45,450
9	United Co	$40,450
10	Cleveland-Cliffs Iron Co	$38,400

* Contributions came from more than one affiliate or subsidiary.

	Top Senate Recipients			
1	Wendell H. Ford (D-Ky)	$61,000	Incumb	W
2	Harry Reid (D-Nev)	$49,900	Incumb	W
3	John McCain (R-Ariz)	$34,617	Incumb	W
4	Arlen Specter (R-Pa)	$34,000	Incumb	W
5	Dick Thornburgh (R-Pa)	$33,650	Chall	L

	Top House Recipients			
1	Harold Rogers (R-Ky)	$60,625	Incumb	W
2	John E. Jones (R-Pa)	$31,500	Open	L
3	Barbara F. Vucanovich (R-Nev)	$25,100	Incumb	W
4	Ron Marlenee (R-Mont)	$23,520	Incumb	L
5	Earl F. Hilliard (D-Ala)	$21,500	Open	W

Electric Utilities ....$4.6 million

Cleaning up their smokestacks in compliance with Clean Air legislation is a major preoccupation of many electric utilities, particularly those whose clouds of pollution have been responsible for much of the acid rain in the Northeast. The federal government's many rules governing the operation of utilities are another important issue, as is the perennial issue of nuclear power and the disposal of nuclear waste.

Big metropolitan area utilities are not the only ones with a strong voice on Capitol Hill. The largest single political contributor in the industry is the Action Committee for Rural Electrification (or ACRE), a PAC that represents the interests of the nation's rural electric cooperatives. The top contributor list also includes a number of holding companies that control smaller state-based utilities. Southern Co., for example, is the parent of Alabama Power, Georgia Power, Gulf Power and Mississippi Power.

Three of the top Senate recipients — Kent Conrad, Wendell Ford and Richard Shelby — sit on the Senate Energy and Natural Resources Committee. All five of the top House recipients hold seats on the House Energy and Commerce Committee, which regulates the electric utility industry.

	Top Contributors	
1	ACRE (Action Cmte for Rural Electric)*	$627,155
2	Southern Co*	$364,541
3	Southern California Edison	$298,650
4	Texas Utilities Co*	$237,000
5	Entergy Corp*	$149,125
6	Pacific Gas & Electric	$147,175
7	American Electric Power*	$130,909
8	Detroit Edison	$103,870
9	Philadelphia Electric	$102,250
10	FPL Group Inc*	$97,950

* Contributions came from more than one affiliate or subsidiary.

	Top Senate Recipients			
1	Kent Conrad (D-ND)	$67,500	Incumb	W
2	Wendell H. Ford (D-Ky)	$64,750	Incumb	W
3	Arlen Specter (R-Pa)	$63,566	Incumb	W
4	Richard C. Shelby (D-Ala)	$53,491	Incumb	W
5	Bob Graham (D-Fla)	$50,750	Incumb	W

	Top House Recipients			
1	Tom McMillen (D-Md)	$53,550	Incumb	L
2	Philip R. Sharp (D-Ind)	$50,675	Incumb	W
3	Joe L. Barton (R-Texas)	$37,400	Incumb	W
4	Ralph M. Hall (D-Texas)	$37,050	Incumb	W
5	Don Ritter (R-Pa)	$33,536	Incumb	L

Finance, Insurance & Real Estate

Where the money came from...

If doctors, lawyers, oil companies and defense contractors are tidy pots of gold to congressional and presidential candidates, the financial sector is the mother lode. The combined giving by banks, insurance companies, real estate interests and other finance-related businesses amounted to more than $71 million in the 1991-92 election cycle — vastly more than any other industry or interest group.

Within the sector, the methods of delivering campaign dollars varied widely. Commercial banks gave two-thirds of their money through political action committees, as did the insurance industry. Securities brokers and real estate agents gave three dollars out of every four through individual contributions. Accountants split the difference equally between PACs and individuals. Wall Street brokerage houses in particular tended to use individual contributions from their executives (and their families) to bundle large sums to favored candidates — much more than they could have given through a single PAC. Federal regulation is a preoccupation for nearly every segment of the financial community. Insurance companies in particular were scrambling to protect their interests as national health insurance began to advance on the nation's political agenda in the '92 elections.

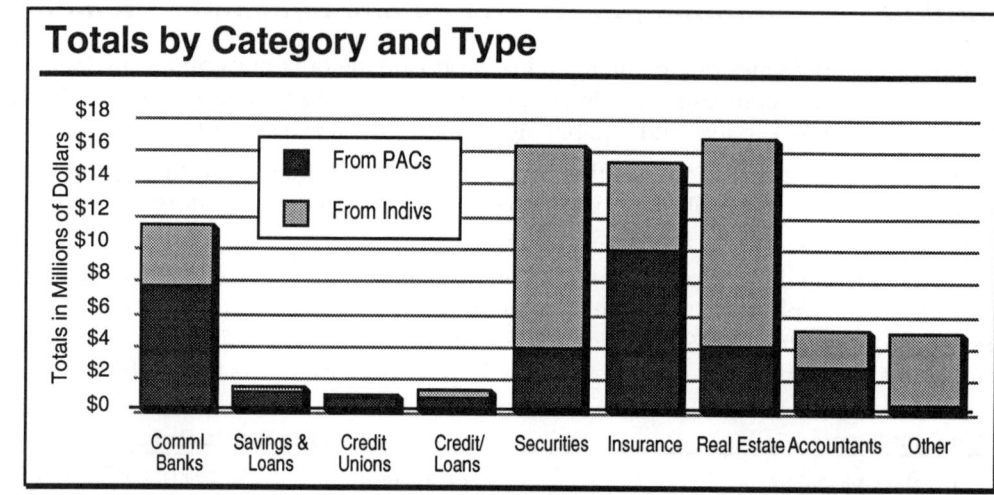

Category	Total	From PACs	PAC Pct	From Indivs	Indiv Pct
Commercial Banks	$11,196,321	$7,411,954	66%	$3,784,367	34%
Savings & Loans	$1,318,827	$927,898	70%	$390,929	30%
Credit Unions	$697,305	$664,910	95%	$32,395	5%
Finance/Credit Companies	$1,042,551	$572,678	55%	$469,873	45%
Securities & Investment	$15,936,222	$3,692,967	23%	$12,243,255	77%
Insurance	$14,944,778	$9,724,432	65%	$5,220,346	35%
Real Estate	$16,472,555	$3,907,233	24%	$12,565,322	76%
Accountants	$4,877,052	$2,481,924	51%	$2,395,128	49%
Other & Unclassified	$4,606,265	$233,357	5%	$4,372,908	95%
TOTAL	$71,091,876	$29,617,353	42%	$41,474,523	58%

Top 20 Finance, Insurance & Real Estate Contributors

Rank	Total	Contributor	Category	PAC Pct	Dem Pct	Repub Pct
1	$2,954,973	National Assn of Realtors	Real Estate	100%	55%	45%
2	$1,692,508	American Bankers Assn*	Comml Banks	99%	50%	49%
3	$1,544,701	American Institute of CPA's	Accountants	100%	56%	44%
4	$1,373,955	National Assn of Life Underwriters	Life Insurance	100%	54%	46%
5	$898,545	Goldman, Sachs & Co	Securities	22%	67%	33%
6	$881,820	American Express*	Stocks/Credit	38%	69%	30%
7	$640,040	Prudential Insurance*	Insurance	63%	59%	41%
8	$627,864	Merrill Lynch*	Securities	30%	51%	48%
9	$589,798	Independent Insurance Agents of America	Insurance	100%	60%	40%
10	$581,880	American Council of Life Insurance	Life Insurance	99%	59%	40%
11	$581,830	Credit Union National Assn*	Credit Unions	100%	67%	33%
12	$550,000	American Family Corp	Health Insur	91%	61%	39%
13	$549,500	Chicago Mercantile Exchange	Commodities	90%	74%	26%
14	$473,175	JP Morgan & Co	Comml Banks	89%	56%	44%
15	$470,781	Morgan Stanley & Co	Securities	47%	54%	46%
16	$453,564	Metropolitan Life Insurance*	Insur/Real Est	81%	57%	43%
17	$453,134	Blue Cross & Blue Shield Assn*	Health Insur	75%	59%	41%
18	$440,377	Arthur Andersen & Co	Accountants	48%	56%	44%
19	$436,867	C&S/Sovran Corp*	Comml Banks	99%	61%	38%
20	$419,653	Ernst & Young	Accountants	56%	55%	45%

* Contributions came from more than one affiliate or subsidiary.

Where the money went . . .

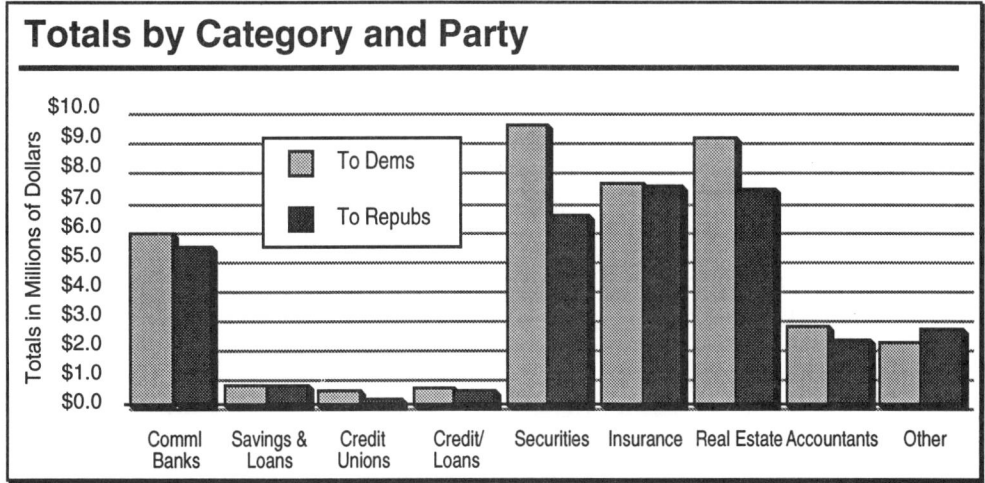

Totals by Category and Party

Category	Total	To Dems	Dem Pct	To Repubs	Repub Pct
Commercial Banks	$11,196,321	$5,827,443	52%	$5,353,698	48%
Savings & Loans	$1,318,827	$697,567	53%	$621,260	47%
Credit Unions	$697,305	$455,030	65%	$242,275	35%
Finance/Credit Companies	$1,042,551	$534,043	51%	$508,508	49%
Securities & Investment	$15,936,222	$9,507,816	60%	$6,389,133	40%
Insurance	$14,944,778	$7,506,107	50%	$7,425,126	50%
Real Estate	$16,472,555	$9,045,991	55%	$7,347,431	45%
Accountants	$4,877,052	$2,680,609	55%	$2,183,101	45%
Other & Unclassified	$4,606,265	$2,066,419	45%	$2,503,680	54%
TOTAL	**$71,091,876**	**$38,321,025**	**54%**	**$32,574,212**	**46%**

Keenly attuned to the value of careful investments, the financial community took pains to spread its dollars widely on both sides of the political aisle. Democrats got a narrow 54 percent majority of the overall dollars. That proportion was fairly consistent throughout the sector. The widest variance came among credit unions, which backed Democrats nearly two-to-one, and in the "other & unclassified" group, which gave a majority of its dollars to Republicans. That group consisted primarily of contributors who identified themselves only as "investors."

New York is the center of the nation's financial community and the 1992 race for the U.S. Senate in that state saw the biggest concentration of finance industry dollars. Robert Abrams, the Democratic loser against Alfonse D'Amato, was the top overall recipient. D'Amato ranked second. Elizabeth Holtzman, who lost to Abrams in the Democratic primary, collected $774,000 — most of it from the securities industry.

Three New Yorkers also showed up on the House's Top 10 list, but the leader there was Missouri's Dick Gephardt, the House Majority Leader who collected more than $575,000 in finance sector contributions for his reelection campaign. Gephardt's money was fairly evenly split between insurance, securities and real estate.

Top 10 Senate Recipients

Rank	Name	Amount	Status	W/L
1	Robert Abrams (D-NY)	$1,222,788	Chall	L
2	Alfonse M. D'Amato (R-NY)	$1,102,983	Incumb	W
3	Christopher J. Dodd (D-Conn)	$949,575	Incumb	W
4	John F. Seymour (R-Calif)	$869,275	Incumb	L
5	Tom Campbell (R-Calif)	$828,631	Open	L
6	Arlen Specter (R-Pa)	$817,527	Incumb	W
7	Dianne Feinstein (D-Calif)	$780,413	Chall	W
8	Elizabeth Holtzman (D-NY)	$774,360	Chall	L
9	Christopher S. Bond (R-Mo)	$650,059	Incumb	W
10	Mel Levine (D-Calif)	$628,700	Open	L

Top 10 House Recipients

Rank	Name	Amount	Status	W/L
1	Richard A. Gephardt (D-Mo)	$575,673	Incumb	W
2	Charles E. Schumer (D-NY)	$407,246	Incumb	W
3	Dan Rostenkowski (D-Ill)	$403,798	Incumb	W
4	Newt Gingrich (R-Ga)	$274,247	Incumb	W
5	Vic Fazio (D-Calif)	$272,781	Incumb	W
6	Marty Russo (D-Ill)	$252,349	Incumb	L
7	Thomas J. Downey (D-NY)	$244,800	Incumb	L
8	Stephen L. Neal (D-NC)	$220,050	Incumb	W
9	Tom McMillen (D-Md)	$210,835	Incumb	L
10	John J. LaFalce (D-NY)	$206,997	Incumb	W

Closeup on Finance, Insurance & Real Estate

Commercial Banks ....$11.2 million

Banking deregulation — allowing banks to operate freely across state lines and offer a wider array of financial services — remains high on the agenda of the nation's largest banks. The proposals have met wide opposition in Congress from competing interests, particularly insurance companies who want to keep the banks out of the securities brokerage business — something that's become a major sideline of insurance companies themselves. Non-industry critics oppose deregulation for different reasons. It was the loosening of rules in the savings & loan industry that led to rampant speculation and the eventual near-collapse of the industry, which is now being bailed out at enormous taxpayer expense.

Four of the five leaders in banking contributions in the House and Senate serve on the banking committees of their respective houses. Dan Coats was the only exception in the Senate. The top House recipient, freshman Republican Michael Castle, served as governor of Delaware before joining Congress.

Top Contributors

1	American Bankers Assn*	$1,692,508
2	JP Morgan & Co	$473,175
3	C&S/Sovran Corp*	$436,867
4	Citicorp*	$409,902
5	Independent Bankers Assn	$401,060
6	BankAmerica Corp*	$377,723
7	Barnett Banks Inc	$335,764
8	Chase Manhattan*	$303,328
9	Chemical Bank	$164,050
10	First Chicago Corp	$136,703

* Contributions came from more than one affiliate or subsidiary.

Top Senate Recipients

#	Recipient	Amount	Status	Result
1	Christopher S. Bond (R-Mo)	$158,918	Incumb	W
2	Richard C. Shelby (D-Ala)	$125,828	Incumb	W
3	Terry Sanford (D-NC)	$125,400	Incumb	L
4	Daniel R. Coats (R-Ind)	$97,035	Incumb	W
5	Christopher J. Dodd (D-Conn)	$96,300	Incumb	W

Top House Recipients

#	Recipient	Amount	Status	Result
1	Michael N. Castle (R-Del)	$123,800	Open	W
2	Stephen L. Neal (D-NC)	$112,900	Incumb	W
3	John J. LaFalce (D-NY)	$103,450	Incumb	W
4	Peter Hoagland (D-Neb)	$92,300	Incumb	W
5	Richard H. Baker (R-La)	$91,900	Incumb	W

Securities & Investment ....$15.9 million

While a number of top Wall Street investment firms do sponsor PACs, the preferred method for handing out contributions in the securities industry is through individual donations — often bundled in large amounts to their favorite candidates. Of the 30 biggest contributors of individual donations in the 1992 elections, 11 were securities firms. Goldman, Sachs was the biggest of all. It was also the single biggest supporter of Bill Clinton's campaign. Elizabeth Holtzman, who as New York City Comptroller was responsible for arranging the city's bond sales, led all other recipients from the industry. She lost in the Democratic primary to Robert Abrams, the number two recipient. Abrams, in turn, lost to incumbent Alfonse D'Amato, number three on the top recipient list.

Top Contributors

1	Goldman, Sachs & Co	$898,545
2	American Express/Shearson Lehman Bros*	$881,820
3	Merrill Lynch*	$627,864
4	Chicago Mercantile Exchange	$549,500
5	Morgan Stanley & Co	$470,781
6	Chicago Board of Trade	$346,750
7	PaineWebber*	$318,847
8	First Boston Corp	$315,621
9	Salomon Brothers	$285,885
10	Bear, Stearns & Co	$267,095

* Contributions came from more than one affiliate or subsidiary.

Top Senate Recipients

#	Recipient	Amount	Status	Result
1	Elizabeth Holtzman (D-NY)	$636,880	Chall	L
2	Robert Abrams (D-NY)	$610,010	Chall	L
3	Alfonse M. D'Amato (R-NY)	$457,151	Incumb	W
4	Christopher J. Dodd (D-Conn)	$341,484	Incumb	W
5	Tom Campbell (R-Calif)	$264,700	Open	L

Top House Recipients

#	Recipient	Amount	Status	Result
1	Charles E. Schumer (D-NY)	$221,996	Incumb	W
2	Richard A. Gephardt (D-Mo)	$141,207	Incumb	W
3	Dan Rostenkowski (D-Ill)	$124,600	Incumb	W
4	Nita M. Lowey (D-NY)	$99,740	Incumb	W
5	Bill Green (R-NY)	$96,000	Incumb	L

Insurance ....$14.9 million

Another giant of the financial world, the nation's insurance industry was one of the biggest contributors to congressional campaigns in the 1992 elections. Two-thirds of its money came from political action committees and much of it was targeted at members of committees concerned with tax policy, and with the redrafting of the nation's health insurance system.

Christopher Dodd, the industry's top recipient in 1992, represents the state that is home to some of the nation's largest insurance firms. Two other Connecticut lawmakers — Barbara Kennelly and Nancy Johnson — made the top 5 list in the House. Both sit on the powerful Ways & Means Committee, whose chairman, Dan Rostenkowski, ranked second on the list. The only non-incumbent on the leading recipients list was Earl Pomeroy, who served as North Dakota's insurance commissioner before his election to Congress.

Top Contributors	
1	National Assn of Life Underwriters $1,373,855
2	Prudential Insurance* $639,540
3	Independent Insurance Agents of America $589,798
4	American Council of Life Insurance $581,880
5	American Family Corp $550,000
6	Metropolitan Life Insurance* $453,564
7	Blue Cross & Blue Shield Assn* $412,359
8	Equitable Life* $308,857
9	Massachusetts Mutual Life Insurance $307,641
10	Northwestern Mutual Life $288,829

* Contributions came from more than one affiliate or subsidiary.

Top Senate Recipients				
1	Christopher J. Dodd (D-Conn) $225,896	Incumb	W
2	Arlen Specter (R-Pa) $199,494	Incumb	W
3	Christopher S. Bond (R-Mo)..............$176,786	Incumb	W
4	Daniel R. Coats (R-Ind) $174,248	Incumb	W
5	Bob Packwood (R-Ore) $164,260	Incumb	W

Top House Recipients				
1	Richard A. Gephardt (D-Mo) $157,889	Incumb	W
2	Dan Rostenkowski (D-Ill) $144,198	Incumb	W
3	Barbara B. Kennelly (D-Conn) $111,305	Incumb	W
4	Earl Pomeroy (D-ND) $98,628	Open	W
5	Nancy L. Johnson (R-Conn)................$95,305	Incumb	W

Real Estate ....$16.5 million

Investing in land and developing it with new and valuable buildings has been a thriving business fueling the American economy since the vast Eastern forests first began to be peeled back to make way for the villages, towns and farms of colonial settlers. The frantic building boom and real estate heyday of the 1980s gave way to a sobering crash in the early 90s in many markets around the nation. Some — particularly in California — have still not recovered, though the industry as a whole is rebounding with the gradually improving economy.

Campaign dollars from the real estate industry poured in heavily in 1991-92. The Realtors PAC gave more money to federal candidates than any other political action committee (though the American Medical Association gave more when state-based affiliates were added in). Despite their giant PAC, however, three-quarters of the real estate industry's money came from individuals.

Top Contributors	
1	National Assn of Realtors $2,954,973
2	Forest City Enterprises Inc $252,833
3	Mortgage Bankers Assn of America $221,200
4	JMB Realty Corp $132,331
5	American Land Title Assn $103,389
6	AKT Development Co $94,982
7	Federal National Mortgage Assn $93,775
8	Henry Crown & Co $85,500
9	Carr-Gottstein Inc $84,976
10	Sudler Companies $82,750

* Contributions came from more than one affiliate or subsidiary.

Top Senate Recipients				
1	John F. Seymour (R-Calif) $414,017	Incumb	L
2	Robert Abrams (D-NY) $270,718	Chall	L
3	Mel Levine (D-Calif) $248,160	Open	L
4	Gray Davis (D-Calif) $245,200	Chall	L
5	Dianne Feinstein (D-Calif) $226,258	Chall	W

Top House Recipients				
1	Richard A. Gephardt (D-Mo) $125,677	Incumb	W
2	Charles E. Schumer (D-NY) $83,000	Incumb	W
3	Bob Filner (D-Calif) $62,950	Open	W
4	Newt Gingrich (R-Ga) $56,459	Incumb	W
5	Bill Baker (R-Calif) $55,567	Open	W

Health

Where the money came from . . .

For years — in fact, for decades — campaign dollars from medical PACs and from thousands of individual doctors, dentists, chiropractors, pharmacists, nursing home operators and all other manner of health care providers have been flowing generously toward Washington. But as the long march toward some form of national health insurance (or an industry acceptable alternative) enters the final stages of political battle, the pace of giving has surged to extraordinary new levels. In the 1991-92 election season, the health care sector gave $31.7 million to federal candidates — nearly double the amount identified by the Center just two years earlier.

Two thirds of that money came from physicians and other health care professionals. The rest came from hospitals, pharmaceutical companies and a variety of other health industry givers. The American Medical Association's political action committee, and its network of state-based affiliates, was the single biggest giver. In fact, the AMA ranked as the overall number one contributor to federal campaigns in the 1992 elections. But as a glance at the chart below makes clear, the AMA is hardly alone. Many other medical professionals — from ophthalmologists to root canal specialists — have national associations with PACs of their own. So do dozens of other health industry corporations.

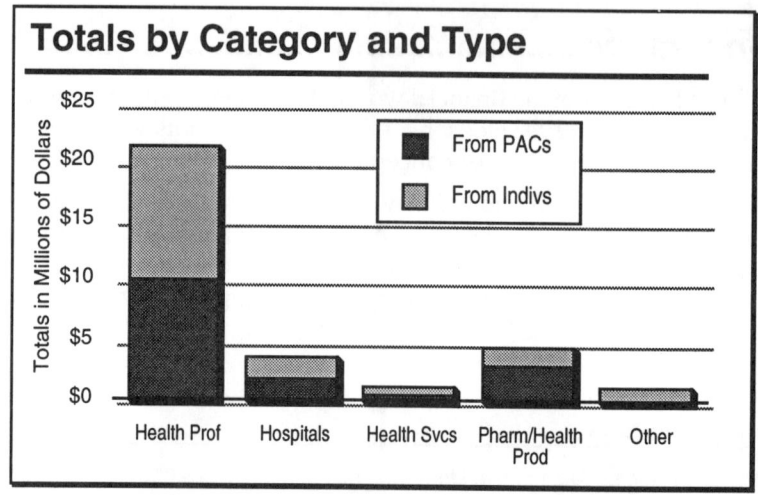

Category	Total	From PACs	PAC Pct	From Indivs	Indiv Pct
Health Professionals	$21,421,791	$9,959,465	46%	$11,462,326	54%
Hospitals/Nursing Homes	$3,638,760	$1,658,859	46%	$1,979,901	54%
Health Services	$1,122,272	$341,563	30%	$780,709	70%
Pharmaceuticals/Health Prod	$4,439,371	$2,972,414	67%	$1,466,957	33%
Other & Unclassified	$1,088,045	$0	0%	$1,088,045	100%
TOTAL	$31,710,239	$14,932,301	47%	$16,777,938	53%

Top 20 Health Contributors

Rank	Total	Contributor	Category	PAC Pct	Dem Pct	Repub Pct
1	$3,245,544	American Medical Assn*	Doctors	100%	49%	51%
2	$1,434,408	American Dental Assn*	Dentists	100%	60%	40%
3	$870,227	American Academy of Ophthalmology	Eye Doctors	100%	63%	37%
4	$658,596	American Chiropractic Assn*	Chiropractors	100%	73%	27%
5	$617,102	American Hospital Assn*	Hospitals	95%	69%	31%
6	$401,000	American Podiatry Assn	Doctors	100%	70%	30%
7	$398,366	American Optometric Assn	Eye Doctors	100%	69%	31%
8	$383,269	American Health Care Assn	Nursing Homes	99%	66%	33%
9	$332,925	American College of Emerg'cy Physicians	Doctors	99%	73%	26%
10	$311,019	American Nurses Assn	Nurses	100%	91%	9%
11	$276,743	Assn for the Advancement of Psychology	Psychology	99%	90%	10%
12	$258,330	Eli Lilly & Co	Pharmaceut	76%	21%	79%
13	$217,780	Pfizer Inc	Pharmaceut	86%	47%	53%
14	$207,331	Schering-Plough Corp	Pharmaceut	90%	51%	49%
15	$199,166	American Physical Therapy Assn	Phys Therapists	100%	73%	27%
16	$196,772	Glaxo Inc	Pharmaceut	89%	57%	43%
17	$182,900	Federation of American Health Systems	Hospitals	98%	59%	41%
18	$180,926	Merck & Co	Pharmaceut	80%	57%	43%
19	$176,475	Bristol-Myers Squibb	Pharmaceut	72%	38%	62%
20	$165,430	American Psychiatric Assn	Psychiatrists	100%	87%	12%

* Contributions came from more than one affiliate or subsidiary.

Where the money went . . .

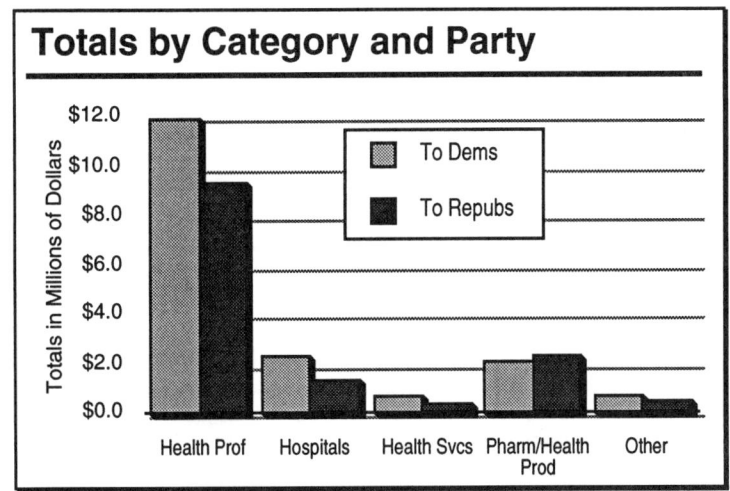

Overall, 54 percent of the medical community's campaign dollars went to Democrats. As with many other sectors, however, there were wide variations within the industry. Psychiatrists, psychologists and nurses were the most heavily Democratic, giving more than 80 percent of their dollars to candidates of that party. Pharmacists and chiropractors gave 70 percent to Democrats. The pharmaceutical industry leaned in the opposite direction, though not as far. Overall, they gave 53 percent of their campaign dollars to Republicans.

Category	Total	To Dems	Dem Pct	To Repubs	Repub Pct
Health Professionals	$21,421,791	$11,932,900	56%	$9,354,345	44%
Hospitals/Nursing Homes	$3,638,760	$2,350,484	65%	$1,279,291	35%
Health Services	$1,122,272	$726,279	65%	$393,428	35%
Pharmaceuticals/Health Prod	$4,439,371	$2,104,593	47%	$2,332,128	53%
Other & Unclassified	$1,088,045	$659,884	61%	$420,893	39%
TOTAL	**$31,710,239**	**$17,774,140**	**56%**	**$13,780,085**	**43%**

Republican Arlen Specter of Pennsylvania led all recipients of health care contributions in the 1992 elections, with $364,000. Bob Packwood, the number three recipient, is ranking Republican on the Senate Finance Committee — one of the key panels overseeing health care reform legislation.

Among House members, the top contributor list was led by Majority Leader Dick Gephardt. He was followed by Democrats Henry Waxman and Pete Stark, chairmen of the two key subcommittees (in the Energy & Commerce and Ways & Means Committees) that will write the new health care legislation.

Top 10 Senate Recipients

Rank	Name	Amount	Status	W/L
1	Arlen Specter (R-Pa)	$364,403	Incumb	W
2	Dianne Feinstein (D-Calif)	$329,029	Chall	W
3	Bob Packwood (R-Ore)	$299,400	Incumb	W
4	Barbara Boxer (D-Calif)	$284,897	Open	W
5	Daniel R. Coats (R-Ind)	$272,394	Incumb	W
6	John McCain (R-Ariz)	$251,989	Incumb	W
7	Tom Daschle (D-SD)	$244,999	Incumb	W
8	Christopher S. Bond (R-Mo)	$230,783	Incumb	W
9	Bob Graham (D-Fla)	$212,571	Incumb	W
10	Tom Campbell (R-Calif)	$208,759	Open	L

Top 10 House Recipients

Rank	Name	Amount	Status	W/L
1	Richard A. Gephardt (D-Mo)	$282,230	Incumb	W
2	Henry A. Waxman (D-Calif)	$203,199	Incumb	W
3	Pete Stark (D-Calif)	$193,401	Incumb	W
4	Vic Fazio (D-Calif)	$124,730	Incumb	W
5	E. Clay Shaw Jr. (R-Fla)	$115,445	Incumb	W
6	Newt Gingrich (R-Ga)	$114,360	Incumb	W
7	Robert G. Torricelli (D-NJ)	$113,600	Incumb	W
8	Gerry Sikorski (D-Minn)	$112,510	Incumb	L
9	Steny H. Hoyer (D-Md)	$109,174	Incumb	W
10	Michael Bilirakis (R-Fla)	$108,830	Incumb	W

Closeup on Health

Health Professionals ....$21.4 million

Doctors, dentists, psychiatrists, pathologists, chiropractors, pharmacists and a host of other health professionals form this segment of the medical industry that is far and away the biggest contributor to political campaigns. And while the political action committees representing these professionals are among the largest in the nation, half the dollars they gave in the 1992 elections came from individuals.

Eclipsing all other groups in this category were physicians and physician specialists. Among those specialties, optometrists and ophthalmologists were the most generous, giving $1.7 million to federal candidates. Psychiatrists and psychologists gave $920,000. Dentists opened their wallets wide and handed out $2.3 million of their own.

Top Contributors

1	American Medical Assn*	$3,225,110
2	American Dental Assn*	$1,434,408
3	American Academy of Ophthalmology	$870,227
4	American Chiropractic Assn*	$658,596
5	American Podiatry Assn	$401,000
6	American Optometric Assn	$398,366
7	American College of Emergency Physicians	$332,925
8	American Nurses Assn	$311,019
9	Assn for the Advancement of Psychology	$276,743
10	American Physical Therapy Assn	$199,166

* Contributions came from more than one affiliate or subsidiary.

Top Senate Recipients

1	Dianne Feinstein (D-Calif)	$222,087	Chall	W
2	Arlen Specter (R-Pa)	$217,685	Incumb	W
3	Barbara Boxer (D-Calif)	$212,294	Open	W
4	Bob Graham (D-Fla)	$154,081	Incumb	W
5	John McCain (R-Ariz)	$149,006	Incumb	W

Top House Recipients

1	Henry A. Waxman (D-Calif)	$126,049	Incumb	W
2	Pete Stark (D-Calif)	$113,401	Incumb	W
3	Richard A. Gephardt (D-Mo)	$98,630	Incumb	W
4	E. Clay Shaw Jr. (R-Fla)	$95,895	Incumb	W
5	Don Weidner (R-Fla)	$95,600	Open	L

Hospitals & Nursing Homes ....$3.6 million

Physicians are not the only ones with a stake in the current and future state of health care. Hospitals and nursing homes are also major players in the industry, with billions of dollars at stake in the details of federal health care policy. During the 1991-92 election cycle, hospital PACs and individual administrators and executives gave nearly $2.4 million to federal candidates. Nursing home operators gave an additional $1.2 million. Both groups gave just under two-thirds of their dollars to Democrats.

Top Contributors

1	American Hospital Assn*	$616,602
2	Federation of American Health Systems	$182,900
3	Hospice Care Inc	$163,150
4	Manor Healthcare Corp	$96,200
5	Natl Assn of Private Psychiatric Hospitals	$92,950

* Contributions came from more than one affiliate or subsidiary.

Top Senate Recipients

1	Bob Packwood (R-Ore)	$68,675	Incumb	W
2	Dianne Feinstein (D-Calif)	$42,750	Chall	W
3	Tom Daschle (D-SD)	$42,700	Incumb	W
4	Bob Kerrey (D-Neb)	$39,100	Incumb	†
5	John F. Seymour (R-Calif)	$36,450	Incumb	L

Top House Recipients

1	Richard A. Gephardt (D-Mo)	$66,500	Incumb	W
2	Carrie Meek (D-Fla)	$44,500	Open	W
3	Pete Stark (D-Calif)	$32,000	Incumb	W
4	Henry A. Waxman (D-Calif)	$31,250	Incumb	W
5	Joseph D. Early (D-Mass)	$25,400	Incumb	L

Health Services ....$1.1 million

The Health Services classification covers a wide variety of health industry companies that provide services of one sort or another to the public at large. The biggest cluster of dollars within the group comes from health maintenance organizations, or HMO's, that offer their clients full medical services from on-staff doctors. (Many of the largest insurance companies also sponsor HMO's; those are not included here. Also in this category are companies providing home care services, and medical laboratories.

Top Contributors

1	Family Health Program Inc	$120,363
2	US Healthcare Inc	$79,868
3	Pacificare Health Systems	$69,100
4	American Ambulance Assn	$55,425
5	National Assn for Home Care	$32,982

Top Senate Recipients

1	Arlen Specter (R-Pa)	$30,118	Incumb	W
2	John F. Seymour (R-Calif)	$29,338	Incumb	L
3	Tom Campbell (R-Calif)	$23,050	Open	L
4	Gray Davis (D-Calif)	$21,800	Chall	L
5	Dianne Feinstein (D-Calif)	$21,042	Chall	W

Top House Recipients

1	Richard A. Gephardt (D-Mo)	$57,950	Incumb	W
2	Pete Stark (D-Calif)	$24,250	Incumb	W
3	Newt Gingrich (R-Ga)	$15,700	Incumb	W
4	Henry A. Waxman (D-Calif)	$15,500	Incumb	W
5	Vic Fazio (D-Calif)	$14,750	Incumb	W

Pharmaceuticals & Health Products ....$4.4 million

Pharmaceutical manufacturers are the one segment of the health care community that gave more money to Republicans in the 1992 elections than to Democrats. In that sense, their pattern of giving more closely reflects that of the manufacturing sector than the health care industry. Drug companies and health products manufacturers contributed $4.4 million to federal candidates. Two-thirds of the dollars came from PACs.

Top Contributors

1	Eli Lilly & Co	$258,330
2	Pfizer Inc	$217,780
3	Merck & Co	$211,943
4	Schering-Plough Corp	$207,331
5	Glaxo Inc	$196,772
6	Bristol-Myers Squibb	$176,475
7	Abbott Laboratories	$165,393
8	Upjohn Co	$151,900
9	Ciba-Geigy Corp	$144,400
10	Warner-Lambert	$142,555

Top Senate Recipients

1	Daniel R. Coats (R-Ind)	$112,850	Incumb	W
2	Frank R. Lautenberg (D-NJ)	$103,500	Incumb	†
3	Bob Packwood (R-Ore)	$96,825	Incumb	W
4	Christopher J. Dodd (D-Conn)	$80,298	Incumb	W
5	John McCain (R-Ariz)	$67,233	Incumb	W

Top House Recipients

1	Dick Zimmer (R-NJ)	$49,250	Incumb	W
2	Dan Rostenkowski (D-Ill)	$45,500	Incumb	W
3	Richard A. Gephardt (D-Mo)	$41,500	Incumb	W
4	Thomas J. Bliley Jr. (R-Va)	$35,000	Incumb	W
5	Charles B. Rangel (D-NY)	$34,200	Incumb	W

Leading Health & Insurance Recipients in Congress

The lists on these two pages show at a glance which members of the House and Senate received the biggest contributions from a combination of health and insurance industry supporters. Though these groups are classified separately in this book (insurance is included under the Finance, Insurance & Real Estate sector), both will be fundamentally affected by the outcome of the current health care debate in Congress and both are lobbying as mightily as they can to preserve their financial interests.

The Senate totals include money received over each member's full six-year term (or less if they were elected after 1988). House totals cover only those contributions received in the 1992 elections.

Top Senate Recipients

Rank	Name	Total	Health	Insurance
1	Phil Gramm (R-Texas)	$869,561	$623,564	$245,997
2	Daniel R. Coats (R-Ind)	$832,593	$516,886	$315,707
3	Arlen Specter (R-Pa)	$796,682	$531,479	$265,203
4	John D. Rockefeller IV (D-WVa)	$639,977	$482,327	$157,650
5	Bill Bradley (D-NJ)	$576,970	$312,586	$264,384
6	Tom Daschle (D-SD)	$507,373	$321,849	$185,524
7	Christopher J. Dodd (D-Conn)	$494,155	$210,797	$283,358
8	Christopher S. Bond (R-Mo)	$481,419	$261,083	$220,336
9	Tom Harkin (D-Iowa)	$475,905	$352,752	$123,153
10	Dave Durenberger (R-Minn)	$467,159	$308,217	$158,942
11	Bob Packwood (R-Ore)	$465,964	$302,600	$163,364
12	Bob Dole (R-Kan)	$444,689	$186,100	$258,589
13	Alfonse M. D'Amato (R-NY)	$430,456	$233,600	$196,856
14	Lloyd Bentsen (D-xTex)	$423,855	$191,705	$232,150
15	Dianne Feinstein (D-Calif)	$401,539	$329,029	$72,510
16	Frank R. Lautenberg (D-NJ)	$373,150	$222,400	$150,750
17	Richard C. Shelby (D-Ala)	$371,150	$226,100	$145,050
18	Max Baucus (D-Mont)	$367,209	$188,435	$178,774
19	Don Nickles (R-Okla)	$365,042	$183,550	$181,492
20	Charles E. Grassley (R-Iowa)	$364,792	$192,569	$172,223
21	Bob Graham (D-Fla)	$357,201	$226,071	$131,130
22	Orrin G. Hatch (R-Utah)	$355,290	$226,798	$128,492
23	John McCain (R-Ariz)	$350,514	$257,139	$93,375
24	Mitch McConnell (R-Ky)	$336,206	$215,050	$121,156
25	Barbara Boxer (D-Calif)	$331,647	$286,897	$44,750
26	John B. Breaux (D-La)	$299,354	$167,042	$132,312
27	Hank Brown (R-Colo)	$297,893	$115,004	$182,889
28	Paul Simon (D-Ill)	$293,849	$236,474	$57,375
29	Harry Reid (D-Nev)	$278,622	$234,622	$44,000
30	Connie Mack (R-Fla)	$277,045	$178,950	$98,095
31	Ernest F. Hollings (D-SC)	$274,575	$142,555	$132,020
32	John H. Chafee (R-RI)	$260,733	$146,400	$114,333
33	Carl Levin (D-Mich)	$260,136	$167,502	$92,634
34	Paul Coverdell (R-Ga)	$257,091	$145,729	$111,362
35	John Glenn (D-Ohio)	$252,301	$173,351	$78,950
36	Al Gore (D-Tenn)	$231,326	$127,750	$103,576
37	Howell Heflin (D-Ala)	$230,646	$111,615	$119,031
38	Harris Wofford (D-Pa)	$227,925	$156,425	$71,500
39	John C. Danforth (R-Mo)	$223,275	$89,650	$133,625
40	Larry Pressler (R-SD)	$220,398	$89,900	$130,498
41	John Kerry (D-Mass)	$219,625	$142,725	$76,900
42	Daniel Patrick Moynihan (D-NY)	$213,147	$119,180	$93,967
43	Jesse Helms (R-NC)	$208,185	$135,245	$72,940
44	Wendell H. Ford (D-Ky)	$205,859	$81,300	$124,559
45	Barbara A. Mikulski (D-Md)	$205,723	$178,723	$27,000
46	Dennis DeConcini (D-Ariz)	$203,056	$97,656	$105,400
47	Donald W. Riegle Jr. (D-Mich)	$197,450	$79,500	$117,950
48	George J. Mitchell (D-Maine)	$196,883	$106,759	$90,124
49	Jim Sasser (D-Tenn)	$196,765	$89,715	$107,050
50	Richard G. Lugar (R-Ind)	$194,365	$119,400	$74,965

It should be emphasized that the health care debate is a complex one. Different segments within both the health and insurance communities have interests that often conflict with others in their industry. Neither group speaks with a single voice, nor do the interests of the health community necessarily coincide with those of insurance carriers. These lists do indicate, however, which members of Congress have gotten the biggest financial support from each industry. These are the members that the industries are counting on the most, and for that reason the combined list is offered here.

Top House Recipients

Rank	Name	Total	Health	Insurance
1	Richard A. Gephardt (D-Mo)	$440,119	$282,230	$157,889
2	Dan Rostenkowski (D-Ill)	$238,598	$94,400	$144,198
3	Henry A. Waxman (D-Calif)	$224,449	$203,199	$21,250
4	Pete Stark (D-Calif)	$221,901	$193,401	$28,500
5	Vic Fazio (D-Calif)	$215,029	$124,730	$90,299
6	Newt Gingrich (R-Ga)	$198,873	$114,360	$84,513
7	E. Clay Shaw Jr. (R-Fla)	$185,545	$115,445	$70,100
8	Nancy L. Johnson (R-Conn)	$171,505	$76,200	$95,305
9	Barbara B. Kennelly (D-Conn)	$151,705	$40,400	$111,305
10	David E. Bonior (D-Mich)	$148,925	$82,650	$66,275
11	Michael A. Andrews (D-Texas)	$147,325	$81,160	$66,165
12	Steny H. Hoyer (D-Md)	$146,924	$109,174	$37,750
13	Sander Levin (D-Mich)	$143,596	$100,597	$42,999
14	Jim Bunning (R-Ky)	$142,632	$67,559	$75,073
15	Charles B. Rangel (D-NY)	$138,570	$84,275	$54,295
16	John D. Dingell (D-Mich)	$136,300	$76,050	$60,250
17	Benjamin L. Cardin (D-Md)	$136,000	$93,800	$42,200
18	Robert G. Torricelli (D-NJ)	$135,050	$113,600	$21,450
19	Michael Bilirakis (R-Fla)	$130,080	$108,830	$21,250
20	Earl Pomeroy (D-ND)	$127,328	$28,700	$98,628
21	J. Roy Rowland (D-Ga)	$123,200	$105,950	$17,250
22	Thomas J. Bliley Jr. (R-Va)	$116,738	$87,050	$29,688
23	Sam M. Gibbons (D-Fla)	$113,999	$53,050	$60,949
24	Bill Richardson (D-NM)	$108,610	$90,260	$18,350
25	Jim Bacchus (D-Fla)	$108,430	$98,530	$9,900
26	Martin Frost (D-Texas)	$107,150	$76,600	$30,550
27	Butler Derrick (D-SC)	$106,550	$49,900	$56,650
28	Don Sundquist (R-Tenn)	$106,011	$53,850	$52,161
29	Ileana Ros-Lehtinen (R-Fla)	$103,813	$88,085	$15,728
30	Jim Slattery (D-Kan)	$101,849	$55,150	$46,699
31	Dick Zimmer (R-NJ)	$101,822	$76,375	$25,447
32	Jim McCrery (R-La)	$100,100	$74,100	$26,000
33	Robert T. Matsui (D-Calif)	$99,273	$68,423	$30,850
34	Fred Grandy (R-Iowa)	$98,346	$40,847	$57,499
35	Bill Paxon (R-NY)	$97,500	$46,900	$50,600
36	J. J. Pickle (D-Texas)	$97,106	$49,397	$47,709
37	Bill Zeliff (R-NH)	$96,152	$53,010	$43,142
38	Bill McCollum (R-Fla)	$94,850	$60,400	$34,450
39	Rosa DeLauro (D-Conn)	$91,168	$61,468	$29,700
40	Peter Deutsch (D-Fla)	$90,750	$38,600	$52,150
41	Jack Kingston (R-Ga)	$89,672	$53,352	$36,320
42	Jim Ramstad (R-Minn)	$88,120	$50,445	$37,675
43	Robert H. Michel (R-Ill)	$86,473	$46,025	$40,448
44	Gary L. Ackerman (D-NY)	$84,650	$63,600	$21,050
45	Sam Johnson (R-Texas)	$83,584	$64,459	$19,125
46	Bill Thomas (R-Calif)	$82,899	$39,050	$43,849
47	Dan Burton (R-Ind)	$82,709	$36,805	$45,904
48	John Bryant (D-Texas)	$81,039	$64,189	$16,850
49	Jerry Lewis (R-Calif)	$80,789	$41,289	$39,500
50	Hamilton Fish Jr. (R-NY)	$80,600	$17,900	$62,700

Lawyers & Lobbyists

Where the money came from . . .

Lawyers, lobbyists and lawmakers have had a long and close relationship ever since modern democracy made its emergence on the world political scene. Indeed, many individuals have passed through all three professions in succession: lawyers winning election and becoming lawmakers, then retiring from office and becoming high-paid lobbyists. Congress has always had more lawyers than members of any other profession, and the number of former lawmakers who make the transition from Capitol Hill to K Street — the heart of Washington's lobbying district — is large and continually growing.

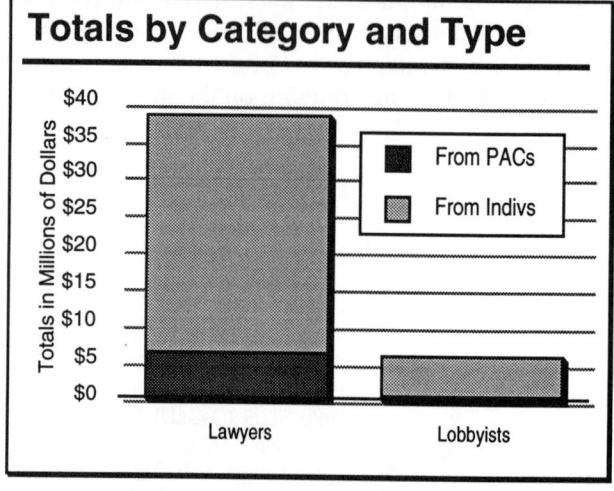

But little of that can be seen from tracking PAC contributions alone. Indeed, compared with other industry sectors, the legal community seems quite small. Legal industry PACs, led by the Association of Trial Lawyers of America, gave just $6.3 million in the 1992 elections. But in this case, following the PACs leads to a misleading conclusion. In fact, lawyers and lobbyists were responsible for $44 million in all — more than any other business sector except finance. But 86

Category	Total	From PACs	PAC Pct	From Indivs	Indiv Pct
Lawyers/Law Firms	$38,237,491	$6,051,042	16%	$32,186,449	84%
Lobbyists/Foreign Agents	$5,821,253	$268,637	5%	$5,552,616	95%
TOTAL	**$44,058,744**	**$6,319,679**	**14%**	**$37,739,065**	**86%**

percent of those dollars were delivered through individual contributions, not PACs. To journalists and other observers keeping a close watch on PAC donations, the full extent of the lawyers' giving was practically invisible.

Even with the research that went into this book, many questions about the role of lawyers and lobbyists are unanswered. Many lawyers failed to put the name of their law firm, simply filling in "attorney" as their employer. And federal lobbying laws are so porous that the number of registered lobbyists is widely understood to be only a fraction of the number of Washington-area lawyers who routinely perform lobbying services for clients.

In this book, contributions from attorneys are classified under the lobbyist category only if the contributor was an officially registered lobbyist. The total lobbying dollars can therefore safely be considered to be extremely conservative. A new classification in this year's *Cash Constituents of Congress* is that of "foreign agent." These are a particular class of Washington lobbyist who represents a foreign government or corporation in dealings with the federal government. Most, but not all registered foreign agents are also lobbyists, just as most, but not all lobbyists are also attorneys.

Top 20 Lawyer & Lobbyist Contributors

Rank	Total	Contributor	Category	PAC Pct	Dem Pct	Repub Pct	To Dems	To Repubs
1	$2,361,135	Assn of Trial Lawyers of America	Trial Lawyers	100%	92%	8%		
2	$538,228	Akin, Gump et al	Law/Lobby	57%	79%	21%		
3	$372,666	Cassidy & Associates	Lobbyists	0%	77%	23%		
4	$350,566	Skadden, Arps et al	Law/Lobby	27%	77%	23%		
5	$344,611	Jones, Day et al	Law/Lobby	51%	57%	43%		
6	$269,264	Williams & Jensen	Law/Lobby	34%	70%	30%		
7	$250,342	Verner, Liipfert et al	Law/Lobby	70%	87%	13%		
8	$203,374	Vinson & Elkins	Law/Lobby	59%	53%	47%		
9	$183,192	Preston, Gates et al	Law/Lobby	63%	68%	32%		
10	$180,389	Latham & Watkins	Law/Lobby	0%	57%	43%		
11	$179,224	Arnold & Porter*	Law/Lobby	60%	81%	19%		
12	$168,596	Manatt, Phelps et al	Law/Lobby	42%	83%	17%		
13	$160,937	Patton, Boggs & Blow	Law/Lobby	0%	80%	20%		
14	$160,509	O'Melveny & Myers	Law/Lobby	0%	56%	44%		
15	$159,619	Powell, Goldstein et al	Law/Lobby	77%	89%	11%		
16	$152,294	Kirkpatrick & Lockhart	Law/Lobby	45%	34%	66%		
17	$148,900	Hogan & Hartson	Law/Lobby	35%	83%	17%		
18	$147,741	Baker & Botts	Law/Lobby	50%	40%	60%		
19	$146,700	Milberg, Weiss et al	Law/Lobby	0%	99%	1%		
20	$145,595	Gibson, Dunn & Crutcher	Law/Lobby	0%	63%	37%		

* Contributions came from more than one affiliate or subsidiary.

Where the money went...

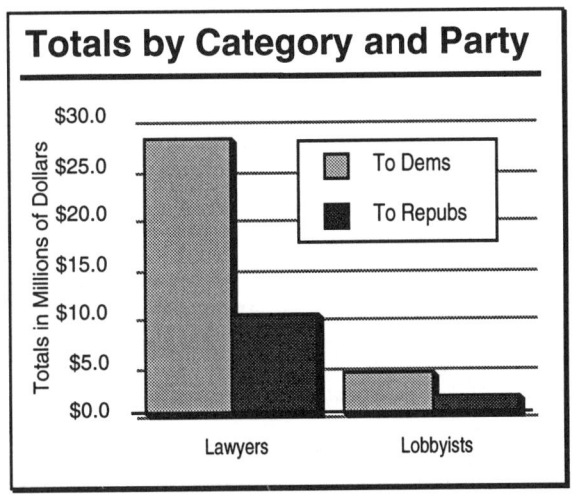

Totals by Category and Party

By nearly a three-to-one margin, individual lawyers and their PACs favored Democrats over Republicans in their contributions. That was the strongest tilt by any business sector to either party.

Category	Total	To Dems	Dem Pct	To Repubs	Repub Pct
Lawyers/Law Firms	$38,237,491	$27,992,570	73%	$10,176,750	27%
Lobbyists/Foreign Agents	$5,821,253	$4,168,327	72%	$1,650,975	28%
TOTAL	**$44,058,744**	**$32,160,897**	**73%**	**$11,827,725**	**27%**

The biggest recipients from the legal community were nearly all Democrats. The only exception was Republican Senator Arlen Specter of Pennsylvania. Specter sits on the Senate Judiciary Committee, a panel of key importance to lawyers.

New York Democrat Robert Abrams was the top overall recipient in Congress. He collected nearly a million dollars from lawyers and lobbyists in his abortive attempt to oust Republican incumbent Alfonse D'Amato. Dick Gephardt led all House members, with nearly $370,000 in contributions.

Because of their heavy reliance on individual contributions, and the fact that many law firms bundled large numbers of contributions to particularly favored candidates, law firms were prominent on the list of the year's biggest individual contributors. In all, 13 law firms ranked among the top 50 individual contributors in the 1992 elections, as did Cassidy & Associates, a Washington lobbying group.

Top 10 Senate Recipients

Rank	Name	Amount	Status	W/L
1	Robert Abrams (D-NY)	$996,806	Chall	L
2	Harris Wofford (D-Pa)	$724,065	Incumb	W
3	Dianne Feinstein (D-Calif)	$707,149	Chall	W
4	Barbara Boxer (D-Calif)	$680,582	Open	W
5	Mel Levine (D-Calif)	$638,625	Open	L
6	Arlen Specter (R-Pa)	$544,605	Incumb	W
7	Wyche Fowler Jr. (D-Ga)	$425,231	Incumb	L
8	Ernest F. Hollings (D-SC)	$412,467	Incumb	W
9	Bob Graham (D-Fla)	$398,539	Incumb	W
10	Richard C. Shelby (D-Ala)	$390,213	Incumb	W

Top 10 House Recipients

Rank	Name	Amount	Status	W/L
1	Richard A. Gephardt (D-Mo)	$369,892	Incumb	W
2	Vic Fazio (D-Calif)	$165,504	Incumb	W
3	Jane Harman (D-Calif)	$148,925	Open	W
4	Mike Synar (D-Okla)	$143,121	Incumb	W
5	Gerry Sikorski (D-Minn)	$140,726	Incumb	L
6	Steny H. Hoyer (D-Md)	$140,217	Incumb	W
7	Lynn Schenk (D-Calif)	$139,642	Open	W
8	Martin Frost (D-Texas)	$137,162	Incumb	W
9	Marty Russo (D-Ill)	$136,265	Incumb	L
10	Robert G. Torricelli (D-NJ)	$131,800	Incumb	W

Miscellaneous Business

Where the money came from...

This catchall category encompasses a wide diversity of businesses from many different industries — from steel manufacturers to travel agents to funeral directors. Most of the industries here have an interest in many different legislative matters, but — aside from tax laws — few of those issues are concentrated under the jurisdiction of a particular committee.

Miscellaneous manufacturers and distributors comprised the biggest single group within the sector, both in PAC and individual contributions. The companies in this group manufacture everything from machine tools to cosmetics. Other large groups were the food & beverage industry (which includes restaurants, soft drink makers and bottlers — but not food manufacturers, who are classified under agriculture); the beer & liquor industry, retail sales, and "business services," which covers such fields as advertising, business consulting and employment agencies. Overall, two-thirds of the dollars in this sector came from individual contributors rather than PACs.

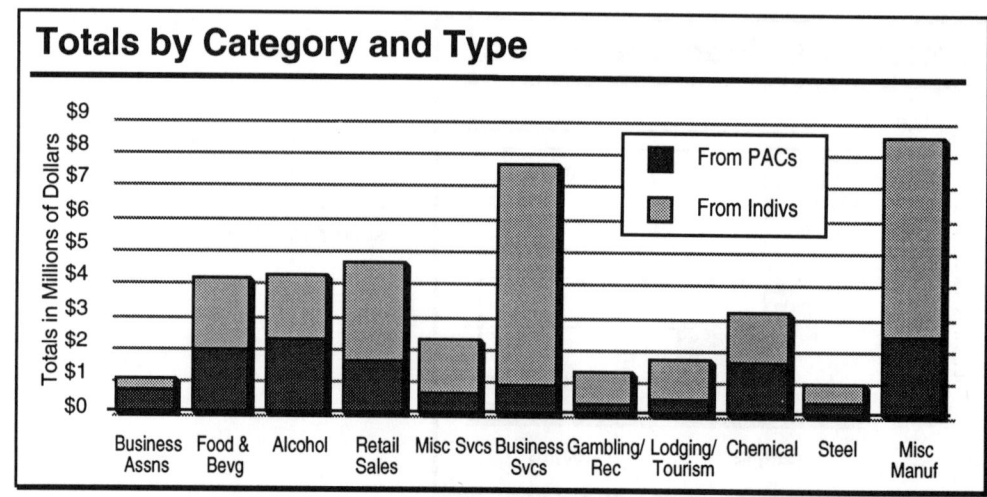

Totals by Category and Type

Category	Total	From PACs	PAC Pct	From Indivs	Indiv Pct
Business Associations	$934,666	$656,618	70%	$278,048	30%
Food & Beverage	$4,064,037	$1,854,399	46%	$2,209,638	54%
Beer, Wine & Liquor	$4,079,617	$2,139,202	52%	$1,940,415	48%
Retail Sales	$4,530,113	$1,500,376	33%	$3,029,737	67%
Misc Services	$2,174,644	$529,793	24%	$1,644,851	76%
Business Services	$7,502,660	$780,951	10%	$6,721,709	90%
Gambling/Live Entertainment	$1,212,097	$251,445	21%	$960,652	79%
Lodging/Tourism	$1,595,139	$401,600	25%	$1,193,539	75%
Chemicals	$3,088,619	$1,517,729	49%	$1,570,890	51%
Steel Production	$870,603	$276,646	32%	$593,957	68%
Misc Manufacturing/Distrib	$8,425,812	$2,326,129	28%	$6,099,683	72%
TOTAL	$38,478,007	$12,234,888	32%	$26,243,119	68%

Top 20 Miscellaneous Business Contributors

Rank	Total	Contributor	Category	PAC Pct	Dem Pct	Repub Pct
1	$977,081	National Beer Wholesalers Assn	Beer Distrib	100%	38%	62%
2	$571,197	National Restaurant Assn*	Restaurants	100%	23%	77%
3	$525,569	Dow Chemical*	Chemicals	82%	22%	78%
4	$452,363	Pepsico*	Soft Drinks/Rest	66%	26%	63%
5	$368,000	Stone Container Corp	Paper Packging	96%	11%	89%
6	$296,434	McDonald's Corp	Restaurants	79%	29%	71%
7	$295,287	National Fedn of Independent Business	Business Assns	99%	13%	86%
8	$284,649	Intl Council of Shopping Centers	Retail Sales	99%	41%	59%
9	$277,260	FMC Corp	Chemicals	94%	36%	64%
10	$267,090	Coca-Cola Co*	Soft Drinks	81%	59%	41%
11	$258,600	Joseph E Seagram & Sons	Liquor/Wine	80%	83%	17%
12	$232,134	Outdoor Advertising Assn of America	Billboards	91%	64%	36%
13	$217,984	Gallo Winery	Wine	0%	68%	32%
14	$198,890	JC Penney Co	Retail Sales	98%	57%	43%
15	$190,800	Hoechst Celanese Corp	Synth Fibers	98%	47%	53%
16	$187,050	Brown-Forman Distillers	Liquor	83%	21%	79%
17	$178,228	Wine & Spirits Wholesalers of America	Liquor Whlsale	100%	66%	33%
18	$176,700	Monsanto Co*	Chemicals	81%	27%	73%
19	$163,075	Burlington Industries	Textiles	91%	77%	23%
20	$152,895	WR Grace & Co	Chemicals	88%	37%	63%

* Contributions came from more than one affiliate or subsidiary.

Where the money went . . .

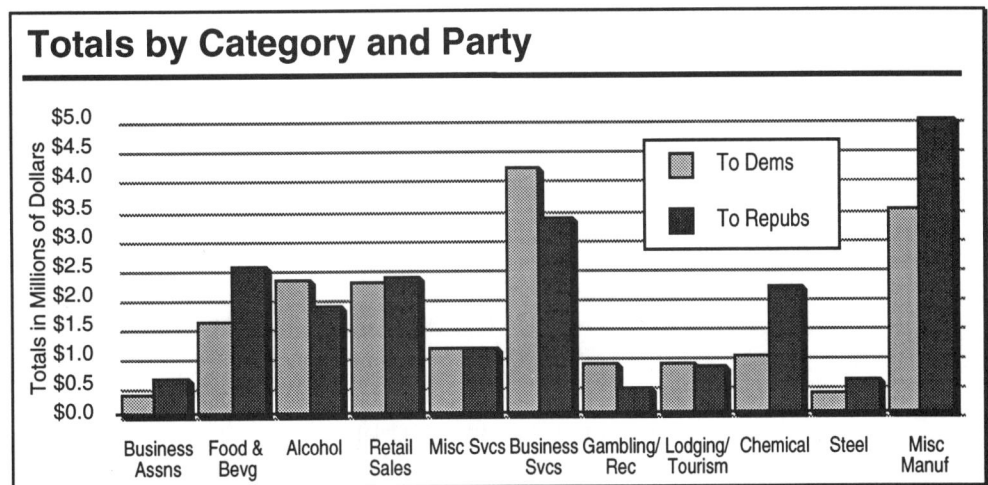

Totals by Category and Party

Democrats fared best among casinos and gambling interests. They also got a majority of the dollars from the liquor industry and from the diverse "business services" category. Republicans collected most of the dollars from everyone else — particularly the chemical, steel and food & beverage industries, and from the wide variety of manufacturing companies.

Category	Total	To Dems	Dem Pct	To Repubs	Repub Pct
Business Associations	$934,666	$310,721	33%	$612,979	66%
Food & Beverage	$4,064,037	$1,551,573	38%	$2,498,459	61%
Beer, Wine & Liquor	$4,079,617	$2,280,813	56%	$1,796,554	44%
Retail Sales	$4,530,113	$2,212,503	49%	$2,299,822	51%
Misc Services	$2,174,644	$1,083,112	50%	$1,084,086	50%
Business Services	$7,502,660	$4,161,485	55%	$3,285,390	44%
Gambling/Live Entertainment	$1,212,097	$807,481	67%	$400,268	33%
Lodging/Tourism	$1,595,139	$804,005	50%	$783,367	49%
Chemicals	$3,088,619	$970,808	31%	$2,110,998	68%
Steel Production	$870,603	$328,442	38%	$540,913	62%
Misc Manufacturing/Distrib	$8,425,812	$3,451,393	41%	$4,941,633	59%
TOTAL	**$38,478,007**	**$17,962,336**	**47%**	**$20,354,469**	**53%**

Leading recipients in this category most typically are candidates who raised large sums from all groups of contributors. House Majority Leader Richard Gephardt, who led all House recipients, was typical in that regard. His campaign raised over $3 million in contributions and his name was at or near the top of the Top 10 recipients list in eight of the 12 sector classifications. Overall, Republicans held seven of the top 10 Senate spots under the Miscellaneous Business sector, and accounted for six of the top 10 in the House of Representatives.

Top 10 Senate Recipients

Rank	Name	Amount	Status	W/L
1	Robert Abrams (D-NY)	$607,115	Chall	L
2	Arlen Specter (R-Pa)	$557,725	Incumb	W
3	Bob Kasten (R-Wis)	$532,099	Incumb	L
4	Alfonse M. D'Amato (R-NY)	$435,505	Incumb	W
5	Christopher S. Bond (R-Mo)	$422,928	Incumb	W
6	Dianne Feinstein (D-Calif)	$405,469	Chall	W
7	Dick Thornburgh (R-Pa)	$396,316	Chall	L
8	John F. Seymour (R-Calif)	$392,389	Incumb	L
9	Paul Coverdell (R-Ga)	$369,908	Chall	W
10	Mel Levine (D-Calif)	$368,898	Open	L

Top 10 House Recipients

Rank	Name	Amount	Status	W/L
1	Richard A. Gephardt (D-Mo)	$378,121	Incumb	W
2	Newt Gingrich (R-Ga)	$244,434	Incumb	W
3	Dan Rostenkowski (D-Ill)	$215,507	Incumb	W
4	Don Ritter (R-Pa)	$151,669	Incumb	L
5	Bud Shuster (R-Pa)	$135,050	Incumb	W
6	Jim Ramstad (R-Minn)	$119,643	Incumb	W
7	Bill Zeliff (R-NH)	$119,254	Incumb	W
8	Vic Fazio (D-Calif)	$116,631	Incumb	W
9	Barbara F. Vucanovich (R-Nev)	$108,745	Incumb	W
10	Robert G. Torricelli (D-NJ)	$104,100	Incumb	W

Closeup on Miscellaneous Business

Food & Beverage .... $4.1 million

This group includes restaurants and drinking establishments, soft drink manufacturers and bottlers, fish processors, candy manufacturers, and companies that make food additives. More general food processors and manufacturers are classified under the Agriculture sector.

Top Contributors

1	National Restaurant Assn*	$569,197
2	Pepsico*	$452,363
3	McDonald's Corp	$296,434
4	Coca-Cola Co*	$267,090
5	S&A Restaurant Corp	$143,500
6	Pepsi-Cola General Bottlers	$79,695
7	Chili's Inc	$70,000
8	National Soft Drink Assn	$64,264
9	ARA Services Inc	$57,947
10	Delaware North Companies	$54,300

* Contributions came from more than one affiliate or subsidiary.

Top Senate Recipients

1	Bob Kasten (R-Wis)	$64,856	Incumb	L
2	Dick Thornburgh (R-Pa)	$58,500	Chall	L
3	Paul Coverdell (R-Ga)	$55,280	Chall	W
4	Arlen Specter (R-Pa)	$50,947	Incumb	W
5	Christopher S. Bond (R-Mo)	$49,235	Incumb	W

Top House Recipients

1	Newt Gingrich (R-Ga)	$72,049	Incumb	W
2	Bill Zeliff (R-NH)	$28,170	Incumb	W
3	John J. LaFalce (D-NY)	$28,094	Incumb	W
4	Dan Rostenkowski (D-Ill)	$28,000	Incumb	W
5	Drew Edmondson (D-Okla)	$22,800	Chall	L

Beer, Wine & Liquor .... $4.1 million

Beer & liquor wholesalers were the biggest contributors in this group, accounting for $2.3 million. Wine & spirit manufacturers gave over $1.3 million. Beer manufacturers, led by Anheuser-Busch, gave a total of $348,000.

Top Contributors

1	National Beer Wholesalers Assn	$977,081
2	Joseph E Seagram & Sons	$258,600
3	Anheuser-Busch	$237,980
4	Gallo Winery	$217,984
5	Brown-Forman Distillers	$187,050
6	Wine & Spirits Wholesalers of America	$178,228
7	Wine Institute	$108,276
8	Smirnoff/Inglenook Distributors	$84,000
9	Distilled Spirits Council	$68,401
10	Southern Wine & Spirits	$64,250

Top Senate Recipients

1	John F. Seymour (R-Calif)	$88,477	Incumb	L
2	Robert Abrams (D-NY)	$66,700	Chall	L
3	Tom Daschle (D-SD)	$61,639	Incumb	W
4	Wendell H. Ford (D-Ky)	$58,050	Incumb	W
5	Christopher S. Bond (R-Mo)	$55,950	Incumb	W

Top House Recipients

1	Richard A. Gephardt (D-Mo)	$151,100	Incumb	W
2	Dan Rostenkowski (D-Ill)	$57,000	Incumb	W
3	Vic Fazio (D-Calif)	$53,750	Incumb	W
4	Frank Riggs (R-Calif)	$35,878	Incumb	L
5	Martin Frost (D-Texas)	$26,750	Incumb	W

Retail Sales .... $4.5 million

Department and variety stores led the spending in this category, which includes retail stores of all types as well as catalog and direct mail houses, vending machine operators and door-to-door sales companies.

Top Contributors

1	Intl Council of Shopping Centers	$284,649
2	Sears*	$220,926
3	JC Penney Co	$198,890
4	May Department Stores	$151,800
5	Amway Corp	$149,121
6	National Assn of Convenience Stores	$106,195
7	National Assn of Chain Drug Stores	$91,050
8	Wal-Mart Stores	$84,725
9	Dayton Hudson Corp	$69,250
10	Spiegel Inc	$68,650

* Contributions came from more than one affiliate or subsidiary.

Top Senate Recipients

1	Robert Abrams (D-NY)	$119,415	Chall	L
2	Arlen Specter (R-Pa)	$76,407	Incumb	W
3	Dianne Feinstein (D-Calif)	$68,300	Chall	W
4	Christopher S. Bond (R-Mo)	$59,017	Incumb	W
5	Bob Packwood (R-Ore)	$55,307	Incumb	W

Top House Recipients

1	Dan Rostenkowski (D-Ill)	$49,507	Incumb	W
2	Bob McEwen (R-Ohio)	$36,650	Incumb	L
3	Richard A. Gephardt (D-Mo)	$30,400	Incumb	W
4	Newt Gingrich (R-Ga)	$21,600	Incumb	W
5	Bill Baker (R-Calif)	$17,750	Open	W

Chemical & Related Manufacturing ....$3.1 million

Because of strict federal regulations on pollution control, clean air standards and hazardous waste cleanup, the chemical industry has long been one of the most politically active segments of the manufacturing sector. It is also one of the most conservative, delivering two-thirds of its campaign dollars to Republicans.

Top Contributors	
1 Dow Chemical*	$525,569
2 FMC Corp	$277,260
3 Monsanto Co*	$175,000
4 WR Grace & Co	$152,895
5 Procter & Gamble	$110,100
6 Air Products & Chemicals Inc	$106,750
7 Dial Corp	$97,200
8 El du Pont de Nemours & Co*	$83,604
9 Philipp Brothers Chemical	$81,660
10 Nalco Chemical Co	$79,550

* Contributions came from more than one affiliate or subsidiary.

Top Senate Recipients			
1 Dick Thornburgh (R-Pa)	$69,350	Chall	L
2 Christopher S. Bond (R-Mo)	$68,165	Incumb	W
3 Bob Kasten (R-Wis)	$56,886	Incumb	L
4 Arlen Specter (R-Pa)	$54,800	Incumb	W
5 Richard Williamson (R-Ill)	$43,400	Chall	L

Top House Recipients			
1 Dave Camp (R-Mich)	$64,819	Incumb	W
2 Don Ritter (R-Pa)	$39,229	Incumb	L
3 James C. Greenwood (R-Pa)	$22,500	Chall	W
4 Jack Fields (R-Texas)	$21,050	Incumb	W
5 W.J. "Billy" Tauzin (D-La)	$20,350	Incumb	W

Misc. Manufacturing & Distributing ....$8.4 million

Once the backbone of American industry, this diverse group of manufacturers and distributors supply everything from office copiers to running shoes, blue jeans to jewelry, light bulbs to tin cans. Its dollars went mainly to Republicans, and its legislative interests range from occupational safety standards to product liability laws to the North American Free Trade Agreement.

Top Contributors	
1 Stone Container Corp	$368,000
2 Hoechst Celanese Corp	$190,800
3 MacAndrews & Forbes Group	$147,750
4 Friedkin Industries	$106,500
5 American Furniture Manufacturers Assn	$86,750
6 Schnitzer Steel Industries	$81,602
7 Minnesota Mining & Manufacturing (3M)	$76,750
8 Nike Inc	$74,099
9 Maytag Co	$59,200
10 National Tooling & Machining Assn	$58,260

Top Senate Recipients			
1 Robert Abrams (D-NY)	$164,750	Chall	L
2 Bob Kasten (R-Wis)	$164,031	Incumb	L
3 Arlen Specter (R-Pa)	$137,000	Incumb	W
4 Alfonse M. D'Amato (R-NY)	$114,984	Incumb	W
5 Daniel R. Coats (R-Ind)	$108,733	Incumb	W

Top House Recipients			
1 Newt Gingrich (R-Ga)	$56,900	Incumb	W
2 Dick Swett (D-NH)	$49,828	Incumb	W
3 Jim Ramstad (R-Minn)	$47,825	Incumb	W
4 Richard A. Gephardt (D-Mo)	$46,750	Incumb	W
5 James M. Talent (R-Mo)	$41,987	Chall	W

Transportation

Where the money came from . . .

In a nation that spans more than 2,000 miles from coast to coast, and another 1,000 from border to border, the transportation of goods, services and people from one location to another has always been a major industry. From the days when the railroads opened up the American West, transportation companies have relied on allies in Congress to keep their business rolling along. Likewise, competing segments within the industry — railroads versus truckers, for example — have often sought to improve their market position at their competitors' expense.

In the 1992 elections the automotive and air transport industries were the biggest contributors to federal candidates, though most of the dollars did not come from airlines and automakers. Rather, it was the two biggest overnight delivery carriers — Federal Express and UPS — that were the leaders in air transport, along with General Electric, whose aerospace division provides its biggest source of revenues. And it was auto dealers — not the manufacturers — who led the way in spending in the automotive sector.

Contributions through political action committees were the most common form of delivering dollars from transportation interests. Two dollars out of every three came from PACs.

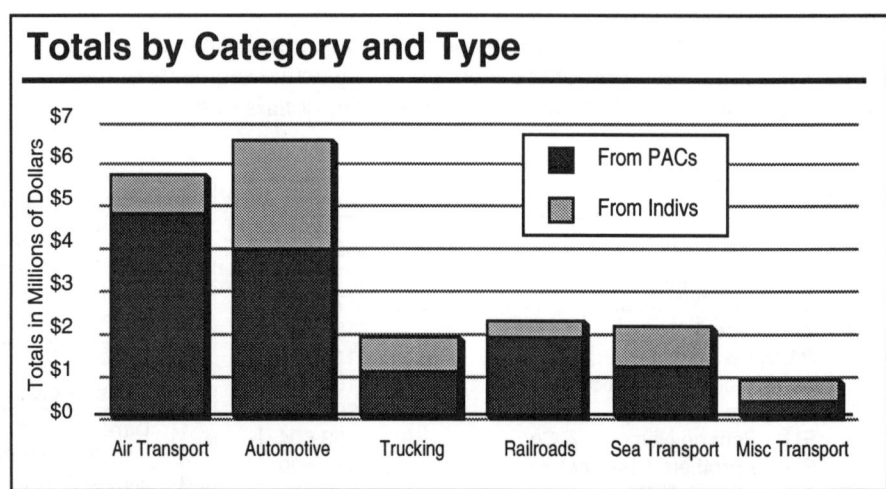

Category	Total	From PACs	PAC Pct	From Indivs	Indiv Pct
Air Transport/Aerospace	$5,655,211	$4,713,363	83%	$941,848	17%
Automotive	$6,494,504	$3,861,991	59%	$2,632,513	41%
Trucking	$1,821,556	$1,019,949	56%	$801,607	44%
Railroads	$2,179,996	$1,780,081	82%	$399,915	18%
Sea Transport	$2,062,351	$1,112,724	54%	$949,627	46%
Misc Transport	$776,072	$278,909	36%	$497,163	64%
TOTAL	**$18,989,690**	**$12,767,017**	**67%**	**$6,222,673**	**33%**

Top 20 Transportation Contributors

Rank	Total	Contributor	Category	PAC Pct	Dem Pct	Repub Pct
1	$1,784,375	National Auto Dealers Assn	Auto Dealers	100%	39%	61%
2	$1,472,357	United Parcel Service	Delivery Svcs	99%	54%	46%
3	$851,852	General Electric*	Aerospace	84%	58%	42%
4	$771,474	General Motors*	Auto Manuf	88%	53%	46%
5	$747,445	Federal Express Corp	Delivery Svcs	99%	68%	32%
6	$713,390	Union Pacific Corp*	Railroads	96%	33%	67%
7	$538,550	Auto Dealers & Drivers for Free Trade	Import Auto Dlrs	100%	38%	62%
8	$482,695	Aircraft Owners & Pilots Assn	Air Transport	100%	56%	44%
9	$475,150	Americans for Free International Trade	Import Auto Dlrs	100%	20%	80%
10	$453,750	CSX Corp*	RR/Sea Trans	93%	53%	47%
11	$385,003	Boeing Co	Aircraft Manuf	87%	54%	46%
12	$380,508	Ford Motor Co	Auto Manuf	85%	54%	46%
13	$359,019	American Trucking Assns	Trucking	99%	62%	38%
14	$316,481	Burlington Northern*	Railroads	93%	71%	29%
15	$298,469	American Airlines	Airlines	86%	70%	30%
16	$239,697	Norfolk Southern Corp*	Railroads	96%	63%	37%
17	$229,876	United Airlines	Airlines	86%	56%	44%
18	$223,850	Eaton Corp	Auto Parts	98%	7%	93%
19	$185,539	Northwest Airlines	Airlines	84%	66%	33%
20	$173,659	Yellow Freight System	Trucking	98%	68%	32%

* Contributions came from more than one affiliate or subsidiary.

Where the money went . . .

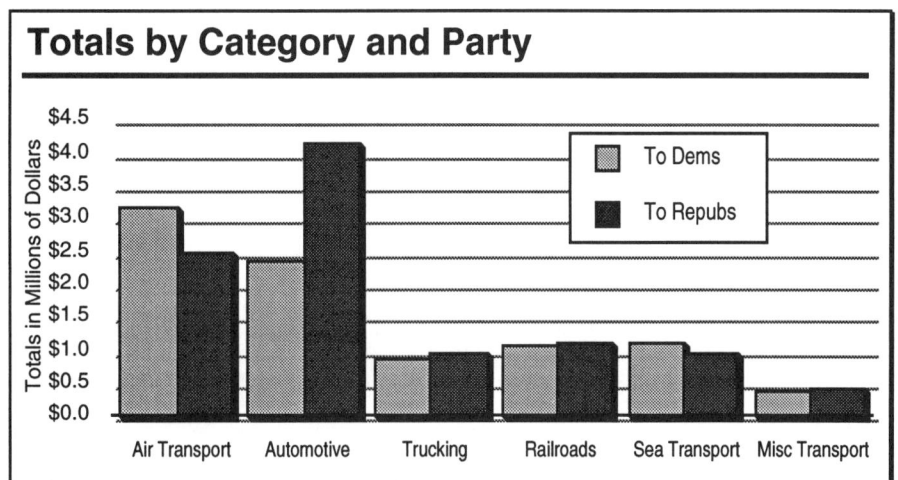

Overall, the transportation sector split its campaign dollars fairly evenly, with Republicans collecting slightly more than half the money. The air transport and sea transport industries tipped slightly in favor of Democrats, while the automotive industry — particularly auto dealers — were the heaviest backers of the GOP.

Category	Total	To Dems	Dem Pct	To Repubs	Repub Pct
Air Transport/Aerospace	$5,655,211	$3,176,333	56%	$2,471,648	44%
Automotive	$6,494,504	$2,345,000	36%	$4,137,394	64%
Trucking	$1,821,556	$872,935	48%	$948,021	52%
Railroads	$2,179,996	$1,051,616	48%	$1,126,374	52%
Sea Transport	$2,062,351	$1,122,733	54%	$939,218	46%
Misc Transport	$776,072	$372,185	48%	$398,235	51%
TOTAL	**$18,989,690**	**$8,940,802**	**47%**	**$10,020,890**	**53%**

Several committees in Congress deal specifically with transportation issues, and their members were among the top recipients from the industry. In the upper chamber, the Senate Commerce and Transportation Committee is the focal point. Five of the top six Senate recipients (all but John Seymour) were members of that committee. So was 10th ranking John McCain.

In the House, the Public Works and Transportation Committee is the industry's chief overseer. The leading House recipient, Norman Mineta, chairs the committee's Surface Transportation Subcommittee. Three others among the top 10 — Pete Geren, Bud Shuster and Robert Roe — also served on the panel in 1992. Roe was chairman of the full committee.

Top 10 Senate Recipients

Rank	Name	Amount	Status	W/L
1	Bob Packwood (R-Ore)	$260,937	Incumb	W
2	John F. Seymour (R-Calif)	$238,746	Incumb	L
3	Bob Kasten (R-Wis)	$236,575	Incumb	L
4	John B. Breaux (D-La)	$205,718	Incumb	W
5	Ernest F. Hollings (D-SC)	$192,875	Incumb	W
6	Wendell H. Ford (D-Ky)	$187,920	Incumb	W
7	Christopher S. Bond (R-Mo)	$168,122	Incumb	W
8	Rod Chandler (R-Wash)	$161,627	Open	L
9	Bob Dole (R-Kan)	$155,937	Incumb	W
10	John McCain (R-Ariz)	$152,191	Incumb	W

Top 10 House Recipients

Rank	Name	Amount	Status	W/L
1	Norman Y. Mineta (D-Calif)	$174,359	Incumb	W
2	Richard A. Gephardt (D-Mo)	$146,996	Incumb	W
3	Bob Carr (D-Mich)	$129,330	Incumb	W
4	John D. Dingell (D-Mich)	$120,050	Incumb	W
5	Pete Geren (D-Texas)	$107,709	Incumb	W
6	Dan Rostenkowski (D-Ill)	$100,750	Incumb	W
7	Newt Gingrich (R-Ga)	$93,365	Incumb	W
8	David E. Bonior (D-Mich)	$88,925	Incumb	W
9	Bud Shuster (R-Pa)	$88,425	Incumb	W
10	Robert A. Roe (D-NJ)	$87,650	Incumb	Ret

Closeup on Transportation

Air Transport ....$5.7 million

Besides being among the most frequent fliers on the domestic airline system, as they wing their way back and forth from their far-flung districts, members of Congress also keep a close eye on the industry, with subcommittees in both the House and Senate dealing specifically with aviation issues. The industry returned the attention, contributing nearly $5.7 million to federal campaigns in the 1992 elections. Topping the list of contributors was UPS, whose PAC ranked just ahead of AT&T as the largest corporate PAC in the nation in 1991-92. Between them, UPS and Federal Express gave more than $2.2 million to federal candidates. That was almost double the amount given by all the nation's airlines.

Top Contributors	
1 United Parcel Service	$1,472,357
2 General Electric*	$785,636
3 Federal Express Corp	$747,445
4 Aircraft Owners & Pilots Assn	$482,695
5 Boeing Co	$385,003
6 American Airlines	$298,469
7 United Airlines	$216,526
8 Northwest Airlines	$185,539
9 Delta Airlines	$151,970
10 Texas Air	$110,550

* Contributions came from more than one affiliate or subsidiary.

Top Senate Recipients			
1 Wendell H. Ford (D-Ky)	$106,745	Incumb	W
2 John McCain (R-Ariz)	$64,615	Incumb	W
3 Bob Kasten (R-Wis)	$61,880	Incumb	L
4 Bob Packwood (R-Ore)	$61,437	Incumb	W
5 Bob Dole (R-Kan)	$59,775	Incumb	W

Top House Recipients			
1 Bob Carr (D-Mich)	$72,940	Incumb	W
2 Pete Geren (D-Texas)	$63,800	Incumb	W
3 Norman Y. Mineta (D-Calif)	$59,944	Incumb	W
4 James M. Inhofe (R-Okla)	$46,725	Incumb	W
5 Newt Gingrich (R-Ga)	$46,615	Incumb	W

Automotive ....$6.5 million

The Big Three automakers took a backseat to auto dealers when it came to handing out federal campaign contributions in the '92 elections. The National Auto Dealers Association more than doubled the dollars of General Motors, giving nearly $1.8 million. Meanwhile, two PACs representing dealers of Japanese imports — Auto Dealers & Drivers for Free Trade, and Americans for Free International Trade — combined for another million dollars in contributions. Though the PACs represent U.S. dealers, they lobby in favor of generous import quotas for Japanese automakers.

In recent years the increasing incursion of Japanese autos on American highways have made bilateral trade issues paramount in the minds of GM, Ford, Chrysler and their numerous suppliers and support industries. Emission controls, safety standards and requirements for fuel economy are other perennial issues that keep the path well-worn between Detroit and Washington.

Top Contributors	
1 National Auto Dealers Assn	$1,784,375
2 General Motors*	$771,474
3 Auto Dealers & Drivers for Free Trade	$538,550
4 Americans for Free International Trade	$475,150
5 Ford Motor Co	$344,904
6 Eaton Corp	$223,850
7 Prince Corp	$58,000
8 Enterprise Rent-a-Car	$55,000
9 Ryder System Inc	$51,961
10 Paccar Inc	$48,450

* Contributions came from more than one affiliate or subsidiary.

Top Senate Recipients			
1 John F. Seymour (R-Calif)	$104,500	Incumb	L
2 Bob Kasten (R-Wis)	$86,679	Incumb	L
3 Daniel R. Coats (R-Ind)	$72,433	Incumb	W
4 Bob Packwood (R-Ore)	$64,400	Incumb	W
5 Lauch Faircloth (R-NC)	$53,600	Chall	W

Top House Recipients			
1 John D. Dingell (D-Mich)	$75,150	Incumb	W
2 Richard A. Gephardt (D-Mo)	$50,500	Incumb	W
3 Don Sundquist (R-Tenn)	$33,400	Incumb	W
4 E. Clay Shaw Jr. (R-Fla)	$29,650	Incumb	W
5 Newt Gingrich (R-Ga)	$29,200	Incumb	W

Trucking ....$1.8 million

Top Contributors

1	American Trucking Assns	$359,019
2	Yellow Freight System	$172,409
3	Roadway Services Inc*	$100,425
4	Consolidated Freightways	$93,400
5	National Assn of Truck Stop Operators	$57,903

* Contributions came from more than one affiliate or subsidiary.

Top Senate Recipients

1	Ernest F. Hollings (D-SC)	$43,629	Incumb	W
2	Bob Kasten (R-Wis)	$30,666	Incumb	L
3	Bob Packwood (R-Ore)	$29,800	Incumb	W
4	Rod Chandler (R-Wash)	$29,150	Open	L
5	Christopher S. Bond (R-Mo)	$26,934	Incumb	W

Top House Recipients

1	Norman Y. Mineta (D-Calif)	$45,665	Incumb	W
2	Richard A. Gephardt (D-Mo)	$26,246	Incumb	W
3	Nick J. Rahall II (D-WVa)	$24,300	Incumb	W
4	Robert A. Roe (D-NJ)	$21,350	Incumb	†
5	Bud Shuster (R-Pa)	$18,750	Incumb	W

† Did not seek reelection in 1992

Trucking companies have an abiding interest in a variety of federal issues, particularly related to the interstate highway system. When the truckers lobbied Congress in 1991 to allow giant triple-trailer rigs on the nation's interstates, they ran into an onslaught of negative publicity from their rivals in the railroad industry. It was an example of the inter-industry competition that is often played out in the halls of Congress. Both sides lobbied heavily, but in the end the truckers' proposal was derailed.

Railroads ....$2.2 million

Top Contributors

1	Union Pacific Corp*	$713,390
2	Burlington Northern*	$316,481
3	Norfolk Southern Corp*	$239,697
4	CSX Corp†	$195,275
5	Southern Pacific Transportation Co	$119,700

* Contributions came from more than one affiliate or subsidiary.
† Does not include CSX's non-railroad subsidiaries.

Top Senate Recipients

1	Bob Packwood (R-Ore)	$43,850	Incumb	W
2	Christopher S. Bond (R-Mo)	$31,250	Incumb	W
3	Ernest F. Hollings (D-SC)	$31,051	Incumb	W
4	Arlen Specter (R-Pa)	$28,677	Incumb	W
5	Charles E. Grassley (R-Iowa)	$28,250	Incumb	W

Top House Recipients

1	Al Swift (D-Wash)	$41,250	Incumb	W
2	Don Ritter (R-Pa)	$32,375	Incumb	L
3	Norman Y. Mineta (D-Calif)	$29,000	Incumb	W
4	Bud Shuster (R-Pa)	$25,954	Incumb	W
5	Dan Rostenkowski (D-Ill)	$25,750	Incumb	W

Sea Transport ....$2.1 million

The American Merchant Marine fleet has seen more prosperous days, but shipping companies still managed to give $2.1 million to federal candidates in the 1992 elections. Sea transport unions gave an additional $3.1 million, often to the same members of Congress. Both labor and management are struggling to keep the merchant marine afloat in the face of fierce foreign competition.

Top Contributors

1	Sea-Land Corp	$175,375
2	American President Lines	$120,282
3	National Marine Manufacturers Assn	$73,000
4	Cruise PAC	$66,500
5	American Waterways Operators	$66,294

Top Senate Recipients

1	John B. Breaux (D-La)	$90,868	Incumb	W
2	Daniel K. Inouye (D-Hawaii)	$51,250	Incumb	W
3	John F. Seymour (R-Calif)	$41,016	Incumb	L
4	Dianne Feinstein (D-Calif)	$39,600	Chall	W
5	Bob Packwood (R-Ore)	$38,200	Incumb	W

Top House Recipients

1	Helen Delich Bentley (R-Md)	$53,230	Incumb	W
2	Gerry E. Studds (D-Mass)	$50,900	Incumb	W
3	W.J. "Billy" Tauzin (D-La)	$34,700	Incumb	W
4	Don Young (R-Alaska)	$33,750	Incumb	W
5	Jack Fields (R-Texas)	$33,000	Incumb	W

Labor

Where the money came from . . .

The 17 million Americans who are members of organized labor unions represent a cross-section of the workforce that is as diverse as one can imagine. Union members drive trucks, deliver mail, build skyscrapers, teach children, print newspapers, and manufacture everything from bombers to safety pins. Even individual unions can be amazingly diverse. Teamsters, for example, can be found not only behind the wheels of tractor-trailers, but in canneries, dairies, building sites and even in police departments.

Despite their diversity, however, the political action committees operated by labor unions have always been rock-solid supporters of the Democratic party. Of the $43.3 million they pumped

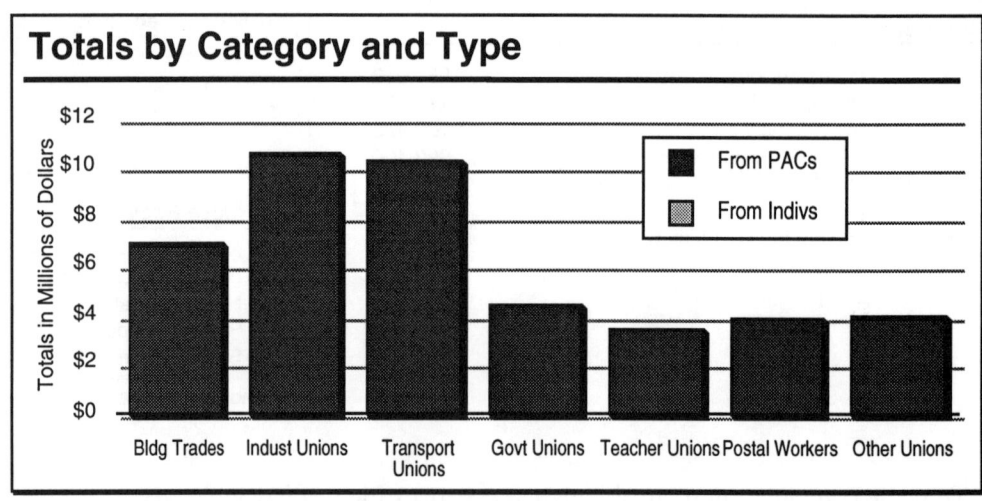

Category	Total	From PACs	PAC Pct	From Indivs	Indiv Pct
Building Trade Unions	$6,904,679	$6,828,879	99%	$75,800	1%
Industrial Unions	$10,505,946	$10,460,319	100%	$45,627	0%
Transportation Unions	$10,220,734	$10,195,513	100%	$25,221	0%
Government Worker Unions	$4,449,066	$4,440,668	100%	$8,398	0%
Teacher Unions	$3,477,117	$3,461,747	100%	$15,370	0%
Postal Service Unions	$3,822,198	$3,815,298	100%	$6,900	0%
Other Unions	$3,919,857	$3,867,229	99%	$52,628	1%
TOTAL	**$43,299,597**	**$43,069,653**	**99%**	**$229,944**	**1%**

into federal campaigns in the 1992 elections, 94 percent went to Democrats. No other sector of the PAC community is as partisan in its distribution of funds. Nor does any sector give as heavily through PACs.

As the 1994 elections approach, however, the unions may be rethinking their strategies. Deeply stung by their defeat in the passage of the North American Free Trade Agreement in 1993, many labor leaders vowed to withhold their traditional support of Democrats who voted for NAFTA. They may also be stung by changes in the campaign finance laws that reduce

Top 20 Labor Contributors

Rank	Total	Contributor	Category	PAC Pct	Dem Pct	Repub Pct
1	$2,532,956	Teamsters Union*	Transpt Unions	100%	94%	5%
2	$2,360,017	National Education Assn*	Teachers	100%	95%	3%
3	$2,251,489	United Auto Workers*	Manuf Unions	100%	98%	1%
4	$1,954,063	American Fedn of St/Cnty/Munic Emps*	Govt Unions	100%	97%	2%
5	$1,661,880	National Assn of Letter Carriers*	Postal Workers	100%	90%	10%
6	$1,641,746	Machinists/Aerospace Workers Union*	Indust Unions	100%	97%	1%
7	$1,605,574	Marine Engineers Union*	Transpt Unions	100%	73%	27%
8	$1,575,999	Intl Brotherhood of Electrical Workers*	Electrical Wrkrs	99%	96%	3%
9	$1,493,572	Carpenters & Joiners Union*	Bldg Trades	98%	94%	5%
10	$1,488,961	Food & Commercial Workers Union	Misc Unions	100%	97%	2%
11	$1,472,681	Laborers Union*	Bldg Trades	100%	94%	5%
12	$1,437,250	National Assn Retired Federal Employees	Govt Unions	100%	80%	19%
13	$1,279,093	Air Line Pilots Assn	Transpt Unions	100%	87%	13%
14	$1,267,774	United Steelworkers	Indust Unions	99%	99%	1%
15	$1,118,214	AFL-CIO*	Misc Unions	99%	97%	2%
16	$1,112,350	American Federation of Teachers	Teachers	100%	99%	2%
17	$1,100,050	United Transportation Union	Transpt Unions	100%	97%	3%
18	$1,012,468	Communications Workers of America*	Indust Unions	100%	98%	1%
19	$992,638	Plumbers/Pipefitters Union*	Bldg Trades	100%	95%	4%
20	$970,476	Seafarers International Union*	Transpt Unions	100%	92%	8%

* Contributions came from more than one affiliate or subsidiary.

Where the money went . . .

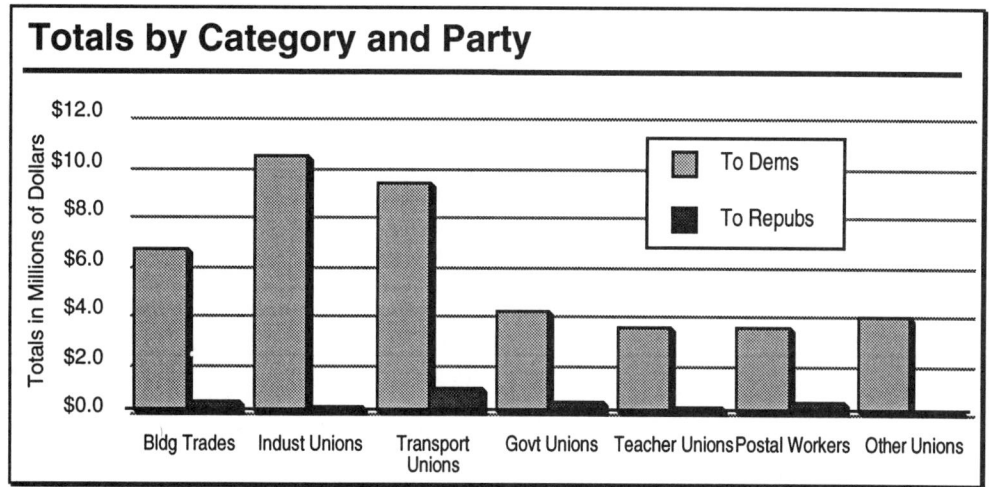

Totals by Category and Party

Category	Total	To Dems	Dem Pct	To Repubs	Repub Pct
Building Trade Unions	$6,904,679	$6,466,973	94%	$385,856	6%
Industrial Unions	$10,505,946	$10,262,774	98%	$172,172	2%
Transportation Unions	$10,220,734	$9,253,260	91%	$945,024	9%
Government Worker Unions	$4,449,066	$4,048,998	91%	$391,568	9%
Teacher Unions	$3,477,117	$3,340,592	96%	$107,325	3%
Postal Service Unions	$3,822,198	$3,419,083	89%	$394,115	10%
Other Unions	$3,919,857	$3,818,433	97%	$75,042	2%
TOTAL	**$43,299,597**	**$40,610,113**	**94%**	**$2,471,102**	**6%**

Within the labor community there was a general consistency in spending patterns, though transport unions were the most likely to cross the aisle and give to Republicans. This was particularly true of the merchant marine unions.

In picking their candidates, labor PACs tend to concentrate their dollars on races where strong pro-union incumbents are facing a serious challenge. Unions are also far more likely than business PACs to underwrite the efforts of promising challengers. Still, 64 percent of the labor PACs' dollars went to incumbents in 1992. The remainder was split evenly between challengers and candidates in open seat races.

Though they tend to give as a bloc, labor unions can be separated into several distinct classes. Public sector unions — representing local, state and federal government workers, postal employees and teachers — are a growing segment of the labor community. Transportation unions are another major sector. Building trades and manufacturing unions are the mainstream of the popular image of union members, though their numbers are dwindling in the face of growing anti-union sentiment among businesses and (before the '92 elections) 12 successive years of Republican administrations.

the power of PACs — the source of nearly 100 percent of their contributions.

In the study undertaken for this book, only $230,000 was identified as individual contributions by labor union members. Partly this reflects the fact that it is virtually impossible to tell who is or is not a union member by looking at their occupation (unless they work for the union itself). But it is also likely, given the economic makeup of the individuals who do make large contributions, that few union members have the resources or the inclination to write $500 or $1,000 checks to politicians.

Indeed, pooling small individual donations into large contributions from political action committees was an invention of labor unions back in the 1940s. Only later did it catch on in the business world.

Top 10 Senate Recipients

Rank	Name	Amount	Status	W/L
1	Harris Wofford (D-Pa)	$463,979	Incumb	W
2	Wyche Fowler Jr. (D-Ga)	$401,649	Incumb	L
3	John Glenn (D-Ohio)	$368,823	Incumb	W
4	Barbara Boxer (D-Calif)	$326,944	Open	W
5	Les AuCoin (D-Ore)	$309,526	Chall	L
6	Dianne Feinstein (D-Calif)	$298,602	Chall	W
7	Joseph H. Hogsett (D-Ind)	$297,940	Chall	L
8	Christopher J. Dodd (D-Conn)	$296,509	Incumb	W
9	Wayne Owens (D-Utah)	$293,699	Open	L
10	Carol Moseley-Braun (D-Ill)	$282,198	Chall	W

Top 10 House Recipients

Rank	Name	Amount	Status	W/L
1	John W. Olver (D-Mass)	$343,599	Incumb	W
2	David E. Bonior (D-Mich)	$286,688	Incumb	W
3	Pat Williams (D-Mont)	$282,709	Incumb	W
4	William D. Ford (D-Mich)	$282,200	Incumb	W
5	Mary Rose Oakar (D-Ohio)	$255,235	Incumb	L
6	Frank Pallone Jr. (D-NJ)	$255,030	Incumb	W
7	Gerry Sikorski (D-Minn)	$247,800	Incumb	L
8	Dale E. Kildee (D-Mich)	$244,135	Incumb	W
9	Dave Nagle (D-Iowa)	$243,563	Incumb	L
10	Vic Fazio (D-Calif)	$242,326	Incumb	W

Closeup on Labor

Building Trades Unions ....$6.9 million

Carpenters, laborers, plumbers, bricklayers — the union names are like job descriptions of the workforce that built much of the American skyline, and transformed the countryside from meadows and forests to cities and superhighways. Like the construction industry that employs them, their jobs are dependent on a healthy and growing economy. They are also dependent on labor laws that cover issues ranging from worksite safety to union organizing rules. Many of the top recipients of the building trades' PAC money come from the Northeastern and Midwest "rust belt" states where union membership is highest.

Top Contributors

1	Carpenters & Joiners Union*	$1,493,572
2	Laborers Union*	$1,472,681
3	Plumbers/Pipefitters Union*	$992,638
4	Sheet Metal Workers Union*	$745,749
5	Operating Engineers Union*	$723,524
6	Ironworkers Union*	$551,480
7	Boilermakers Union*	$425,054
8	Painters & Allied Trades Union*	$283,252
9	Bricklayers Union	$239,200
10	Heat/Frost/Asbestos Workers Union	$40,800

* Contributions came from more than one affiliate or subsidiary.

Top Senate Recipients

#	Recipient	Amount	Status	Result
1	Harris Wofford (D-Pa)	$86,350	Incumb	W
2	John Glenn (D-Ohio)	$63,625	Incumb	W
3	Joseph H. Hogsett (D-Ind)	$58,250	Chall	L
4	Wayne Owens (D-Utah)	$57,250	Open	L
5	Dianne Feinstein (D-Calif)	$54,502	Chall	W

Top House Recipients

#	Recipient	Amount	Status	Result
1	John W. Olver (D-Mass)	$86,000	Incumb	W
2	Pat Williams (D-Mont)	$60,750	Incumb	W
3	Frank Pallone Jr. (D-NJ)	$58,350	Incumb	W
4	Robert E. Andrews (D-NJ)	$56,123	Incumb	W
5	Dale E. Kildee (D-Mich)	$51,240	Incumb	W

Industrial Unions ....$10.5 million

Of all the sectors within organized labor, none had more at stake in the NAFTA debate than the manufacturing and industrial workers whose jobs may exported to Mexico as their employers try to compete with foreign exports by cutting labor costs. Many jobs in this sector have already headed south — from rustbelt states to the non-union sunbelt, leaving thousands of union workers in states like Michigan and Pennsylvania with little alternative but to pack up and follow along, and take whatever work they can find.

Like all other unions, their contributions have always been heavily Democratic, but the NAFTA loss may prompt a second look at the way they invest their campaign cash in 1994.

Top Contributors

1	United Auto Workers*	$2,251,489
2	Machinists/Aerospace Workers Union*	$1,641,746
3	Intl Brotherhood of Electrical Workers*	$1,575,999
4	United Steelworkers	$1,267,774
5	Communications Workers of America*	$1,012,468
6	Rubber Cork Linoleum & Plastic Workers	$505,730
7	United Mine Workers	$459,600
8	Electronic Machine Furniture Workers	$307,102
9	Amalgamated Clothing & Textile Workers*	$297,242
10	Ladies Garment Workers Union	$296,301

* Contributions came from more than one affiliate or subsidiary.

Top Senate Recipients

#	Recipient	Amount	Status	Result
1	Harris Wofford (D-Pa)	$154,600	Incumb	W
2	Wyche Fowler Jr. (D-Ga)	$102,500	Incumb	L
3	Joseph H. Hogsett (D-Ind)	$100,850	Chall	L
4	Les AuCoin (D-Ore)	$98,500	Chall	L
5	Robert Abrams (D-NY)	$92,342	Chall	L

Top House Recipients

#	Recipient	Amount	Status	Result
1	Gene Green (D-Texas)	$78,000	Open	W
2	John W. Olver (D-Mass)	$74,250	Incumb	W
3	Pat Williams (D-Mont)	$73,190	Incumb	W
4	Mary Rose Oakar (D-Ohio)	$72,700	Incumb	L
5	David E. Bonior (D-Mich)	$67,978	Incumb	W

Transportation Unions ......$10.2 million

The Teamsters is the largest and best known of the transportation unions, but it's got plenty of company from unions that represent longshoremen, transit workers, railroad employees, airline pilots and a host of other transport workers who move people and goods across the nation's land, sea and air lanes. This is the one sector of the labor community most likely to give to Republicans, particularly if they sit on committees important to the transportation industry. That support is relative, however. Even the merchant marine unions, which gave the most to Republicans, still gave 82 percent of their dollars to Democrats.

Top Contributors

1	Teamsters Union*	$2,532,956
2	Marine Engineers Union*	$1,605,574
3	Air Line Pilots Assn	$1,279,093
4	United Transportation Union	$1,100,050
5	Seafarers International Union*	$970,476
6	Amalgamated Transit Union	$428,690
7	Transport Workers Union*	$422,730
8	Trans Comm International Union	$421,230
9	Brotherhood of Locomotive Engineers*	$262,969
10	Assn of Flight Attendants	$221,100

* Contributions came from more than one affiliate or subsidiary.

Top Senate Recipients

1	Barbara Boxer (D-Calif)	$105,250	Open	W
2	Dianne Feinstein (D-Calif)	$103,550	Chall	W
3	Les AuCoin (D-Ore)	$93,901	Chall	L
4	Wyche Fowler Jr. (D-Ga)	$91,300	Incumb	L
5	Patty Murray (D-Wash)	$82,500	Open	W

Top House Recipients

1	Gerry Sikorski (D-Minn)	$75,500	Incumb	L
2	David E. Bonior (D-Mich)	$73,400	Incumb	W
3	Frank Pallone Jr. (D-NJ)	$67,630	Incumb	W
4	Dave Nagle (D-Iowa)	$63,184	Incumb	L
5	Bob Carr (D-Mich)	$60,750	Incumb	W

Public Sector Unions ......$11.7 million

The one segment of the labor community that is actually growing, public sector workers hold down jobs in government offices, classrooms, post offices, fire houses and precinct stations that stretch from coast to coast and extend to all levels of government — state, federal and local. The one thing they have in common is that their paychecks ultimately are paid by taxpayers' money. Postal workers gave the most from within this group in 1991-92, a total of $3.8 million. Not far behind were teachers' unions that gave a combined $3.5 million.

Top Contributors

1	National Education Assn*	$2,360,017
2	American Fedn of St/Cnty/Munic Employ's*	$1,954,063
3	National Assn of Letter Carriers*	$1,661,880
4	National Assn Retired Federal Employees	$1,437,250
5	American Federation of Teachers	$1,092,600
6	American Postal Workers Union*	$900,390
7	International Assn of Firefighters*	$565,353
8	National Rural Letter Carriers Assn	$526,528
9	National Assn of Postmasters	$340,695
10	National League of Postmasters	$216,400

* Contributions came from more than one affiliate or subsidiary.

Top Senate Recipients

1	Wyche Fowler Jr. (D-Ga)	$94,750	Incumb	L
2	Terry Sanford (D-NC)	$74,793	Incumb	L
3	Wayne Owens (D-Utah)	$71,250	Open	L
4	Les AuCoin (D-Ore)	$65,425	Chall	L
5	Robert Abrams (D-NY)	$63,450	Chall	L

Top House Recipients

1	Gerry Sikorski (D-Minn)	$78,900	Incumb	L
2	Mary Rose Oakar (D-Ohio)	$78,850	Incumb	L
3	Dave Nagle (D-Iowa)	$63,780	Incumb	L
4	Peter H. Kostmayer (D-Pa)	$53,277	Incumb	L
5	John W. Olver (D-Mass)	$52,500	Incumb	W

Ideological/Single-Issue

Where the money came from...

A world apart from the pragmatic and largely bipartisan business PACs and the Democratically-aligned labor PACs are the third family of political givers — those organized not around a business or union, but an idea, cause or political party. Ideological and single-issue PACs have become significant players on the political landscape, as the women's rights PACs proved in the last election. In all, ideological PACs and their supporters delivered $29.3 million in the 1992 elections. Within this diverse community are political activists who represent every shade of political viewpoint, and many of them spend much of their money and time working to counteract the efforts of their adversaries. For issues which stir deep divisions among the American public — such as abortion, gun control, or defense spending — PACs have coalesced around both sides.

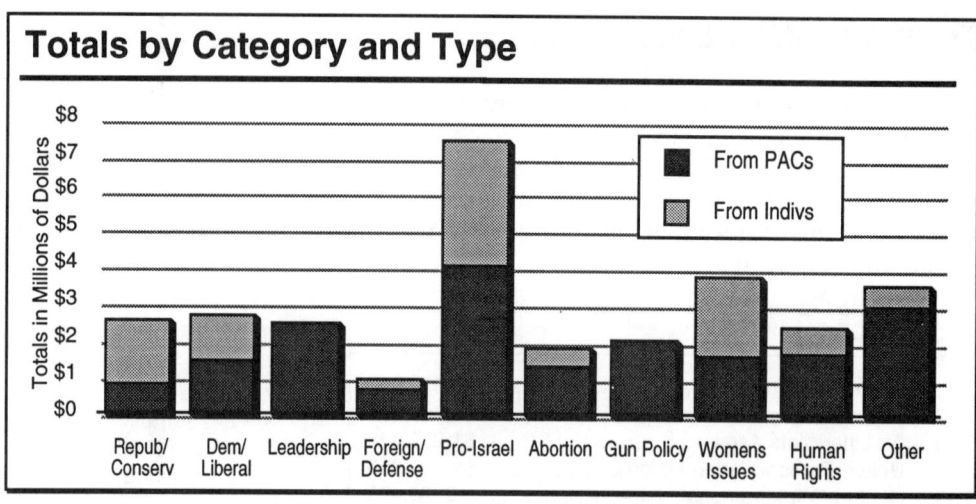

Totals by Category and Type

Category	Total	From PACs	PAC Pct	From Indivs	Indiv Pct
Republican/Conservative	$2,479,934	$794,031	32%	$1,685,903	68%
Democratic/Liberal	$2,658,027	$1,389,680	52%	$1,268,347	48%
Leadership PACs	$2,440,935	$2,428,435	99%	$12,500	1%
Foreign & Defense Policy	$918,162	$611,010	67%	$307,152	33%
Pro-Israel	$7,401,113	$4,022,677	54%	$3,378,436	46%
Abortion Policy	$1,804,175	$1,276,900	71%	$527,275	29%
Gun Policy	$2,024,067	$1,987,192	98%	$36,875	2%
Women's Issues	$3,725,735	$1,566,491	42%	$2,159,244	58%
Human Rights	$2,335,435	$1,623,606	70%	$711,829	30%
Other Issues	$3,544,331	$2,943,340	83%	$600,991	17%
TOTAL	$29,331,914	$18,643,362	64%	$10,688,552	36%

In addition to the PACs, the study that led to this book examined giving by individuals aligned with PACs who made individual contributions of their own directly to candidates. To be classified as an "ideological" giver, a contributor had to

Top 20 Ideological/Single-Issue Contributors

Rank	Total	Contributor	Category	PAC Pct	Dem Pct	Repub Pct
1	$1,736,446	National Rifle Assn	Pro-Guns	100%	36%	63%
2	$999,755	Emily's List	Womens Issues	37%	98%	0%
3	$941,650	Natl Cmte to Preserve Social Security	Sr Citizens	100%	88%	13%
4	$718,590	Human Rights Campaign Fund	Gay/Lesbian	99%	92%	6%
5	$684,000	National PAC	Pro-Israel	100%	65%	35%
6	$651,250	National Cmte for an Effective Congress	Dem/Liberal	100%	100%	0%
7	$612,130	Sierra Club	Environment	99%	96%	3%
8	$517,705	National Abortion Rights Action League*	Pro-Choice	100%	94%	8%
9	$513,067	Women's Campaign Fund	Womens Issues	100%	76%	22%
10	$443,062	League of Conservation Voters*	Environment	97%	93%	7%
11	$440,600	KidsPAC	Child Rights	100%	95%	4%
12	$400,736	Campaign America (Bob Dole)	Repub Leaders	97%	0%	100%
13	$329,451	National Organization for Women	Womens Issues	98%	89%	8%
14	$290,934	Right to Life*	Pro-Life	100%	13%	87%
15	$286,200	Voters for Choice	Pro-Choice	93%	89%	10%
16	$279,750	Hollywood Women's Political Cmte	Dem/Liberal	100%	99%	0%
17	$266,965	Hudson Valley PAC	Pro-Israel	100%	65%	35%
18	$244,056	House Leadership Fund (Tom Foley)	Dem Leaders	100%	100%	0%
19	$230,829	Council for a Livable World	Pro-Peace	56%	99%	0%
20	$221,950	National Council of Senior Citizens	Sr Citizens	100%	100%	0%

* Contributions came from more than one affiliate or subsidiary.

Where the money went . . .

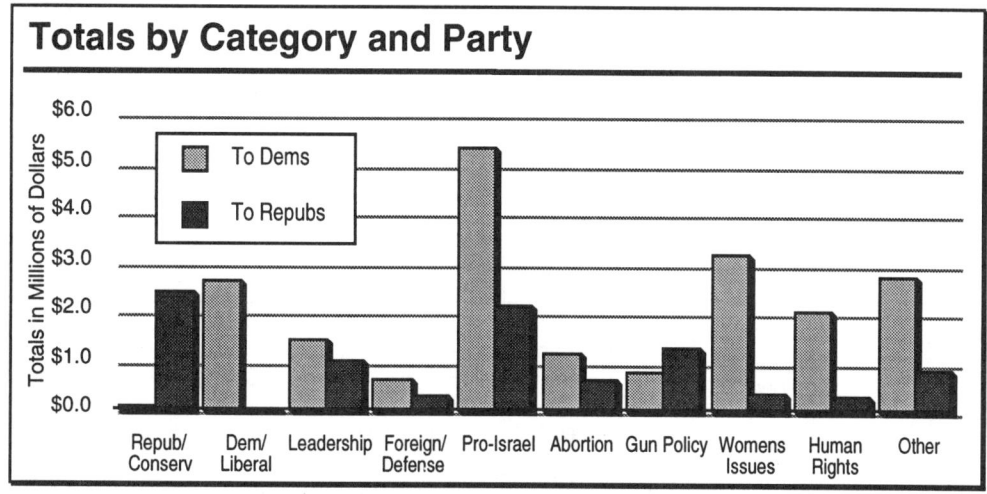

Category	Total	To Dems	Dem Pct	To Repubs	Repub Pct
Republican/Conservative	$2,479,934	$61,683	2%	$2,406,051	97%
Democratic/Liberal	$2,658,027	$2,612,692	98%	$25,700	1%
Leadership PACs	$2,440,935	$1,429,723	59%	$1,010,712	41%
Foreign & Defense Policy	$918,162	$607,997	66%	$279,696	30%
Pro-Israel	$7,401,113	$5,289,881	71%	$2,110,670	29%
Abortion Policy	$1,804,175	$1,162,980	64%	$630,595	35%
Gun Policy	$2,024,067	$786,554	39%	$1,232,563	61%
Women's Issues	$3,725,735	$3,138,406	84%	$339,488	9%
Human Rights	$2,335,435	$2,000,217	86%	$312,818	13%
Other Issues	$3,544,331	$2,700,329	76%	$813,246	23%
TOTAL	$29,331,914	$19,790,462	67%	$9,161,539	31%

give $200 or more both to an ideological or single-issue PAC and to a candidate who received funds from that PAC. Using that conservative criteria, the Center was able to identify another $10.7 million of ideological contributions.

The single biggest interest group within this community — in terms of dollars delivered to candidates — were those interested in strong U.S. ties with Israel. Pro-Israel PACs and individuals gave a combined $7.4 million to federal candidates in the 1992 elections, twice as much as any other ideological group. Women's rights PACs were second, dramatically increasing their giving from 1990 and in the process helping elect four new women to the U.S. Senate.

Other major contribution groups included broad-based conservative and liberal PACs, "leadership PACs" run by members of Congress and other political figures, PACs supporting environmental issues, groups opposing organized labor, defending the rights of gays and lesbians, supporting or attacking the right to legal abortions, and groups involved in every issue from gun control to animal rights. There were also a variety of ethnic and minority PACs whose interests revolve around a specific segment of the American population, as well as the interests of the citizens in their homelands. Hispanic-Americans support no fewer than five individual PACs. Others promote the interests of Armenian-, Albanian-, Greek-, Korean-, Turkish-, Italian- and African-Americans; and there are PACs representing both American Indians and Indo-Americans from India.

Though they may represent every issue under the sun (and a few, like the SpacePAC, *beyond* the sun) one thing most single-issue and ideological PACs do have in common is a tendency to back candidates from one political party or the other. They also have a higher-than-normal tendency to give money to challengers — something the more pragmatic business PACs do only a tiny proportion of the time.

Top 10 Senate Recipients

Rank	Name	Amount	Status	W/L
1	Barbara Boxer (D-Calif)	$843,555	Open	W
2	Dianne Feinstein (D-Calif)	$542,956	Chall	W
3	Carol Moseley-Braun (D-Ill)	$451,135	Chall	W
4	Robert Abrams (D-NY)	$409,964	Chall	L
5	Lynn Yeakel (D-Pa)	$394,285	Chall	L
6	Harris Wofford (D-Pa)	$390,625	Incumb	W
7	Mel Levine (D-Calif)	$358,125	Open	L
8	Arlen Specter (R-Pa)	$337,153	Incumb	W
9	Bob Packwood (R-Ore)	$305,102	Incumb	W
10	Wyche Fowler Jr. (D-Ga)	$295,850	Incumb	L

Top 10 House Recipients

Rank	Name	Amount	Status	W/L
1	Anna G. Eshoo (D-Calif)	$169,441	Open	W
2	Elizabeth Furse (D-Ore)	$150,439	Open	W
3	Rosa DeLauro (D-Conn)	$149,893	Incumb	W
4	John W. Olver (D-Mass)	$136,683	Incumb	W
5	Gerry E. Studds (D-Mass)	$133,918	Incumb	W
6	Joan Kelly Horn (D-Mo)	$131,028	Incumb	L
7	Sam Gejdenson (D-Conn)	$129,360	Incumb	W
8	Peter H. Kostmayer (D-Pa)	$128,947	Incumb	L
9	Vic Fazio (D-Calif)	$128,450	Incumb	W
10	Anita Perez Ferguson (D-Calif)	$123,676	Chall	L

Closeup on Ideology/Single-Issue

Pro-Israel .... $7.4 million

The biggest single source of contributions among ideological groups came from PACs supporting strong U.S. relations with Israel. In all, some 55 pro-Israel PACs contributed to federal campaigns in the 1992 elections, as did many more individuals who gave to the PACs and also gave to favored candidates in tight races. The money went mainly, but not exclusively to Democrats. Indeed, three of the biggest recipients in 1992 — Arlen Specter, Bob Packwood and Bob Kasten — were Republicans. Instead of spreading token payments to dozens of candidates, the pro-Israel groups tend to concentrate their contributions in a handful of key races — generally in the Senate.

Top Contributors

1	National PAC	$684,000
2	Hudson Valley PAC	$266,965
3	Women's Alliance for Israel	$209,000
4	Joint Action Cmte for Political Affairs	$205,000
5	Washington PAC	$202,020
6	Citizens Organized PAC	$192,750
7	Desert Caucus	$178,550
8	Americans for Good Government Inc	$166,750
9	Florida Congressional Committee	$158,250
10	Women's Pro-Israel National PAC	$155,550

Top Senate Recipients

1	Mel Levine (D-Calif)	$285,525	Open	L
2	Arlen Specter (R-Pa)	$249,210	Incumb	W
3	Bob Packwood (R-Ore)	$241,636	Incumb	W
4	Bob Kasten (R-Wis)	$198,599	Incumb	L
5	Daniel K. Inouye (D-Hawaii)	$190,155	Incumb	W

Top House Recipients

1	Sam Gejdenson (D-Conn)	$88,060	Incumb	W
2	Mel Reynolds (D-Ill)	$80,671	Chall	W
3	Les Aspin (D-Wis)	$79,850	Incumb	W
4	Eric D. Fingerhut (D-Ohio)	$72,950	Open	W
5	Dick Swett (D-NH)	$60,157	Incumb	W

Womens Issues .... $3.7 million

The much-trumpeted "Year of the Woman" in 1992 was helped along significantly by a virtual explosion in funds directed to and by women's rights PACs that aimed their considerable financial resources at electing a record new crop of women to the U.S. Congress. Leading the charge, and organizing the most money, was Emily's List, a Washington-based PAC that aims to elect Democratic women not just through direct PAC contributions, but by "bundling" hundreds and even thousands of individual donations from around the country and delivering them to the women with the most likely chances of winning. Though Emily's List claimed to have raised $6 million in contributions, the Center was able to confirm only $1 million in contributions using the conservative criteria outlined on the previous two pages. One reason that so much of the money was "invisible" was likely that most of it came in small contributions. Federal election law requires itemization only of contributions of $200 and above. Candidates receiving gifts below that amount need not identify the source; they only need to give the total.

Whatever their financial impact however, Emily's List and the rest of the women's issue PACs emerged as a major political force in 1992. Their impact is not likely to fade any time soon.

Top Contributors

1	Emily's List	$999,755
2	Women's Campaign Fund	$513,067
3	National Organization for Women	$329,451
4	National Womens Political Caucus	$207,520
5	Wish List	$86,509

Top Senate Recipients

1	Barbara Boxer (D-Calif)	$378,286	Open	W
2	Dianne Feinstein (D-Calif)	$223,878	Chall	W
3	Carol Moseley-Braun (D-Ill)	$185,717	Chall	W
4	Lynn Yeakel (D-Pa)	$142,211	Chall	L
5	Patty Murray (D-Wash)	$100,783	Open	W

Top House Recipients

1	Anna G. Eshoo (D-Calif)	$93,751	Open	W
2	Elizabeth Furse (D-Ore)	$60,305	Open	W
3	Elaine Baxter (D-Iowa)	$53,956	Chall	L
4	Karen Shepherd (D-Utah)	$48,255	Open	W
5	Lynn H. Taborsak (I-Conn)	$45,316	Chall	L

1992 Leadership PAC Roster

Since members of Congress often raise funds for their Leadership PACs at the same time they're collecting money for their reelection campaigns, it may be instructive to know which members have PACs and how much they give out. The list below shows all leadership PACs operated by members of Congress and other prominent party officials that made contributions to candidates in the 1992 elections.

Members of Congress

PAC Name	Sponsor	1992 Contributions
15th District Committee	Rep Edward Madigan (R-Ill)	$225
24th Congressional District of California PAC	Rep Henry Waxman (D-Calif)	$79,000
America's Leaders' Fund	Rep Dan Rostenkowski (D-Ill)	$120,703
AmeriPAC: The Fund for a Greater America	Rep Steny Hoyer (D-Md)	$31,500
Arizona Leadership for America	Sen Dennis DeConcini (D-Ariz)	$5,523
Bluegrass Committee	Sen Mitch McConnell (R-Ky)	$5,750
Campaign America	Sen Bob Dole (R-Kans)	$400,736
Campaign for America	Sen Frank Lautenberg (D-NJ)	$26,000
Catch the Spirit PAC	Sen Bob Kasten (R-Wisc)	$10,000
Citizens for Competitive America	Sen Ernest Hollings (D-SC)	$6,000
Committee for a Demoratic Consensus	Sen Alan Cranston (D-Calif)	$89,446
Committee for a Progressive Congress	Rep David Obey (D-Wis)	$500
Committee for America's Future	Sen Robert Byrd (D-WVa)	$47,000
Committee for Democratic Action	Sen Howard Metzenbaum (D-Ohio)	$17,250
Committee for Democratic Opportunity	Rep William Gray III (D-Pa)	$3,500
Congressional Black Caucus	Rep William Clay (D-Mo)	$6,500
Conservative Democratic PAC	Rep Charles Stenholm (D-Tex)	$16,250
Conservative Opportunities Society	Rep Newt Gingrich (R-Ga)	$1,000
Conservative Victory Fund	Sen Steve Symms (R-Idaho)	$19,298
Democratic Congressional Fund	Rep Joe Moakley (D-Mass)	$870
Democrats for the Future	Rep Beryl Anthony (D-Ark)	$11,000
Effective Government Committee	Rep Richard Gephardt (D-Mo)	$204,425
Fund for a Democratic Majority	Sen Edward Kennedy (D-Mass)	$185,530
Fund for a Republican Majority	Sen Ted Stevens (R-Alaska)	$3,000
Fund for Effective Leadership	Rep Neal Smith (D-Iowa)	$3,000
Fund for the Future Committee	Sen John Danforth (R-Mo)	$6,999
Future Leaders PAC	Rep Jerry Lewis (R-Calif)	$22,205
GOPAC	Rep Newt Gingrich (R-Ga)	$10,614
House Leadership Fund	Rep Thomas Foley (D-Wash)	$244,056
Lone Star Fund	Rep Martin Frost (D-Texas)	$38,500
Modern PAC	Rep Bill Green (R-NY)	$7,100
National Congressional Club	Sen Jesse Helms (R-NC)	$34,476
New Frontier Leadership PAC	Rep Norman Lent (R-NY)	$21,550
New Majority Leadership PAC	Rep Vin Weber (R-Minn)	$38,054
New Republican Majority Fund	Sen Trent Lott (R-Miss)	$4,500
Pelican PAC	Sen Bennett Johnston (D-La)	$93,284
People Helping People	Rep Maxine Waters (D-Calif)	$13,000
Policy Innovation PAC	Rep Dick Armey (R-Texas)	$1,000
Republican Leader's Fund	Rep Bob Michel (R-Ill)	$169,000
Senate Majority Fund	Sen Daniel Inouye (D-Hawaii)	$8,000
Senate Victory Fund	Sen Thad Cochran (R-Miss)	$107,000
Victory USA	Rep Vic Fazio (D-Calif)	$91,100

Other Notable Officials

PAC Name	Sponsor	1992 Contributions
America 2000 Fund	Former Gov Jim Thompson (R-Ill)	$19,950
America First PAC	Pat Buchanan	$2,750
Americans Concerned for Tomorrow	Geraldine Ferraro	$1,510
Americans for the Republic	Pat Robertson	$1,000
Citizens for the Republic	Ronald Reagan	$6,000
Committee for an Affordable New Jersey	Gov Christine Todd Whitman (R-NJ)	$61,500
DC Montana Committee	Former Sen Lee Metcalf (D-Mont)	$1,000
Democratic Candidate Fund	Former Rep Tip O'Neill (D-Mass)	$14,950
Fund for Southern Progress	Gov Carroll Campbell (R-SC)	$42,500
Majority Congress Committee	Former Rep Jim Wright (D-Texas)	$100
Participation 2000	Gov Richard Celeste (D-Ohio)	$8,824
San Franciscans Getting Things Done	Art Agnos (former SF Mayor)	$2,500

A Potpourri of Issue PACs

Like metal filings drawn to a magnet, political action committees have coalesced around virtually every issue of interest — or dispute — among Americans. The amounts spent by one group versus another, and the proportions within each camp that go to Democrats versus Republicans, offer a fascinating glimpse at the political strategies of these specialized interest groups. The following mini-profiles present the highlights, combining dollars that came both from PACs and from individuals supporting the PACs' policies through direct contributions to candidates.

Abortion

A total of 27 Pro-Life PACs and 13 Pro-Choice PACs contributed to federal candidates in the 1992 elections. Most of the Pro-Life PACs were organized under the national Right to Life organization, and that group's national PAC gave the biggest share of the group's money.

As can be seen from the chart at right, the Pro-Choice forces were decidedly Democratic in their contributions. Pro-Life groups mainly supported Republicans.

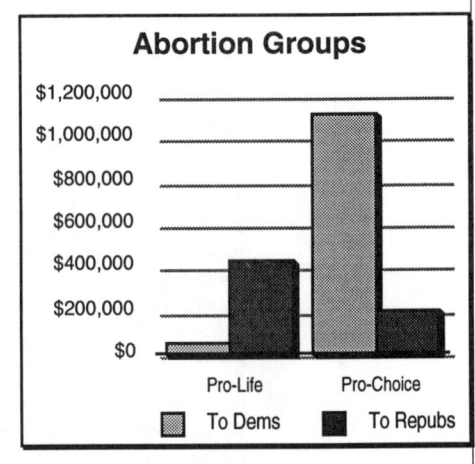

Pro-Life	
Right to Life*	$290,934
Pro-Choice	
National Abortion Rights Action League*	$517,705
Voters for Choice	$286,200

* Contributions came from more than one affiliate or subsidiary.

Gun Control vs. Gun Ownership

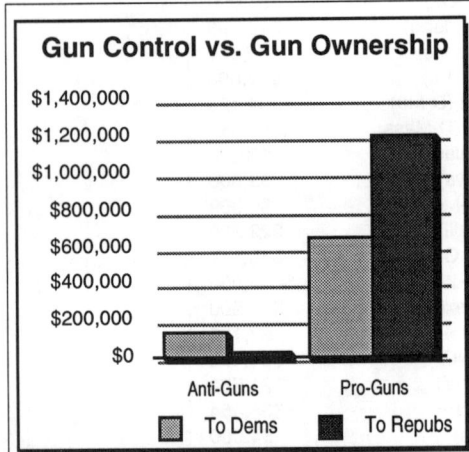

The National Rifle Association had the strongest presence by far among PACs dealing with the issue of gun control vs. gun owners' rights. Long an influential lobby on Capitol Hill, the NRA Political Victory Fund was the biggest ideological PAC in the nation in 1992, delivering over $1.7 million to 346 candidates — more than double what they gave two years earlier. Playing David to the NRA's Goliath was Handgun Control Inc., the anti-gun PAC organized by Sarah and Jim Brady. Despite the huge NRA financial advantage, the Brady Bill finally became law in 1993, requiring a seven-day waiting period for purchasers of firearms.

Pro-Guns	
National Rifle Assn	$1,736,446
Anti-Guns	
Handgun Control Inc	$156,112

The Left and the Right

A total of 101 ideological PACs on both the left and right of the political spectrum contributed to federal candidates in the 1992 election. Along with Leadership PACs operated by members of Congress, these tend to be the most partisan of all PACs, giving virtually all their funds to candidates of one party or the other.

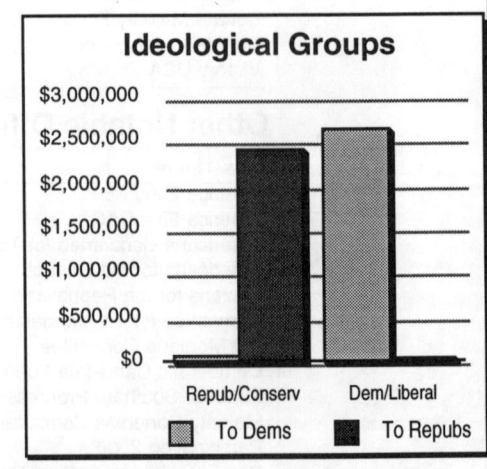

Republican/Conservative PACs	
Eagle Forum	$148,361
Conservative Victory Committee	$96,022
Democratic/Liberal PACs	
National Cmte for an Effective Congress	$650,750
Hollywood Women's Political Cmte	$278,500
Independent Action	$116,318
Fifth Horseman PAC	$109,000

Human Rights

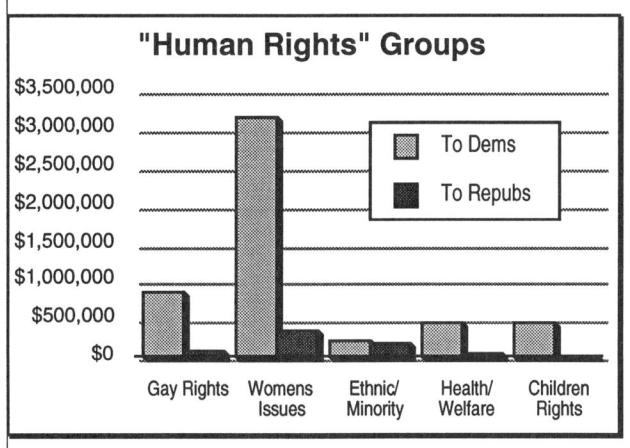

Groups seeking to improve the lot of the women, children, gays and ethnic minorities were all active with political contributions in the 1992 elections — none more so than the women's groups whose spending helped elect a record crop of women to Congress. Democrats were by far the biggest beneficiaries of the human rights groups' spending.

Gay/Lesbian Rights
  Human Rights Campaign Fund $713,040
Womens Issues (see list on page 90) $3,725,735
Ethnic/Minority $365,619
Children's Rights
  KidsPAC $440,600
Health/Welfare
  National Community Action Foundation $120,350

War and Peace

The end of the Cold War and the dissolution of the Soviet Union greatly diminished the threat of global nuclear war, shifting the focus of debate between the pro-military and pro-peace PACs. The level of defense spending in the post Cold War era remains a concern of both groups, though their perspectives — and the distribution of their dollars — are at opposite poles.

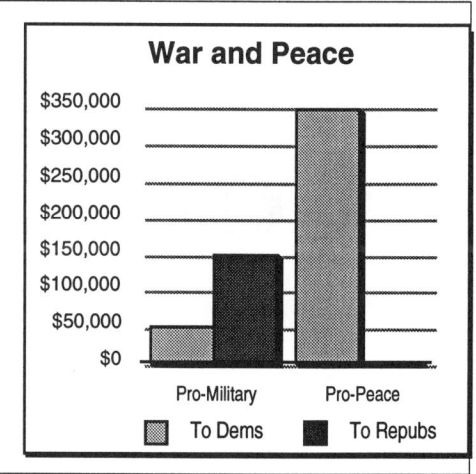

Pro-Military
  Veterans of Foreign Wars $102,675
  Council for National Defense $55,995
Pro-Peace
  Council for a Livable World* $230,829

* Contributions came from more than one affiliate or subsidiary.

Other Single-Issue Groups

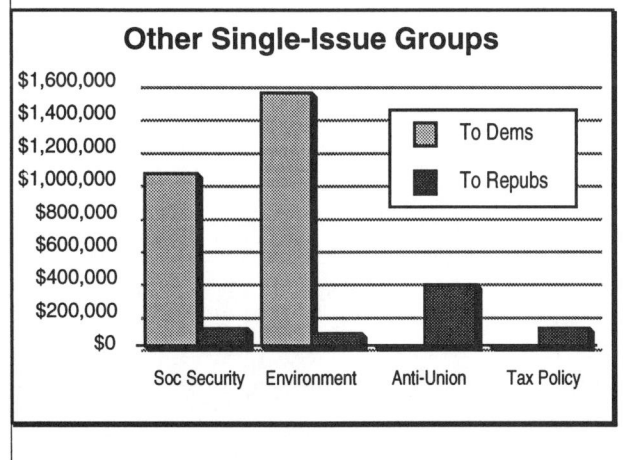

Of the remaining single-issue groups the largest are those advocating protection of the social security and medicare programs for senior citizens, along with environmental PACs and organizations seeking to reduce the influence of labor unions in the American workplace. Among the anti-union PACs, the Public Service Research Council specifically opposes unionism among public employees.

Elderly/Social Security
  National Cmte to Preserve Social Security $941,650
  National Council of Senior Citizens $221,750
Environmental Issues
  Sierra Club $608,680
  League of Conservation Voters $413,139
Anti-Union
  Right to Work PAC $205,151
  Public Service Research Council $140,553
Tax Policy $111,404

3. Committee Profiles

Cash Constituents of Congress

Introduction to the Committee Profiles

Most of the work that Congress does in shaping legislation takes place not on the floor of the House and Senate, but in meetings of committees and subcommittees. It is at this level that the language of bills is crafted, revised and debated, that congressional hearings are held and investigations directed. For all these reasons, much of the attention of industry and interest group lobbyists — and contributors — is focused on deliberations within the specific committees that oversee their particular industry or interest. The section which follows examines the patterns in political contributions made in 1991-92 to members of each of the 37 standing committees of the House and Senate.

What the profiles contain

• Names of the chairman and ranking minority member of each committee and the ratio of seats between Democrats and Republicans.

• A full description of the committee's jurisdiction.

• A listing of each subcommittee, with its chairman and ranking minority member.

• A roster listing each committee member, and showing the totals they received in 1991-92 from PACs and from individual contributors giving $200 or more. The members are arranged in descending order of the amount they received. The rosters include all members who served on the committee during the 102nd Congress — whether or not they ran for reelection in 1992.

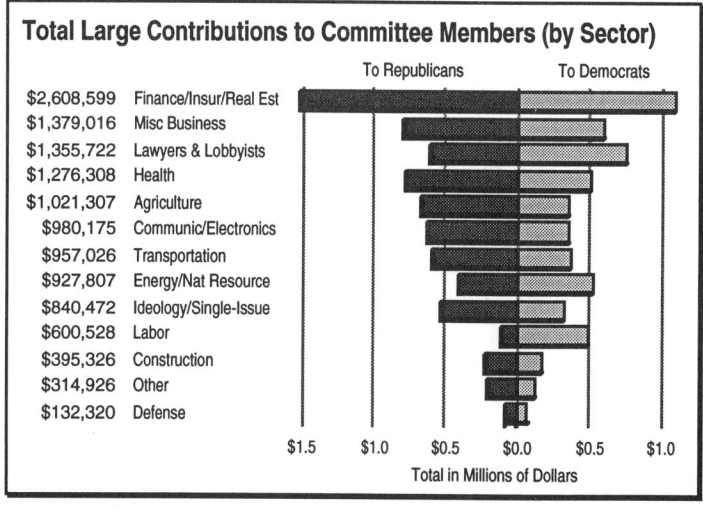

• Top 20 contributors to members of that committee, including both PACs and individual contributors of $200 and more.

• Total contributions to all members of that committee from 13 broad categories of industries and interests.

• A spotlight on the 15 largest industry and interest group sectors that contributed to committee members during 1991-92. This is a more detailed breakdown of the general categories. For example, the general chart groups all finance, insurance and real estate contributors into one broad category. The spotlight chart breaks them down further, into commercial banks, insurance companies, real estate, etc.

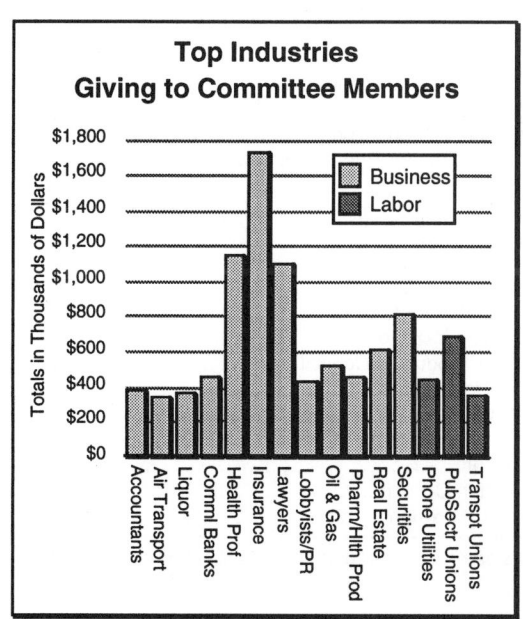

"Generic" Committees and "Specific" Committees

The format and information shown on the committee pages varies with the jurisdictional scope of the committee. Some "generic" committees (for example, the tax-writing committees or those dealing with foreign relations, veterans' affairs, or government operations) affect a broad range of industries and interest groups more or less equally. Other committees — such as Agriculture, Armed Services, or Banking — have jurisdictions which focus on specific industries.

In generic committees, the contribution totals shown for committee members refer to the total dollars received by that member from *all* PACs and *all* individual contributors giving $200 or more. In the specific committees, the figure refers to the total received *only from those contributors whose interests coincide with the committee's jurisdiction.*

"Specific" committees also include one additional chart, highlighting those interests most directly affected by the committee's actions.

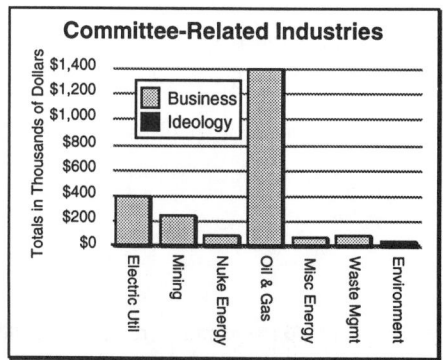

Senate Agriculture, Nutrition and Forestry Committee

Patrick J. Leahy (D-Vt), Chairman
Richard G. Lugar (R-Ind), Ranking Republican

Party Ratio: 10 Democrats
8 Republicans

Jurisdiction: (1) Agricultural economics and research; (2) Agricultural extension services and experiment stations; (3) Agricultural production, marketing and stabilization of prices; (4) Agriculture and agricultural commodities; (5) Animal industry and diseases; (6) Crop insurance and soil conservation; (7) Farm credit and farm security; (8) Food from fresh waters; (9) Food stamp programs; (10) Forestry and forest reserves and wilderness areas other than those created from the public domain; (11) Home economics; (12) Home nutrition; (13) Inspection of livestock, meat and agricultural products; (14) Pests and pesticides; (15) Plant industry, soils and agricultural engineering; (16) Rural development, rural electrification and watershed; (17) School nutrition programs. In addition, the committee is mandated to study and review matters relating to food, nutrition and hunger — both in the U.S. and in foreign countries — and rural areas, and to report on these matters periodically.

Subcommittees

Agricultural Credit
Kent Conrad (D-ND), Chairman
Charles E. Grassley (R-Iowa), Ranking Republican

Agricultural Production and Stabilization of Prices
David Pryor (D-Ark), Chairman
Jesse Helms (R-NC), Ranking Republican

Agricultural Research and General Legislation
Tom Daschle (D-SD), Chairman
John Seymour (R-Calif), Ranking Republican

Conservation and Forestry
Wyche Fowler Jr. (D-Ga), Chairman
Larry E. Craig (R-Idaho), Ranking Republican

Domestic and Foreign Marketing and Product Promotion
David L. Boren (D-Okla), Chairman
Thad Cochran (R-Miss), Ranking Republican

Nutrition and Investigations
Tom Harkin (D-Iowa), Chairman
Mitch McConnell (R-Ky), Ranking Republican

Rural Development and Rural Electrification
Howell Heflin (D-Ala), Chairman
Thad Cochran (R-Miss), Ranking Republican

Total Agriculture-Related Contributions to Committee Members

	Total from Cmte-Related Contribs	Pct of Member's Lg Contribs
John F. Seymour (R-Calif)	$567,003	11%
Wyche Fowler Jr. (D-Ga)	$432,449	12%
Bob Dole (R-Kan)	$262,381	13%
Charles E. Grassley (R-Iowa)	$221,752	14%
Tom Daschle (D-SD)	$204,694	9%
Kent Conrad (D-ND)	$183,780	15%
Bob Kerrey (D-Neb)†	$139,379	4%
Tom Harkin (D-Iowa)†	$87,099	4%
Richard G. Lugar (R-Ind)	$78,750	13%
Patrick J. Leahy (D-Vt)	$74,160	11%
Thad Cochran (R-Miss)	$30,750	58%
Jesse Helms (R-NC)	$29,088	13%
Larry E. Craig (R-Idaho)	$13,750	53%
David L. Boren (D-Okla)	$5,500	16%
Howell Heflin (D-Ala)	$3,250	18%
Mitch McConnell (R-Ky)	$3,125	4%
Max Baucus (D-Mont)	$1,000	14%

† Includes contributions to his 1992 presidential campaign

Top 20 Agriculture-Related Contributors to Committee Members in 1991-92

1	Archer-Daniels-Midland Corp	$55,000
2	Chicago Board of Trade	$54,500
3	Chicago Mercantile Exchange	$53,750
4	Philip Morris*	$53,000
5	American Assn of Crop Insurers	$51,976
6	ACRE (Action Cmte for Rural Electrification)*	$48,000
7	ConAgra Inc	$43,500
8	Associated Milk Producers	$37,000
9	US Tobacco Co	$36,500
10	Sun-Diamond Growers*	$34,000
11	Tyson Foods	$32,500
12	American Crystal Sugar Corp	$32,000
13	Food Marketing Institute	$29,500
14	National Pork Producers Council	$27,603
15	National Cattlemen's Assn*	$26,500
16	RJR Nabisco	$24,000
17	American Sugarbeet Growers Assn	$23,766
18	Okeelanta Corp	$23,500
19	National Cotton Council	$23,451
20	Mid-America Dairymen	$23,000

* Contributions came from more than one affiliate or subsidiary.

Members in **bold italics** ran for reelection in 1992

Summary

Dairy, sugar, tobacco and a variety of other agricultural subsidies and programs come under the jurisdiction of the Senate Agriculture Committee, making this panel crucially important to the nation's agriculture and food processing industries.

Like other Senate committees, however, the contribution patterns to committee members do not always draw a direct line between the industries and committee members. Since most Senators have four committee assignments, no one committee tends to dominate their contribution profiles. Likewise, the amount of money going to committee members varies greatly from year to year, depending on how many members are up for reelection and whether they come from big (high-budget) states, or small ones. Nevertheless, as seen in the chart at right, the agriculture industry was one of the leading sources of funds for committee members in 1991-92.

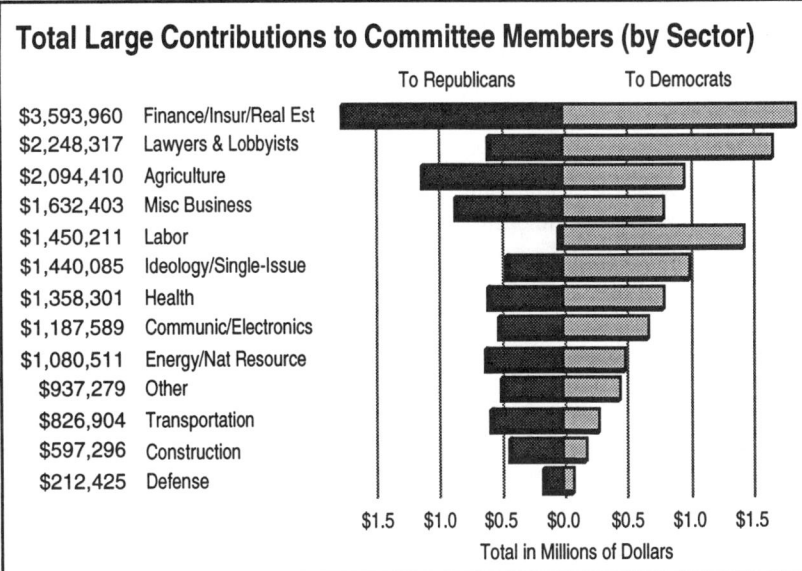

Total Large Contributions to Committee Members (by Sector)

Amount	Sector
$3,593,960	Finance/Insur/Real Est
$2,248,317	Lawyers & Lobbyists
$2,094,410	Agriculture
$1,632,403	Misc Business
$1,450,211	Labor
$1,440,085	Ideology/Single-Issue
$1,358,301	Health
$1,187,589	Communic/Electronics
$1,080,511	Energy/Nat Resource
$937,279	Other
$826,904	Transportation
$597,296	Construction
$212,425	Defense

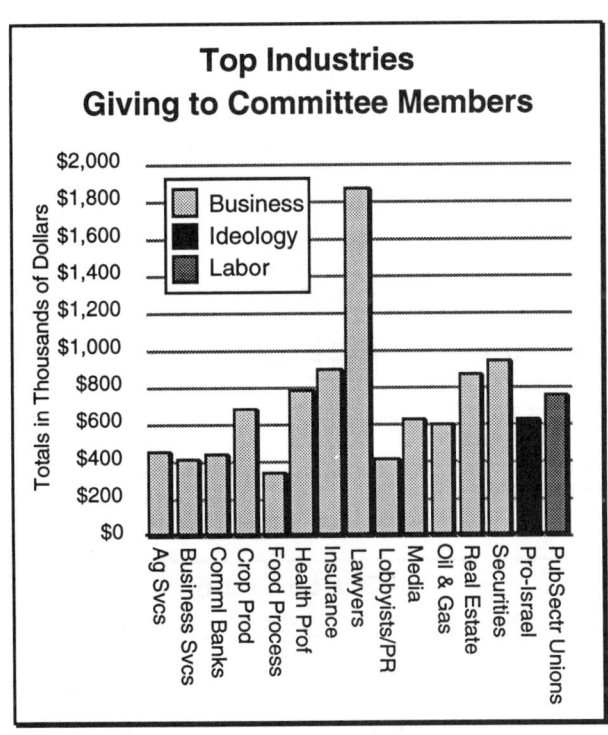

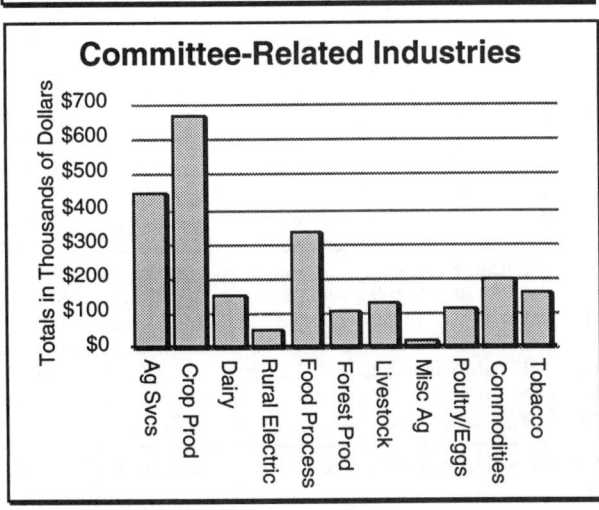

Leading Industries Giving to Committee Members

Business
- Agricultural Services/Products $444,213
- Business Services $393,448
- Commercial Banks $428,138
- Crop Production & Basic Processing $661,671
- Food Processing & Sales $330,141
- Health Professionals $767,074
- Insurance $881,578
- Lawyers/Law Firms $1,848,698
- Lobbyists/PR $399,619
- Media/Entertainment $612,899
- Oil & Gas $578,346
- Real Estate $856,523
- Securities & Investment $928,370

Ideological/Single-Issue
- Pro-Israel $609,358

Labor
- Public Sector Unions $731,053

Leading Committee-Related Industries Giving to Committee Members

Business
- Agricultural Services/Products $444,213
- Crop Production & Basic Processing $661,671
- Dairy $145,290
- Rural Electric Utilities $50,000
- Food Processing & Sales $330,141
- Forestry & Forest Products $103,675
- Livestock $125,780
- Poultry & Eggs $112,400
- Commodity Trading $193,000
- Tobacco $151,500
- Misc Agriculture $19,740

Senate Appropriations Committee

Robert C. Byrd (D-WVa), Chairman
Mark O. Hatfield (R-Ore), Ranking Republican

Party Ratio: 16 Democrats
13 Republicans

Jurisdiction: (1) Appropriation of the revenue for the support of the Government; (2) Rescission of appropriations contained in appropriation acts; (3) The amount of new spending authority . . . which is to be effective for a fiscal year. Other committees of Congress may *authorize* the government to spend money on various projects and programs, but only the Appropriations committees of the House and Senate *appropriate* the funds.

Subcommittees

Agriculture, Rural Development and Related Agencies
Dale Bumpers (D-Ark), Chairman
Thad Cochran (R-Miss), Ranking Republican

Commerce, Justice and State, the Judiciary and Related Agencies
Ernest F. Hollings (D-SC), Chairman
Warren B. Rudman (R-NH), Ranking Republican

Defense
Daniel K. Inouye (D-Hawaii), Chairman
Ted Stevens (R-Alaska), Ranking Republican

District of Columbia
Brock Adams (D-Wash), Chairman
Christopher S. Bond (R-Mo), Ranking Republican

Energy and Water Development
J. Bennett Johnston (D-La), Chairman
Mark O. Hatfield (R-Ore), Ranking Republican

Foreign Operations
Patrick J. Leahy (D-Vt), Chairman
Bob Kasten (R-Wis), Ranking Republican

Interior and Related Agencies
Robert C. Byrd (D-WVa), Chairman
Don Nickles (R-Okla), Ranking Republican

Labor, Health and Human Services, Education and Related Agencies
Tom Harkin (D-Iowa), Chairman
Arlen Specter (R-Pa), Ranking Republican

Legislative Branch
Harry Reid (D-Nev), Chairman
Slade Gorton (R-Wash), Ranking Republican

Military Construction
Jim Sasser (D-Tenn), Chairman
Phil Gramm (R-Texas), Ranking Republican

Transportation and Related Agencies
Frank Lautenberg (D-NJ), Chairman
Alfonse M. D'Amato (R-NY), Ranking Republican

Treasury, Postal Service and General Government
Dennis DeConcini (D-Ariz), Chairman
Pete V. Domenici (R-NM), Ranking Republican

VA, HUD and Independent Agencies
Barbara A. Mikulski (D-Md), Chairwoman
Jake Garn (R-Utah), Ranking Republican

Total PAC and Large Individual Contributions to Committee Members

Arlen Specter (R-Pa) $5,296,607
Alfonse M. D'Amato (R-NY) $4,607,894
Bob Kasten (R-Wis) $4,009,220
Wyche Fowler Jr. (D-Ga) $3,516,212
Bob Kerrey (D-Neb)† $3,409,573
Christopher S. Bond (R-Mo) $3,232,383
Don Nickles (R-Okla) $2,591,195
Daniel K. Inouye (D-Hawaii) $2,398,729
Ernest F. Hollings (D-SC) $2,318,965
Tom Harkin (D-Iowa)† $2,149,567
Phil Gramm (R-Texas) $1,964,503
Harry Reid (D-Nev) $1,845,018
Dale Bumpers (D-Ark) $1,648,431
Barbara A. Mikulski (D-Md) $1,578,220
Kent Conrad (D-ND) $1,238,407
Frank R. Lautenberg (D-NJ) $1,129,924
Brock Adams (D-Wash) $701,536
Patrick J. Leahy (D-Vt) $662,722
Dennis DeConcini (D-Ariz) $362,639
Slade Gorton (R-Wash) $280,422
Jim Sasser (D-Tenn) $152,231
Robert C. Byrd (D-WVa) $139,000
Mark O. Hatfield (R-Ore) $96,200
Thad Cochran (R-Miss) $52,600
J. Bennett Johnston (D-La) $43,950
Pete V. Domenici (R-NM) $17,700

Ted Stevens (R-Alaska) $8,050
Jake Garn (R-Utah) $1,000
Warren B. Rudman (R-NH) $0
Quentin N. Burdick (D-ND) .... -$900

Members in **bold italics** ran for reelection in 1992

† Includes contributions to his 1992 presidential campaign

Top 20 Contributors to Committee Members in 1991-92

1	American Bankers Assn*	$108,450
2	General Electric*	$105,825
3	Time Warner*	$99,250
4	American Dental Assn	$98,100
5	American Federation of Teachers	$97,000
6	Assn of Trial Lawyers of America	$97,000
7	United Parcel Service	$94,550
8	Merrill Lynch*	$93,214
9	National Assn of Realtors	$90,450
10	National Assn of Letter Carriers*	$90,040
11	National PAC	$90,000
12	National Assn of Life Underwriters	$87,000
13	National Cable Television Assn	$86,750
14	American Express*	$86,100
15	National Beer Wholesalers Assn	$85,700
16	National Assn of Broadcasters	$85,186
17	United Transportation Union	$83,800
18	Goldman, Sachs & Co	$83,501
19	US Tobacco*	$82,270
20	Philip Morris*	$80,980

* Contributions came from more than one affiliate or subsidiary.

Summary

The Appropriations Committee is the largest committee in the U.S. Senate; its 29 members have the job of doling out the dollars it takes to keep the government running. This makes its decisions especially important to those businesses that rely heavily on government contracts.

As seen dramatically in the chart below, contributions from lawyers and law firms towered over those of all other industries giving to members of the committee. That pattern was not specifically related to the Appropriations Committee — in fact the same pattern can be found in nearly every Senate committee. The reason has less to do with the effect of committee decisions on the legal profession than it does with the fact that lawyers and lobbyists represent a diverse collection of clients whose interests *are* affected by congressional decisions.

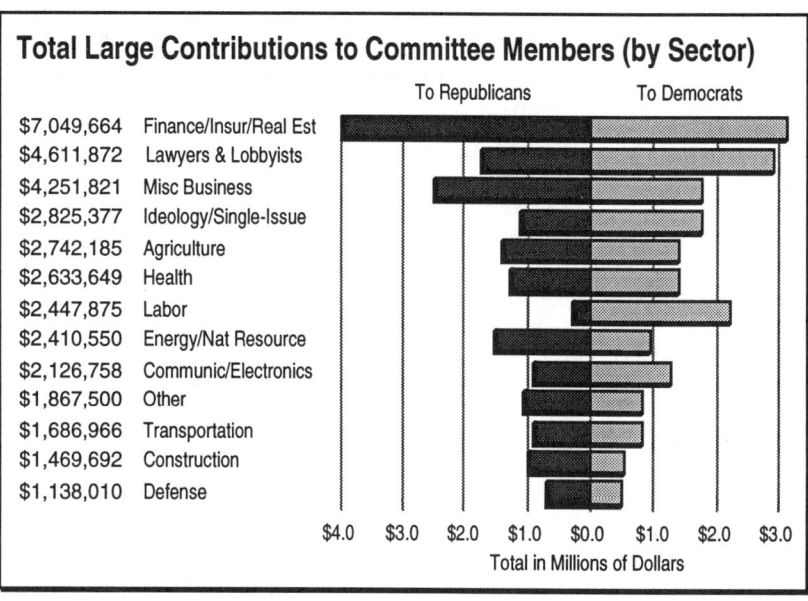

Total Large Contributions to Committee Members (by Sector)

Amount	Sector
$7,049,664	Finance/Insur/Real Est
$4,611,872	Lawyers & Lobbyists
$4,251,821	Misc Business
$2,825,377	Ideology/Single-Issue
$2,742,185	Agriculture
$2,633,649	Health
$2,447,875	Labor
$2,410,550	Energy/Nat Resource
$2,126,758	Communic/Electronics
$1,867,500	Other
$1,686,966	Transportation
$1,469,692	Construction
$1,138,010	Defense

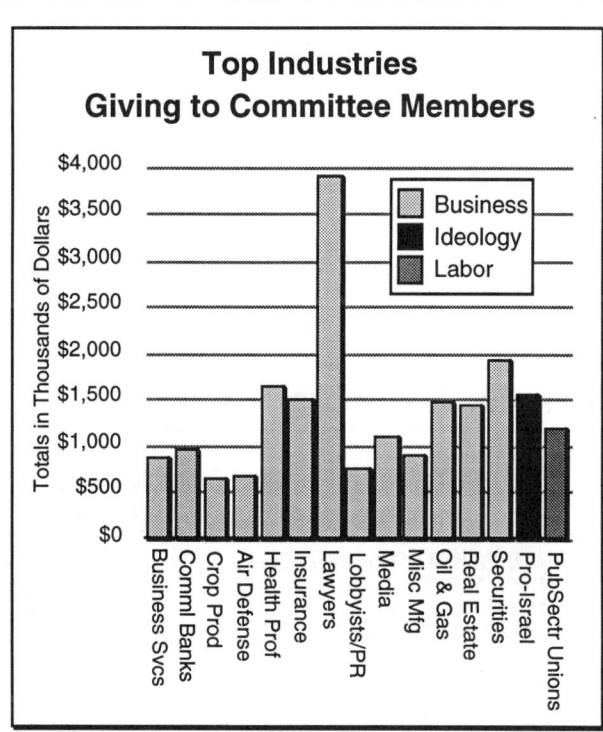

Leading Industries Giving to Committee Members

Business

Business Services	$840,036
Commercial Banks	$939,786
Crop Production & Basic Processing	$628,261
Defense Aerospace	$655,178
Health Professionals	$1,620,535
Insurance	$1,489,334
Lawyers/Law Firms	$3,878,193
Lobbyists/PR	$733,679
Media/Entertainment	$1,077,620
Misc Manufacturing & Distributing	$871,653
Oil & Gas	$1,444,090
Real Estate	$1,410,402
Securities & Investment	$1,906,250

Ideological/Single-Issue

Pro-Israel	$1,545,837

Labor

Public Sector Unions	$1,156,886

Senate Armed Services Committee

Sam Nunn (D-Ga), Chairman
John W. Warner (R-Va), Ranking Republican

Party Ratio: 11 Democrats
9 Republicans

Jurisdiction: (1) Aeronautical and space activities peculiar to or primarily associated with the development of weapons systems or military operations; (2) The common defense; (3) The Department of Defense, the Department of the Army, the Department of the Navy and the Department of the Air Force, generally; (4) Maintenance and operation of the Panama Canal, including administration, sanitation and government of the Canal Zone; (5) Military research and development; (6) National security aspects of nuclear energy; (7) Naval petroleum reserves, except those in Alaska; (8) Pay, promotion, retirement and other benefits and privileges of members of the Armed Forces, including overseas education of civilian and military dependents; (9) Selective Service System; and (10) Strategic and critical materials necessary for the common defense. In addition, the committee is mandated to study and review, on a comprehensive basis, matters relating to the common defense policy of the United States and to report on them from time to time.

Subcommittees

Conventional Forces and Alliance Defense
Carl Levin (D-Mich), Chairman
Malcolm Wallop (R-Wyo), Ranking Republican

Defense Industry and Technology
Jeff Bingaman (D-NM), Chairman
Daniel R. Coats (R-Ind), Ranking Republican

Manpower and Personnel
John Glenn (D-Ohio), Chairman
John McCain (R-Ariz), Ranking Republican

Projection Forces and Regional Defense
Edward M. Kennedy (D-Mass), Chairman
William S. Cohen (R-Maine), Ranking Republican

Readiness, Sustainability and Support
Alan J. Dixon (D-Ill), Chairman
Trent Lott (R-Miss), Ranking Republican

Strategic Forces and Nuclear Deterrence
Jim Exon (D-Neb), Chairman
Strom Thurmond (R-SC), Ranking Republican

Total Defense-Related Contributions to Committee Members

	Total from Cmte-Related Contribs	Pct of Member's Lg Contribs
Daniel R. Coats (R-Ind)	$175,998	6%
John Glenn (D-Ohio)	$151,572	6%
Richard C. Shelby (D-Ala)	$142,175	6%
John McCain (R-Ariz)	$138,821	6%
Alan J. Dixon (D-Ill)	$93,312	7%
Tim Wirth (D-Colo)	$48,214	5%
Trent Lott (R-Miss)	$20,750	6%
Robert C. Byrd (D-WVa)	$11,500	8%
Connie Mack (R-Fla)	$8,000	1%
Malcolm Wallop (R-Wyo)	$6,000	11%
John W. Warner (R-Va)	$2,850	58%
William S. Cohen (R-Maine)	$2,000	4%
Robert C. Smith (R-NH)	$1,250	26%
Strom Thurmond (R-SC)	$1,000	31%
Sam Nunn (D-Ga)	$695	0%
Jim Exon (D-Neb)	$426	4%

Top 20 Defense-Related Contributors to Committee Members in 1991-92

1	Martin Marietta Corp	$43,750
2	General Motors*	$35,500
3	Northrop Corp	$29,300
4	Rockwell International	$29,050
5	United Technologies	$27,400
6	Loral Corp	$27,000
7	General Dynamics	$26,101
8	Allied-Signal	$25,750
9	McDonnell Douglas*	$25,500
10	Boeing Co	$23,500
11	Grumman Corp	$22,800
12	Lockheed Corp	$22,750
13	General Electric	$20,500
14	GTE Corp	$20,000
15	Litton Industries	$19,000
16	BDM International	$18,300
17	Textron Inc	$18,000
18	FMC Corp	$17,500
19	AT&T	$14,500
20	Gencorp Inc	$14,100

* Contributions came from more than one affiliate or subsidiary.

Members in **bold italics** ran for reelection in 1992

Summary

Defense aerospace and electronics contractors were the biggest defense-related contributors to members of the Senate Armed Services Committee, but the chart at right reveals that overall the defense industry was not one of the top sources of campaign cash for committee members. This is due partly to the fact that senators routinely sit on three or four major committees, and as many as a dozen subcommittees. That tends to broaden the spectrum of interests that contribute to their campaigns.

The defense industry also gives much less to Congress as a whole than any other business sector. The $8.3 million that defense contractors gave in 1991-92 compares with $44 million from lawyers and lobbyists, for example, $24 million from agriculture interests, and more than $71 million from the finance/insurance/real estate sector.

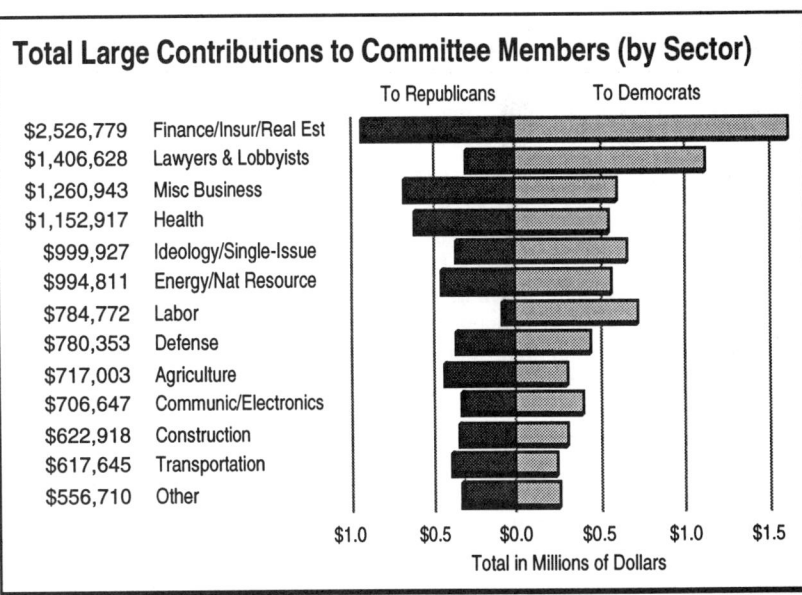

Total Large Contributions to Committee Members (by Sector)

$2,526,779	Finance/Insur/Real Est
$1,406,628	Lawyers & Lobbyists
$1,260,943	Misc Business
$1,152,917	Health
$999,927	Ideology/Single-Issue
$994,811	Energy/Nat Resource
$784,772	Labor
$780,353	Defense
$717,003	Agriculture
$706,647	Communic/Electronics
$622,918	Construction
$617,645	Transportation
$556,710	Other

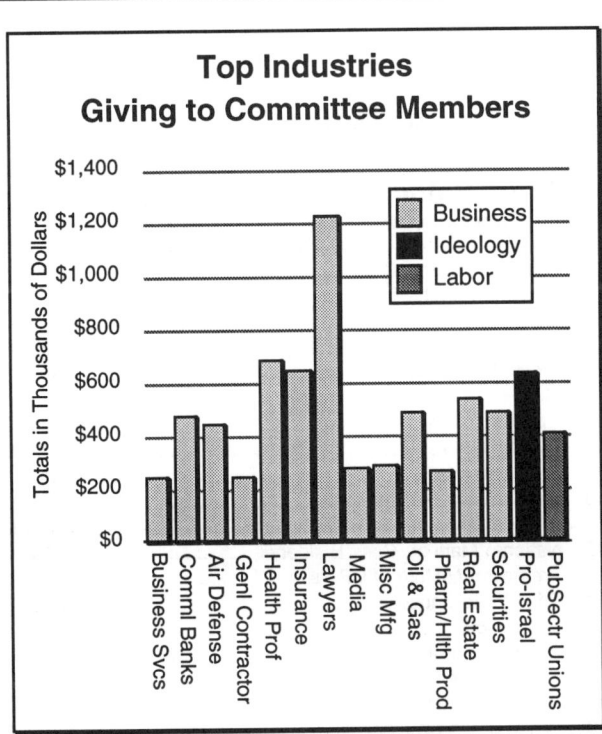

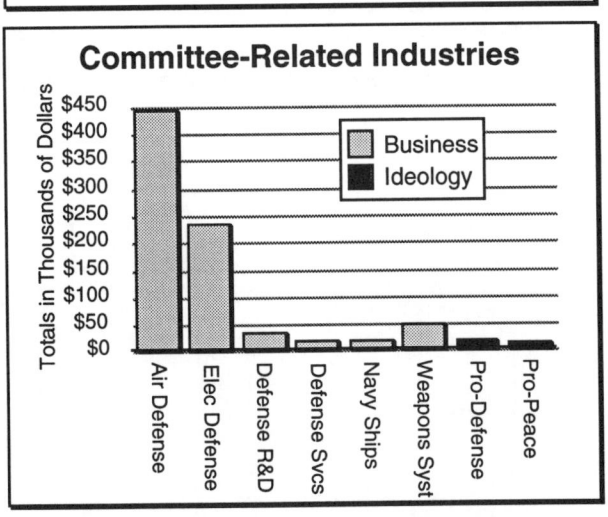

Leading Industries Giving to Committee Members

Business
- Business Services $234,221
- Commercial Banks $465,963
- Defense Aerospace $438,147
- General Contractors $237,911
- Health Professionals $678,861
- Insurance $639,372
- Lawyers/Law Firms $1,216,367
- Media/Entertainment $271,212
- Misc Manufacturing & Distributing $275,017
- Oil & Gas $480,425
- Pharmaceuticals/Health Products $254,662
- Real Estate $525,084
- Securities & Investment $477,011

Ideological/Single-Issue
- Pro-Israel $625,228

Labor
- Public Sector Unions $393,801

Leading Industries Giving to Committee Members

Business
- Defense Aerospace $438,147
- Defense Electronics $230,520
- Defense R&D $32,500
- Defense Services $15,294
- Defense Shipbuilders $16,500
- Weapons Systems $47,392

Ideological/Single-Issue
- Pro-Defense $15,569
- Pro-Peace $8,641

Senate Banking, Housing & Urban Affairs Committee

Donald W. Riegle Jr. (D-Mich), Chairman
Jake Garn (R-Utah), Ranking Republican

Party Ratio: 12 Democrats
9 Republicans

Jurisdiction: (1) Banks, banking and financial institutions; (2) Financial aid to commerce and industry; (3) Deposit insurance; (4) Public and private housing (including veterans' housing); (5) Federal monetary policy (including Federal Reserve System); (6) Money and credit, including currency and coinage; (7) Issuance and redemption of notes; (8) Control of prices of commodities, rents and services; (9) Urban development and urban mass transit; (10) Economic stabilization and defense production; (11) Export controls; (12) Export and foreign trade promotion; (13) Nursing home construction; (14) Renegotiation of Government contracts. In addition, the committee is mandated to study and review matters relating to international economic policy as it affects U.S. monetary affairs, credit, and financial institutions, economic growth, urban affairs and credit and to report on these matters periodically.

Subcommittees

Consumer and Regulatory Affairs
Alan J. Dixon (D-Ill), Chairman
Christopher S. Bond (R-Mo), Ranking Republican

Housing and Urban Affairs
Alan Cranston (D-Calif), Chairman
Alfonse M. D'Amato (R-NY), Ranking Republican

International Finance and Monetary Policy
Paul S. Sarbanes (D-Md), Chairman
Connie Mack (R-Fla), Ranking Republican

Securities
Christopher J. Dodd (D-Conn), Chairman
Phil Gramm (R-Texas), Ranking Republican

Total Committee-Related Contributions to Committee Members

	Total from Cmte-Related Contribs	Pct of Member's Lg Contribs
Alfonse M. D'Amato (R-NY)	$1,143,033	25%
Christopher J. Dodd (D-Conn)	$967,075	31%
Arlen Specter (R-Pa)	$844,347	16%
Christopher S. Bond (R-Mo)	$683,648	21%
Richard C. Shelby (D-Ala)	$453,828	18%
Bob Graham (D-Fla)	$432,157	17%
Alan J. Dixon (D-Ill)	$385,379	28%
Terry Sanford (D-NC)	$378,974	21%
Phil Gramm (R-Texas)	$344,374	18%
Tim Wirth (D-Colo)	$260,446	24%
John Kerry (D-Mass)	$130,524	27%
Connie Mack (R-Fla)	$125,703	17%
Jim Sasser (D-Tenn)	$47,806	31%
Richard H. Bryan (D-Nev)	$33,900	12%
Donald W. Riegle Jr. (D-Mich)	$27,000	15%
William V. Roth Jr. (R-Del)	$9,500	34%
Pete V. Domenici (R-NM)	$7,300	41%
Paul S. Sarbanes (D-Md)	$750	4%
Nancy Landon Kassebaum (R-Kan)	-$750	7%
Alan Cranston (D-Calif)	-$48,000	18%

Top 20 Commitee-Related Contributors to Committee Members in 1991-92

1	American Express*	$88,725
2	Goldman, Sachs & Co	$84,766
3	Bear, Stearns & Co	$80,951
4	Arthur Andersen & Co	$70,199
5	Merrill Lynch	$69,679
6	Coopers & Lybrand	$63,840
7	Ernst & Young	$60,396
8	Morgan Stanley & Co	$58,450
9	Equitable Life*	$56,575
10	National Assn of Realtors	$56,100
11	National Assn of Life Underwriters	$56,000
12	National Assn of Home Builders	$55,250
13	American Institute of CPA's	$51,000
14	Price Waterhouse	$46,775
15	Cigna Corp	$44,950
16	American Bankers Assn	$44,000
17	Independent Insurance Agents of America	$42,999
18	American Council of Life Insurance	$42,069
19	Credit Union National Assn*	$41,500
20	Smith Barney	$41,256

* Contributions came from more than one affiliate or subsidiary.

Members in **bold italics** ran for reelection in 1992

Summary

The banking industry, a heavily regulated sector of American business, has become much more diversified in recent years, offering an ever-widening array of financial services. This diversification has come about as Congress (and the banking committees in particular) have gradually lifted many restrictions governing the industry. But banks are anxious for considerably more freedom — the ability to branch into stock brokerage services, for example — and the Senate Banking Committee is one of the central battlegrounds for the ongoing debate.

The issue of bank deregulation, of course, concerns not only banks but also their competitors — particularly major insurance companies who have become increasingly active in the securities field themselves. And, like many other committees in the Senate, contributions from lawyers and lobbyists (representing either their own interests or those of their clients) were substantial.

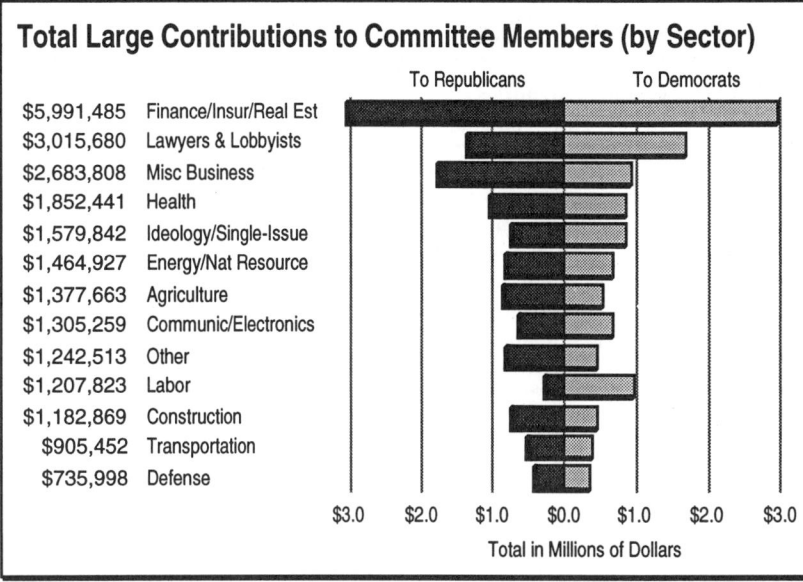

Total Large Contributions to Committee Members (by Sector)

Amount	Sector
$5,991,485	Finance/Insur/Real Est
$3,015,680	Lawyers & Lobbyists
$2,683,808	Misc Business
$1,852,441	Health
$1,579,842	Ideology/Single-Issue
$1,464,927	Energy/Nat Resource
$1,377,663	Agriculture
$1,305,259	Communic/Electronics
$1,242,513	Other
$1,207,823	Labor
$1,182,869	Construction
$905,452	Transportation
$735,998	Defense

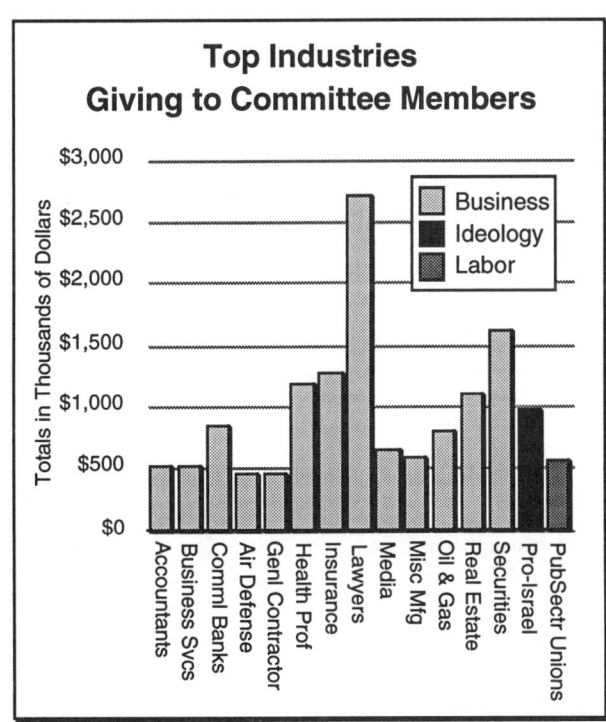

Top Industries Giving to Committee Members

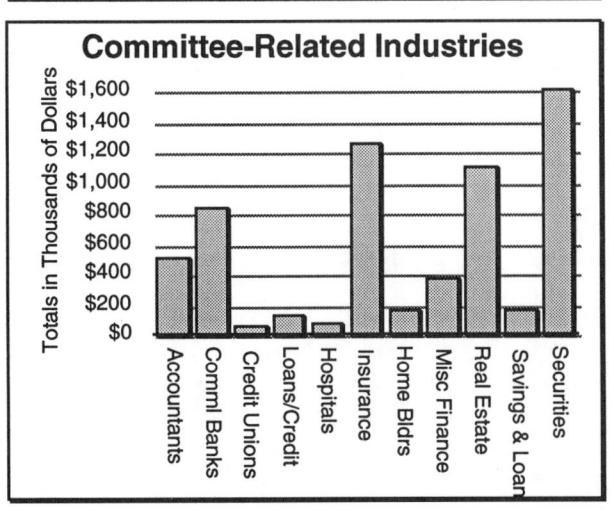

Committee-Related Industries

Leading Industries Giving to Committee Members

Business
- Accountants $505,919
- Business Services $505,605
- Commercial Banks $833,476
- Defense Aerospace $452,499
- General Contractors $451,194
- Health Professionals $1,166,535
- Insurance $1,255,163
- Lawyers/Law Firms $2,700,544
- Media/Entertainment $628,115
- Misc Manufacturing & Distributing $567,322
- Oil & Gas $779,616
- Real Estate $1,095,443
- Securities & Investment $1,590,906

Ideological/Single-Issue
- Pro-Israel $961,088

Labor
- Public Sector Unions $555,353

Leading Committee-Related Industries Giving to Committee Members

Business
- Accountants $505,919
- Commercial Banks $833,476
- Credit Unions $50,000
- Finance/Credit Companies $131,371
- Hospitals/Nursing Homes $79,070
- Insurance $1,255,163
- Home Builders $156,439
- Misc Finance $375,180
- Real Estate $1,095,443
- Savings & Loans $154,027
- Securities & Investment $1,590,906

Senate Budget Committee

Jim Sasser (D-Tenn), Chairman
Pete V. Domenici (R-NM), Ranking Republican

Party Ratio: 12 Democrats
9 Republicans

Jurisdiction: (1) To report the matters needing to be reported by it under Titles III and IV of the Congressional Budget Act of 1974; (2) To make continuing studies of the effect on budget outlays of relevant existing and proposed legislation and to report the results of such studies to the Senate on a recurring basis; (3) To request and evaluate continuing studies of tax expenditures, to devise methods of coordinating tax expenditures, policies and programs with direct budget outlays, and to report the results of such studies to the Senate on a recurring basis; (4) To review, on a continuing basis, the conduct by the Congressional Budget Office of its functions and duties; (5) To consider impoundment legislation required to be jointly referred to it, the Appropriations Committee, and other Senate Committees . . . and (6) To consider matters affecting the Congressional Budget process required to be referred to it and the Governmental Affairs Committee.

No Subcommittees

Total PAC and Large Individual Contributions to Committee Members

Bob Kasten (R-Wis)	$4,009,220
Wyche Fowler Jr. (D-Ga)	$3,516,212
Christopher S. Bond (R-Mo)	$3,232,383
Christopher J. Dodd (D-Conn)	$3,167,767
Don Nickles (R-Okla)	$2,591,195
Ernest F. Hollings (D-SC)	$2,318,965
Phil Gramm (R-Texas)	$1,964,503
Terry Sanford (D-NC)	$1,803,161
Charles E. Grassley (R-Iowa)	$1,593,319
Kent Conrad (D-ND)	$1,238,407
Frank R. Lautenberg (D-NJ)	$1,129,924
Tim Wirth (D-Colo)	$1,067,928
Trent Lott (R-Miss)	$372,060
Steve Symms (R-Idaho)	$188,078
Donald W. Riegle Jr. (D-Mich)	$180,405
Jim Sasser (D-Tenn)	$152,231
Paul Simon (D-Ill)	$59,392
J. Bennett Johnston (D-La)	$43,950
Pete V. Domenici (R-NM)	$17,700
Jim Exon (D-Neb)	$10,176
Hank Brown (R-Colo)	-$1,813

Top 20 Contributors to Committee Members in 1991-92

1	US Tobacco*	$102,770
2	Merrill Lynch*	$99,919
3	Time Warner*	$92,450
4	American Bankers Assn*	$84,700
5	American Dental Assn	$76,000
6	United Parcel Service	$75,050
7	General Electric*	$72,950
8	BellSouth Corp*	$71,669
9	Philip Morris*	$70,530
10	National Assn of Life Underwriters	$69,500
11	American Institute of CPA's	$67,750
12	Goldman, Sachs & Co	$66,700
13	RJR Nabisco*	$66,500
14	American Express*	$66,375
15	American Federation of Teachers	$65,000
16	Federal Express Corp	$65,000
17	National Rifle Assn	$64,850
18	National Assn of Broadcasters	$63,336
19	National Beer Wholesalers Assn	$62,200
20	Citizens Organized PAC	$61,000

* Contributions came from more than one affiliate or subsidiary.

Members in **bold italics** ran for reelection in 1992

Summary

Perhaps no other document in the Western World is so important to so many people, yet understood by so few, as the federal government's annual budget. Weighty, befuddling, sometimes self-contradictory, and inevitably the subject of political wrangling and intense negotiation between Congress and the administration, the budget is the blueprint for federal spending and programs for the coming fiscal year. This is the committee charged with shaping that budget into something both sides can live with.

In recent years the budget deficit has been an ever-growing preoccupation of this committee. Finding ways to reduce it — at least on paper — has been a sometimes all-consuming task. Since federal spending — and the deficit in particular — affects the overall American economy, many industries have a more than casual interest in the committee's work. Not surprisingly, the financial sector was the biggest overall contributor to committee members.

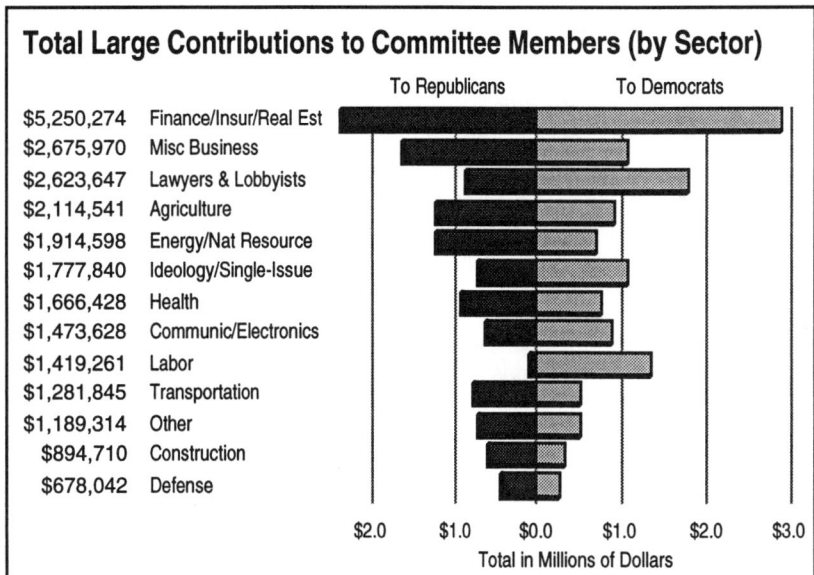

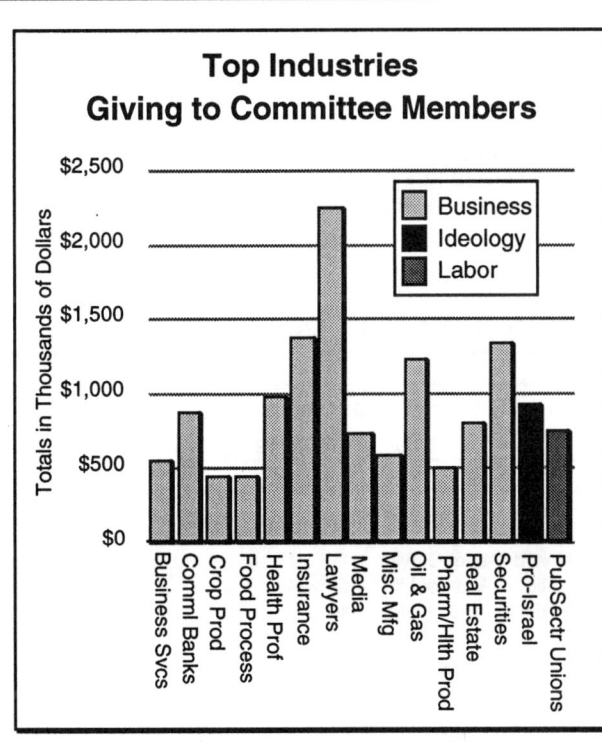

Leading Industries Giving to Committee Members

Business
- Business Services $520,920
- Commercial Banks $857,697
- Crop Production & Basic Processing $423,700
- Food Processing & Sales $418,920
- Health Professionals $951,550
- Insurance $1,353,599
- Lawyers/Law Firms $2,232,021
- Media/Entertainment $702,259
- Misc Manufacturing & Distributing $572,722
- Oil & Gas $1,205,804
- Pharmaceuticals/Health Products $472,161
- Real Estate $777,678
- Securities & Investment $1,309,114

Ideological/Single-Issue
- Pro-Israel $908,735

Labor
- Public Sector Unions $733,819

105

Senate Commerce, Science and Transportation Committee

Ernest F. Hollings (D-SC), Chairman
John C. Danforth (R-Mo), Ranking Republican

Party Ratio: 11 Democrats
9 Republicans

Jurisdiction: (1) Interstate commerce; (2) Transportation; (3) Regulation of interstate common carriers, including railroads, buses, trucks, vessels, pipelines and civil aviation; (4) Merchant marine and navigation; (5) Marine and ocean navigation, safety, and transportation, including navigational aspects of deepwater ports; (6) Coast Guard; (7) Inland waterways, except construction; (8) Communications; (9) Regulation of consumer products and services, including testing related to toxic substances, other than pesticides, and except for credit, financial services and housing; (10) The Panama Canal and interoceanic canals generally, except as referred to the Committee on Armed Services; (11) Standards and measurement; (12) Highway safety; (13) Science, engineering, and technology research and development and policy; (14) Nonmilitary aeronautical and space sciences; (15) Transportation and commerce aspects of Outer Continental Shelf lands; (16) Marine fisheries; (17) Coastal Zone Management; (18) Oceans, weather and atmospheric activities; (19) Sports. In addition, the committee is mandated to study and review all matters relating to science and technology, oceans policy, transportation, communications and consumer affairs, and to report on these matters periodically.

Subcommittees

Aviation
Wendell H. Ford (D-Ky), Chairman
John McCain (R-Ariz), Ranking Republican

Communications
Daniel K. Inouye (D-Hawaii), Chairman
Bob Packwood (R-Ore), Ranking Republican

Consumer
Richard H. Bryan (D-Nev), Chairman
Slade Gorton (R-Wash), Ranking Republican

Foreign Commerce and Tourism
John D. Rockefeller IV (D-WVa), Chairman
Conrad Burns (R-Mont), Ranking Republican

Merchant Marine
John B. Breaux (D-La), Chairman
Trent Lott (R-Miss), Ranking Republican

Science, Technology and Space
Al Gore (D-Tenn), Chairman
Larry Pressler (R-SD), Ranking Republican

Surface Transportation
Jim Exon (D-Neb), Chairman
Bob Kasten (R-Wis), Ranking Republican

National Ocean Policy Study
Ernest F. Hollings (D-SC), Chairman
Ted Stevens (R-Alaska), Ranking Republican

Total Committee-Related Contributions to Committee Members

	Total from Cmte-Related Contribs	Pct of Member's Lg Contribs
Bob Packwood (R-Ore)	$922,144	28%
Ernest F. Hollings (D-SC)	$917,053	40%
John B. Breaux (D-La)	$776,464	35%
Wendell H. Ford (D-Ky)	$648,886	33%
Bob Kasten (R-Wis)	$634,030	16%
Daniel K. Inouye (D-Hawaii)	$487,600	20%
John McCain (R-Ariz)	$439,106	20%
Lloyd Bentsen (D-Tex)	$265,409	34%
John Kerry (D-Mass)	$145,573	30%
Trent Lott (R-Miss)	$127,700	34%
Conrad Burns (R-Mont)	$102,868	40%
Slade Gorton (R-Wash)	$88,448	32%
Richard H. Bryan (D-Nev)	$51,890	18%
Larry Pressler (R-SD)	$31,000	29%
John D. Rockefeller IV (D-WVa)	$20,000	10%
John C. Danforth (R-Mo)	$17,500	55%
Charles S. Robb (D-Va)	$7,100	54%
Jim Exon (D-Neb)	$5,750	57%
Ted Stevens (R-Alaska)	$5,250	65%
Al Gore (D-Tenn)	$500	5%

Top 20 Committee-Related Contributors to Committee Members in 1991-92

1	National Assn of Broadcasters	$82,386
2	Marine Engineers Union*	$65,500
3	CSX Corp*	$55,500
4	United Parcel Service	$55,050
5	National Assn of Life Underwriters	$54,500
6	National Auto Dealers Assn	$54,000
7	General Electric*	$51,900
8	Federal Express Corp	$51,000
9	Time Warner*	$50,500
10	GTE Corp*	$49,800
11	American Trucking Assns	$49,243
12	Union Pacific Corp	$48,951
13	Aircraft Owners & Pilots Assn	$46,000
14	American Family Corp	$45,500
15	National Cable Television Assn	$44,250
16	Auto Dealers & Drivers for Free Trade	$44,000
17	Air Line Pilots Assn	$42,500
18	American Council of Life Insurance	$40,783
19	BellSouth Corp*	$39,850
20	Americans for Free International Trade	$39,000

* Contributions came from more than one affiliate or subsidiary.

Members in **bold italics** ran for reelection in 1992

Summary

Under the wide umbrella of the Senate Commerce Committee's jurisdiction falls a variety of industries and interests ranging from cable TV operators to telephone utilities, railroads to barge lines to interstate truckers. Disputes between competing segments within those industries ensure a perennially heavy schedule on the committee's agenda. This is also the committee that wrestles with the issue of product liability laws, pitting lawyers on the one side against manufacturers on the other — with a host of other groups falling somewhere in between.

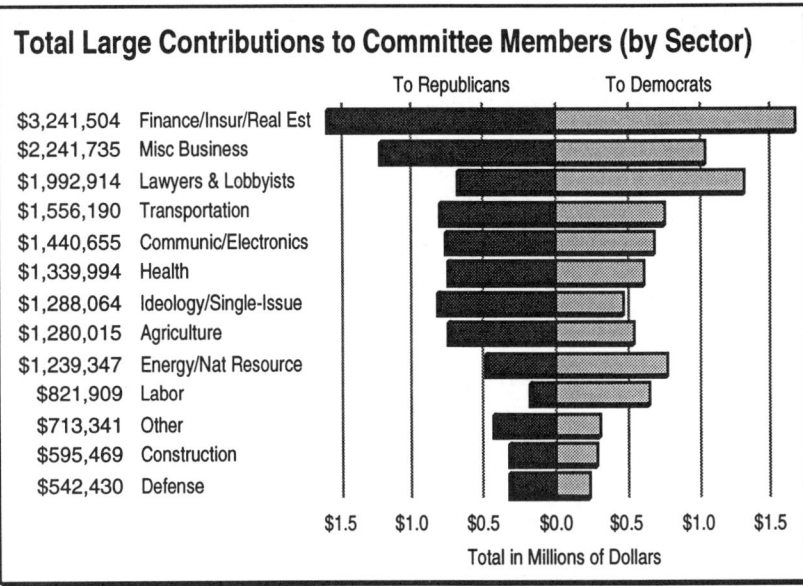

Total Large Contributions to Committee Members (by Sector)

Amount	Sector
$3,241,504	Finance/Insur/Real Est
$2,241,735	Misc Business
$1,992,914	Lawyers & Lobbyists
$1,556,190	Transportation
$1,440,655	Communic/Electronics
$1,339,994	Health
$1,288,064	Ideology/Single-Issue
$1,280,015	Agriculture
$1,239,347	Energy/Nat Resource
$821,909	Labor
$713,341	Other
$595,469	Construction
$542,430	Defense

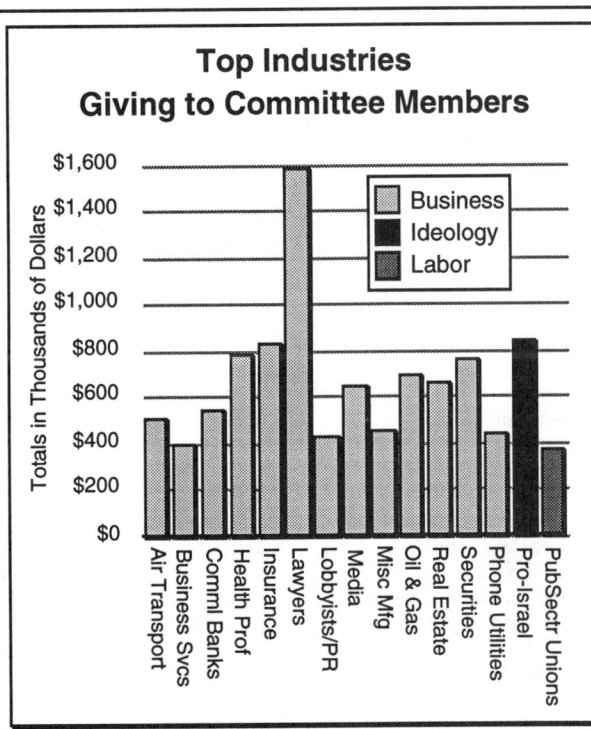

Leading Industries Giving to Committee Members

Business
- Air Transport $500,362
- Business Services $388,197
- Commercial Banks $531,428
- Health Professionals $771,020
- Insurance $822,470
- Lawyers/Law Firms $1,575,445
- Lobbyists/PR $417,469
- Media/Entertainment $634,986
- Misc Manufacturing & Distributing $444,621
- Oil & Gas $683,819
- Real Estate $643,205
- Securities & Investment $749,909
- Telephone Utilities $431,616

Ideological/Single-Issue
- Pro-Israel $829,757

Labor
- Public Sector Unions $364,373

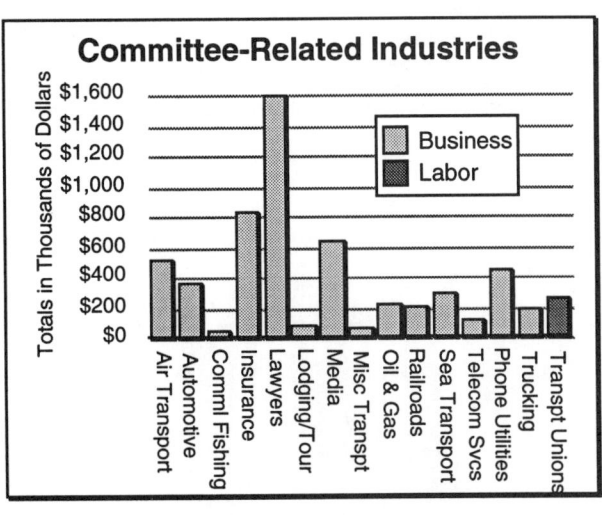

Leading Committee-Related Industries Giving to Committee Members

Business
- Air Transport $500,362
- Automotive $347,774
- Commercial Fishing $38,783
- Insurance $822,470
- Lawyers/Law Firms $1,575,445
- Lodging/Tourism $75,850
- Media/Entertainment $634,986
- Misc Transport $48,800
- Oil & Gas $210,153
- Railroads $187,227
- Sea Transport $274,518
- Telecom Services & Equipment $109,103
- Telephone Utilities $431,616
- Trucking $178,309

Labor
- Transportation Unions $253,250

Senate Energy and Natural Resources Committee

J. Bennett Johnston (D-La), Chairman
Malcolm Wallop (R-Wyo), Ranking Republican

Party Ratio: 11 Democrats
9 Republicans

Jurisdiction: Oversight and legislative responsibilities, including (1) Strategic petroleum reserves; (2) Intergovernmental Relations; (3) Outer continental shelf leasing; (4) Investigation and oversight; (5) International energy affairs; (6) Global climate change; (7) Natural gas pricing and regulation; (8) Utility policy; (9) Nuclear waste and insurance programs; (10) Territorial affairs, including commonwealths; (11) Free Associated States; and (12) Antarctica.

Subcommittees

Energy Regulation and Conservation
Tim Wirth (D-Colo), Chairman
Don Nickles (R-Okla), Ranking Republican

Energy Research and Development
Wendell H. Ford (D-Ky), Chairman
Pete V. Domenici (R-NM), Ranking Republican

Mineral Resources Development and Production
Jeff Bingaman (D-NM), Chairman
Larry E. Craig (R-Idaho), Ranking Republican

Public Lands, National Parks and Forests
Dale Bumpers (D-Ark), Chairman
Frank H. Murkowski (R-Alaska), Ranking Republican

Water and Power
Bill Bradley (D-NJ), Chairman
Conrad Burns (R-Mont), Ranking Republican

Total Committee-Related Contributions to Committee Members

	Total from Cmte-Related Contribs	Pct of Member's Lg Contribs
Don Nickles (R-Okla)	$572,766	22%
John F. Seymour (R-Calif)	$271,625	5%
Wendell H. Ford (D-Ky)	$259,950	13%
Richard C. Shelby (D-Ala)	$241,889	10%
Frank H. Murkowski (R-Alaska)	$204,227	15%
Kent Conrad (D-ND)	$185,172	15%
Wyche Fowler Jr. (D-Ga)	$170,534	5%
Dale Bumpers (D-Ark)	$170,366	10%
Tim Wirth (D-Colo)	$92,203	9%
Conrad Burns (R-Mont)	$32,850	13%
Malcolm Wallop (R-Wyo)	$19,965	38%
Daniel K. Akaka (D-Hawaii)	$13,650	3%
Jeff Bingaman (D-NM)	$8,818	5%
Mark O. Hatfield (R-Ore)	$8,500	9%
J. Bennett Johnston (D-La)	$7,500	17%
Paul Wellstone (D-Minn)	$6,100	4%
Larry E. Craig (R-Idaho)	$1,500	6%
Pete V. Domenici (R-NM)	$500	3%
Bill Bradley (D-NJ)	-$150	0%

Top 20 Committee-Related Contributors to Committee Members in 1991-92

1	Atlantic Richfield	$55,633
2	General Atomics	$52,750
3	ACRE (Action Cmte for Rural Electrification)*	$48,500
4	Chevron Corp	$44,000
5	Southern California Edison	$42,000
6	Arkla Inc	$38,200
7	Southern Co*	$34,250
8	Mobil Oil	$32,000
9	National Coal Assn	$31,499
10	Waste Management Inc	$30,650
11	Coastal Corp	$30,000
12	Exxon Corp	$28,700
13	Pacific Gas & Electric	$28,500
14	Southern Natural Resources	$27,300
15	Union Pacific Corp	$27,000
16	Columbia Gas System*	$25,600
17	Amoco Corp	$25,500
18	Halliburton Co*	$25,500
19	Phillips Petroleum	$25,446
20	Pacific Enterprises	$24,500
20	Petroleum Marketers Assn	$24,500

* Contributions came from more than one affiliate or subsidiary.

Members in **bold italics** ran for reelection in 1992

Summary

Oil & gas policies, the interstate transportation of natural gas, the ever-deepening problem of nuclear waste disposal and a host of other energy-related issues are the primary concern of the Senate Energy and Natural Resources Committee. Its domain, and the scope of its jurisdiction, range from oilfields on the North Slope of Alaska to the ice fields of Antarctica and the oil and mineral-rich deposits beneath the seabeds of the outer continental shelf.

As the world's largest consumer of energy, and one of its largest producers, America's economic health has long been tied to the fortunes of the oil & gas industry — though the interests of the nation and the industry do not always coincide. Balancing those interests, and setting the nation's energy policy, is the charge of this committee.

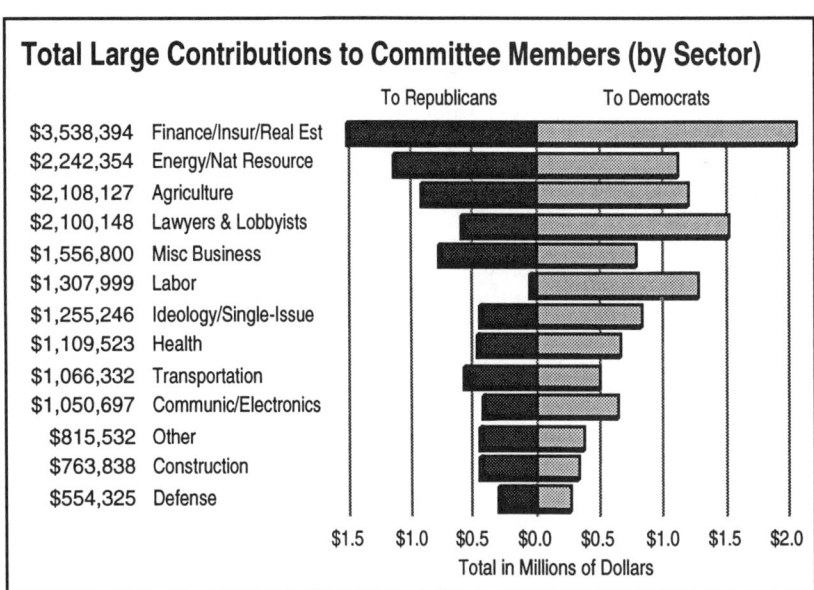

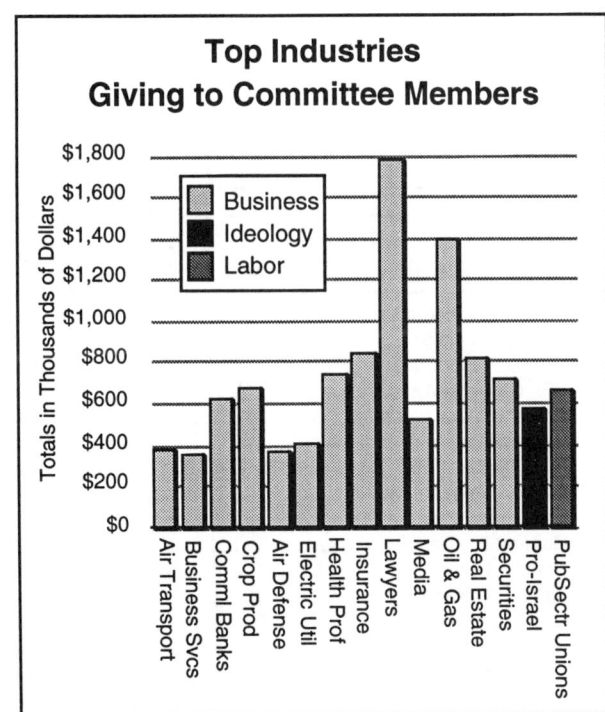

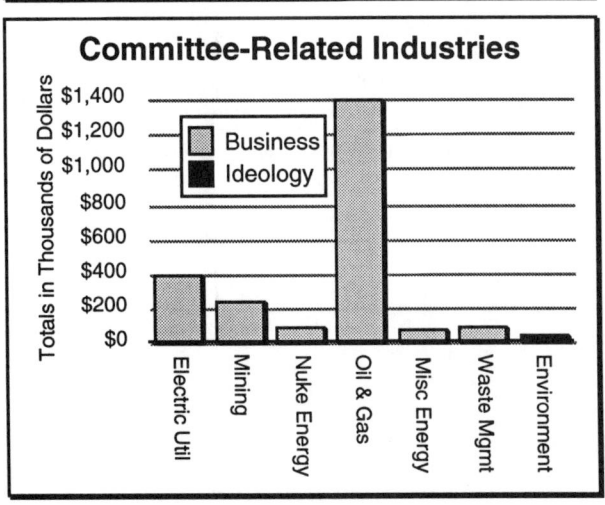

Leading Industries Giving to Committee Members

Business

Air Transport	$361,979
Business Services	$347,726
Commercial Banks	$614,187
Crop Production & Basic Processing	$665,323
Defense Aerospace	$354,775
Electric Utilities	$390,318
Health Professionals	$728,162
Insurance	$827,114
Lawyers/Law Firms	$1,766,978
Media/Entertainment	$511,881
Oil & Gas	$1,380,334
Real Estate	$806,213
Securities & Investment	$705,082

Ideological/Single-Issue

Pro-Israel	$566,321

Labor

Public Sector Unions	$649,561

Leading Committee-Related Industries Giving to Committee Members

Business

Electric Utilities	$390,318
Mining	$227,794
Nuclear Energy	$72,750
Oil & Gas	$1,380,334
Misc Energy	$72,225
Waste Management	$81,400

Ideological/Single-Issue

Environmental Issues	$37,211

Senate Environment and Public Works Committee

Daniel Patrick Moynihan (D-NY), Chairman
John H. Chafee (R-RI), Ranking Republican

Party Ratio: 10 Democrats
7 Republicans

Jurisdiction: (1) Environmental policy; (2) Environmental research and development; (3) Ocean dumping; (4) Fisheries and wildlife; (5) Environmental aspects of Outer Continental Shelf lands; (6) Solid waste disposal and recycling; (7) Environmental effects of toxic substances, other than pesticides; (8) Water resources; (9) Flood control and improvements of rivers and harbors, including environmental aspects of deepwater ports; (10) Public works, bridges and dams; (11) Water pollution; (12) Air pollution; (13) Noise pollution; (14) Nonmilitary environmental regulation and control of nuclear energy; (15) Regional economic development; (16) Construction and maintenance of highways; (17) Public buildings and improved grounds of the United States generally, including Federal buildings in the District of Columbia. In addition, the committee is mandated to study and review matters relating to environmental protection, resource utilization and conservation, and to report on these matters periodically.

Subcommittees

Environmental Protection
Max Baucus (D-Mont), Chairman
John H. Chafee (R-RI), Ranking Republican

Nuclear Regulation
Bob Graham (D-Fla), Chairman
Alan K. Simpson (R-Wyo), Ranking Republican

Superfund, Ocean and Water Protection
Frank Lautenberg (D-NJ), Chairman
Dave Durenberger (R-Minn), Ranking Republican

Toxic Substances, Environmental Oversight, Research and Development
Harry Reid (D-Nev), Chairman
John W. Warner (R-Va), Ranking Republican

Water Resources, Transportation and Infrastructure
Daniel Patrick Moynihan (D-NY), Chairman
Steve Symms (R-Idaho), Ranking Republican

Total Committee-Related Contributions to Committee Members

	Total from Cmte-Related Contribs	Pct of Member's Lg Contribs
Bob Graham (D-Fla)	$286,175	11%
Harry Reid (D-Nev)	$270,594	15%
Harris Wofford (D-Pa)†	$214,048	6%
Frank R. Lautenberg (D-NJ)	$107,374	10%
Daniel Patrick Moynihan (D-NY)	$92,987	16%
Joseph I. Lieberman (D-Conn)	$83,660	9%
Steve Symms (R-Idaho)	$34,250	18%
John H. Chafee (R-RI)	$15,050	12%
Dave Durenberger (R-Minn)	$13,050	5%
Alan K. Simpson (R-Wyo)	$3,000	21%
Robert C. Smith (R-NH)	$1,500	32%
Max Baucus (D-Mont)	$1,000	14%
James M. Jeffords (R-Vt)	$1,000	14%
John W. Warner (R-Va)	$1,000	20%

† Wofford's election was in 1991

Top 20 Committee Related Contributors to Committee Members in 1991-92

1	Marine Engineers Union*	$31,000
2	Teamsters Union	$27,500
3	United Transportation Union	$26,500
4	FPL Group Inc*	$26,250
5	Chambers Development Co	$25,000
6	Seafarers International Union	$18,000
7	Auto Dealers & Drivers for Free Trade	$15,000
8	Waste Management Inc	$14,500
9	Browning-Ferris Industries	$13,640
10	General Electric	$13,400
11	Coastal Corp	$13,000
12	Amerada Hess Corp	$12,000
13	Cyprus Minerals Co	$11,500
14	General Public Utilities	$11,500
15	Yellow Freight System	$11,500
16	ACRE (Action Cmte for Rural Electrification)	$11,000
17	ITEL Corp	$11,000
18	WR Grace & Co	$11,000
19	American Trucking Assns	$10,081
20	Occidental Petroleum	$10,000
20	Sierra Pacific Resources	$10,000

* Contributions came from more than one affiliate or subsidiary.

Members in **bold italics** ran for reelection in 1992

Summary

"Infrastructure" is not a glamorous word or a particularly inspiring political cause, but it is crucial to the health of the nation. The building and maintenance of the nation's highways, waterways and other public facilities is a central concern of this committee — and of many of the industries that supply campaign dollars to committee members.

But there is another side to development, one that often *does* inspire political action — the effect that our modern industrial infrastructure has on the environment of the planet. That too is a major preoccupation of this committee.

The heavy Democratic tilt in contributors to the committee (as seen in the chart at right) is due to the fact that the only three committee members who faced election campaigns in 1991-92 were all Democrats.

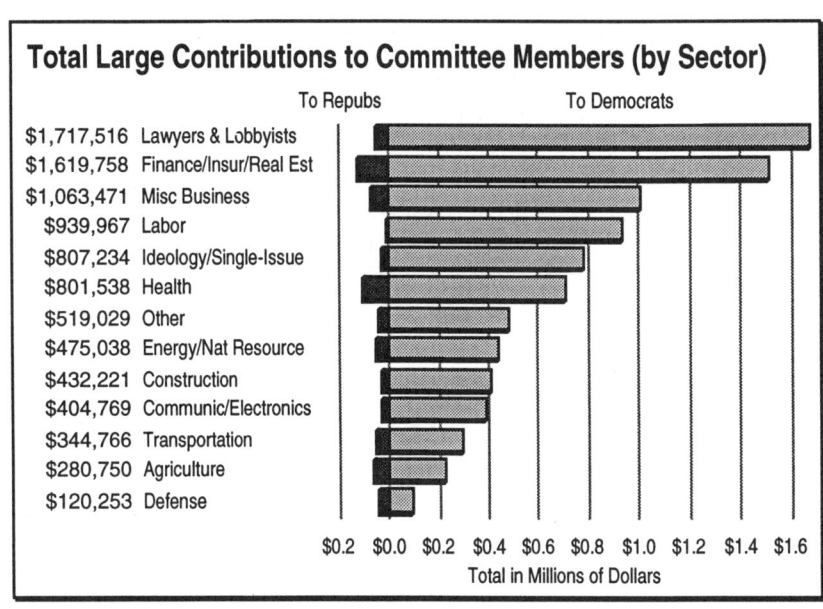

Total Large Contributions to Committee Members (by Sector)

Amount	Sector
$1,717,516	Lawyers & Lobbyists
$1,619,758	Finance/Insur/Real Est
$1,063,471	Misc Business
$939,967	Labor
$807,234	Ideology/Single-Issue
$801,538	Health
$519,029	Other
$475,038	Energy/Nat Resource
$432,221	Construction
$404,769	Communic/Electronics
$344,766	Transportation
$280,750	Agriculture
$120,253	Defense

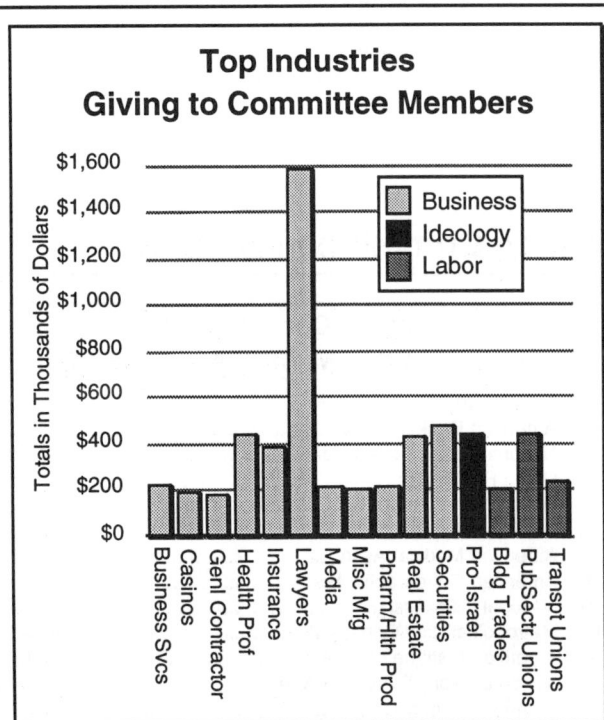

Leading Industries Giving to Committee Members

Business
- Business Services $218,531
- Casinos/Gambling $175,909
- General Contractors $171,498
- Health Professionals $433,148
- Insurance $367,919
- Lawyers/Law Firms $1,574,065
- Media/Entertainment $199,000
- Misc Manufacturing & Distributing $185,710
- Pharmaceuticals/Health Products $201,750
- Real Estate $422,250
- Securities & Investment $460,158

Ideological/Single-Issue
- Pro-Israel $433,176

Labor
- Building Trade Unions $191,629
- Public Sector Unions $424,399
- Transportation Unions $227,350

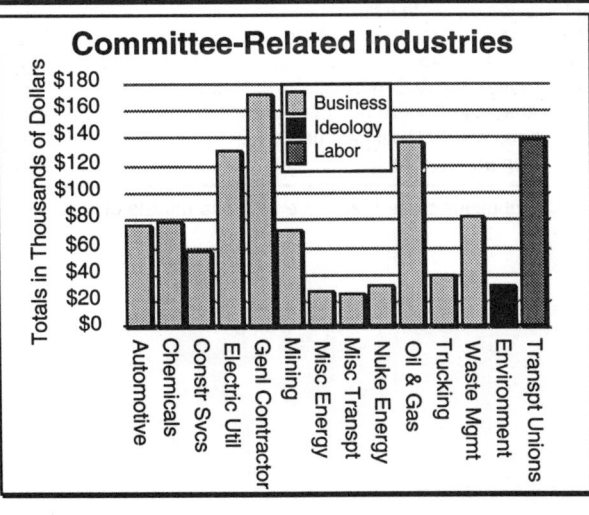

Leading Committee-Related Industries Giving to Committee Members

Business
- Automotive $73,750
- Chemical & Related Manufacturing $76,950
- Construction Services $54,773
- Electric Utilities $129,100
- General Contractors $171,498
- Mining $70,650
- Misc Energy $24,912
- Misc Transport $22,750
- Nuclear Energy $28,650
- Oil & Gas $136,386
- Trucking $37,981
- Waste Management $79,840

Ideological/Single-Issue
- Environmental Issues $29,248

Labor
- Transportation Unions $137,100

Senate Finance Committee

Lloyd Bentsen (D-Texas), Chairman
Bob Packwood (R-Ore), Ranking Republican

Party Ratio: 11 Democrats
9 Republicans

Jurisdiction: (1) Except as provided in the Congressional Budget Act of 1974, revenue measures generally; (2) Except as provided in the Congressional Budget Act of 1974, the bonded debt of the United States; (3) The deposit of public moneys; (4) Customs, collection districts and ports of entry and delivery; (5) Reciprocal trade agreements; (6) Transportation of dutiable goods; (7) Revenue measures relating to the insular possessions; (8) Tariffs and import quotas, and matters related thereto; (9) National social security; (10) General revenue sharing; (11) Health programs under the Social Security Act and health programs financed by a specific tax or trust fund.

Subcommittees

Energy and Agricultural Taxation
Tom Daschle (D-SD), Chairman
Steve Symms (R-Idaho), Ranking Republican

Health for Families and the Uninsured
Donald W. Riegle Jr. (D-Mich), Chairman
John H. Chafee (R-RI), Ranking Republican

Deficits, Debt Management and International Debt
Bill Bradley (D-NJ), Chairman
Orrin G. Hatch (R-Utah), Ranking Republican

International Trade
Max Baucus (D-Mont), Chairman
John C. Danforth (R-Mo), Ranking Republican

Medicare and Long-Term Care
John D. Rockefeller IV (D-WVa), Chairman
Dave Durenberger (R-Minn), Ranking Republican

Private Retirement Plans and Oversight of the Internal Revenue Service
David Pryor (D-Ark), Chairman
Charles E. Grassley (R-Iowa), Ranking Republican

Social Security and Family Policy
Daniel Patrick Moynihan (D-NY), Chairman
Bob Dole (R-Kan), Ranking Republican

Taxation
David L. Boren (D-Okla), Chairman
William V. Roth Jr. (R-Del), Ranking Republican

Total PAC and Large Individual Contributions to Committee Members

Bob Packwood (R-Ore) $3,300,513
John B. Breaux (D-La) $2,225,056
Tom Daschle (D-SD) $2,157,690
Bob Dole (R-Kan) $1,949,015
Charles E. Grassley (R-Iowa) $1,593,319
Lloyd Bentsen (D-Tex) $774,065
Daniel Patrick Moynihan (D-NY) $584,201
Orrin G. Hatch (R-Utah) $364,798
Dave Durenberger (R-Minn) $275,339
John D. Rockefeller IV (D-WVa) $191,950
Steve Symms (R-Idaho) $188,078
Donald W. Riegle Jr. (D-Mich) $180,405
John H. Chafee (R-RI) $128,550
David L. Boren (D-Okla) $34,306
John C. Danforth (R-Mo) $31,975
William V. Roth Jr. (R-Del) $28,210
Max Baucus (D-Mont) $7,000
George J. Mitchell (D-Maine) $4,000
Bill Bradley (D-NJ) $1,215

Top 20 Contributors to Committee Members in 1991-92

1	Time Warner*	$61,500
2	American Bankers Assn	$51,300
3	National Assn of Life Underwriters	$50,500
4	Union Pacific Corp	$50,449
5	Waste Management Inc	$44,687
6	American Express*	$44,250
7	American Medical Assn*	$43,790
8	American Chiropractic Assn*	$42,747
9	National Rifle Assn	$42,600
10	Metropolitan Life/Century 21*	$42,490
11	American Institute of CPA's	$41,000
12	National Cable Television Assn	$41,000
13	American Family Corp	$40,500
14	Salomon Brothers	$40,500
15	American Health Care Assn	$39,750
16	Coastal Corp	$39,000
17	United Parcel Service	$39,000
18	American Council of Life Insurance	$38,782
19	Laborers' Political League	$37,500
20	General Electric	$37,175

* Contributions came from more than one affiliate or subsidiary.

Members in **bold italics** ran for reelection in 1992

Summary

As the Senate committee charged with debating and defining the nation's tax laws, the Senate Finance Committee is one of the most important panels in Congress to virtually every industry in America. It is also one of the most heavily lobbied committees, particularly when major revisions to the tax code are under consideration.

These days, however, the committee's most notable assignment has to do not with taxes, but with health care. As one of the Senate's lead committees charged with remaking the nation's health insurance system, the committee is at the center of the biggest political firestorm to engulf Capitol Hill in years. Even in 1992, before the election of Bill Clinton brought health care reform firmly onto Congress's front burner, the money from health professionals and insurance firms was on the rise. It will undoubtedly continue to flow generously to committee members as the debate intensifies.

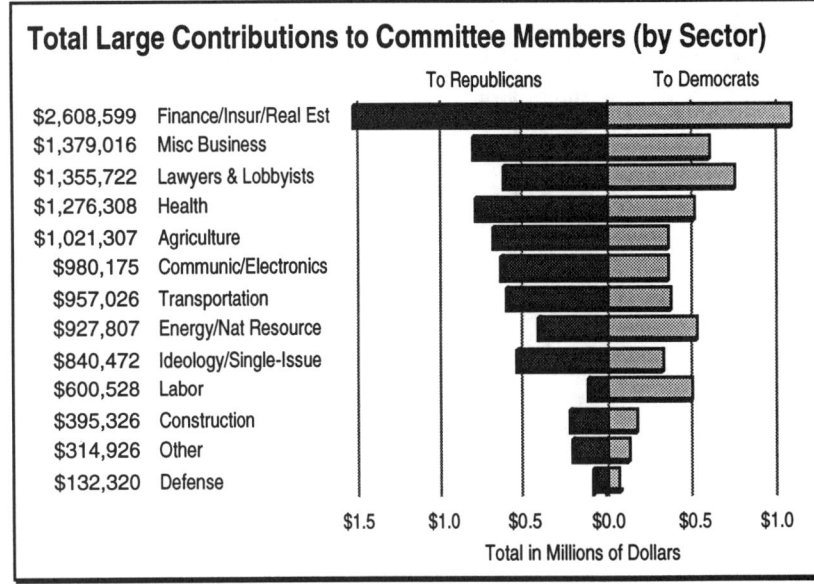

Total Large Contributions to Committee Members (by Sector)

Amount	Sector
$2,608,599	Finance/Insur/Real Est
$1,379,016	Misc Business
$1,355,722	Lawyers & Lobbyists
$1,276,308	Health
$1,021,307	Agriculture
$980,175	Communic/Electronics
$957,026	Transportation
$927,807	Energy/Nat Resource
$840,472	Ideology/Single-Issue
$600,528	Labor
$395,326	Construction
$314,926	Other
$132,320	Defense

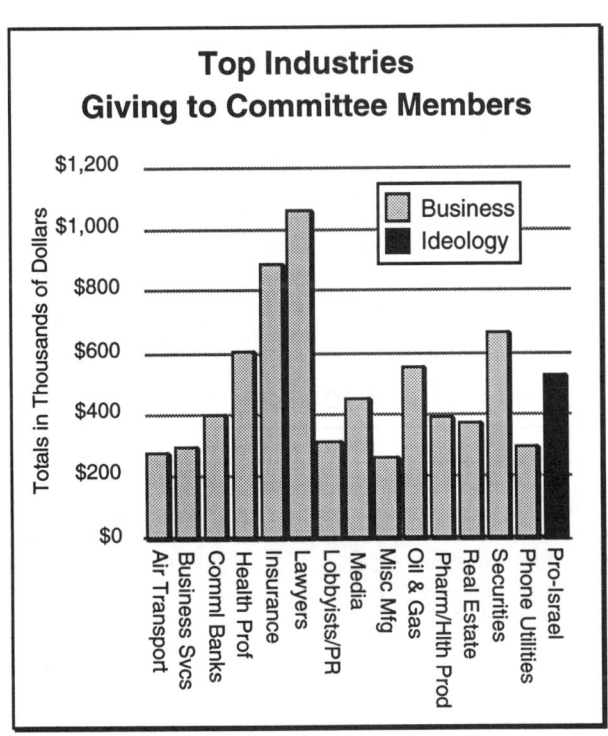

Leading Industries
Giving to Committee Members

Business

Air Transport	$268,577
Business Services	$286,203
Commercial Banks	$387,203
Health Professionals	$600,629
Insurance	$877,060
Lawyers/Law Firms	$1,050,623
Lobbyists/PR	$305,099
Media/Entertainment	$438,725
Misc Manufacturing & Distributing	$251,316
Oil & Gas	$542,517
Pharmaceuticals/Health Products	$380,104
Real Estate	$363,291
Securities & Investment	$657,633
Telephone Utilities	$290,275

Ideological/Single-Issue

Pro-Israel	$521,597

Senate Foreign Relations Committee

Claiborne Pell (D-RI), Chairman
Jesse Helms (R-NC), Ranking Republican

Party Ratio: 11 Democrats
8 Republicans

Jurisdiction: (1) Relations of the United States with foreign nations generally; (2) Treaties and executive agreements, except reciprocal trade agreements; (3) Boundaries of the United States; (4) Protection of United States citizens abroad and expatriation; (5) Intervention abroad and declarations of war; (6) Foreign economic, military, technical and humanitarian assistance;(7) United Nations and its affiliated organizations; (8) International conferences and congresses; (9) Diplomatic service; (10) International law as it relates to foreign policy; (11) Oceans and international environmental and scientific affairs as they relate to foreign policy; (12) International activities of the American National Red Cross and the International Committee of the Red Cross; (13) International aspects of nuclear energy, including nuclear transfer policy; (14) Foreign loans; (15) Measures to foster commercial intercourse with foreign nations and to safeguard American business interests abroad; (16) The World Bank group, the regional development banks and other international organizations established primarily for development assistance purposes; (17) The International Monetary Fund and other international organizations established primarily for international monetary purposes (except that, at the request of the Committee on Banking, Housing and Urban Affairs, any proposed legislation relating to such subjects reported by the Committee on Foreign Relations shall be referred to the Committee on Banking, Housing and Urban Affairs); (18) Acquisition of land and buildings for embassies and legations in foreign countries; (19) National security and international aspects of trusteeships of the United States. In addition, the committee is mandated to study and review matters relating to the national security policy, foreign policy, and international economic policy as it relates to foreign policy of the U.S., and matters relating to food, hunger and nutrition in foreign countries, and to report on these matters periodically.

Subcommittees

African Affairs
Paul Simon (D-Ill), Chairman
Nancy Landon Kassebaum (R-Kan), Ranking Republican

East Asian and Pacific Affairs
Alan Cranston (D-Calif), Chairman
Frank H. Murkowski (R-Alaska), Ranking Republican

European Affairs
Joseph R. Biden Jr. (D-Del), Chairman
Larry Pressler (R-SD), Ranking Republican

International Economic Policy, Trade, Oceans and Environment
Paul S. Sarbanes (D-Md), Chairman
Mitch McConnell (R-Ky), Ranking Republican

Near Eastern and South Asian Affairs
Terry Sanford (D-NC), Chairman
James M. Jeffords (R-Vt), Ranking Republican

Terrorism, Narcotics and International Operations
John Kerry (D-Mass), Chairman
Hank Brown (R-Colo), Ranking Republican

Western Hemisphere and Peace Corps Affairs
Christopher J. Dodd (D-Conn), Chairman
Richard G. Lugar (R-Ind), Ranking Republican

Total PAC and Large Individual Contributions to Committee Members

Harris Wofford (D-Pa) †	$3,309,396
Christopher J. Dodd (D-Conn)	$3,167,767
Terry Sanford (D-NC)	$1,803,161
Frank H. Murkowski (R-Alaska)	$1,362,732
Richard G. Lugar (R-Ind)	$607,269
Daniel Patrick Moynihan (D-NY)	$584,201
John Kerry (D-Mass)	$483,997
Jesse Helms (R-NC)	$224,478
Larry Pressler (R-SD)	$105,350
Mitch McConnell (R-Ky)	$75,650
Paul Simon (D-Ill)	$59,392
Paul S. Sarbanes (D-Md)	$17,148
Charles S. Robb (D-Va)	$13,100
James M. Jeffords (R-Vt)	$6,950
Joseph R. Biden Jr. (D-Del)	$4,000
Hank Brown (R-Colo)	-$1,813
Claiborne Pell (D-RI)	-$4,100
Nancy Landon Kassebaum (R-Kan)	-$10,250
Alan Cranston (D-Calif)	-$272,198

† Wofford's election was in 1991

Members in **bold italics** ran for reelection in 1992

Top 20 Contributors to Committee Members in 1991-92

1	Goldman, Sachs & Co	$43,100
2	Marine Engineers Union*	$41,500
3	American Express*	$40,625
4	Laborers Union*	$39,300
5	Time Warner*	$37,500
6	General Electric*	$36,950
7	US Tobacco	$34,700
8	AT&T	$32,693
9	American Fedn of St/Cnty/Munic Employees	$32,500
10	Federal Express Corp	$32,500
11	Mintz, Levin et al	$31,471
12	Greenwich Capital Markets	$30,250
13	American Federation of Teachers	$30,000
14	MacAndrews & Forbes Group	$29,250
15	American Bankers Assn*	$29,000
16	United Auto Workers	$28,000
17	Barrack, Rodos & Bacine	$27,500
18	Chicago Mercantile Exchange	$27,000
19	National Education Assn	$27,000
20	Merrill Lynch	$26,930

* Contributions came from more than one affiliate or subsidiary.

Summary

The Senate Foreign Relations Committee may be the one committee in Congress that is more important to the world at large than to the community of PACs and other high-level contributors here at home. Since foreign nationals and their governments are prohibited from making direct contributions to U.S. candidates, they must find other means to make their voices heard when the committee debates such issues as the level and focus of American foreign aid.

One group of major contributors that is squarely focused on the committee's deliberations, however, is the community of Pro-Israel PACs and their individual supporters. In all, they delivered over $400,000 to committee members in 1991-92. The two biggest recipients during the last election were Harris Wofford, who collected $172,000 from Pro-Israel groups, and Christopher Dodd, who got $150,000.

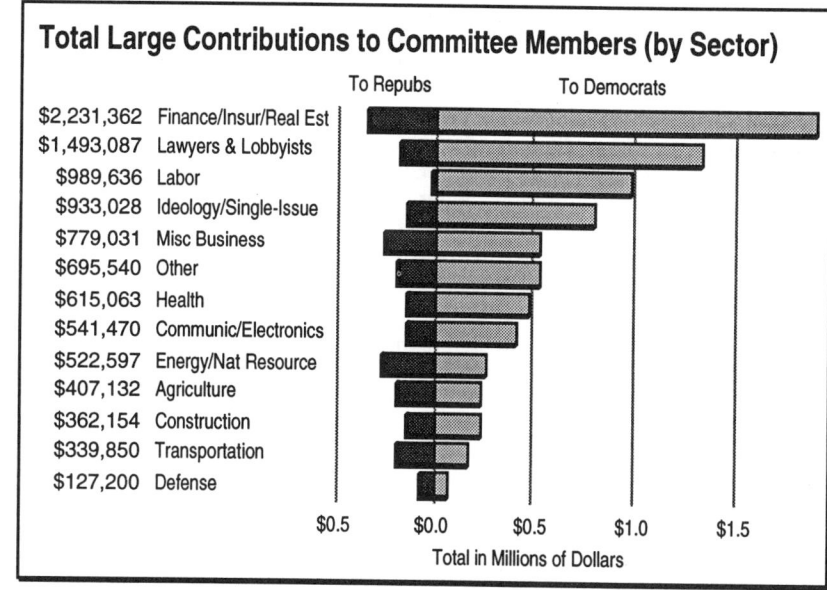

Total Large Contributions to Committee Members (by Sector)

Amount	Sector
$2,231,362	Finance/Insur/Real Est
$1,493,087	Lawyers & Lobbyists
$989,636	Labor
$933,028	Ideology/Single-Issue
$779,031	Misc Business
$695,540	Other
$615,063	Health
$541,470	Communic/Electronics
$522,597	Energy/Nat Resource
$407,132	Agriculture
$362,154	Construction
$339,850	Transportation
$127,200	Defense

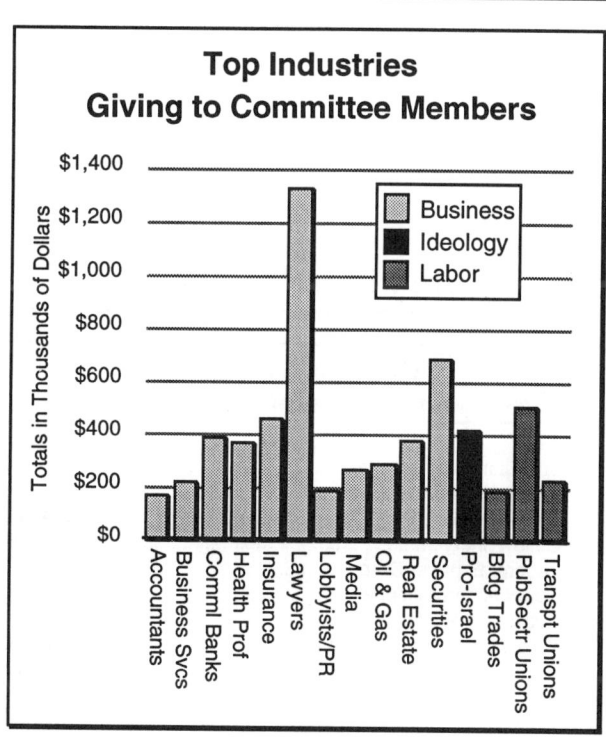

Top Industries Giving to Committee Members

Leading Industries Giving to Committee Members

Business

Accountants	$157,089
Business Services	$209,959
Commercial Banks	$375,670
Health Professionals	$360,289
Insurance	$441,760
Lawyers/Law Firms	$1,319,910
Lobbyists/PR	$173,177
Media/Entertainment	$252,696
Oil & Gas	$274,263
Real Estate	$364,362
Securities & Investment	$677,695

Ideological/Single-Issue

Pro-Israel	$404,800

Labor

Building Trade Unions	$174,550
Public Sector Unions	$500,958
Transportation Unions	$212,456

Senate Governmental Affairs Committee

John Glenn (D-Ohio), Chairman
William V. Roth Jr. (R-Del), Ranking Republican

Party Ratio: 8 Democrats
6 Republicans

Jurisdiction: (1) Except as provided in the Congressional Budget Act of 1974, budget and accounting measures, other than appropriations; (2) Organization and reorganization of the executive branch of the Government; (3) Intergovernmental relations; (4) Government information; (5) Municipal affairs of the District of Columbia, except appropriations therefor; (6) Federal Civil Service; (7) Status of officers and employees of the United States, including their classification, compensation and benefits; (8) Postal Service; (9) Census and collection of statistics, including economic and social statistics; (10) Archives of the United States; (11) Organization and management of United States nuclear export policy; (12) Congressional organization, except for any part of the matter that amends the rules or orders of the Senate. In addition, the committee is mandated to (a) receive and examine reports of the U.S. Comptroller General and submit to the Senate recommendations relating thereto; (b) study the efficiency, economy and effectiveness of the Government's agencies and departments; (c) evaluate the effects of laws enacted to reorganize the legislative and executive branches of the Government; (d) study the intergovernmental relationships between the U.S. and the states and municipalities, and between the U.S. and international organizations of which the U.S. is a member.

Subcommittees

Federal Service, Post Office and Civil Service
David Pryor (D-Ark), Chairman
Ted Stevens (R-Alaska), Ranking Republican

General Service, Federalism and the District of Columbia
Jim Sasser (D-Tenn), Chairman
John Seymour (R-Calif), Ranking Republican

Government Information and Regulation
Herb Kohl (D-Wis), Chairman
Warren B. Rudman (R-NH), Ranking Republican

Oversight of Government Management
Carl Levin (D-Mich), Chairman
William S. Cohen (R-Maine), Ranking Republican

Permanent Subcommittee on Investigations
Sam Nunn (D-Ga), Chairman
William V. Roth Jr. (R-Del), Ranking Republican

Total PAC and Large Individual Contributions to Committee Members

John F. Seymour (R-Calif) $5,126,165
John Glenn (D-Ohio) $2,486,349
Joseph I. Lieberman (D-Conn) $906,337
Daniel K. Akaka (D-Hawaii) $415,958
Jim Sasser (D-Tenn) $152,231
William S. Cohen (R-Maine) $46,200
William V. Roth Jr. (R-Del) $28,210
Ted Stevens (R-Alaska) $8,050
Carl Levin (D-Mich) $2,400
Herb Kohl (D-Wis) $0
Warren B. Rudman (R-NH) $0
Sam Nunn (D-Ga) .... -$35,089

Top 20 Contributors to Committee Members in 1991-92

1	AT&T	$30,900
2	Sun-Diamond Growers*	$27,000
3	Atlantic Richfield	$26,650
4	General Motors*	$24,000
5	Gallo Winery	$22,482
6	Federal Express Corp	$21,000
7	Rockwell International	$20,750
8	Occidental Petroleum	$20,500
9	Forest City Enterprises Inc	$20,000
10	Hudson Valley PAC	$20,000
11	Procter & Gamble	$19,800
12	Walt Disney Co*	$18,750
13	American Dental Assn	$18,500
14	National Assn of Home Builders	$18,500
15	Plumbers/Pipefitters Union*	$18,500
16	Lockheed Corp	$17,900
17	Teamsters Union	$17,500
18	General Electric	$17,450
19	Waste Management Inc	$17,150
20	United Parcel Service	$16,700

* Contributions came from more than one affiliate or subsidiary.

Members in **bold italics** ran for reelection in 1992

Summary

Other committees of Congress have more direct relevance to particular industries or interest groups than Senate Governmental Affairs, which focuses more on the government itself. The federal civil service and postal system do fall within its purview, as does reorganization of executive branch agencies. Affairs relating to the District of Columbia are also debated here.

With the exception of money that came from PACs representing postal workers, the breakdown of contributions by industry and sector among Government Affairs members is more likely affected by the members' other committee assignments than by work specifically done on this committee.

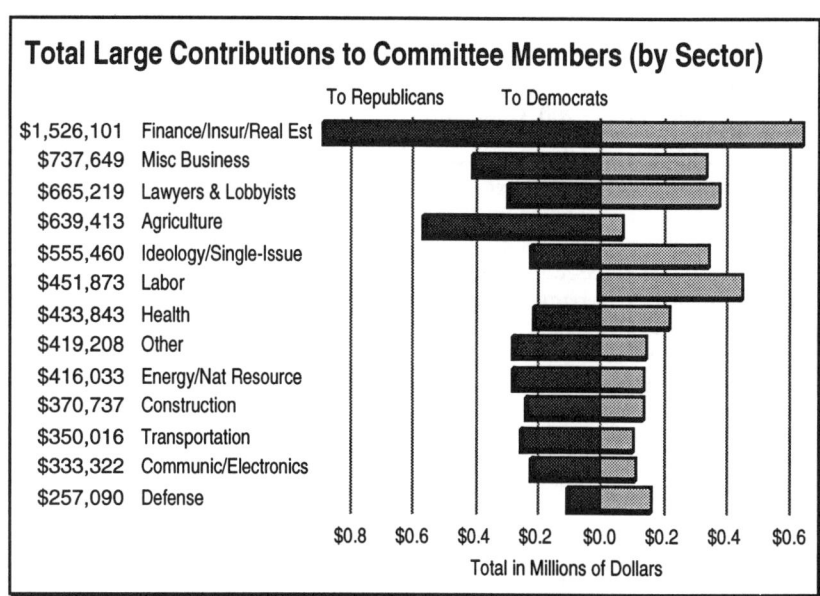

Total Large Contributions to Committee Members (by Sector)

$1,526,101	Finance/Insur/Real Est
$737,649	Misc Business
$665,219	Lawyers & Lobbyists
$639,413	Agriculture
$555,460	Ideology/Single-Issue
$451,873	Labor
$433,843	Health
$419,208	Other
$416,033	Energy/Nat Resource
$370,737	Construction
$350,016	Transportation
$333,322	Communic/Electronics
$257,090	Defense

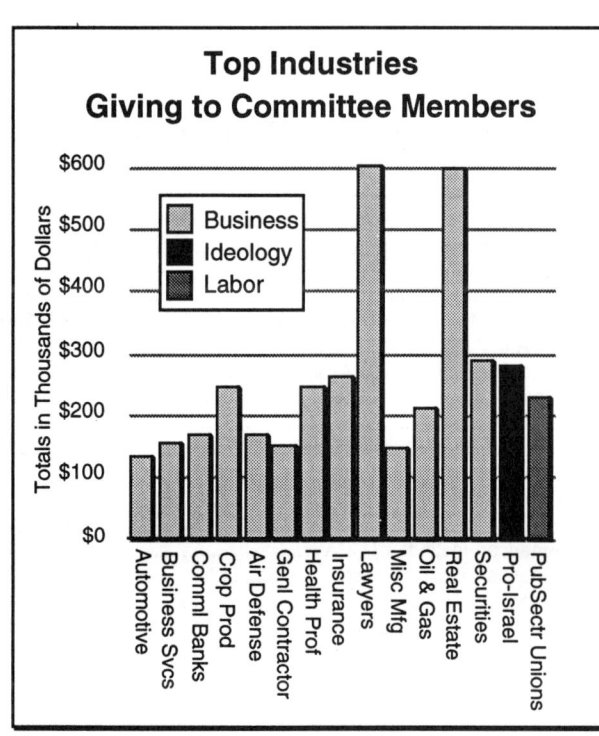

Leading Industries Giving to Committee Members

Business
- Automotive $131,100
- Business Services $153,950
- Commercial Banks $166,367
- Crop Production & Basic Processing $243,087
- Defense Aerospace $166,146
- General Contractors $146,891
- Health Professionals $243,906
- Insurance $259,099
- Lawyers/Law Firms $598,449
- Misc Manufacturing & Distributing $144,700
- Oil & Gas $208,150
- Real Estate $595,467
- Securities & Investment $284,831

Ideological/Single-Issue
- Pro-Israel $275,112

Labor
- Public Sector Unions $223,950

Senate Judiciary Committee

Joseph R. Biden Jr. (D-Del), Chairman
Strom Thurmond (R-SC), Ranking Republican

Party Ratio: 8 Democrats
6 Republicans

Jurisdiction: All areas not delegated to the subcommittees, including but not limited to: (1) Nominations; (2) Holidays, commemorations, Federal charters and celebrations; (3) Department of Justice oversight, authorization and budget; (4) Revision and codification of the statutes of the United States; (5) Criminal justice, including (a) criminal laws, (b) criminal judicial proceedings, (c) Rules of Criminal Procedure, (d) national penitentiaries, (e) Bureau of Prisons, (f) U.S. Parole Commission, (g) oversight of the Criminal Division of the U.S. Department of Justice, (h) juvenile justice, (i) Youthful Offenders Act, (j) oversight of the Office of Justice Programs. (Excluded from (5) above is criminal legislation delegated to the Subcommittee on the Constitution.)

Subcommittees

Antitrust, Monopolies and Business Rights
Howard M. Metzenbaum (D-Ohio), Chairman
Strom Thurmond (R-SC), Ranking Republican

Constitution
Paul Simon (D-Ill), Chairman
Arlen Specter (R-Pa), Ranking Republican

Courts and Administrative Practice
Howell Heflin (D-Ala), Chairman
Charles E. Grassley (R-Iowa), Ranking Republican

Immigration and Refugee Affairs
Edward M. Kennedy (D-Mass), Chairman
Alan K. Simpson (R-Wyo), Ranking Republican

Patents, Copyrights and Trademarks
Dennis DeConcini (D-Ariz), Chairman
Orrin G. Hatch (R-Utah), Ranking Republican

Technology and the Law
Patrick J. Leahy (D-Vt), Chairman
Hank Brown (R-Colo), Ranking Republican

Total PAC and Large Individual Contributions to Committee Members

Arlen Specter (R-Pa)	$5,296,607
Charles E. Grassley (R-Iowa)	$1,593,319
Edward M. Kennedy (D-Mass)	$797,580
Patrick J. Leahy (D-Vt)	$662,722
Orrin G. Hatch (R-Utah)	$364,798
Dennis DeConcini (D-Ariz)	$362,639
Paul Simon (D-Ill)	$59,392
Howell Heflin (D-Ala)	$18,200
Alan K. Simpson (R-Wyo)	$14,000
Joseph R. Biden Jr. (D-Del)	$4,000
Strom Thurmond (R-SC)	$3,230
Herb Kohl (D-Wis)	$0
Hank Brown (R-Colo)	-$1,813

Top 20 Contributors to Committee Members in 1991-92

1	Walt Disney Co*	$38,750
2	National Assn of Independent Insurers	$30,500
3	MCA Inc*	$27,200
4	American Chiropractic Assn	$24,998
5	Morgan, Lewis & Bockius	$23,000
6	General Electric	$22,675
7	National Beer Wholesalers Assn	$22,000
8	Reed, Smith et al	$21,800
9	ConAgra Inc	$21,500
10	Sears*	$21,200
11	American Institute of CPA's	$21,100
12	American Bankers Assn*	$21,000
13	Union Pacific Corp	$20,750
14	National Assn of Realtors	$20,509
15	Citizens Concerned for the Natl Interest	$20,000
16	Citizens Organized PAC	$20,000
17	General Motors*	$20,000
18	National Cable Television Assn	$20,000
19	National Rifle Assn	$19,800
20	Dechert, Price & Rhoads	$19,125

* Contributions came from more than one affiliate or subsidiary.

Members in **bold italics** ran for reelection in 1992

Summary

Though it is most known to the public for its sometimes dramatic hearings on the confirmation of presidential appointments to the Supreme Court, cabinet positions and other top government posts, the Senate Judiciary Committee is also important to a wide range of businesses and industries — none more so than lawyers. From the criminal justice system to antitrust legislation to copyright and patent law, to new areas of the law arising from the birth of new high-tech industries, the committee plays a major role in defining the system of laws that governs the nation.

All that was overshadowed during 1991-92, however, by the committee's nationally televised hearings on the confirmation of Clarence Thomas to the Supreme Court — and most

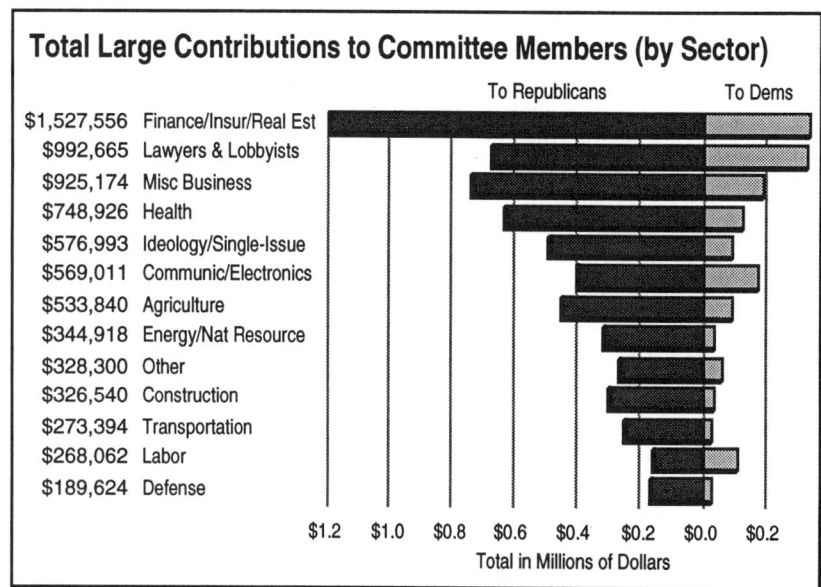

particularly by several members' heavy-handed treatment of witness Anita Hill. The committee's treatment of Hill ignited a firestorm of outrage among women across the nation, and was a catalyst in the decision of a record number of women to seek office themselves. The controversy also helped bring about a massive increase in fund-raising for women's issue PACs — money that helped elect four new women to the U.S. Senate in 1992.

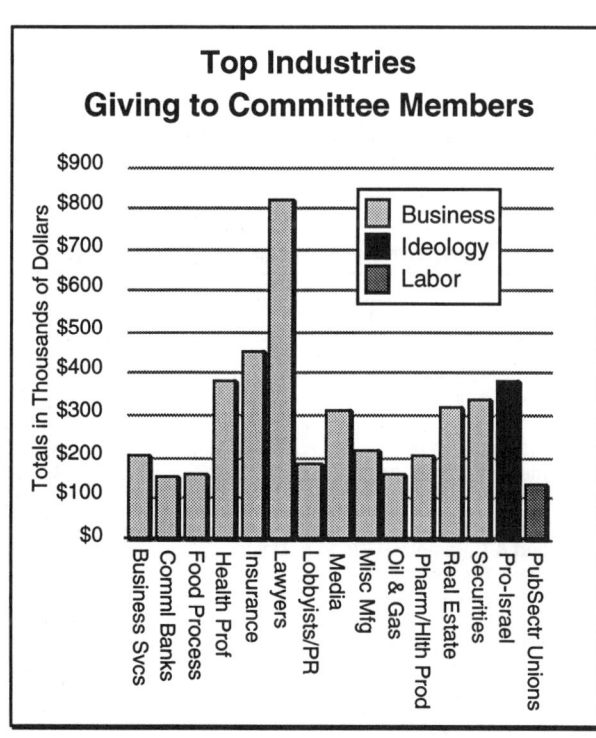

Leading Industries Giving to Committee Members

Business
- Business Services $195,105
- Commercial Banks $142,424
- Food Processing & Sales $151,828
- Health Professionals $377,673
- Insurance $448,567
- Lawyers/Law Firms $813,458
- Lobbyists/PR $179,207
- Media/Entertainment $306,805
- Misc Manufacturing & Distributing $211,627
- Oil & Gas $149,102
- Pharmaceuticals/Health Products $194,860
- Real Estate $311,248
- Securities & Investment $331,869

Ideological/Single-Issue
- Pro-Israel $378,107

Labor
- Public Sector Unions $128,126

Senate Labor and Human Resources Committee

Edward M. Kennedy (D-Mass), Chairman
Orrin G. Hatch (R-Utah), Ranking Republican

Party Ratio: 10 Democrats
7 Republicans

Jurisdiction: (1) Education, labor, health and public welfare; (2) Labor standards and labor statistics; (3) Wages and hours of labor; (4) Child labor; (5) Mediation and arbitration of labor disputes; (6) Convict labor and the entry of goods made by convicts into interstate commerce; (7) Regulation of foreign laborers; (8) Handicapped individuals; (9) Equal employment opportunity; (10) Occupational safety and health, including the welfare of miners; (11) Private pension plans; (12) Aging; (13) Railway labor and retirement; (14) Public health; (15) Arts and humanities; (16) Gallaudet College, Howard University and Saint Elizabeths Hospital; (17) Biomedical research and development; (18) Student loans; (19) Agricultural colleges; (20) Domestic activities of the American Red Cross. The committee is also mandated to study and review matters relating to health, education and training, and public welfare, and to report thereon from time to time.

Subcommittees

Aging
Brock Adams (D-Wash), Chairman
Thad Cochran (R-Miss), Ranking Republican

Children, Family, Drugs and Alcoholism
Christopher J. Dodd (D-Conn), Chairman
Daniel R. Coats (R-Ind), Ranking Republican

Education, Arts and Humanities
Claiborne Pell (D-RI), Chairman
Nancy Landon Kassebaum (R-Kan), Ranking Republican

Employment and Productivity
Paul Simon (D-Ill), Chairman
Strom Thurmond (R-SC), Ranking Republican

Disability Policy
Tom Harkin (D-Iowa), Chairman
Dave Durenberger (R-Minn), Ranking Republican

Labor
Howard M. Metzenbaum (D-Ohio), Chairman
James M. Jeffords (R-Vt), Ranking Republican

Total PAC and Large Individual Contributions to Committee Members

Christopher J. Dodd (D-Conn)	$3,167,767
Daniel R. Coats (R-Ind)	$2,825,825
Tom Harkin (D-Iowa)†	$2,149,567
Barbara A. Mikulski (D-Md)	$1,578,220
Edward M. Kennedy (D-Mass)	$797,580
Brock Adams (D-Wash)	$701,536
Orrin G. Hatch (R-Utah)	$364,798
Dave Durenberger (R-Minn)	$275,339
Jeff Bingaman (D-NM)	$192,522
Paul Wellstone (D-Minn)	$142,017
Paul Simon (D-Ill)	$59,392
Thad Cochran (R-Miss)	$52,600
James M. Jeffords (R-Vt)	$6,950
Strom Thurmond (R-SC)	$3,230
Claiborne Pell (D-RI)	-$4,100
Nancy Landon Kassebaum (R-Kan)	-$10,250

† Includes contributions to his 1992 presidential campaign

Top 20 Contributors to Committee Members in 1991-92

1	Eli Lilly & Co	$49,650
2	American Chiropractic Assn*	$45,698
3	National Assn of Letter Carriers*	$36,040
4	US Tobacco Co	$35,200
5	Time Warner*	$34,500
6	Intl Brotherhood of Electrical Workers	$34,450
7	American Express*	$33,375
8	American Dental Assn	$33,100
9	Seafarers International Union*	$32,150
10	Merrill Lynch	$31,730
11	Food & Commercial Workers Union	$31,500
12	United Technologies*	$31,100
13	United Transportation Union	$31,000
14	American Federation of Teachers	$30,000
15	Bricklayers Union	$30,000
16	Marine Engineers Union*	$30,000
17	Aetna Life & Casualty	$29,350
18	American Council of Life Insurance	$29,284
19	Greenwich Capital Markets	$29,250
20	United Auto Workers	$28,807

* Contributions came from more than one affiliate or subsidiary.

Members in **bold italics** ran for reelection in 1992

Summary

The Senate Labor Committee is the birthplace for many of the standards and rules that govern the American workplace. As such, it is of natural interest to the nation's labor unions, which gave more than a million dollars in contributions to its members in 1991-92. But decisions about labor conditions affect not only workers, but also their employers, who must live by the rules. Consequently, many of the issues discussed and debated by the committee are closely followed by a wide cross-section of business interests. And those businesses delivered substantial campaign contributions to committee members.

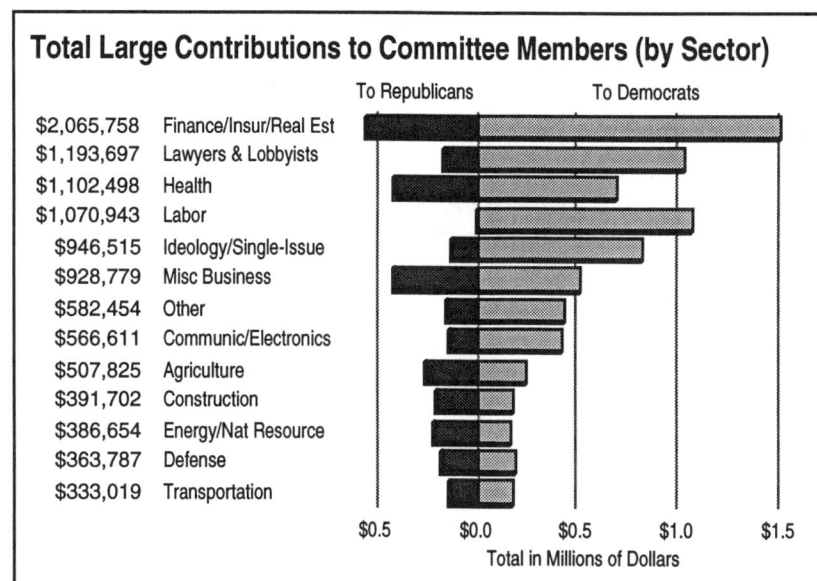

The Labor committee's cash profile reveals another important fact about the relationship between business and labor contributors: if PACs alone are counted, organized labor ranks as the single largest industry group giving to committee members (followed closely by ideological PACs). But if *all* contributors are included — PACs *and* individuals giving $200 or more — labor falls to fourth place. This illustrates the fact that business contributors give heavily both through PACs and individuals, while labor gives almost all its contributions through PACs. Because of that, looking at PAC contributions alone substantially overstates the cash clout of organized labor in American politics and understates the clout of business interests.

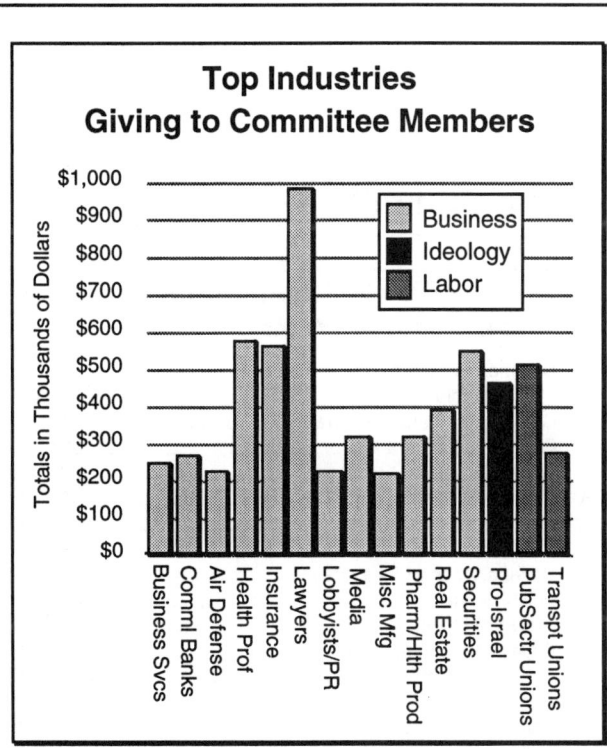

Leading Industries Giving to Committee Members

Business
- Business Services $236,999
- Commercial Banks $258,625
- Defense Aerospace $216,917
- Health Professionals $566,633
- Insurance $556,008
- Lawyers/Law Firms $973,678
- Lobbyists/PR $220,019
- Media/Entertainment $308,203
- Misc Manufacturing & Distributing $212,985
- Pharmaceuticals/Health Products $309,427
- Real Estate $381,554
- Securities & Investment $539,303

Ideological/Single-Issue
- Pro-Israel $452,950

Labor
- Public Sector Unions $507,217
- Transportation Unions $271,256

Senate Rules and Administration Committee

Wendell H. Ford (D-Ky), Chairman
Ted Stevens (R-Alaska), Ranking Republican

Party Ratio: 9 Democrats
7 Republicans

Jurisdiction: (1) Administration of the Senate Office Buildings and the Senate wing of the Capitol, including the assignment of office space; (2) Congressional organization relative to rules and procedures, and Senate rules and regulations, including floor and gallery rules; (3) Corrupt practices; (4) Credentials and qualifications of Members of the Senate, contested elections, and acceptance of incompatible offices; (5) Federal elections generally, including the election of the President, Vice President, and Members of the Congress; (6) Government Printing Office and the printing and correction of the *Congressional Record*, as well as those matters provided for under rule XI; (7) Meetings of the Congress and attendance of Members; (8) Payment of money out of the contingent fund of the Senate or creating a charge upon the same (except that any resolution relating to substantive matter within the jurisdiction of any other standing committee of the Senate shall be first referred to such committee); (9) Presidential succession; (10) Purchase of books and manuscripts and erection of monuments to the memory of individuals; (11) Senate Library and statuary, art and pictures in the Capitol and Senate Office Buildings; (12) Services to the Senate, including the Senate restaurant; (13) United States Capitol and congressional office buildings, the Library of Congress, the Smithsonian Institution (and the incorporation of similar institutions), and the Botanic Garden. The committee is also mandated to (A) make a continuing study of the organization and operation of the Congress of the United States and recommend improvements in such organization and operation with a view toward strengthening the Congress, simplifying its operations, improving its relationships with other branches of the U.S. Government, and enabling it to better meet its responsibilities under the Constitution of the United States; and (B) identify any court proceeding or action which, in its opinion, is of vital interest to the Congress as a constitutionally established institution of the Federal Government and call such proceeding or action to the attention of the Senate.

No Subcommittees

Total PAC and Large Individual Contributions to Committee Members

Christopher J. Dodd (D-Conn) $3,167,767
Daniel K. Inouye (D-Hawaii) $2,398,729
Bob Dole (R-Kan) $1,949,015
Wendell H. Ford (D-Ky) $1,981,781
Brock Adams (D-Wash) $701,536
Daniel Patrick Moynihan (D-NY) $584,201
Dennis DeConcini (D-Ariz) $362,639
Jesse Helms (R-NC) $224,478
Robert C. Byrd (D-WVa) $139,000
Mark O. Hatfield (R-Ore) $96,200
Mitch McConnell (R-Ky) $75,650
Al Gore (D-Tenn) $10,112
Ted Stevens (R-Alaska) $8,050
John W. Warner (R-Va) $4,925
Jake Garn (R-Utah) $1,000
Claiborne Pell (D-RI) ....-$4,100

Top 20 Contributors to Committee Members in 1991-92

1	Salomon Brothers	$51,000
2	Marine Engineers Union*	$46,000
3	Chicago Mercantile Exchange	$44,250
4	Goldman, Sachs & Co	$42,000
5	Time Warner*	$40,500
6	Cassidy & Associates	$40,060
7	American Bankers Assn	$39,500
8	US Tobacco Co	$39,200
9	National Assn of Realtors	$39,100
10	Philip Morris*	$38,848
11	Laborers Union*	$37,800
12	Waste Management Inc	$37,687
13	American Express*	$37,625
14	General Electric	$36,350
15	United Parcel Service	$36,250
16	Federal Express Corp	$36,000
17	Teamsters Union	$35,000
18	Akin, Gump et al	$34,349
19	AFL-CIO*	$33,950
20	American Institute of CPA's	$32,250

* Contributions came from more than one affiliate or subsidiary.

Members in **bold italics** ran for reelection in 1992

Summary

In any legislative body, the key to success often lies in a mastery of the body's rules and procedures. Those rules — from the assignment of office space to the conducting of business on the Senate floor and even the rules governing federal elections — are debated within this committee.

As part of its role in setting election procedures, the committee is also at center stage in revising the laws governing campaign financing. The rules governing PACs, the spending limits and reporting requirements of contributors to federal campaigns, the oversight of the process by the Federal Election Commission — all these elements of American elections fall within the jurisdiction of the Senate Rules Committee.

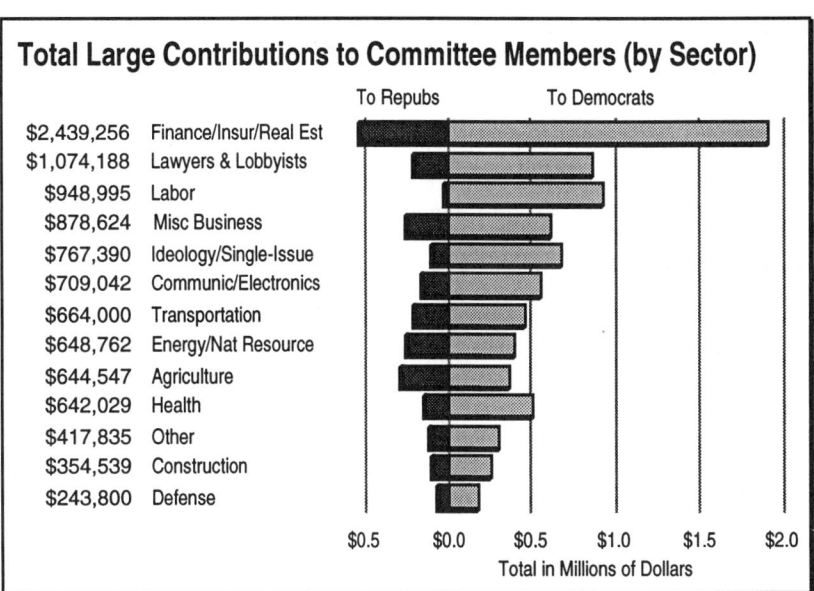

Total Large Contributions to Committee Members (by Sector)

Amount	Sector
$2,439,256	Finance/Insur/Real Est
$1,074,188	Lawyers & Lobbyists
$948,995	Labor
$878,624	Misc Business
$767,390	Ideology/Single-Issue
$709,042	Communic/Electronics
$664,000	Transportation
$648,762	Energy/Nat Resource
$644,547	Agriculture
$642,029	Health
$417,835	Other
$354,539	Construction
$243,800	Defense

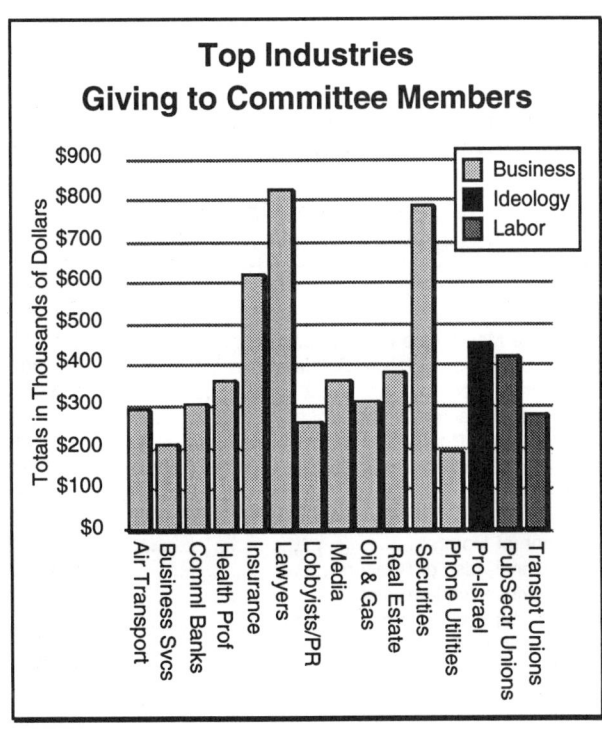

Leading Industries Giving to Committee Members

Business
- Air Transport $284,270
- Business Services $202,988
- Commercial Banks $302,365
- Health Professionals $360,254
- Insurance $615,401
- Lawyers/Law Firms $818,078
- Lobbyists/PR $256,110
- Media/Entertainment $359,460
- Oil & Gas $308,536
- Real Estate $377,629
- Securities & Investment $778,749
- Telephone Utilities $181,272

Ideological/Single-Issue
- Pro-Israel $448,455

Labor
- Public Sector Unions $417,979
- Transportation Unions $272,600

Senate Small Business Committee

Dale Bumpers (D-Ark), Chairman
Bob Kasten (R-Wis), Ranking Republican

Party Ratio: 11 Democrats
8 Republicans

Jurisdiction: (1) All legislation referred to the committee; (2) Jurisdiction over all matters related to the Small Business Administration; (3) Study and survey, through research and investigation, of all problems of American small business enterprises.

Subcommittees

Competition and Economic Opportunity
Joseph I. Lieberman (D-Conn), Chairman
Connie Mack (R-Fla), Ranking Republican

Export Expansion
Barbara A. Mikulski (D-Md), Chairwoman
Larry Pressler (R-SD), Ranking Republican

Government Contracting and Paperwork Reduction
Alan J. Dixon (D-Ill), Chairman
Christopher S. Bond (R-Mo), Ranking Republican

Innovation, Technology and Productivity
Carl Levin (D-Mich), Chairman
Ted Stevens (R-Alaska), Ranking Republican

Rural Economy and Family Farming
Max Baucus (D-Mont), Chairman
Bob Kasten (R-Wis), Ranking Republican

Urban and Minority-Owned Business Development
John Kerry (D-Mass), Chairman
Conrad Burns (R-Mont), Ranking Republican

Total PAC and Large Individual Contributions to Committee Members

John F. Seymour (R-Calif)	$5,126,165
Bob Kasten (R-Wis)	$4,009,220
Harris Wofford (D-Pa)[1]	$3,309,396
Christopher S. Bond (R-Mo)	$3,232,383
Tom Harkin (D-Iowa)[2]	$2,149,567
Dale Bumpers (D-Ark)	$1,648,431
Barbara A. Mikulski (D-Md)	$1,578,220
Alan J. Dixon (D-Ill)	$1,383,511
Joseph I. Lieberman (D-Conn)	$906,337
Connie Mack (R-Fla)	$726,909
John Kerry (D-Mass)	$483,997
Conrad Burns (R-Mont)	$256,346
Paul Wellstone (D-Minn)	$142,017
Larry Pressler (R-SD)	$105,350
Malcolm Wallop (R-Wyo)	$53,215
Ted Stevens (R-Alaska)	$8,050
Max Baucus (D-Mont)	$7,000
Carl Levin (D-Mich)	$2,400
Sam Nunn (D-Ga)	-$35,089

[1] Wofford's election was in 1991
[2] Includes contributions to his 1992 presidential campaign

Top 20 Contributors to Committee Members in 1991-92

1	American Dental Assn	$57,000
2	US Tobacco*	$55,570
3	Waste Management Inc	$55,150
4	National Assn of Home Builders	$55,000
5	General Electric*	$54,200
6	Chicago Mercantile Exchange	$51,650
7	McDonnell Douglas*	$50,435
8	National Assn of Letter Carriers*	$50,040
9	Federal Express Corp	$47,300
10	Assn of Trial Lawyers of America	$46,000
11	General Motors*	$44,750
12	National Assn of Realtors	$44,699
13	American Bankers Assn*	$44,450
14	National Beer Wholesalers Assn	$44,200
15	Associated General Contractors	$42,000
16	Philip Morris*	$41,532
17	Anheuser-Busch	$41,250
18	AT&T	$40,200
19	National Assn of Life Underwriters	$40,000
20	National PAC	$40,000

* Contributions came from more than one affiliate or subsidiary.

Members in ***bold italics*** ran for reelection in 1992

Summary

Its statement of jurisdiction is the shortest of all Senate committees, but the expanse of that jurisdiction reaches into every city and town across America. Overseeing the concerns of small business — from the corner grocery to the family farm — is the committee's charge, and considering the fact that both the corner grocery and the family farm are endangered species in America today, the concerns of small business are large indeed.

As with most committees in the Senate, the single biggest source of campaign funds to committee members came from the Finance/Insurance/Real Estate sector, while lawyers and law firms, as seen in the chart below, were the top-ranking industry.

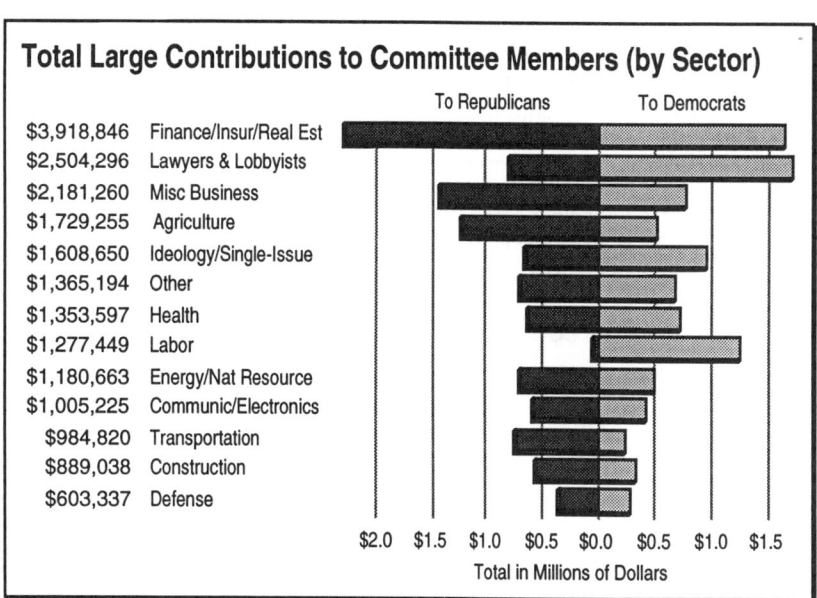

Total Large Contributions to Committee Members (by Sector)

Amount	Sector
$3,918,846	Finance/Insur/Real Est
$2,504,296	Lawyers & Lobbyists
$2,181,260	Misc Business
$1,729,255	Agriculture
$1,608,650	Ideology/Single-Issue
$1,365,194	Other
$1,353,597	Health
$1,277,449	Labor
$1,180,663	Energy/Nat Resource
$1,005,225	Communic/Electronics
$984,820	Transportation
$889,038	Construction
$603,337	Defense

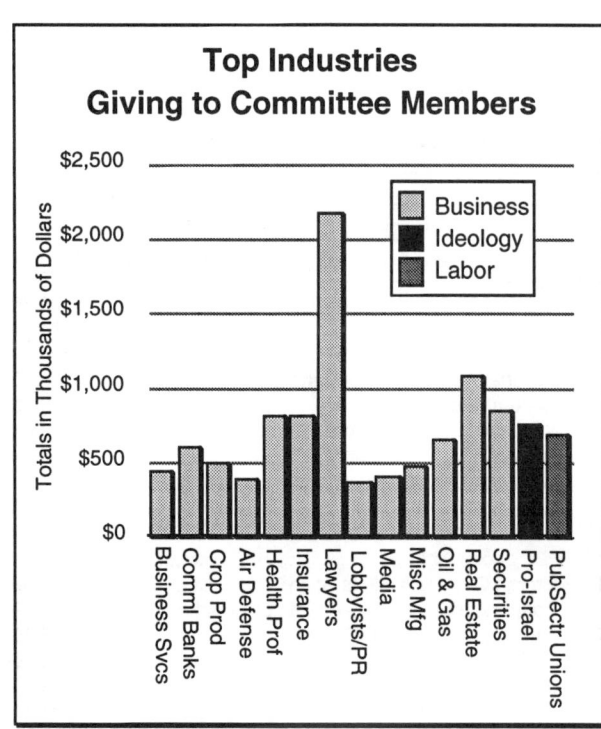

Leading Industries Giving to Committee Members

Business
- Business Services $421,158
- Commercial Banks $581,747
- Crop Production & Basic Processing $472,052
- Defense Aerospace $371,657
- Health Professionals $798,840
- Insurance $795,009
- Lawyers/Law Firms $2,159,383
- Lobbyists/PR $344,913
- Media/Entertainment $388,310
- Misc Manufacturing & Distributing $456,494
- Oil & Gas $630,754
- Real Estate $1,057,133
- Securities & Investment $834,177

Ideological/Single-Issue
- Pro-Israel $747,366

Labor
- Public Sector Unions $665,052

Senate Veterans' Affairs Committee

Alan Cranston (D-Calif), Chairman
Arlen Specter (R-Pa), Ranking Republican

Party Ratio: 7 Democrats
5 Republicans

Jurisdiction: Veterans' measures generally; (2) Pensions of all wars of the U.S., general and special; (3) Life insurance issued by the Government on account of service in the Armed Forces; (4) Compensation of veterans; (5) Vocational rehabilitation and education of veterans; (6) Veterans' hospitals, medical care and treatment of veterans; (7) Soldiers' and sailors' civil relief; (8) Readjustment of servicemen to civil life; (9) National cemeteries.

No Subcommittees

Total PAC and Large Individual Contributions to Committee Members

Arlen Specter (R-Pa) $5,296,607
Bob Graham (D-Fla) $2,508,277
Tom Daschle (D-SD) $2,157,690
Frank H. Murkowski (R-Alaska) $1,362,732
Daniel K. Akaka (D-Hawaii) $415,958
Dennis DeConcini (D-Ariz) $362,639
John D. Rockefeller IV (D-WVa) $191,950
Alan K. Simpson (R-Wyo) $14,000
James M. Jeffords (R-Vt) $6,950
George J. Mitchell (D-Maine) $4,000
Strom Thurmond (R-SC) $3,230
Alan Cranston (D-Calif) .... -$272,198

Top 20 Contributors to Committee Members in 1991-92

1	National Cable Television Assn	$35,000
2	American Dental Assn	$34,500
3	Marine Engineers Union*	$34,000
4	National Assn of Life Underwriters	$33,000
5	General Electric	$30,100
6	National Assn of Realtors	$29,350
7	American Medical Assn*	$28,224
8	American Bankers Assn*	$27,900
9	Laborers Union*	$27,500
10	National Assn of Home Builders	$27,500
11	FPL Group Inc*	$26,750
12	Aircraft Owners & Pilots Assn	$25,500
13	Independent Insurance Agents of America	$25,499
14	American Institute of CPA's	$25,250
15	Desert Caucus	$25,000
16	United Transportation Union	$25,000
17	Barnett Banks Inc	$24,676
18	American Federation of Teachers	$24,500
19	Assn of Trial Lawyers of America	$24,500
20	National Venture Capital Assn	$24,500

* Contributions came from more than one affiliate or subsidiary.

Members in ***bold italics*** ran for reelection in 1992

Summary

Insurance companies and health professionals were among the major contributors to the Senate Veterans Affairs Committee in 1991-92, ranking only behind lawyers and law firms among business groups. While government life insurance to veterans does fall within its jurisdiction, as does the VA hospital system, most of the committee's work does not directly affect any particular segments of American business in a major way. Perhaps because of this, the Veterans Affairs Committee has never been a central focus of political fundraising on Capitol Hill.

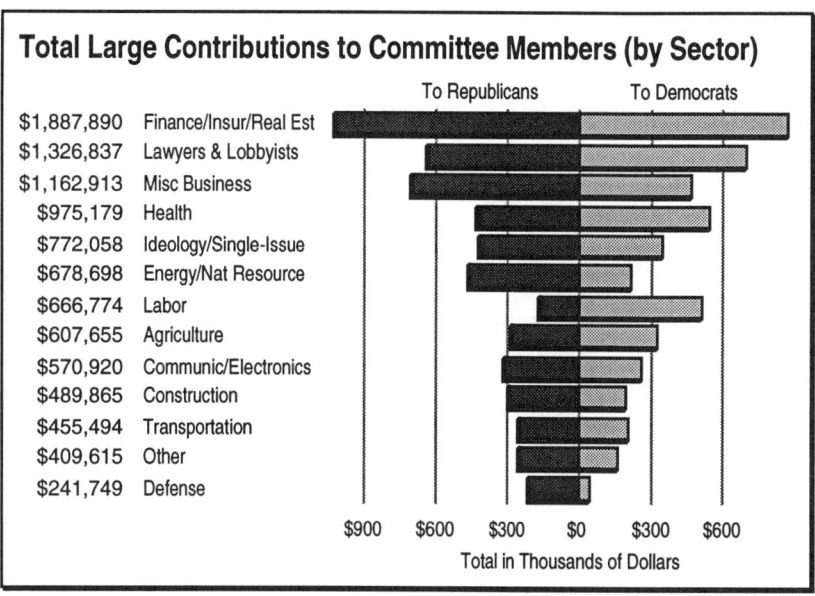

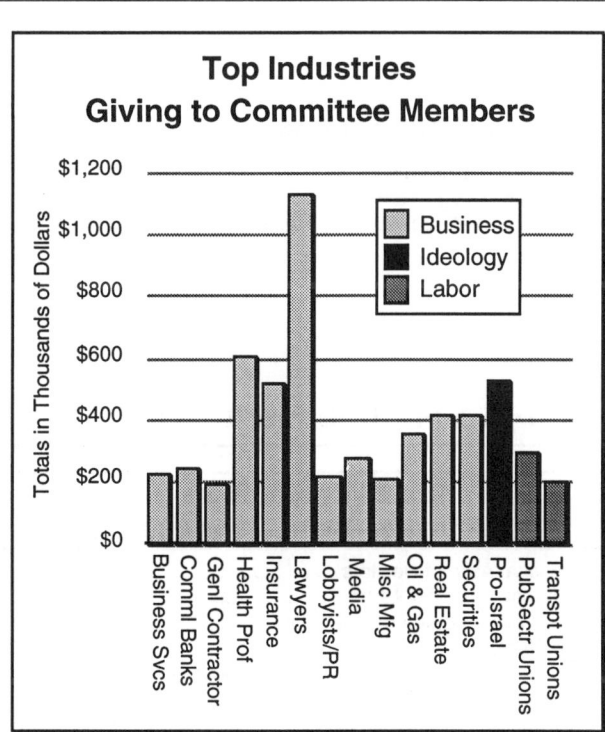

Leading Industries Giving to Committee Members

Business

Business Services	$221,572
Commercial Banks	$236,427
General Contractors	$187,451
Health Professionals	$592,640
Insurance	$510,449
Lawyers/Law Firms	$1,115,646
Lobbyists/PR	$211,191
Media/Entertainment	$268,331
Misc Manufacturing & Distributing	$204,500
Oil & Gas	$345,727
Real Estate	$405,991
Securities & Investment	$408,255

Ideological/Single-Issue

Pro-Israel	$522,171

Labor

Public Sector Unions	$292,020
Transportation Unions	$193,500

House Administration Committee

Charlie Rose (D-NC), Chairman
Bill Thomas (R-Calif), Ranking Republican

Party Ratio: 15 Democrats
9 Republicans

Jurisdiction: (1) Appropriations from the contingent fund; (2) Auditing and settling of all accounts which may be charged to the contingent fund; (3) Employment of persons by the House, including clerks for Members and committees, and reporters of debates; (4) Matters relating to the Library of Congress and the House Library; statuary and pictures; acceptance or purchase of works of art for the Capitol; the Botanic Gardens; management of the Library of Congress, purchase of books and manuscripts; erection of monuments to the memory of individuals; (5) Matters relating to the Smithsonian Institution and the incorporation of similar institutions; (6) Expenditure of contingent fund of the House; (7) Matters relating to printing and correction of the Congressional Record; (8) Measures relating to accounts of the House generally; (9) Measures relating to assignment of office space for Members and committees; (10) measures relating to the disposition of useless executive papers; (11) Measures relating to the election of the President, Vice President or Members of Congress; corrupt practices; contested elections; credentials and qualifications; and Federal elections generally; (12) Measures relating to services to the House, including the House Restaurant, parking facilities and administration of the House office Buildings and of the House wing of the Capitol; (13) Measures relating to the travel of Members of the House; (14) Measures relating to the raising, reporting and use of campaign contributions for candidates for office of Representative in the House of Representatives and of Resident Commissioner to the United States from Puerto Rico; (15) Measures relating to the compensation, retirement and other benefits of the Members, officers and employees of the Congress.

Subcommittees

Accounts
Joseph M. Gaydos (D-Pa), Chairman
Paul E. Gillmor (R-Ohio), Ranking Republican

Elections
Al Swift (D-Wash), Chairman
Bob Livingston (R-La), Ranking Republican

Libraries and Memorials
William L. Clay (D-Mo), Chairman
Bill Barrett (R-Neb), Ranking Republican

Office Systems
Sam Gejdenson (D-Conn), Chairman
James T. Walsh (R-NY), Ranking Republican

Personnel and Police
Mary Rose Oakar (D-Ohio), Chairwoman
Pat Roberts (R-Kan), Ranking Republican

Procurement and Printing
Frank Annunzio (D-Ill), Chairman
Mickey Edwards (R-Okla), Ranking Republican

Total PAC and Large Individual Contributions to Committee Members

Newt Gingrich (R-Ga)	$1,419,505
Steny H. Hoyer (D-Md)	$1,091,486
Martin Frost (D-Texas)	$1,079,404
Marty Russo (D-Ill)	$990,657
Mary Rose Oakar (D-Ohio)	$860,393
Al Swift (D-Wash)	$781,229
Sam Gejdenson (D-Conn)	$571,167
Dale E. Kildee (D-Mich)	$558,660
Thomas J. Manton (D-NY)	$516,378
Bill Thomas (R-Calif)	$469,226
Mickey Edwards (R-Okla)	$388,827
Charlie Rose (D-NC)	$323,975
Bill Barrett (R-Neb)	$301,454
Leon E. Panetta (D-Calif)	$300,800
William L. Clay (D-Mo)	$282,938
William H. Gray III (D-Pa)†	$267,995
Gerald D. Kleczka (D-Wis)	$261,040
Robert L. Livingston (R-La)	$231,250
Pat Roberts (R-Kan)	$223,912
Paul E. Gillmor (R-Ohio)	$205,782
James T. Walsh (R-NY)	$136,553
Joe Kolter (D-Pa)	$117,475
Bill Dickinson (R-Ala)	$54,780
Joseph M. Gaydos (D-Pa)	$45,800
Frank Annunzio (D-Ill)	$42,720

† Resigned in September 1991

Top 20 Contributors to Committee Members in 1991-92

1	National Assn of Realtors	$127,780
2	American Medical Assn*	$122,950
3	Assn of Trial Lawyers of America	$110,500
4	Teamsters Union*	$107,000
5	American Fedn of St/Cnty/Munic Employees	$89,600
6	National Assn of Letter Carriers	$89,475
7	United Auto Workers	$81,000
8	National Education Assn	$78,500
9	Carpenters & Joiners Union*	$78,000
10	National Assn Retired Federal Employees	$76,500
11	American Bankers Assn*	$74,170
12	Air Line Pilots Assn	$70,500
13	Laborers Union*	$69,450
14	United Parcel Service	$65,925
15	Marine Engineers Union*	$63,500
16	American Postal Workers Union	$63,000
17	American Institute of CPA's	$62,100
18	Machinists/Aerospace Workers Union	$62,000
19	AT&T	$61,000
20	National Assn of Life Underwriters	$60,000

* Contributions came from more than one affiliate or subsidiary.

Summary

Since the Committee on House Administration is more concerned with matters internal to the House than to the world of industry and commerce beyond it, the pattern of contributions to its members closely parallels that of the rest of Congress. In fact, 16 of the Top 20 contributors to committee members also rank among the top 20 contributors to Congress as a whole.

In one respect, the committee does figure prominently in the world of money and politics on Capital Hill. Its subcommittee on Elections is the panel that oversees the drafting of changes in the nation's campaign finance laws.

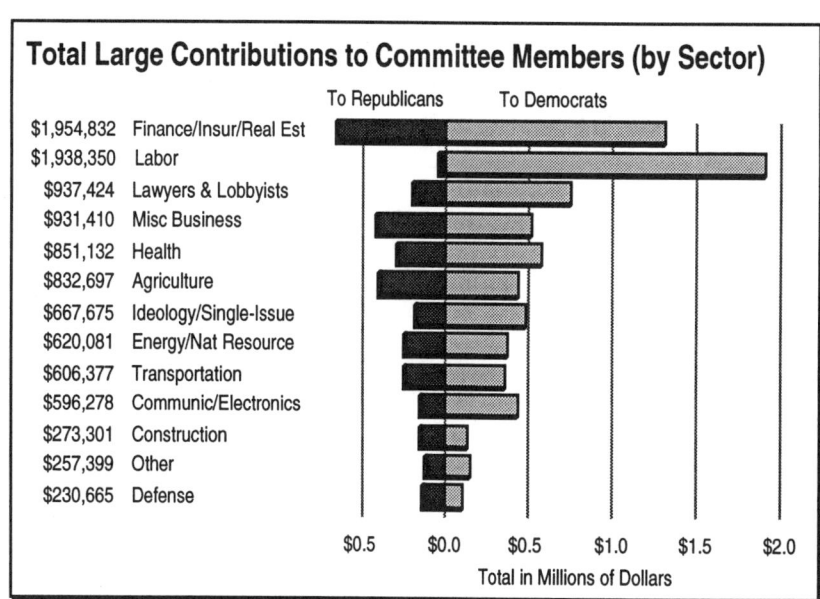

Total Large Contributions to Committee Members (by Sector)

$1,954,832	Finance/Insur/Real Est
$1,938,350	Labor
$937,424	Lawyers & Lobbyists
$931,410	Misc Business
$851,132	Health
$832,697	Agriculture
$667,675	Ideology/Single-Issue
$620,081	Energy/Nat Resource
$606,377	Transportation
$596,278	Communic/Electronics
$273,301	Construction
$257,399	Other
$230,665	Defense

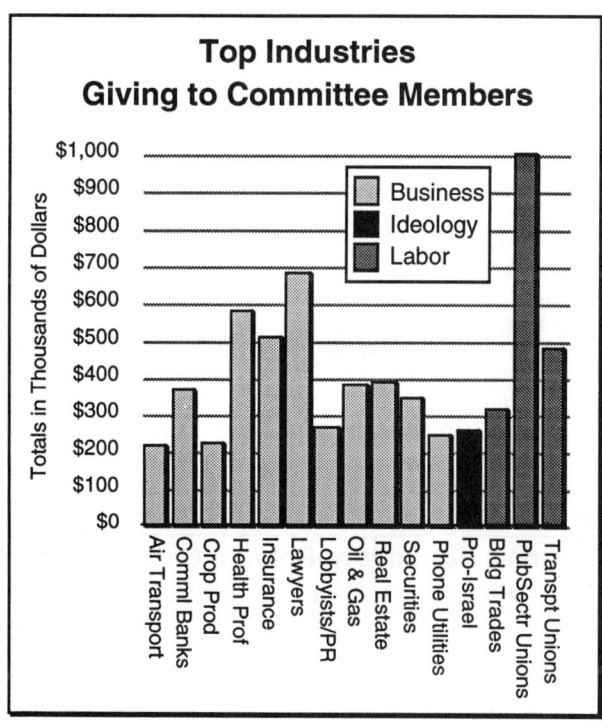

Leading Industries
Giving to Committee Members

Business
- Air Transport $211,549
- Commercial Banks $358,416
- Crop Production & Basic Processing $219,275
- Health Professionals $573,407
- Insurance $504,013
- Lawyers/Law Firms $677,887
- Lobbyists/PR $259,537
- Oil & Gas $376,093
- Real Estate $386,228
- Securities & Investment $338,133
- Telephone Utilities $238,870

Ideological/Single-Issue
- Pro-Israel $256,537

Labor
- Building Trade Unions $309,500
- Public Sector Unions $1,000,666
- Transportation Unions $474,330

House Agriculture Committee

Kika de la Garza (D-Texas), Chairman
Tom Coleman (R-Mo), Ranking Republican

Party Ratio: 27 Democrats
18 Republicans

Jurisdiction: (1) Adulteration of seeds, insect pests, and protection of birds and animals in forest reserves; (2) Agriculture generally; (3) Agricultural and industrial chemistry; (4) Agricultural colleges and experimental stations; (5) Agricultural economics and research; (6) Agricultural education extension services; (7) Agricultural production and marketing and stabilization of prices of agricultural products and commodities (not including distribution outside the United States); (8) Animal industry and diseases of animals; (9) Crop insurance and soil conservation; (10) Dairy industry; (11) Entomology and plant quarantine; (12) Extension of farm credit and farm security; (13) Forestry in general, and forest reserves other than those created from the public domain; (14) Human nutrition and home economics; (15) Inspection of livestock and meat products; (16) Plant industry, soils, and agricultural engineering; (17) Rural electrification; (18) Commodities exchanges; (19) Rural development.

Subcommittees

Conservation, Credit and Rural Development
Glenn English (D-Okla), Chairman
Bob Smith (R-Ore), Ranking Republican

Cotton, Rice and Sugar
Jerry Huckaby (D-La), Chairman
Bill Emerson (R-Mo), Ranking Republican

Department Operations, Research and Foreign Agriculture
Charlie Rose (D-NC), Chairman
Pat Roberts (R-Kan), Ranking Republican

Livestock, Dairy and Poultry
Charles W. Stenholm (D-Texas), Chairman
Steve Gunderson (R-Wis), Ranking Republican

Tobacco and Peanuts
Charlie Hatcher (D-Ga), Chairman
Larry J. Hopkins (R-Ky), Ranking Republican

Wheat, Soybeans and Feed Grains
Dan Glickman (D-Kan), Chairman
Ron Marlenee (R-Mont), Ranking Republican

Total Agriculture-Related Contributions to Committee Members

	Total from Cmte-Related Contribs	Pct of Member's Lg Contribs
Ron Marlenee (R-Mont)	$191,805	24%
Jerry Huckaby (D-La)	$189,374	48%
Charles Hatcher (D-Ga)	$180,121	52%
Wally Herger (R-Calif)	$159,098	39%
E. "Kika" de la Garza (D-Texas)	$157,599	72%
Tom Coleman (R-Mo)	$148,475	36%
Calvin Dooley (D-Calif)	$148,223	39%
Charles W. Stenholm (D-Texas)	$148,003	44%
Bill Emerson (R-Mo)	$146,925	36%
Ben Nighthorse Campbell (D-Colo)†	$121,574	9%
Bob Smith (R-Ore)	$118,487	47%
Bill Sarpalius (D-Texas)	$114,781	25%
Jim Nussle (R-Iowa)	$97,682	18%
Pat Roberts (R-Kan)	$97,525	44%
Richard Stallings (D-Idaho)†	$96,430	12%
Steve Gunderson (R-Wis)	$93,316	30%
Glenn English (D-Okla)	$92,550	32%
Wayne Allard (R-Colo)	$90,038	23%
Charlie Rose (D-NC)	$89,275	28%
Gary Condit (D-Calif)	$89,272	38%
Tom Lewis (R-Fla)	$87,793	41%
Dan Glickman (D-Kan)	$71,100	10%
Mike Espy (D-Miss)	$68,350	24%
Collin C. Peterson (D-Minn)	$68,267	20%
John A. Boehner (R-Ohio)	$67,538	20%
Dave Camp (R-Mich)	$67,255	19%
Harold L. Volkmer (D-Mo)	$67,008	25%
Thomas W. Ewing (R-Ill)	$65,189	17%
Bill Barrett (R-Neb)	$64,890	22%
Jill L. Long (D-Ind)	$61,500	21%
Larry Combest (R-Texas)	$57,380	33%
Dave Nagle (D-Iowa)	$56,555	10%
Leon E. Panetta (D-Calif)	$55,900	19%
Tim Johnson (D-SD)	$54,775	20%
George E. Brown Jr. (D-Calif)	$52,550	8%
Jim Jontz (D-Ind)	$50,450	12%
Mike Kopetski (D-Ore)	$41,337	12%
Robin Tallon (D-SC)	$38,950	41%
Timothy J. Penny (D-Minn)	$35,450	34%
Harley O. Staggers Jr. (D-WVa)	$20,000	11%
James T. Walsh (R-NY)	$16,100	12%
Jim Olin (D-Va)	$10,075	38%
Richard Stallings (D-Idaho)	$9,850	15%
Larry J. Hopkins (R-Ky)	$5,500	100%
Sid Morrison (R-Wash)	$4,000	39%
Walter B. Jones (D-NC)	$3,650	22%

† Ran for US Senate in 1992

Top 20 Agriculture-Related Contributors to Committee Members in 1991-92

1	Associated Milk Producers	$165,300
2	ConAgra Inc	$98,450
3	National Cattlemen's Assn*	$92,550
4	ACRE (Action Cmte for Rural Electrification)*	$82,750
5	American Crystal Sugar Corp	$80,400
6	Chicago Mercantile Exchange	$78,950
7	RJR Nabisco	$72,250
8	Mid-America Dairymen	$72,150
9	Food Marketing Institute	$68,970
10	American Veterinary Medical Assn	$68,500
11	American Sugarbeet Growers Assn	$68,150
12	American Assn of Crop Insurers	$63,900
13	National Cotton Council	$63,105
14	Philip Morris*	$62,345
15	National Broiler Council	$48,200
16	Chicago Board of Trade	$46,850
17	Farm Credit Council	$46,755
18	American Meat Institute	$41,581
19	National Council of Farmer Co-ops	$39,400
20	National Pork Producers Council	$38,551

* Contributions came from more than one affiliate or subsidiary.

Summary

Farmers and agribusiness corporations involved in the production of crops were the leading source of campaign funds for members of the House Agriculture committee, but committee members also drew contributions from many other agriculture-related industries. Dairy farmers, agricultural chemical manufacturers, and a wide variety of agricultural service companies were also major sources of cash, as were livestock and poultry producers, commodities brokers, tobacco companies and timber and paper producers. Within the crop production sector, sugar growers led all other groups by a wide margin — a reflection of the importance of sugar in the American diet and also the role of federal subsidies in sweetening the growers' profits.

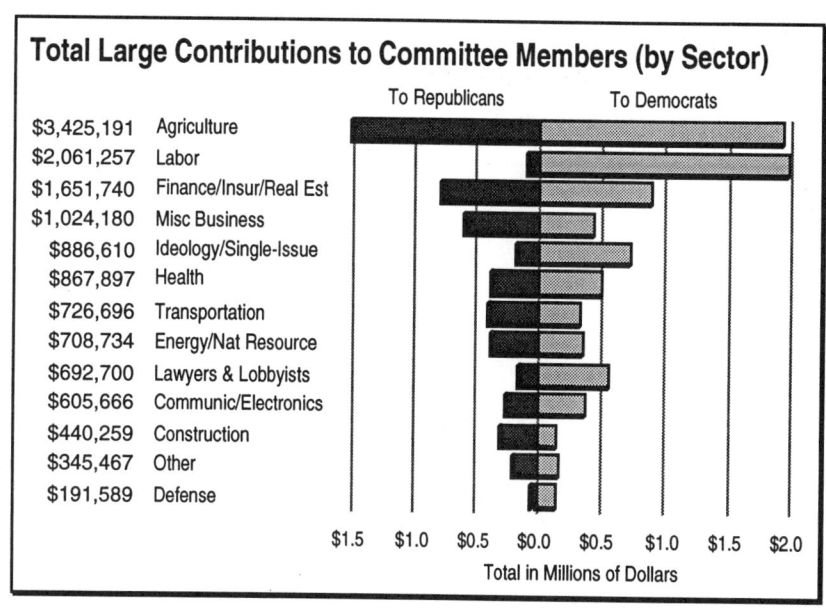

Total Large Contributions to Committee Members (by Sector)

Amount	Sector
$3,425,191	Agriculture
$2,061,257	Labor
$1,651,740	Finance/Insur/Real Est
$1,024,180	Misc Business
$886,610	Ideology/Single-Issue
$867,897	Health
$726,696	Transportation
$708,734	Energy/Nat Resource
$692,700	Lawyers & Lobbyists
$605,666	Communic/Electronics
$440,259	Construction
$345,467	Other
$191,589	Defense

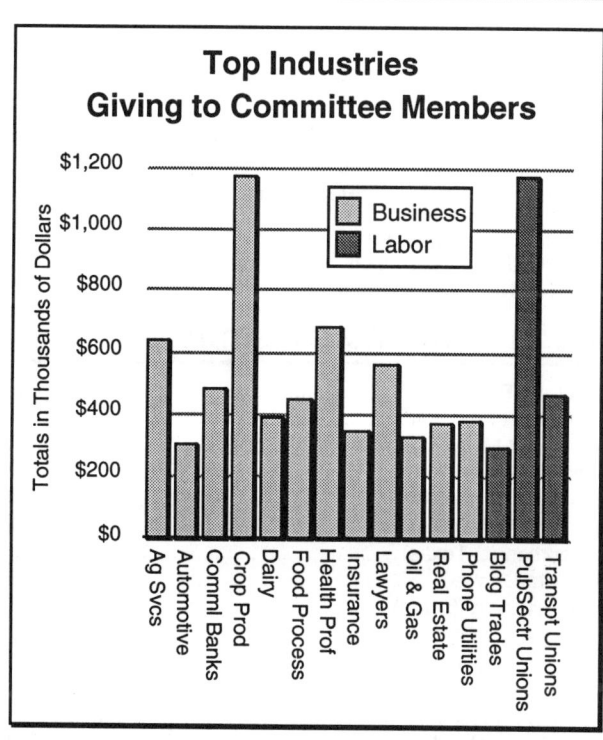

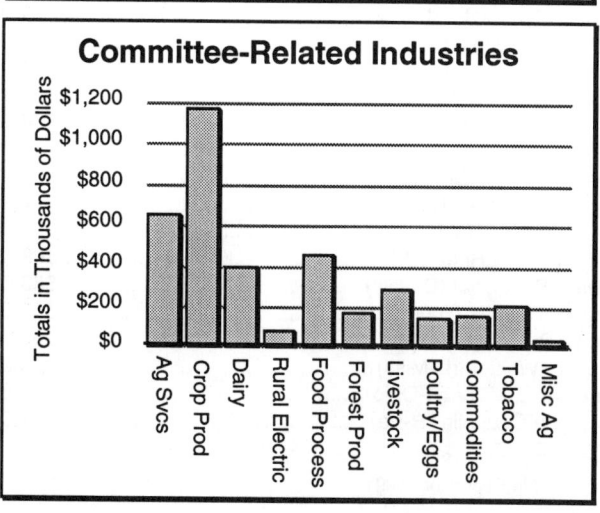

Leading Industries Giving to Committee Members

Business

Industry	Amount
Agricultural Services/Products	$635,119
Automotive	$299,553
Commercial Banks	$473,528
Crop Production & Basic Processing	$1,159,173
Dairy	$386,841
Food Processing & Sales	$445,664
Health Professionals	$673,127
Insurance	$336,975
Lawyers/Law Firms	$550,513
Oil & Gas	$318,900
Real Estate	$367,019
Telephone Utilities	$377,720

Labor

Industry	Amount
Building Trade Unions	$287,345
Public Sector Unions	$1,159,005
Transportation Unions	$458,234

Leading Committee-Related Industries Giving to Committee Members

Business

Industry	Amount
Agricultural Services/Products	$635,119
Crop Production & Basic Processing	$1,159,173
Dairy	$386,841
Rural Electric Utilities	$74,050
Food Processing & Sales	$445,664
Forestry & Forest Products	$163,214
Livestock	$278,092
Poultry & Eggs	$135,050
Commodity Trading	$150,150
Tobacco	$196,346
Misc Agriculture	$25,692

House Appropriations Committee

Jamie L. Whitten (D-Miss), Chairman
Joseph M. McDade (R-Pa), Ranking Republican

Party Ratio: 37 Democrats
22 Republicans

Jurisdiction: (1) Appropriation of the revenue for the support of the Government; (2) Rescissions of appropriations contained in appropriation acts; (3) Transfers of unexpended balances, and a variety of other duties involving the appropriation of government funds. Other committees of Congress may *authorize* the government to spend money on various projects and programs, but only the Appropriations committee *appropriates* the funds.

Subcommittees

Agriculture, Rural Development, FDA and Related Agencies
Jamie L. Whitten (D-Miss), Chairman
Joe Skeen (R-NM), Ranking Republican

Commerce, Justice, and State, the Judiciary and Related Agencies
Neal Smith (D-Iowa), Chairman
Harold Rogers (R-Ky), Ranking Republican

Defense
John P. Murtha (D-Pa), Chairman
Joseph M. McDade (R-Pa), Ranking Republican

District of Columbia
Julian C. Dixon (D-Calif), Chairman
Dean A. Gallo (R-NJ), Ranking Republican

Energy and Water Development
Tom Bevill (D-Ala), Chairman
John T. Myers (R-Ind), Ranking Republican

Foreign Operations, Export Financing and Related Programs
David R. Obey (D-Wis), Chairman
Mickey Edwards (R-Okla), Ranking Republican

Interior and Related Agencies
Sidney R. Yates (D-Ill), Chairman
Ralph Regula (R-Ohio), Ranking Republican

Labor, Health and Human Services, Education and Related Agencies
William H. Natcher (D-Ky), Chairman
Carl D. Pursell (R-Mich), Ranking Republican

Legislative Branch
Vic Fazio (D-Calif), Chairman
Jerry Lewis (R-Calif), Ranking Republican

Military Construction
W. G. "Bill" Hefner (D-NC), Chairman
Bill Lowery (R-Calif), Ranking Republican

Transportation and Related Agencies
William Lehman (D-Fla), Chairman
Lawrence Coughlin (R-Pa), Ranking Republican

Treasury, Postal Service and General Government
Edward R. Roybal (D-Calif), Chairman
Frank R. Wolf (R-Va), Ranking Republican

VA, HUD and Independent Agencies
Bob Traxler (D-Mich), Chairman
Bill Green (R-NY), Ranking Republican

Total PAC and Large Individual Contributions to Committee Members

Vic Fazio (D-Calif)	$1,715,706
Les AuCoin (D-Ore)[1]	$1,672,141
Steny H. Hoyer (D-Md)	$1,091,486
Charles Wilson (D-Texas)	$1,089,956
Bob Carr (D-Mich)	$951,370
John P. Murtha (D-Pa)	$876,783
Robert J. Mrazek (D-NY)	$788,458
Bill Green (R-NY)	$635,158
Joseph D. Early (D-Mass)	$595,518
Ronald D. Coleman (D-Texas)	$590,272
Chester G. Atkins (D-Mass)	$526,348
Harold Rogers (R-Ky)	$505,082
Richard J. Durbin (D-Ill)	$493,702
Barbara F. Vucanovich (R-Nev)	$471,113
Norm Dicks (D-Wash)	$469,728
W. G. "Bill" Hefner (D-NC)	$457,667
David E. Skaggs (D-Colo)	$454,221
Jerry Lewis (R-Calif)	$435,220
Dean A. Gallo (R-NJ)	$427,809
Bill Lowery (R-Calif)	$423,953
Alan B. Mollohan (D-WVa)	$393,925
Mickey Edwards (R-Okla)	$388,827
Nancy Pelosi (D-Calif)	$387,813
Bill Alexander (D-Ark)	$371,886
David R. Obey (D-Wis)	$346,125
John Porter (R-Ill)	$341,385
Jim Ross Lightfoot (R-Iowa)	$340,475
Joseph M. McDade (R-Pa)	$334,623
David Price (D-NC)	$323,455
Frank R. Wolf (R-Va)	$312,158
Tom DeLay (R-Texas)	$307,744
Martin Olav Sabo (D-Minn)	$290,309
Vin Weber (R-Minn)	$282,753
Jim Kolbe (R-Ariz)	$273,343
William H. Gray III (D-Pa)[2]	$267,995
William Lehman (D-Fla)	$264,643
Jim Chapman (D-Texas)	$263,149
Neal Smith (D-Iowa)	$262,542
Peter J. Visclosky (D-Ind)	$262,476
Louis Stokes (D-Ohio)	$260,657
Joe Skeen (R-NM)	$240,363
Robert L. Livingston (R-La)	$231,250
Marcy Kaptur (D-Ohio)	$222,325
John T. Myers (R-Ind)	$215,708
C. W. Bill Young (R-Fla)	$207,150
Sidney R. Yates (D-Ill)	$189,164
Tom Bevill (D-Ala)	$187,810
Bob Traxler (D-Mich)	$126,528
Lawrence J. Smith (D-Fla)	$84,743
Julian C. Dixon (D-Calif)	$82,489
Bernard J. Dwyer (D-NJ)	$77,875
Ralph Regula (R-Ohio)	$69,513
Matthew F. McHugh (D-NY)	$68,890
Edward R. Roybal (D-Calif)	$68,625
Lindsay Thomas (D-Ga)	$67,278
Carl D. Pursell (R-Mich)	$63,000
Jamie L. Whitten (D-Miss)	$29,300
Clarence E. Miller (R-Ohio)	$18,800
Lawrence Coughlin (R-Pa)	-$1,045

[1] Ran for Senate in 1992
[2] Resigned in September 1991

Summary

Businesses and industries that rely heavily on government contracts keep a sharp eye on the activities of the congressional appropriations committees — particularly defense contractors, whose fortunes may rise or fall depending on decisions reached by these panels. John Murtha, the Pennsylvania Democrat who chairs the Defense Appropriations subcommittee, collected over $230,000 from defense contractors in 1991-92, once again leading all other House recipients in defense dollars. Democrat Charles Wilson of Texas wasn't far behind, with over $210,000 from the defense sector. In all, eight of the 13 members of Murtha's subcommittee drew $50,000 or more from defense industry contributors.

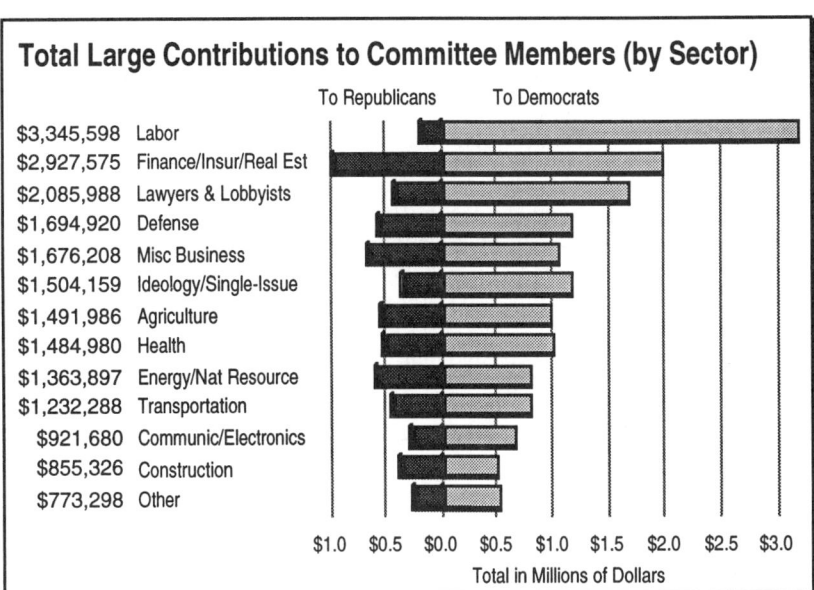

Total Large Contributions to Committee Members (by Sector)

Amount	Sector
$3,345,598	Labor
$2,927,575	Finance/Insur/Real Est
$2,085,988	Lawyers & Lobbyists
$1,694,920	Defense
$1,676,208	Misc Business
$1,504,159	Ideology/Single-Issue
$1,491,986	Agriculture
$1,484,980	Health
$1,363,897	Energy/Nat Resource
$1,232,288	Transportation
$921,680	Communic/Electronics
$855,326	Construction
$773,298	Other

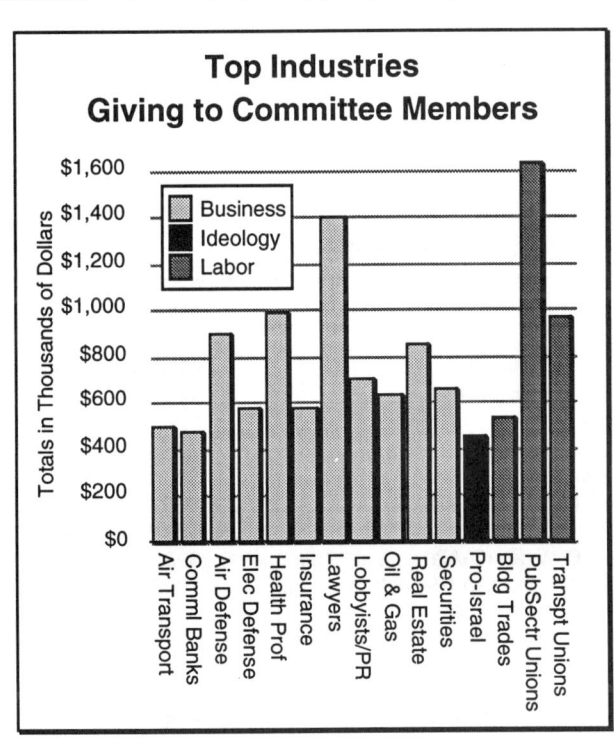

Top 20 Contributors to Committee Members in 1991-92

1	National Assn of Realtors	$276,510
2	American Medical Assn*	$246,599
3	Teamsters Union*	$217,670
4	United Auto Workers	$169,650
5	Air Line Pilots Assn	$165,000
6	National Education Assn*	$162,250
7	American Dental Assn	$148,289
8	Marine Engineers Union*	$147,250
9	National Rifle Assn	$143,550
10	Assn of Trial Lawyers of America	$139,350
11	American Fedn of St/Cnty/Munic Employees	$138,950
12	AT&T*	$137,995
13	United Parcel Service	$136,174
14	Laborers Union*	$128,750
15	National Assn Retired Federal Employees	$128,500
16	Carpenters & Joiners Union	$121,950
17	National Assn of Letter Carriers*	$121,800
18	United Transportation Union	$116,100
19	National Auto Dealers Assn	$108,000
20	General Motors*	$107,250

* Contributions came from more than one affiliate or subsidiary.

Leading Industries Giving to Committee Members

Business
Industry	Amount
Air Transport	$487,543
Commercial Banks	$459,294
Defense Aerospace	$888,875
Defense Electronics	$568,250
Health Professionals	$983,543
Insurance	$567,517
Lawyers/Law Firms	$1,390,579
Lobbyists/PR	$695,409
Oil & Gas	$628,613
Real Estate	$839,331
Securities & Investment	$649,279

Ideological/Single-Issue
Pro-Israel	$439,055

Labor
Building Trade Unions	$527,046
Public Sector Unions	$1,617,281
Transportation Unions	$960,681

House Armed Services Committee

Les Aspin (D-Wis), Chairman
Bill Dickinson (R-Ala), Ranking Republican

Party Ratio: 32 Democrats
21 Republicans

Jurisdiction: (1) Common defense generally; (2) The Department of Defense generally, including the Departments of the Army, Navy, and Air Force; (3) Ammunition depots, forts, arsenals, Army, Navy, and Air Force reservations and establishments; (4) Conservation, development, and use of naval petroleum and oil shale reserves; (5) Pay, promotion, retirement, and other benefits and privileges of members of the armed forces; (6) Scientific research and development in support of the armed services; (7) Selective service; (8) Size and composition of the Army, Navy and Air Force; (9) Soldiers' and sailors' homes; (10) Strategic and critical materials necessary for the common defense; (11) Military applications of nuclear energy. The committee also has oversight duties with respect to international arms control and disarmament, and military dependents' education.

Subcommittees

Investigations
Nicholas Mavroules (D-Mass), Chairman
Larry J. Hopkins (R-Ky), Ranking Republican

Military Installations and Facilities
Patricia Schroeder (D-Colo), Chairwoman
David O'B. Martin (R-NY), Ranking Republican

Military Personnel and Compensation
Beverly B. Byron (D-Md), Chairwoman
Herbert H. Bateman (R-Va), Ranking Republican

Procurement and Military Nuclear Systems
Les Aspin (D-Wis), Chairman
Bill Dickinson (R-Ala), Ranking Republican

Readiness
Earl Hutto (D-Fla), Chairman
John R. Kasich (R-Ohio), Ranking Republican

Research and Development
Ronald V. Dellums (D-Calif), Chairman
Robert W. Davis (R-Mich), Ranking Republican

Seapower and Strategic and Critical Materials
Charles E. Bennett (D-Fla), Chairman
Floyd D. Spence (R-SC), Ranking Republican

Total Defense-Related Contributions to Committee Members

Member	Total from Cmte-Related Contribs	Pct of Member's Lg Contribs
Les Aspin (D-Wis)	$222,125	21%
Dave McCurdy (D-Okla)	$129,450	27%
Herbert H. Bateman (R-Va)	$103,750	19%
Richard Ray (D-Ga)	$92,800	17%
Duncan Hunter (R-Calif)	$81,167	19%
Nicholas Mavroules (D-Mass)	$77,200	15%
Randy "Duke" Cunningham (R-Calif)	$72,055	14%
Chet Edwards (D-Texas)	$58,950	13%
Gary Franks (R-Conn)	$54,959	11%
Marilyn Lloyd (D-Tenn)	$51,750	15%
Ike Skelton (D-Mo)	$49,700	20%
Beverly B. Byron (D-Md)	$49,500	32%
H. Martin Lancaster (D-NC)	$47,000	10%
Barbara Boxer (D-Calif)†	$45,720	1%
George "Buddy" Darden (D-Ga)	$44,700	14%
Albert G. Bustamante (D-Texas)	$43,200	11%
H. James Saxton (R-NJ)	$41,955	10%
Norman Sisisky (D-Va)	$39,550	20%
Jim McCrery (R-La)	$39,300	7%
Robert W. Davis (R-Mich)	$38,250	27%
Ronald K. Machtley (R-RI)	$38,025	11%
James V. Hansen (R-Utah)	$36,750	20%
Bill Dickinson (R-Ala)	$36,700	67%
Curt Weldon (R-Pa)	$36,323	13%
Earl Hutto (D-Fla)	$34,850	18%
Bob Stump (R-Ariz)	$34,065	18%
Floyd D. Spence (R-SC)	$32,850	27%
Jon Kyl (R-Ariz)	$31,920	7%
George J. Hochbrueckner (D-NY)	$30,300	8%
Gene Taylor (D-Miss)	$29,270	12%
Frank McCloskey (D-Ind)	$26,400	8%
Dennis M. Hertel (D-Mich)	$26,045	15%
James Bilbray (D-Nev)	$23,950	6%
John M. Spratt Jr. (D-SC)	$23,900	10%
Owen B. Pickett (D-Va)	$22,650	10%
Glen Browder (D-Ala)	$22,500	14%
Robert K. Dornan (R-Calif)	$20,350	6%
Joel Hefley (R-Colo)	$18,000	16%
G. V. "Sonny" Montgomery (D-Miss)	$17,750	13%
Thomas H. Andrews (D-Maine)	$17,161	3%
John R. Kasich (R-Ohio)	$16,850	7%
John Tanner (D-Tenn)	$16,450	8%
Michael R. McNulty (D-NY)	$13,650	11%
Arthur Ravenel Jr. (R-SC)	$13,000	7%
Thomas M. Foglietta (D-Pa)	$12,000	4%
Solomon P. Ortiz (D-Texas)	$10,950	5%
Andy Ireland (R-Fla)	$7,100	9%
Ben Blaz (R-Guam)	$4,950	7%
Patricia Schroeder (D-Colo)	$4,500	2%
Lane Evans (D-Ill)	$3,500	2%
Neil Abercrombie (D-Hawaii)	$1,750	1%
Ronald V. Dellums (D-Calif)	$1,000	1%
David O'B. Martin (R-NY)	$0	0%
Charles E. Bennett (D-Fla)	-$1,000	0%

† Ran for US Senate in 1992

Summary

The demise of the Soviet Union and a general warming in international relations may be welcome news to most Americans, but it also signals hard times for the nation's defense industry. The House and Senate Armed Services and Appropriations committees are the key congressional panels wrestling with the problem of downsizing the military without crippling the American defense industry.

The patterns of contributions within the committee reflects the industry's concern. Defense contractors delivered nearly $2 million in contributions to House Armed Services members in the 1992 elections, and the Top 20 list of contributors bears a close resemblance to the Pentagon's list of top contractors.

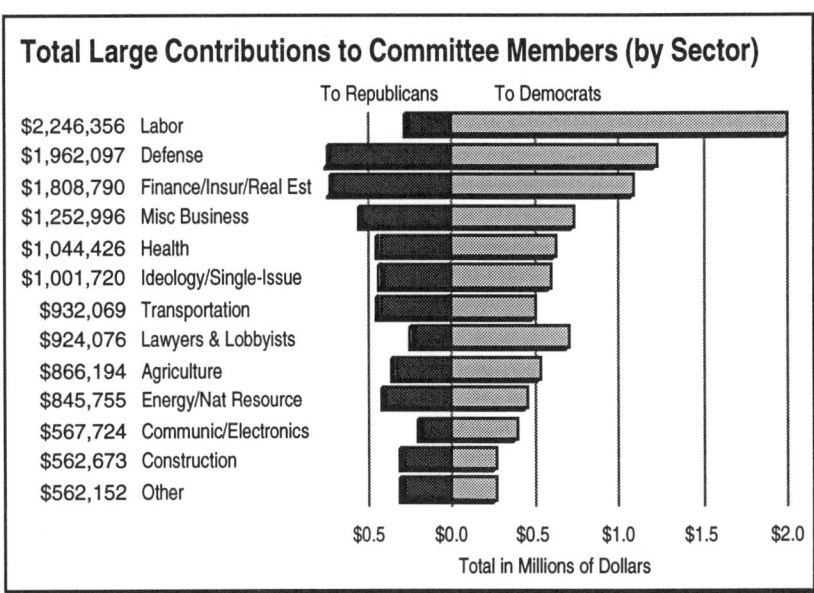

Total Large Contributions to Committee Members (by Sector)

Amount	Sector
$2,246,356	Labor
$1,962,097	Defense
$1,808,790	Finance/Insur/Real Est
$1,252,996	Misc Business
$1,044,426	Health
$1,001,720	Ideology/Single-Issue
$932,069	Transportation
$924,076	Lawyers & Lobbyists
$866,194	Agriculture
$845,755	Energy/Nat Resource
$567,724	Communic/Electronics
$562,673	Construction
$562,152	Other

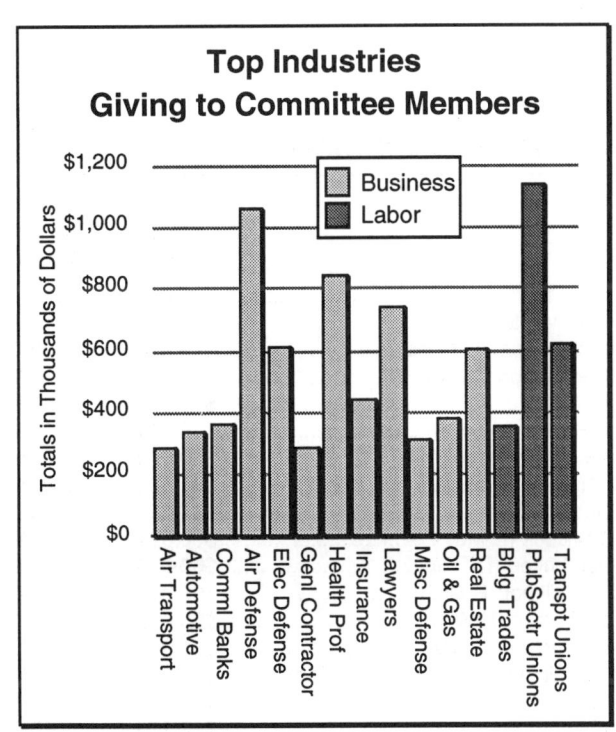

Top 20 Defense-Related Contributors to Committee Members in 1991-92

1	General Dynamics	$105,600
2	Textron Inc	$104,250
3	Martin Marietta Corp	$97,700
4	AT&T	$79,200
5	McDonnell Douglas*	$78,275
6	Lockheed Corp	$76,720
7	Grumman Corp	$72,775
8	Raytheon	$72,525
9	General Electric	$69,500
10	Rockwell International	$67,250
11	General Motors*	$62,450
12	General Atomics	$59,900
13	Northrop Corp	$54,400
14	LTV Aerospace & Defense Co	$52,000
15	Tenneco Inc	$48,000
16	United Technologies	$45,600
17	Boeing Co	$45,000
18	E-Systems*	$44,400
19	Colt Industries	$41,400
20	GTE Corp	$39,900

* Contributions came from more than one affiliate or subsidiary.

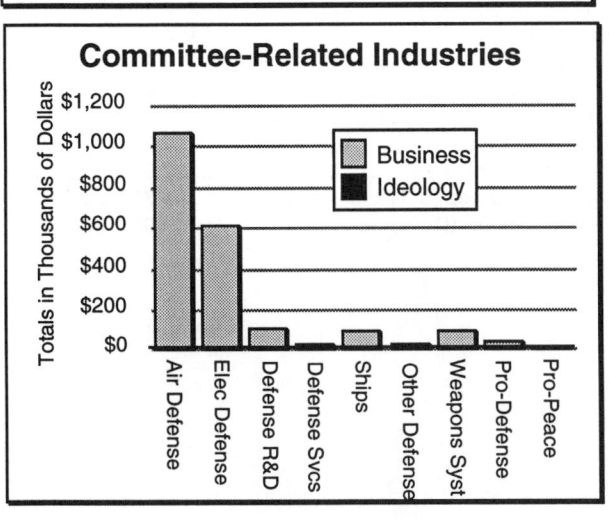

Leading Industries Giving to Committee Members

Business
Defense Aerospace	$1,054,470
Defense Electronics	$603,482
Defense R&D	$97,200
Defense Services	$20,600
Naval Ships	$86,645
Weapons Systems	$84,500
Other Defense	$15,200

Ideological/Single-Issue
Pro-Defense	$35,462
Pro-Peace	$4,261

House Banking, Finance & Urban Affairs Committee

Henry B. Gonzalez (D-Texas), Chairman
Chalmers P. Wylie (R-Ohio), Ranking Republican

Party Ratio: 31 Democrats
20 Republicans

Jurisdiction: (1) Banks and banking, including deposit insurance and Federal monetary policy; (2) money and credit, including currency and the issuance of notes and redemption thereof; gold and silver, including the coinage thereof; valuation and revaluation of the dollar; (3) Urban development; (4) Public and private housing; (5) Economic stabilization, defense production, renegotiation, and control of the price of commodities, rents and services; (6) International finance; (7) Financial aid to commerce and industry; (8) International financial and monetary organizations.

Subcommittees

Consumer Affairs and Coinage
Esteban E. Torres (D-Calif), Chairman
Al McCandless (R-Calif), Ranking Republican

Domestic Monetary Policy
Stephen L. Neal (D-NC), Chairman
Toby Roth (R-Wis), Ranking Republican

Economic Stabilization
Thomas R. Carper (D-Del), Chairman
Tom Ridge (R-Pa), Ranking Republican

Financial Institutions Supervision, Regulation and Insurance
Frank Annunzio (D-Ill), Chairman
Chalmers P. Wylie (R-Ohio), Ranking Republican

General Oversight and Investigations
Carroll Hubbard Jr. (D-Ky), Chairman
Bill McCullum (R-Fla), Ranking Republican

Housing and Community Development
Henry B. Gonzalez (D-Texas), Chairman
Marge Roukema (R-NJ), Ranking Republican

International Development, Finance, Trade and Monetary Policy
Mary Rose Oakar (D-Ohio), Chairwoman
Jim Leach (R-Iowa), Ranking Republican

Policy Research and Insurance
Ben Erdreich (D-Ala), Chairman
Doug Bereuter (R-Neb), Ranking Republican

Total Committee-Related Contributions to Committee Members

Member	Total from Cmte-Related Contribs	Pct of Member's Lg Contribs
Tom Campbell (R-Calif)†	$842,114	23%
Charles E. Schumer (D-NY)	$407,746	60%
Stephen L. Neal (D-NC)	$223,550	52%
Richard H. Baker (R-La)	$209,775	36%
John J. LaFalce (D-NY)	$208,997	43%
Bill Paxon (R-NY)	$197,392	31%
Mary Rose Oakar (D-Ohio)	$192,061	22%
Peter Hoagland (D-Neb)	$191,329	32%
Ben Erdreich (D-Ala)	$170,600	30%
Larry LaRocco (D-Idaho)	$155,197	33%
Toby Roth (R-Wis)	$149,475	37%
James P. Moran Jr. (D-Va)	$148,558	21%
Sam Johnson (R-Texas)	$143,975	24%
Tom Ridge (R-Pa)	$143,410	34%
Jim Bacchus (D-Fla)	$143,300	19%
Bill McCollum (R-Fla)	$141,600	28%
Joseph P. Kennedy II (D-Mass)	$137,536	23%
Marge Roukema (R-NJ)	$133,485	38%
Jim Nussle (R-Iowa)	$132,525	24%
Frank Riggs (R-Calif)	$132,139	27%
Jim Slattery (D-Kan)	$122,894	20%
Gary L. Ackerman (D-NY)	$121,975	21%
Al McCandless (R-Calif)	$119,799	44%
Paul E. Kanjorski (D-Pa)	$111,400	42%
Barney Frank (D-Mass)	$109,293	36%
Doug Bereuter (R-Neb)	$105,931	47%
Chalmers P. Wylie (R-Ohio)	$102,520	77%
Cliff Stearns (R-Fla)	$97,888	37%
Bruce F. Vento (D-Minn)	$97,375	43%
Richard E. Neal (D-Mass)	$92,318	33%
Liz J. Patterson (D-SC)	$90,720	34%
John W. Cox Jr. (D-Ill)	$80,570	21%
Floyd H. Flake (D-NY)	$76,264	39%
Gerald D. Kleczka (D-Wis)	$73,000	28%
Dick Armey (R-Texas)	$71,500	24%
Bill Orton (D-Utah)	$67,294	26%
Mel Hancock (R-Mo)	$66,324	23%
Charles Luken (D-Ohio)	$66,025	36%
Paul E. Gillmor (R-Ohio)	$65,342	32%
Craig Thomas (R-Wyo)	$63,675	20%
Carroll Hubbard Jr. (D-Ky)	$61,950	50%
John J. "Jimmy" Duncan Jr. (R-Tenn)	$57,615	28%
Kweisi Mfume (D-Md)	$52,390	28%
Frank Annunzio (D-Ill)	$32,220	75%
Ted Weiss (D-NY)	$30,450	11%
Esteban E. Torres (D-Calif)	$27,600	21%
Maxine Waters (D-Calif)	$20,475	12%
Thomas R. Carper (D-Del)	$9,063	85%
Jim Leach (R-Iowa)	$7,800	13%
Bernard Sanders (I-Vt)	$2,950	1%
Henry B. Gonzalez (D-Texas)	$1,700	6%
Doug Barnard Jr. (D-Ga)	$900	22%

† Ran for U.S. Senate in 1992

Summary

Commercial banks were the leading (but hardly the only) major contributor to members of the House Banking Committee in 1991-92, since no committee in the House is as important to the heavily-regulated banking industry. The issue of bank deregulation has been high on the committee's agenda in recent years, as Congress tries to shore up the sagging fortunes of many of the nation's leading financial institutions. This is the same committee that in the early 1980s loosened the rules governing savings & loans — thereby setting the stage for what became the most expensive political scandal (and subsequent bailout) in American history.

Aside from banking and financial interests, the committee also deals with housing issues — a fact that helped attract nearly $1.3 million dollars in contributions from the real estate and home building industries.

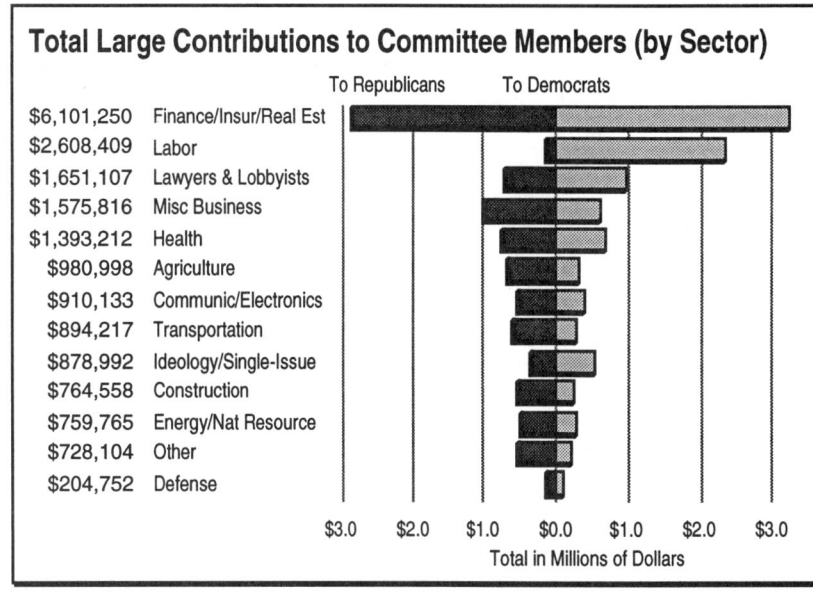

Total Large Contributions to Committee Members (by Sector)

Amount	Sector
$6,101,250	Finance/Insur/Real Est
$2,608,409	Labor
$1,651,107	Lawyers & Lobbyists
$1,575,816	Misc Business
$1,393,212	Health
$980,998	Agriculture
$910,133	Communic/Electronics
$894,217	Transportation
$878,992	Ideology/Single-Issue
$764,558	Construction
$759,765	Energy/Nat Resource
$728,104	Other
$204,752	Defense

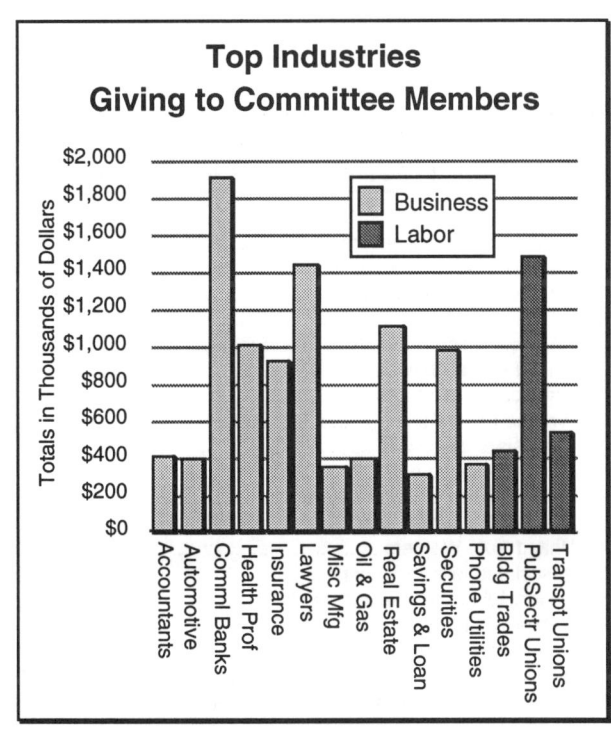

Top Industries Giving to Committee Members

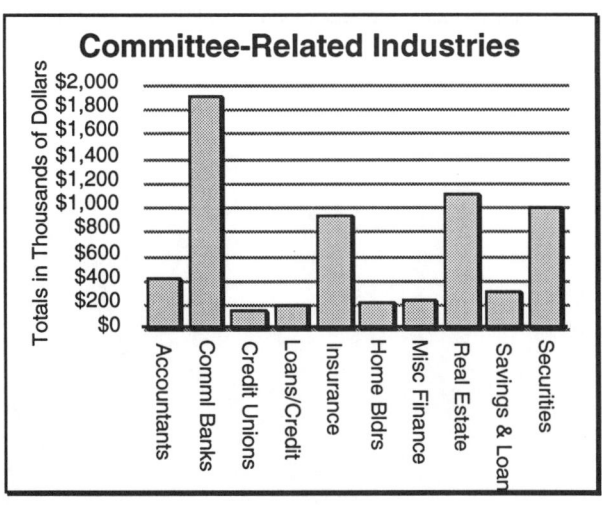

Committee-Related Industries

Top 20 Committee-Related Contributors to Committee Members in 1991-92

1	National Assn of Realtors	$316,733
2	American Bankers Assn*	$305,965
3	American Institute of CPA's	$224,350
4	JP Morgan & Co	$153,500
5	National Assn of Life Underwriters	$120,000
6	National Assn of Home Builders	$110,196
7	Credit Union National Assn*	$108,450
8	Chase Manhattan	$100,650
9	Citicorp	$99,900
10	US League of Savings Assns*	$94,169
11	Citizens & Southern National Bank	$92,850
12	Barnett Banks Inc	$75,950
13	BankAmerica Corp*	$66,750
14	Independent Bankers Assn	$64,807
15	American Council of Life Insurance	$60,769
16	American Express*	$59,900
17	Goldman, Sachs & Co	$55,358
18	Household International Inc	$54,650
19	Bankers Trust	$54,400
20	Associated Credit Bureaus	$51,950

* Contributions came from more than one affiliate or subsidiary.

Leading Committee-Related Industries Giving to Committee Members

Business

Accountants	$390,834
Commercial Banks	$1,893,409
Credit Unions	$144,446
Finance/Credit Companies	$188,900
Insurance	$912,372
Home Builders	$210,734
Misc Finance	$217,307
Real Estate	$1,092,077
Savings & Loans	$290,739
Securities & Investment	$971,166

House Budget Committee

Leon E. Panetta (D-Calif), Chairman
Bill Gradison (R-Ohio), Ranking Republican

Party Ratio: 23 Democrats
14 Republicans

Jurisdiction: (1) To report the matters required to be reported by it under titles III and IV of the Congressional Budget Act of 1974; (2) To make continuing studies of the effect on budget outlays of relevant existing and proposed legislation and to report the results of such studies to the House on a recurring basis; (3) To request and evaluate continuing studies of tax expenditures, to devise methods of coordinating tax expenditures, policies, and programs with direct budget outlays, and to report the results of such studies to the House on a recurring basis; and (4) To review, on a continuing basis, the conduct by the Congressional Budget Office of its functions and duties.

Subcommittees

Budget Process, Reconciliation and Enforcement
Anthony C. Beilenson (D-Calif), Chairman
Bill Thomas (R-Calif), Ranking Republican

Community Development and Natural Resources
Mike Espy (D-Miss), Chairman
Helen Delich Bentley (R-Md), Ranking Republican

Defense, Foreign Policy and Space
Richard J. Durbin (D-Ill), Chairman
Jim McCrery (R-La), Ranking Republican

Economic Policy, Projections and Revenues
Dale E. Kildee (D-Mich), Chairman
Amo Houghton (R-NY), Ranking Republican

Human Resources
James L. Oberstar (D-Minn), Chairman
John R. Kasich (R-Ohio), Ranking Republican

Urgent Fiscal Issues
Frank J. Guarini (D-NY), Chairman
Harold Rogers (R-Ky), Ranking Republican

Total PAC and Large Individual Contributions to Committee Members

Richard A. Gephardt (D-Mo)	$2,870,796
Helen Delich Bentley (R-Md)	$657,606
Bill Paxon (R-NY)	$640,187
Jim McCrery (R-La)	$565,170
Dale E. Kildee (D-Mich)	$558,660
John Bryant (D-Texas)	$525,038
Robert T. Matsui (D-Calif)	$521,339
Harold Rogers (R-Ky)	$505,082
Howard L. Berman (D-Calif)	$498,862
Anthony C. Beilenson (D-Calif)	$497,109
Rick Santorum (R-Pa)	$494,739
Richard J. Durbin (D-Ill)	$493,702
Bill Thomas (R-Calif)	$469,226
Jerry Huckaby (D-La)	$392,884
Lewis F. Payne Jr. (D-Va)	$364,257
Louise M. Slaughter (D-NY)	$357,247
Mike Parker (D-Miss)	$339,891
William E. Dannemeyer (R-Calif)†	$339,067
Charles W. Stenholm (D-Texas)	$335,166
Barney Frank (D-Mass)	$304,428
Alex McMillan (R-NC)	$301,050
Leon E. Panetta (D-Calif)	$300,800
Martin Olav Sabo (D-Minn)	$290,309
Amo Houghton (R-NY)	$288,678
Mike Espy (D-Miss)	$280,598
Jim Kolbe (R-Ariz)	$273,343
John R. Kasich (R-Ohio)	$255,254
James L. Oberstar (D-Minn)	$247,230
John M. Spratt Jr. (D-SC)	$238,600
Bob Wise (D-WVa)	$219,450
Christopher Shays (R-Conn)	$214,388
Frank J. Guarini (D-NJ)	$81,498
Bernard J. Dwyer (D-NJ)	$77,875
Jim Cooper (D-Tenn)	$65,275
John Miller (R-Wash)	$65,000
Bill Gradison (R-Ohio)	$40,509
Don J. Pease (D-Ohio)	-$9,849

Top 20 Contributors to Committee Members in 1991-92

1	American Medical Assn*	$180,624
2	National Assn of Realtors	$154,559
3	Assn of Trial Lawyers of America	$93,000
4	National Auto Dealers Assn	$89,700
5	AT&T	$85,075
6	American Fedn of St/Cnty/Munic Employees	$84,000
7	United Parcel Service	$82,490
8	American Bankers Assn*	$81,250
9	Air Line Pilots Assn	$81,000
10	Teamsters Union	$79,300
11	American Institute of CPA's	$78,000
12	National Assn of Letter Carriers*	$77,925
13	National Education Assn	$75,000
14	United Auto Workers	$72,850
15	Associated Milk Producers	$70,500
16	National Assn of Life Underwriters	$70,500
17	National Rifle Assn	$68,100
18	American Federation of Teachers	$65,000
19	BellSouth Corp*	$60,150
20	National Assn Retired Federal Employees	$57,500

* Contributions came from more than one affiliate or subsidiary.

† Ran for U.S. Senate in 1992

Summary

Along with its counterpart in the Senate, the House Budget Committee is the panel in Congress chiefly responsible for putting together the federal government's annual budget. That assignment, though important to the nation as a whole, is not focused directly on any one industry or interest group — so the patterns in campaign contributions are typical of Congress as a whole. The financial sector was the biggest funder of committee members' 1992 campaigns. Organized labor was second, delivering its dollars overwhelmingly to Democrats.

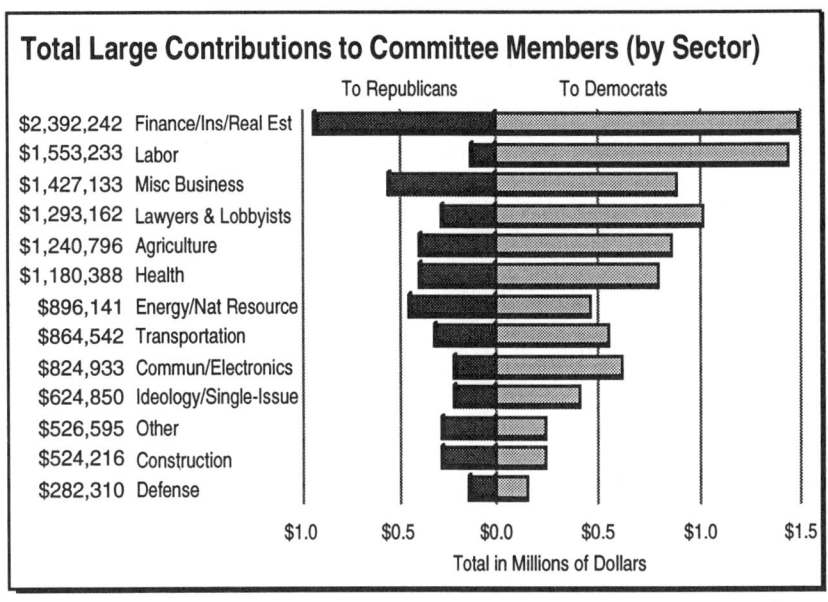

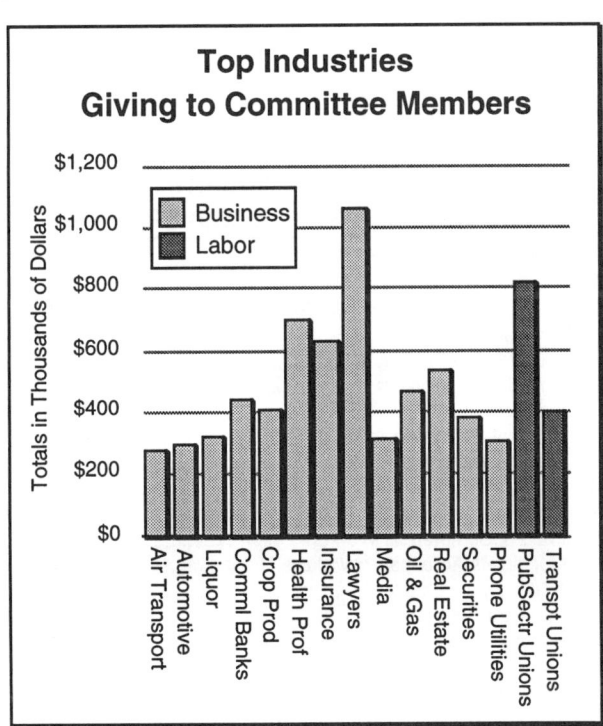

Leading Industries
Giving to Committee Members

Business

Air Transport	$272,201
Automotive	$291,547
Beer, Wine & Liquor	$310,540
Commercial Banks	$430,649
Crop Production & Basic Processing	$401,774
Health Professionals	$690,414
Insurance	$621,265
Lawyers/Law Firms	$1,051,616
Media/Entertainment	$301,855
Oil & Gas	$456,957
Real Estate	$529,925
Securities & Investment	$377,447
Telephone Utilities	$297,410

Labor

Public Sector Unions	$811,129
Transportation Unions	$393,970

House District of Columbia Committee

Ronald V. Dellums (D-Calif), Chairman
Thomas J. Bliley Jr. (R-Va), Ranking Republican

Party Ratio: 7 Democrats
4 Republicans

Jurisdiction: (1) Local government, delegated authority, form, finances, operations and programs, of local government bodies, as authorized by . . . the U.S. Constitution—"Congress shall have the power to exercise exclusive legislation in all cases whatsoever over such District . . ."; (2) Political status, jurisdiction and boundaries of the District of Columbia; (3) The annual federal payment—pension fund financing for police, firefighters and teachers; (4) Delegate to the House of Representatives; courts: organization, operations; appointment and removal mechanisms and term of judges; (5) Organizations chartered by Congress: determination of tax-exempt status; (6) Planning and design of the national capital: (a) building height limitation, National Capital Planning Commission, protection of Old Georgetown, the Commission of Fine Arts; (7) Metropolitan regional affairs: (a) Washington Metropolitan Area Transit Authority, (b) emergency planning and procedures, Potomac River shoreline and water quality improvement; (8) The International Community.

Subcommittees

Fiscal Affairs and Health
Pete Stark (D-Calif), Chairman
Dana Rohrabacher (R-Calif), Ranking Republican

Government Operations and Metropolitan Affairs
Alan Wheat (D-Mo), Chairman
Larry Combest (R-Texas), Ranking Republican

Judiciary and Education
Mervyn M. Dymally (D-Calif), Chairman
Bill Lowery (R-Calif), Ranking Republican

Total PAC and Large Individual Contributions to Committee Members

Sander Levin (D-Mich)	$791,756
Thomas J. Bliley Jr. (R-Va)	$557,531
Pete Stark (D-Calif)	$455,572
Bill Lowery (R-Calif)	$423,953
Alan Wheat (D-Mo)	$414,621
Dana Rohrabacher (R-Calif)	$282,873
William H. Gray III (D-Pa)†	$267,995
Jim McDermott (D-Wash)	$213,735
Ronald V. Dellums (D-Calif)	$196,021
Larry Combest (R-Texas)	$175,084
Mervyn M. Dymally (D-Calif)	$144,911
Eleanor Holmes Norton (D-DC)	$136,975

† Resigned in September 1991

Top 20 Contributors to Committee Members in 1991-92

1	American Medical Assn*	$64,450
2	Assn of Trial Lawyers of America	$45,000
3	American Fedn of St/Cnty/Munic Employees	$41,000
4	Teamsters Union	$41,000
5	National Assn of Realtors	$38,825
6	United Auto Workers	$35,900
7	American Institute of CPA's	$32,000
8	National Education Assn	$29,350
9	Air Line Pilots Assn	$28,000
10	American Federation of Teachers	$24,500
11	American Chiropractic Assn	$23,000
12	Food & Commercial Workers Union	$23,000
13	Machinists/Aerospace Workers Union	$22,800
14	AT&T	$21,975
15	American Bankers Assn	$21,500
16	National Assn Retired Federal Employees	$21,500
17	American Postal Workers Union	$20,500
18	Laborers' Political League	$20,400
19	Intl Brotherhood of Electrical Workers	$20,100
20	American Podiatry Assn	$20,000

* Contributions came from more than one affiliate or subsidiary.

Summary

Unlike every other city in America, the nation's capital is governed only partly by its own elected officials, and partly by the U.S. Congress, which has overseen the city's affairs since the District of Columbia was created in 1790. The degree of congressional control has lessened over the years and the city now enjoys most benefits of home rule. But the Congress still controls a major part of the city's purse strings, and decisions made in this committee affect the lives of every resident of Washington.

Since D.C. is not a state, its residents do not elect their own representative, but rather a "delegate," like those who represent Puerto Rico, the Virgin Islands, Guam and American Samoa. Delegates do not have full voting rights on the House floor, but they are entitled to debate and vote on issues within the committees on which they serve.

This second-class status has long rankled D.C. residents. In 1990, in addition to electing their delegate to Congress, the district's voters also elected two "shadow Senators" — one of them the Rev. Jesse Jackson — to lobby for statehood. Unlike the D.C. delegate, the shadow Senators enjoy no official status in Congress, formal or otherwise.

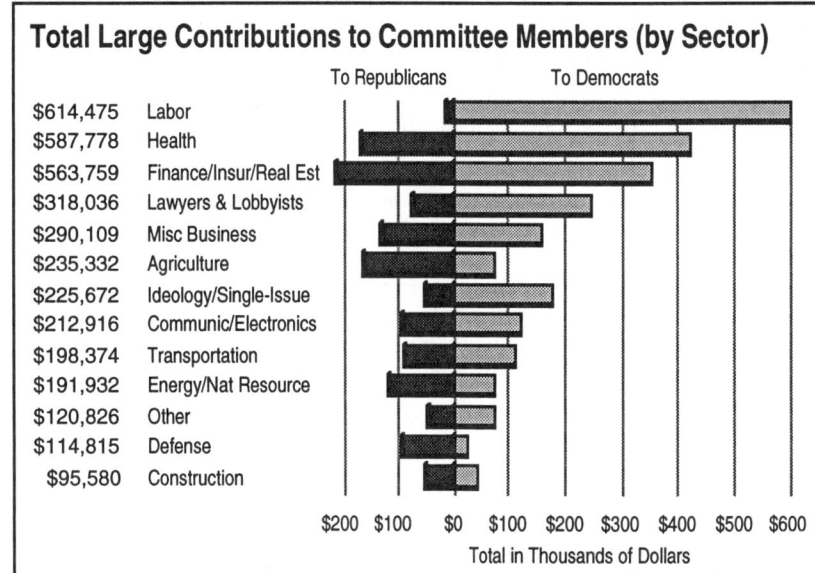

Total Large Contributions to Committee Members (by Sector)

Amount	Sector
$614,475	Labor
$587,778	Health
$563,759	Finance/Insur/Real Est
$318,036	Lawyers & Lobbyists
$290,109	Misc Business
$235,332	Agriculture
$225,672	Ideology/Single-Issue
$212,916	Communic/Electronics
$198,374	Transportation
$191,932	Energy/Nat Resource
$120,826	Other
$114,815	Defense
$95,580	Construction

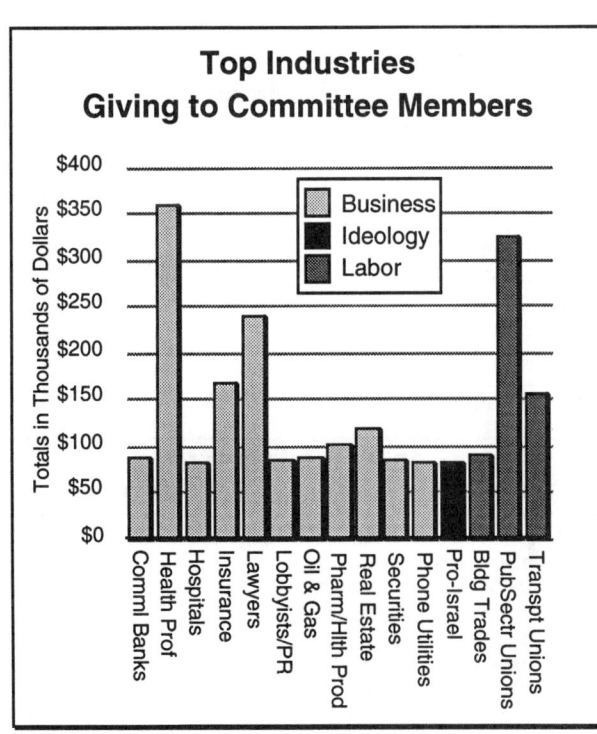

Leading Industries Giving to Committee Members

Business
- Commercial Banks $83,590
- Health Professionals $356,163
- Hospitals/Nursing Homes $79,600
- Insurance $164,087
- Lawyers/Law Firms $237,201
- Lobbyists/PR $80,835
- Oil & Gas $83,875
- Pharmaceuticals/Health Products $99,150
- Real Estate $116,829
- Securities & Investment $83,125
- Telephone Utilities $77,985

Ideological/Single-Issue
- Pro-Israel $77,750

Labor
- Building Trade Unions $86,540
- Public Sector Unions $321,700
- Transportation Unions $154,050

House Education and Labor Committee

William D. Ford (D-Mich), Chairman
Bill Goodling (R-Pa), Ranking Republican

Party Ratio: 24 Democrats
15 Republicans

Jurisdiction: (1) Measures relating to education or labor generally; (2) Child labor; (3) Columbia Institution for the Deaf, Dumb and Blind; Howard University; Freedman's Hospital; (4) Convict labor and the entry of goods made by convicts into interstate commerce; (5) Labor standards; (6) Labor statistics; (7) Mediation and arbitration of labor disputes; (8) Regulation or prevention of importation of foreign laborers under contract; (9) Food programs for children in schools; (10) United States Employees' Compensation Commission; (11) Vocational rehabilitation; (12) Wages and hours of labor; (13) Welfare of miners; (14) Work incentives programs. The committee also has a special oversight function with respect to domestic educational programs and institutions, and programs of student assistance, which are within the Jurisdiction of other committees.

Subcommittees

Elementary, Secondary and Vocational Education
Dale E. Kildee (D-Mich), Chairman
Bill Goodling (R-Pa), Ranking Republican

Employment Opportunities
Carl C. Perkins (D-Ky), Chairman
Steve Gunderson (R-Wis), Ranking Republican

Health and Safety
Joseph M. Gaydos (D-Pa), Chairman
Paul B. Henry (R-Mich), Ranking Republican

Human Resources
Matthew G. Martinez (D-Calif), Chairman
Harris W. Fawell (R-Ill), Ranking Republican

Labor-Management Relations
Pat Williams (D-Mont), Chairman
Marge Roukema (R-NJ), Ranking Republican

Labor Standards
Austin J. Murphy (D-Pa), Chairman
Thomas E. Petri (R-Wis), Ranking Republican

Postsecondary Education
William D. Ford (D-Mich), Chairman
Tom Coleman (R-Mo), Ranking Republican

Total PAC and Large Individual Contributions to Committee Members

John W. Olver (D-Mass)	$859,467
Nita M. Lowey (D-NY)	$831,320
Pat Williams (D-Mont)	$730,984
Ed Pastor (D-Ariz)	$695,569
William D. Ford (D-Mich)	$585,175
John F. Reed (D-RI)	$580,186
Dale E. Kildee (D-Mich)	$558,660
Scott L. Klug (R-Wis)	$528,430
Randy "Duke" Cunningham (R-Calif)	$498,935
Jolene Unsoeld (D-Wash)	$476,934
Robert E. Andrews (D-NJ)	$473,741
Harris W. Fawell (R-Ill)	$428,241
Tom Coleman (R-Mo)	$417,087
Susan Molinari (R-NY)	$415,370
Tim Roemer (D-Ind)	$411,948
George Miller (D-Calif)	$393,005
Mickey Edwards (R-Okla)	$388,827
William J. Jefferson (D-La)	$350,974
Marge Roukema (R-NJ)	$349,324
John A. Boehner (R-Ohio)	$343,332
Steve Gunderson (R-Wis)	$310,242
Bill Barrett (R-Neb)	$301,454
Dick Armey (R-Texas)	$294,990
William L. Clay (D-Mo)	$282,938
Donald M. Payne (D-NJ)	$262,191
Cass Ballenger (R-NC)	$253,875
Tom Petri (R-Wis)	$237,318
Charles A. Hayes (D-Ill)	$223,251
Austin J. Murphy (D-Pa)	$191,323
Paul B. Henry (R-Mich)	$187,298
Craig Washington (D-Texas)	$171,250
Tom Sawyer (D-Ohio)	$169,407
Patsy T. Mink (D-Hawaii)	$168,358
Carl C. Perkins (D-Ky)	$160,275
Matthew G. Martinez (D-Calif)	$110,291
Major R. Owens (D-NY)	$109,744
Jose E. Serrano (D-NY)	$108,900
Bill Goodling (R-Pa)	$95,579
Joseph M. Gaydos (D-Pa)	$45,800
Ron de Lugo (D-Virgin Is)	$44,050
Steve Bartlett (R-Texas)†	$4,592

† Resigned in March 1991

Top 20 Contributors to Committee Members in 1991-92

1	American Medical Assn*	$207,800
2	Teamsters Union*	$195,600
3	American Fedn of St/Cnty/Munic Employees	$174,197
4	National Assn of Realtors	$173,960
5	United Auto Workers	$163,900
6	National Education Assn	$147,750
7	Assn of Trial Lawyers of America	$145,500
8	Carpenters & Joiners Union*	$142,700
9	Laborers Union*	$140,800
10	Machinists/Aerospace Workers Union	$133,875
11	Intl Brotherhood of Electrical Workers*	$129,800
12	American Federation of Teachers	$126,475
13	National Assn Retired Federal Employees	$119,750
14	Food & Commercial Workers Union	$118,791
15	Marine Engineers Union*	$115,774
16	National Assn of Letter Carriers*	$111,950
17	Air Line Pilots Assn	$109,000
18	American Postal Workers Union	$106,300
19	United Parcel Service	$96,055
20	Plumbers/Pipefitters Union*	$94,850

* Contributions came from more than one affiliate or subsidiary.

Summary

Not surprisingly, labor unions dominate the political contributions to members of the Education and Labor Committee, giving twice as much as any other sector. But decisions made by this panel affect virtually every American business, whether or not they employ union workers. Minimum wage laws, safety rules, and dozens of other labor-related standards and regulations fall within the purview of this committee.

Organized unions do have an enormous stake in the issues debated here and they accounted for 16 of the top 20 contributors to the committee and $3.4 million in contributions overall to committee members. Still, despite the tens of millions of dollars that labor groups donate to Congress every election cycle, their political clout has been in serious decline in recent years. The unions' embarrassing defeat on the North American Free Trade Agreement in November 1993 was a particularly painful one for labor leaders, as many of their Democratic allies sided against them and voted yes on NAFTA. Many unions vowed retribution against those Democrats in the 1994 elections.

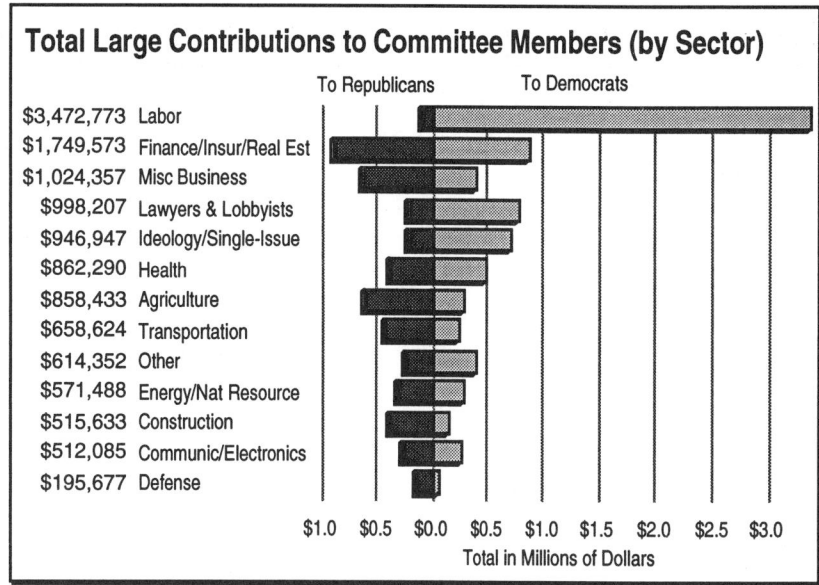

Total Large Contributions to Committee Members (by Sector)

Amount	Sector
$3,472,773	Labor
$1,749,573	Finance/Insur/Real Est
$1,024,357	Misc Business
$998,207	Lawyers & Lobbyists
$946,947	Ideology/Single-Issue
$862,290	Health
$858,433	Agriculture
$658,624	Transportation
$614,352	Other
$571,488	Energy/Nat Resource
$515,633	Construction
$512,085	Communic/Electronics
$195,677	Defense

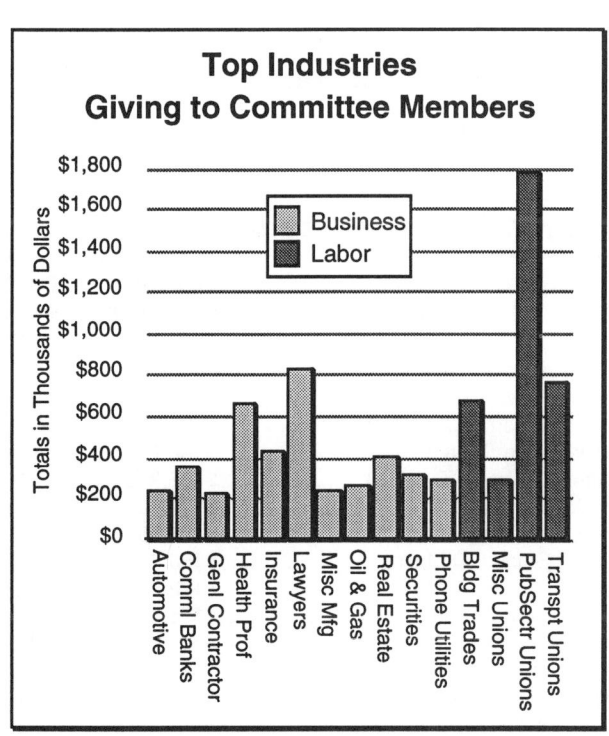

Top Industries Giving to Committee Members

Leading Industries Giving to Committee Members

Business

Automotive	$222,089
Commercial Banks	$344,860
General Contractors	$214,473
Health Professionals	$652,356
Insurance	$418,607
Lawyers/Law Firms	$822,477
Misc Manufacturing & Distributing	$224,785
Oil & Gas	$250,576
Real Estate	$399,967
Securities & Investment	$298,068
Telephone Utilities	$280,953

Labor

Building Trade Unions	$663,118
Misc Unions	$284,096
Public Sector Unions	$1,768,015
Transportation Unions	$757,544

House Energy and Commerce Committee

John D. Dingell (D-Mich), Chairman
Norman F. Lent (R-NY), Ranking Republican

Party Ratio: 27 Democrats
16 Republicans

Jurisdiction: (1) Interstate and foreign commerce generally; (2) National energy policy generally; (3) Measures relating to the exploration, production, storage, supply, marketing, pricing, and regulation of energy resources, including all fossil fuels, solar energy, and other unconventional or renewable energy resources; (4) Measures relating to the conservation of energy resources; (5) Measures relating to the commercial application of energy technology; (6) Measures relating to energy information generally; (7) Measures relating to (A) the generation and marketing of power (except by federally chartered or Federal regional power marketing authorities), (B) the reliability and interstate transmission of, and rate making for, all power, and (C) the siting of generation facilities; except the installation of interconnections between Government waterpower projects. (The committee's jurisdiction extends both to nuclear and nonnuclear facilities and energy). (8) Interstate energy compacts; (9) Measures relating to general management of the Department of Energy, and the management and all functions of the Federal Energy Regulatory Commission; (10) Inland waterways; (11) Railroads, including railroad labor, railroad retirement and unemployment, except revenue measures related thereto; (12) Regulation of interstate and foreign communication; (13) Securities and exchanges; (14) Consumer affairs and consumer protection; (15) Travel and tourism; (16) Public health and quarantine; (17) Health and health facilities, except health care supported by payroll deductions; (18) Biomedical research and development. The committee also has special oversight functions with respect to all laws, programs, and Government activities affecting nuclear and other energy.

Subcommittees

Commerce, Consumer Protection and Competitiveness
Cardiss Collins(D-Ill), Chairwoman
Alex McMillan (R-NC), Ranking Republican

Energy and Power
Philip R. Sharp (D-Ind), Chairman
Carlos J. Moorhead (R-Calif), Ranking Republican

Health and the Environment
Henry A. Waxman (D-Calif), Chairman
William E. Dannemeyer (R-Calif), Ranking Republican

Oversight and Investigations
John D. Dingell (D-Mich), Chairman
Thomas J. Bliley Jr. (R-Va), Ranking Republican

Telecommunications and Finance
Edward J. Markey (D-Mass), Chairman
Matthew J. Rinaldo (R-NJ), Ranking Republican

Transportation and Hazardous Materials
Al Swift (D-Wash), Chairman
Don Ritter (R-Pa), Ranking Republican

Total Committee-Related Contributions to Committee Members

	Total from Cmte-Related Contribs	Pct of Member's Lg Contribs
John D. Dingell (D-Mich)	$592,072	59%
Mike Synar (D-Okla)	$477,411	55%
Tom McMillen (D-Md)	$462,755	43%
Joe L. Barton (R-Texas)	$390,781	52%
Don Ritter (R-Pa)	$387,889	51%
Jack Fields (R-Texas)	$387,707	57%
Al Swift (D-Wash)	$386,873	50%
Henry A. Waxman (D-Calif)	$375,949	64%
Gerry Sikorski (D-Minn)	$346,842	45%
Jim Slattery (D-Kan)	$334,348	55%
Thomas J. Bliley Jr. (R-Va)	$320,443	57%
Bill Richardson (D-NM)	$310,231	57%
Peter H. Kostmayer (D-Pa)	$309,646	33%
W.J. "Billy" Tauzin (D-La)	$298,791	54%
Rick Boucher (D-Va)	$282,400	57%
Philip R. Sharp (D-Ind)	$278,241	54%
John Bryant (D-Texas)	$274,391	52%
Thomas J. Manton (D-NY)	$264,282	51%
Michael Bilirakis (R-Fla)	$262,073	52%
Ralph M. Hall (D-Texas)	$261,913	61%
Richard H. Lehman (D-Calif)	$255,340	36%
Michael G. Oxley (R-Ohio)	$229,750	61%
Dennis Hastert (R-Ill)	$212,996	50%
J. Roy Rowland (D-Ga)	$206,702	62%
Edolphus Towns (D-NY)	$191,874	45%
Carlos J. Moorhead (R-Calif)	$190,000	64%
Alex McMillan (R-NC)	$186,150	62%
Edward J. Markey (D-Mass)	$185,325	56%
Dan Schaefer (R-Colo)	$177,424	57%
Sonny Callahan (R-Ala)	$168,650	48%
Gerry E. Studds (D-Mass)	$166,730	22%
Norman F. Lent (R-NY)	$163,394	69%
Cardiss Collins (D-Ill)	$156,312	62%
James H. Scheuer (D-NY)	$136,435	62%
Clyde C. Holloway (R-La)	$126,075	47%
Fred Upton (R-Mich)	$125,370	38%
Terry L. Bruce (D-Ill)	$123,497	56%
Dennis E. Eckart (D-Ohio)	$98,548	53%
Ron Wyden (D-Ore)	$78,575	56%
Matthew J. Rinaldo (R-NJ)	$72,592	58%
Claude Harris (D-Ala)	$68,209	59%
William E. Dannemeyer (R-Calif)†	$38,230	11%
Jim Cooper (D-Tenn)	$27,556	42%

† Ran for Senate in 1992

Summary

One glance at the volume of campaign dollars flowing into the reelection campaigns of Energy and Commerce Committee members is enough to see why a seat on this committee is considered a plum assignment on Capitol Hill. Its jurisdiction gives it important influence over some of the most politically active industries in America: oil & gas, health care, telecommunications, finance and a host of smaller industries and interests.

After the election of Bill Clinton in 1992 and the elevation of health care reform to the top of the political agenda, the committee became even more important to American business. Along with the Ways & Means Committee, it is the lead panel charged with drafting the details of the nation's new health care policy.

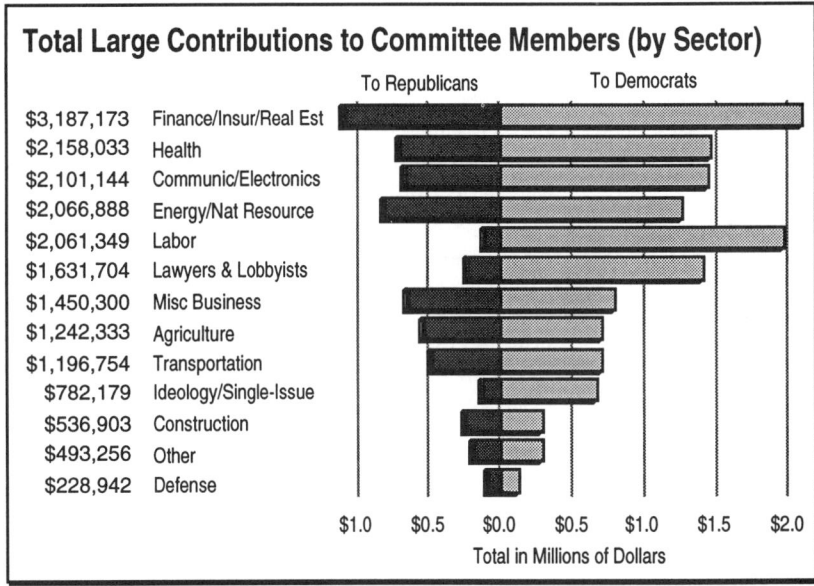

Total Large Contributions to Committee Members (by Sector)

Amount	Sector
$3,187,173	Finance/Insur/Real Est
$2,158,033	Health
$2,101,144	Communic/Electronics
$2,066,888	Energy/Nat Resource
$2,061,349	Labor
$1,631,704	Lawyers & Lobbyists
$1,450,300	Misc Business
$1,242,333	Agriculture
$1,196,754	Transportation
$782,179	Ideology/Single-Issue
$536,903	Construction
$493,256	Other
$228,942	Defense

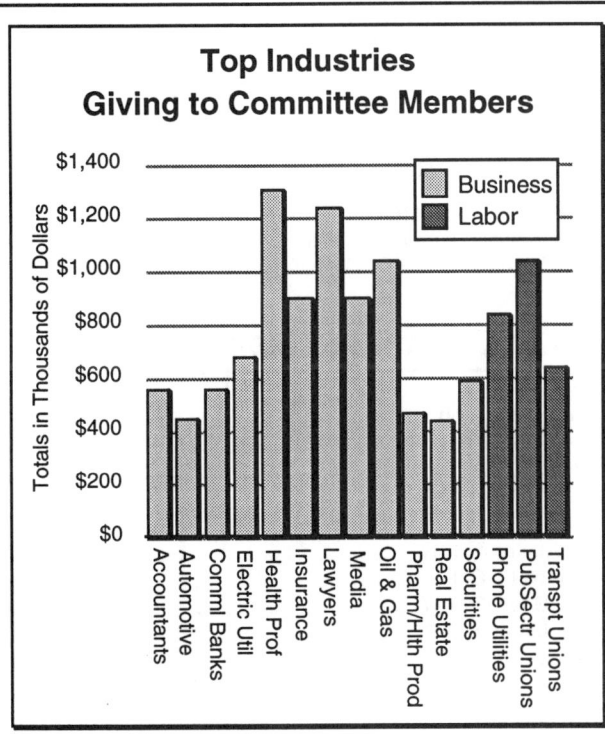

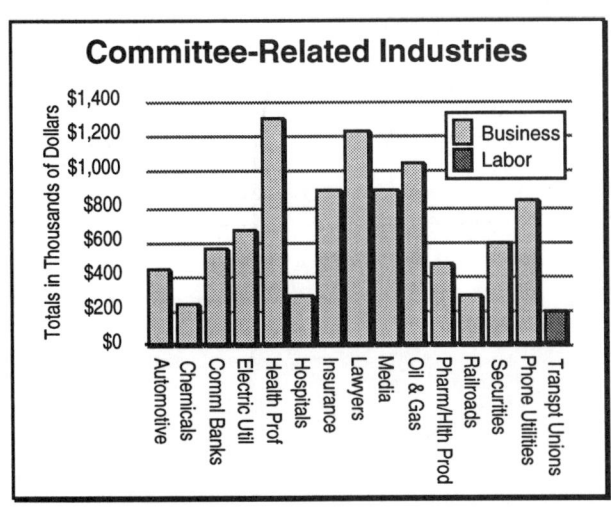

Top 20 Committe-Related Contributors to Committee Members in 1991-92

1	American Medical Assn*	$255,196
2	National Cable Television Assn	$186,049
3	American Dental Assn	$148,750
4	Assn of Trial Lawyers of America	$143,500
5	AT&T	$132,975
6	National Assn of Broadcasters	$127,150
7	National Auto Dealers Assn	$119,250
8	American Bankers Assn*	$118,850
9	United Transportation Union	$116,200
10	American Family Corp	$104,250
11	Ameritech Corp*	$99,950
12	BellSouth Corp*	$94,350
13	American Hospital Assn	$90,836
14	American Academy of Ophthalmology	$86,500
15	National Assn of Life Underwriters	$78,000
16	Burlington Northern*	$76,099
17	Union Pacific Corp	$68,499
18	GTE Corp	$66,220
19	Pacific Telesis Group	$65,550
20	Viacom International	$63,550

* Contributions came from more than one affiliate or subsidiary.

Leading Committee-Related Industries Giving to Committee Members

Business
Automotive	$435,365
Chemical & Related Manufacturing	$238,434
Commercial Banks	$550,395
Electric Utilities	$662,184
Health Professionals	$1,300,449
Hospitals/Nursing Homes	$277,402
Insurance	$888,736
Lawyers/Law Firms	$1,221,667
Media/Entertainment	$885,435
Oil & Gas	$1,028,721
Pharmaceuticals/Health Products	$453,079
Railroads	$271,323
Securities & Investment	$578,953
Telephone Utilities	$826,335

Labor
Transportation Unions	$181,450

House Foreign Affairs Committee

Dante B. Fascell (D-Fla), Chairman
William S. Broomfield (R-Mich), Ranking Republican

Party Ratio: 26 Democrats
17 Republicans

Jurisdiction: (1) Relations of the United States with foreign nations generally; (2) Acquisition of land and buildings for embassies and legations in foreign countries; (3) Establishment of boundary lines between the United States and foreign nations; (4) Foreign loans; (5) International conferences and congresses; (6) Intervention abroad and declarations of war; (7) Measures relating to the diplomatic service; (8) Measures to foster commercial intercourse with foreign nations and to safeguard American business interests abroad; (9) Neutrality; (10) Protection of American citizens abroad and expatriation; (11) The American National Red Cross; (12) United Nations Organizations; (13) Measures relating to international economic policy; (14) Export controls, including non-proliferation of nuclear technology and nuclear hardware; (15) International commodity agreements (other than those involving sugar), including all agreements for cooperation in the export of nuclear technology and nuclear hardware; (16) Trading with the enemy; (17) International education. The committee also has special oversight functions with respect to customs administration, intelligence activities relating to foreign policy, international financial and monetary organizations, and international fishing agreements.

Subcommittees

Africa
Mervyn M. Dymally (D-Calif), Chairman
Dan Burton (R-Ind), Ranking Republican

Arms Control, International Security and Science
Dante B. Fascell (D-Fla), Chairman
William S. Broomfield (R-Mich), Ranking Republican

Asian and Pacific Affairs
Stephen J. Solarz (D-NY), Chairman
Jim Leach (R-Iowa), Ranking Republican

Europe and the Middle East
Lee H. Hamilton (D-Ind), Chairman
Benjamin A. Gilman (R-NY), Ranking Republican

Human Rights and International Organizations
Gus Yatron (D-Pa), Chairman
Doug Bereuter (R-Neb), Ranking Republican

International Economic Policy and Trade
Sam Gejdenson (D-Conn), Chairman
Toby Roth (R-Wis), Ranking Republican

International Operations
Howard L. Berman (D-Calif), Chairman
Olympia J. Snowe (R-Maine), Ranking Republican

Western Hemisphere Affairs
Robert G. Torricelli (D-NJ), Chairman
Robert J. Lagomarsino (R-Calif), Ranking Republican

Total PAC and Large Individual Contributions to Committee Members

Mel Levine (D-Calif)†	$4,106,254
Wayne Owens (D-Utah)†	$1,507,026
Robert G. Torricelli (D-NJ)	$940,467
Peter H. Kostmayer (D-Pa)	$936,117
Gerry E. Studds (D-Mass)	$758,331
Sam Gejdenson (D-Conn)	$571,167
Gary L. Ackerman (D-NY)	$570,150
Stephen J. Solarz (D-NY)	$500,753
Howard L. Berman (D-Calif)	$498,862
Ileana Ros-Lehtinen (R-Fla)	$483,059
Elton Gallegly (R-Calif)	$458,469
Dan Burton (R-Ind)	$447,425
Olympia J. Snowe (R-Maine)	$444,140
Benjamin A. Gilman (R-NY)	$400,750
Toby Roth (R-Wis)	$399,470
Eliot L. Engel (D-NY)	$366,480
Lee H. Hamilton (D-Ind)	$352,150
Frank McCloskey (D-Ind)	$339,669
Thomas M. Foglietta (D-Pa)	$334,781
Harry A. Johnston (D-Fla)	$303,042
Robert J. Lagomarsino (R-Calif)	$299,079
Antonio J. Colorado-Laguna (D-Puerto Rico)	$297,325
Amo Houghton (R-NY)	$288,678
Henry J. Hyde (R-Ill)	$278,227
Jan Meyers (R-Kan)	$265,614
Ted Weiss (D-NY)	$264,980
Donald M. Payne (D-NJ)	$262,191
Bill Orton (D-Utah)	$255,564
Doug Bereuter (R-Neb)	$223,833
Tom Lantos (D-Calif)	$219,848
Porter J. Goss (R-Fla)	$212,049
Austin J. Murphy (D-Pa)	$191,323
Tom Sawyer (D-Ohio)	$169,407
Christopher H. Smith (R-NJ)	$149,555
Mervyn M. Dymally (D-Calif)	$144,911
Howard Wolpe (D-Mich)	$134,215
Bill Goodling (R-Pa)	$95,579
Edward F. Feighan (D-Ohio)	$83,348
Ben Blaz (R-Guam)	$69,200
John Miller (R-Wash)	$65,000
Jim Leach (R-Iowa)	$59,058
William S. Broomfield (R-Mich)	$33,950
Dante B. Fascell (D-Fla)	$32,565
Eni F. H. Faleomavaega (D-Amer Samoa)	$24,703
Gus Yatron (D-Pa)	$18,500

† Ran for U.S. Senate in 1992

Summary

Though its agenda spans foreign policy issues around the world, the House Foreign Affairs Committee is not a center of great interest for a majority of the PAC community or among other major political contributors. There is one important exception, however — ideological and single-issue groups whose main focus is foreign policy. Within that group, none is more formidable on Capitol Hill than supporters of strong U.S. ties to Israel. Pro-Israel PACs and their members are heavy contributors to Congress as a whole (giving more than $7.4 million in the 1992 elections), and to this committee in particular. Foreign Affairs members received a combined $827,000 from pro-Israel contributors in the last election cycle — an average of more than $19,000 per member. Overall, however, most of the pro-Israel dollars went not to House members, but to Senators.

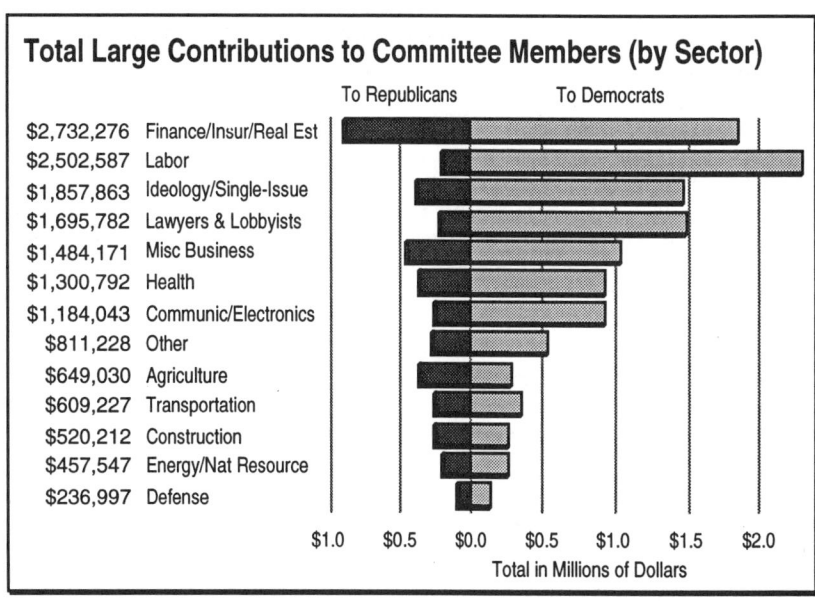

Total Large Contributions to Committee Members (by Sector)

Amount	Sector
$2,732,276	Finance/Insur/Real Est
$2,502,587	Labor
$1,857,863	Ideology/Single-Issue
$1,695,782	Lawyers & Lobbyists
$1,484,171	Misc Business
$1,300,792	Health
$1,184,043	Communic/Electronics
$811,228	Other
$649,030	Agriculture
$609,227	Transportation
$520,212	Construction
$457,547	Energy/Nat Resource
$236,997	Defense

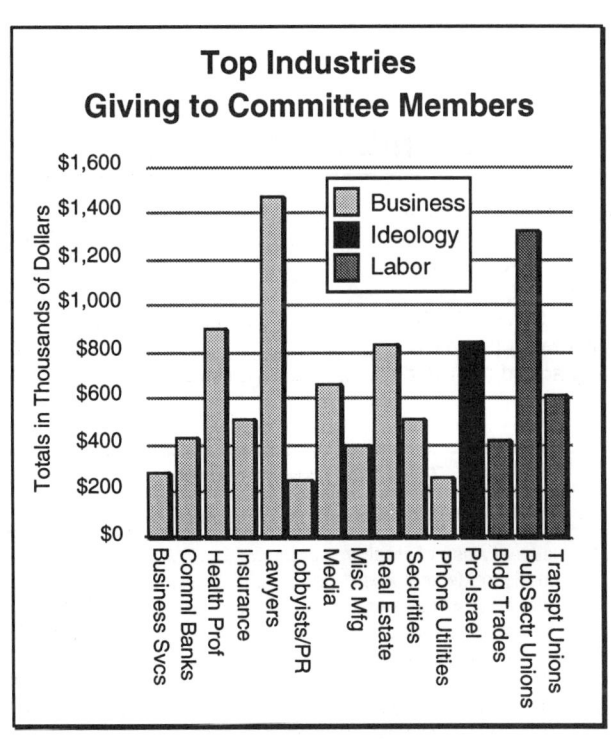

Top Industries Giving to Committee Members

Top 20 Contributors to Committee Members in 1991-92

1	National Assn of Realtors	$193,144
2	American Medical Assn*	$172,200
3	Teamsters Union*	$162,175
4	United Auto Workers	$145,755
5	American Fedn of St/Cnty/Munic Employees	$136,777
6	Assn of Trial Lawyers of America	$132,500
7	Marine Engineers Union*	$125,500
8	National PAC	$117,000
9	National Education Assn	$115,525
10	National Assn Retired Federal Employees	$112,000
11	National Assn of Letter Carriers	$107,225
12	AT&T*	$90,780
13	Laborers Union*	$89,750
14	Air Line Pilots Assn	$87,000
15	Carpenters & Joiners Union*	$85,300
16	Intl Brotherhood of Electrical Workers*	$80,492
17	Machinists/Aerospace Workers Union	$78,425
18	Food & Commercial Workers Union	$76,199
19	American Federation of Teachers	$75,750
20	American Postal Workers Union	$71,750

* Contributions came from more than one affiliate or subsidiary.

Leading Industries Giving to Committee Members

Business
Business Services	$274,146
Commercial Banks	$421,996
Health Professionals	$892,199
Insurance	$495,788
Lawyers/Law Firms	$1,461,148
Lobbyists/PR	$234,634
Media/Entertainment	$642,494
Misc Manufacturing & Distributing	$378,944
Real Estate	$820,108
Securities & Investment	$493,368
Telephone Utilities	$250,197

Ideological/Single-Issue
Pro-Israel	$827,012

Labor
Building Trade Unions	$408,150
Public Sector Unions	$1,311,935
Transportation Unions	$605,850

House Government Operations Committee

John Conyers Jr. (D-Mich), Chairman
Frank Horton (R-NY), Ranking Republican

Party Ratio: 24 Democrats
15 Republicans

Jurisdiction: (1) Budget and accounting measures, other than appropriations; (2) The overall economy and efficiency of Government operations and activities, including Federal procurement; (3) Reorganizations in the executive branch of the Government; (4) Intergovernmental relationships between the United States and the States and municipalities, and general revenue sharing; (5) National archives; (6) Measures providing for off-budget treatment of Federal agencies or programs.

Subcommittees

Commerce, Consumer and Monetary Affairs
Doug Barnard Jr. (D-Ga), Chairman
Dennis Hastert (R-Ill), Ranking Republican

Employment and Housing
Tom Lantos (D-Calif), Chairman
Ronald K. Machtley (R-RI), Ranking Republican

Environment, Energy and Natural Resources
Mike Synar (D-Okla), Chairman
William F. Clinger Jr. (R-Pa), Ranking Republican

Government Activities and Transportation
Barbara Boxer (D-Calif), Chairwoman
C. Christopher Cox (R-Calif), Ranking Republican

Government Information, Justice and Agriculture
Bob Wise (D-WVa), Chairman
Al McCandless (R-Calif), Ranking Republican

Human Resources and Intergovernmental Relations
Edolphus Towns (D-NY), Chairman
Craig Thomas (R-Wyo), Ranking Republican

Legislation and National Security
John Conyers Jr. (D-Mich), Chairman
Frank Horton (R-NY), Ranking Republican

Total PAC and Large Individual Contributions to Committee Members

Barbara Boxer (D-Calif)†	$4,591,641
Mike Synar (D-Okla)	$862,475
Rosa DeLauro (D-Conn)	$811,235
Dick Zimmer (R-NJ)	$752,478
Bill Zeliff (R-NH)	$621,554
Henry A. Waxman (D-Calif)	$584,505
Ben Erdreich (D-Ala)	$573,700
Scott L. Klug (R-Wis)	$528,430
Jon Kyl (R-Ariz)	$486,876
Ileana Ros-Lehtinen (R-Fla)	$483,059
C. Christopher Cox (R-Calif)	$480,795
Dennis Hastert (R-Ill)	$429,221
Stephen L. Neal (D-NC)	$428,370
Edolphus Towns (D-NY)	$424,274
Albert G. Bustamante (D-Texas)	$399,962
John W. Cox Jr. (D-Ill)	$389,715
Ronald K. Machtley (R-RI)	$355,191
Collin C. Peterson (D-Minn)	$342,787
Craig Thomas (R-Wyo)	$312,050
Steven H. Schiff (R-NM)	$297,300
Glenn English (D-Okla)	$289,271
Ray Thornton (D-Ark)	$280,048
John Conyers Jr. (D-Mich)	$273,450
Al McCandless (R-Calif)	$271,107
Ted Weiss (D-NY)	$264,980
Donald M. Payne (D-NJ)	$262,191
Gerald D. Kleczka (D-Wis)	$261,040
David L. Hobson (R-Ohio)	$251,230
Cardiss Collins (D-Ill)	$250,761
Gary Condit (D-Calif)	$233,244
Tom Lantos (D-Calif)	$219,848
Bob Wise (D-WVa)	$219,450
Christopher Shays (R-Conn)	$214,388
Bernard Sanders (I-Vt)	$209,885
Charles Luken (D-Ohio)	$181,600
William F. Clinger (R-Pa)	$170,817
Patsy T. Mink (D-Hawaii)	$168,358
Matthew G. Martinez (D-Calif)	$110,291
Major R. Owens (D-NY)	$109,744
Frank Horton (R-NY)	$66,481
Doug Barnard Jr. (D-Ga)	$4,150

† Ran for US Senate in 1992

Top 20 Contributors to Committee Members in 1991-92

1	National Assn of Realtors	$220,625
2	American Medical Assn*	$178,745
3	American Institute of CPA's	$173,400
4	Teamsters Union*	$149,250
5	United Auto Workers	$139,550
6	Emily's List	$136,995
7	National Education Assn	$135,005
8	Assn of Trial Lawyers of America	$123,350
9	National Assn Retired Federal Employees	$120,000
10	American Fedn of St/Cnty/Munic Employees	$118,397
11	American Bankers Assn*	$108,150
12	United Parcel Service	$102,580
13	Machinists/Aerospace Workers Union	$97,000
14	AT&T*	$93,885
15	National Auto Dealers Assn	$91,700
16	Marine Engineers Union*	$86,500
16	Air Line Pilots Assn	$86,500
18	Food & Commercial Workers Union	$86,098
19	Associated Milk Producers	$80,900
20	Laborers Union*	$79,000
20	National Assn of Letter Carriers	$79,000

* Contributions came from more than one affiliate or subsidiary.

Summary

Despite a name which might make it seem preoccupied with affairs inside the federal bureaucracy, the Government Operations Committee has a wide-ranging jurisdiction that touches upon large segments of American business. Among other things, this committee has an important say in the reorganization of executive branch agencies — something that can have important repercussions on heavily-regulated industries.

Banking and other financial interests were an important element in the members' contribution profile. The panel's Commerce, Consumer and Monetary Affairs subcommittee is of particular interest to that industry.

Lawyers, doctors and labor unions representing public employees were also important sources of contributions.

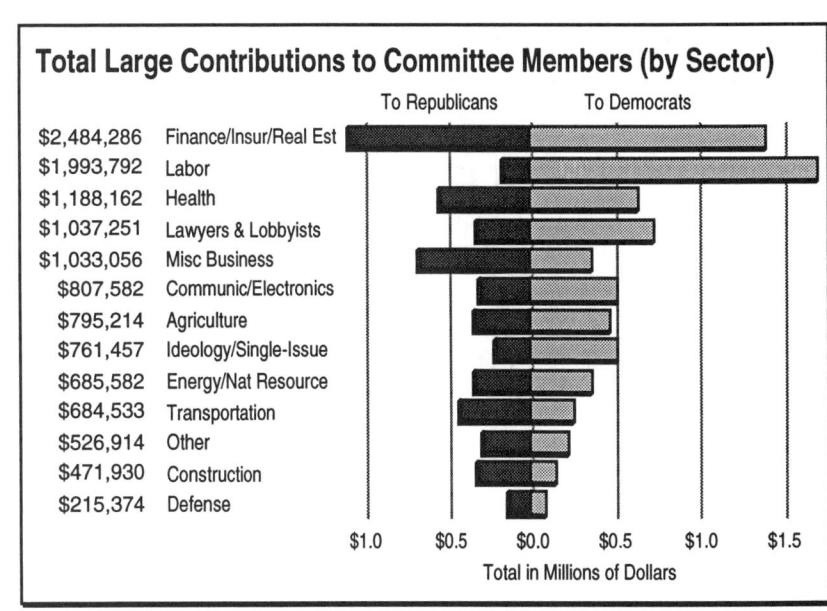

Total Large Contributions to Committee Members (by Sector)

Amount	Sector
$2,484,286	Finance/Insur/Real Est
$1,993,792	Labor
$1,188,162	Health
$1,037,251	Lawyers & Lobbyists
$1,033,056	Misc Business
$807,582	Communic/Electronics
$795,214	Agriculture
$761,457	Ideology/Single-Issue
$685,582	Energy/Nat Resource
$684,533	Transportation
$526,914	Other
$471,930	Construction
$215,374	Defense

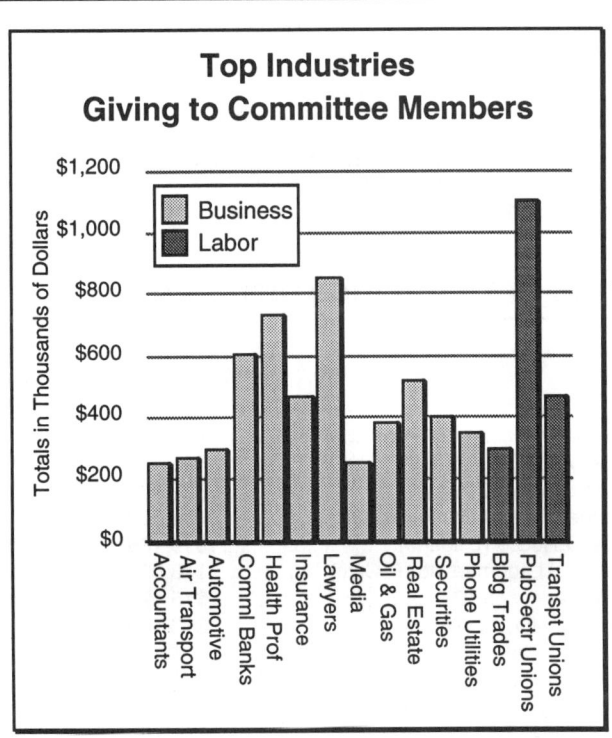

Leading Industries Giving to Committee Members

Business

Accountants	$249,080
Air Transport	$260,930
Automotive	$288,621
Commercial Banks	$596,030
Health Professionals	$724,579
Insurance	$459,905
Lawyers/Law Firms	$844,450
Media/Entertainment	$243,024
Oil & Gas	$376,510
Real Estate	$509,681
Securities & Investment	$388,500
Telephone Utilities	$337,088

Labor

Building Trade Unions	$287,120
Public Sector Unions	$1,091,179
Transportation Unions	$462,375

House Interior and Insular Affairs Committee

George Miller (D-Calif), Chairman
Don Young (R-Alaska), Ranking Republican

Party Ratio: 26 Democrats
16 Republicans

Jurisdiction: (1) Forest reserves and national parks created from the public domain; (2) Forfeiture of land grants and alien ownership, including alien ownership of mineral lands; (3) Geological survey; (4) Interstate compacts relating to apportionment of waters for irrigation purposes; (5) Irrigation and reclamation, including water supply for reclamation projects, and easements of public lands for irrigation projects, and acquisition of private lands when necessary to complete irrigation project; (6) Measures relating to the care and management of Indians, including the care and allotment of Indian lands and general and special measures relating to claims which are paid out of Indian funds; (7) Measures relating generally to the insular possessions of the United States, except those affecting the revenue and appropriations; (8) Military parks and battlefields; national cemeteries administered by the Secretary of the Interior, and parks within the District of Columbia; (9) Mineral land laws and claims and entries thereunder; (10) Mineral resources of the public lands; (11) Mining interest generally; (12) Mining schools and experimental stations; (13) Petroleum conservation on the public lands and conservation of the radium supply in the United States; (14) Preservation of historic ruins and objects of interest on the public domain; (15) Public lands generally, including entry, easements, and grazing thereon; (16) Relations of the United States with the Indians and the Indian tribes; (17) Regulation of the domestic nuclear energy industry, including regulation of research and development reactors and nuclear regulatory research. The committee also has special oversight functions with respect to all programs affecting Indians and nonmilitary nuclear energy and research and development including the disposal of nuclear waste.

Subcommittees

Energy and the Environment
Peter H. Kostmayer (D-Pa), Chairman
John J. Rhodes III (R-Ariz), Ranking Republican

General Oversight and Investigations
Richard H. Lehman (D-Calif), Chairman
Ben Blaz (R-Guam), Ranking Republican

Insular and International Affairs
Ron de Lugo (D-Virgin Islands), Chairman
Robert J. Lagomarsino (R-Calif), Ranking Republican

Mining and Natural Resources
Nick J. Rahall II (D-WVa), Chairman
Barbara Vucanocich (R-Nev), Ranking Republican

National Parks and Public Lands
Bruce F. Vento (D-Minn), Chairman
Ron Marlenee (R-Mont), Ranking Republican

Water, Power and Offshore Energy Resources
George Miller (D-Calif), Chairman
James V. Hansen (R-Utah), Ranking Republican

Total PAC and Large Individual Contributions to Committee Members

	Total from Cmte-Related Contribs	Pct of Member's Lg Contribs		Total from Cmte-Related Contribs	Pct of Member's Lg Contribs
Don Young (R-Alaska)	$174,251	26%	James V. Hansen (R-Utah)	$27,125	14%
Ron Marlenee (R-Mont)	$130,069	16%	Beverly B. Byron (D-Md)	$24,450	16%
Philip R. Sharp (D-Ind)	$114,641	22%	Dick Schulze (R-Pa)	$22,400	13%
Ben Nighthorse Campbell (D-Colo)†	$112,166	9%	George "Buddy" Darden (D-Ga)	$20,350	6%
Charles H. Taylor (R-NC)	$70,475	15%	Larry LaRocco (D-Idaho)	$19,186	4%
Wayne Owens (D-Utah)†	$68,959	5%	Robert J. Lagomarsino (R-Calif)	$18,050	6%
Craig Thomas (R-Wyo)	$66,050	21%	Sam Gejdenson (D-Conn)	$15,125	3%
John J. Rhodes III (R-Arizona)	$59,700	14%	Austin J. Murphy (D-Pa)	$13,500	7%
Bob Smith (R-Ore)	$58,012	23%	Edward J. Markey (D-Mass)	$11,475	3%
Barbara F. Vucanovich (R-Nev)	$55,200	12%	Peter Hoagland (D-Neb)	$11,000	2%
Pat Williams (D-Mont)	$52,526	7%	John J. "Jimmy" Duncan Jr. (R-Tenn)	$10,800	5%
John T. Doolittle (R-Calif)	$52,200	12%	Joel Hefley (R-Colo)	$10,150	9%
George Miller (D-Calif)	$48,341	12%	Calvin Dooley (D-Calif)	$9,780	3%
Richard H. Lehman (D-Calif)	$47,750	7%	John Lewis (D-Ga)	$8,250	3%
Bill Richardson (D-NM)	$47,062	9%	Harry A. Johnston (D-Fla)	$7,150	2%
Mel Levine (D-Calif)†	$45,084	1%	Peter A. DeFazio (D-Ore)	$6,750	4%
Wayne Allard (R-Colo)	$38,288	10%	Neil Abercrombie (D-Hawaii)	$4,300	2%
Peter H. Kostmayer (D-Pa)	$37,443	4%	Bruce F. Vento (D-Minn)	$4,296	2%
Elton Gallegly (R-Calif)	$35,222	8%	Antonio J. Colorado-Laguna (D-Puerto Rico)	$3,500	1%
Richard H. Baker (R-La)	$34,000	6%	Tim Johnson (D-SD)	$3,500	1%
Jim Jontz (D-Ind)	$29,318	7%	Eni F. H. Faleomavaega (D-Amer Samoa)	$2,000	8%
Nick J. Rahall II (D-WVa)	$27,325	8%	Ron de Lugo (D-Virgin Is)	$1,500	3%
			Charles E. Schumer (D-NY)	$1,400	0%

† Ran for US Senate in 1992

Summary

Debates over the use and disposal of public lands are a central focus of the House Interior Committee — a focus that makes it vitally important to states in the western U.S., where much of the land is still federally owned. The committee is also vital to mining, oil & gas and other industries that extract natural resources from public lands through federal leases. In recent years the committee has been a battleground for issues that pit the interests of industry versus those of environmentalists. The committee is also important to American territories and possessions, from Puerto Rico to American Samoa.

With the opening of the 103rd Congress in 1993, the committee officially changed its name to the House Natural Resources Committee. Its jurisdiction remains the same.

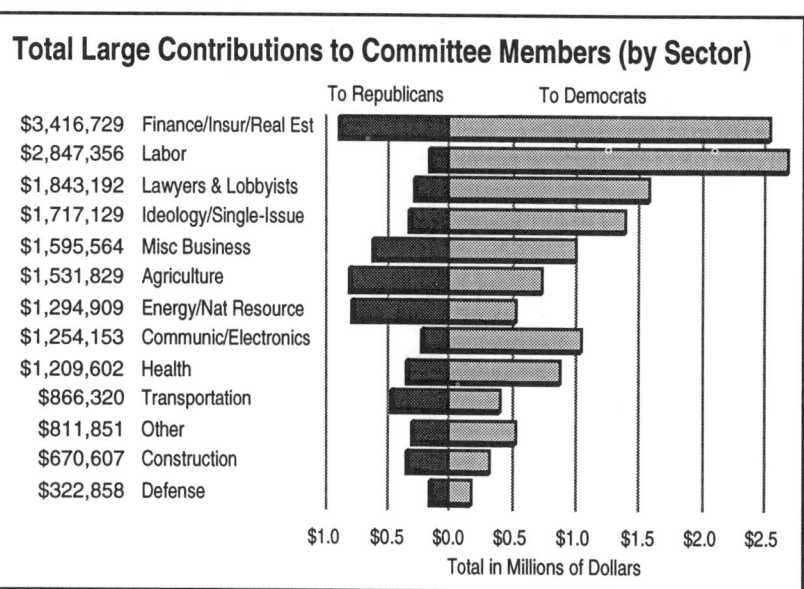

Total Large Contributions to Committee Members (by Sector)

Amount	Sector
$3,416,729	Finance/Insur/Real Est
$2,847,356	Labor
$1,843,192	Lawyers & Lobbyists
$1,717,129	Ideology/Single-Issue
$1,595,564	Misc Business
$1,531,829	Agriculture
$1,294,909	Energy/Nat Resource
$1,254,153	Communic/Electronics
$1,209,602	Health
$866,320	Transportation
$811,851	Other
$670,607	Construction
$322,858	Defense

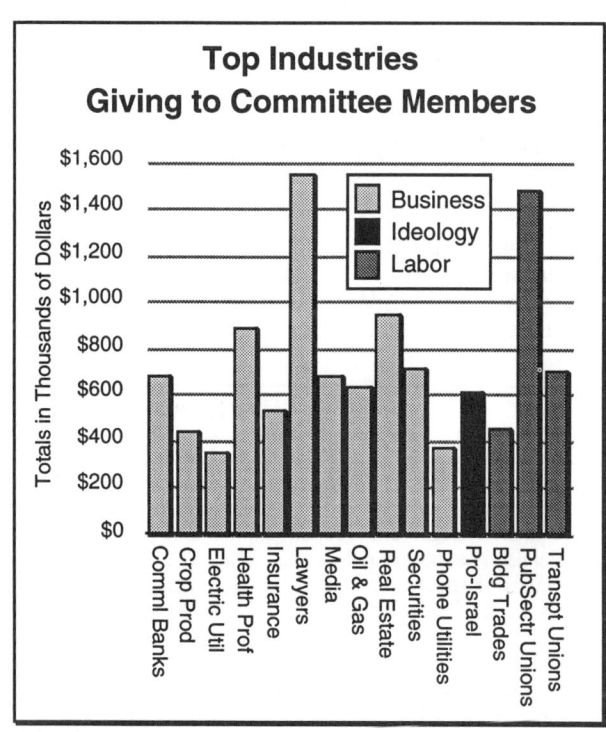

Top Industries Giving to Committee Members

Top 20 Committe-Related Contributors to Committee Members in 1991-92

1	Sierra Club	$61,752
2	Atlantic Richfield	$53,283
3	ACRE (Action Cmte for Rural Electrification)*	$51,651
4	Chevron Corp	$45,400
5	United Mine Workers	$42,100
6	Southern California Edison	$39,230
7	League of Conservation Voters	$34,207
8	Exxon Corp	$31,300
9	Veco International Inc	$27,790
10	Pacific Gas & Electric	$27,600
11	Amoco Corp	$25,050
12	National Coal Assn	$24,400
13	Southern Co*	$20,775
14	Coastal Corp	$20,000
15	Phelps Dodge Corp	$17,100
16	Louisiana-Pacific Corp	$16,600
17	Cyprus Minerals Co	$16,500
18	Occidental Petroleum*	$15,350
18	Shell Oil	$15,350
20	Columbia Gas System*	$15,100

* Contributions came from more than one affiliate or subsidiary.

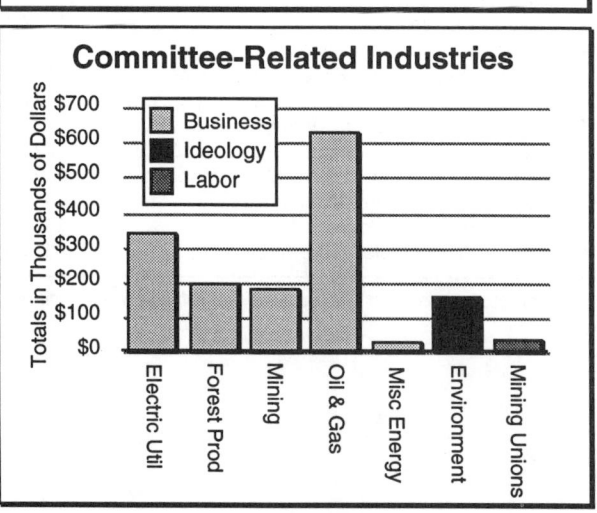

Committee-Related Industries

Leading Committee-Related Industries Giving to Committee Members

Business
- Electric Utilities $337,268
- Forestry & Forest Products $189,343
- Mining $177,569
- Oil & Gas $626,932
- Misc Energy $28,500

Ideological/Single-Issue
- Environmental Issues $153,741

Labor
- Mining Unions $34,600

House Judiciary Committee

Jack Brooks (D-Texas), Chairman
Hamilton Fish Jr. (R-NY), Ranking Republican

Party Ratio: 21 Democrats
13 Republicans

Jurisdiction: (1) Judicial proceedings, civil and criminal generally; (2) Apportionment of Representatives; (3) Bankruptcy, mutiny, espionage and counterfeiting; (4) Civil liberties; (5) Constitutional amendments; (6) Federal courts and judges; (7) Immigration and naturalization; (8) Interstate compacts generally; (9) Local courts in the Territories and possessions; (10) Measures relating to claims against the United States; (11) Meetings of Congress, attendance of Members and their acceptance of incompatible offices; (12) National penitentiaries; (13) Patent Office; (14) Patents, copyrights, and trademarks; (15) Presidential succession; (16) Protection of trade and commerce against unlawful restraints and monopolies; (17) Revision and codification of the Statutes of the United States; (18) State and territorial boundary lines; (19) Communist and other subversive activities affecting the internal security of the United States.

Subcommittees

Administrative Law and Governmental Relations
Barney Frank (D-Mass), Chairman
George W. Gekas (R-Pa), Ranking Republican

Civil and Constitutional Rights
Don Edwards (D-Calif), Chairman
Henry J. Hyde (R-Ill), Ranking Republican

Intellectual Property and Judicial Administration
William J. Hughes (D-NJ), Chairman
Carlos J. Moorhead (R-Calif), Ranking Republican

Criminal Justice
Charles E. Schumer (D-NY), Chairman
F. James Sensenbrenner Jr. (R-Wis), Ranking Republican

Economic and Commercial Law
Jack Brooks (D-Texas), Chairman
Hamilton Fish Jr. (R-NY), Ranking Republican

International Law, Immigration and Refugees
Romano L. Mazzoli (D-Ky), Chairman
Bill McCollum (R-Fla), Ranking Republican

Total PAC and Large Individual Contributions to Committee Members

Mel Levine (D-Calif)[1]	$4,106,254
Tom Campbell (R-Calif)[1]	$3,593,778
Mike Synar (D-Okla)	$862,475
Dan Glickman (D-Kan)	$730,001
Jim Ramstad (R-Minn)	$712,432
Charles E. Schumer (D-NY)	$677,473
Peter Hoagland (D-Neb)	$605,817
John F. Reed (D-RI)	$580,186
Jack Brooks (D-Texas)	$540,283
John Bryant (D-Texas)	$525,038
Bill McCollum (R-Fla)	$514,575
Howard L. Berman (D-Calif)	$498,862
Rick Boucher (D-Va)	$493,959
Hamilton Fish Jr. (R-NY)	$401,550
William J. Hughes (D-NJ)	$362,262
George F. Allen (R-Va)	$357,906
Mike Kopetski (D-Ore)	$351,542
Lamar Smith (R-Texas)	$329,635
J. Howard Coble (R-NC)	$307,546
Barney Frank (D-Mass)	$304,428
Steven H. Schiff (R-NM)	$297,300
Carlos J. Moorhead (R-Calif)	$294,740
George E. Sangmeister (D-Ill)	$278,286
Henry J. Hyde (R-Ill)	$278,227
Patricia Schroeder (D-Colo)	$278,131
John Conyers Jr. (D-Mich)	$273,450
Don Edwards (D-Calif)	$221,785
Harley O. Staggers Jr. (D-WVa)	$188,168
Craig Washington (D-Texas)	$171,250
F. James Sensenbrenner Jr. (R-Wis)	$131,020
Craig T. James (R-Fla)	$116,087
Edward F. Feighan (D-Ohio)	$83,348
George W. Gekas (R-Pa)	$80,810
D. French Slaughter Jr. (R-Va)[2]	$43,525
Romano L. Mazzoli (D-Ky)	$14,923

Top 20 Contributors to Committee Members in 1991-92

1	American Institute of CPA's	$181,800
2	National Assn of Realtors	$167,749
3	Assn of Trial Lawyers of America	$159,500
4	American Medical Assn*	$141,084
5	Teamsters Union	$124,000
6	American Bankers Assn*	$113,075
7	AT&T	$108,520
8	National Education Assn*	$106,685
9	American Fedn of St/Cnty/Munic Employees	$103,600
10	National Cable Television Assn	$102,650
11	United Auto Workers	$97,600
12	National Auto Dealers Assn	$94,700
13	National Assn Retired Federal Employees	$79,500
14	Time Warner*	$78,200
15	National Assn of Letter Carriers*	$73,775
16	Walt Disney Co*	$72,599
17	Intl Brotherhood of Electrical Workers	$69,450
18	Carpenters & Joiners Union	$68,300
19	Marine Engineers Union*	$63,850
20	National Assn of Life Underwriters	$63,000

* Contributions came from more than one affiliate or subsidiary.

[1] Ran for U.S. Senate in 1992
[2] Resigned in November 1991

Summary

The shape of the American judicial and criminal justice system is the central focus of the House Judiciary Committee. It is a role that makes it important not only to lawyers, but to every sector of the American business community as well. As is true in most committees of Congress, the financial industry provided the biggest level of support to committee members — nearly $3.9 million in 1991-92. But attorneys and lobbyists were particularly active in this committee, delivering a combined $2.2 million, mostly through individual contributions as opposed to PACs. The average committee member received nearly $65,000 from lawyers and lobbyists in the 1992 elections — the highest average from the legal community to any House committee.

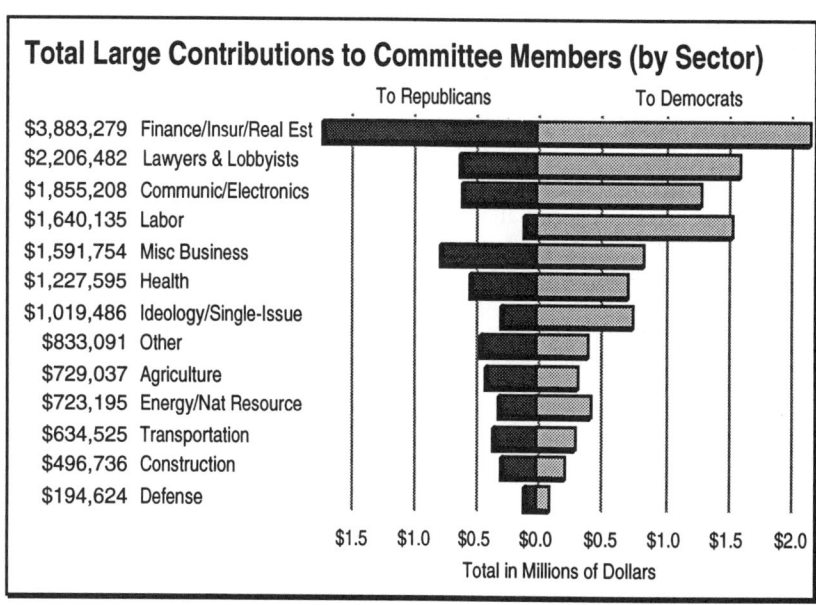

Total Large Contributions to Committee Members (by Sector)

Amount	Sector
$3,883,279	Finance/Insur/Real Est
$2,206,482	Lawyers & Lobbyists
$1,855,208	Communic/Electronics
$1,640,135	Labor
$1,591,754	Misc Business
$1,227,595	Health
$1,019,486	Ideology/Single-Issue
$833,091	Other
$729,037	Agriculture
$723,195	Energy/Nat Resource
$634,525	Transportation
$496,736	Construction
$194,624	Defense

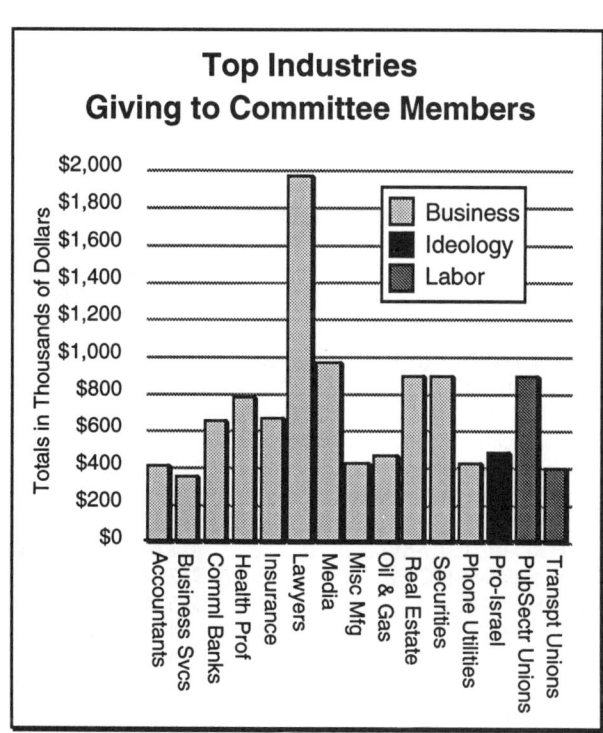

Leading Industries Giving to Committee Members

Business
- Accountants $396,210
- Business Services $341,340
- Commercial Banks $635,557
- Health Professionals $761,747
- Insurance $653,673
- Lawyers/Law Firms $1,948,788
- Media/Entertainment $951,484
- Misc Manufacturing & Distributing $406,994
- Oil & Gas $458,554
- Real Estate $880,096
- Securities & Investment $881,061
- Telephone Utilities $415,155

Ideological/Single-Issue
- Pro-Israel $464,539

Labor
- Public Sector Unions $885,274
- Transportation Unions $382,789

House Merchant Marine and Fisheries Committee

Gerry E. Studds (D-Mass), Chairman
Robert W. Davis (R-Mich), Ranking Republican

Party Ratio: 28 Democrats
17 Republicans

Jurisdiction: (1) Merchant marine generally; (2) Oceanography and marine affairs, including coastal zone management; (3) Coast Guard, including lifesaving service, lighthouses, lightships and ocean derelicts; (4) Fisheries and wildlife, including research, restoration, refuges and conservation; (5) Measures relating to the regulation of common carriers by water (except matters subject to the jurisdiction of the Interstate Commerce Commission) and to the inspection of merchant marine vessels, lights and signals, lifesaving equipment and fire protection on such vessels; (6) Merchant marine officers and seamen; (7) Navigation and the laws relating thereto, including pilotage; (8) Panama Canal and the maintenance and operation of the Panama Canal, including the administration, sanitation and government of the Canal Zone; and interoceanic canals generally; (9) Registering and licensing of vessels and small boats; (10) Rules and international arrangements to prevent collisions at sea; (11) United States Coast Guard and Merchant Marine Academies, and State maritime academies; (12) International fishing agreements. The committee also oversees offshore oil and gas matters on the U.S. Outer Continental Shelf.

Subcommittees

Coast Guard and Navigation
W. J. "Billy" Tauzin (D-La), Chairman
Jack Fields (R-Texas), Ranking Republican

Fisheries and Wildlife Conservation and Environment
Gerry E. Studds (D-Mass), Chairman
Don Young (R-Alaska), Ranking Republican

Merchant Marine
Carroll Hubbard Jr. (D-Ky), Acting Chairman
Norman F. Lent (R-NY), Ranking Republican

Oceanography and Great Lakes
Dennis M. Hertel (D-Mich), Chairman
Herbert H. Bateman (R-Va), Ranking Republican

Oversight and Investigations
William O. Lipinski (D-Ill), Chairman
H. James Saxton (R-NJ), Ranking Republican

Total Committee-Related Contributions to Committee Members

Member	Total from Cmte-Related Contribs	Pct of Member's Lg Contribs
Don Young (R-Alaska)	$171,797	25%
Gerry E. Studds (D-Mass)	$125,454	17%
Jack Fields (R-Texas)	$107,105	16%
Helen Delich Bentley (R-Md)	$88,630	13%
Jolene Unsoeld (D-Wash)	$78,952	17%
W.J. "Billy" Tauzin (D-La)	$70,700	13%
Frank Pallone Jr. (D-NJ)	$66,635	9%
Randy "Duke" Cunningham (R-Calif)	$61,848	12%
Greg Laughlin (D-Texas)	$44,338	8%
James M. Inhofe (R-Okla)	$43,305	12%
Herbert H. Bateman (R-Va)	$38,700	7%
H. James Saxton (R-NJ)	$33,748	8%
Nita M. Lowey (D-NY)	$33,050	4%
William J. Jefferson (D-La)	$32,400	9%
Gene Taylor (D-Miss)	$31,050	12%
William J. Hughes (D-NJ)	$30,300	8%
George J. Hochbrueckner (D-NY)	$29,850	8%
John T. Doolittle (R-Calif)	$29,050	7%
Thomas J. Manton (D-NY)	$28,533	6%
Robert W. Davis (R-Mich)	$27,600	19%
H. Martin Lancaster (D-NC)	$26,700	6%
John F. Reed (D-RI)	$26,500	5%
Wally Herger (R-Calif)	$24,150	6%
Thomas M. Foglietta (D-Pa)	$24,050	7%
Robert A. Borski (D-Pa)	$23,550	5%
Owen B. Pickett (D-Va)	$23,232	10%
William O. Lipinski (D-Ill)	$21,000	4%
Sonny Callahan (R-Ala)	$20,700	6%
Solomon P. Ortiz (D-Texas)	$19,300	9%
Earl Hutto (D-Fla)	$18,750	10%
Carroll Hubbard Jr. (D-Ky)	$17,600	14%
Lucien E. Blackwell (D-Pa)	$17,500	6%
Curt Weldon (R-Pa)	$16,250	6%
Arthur Ravenel Jr. (R-SC)	$14,425	8%
Norman F. Lent (R-NY)	$14,300	6%
Dennis M. Hertel (D-Mich)	$14,250	8%
Wayne T. Gilchrest (R-Md)	$11,973	6%
J. Howard Coble (R-NC)	$11,300	4%
Bob Clement (D-Tenn)	$8,750	2%
Robin Tallon (D-SC)	$8,050	9%
Stephen J. Solarz (D-NY)	$5,350	1%
Glenn M. Anderson (D-Calif)	$5,000	17%
Walter B. Jones (D-NC)	$3,750	23%
Charles E. Bennett (D-Fla)	$3,000	18%
Eni F. H. Faleomavaega (D-Amer Samoa)	$2,600	11%
Porter J. Goss (R-Fla)	$1,000	0%

Summary

The House Merchant Marine and Fisheries Committee presents an interesting example of one of the often-overlooked realities of PAC giving in Congress — that the interests of labor unions and businesses are not always in conflict. Foreign competition and a dwindling American presence on the open seas have put labor and business together in trying to preserve what is left of the increasingly imperiled U.S. merchant marine. While the two sides do have their differences, they often work to achieve consensus on issues of basic interest to the survival of the industry.

Oil & gas producers and exploration companies also pay close attention to this committee's deliberations, as this is the panel that wrangles over the economic and environmental repercussions of offshore oil drilling.

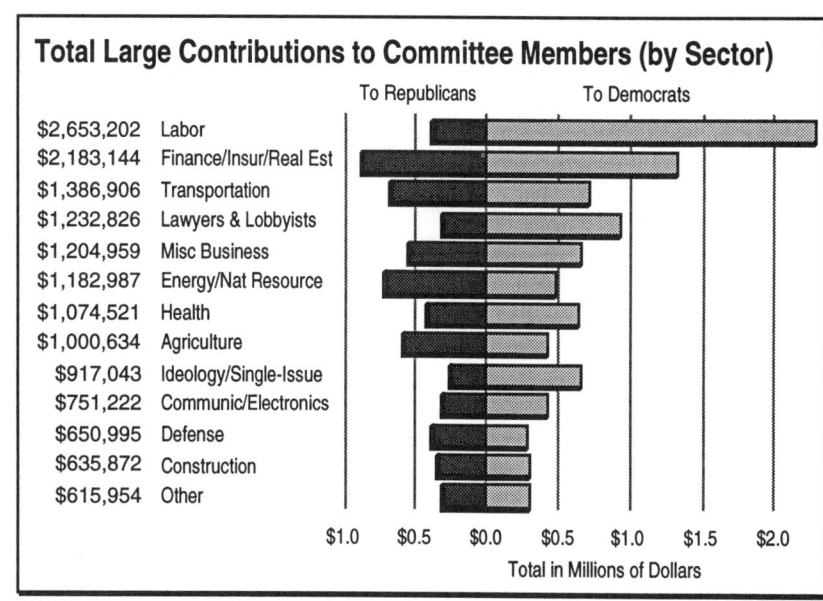

Total Large Contributions to Committee Members (by Sector)

Amount	Sector
$2,653,202	Labor
$2,183,144	Finance/Insur/Real Est
$1,386,906	Transportation
$1,232,826	Lawyers & Lobbyists
$1,204,959	Misc Business
$1,182,987	Energy/Nat Resource
$1,074,521	Health
$1,000,634	Agriculture
$917,043	Ideology/Single-Issue
$751,222	Communic/Electronics
$650,995	Defense
$635,872	Construction
$615,954	Other

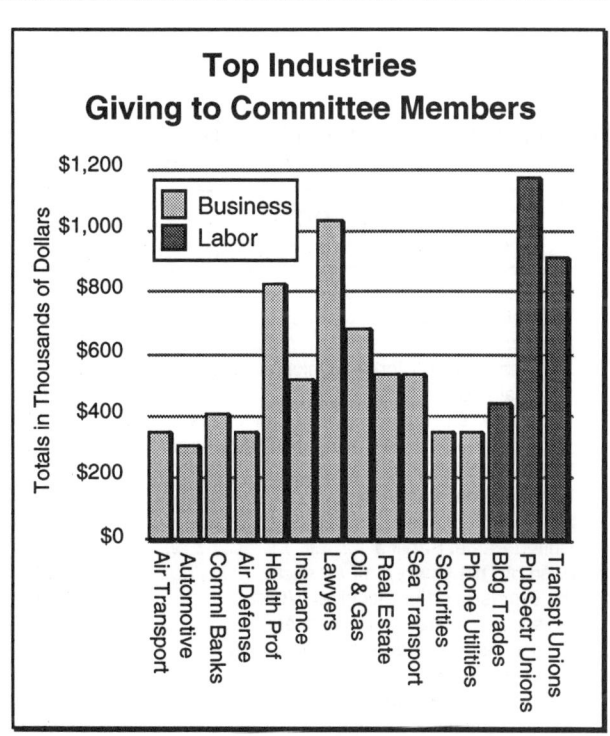

Top 20 Committee-Related Contributors to Committee Members in 1991-92

1	Marine Engineers Union*	$232,974
2	Seafarers International Union*	$161,700
3	CSX Corp*	$89,375
4	Sierra Club	$45,144
5	Atlantic Richfield	$41,950
6	International Longshoremens Assn	$39,050
7	Exxon Corp	$33,450
8	Chevron Corp	$33,200
9	American Pilots Assn	$28,700
10	Masters, Mates & Pilots Union	$27,900
11	Veco International Inc	$27,790
12	American President Lines	$27,200
13	American Waterways Operators	$20,500
14	BP America	$20,050
15	Matson Navigation	$19,600
16	Crowley Maritime	$19,050
17	Shell Oil	$17,950
18	Occidental Petroleum*	$17,600
19	Cruise PAC	$17,500
20	Amoco Corp	$17,250

* Contributions came from more than one affiliate or subsidiary.

Leading Committee-Related Industries Giving to Committee Members

Business
- Commercial Fishing $81,084
- Oil & Gas $383,493
- Sea Transport $530,799

Ideological/Single-Issue
- Environmental Issues $80,075

Labor
- Sea Transport Unions $480,624

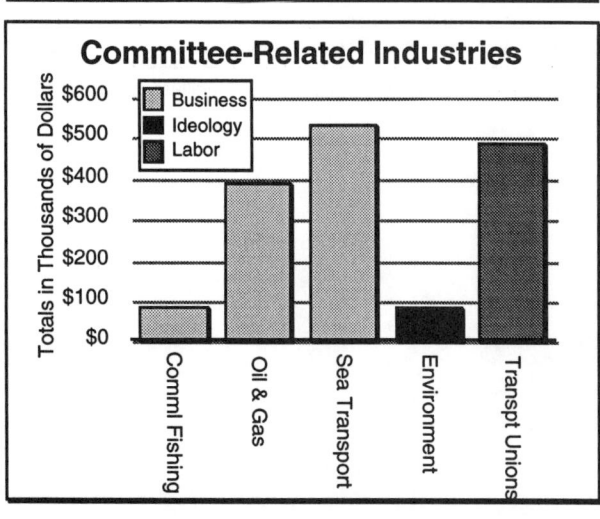

House Post Office and Civil Service Committee

William L. Clay (D-Mo), Chairman
Benjamin A. Gilman (R-NY), Ranking Republican

Party Ratio: 14 Democrats
8 Republicans

Jurisdiction: (1) Census and the collection of statistics generally; (2) All Federal Civil Service, including intergovernmental personnel; (3) Postal-savings banks; (4) Postal Service generally, including the railway mail service, and measures relating to ocean mail and pneumatic-tube service; but excluding post roads; (5) Status of officers and employees of the United States, including their compensation, classification and retirement; (6) Hatch Act; (7) Holidays and celebrations; (8) Population and demography.

Subcommittees

Census and Population
Thomas C. Sawyer (D-Ohio), Chairman
Tom Ridge (R-Pa), Ranking Republican

Civil Service
Gerry Sikorski (D-Minn), Chairman
Constance A. Morella (R-Md), Ranking Republican

Compensation and Employee Benefits
Gary L. Ackerman (D-NY), Chairman
John T. Myers (R-Ind), Ranking Republican

Human Resources
Paul E. Kanjorski (D-Pa), Chairman
Dan Burton (R-Ind), Ranking Republican

Investigations
William L. Clay (D-Mo), Chairman
Rod Chandler (R-Wash), Ranking Republican

Postal Operations and Services
Frank McCloskey (D-Ind), Chairman
Frank Horton (R-NY), Ranking Republican

Postal Personnel and Modernization
Charles A. Hayes (D-Ill), Chairman
Don Young (R-Alaska), Ranking Republican

Total PAC and Large Individual Contributions to Committee Members

Rod Chandler (R-Wash)† $2,094,096
Mary Rose Oakar (D-Ohio) $860,393
Gerry Sikorski (D-Minn) $775,497
James P. Moran Jr. (D-Va) $715,363
Don Young (R-Alaska) $679,879
Gary L. Ackerman (D-NY) $570,150
Dan Burton (R-Ind) $447,425
Tom Ridge (R-Pa) $416,370
Benjamin A. Gilman (R-NY) $400,750
Frank McCloskey (D-Ind) $339,669
William L. Clay (D-Mo) $282,938
Constance A. Morella (R-Md) $282,091
Patricia Schroeder (D-Colo) $278,131
Paul E. Kanjorski (D-Pa) $265,662
Charles A. Hayes (D-Ill) $223,251
Barbara-Rose Collins (D-Mich) $217,646
John T. Myers (R-Ind) $215,708
Tom Sawyer (D-Ohio) $169,407
Mervyn M. Dymally (D-Calif) $144,911
Eleanor Holmes Norton (D-DC) $136,975
Michael R. McNulty (D-NY) $126,126
Frank Horton (R-NY) $66,481
Gus Yatron (D-Pa) $18,500

† Ran for U.S. Senate in 1992

Top 20 Contributors to Committee Members in 1991-92

1	National Assn of Letter Carriers	$140,000
2	Teamsters Union*	$120,025
3	American Medical Assn*	$103,900
4	American Postal Workers Union*	$102,700
5	National Assn of Realtors	$100,890
6	National Assn Retired Federal Employees	$94,500
7	American Fedn of St/Cnty/Munic Employees	$92,500
8	United Auto Workers	$78,705
9	National Education Assn	$77,975
10	Air Line Pilots Assn	$77,500
11	United Parcel Service	$71,280
12	Assn of Trial Lawyers of America	$69,500
13	Intl Brotherhood of Electrical Workers*	$63,992
14	American Federation of Teachers	$61,100
15	Machinists/Aerospace Workers Union*	$60,925
16	Laborers' Political League	$59,000
17	Marine Engineers Union*	$56,750
18	American Institute of CPA's	$56,600
19	American Bankers Assn*	$55,225
20	Food & Commercial Workers Union	$52,843

* Contributions came from more than one affiliate or subsidiary.

Summary

Steelworkers, teamsters and assembly line operators may be popularly thought of as the mainstream of organized labor, but government employees and postal workers are an increasingly powerful segment of the labor community — and one which has weighed in heavily with PAC contributions to members of Congress. The Post Office and Civil Service Committee is of particular interest to government and postal PACs, since it debates crucial issues ranging from salaries to government workers' participation in political activities.

Public sector unions (which includes postal workers, government unions and teacher unions) gave an average of nearly $56,000 to committee members — far more than to any other House committee. Non-government unions were also generous to committee members. In all, committee members received an average of more than $95,000 from labor unions.

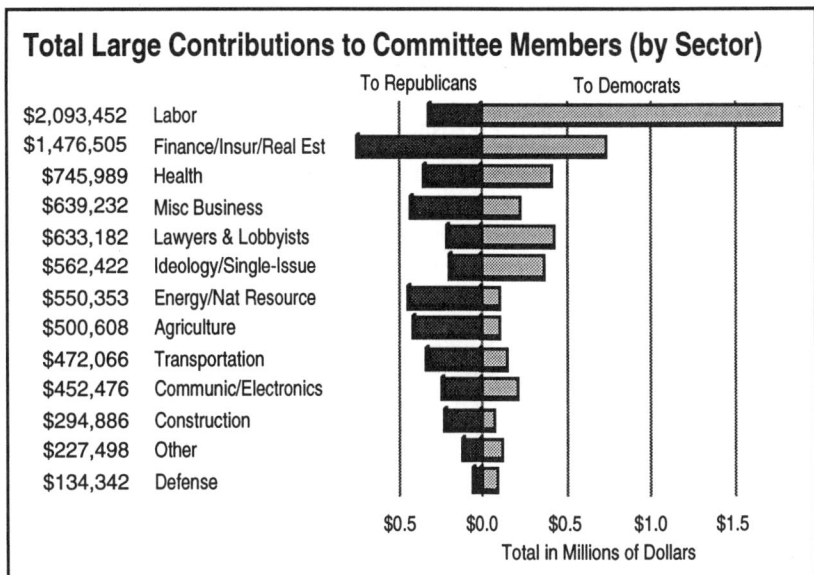

Total Large Contributions to Committee Members (by Sector)

Amount	Sector
$2,093,452	Labor
$1,476,505	Finance/Insur/Real Est
$745,989	Health
$639,232	Misc Business
$633,182	Lawyers & Lobbyists
$562,422	Ideology/Single-Issue
$550,353	Energy/Nat Resource
$500,608	Agriculture
$472,066	Transportation
$452,476	Communic/Electronics
$294,886	Construction
$227,498	Other
$134,342	Defense

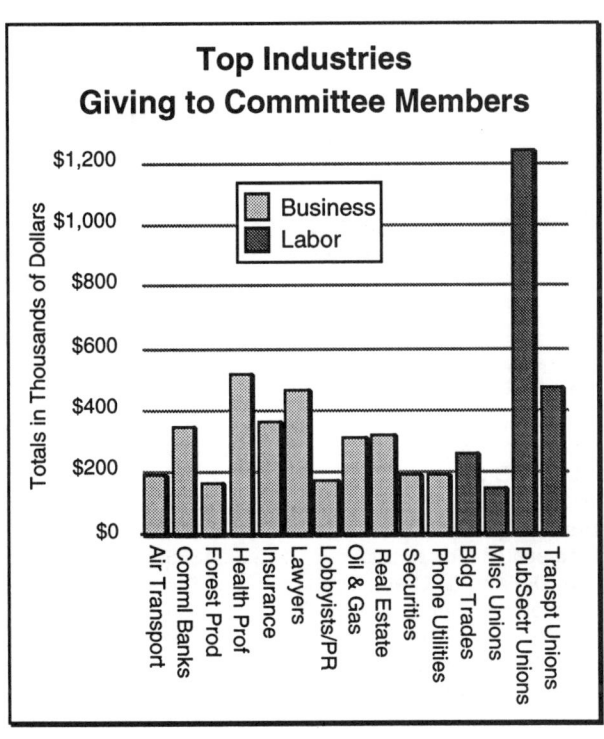

Top Industries Giving to Committee Members

Leading Industries Giving to Committee Members

Business
- Air Transport $183,702
- Commercial Banks $337,929
- Forestry & Forest Products $162,424
- Health Professionals $511,800
- Insurance $359,428
- Lawyers/Law Firms $462,893
- Lobbyists/PR $170,289
- Oil & Gas $305,630
- Real Estate $313,400
- Securities & Investment $188,170
- Telephone Utilities $186,035

Labor
- Building Trade Unions $258,185
- Misc Unions $138,535
- Public Sector Unions $1,230,032
- Transportation Unions $466,700

157

House Public Works and Transportation Committee

Robert A. Roe (D-NJ), Chairman
John Paul Hammerschmidt (R-Ark), Ranking Republican

Party Ratio: 34 Democrats
21 Republicans

Jurisdiction: (1) Flood control and improvement of rivers and harbors; (2) Measures relating to the Capitol Building and the Senate and the House Office Buildings; (3) Measures relating to the construction or maintenance of roads and post roads, other than appropriations therefor; but no bill providing general legislation in relation to roads may contain any provision for any specific road, nor may any bill in relation to a specific road embrace a provision in relation to any other specific road; (4) Measures relating to the construction or reconstruction, maintenance and care of the buildings and grounds of the Botanic Garden, the Library of Congress, and the Smithsonian Institution; (5) Measures relating to the purchase of sites and construction of post offices, customhouses, Federal courthouses, and Government buildings within the District of Columbia; (6) Oil and other pollution of navigable waters; (7) Public buildings and occupied or improved grounds of the United States generally; (8) Public works for the benefit of navigation, including bridges and dams (other than international bridges and dams); (9) Water power; (10) Transportation, including civil aviation except railroads, railroad labor and pensions; (11) Roads and the safety thereof; (12) Water transportation subject to the jurisdiction of the Interstate Commerce Commission; (13) Related transportation regulatory agencies, except (A) the Interstate Commerce Commission as it relates to railroads, (B) Federal Railroad Administration, and (C) Amtrak.

Subcommittees

Aviation
James L. Oberstar (D-Minn), Chairman
William F. Clinger Jr. (R-Pa), Ranking Republican

Economic Development
Joe Kolter (D-Pa), Chairman
Helen Delich Bentley (R-Md), Ranking Republican

Investigations and Oversight
Robert A. Borski (D-Pa), Chairman
Ron Packard (R-Calif), Ranking Republican

Public Buildings and Grounds
Gus Savage (D-Ill), Chairman
James M. Inhofe (R-Okla), Ranking Republican

Surface Transportation
Norman Y. Mineta (D-Calif), Chairman
Bud Shuster (R-Pa), Ranking Republican

Water Resources
Henry J. Nowak (D-NY), Chairman
Thomas E. Petri (R-Wis), Ranking Republican

Total Committee-Related Contributions to Committee Members

	Total from Cmte-Related Contribs	Pct of Member's Lg Contribs
Norman Y. Mineta (D-Calif)	$297,809	36%
Bud Shuster (R-Pa)	$196,925	38%
Robert A. Roe (D-NJ)	$180,300	43%
Frank Pallone Jr. (D-NJ)	$163,871	22%
Pete Geren (D-Texas)	$155,138	21%
Helen Delich Bentley (R-Md)	$150,290	23%
Greg Laughlin (D-Texas)	$137,529	25%
William O. Lipinski (D-Ill)	$120,650	26%
Nick J. Rahall II (D-WVa)	$107,840	33%
Robert A. Borski (D-Pa)	$103,545	24%
Bob Clement (D-Tenn)	$101,566	22%
James L. Oberstar (D-Minn)	$97,680	40%
James M. Inhofe (R-Okla)	$97,575	28%
Rosa DeLauro (D-Conn)	$97,361	12%
Ron Packard (R-Calif)	$96,023	44%
Joan Kelly Horn (D-Mo)	$93,950	17%
Bill Zeliff (R-NH)	$93,500	15%
Jimmy Hayes (D-La)	$93,130	26%
Dick Swett (D-NH)	$91,910	12%
C. Christopher Cox (R-Calif)	$83,790	17%
Jerry F. Costello (D-Ill)	$83,700	21%
Pete Peterson (D-Fla)	$81,957	24%
Lewis F. Payne Jr. (D-Va)	$80,700	22%
Susan Molinari (R-NY)	$72,150	17%
Frank Riggs (R-Calif)	$69,924	14%
Charles H. Taylor (R-NC)	$68,172	15%
Mike Parker (D-Miss)	$66,755	20%
William F. Clinger (R-Pa)	$65,325	38%
Tim Valentine (D-NC)	$64,550	19%
Tom Petri (R-Wis)	$63,390	27%
Bud Cramer (D-Ala)	$60,200	19%
Mel Hancock (R-Mo)	$59,400	21%
John Lewis (D-Ga)	$59,250	19%
Sherwood Boehlert (R-NY)	$57,270	21%
Bill Brewster (D-Okla)	$56,000	15%
Bill Emerson (R-Mo)	$55,260	14%
Peter A. DeFazio (D-Ore)	$54,550	29%
Dick Nichols (R-Kan)	$53,324	22%
Thomas W. Ewing (R-Ill)	$50,760	13%
John J. "Jimmy" Duncan Jr. (R-Tenn)	$49,400	24%
Barbara-Rose Collins (D-Mich)	$48,450	22%
Ben Jones (D-Ga)	$45,250	21%
George E. Sangmeister (D-Ill)	$45,190	16%
David L. Hobson (R-Ohio)	$44,400	18%
Lucien E. Blackwell (D-Pa)	$44,370	16%
Joe Kolter (D-Pa)	$38,950	33%
Cass Ballenger (R-NC)	$37,350	15%
Paul E. Gillmor (R-Ohio)	$34,100	17%
Gus Savage (D-Ill)	$32,550	32%
Douglas Applegate (D-Ohio)	$24,368	29%
James A. Traficant Jr. (D-Ohio)	$23,500	19%
Eleanor Holmes Norton (D-DC)	$19,300	14%
Glenn M. Anderson (D-Calif)	$16,050	55%
Ron de Lugo (D-Virgin Is)	$15,750	36%
Glenn Poshard (D-Ill)	$3,650	8%
John Paul Hammerschmidt (R-Ark)	$1,524	100%
Henry J. Nowak (D-NY)	$0	0%

Summary

The biggest contributors on this committee are related to the transportation industry — and those interests are represented not only by the airlines, trucking companies, railroads and freight services, but by the labor unions representing the people who drive the trucks, pilot the planes and ride the rails across America. Together, transportation companies and transport unions gave nearly $3.3 million to the committee's members during the 1991-92 election cycle.

The committee also earmarks billions of dollars in federally-funded public works projects that are built each year in every congressional district in the nation — projects that employ thousands of construction workers and supply important revenues to the nation's builders and other construction-related businesses. Here too the contributions came both from the business and labor sectors, though most businesses gave more to Republicans and the labor PACs heavily favored Democrats.

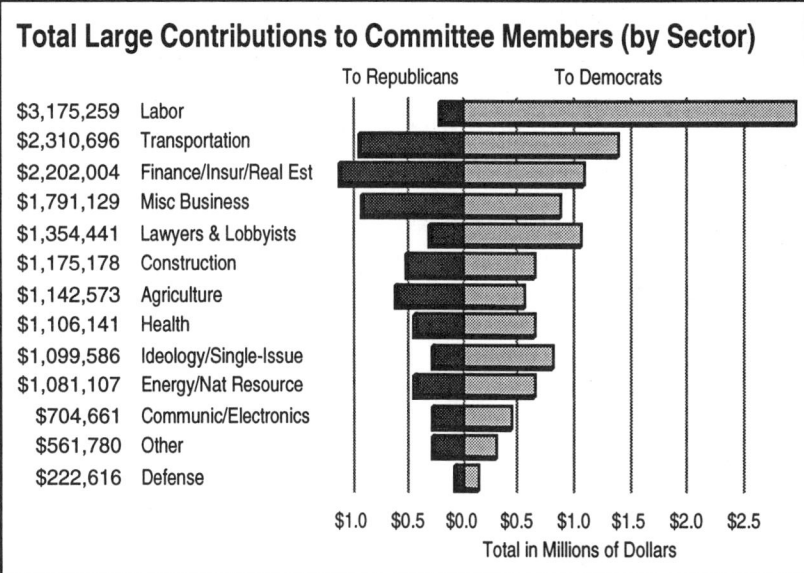

Total Large Contributions to Committee Members (by Sector)

Amount	Sector
$3,175,259	Labor
$2,310,696	Transportation
$2,202,004	Finance/Insur/Real Est
$1,791,129	Misc Business
$1,354,441	Lawyers & Lobbyists
$1,175,178	Construction
$1,142,573	Agriculture
$1,106,141	Health
$1,099,586	Ideology/Single-Issue
$1,081,107	Energy/Nat Resource
$704,661	Communic/Electronics
$561,780	Other
$222,616	Defense

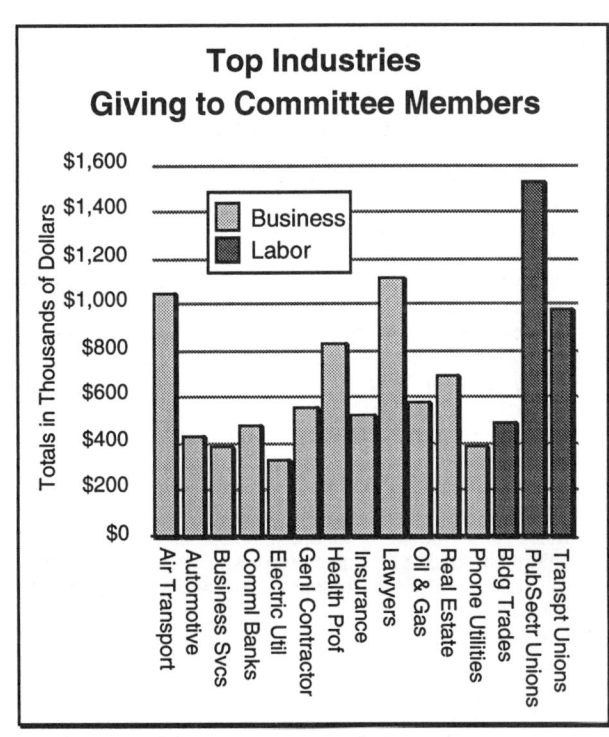

Top 20 Committee-Related Contributors to Committee Members in 1991-92

1	United Parcel Service	$241,000
2	Federal Express Corp	$211,145
3	Air Line Pilots Assn	$208,000
4	Teamsters Union*	$186,898
5	National Auto Dealers Assn	$181,900
6	Marine Engineers Union*	$134,850
7	Aircraft Owners & Pilots Assn	$128,000
8	Associated General Contractors*	$84,399
9	American Airlines	$77,150
10	United Transportation Union	$76,348
11	Seafarers International Union	$70,500
12	National Utility Contractors Assn	$62,330
13	CSX Corp*	$61,250
14	American Trucking Assns	$59,875
15	Norfolk Southern*	$59,500
16	Amalgamated Transit Union	$54,750
17	Auto Dealers & Drivers for Free Trade	$53,500
18	Union Pacific Corp	$51,359
19	Transport Workers Union	$51,280
20	United Airlines	$48,600

* Contributions came from more than one affiliate or subsidiary.

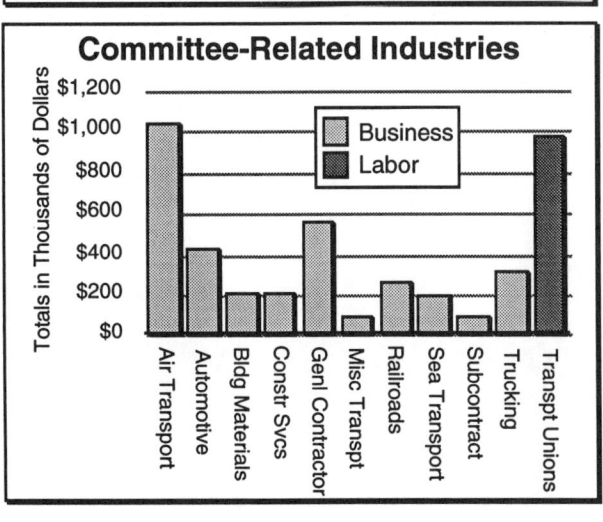

Leading Committee-Related Industries Giving to Committee Members

Business
- Air Transport $1,037,213
- Automotive $422,482
- Building Materials & Equipment $195,229
- Construction Services $202,970
- General Contractors $543,595
- Misc Transport $87,525
- Railroads $247,036
- Sea Transport $188,468
- Special Trade Contractors $82,456
- Trucking $307,271

Labor
- Transportation Unions $965,126

House Rules Committee

Joe Moakley (D-Mass), Chairman
Gerald B. H. Solomon (R-NY), Ranking Republican

Party Ratio: 9 Democrats
4 Republicans

Jurisdiction: (1) The rules and joint rules (other than rules or joint rules relating to the Code of Official Conduct), and order of business of the House; (2) Emergency waivers (under the Congressional Budget Act of 1974) of the required reporting date for bills and resolutions authorizing new budget authority; (3) Recesses and final adjournments of Congress.

Subcommittees

Rules of the House
Anthony C. Beilenson (D-Calif), Chairman
David Dreier (R-Calif), Ranking Republican

The Legislative Process
Butler Derrick (D-SC), Chairman
James H. Quillen (R-Tenn), Ranking Republican

Total PAC and Large Individual Contributions to Committee Members

David E. Bonior (D-Mich)	$1,113,713
Martin Frost (D-Texas)	$1,079,404
Joe Moakley (D-Mass)	$649,823
Butler Derrick (D-SC)	$581,380
Anthony C. Beilenson (D-Calif)	$497,109
Bob McEwen (R-Ohio)	$462,448
Alan Wheat (D-Mo)	$414,621
Bart Gordon (D-Tenn)	$403,510
Louise M. Slaughter (D-NY)	$357,247
David Dreier (R-Calif)	$346,008
James H. Quillen (R-Tenn)	$334,744
Gerald B. H. Solomon (R-NY)	$315,143
Tony P. Hall (D-Ohio)	$256,344

Top 20 Contributors to Committee Members in 1991-92

1	Assn of Trial Lawyers of America	$105,000
2	National Assn of Realtors	$91,879
3	American Medical Assn*	$86,200
4	National Assn of Letter Carriers	$76,390
5	American Institute of CPA's	$65,000
6	American Bankers Assn*	$59,450
7	Air Line Pilots Assn	$57,500
8	Marine Engineers Union*	$54,200
9	National Education Assn	$53,900
10	American Fedn of St/Cnty/Munic Employees	$53,000
11	National Assn of Life Underwriters	$52,500
12	United Transportation Union	$51,640
13	Federal Express Corp	$50,000
14	United Auto Workers	$49,760
15	Intl Brotherhood of Electrical Workers	$47,500
16	National Assn Retired Federal Employees	$47,500
17	BellSouth Corp*	$45,500
18	Teamsters Union*	$45,500
19	Associated Milk Producers	$44,000
20	Seafarers International Union	$42,500
20	United Steelworkers	$42,500

* Contributions came from more than one affiliate or subsidiary.

Summary

On the floor of the U.S. Senate, any Senator can offer an amendment to a bill under discussion, whether or not the amendment is germane to the bill itself. In the House, with its 435 members, such a policy could lead to a nightmare of legislative gridlock. To prevent that, the House is far more structured in its legislative procedures. Before any bill is brought to the House floor, specific rules are determined over whether amendments can be offered, and if so what type. Those rules — and a variety of other important legislative guidelines — are determined by the House Rules Committee.

While the shape of those rules can be important to a bill's passage, they do not specifically affect any particular industry or interest group more than any other. Correspondingly, PAC contributions to the committee came from a diversity of sources and were reflective of the overall patterns of PAC giving to members of Congress in general.

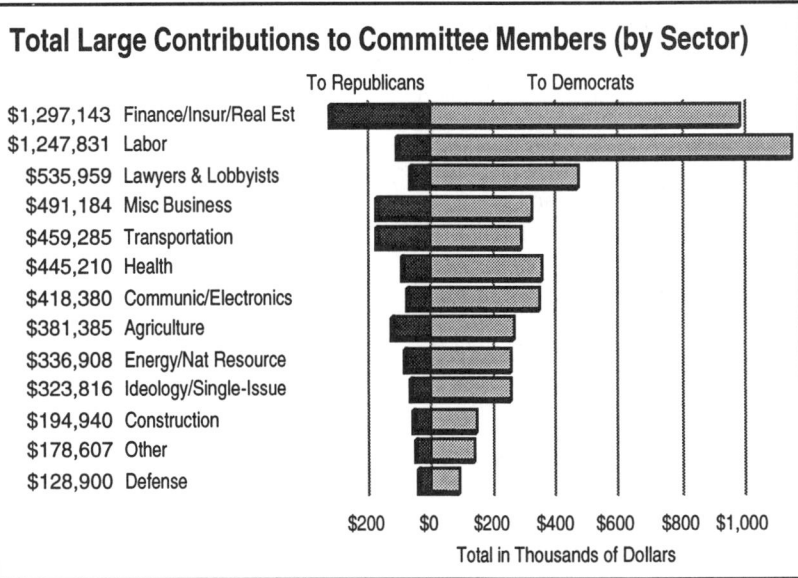

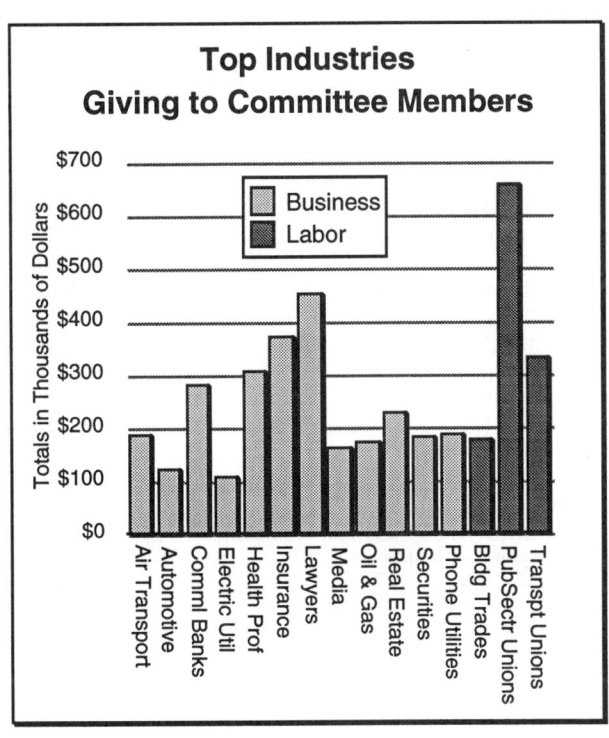

Leading Industries Giving to Committee Members

Business
- Air Transport $182,605
- Automotive $115,950
- Commercial Banks $276,589
- Electric Utilities $101,490
- Health Professionals $301,960
- Insurance $367,263
- Lawyers/Law Firms $448,730
- Media/Entertainment $156,130
- Oil & Gas $169,570
- Real Estate $224,079
- Securities & Investment $177,500
- Telephone Utilities $183,900

Labor
- Building Trade Unions $172,600
- Public Sector Unions $653,838
- Transportation Unions $329,710

House Science, Space and Technology Committee

George E. Brown Jr. (D-Calif), Chairman
Robert S. Walker (R-Pa), Ranking Republican

Party Ratio: 33 Democrats
20 Republicans

Jurisdiction: (1) Astronautical research and development, including resources, personnel, equipment and facilities; (2) Bureau of Standards, standardization of weights and measures and the metric system; (3) National Aeronautics and Space Administration; (4) National Aeronautics and Space Council; (5) National Science Foundation; (6) Outer space, including exploration and control thereof; (7) Science scholarships; (8) Scientific research, development, and demonstration, and projects therefor, and all federally owned or operated nonmilitary energy laboratories; (9) Civil aviation research and development; (10) Environmental research and development; (11) All energy research, development, and demonstration, and projects therefor, and all federally owned or operated nonmilitary energy laboratories; (12) National Weather Service. The committee also has oversight with respect to all nonmilitary research and development.

Subcommittees

Energy
Marilyn Lloyd (D-Tenn), Chairwoman
Sid Morrison (R-Wash), Ranking Republican

Environment
James H. Scheuer (D-NY), Chairman
Don Ritter (R-Pa), Ranking Republican

Investigations and Oversight
Howard Wolpe (D-Mich), Chairman
Sherwood Boehlert (R-NY), Ranking Republican

Science
Rick Boucher (D-Va), Chairman
Ron Packard (R-Calif), Ranking Republican

Space
Ralph M. Hall (D-Texas), Chairman
F. James Sensenbrenner Jr. (R-Wis), Ranking Republican

Technology and Competitiveness
Tim Valentine (D-NC), Chairman
Tom Lewis (R-Fla), Ranking Republican

Total PAC and Large Individual Contributions to Committee Members

Tom Campbell (R-Calif)[1]	$3,593,778
Tom McMillen (D-Md)	$1,065,639
Robert G. Torricelli (D-NJ)	$940,467
John W. Olver (D-Mass)	$859,467
Norman Y. Mineta (D-Calif)	$818,018
Richard Stallings (D-Idaho)[1]	$810,812
Dick Swett (D-NH)	$766,645
Don Ritter (R-Pa)	$764,400
Jim Bacchus (D-Fla)	$759,216
Dick Zimmer (R-NJ)	$752,478
Joe L. Barton (R-Texas)	$746,490
Dan Glickman (D-Kan)	$730,001
Pete Geren (D-Texas)	$725,500
George E. Brown Jr. (D-Calif)	$671,601
Sam Johnson (R-Texas)	$608,534
Joan Kelly Horn (D-Mo)	$567,392
Dave Nagle (D-Iowa)	$547,441
Rick Boucher (D-Va)	$493,959
Dave McCurdy (D-Okla)	$484,850
Ralph M. Hall (D-Texas)	$431,623
John J. Rhodes III (R-Ariz)	$429,710
Harris W. Fawell (R-Ill)	$428,241
Tim Roemer (D-Ind)	$411,948
Jerry F. Costello (D-Ill)	$404,080
Eliot L. Engel (D-NY)	$366,480
George F. Allen (R-Va)	$357,906
Jimmy Hayes (D-La)	$356,638
Marilyn Lloyd (D-Tenn)	$353,972
Mike Kopetski (D-Ore)	$351,542
Tim Valentine (D-NC)	$345,522
Lamar Smith (R-Texas)	$329,635
Bud Cramer (D-Ala)	$323,585
Steven H. Schiff (R-NM)	$297,300
Dana Rohrabacher (R-Calif)	$282,873
Constance A. Morella (R-Md)	$282,091
Ray Thornton (D-Ark)	$280,048
Sherwood Boehlert (R-NY)	$278,396
Harold L. Volkmer (D-Mo)	$265,808
Terry L. Bruce (D-Ill)	$220,147
James H. Scheuer (D-NY)	$218,318
Ron Packard (R-Calif)	$217,119
Tom Lewis (R-Fla)	$215,067
John Tanner (D-Tenn)	$195,689
Wayne T. Gilchrest (R-Md)	$191,810
Paul B. Henry (R-Mich)	$187,298
Glen Browder (D-Ala)	$166,713
Carl C. Perkins (D-Ky)	$160,275
Howard Wolpe (D-Mich)	$134,215
F. James Sensenbrenner Jr. (R-Wis)	$131,020
James A. Traficant Jr. (D-Ohio)	$120,870
Robert S. Walker (R-Pa)	$103,416
Richard Stallings (D-Idaho)	$63,868
D. French Slaughter Jr. (R-Va)[2]	$43,525
Sid Morrison (R-Wash)	$10,340
Henry J. Nowak (D-NY)	$573

[1] Ran for U.S. Senate in 1992
[2] Resigned in November 1991

Summary

As the mainstream of the American economy has shifted away from the old heavy industrial base and into new high-tech and information industries, the attention of Congress has come to focus more and more on the legal and political ramifications of emerging technologies and the post-industrial economy. Much of the legislative debate on these new industries — and the unique new problems and legal challenges they present — has fallen under the jurisdiction of the Science, Space and Technology Committee. Formed in 1959, a year after the Russians launched Sputnik, the committee has also been deeply involved with the U.S. space program and NASA.

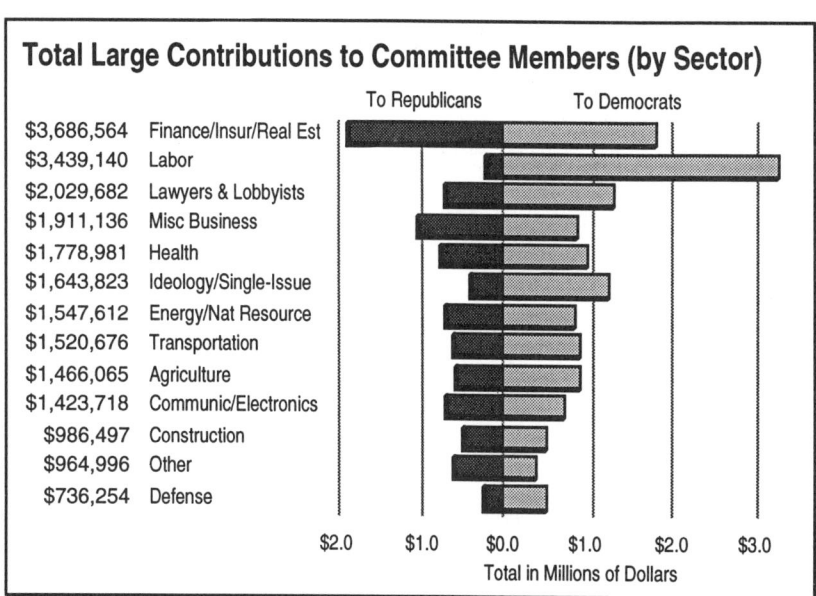

Total Large Contributions to Committee Members (by Sector)

Amount	Sector
$3,686,564	Finance/Insur/Real Est
$3,439,140	Labor
$2,029,682	Lawyers & Lobbyists
$1,911,136	Misc Business
$1,778,981	Health
$1,643,823	Ideology/Single-Issue
$1,547,612	Energy/Nat Resource
$1,520,676	Transportation
$1,466,065	Agriculture
$1,423,718	Communic/Electronics
$986,497	Construction
$964,996	Other
$736,254	Defense

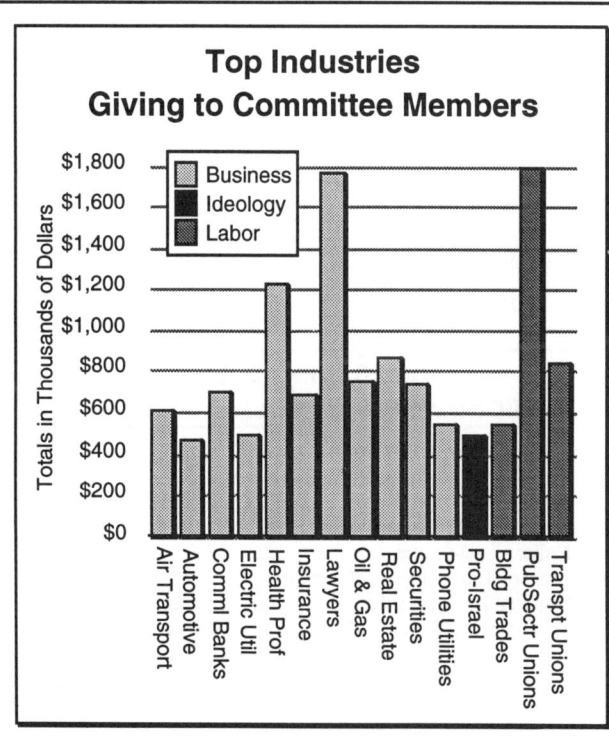

Top 20 Contributors to Committee Members in 1991-92

1	American Medical Assn*	$304,029
2	National Assn of Realtors	$250,675
3	Assn of Trial Lawyers of America	$223,650
4	Teamsters Union*	$206,250
5	National Education Assn*	$200,650
6	National Auto Dealers Assn	$183,300
7	United Auto Workers	$179,700
8	National Assn Retired Federal Employees	$162,000
9	Machinists/Aerospace Workers Union*	$155,900
10	Marine Engineers Union*	$147,500
11	Intl Brotherhood of Electrical Workers*	$145,482
12	American Fedn of St/Cnty/Munic Employees	$143,899
13	American Bankers Assn*	$143,690
14	National Assn of Letter Carriers*	$138,015
15	Food & Commercial Workers Union	$134,985
16	Air Line Pilots Assn	$133,500
17	AT&T*	$127,800
18	United Parcel Service	$121,990
19	Carpenters & Joiners Union*	$116,815
20	Laborers Union*	$113,000

* Contributions came from more than one affiliate or subsidiary.

Leading Industries Giving to Committee Members

Business

Air Transport	$602,283
Automotive	$455,353
Commercial Banks	$683,715
Electric Utilities	$486,997
Health Professionals	$1,217,447
Insurance	$677,888
Lawyers/Law Firms	$1,759,927
Oil & Gas	$747,143
Real Estate	$854,953
Securities & Investment	$729,083
Telephone Utilities	$532,785

Ideological/Single-Issue

Pro-Israel	$478,667

Labor

Building Trade Unions	$533,010
Public Sector Unions	$1,782,651
Transportation Unions	$828,934

House Small Business Committee

John J. LaFalce (D-NY), Chairman
Andy Ireland (R-Fla), Ranking Republican

Party Ratio: 27 Democrats
17 Republicans

Jurisdiction: (1) Assistance to and protection of small business, including financial aid; (2) Participation of small-business enterprises in Federal procurement and Government contracts. The committee also has oversight with respect to the problems of small business.

Subcommittees

Antitrust, Impact of Deregulation and Privatization
Dennis E. Eckart (D-Ohio), Chairman
Joel Hefley (R-Colo), Ranking Republican

Environment and Employment
Jim Olin (D-Va), Chairman
Richard H. Baker (R-La), Ranking Republican

Procurement, Tourism and Rural Development
Ike Skelton (D-Mo), Chairman
Mel Hancock (R-Mo), Ranking Republican

Regulation, Business Opportunities and Energy
Ron Wyden (D-Ore), Chairman
Jan Meyers (R-Kan), Ranking Republican

SBA, the General Economy and Minority Enterprise Development
John J. LaFalce (D-NY), Chairman
Andy Ireland (R-Fla), Ranking Republican

Total PAC and Large Individual Contributions to Committee Members

Jim Ramstad (R-Minn)	$712,432
Ed Pastor (D-Ariz)	$695,569
Thomas H. Andrews (D-Maine)	$623,990
Bill Zeliff (R-NH)	$621,554
Sam Johnson (R-Texas)	$608,534
Richard H. Baker (R-La)	$589,721
Richard Ray (D-Ga)	$531,178
Gary Franks (R-Conn)	$518,787
Nicholas Mavroules (D-Mass)	$498,298
John J. LaFalce (D-NY)	$483,431
H. Martin Lancaster (D-NC)	$478,515
Robert E. Andrews (D-NJ)	$473,741
Bill Sarpalius (D-Texas)	$456,536
James Bilbray (D-Nev)	$413,557
Wayne Allard (R-Colo)	$392,891
George F. Allen (R-Va)	$357,906
Ronald K. Machtley (R-RI)	$355,191
Dave Camp (R-Mich)	$354,181
Charles Hatcher (D-Ga)	$349,500
John A. Boehner (R-Ohio)	$343,332
Joseph M. McDade (R-Pa)	$334,623
Mel Hancock (R-Mo)	$282,537
Richard E. Neal (D-Mass)	$279,091
John Conyers Jr. (D-Mich)	$273,450
Jan Meyers (R-Kan)	$265,614
Neal Smith (D-Iowa)	$262,542
Bill Orton (D-Utah)	$255,564
Ike Skelton (D-Mo)	$242,876
Norman Sisisky (D-Va)	$200,384
Floyd H. Flake (D-NY)	$194,650
Kweisi Mfume (D-Md)	$188,034
Dennis E. Eckart (D-Ohio)	$186,930
Larry Combest (R-Texas)	$175,084
Ron Wyden (D-Ore)	$141,075
Esteban E. Torres (D-Calif)	$133,106
Joel Hefley (R-Colo)	$113,075
Jose E. Serrano (D-NY)	$108,900
Gus Savage (D-Ill)	$100,500
Andy Ireland (R-Fla)	$82,488
Glenn Poshard (D-Ill)	$47,862
D. French Slaughter Jr. (R-Va)†	$43,525
William S. Broomfield (R-Mich)	$33,950
Jim Olin (D-Va)	$26,350
Romano L. Mazzoli (D-Ky)	$14,923

† Resigned in November 1991

Top 20 Contributors to Committee Members in 1991-92

1	National Assn of Realtors	$262,138
2	American Medical Assn*	$220,348
3	Teamsters Union*	$134,000
4	National Auto Dealers Assn	$130,700
5	National Rifle Assn	$124,750
6	Assn of Trial Lawyers of America	$124,000
7	National Education Assn*	$104,300
8	American Institute of CPA's	$101,804
9	American Bankers Assn*	$94,615
10	United Auto Workers	$93,450
11	National Assn Retired Federal Employees	$89,500
12	National Assn of Home Builders	$87,649
13	Laborers Union*	$85,275
14	AT&T	$85,225
15	Dow Chemical*	$82,519
16	Marine Engineers Union*	$78,250
17	National Beer Wholesalers Assn	$78,100
18	American Fedn of St/Cnty/Munic Employees	$71,300
19	United Parcel Service	$71,270
20	Food & Commercial Workers Union	$70,448

* Contributions came from more than one affiliate or subsidiary.

Summary

Small businesses have always been an important constituency of Congress. Every congressional district in the land has its local chamber of commerce, with its bankers, lawyers, doctors, insurance agents and real estate brokers — many of whom take a keen interest in those items of federal government policy that affect their businesses.

Judging by the patterns in contributions to committee members, those doctors, lawyers, bankers and brokers paid the closest attention of all. Financial industry contributors led all others overall, just as they did in contributions to Congress as a whole. And as on most committees, organized labor PACs were a major source of funds for Democrats.

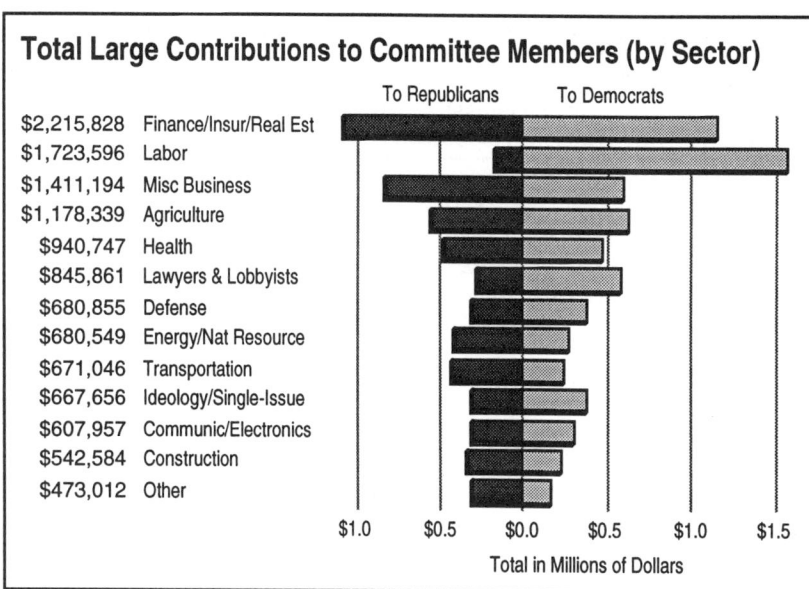

Total Large Contributions to Committee Members (by Sector)

Amount	Sector
$2,215,828	Finance/Insur/Real Est
$1,723,596	Labor
$1,411,194	Misc Business
$1,178,339	Agriculture
$940,747	Health
$845,861	Lawyers & Lobbyists
$680,855	Defense
$680,549	Energy/Nat Resource
$671,046	Transportation
$667,656	Ideology/Single-Issue
$607,957	Communic/Electronics
$542,584	Construction
$473,012	Other

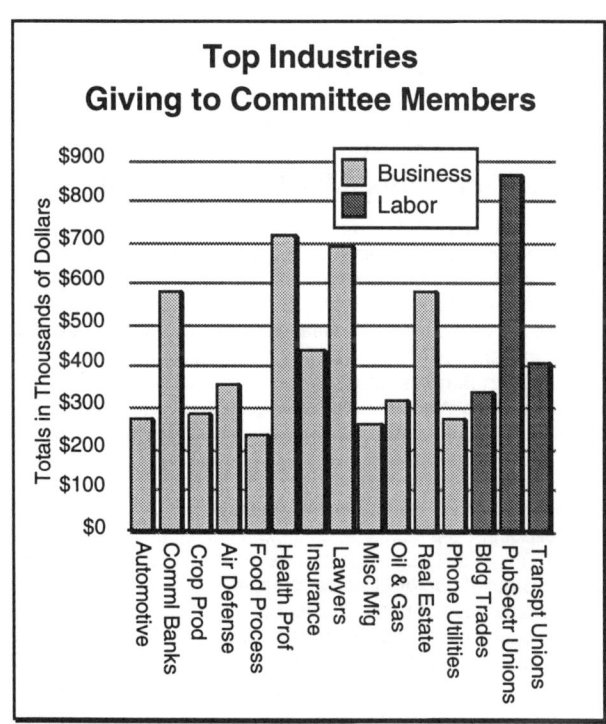

Top Industries Giving to Committee Members

Leading Industries Giving to Committee Members

Business

Automotive	$268,098
Commercial Banks	$579,373
Crop Production & Basic Processing	$278,416
Defense Aerospace	$352,305
Food Processing & Sales	$230,312
Health Professionals	$708,427
Insurance	$433,744
Lawyers/Law Firms	$686,867
Misc Manufacturing & Distributing	$252,299
Oil & Gas	$312,679
Real Estate	$576,209
Telephone Utilities	$267,252

Labor

Building Trade Unions	$331,599
Public Sector Unions	$860,843
Transportation Unions	$403,056

House Veterans' Affairs Committee

G. V. "Sonny" Montgomery (D-Miss), Chairman
Bob Stump (R-Ariz), Ranking Republican

Party Ratio: 21 Democrats
13 Republicans

Jurisdiction: (1) Veterans' measures generally; (2) Cemeteries of the United States in which veterans of any war or conflict are or may be buried, whether in the United States or abroad, except cemeteries administered by the Secretary of the Interior; (3) Compensation, vocational rehabilitation and education of veterans; (4) Life insurance issued by the Government on account of service in the Armed Forces; (5) Pensions of all the wars of the United States, general and special; (6) Compensation for service-related disability; (7) Readjustment of servicemen to civil life; (8) Soldiers' and sailors' civil relief; (9) Veterans' hospitals, medical care, and treatment of veterans.

Subcommittees

Compensation, Pension and Insurance
Douglas Applegate (D-Ohio), Chairman
Bob Stump (R-Ariz), Ranking Republican

Education, Training and Employment
Timothy J. Penny (D-Minn), Chairman
Christopher H. Smith (R-NJ), Ranking Republican

Hospitals and Health Care
G. V. "Sonny" Montgomery (D-Miss), Chairman
John Paul Hammerschmidt (R-Ark), Ranking Republican

Housing and Memorial Affairs
Harley O. Staggers Jr. (D-WVa), Chairman
Dan Burton (R-Ind), Ranking Republican

Oversight and Investigations
Lane Evans (D-Ill), Chairman
Michael Bilirakis (R-Fla), Ranking Republican

Total PAC and Large Individual Contributions to Committee Members

Pete Geren (D-Texas)	$725,500
Bill Paxon (R-NY)	$640,187
Jim Slattery (D-Kan)	$611,113
Joseph P. Kennedy II (D-Mass)	$598,296
Michael Bilirakis (R-Fla)	$506,808
Rick Santorum (R-Pa)	$494,739
Bob Clement (D-Tenn)	$466,453
Dan Burton (R-Ind)	$447,425
Chet Edwards (D-Texas)	$439,199
Tom Ridge (R-Pa)	$416,370
Bill Brewster (D-Okla)	$368,096
Pete Peterson (D-Fla)	$335,730
J. Roy Rowland (D-Ga)	$332,098
Jill L. Long (D-Ind)	$291,363
George E. Sangmeister (D-Ill)	$278,286
Liz J. Patterson (D-SC)	$266,558
Cliff Stearns (R-Fla)	$261,910
Dick Nichols (R-Kan)	$247,150
Owen B. Pickett (D-Va)	$225,835
Lane Evans (D-Ill)	$222,293
Don Edwards (D-Calif)	$221,785
Ben Jones (D-Ga)	$218,345
Bob Stump (R-Ariz)	$192,525
Harley O. Staggers Jr. (D-WVa)	$188,168
Maxine Waters (D-Calif)	$171,652
Christopher H. Smith (R-NJ)	$149,555
G. V. "Sonny" Montgomery (D-Miss)	$140,243
Chalmers P. Wylie (R-Ohio)	$132,770
Floyd D. Spence (R-SC)	$120,600
Craig T. James (R-Fla)	$116,087
Claude Harris (D-Ala)	$114,701
Timothy J. Penny (D-Minn)	$104,943
Douglas Applegate (D-Ohio)	$84,591
John Paul Hammerschmidt (R-Ark)	$1,524

Top 20 Contributors to Committee Members in 1991-92

1	National Assn of Realtors	$187,250
2	American Medical Assn*	$165,660
3	National Auto Dealers Assn	$126,850
4	American Institute of CPA's	$100,950
5	Assn of Trial Lawyers of America	$92,000
6	Teamsters Union*	$91,098
7	American Bankers Assn*	$89,200
8	United Auto Workers	$87,750
9	National Rifle Assn	$86,850
10	United Parcel Service	$86,700
11	National Education Assn*	$79,600
12	National Assn Retired Federal Employees	$77,000
13	BellSouth Corp*	$73,200
14	AT&T	$69,950
15	Intl Brotherhood of Electrical Workers	$64,750
16	National Assn of Home Builders	$64,699
17	National Assn of Life Underwriters	$64,500
18	National Assn of Letter Carriers*	$62,950
19	Marine Engineers Union*	$58,250
20	American Fedn of St/Cnty/Munic Employees	$58,000

* Contributions came from more than one affiliate or subsidiary.

Summary

The profile — and problems — of America's veterans have changed considerably over the past generation. The postwar boom of the late 1940s and early 50s, when veterans of World War II and Korea came home to raise new families, build new suburbs and go on to college with the G.I. Bill has been replaced by the postwar trauma of Vietnam era vets, many of whom have still not been able to shake off the war's lingering effects.

The Gulf War added a new class of combat veterans, many of whom came not from the regular ranks of active services but from reserve units all around the nation. They have since been joined by yet another group of veterans — those whose military careers are ending prematurely due to the post-Cold War downsizing of the active military. The Veterans Affairs committee pays close attention to the needs of all these ex-servicemen and women, but the scope of its political contributions reflect no special patterns apart from those of Congress as a whole.

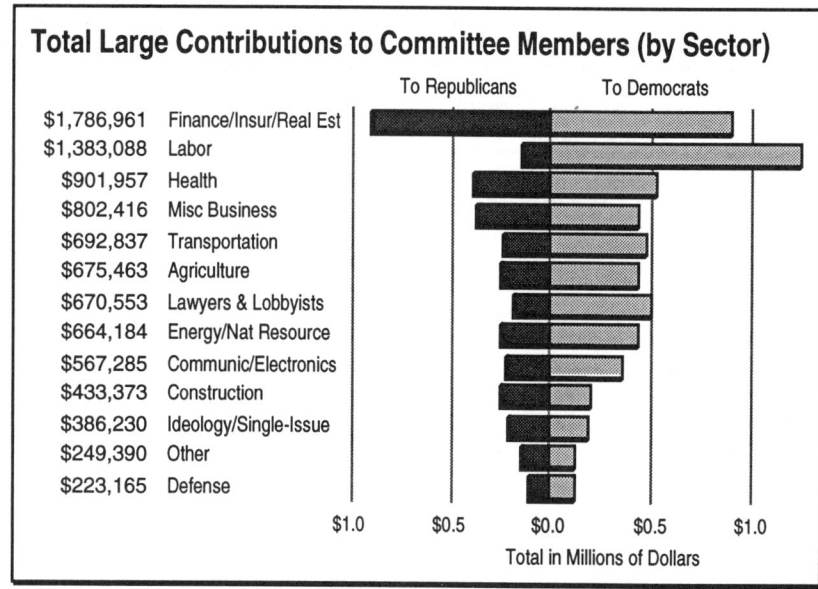

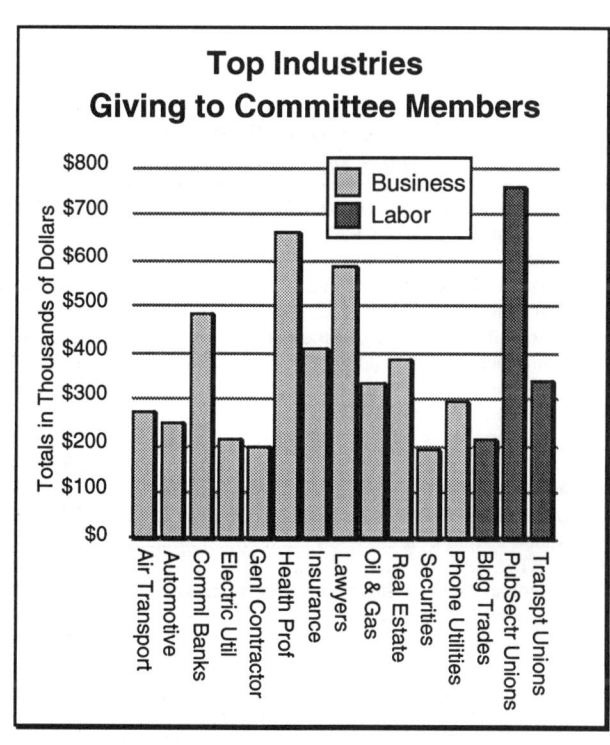

Leading Industries Giving to Committee Members

Business

Air Transport	$268,739
Automotive	$243,824
Commercial Banks	$478,062
Electric Utilities	$210,830
General Contractors	$194,920
Health Professionals	$654,216
Insurance	$401,298
Lawyers/Law Firms	$582,055
Oil & Gas	$330,677
Real Estate	$379,317
Securities & Investment	$186,025
Telephone Utilities	$291,860

Labor

Building Trade Unions	$207,585
Public Sector Unions	$750,781
Transportation Unions	$333,572

House Ways and Means Committee

Dan Rostenkowski (D-Ill), Chairman
Bill Archer (R-Texas), Ranking Republican

Party Ratio: 23 Democrats
13 Republicans

Jurisdiction: (1) Customs, collection districts, and ports of entry and delivery; (2) Reciprocal trade agreements; (3) Revenue measures generally; (4) Revenue measures relating to the insular possessions; (5) The bonded debt of the United States; (6) The deposit of public moneys; (7) Transportation of dutiable goods; (8) Tax-exempt foundations and charitable trusts; (9) National social security, except (a) health care and facilities programs that are supported form general revenues as opposed to payroll deductions, and (b) work incentive programs.

Subcommittees

Health
Pete Stark (D-Calif), Chairman
Bill Gradison (R-Ohio), Ranking Republican

Human Resources
Harold E. Ford (D-Tenn), Chairman
E. Clay Shaw Jr. (R-Fla), Ranking Republican

Oversight
J. J. Pickle (D-Texas), Chairman
Dick Schulze (R-Pa), Ranking Republican

Select Revenue Measures
Charles B. Rangel (D-NY), Chairman
Guy Vander Jagt (R-Mich), Ranking Republican

Social Security
Andrew Jacobs Jr. (D-Ind), Chairman
Jim Bunning (R-Ky), Ranking Republican

Trade
Sam M. Gibbons (D-Fla), Chairman
Philip M. Crane (R-Ill), Ranking Republican

Total PAC and Large Individual Contributions to Committee Members

Rod Chandler (R-Wash)†	$2,094,096
Jim Moody (D-Wis)†	$1,448,240
Dan Rostenkowski (D-Ill)	$1,302,759
Marty Russo (D-Ill)	$990,657
Byron Dorgan (D-ND)†	$870,676
Thomas J. Downey (D-NY)	$864,993
Michael A. Andrews (D-Texas)	$802,333
Sander Levin (D-Mich)	$791,756
E. Clay Shaw Jr. (R-Fla)	$773,302
Beryl Anthony Jr. (D-Ark)	$769,360
Jim Bunning (R-Ky)	$713,831
Sam M. Gibbons (D-Fla)	$617,249
Don Sundquist (R-Tenn)	$590,627
Guy Vander Jagt (R-Mich)	$537,329
Robert T. Matsui (D-Calif)	$521,339
Charles B. Rangel (D-NY)	$491,425
Bill Thomas (R-Calif)	$469,226
Nancy L. Johnson (R-Conn)	$467,506
Benjamin L. Cardin (D-Md)	$466,793
Pete Stark (D-Calif)	$455,572
Barbara B. Kennelly (D-Conn)	$436,004
J. J. Pickle (D-Texas)	$373,514
Fred Grandy (R-Iowa)	$351,733
Raymond J. McGrath (R-NY)	$257,974
William J. Coyne (D-Pa)	$229,882
Jim McDermott (D-Wash)	$213,735
Harold E. Ford (D-Tenn)	$189,768
Dick Schulze (R-Pa)	$170,375
Philip M. Crane (R-Ill)	$137,894
Frank J. Guarini (D-NJ)	$81,498
Brian Donnelly (D-Mass)	$62,450
Bill Archer (R-Texas)	$44,679
Bill Gradison (R-Ohio)	$40,509
Ed Jenkins (D-Ga)	$9,440
Andrew Jacobs Jr. (D-Ind)	$3,050
Don J. Pease (D-Ohio)	-$9,849

† U.S. Senate candidate in 1992

Top 20 Contributors to Committee Members in 1991-92

1	National Assn of Life Underwriters	$185,755
2	American Institute of CPA's	$172,347
3	National Assn of Realtors	$161,600
4	American Medical Assn*	$150,529
5	American Dental Assn	$126,850
6	Assn of Trial Lawyers of America	$113,500
7	Metropolitan Life/Century 21*	$103,030
8	American Family Corp	$95,500
9	American Hospital Assn*	$93,100
10	American Council of Life Insurance	$92,994
11	National Education Assn	$91,300
12	Air Line Pilots Assn	$88,093
13	United Parcel Service	$86,255
14	National Auto Dealers Assn	$86,000
15	AT&T	$79,050
15	American Fedn of St/Cnty/Munic Employees	$79,050
17	American Bankers Assn*	$77,000
18	US Tobacco*	$76,250
19	National Assn of Letter Carriers	$70,800
20	Massachusetts Mutual Life Insurance	$70,200

* Contributions came from more than one affiliate or subsidiary.

Summary

No committee in the House of Representatives — and possibly in all of Congress — is more important to as wide a breath of industries, interests and political contributors as Ways and Means. Along with its counterpart, the Senate Finance Committee, this is where the first drafts of the nation's tax laws are written and where the final chapters (along with footnotes, abridgments and special exceptions) are hammered into shape. Ways and Means operates in an arcane world of lawyers and tax accountants, where every comma, semicolon and parenthetical addendum can mean millions or billions of dollars to individual companies and industries.

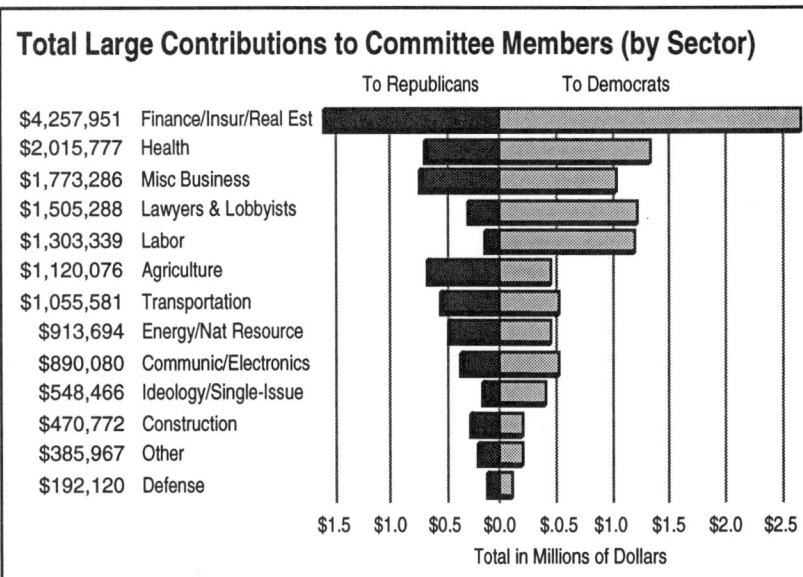

A quick glance at the Top Industries chart below spotlights another crucial jurisdiction of the committee. Along with the Energy & Commerce Committee, it is the lead panel in redrafting federal health care policy — and thus is of extreme interest to insurance companies and doctors' groups. The insurance industry, which has been a consistent supporter of Ways and Means members over the years, gave its members an average of more than $47,000 in the 1992 elections.

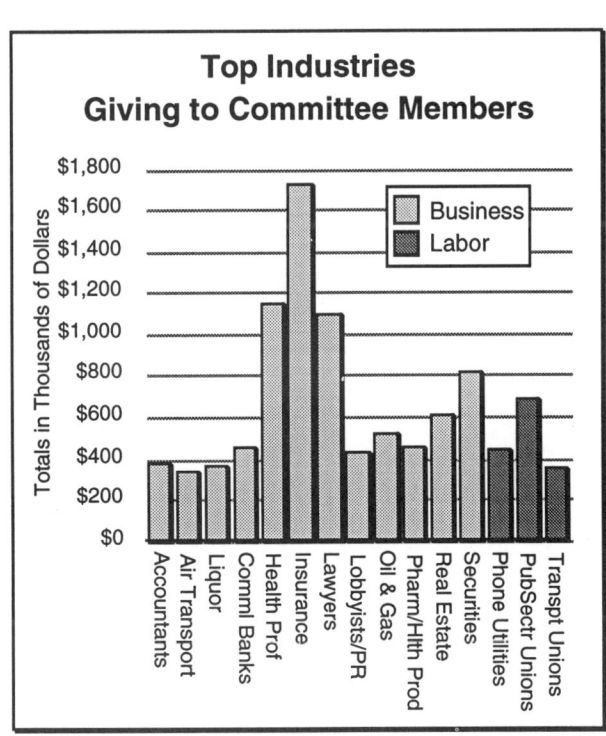

Leading Industries Giving to Committee Members

Business

Accountants	$362,317
Air Transport	$335,191
Beer, Wine & Liquor	$361,664
Commercial Banks	$440,980
Health Professionals	$1,138,791
Insurance	$1,713,765
Lawyers/Law Firms	$1,090,096
Lobbyists/PR	$415,192
Oil & Gas	$511,136
Pharmaceuticals/Health Products	$447,454
Real Estate	$594,532
Securities & Investment	$803,065
Telephone Utilities	$438,110

Labor

Public Sector Unions	$671,346
Transportation Unions	$338,403

4. Member Profiles

Cash Constituents of Congress

What's included in the Member Profiles...

These mini-profiles aim to convey a sense of each member's financial supporters. Readers may particularly note the correlation (or lack of it) between a member's "cash constituents" and his or her committee assigments.

For senators, this shows the period of the fundraising shown below and in the category chart at right. For House members, the fundraising period is 1991-92 and the dates are not shown.

District number (or office, in the case of senators)

Sen. Joseph R. Biden Jr. (D)
1992 Committees: Foreign Relations Judiciary
First elected: 1972

1987-92 Total Rcpts: $2,160,291
1992 Year-end cash: $46,943

Source of Funds
- PACs 31%
- Lg Individuals ($200+) 36%
- Individuals under $200 ....20%
- Other 14%

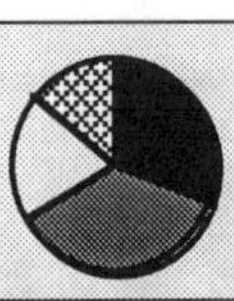

1987-92†
Top Industries & Interest Groups
Lawyers & Lobbyists $233,650
Pro-Israel $99,900
Transportation Unions $86,000
Industrial Unions $85,500
Media/Entertainment $79,754

Unidentified $179,205

Totals in Thousands of Dollars

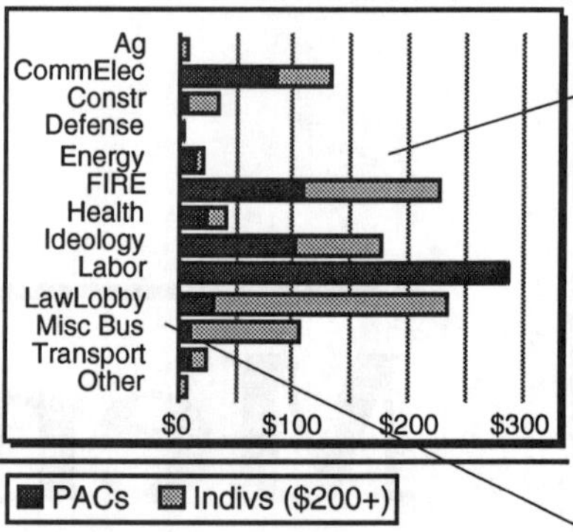

Bar chart categories: Ag, CommElec, Constr, Defense, Energy, FIRE, Health, Ideology, Labor, LawLobby, Misc Bus, Transport, Other — scale $0 to $300

■ PACs ▩ Indivs ($200+)

Sources of Campaign Revenues

This box and pie chart gives the broad breakdown of where each member's campaign funds came from. In the case of House members, the percentages cover funds raised in the 1991-92 election cycle. For senators, the figures cover the past six years (less if they were elected more recently). The sources include:

PACs. Contributions from political action committees.

Indivs $200+. These are contributions of $200 or more made by individuals. Under federal law, each of these contributions must be itemized and the contributor identified by name, address, employer and occupation.

Indivs under $200. Contributions from individuals who gave $200 or less. The FEC does not require that these contributions be itemized, but only reported in the aggregate. This figure was derived by subtracting the itemized contributions from the total individual contributions reported by the member.

Other. This covers funds from all other sources including, but not limited to, party contributions and funds from the candidate's own pocket. This figure was calculated by subtracting the member's total contributions from the total they received from PACs and individuals.

This is a more detailed breakdown of the industries and interest groups that contributed the most money to the member's campaign. Each member's five leading contributor groups are listed.

This is the total of contributions from PACs and large individual donations that the center was not able to identify or classify into any of the other categories.

Committee Abbreviations

Senate Committees

Agric	Senate Agriculture, Nutrition & Forestry Committee
Approp	Senate Appropriations Committee
ArmServ	Senate Armed Services Committee
Banking	Senate Banking, Housing & Urban Affairs Committee
Budget	Senate Budget Committee
Commerce	Senate Commerce, Science & Transportation Committee
Energy	Senate Energy & Natural Resources Committee
Envir	Senate Environment & Public Works Committee
Finance	Senate Finance Committee
ForRel	Senate Foreign Relations Committee
GovAff	Senate Governmental Affairs Committee
Judiciary	Senate Judiciary Committee
Labor	Senate Labor & Human Resources Committee
Rules	Senate Rules & Administration Committee
SmBus	Senate Small Business Committee
Vet Affairs	Senate Veterans' Affairs Committee

House Committees

Admin	House Administration Committee
Agric	House Agriculture Committee
Approp	House Appropriations Committee
ArmServ	House Armed Services Committee
Banking	House Banking, Finance & Urban Affairs Committee
Budget	House Budget Committee
DC	House District of Columbia Committee
Educ/Labor	House Education & Labor Committee
Energy/Commerce	House Energy & Commerce Committee
ForAff	House Foreign Affairs Committee
Govt Ops	House Government Operations Committee
Interior*	House Interior & Insular Affairs Committee*
Judiciary	House Judiciary Committee
MerchMarine	House Merchant Marine & Fisheries Committee
NatResources*	House Natural Resources Committee*
Post Office	House Post Office & Civil Service Committee
PubWorks	House Public Works & Transportation Committee
Rules	House Rules Committee
Science	House Science, Space & Technology Committee
SmBus	House Small Business Committee
VetAffairs	House Veterans' Affairs Committee
Ways & Means	House Ways & Means Committee

Contribution Totals by Category

To allow for easy comparison of the sources of campaign funds among different candidates, each contribution was grouped into one of 13 broad categories. This chart shows how much the member got from each, as well as the proportion of funds from PACs and individuals within each group. The categories are described below.

Categories

Agriculture (Ag). Includes farmers and all other segments of the agriculture industry, including food processors and supermarkets. Also covers timber companies and paper manufacturers.

Communications/Electronics (Comm Elec). This includes telecommunications, broadcasting, TV & movie production, printing and publishing, and the computer and electronics industries.

Construction (Const) and related services, materials and equipment.

Defense. Defense contractors (like Boeing and General Motors) that earn most of their revenues from non-defense activities are *not* classified as defense unless the member sits on a defense related committee.

Energy & Natural Resources (Energy). Besides the oil & gas industry, this includes electric utilities, mining companies, waste management and related industries.

Finance, Insurance & Real Estate (FIRE). Includes banks, stock brokerage and investment firms, insurance and real estate companies, accountants, commodities brokers and all other financial services.

Health. Includes health professionals, hospitals, nursing homes, pharmaceutical companies and others providing health services or products.

Ideology/Single Issue (Ideology). Also includes "leadership" PACs.

Labor. Includes all varieties of labor union PACs.

Lawyers & Lobbyists (LawLobby). Includes law firms and lawyers' professional associations, as well as other firms specializing in lobbying and public relations counseling.

Miscellaneous Businesses (Misc Bus). This includes a variety of manufacturing, sales and service-related companies not classified elsewhere.

Transportation (Transport). Also includes non-defense aerospace manufacturers.

Other. Includes companies that do not fit easily into the other categories, as well as groups (such as retirees) who have no specific financial interest.

---

* Beginning in 1993, the House Interior & Insular Affairs Committee changed its name to the House Natural Resources Committee.

Alabama

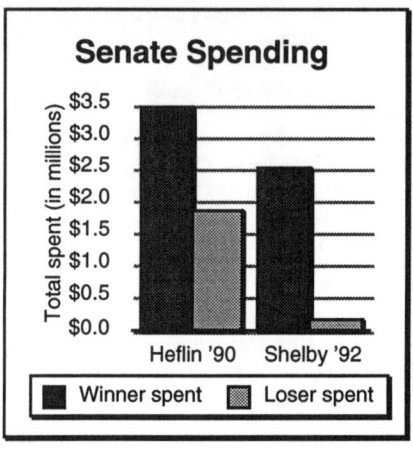

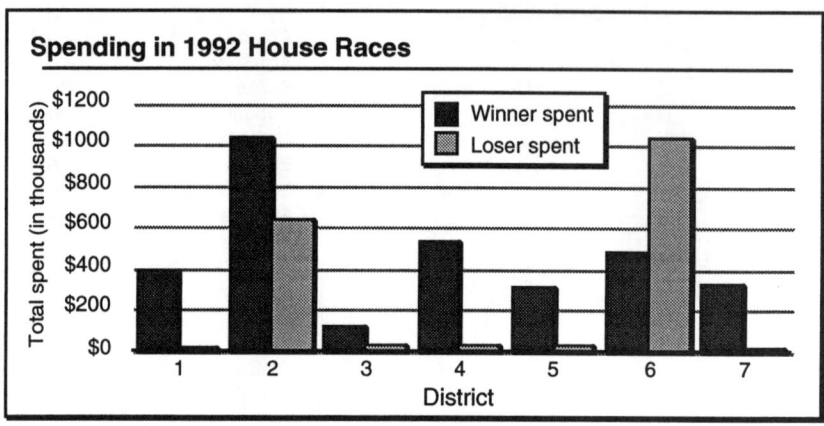

1992 Elections at a Glance

Dist	Name	Party	Vote Pct	Race Type
Sen	Howell Heflin (1990)	Dem	61%	Reelected
Sen	Richard C. Shelby (1992)	Dem	65%	Reelected
1	Sonny Callahan	Rep	60%	Reelected
2	Terry Everett	Rep	50%	Open Seat
3	Glen Browder	Dem	60%	Reelected
4	Tom Bevill	Dem	68%	Reelected
5	Bud Cramer	Dem	66%	Reelected
6	Spencer Bachus	Rep	52%	Beat Incumb
7	Earl F. Hilliard	Dem	70%	Open Seat

Totals in Thousands of Dollars

Sen. Howell Heflin (D)

1992 Committees: Agric Judiciary
First elected: 1978

1987-92 Total Rcpts: $4,103,630
1990 Year-end cash: $962,661

Source of Funds
- PACs 35%
- Lg Individuals ($200+) 40%
- Individuals under $200 ....8%
- Other 17%

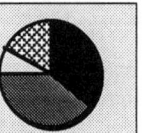

1987-92 †
Top Industries & Interest Groups

Lawyers & Lobbyists	$496,064
Pro-Israel	$169,986
Crop Production/Processing	$162,361
Oil & Gas	$149,615
Insurance	$119,031
Unidentified	$230,323

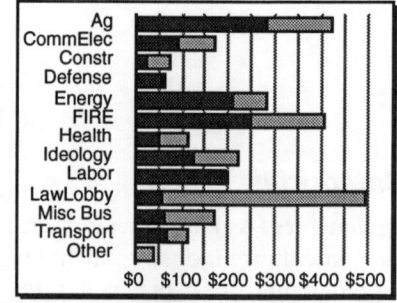

Sen. Richard C. Shelby (D)

1992 Committees: ArmServ Banking Energy
First elected: 1986

1987-92 Total Rcpts: $3,778,582
1990 Year-end cash: $1,112,139

Source of Funds
- PACs 43%
- Lg Individuals ($200+) 38%
- Individuals under $200 ....6%
- Other 12%

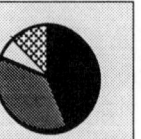

1987-92†
Top Industries & Interest Groups

Lawyers & Lobbyists	$423,147
Commercial Banks	$208,324
Health Professionals	$150,050
Oil & Gas	$149,148
Pro-Israel	$148,330
Unidentified	$162,065

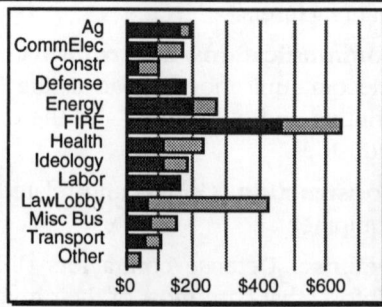

1. Sonny Callahan (R)

1992 Committees: Energy/Commerce MerchMarine
First elected: 1984

1991-92 Total Rcpts: $376,087
1990 Year-end cash: $228,837

Source of Funds
- PACs 55%
- Lg Individuals ($200+) 31%
- Individuals under $200 ....6%
- Other 7%

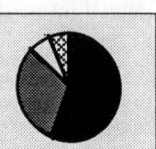

Top Industries & Interest Groups

Health Professionals	$28,650
Insurance	$22,800
Oil & Gas	$22,600
Forestry & Forest Products	$19,249
Commercial Banks	$16,150
Unidentified	$14,750

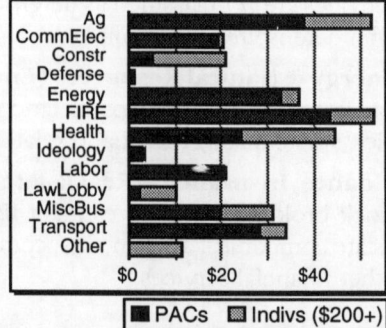

Key to committee & category abbreviations is on page 173

2. Terry Everett (R)

1993-94 Committees: ArmServ VetAffairs
First elected: 1992

1991-92 Total Rcpts: $1,054,982
1990 Year-end cash: $27,228

Source of Funds
- PACs 0%
- Lg Individuals ($200+) 9%
- Individuals under $200 .... 3%
- Other 89%

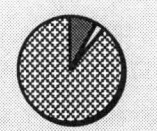

Top Industries & Interest Groups

Accountants $11,125
Automotive $11,050
General Contractors $9,650
Retail Sales $5,400
Retired $4,250

Unidentified $25,007

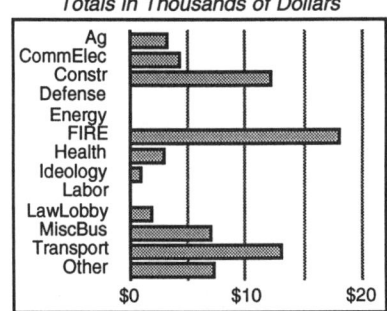

3. Glen Browder (D)

1992 Committees: ArmServ Science
First elected: 1989

1991-92 Total Rcpts: $231,325
1990 Year-end cash: $242,422

Source of Funds
- PACs 45%
- Lg Individuals ($200+) 26%
- Individuals under $200 .... 21%
- Other 8%

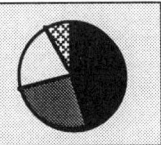

Top Industries & Interest Groups

Lawyers & Lobbyists $14,450
Health Professionals $11,450
Defense Aerospace $9,500
Industrial Unions $9,400
Retired $7,250

Unidentified $13,163

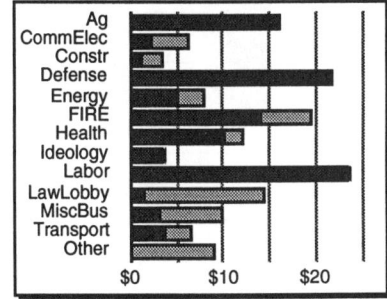

4. Tom Bevill (D)

1992 Committees: Appropriations
First elected: 1966

1991-92 Total Rcpts: $318,198
1990 Year-end cash: $365,281

Source of Funds
- PACs 32%
- Lg Individuals ($200+) 25%
- Individuals under $200 .... 15%
- Other 28%

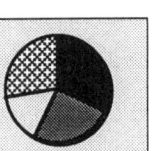

Top Industries & Interest Groups

Lawyers & Lobbyists $21,675
Nuclear Energy $11,500
Oil & Gas $10,600
Electric Utilities $9,750
General Contractors $9,500

Unidentified $14,813

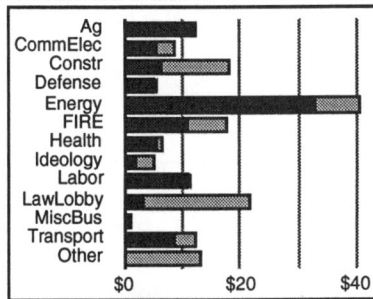

5. Bud Cramer (D)

1992 Committees: PubWorks Science
First elected: 1990

1991-92 Total Rcpts: $400,693
1990 Year-end cash: $32,112

Source of Funds
- PACs 53%
- Lg Individuals ($200+) 25%
- Individuals under $200 .... 16%
- Other 6%

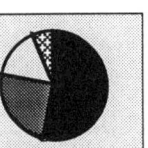

Top Industries & Interest Groups

Health Professionals $27,462
Industrial Unions $21,900
Air Transport $21,200
Lawyers & Lobbyists $15,598
Transportation Unions $13,500

Unidentified $27,450

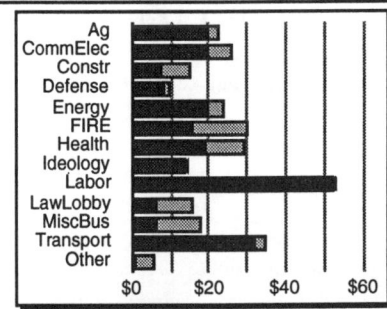

6. Spencer Bachus (R)

1993-94 Committees: Banking VetAffairs
First elected: 1992

1991-92 Total Rcpts: $499,206
1990 Year-end cash: $15,660

Source of Funds
- PACs 28%
- Lg Individuals ($200+) 56%
- Individuals under $200 .... 4%
- Other 12%

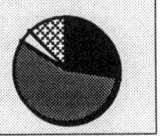

Top Industries & Interest Groups

Commercial Banks $42,500
Lawyers & Lobbyists $37,274
General Contractors $30,425
Real Estate $29,236
Health Professionals $25,625

Unidentified $72,145

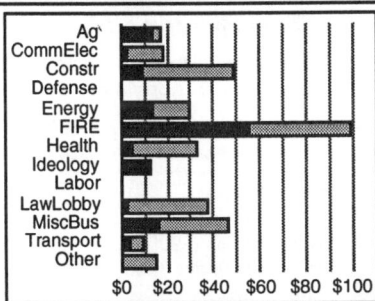

7. Earl F. Hilliard (D)

1993-94 Committees: Agric SmBus
First elected: 1992

1991-92 Total Rcpts: $333,362
1990 Year-end cash: $13,922

Source of Funds
- PACs 29%
- Lg Individuals ($200+) 31%
- Individuals under $200 .... 9%
- Other 30%

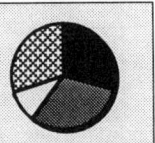

Top Industries & Interest Groups

Lawyers & Lobbyists $39,521
Mining $21,500
Industrial Unions $14,000
Pro-Israel $12,000
Commercial Banks $11,550

Unidentified $32,775

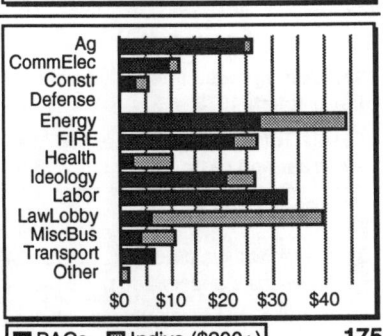

† Does not include individual contributions from 1987-88

Alaska

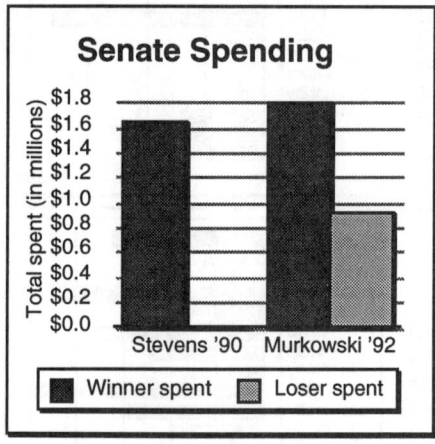
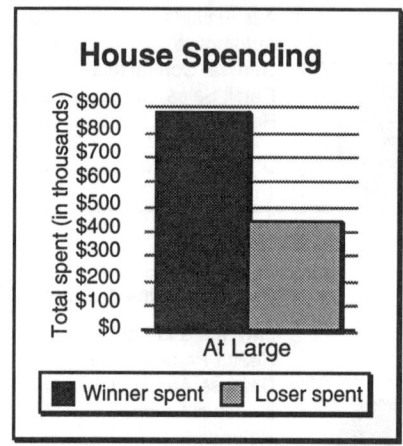

1992 Elections at a Glance

Dist	Name	Party	Vote Pct	Race Type
Sen	Frank H. Murkowski (1992)	Rep	53%	Reelected
Sen	Ted Stevens (1990)	Rep	66%	Reelected
1	Don Young	Rep	47%	Reelected

Totals in Thousands of Dollars

Sen. Frank H. Murkowski (R)

1992 Committees: Energy ForRel VetAffairs
First elected: 1980

1987-92 Total Rcpts: $1,887,991
1990 Year-end cash: $31,081

Source of Funds
- PACs...38%
- Lg Individuals ($200+) 33%
- Individuals under $200 ....11%
- Other..18%

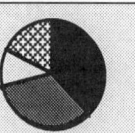

1987-92†
Top Industries & Interest Groups

Oil & Gas $166,327
Lawyers & Lobbyists................$103,486
Commercial Banks $70,750
Air Transport $58,244
General Contractors $53,550

Unidentified $151,145

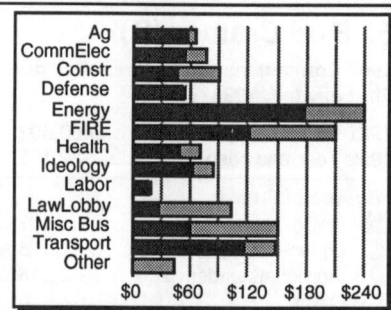

Sen. Ted Stevens (R)

1992 Committees: Approp Comm GovAff Rules SmBus
First elected: 1970 (Appointed 1968)

1987-92 Total Rcpts: $1,709,700
1990 Year-end cash: $45,715

Source of Funds
- PACs...51%
- Lg Individuals ($200+) 24%
- Individuals under $200 ....5%
- Other..20%

1987-92†
Top Industries & Interest Groups

Defense Aerospace $113,275
Lawyers & Lobbyists................$103,750
Oil & Gas $100,100
Media/Entertainment $90,610
Defense Electronics $59,000

Unidentified $68,399

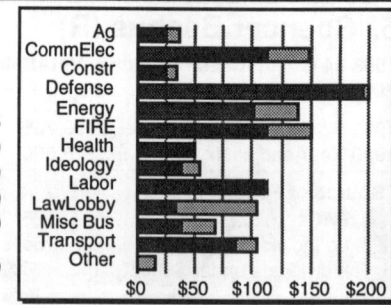

1. Don Young (R)

1992 Committees: Interior MerchMarine Post Office
First elected: 1973

1991-92 Total Rcpts: $867,848
1990 Year-end cash: ....$-94

Source of Funds
- PACs...40%
- Lg Individuals ($200+) 34%
- Individuals under $200 ....14%
- Other..11%

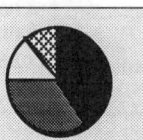

Top Industries & Interest Groups

Oil & Gas $118,495
Lawyers & Lobbyists $53,055
Sea Transport $33,750
Transportation Unions $32,050
General Contractors $28,250

Unidentified $59,089

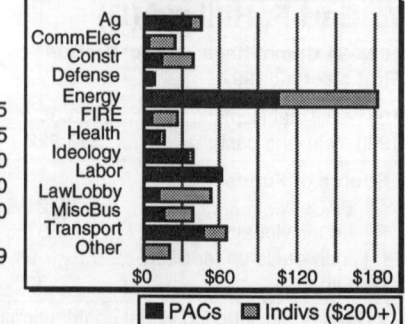

Key to committee & category abbreviations is on page 173

Arizona

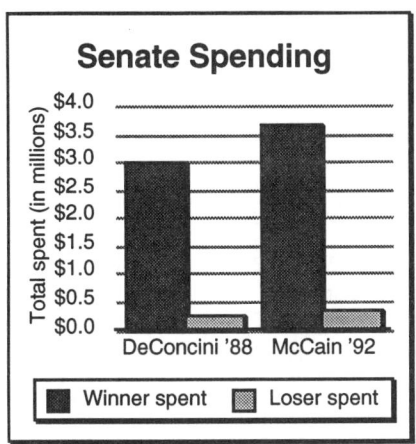

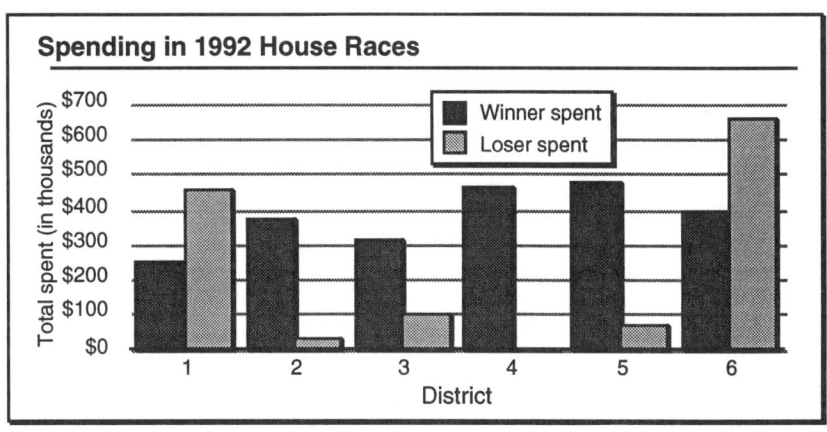

1992 Elections at a Glance

Dist	Name	Party	Vote Pct	Race Type
Sen	Dennis DeConcini (1988)	Dem	57%	Reelected
Sen	John McCain (1992)	Rep	56%	Reelected
1	Sam Coppersmith	Dem	51%	Beat Incumb
2	Ed Pastor	Dem	66%	Reelected
3	Bob Stump	Rep	62%	Reelected
4	Jon Kyl	Rep	59%	Reelected
5	Jim Kolbe	Rep	66%	Reelected
6	Karan English	Dem	53%	Open Seat

Totals in Thousands of Dollars

Sen. Dennis DeConcini (D)

1992 Committees: Approp Judiciary Rules VetAffairs
First elected: 1976

1987-92 Total Rcpts: $3,487,272
1990 Year-end cash: $269,245

Source of Funds
- PACs 36%
- Lg Individuals ($200+) 38%
- Individuals under $200 ....16%
- Other 10%

1987-92†
Top Industries & Interest Groups

Lawyers & Lobbyists $121,212
Insurance $105,400
Media/Entertainment $84,972
Defense Aerospace $77,800
Public Sector Unions $70,070

Unidentified $80,479

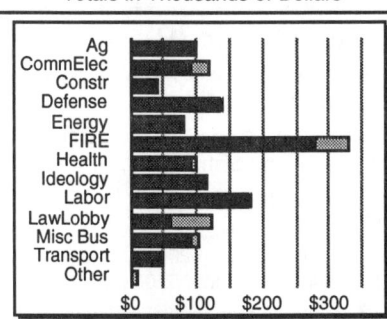

Sen. John McCain (R)

1992 Committees: ArmServ Commerce
First elected: 1986

1987-92 Total Rcpts: $3,623,397
1990 Year-end cash: $5,927

Source of Funds
- PACs 31%
- Lg Individuals ($200+) 27%
- Individuals under $200 ....27%
- Other 14%

1987-92†
Top Industries & Interest Groups

Health Professionals $152,756
Pro-Israel $110,802
Lawyers & Lobbyists $102,970
Insurance $93,375
Oil & Gas $88,305

Unidentified $275,557

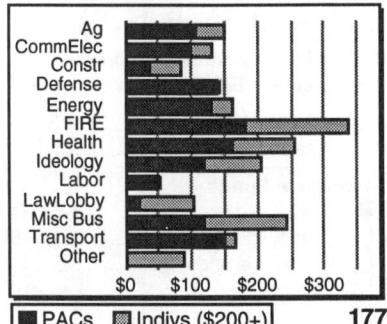

† Does not include individual contributions from 1987-88

1. Sam Coppersmith (D)
1993-94 Committees: PubWorks Science
First elected: 1992

1991-92 Total Rcpts: $248,108
1990 Year-end cash: $3,474

Source of Funds
- PACs 24%
- Lg Individuals ($200+) 36%
- Individuals under $200 .... 16%
- Other 24%

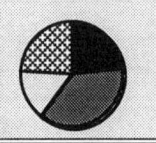

Top Industries & Interest Groups

Lawyers & Lobbyists $46,675
Public Sector Unions $13,500
Misc Issues $8,183
Transportation Unions $6,500
Industrial Unions $6,499

Unidentified $17,400

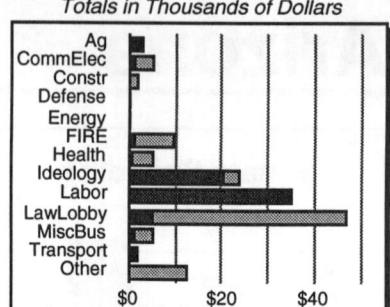

2. Ed Pastor (D)
1992 Committees: Educ/Labor SmBus
First elected: 1991

1991-92 Total Rcpts: $928,664
1990 Year-end cash: $33,368

Source of Funds
- PACs 36%
- Lg Individuals ($200+) 34%
- Individuals under $200 .... 21%
- Other 8%

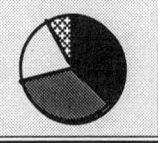

Top Industries & Interest Groups

Lawyers & Lobbyists $65,309
Public Sector Unions $51,644
Industrial Unions $47,499
Transportation Unions $39,800
Real Estate $29,300

Unidentified $103,529

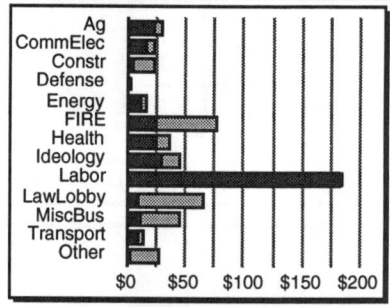

3. Bob Stump (R)
1992 Committees: ArmServ VetAffairs
First elected: 1976

1991-92 Total Rcpts: $233,476
1990 Year-end cash: $43,638

Source of Funds
- PACs 58%
- Lg Individuals ($200+) 25%
- Individuals under $200 .... 9%
- Other 8%

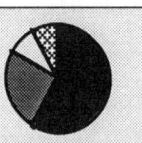

Top Industries & Interest Groups

Defense Aerospace $18,415
Defense Electronics $13,750
Crop Production/Processing $13,550
Health Professionals $13,350
Gun Rights/Gun Control $9,900

Unidentified $8,000

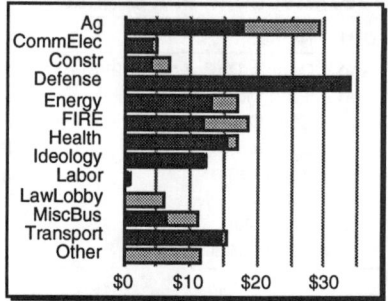

4. Jon Kyl (R)
1992 Committees: ArmServ GovtOps
First elected: 1986

1991-92 Total Rcpts: $616,154
1990 Year-end cash: $493,753

Source of Funds
- PACs 26%
- Lg Individuals ($200+) 53%
- Individuals under $200 .... 12%
- Other 8%

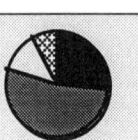

Top Industries & Interest Groups

Lawyers & Lobbyists $46,550
Health Professionals $35,740
Retired $33,910
Real Estate $27,900
Defense Aerospace $18,170

Unidentified $60,360

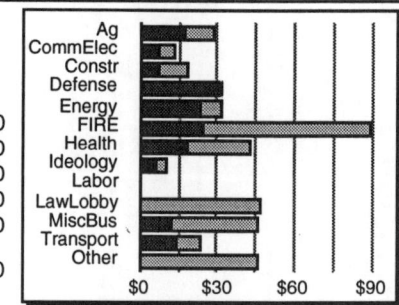

5. Jim Kolbe (R)
1992 Committees: Approp Budget
First elected: 1984

1991-92 Total Rcpts: $409,883
1990 Year-end cash: $21,918

Source of Funds
- PACs 35%
- Lg Individuals ($200+) 33%
- Individuals under $200 .... 28%
- Other 4%

Top Industries & Interest Groups

Retired $18,405
Automotive $15,650
Lawyers & Lobbyists $14,357
Livestock $14,150
Real Estate $13,600

Unidentified $22,771

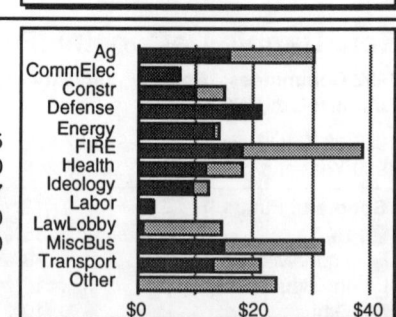

6. Karan English (D)
1993-94 Committees: Educ/Labor
First elected: 1992

1991-92 Total Rcpts: $392,253
1990 Year-end cash: $3,238

Source of Funds
- PACs 34%
- Lg Individuals ($200+) 15%
- Individuals under $200 .... 41%
- Other 10%

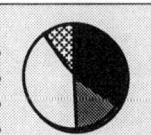

Top Industries & Interest Groups

Womens Issues $36,046
Health Professionals $15,800
Public Sector Unions $14,700
Misc Issues $10,929
Lawyers & Lobbyists $10,557

Unidentified $12,290

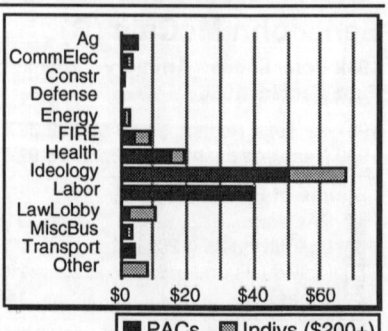

Arkansas

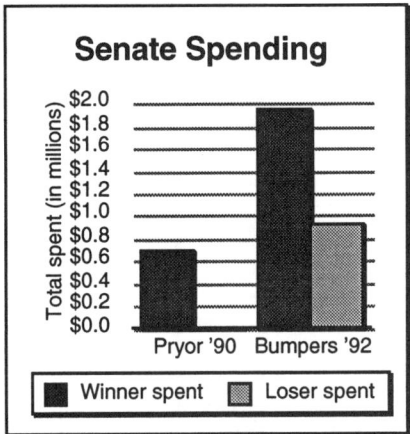

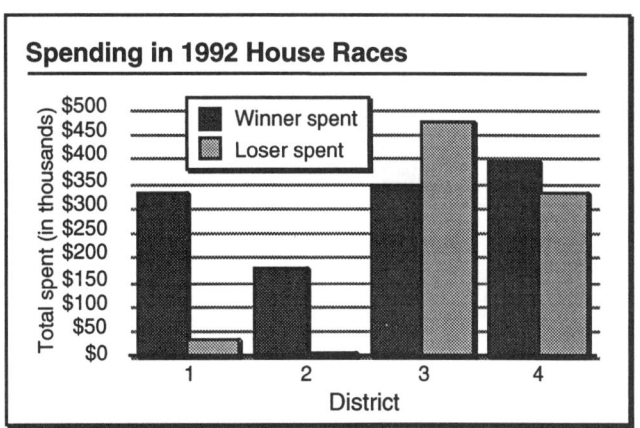

1992 Elections at a Glance

Dist	Name	Party	Vote Pct	Race Type
Sen	Dale Bumpers (1992)	Dem	60%	Reelected
Sen	David Pryor (1990)	Dem	100%	Reelected
1	Blanche Lambert	Dem	70%	Open Seat
2	Ray Thornton	Dem	74%	Reelected
3	Tim Hutchinson	Rep	50%	Open Seat
4	Jay Dickey	Rep	52%	Open Seat

Totals in Thousands of Dollars

Sen. Dale Bumpers (D)

1992 Committees: Approp Energy SmBus
First elected: 1974

1987-92 Total Rcpts: $2,063,717
1990 Year-end cash: $172,582

Source of Funds
- PACs 34%
- Lg Individuals ($200+) 48%
- Individuals under $200 .... 9%
- Other 8%

1987-92†
Top Industries & Interest Groups

Lawyers & Lobbyists $213,550
Oil & Gas $101,300
Crop Production/Processing $79,970
Commercial Banks $76,050
Poultry & Eggs $69,750

Unidentified $147,799

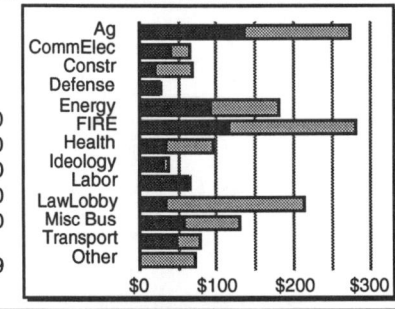

Sen. David Pryor (D)

1992 Committees: Agric Finance GovAff
First elected: 1978

1987-92 Total Rcpts: $1,513,481
1990 Year-end cash: $804,911

Source of Funds
- PACs 38%
- Lg Individuals ($200+) 42%
- Individuals under $200 .... 3%
- Other 16%

1987-92†
Top Industries & Interest Groups

Lawyers & Lobbyists $118,817
Crop Production/Processing $87,383
Insurance $83,762
Securities & Investment $62,890
Health Professionals $57,000

Unidentified $96,299

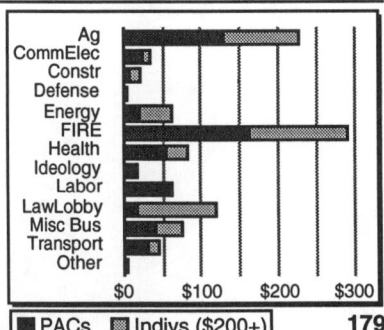

† Does not include individual contributions from 1987-88

1. Blanche Lambert (D)

1993-94 Committees: Agric Energy/Comm MerchMarine
First elected: 1992

1991-92 Total Rcpts: $439,343
1990 Year-end cash: $112,243

Source of Funds
- PACs..38%
- Lg Individuals ($200+) 28%
- Individuals under $200 ....26%
- Other..8%

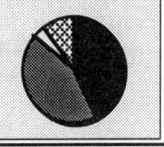

Top Industries & Interest Groups

Lawyers & Lobbyists $23,432
Crop Production/Processing $19,925
Oil & Gas $16,200
Insurance $15,300
Health Professionals $13,800

Unidentified $25,440

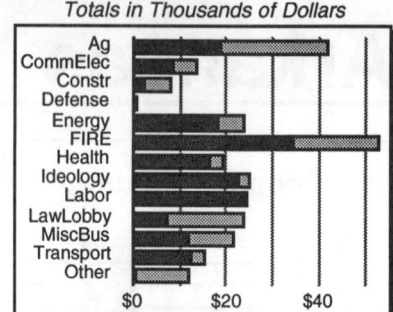

2. Ray Thornton (D)

1992 Committees: GovtOps Science
First elected: 1990

1991-92 Total Rcpts: $303,430
1990 Year-end cash: $115,739

Source of Funds
- PACs..43%
- Lg Individuals ($200+) 43%
- Individuals under $200 ....4%
- Other..10%

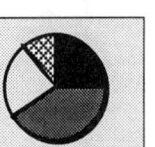

Top Industries & Interest Groups

Securities & Investment $44,750
Lawyers & Lobbyists $19,050
Industrial Unions $19,000
Transportation Unions $15,100
Health Professionals $12,350

Unidentified $12,050

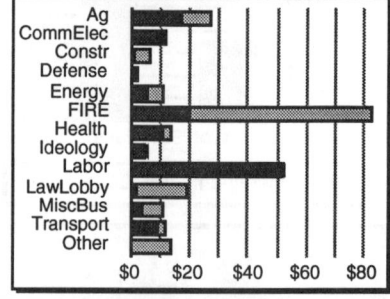

3. Tim Hutchinson (R)

1993-94 Committees: PubWorks VetAffairs
First elected: 1992

1991-92 Total Rcpts: $344,017
1990 Year-end cash: $4,246

Source of Funds
- PACs..25%
- Lg Individuals ($200+) 41%
- Individuals under $200 ....23%
- Other..11%

Top Industries & Interest Groups

Health Professionals $31,800
Real Estate $12,500
Oil & Gas $12,250
Retail Sales..................................$9,200
Food Processing & Sales $9,000

Unidentified $39,558

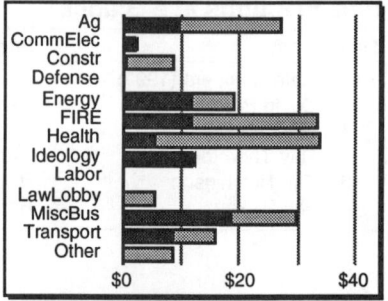

4. Jay Dickey (R)

1993-94 Committees: Agriculture
First elected: 1992

1991-92 Total Rcpts: $405,965
1990 Year-end cash: $14,621

Source of Funds
- PACs..0%
- Lg Individuals ($200+) 34%
- Individuals under $200 ....24%
- Other..42%

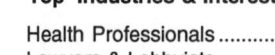

Top Industries & Interest Groups

Health Professionals $14,524
Lawyers & Lobbyists $12,100
Retired $10,580
Forestry & Forest Products $9,867
Commercial Banks $9,000

Unidentified $27,749

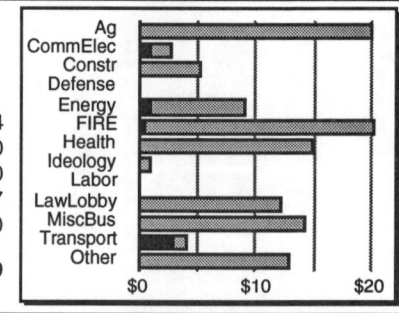

■ PACs   ▨ Indivs ($200+)

Totals in Thousands of Dollars

California

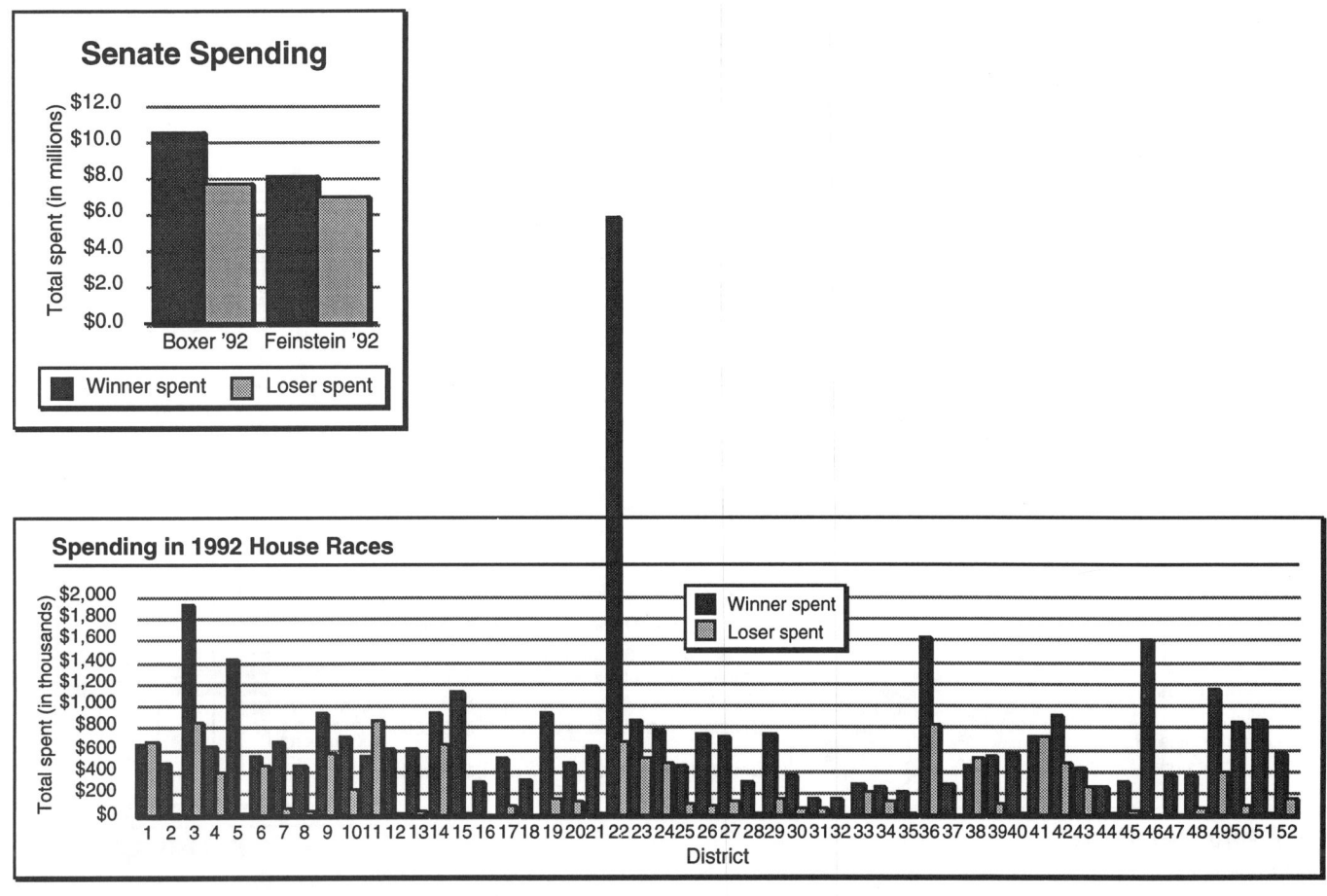

1992 Elections at a Glance

Dist	Name	Party	Vote Pct	Race Type
Sen	Barbara Boxer (1992)	Dem	48%	Open Seat
Sen	Dianne Feinstein (1992)	Dem	54%	Beat Incumb
1	Dan Hamburg	Dem	48%	Beat Incumb
2	Wally Herger	Rep	65%	Reelected
3	Vic Fazio	Dem	51%	Reelected
4	John T. Doolittle	Rep	50%	Reelected
5	Robert T. Matsui	Dem	69%	Reelected
6	Lynn Woolsey	Dem	65%	Open Seat
7	George Miller	Dem	70%	Reelected
8	Nancy Pelosi	Dem	82%	Reelected
9	Ronald V. Dellums	Dem	72%	Reelected
10	Bill Baker	Rep	52%	Open Seat
11	Richard W. Pombo	Rep	48%	Open Seat
12	Tom Lantos	Dem	69%	Reelected
13	Pete Stark	Dem	60%	Reelected
14	Anna G. Eshoo	Dem	57%	Open Seat
15	Norman Y. Mineta	Dem	64%	Reelected
16	Don Edwards	Dem	62%	Reelected
17	Leon E. Panetta	Dem	72%	Reelected
18	Gary Condit	Dem	85%	Reelected
19	Richard H. Lehman	Dem	47%	Reelected
20	Calvin Dooley	Dem	65%	Reelected
21	Bill Thomas	Rep	65%	Reelected
22	Michael Huffington	Rep	52%	Open Seat
23	Elton Gallegly	Rep	54%	Reelected
24	Anthony C. Beilenson	Dem	56%	Reelected
25	Howard "Buck" McKeon	Rep	52%	Open Seat
26	Howard L. Berman	Dem	61%	Reelected
27	Carlos J. Moorhead	Rep	50%	Reelected
28	David Dreier	Rep	58%	Reelected
29	Henry A. Waxman	Dem	61%	Reelected
30	Xavier Becerra	Dem	58%	Open Seat
31	Matthew G. Martinez	Dem	63%	Reelected
32	Julian C. Dixon	Dem	87%	Reelected
33	Lucille Roybal-Allard	Dem	63%	Open Seat
34	Esteban E. Torres	Dem	61%	Reelected
35	Maxine Waters	Dem	82%	Reelected
36	Jane Harman	Dem	48%	Open Seat
37	Walter R. Tucker	Dem	86%	Open Seat
38	Steve Horn	Rep	49%	Open Seat
39	Ed Royce	Rep	57%	Open Seat
40	Jerry Lewis	Rep	63%	Reelected
41	Jay C. Kim	Rep	60%	Open Seat
42	George E. Brown Jr.	Dem	51%	Reelected
43	Ken Calvert	Rep	47%	Open Seat
44	Al McCandless	Rep	54%	Reelected
45	Dana Rohrabacher	Rep	54%	Reelected
46	Robert K. Dornan	Rep	50%	Reelected
47	C. Christopher Cox	Rep	65%	Reelected
48	Ron Packard	Rep	61%	Reelected
49	Lynn Schenk	Dem	51%	Open Seat
50	Bob Filner	Dem	57%	Open Seat
51	Randy "Duke" Cunningham	Rep	56%	Reelected
52	Duncan Hunter	Rep	53%	Reelected

Sen. Barbara Boxer (D)
1992 House Committees: ArmServ Gov Ops
First elected: 1992

1991-92 Total Rcpts: $10,348,571
1990 Year-end cash: $18,459

Source of Funds
- PACs 7%
- Lg Individuals ($200+) 31%
- Individuals under $200 .... 41%
- Other 20%

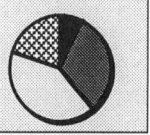

1991-92
Top Industries & Interest Groups

Lawyers & Lobbyists $687,082
Media/Entertainment $386,395
Womens Issues $379,286
Health Professionals $214,294
Retired $147,026

Unidentified $880,013

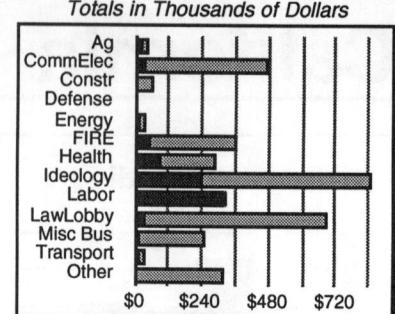

Sen. Dianne Feinstein (D)
1993-94 Committees: Approp Judiciary Rules
First elected: 1992

1991-92 Total Rcpts: $8,114,032
1990 Year-end cash: $60,645

Source of Funds
- PACs 10%
- Lg Individuals ($200+) 41%
- Individuals under $200 .... 29%
- Other 20%

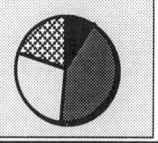

1991-92
Top Industries & Interest Groups

Lawyers & Lobbyists $707,149
Media/Entertainment $277,250
Securities & Investment $235,553
Real Estate $226,258
Womens Issues $223,878

Unidentified $676,787

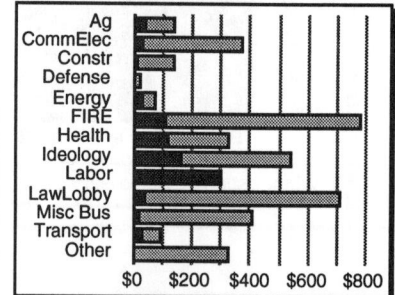

1. Dan Hamburg (D)
1993-94 Committees: MerchMarine PubWorks
First elected: 1992

1991-92 Total Rcpts: $642,592
1990 Year-end cash: $5,057

Source of Funds
- PACs 28%
- Lg Individuals ($200+) 10%
- Individuals under $200 .... 51%
- Other 11%

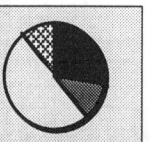

Top Industries & Interest Groups

Public Sector Unions $30,000
Industrial Unions $29,300
Transportation Unions $20,500
Misc Unions $19,300
Building Trade Unions $16,250

Unidentified $29,993

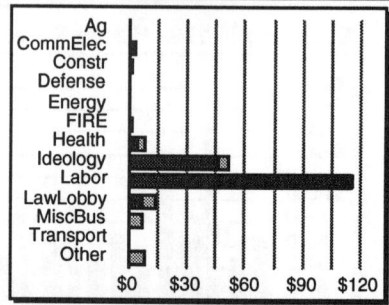

2. Wally Herger (R)
1992 Committees: Agric MerchMarine
First elected: 1986

1991-92 Total Rcpts: $615,832
1990 Year-end cash: $225,763

Source of Funds
- PACs 36%
- Lg Individuals ($200+) 30%
- Individuals under $200 .... 28%
- Other 6%

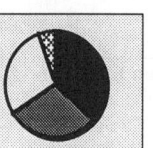

Top Industries & Interest Groups

Crop Production/Processing $76,165
Health Professionals $24,600
Retired $18,375
Food Processing & Sales $18,054
Livestock $16,975

Unidentified $31,100

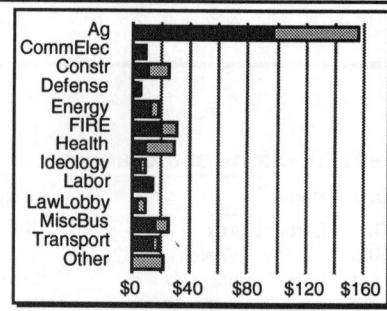

3. Vic Fazio (D)
1992 Committees: Appropriations
First elected: 1978

1991-92 Total Rcpts: $1,993,452
1990 Year-end cash: $281,802

Source of Funds
- PACs 57%
- Lg Individuals ($200+) 29%
- Individuals under $200 .... 10%
- Other 3%

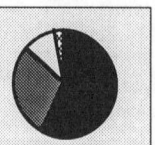

Top Industries & Interest Groups

Lawyers & Lobbyists $165,504
Crop Production/Processing $95,774
Insurance $90,299
Public Sector Unions $74,650
Health Professionals $73,225

Unidentified $114,965

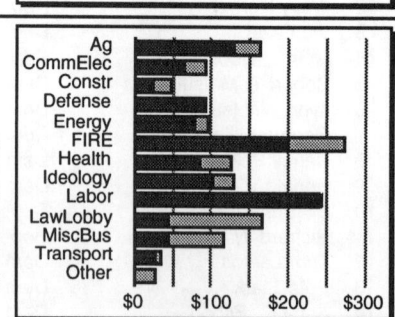

4. John T. Doolittle (R)
1992 Committees: Interior MerchMarine
First elected: 1990

1991-92 Total Rcpts: $610,104
1990 Year-end cash: $217

Source of Funds
- PACs 38%
- Lg Individuals ($200+) 31%
- Individuals under $200 .... 22%
- Other 9%

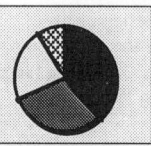

Top Industries & Interest Groups

Oil & Gas $23,000
Retired $22,025
Commercial Banks $21,825
Health Professionals $18,700
Automotive $17,150

Unidentified $72,380

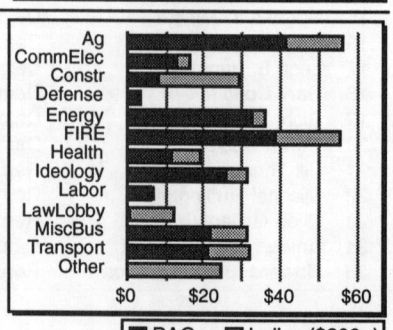

Key to committee & category abbreviations is on page 173

5. Robert T. Matsui (D)

1992 Committees: Budget Ways & Means
First elected: 1978

1991-92 Total Rcpts: $656,875
1990 Year-end cash: $384,523

Source of Funds
- PACs 55%
- Lg Individuals ($200+) 13%
- Individuals under $200 .... 14%
- Other 18%

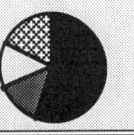

Top Industries & Interest Groups

Lawyers & Lobbyists $65,875
Health Professionals $31,100
Insurance $30,850
Real Estate $23,100
Public Sector Unions $23,050

Unidentified $6,250

Totals in Thousands of Dollars

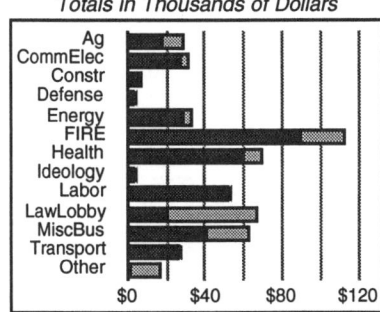

6. Lynn Woolsey (D)

1993-94 Committees: Budget Educ/Labor GovtOps
First elected: 1992

1991-92 Total Rcpts: $523,181
1990 Year-end cash: $3,112

Source of Funds
- PACs 36%
- Lg Individuals ($200+) 16%
- Individuals under $200 .... 41%
- Other 7%

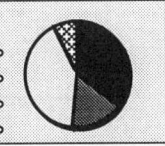

Top Industries & Interest Groups

Womens Issues $36,583
Public Sector Unions $27,500
Lawyers & Lobbyists $22,750
Building Trade Unions $19,000
Transportation Unions $19,000

Unidentified $18,140

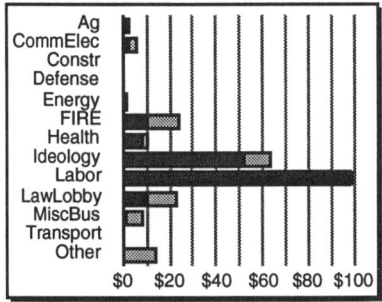

7. George Miller (D)

1992 Committees: Educ/Labor Interior
First elected: 1974

1991-92 Total Rcpts: $542,532
1990 Year-end cash: $328,659

Source of Funds
- PACs 48%
- Lg Individuals ($200+) 25%
- Individuals under $200 .... 15%
- Other 12%

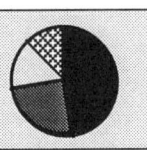

Top Industries & Interest Groups

Lawyers & Lobbyists $58,424
Transportation Unions $31,350
Electric Utilities $21,875
Industrial Unions $21,525
Building Trade Unions $20,675

Unidentified $13,450

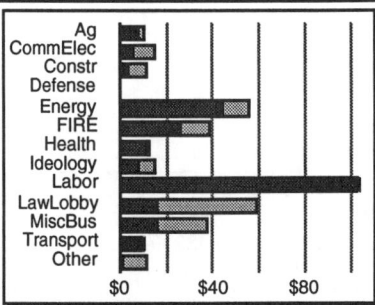

8. Nancy Pelosi (D)

1992 Committees: Appropriations
First elected: 1987

1991-92 Total Rcpts: $417,254
1990 Year-end cash: $74,704

Source of Funds
- PACs 48%
- Lg Individuals ($200+) 43%
- Individuals under $200 .... 3%
- Other 6%

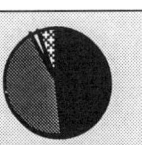

Top Industries & Interest Groups

Lawyers & Lobbyists $40,525
Transportation Unions $37,300
Public Sector Unions $29,750
Real Estate $25,000
Health Professionals $22,900

Unidentified $23,050

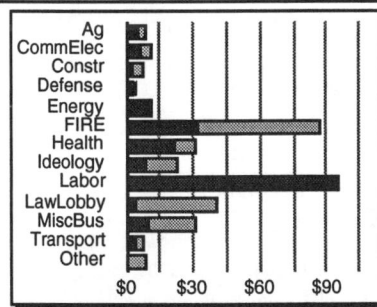

9. Ronald V. Dellums (D)

1992 Committees: ArmServ DC
First elected: 1970

1991-92 Total Rcpts: $854,478
1990 Year-end cash: $15,335

Source of Funds
- PACs 9%
- Lg Individuals ($200+) 12%
- Individuals under $200 .... 62%
- Other 17%

Top Industries & Interest Groups

Transportation Unions $26,150
Retired $21,456
Lawyers & Lobbyists $17,506
Public Sector Unions $10,350
Industrial Unions $9,100

Unidentified $25,399

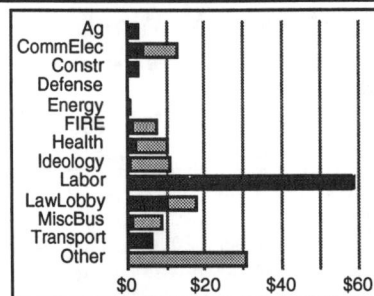

10. Bill Baker (R)

1993-94 Committees: PubWorks Science
First elected: 1992

1991-92 Total Rcpts: $708,485
1990 Year-end cash: $1,704

Source of Funds
- PACs 25%
- Lg Individuals ($200+) 44%
- Individuals under $200 .... 20%
- Other 11%

Top Industries & Interest Groups

Real Estate $55,567
Health Professionals $28,375
Insurance $21,150
General Contractors $19,250
Retired $18,153

Unidentified $94,565

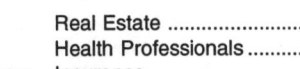
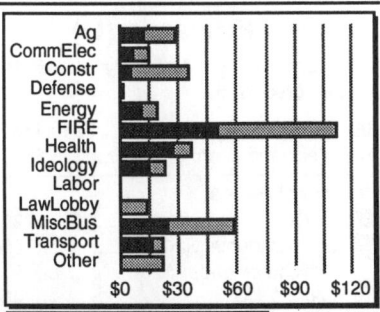

11. Richard W. Pombo (R)

1993-94 Committees: Agric MerchMarine
First elected: 1992

1991-92 Total Rcpts: $532,902
1990 Year-end cash: $3,911

Source of Funds
- PACs 26%
- Lg Individuals ($200+) 37%
- Individuals under $200 ....25%
- Other 13%

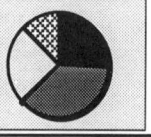

Top Industries & Interest Groups

Crop Production/Processing $43,030
Real Estate $24,750
Commercial Banks $16,650
Republican/Conservative $13,674
Retired $12,975

Unidentified $58,490

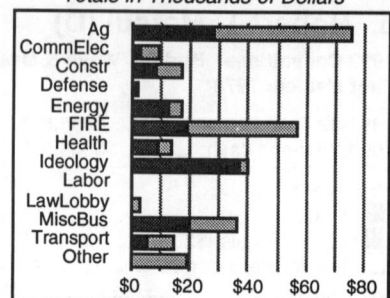

12. Tom Lantos (D)

1992 Committees: ForAff GovtOps
First elected: 1980

1991-92 Total Rcpts: $499,867
1990 Year-end cash: $510,190

Source of Funds
- PACs 22%
- Lg Individuals ($200+) 21%
- Individuals under $200 ....45%
- Other 11%

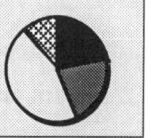

Top Industries & Interest Groups

Transportation Unions $28,050
Pro-Israel $23,300
Real Estate $21,500
Public Sector Unions $12,250
Building Trade Unions $11,000

Unidentified $17,750

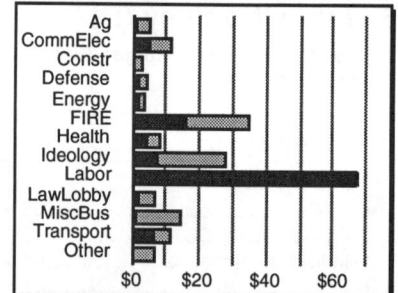

13. Pete Stark (D)

1992 Committees: DC Ways & Means
First elected: 1972

1991-92 Total Rcpts: $634,494
1990 Year-end cash: $400,792

Source of Funds
- PACs 55%
- Lg Individuals ($200+) 17%
- Individuals under $200 ....11%
- Other 17%

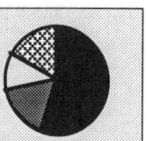

Top Industries & Interest Groups

Health Professionals $113,401
Lawyers & Lobbyists $61,210
Hospitals/Nursing Homes $32,000
Insurance $28,500
Public Sector Unions $25,600

Unidentified $6,450

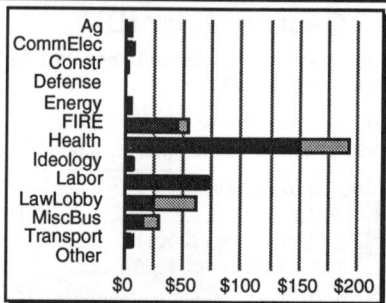

14. Anna G. Eshoo (D)

1993-94 Committees: MerchMarine Science
First elected: 1992

1991-92 Total Rcpts: $917,346
1990 Year-end cash: $7,774

Source of Funds
- PACs 32%
- Lg Individuals ($200+) 35%
- Individuals under $200 ....32%
- Other 2%

Top Industries & Interest Groups

Womens Issues $93,751
Public Sector Unions $43,000
Lawyers & Lobbyists $39,850
Real Estate $34,650
Industrial Unions $30,000

Unidentified $59,897

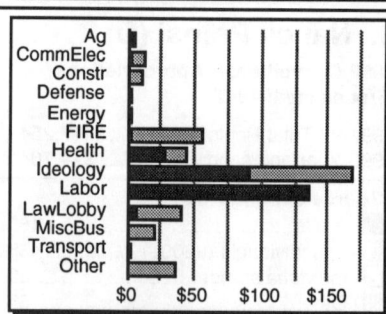

15. Norman Y. Mineta (D)

1992 Committees: PubWorks Science
First elected: 1974

1991-92 Total Rcpts: $967,049
1990 Year-end cash: $197,336

Source of Funds
- PACs 56%
- Lg Individuals ($200+) 27%
- Individuals under $200 ....11%
- Other 5%

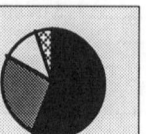

Top Industries & Interest Groups

Lawyers & Lobbyists $80,335
Air Transport $59,944
Transportation Unions $56,300
Trucking $45,665
Public Sector Unions $37,828

Unidentified $52,444

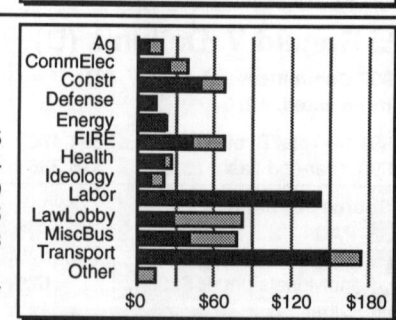

16. Don Edwards (D)

1992 Committees: Judiciary VetAffairs
First elected: 1962

1991-92 Total Rcpts: $249,478
1990 Year-end cash: $13,687

Source of Funds
- PACs 72%
- Lg Individuals ($200+) 16%
- Individuals under $200 ....9%
- Other 4%

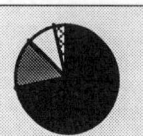

Top Industries & Interest Groups

Lawyers & Lobbyists $30,450
Public Sector Unions $30,375
Transportation Unions $16,300
Building Trade Unions $15,200
Telephone Utilities $14,300

Unidentified $3,850

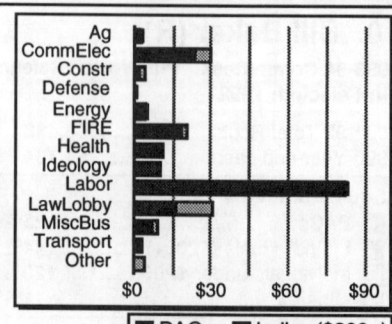

Key to committee & category abbreviations is on page 173

Totals in Thousands of Dollars

17. Leon E. Panetta (D)
1992 Committees: Admin Agric Budget
First elected: 1976

1991-92 Total Rcpts: $410,124
1990 Year-end cash: $100,272

Source of Funds
- PACs 56%
- Lg Individuals ($200+) 15%
- Individuals under $200 .... 20%
- Other 9%

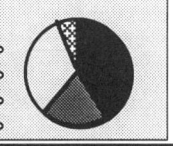

Top Industries & Interest Groups

Public Sector Unions $31,000
Beer, Wine & Liquor $25,750
Crop Production/Processing $22,650
Lawyers & Lobbyists $17,850
Hospitals/Nursing Homes $16,750

Unidentified $4,750

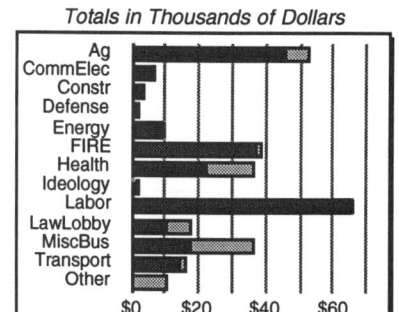

18. Gary Condit (D)
1992 Committees: Agric GovtOps
First elected: 1989

1991-92 Total Rcpts: $371,990
1990 Year-end cash: $66,029

Source of Funds
- PACs 41%
- Lg Individuals ($200+) 20%
- Individuals under $200 .... 32%
- Other 7%

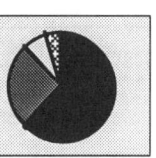

Top Industries & Interest Groups

Crop Production/Processing $44,975
Dairy $13,302
Industrial Unions $11,500
Transportation Unions $10,800
Agricultural Services/Products ..$10,780

Unidentified $14,407

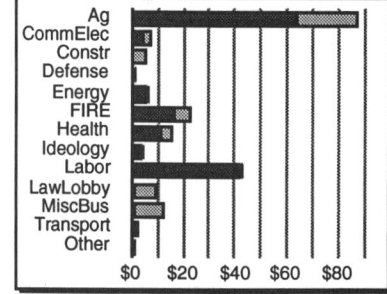

19. Richard H. Lehman (D)
1992 Committees: Energy/Commerce Interior
First elected: 1982

1991-92 Total Rcpts: $826,532
1990 Year-end cash: $7,171

Source of Funds
- PACs 62%
- Lg Individuals ($200+) 26%
- Individuals under $200 .... 8%
- Other 4%

Top Industries & Interest Groups

Crop Production/Processing $52,470
Real Estate $50,100
Lawyers & Lobbyists $48,493
Public Sector Unions $39,210
Industrial Unions $34,750

Unidentified $43,705

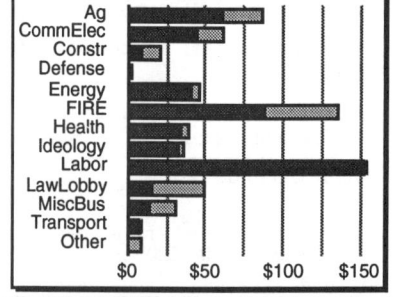

20. Calvin Dooley (D)
1992 Committees: Agric Interior
First elected: 1990

1991-92 Total Rcpts: $496,485
1990 Year-end cash: $1,544

Source of Funds
- PACs 49%
- Lg Individuals ($200+) 29%
- Individuals under $200 .... 20%
- Other 2%

Top Industries & Interest Groups

Crop Production/Processing $82,122
Lawyers & Lobbyists $22,023
Health Professionals $17,950
Agricultural Services/Products ..$17,550
Building Trade Unions $15,600

Unidentified $44,670

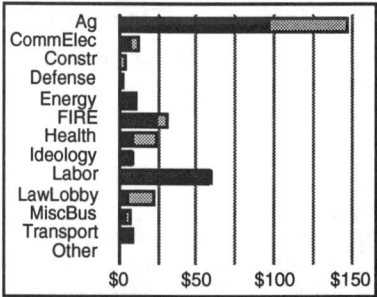

21. Bill Thomas (R)
1992 Committees: Admin Budget Ways & Means
First elected: 1978

1991-92 Total Rcpts: $603,169
1990 Year-end cash: $95,932

Source of Funds
- PACs 47%
- Lg Individuals ($200+) 32%
- Individuals under $200 .... 10%
- Other 11%

Top Industries & Interest Groups

Crop Production/Processing $56,490
Insurance $43,849
Lawyers & Lobbyists $32,275
Oil & Gas $28,144
Health Professionals $27,050

Unidentified $52,476

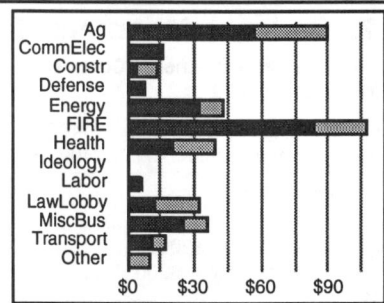

22. Michael Huffington (R)
1993-94 Committees: Banking SmBus
First elected: 1992

1991-92 Total Rcpts: $5,443,247
1990 Year-end cash: $8,071

Source of Funds
- PACs 0%
- Lg Individuals ($200+) 3%
- Individuals under $200 .... 1%
- Other 95%

Top Industries & Interest Groups

Retired $19,560
Oil & Gas $17,650
Securities & Investment $16,700
Real Estate $14,050
Misc Finance $12,200

Unidentified $28,950

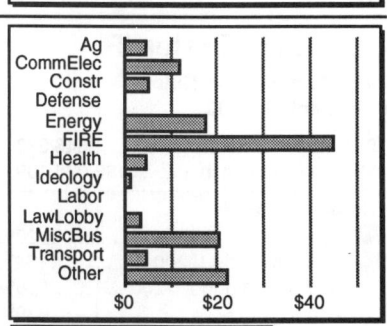

■ PACs   ▨ Indivs ($200+)

185

23. Elton Gallegly (R)

1992 Committees: ForAff Interior
First elected: 1986

1991-92 Total Rcpts: $679,886
1990 Year-end cash: $49,095

Source of Funds
- PACs 27%
- Lg Individuals ($200+) 36%
- Individuals under $200 .... 21%
- Other 16%

Top Industries & Interest Groups

Real Estate $54,038
Oil & Gas $22,692
General Contractors $17,726
Insurance $17,597
Retired $16,520

Unidentified $65,333

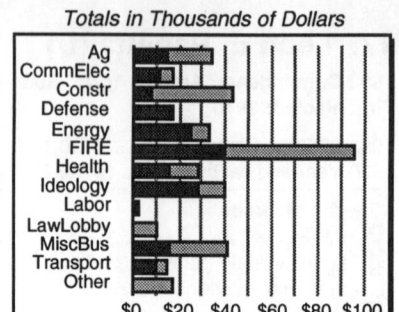

24. Anthony C. Beilenson (D)

1992 Committees: Budget Rules
First elected: 1976

1991-92 Total Rcpts: $739,415
1990 Year-end cash: $12,478

Source of Funds
- PACs 0%
- Lg Individuals ($200+) 63%
- Individuals under $200 .... 24%
- Other 14%

Top Industries & Interest Groups

Lawyers & Lobbyists $76,650
Retired $59,167
Media/Entertainment $50,150
Real Estate $27,950
Misc Finance $26,700

Unidentified $91,896

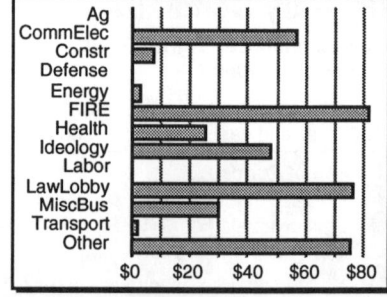

25. Howard "Buck" McKeon (R)

1993-94 Committees: Educ/Labor PubWorks
First elected: 1992

1991-92 Total Rcpts: $457,650
1990 Year-end cash: $4,858

Source of Funds
- PACs 21%
- Lg Individuals ($200+) 36%
- Individuals under $200 .... 14%
- Other 29%

Top Industries & Interest Groups

Real Estate $24,686
Automotive $24,600
Health Professionals $24,350
Retail Sales $17,350
Retired $11,950

Unidentified $48,855

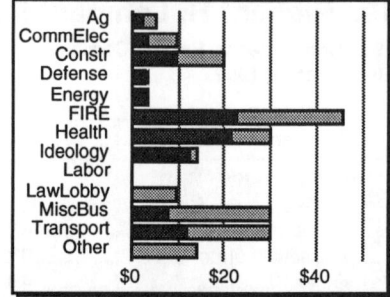

26. Howard L. Berman (D)

1992 Committees: Budget ForAff Judiciary
First elected: 1982

1991-92 Total Rcpts: $548,212
1990 Year-end cash: $26,077

Source of Funds
- PACs 39%
- Lg Individuals ($200+) 51%
- Individuals under $200 .... 3%
- Other 7%

Top Industries & Interest Groups

Media/Entertainment $82,650
Lawyers & Lobbyists $81,700
Building Trade Unions $26,000
Real Estate $25,900
Public Sector Unions $23,800

Unidentified $35,550

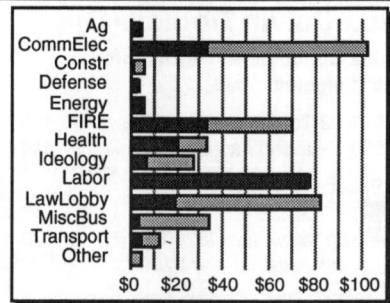

27. Carlos J. Moorhead (R)

1992 Committees: Energy/Commerce Judiciary
First elected: 1972

1991-92 Total Rcpts: $448,791
1990 Year-end cash: $409,659

Source of Funds
- PACs 57%
- Lg Individuals ($200+) 8%
- Individuals under $200 .... 13%
- Other 22%

Top Industries & Interest Groups

Media/Entertainment $27,300
Oil & Gas $23,150
Health Professionals $21,350
Insurance $19,100
Electric Utilities $17,150

Unidentified $8,600

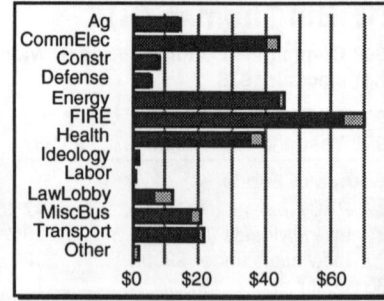

28. David Dreier (R)

1992 Committees: Rules
First elected: 1980

1991-92 Total Rcpts: $646,323
1990 Year-end cash: $2,026,109

Source of Funds
- PACs 20%
- Lg Individuals ($200+) 34%
- Individuals under $200 .... 6%
- Other 39%

Top Industries & Interest Groups

Commercial Banks $29,750
Retired $27,450
Real Estate $21,000
Lawyers & Lobbyists $18,050
Health Professionals $17,000

Unidentified $34,947

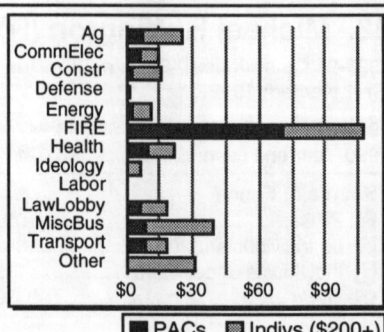

Key to committee & category abbreviations is on page 173

29. Henry A. Waxman (D)
1992 Committees: Energy/Commerce GovtOps
First elected: 1974

1991-92 Total Rcpts: $682,214
1990 Year-end cash: $432,414

Source of Funds
- PACs..58%
- Lg Individuals ($200+) 28%
- Individuals under $200 ....5%
- Other...9%

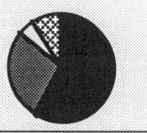

Top Industries & Interest Groups

Health Professionals $126,049
Lawyers & Lobbyists $65,350
Media/Entertainment $44,750
Hospitals/Nursing Homes $31,250
Pharmaceuticals/Health Prod $25,600

Unidentified $20,792

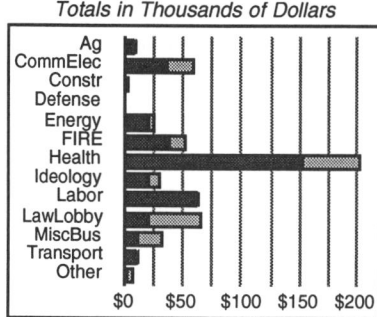

30. Xavier Becerra (D)
1993-94 Committees: Educ/Labor Judiciary Science
First elected: 1992

1991-92 Total Rcpts: $367,385
1990 Year-end cash: $13,833

Source of Funds
- PACs..26%
- Lg Individuals ($200+) 26%
- Individuals under $200 ....24%
- Other...24%

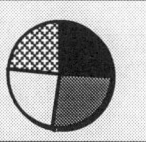

Top Industries & Interest Groups

Lawyers & Lobbyists $22,800
Industrial Unions $15,500
Health Professionals $15,250
Public Sector Unions $14,700
Real Estate $9,950

Unidentified $29,950

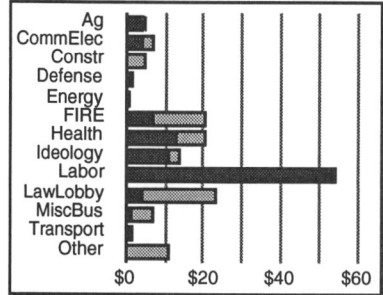

31. Matthew G. Martinez (D)
1992 Committees: Educ/Labor GovtOps
First elected: 1982

1991-92 Total Rcpts: $119,807
1990 Year-end cash: $13,570

Source of Funds
- PACs..59%
- Lg Individuals ($200+) 27%
- Individuals under $200 ....5%
- Other...9%

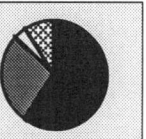

Top Industries & Interest Groups

Real Estate $16,050
Public Sector Unions $10,000
Human Rights $10,000
Industrial Unions $8,500
Building Trade Unions $5,500

Unidentified $8,500

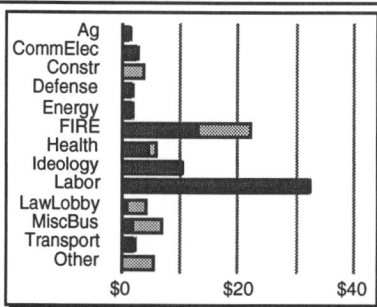

32. Julian C. Dixon (D)
1992 Committees: Appropriations
First elected: 1978

1991-92 Total Rcpts: $83,583
1990 Year-end cash: $80,101

Source of Funds
- PACs..58%
- Lg Individuals ($200+) 29%
- Individuals under $200 ....2%
- Other...11%

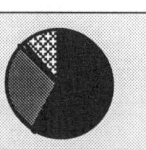

Top Industries & Interest Groups

Real Estate $7,750
Public Sector Unions $5,500
Pro-Israel $5,500
Health Professionals $5,000
Transportation Unions $5,000

Unidentified $3,950

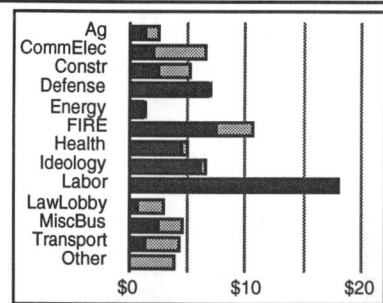

33. Lucille Roybal-Allard (D)
1993-94 Committees: Banking SmBus
First elected: 1992

1991-92 Total Rcpts: $283,770
1990 Year-end cash: $19,015

Source of Funds
- PACs..47%
- Lg Individuals ($200+) 26%
- Individuals under $200 ....24%
- Other...3%

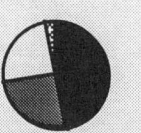

Top Industries & Interest Groups

Womens Issues $21,105
Real Estate $16,500
Health Professionals $14,500
Lawyers & Lobbyists $14,450
Beer, Wine & Liquor $10,500

Unidentified $10,800

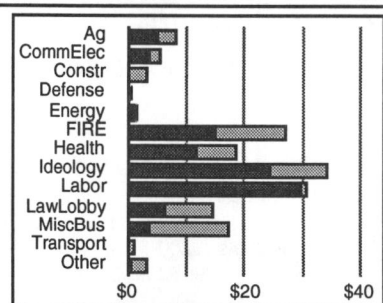

34. Esteban E. Torres (D)
1992 Committees: Banking SmBus
First elected: 1982

1991-92 Total Rcpts: $169,451
1990 Year-end cash: $63,139

Source of Funds
- PACs..27%
- Lg Individuals ($200+) 43%
- Individuals under $200 ....12%
- Other...17%

Top Industries & Interest Groups

Lawyers & Lobbyists $21,100
Real Estate $13,250
Industrial Unions $6,500
Public Sector Unions $6,500
Telecom Services & Equipment ..$5,505

Unidentified $18,493

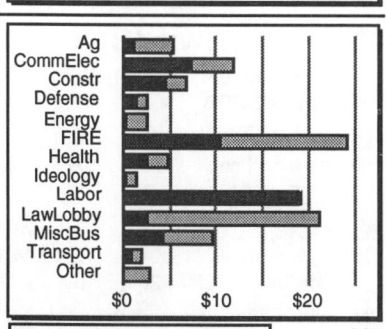

35. Maxine Waters (D)

1992 Committees: Banking VetAffairs
First elected: 1990

1991-92 Total Rcpts: $191,510
1990 Year-end cash: $11,274

Source of Funds
- PACs 46%
- Lg Individuals ($200+) 39%
- Individuals under $200 .... 8%
- Other 8%

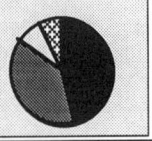

Top Industries & Interest Groups

Public Sector Unions $18,800
Lawyers & Lobbyists $11,800
Health Professionals $11,625
Industrial Unions $11,550
Transportation Unions $9,000

Unidentified $18,756

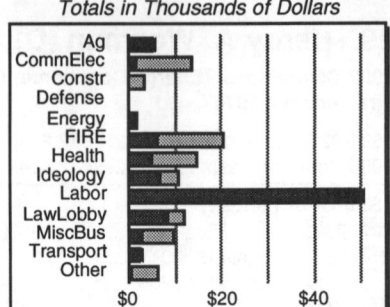

36. Jane Harman (D)

1993-94 Committees: ArmServ Science
First elected: 1992

1991-92 Total Rcpts: $1,628,376
1990 Year-end cash: $16,019

Source of Funds
- PACs 12%
- Lg Individuals ($200+) 27%
- Individuals under $200 .... 9%
- Other 51%

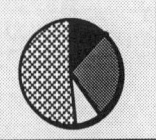

Top Industries & Interest Groups

Lawyers & Lobbyists $148,925
Securities & Investment $45,300
Womens Issues $40,932
Media/Entertainment $28,400
Defense Aerospace $23,184

Unidentified $67,900

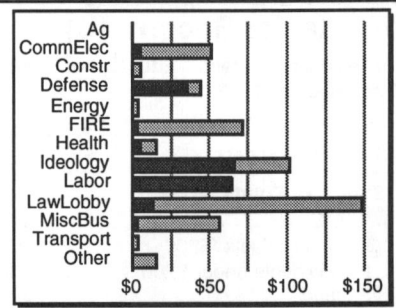

37. Walter R. Tucker (D)

1993-94 Committees: PubWorks SmBus
First elected: 1992

1991-92 Total Rcpts: $283,230
1990 Year-end cash: $5,644

Source of Funds
- PACs 19%
- Lg Individuals ($200+) 39%
- Individuals under $200 .... 15%
- Other 27%

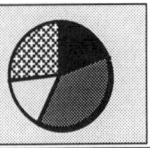

Top Industries & Interest Groups

Health Professionals $13,500
Industrial Unions $12,250
Transportation Unions $8,050
Pro-Israel $7,250
Real Estate $6,750

Unidentified $88,682

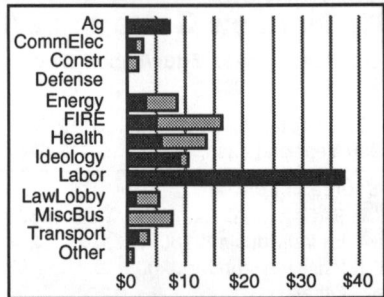

38. Steve Horn (R)

1993-94 Committees: GovtOps PubWorks
First elected: 1992

1991-92 Total Rcpts: $436,093
1990 Year-end cash: $493

Source of Funds
- PACs 0%
- Lg Individuals ($200+) 56%
- Individuals under $200 .... 18%
- Other 25%

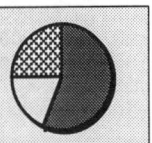

Top Industries & Interest Groups

Retired $36,863
Health Professionals $24,966
Education $24,224
Lawyers & Lobbyists $17,250
Real Estate $16,200

Unidentified $66,686

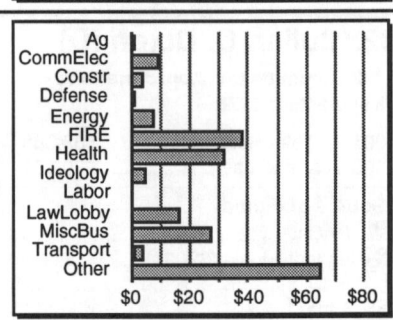

39. Ed Royce (R)

1993-94 Committees: ForAff Science
First elected: 1992

1991-92 Total Rcpts: $499,264
1990 Year-end cash: $6,772

Source of Funds
- PACs 37%
- Lg Individuals ($200+) 36%
- Individuals under $200 .... 12%
- Other 15%

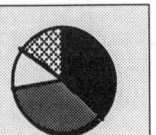

Top Industries & Interest Groups

Health Professionals $39,667
Lawyers & Lobbyists $28,950
Insurance $23,800
Real Estate $21,780
Republican/Conservative $15,997

Unidentified $45,811

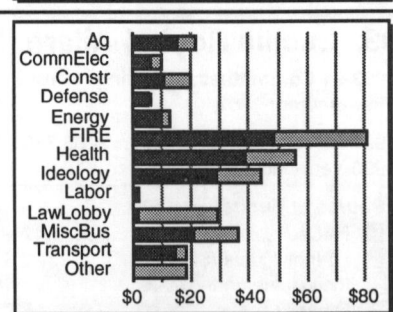

40. Jerry Lewis (R)

1992 Committees: Appropriations
First elected: 1978

1991-92 Total Rcpts: $471,956
1990 Year-end cash: $264,213

Source of Funds
- PACs 76%
- Lg Individuals ($200+) 16%
- Individuals under $200 .... 3%
- Other 5%

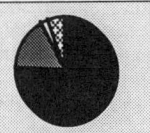

Top Industries & Interest Groups

Defense Aerospace $39,945
Insurance $39,500
Health Professionals $24,539
Defense Electronics $19,250
Lawyers & Lobbyists $18,500

Unidentified $12,250

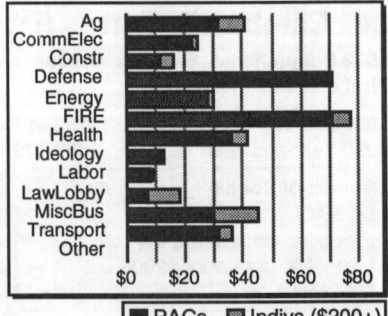

Key to committee & category abbreviations is on page 173

41. Jay C. Kim (R)

1993-94 Committees: PubWorks SmBus
First elected: 1992

1991-92 Total Rcpts: $735,483
1990 Year-end cash: $28,312

Source of Funds
- PACs 12%
- Lg Individuals ($200+) 44%
- Individuals under $200 ....26%
- Other 17%

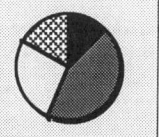

Top Industries & Interest Groups

Health Professionals $45,295
Real Estate $21,750
Construction Services $9,800
Commercial Banks $9,150
Insurance $8,700

Unidentified $192,640

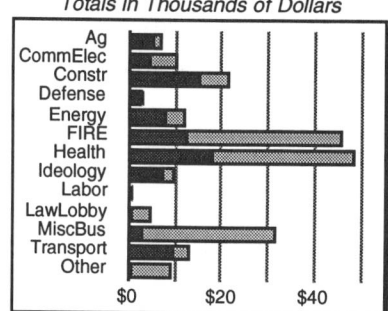

42. George E. Brown Jr. (D)

1992 Committees: Agric Science
First elected: 1962

1991-92 Total Rcpts: $908,348
1990 Year-end cash: $5,564

Source of Funds
- PACs 54%
- Lg Individuals ($200+) 20%
- Individuals under $200 ....20%
- Other 6%

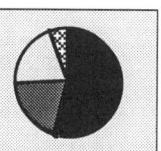

Top Industries & Interest Groups

Public Sector Unions $50,250
Defense Aerospace $43,062
Industrial Unions $42,850
Lawyers & Lobbyists $42,675
Transportation Unions $31,000

Unidentified $32,900

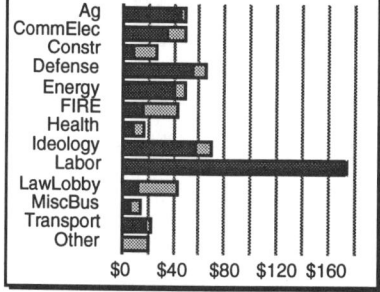

43. Ken Calvert (D)

1993-94 Committees: NatResources Science
First elected: 1992

1991-92 Total Rcpts: $423,001
1990 Year-end cash: $934

Source of Funds
- PACs 29%
- Lg Individuals ($200+) 47%
- Individuals under $200 ....9%
- Other 15%

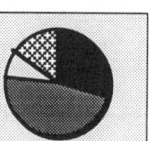

Top Industries & Interest Groups

Real Estate $36,921
Retired $30,500
Health Professionals $19,335
Automotive $19,250
Lawyers & Lobbyists $16,500

Unidentified $54,225

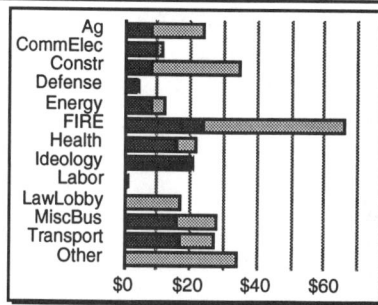

44. Al McCandless (R)

1992 Committees: Banking GovtOps
First elected: 1982

1991-92 Total Rcpts: $318,312
1990 Year-end cash: $45,027

Source of Funds
- PACs 61%
- Lg Individuals ($200+) 24%
- Individuals under $200 ....14%
- Other 1%

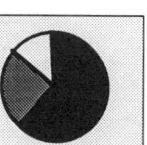

Top Industries & Interest Groups

Commercial Banks $52,799
Real Estate $17,250
Crop Production/Processing $17,056
Automotive $13,000
Retired $12,953

Unidentified $11,250

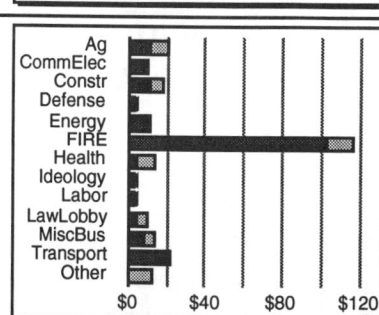

45. Dana Rohrabacher (R)

1992 Committees: DC Science
First elected: 1988

1991-92 Total Rcpts: $311,608
1990 Year-end cash: $52,281

Source of Funds
- PACs 35%
- Lg Individuals ($200+) 55%
- Individuals under $200 ....9%
- Other 1%

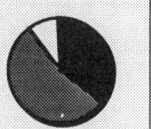

Top Industries & Interest Groups

Health Professionals $33,110
Real Estate $16,215
Lawyers & Lobbyists $13,750
Republican/Conservative $13,150
Automotive $12,150

Unidentified $50,226

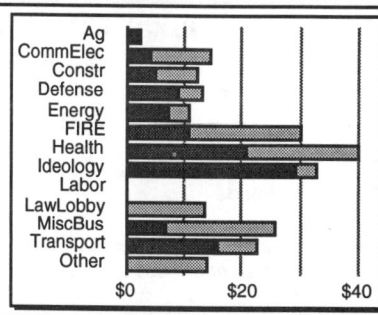

46. Robert K. Dornan (R)

1992 Committees: Armed Services
First elected: 1976

1991-92 Total Rcpts: $1,443,564
1990 Year-end cash: $47,253

Source of Funds
- PACs 5%
- Lg Individuals ($200+) 18%
- Individuals under $200 ....76%
- Other 1%

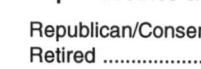

Top Industries & Interest Groups

Republican/Conservative $81,304
Retired $72,813
Defense Aerospace $13,500
Automotive $11,250
Abortion Policy $9,750

Unidentified $24,145

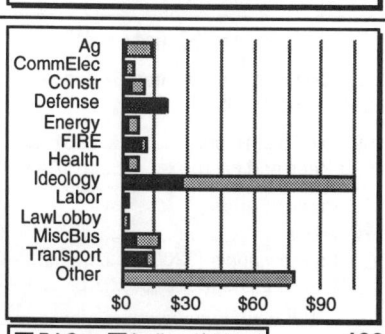

Totals in Thousands of Dollars

47. C. Christopher Cox (R)
1992 Committees: GovtOps PubWorks
First elected: 1988

1991-92 Total Rcpts: $515,754
1990 Year-end cash: $118,668

Source of Funds
- PACs 30%
- Lg Individuals ($200+) 62%
- Individuals under $200 .... 6%
- Other 1%

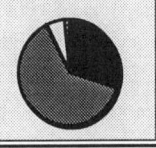

Top Industries & Interest Groups

Lawyers & Lobbyists $60,300
Real Estate $35,000
General Contractors $25,700
Air Transport $24,690
Republican/Conservative $24,450

Unidentified $68,575

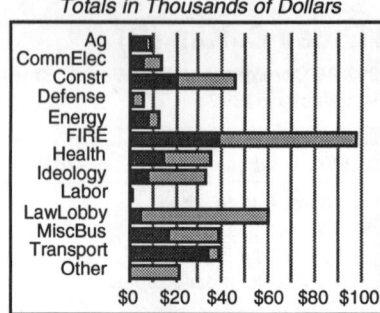

48. Ron Packard (R)
1992 Committees: PubWorks Science
First elected: 1982

1991-92 Total Rcpts: $292,021
1990 Year-end cash: $105,268

Source of Funds
- PACs 66%
- Lg Individuals ($200+) 12%
- Individuals under $200 .... 13%
- Other 9%

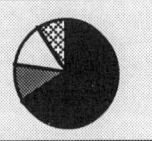

Top Industries & Interest Groups

Air Transport $40,373
Health Professionals $13,600
Automotive $12,500
General Contractors $11,500
Real Estate $9,750

Unidentified $1,546

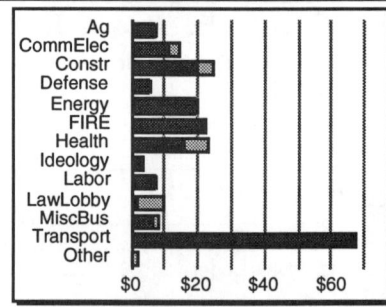

49. Lynn Schenk (D)
1993-94 Committees: Energy/Commerce MerchMarine
First elected: 1992

1991-92 Total Rcpts: $1,150,104
1990 Year-end cash: $23,509

Source of Funds
- PACs 26%
- Lg Individuals ($200+) 42%
- Individuals under $200 .... 15%
- Other 18%

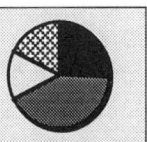

Top Industries & Interest Groups

Lawyers & Lobbyists $139,642
Womens Issues $42,163
Health Professionals $37,415
Real Estate $37,025
Public Sector Unions $33,000

Unidentified $92,835

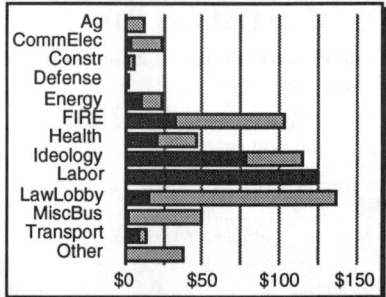

50. Bob Filner (D)
1993-94 Committees: PubWorks VetAffairs
First elected: 1992

1991-92 Total Rcpts: $842,594
1990 Year-end cash: $822

Source of Funds
- PACs 32%
- Lg Individuals ($200+) 38%
- Individuals under $200 .... 11%
- Other 20%

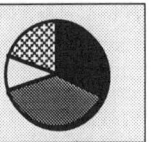

Top Industries & Interest Groups

Real Estate $62,950
Lawyers & Lobbyists $49,000
Pro-Israel $45,350
Health Professionals $39,700
Public Sector Unions $38,750

Unidentified $79,070

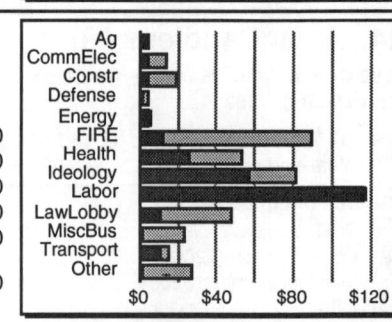

51. Randy "Duke" Cunningham (R)
1992 Committees: ArmServ Educ/Labor MerchMarine
First elected: 1990

1991-92 Total Rcpts: $907,606
1990 Year-end cash: $19,196

Source of Funds
- PACs 29%
- Lg Individuals ($200+) 27%
- Individuals under $200 .... 41%
- Other 4%

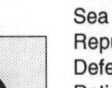

Top Industries & Interest Groups

Defense Aerospace $35,533
Sea Transport $30,424
Republican/Conservative $22,643
Defense Electronics $22,422
Retired $21,250

Unidentified $66,655

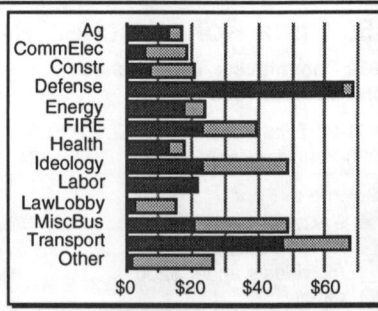

52. Duncan Hunter (R)
1992 Committees: Armed Services
First elected: 1980

1991-92 Total Rcpts: $561,203
1990 Year-end cash: $7,460

Source of Funds
- PACs 39%
- Lg Individuals ($200+) 34%
- Individuals under $200 .... 15%
- Other 11%

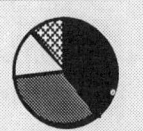

Top Industries & Interest Groups

Defense Aerospace $37,467
General Contractors $29,200
Defense Electronics $26,600
Sea Transport $21,750
Textiles $15,500

Unidentified $49,808

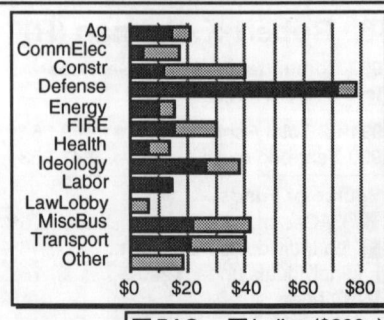

Key to committee & category abbreviations is on page 173

■ PACs   ▩ Indivs ($200+)

Colorado

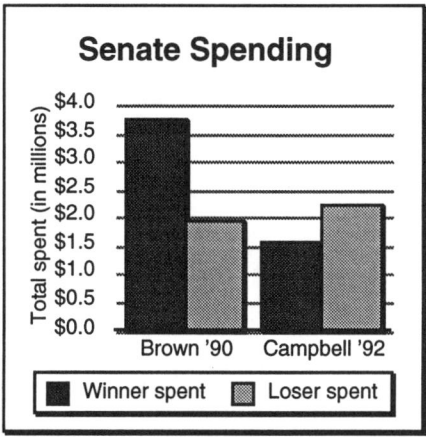

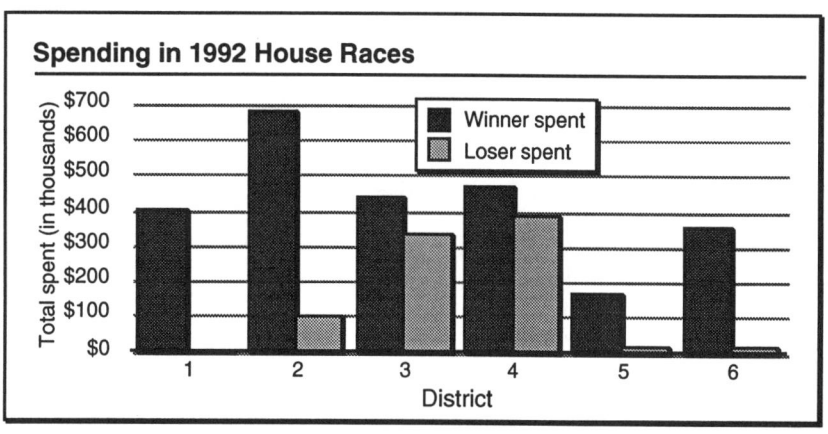

1992 Elections at a Glance

Dist	Name	Party	Vote Pct	Race Type
Sen	Hank Brown (1990)	Rep	56%	Open Seat
Sen	Ben Nighthorse Campbell (1992)	Dem	52%	Open Seat
1	Patricia Schroeder	Dem	69%	Reelected
2	David E. Skaggs	Dem	61%	Reelected
3	Scott McInnis	Rep	55%	Open Seat
4	Wayne Allard	Rep	58%	Reelected
5	Joel Hefley	Rep	71%	Reelected
6	Dan Schaefer	Rep	61%	Reelected

Totals in Thousands of Dollars

Sen. Hank Brown (R)

1992 Committees: Budget ForRel Judiciary
First elected: 1990

1989-92 Total Rcpts: $4,288,022
1990 Year-end cash: $426,326

Source of Funds
- PACs 30%
- Lg Individuals ($200+) 31%
- Individuals under $200 ....13%
- Other 26%

1989-92
Top Industries & Interest Groups

Insurance $182,889
Lawyers & Lobbyists................$167,010
Oil & Gas $153,991
Securities & Investment $117,101
Real Estate $102,625

Unidentified $451,735

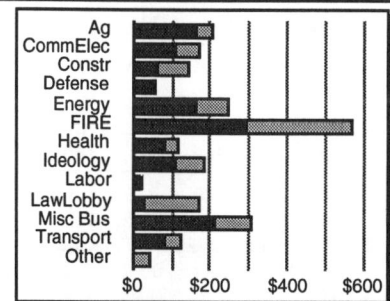

Sen. Ben Nighthorse Campbell (D)

1992 House Committees: Agric Interior
First elected: 1992

1991-92 Total Rcpts: $1,594,544
1990 Year-end cash: $46,741

Source of Funds
- PACs 40%
- Lg Individuals ($200+) 30%
- Individuals under $200 ....14%
- Other 15%

1991-92
Top Industries & Interest Groups

Lawyers & Lobbyists................$129,763
Industrial Unions $72,650
Transportation Unions $68,350
Oil & Gas $58,918
Health Professionals $56,500

Unidentified $156,350

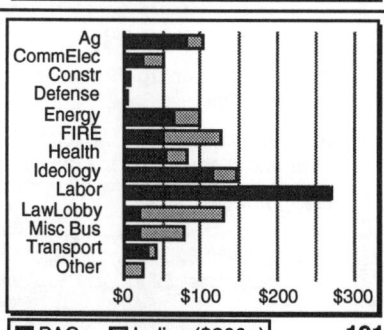

■ PACs   ▨ Indivs ($200+)

1. Patricia Schroeder (D)

1992 Committees: ArmServ Judiciary Post Office
First elected: 1972

1991-92 Total Rcpts: $361,845
1990 Year-end cash: $612,243

Source of Funds
- PACs 36%
- Lg Individuals ($200+) 39%
- Individuals under $200 .... 6%
- Other 19%

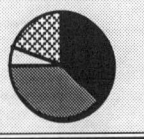

Top Industries & Interest Groups

Lawyers & Lobbyists $32,906
Media/Entertainment $30,250
Public Sector Unions $19,250
Transportation Unions $16,000
Printing & Publishing $14,281

Unidentified $30,028

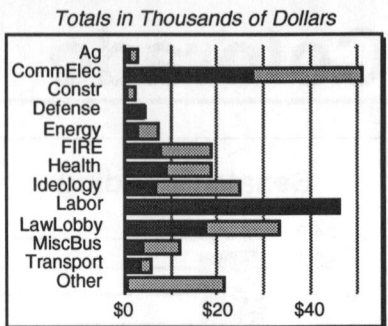

2. David E. Skaggs (D)

1992 Committees: Appropriations
First elected: 1986

1991-92 Total Rcpts: $659,719
1990 Year-end cash: $17,460

Source of Funds
- PACs 45%
- Lg Individuals ($200+) 22%
- Individuals under $200 .... 26%
- Other 8%

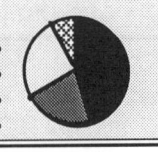

Top Industries & Interest Groups

Lawyers & Lobbyists $45,222
Public Sector Unions $39,500
Industrial Unions $35,550
Transportation Unions $35,150
Health Professionals $18,700

Unidentified $24,576

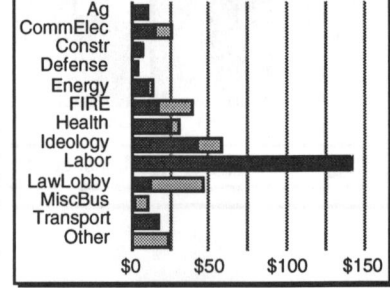

3. Scott McInnis (R)

1993-94 Committees: NatResources SmBus
First elected: 1992

1991-92 Total Rcpts: $438,090
1990 Year-end cash: $3,638

Source of Funds
- PACs 29%
- Lg Individuals ($200+) 51%
- Individuals under $200 .... 4%
- Other 16%

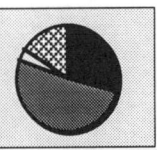

Top Industries & Interest Groups

Oil & Gas $46,228
Real Estate $21,200
Retired $19,900
Automotive $15,750
Health Professionals $15,500

Unidentified $76,966

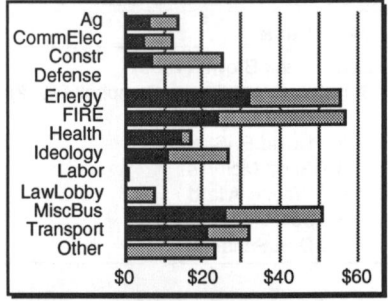

4. Wayne Allard (R)

1992 Committees: Agric Interior SmBus
First elected: 1990

1991-92 Total Rcpts: $474,315
1990 Year-end cash: $6,808

Source of Funds
- PACs 47%
- Lg Individuals ($200+) 29%
- Individuals under $200 .... 9%
- Other 15%

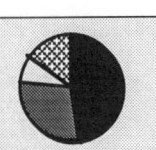

Top Industries & Interest Groups

Oil & Gas $28,638
Agricultural Services/Products .. $25,850
Dairy $21,100
Health Professionals $20,944
Real Estate $17,650

Unidentified $35,833

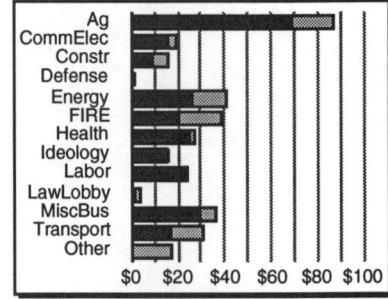

5. Joel Hefley (R)

1992 Committees: ArmServ Interior SmBus
First elected: 1986

1991-92 Total Rcpts: $137,757
1990 Year-end cash: $60,257

Source of Funds
- PACs 72%
- Lg Individuals ($200+) 10%
- Individuals under $200 .... 10%
- Other 7%

Top Industries & Interest Groups

Defense Aerospace $10,500
Air Transport $6,500
Real Estate $5,950
Defense Electronics $5,000
Automotive $5,000

Unidentified $2,070

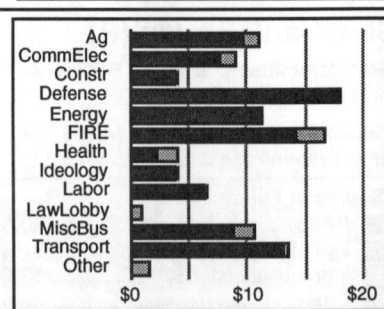

6. Dan Schaefer (R)

1992 Committees: Energy/Commerce
First elected: 1983

1991-92 Total Rcpts: $360,676
1990 Year-end cash: $130,660

Source of Funds
- PACs 76%
- Lg Individuals ($200+) 10%
- Individuals under $200 .... 9%
- Other 5%

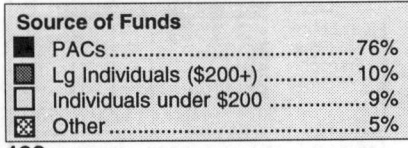
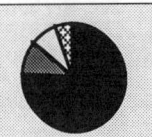

Top Industries & Interest Groups

Media/Entertainment $26,250
Insurance $24,800
Oil & Gas $19,159
Accountants $17,000
Health Professionals $14,500

Unidentified $5,030

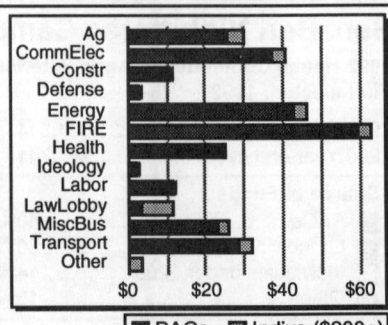

Key to committee & category abbreviations is on page 173

■ PACs ▨ Indivs ($200+)

Connecticut

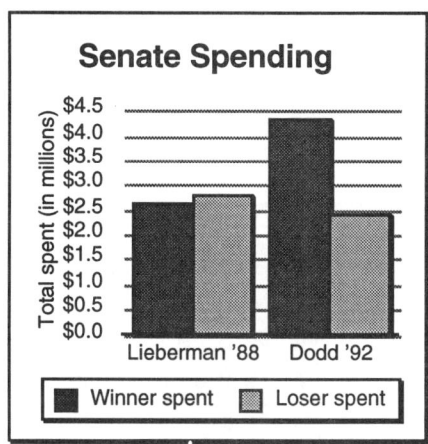

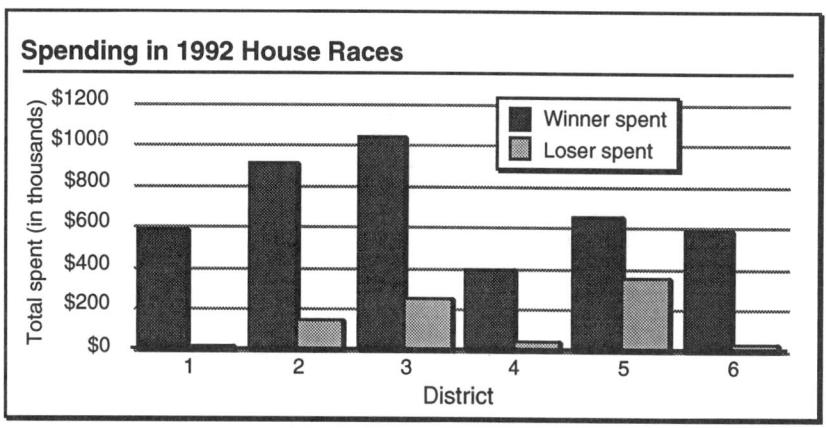

1992 Elections at a Glance

Dist	Name	Party	Vote Pct	Race Type
Sen	Christopher J. Dodd (1992)	Dem	59%	Reelected
Sen	Joseph I. Lieberman (1988)	Dem	50%	Beat Incumb
1	Barbara B. Kennelly	Dem	67%	Reelected
2	Sam Gejdenson	Dem	51%	Reelected
3	Rosa DeLauro	Dem	66%	Reelected
4	Christopher Shays	Rep	67%	Reelected
5	Gary Franks	Rep	44%	Reelected
6	Nancy L. Johnson	Rep	70%	Reelected

Totals in Thousands of Dollars

Sen. Christopher J. Dodd (D)

1992 Committees: Banking Budget ForRel Labor Rules
First elected: 1980

1987-92 Total Rcpts: $4,342,880
1990 Year-end cash: $62,777

Source of Funds
- PACs 33%
- Lg Individuals ($200+) 45%
- Individuals under $200 .... 12%
- Other 10%

1987-92†
Top Industries & Interest Groups

Securities & Investment $394,750
Lawyers & Lobbyists $339,250
Insurance $283,358
Real Estate $153,503
Pro-Israel $150,750

Unidentified $408,607

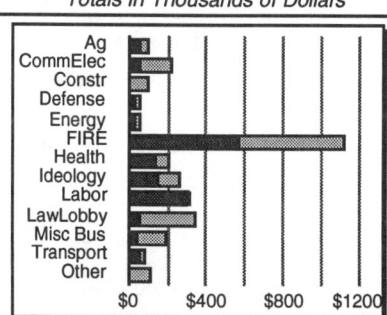

Sen. Joseph I. Lieberman (D)

1992 Committees: Envir GovAff SmBus
First elected: 1988

1987-92 Total Rcpts: $4,052,725
1990 Year-end cash: $702,453

Source of Funds
- PACs 11%
- Lg Individuals ($200+) 55%
- Individuals under $200 .... 24%
- Other 10%

1987-92†
Top Industries & Interest Groups

Lawyers & Lobbyists $150,623
Securities & Investment $130,716
Real Estate $94,200
Pro-Israel $81,818
Insurance $70,400

Unidentified $205,060

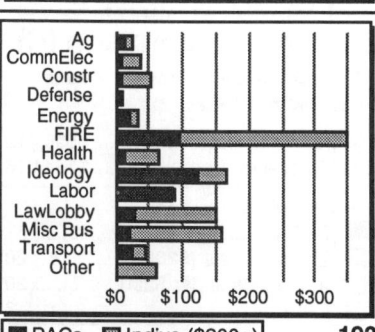

† Does not include individual contributions from 1987-88

193

1. Barbara B. Kennelly (D)

1992 Committees: Ways & Means
First elected: 1982

1991-92 Total Rcpts: $523,025
1990 Year-end cash: $127,166

Source of Funds
- PACs 63%
- Lg Individuals ($200+) 19%
- Individuals under $200 .... 11%
- Other 7%

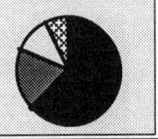

Top Industries & Interest Groups

Insurance $111,305
Lawyers & Lobbyists $30,375
Health Professionals $22,700
Public Sector Unions $17,650
Business Services $15,600

Unidentified $12,200

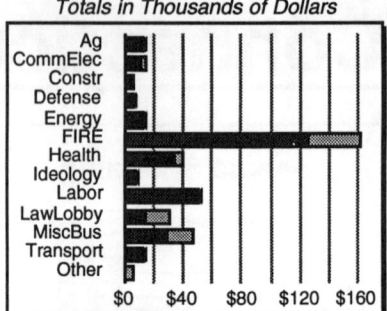

2. Sam Gejdenson (D)

1992 Committees: Admin ForAff Interior
First elected: 1980

1991-92 Total Rcpts: $909,091
1990 Year-end cash: $11,333

Source of Funds
- PACs 36%
- Lg Individuals ($200+) 28%
- Individuals under $200 .... 23%
- Other 14%

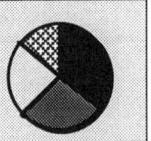

Top Industries & Interest Groups

Pro-Israel $88,060
Public Sector Unions $43,331
Lawyers & Lobbyists $38,085
Industrial Unions $26,950
Transportation Unions $20,250

Unidentified $71,013

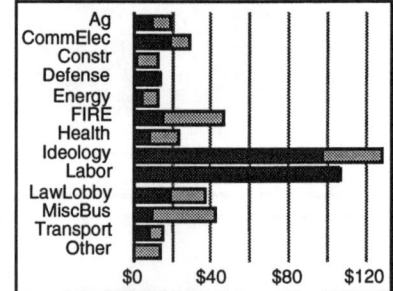

3. Rosa DeLauro (D)

1992 Committees: GovtOps PubWorks
First elected: 1990

1991-92 Total Rcpts: $1,026,034
1990 Year-end cash: $19,545

Source of Funds
- PACs 47%
- Lg Individuals ($200+) 30%
- Individuals under $200 .... 19%
- Other 4%

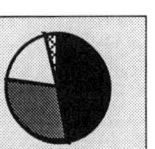

Top Industries & Interest Groups

Lawyers & Lobbyists $76,263
Public Sector Unions $63,950
Industrial Unions $58,800
Womens Issues $41,122
Transportation Unions $39,150

Unidentified $62,583

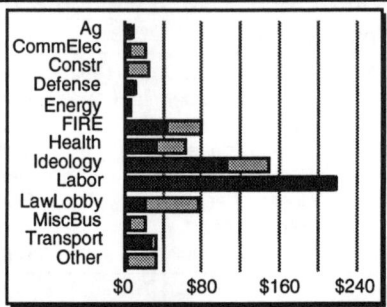

4. Christopher Shays (R)

1992 Committees: Budget GovtOps
First elected: 1987

1991-92 Total Rcpts: $402,120
1990 Year-end cash: $93,866

Source of Funds
- PACs 13%
- Lg Individuals ($200+) 41%
- Individuals under $200 .... 41%
- Other 5%

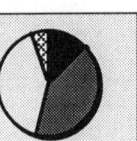

Top Industries & Interest Groups

Securities & Investment $20,750
Business Services $14,800
Retired $14,350
Real Estate $12,950
Misc Manufacturing & Distrib $11,349

Unidentified $34,600

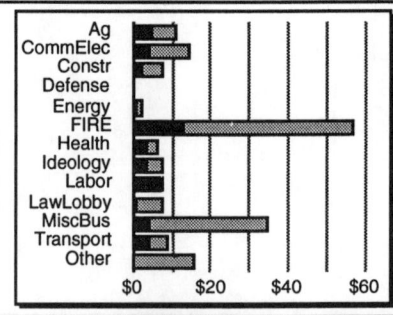

5. Gary Franks (R)

1992 Committees: ArmServ SmBus
First elected: 1990

1991-92 Total Rcpts: $650,466
1990 Year-end cash: $18,140

Source of Funds
- PACs 42%
- Lg Individuals ($200+) 33%
- Individuals under $200 .... 11%
- Other 15%

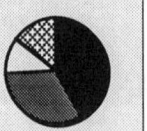

Top Industries & Interest Groups

Defense Aerospace $29,000
Insurance $27,222
Health Professionals $26,259
Defense Electronics $17,500
Oil & Gas $16,300

Unidentified $92,697

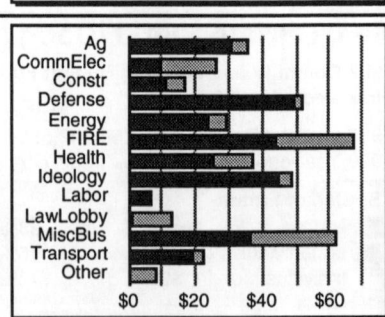

6. Nancy L. Johnson (R)

1992 Committees: Ways & Means
First elected: 1982

1991-92 Total Rcpts: $596,412
1990 Year-end cash: $144,036

Source of Funds
- PACs 57%
- Lg Individuals ($200+) 20%
- Individuals under $200 .... 20%
- Other 3%

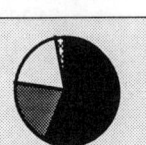

Top Industries & Interest Groups

Insurance $95,305
Health Professionals $44,050
General Contractors $16,550
Telephone Utilities $15,770
Pharmaceuticals/Health Prod $15,200

Unidentified $24,434

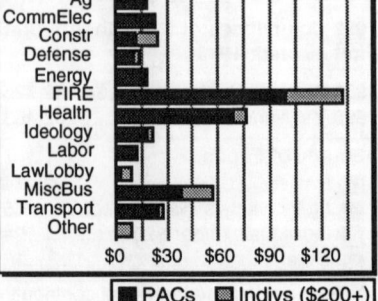

Key to committee & category abbreviations is on page 173

Delaware

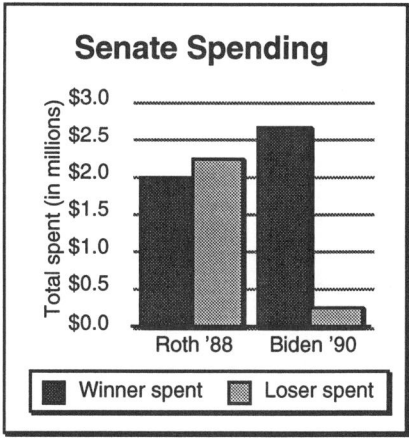
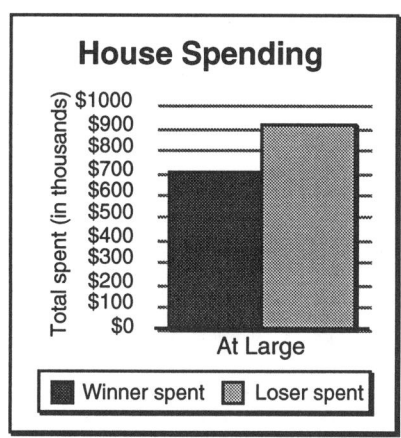

1992 Elections at a Glance

Dist	Name	Party	Vote Pct	Race Type
Sen	Joseph R. Biden Jr. (1990)	Dem	63%	Reelected
Sen	William V. Roth Jr. (1988)	Rep	62%	Reelected
1	Michael N. Castle	Rep	55%	Open Seat

Totals in Thousands of Dollars

Sen. Joseph R. Biden Jr. (D)

1992 Committees: ForRel Judiciary
First elected: 1972

1987-92 Total Rcpts: $2,160,291
1990 Year-end cash: $46,943

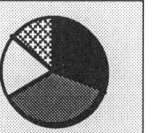

Source of Funds
- PACs 31%
- Lg Individuals ($200+) 36%
- Individuals under $200 ......20%
- Other 14%

1987-92†
Top Industries & Interest Groups

Lawyers & Lobbyists $233,650
Pro-Israel $99,900
Transportation Unions $86,000
Industrial Unions $85,500
Media/Entertainment $79,754

Unidentified $179,205

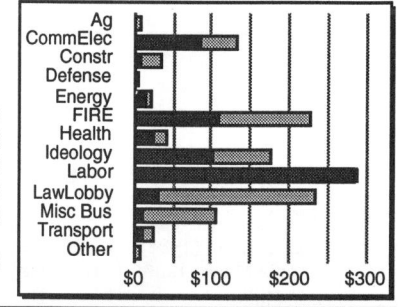

Sen. William V. Roth Jr. (R)

1992 Committees: Banking Finance GovAff
First elected: 1970

1987-92 Total Rcpts: $1,945,816
1990 Year-end cash: $69,658

Source of Funds
- PACs 39%
- Lg Individuals ($200+) 32%
- Individuals under $200 ......19%
- Other 10%

1987-92†
Top Industries & Interest Groups

Insurance $83,800
Securities & Investment $59,750
Commercial Banks $53,450
Oil & Gas $51,950
Health Professionals $38,500

Unidentified $1,313

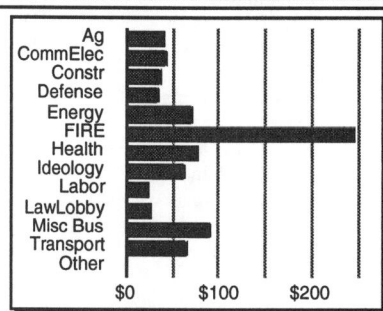

1. Michael N. Castle (R)

1993-94 Committees: Banking MerchMarine
First elected: 1992

1991-92 Total Rcpts: $708,671
1990 Year-end cash: $17,929

Source of Funds
- PACs 27%
- Lg Individuals ($200+) 48%
- Individuals under $200 ......13%
- Other 12%

Top Industries & Interest Groups

Commercial Banks $123,800
Retired $52,890
Lawyers & Lobbyists $47,275
Finance/Credit Companies $24,750
Health Professionals $21,820

Unidentified $71,925

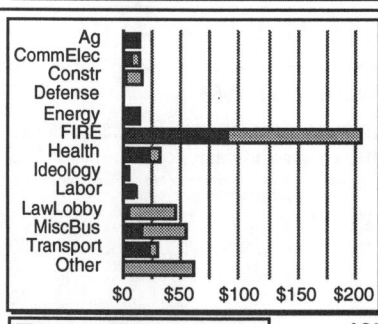

† Does not include individual contributions from 1987-88

■ PACs ▩ Indivs ($200+)

Florida

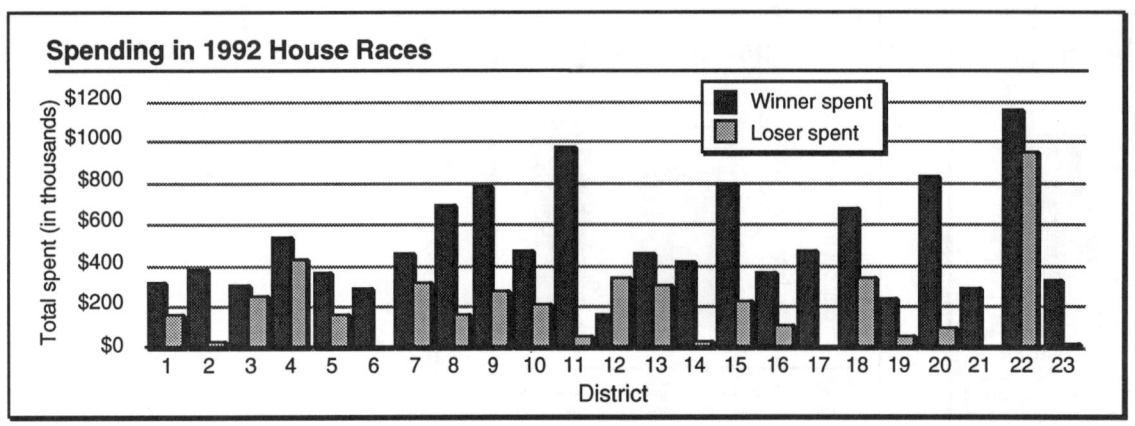

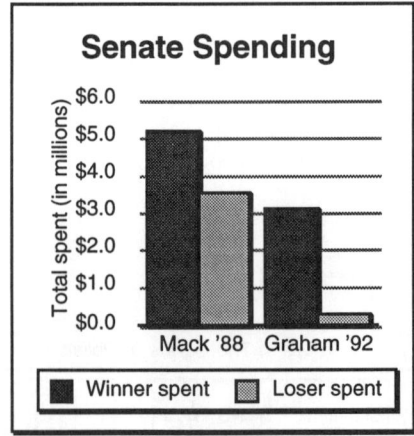

1992 Elections at a Glance

Dist	Name	Party	Vote Pct	Race Type	Dist	Name	Party	Vote Pct	Race Type
Sen	Bob Graham (1992)	Dem	65%	Reelected	12	Charles T. Canady	Rep	52%	Open Seat
Sen	Connie Mack (1988)	Rep	50%	Open Seat	13	Dan Miller	Rep	58%	Open Seat
1	Earl Hutto	Dem	52%	Reelected	14	Porter J. Goss	Rep	82%	Reelected
2	Pete Peterson	Dem	73%	Reelected	15	Jim Bacchus	Dem	51%	Reelected
3	Corrine Brown	Dem	59%	Open Seat	16	Tom Lewis	Rep	61%	Reelected
4	Tillie Fowler	Rep	57%	Open Seat	17	Carrie Meek	Dem	100%	Open Seat
5	Karen L. Thurman	Dem	49%	Open Seat	18	Ileana Ros-Lehtinen	Rep	67%	Reelected
6	Cliff Stearns	Rep	65%	Reelected	19	Harry A. Johnston	Dem	63%	Reelected
7	John L. Mica	Rep	56%	Open Seat	20	Peter Deutsch	Dem	55%	Open Seat
8	Bill McCollum	Rep	68%	Reelected	21	Lincoln Diaz-Balart	Rep	100%	Open Seat
9	Michael Bilirakis	Rep	59%	Reelected	22	E. Clay Shaw Jr.	Rep	52%	Reelected
10	C. W. Bill Young	Rep	57%	Reelected	23	Alcee L. Hastings	Dem	59%	Open Seat
11	Sam M. Gibbons	Dem	53%	Reelected					

Totals in Thousands of Dollars

Sen. Bob Graham (D)

1992 Committees: Banking Envir VetAffairs
First elected: 1986

1987-92 Total Rcpts: $3,696,833
1990 Year-end cash: $354,763

Source of Funds
- PACs 31%
- Lg Individuals ($200+) 50%
- Individuals under $200 .... 9%
- Other 10%

1987-92†
Top Industries & Interest Groups

Lawyers & Lobbyists	$463,670
Health Professionals	$163,581
Real Estate	$140,950
Insurance	$131,130
Securities & Investment	$114,816
Unidentified	$373,279

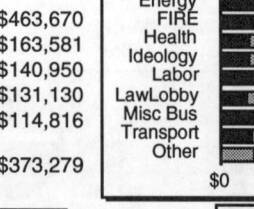

Key to committee & category abbreviations is on page 173

Sen. Connie Mack (R)

1992 Committees: ArmServ Banking SmBus
First elected: 1988

1987-92 Total Rcpts: $7,589,143
1990 Year-end cash: $413,863

Source of Funds
- PACs 17%
- Lg Individuals ($200+) 36%
- Individuals under $200 .... 31%
- Other 16%

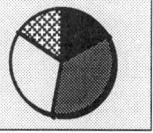

1987-92†

Top Industries & Interest Groups

Health Professionals $130,860
Lawyers & Lobbyists $117,454
Retired $109,240
Oil & Gas $108,260
Commercial Banks $104,990

Unidentified $420,051

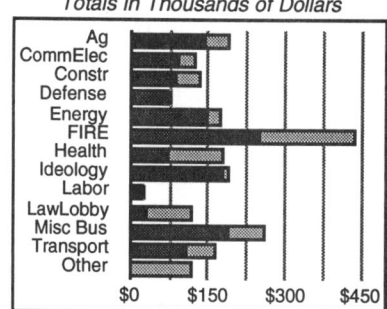

1. Earl Hutto (D)

1992 Committees: ArmServ MerchMarine
First elected: 1978

1991-92 Total Rcpts: $298,700
1990 Year-end cash: $94,485

Source of Funds
- PACs 48%
- Lg Individuals ($200+) 15%
- Individuals under $200 .... 27%
- Other 11%

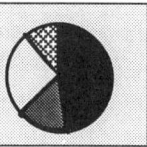

Top Industries & Interest Groups

Defense Aerospace $23,650
Health Professionals $17,550
Real Estate $12,550
Commercial Banks $10,770
Electric Utilities $8,900

Unidentified $7,150

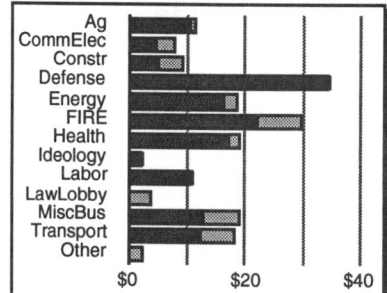

2. Pete Peterson (D)

1992 Committees: PubWorks VetAffairs
First elected: 1990

1991-92 Total Rcpts: $400,867
1990 Year-end cash: $25,352

Source of Funds
- PACs 69%
- Lg Individuals ($200+) 16%
- Individuals under $200 .... 13%
- Other 3%

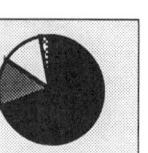

Top Industries & Interest Groups

Transportation Unions $32,750
Public Sector Unions $30,100
Industrial Unions $29,500
Health Professionals $21,700
Air Transport $21,150

Unidentified $8,451

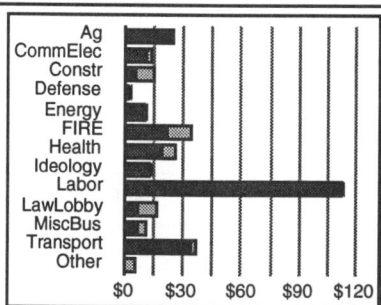

3. Corrine Brown (D)

1993-94 Committees: GovtOps PubWorks VetAffairs
First elected: 1992

1991-92 Total Rcpts: $293,084
1990 Year-end cash: $1,398

Source of Funds
- PACs 56%
- Lg Individuals ($200+) 12%
- Individuals under $200 .... 28%
- Other 4%

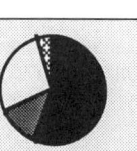

Top Industries & Interest Groups

Public Sector Unions $33,000
Womens Issues $26,745
Lawyers & Lobbyists $14,750
Transportation Unions $10,765
Telephone Utilities $9,750
Health Professionals $9,750

Unidentified $14,428

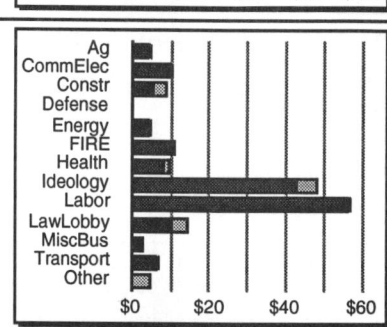

4. Tillie Fowler (R)

1993-94 Committees: ArmServ MerchMarine
First elected: 1992

1991-92 Total Rcpts: $525,279
1990 Year-end cash: $2,329

Source of Funds
- PACs 20%
- Lg Individuals ($200+) 53%
- Individuals under $200 .... 14%
- Other 13%

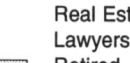

Top Industries & Interest Groups

Real Estate $33,240
Lawyers & Lobbyists $30,207
Retired $23,434
Insurance $22,650
Food Processing & Sales $21,150

Unidentified $83,564

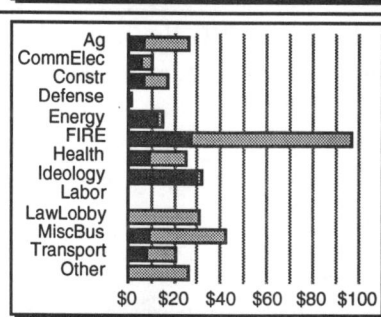

5. Karen L. Thurman (D)

1993-94 Committees: Agric GovtOps
First elected: 1992

1991-92 Total Rcpts: $360,160
1990 Year-end cash: $7,553

Source of Funds
- PACs 56%
- Lg Individuals ($200+) 16%
- Individuals under $200 .... 19%
- Other 8%

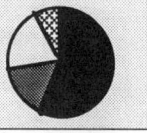

Top Industries & Interest Groups

Health Professionals $30,654
Public Sector Unions $28,500
Industrial Unions $24,200
Womens Issues $22,878
Crop Production/Processing $14,925

Unidentified $7,412

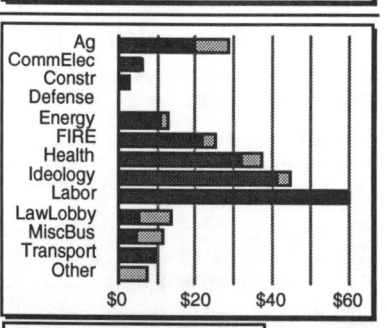

† Does not include individual contributions from 1987-88

Totals in Thousands of Dollars

6. Cliff Stearns (R)

1992 Committees: Banking VetAffairs
First elected: 1988

1991-92 Total Rcpts: $374,016
1990 Year-end cash: $112,117

Source of Funds
- PACs 46%
- Lg Individuals ($200+) 25%
- Individuals under $200 .... 18%
- Other 11%

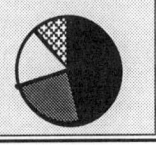

Top Industries & Interest Groups

Health Professionals $37,063
Commercial Banks $28,804
Insurance $24,204
Real Estate $15,380
Automotive $9,819

Unidentified $21,325

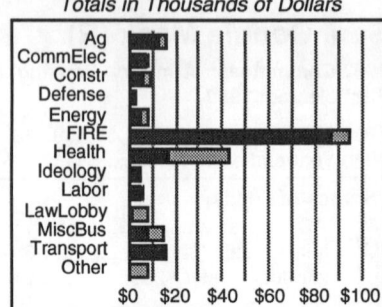

7. John L. Mica (R)

1993-94 Committees: GovtOps PubWorks
First elected: 1992

1991-92 Total Rcpts: $598,764
1990 Year-end cash: $4,609

Source of Funds
- PACs 24%
- Lg Individuals ($200+) 16%
- Individuals under $200 .... 17%
- Other 44%

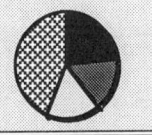

Top Industries & Interest Groups

Health Professionals $24,110
Insurance $22,749
Lawyers & Lobbyists $14,515
Crop Production/Processing $11,600
Real Estate $9,350

Unidentified $28,010

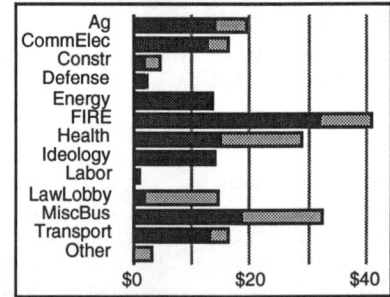

8. Bill McCollum (R)

1992 Committees: Banking Judiciary
First elected: 1980

1991-92 Total Rcpts: $642,785
1990 Year-end cash: $68,837

Source of Funds
- PACs 47%
- Lg Individuals ($200+) 33%
- Individuals under $200 .... 13%
- Other 7%

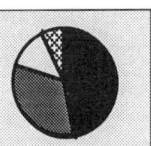

Top Industries & Interest Groups

Commercial Banks $48,800
Health Professionals $48,400
Lawyers & Lobbyists $41,600
Insurance $34,450
Real Estate $24,100

Unidentified $43,325

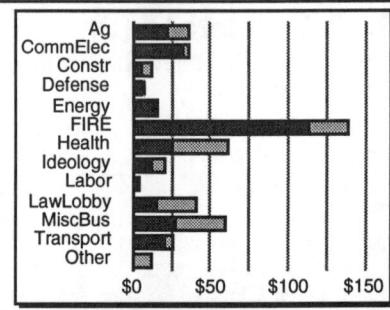

9. Michael Bilirakis (R)

1992 Committees: Energy/Commerce VetAffairs
First elected: 1982

1991-92 Total Rcpts: $779,124
1990 Year-end cash: $1,923

Source of Funds
- PACs 38%
- Lg Individuals ($200+) 23%
- Individuals under $200 .... 31%
- Other 8%

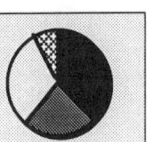

Top Industries & Interest Groups

Health Professionals $77,994
Media/Entertainment $25,300
Electric Utilities $25,300
Insurance $21,250
Telephone Utilities $17,250

Unidentified $35,752

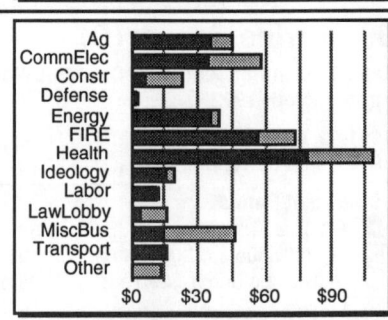

10. C. W. Bill Young (R)

1992 Committees: Appropriations
First elected: 1970

1991-92 Total Rcpts: $274,122
1990 Year-end cash: $156,032

Source of Funds
- PACs 60%
- Lg Individuals ($200+) 11%
- Individuals under $200 .... 12%
- Other 17%

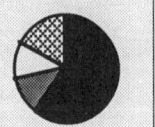

Top Industries & Interest Groups

Defense Aerospace $47,750
Defense Electronics $35,000
Health Professionals $22,350
Real Estate $16,000
Lawyers & Lobbyists $9,950

Unidentified $5,600

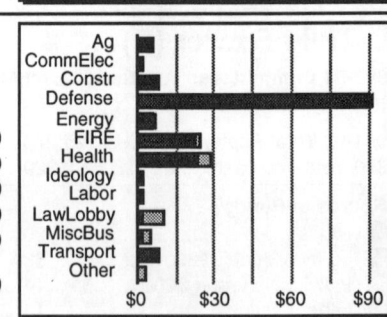

11. Sam M. Gibbons (D)

1992 Committees: Ways & Means
First elected: 1962

1991-92 Total Rcpts: $722,678
1990 Year-end cash: $41,127

Source of Funds
- PACs 59%
- Lg Individuals ($200+) 24%
- Individuals under $200 .... 10%
- Other 7%

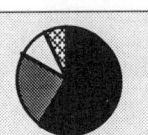

Top Industries & Interest Groups

Lawyers & Lobbyists $75,100
Insurance $60,949
Health Professionals $26,050
Beer, Wine & Liquor $25,750
Tobacco $25,250

Unidentified $22,424

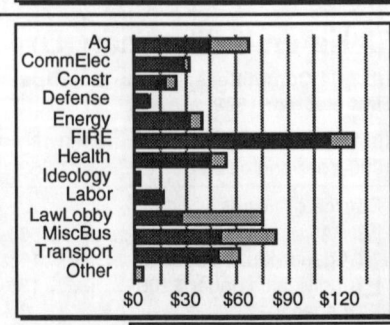

■ PACs ▨ Indivs ($200+)

Key to committee & category abbreviations is on page 173

12. Charles T. Canady (R)

1993-94 Committees: Agric Judiciary
First elected: 1992

1991-92 Total Rcpts: $158,527
1990 Year-end cash: $1,792

Source of Funds
- PACs 25%
- Lg Individuals ($200+) 22%
- Individuals under $200 .... 22%
- Other 30%

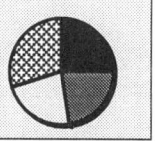

Top Industries & Interest Groups

Food Processing & Sales $7,400
Crop Production/Processing $7,200
Real Estate $5,600
Gun Rights/Gun Control $4,950
Lawyers & Lobbyists $4,900

Unidentified $10,837

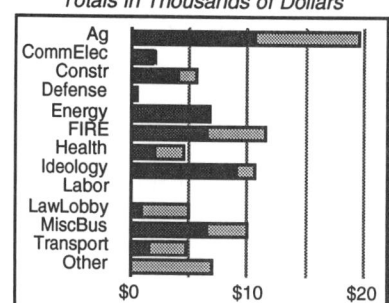

13. Dan Miller (R)

1993-94 Committees: Budget Educ/Labor
First elected: 1992

1991-92 Total Rcpts: $453,193
1990 Year-end cash: $3,980

Source of Funds
- PACs 16%
- Lg Individuals ($200+) 35%
- Individuals under $200 .... 22%
- Other 27%

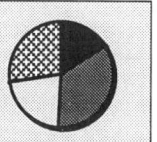

Top Industries & Interest Groups

Health Professionals $27,350
Real Estate $20,850
Retired $11,585
Food Processing & Sales $10,250
Commercial Banks $8,600

Unidentified $38,690

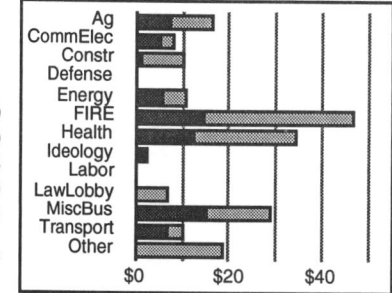

14. Porter J. Goss (R)

1992 Committees: ForAff MerchMarine
First elected: 1988

1991-92 Total Rcpts: $419,508
1990 Year-end cash: $106,397

Source of Funds
- PACs 8%
- Lg Individuals ($200+) 42%
- Individuals under $200 .... 47%
- Other 3%

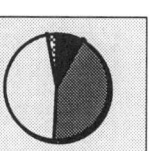

Top Industries & Interest Groups

Retired $47,000
Health Professionals $18,000
Real Estate $17,985
Misc Finance $6,500
Lawyers & Lobbyists $6,461

Unidentified $39,851

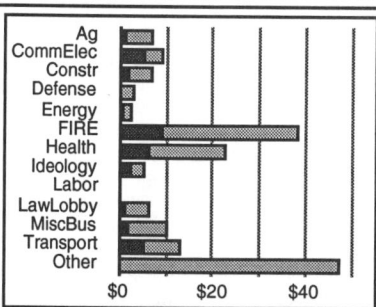

15. Jim Bacchus (D)

1992 Committees: Banking Science
First elected: 1990

1991-92 Total Rcpts: $842,030
1990 Year-end cash: $23,893

Source of Funds
- PACs 54%
- Lg Individuals ($200+) 32%
- Individuals under $200 .... 8%
- Other 6%

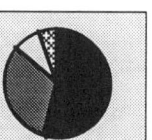

Top Industries & Interest Groups

Health Professionals $86,480
Lawyers & Lobbyists $72,296
Commercial Banks $62,650
Public Sector Unions $53,549
Transportation Unions $43,000

Unidentified $50,735

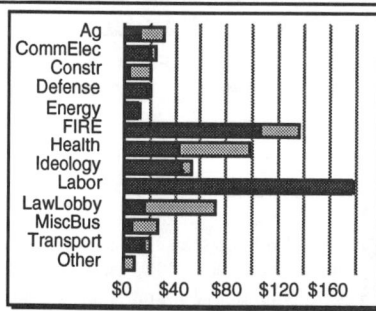

16. Tom Lewis (R)

1992 Committees: Agric Science
First elected: 1982

1991-92 Total Rcpts: $296,405
1990 Year-end cash: $53,970

Source of Funds
- PACs 43%
- Lg Individuals ($200+) 27%
- Individuals under $200 .... 23%
- Other 8%

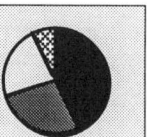

Top Industries & Interest Groups

Crop Production/Processing $58,193
Air Transport $11,000
Electric Utilities $10,100
Real Estate $9,907
Telephone Utilities $9,750

Unidentified $19,634

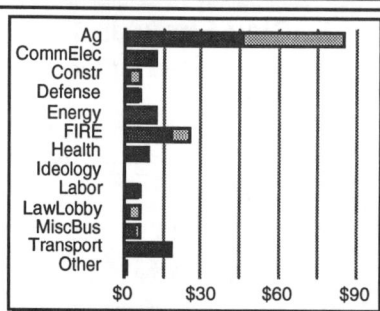

17. Carrie Meek (D)

1993-94 Committees: Appropriations
First elected: 1992

1991-92 Total Rcpts: $574,719
1990 Year-end cash: $113,605

Source of Funds
- PACs 27%
- Lg Individuals ($200+) 32%
- Individuals under $200 .... 39%
- Other 2%

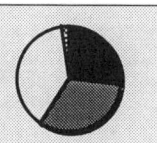

Top Industries & Interest Groups

Hospitals/Nursing Homes $44,500
Lawyers & Lobbyists $33,550
Public Sector Unions $26,250
Womens Issues $17,415
Industrial Unions $17,000

Unidentified $40,784

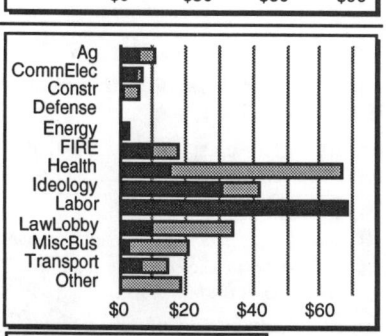

18. Ileana Ros-Lehtinen (R)

1992 Committees: ForAff GovtOps
First elected: 1989

1991-92 Total Rcpts: $662,069
1990 Year-end cash: $7,076

Source of Funds
- PACs 22%
- Lg Individuals ($200+) 51%
- Individuals under $200 .... 23%
- Other 4%

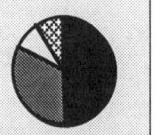

Top Industries & Interest Groups

Health Professionals $42,617
Lawyers & Lobbyists $25,558
Real Estate $23,856
Pro-Israel $23,680
Hospitals/Nursing Homes $16,189

Unidentified $90,754

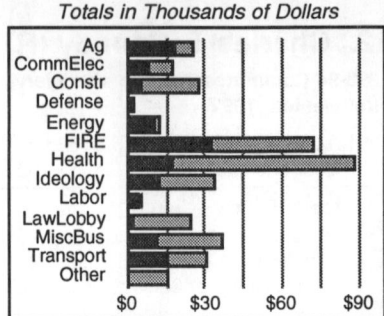

19. Harry A. Johnston (D)

1992 Committees: ForAff Interior
First elected: 1988

1991-92 Total Rcpts: $348,039
1990 Year-end cash: $155,908

Source of Funds
- PACs 49%
- Lg Individuals ($200+) 33%
- Individuals under $200 .... 9%
- Other 9%

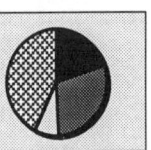

Top Industries & Interest Groups

Lawyers & Lobbyists $38,150
Transportation Unions $24,650
Industrial Unions $24,500
Public Sector Unions $21,400
Crop Production/Processing $19,050

Unidentified $16,446

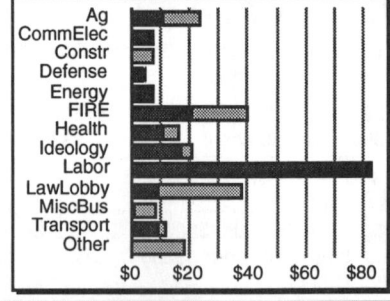

20. Peter Deutsch (D)

1993-94 Committees: Banking ForAff MerchMarine
First elected: 1992

1991-92 Total Rcpts: $835,010
1990 Year-end cash: $17,277

Source of Funds
- PACs 20%
- Lg Individuals ($200+) 28%
- Individuals under $200 .... 8%
- Other 42%

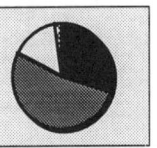

Top Industries & Interest Groups

Lawyers & Lobbyists $44,700
Insurance $38,650
Public Sector Unions $29,750
Health Professionals $27,350
Transportation Unions $22,350

Unidentified $66,560

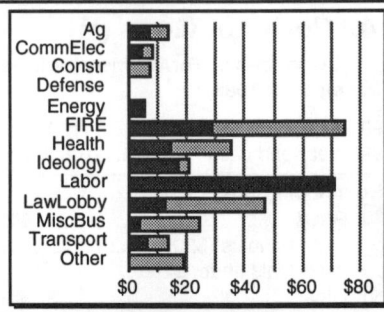

21. Lincoln Diaz-Balart (R)

1993-94 Committees: ForAff MerchMarine
First elected: 1992

1991-92 Total Rcpts: $279,773
1990 Year-end cash: $292

Source of Funds
- PACs 30%
- Lg Individuals ($200+) 52%
- Individuals under $200 .... 16%
- Other 2%

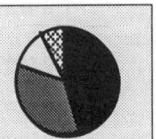

Top Industries & Interest Groups

Lawyers & Lobbyists $21,200
Health Professionals $16,450
Foreign & Defense Policy $14,750
Real Estate $12,500
Crop Production/Processing $10,000

Unidentified $39,920

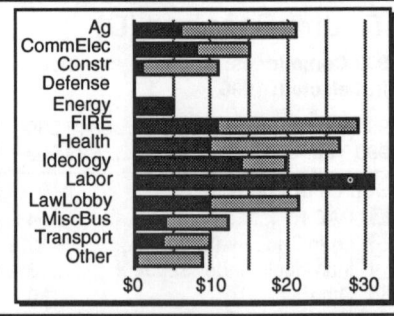

22. E. Clay Shaw Jr. (R)

1992 Committees: Ways & Means
First elected: 1980

1991-92 Total Rcpts: $948,514
1990 Year-end cash: $116,312

Source of Funds
- PACs 45%
- Lg Individuals ($200+) 34%
- Individuals under $200 .... 12%
- Other 8%

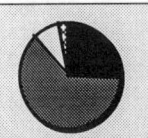

Top Industries & Interest Groups

Health Professionals $95,895
Insurance $70,100
Lawyers & Lobbyists $48,163
Accountants $42,037
Real Estate $32,900

Unidentified $65,336

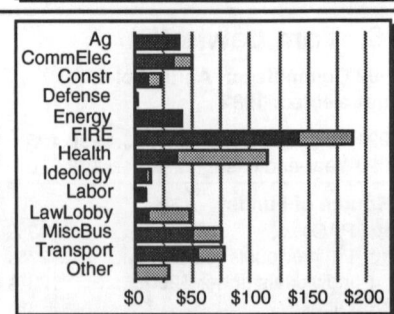

23. Alcee L. Hastings (D)

1993-94 Committees: ForAff MerchMarine Post Office
First elected: 1992

1991-92 Total Rcpts: $191,142
1990 Year-end cash: $11,428

Source of Funds
- PACs 19%
- Lg Individuals ($200+) 48%
- Individuals under $200 .... 26%
- Other 7%

Top Industries & Interest Groups

Lawyers & Lobbyists $57,920
Transportation Unions $25,500
Health Professionals $15,550
Public Sector Unions $12,500
Industrial Unions $9,000

Unidentified $63,100

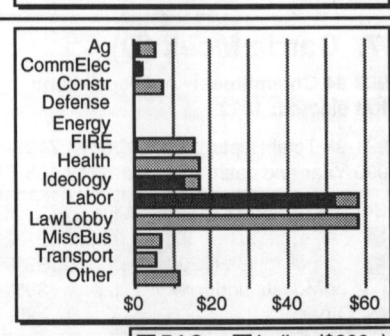

Key to committee & category abbreviations is on page 173

Georgia

Spending in 1992 House Races

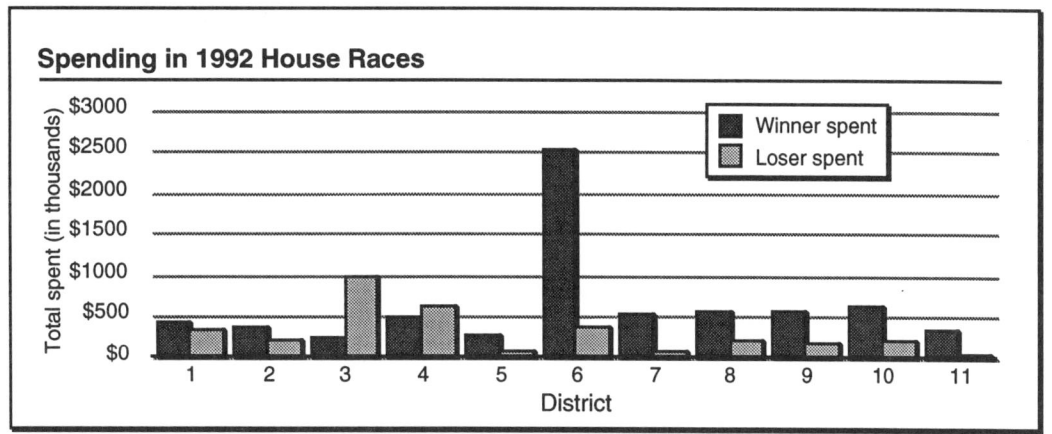

1992 Elections at a Glance

Dist	Name	Party	Vote Pct	Race Type
Sen	Paul Coverdell (1992)	Rep	51%	Beat Incumb
Sen	Sam Nunn (1990)	Dem	100%	Reelected
1	Jack Kingston	Rep	58%	Open Seat
2	Sanford Bishop	Dem	64%	Open Seat
3	Mac Collins	Rep	55%	Beat Incumb
4	John Linder	Rep	50%	Open Seat
5	John Lewis	Dem	72%	Reelected
6	Newt Gingrich	Rep	58%	Reelected
7	George "Buddy" Darden	Dem	57%	Reelected
8	J. Roy Rowland	Dem	56%	Reelected
9	Nathan Deal	Dem	59%	Open Seat
10	Don Johnson	Dem	54%	Open Seat
11	Cynthia McKinney	Dem	73%	Open Seat

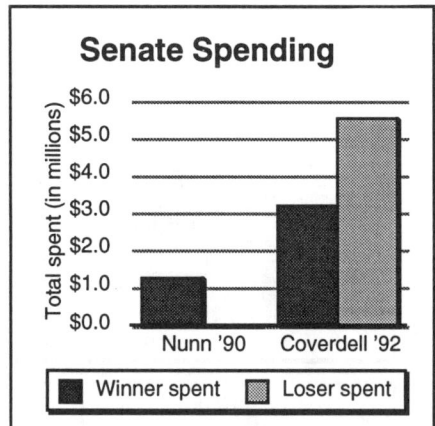

Totals in Thousands of Dollars

Sen. Paul Coverdell (R)

1993-94 Committees: Agric ForAff SmBus
First elected: 1992

1991-92 Total Rcpts: $3,297,110
1990 Year-end cash: $136,055

Source of Funds
- PACs...15%
- Lg Individuals ($200+) 45%
- Individuals under $200 ....14%
- Other..26%

1991-92
Top Industries & Interest Groups

Lawyers & Lobbyists.................$226,287
Securities & Investment $114,115
Insurance $111,362
Real Estate $107,600
Health Professionals $103,358

Unidentified $430,204

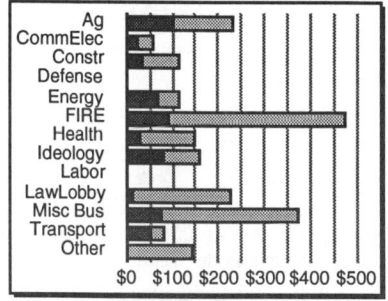

Sen. Sam Nunn (D)

1992 Committees: ArmServ GovAff SmBus
First elected: 1972

1987-92 Total Rcpts: $2,245,900
1990 Year-end cash: $1,381,700

Source of Funds
- PACs...27%
- Lg Individuals ($200+) 46%
- Individuals under $200 ....5%
- Other..22%

1987-92†
Top Industries & Interest Groups

Lawyers & Lobbyists.................$178,654
Securities & Investment $122,220
Real Estate $101,500
Defense Aerospace $69,499
Commercial Banks $67,995

Unidentified $173,639

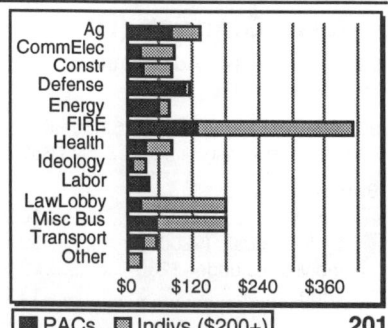

† Does not include individual contributions from 1987-88

1. Jack Kingston (R)

1993-94 Committees: Agric MerchMarine
First elected: 1992

1991-92 Total Rcpts: $439,846
1990 Year-end cash: $20,963

Source of Funds
- PACs 25%
- Lg Individuals ($200+) 44%
- Individuals under $200 ....22%
- Other 10%

Top Industries & Interest Groups

Health Professionals $51,302
Insurance $36,320
Retired $16,250
Food Processing & Sales $10,300
Misc Manufacturing & Distrib $9,548

Unidentified $53,267

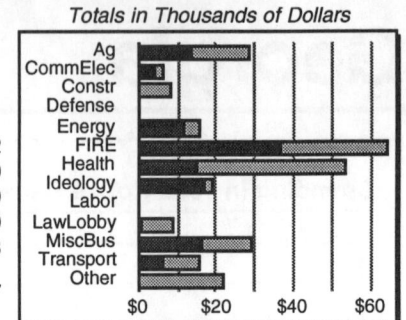

2. Sanford Bishop (D)

1993-94 Committees: Agric Post Office VetAffairs
First elected: 1992

1991-92 Total Rcpts: $354,989
1990 Year-end cash: $3,737

Source of Funds
- PACs 40%
- Lg Individuals ($200+) 27%
- Individuals under $200 ....17%
- Other 16%

Top Industries & Interest Groups

Commercial Banks $28,000
Insurance $21,640
Health Professionals $20,150
Lawyers & Lobbyists $18,100
Public Sector Unions $11,500

Unidentified $22,137

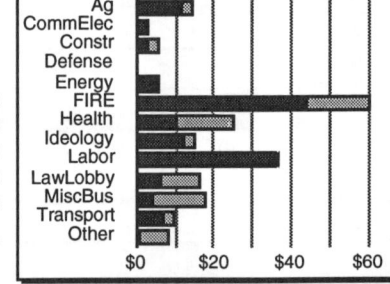

3. Mac Collins (R)

1993-94 Committees: PubWorks SmBus
First elected: 1992

1991-92 Total Rcpts: $241,783
1990 Year-end cash: $9,676

Source of Funds
- PACs 17%
- Lg Individuals ($200+) 30%
- Individuals under $200 ....16%
- Other 37%

Top Industries & Interest Groups

Health Professionals $8,650
Forestry & Forest Products $8,200
Insurance $8,125
Misc Manufacturing & Distrib $6,000
Lawyers & Lobbyists $5,946

Unidentified $31,339

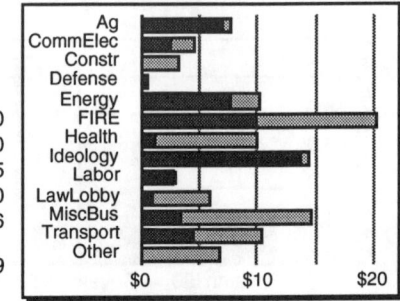

4. John Linder (R)

1993-94 Committees: Banking Science VetAffairs
First elected: 1992

1991-92 Total Rcpts: $516,357
1990 Year-end cash: $1,219

Source of Funds
- PACs 35%
- Lg Individuals ($200+) 30%
- Individuals under $200 ....22%
- Other 13%

Top Industries & Interest Groups

Health Professionals $28,050
Insurance $23,250
Lawyers & Lobbyists $20,750
Republican/Conservative $20,391
Commercial Banks $16,917

Unidentified $44,150

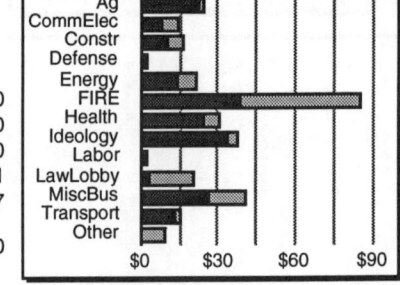

5. John Lewis (D)

1992 Committees: Interior PubWorks
First elected: 1986

1991-92 Total Rcpts: $307,636
1990 Year-end cash: $324,123

Source of Funds
- PACs 71%
- Lg Individuals ($200+) 16%
- Individuals under $200 ....7%
- Other 6%

Top Industries & Interest Groups

Industrial Unions $30,350
Public Sector Unions $27,400
Transportation Unions $25,850
Insurance $22,250
Air Transport $21,550

Unidentified $11,250

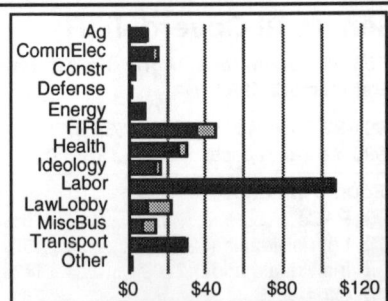

6. Newt Gingrich (R)

1992 Committees: Administration
First elected: 1978

1991-92 Total Rcpts: $2,507,668
1990 Year-end cash: $25,365

Source of Funds
- PACs 30%
- Lg Individuals ($200+) 30%
- Individuals under $200 ....27%
- Other 13%

Top Industries & Interest Groups

Insurance $84,513
Health Professionals $75,510
Lawyers & Lobbyists $73,759
Food & Beverage $72,049
Securities & Investment $63,375

Unidentified $166,192

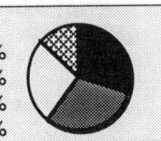

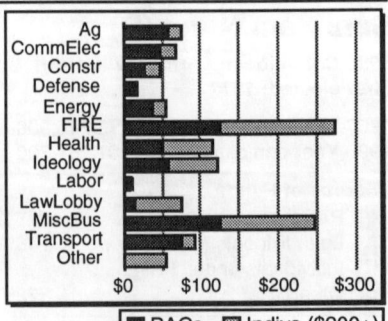

Key to committee & category abbreviations is on page 173

■ PACs ▫ Indivs ($200+)

7. George "Buddy" Darden (D)

1992 Committees: ArmServ Interior
First elected: 1983

1991-92 Total Rcpts: $410,958
1990 Year-end cash: $650

Source of Funds
- PACs 55%
- Lg Individuals ($200+) 22%
- Individuals under $200 .... 17%
- Other 6%

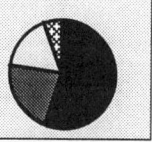

Top Industries & Interest Groups

Defense Aerospace	$24,950
Lawyers & Lobbyists	$21,900
Health Professionals	$20,475
Industrial Unions	$19,000
Defense Electronics	$17,750
Unidentified	$19,410

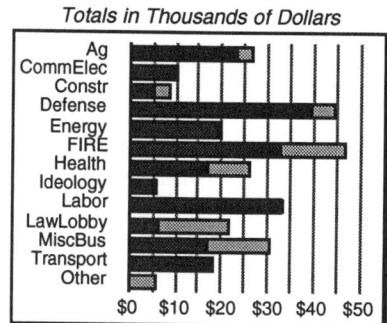

8. J. Roy Rowland (D)

1992 Committees: Energy/Commerce VetAffairs
First elected: 1982

1991-92 Total Rcpts: $454,319
1990 Year-end cash: $120,061

Source of Funds
- PACs 62%
- Lg Individuals ($200+) 12%
- Individuals under $200 .... 13%
- Other 13%

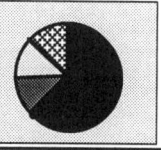

Top Industries & Interest Groups

Health Professionals	$72,200
Pharmaceuticals/Health Prod	$19,950
Insurance	$17,250
Accountants	$16,500
Telephone Utilities	$13,250
Unidentified	$5,335

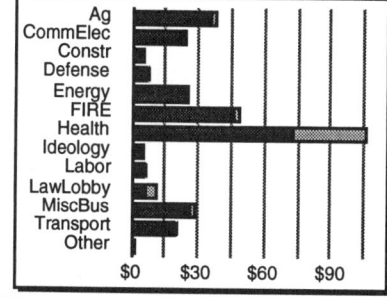

9. Nathan Deal (D)

1993-94 Committees: NatResources PubWorks Science
First elected: 1992

1991-92 Total Rcpts: $543,942
1990 Year-end cash: $1,461

Source of Funds
- PACs 25%
- Lg Individuals ($200+) 25%
- Individuals under $200 .... 17%
- Other 33%

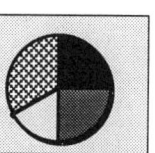

Top Industries & Interest Groups

Health Professionals	$34,750
Retired	$22,400
Commercial Banks	$19,200
Insurance	$13,625
Public Sector Unions	$13,000
Unidentified	$36,991

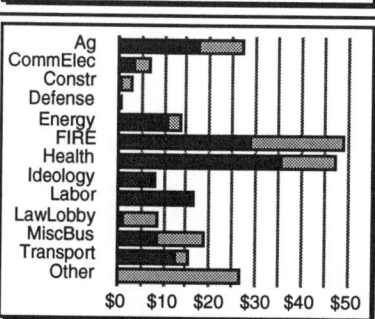

10. Don Johnson (D)

1993-94 Committees: ArmServ Science
First elected: 1992

1991-92 Total Rcpts: $610,154
1990 Year-end cash: $7,016

Source of Funds
- PACs 27%
- Lg Individuals ($200+) 30%
- Individuals under $200 .... 28%
- Other 15%

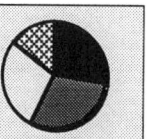

Top Industries & Interest Groups

Lawyers & Lobbyists	$34,099
Commercial Banks	$33,675
Health Professionals	$23,900
Beer, Wine & Liquor	$15,245
Public Sector Unions	$14,800
Unidentified	$52,889

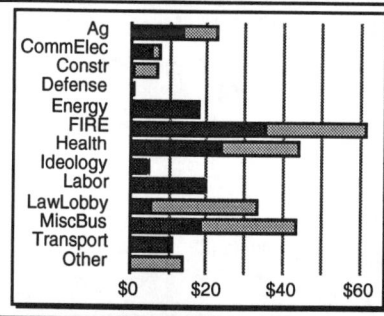

11. Cynthia McKinney (D)

1993-94 Committees: Agric ForAff
First elected: 1992

1991-92 Total Rcpts: $316,990
1990 Year-end cash: $4,066

Source of Funds
- PACs 51%
- Lg Individuals ($200+) 22%
- Individuals under $200 .... 19%
- Other 8%

Top Industries & Interest Groups

Womens Issues	$27,500
Health Professionals	$24,250
Public Sector Unions	$21,000
Lawyers & Lobbyists	$18,250
Industrial Unions	$13,700
Unidentified	$22,020

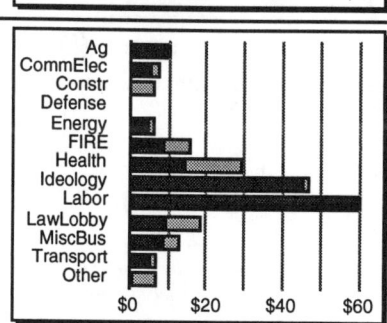

■ PACs   ▨ Indivs ($200+)

Hawaii

1992 Elections at a Glance

Dist	Name	Party	Vote Pct	Race Type
Sen	Daniel K. Inouye (1992)	Dem	57%	Reelected
Sen	Daniel K. Akaka (1990)	Dem	54%	Reelected
1	Neil Abercrombie	Dem	73%	Reelected
2	Patsy T. Mink	Dem	73%	Reelected

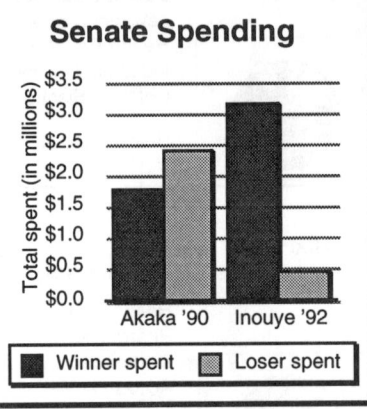

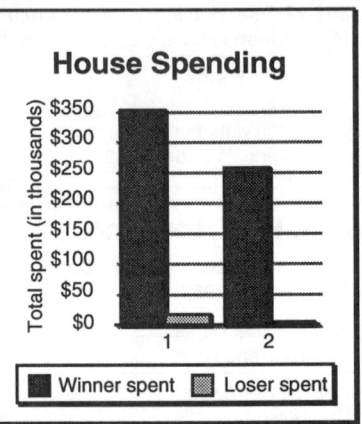

Totals in Thousands of Dollars

Sen. Daniel K. Akaka (D)

1992 Committees: Energy GovAff VetAffairs
First elected: 1990

1989-92 Total Rcpts: $2,237,549
1990 Year-end cash: $69,280

Source of Funds
- PACs 43%
- Lg Individuals ($200+) 37%
- Individuals under $200 .... 12%
- Other 8%

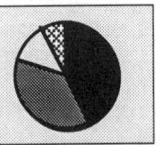

1989-92
Top Industries & Interest Groups

Pro-Israel	$107,900
Transportation Unions	$107,500
Public Sector Unions	$97,150
Construction Services	$95,185
Industrial Unions	$93,000
Unidentified	$342,038

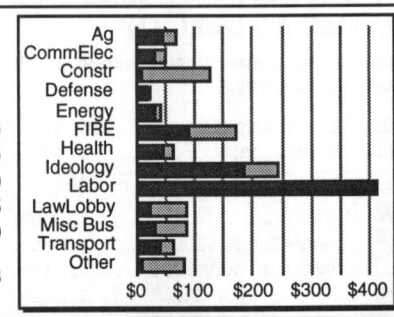

Sen. Daniel K. Inouye (D)

1992 Committees: Approp Commerce Rules
First elected: 1962

1987-92 Total Rcpts: $2,936,821
1990 Year-end cash: $11,907

Source of Funds
- PACs 29%
- Lg Individuals ($200+) 54%
- Individuals under $200 .... 9%
- Other 8%

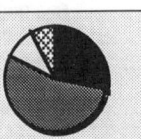

1987-92†
Top Industries & Interest Groups

Pro-Israel	$190,155
Lawyers & Lobbyists	$171,330
Securities & Investment	$138,550
Health Professionals	$104,555
Real Estate	$102,398
Unidentified	$482,878

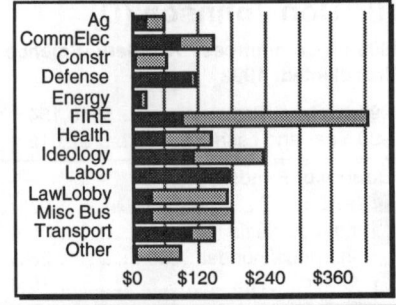

1. Neil Abercrombie (D)

1992 Committees: ArmServ Interior
First elected: 1990

1991-92 Total Rcpts: $359,336
1990 Year-end cash: $33,907

Source of Funds
- PACs 48%
- Lg Individuals ($200+) 13%
- Individuals under $200 .... 19%
- Other 20%

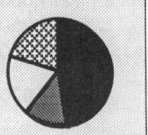

Top Industries & Interest Groups

Transportation Unions	$30,100
Industrial Unions	$29,250
Public Sector Unions	$26,300
Building Trade Unions	$20,150
Real Estate	$16,200
Unidentified	$12,550

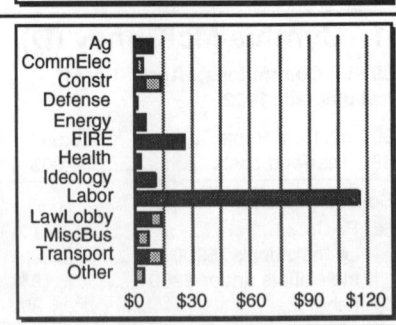

2. Patsy T. Mink (D)

1992 Committees: Educ/Labor GovtOps
First elected: 1990 (also served 1965-77)

1991-92 Total Rcpts: $332,881
1990 Year-end cash: $49,359

Source of Funds
- PACs 34%
- Lg Individuals ($200+) 17%
- Individuals under $200 .... 45%
- Other 5%

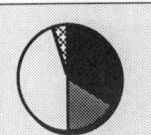

Top Industries & Interest Groups

Building Trade Unions	$21,000
Industrial Unions	$19,000
Public Sector Unions	$18,699
Transportation Unions	$13,700
Retired	$11,850
Unidentified	$13,250

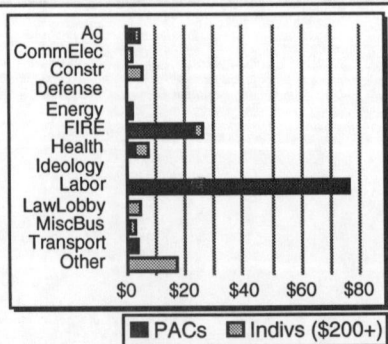

Idaho

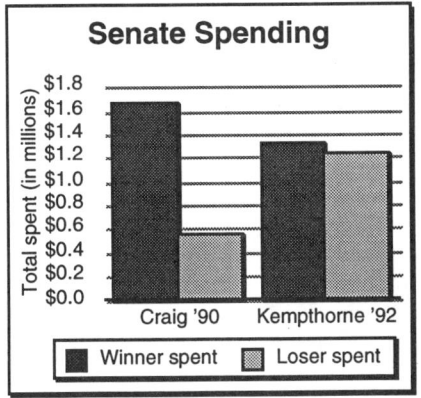
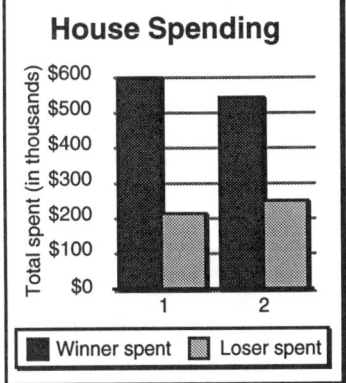

1992 Elections at a Glance

Dist	Name	Party	Vote Pct	Race Type
Sen	Dirk Kempthorne (1992)	Rep	56%	Open Seat
Sen	Larry E. Craig (1990)	Rep	61%	Open Seat
1	Larry LaRocco	Dem	58%	Reelected
2	Michael D. Crapo	Rep	61%	Open Seat

Totals in Thousands of Dollars

Sen. Larry E. Craig (R)
1992 Committees: Agric Energy
First elected: 1990

1989-92 Total Rcpts: $1,784,600
1990 Year-end cash: $58,562

Source of Funds
- PACs 43%
- Lg Individuals ($200+) 19%
- Individuals under $200 .... 20%
- Other 18%

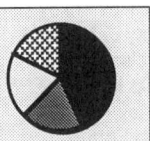

1989-92
Top Industries & Interest Groups

Oil & Gas	$122,308
Forest Products	$80,320
Mining	$58,456
Food Processing & Sales	$53,309
Insurance	$52,800
Unidentified	$74,855

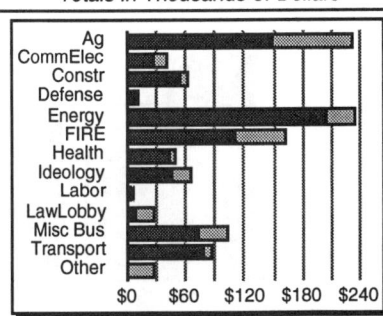

Sen. Dirk Kempthorne (R)
1993-94 Committees: ArmServ Envir SmBus
First elected: 1992

1991-92 Total Rcpts: $1,351,127
1990 Year-end cash: $45,789

Source of Funds
- PACs 40%
- Lg Individuals ($200+) 25%
- Individuals under $200 .... 23%
- Other 13%

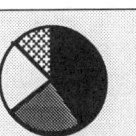

1987-92†
Top Industries & Interest Groups

Forest Products	$83,554
Food Processing & Sales	$79,982
Oil & Gas	$75,507
Insurance	$46,504
Automotive	$33,060
Unidentified	$92,798

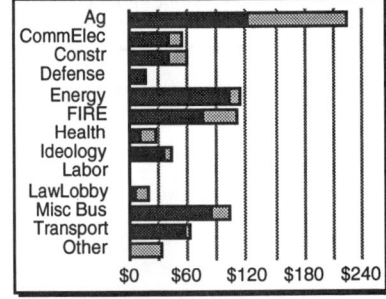

1. Larry LaRocco (D)
1992 Committees: Banking Interior
First elected: 1990

1991-92 Total Rcpts: $598,847
1990 Year-end cash: $2,042

Source of Funds
- PACs 67%
- Lg Individuals ($200+) 12%
- Individuals under $200 .... 18%
- Other 4%

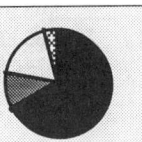

Top Industries & Interest Groups

Commercial Banks	$72,350
Public Sector Unions	$29,250
Lawyers & Lobbyists	$29,095
Industrial Unions	$28,500
Securities & Investment	$26,225
Unidentified	$9,650

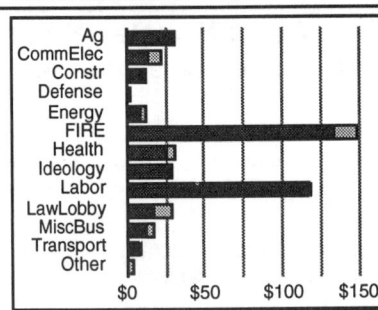

2. Michael D. Crapo (R)
1993-94 Committees: Energy/Commerce
First elected: 1992

1991-92 Total Rcpts: $537,519
1990 Year-end cash: $2,568

Source of Funds
- PACs 40%
- Lg Individuals ($200+) 26%
- Individuals under $200 .... 21%
- Other 12%

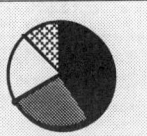

Top Industries & Interest Groups

Food Processing & Sales	$38,750
Health Professionals	$33,296
Forestry & Forest Products	$21,700
Oil & Gas	$19,100
Commercial Banks	$13,750
Unidentified	$31,837

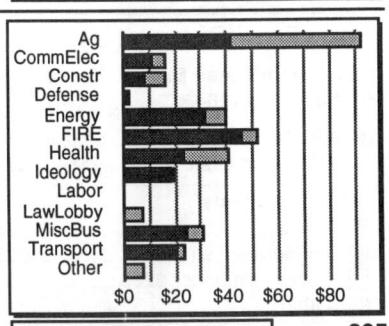

† Does not include individual contributions from 1987-88

Illinois

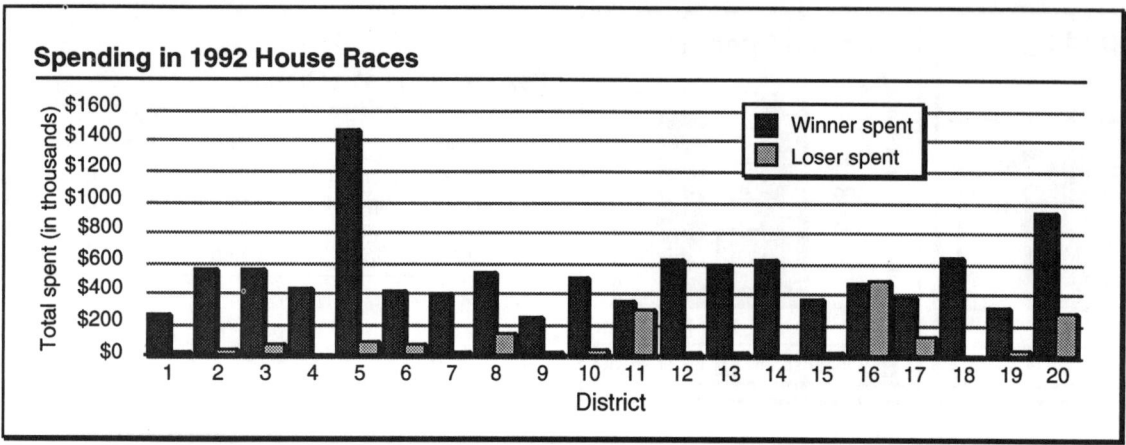

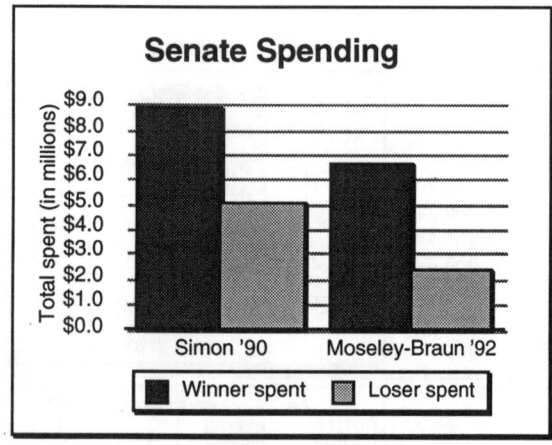

1992 Elections at a Glance

Dist	Name	Party	Vote Pct	Race Type
Sen	Carol Moseley-Braun (1992)	Dem	53%	Open Seat
Sen	Paul Simon (1990)	Dem	65%	Reelected
1	Bobby L. Rush	Dem	83%	Open Seat
2	Mel Reynolds	Dem	78%	Open Seat
3	William O. Lipinski	Dem	64%	Reelected
4	Luis V. Gutierrez	Dem	78%	Open Seat
5	Dan Rostenkowski	Dem	57%	Reelected
6	Henry J. Hyde	Rep	66%	Reelected
7	Cardiss Collins	Dem	81%	Reelected
8	Philip M. Crane	Rep	56%	Reelected
9	Sidney R. Yates	Dem	68%	Reelected
10	John Porter	Rep	64%	Reelected
11	George E. Sangmeister	Dem	56%	Reelected
12	Jerry F. Costello	Dem	71%	Reelected
13	Harris W. Fawell	Rep	68%	Reelected
14	Dennis Hastert	Rep	67%	Reelected
15	Thomas W. Ewing	Rep	59%	Reelected
16	Donald Manzullo	Rep	56%	Beat Incumb
17	Lane Evans	Dem	60%	Reelected
18	Robert H. Michel	Rep	58%	Reelected
19	Glenn Poshard	Dem	69%	Reelected
20	Richard J. Durbin	Dem	56%	Reelected

Totals in Thousands of Dollars

Sen. Carol Moseley-Braun (D)

1993-94 Committees: Banking Judiciary SmBus
First elected: 1992

1991-92 Total Rcpts: $6,774,890
1990 Year-end cash: $30,144

Source of Funds
- PACs 11%
- Lg Individuals ($200+) 25%
- Individuals under $200 ....53%
- Other 11%

1991-92
Top Industries & Interest Groups

Lawyers & Lobbyists................$356,893
Womens Issues $185,717
Health Professionals $98,912
Securities & Investment $85,560
Industrial Unions $74,998

Unidentified $736,717

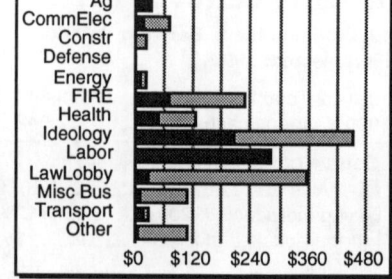

Sen. Paul Simon (D)

1992 Committees: Budget ForRel Judiciary Labor
First elected: 1984

1987-92 Total Rcpts: $9,018,774
1990 Year-end cash: $540,483

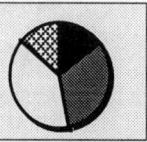

Source of Funds
- PACs 15%
- Lg Individuals ($200+) 32%
- Individuals under $200 ....40%
- Other 14%

1987-92†
Top Industries & Interest Groups

Lawyers & Lobbyists................$644,496
Pro-Israel $466,567
Real Estate $210,434
Industrial Unions $193,891
Democratic/Liberal $174,434

Unidentified $841,751

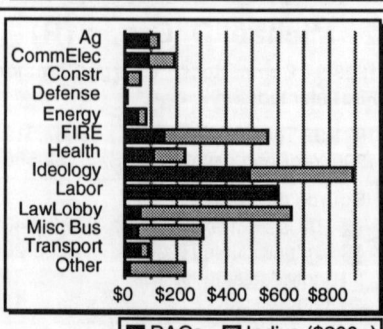

Key to committee & category abbreviations is on page 173

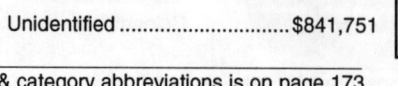

1. Bobby L. Rush (D)

1993-94 Committees: Banking GovtOps
First elected: 1992

1991-92 Total Rcpts: $257,455
1990 Year-end cash: $112

Source of Funds	
■ PACs	51%
▨ Lg Individuals ($200+)	37%
☐ Individuals under $200	12%
▧ Other	2%

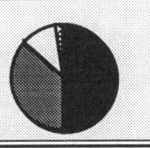

Top Industries & Interest Groups

Lawyers & Lobbyists $28,550
Health Professionals $10,550
Securities & Investment $10,050
Industrial Unions $9,750
Public Sector Unions $9,500

Unidentified $45,000

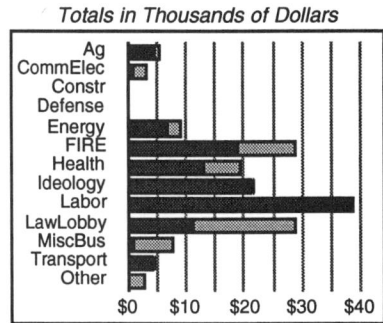

2. Mel Reynolds (D)

1993-94 Committees: Ways & Means
First elected: 1992

1991-92 Total Rcpts: $532,031
1990 Year-end cash: $1,032

Source of Funds	
■ PACs	37%
▨ Lg Individuals ($200+)	34%
☐ Individuals under $200	27%
▧ Other	2%

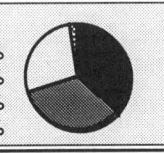

Top Industries & Interest Groups

Pro-Israel $80,671
Lawyers & Lobbyists $31,150
Public Sector Unions $30,600
Health Professionals $21,700
Real Estate $17,650

Unidentified $46,435

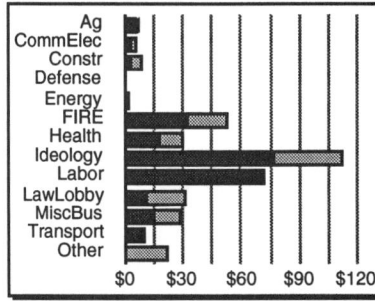

3. William O. Lipinski (D)

1992 Committees: MerchMarine PubWorks
First elected: 1982

1991-92 Total Rcpts: $556,335
1990 Year-end cash: $23,597

Source of Funds	
■ PACs	57%
▨ Lg Individuals ($200+)	31%
☐ Individuals under $200	10%
▧ Other	2%

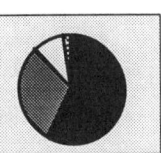

Top Industries & Interest Groups

Lawyers & Lobbyists $50,000
Transportation Unions $49,400
Air Transport $31,000
Civil Servants/Public Officials $30,375
Building Trade Unions $25,500

Unidentified $43,200

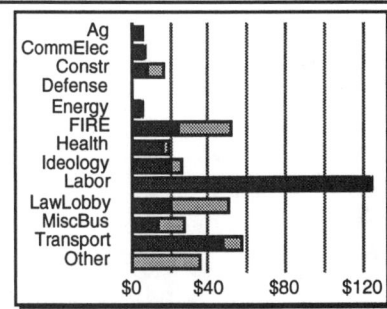

4. Luis V. Gutierrez (D)

1993-94 Committees: Banking VetAffairs
First elected: 1992

1991-92 Total Rcpts: $438,253
1990 Year-end cash: $18,024

Source of Funds	
■ PACs	43%
▨ Lg Individuals ($200+)	44%
☐ Individuals under $200	12%
▧ Other	2%

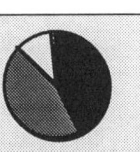

Top Industries & Interest Groups

Lawyers & Lobbyists $38,750
Real Estate $28,680
Misc Unions $21,500
Public Sector Unions $19,000
Pro-Israel $17,250

Unidentified $57,250

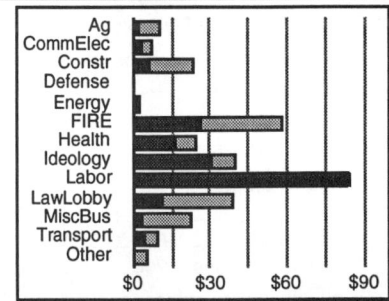

5. Dan Rostenkowski (D)

1992 Committees: Ways & Means
First elected: 1958

1991-92 Total Rcpts: $1,587,234
1990 Year-end cash: $1,245,721

Source of Funds	
■ PACs	60%
▨ Lg Individuals ($200+)	22%
☐ Individuals under $200	1%
▧ Other	17%

Top Industries & Interest Groups

Insurance $144,198
Securities & Investment $124,600
Lawyers & Lobbyists $70,081
Beer, Wine & Liquor $57,000
Real Estate $51,750

Unidentified $58,850

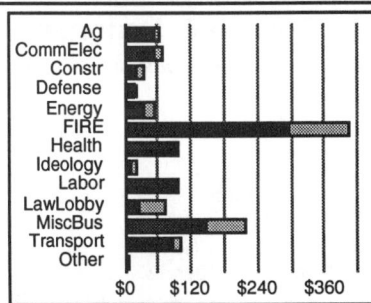

6. Henry J. Hyde (R)

1992 Committees: ForAff Judiciary
First elected: 1974

1991-92 Total Rcpts: $355,851
1990 Year-end cash: $134,632

Source of Funds	
■ PACs	47%
▨ Lg Individuals ($200+)	32%
☐ Individuals under $200	13%
▧ Other	8%

Top Industries & Interest Groups

Commercial Banks $19,500
Real Estate $18,900
Insurance $18,500
Lawyers & Lobbyists $17,600
Health Professionals $15,400

Unidentified $20,300

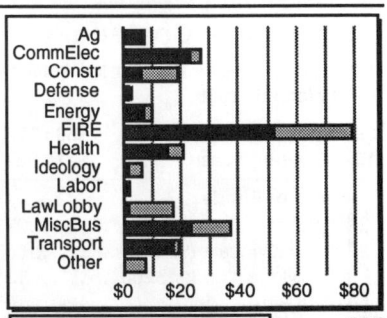

† Does not include individual contributions from 1987-88

7. Cardiss Collins (D)

1992 Committees: Energy/Commerce GovtOps
First elected: 1973

1991-92 Total Rcpts: $344,933
1990 Year-end cash: $49,167

Source of Funds
- PACs 82%
- Lg Individuals ($200+) 7%
- Individuals under $200 .... 1%
- Other 11%

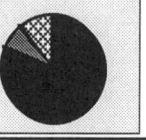

Top Industries & Interest Groups

Insurance $60,000
Lawyers & Lobbyists $33,912
Public Sector Unions $21,500
Transportation Unions $16,650
Telephone Utilities $13,850

Unidentified $500

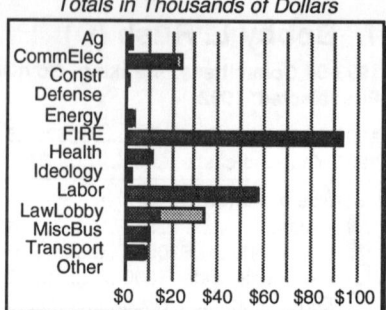

8. Philip M. Crane (R)

1992 Committees: Ways & Means
First elected: 1969

1991-92 Total Rcpts: $477,110
1990 Year-end cash: $64,211

Source of Funds
- PACs 0%
- Lg Individuals ($200+) 29%
- Individuals under $200 .... 65%
- Other 6%

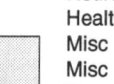

Top Industries & Interest Groups

Retired $22,150
Health Professionals $8,450
Misc Manufacturing & Distrib $6,075
Misc Finance $5,000
Republican/Conservative $4,750

Unidentified $54,726

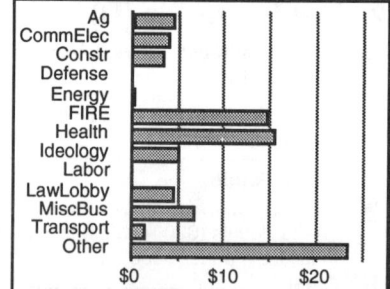

9. Sidney R. Yates (D)

1992 Committees: Appropriations
First elected: 1948

1991-92 Total Rcpts: $227,671
1990 Year-end cash: $52,684

Source of Funds
- PACs 15%
- Lg Individuals ($200+) 69%
- Individuals under $200 .... 15%
- Other 1%

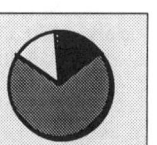

Top Industries & Interest Groups

Real Estate $29,800
Lawyers & Lobbyists $23,750
Pro-Israel $18,750
Non-Profit Institutions $11,550
Public Sector Unions $11,500

Unidentified $22,264

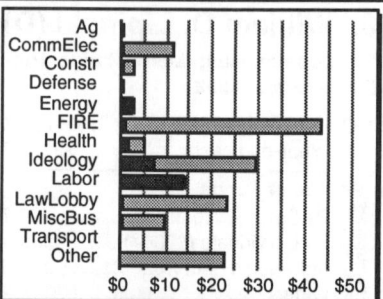

10. John Porter (R)

1992 Committees: Appropriations
First elected: 1980

1991-92 Total Rcpts: $453,794
1990 Year-end cash: $40,011

Source of Funds
- PACs 35%
- Lg Individuals ($200+) 40%
- Individuals under $200 .... 23%
- Other 2%

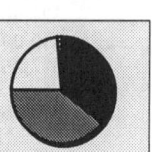

Top Industries & Interest Groups

Health Professionals $42,061
Retired $18,910
Pharmaceuticals/Health Prod ... $15,350
Pro-Israel $15,300
Real Estate $14,850

Unidentified $36,681

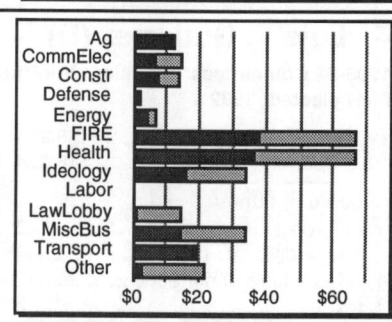

11. George E. Sangmeister (D)

1992 Committees: Judiciary PubWorks VetAffairs
First elected: 1988

1991-92 Total Rcpts: $339,478
1990 Year-end cash: $17,831

Source of Funds
- PACs 69%
- Lg Individuals ($200+) 8%
- Individuals under $200 .... 10%
- Other 13%

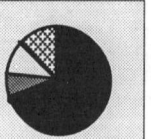

Top Industries & Interest Groups

Public Sector Unions $48,800
Industrial Unions $35,300
Transportation Unions $24,900
Building Trade Unions $18,800
Lawyers & Lobbyists $17,500

Unidentified $3,775

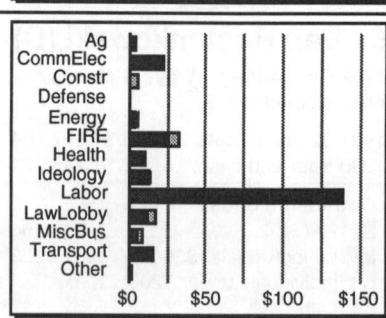

12. Jerry F. Costello (D)

1992 Committees: PubWorks Science
First elected: 1988

1991-92 Total Rcpts: $503,778
1990 Year-end cash: $171,227

Source of Funds
- PACs 27%
- Lg Individuals ($200+) 50%
- Individuals under $200 .... 13%
- Other 10%

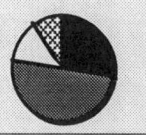

Top Industries & Interest Groups

Lawyers & Lobbyists $85,000
Industrial Unions $27,100
General Contractors $20,875
Transportation Unions $17,900
Health Professionals $17,200

Unidentified $43,400

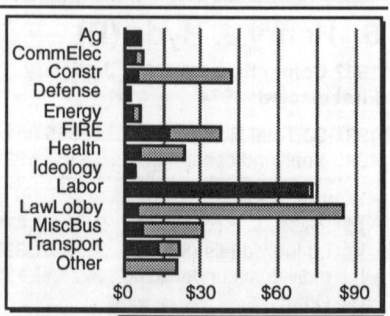

Key to committee & category abbreviations is on page 173

■ PACs ▨ Indivs ($200+)

13. Harris W. Fawell (R)

1992 Committees: Educ/Labor Science
First elected: 1984

1991-92 Total Rcpts: $498,465
1990 Year-end cash: $30,674

Source of Funds
- PACs 36%
- Lg Individuals ($200+) 54%
- Individuals under $200 .... 6%
- Other 4%

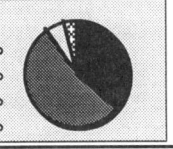

Top Industries & Interest Groups

Health Professionals	$30,225
Insurance	$27,100
Retired	$22,200
Building Materials & Equipment	$16,674
General Contractors	$15,950
Unidentified	$69,929

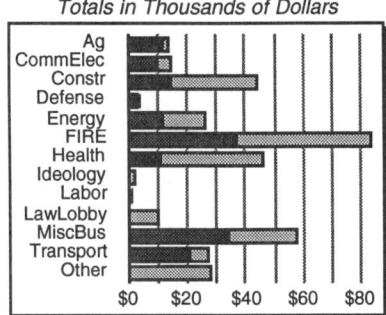

14. Dennis Hastert (R)

1992 Committees: Energy/Commerce GovtOps
First elected: 1986

1991-92 Total Rcpts: $601,812
1990 Year-end cash: $177,247

Source of Funds
- PACs 53%
- Lg Individuals ($200+) 19%
- Individuals under $200 .... 22%
- Other 5%

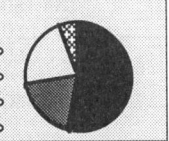

Top Industries & Interest Groups

Health Professionals	$34,350
Telephone Utilities	$30,200
Accountants	$23,200
Commercial Banks	$19,690
Misc Manufacturing & Distrib	$17,900
Unidentified	$23,683

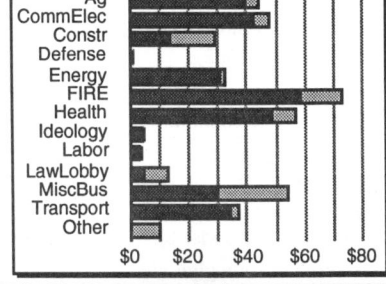

15. Thomas W. Ewing (R)

1992 Committees: Agric PubWorks
First elected: 1991

1991-92 Total Rcpts: $700,864
1990 Year-end cash: $123,473

Source of Funds
- PACs 45%
- Lg Individuals ($200+) 13%
- Individuals under $200 .... 32%
- Other 11%

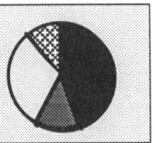

Top Industries & Interest Groups

Health Professionals	$34,500
Agricultural Services/Products ..	$23,039
Real Estate	$23,000
Telephone Utilities	$19,850
Commercial Banks	$16,350
Unidentified	$34,700

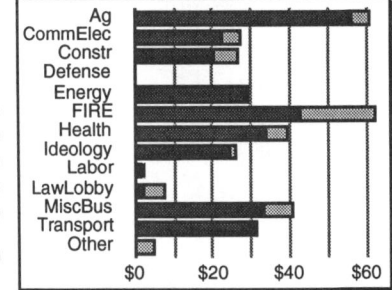

16. Donald Manzullo (R)

1993-94 Committees: ForAff SmBus
First elected: 1992

1991-92 Total Rcpts: $465,348
1990 Year-end cash: $5,908

Source of Funds
- PACs 24%
- Lg Individuals ($200+) 30%
- Individuals under $200 .... 23%
- Other 23%

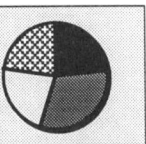

Top Industries & Interest Groups

Misc Manufacturing & Distrib	$22,000
Health Professionals	$21,700
Retired	$14,875
Air Transport	$12,182
Lawyers & Lobbyists	$11,044
Unidentified	$50,103

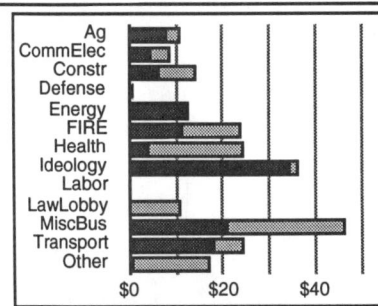

17. Lane Evans (D)

1992 Committees: ArmServ VetAffairs
First elected: 1982

1991-92 Total Rcpts: $370,096
1990 Year-end cash: $25,957

Source of Funds
- PACs 49%
- Lg Individuals ($200+) 9%
- Individuals under $200 .... 36%
- Other 6%

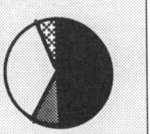

Top Industries & Interest Groups

Industrial Unions	$36,750
Public Sector Unions	$36,400
Building Trade Unions	$28,010
Lawyers & Lobbyists	$20,533
Transportation Unions	$18,025
Unidentified	$2,750

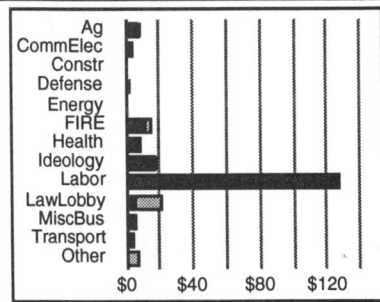

18. Robert H. Michel (R)

1992 Committees: House Minority Leader
First elected: 1956

1991-92 Total Rcpts: $646,637
1990 Year-end cash: $252,205

Source of Funds
- PACs 62%
- Lg Individuals ($200+) 18%
- Individuals under $200 .... 16%
- Other 4%

Top Industries & Interest Groups

Insurance	$40,448
Health Professionals	$30,100
Commercial Banks	$29,650
Agricultural Services/Products ..	$26,982
Telephone Utilities	$18,785
Unidentified	$23,870

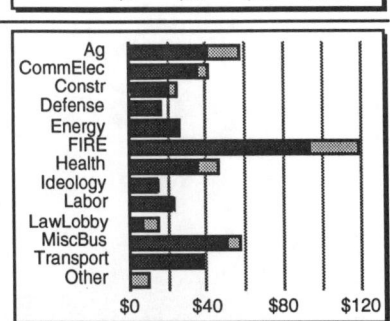

19. Glenn Poshard (D)

1992 Committees: PubWorks SmBus
First elected: 1988

1991-92 Total Rcpts: $304,026
1990 Year-end cash: $6,650

Source of Funds
- PACs 0%
- Lg Individuals ($200+) 14%
- Individuals under $200 .... 78%
- Other 9%

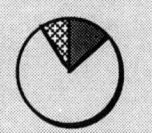

Top Industries & Interest Groups

Public Sector Unions $4,000
Lawyers & Lobbyists $3,540
Health Professionals $2,800
Civil Servants/Public Officials $2,750
Education $1,775

Unidentified $16,789

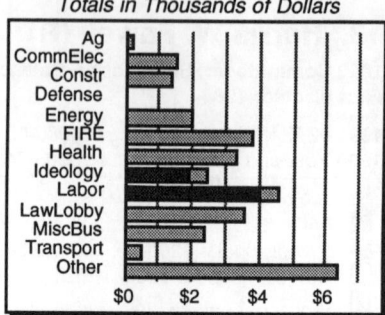

Totals in Thousands of Dollars

20. Richard J. Durbin (D)

1992 Committees: Approp Budget
First elected: 1982

1991-92 Total Rcpts: $666,110
1990 Year-end cash: $51,822

Source of Funds
- PACs 61%
- Lg Individuals ($200+) 12%
- Individuals under $200 .... 18%
- Other 9%

Top Industries & Interest Groups

Public Sector Unions $44,250
Transportation Unions $39,000
Lawyers & Lobbyists $34,150
Industrial Unions $33,250
Health Professionals $26,900

Unidentified $14,450

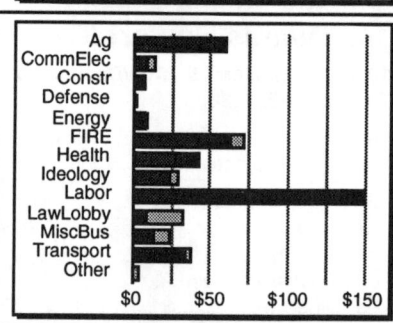

■ PACs   ▦ Indivs ($200+)

Key to committee & category abbreviations is on page 173

Indiana

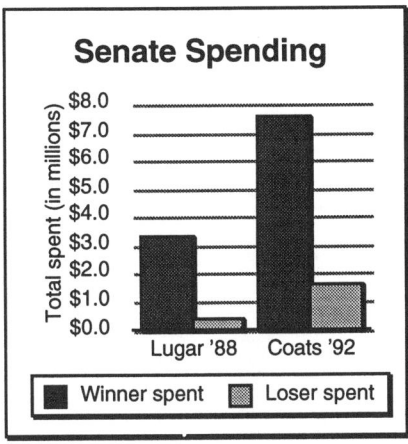

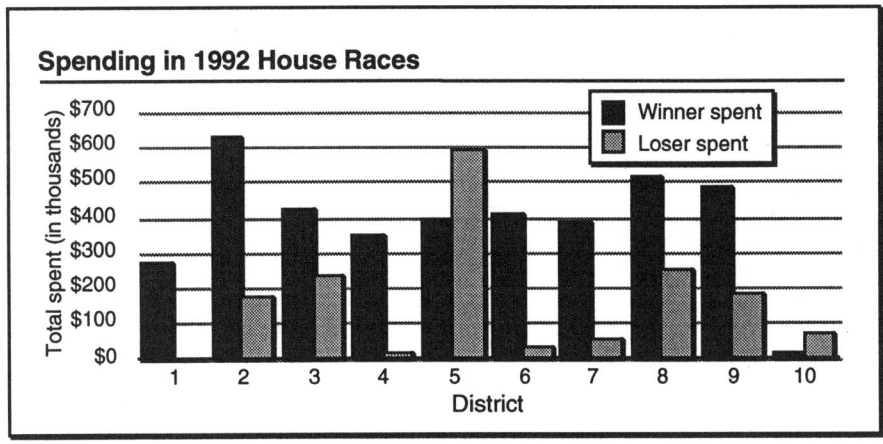

1992 Elections at a Glance

Dist	Name	Party	Vote Pct	Race Type
Sen	Daniel R. Coats (1992)	Rep	57%	Reelected
Sen	Richard G. Lugar (1988)	Rep	68%	Reelected
1	Peter J. Visclosky	Dem	69%	Reelected
2	Philip R. Sharp	Dem	57%	Reelected
3	Tim Roemer	Dem	57%	Reelected
4	Jill L. Long	Dem	62%	Reelected
5	Steve Buyer	Rep	51%	Beat Incumb
6	Dan Burton	Rep	72%	Reelected
7	John T. Myers	Rep	60%	Reelected
8	Frank McCloskey	Dem	52%	Reelected
9	Lee H. Hamilton	Dem	70%	Reelected
10	Andrew Jacobs Jr.	Dem	64%	Reelected

Totals in Thousands of Dollars

Sen. Daniel R. Coats (R)

1992 Committees: ArmServ Labor
First elected: 1990 (appointed 1988)

1989-92 Total Rcpts: $7,727,256
1990 Year-end cash: $183,495

Source of Funds
- PACs 27%
- Lg Individuals ($200+) 35%
- Individuals under $200 .... 19%
- Other 19%

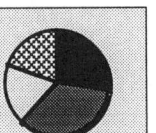

1988-92†
Top Industries & Interest Groups

Insurance $315,707
Health Professionals $239,412
Pharmaceuticals/Health Prod ..$219,820
Oil & Gas $210,000
Defense Aerospace $203,745

Unidentified $966,766

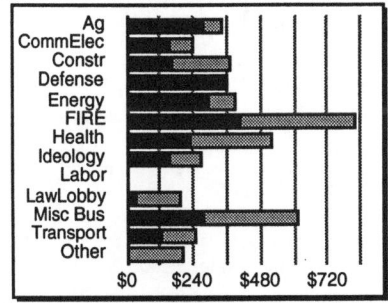

Sen. Richard G. Lugar (R)

1992 Committees: Agric ForRel
First elected: 1976

1987-92 Total Rcpts: $4,583,235
1990 Year-end cash: $1,346,212

Source of Funds
- PACs 20%
- Lg Individuals ($200+) 33%
- Individuals under $200 .... 35%
- Other 11%

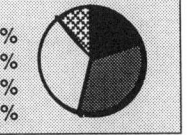

1987-92†
Top Industries & Interest Groups

Food Processing & Sales $97,135
Agric Services/Products $90,820
Health Professionals $86,400
Lawyers & Lobbyists $76,140
Insurance $74,965

Unidentified $226,875

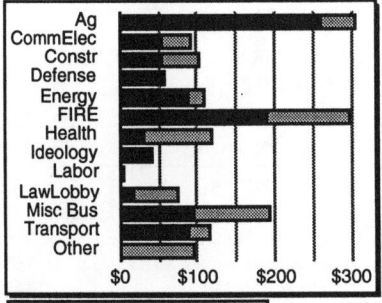

† Does not include individual contributions from 1987-88

1. Peter J. Visclosky (D)
1992 Committees: Appropriations
First elected: 1984

1991-92 Total Rcpts: $276,028
1990 Year-end cash: $50,939

Source of Funds
- PACs 69%
- Lg Individuals ($200+) 19%
- Individuals under $200 .... 11%
- Other 1%

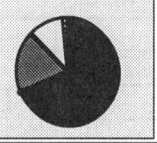

Top Industries & Interest Groups

Industrial Unions $40,500
Public Sector Unions $25,800
Building Trade Unions $25,300
Transportation Unions $24,950
Health Professionals $22,850

Unidentified $8,725

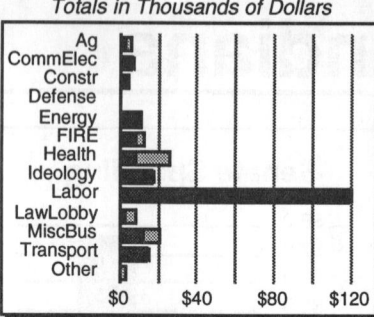

2. Philip R. Sharp (D)
1992 Committees: Energy/Commerce Interior
First elected: 1974

1991-92 Total Rcpts: $624,265
1990 Year-end cash: $30,810

Source of Funds
- PACs 72%
- Lg Individuals ($200+) 10%
- Individuals under $200 .... 14%
- Other 3%

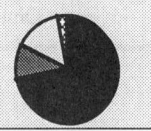

Top Industries & Interest Groups

Electric Utilities $50,675
Oil & Gas $43,416
Lawyers & Lobbyists $43,228
Public Sector Unions $29,500
Telephone Utilities $26,400

Unidentified $5,600

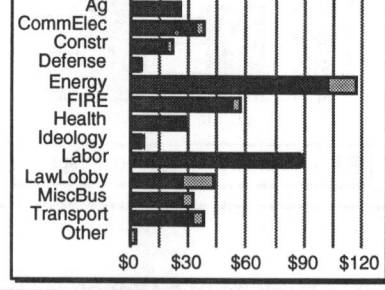

3. Tim Roemer (D)
1992 Committees: Educ/Labor Science
First elected: 1990

1991-92 Total Rcpts: $467,094
1990 Year-end cash: $73,596

Source of Funds
- PACs 64%
- Lg Individuals ($200+) 21%
- Individuals under $200 .... 5%
- Other 10%

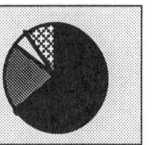

Top Industries & Interest Groups

Industrial Unions $55,600
Lawyers & Lobbyists $45,270
Building Trade Unions $29,250
Public Sector Unions $29,000
Transportation Unions $17,300

Unidentified $24,837

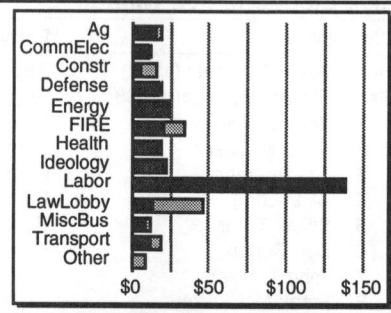

4. Jill L. Long (D)
1992 Committees: Agric VetAffairs
First elected: 1989

1991-92 Total Rcpts: $375,147
1990 Year-end cash: $15,090

Source of Funds
- PACs 69%
- Lg Individuals ($200+) 8%
- Individuals under $200 .... 17%
- Other 7%

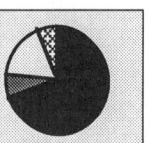

Top Industries & Interest Groups

Public Sector Unions $44,000
Industrial Unions $39,800
Dairy $23,500
Transportation Unions $19,550
Health Professionals $16,508

Unidentified $4,450

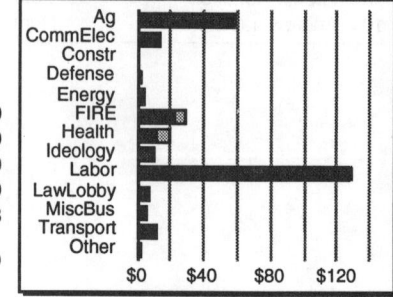

5. Steve Buyer (R)
1993-94 Committees: ArmServ VetAffairs
First elected: 1992

1991-92 Total Rcpts: $392,885
1990 Year-end cash: $2,902

Source of Funds
- PACs 31%
- Lg Individuals ($200+) 24%
- Individuals under $200 .... 21%
- Other 24%

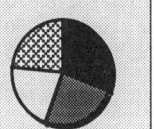

Top Industries & Interest Groups

Forestry & Forest Products $39,698
Misc Manufacturing & Distrib $15,250
Building Materials & Equipment $15,240
Real Estate $13,800
Agricultural Services/Products .. $11,500

Unidentified $26,949

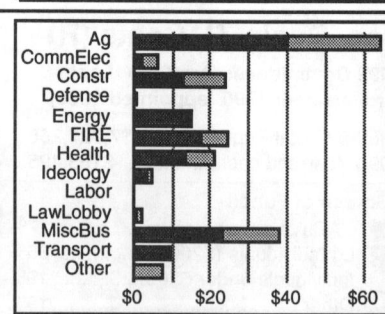

6. Dan Burton (R)
1992 Committees: ForAff Post Office VetAffairs
First elected: 1982

1991-92 Total Rcpts: $629,390
1990 Year-end cash: $622,881

Source of Funds
- PACs 33%
- Lg Individuals ($200+) 38%
- Individuals under $200 .... 18%
- Other 11%

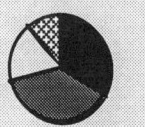

Top Industries & Interest Groups

Insurance $45,904
Health Professionals $32,050
Pro-Israel $19,500
Automotive $17,000
Foreign & Defense Policy $13,150

Unidentified $77,047

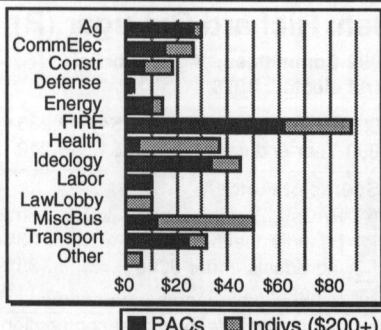

7. John T. Myers (R)

1992 Committees: Approp Post Office
First elected: 1966

1991-92 Total Rcpts: $340,979
1990 Year-end cash: $62,387

Source of Funds
- PACs 59%
- Lg Individuals ($200+) 8%
- Individuals under $200 .... 20%
- Other 13%

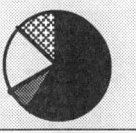

Top Industries & Interest Groups

Public Sector Unions $19,750
Electric Utilities $12,500
Automotive $10,300
Lawyers & Lobbyists $10,150
Agricultural Services/Products $9,500

Unidentified $3,609

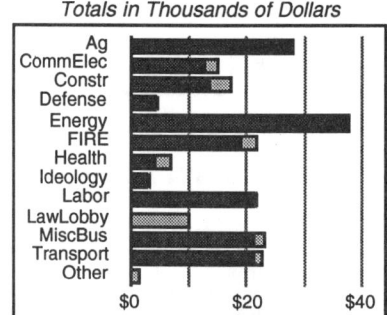

8. Frank McCloskey (D)

1992 Committees: ArmServ ForAff Post Office
First elected: 1982

1991-92 Total Rcpts: $498,192
1990 Year-end cash: $8,622

Source of Funds
- PACs 62%
- Lg Individuals ($200+) 5%
- Individuals under $200 .... 22%
- Other 11%

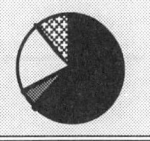

Top Industries & Interest Groups

Public Sector Unions $71,200
Industrial Unions $59,000
Building Trade Unions $25,700
Transportation Unions $19,850
Defense Aerospace $18,000

Unidentified $2,700

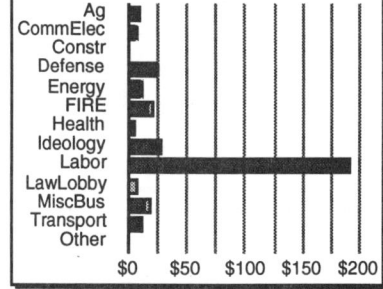

9. Lee H. Hamilton (D)

1992 Committees: Foreign Affairs
First elected: 1964

1991-92 Total Rcpts: $485,788
1990 Year-end cash: $66,788

Source of Funds
- PACs 41%
- Lg Individuals ($200+) 31%
- Individuals under $200 .... 25%
- Other 3%

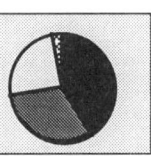

Top Industries & Interest Groups

Lawyers & Lobbyists $28,750
Real Estate $24,850
Pro-Israel $21,800
Securities & Investment $13,250
Public Sector Unions $12,600

Unidentified $29,150

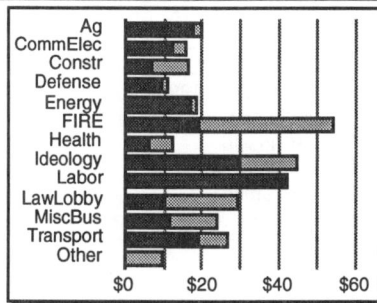

10. Andrew Jacobs Jr. (D)

1992 Committees: Ways & Means
First elected: 1964

1991-92 Total Rcpts: $15,690
1990 Year-end cash: $33,505

Source of Funds
- PACs 0%
- Lg Individuals ($200+) 19%
- Individuals under $200 .... 61%
- Other 19%

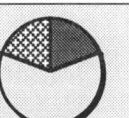

Top Industries & Interest Groups

Insurance $1,200
Retired $700
Lawyers & Lobbyists $450
Education $250
Retail Sales $200

Unidentified $250

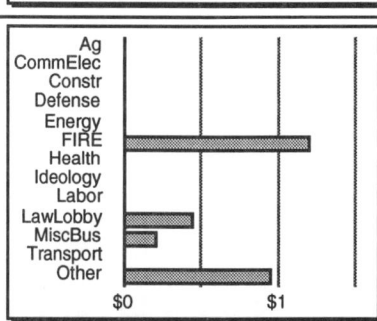

■ PACs   ▦ Indivs ($200+)

Iowa

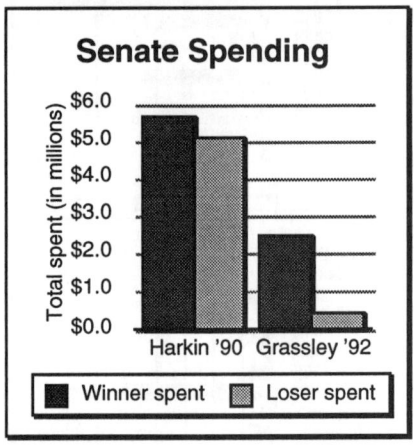

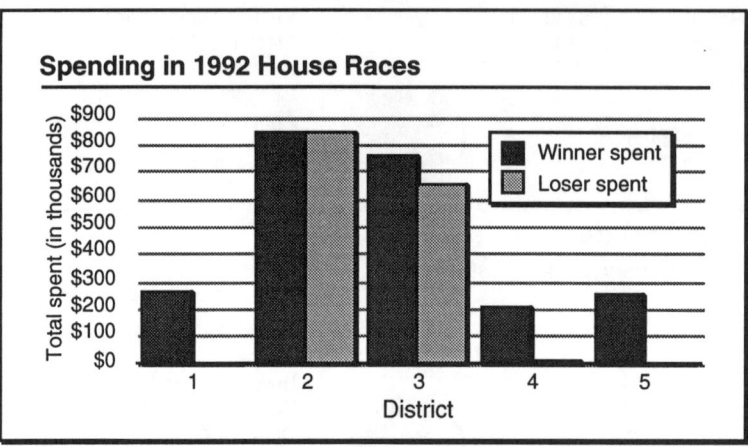

1992 Elections at a Glance

Dist	Name	Party	Vote Pct	Race Type
Sen	Charles E. Grassley (1992)	Rep	70%	Reelected
Sen	Tom Harkin (1990)	Dem	54%	Reelected
1	Jim Leach	Rep	68%	Reelected
2	Jim Nussle	Rep	50%	Reelected
3	Jim Ross Lightfoot	Rep	49%	Reelected
4	Neal Smith	Dem	62%	Reelected
5	Fred Grandy	Rep	99%	Reelected

Totals in Thousands of Dollars

Sen. Charles E. Grassley (R)

1992 Committees: Agric Budget Finance Judiciary
First elected: 1980

1987-92 Total Rcpts: $2,833,489
1990 Year-end cash: $821,030

Source of Funds
- PACs 33%
- Lg Individuals ($200+) 19%
- Individuals under $200 .... 26%
- Other 22%

1987-92†
Top Industries & Interest Groups

Insurance $172,223
Health Professionals $101,540
Lawyers & Lobbyists $87,670
Pro-Israel $82,600
Agric Services/Products $64,429

Unidentified $144,888

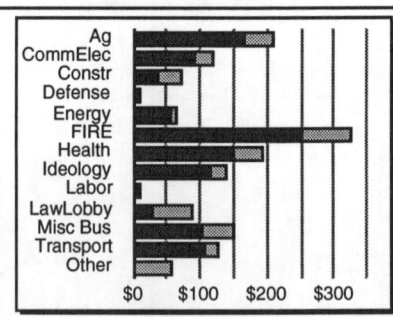

Sen. Tom Harkin (D)

1992 Committees: Agric Approp Labor SmBus
First elected: 1984

1987-92 Total Rcpts: $5,867,588
1990 Year-end cash: $78,831

Source of Funds
- PACs 30%
- Lg Individuals ($200+) 29%
- Individuals under $200 .... 33%
- Other 9%

1987-92†
Top Industries & Interest Groups

Pro-Israel $353,450
Lawyers & Lobbyists $311,294
Health Professionals $244,127
Industrial Unions $182,150
Transportation Unions $164,560

Unidentified $403,094

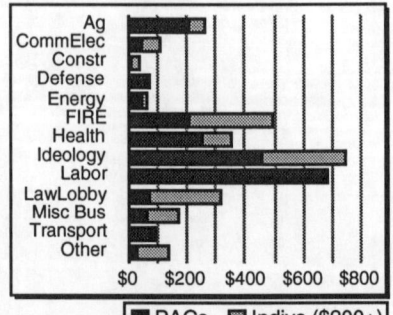

Key to committee & category abbreviations is on page 173

1. Jim Leach (R)
1992 Committees: Banking ForAff
First elected: 1976

1991-92 Total Rcpts: $213,649
1990 Year-end cash: $759

Source of Funds
- PACs .... -0%
- Lg Individuals ($200+) 28%
- Individuals under $200 .... 64%
- Other 8%

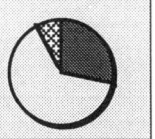

Top Industries & Interest Groups

Health Professionals $5,550
Retired $5,236
Printing & Publishing $3,000
Lawyers & Lobbyists $2,700
Commercial Banks $2,550

Unidentified $18,180

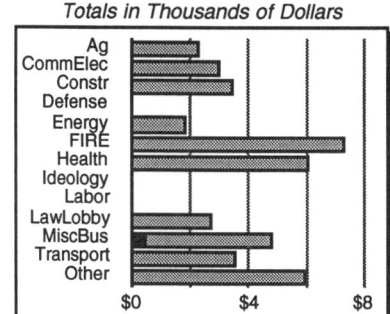

2. Jim Nussle (R)
1992 Committees: Agric Banking
First elected: 1990

1991-92 Total Rcpts: $867,359
1990 Year-end cash: $5,194

Source of Funds
- PACs 38%
- Lg Individuals ($200+) 23%
- Individuals under $200 .... 28%
- Other 11%

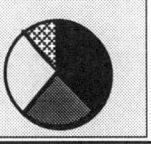

Top Industries & Interest Groups

Commercial Banks $43,150
Insurance $33,800
Health Professionals $32,500
Misc Manufacturing & Distrib $27,850
Automotive $26,750

Unidentified $35,488

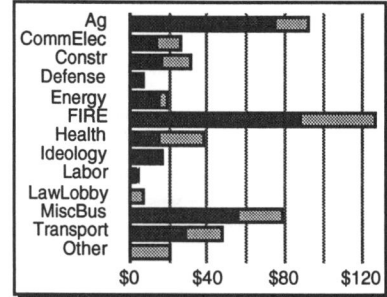

3. Jim Ross Lightfoot (R)
1992 Committees: Appropriations
First elected: 1984

1991-92 Total Rcpts: $623,098
1990 Year-end cash: $8,356

Source of Funds
- PACs 38%
- Lg Individuals ($200+) 13%
- Individuals under $200 .... 34%
- Other 16%

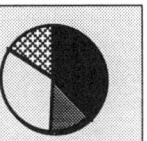

Top Industries & Interest Groups

Health Professionals $24,346
Agricultural Services/Products .. $21,298
Air Transport $19,600
Automotive $18,000
Crop Production/Processing $15,525

Unidentified $11,213

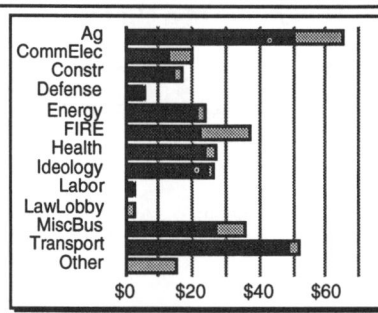

4. Neal Smith (D)
1992 Committees: Approp SmBus
First elected: 1958

1991-92 Total Rcpts: $324,231
1990 Year-end cash: $502,580

Source of Funds
- PACs 61%
- Lg Individuals ($200+) 16%
- Individuals under $200 .... 2%
- Other 22%

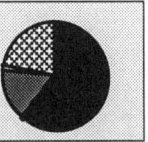

Top Industries & Interest Groups

Lawyers & Lobbyists $28,743
Public Sector Unions $21,000
Health Professionals $15,600
Building Trade Unions $12,500
Real Estate $10,750

Unidentified $8,450

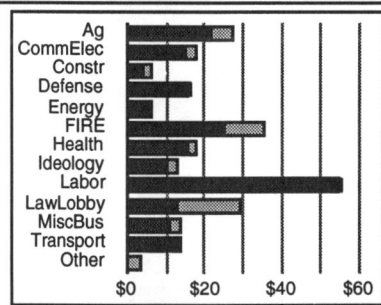

5. Fred Grandy (R)
1992 Committees: Ways & Means
First elected: 1986

1991-92 Total Rcpts: $382,626
1990 Year-end cash: $174,722

Source of Funds
- PACs 77%
- Lg Individuals ($200+) 15%
- Individuals under $200 .... 5%
- Other 3%

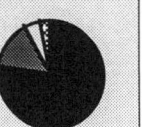

Top Industries & Interest Groups

Insurance $57,499
Health Professionals $28,397
Telephone Utilities $22,600
Agricultural Services/Products .. $19,750
Food Processing & Sales $15,750

Unidentified $20,750

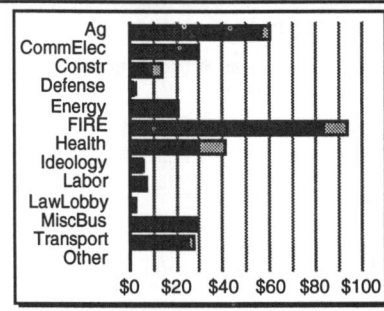

■ PACs   ▨ Indivs ($200+)

† Does not include individual contributions from 1987-88

Kansas

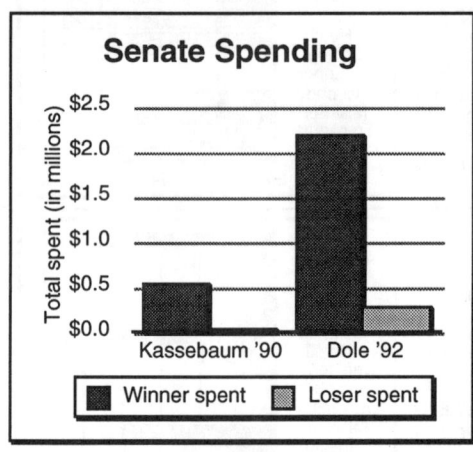

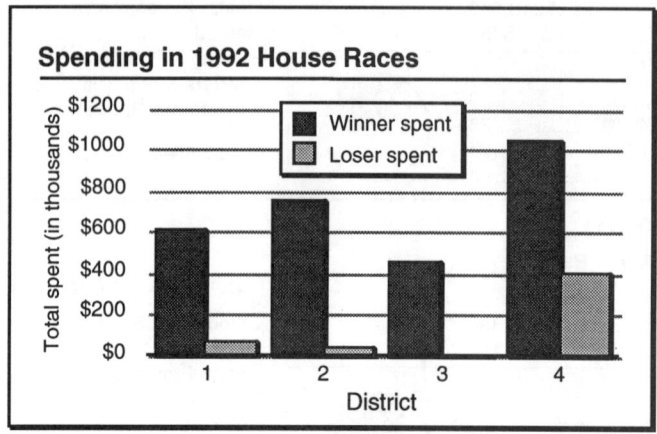

1992 Elections at a Glance

Dist	Name	Party	Vote Pct	Race Type
Sen	Bob Dole (1992)	Rep	63%	Reelected
Sen	Nancy Kassebaum (1990)	Rep	74%	Reelected
1	Pat Roberts	Rep	68%	Reelected
2	Jim Slattery	Dem	56%	Reelected
3	Jan Meyers	Rep	58%	Reelected
4	Dan Glickman	Dem	52%	Reelected

Totals in Thousands of Dollars

Sen. Bob Dole (R)

1992 Committees: Agric Finance Rules
First elected: 1968

1987-92 Total Rcpts: $3,143,115
1990 Year-end cash: $1,756,483

Source of Funds
- PACs 50%
- Lg Individuals ($200+) 29%
- Individuals under $200 .... 4%
- Other 17%

1987-92†
Top Industries & Interest Groups

Lawyers & Lobbyists $267,617
Insurance $258,589
Securities & Investment $205,050
Oil & Gas $204,000
Commercial Banks $130,340

Unidentified $117,518

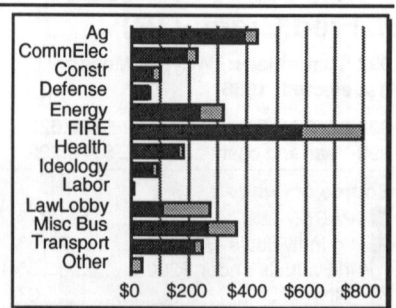

Sen. Nancy Landon Kassebaum (R)

1992 Committees: Banking ForRel Labor
First elected: 1978

1987-92 Total Rcpts: $529,612
1990 Year-end cash: $172,579

Source of Funds
- PACs 29%
- Lg Individuals ($200+) 26%
- Individuals under $200 .... 14%
- Other 30%

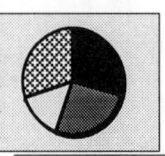

1987-92†
Top Industries & Interest Groups

Commercial Banks $33,850
Oil & Gas $18,208
Insurance $11,930
Health Professionals $11,700
Securities & Investment $11,250

Unidentified $40,449

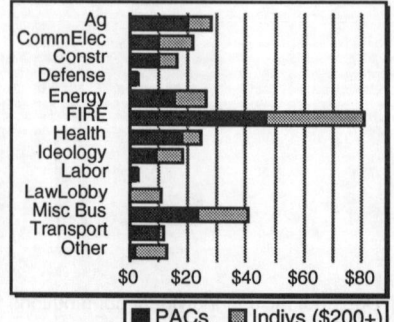

Key to committee & category abbreviations is on page 173

■ PACs ▨ Indivs ($200+)

1. Pat Roberts (R)

1992 Committees: Admin Agric
First elected: 1980

1991-92 Total Rcpts: $313,020
1990 Year-end cash: $110,891

Source of Funds
- PACs 59%
- Lg Individuals ($200+) 12%
- Individuals under $200 .... 14%
- Other 15%

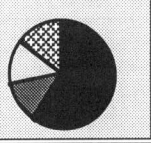

Top Industries & Interest Groups

Agricultural Services/Products ..$27,500
Food Processing & Sales $21,350
Crop Production/Processing $17,425
Commercial Banks $14,500
Securities & Investment $11,000

Unidentified $7,850

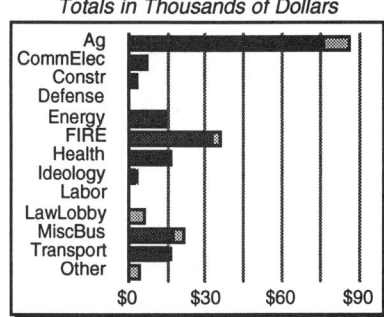

2. Jim Slattery (D)

1992 Committees: Banking Energy/Comm VetAffairs
First elected: 1982

1991-92 Total Rcpts: $701,965
1990 Year-end cash: $12,748

Source of Funds
- PACs 62%
- Lg Individuals ($200+) 24%
- Individuals under $200 .... 11%
- Other 3%

Top Industries & Interest Groups

Lawyers & Lobbyists $53,300
Insurance $46,699
Telephone Utilities $46,050
Health Professionals $34,650
Industrial Unions $28,250

Unidentified $38,915

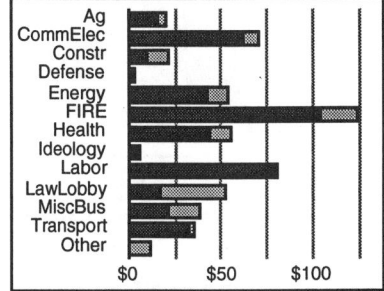

3. Jan Meyers (R)

1992 Committees: ForAff SmBus
First elected: 1984

1991-92 Total Rcpts: $440,290
1990 Year-end cash: $403

Source of Funds
- PACs 48%
- Lg Individuals ($200+) 14%
- Individuals under $200 .... 33%
- Other 6%

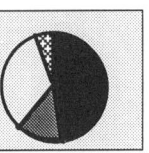

Top Industries & Interest Groups

Health Professionals $20,350
Telephone Utilities $14,875
Automotive $13,925
Insurance $13,450
Food & Beverage $12,050

Unidentified $15,165

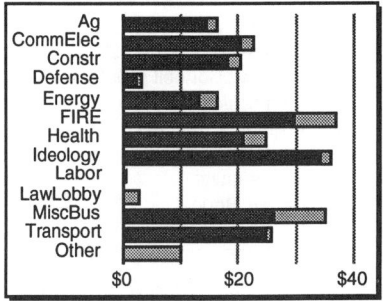

4. Dan Glickman (D)

1992 Committees: Agric Judiciary Science
First elected: 1976

1991-92 Total Rcpts: $873,194
1990 Year-end cash: $18,743

Source of Funds
- PACs 48%
- Lg Individuals ($200+) 35%
- Individuals under $200 .... 11%
- Other 6%

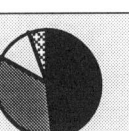

Top Industries & Interest Groups

Lawyers & Lobbyists $86,903
Pro-Israel $59,639
Securities & Investment $45,450
Insurance $39,939
Industrial Unions $33,550

Unidentified $51,708

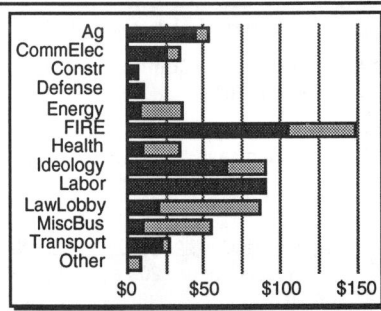

■ PACs ▩ Indivs ($200+)

† Does not include individual contributions from 1987-88

Kentucky

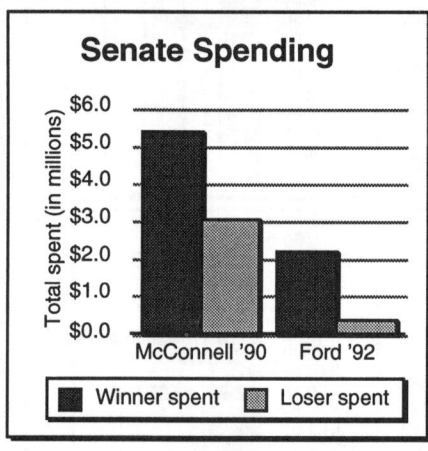

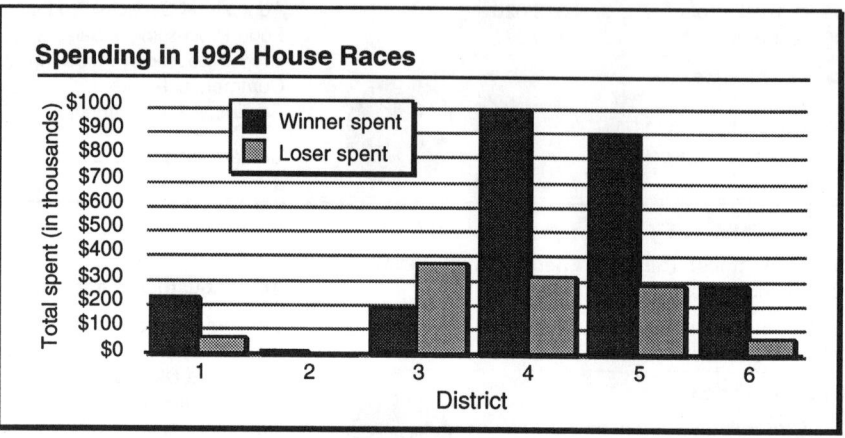

1992 Elections at a Glance

Dist	Name	Party	Vote Pct	Race Type
Sen	Wendell H. Ford (1992)	Dem	63%	Reelected
Sen	Mitch McConnell (1990)	Rep	52%	Reelected
1	Tom Barlow	Dem	60%	Open Seat
2	William H. Natcher	Dem	61%	Reelected
3	Romano L. Mazzoli	Dem	53%	Reelected
4	Jim Bunning	Rep	62%	Reelected
5	Harold Rogers	Rep	55%	Reelected
6	Scotty Baesler	Dem	61%	Open Seat

Totals in Thousands of Dollars

Sen. Wendell H. Ford (D)

1992 Committees: Commerce Energy Rules
First elected: 1974

1987-92 Total Rcpts: $2,386,966
1990 Year-end cash: $438,224

Source of Funds
- PACs 55%
- Lg Individuals ($200+) 29%
- Individuals under $200 .... 5%
- Other 11%

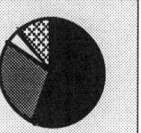

1987-92†
Top Industries & Interest Groups

Lawyers & Lobbyists $188,057
Insurance $124,559
Air Transport $111,745
Oil & Gas $108,700
Electric Utilities $69,250

Unidentified $106,704

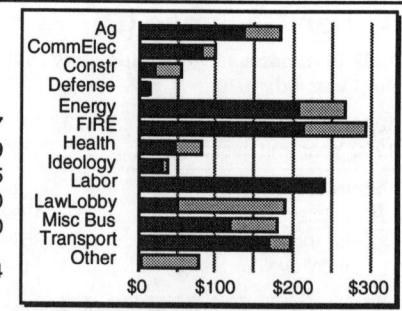

Sen. Mitch McConnell (R)

1992 Committees: Agric ForRel Rules
First elected: 1984

1987-92 Total Rcpts: $5,108,185
1990 Year-end cash: $233,458

Source of Funds
- PACs 22%
- Lg Individuals ($200+) 42%
- Individuals under $200 .... 17%
- Other 19%

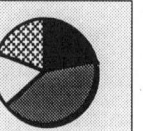

1987-92†
Top Industries & Interest Groups

Pro-Israel $230,400
Oil & Gas $199,292
Lawyers & Lobbyists $189,218
Health Professionals $181,875
Insurance $121,156

Unidentified $548,166

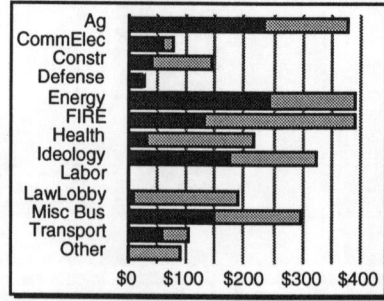

1. Tom Barlow (D)

1993-94 Committees: Agric MerchMarine
First elected: 1992

1991-92 Total Rcpts: $220,396
1990 Year-end cash: $6,864

Source of Funds
- PACs 48%
- Lg Individuals ($200+) 10%
- Individuals under $200 .... 14%
- Other 28%

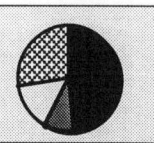

Top Industries & Interest Groups

Industrial Unions $26,000
Public Sector Unions $13,500
Transportation Unions $9,000
Lawyers & Lobbyists $5,650
Health Professionals $5,500

Unidentified $5,800

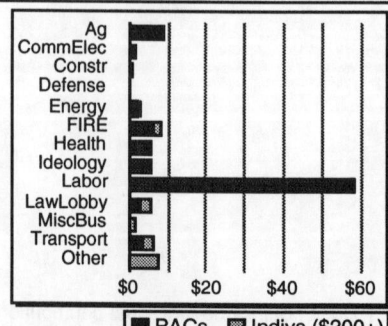

Key to committee & category abbreviations is on page 173

2. William H. Natcher (D)

1992 Committees: Appropriations
First elected: 1953

1991-92 Total Rcpts: $6,623
1990 Year-end cash: $0

Source of Funds
- PACs 0%
- Lg Individuals ($200+) 0%
- Individuals under $200 .... 0%
- Other 100%

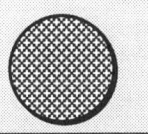

Top Industries & Interest Groups

NOTE: Natcher financed his own campaign in 1990, as is his custom. It was the least expensive winning campaign of the year, by far.

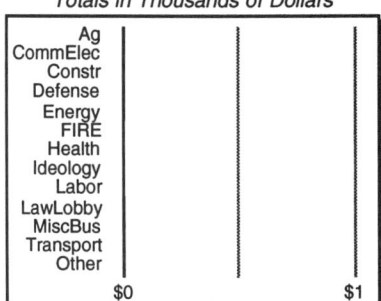

3. Romano L. Mazzoli (D)

1992 Committees: Judiciary SmBus
First elected: 1970

1991-92 Total Rcpts: $223,091
1990 Year-end cash: $6,743

Source of Funds
- PACs 0%
- Lg Individuals ($200+) 7%
- Individuals under $200 .... 91%
- Other 2%

Top Industries & Interest Groups

Lawyers & Lobbyists $2,900
Health Professionals $2,100
Commercial Banks $1,400
Real Estate $1,000
Hospitals/Nursing Homes $800

Unidentified $1,300

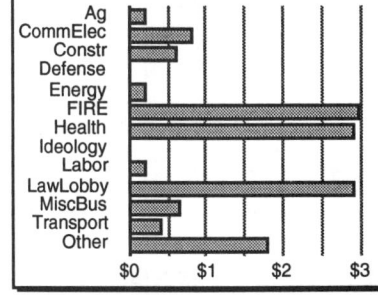

4. Jim Bunning (R)

1992 Committees: Ways & Means
First elected: 1986

1991-92 Total Rcpts: $946,781
1990 Year-end cash: $59,618

Source of Funds
- PACs 45%
- Lg Individuals ($200+) 29%
- Individuals under $200 .... 18%
- Other 8%

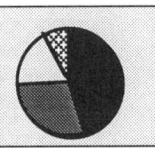

Top Industries & Interest Groups

Insurance $75,073
Health Professionals $52,809
Commercial Banks $39,600
Telephone Utilities $33,550
Oil & Gas $31,840

Unidentified $61,850

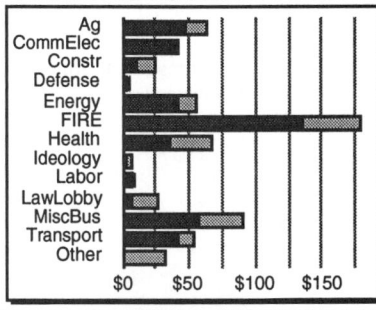

5. Harold Rogers (R)

1992 Committees: Approp Budget
First elected: 1980

1991-92 Total Rcpts: $651,821
1990 Year-end cash: $32,933

Source of Funds
- PACs 34%
- Lg Individuals ($200+) 42%
- Individuals under $200 .... 13%
- Other 11%

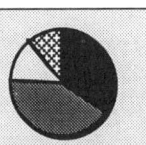

Top Industries & Interest Groups

Mining $60,625
Oil & Gas $37,050
Lawyers & Lobbyists $29,050
Health Professionals $20,900
Beer, Wine & Liquor $19,750

Unidentified $50,500

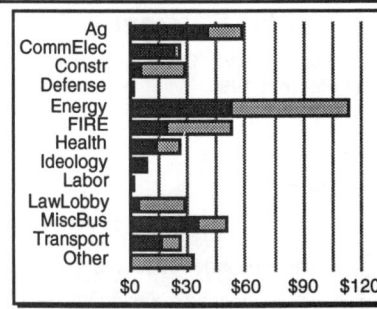

6. Scotty Baesler (D)

1993-94 Committees: Agric Educ/Labor VetAffairs
First elected: 1992

1991-92 Total Rcpts: $301,557
1990 Year-end cash: $27,830

Source of Funds
- PACs 0%
- Lg Individuals ($200+) 58%
- Individuals under $200 .... 35%
- Other 7%

Top Industries & Interest Groups

Health Professionals $18,850
Lawyers & Lobbyists $18,671
General Contractors $10,950
Real Estate $8,650
Crop Production/Processing $6,752

Unidentified $61,850

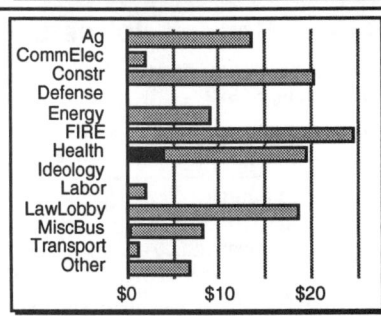

■ PACs   ▨ Indivs ($200+)

† Does not include individual contributions from 1987-88

Louisiana

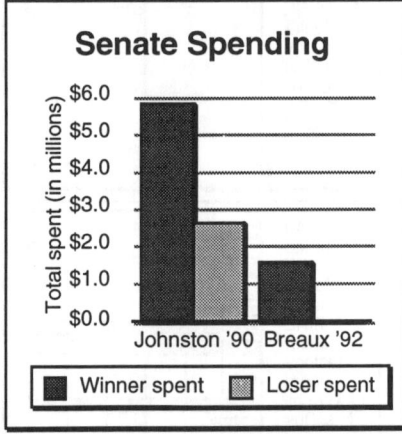

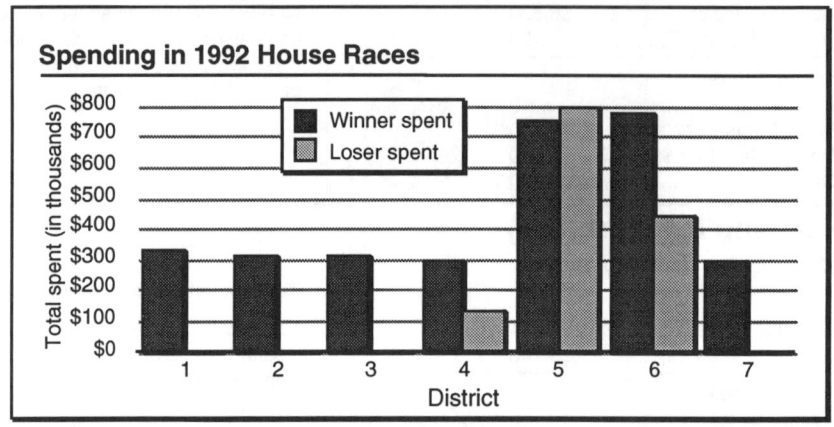

1992 Elections at a Glance

Dist	Name	Party	Vote Pct	Race Type
Sen	John B. Breaux (1992)	Dem	100%	Reelected
Sen	J. Bennett Johnston (1990)	Dem	54%	Reelected
1	Robert L. Livingston	Rep	100%	Reelected
2	William J. Jefferson	Dem	100%	Reelected
3	W.J. "Billy" Tauzin	Dem	100%	Reelected
4	Cleo Fields	Dem	74%	Open Seat
5	Jim McCrery	Rep	63%	Reelected
6	Richard H. Baker	Rep	51%	Reelected
7	Jimmy Hayes	Dem	100%	Reelected

Totals in Thousands of Dollars

Sen. John B. Breaux (D)

1992 Committees: Commerce Finance
First elected: 1986

1987-92 Total Rcpts: $3,481,494
1990 Year-end cash: $1,522,344

Source of Funds
- PACs 48%
- Lg Individuals ($200+) 33%
- Individuals under $200 .... 12%
- Other 8%

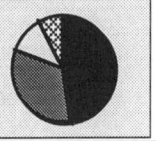

1987-92†
Top Industries & Interest Groups

Lawyers & Lobbyists	$282,631
Oil & Gas	$211,675
Insurance	$132,312
Sea Transport	$116,098
Securities & Investment	$112,899
Unidentified	$179,774

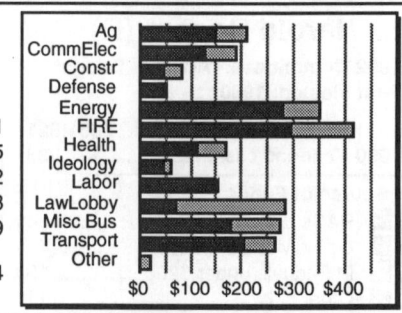

Sen. J. Bennett Johnston (D)

1992 Committees: Approp Budget Energy
First elected: 1972

1987-92 Total Rcpts: $4,671,888
1990 Year-end cash: $874,800

Source of Funds
- PACs 30%
- Lg Individuals ($200+) 28%
- Individuals under $200 .... 19%
- Other 22%

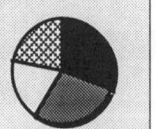

1987-92†
Top Industries & Interest Groups

Oil & Gas	$344,750
Lawyers & Lobbyists	$305,150
Electric Utilities	$176,950
Pro-Israel	$129,802
Defense Aerospace	$106,950
Unidentified	$255,245

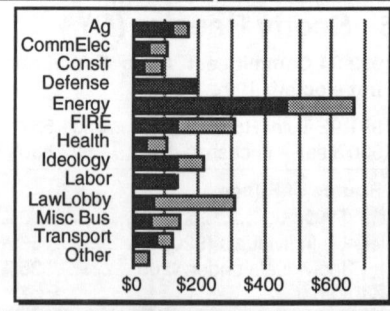

1. Robert L. Livingston (R)

1992 Committees: Admin Approp
First elected: 1977

1991-92 Total Rcpts: $337,316
1990 Year-end cash: $295,908

Source of Funds
- PACs 40%
- Lg Individuals ($200+) 30%
- Individuals under $200 .... 21%
- Other 10%

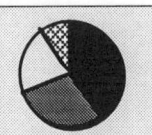

1985-90
Top Industries & Interest Groups

Defense Aerospace	$24,000
Lawyers & Lobbyists	$21,100
Defense Electronics	$21,000
Oil & Gas	$19,600
Health Professionals	$12,800
Unidentified	$27,750

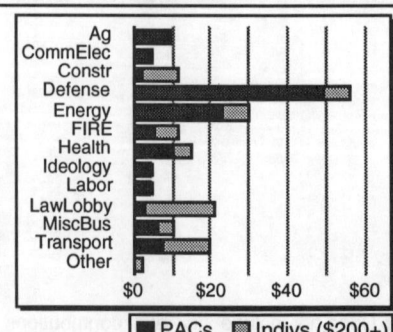

Key to committee & category abbreviations is on page 173

2. William J. Jefferson (D)

1992 Committees: Educ/Labor MerchMarine
First elected: 1990

1991-92 Total Rcpts: $398,154
1990 Year-end cash: $25,522

Source of Funds
- PACs 55%
- Lg Individuals ($200+) 32%
- Individuals under $200 .... 4%
- Other 10%

Top Industries & Interest Groups

Lawyers & Lobbyists $58,300
Public Sector Unions $33,500
Transportation Unions $23,600
Industrial Unions $20,000
Real Estate $16,500

Unidentified $35,425

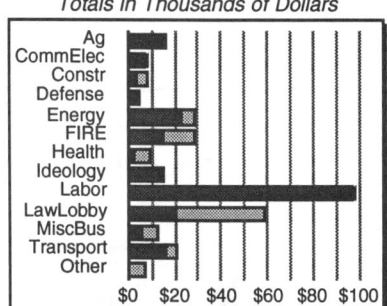

3. W.J. "Billy" Tauzin (D)

1992 Committees: Energy/Commerce MerchMarine
First elected: 1980

1991-92 Total Rcpts: $590,179
1990 Year-end cash: $327,478

Source of Funds
- PACs 74%
- Lg Individuals ($200+) 18%
- Individuals under $200 .... 4%
- Other 5%

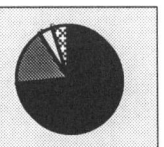

Top Industries & Interest Groups

Accountants $50,750
Oil & Gas $49,850
Lawyers & Lobbyists $45,850
Sea Transport $34,700
Telephone Utilities $33,550

Unidentified $20,750

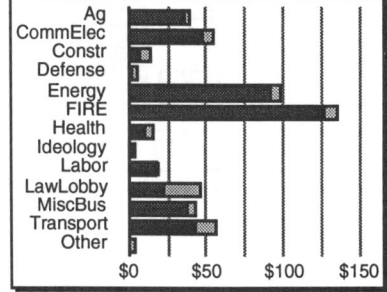

4. Cleo Fields (D)

1993-94 Committees: Banking SmBus
First elected: 1992

1991-92 Total Rcpts: $291,225
1990 Year-end cash: $1,044

Source of Funds
- PACs 17%
- Lg Individuals ($200+) 68%
- Individuals under $200 .... 4%
- Other 11%

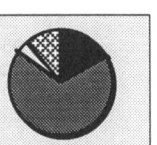

Top Industries & Interest Groups

Lawyers & Lobbyists $50,420
Health Professionals $8,700
Civil Servants/Public Officials $8,200
Education $7,050
Transportation Unions $6,800

Unidentified $90,200

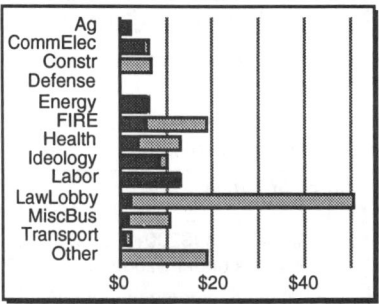

5. Jim McCrery (R)

1992 Committees: ArmServ Budget
First elected: 1988

1991-92 Total Rcpts: $768,933
1990 Year-end cash: $63,367

Source of Funds
- PACs 27%
- Lg Individuals ($200+) 41%
- Individuals under $200 .... 20%
- Other 11%

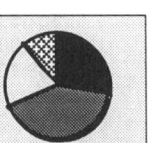

Top Industries & Interest Groups

Health Professionals $62,100
Oil & Gas $49,950
Insurance $26,000
Defense Aerospace $23,600
Pro-Israel $23,250

Unidentified $82,072

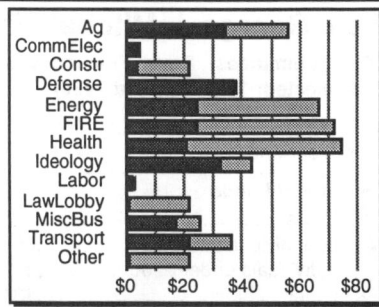

6. Richard H. Baker (R)

1992 Committees: Banking Interior SmBus
First elected: 1986

1991-92 Total Rcpts: $711,147
1990 Year-end cash: $7,999

Source of Funds
- PACs 38%
- Lg Individuals ($200+) 44%
- Individuals under $200 .... 16%
- Other 2%

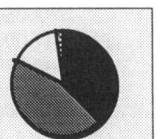

Top Industries & Interest Groups

Commercial Banks $91,900
Lawyers & Lobbyists $61,400
Health Professionals $33,150
Real Estate $27,800
Retired $27,350

Unidentified $62,496

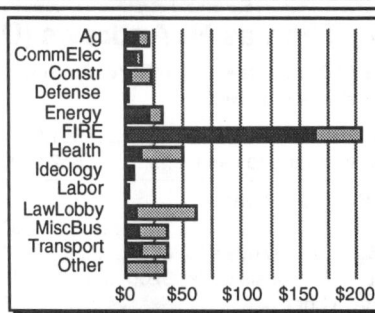

7. Jimmy Hayes (D)

1992 Committees: PubWorks Science
First elected: 1986

1991-92 Total Rcpts: $507,046
1990 Year-end cash: $42,064

Source of Funds
- PACs 47%
- Lg Individuals ($200+) 16%
- Individuals under $200 .... 7%
- Other 29%

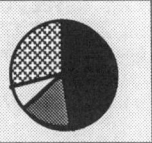

Top Industries & Interest Groups

Lawyers & Lobbyists $39,425
Oil & Gas $37,675
Air Transport $26,300
Transportation Unions $18,800
Real Estate $17,850

Unidentified $12,300

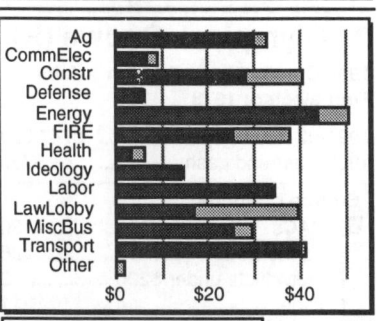

† Does not include individual contributions from 1987-88

Maine

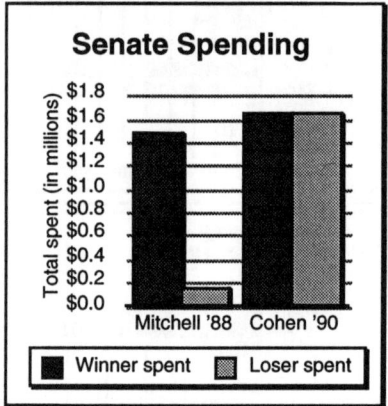
Senate Spending

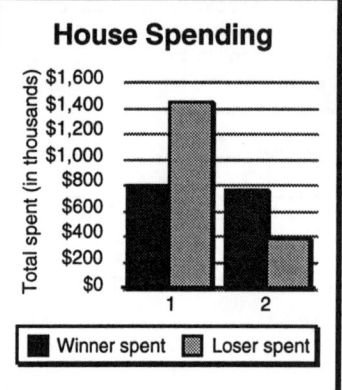
House Spending

1992 Elections at a Glance

Dist	Name	Party	Vote Pct	Race Type
Sen	William S. Cohen (1990)	Rep	61%	Reelected
Sen	George J. Mitchell (1988)	Dem	81%	Reelected
1	Thomas H. Andrews	Dem	65%	Reelected
2	Olympia J. Snowe	Rep	49%	Reelected

Totals in Thousands of Dollars

Sen. William S. Cohen (R)
1992 Committees: ArmServ GovAff
First elected: 1978

1987-92 Total Rcpts: $1,557,640
1990 Year-end cash: $26,547

Source of Funds
- PACs 33%
- Lg Individuals ($200+) 34%
- Individuals under $200 ....15%
- Other 18%

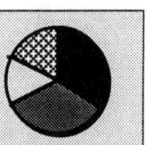

1987-92†
Top Industries & Interest Groups

Pro-Israel $114,750
Securities & Investment $71,900
Lawyers & Lobbyists $64,200
Real Estate $61,350
Health Professionals $53,200

Unidentified $97,291

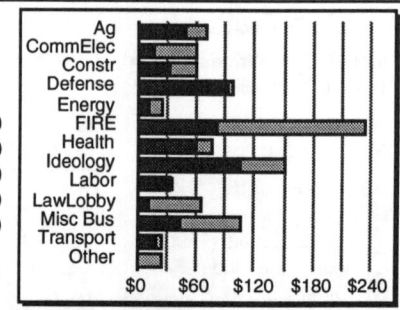

Sen. George J. Mitchell (D)
1992 Committees: Envir Finance VetAffairs
First elected: 1982 (App'ted 1980)

1987-92 Total Rcpts: $1,966,727
1990 Year-end cash: $477,648

Source of Funds
- PACs 37%
- Lg Individuals ($200+) 30%
- Individuals under $200 ....19%
- Other 13%

1987-92†
Top Industries & Interest Groups

Insurance $90,124
Pro-Israel $58,500
Health Professionals $52,509
Transportation Unions $41,000
Public Sector Unions $36,300

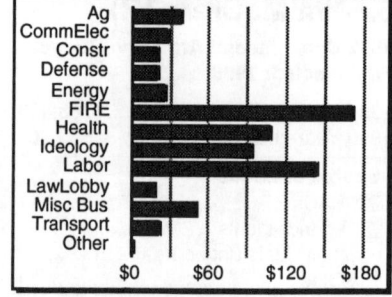

1. Thomas H. Andrews (D)
1992 Committees: ArmServ SmBus
First elected: 1990

1991-92 Total Rcpts: $861,034
1990 Year-end cash: $52,269

Source of Funds
- PACs 43%
- Lg Individuals ($200+) 26%
- Individuals under $200 ....24%
- Other 7%

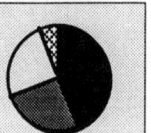

Top Industries & Interest Groups

Industrial Unions $58,800
Lawyers & Lobbyists $54,500
Public Sector Unions $52,350
Transportation Unions $47,000
Misc Issues $40,860

Unidentified $50,705

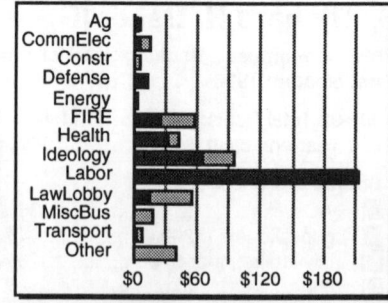

2. Olympia J. Snowe (R)
1992 Committees: Foreign Affairs
First elected: 1978

1991-92 Total Rcpts: $747,300
1990 Year-end cash: $799

Source of Funds
- PACs 30%
- Lg Individuals ($200+) 26%
- Individuals under $200 ....33%
- Other 11%

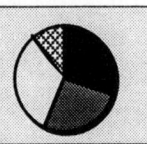

Top Industries & Interest Groups

Lawyers & Lobbyists $31,950
Real Estate $29,000
Health Professionals $28,200
Womens Issues $27,172
Forestry & Forest Products $24,873

Unidentified $33,975

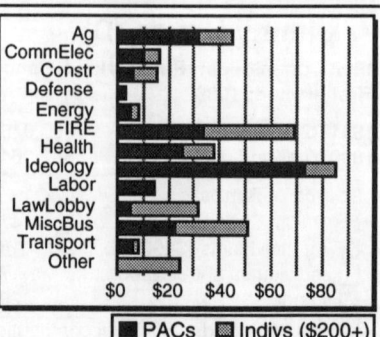

Key to committee & category abbreviations is on page 173

■ PACs ■ Indivs ($200+)

Maryland

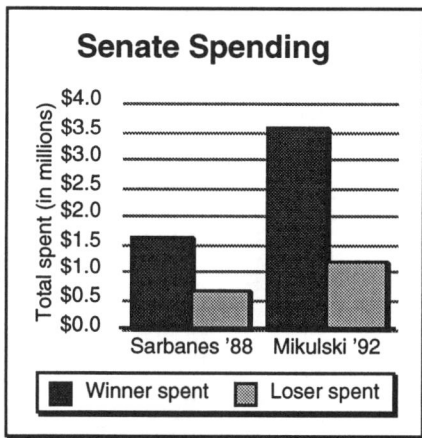

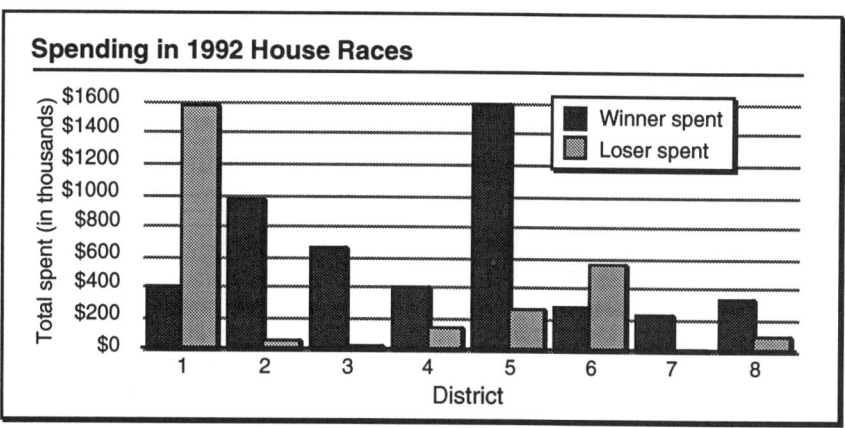

1992 Elections at a Glance

Dist	Name	Party	Vote Pct	Race Type
Sen	Barbara A. Mikulski (1992)	Dem	71%	Reelected
Sen	Paul S. Sarbanes (1988)	Dem	62%	Reelected
1	Wayne T. Gilchrest	Rep	52%	Reelected
2	Helen Delich Bentley	Rep	65%	Reelected
3	Benjamin L. Cardin	Dem	74%	Reelected
4	Albert R. Wynn	Dem	75%	Open Seat
5	Steny H. Hoyer	Dem	53%	Reelected
6	Roscoe G. Bartlett	Rep	54%	Open Seat
7	Kweisi Mfume	Dem	85%	Reelected
8	Constance A. Morella	Rep	72%	Reelected

Totals in Thousands of Dollars

Sen. Barbara A. Mikulski (D)

1992 Committees: Approp Labor SmBus
First elected: 1986

1987-92 Total Rcpts: $3,789,523
1990 Year-end cash: $269,145

Source of Funds
- PACs 28%
- Lg Individuals ($200+) 27%
- Individuals under $200 .... 37%
- Other 8%

1987-92†
Top Industries & Interest Groups

Lawyers & Lobbyists $180,150
Pro-Israel $118,950
Health Professionals $115,735
Defense Aerospace $95,237
Public Sector Unions $93,087

Unidentified $241,281

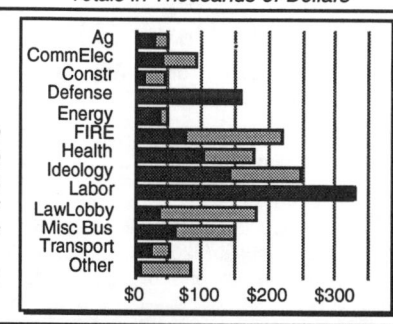

Sen. Paul S. Sarbanes (D)

1992 Committees: Banking ForRel
First elected: 1976

1987-92 Total Rcpts: $1,547,244
1990 Year-end cash: $12,862

Source of Funds
- PACs 38%
- Lg Individuals ($200+) 33%
- Individuals under $200 .... 21%
- Other 7%

1987-92†
Top Industries & Interest Groups

Transportation Unions $84,000
Industrial Unions $81,225
Public Sector Unions $54,950
Building Trade Unions $45,200
Pro-Israel $37,000

Unidentified $12,600

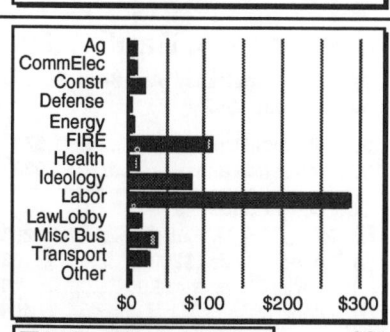

† Does not include individual contributions from 1987-88

1. Wayne T. Gilchrest (R)

1992 Committees: MerchMarine Science
First elected: 1990

1991-92 Total Rcpts: $394,794
1990 Year-end cash: $2,582

Source of Funds
- PACs.................................22%
- Lg Individuals ($200+)................22%
- Individuals under $200................36%
- Other.................................20%

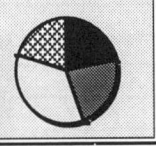

Top Industries & Interest Groups

Retired $26,934
General Contractors $10,250
Textiles $10,000
Automotive $8,250
Air Transport $7,250

Unidentified $20,040

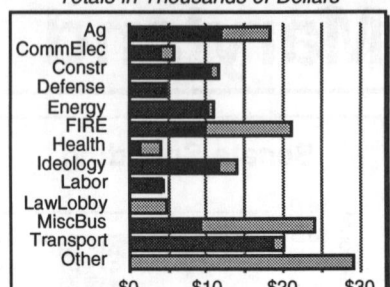

Totals in Thousands of Dollars

2. Helen Delich Bentley (R)

1992 Committees: Budget MerchMarine PubWorks
First elected: 1984

1991-92 Total Rcpts: $959,100
1990 Year-end cash: $130,463

Source of Funds
- PACs.................................25%
- Lg Individuals ($200+)................44%
- Individuals under $200................29%
- Other..................................2%

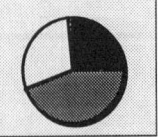

Top Industries & Interest Groups

Sea Transport $55,230
Lawyers & Lobbyists $51,270
Transportation Unions $33,400
Retired $26,705
Real Estate $24,570

Unidentified $111,495

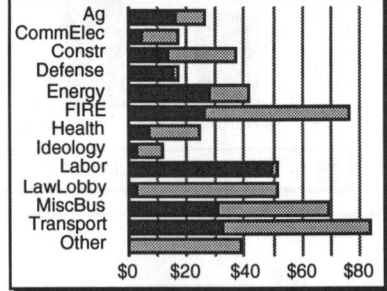

3. Benjamin L. Cardin (D)

1992 Committees: Ways & Means
First elected: 1986

1991-92 Total Rcpts: $591,234
1990 Year-end cash: $195,084

Source of Funds
- PACs.................................48%
- Lg Individuals ($200+)................29%
- Individuals under $200.................7%
- Other.................................16%

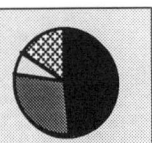

Top Industries & Interest Groups

Health Professionals $50,400
Insurance $42,200
Lawyers & Lobbyists $36,472
Securities & Investment $28,072
Pharmaceuticals/Health Prod $20,750

Unidentified $31,978

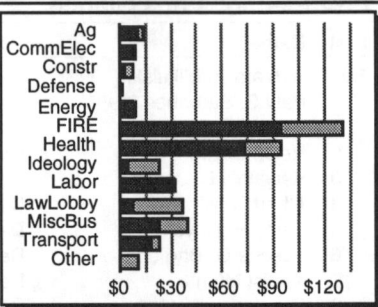

4. Albert R. Wynn (D)

1993-94 Committees: Banking ForAff Post Office
First elected: 1992

1991-92 Total Rcpts: $565,665
1990 Year-end cash: $185,179

Source of Funds
- PACs.................................41%
- Lg Individuals ($200+)................21%
- Individuals under $200................10%
- Other.................................28%

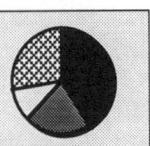

Top Industries & Interest Groups

Public Sector Unions $39,500
Lawyers & Lobbyists $35,750
Industrial Unions $34,500
Health Professionals $26,600
Building Trade Unions $26,250

Unidentified $60,336

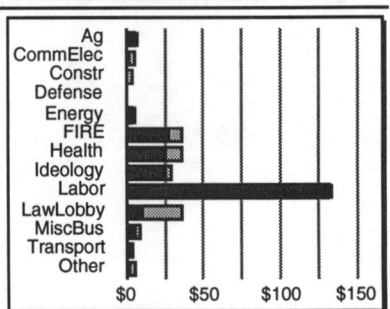

5. Steny H. Hoyer (D)

1992 Committees: Admin Approp
First elected: 1981

1991-92 Total Rcpts: $1,304,867
1990 Year-end cash: $41,000

Source of Funds
- PACs.................................53%
- Lg Individuals ($200+)................29%
- Individuals under $200................12%
- Other..................................7%

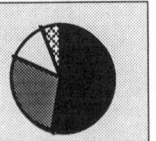

Top Industries & Interest Groups

Lawyers & Lobbyists $140,217
Public Sector Unions $90,000
Health Professionals $76,249
Transportation Unions $56,010
Pro-Israel $45,575

Unidentified $65,925

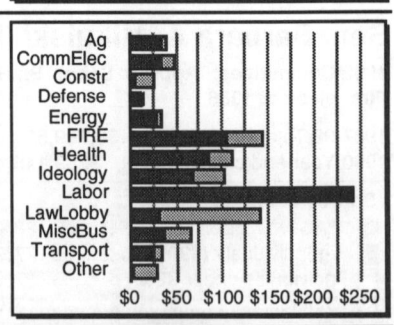

6. Roscoe G. Bartlett (R)

1993-94 Committees: ArmServ Science
First elected: 1992

1991-92 Total Rcpts: $271,371
1990 Year-end cash: $3,933

Source of Funds
- PACs.................................28%
- Lg Individuals ($200+)................15%
- Individuals under $200................17%
- Other.................................40%

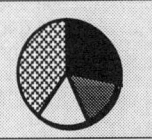

Top Industries & Interest Groups

Electric Utilities $10,450
Automotive $8,300
Retail Sales $7,690
Oil & Gas $6,760
Misc Energy $6,000

Unidentified $10,530

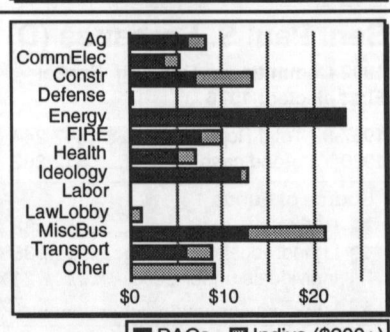

Key to committee & category abbreviations is on page 173

■ PACs   ▨ Indivs ($200+)

7. Kweisi Mfume (D)

1992 Committees: Banking SmBus
First elected: 1986

1991-92 Total Rcpts: $255,269
1990 Year-end cash: $123,136

Source of Funds
- PACs 50%
- Lg Individuals ($200+) 24%
- Individuals under $200 .... 20%
- Other 7%

Top Industries & Interest Groups

Industrial Unions $18,650
Commercial Banks $17,190
Public Sector Unions $14,000
Transportation Unions $13,000
Lawyers & Lobbyists $11,220

Unidentified $12,594

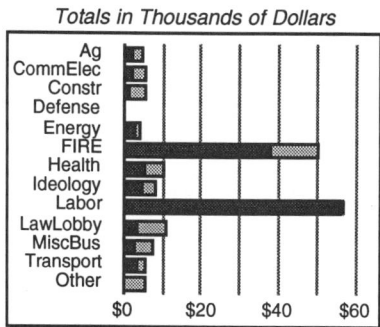

8. Constance A. Morella (R)

1992 Committees: Post Office Science
First elected: 1986

1991-92 Total Rcpts: $430,301
1990 Year-end cash: $303,167

Source of Funds
- PACs 43%
- Lg Individuals ($200+) 24%
- Individuals under $200 .... 29%
- Other 4%

Top Industries & Interest Groups

Public Sector Unions $35,400
Lawyers & Lobbyists $25,970
Health Professionals $25,600
Real Estate $12,550
Insurance $11,150

Unidentified $19,435

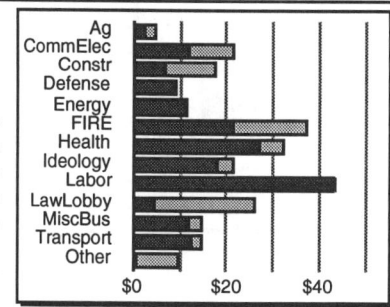

■ PACs   ▥ Indivs ($200+)

Massachusetts

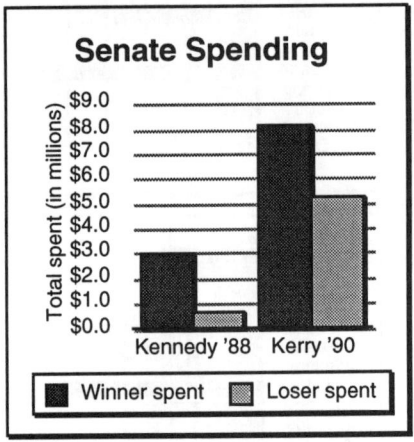

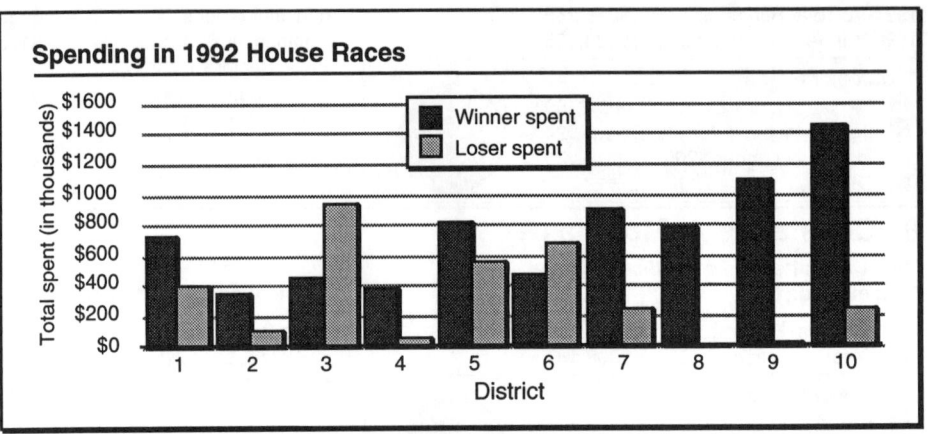

1992 Elections at a Glance

Dist	Name	Party	Vote Pct	Race Type
Sen	Edward M. Kennedy (1988)	Dem	65%	Reelected
Sen	John Kerry (1990)	Dem	57%	Reelected
1	John W. Olver	Dem	52%	Reelected
2	Richard E. Neal	Dem	53%	Reelected
3	Peter Blute	Rep	50%	Beat Incumb
4	Barney Frank	Dem	68%	Reelected
5	Martin T. Meehan	Dem	52%	Open Seat
6	Peter Torkildsen	Rep	55%	Beat Incumb
7	Edward J. Markey	Dem	62%	Reelected
8	Joseph P. Kennedy II	Dem	83%	Reelected
9	Joe Moakley	Dem	69%	Reelected
10	Gerry E. Studds	Dem	61%	Reelected

Totals in Thousands of Dollars

Sen. Edward M. Kennedy (D)

1992 Committees: ArmServ Judiciary Labor
First elected: 1962

1987-92 Total Rcpts: $4,270,784
1990 Year-end cash: $748,063

Source of Funds
- PACs..8%
- Lg Individuals ($200+) 63%
- Individuals under $200 ....23%
- Other..6%

1987-92†
Top Industries & Interest Groups

Lawyers & Lobbyists $177,809
Real Estate $73,889
Securities & Investment $47,133
Industrial Unions $40,500
Health Professionals $40,000
Hospitals/Nursing Homes $40,000

Unidentified $120,640

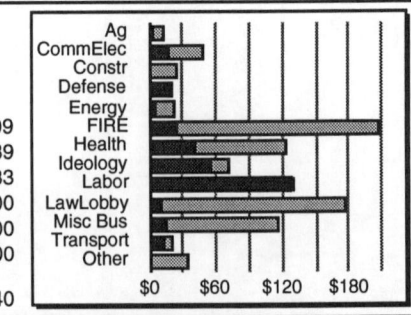

Sen. John Kerry (D)

1992 Committees: Banking Commerce ForRel SmBus
First elected: 1984

1987-92 Total Rcpts: $7,573,317
1990 Year-end cash: $119,651

Source of Funds
- PACs..0%
- Lg Individuals ($200+) 55%
- Individuals under $200 ....36%
- Other..10%

1987-92†
Top Industries & Interest Groups

Lawyers & Lobbyists $670,205
Real Estate $335,497
Media/Entertainment $256,125
Securities & Investment $209,092
Pro-Israel $121,045

Unidentified $959,841

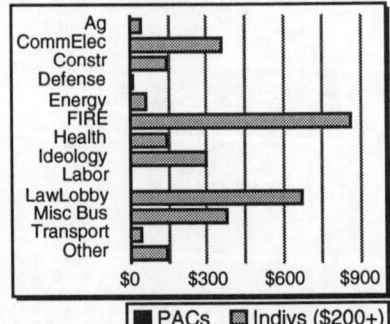

Key to committee & category abbreviations is on page 173

1. John W. Olver (D)

1992 Committees: Educ/Labor Science
First elected: 1991

1991-92 Total Rcpts: $1,416,201
1990 Year-end cash: $3,502

Source of Funds
- PACs 40%
- Lg Individuals ($200+) 24%
- Individuals under $200 .... 22%
- Other 15%

Top Industries & Interest Groups

Public Sector Unions $96,350
Building Trade Unions $86,000
Industrial Unions $74,250
Lawyers & Lobbyists $68,095
Transportation Unions $49,700

Unidentified $55,137

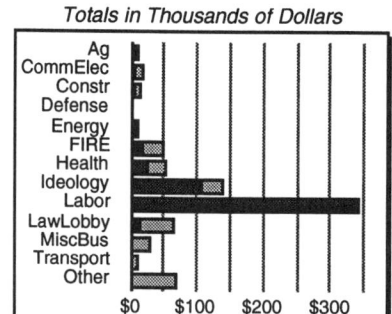

2. Richard E. Neal (D)

1992 Committees: Banking SmBus
First elected: 1988

1991-92 Total Rcpts: $384,741
1990 Year-end cash: $41,868

Source of Funds
- PACs 54%
- Lg Individuals ($200+) 20%
- Individuals under $200 .... 24%
- Other 1%

Top Industries & Interest Groups

Insurance $50,418
Lawyers & Lobbyists $23,050
Building Trade Unions $19,000
Industrial Unions $18,900
Public Sector Unions $14,900

Unidentified $27,450

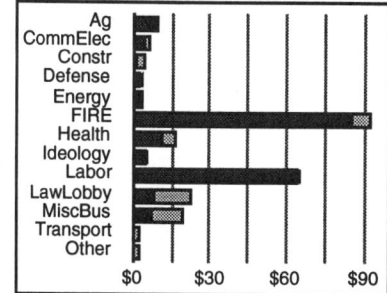

3. Peter Blute (R)

1993-94 Committees: PubWorks Science
First elected: 1992

1991-92 Total Rcpts: $446,908
1990 Year-end cash: $4,753

Source of Funds
- PACs 9%
- Lg Individuals ($200+) 37%
- Individuals under $200 .... 40%
- Other 14%

Top Industries & Interest Groups

Health Professionals $24,685
Lawyers & Lobbyists $13,700
Retired $10,450
Insurance $8,850
Securities & Investment $7,250

Unidentified $65,275

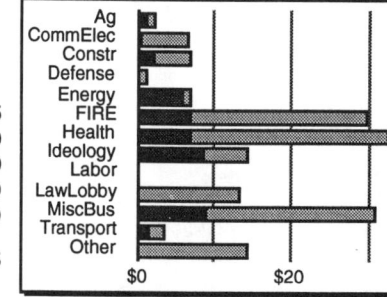

4. Barney Frank (D)

1992 Committees: Banking Budget Judiciary
First elected: 1980

1991-92 Total Rcpts: $498,997
1990 Year-end cash: $175,056

Source of Funds
- PACs 37%
- Lg Individuals ($200+) 24%
- Individuals under $200 .... 37%
- Other 2%

Top Industries & Interest Groups

Lawyers & Lobbyists $40,175
Commercial Banks $35,200
Real Estate $27,750
Public Sector Unions $22,050
Insurance $14,700

Unidentified $14,675

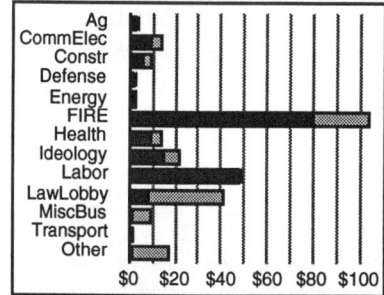

5. Martin T. Meehan (D)

1993-94 Committees: ArmServ SmBus
First elected: 1992

1991-92 Total Rcpts: $812,181
1990 Year-end cash: $721

Source of Funds
- PACs 0%
- Lg Individuals ($200+) 53%
- Individuals under $200 .... 22%
- Other 26%

Top Industries & Interest Groups

Lawyers & Lobbyists $99,249
Civil Servants/Public Officials $27,925
Real Estate $26,785
Retired $17,924
Business Services $13,500

Unidentified $129,276

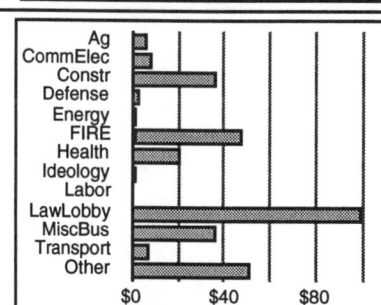

6. Peter Torkildsen (R)

1993-94 Committees: ArmServ SmBus
First elected: 1992

1991-92 Total Rcpts: $453,507
1990 Year-end cash: $2,072

Source of Funds
- PACs 0%
- Lg Individuals ($200+) 50%
- Individuals under $200 .... 37%
- Other 12%

Top Industries & Interest Groups

Real Estate $24,032
Retired $22,349
Securities & Investment $18,700
Business Services $15,040
Lawyers & Lobbyists $12,829

Unidentified $66,453

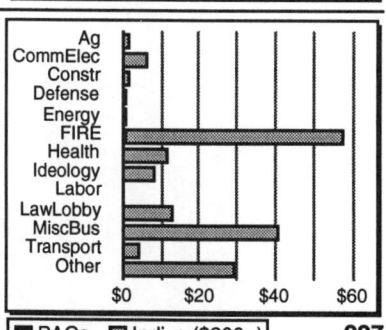

† Does not include individual contributions from 1987-88

7. Edward J. Markey (D)

1992 Committees: Energy/Commerce Interior
First elected: 1976

1991-92 Total Rcpts: $444,628
1990 Year-end cash: $131,110

Source of Funds
- PACs 0%
- Lg Individuals ($200+) 75%
- Individuals under $200 .... 13%
- Other 11%

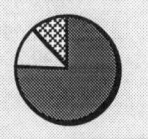

Top Industries & Interest Groups

Lawyers & Lobbyists $81,750
Securities & Investment $42,250
Media/Entertainment $34,200
Telephone Utilities $18,900
Business Services $14,000

Unidentified $45,450

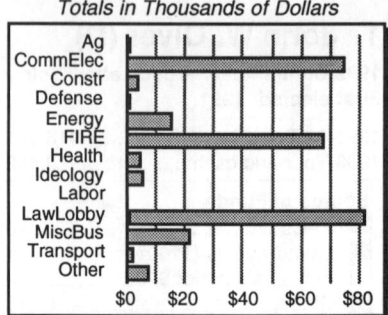

Totals in Thousands of Dollars

8. Joseph P. Kennedy II (D)

1992 Committees: Banking VetAffairs
First elected: 1986

1991-92 Total Rcpts: $769,635
1990 Year-end cash: $228,528

Source of Funds
- PACs 19%
- Lg Individuals ($200+) 59%
- Individuals under $200 .... 17%
- Other 5%

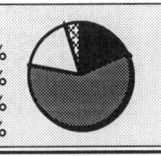

Top Industries & Interest Groups

Lawyers & Lobbyists $82,521
Real Estate $50,389
Securities & Investment $32,150
Business Services $21,829
Building Trade Unions $20,750

Unidentified $88,353

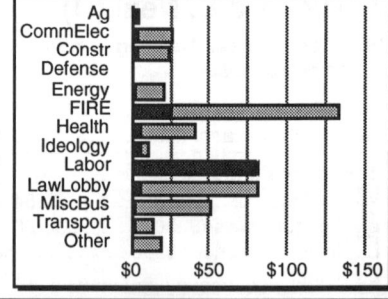

9. Joe Moakley (D)

1992 Committees: Rules
First elected: 1972

1991-92 Total Rcpts: $869,410
1990 Year-end cash: $287,002

Source of Funds
- PACs 50%
- Lg Individuals ($200+) 26%
- Individuals under $200 .... 18%
- Other 6%

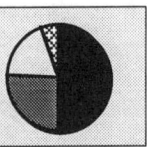

Top Industries & Interest Groups

Lawyers & Lobbyists $72,175
Transportation Unions $48,600
Insurance $48,150
Commercial Banks $41,250
Securities & Investment $34,100

Unidentified $50,450

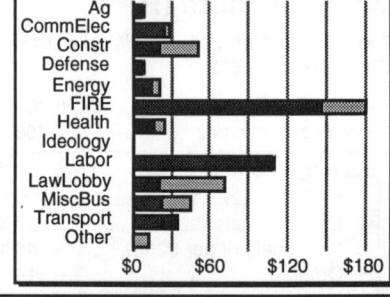

10. Gerry E. Studds (D)

1992 Committees: Energy/Comm ForAff MerchMarine
First elected: 1972

1991-92 Total Rcpts: $1,438,264
1990 Year-end cash: $19,799

Source of Funds
- PACs 28%
- Lg Individuals ($200+) 23%
- Individuals under $200 .... 45%
- Other 3%

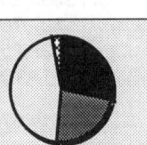

Top Industries & Interest Groups

Lawyers & Lobbyists $61,150
Sea Transport $51,900
Public Sector Unions $49,600
Transportation Unions $48,300
Human Rights $43,179

Unidentified $82,615

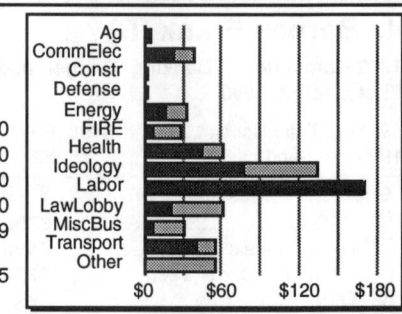

■ PACs ▨ Indivs ($200+)

Key to committee & category abbreviations is on page 173

Michigan

Spending in 1992 House Races

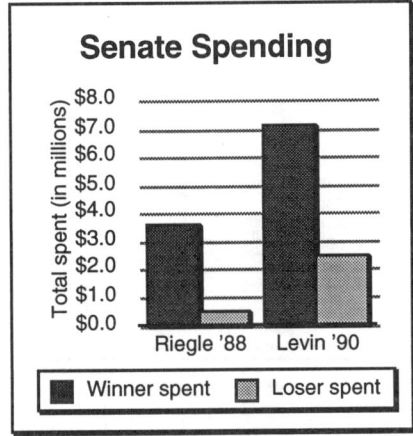

Senate Spending

1992 Elections at a Glance

Dist	Name	Party	Vote Pct	Race Type
Sen	Carl Levin (1990)	Dem	58%	Reelected
Sen	Donald W. Riegle Jr. (1988)	Dem	60%	Reelected
1	Bart Stupak	Dem	54%	Open Seat
2	Peter Hoekstra	Rep	63%	Open Seat
3	Paul B. Henry	Rep	61%	Reelected
4	Dave Camp	Rep	62%	Reelected
5	James A. Barcia	Dem	60%	Open Seat
6	Fred Upton	Rep	62%	Reelected
7	Nick Smith	Rep	88%	Open Seat
8	Bob Carr	Dem	48%	Reelected
9	Dale E. Kildee	Dem	54%	Reelected
10	David E. Bonior	Dem	53%	Reelected
11	Joseph K. Knollenberg	Rep	58%	Open Seat
12	Sander Levin	Dem	53%	Reelected
13	William D. Ford	Dem	52%	Reelected
14	John Conyers Jr.	Dem	82%	Reelected
15	Barbara-Rose Collins	Dem	80%	Reelected
16	John D. Dingell	Dem	65%	Reelected

Totals in Thousands of Dollars

Sen. Carl Levin (D)

1992 Committees: ArmServ GovAff SmBus
First elected: 1978

1987-92 Total Rcpts: $7,232,932
1990 Year-end cash: $92,319

Source of Funds
- PACs 18%
- Lg Individuals ($200+) 39%
- Individuals under $200 ....30%
- Other 13%

1987-92†
Top Industries & Interest Groups

Pro-Israel $572,648
Lawyers & Lobbyists $507,808
Real Estate $287,000
Democratic/Liberal $127,580
Health Professionals $116,407

Unidentified $603,488

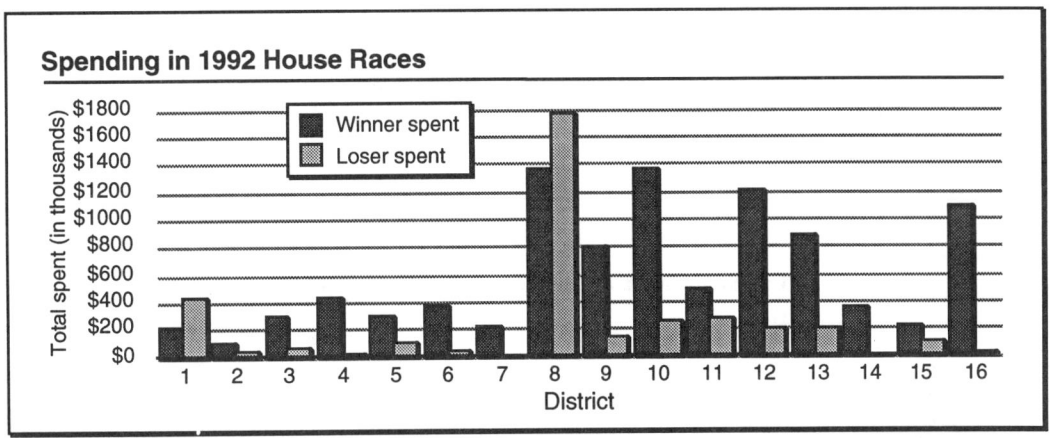

Sen. Donald W. Riegle Jr. (D)

1992 Committees: Banking Budget Finance
First elected: 1976

1987-92 Total Rcpts: $3,776,831
1990 Year-end cash: $544,242

Source of Funds
- PACs 37%
- Lg Individuals ($200+) 34%
- Individuals under $200 ....14%
- Other 16%

1987-92†
Top Industries & Interest Groups

Insurance $117,950
Commercial Banks $103,825
Securities & Investment $88,949
Industrial Unions $84,200
Lawyers & Lobbyists $75,292

Unidentified $10,575

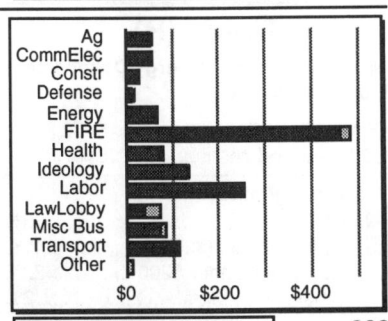

† Does not include individual contributions from 1987-88

1. Bart Stupak (D)

1993-94 Committees: ArmServ MerchMarine
First elected: 1992

1991-92 Total Rcpts: $216,699
1990 Year-end cash: $125

Source of Funds
- PACs 46%
- Lg Individuals ($200+) 17%
- Individuals under $200 ....18%
- Other 19%

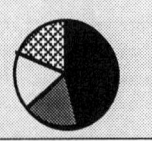

Top Industries & Interest Groups

Industrial Unions $23,500
Building Trade Unions $18,450
Lawyers & Lobbyists $16,000
Transportation Unions $9,500
Misc Unions $9,500

Unidentified $8,900

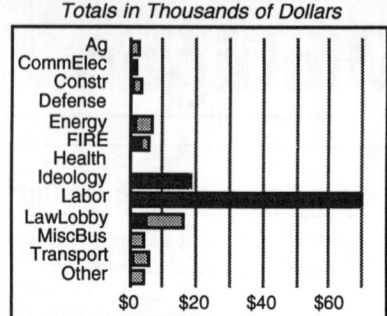

2. Peter Hoekstra (R)

1993-94 Committees: Educ/Labor PubWorks
First elected: 1992

1991-92 Total Rcpts: $101,362
1990 Year-end cash: $4,582

Source of Funds
- PACs 0%
- Lg Individuals ($200+) 25%
- Individuals under $200 ....36%
- Other 39%

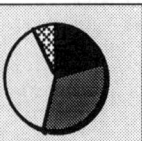

Top Industries & Interest Groups

Automotive $3,000
Retired $2,900
Health Professionals $1,950
Insurance $1,700
Retail Sales $1,650

Unidentified $10,380

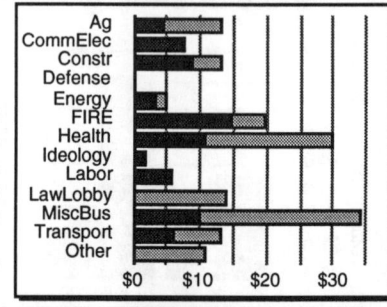

3. Paul B. Henry (R)

1992 Committees: Educ/Labor Science
First elected: 1984

1991-92 Total Rcpts: $349,444
1990 Year-end cash: $342,492

Source of Funds
- PACs 21%
- Lg Individuals ($200+) 33%
- Individuals under $200 ....39%
- Other 8%

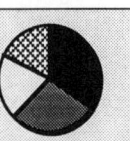

Top Industries & Interest Groups

Health Professionals $23,950
Misc Manufacturing & Distrib $15,950
Lawyers & Lobbyists $14,050
Retired $9,525
Automotive $9,250

Unidentified $20,100

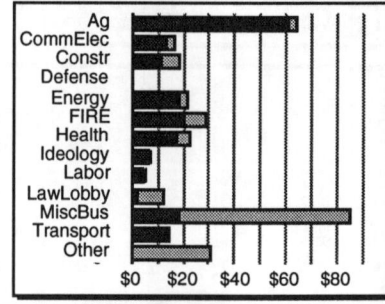

4. Dave Camp (R)

1992 Committees: Agric SmBus
First elected: 1990

1991-92 Total Rcpts: $586,892
1990 Year-end cash: $218

Source of Funds
- PACs 34%
- Lg Individuals ($200+) 28%
- Individuals under $200 ....20%
- Other 17%

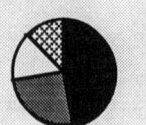

Top Industries & Interest Groups

Chemicals $64,819
Retired $25,850
Health Professionals $18,400
Crop Production/Processing $15,105
Lawyers & Lobbyists $12,795

Unidentified $27,526

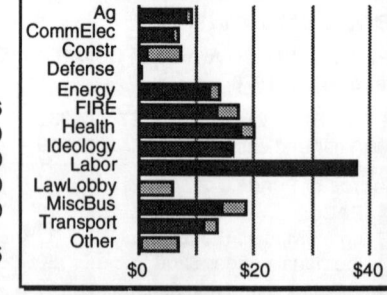

5. James A. Barcia (D)

1993-94 Committees: PubWorks Science
First elected: 1992

1991-92 Total Rcpts: $283,843
1990 Year-end cash: $689

Source of Funds
- PACs 47%
- Lg Individuals ($200+) 26%
- Individuals under $200 ....15%
- Other 13%

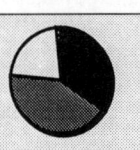

Top Industries & Interest Groups

Health Professionals $17,816
Building Trade Unions $12,300
Oil & Gas $9,500
Industrial Unions $9,000
Real Estate $7,800

Unidentified $32,635

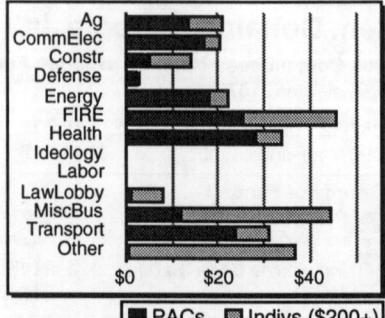

6. Fred Upton (R)

1992 Committees: Energy/Commerce
First elected: 1986

1991-92 Total Rcpts: $432,851
1990 Year-end cash: $107,399

Source of Funds
- PACs 35%
- Lg Individuals ($200+) 41%
- Individuals under $200 ....22%
- Other 2%

Top Industries & Interest Groups

Retired $32,370
Misc Manufacturing & Distrib $28,500
Health Professionals $23,000
Automotive $15,500
Insurance $12,320

Unidentified $46,961

7. Nick Smith (R)

1993-94 Committees: Budget Science
First elected: 1992

1991-92 Total Rcpts: $228,408
1990 Year-end cash: $11,862

Source of Funds
- PACs 0%
- Lg Individuals ($200+) 34%
- Individuals under $200 .... 22%
- Other 44%

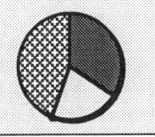

Top Industries & Interest Groups

Retired $9,650
Health Professionals $8,700
Automotive $5,400
Accountants $4,500
Insurance $2,550

Unidentified $28,000

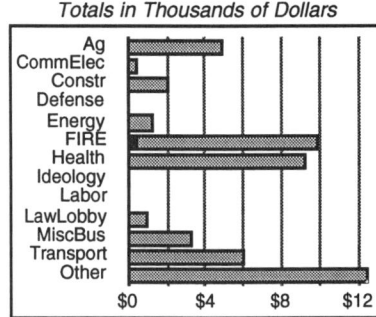

8. Bob Carr (D)

1992 Committees: Appropriations
First elected: 1974

1991-92 Total Rcpts: $1,107,973
1990 Year-end cash: $9,399

Source of Funds
- PACs 50%
- Lg Individuals ($200+) 35%
- Individuals under $200 .... 8%
- Other 7%

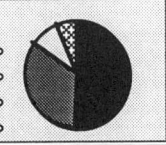

Top Industries & Interest Groups

Lawyers & Lobbyists $119,403
Air Transport $72,940
Transportation Unions $60,750
Real Estate $29,250
Defense Aerospace $28,643

Unidentified $106,109

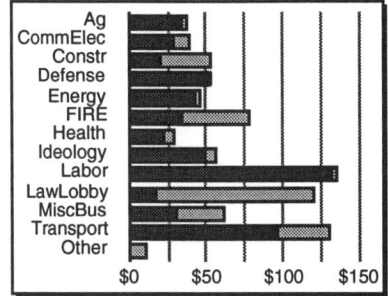

9. Dale E. Kildee (D)

1992 Committees: Admin Budget Educ/Labor
First elected: 1976

1991-92 Total Rcpts: $762,558
1990 Year-end cash: $5,733

Source of Funds
- PACs 59%
- Lg Individuals ($200+) 13%
- Individuals under $200 .... 18%
- Other 11%

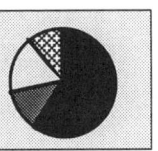

Top Industries & Interest Groups

Public Sector Unions $71,075
Industrial Unions $55,800
Building Trade Unions $51,240
Transportation Unions $40,170
Lawyers & Lobbyists $39,366

Unidentified $30,997

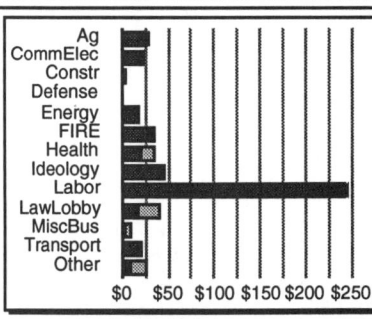

10. David E. Bonior (D)

1992 Committees: Rules
First elected: 1976

1991-92 Total Rcpts: $1,295,553
1990 Year-end cash: $40,391

Source of Funds
- PACs 70%
- Lg Individuals ($200+) 13%
- Individuals under $200 .... 8%
- Other 8%

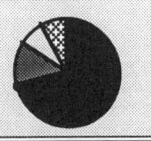

Top Industries & Interest Groups

Transportation Unions $73,400
Public Sector Unions $70,160
Industrial Unions $67,978
Insurance $66,275
Lawyers & Lobbyists $55,540

Unidentified $25,075

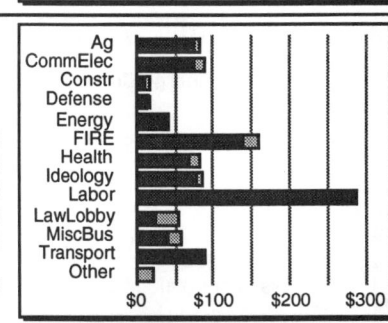

11. Joseph K. Knollenberg (R)

1993-94 Committees: Banking SmBus
First elected: 1992

1991-92 Total Rcpts: $476,906
1990 Year-end cash: $4,058

Source of Funds
- PACs 23%
- Lg Individuals ($200+) 36%
- Individuals under $200 .... 27%
- Other 13%

Top Industries & Interest Groups

Insurance $35,138
Health Professionals $29,400
Automotive $23,872
Lawyers & Lobbyists $17,037
Misc Manufacturing & Distrib $13,000

Unidentified $55,243

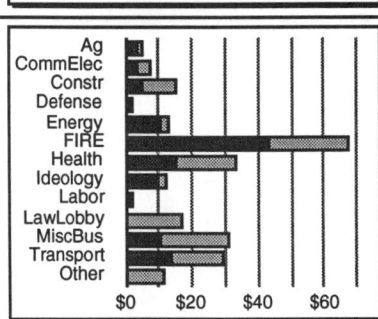

12. Sander Levin (D)

1992 Committees: DC Ways & Means
First elected: 1982

1991-92 Total Rcpts: $1,028,481
1990 Year-end cash: $98,288

Source of Funds
- PACs 47%
- Lg Individuals ($200+) 27%
- Individuals under $200 .... 15%
- Other 11%

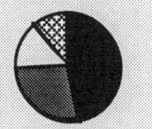

Top Industries & Interest Groups

Lawyers & Lobbyists $93,295
Health Professionals $56,747
Pro-Israel $55,150
Public Sector Unions $49,450
Insurance $42,999

Unidentified $24,850

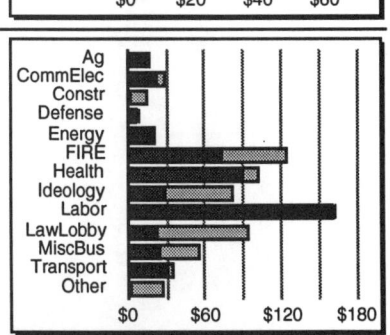

13. William D. Ford (D)

1992 Committees: Education & Labor
First elected: 1964

1991-92 Total Rcpts: $681,981
1990 Year-end cash: $6,768

Source of Funds
- PACs 74%
- Lg Individuals ($200+) 11%
- Individuals under $200 .... 7%
- Other 8%

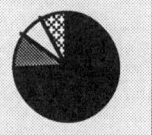

Top Industries & Interest Groups

Public Sector Unions $85,650
Industrial Unions $67,400
Transportation Unions $55,850
Building Trade Unions $48,750
Lawyers & Lobbyists $42,400

Unidentified $15,250

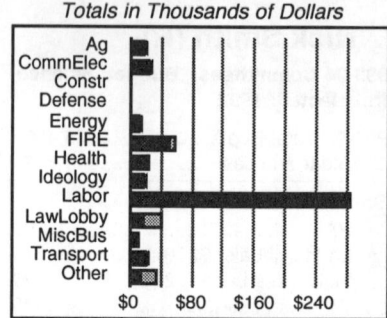

14. John Conyers Jr. (D)

1992 Committees: GovtOps Judiciary SmBus
First elected: 1964

1991-92 Total Rcpts: $380,072
1990 Year-end cash: $35,601

Source of Funds
- PACs 52%
- Lg Individuals ($200+) 15%
- Individuals under $200 .... 13%
- Other 20%

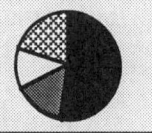

Top Industries & Interest Groups

Lawyers & Lobbyists $40,180
Public Sector Unions $33,775
Transportation Unions $20,625
Computer Equipment & Services $18,750
Industrial Unions $16,550

Unidentified $11,200

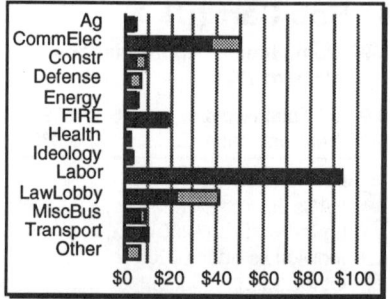

15. Barbara-Rose Collins (D)

1992 Committees: Post Office PubWorks
First elected: 1990

1991-92 Total Rcpts: $222,662
1990 Year-end cash: $55,717

Source of Funds
- PACs 37%
- Lg Individuals ($200+) 24%
- Individuals under $200 .... 6%
- Other 33%

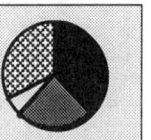

Top Industries & Interest Groups

Transportation Unions $25,600
Public Sector Unions $25,350
Industrial Unions $19,600
Building Trade Unions $11,550
Leadership PACs $7,500

Unidentified $35,650

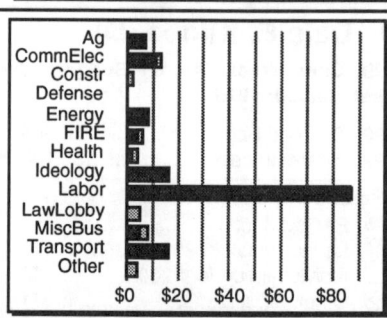

16. John D. Dingell (D)

1992 Committees: Energy/Commerce
First elected: 1955

1991-92 Total Rcpts: $1,112,141
1990 Year-end cash: $523,361

Source of Funds
- PACs 68%
- Lg Individuals ($200+) 21%
- Individuals under $200 .... 4%
- Other 7%

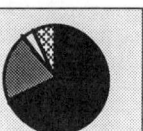

Top Industries & Interest Groups

Lawyers & Lobbyists $98,322
Automotive $75,150
Insurance $60,250
Media/Entertainment $59,050
Securities & Investment $56,350

Unidentified $23,850

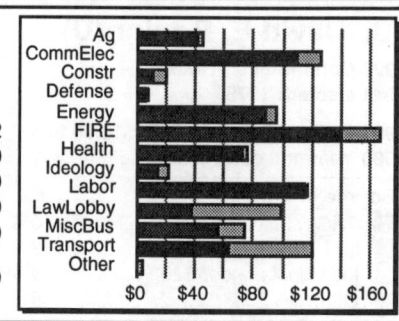

■ PACs ▨ Indivs ($200+)

Key to committee & category abbreviations is on page 173

Minnesota

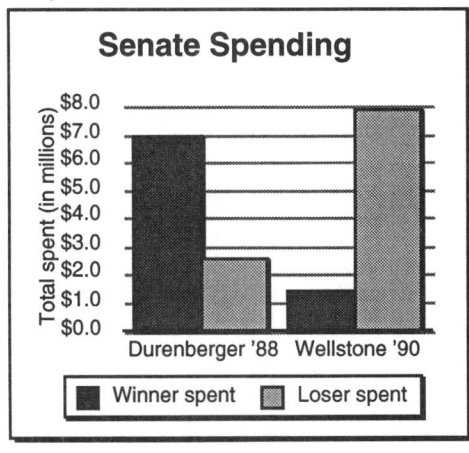

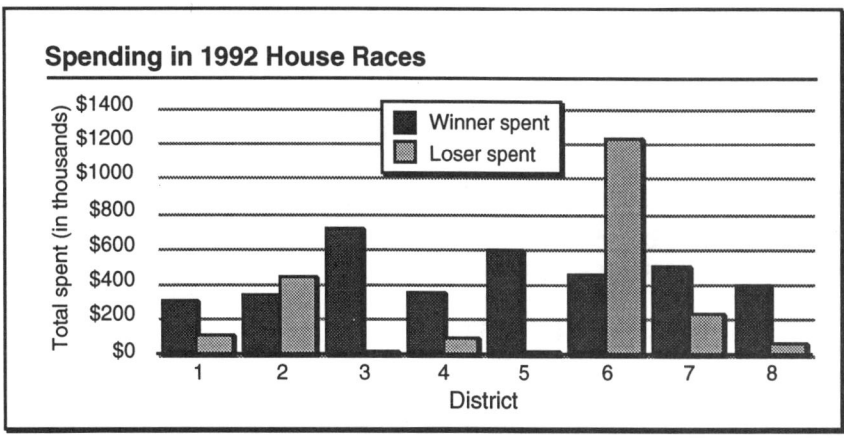

1992 Elections at a Glance

Dist	Name	Party	Vote Pct	Race Type
Sen	Dave Durenberger (1988)	Rep	56%	Reelected
Sen	Paul Wellstone (1990)	Dem	50%	Beat Incumb
1	Timothy J. Penny	Dem	74%	Reelected
2	David Minge	Rep	48%	Open Seat
3	Jim Ramstad	Rep	64%	Reelected
4	Bruce F. Vento	Dem	58%	Reelected
5	Martin Olav Sabo	Dem	63%	Reelected
6	Rod Grams	Rep	44%	Beat Incumb
7	Collin C. Peterson	Dem	51%	Reelected
8	James L. Oberstar	Dem	59%	Reelected

Totals in Thousands of Dollars

Sen. Dave Durenberger (R)

1992 Committees: Envir Finance Labor
First elected: 1978

1987-92 Total Rcpts: $6,388,791
1990 Year-end cash: $27,191

Source of Funds
- PACs......................................26%
- Lg Individuals ($200+) 18%
- Individuals under $200 ....48%
- Other..8%

1987-92†
Top Industries & Interest Groups

Pro-Israel $168,000
Insurance $158,942
Health Professionals $122,896
Pharmaceuticals/Health Prod $97,750
Securities & Investment $81,680

Unidentified $132,005

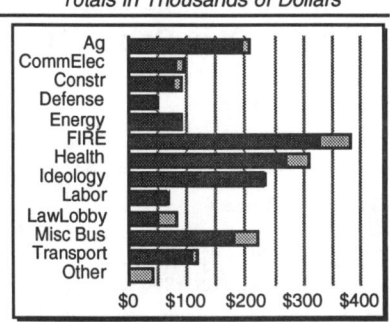

Sen. Paul Wellstone (D)

1992 Committees: Energy Labor SmBus
First elected: 1990

1989-92 Total Rcpts: $2,063,410
1990 Year-end cash: $3,390

Source of Funds
- PACs......................................19%
- Lg Individuals ($200+) 12%
- Individuals under $200 ....59%
- Other......................................10%

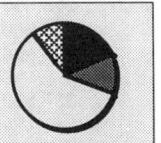

1989-92
Top Industries & Interest Groups

Industrial Unions $98,050
Public Sector Unions $62,036
Transportation Unions $46,750
Lawyers & Lobbyists $41,606
Democratic/Liberal $35,742

Unidentified $111,918

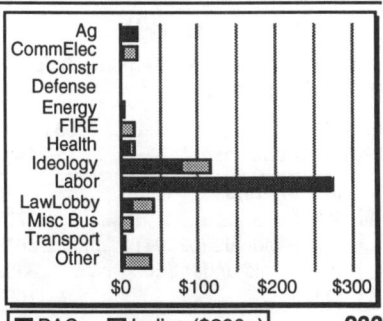

† Does not include individual contributions from 1987-88

1. Timothy J. Penny (D)

1992 Committees: Agric VetAffairs
First elected: 1982

1991-92 Total Rcpts: $244,518
1990 Year-end cash: $207,789

Source of Funds
- PACs 38%
- Lg Individuals ($200+) 5%
- Individuals under $200 .... 43%
- Other 14%

Top Industries & Interest Groups

Health Professionals $11,150
Retail Sales $10,893
Agricultural Services/Products $9,250
Crop Production/Processing $7,100
Dairy $6,500

Unidentified $200

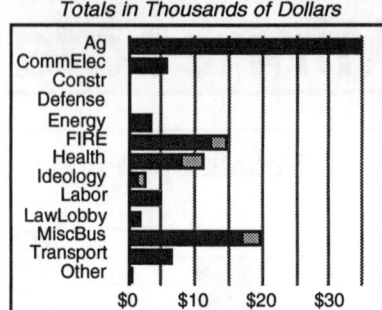

2. David Minge (D)

1993-94 Committees: Agric Science
First elected: 1992

1991-92 Total Rcpts: $331,983
1990 Year-end cash: $7,499

Source of Funds
- PACs 48%
- Lg Individuals ($200+) 17%
- Individuals under $200 .... 25%
- Other 10%

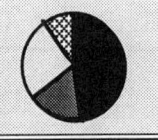

Top Industries & Interest Groups

Public Sector Unions $39,750
Industrial Unions $31,850
Transportation Unions $15,850
Misc Unions $13,100
Lawyers & Lobbyists $11,686

Unidentified $20,040

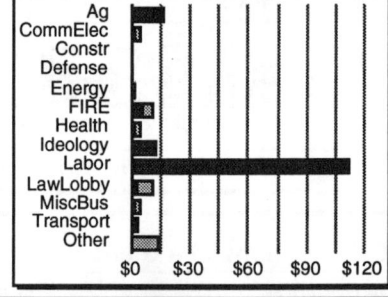

3. Jim Ramstad (R)

1992 Committees: Judiciary SmBus
First elected: 1990

1991-92 Total Rcpts: $1,010,791
1990 Year-end cash: $317,719

Source of Funds
- PACs 25%
- Lg Individuals ($200+) 46%
- Individuals under $200 .... 27%
- Other 2%

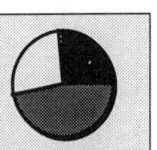

Top Industries & Interest Groups

Misc Manufacturing & Distrib $47,825
Lawyers & Lobbyists $42,900
Retired $42,525
Insurance $37,675
Real Estate $37,100

Unidentified $82,092

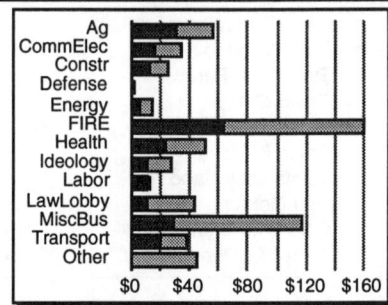

4. Bruce F. Vento (D)

1992 Committees: Banking Interior
First elected: 1976

1991-92 Total Rcpts: $280,123
1990 Year-end cash: $86,382

Source of Funds
- PACs 71%
- Lg Individuals ($200+) 7%
- Individuals under $200 .... 11%
- Other 11%

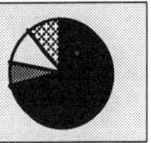

Top Industries & Interest Groups

Securities & Investment $29,950
Public Sector Unions $22,825
Commercial Banks $19,575
Lawyers & Lobbyists $17,388
Transportation Unions $15,150

Unidentified $570

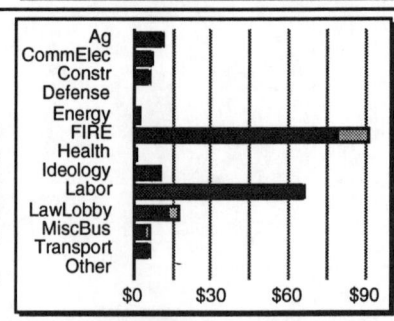

5. Martin Olav Sabo (D)

1992 Committees: Approp Budget
First elected: 1978

1991-92 Total Rcpts: $408,981
1990 Year-end cash: $39,370

Source of Funds
- PACs 61%
- Lg Individuals ($200+) 12%
- Individuals under $200 .... 16%
- Other 12%

Top Industries & Interest Groups

Lawyers & Lobbyists $36,981
Public Sector Unions $31,900
Transportation Unions $28,750
Defense Aerospace $20,000
Defense Electronics $17,750

Unidentified $7,450

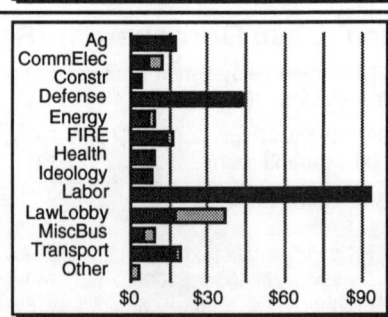

6. Rod Grams (R)

1993-94 Committees: Banking Science
First elected: 1992

1991-92 Total Rcpts: $453,643
1990 Year-end cash: ....$-244

Source of Funds
- PACs 27%
- Lg Individuals ($200+) 26%
- Individuals under $200 .... 33%
- Other 14%

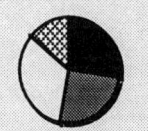

Top Industries & Interest Groups

Oil & Gas $20,200
Retired $16,800
Misc Manufacturing & Distrib $15,850
Chemicals $12,600
Railroads $9,626

Unidentified $37,589

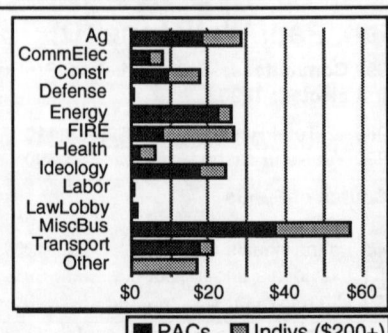

Key to committee & category abbreviations is on page 173

7. Collin C. Peterson (D)

1992 Committees: Agric GovtOps
First elected: 1990

1991-92 Total Rcpts: $497,021
1990 Year-end cash: $2,281

Source of Funds
- PACs 64%
- Lg Individuals ($200+) 4%
- Individuals under $200 ....20%
- Other 12%

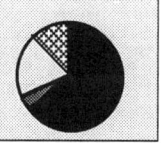

Top Industries & Interest Groups

Public Sector Unions $43,499
Industrial Unions $40,950
Crop Production/Processing $29,450
Transportation Unions $28,350
Building Trade Unions $19,500

Unidentified $6,350

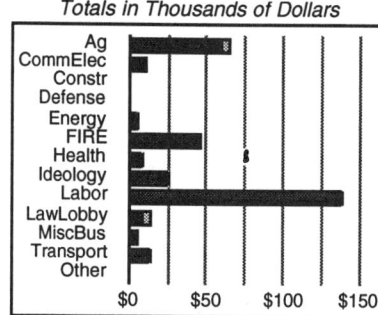

8. James L. Oberstar (D)

1992 Committees: Budget PubWorks
First elected: 1974

1991-92 Total Rcpts: $340,642
1990 Year-end cash: $347,548

Source of Funds
- PACs 57%
- Lg Individuals ($200+) 13%
- Individuals under $200 ....8%
- Other 22%

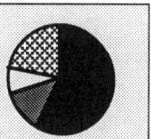

Top Industries & Interest Groups

Air Transport $39,905
Transportation Unions $34,700
Public Sector Unions $19,500
Lawyers & Lobbyists $18,850
Industrial Unions $14,400

Unidentified $11,150

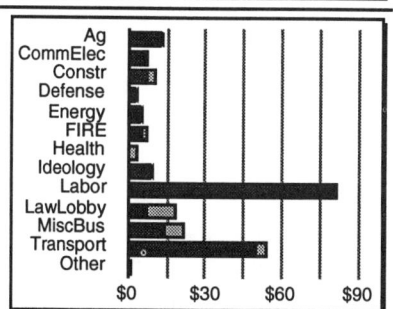

■ PACs ▩ Indivs ($200+)

Totals in Thousands of Dollars

235

Mississippi

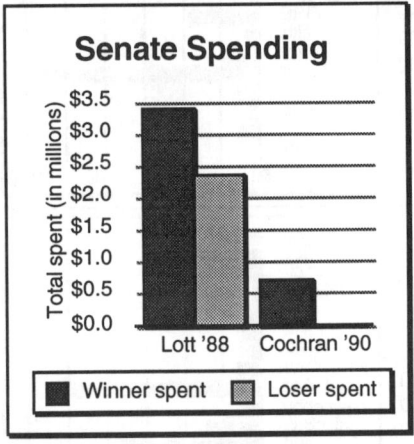

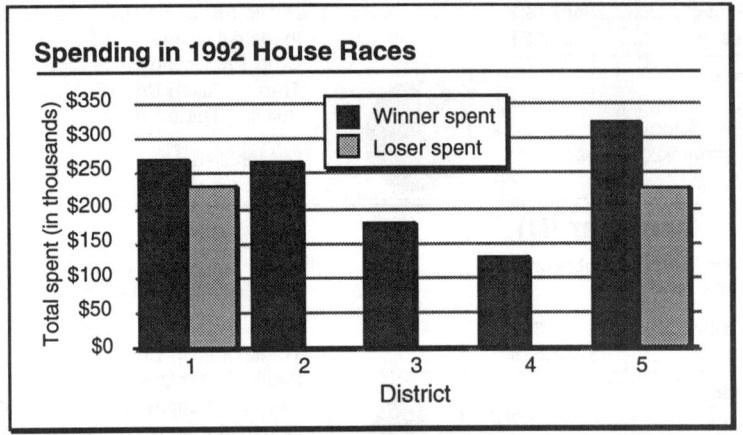

1992 Elections at a Glance

Dist	Name	Party	Vote Pct	Race Type
Sen	Thad Cochran (1990)	Rep	100%	Reelected
Sen	Trent Lott (1988)	Rep	54%	Open Seat
1	Jamie L. Whitten	Dem	60%	Reelected
2	Mike Espy	Dem	76%	Reelected
3	G. V. "Sonny" Montgomery	Dem	81%	Reelected
4	Mike Parker	Dem	67%	Reelected
5	Gene Taylor	Dem	63%	Reelected

Totals in Thousands of Dollars

Sen. Thad Cochran (R)

1992 Committees: Agric Approp Labor
First elected: 1978

1987-92 Total Rcpts: $1,491,775
1990 Year-end cash: $764,610

Source of Funds
- PACs 45%
- Lg Individuals ($200+) 26%
- Individuals under $200 ....10%
- Other 20%

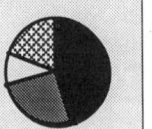

1987-92†
Top Industries & Interest Groups

Crop Production/Processing $136,125
Lawyers & Lobbyists $71,950
Oil & Gas $59,350
Health Professionals $55,850
Insurance $53,232

Unidentified $62,584

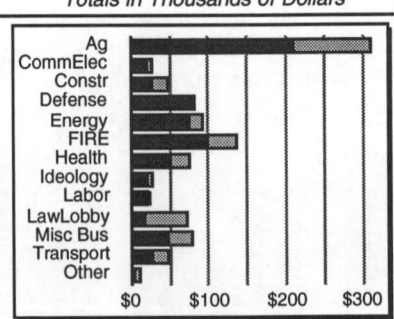

Sen. Trent Lott (R)

1992 Committees: ArmServ Budget Commerce
First elected: 1988

1987-92 Total Rcpts: $4,162,080
1990 Year-end cash: $379,192

Source of Funds
- PACs 29%
- Lg Individuals ($200+) 32%
- Individuals under $200 ....19%
- Other 20%

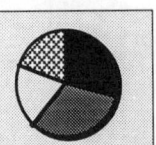

1987-92†
Top Industries & Interest Groups

Oil & Gas $83,250
Insurance $67,500
Food Processing & Sales $62,200
Leadership PACs $52,627
Defense Aerospace $50,000

Unidentified $31,460

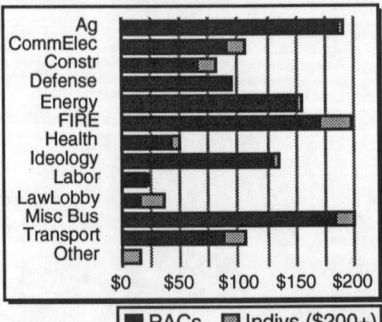

Key to committee & category abbreviations is on page 173

Totals in Thousands of Dollars

1. Jamie L. Whitten (D)
1992 Committees: Appropriations
First elected: 1941

1991-92 Total Rcpts: $82,667
1990 Year-end cash: $251,170

Source of Funds
- PACs 37%
- Lg Individuals ($200+) 1%
- Individuals under $200 .... 7%
- Other 56%

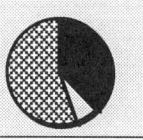

Top Industries & Interest Groups

Lawyers & Lobbyists $5,000
Agricultural Services/Products $4,300
Dairy $3,000
Forestry & Forest Products $2,000
Telephone Utilities $2,000

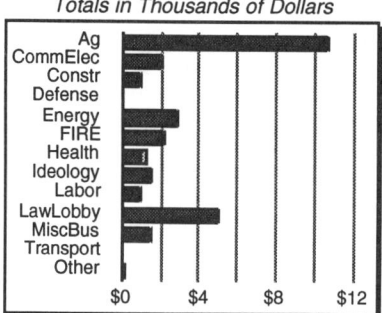

2. Mike Espy (D)
1992 Committees: Agric Budget
First elected: 1986

1991-92 Total Rcpts: $299,560
1990 Year-end cash: $113,887

Source of Funds
- PACs 79%
- Lg Individuals ($200+) 14%
- Individuals under $200 .... 7%
- Other 0%

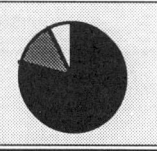

Top Industries & Interest Groups

Public Sector Unions $25,900
Industrial Unions $20,850
Crop Production/Processing $20,675
Telephone Utilities $13,850
Lawyers & Lobbyists $12,140

Unidentified $5,550

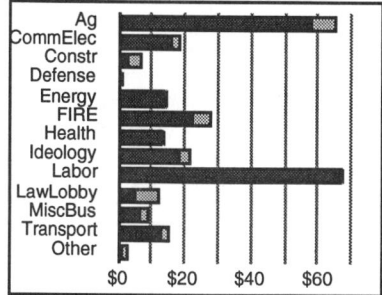

3. G. V. "Sonny" Montgomery (D)
1992 Committees: ArmServ VetAffairs
First elected: 1966

1991-92 Total Rcpts: $172,603
1990 Year-end cash: $170,345

Source of Funds
- PACs 56%
- Lg Individuals ($200+) 25%
- Individuals under $200 .... 10%
- Other 8%

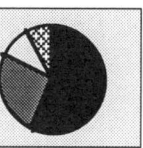

Top Industries & Interest Groups

Health Professionals $12,550
Electric Utilities $10,050
Defense Aerospace $9,750
Oil & Gas $6,950
Retired $6,200

Unidentified $5,900

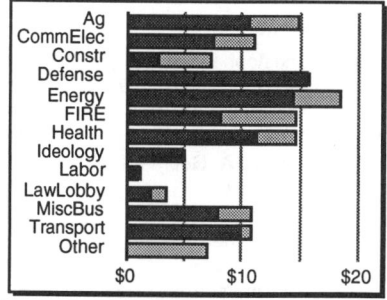

4. Mike Parker (D)
1992 Committees: Budget PubWorks
First elected: 1988

1991-92 Total Rcpts: $386,677
1990 Year-end cash: $307,872

Source of Funds
- PACs 62%
- Lg Individuals ($200+) 27%
- Individuals under $200 .... 7%
- Other 4%

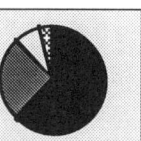

Top Industries & Interest Groups

Air Transport $35,056
Misc Services $27,500
Insurance $24,850
Oil & Gas $22,400
Electric Utilities $18,600

Unidentified $20,489

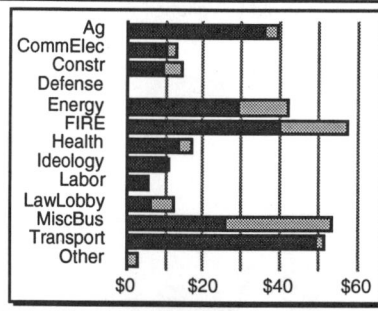

5. Gene Taylor (D)
1992 Committees: ArmServ MerchMarine
First elected: 1988

1991-92 Total Rcpts: $330,357
1990 Year-end cash: $2,918

Source of Funds
- PACs 47%
- Lg Individuals ($200+) 30%
- Individuals under $200 .... 20%
- Other 3%

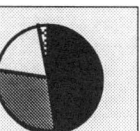

Top Industries & Interest Groups

Health Professionals $22,070
Lawyers & Lobbyists $18,750
Sea Transport $17,250
Defense Aerospace $16,210
Air Transport $11,000

Unidentified $32,625

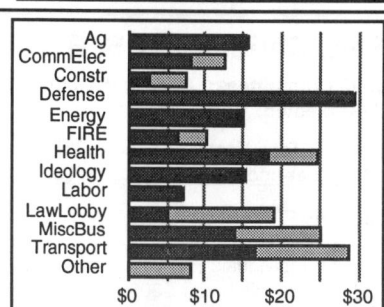

■ PACs ▨ Indivs ($200+)

† Does not include individual contributions from 1987-88

Missouri

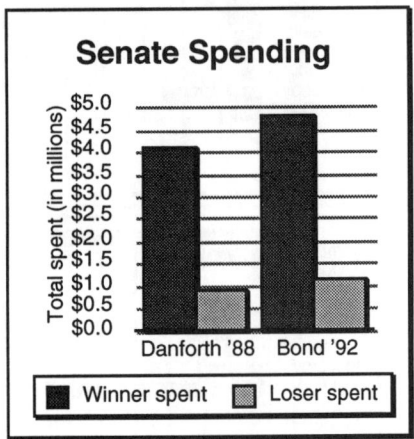

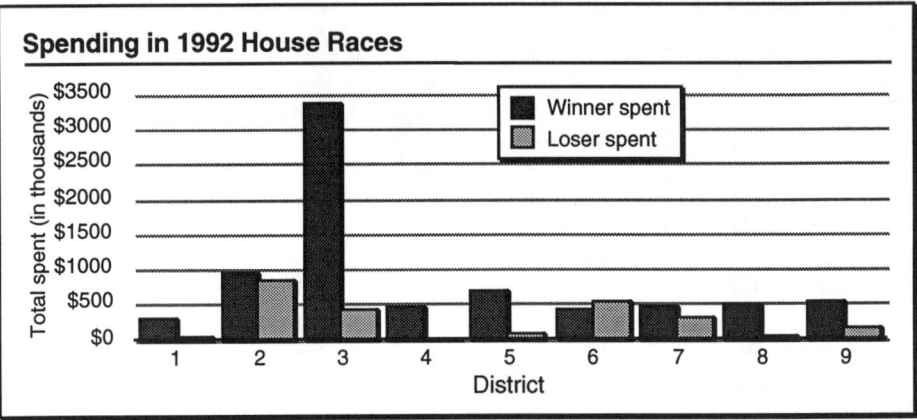

1992 Elections at a Glance

Dist	Name	Party	Vote Pct	Race Type
Sen	Christopher S. Bond (1992)	Rep	52%	Reelected
Sen	John C. Danforth (1988)	Rep	68%	Reelected
1	William L. Clay	Dem	68%	Reelected
2	James M. Talent	Rep	50%	Beat Incumb
3	Richard A. Gephardt	Dem	64%	Reelected
4	Ike Skelton	Dem	70%	Reelected
5	Alan Wheat	Dem	59%	Reelected
6	Pat Danner	Dem	55%	Beat Incumb
7	Mel Hancock	Rep	62%	Reelected
8	Bill Emerson	Rep	63%	Reelected
9	Harold L. Volkmer	Dem	48%	Reelected

Totals in Thousands of Dollars

Sen. Christopher S. Bond (R)

1992 Committees: Approp Banking Budget SmBus
First elected: 1986

1987-92 Total Rcpts: $5,087,184
1990 Year-end cash: $106,621

Source of Funds
- PACs 31%
- Lg Individuals ($200+) 40%
- Individuals under $200 .... 15%
- Other 14%

1987-92†
Top Industries & Interest Groups

Lawyer & Lobbyists	$248,961
Commercial Banks	$226,543
Insurance	$220,336
Securities & Investment	$142,795
Oil & Gas	$142,701
Unidentified	$539,217

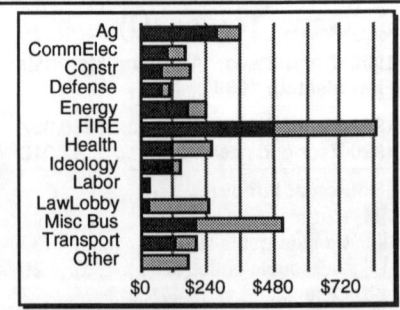

Sen. John C. Danforth (R)

1992 Committees: Commerce Finance
First elected: 1976

1987-92 Total Rcpts: $4,268,154
1990 Year-end cash: $645,961

Source of Funds
- PACs 26%
- Lg Individuals ($200+) 34%
- Individuals under $200 .... 24%
- Other 15%

1987-92†
Top Industries & Interest Groups

Insurance	$133,625
Oil & Gas	$52,455
Securities & Investment	$50,084
Telephone Utilities	$47,571
Air Transport	$47,500
Unidentified	$1,089

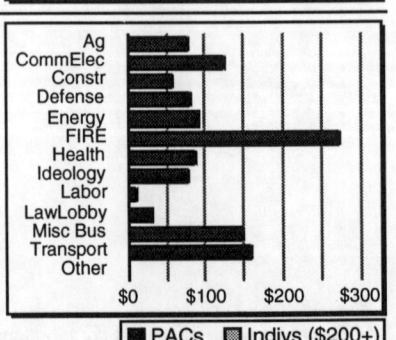

Key to committee & category abbreviations is on page 173

1. William L. Clay (D)

1992 Committees: Admin Educ/Labor Post Office
First elected: 1968

1991-92 Total Rcpts: $328,937
1990 Year-end cash: $124,500

Source of Funds
- PACs 74%
- Lg Individuals ($200+) 8%
- Individuals under $200 .... 4%
- Other 14%

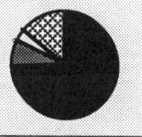

Top Industries & Interest Groups

Public Sector Unions $70,150
Transportation Unions $39,750
Industrial Unions $20,600
Building Trade Unions $20,200
Lawyers & Lobbyists $18,300

Unidentified $4,850

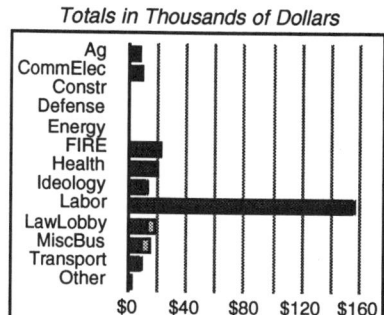

2. James M. Talent (R)

1993-94 Committees: ArmServ SmBus
First elected: 1992

1991-92 Total Rcpts: $924,820
1990 Year-end cash: $10,004

Source of Funds
- PACs 22%
- Lg Individuals ($200+) 41%
- Individuals under $200 .... 26%
- Other 11%

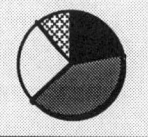

Top Industries & Interest Groups

Misc Manufacturing & Distrib $41,987
Health Professionals $38,100
Retired $36,510
Lawyers & Lobbyists $35,719
Commercial Banks $21,550

Unidentified $121,120

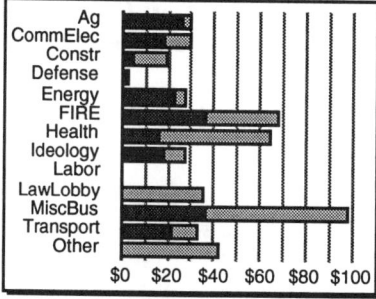

3. Richard A. Gephardt (D)

1992 Committees: Budget
First elected: 1976

1991-92 Total Rcpts: $3,238,479
1990 Year-end cash: $114,236

Source of Funds
- PACs 38%
- Lg Individuals ($200+) 50%
- Individuals under $200 .... 8%
- Other 4%

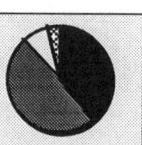

Top Industries & Interest Groups

Lawyers & Lobbyists $369,892
Insurance $157,889
Beer, Wine & Liquor $151,100
Securities & Investment $141,207
Real Estate $125,677

Unidentified $205,782

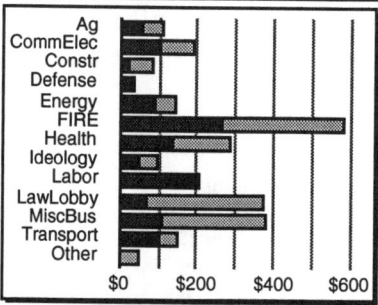

4. Ike Skelton (D)

1992 Committees: ArmServ SmBus
First elected: 1976

1991-92 Total Rcpts: $310,017
1990 Year-end cash: $194,795

Source of Funds
- PACs 66%
- Lg Individuals ($200+) 10%
- Individuals under $200 .... 21%
- Other 3%

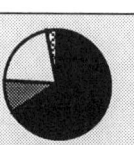

Top Industries & Interest Groups

Defense Aerospace $30,500
Health Professionals $18,000
Defense Electronics $12,700
Commercial Banks $10,725
Lawyers & Lobbyists $9,550

Unidentified $6,450

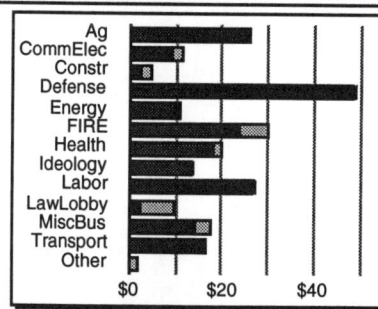

5. Alan Wheat (D)

1992 Committees: DC Rules
First elected: 1982

1991-92 Total Rcpts: $488,439
1990 Year-end cash: $76,049

Source of Funds
- PACs 70%
- Lg Individuals ($200+) 15%
- Individuals under $200 .... 9%
- Other 6%

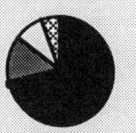

Top Industries & Interest Groups

Public Sector Unions $46,600
Industrial Unions $44,400
Transportation Unions $29,200
Lawyers & Lobbyists $29,110
Building Trade Unions $21,900

Unidentified $8,300

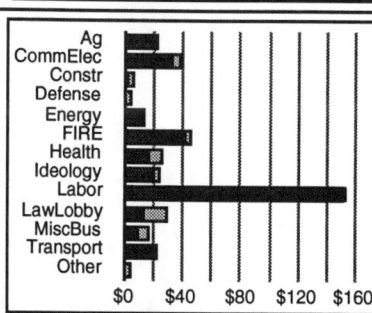

6. Pat Danner (D)

1993-94 Committees: PubWorks SmBus
First elected: 1992

1991-92 Total Rcpts: $417,277
1990 Year-end cash: $3,291

Source of Funds
- PACs 41%
- Lg Individuals ($200+) 23%
- Individuals under $200 .... 10%
- Other 25%

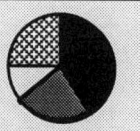

Top Industries & Interest Groups

Health Professionals $34,450
Industrial Unions $25,142
Lawyers & Lobbyists $22,250
Transportation Unions $20,550
Building Trade Unions $14,350

Unidentified $19,868

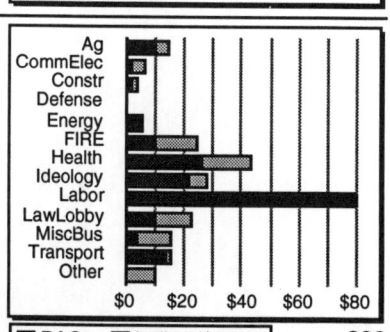

† Does not include individual contributions from 1987-88

7. Mel Hancock (R)

1992 Committees: Banking PubWorks SmBus
First elected: 1988

1991-92 Total Rcpts: $393,638
1990 Year-end cash: $96,147

Source of Funds
- PACs 42%
- Lg Individuals ($200+) 31%
- Individuals under $200 .... 20%
- Other 7%

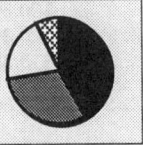

Top Industries & Interest Groups

Commercial Banks $19,549
Retired $19,000
Real Estate $17,150
Automotive $13,850
Air Transport $13,750

Unidentified $15,054

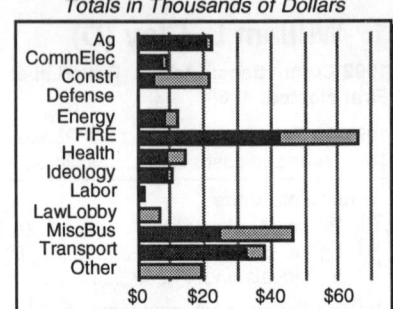

8. Bill Emerson (R)

1992 Committees: Agric PubWorks
First elected: 1980

1991-92 Total Rcpts: $518,998
1990 Year-end cash: $36,538

Source of Funds
- PACs 58%
- Lg Individuals ($200+) 19%
- Individuals under $200 .... 23%
- Other 1%

Top Industries & Interest Groups

Crop Production/Processing $55,440
Agricultural Services/Products .. $22,735
Food Processing & Sales $21,500
Health Professionals $18,600
Forestry & Forest Products $17,250

Unidentified $16,950

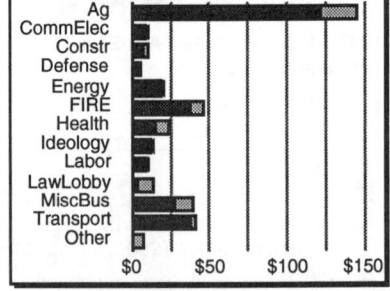

9. Harold L. Volkmer (D)

1992 Committees: Agric Science
First elected: 1976

1991-92 Total Rcpts: $354,612
1990 Year-end cash: $2,883

Source of Funds
- PACs 66%
- Lg Individuals ($200+) 6%
- Individuals under $200 .... 16%
- Other 12%

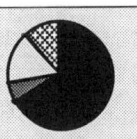

Top Industries & Interest Groups

Industrial Unions $29,150
Public Sector Unions $25,050
Building Trade Unions $20,900
Dairy $20,500
Agricultural Services/Products .. $12,683

Unidentified $2,350

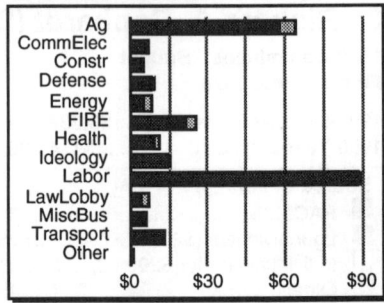

Totals in Thousands of Dollars

■ PACs   ▨ Indivs ($200+)

Montana

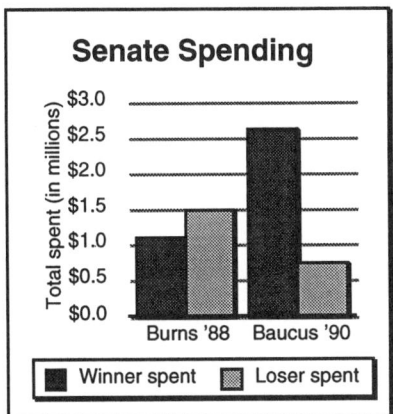

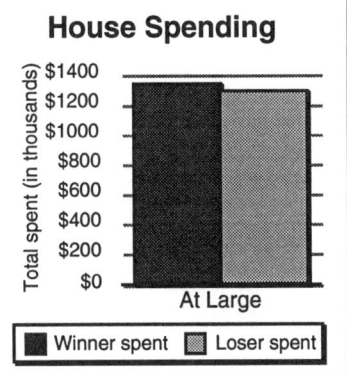

1992 Elections at a Glance

Dist	Name	Party	Vote Pct	Race Type
Sen	Max Baucus (1990)	Dem	68%	Reelected
Sen	Conrad Burns (1988)	Rep	52%	Beat Incumb
1	Pat Williams	Dem	50%	Reelected

Totals in Thousands of Dollars

Sen. Max Baucus (D)

1992 Committees: Agric Envir Finance SmBus
First elected: 1978

1987-92 Total Rcpts: $3,104,032
1990 Year-end cash: $311,797

Source of Funds
- PACs 51%
- Lg Individuals ($200+) 27%
- Individuals under $200 ....12%
- Other 10%

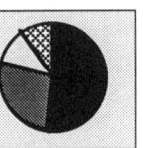

1987-92†
Top Industries & Interest Groups

Lawyer & Lobbyists $263,745
Insurance $178,774
Securities & Investment $143,366
Pro-Israel $115,100
Health Professionals $101,890

Unidentified $115,709

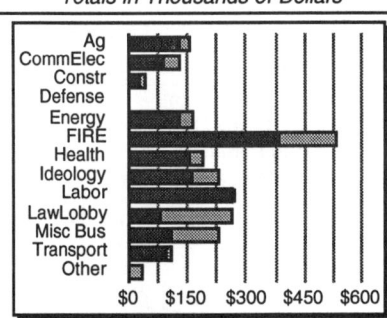

Sen. Conrad Burns (R)

1992 Committees: Commerce Energy SmBus
First elected: 1988

1987-92 Total Rcpts: $1,641,252
1990 Year-end cash: $205,240

Source of Funds
- PACs 38%
- Lg Individuals ($200+) 25%
- Individuals under $200 ....17%
- Other 21%

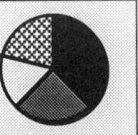

1987-92†
Top Industries & Interest Groups

Leadership PACs $56,000
Telephone Utilities $41,500
Oil & Gas $39,850
Pro-Israel $36,005
Insurance $35,661

Unidentified $51,104

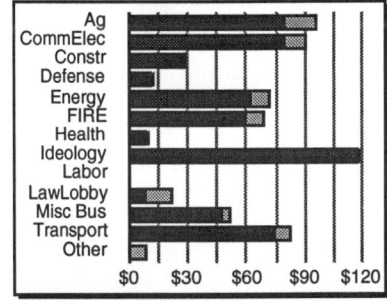

1. Pat Williams (D)

1992 Committees: Educ/Labor Interior
First elected: 1978

1991-92 Total Rcpts: $1,208,424
1990 Year-end cash: $68,395

Source of Funds
- PACs 39%
- Lg Individuals ($200+) 19%
- Individuals under $200 ....30%
- Other 13%

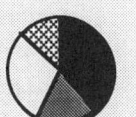

Top Industries & Interest Groups

Industrial Unions $73,190
Public Sector Unions $61,469
Building Trade Unions $60,750
Transportation Unions $53,800
Lawyers & Lobbyists $50,927

Unidentified $48,703

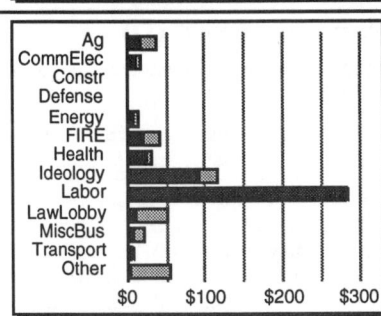

■ PACs ▨ Indivs ($200+)

† Does not include individual contributions from 1987-88

Nebraska

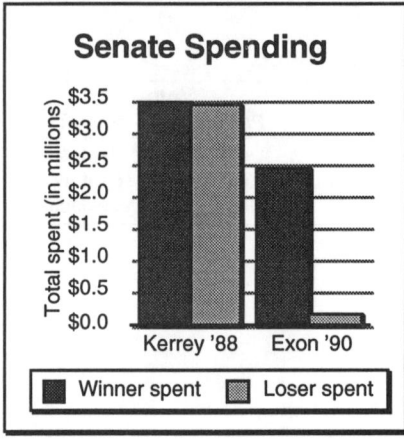

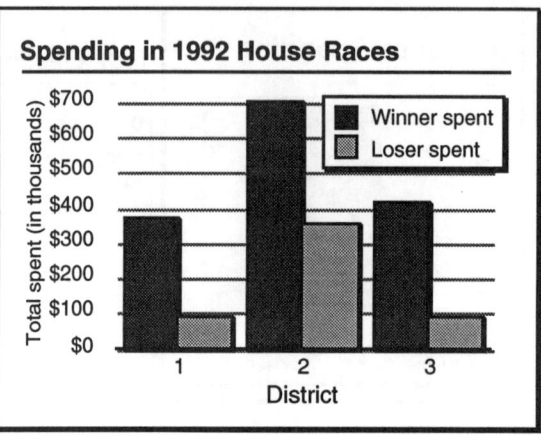

1992 Elections at a Glance

Dist	Name	Party	Vote Pct	Race Type
Sen	Jim Exon (1990)	Dem	59%	Reelected
Sen	Bob Kerrey (1988)	Dem	57%	Beat Incumb
1	Doug Bereuter	Rep	60%	Reelected
2	Peter Hoagland	Dem	51%	Reelected
3	Bill Barrett	Rep	72%	Reelected

Totals in Thousands of Dollars

Sen. Jim Exon (D)

1992 Committees: ArmServ Budget Commerce
First elected: 1978

1987-92 Total Rcpts: $2,705,658
1990 Year-end cash: $250,308

Source of Funds
PACs 53%
Lg Individuals ($200+) 19%
Individuals under $200 ....17%
Other 11%

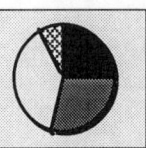

1987-92†
Top Industries & Interest Groups

Insurance $145,973
Lawyer & Lobbyists $138,104
Transportation Unions $109,300
Railroads....................................$101,315
Defense Aerospace $96,837

Unidentified $94,074

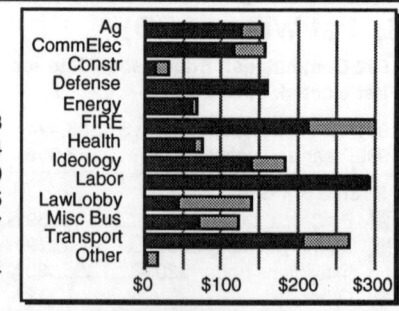

Sen. Bob Kerrey (D)

1992 Committees: Agric Approp
First elected: 1988

1987-92 Total Rcpts: $4,091,163
1990 Year-end cash: $91,304

Source of Funds
PACs 25%
Lg Individuals ($200+) 28%
Individuals under $200 ....39%
Other 8%

1987-92†
Top Industries & Interest Groups

Lawyers & Lobbyists................$546,039
Securities & Investment $215,825
Pro Israel $133,750
Media Entertainment $121,950
Real Estate $116,060

Unidentified $1,204,683

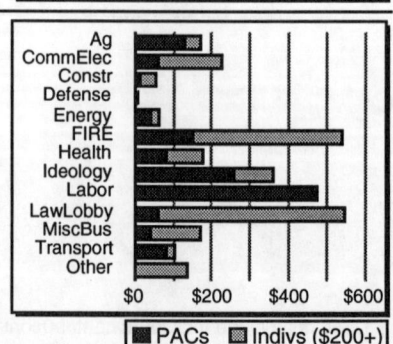

242 Key to committee & category abbreviations is on page 173

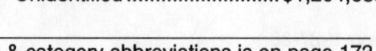

1. Doug Bereuter (R)

1992 Committees: Banking ForAff
First elected: 1978

1991-92 Total Rcpts: $315,824
1990 Year-end cash: $5,167

Source of Funds
- PACs 62%
- Lg Individuals ($200+) 9%
- Individuals under $200 .... 26%
- Other 3%

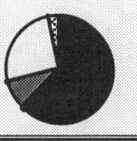

Top Industries & Interest Groups

Commercial Banks $52,732
Insurance $27,899
Food Processing & Sales $11,900
Crop Production/Processing $9,100
Accountants $8,500

Unidentified $6,050

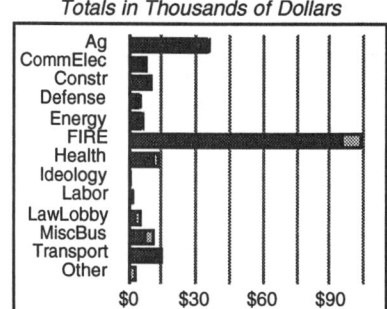

2. Peter Hoagland (D)

1992 Committees: Banking Interior Judiciary
First elected: 1988

1991-92 Total Rcpts: $711,298
1990 Year-end cash: $13,744

Source of Funds
- PACs 64%
- Lg Individuals ($200+) 21%
- Individuals under $200 .... 11%
- Other 5%

Top Industries & Interest Groups

Commercial Banks $92,300
Lawyers & Lobbyists $79,450
Industrial Unions $55,889
Public Sector Unions $44,200
Insurance $33,900

Unidentified $20,000

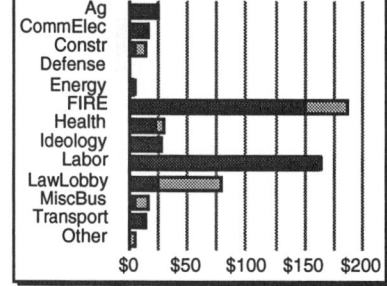

3. Bill Barrett (R)

1992 Committees: Admin Agric Educ/Labor
First elected: 1990

1991-92 Total Rcpts: $454,589
1990 Year-end cash: $17,315

Source of Funds
- PACs 43%
- Lg Individuals ($200+) 24%
- Individuals under $200 .... 31%
- Other 2%

Top Industries & Interest Groups

Insurance $28,049
Commercial Banks $27,741
Food Processing & Sales $19,400
Health Professionals $19,400
Retired $17,800

Unidentified $22,099

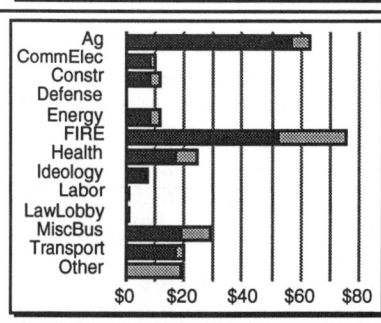

■ PACs   ▨ Indivs ($200+)

† Does not include individual contributions from 1987-88

Nevada

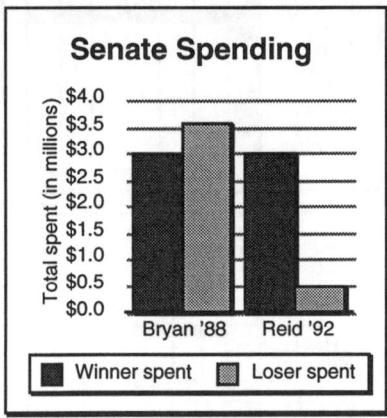

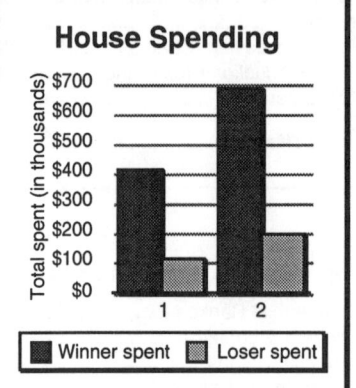

1992 Elections at a Glance

Dist	Name	Party	Vote Pct	Race Type
Sen	Harry Reid (1992)	Dem	51%	Reelected
Sen	Richard H. Bryan (1988)	Dem	50%	Beat Incumb
1	James Bilbray	Dem	58%	Reelected
2	Barbara F. Vucanovich	Rep	48%	Reelected

Totals in Thousands of Dollars

Sen. Richard H. Bryan (D)
1992 Committees: Banking Commerce
First elected: 1988

1987-92 Total Rcpts: $3,482,447
1990 Year-end cash: $201,859

Source of Funds
- PACs 26%
- Lg Individuals ($200+) 55%
- Individuals under $200 ....11%
- Other 9%

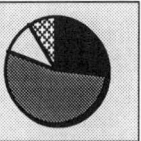

1987-92†
Top Industries & Interest Groups

Transportation Unions $88,250
Pro-Israel $85,660
Casinos/Gambling $84,016
Industrial Unions $77,300
Health Professionals $74,667

Unidentified $74,900

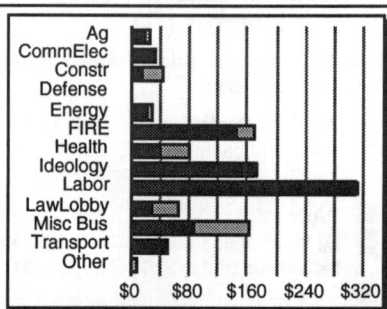

Sen. Harry Reid (D)
1992 Committees: Approp Envir
First elected: 1986

1987-92 Total Rcpts: $3,371,146
1990 Year-end cash: $144,835

Source of Funds
- PACs 31%
- Lg Individuals ($200+) 50%
- Individuals under $200 ....4%
- Other 14%

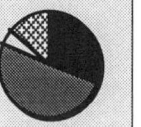

1987-92†
Top Industries & Interest Groups

Lawyer & Lobbyists $271,153
Casinos/Gambling $259,177
Health Professionals $185,272
Pro-Israel $104,574
Real Estate $94,200

Unidentified $377,276

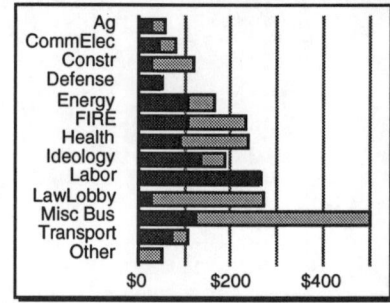

1. James Bilbray (D)
1992 Committees: ArmServ SmBus
First elected: 1986

1991-92 Total Rcpts: $443,431
1990 Year-end cash: $32,519

Source of Funds
- PACs 49%
- Lg Individuals ($200+) 40%
- Individuals under $200 ....3%
- Other 9%

Top Industries & Interest Groups

Health Professionals $44,700
Casinos/Gambling $38,227
Lawyers & Lobbyists $37,050
Building Trade Unions $33,000
Real Estate $28,200

Unidentified $19,295

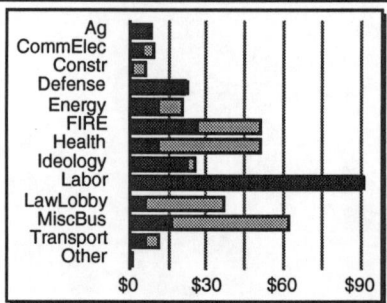

2. Barbara F. Vucanovich (R)
1992 Committees: Approp Interior
First elected: 1982

1991-92 Total Rcpts: $684,022
1990 Year-end cash: $3,849

Source of Funds
- PACs 35%
- Lg Individuals ($200+) 29%
- Individuals under $200 ....20%
- Other 17%

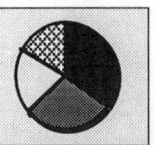

Top Industries & Interest Groups

Casinos/Gambling $52,000
Retired $39,640
Real Estate $27,740
Mining $25,100
Oil & Gas $19,600

Unidentified $28,000

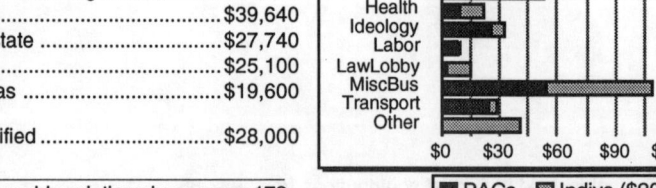

Key to committee & category abbreviations is on page 173

New Hampshire

Senate Spending

House Spending

1992 Elections at a Glance

Dist	Name	Party	Vote Pct	Race Type
Sen	Judd Gregg (1992)	Rep	48%	Open Seat
Sen	Robert C. Smith (1990)	Rep	65%	Open Seat
1	Bill Zeliff	Rep	53%	Reelected
2	Dick Swett	Dem	62%	Reelected

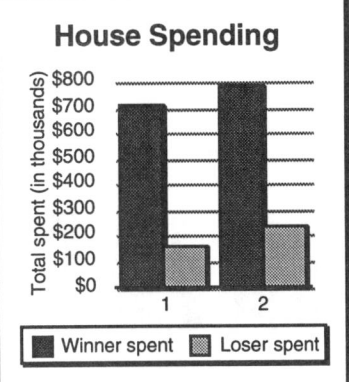

Totals in Thousands of Dollars

Sen. Judd Gregg (R)

1993-94 Committees: Budget Science Educ/Labor
First elected: 1992

1991-92 Total Rcpts: $991,938
1990 Year-end cash: $115,162

Source of Funds
- PACs 33%
- Lg Individuals ($200+) 37%
- Individuals under $200 .... 14%
- Other 16%

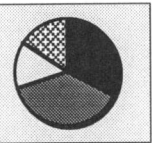

1991-92
Top Industries & Interest Groups

Insurance	$68,909
Pharmaceuticals/Health Prod	$42,600
Lawyer & Lobbyists	$34,900
Health Professionals	$33,301
Retired	$32,650
Unidentified	$118,637

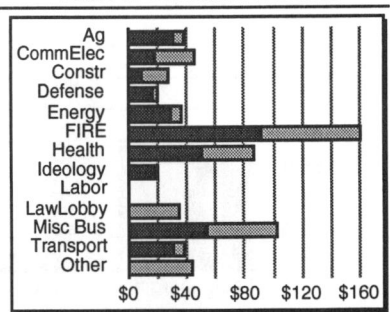

Sen. Robert C. Smith (R)

1992 Committees: ArmServ Envir
First elected: 1990

1989-92 Total Rcpts: $1,537,492
1990 Year-end cash: $46,190

Source of Funds
- PACs 39%
- Lg Individuals ($200+) 25%
- Individuals under $200 .... 14%
- Other 21%

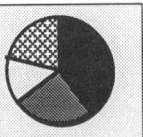

1989-92
Top Industries & Interest Groups

Insurance	$74,675
Defense Aerospace	$55,000
General Contractors	$46,600
Real Estate	$44,225
Oil & Gas	$42,800
Unidentified	$96,680

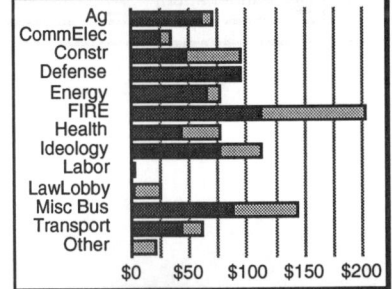

1. Bill Zeliff (R)

1992 Committees: GovtOps PubWorks SmBus
First elected: 1990

1991-92 Total Rcpts: $762,283
1990 Year-end cash: $2,691

Source of Funds
- PACs 41%
- Lg Individuals ($200+) 39%
- Individuals under $200 .... 13%
- Other 8%

Top Industries & Interest Groups

Insurance	$43,142
Real Estate	$42,050
Computer Equipment & Svcs	$28,940
Air Transport	$28,850
Retired	$28,504
Unidentified	$48,000

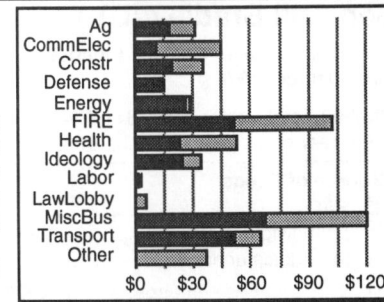

2. Dick Swett (D)

1992 Committees: PubWorks Science
First elected: 1990

1991-92 Total Rcpts: $877,187
1990 Year-end cash: $96,407

Source of Funds
- PACs 46%
- Lg Individuals ($200+) 42%
- Individuals under $200 .... 8%
- Other 5%

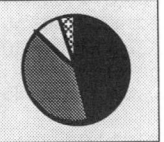

Top Industries & Interest Groups

Pro-Israel	$60,157
Public Sector Unions	$59,050
Lawyers & Lobbyists	$55,177
Misc Manufacturing & Distrib	$49,828
Industrial Unions	$47,000
Unidentified	$63,899

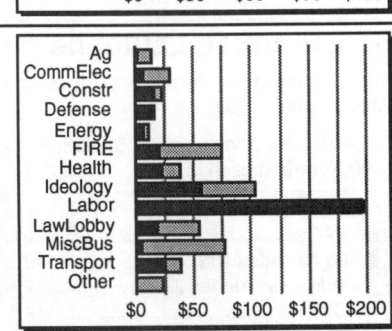

† Does not include individual contributions from 1987-88

New Jersey

Spending in 1992 House Races

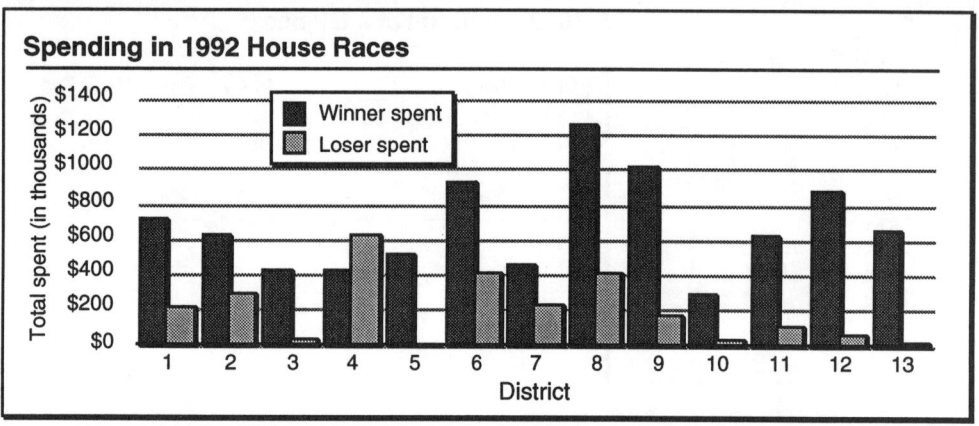

Senate Spending

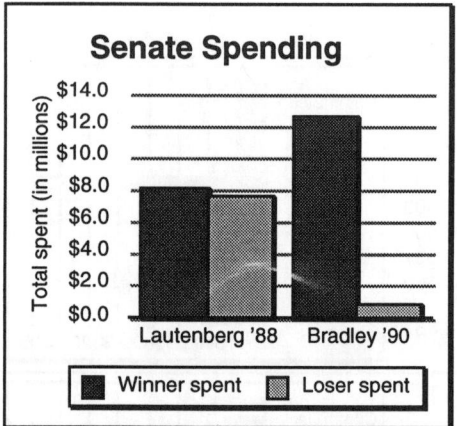

1992 Elections at a Glance

Dist	Name	Party	Vote Pct	Race Type
Sen	Bill Bradley (1990)	Dem	50%	Reelected
Sen	Frank R. Lautenberg (1988)	Dem	54%	Reelected
1	Robert E. Andrews	Dem	67%	Reelected
2	William J. Hughes	Dem	56%	Reelected
3	H. James Saxton	Rep	59%	Reelected
4	Christopher H. Smith	Rep	62%	Reelected
5	Marge Roukema	Rep	72%	Reelected
6	Frank Pallone Jr.	Dem	52%	Reelected
7	Bob Franks	Rep	53%	Open Seat
8	Herbert C. Klein	Dem	47%	Open Seat
9	Robert G. Torricelli	Dem	58%	Reelected
10	Donald M. Payne	Dem	78%	Reelected
11	Dean A. Gallo	Rep	70%	Reelected
12	Dick Zimmer	Rep	64%	Reelected
13	Robert Menendez	Dem	64%	Open Seat

Totals in Thousands of Dollars

Sen. Bill Bradley (D)

1992 Committees: Energy Finance
First elected: 1978

1987-92 Total Rcpts: $11,674,727
1990 Year-end cash: $53,941

Source of Funds
- PACs 11%
- Lg Individuals ($200+) 66%
- Individuals under $200 .... 13%
- Other 11%

1987-92†

Top Industries & Interest Groups

Lawyer & Lobbyists $1,059,963
Securities & Investment $959,048
Media/Entertainment $341,142
Real Estate $311,008
Insurance $264,384

Unidentified $1,311,316

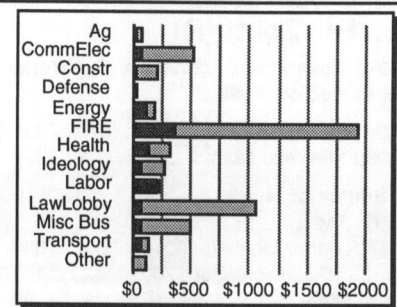

Sen. Frank R. Lautenberg (D)

1992 Committees: Approp Budget Envir
First elected: 1982

1987-92 Total Rcpts: $9,033,987
1990 Year-end cash: $902,271

Source of Funds
- PACs 20%
- Lg Individuals ($200+) 49%
- Individuals under $200 .... 17%
- Other 14%

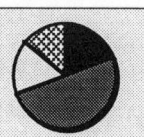

1987-92†

Top Industries & Interest Groups

Lawyer & Lobbyists $321,450
Pro-Israel $250,250
Pharmaceuticals/Health Prod .. $186,400
Insurance $150,750
Real Estate $109,400

Unidentified $304,185

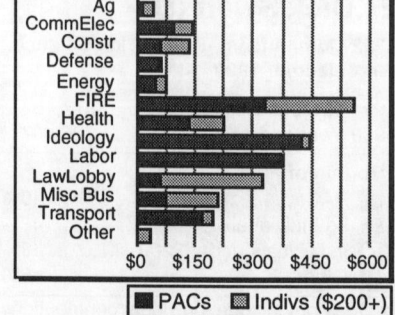

Key to committee & category abbreviations is on page 173

1. Robert E. Andrews (D)

1992 Committees: Educ/Labor SmBus
First elected: 1990

1991-92 Total Rcpts: $738,301
1990 Year-end cash: $1,284

Source of Funds
- PACs 46%
- Lg Individuals ($200+) 19%
- Individuals under $200 .... 25%
- Other 10%

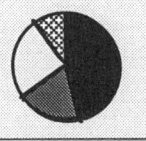

Top Industries & Interest Groups

Building Trade Unions $56,123
Lawyers & Lobbyists $46,650
Public Sector Unions $37,600
Transportation Unions $36,950
Health Professionals $31,650

Unidentified $29,325

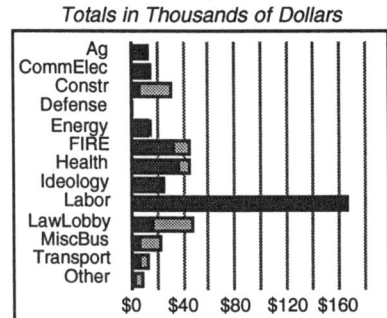

Totals in Thousands of Dollars

2. William J. Hughes (D)

1992 Committees: Judiciary MerchMarine
First elected: 1974

1991-92 Total Rcpts: $513,720
1990 Year-end cash: $116,489

Source of Funds
- PACs 42%
- Lg Individuals ($200+) 29%
- Individuals under $200 .... 20%
- Other 9%

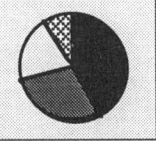

Top Industries & Interest Groups

Lawyers & Lobbyists $40,200
Media/Entertainment $34,850
Transportation Unions $20,350
Building Trade Unions $16,700
Public Sector Unions $16,500

Unidentified $40,053

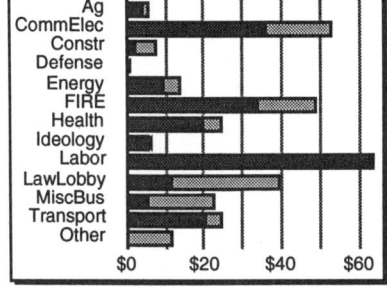

3. H. James Saxton (R)

1992 Committees: ArmServ MerchMarine
First elected: 1984

1991-92 Total Rcpts: $647,329
1990 Year-end cash: $279,382

Source of Funds
- PACs 43%
- Lg Individuals ($200+) 25%
- Individuals under $200 .... 29%
- Other 4%

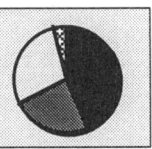

Top Industries & Interest Groups

Insurance $41,840
Health Professionals $27,070
Lawyers & Lobbyists $23,619
Defense Aerospace $20,900
Real Estate $18,850

Unidentified $41,824

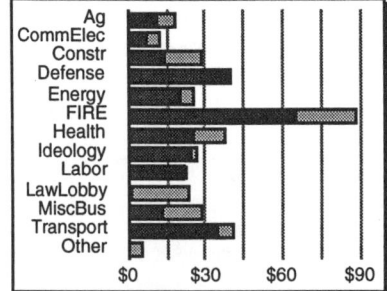

4. Christopher H. Smith (R)

1992 Committees: ForAff VetAffairs
First elected: 1980

1991-92 Total Rcpts: $369,949
1990 Year-end cash: $20,850

Source of Funds
- PACs 29%
- Lg Individuals ($200+) 15%
- Individuals under $200 .... 44%
- Other 13%

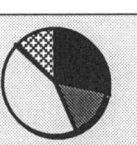

Top Industries & Interest Groups

Abortion Policy $13,875
Transportation Unions $11,500
Real Estate $9,500
Building Trade Unions $9,475
Health Professionals $6,975

Unidentified $20,093

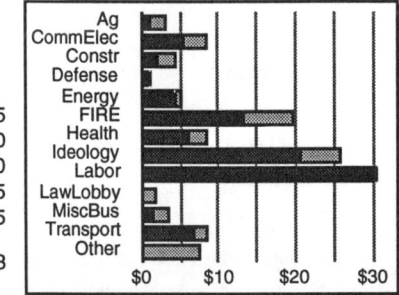

5. Marge Roukema (R)

1992 Committees: Banking Educ/Labor
First elected: 1980

1991-92 Total Rcpts: $439,150
1990 Year-end cash: $32,842

Source of Funds
- PACs 51%
- Lg Individuals ($200+) 28%
- Individuals under $200 .... 17%
- Other 3%

Top Industries & Interest Groups

Securities & Investment $30,062
Commercial Banks $23,950
Insurance $21,704
Health Professionals $19,950
Real Estate $17,150

Unidentified $17,660

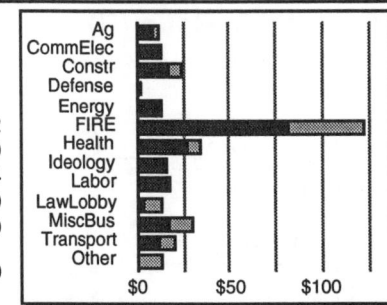

6. Frank Pallone Jr. (D)

1992 Committees: MerchMarine PubWorks
First elected: 1988

1991-92 Total Rcpts: $924,079
1990 Year-end cash: $3,297

Source of Funds
- PACs 57%
- Lg Individuals ($200+) 24%
- Individuals under $200 .... 16%
- Other 3%

Top Industries & Interest Groups

Transportation Unions $67,630
Building Trade Unions $58,350
Public Sector Unions $55,300
Industrial Unions $55,000
Health Professionals $49,850

Unidentified $71,242

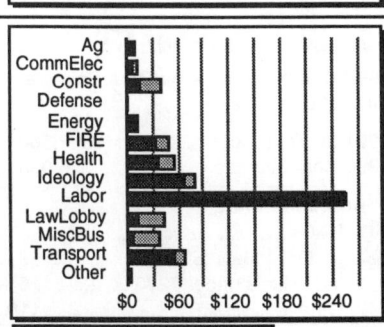

† Does not include individual contributions from 1987-88

7. Bob Franks (R)

1993-94 Committees: Budget PubWorks
First elected: 1992

1991-92 Total Rcpts: $460,998
1990 Year-end cash: $7,007

Source of Funds
- PACs 25%
- Lg Individuals ($200+) 50%
- Individuals under $200 ....9%
- Other 16%

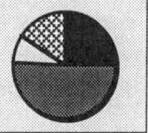

Top Industries & Interest Groups

Securities & Investment $30,600
Lawyers & Lobbyists $30,100
Health Professionals $27,600
Pharmaceuticals/Health Prod $15,400
Insurance $13,817

Unidentified $55,960

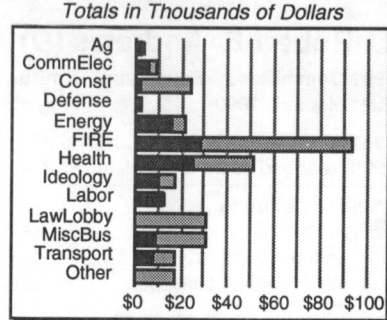

8. Herbert C. Klein (D)

1993-94 Committees: Banking Science
First elected: 1992

1991-92 Total Rcpts: $1,291,518
1990 Year-end cash: $56,646

Source of Funds
- PACs 13%
- Lg Individuals ($200+) 18%
- Individuals under $200 ....14%
- Other 54%

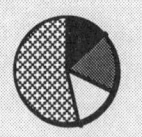

Top Industries & Interest Groups

Lawyers & Lobbyists $49,792
Real Estate $45,300
Industrial Unions $23,650
Building Trade Unions $20,200
Securities & Investment $13,350

Unidentified $46,575

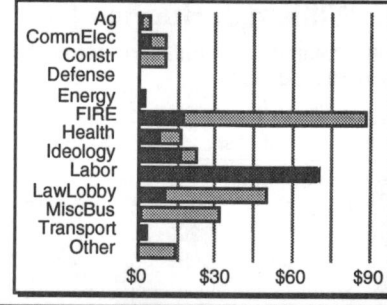

9. Robert G. Torricelli (D)

1992 Committees: ForAff Science
First elected: 1982

1991-92 Total Rcpts: $1,190,045
1990 Year-end cash: $1,035,163

Source of Funds
- PACs 29%
- Lg Individuals ($200+) 51%
- Individuals under $200 ....8%
- Other 13%

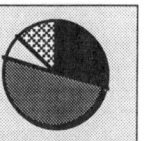

Top Industries & Interest Groups

Lawyers & Lobbyists $131,800
Health Professionals $75,500
Transportation Unions $38,500
Misc Manufacturing & Distrib $34,800
Pro-Israel $33,150

Unidentified $119,099

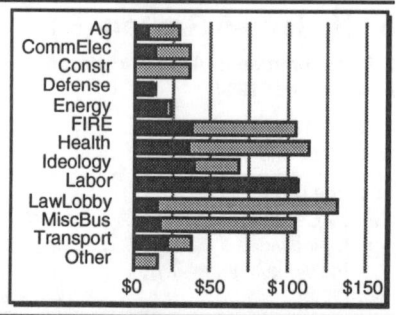

10. Donald M. Payne (D)

1992 Committees: Educ/Labor ForAff GovtOps
First elected: 1988

1991-92 Total Rcpts: $358,688
1990 Year-end cash: $339,836

Source of Funds
- PACs 50%
- Lg Individuals ($200+) 22%
- Individuals under $200 ....17%
- Other 11%

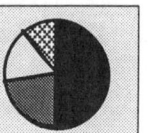

Top Industries & Interest Groups

Lawyers & Lobbyists $28,150
Industrial Unions $21,990
Building Trade Unions $21,580
Transportation Unions $19,700
Public Sector Unions $16,500

Unidentified $10,020

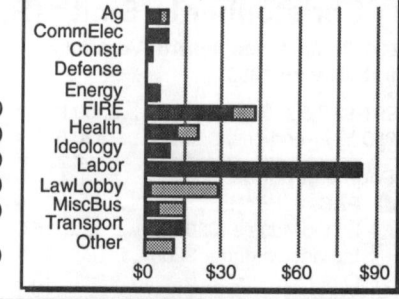

11. Dean A. Gallo (R)

1992 Committees: Appropriations
First elected: 1984

1991-92 Total Rcpts: $567,280
1990 Year-end cash: $20,723

Source of Funds
- PACs 33%
- Lg Individuals ($200+) 43%
- Individuals under $200 ....23%
- Other 1%

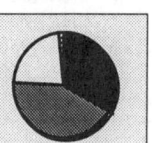

Top Industries & Interest Groups

Pharmaceuticals/Health Prod $24,300
Lawyers & Lobbyists $23,600
Real Estate $19,850
Building Trade Unions $15,950
Insurance $15,300

Unidentified $84,670

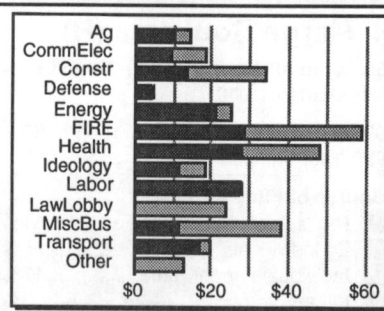

12. Dick Zimmer (R)

1992 Committees: GovtOps Science
First elected: 1990

1991-92 Total Rcpts: $929,560
1990 Year-end cash: $35,038

Source of Funds
- PACs 23%
- Lg Individuals ($200+) 57%
- Individuals under $200 ....10%
- Other 11%

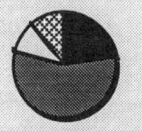

Top Industries & Interest Groups

Securities & Investment $64,500
Lawyers & Lobbyists $59,375
Pharmaceuticals/Health Prod $49,250
Retired $44,200
Real Estate $25,800

Unidentified $117,309

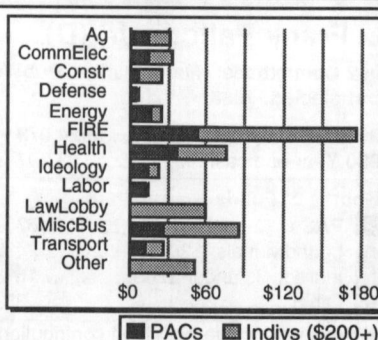

Key to committee & category abbreviations is on page 173

13. Robert Menendez (D)

1993-94 Committees: ForAff PubWorks
First elected: 1992

1991-92 Total Rcpts: $668,659
1990 Year-end cash: $23,018

Source of Funds
- PACs 33%
- Lg Individuals ($200+) 54%
- Individuals under $200 .... 11%
- Other 2%

Top Industries & Interest Groups

Lawyers & Lobbyists $60,200
Civil Servants/Public Officials $38,900
Education $37,550
Health Professionals $26,700
Transportation Unions $25,781

Unidentified $107,421

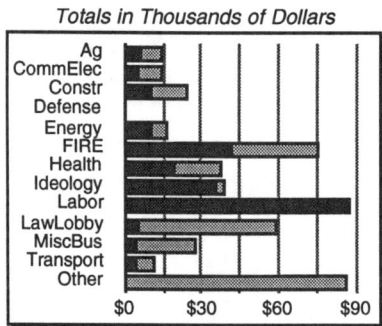

Totals in Thousands of Dollars

■ PACs ▥ Indivs ($200+)

New Mexico

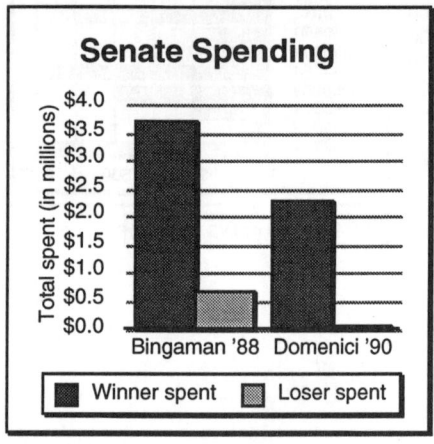

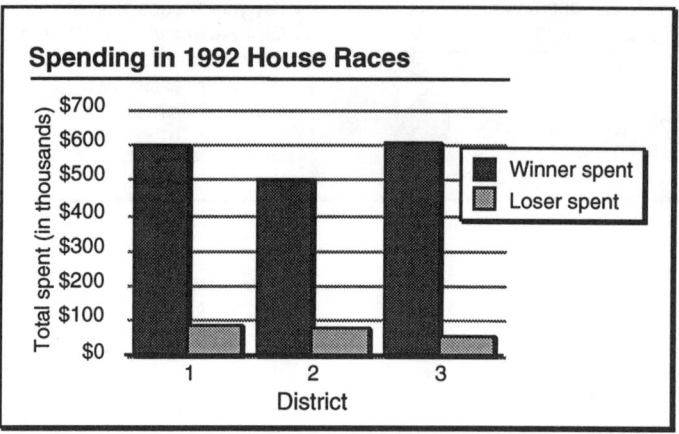

1992 Elections at a Glance

Dist	Name	Party	Vote Pct	Race Type
Sen	Jeff Bingaman (1988)	Dem	63%	Reelected
Sen	Pete V. Domenici (1990)	Rep	73%	Reelected
1	Steven H. Schiff	Rep	63%	Reelected
2	Joe Skeen	Rep	56%	Reelected
3	Bill Richardson	Dem	67%	Reelected

Totals in Thousands of Dollars

Sen. Jeff Bingaman (D)

1992 Committees: ArmServ Energy Labor
First elected: 1982

1987-92 Total Rcpts: $3,697,569
1990 Year-end cash: $466,031

Source of Funds
- PACs 29%
- Lg Individuals ($200+) 26%
- Individuals under $200 .... 34%
- Other 11%

1987-92†
Top Industries & Interest Groups

Pro-Israel $137,100
Lawyer & Lobbyists $120,789
Oil & Gas $88,313
Transportation Unions $72,250
Industrial Unions $66,450

Unidentified $111,864

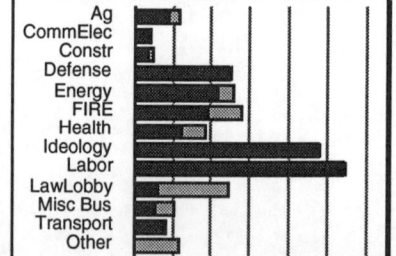

Sen. Pete V. Domenici (R)

1992 Committees: Approp Banking Budget Energy
First elected: 1972

1987-92 Total Rcpts: $2,231,577
1990 Year-end cash: $111,153

Source of Funds
- PACs 38%
- Lg Individuals ($200+) 29%
- Individuals under $200 .... 18%
- Other 14%

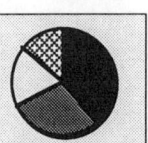

1987-92†
Top Industries & Interest Groups

Oil & Gas $232,435
Lawyer & Lobbyists $106,523
Securities & Investment $102,235
Insurance $61,682
Real Estate $59,118

Unidentified $121,380

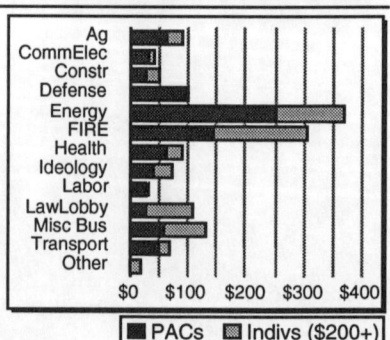

Key to committee & category abbreviations is on page 173

1. Steven H. Schiff (R)

1992 Committees: GovtOps Judiciary Science
First elected: 1988

1991-92 Total Rcpts: $573,884
1990 Year-end cash: $4,682

Source of Funds
- PACs 32%
- Lg Individuals ($200+) 19%
- Individuals under $200 .... 47%
- Other 2%

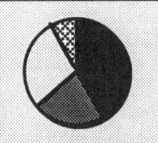

Top Industries & Interest Groups

Lawyers & Lobbyists $23,000
Health Professionals $21,150
Pro-Israel $15,000
Oil & Gas $14,950
Retired $13,000

Unidentified $28,045

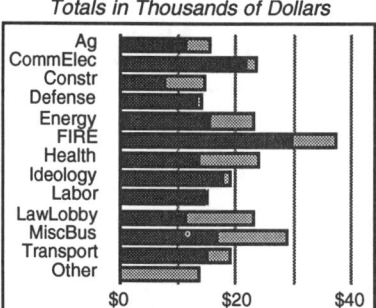

2. Joe Skeen (R)

1992 Committees: Appropriations
First elected: 1980

1991-92 Total Rcpts: $387,893
1990 Year-end cash: $91,360

Source of Funds
- PACs 41%
- Lg Individuals ($200+) 22%
- Individuals under $200 .... 28%
- Other 8%

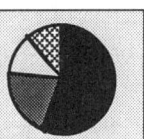

Top Industries & Interest Groups

Crop Production/Processing $24,131
Oil & Gas $24,002
Agricultural Services/Products .. $18,200
Livestock $15,550
Health Professionals $13,182

Unidentified $9,822

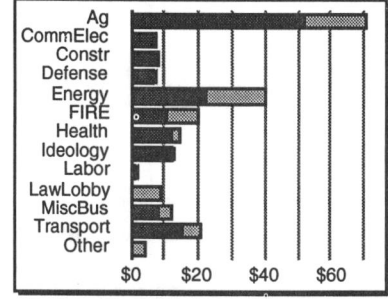

3. Bill Richardson (D)

1992 Committees: Energy/Commerce Interior
First elected: 1982

1991-92 Total Rcpts: $680,154
1990 Year-end cash: $409,373

Source of Funds
- PACs 56%
- Lg Individuals ($200+) 20%
- Individuals under $200 .... 13%
- Other 10%

Top Industries & Interest Groups

Health Professionals $53,482
Lawyers & Lobbyists $45,587
Media/Entertainment $36,250
Oil & Gas $31,812
Telephone Utilities $31,250

Unidentified $19,150

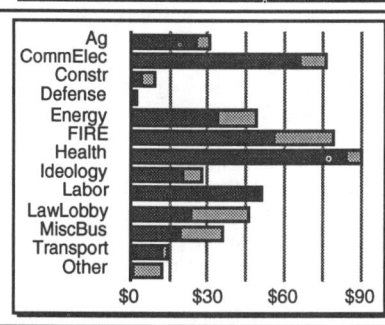

■ PACs   ▨ Indivs ($200+)

† Does not include individual contributions from 1987-88

New York

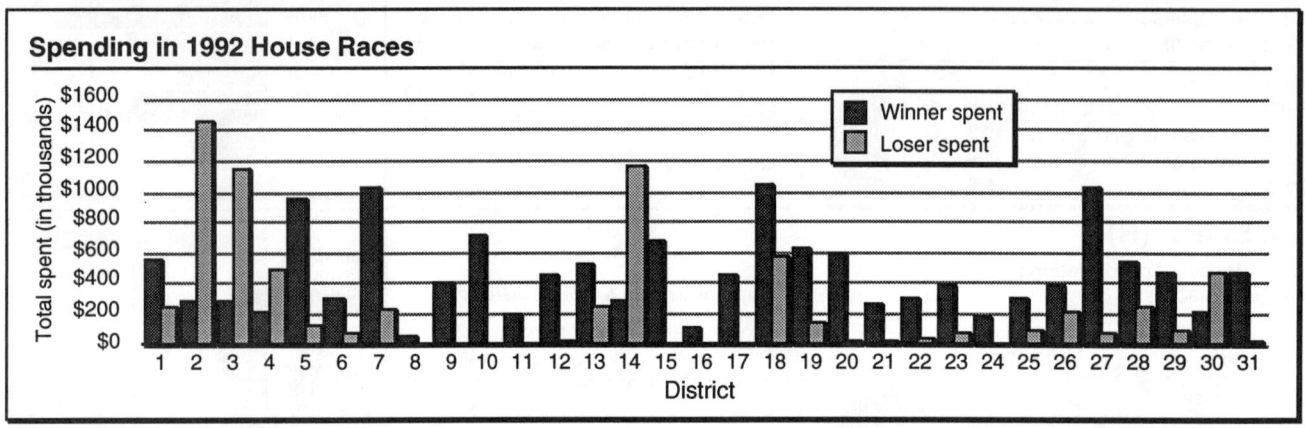

1992 Elections at a Glance

Dist	Name	Party	Vote Pct	Race Type
Sen	Alfonse M. D'Amato (1992)	Rep	49%	Reelected
Sen	Daniel P. Moynihan (1988)	Dem	67%	Reelected
1	George J. Hochbrueckner	Dem	52%	Reelected
2	Rick A. Lazio	Rep	53%	Beat Incumb
3	Peter T. King	Rep	50%	Open Seat
4	David A. Levy	Rep	50%	Open Seat
5	Gary L. Ackerman	Dem	52%	Reelected
6	Floyd H. Flake	Dem	81%	Reelected
7	Thomas J. Manton	Dem	57%	Reelected
8	Jerrold Nadler	Dem	81%	Open Seat
9	Charles E. Schumer	Dem	89%	Reelected
10	Edolphus Towns	Dem	96%	Reelected
11	Major R. Owens	Dem	94%	Reelected
12	Nydia M. Velazquez	Dem	76%	Open Seat
13	Susan Molinari	Rep	56%	Reelected
14	Carolyn B. Maloney	Dem	50%	Beat Incumb
15	Charles B. Rangel	Dem	95%	Reelected
16	Jose E. Serrano	Dem	91%	Reelected
17	Eliot L. Engel	Dem	80%	Reelected
18	Nita M. Lowey	Dem	56%	Reelected
19	Hamilton Fish Jr.	Rep	60%	Reelected
20	Benjamin A. Gilman	Rep	66%	Reelected
21	Michael R. McNulty	Dem	63%	Reelected
22	Gerald B. H. Solomon	Rep	65%	Reelected
23	Sherwood Boehlert	Rep	64%	Reelected

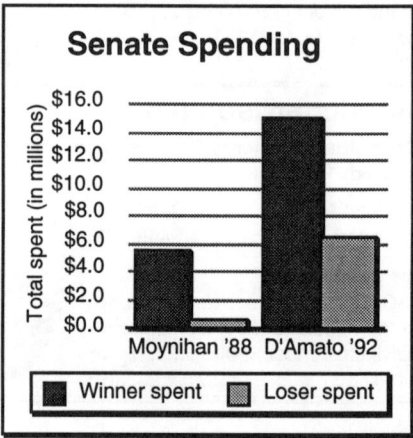

Dist	Name	Party	Vote Pct	Race Type
24	John M. McHugh	Rep	61%	Open Seat
25	James T. Walsh	Rep	56%	Reelected
26	Maurice D. Hinchey	Dem	50%	Open Seat
27	Bill Paxon	Rep	64%	Reelected
28	Louise M. Slaughter	Dem	55%	Reelected
29	John J. LaFalce	Dem	54%	Reelected
30	Jack Quinn	Rep	52%	Open Seat
31	Amo Houghton	Rep	71%	Reelected

Sen. Alfonse M. D'Amato (R)
1992 Committees: Approp Banking
First elected: 1980

1987-92 Total Rcpts: $11,246,373
1990 Year-end cash: $144,716

Source of Funds
- PACs 11%
- Lg Individuals ($200+) 51%
- Individuals under $200 .... 17%
- Other 22%

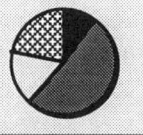

1987-92†
Top Industries & Interest Groups

Securities & Investment $610,651
Lawyer & Lobbyists $505,035
Real Estate $328,973
Insurance $196,856
Health Professionals $140,450

Unidentified $1,810,977

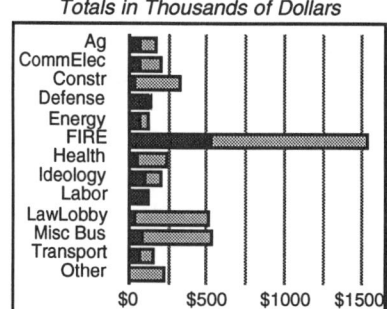

Sen. Daniel Patrick Moynihan (D)
1992 Committees: Envir Finance ForRel Rules
First elected: 1976

1987-92 Total Rcpts: $5,665,268
1990 Year-end cash: $854,325

Source of Funds
- PACs 19%
- Lg Individuals ($200+) 28%
- Individuals under $200 .... 46%
- Other 8%

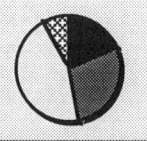

1987-92†
Top Industries & Interest Groups

Securities & Investment $191,178
Lawyer & Lobbyists $140,056
Insurance $93,967
Commercial Banks $69,575
Health Professionals $67,930

Unidentified $122,718

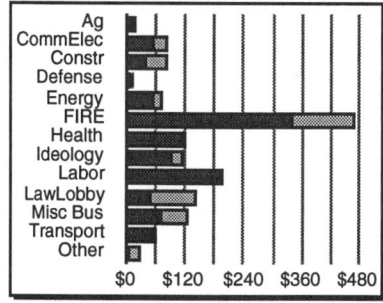

1. George J. Hochbrueckner (D)
1992 Committees: ArmServ MerchMarine
First elected: 1986

1991-92 Total Rcpts: $530,966
1990 Year-end cash: $1,850

Source of Funds
- PACs 54%
- Lg Individuals ($200+) 16%
- Individuals under $200 .... 21%
- Other 10%

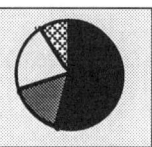

Top Industries & Interest Groups

Public Sector Unions $56,400
Transportation Unions $46,200
Industrial Unions $33,050
Building Trade Unions $28,100
Health Professionals $22,325

Unidentified $30,175

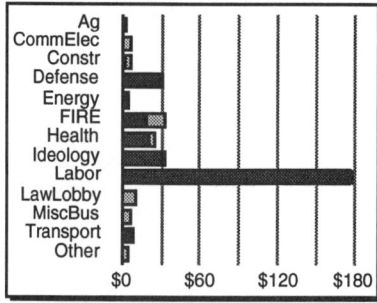

2. Rick A. Lazio (R)
1993-94 Committees: Banking Budget
First elected: 1992

1991-92 Total Rcpts: $283,788
1990 Year-end cash: $223

Source of Funds
- PACs 13%
- Lg Individuals ($200+) 27%
- Individuals under $200 .... 31%
- Other 30%

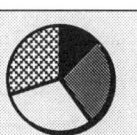

Top Industries & Interest Groups

Lawyers & Lobbyists $16,490
Real Estate $8,485
Transportation Unions $7,500
Health Professionals $5,850
Food Processing & Sales $4,500

Unidentified $26,050

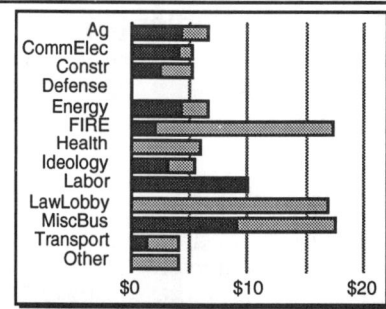

3. Peter T. King (R)
1993-94 Committees: Banking MerchMarine
First elected: 1992

1991-92 Total Rcpts: $244,526
1990 Year-end cash: $8,079

Source of Funds
- PACs 39%
- Lg Individuals ($200+) 26%
- Individuals under $200 .... 15%
- Other 20%

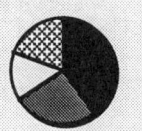

Top Industries & Interest Groups

Health Professionals $12,800
Leadership PACs $12,200
Civil Servants/Public Officials $10,750
Lawyers & Lobbyists $10,150
Securities & Investment $8,700

Unidentified $17,710

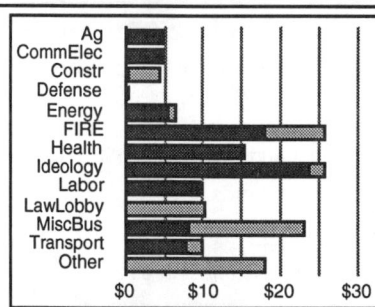

4. David A. Levy (R)
1993-94 Committees: ForAff PubWorks
First elected: 1992

1991-92 Total Rcpts: $217,319
1990 Year-end cash: $8,092

Source of Funds
- PACs 23%
- Lg Individuals ($200+) 31%
- Individuals under $200 .... 21%
- Other 26%

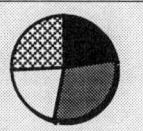

Top Industries & Interest Groups

Retail Sales $13,450
Printing & Publishing $9,225
Lawyers & Lobbyists $7,750
Business Services $6,600
Insurance $6,475

Unidentified $22,350

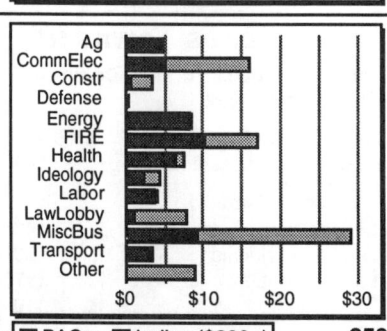

† Does not include individual contributions from 1987-88

5. Gary L. Ackerman (D)

1992 Committees: Banking ForAff Post Office
First elected: 1983

1991-92 Total Rcpts: $688,551
1990 Year-end cash: $28,412

Source of Funds
- PACs 52%
- Lg Individuals ($200+) 31%
- Individuals under $200 .... 7%
- Other 10%

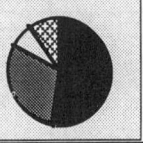

Top Industries & Interest Groups

Public Sector Unions $87,250
Health Professionals $45,350
Securities & Investment $38,000
Transportation Unions $37,000
Industrial Unions $28,750

Unidentified $39,601

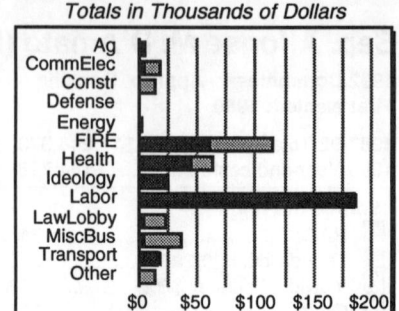

6. Floyd H. Flake (D)

1992 Committees: Banking SmBus
First elected: 1986

1991-92 Total Rcpts: $272,263
1990 Year-end cash: $39,483

Source of Funds
- PACs 52%
- Lg Individuals ($200+) 11%
- Individuals under $200 .... 19%
- Other 18%

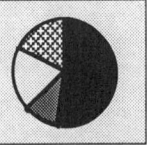

Top Industries & Interest Groups

Commercial Banks $32,450
Public Sector Unions $20,900
Transportation Unions $17,600
Industrial Unions $16,700
Securities & Investment $11,750

Unidentified $4,945

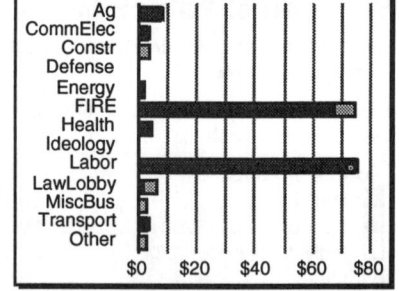

7. Thomas J. Manton (D)

1992 Committees: Admin Energy/Comm MerchMarine
First elected: 1984

1991-92 Total Rcpts: $643,780
1990 Year-end cash: $108,919

Source of Funds
- PACs 66%
- Lg Individuals ($200+) 14%
- Individuals under $200 .... 8%
- Other 11%

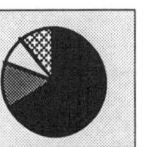

Top Industries & Interest Groups

Lawyers & Lobbyists $45,749
Insurance $45,499
Transportation Unions $42,300
Media/Entertainment $27,500
Public Sector Unions $26,500

Unidentified $13,175

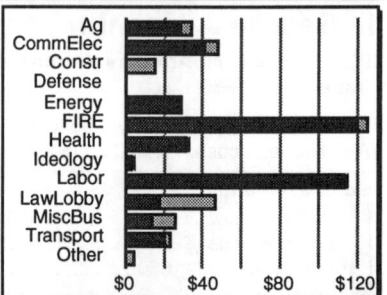

8. Jerrold Nadler (D)

1993-94 Committees: Judiciary PubWorks
First elected: 1992

1991-92 Total Rcpts: $49,685
1990 Year-end cash: $9,178

Source of Funds
- PACs 67%
- Lg Individuals ($200+) 24%
- Individuals under $200 .... 1%
- Other 7%

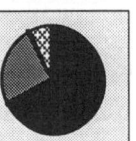

Top Industries & Interest Groups

Health Professionals $7,000
Public Sector Unions $5,500
Commercial Banks $3,500
Securities & Investment $2,750
Industrial Unions $2,500
Transportation Unions $2,500

Unidentified $1,250

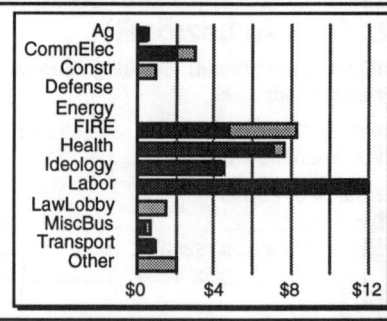

9. Charles E. Schumer (D)

1992 Committees: Banking Interior Judiciary
First elected: 1980

1991-92 Total Rcpts: $923,272
1990 Year-end cash: $2,116,689

Source of Funds
- PACs 20%
- Lg Individuals ($200+) 53%
- Individuals under $200 .... 5%
- Other 22%

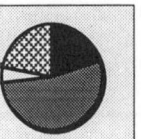

Top Industries & Interest Groups

Securities & Investment $221,996
Real Estate $83,000
Lawyers & Lobbyists $40,750
Misc Manufacturing & Distrib $40,750
Commercial Banks $40,250

Unidentified $54,000

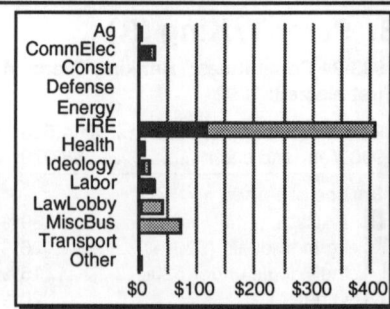

10. Edolphus Towns (D)

1992 Committees: Energy/Commerce GovtOps
First elected: 1982

1991-92 Total Rcpts: $560,977
1990 Year-end cash: $3,803

Source of Funds
- PACs 43%
- Lg Individuals ($200+) 30%
- Individuals under $200 .... 17%
- Other 10%

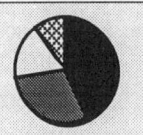

Top Industries & Interest Groups

Media/Entertainment $40,400
Health Professionals $33,761
Lawyers & Lobbyists $27,150
Tobacco $21,245
Transportation Unions $19,300

Unidentified $61,585

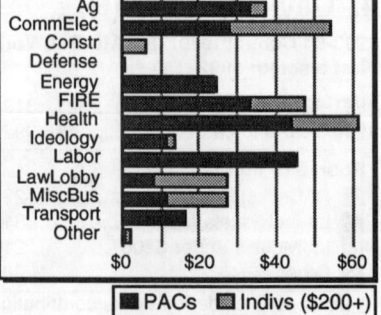

Key to committee & category abbreviations is on page 173

11. Major R. Owens (D)

1992 Committees: Educ/Labor GovtOps
First elected: 1982

1991-92 Total Rcpts: $181,650
1990 Year-end cash: $4,201

Source of Funds
- PACs 49%
- Lg Individuals ($200+) 11%
- Individuals under $200 ....30%
- Other 10%

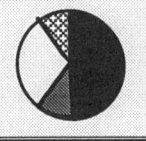

Top Industries & Interest Groups

Transportation Unions $21,750
Public Sector Unions $15,624
Industrial Unions $13,125
Misc Unions $12,100
Building Trade Unions $6,750

Unidentified $10,050

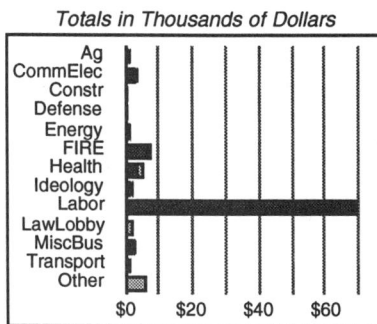

12. Nydia M. Velazquez (D)

1993-94 Committees: Banking SmBus
First elected: 1992

1991-92 Total Rcpts: $477,373
1990 Year-end cash: $14,698

Source of Funds
- PACs 33%
- Lg Individuals ($200+) 23%
- Individuals under $200 ....21%
- Other 23%

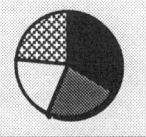

Top Industries & Interest Groups

Industrial Unions $26,300
Transportation Unions $20,350
Womens Issues $17,641
Public Sector Unions $15,500
Lawyers & Lobbyists $11,515

Unidentified $62,300

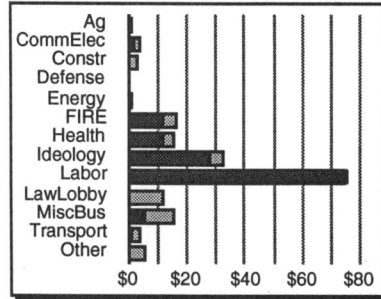

13. Susan Molinari (R)

1992 Committees: Educ/Labor PubWorks
First elected: 1980

1991-92 Total Rcpts: $524,112
1990 Year-end cash: $33,045

Source of Funds
- PACs 44%
- Lg Individuals ($200+) 37%
- Individuals under $200 ....16%
- Other 4%

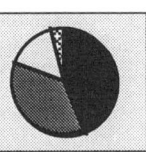

Top Industries & Interest Groups

Health Professionals $34,825
Lawyers & Lobbyists $28,112
Air Transport $19,150
Securities & Investment $18,080
Real Estate $16,650

Unidentified $53,850

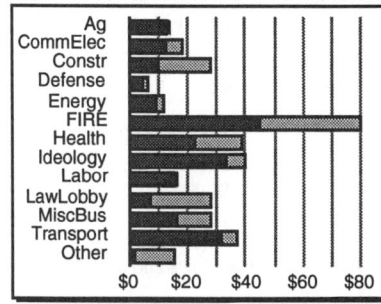

14. Carolyn B. Maloney (D)

1993-94 Committees: Banking GovtOps
First elected: 1992

1991-92 Total Rcpts: $279,980
1990 Year-end cash: $3,786

Source of Funds
- PACs 23%
- Lg Individuals ($200+) 53%
- Individuals under $200 ....7%
- Other 18%

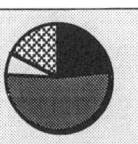

Top Industries & Interest Groups

Securities & Investment $22,850
Industrial Unions $22,000
Real Estate $21,750
Lawyers & Lobbyists $18,150
Building Trade Unions $12,000

Unidentified $41,625

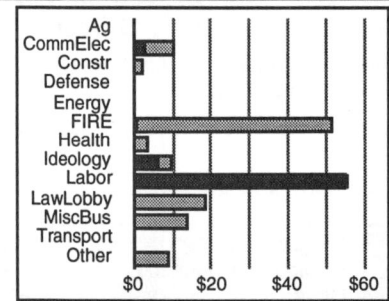

15. Charles B. Rangel (D)

1992 Committees: Ways & Means
First elected: 1970

1991-92 Total Rcpts: $539,183
1990 Year-end cash: $174,093

Source of Funds
- PACs 60%
- Lg Individuals ($200+) 28%
- Individuals under $200 ....10%
- Other 2%

Top Industries & Interest Groups

Insurance $54,295
Lawyers & Lobbyists $47,414
Pharmaceuticals/Health Prod $34,200
Health Professionals $27,900
Public Sector Unions $26,000

Unidentified $30,200

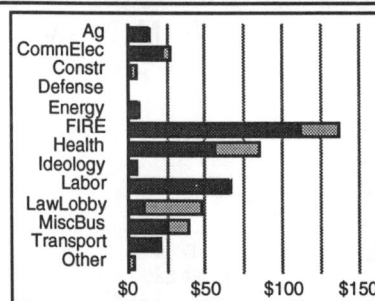

16. Jose E. Serrano (D)

1992 Committees: Educ/Labor SmBus
First elected: 1989

1991-92 Total Rcpts: $116,483
1990 Year-end cash: $41,830

Source of Funds
- PACs 77%
- Lg Individuals ($200+) 13%
- Individuals under $200 ....3%
- Other 7%

Top Industries & Interest Groups

Public Sector Unions $17,000
Transportation Unions $11,250
Building Trade Unions $8,550
Education $8,500
Health Professionals $7,500

Unidentified $2,000

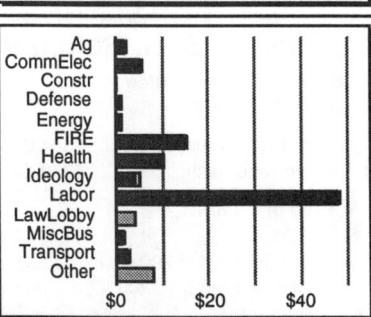

17. Eliot L. Engel (D)

1992 Committees: ForAff Science
First elected: 1988

1991-92 Total Rcpts: $440,835
1990 Year-end cash: $8,107

Source of Funds
- PACs 65%
- Lg Individuals ($200+) 18%
- Individuals under $200 .... 15%
- Other 2%

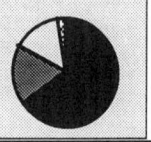

Top Industries & Interest Groups

Public Sector Unions $41,650
Transportation Unions $33,000
Health Professionals $29,130
Industrial Unions $27,100
Pro-Israel $25,870

Unidentified $14,635

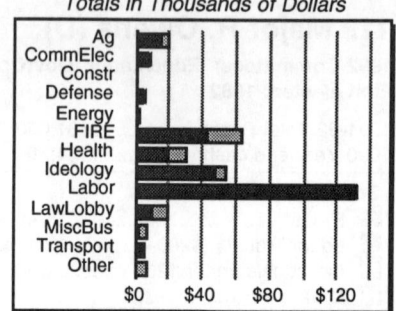

Totals in Thousands of Dollars

---

18. Nita M. Lowey (D)

1992 Committees: Educ/Labor MerchMarine
First elected: 1988

1991-92 Total Rcpts: $1,153,196
1990 Year-end cash: $215,816

Source of Funds
- PACs 27%
- Lg Individuals ($200+) 46%
- Individuals under $200 .... 21%
- Other 7%

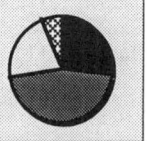

Top Industries & Interest Groups

Lawyers & Lobbyists $126,350
Securities & Investment $99,740
Real Estate $52,000
Public Sector Unions $51,000
Transportation Unions $37,500

Unidentified $75,890

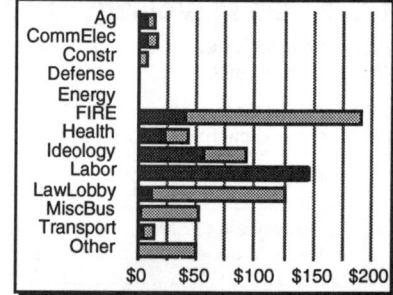

---

19. Hamilton Fish Jr. (R)

1992 Committees: Judiciary
First elected: 1968

1991-92 Total Rcpts: $489,831
1990 Year-end cash: $6,830

Source of Funds
- PACs 46%
- Lg Individuals ($200+) 25%
- Individuals under $200 .... 13%
- Other 16%

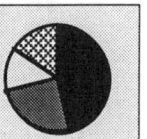

Top Industries & Interest Groups

Insurance $62,700
Media/Entertainment $29,900
Telephone Utilities $26,350
Lawyers & Lobbyists $25,400
Securities & Investment $24,150

Unidentified $26,200

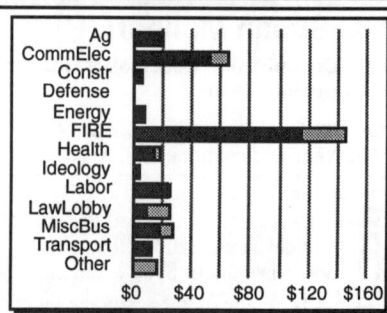

---

20. Benjamin A. Gilman (R)

1992 Committees: ForAff Post Office
First elected: 1972

1991-92 Total Rcpts: $566,773
1990 Year-end cash: $58,491

Source of Funds
- PACs 37%
- Lg Individuals ($200+) 34%
- Individuals under $200 .... 26%
- Other 2%

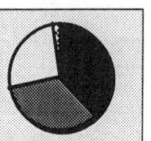

Top Industries & Interest Groups

Public Sector Unions $49,500
Transportation Unions $24,250
Lawyers & Lobbyists $24,000
Health Professionals $18,700
Building Trade Unions $14,475

Unidentified $71,873

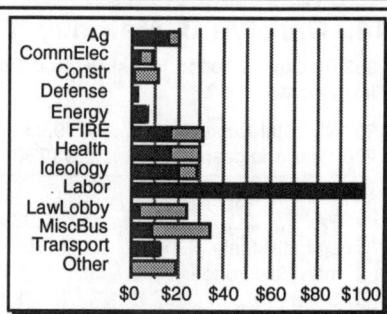

---

21. Michael R. McNulty (D)

1992 Committees: ArmServ Post Office
First elected: 1988

1991-92 Total Rcpts: $220,997
1990 Year-end cash: $68,572

Source of Funds
- PACs 56%
- Lg Individuals ($200+) 6%
- Individuals under $200 .... 29%
- Other 9%

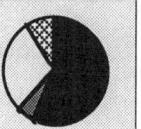

Top Industries & Interest Groups

Public Sector Unions $25,000
Transportation Unions $17,900
Building Trade Unions $11,100
Defense Aerospace $10,200
Industrial Unions $9,000

Unidentified $2,700

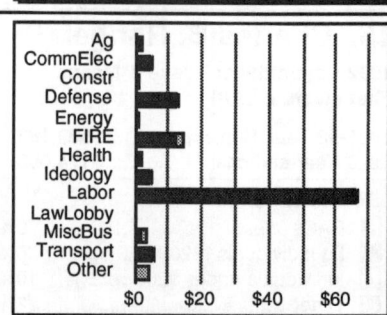

---

22. Gerald B. H. Solomon (R)

1992 Committees: Rules
First elected: 1978

1991-92 Total Rcpts: $384,095
1990 Year-end cash: $210,627

Source of Funds
- PACs 74%
- Lg Individuals ($200+) 9%
- Individuals under $200 .... 14%
- Other 3%

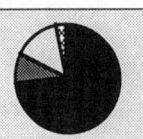

Top Industries & Interest Groups

Insurance $42,123
Transportation Unions $33,210
Air Transport $21,980
Health Professionals $17,410
Public Sector Unions $15,250

Unidentified $10,520

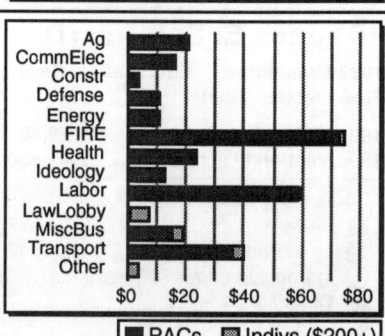

Key to committee & category abbreviations is on page 173

23. Sherwood Boehlert (R)

1992 Committees: PubWorks Science
First elected: 1982

1991-92 Total Rcpts: $368,179
1990 Year-end cash: $185,722

Source of Funds
- PACs 53%
- Lg Individuals ($200+) 25%
- Individuals under $200 .... 13%
- Other 9%

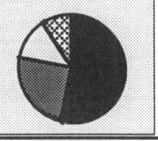

Top Industries & Interest Groups

Transportation Unions $19,250
Health Professionals $18,300
Building Trade Unions $12,500
Public Sector Unions $12,330
Insurance $11,900

Unidentified $20,150

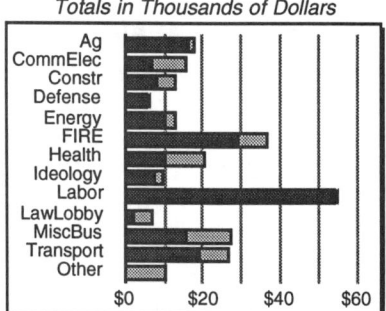

24. John M. McHugh (R)

1993-94 Committees: ArmServ GovtOps
First elected: 1992

1991-92 Total Rcpts: $177,433
1990 Year-end cash: $6,282

Source of Funds
- PACs 48%
- Lg Individuals ($200+) 15%
- Individuals under $200 .... 10%
- Other 27%

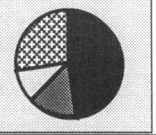

Top Industries & Interest Groups

Health Professionals $15,395
Real Estate $13,150
Gun Rights/Gun Control $9,900
Industrial Unions $9,000
Commercial Banks $6,981

Unidentified $8,695

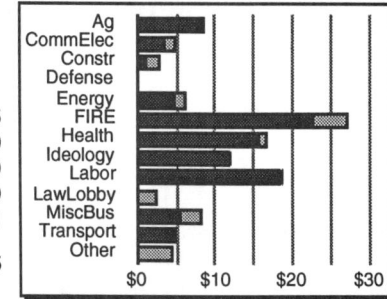

25. James T. Walsh (R)

1992 Committees: Admin Agric
First elected: 1988

1991-92 Total Rcpts: $284,162
1990 Year-end cash: $30,264

Source of Funds
- PACs 27%
- Lg Individuals ($200+) 18%
- Individuals under $200 .... 44%
- Other 12%

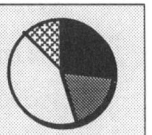

Top Industries & Interest Groups

Health Professionals $15,900
Real Estate $11,900
Insurance $11,666
Lawyers & Lobbyists $8,100
Air Transport $7,925

Unidentified $14,750

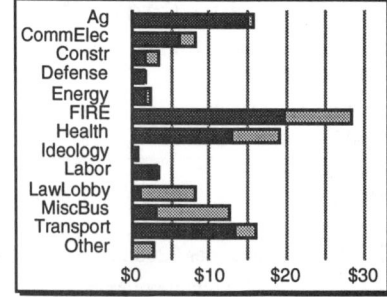

26. Maurice D. Hinchey (D)

1993-94 Committees: Banking
First elected: 1992

1991-92 Total Rcpts: $374,264
1990 Year-end cash: $5,484

Source of Funds
- PACs 38%
- Lg Individuals ($200+) 29%
- Individuals under $200 .... 23%
- Other 10%

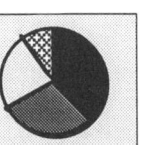

Top Industries & Interest Groups

Public Sector Unions $28,550
Misc Issues $16,484
Lawyers & Lobbyists $16,275
Building Trade Unions $12,930
Building Materials & Equipment $12,000

Unidentified $28,977

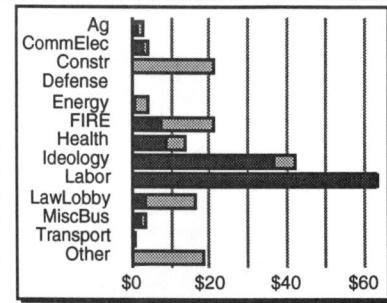

27. Bill Paxon (R)

1992 Committees: Banking Budget VetAffairs
First elected: 1988

1991-92 Total Rcpts: $845,163
1990 Year-end cash: $5,784

Source of Funds
- PACs 39%
- Lg Individuals ($200+) 36%
- Individuals under $200 .... 20%
- Other 5%

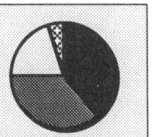

Top Industries & Interest Groups

Commercial Banks $54,550
Insurance $50,600
Real Estate $36,812
Health Professionals $32,800
General Contractors $31,950

Unidentified $64,525

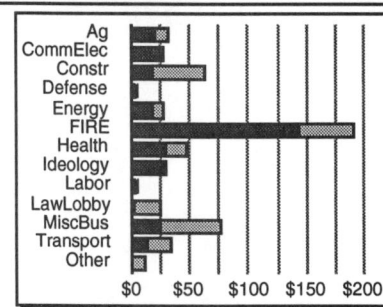

28. Louise M. Slaughter (D)

1992 Committees: Budget Rules
First elected: 1986

1991-92 Total Rcpts: $473,871
1990 Year-end cash: $76,805

Source of Funds
- PACs 58%
- Lg Individuals ($200+) 13%
- Individuals under $200 .... 18%
- Other 10%

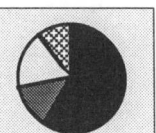

Top Industries & Interest Groups

Public Sector Unions $56,200
Industrial Unions $35,200
Transportation Unions $31,350
Health Professionals $26,200
Building Trade Unions $22,500

Unidentified $18,946

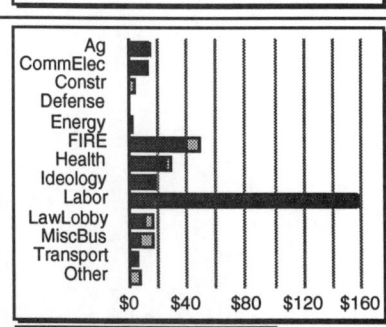

29. John J. LaFalce (D)

1992 Committees: Banking SmBus
First elected: 1974

1991-92 Total Rcpts: $588,616
1990 Year-end cash: $765,913

Source of Funds
- PACs 52%
- Lg Individuals ($200+) 28%
- Individuals under $200 .... 5%
- Other 15%

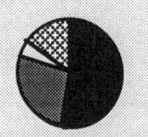

Top Industries & Interest Groups

Commercial Banks $103,450
Lawyers & Lobbyists $43,250
Food & Beverage $28,094
Accountants $23,497
Real Estate $22,700

Unidentified $39,458

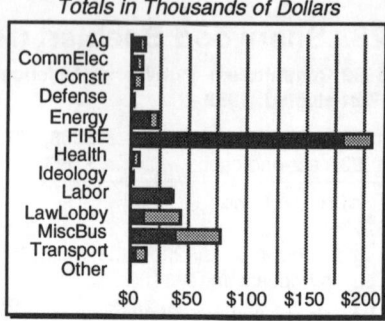

Totals in Thousands of Dollars

30. Jack Quinn (R)

1993-94 Committees: PubWorks VetAffairs
First elected: 1992

1991-92 Total Rcpts: $206,843
1990 Year-end cash: $7,583

Source of Funds
- PACs 4%
- Lg Individuals ($200+) 48%
- Individuals under $200 .... 22%
- Other 26%

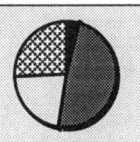

Top Industries & Interest Groups

Automotive $10,200
Lawyers & Lobbyists $8,595
Real Estate $7,900
Trucking $5,450
General Contractors $5,250

Unidentified $50,865

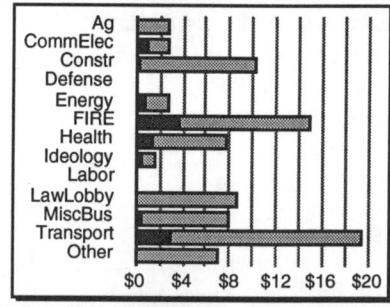

31. Amo Houghton (R)

1992 Committees: Budget ForAff
First elected: 1986

1991-92 Total Rcpts: $363,139
1990 Year-end cash: $213,487

Source of Funds
- PACs 32%
- Lg Individuals ($200+) 50%
- Individuals under $200 .... 11%
- Other 6%

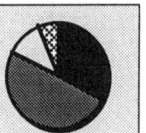

Top Industries & Interest Groups

Retired $33,850
Telecom Services & Equipment $32,250
Misc Manufacturing & Distrib $25,248
Oil & Gas $15,400
Securities & Investment $14,600

Unidentified $30,200

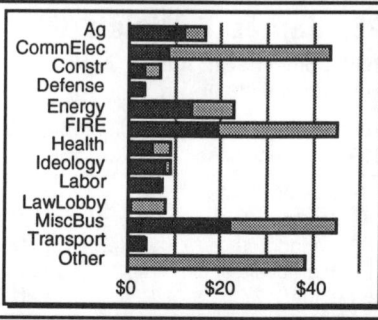

■ PACs ☒ Indivs ($200+)

North Carolina

Spending in 1992 House Races

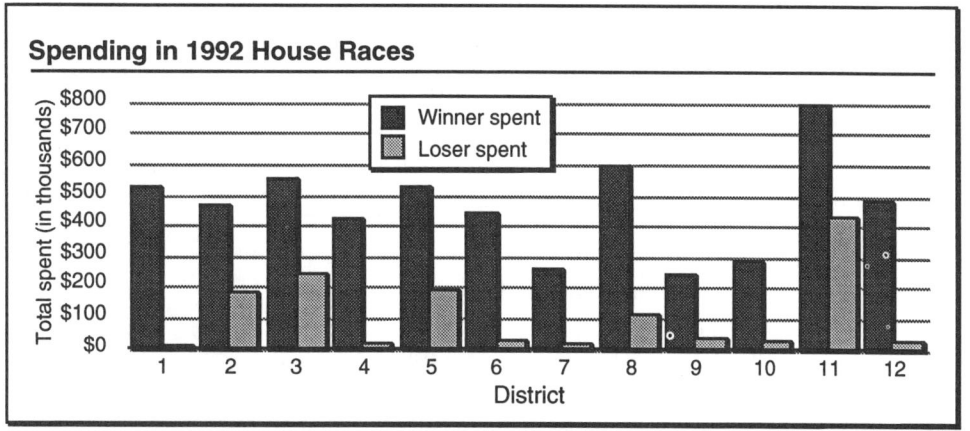

Senate Spending

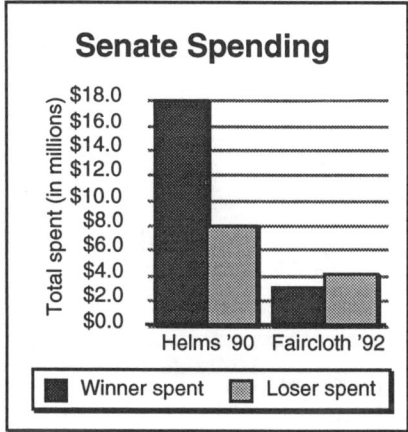

1992 Elections at a Glance

Dist	Name	Party	Vote Pct	Race Type
Sen	Lauch Faircloth (1992)	Rep	50%	Beat Incumb
Sen	Jesse Helms (1990)	Rep	53%	Reelected
1	Eva Clayton	Dem	67%	Open Seat
2	Tim Valentine	Dem	54%	Reelected
3	H. Martin Lancaster	Dem	54%	Reelected
4	David Price	Dem	65%	Reelected
5	Stephen L. Neal	Dem	53%	Reelected
6	J. Howard Coble	Rep	71%	Reelected
7	Charlie Rose	Dem	57%	Reelected
8	W. G. "Bill" Hefner	Dem	58%	Reelected
9	Alex McMillan	Rep	67%	Reelected
10	Cass Ballenger	Rep	63%	Reelected
11	Charles H. Taylor	Rep	55%	Reelected
12	Melvin Watt	Dem	70%	Open Seat

Totals in Thousands of Dollars

Sen. Lauch Faircloth (R)

1993-94 Committees: ArmServ Banking PubWorks
First elected: 1992

1991-92 Total Rcpts: $2,960,437
1990 Year-end cash: $9,762

Source of Funds
- PACs 11%
- Lg Individuals ($200+) 28%
- Individuals under $200 ....22%
- Other 39%

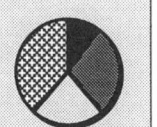

1991-92
Top Industries & Interest Groups

Retired	$99,013
Insurance	$63,300
Health Professionals	$63,006
Misc Manufacturing & Distrib	$53,600
Automotive	$53,600
Unidentified	$215,621

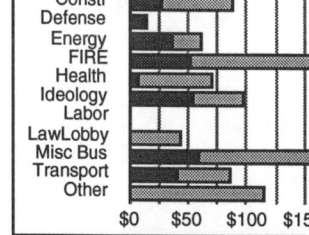

Sen. Jesse Helms (R)

1992 Committees: Agric ForRel Rules
First elected: 1972

1987-92 Total Rcpts: $20,382,361
1990 Year-end cash: $1,387

Source of Funds
- PACs 4%
- Lg Individuals ($200+) 14%
- Individuals under $200 ....77%
- Other 5%

† Does not include individual contributions from 1987-88

1987-92†
Top Industries & Interest Groups

Republican/Conservative	$198,999
Retired	$172,273
Health Professionals	$115,269
Lawyer & Lobbyists	$82,675
Misc Manufacturing & Distrib	$80,540
Unidentified	$1,547,973

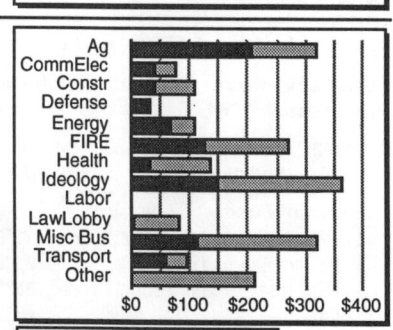

■ PACs ■ Indivs ($200+)

1. Eva Clayton (D)

1993-94 Committees: Agric SmBus
First elected: 1992

1991-92 Total Rcpts: $521,382
1990 Year-end cash: $258

Source of Funds
- PACs 54%
- Lg Individuals ($200+) 12%
- Individuals under $200 .... 26%
- Other 8%

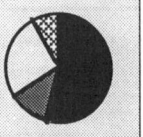

Top Industries & Interest Groups

Industrial Unions $47,800
Womens Issues $39,096
Public Sector Unions $36,500
Health Professionals $25,550
Misc Unions $23,500

Unidentified $17,621

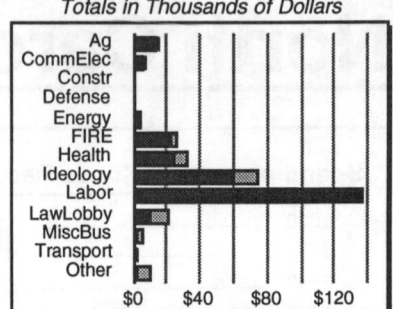

Totals in Thousands of Dollars

2. Tim Valentine (D)

1992 Committees: PubWorks Science
First elected: 1982

1991-92 Total Rcpts: $443,499
1990 Year-end cash: $5,853

Source of Funds
- PACs 52%
- Lg Individuals ($200+) 22%
- Individuals under $200 .... 16%
- Other 11%

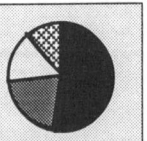

Top Industries & Interest Groups

Air Transport $27,850
Lawyers & Lobbyists $27,820
Tobacco $19,850
Telephone Utilities $15,900
Electric Utilities $15,100

Unidentified $18,850

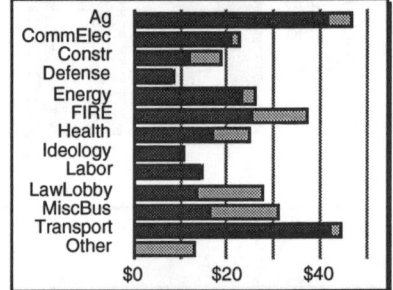

3. H. Martin Lancaster (D)

1992 Committees: ArmServ MerchMarine SmBus
First elected: 1986

1991-92 Total Rcpts: $588,664
1990 Year-end cash: $60,660

Source of Funds
- PACs 50%
- Lg Individuals ($200+) 29%
- Individuals under $200 .... 16%
- Other 4%

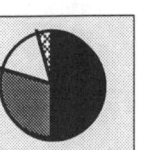

Top Industries & Interest Groups

Health Professionals $37,503
Food Processing & Sales $28,550
Lawyers & Lobbyists $25,200
Tobacco $22,198
Defense Aerospace $20,800

Unidentified $63,478

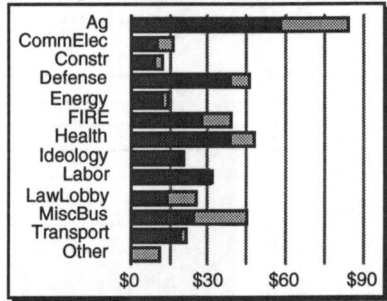

4. David Price (D)

1992 Committees: Appropriations
First elected: 1986

1991-92 Total Rcpts: $474,273
1990 Year-end cash: $56,753

Source of Funds
- PACs 57%
- Lg Individuals ($200+) 9%
- Individuals under $200 .... 29%
- Other 5%

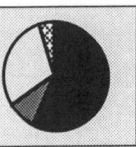

Top Industries & Interest Groups

Transportation Unions $45,050
Public Sector Unions $19,850
Health Professionals $19,150
Commercial Banks $19,050
Lawyers & Lobbyists $17,700

Unidentified $14,550

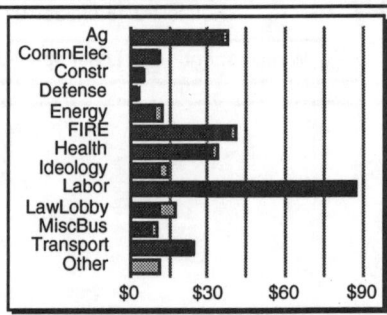

5. Stephen L. Neal (D)

1992 Committees: Banking GovtOps
First elected: 1974

1991-92 Total Rcpts: $493,627
1990 Year-end cash: $3,697

Source of Funds
- PACs 67%
- Lg Individuals ($200+) 16%
- Individuals under $200 .... 11%
- Other 6%

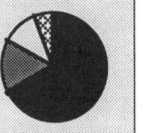

Top Industries & Interest Groups

Commercial Banks $112,900
Public Sector Unions $28,550
Lawyers & Lobbyists $28,400
Securities & Investment $21,950
Insurance $21,850

Unidentified $12,150

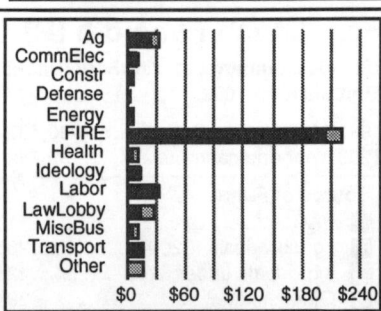

6. J. Howard Coble (R)

1992 Committees: Judiciary MerchMarine
First elected: 1984

1991-92 Total Rcpts: $504,213
1990 Year-end cash: $84,967

Source of Funds
- PACs 41%
- Lg Individuals ($200+) 20%
- Individuals under $200 .... 35%
- Other 3%

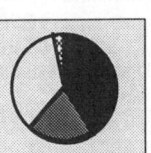

Top Industries & Interest Groups

Insurance $25,650
Textiles $19,675
Telephone Utilities $17,380
Tobacco $16,640
Misc Manufacturing & Distrib $16,169

Unidentified $15,530

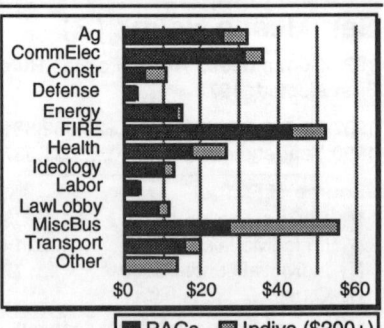

Key to committee & category abbreviations is on page 173

■ PACs ▨ Indivs ($200+)

7. Charlie Rose (D)

1992 Committees: Admin Agric
First elected: 1972

1991-92 Total Rcpts: $395,280
1990 Year-end cash: $681,533

Source of Funds
- PACs 60%
- Lg Individuals ($200+) 15%
- Individuals under $200 .... 5%
- Other 20%

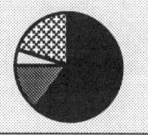

Top Industries & Interest Groups

Lawyers & Lobbyists $22,200
Crop Production/Processing $21,575
Public Sector Unions $21,000
Tobacco $19,500
Dairy $16,000

Unidentified $10,850

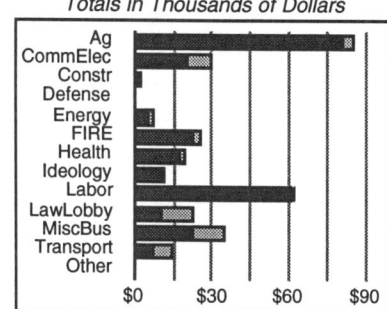

8. W. G. "Bill" Hefner (D)

1992 Committees: Appropriations
First elected: 1974

1991-92 Total Rcpts: $566,690
1990 Year-end cash: $83,385

Source of Funds
- PACs 62%
- Lg Individuals ($200+) 20%
- Individuals under $200 .... 10%
- Other 8%

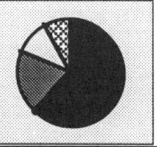

Top Industries & Interest Groups

Defense Electronics $44,550
Defense Aerospace $38,500
Public Sector Unions $35,550
Transportation Unions $25,500
Lawyers & Lobbyists $25,250

Unidentified $19,695

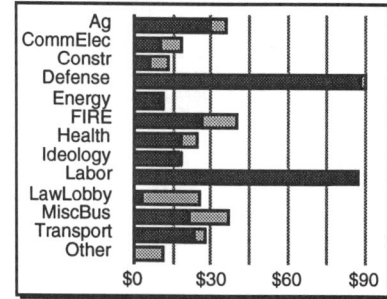

9. Alex McMillan (R)

1992 Committees: Budget Energy/Commerce
First elected: 1984

1991-92 Total Rcpts: $345,961
1990 Year-end cash: $212,977

Source of Funds
- PACs 77%
- Lg Individuals ($200+) 9%
- Individuals under $200 .... 8%
- Other 5%

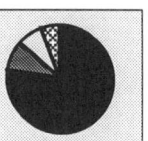

Top Industries & Interest Groups

Commercial Banks $34,450
Insurance $28,650
Health Professionals $25,750
Pharmaceuticals/Health Prod $19,450
Telephone Utilities $13,250

Unidentified $5,800

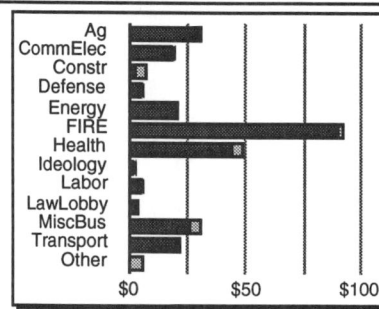

10. Cass Ballenger (R)

1992 Committees: Educ/Labor PubWorks
First elected: 1986

1991-92 Total Rcpts: $277,122
1990 Year-end cash: $19,700

Source of Funds
- PACs 61%
- Lg Individuals ($200+) 32%
- Individuals under $200 .... 4%
- Other 4%

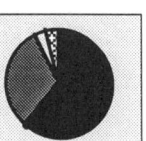

Top Industries & Interest Groups

Misc Manufacturing & Distrib $18,750
Textiles $15,950
Air Transport $12,500
Tobacco $12,250
Telephone Utilities $12,000

Unidentified $22,750

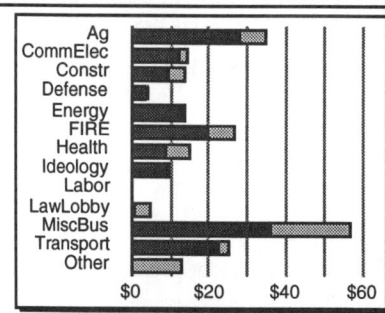

11. Charles H. Taylor (R)

1992 Committees: Interior PubWorks
First elected: 1990

1991-92 Total Rcpts: $788,360
1990 Year-end cash: $4,035

Source of Funds
- PACs 36%
- Lg Individuals ($200+) 20%
- Individuals under $200 .... 28%
- Other 17%

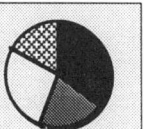

Top Industries & Interest Groups

Forestry & Forest Products $27,925
Health Professionals $23,750
Real Estate $23,125
Electric Utilities $21,000
Retired $19,389

Unidentified $30,325

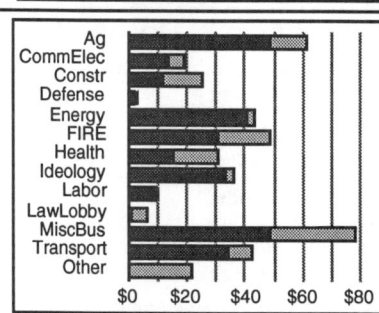

12. Melvin Watt (D)

1993-94 Committees: Banking Judiciary Post Office
First elected: 1992

1991-92 Total Rcpts: $483,601
1990 Year-end cash: $2,887

Source of Funds
- PACs 41%
- Lg Individuals ($200+) 28%
- Individuals under $200 .... 19%
- Other 12%

Top Industries & Interest Groups

Lawyers & Lobbyists $44,550
Public Sector Unions $23,500
Health Professionals $22,000
Real Estate $21,000
Commercial Banks $16,150

Unidentified $59,640

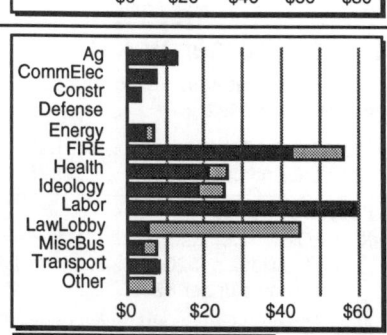

North Dakota

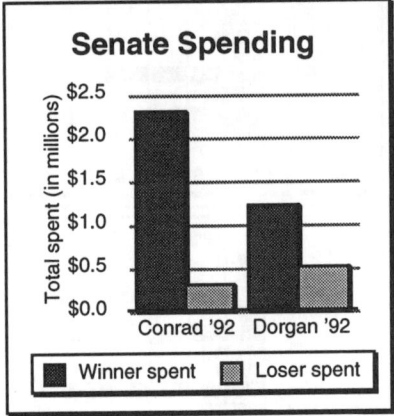

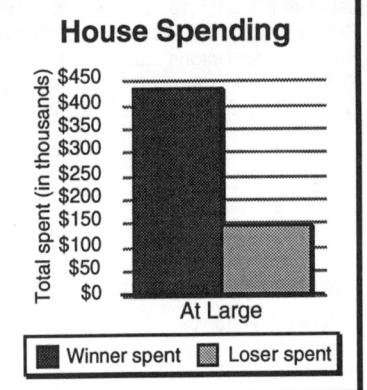

1992 Elections at a Glance

Dist	Name	Party	Vote Pct	Race Type
Sen	Byron L. Dorgan (1992)	Dem	59%	Open Seat
Sen	Kent Conrad (1992)	Dem	63%	Reelected
1	Earl Pomeroy	Dem	57%	Open Seat

Totals in Thousands of Dollars

Sen. Kent Conrad (D)
1992 Committees: Agric Budget Energy Approp
First elected: 1986

1987-92 Total Rcpts: $2,524,425
1990 Year-end cash: $132,101

Source of Funds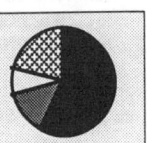
- PACs 57%
- Lg Individuals ($200+) 14%
- Individuals under $200 .... 8%
- Other 21%

1987-92†
Top Industries & Interest Groups

Lawyer & Lobbyists $169,862
Crop Production/Processing $125,555
Oil & Gas $121,649
Public Sector Unions $107,360
Electric Utilities $99,425

Unidentified $52,453

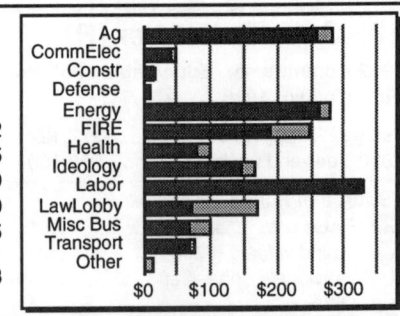

Sen. Byron L. Dorgan (D)
1992 House Committees: Ways & Means
First elected: 1992

1991-92 Total Rcpts: $1,061,651
1990 Year-end cash: $107,654

Source of Funds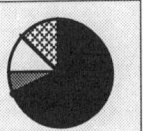
- PACs 68%
- Lg Individuals ($200+) 7%
- Individuals under $200 .... 12%
- Other 13%

1991-92
Top Industries & Interest Groups

Insurance $95,101
Public Sector Unions $68,000
Lawyer & Lobbyists $54,249
Transportation Unions $52,250
Industrial Unions $46,750

Unidentified $12,700

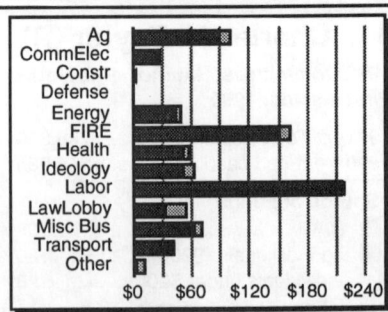

1. Earl Pomeroy (D)
1993-94 Committees: Agric Budget
First elected: 1992

1991-92 Total Rcpts: $431,979
1990 Year-end cash: $1,750

Source of Funds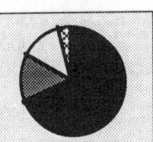
- PACs 69%
- Lg Individuals ($200+) 14%
- Individuals under $200 .... 13%
- Other 4%

Top Industries & Interest Groups

Insurance $98,628
Industrial Unions $30,450
Lawyers & Lobbyists $29,312
Public Sector Unions $28,700
Health Professionals $20,750

Unidentified $10,122

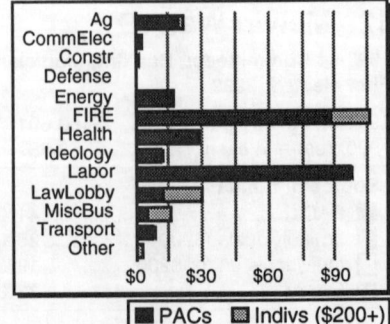

Key to committee & category abbreviations is on page 173

Ohio

Spending in 1992 House Races

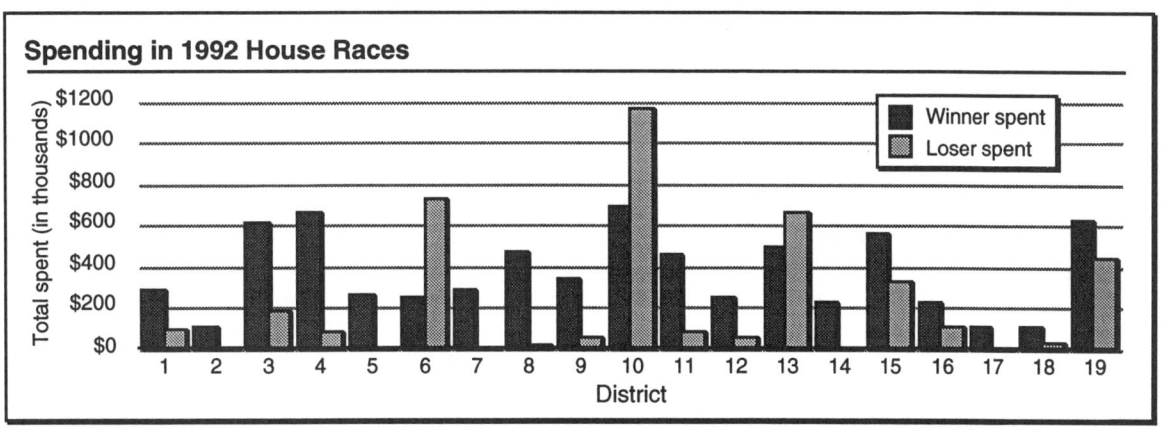

1992 Elections at a Glance

Dist	Name	Party	Vote Pct	Race Type
Sen	John Glenn (1992)	Dem	51%	Reelected
Sen	Howard Metzenbaum (1988)	Dem	57%	Reelected
1	David Mann	Dem	51%	Open Seat
2	Bill Gradison	Rep	70%	Reelected
3	Tony P. Hall	Dem	60%	Reelected
4	Michael G. Oxley	Rep	61%	Reelected
5	Paul E. Gillmor	Rep	100%	Reelected
6	Ted Strickland	Dem	51%	Beat Incumb
7	David L. Hobson	Rep	71%	Reelected
8	John A. Boehner	Rep	74%	Reelected
9	Marcy Kaptur	Dem	74%	Reelected
10	Martin R. Hoke	Rep	57%	Beat Incumb
11	Louis Stokes	Dem	69%	Reelected
12	John R. Kasich	Rep	71%	Reelected
13	Sherrod Brown	Dem	53%	Open Seat
14	Tom Sawyer	Dem	68%	Reelected
15	Deborah Pryce	Rep	44%	Open Seat
16	Ralph Regula	Rep	64%	Reelected
17	James A. Traficant Jr.	Dem	84%	Reelected
18	Douglas Applegate	Dem	68%	Reelected
19	Eric D. Fingerhut	Dem	53%	Open Seat

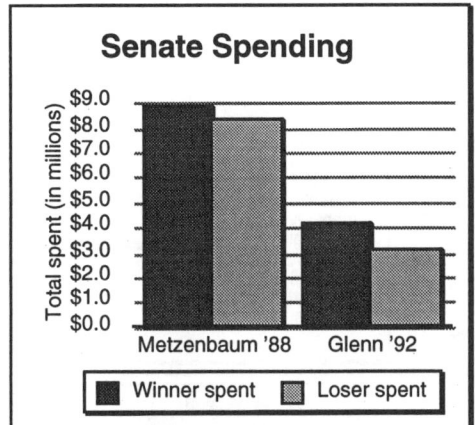

Senate Spending

Totals in Thousands of Dollars

Sen. John Glenn (D)

1992 Committees: ArmServ GovAff
First elected: 1974

1987-92 Total Rcpts: $4,245,138
1990 Year-end cash: $109,668

Source of Funds
- PACs..26%
- Lg Individuals ($200+) 31%
- Individuals under $200 ....11%
- Other 32%

1987-92†
Top Industries & Interest Groups

Lawyer & Lobbyists $251,131
Pro-Israel $182,400
Health Professionals................$121,951
Public Sector Unions $121,200
Real Estate $120,500

Unidentified $455,305

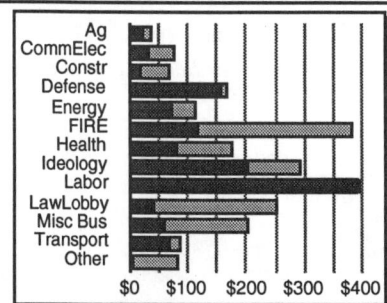

Sen. Howard M. Metzenbaum (D)

1992 Committees: Envir Judiciary Labor
First elected: 1976*

1987-92 Total Rcpts: $7,312,533
1990 Year-end cash: $0

Source of Funds
- PACs..13%
- Lg Individuals ($200+) 37%
- Individuals under $200 ....36%
- Other 15%

1987-92†
Top Industries & Interest Groups

Pro-Israel $245,085
Industrial Unions $126,450
Transportation Unions $90,800
Building Trade Unions $56,480
Leadership PACs $51,500

Unidentified $250

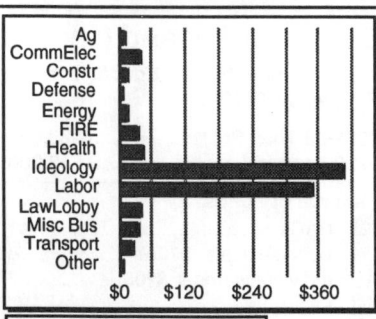

† Does not include individual contributions from 1987-88

263

Totals in Thousands of Dollars

1. David Mann (D)
1993-94 Committees: ArmServ Judiciary
First elected: 1992

1991-92 Total Rcpts: $281,158
1990 Year-end cash: $2,863

Source of Funds
- PACs 38%
- Lg Individuals ($200+) 36%
- Individuals under $200 ....22%
- Other 3%

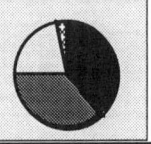

Top Industries & Interest Groups

Lawyers & Lobbyists $25,768
Industrial Unions $22,650
Public Sector Unions $16,000
Health Professionals $14,750
Securities & Investment $14,250

Unidentified $25,250

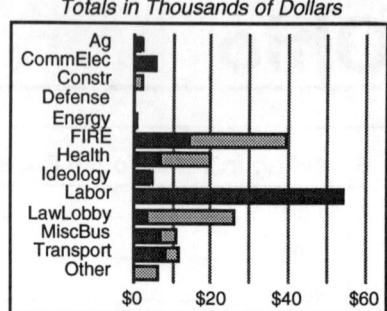

2. Bill Gradison (R)
1992 Committees: Budget Ways & Means
First elected: 1974

1991-92 Total Rcpts: $111,258
1990 Year-end cash: $458,452

Source of Funds
- PACs 0%
- Lg Individuals ($200+) 33%
- Individuals under $200 ....29%
- Other 38%

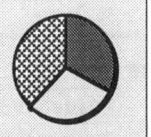

Top Industries & Interest Groups

Lawyers & Lobbyists $9,000
Insurance $5,000
Accountants $4,000
Health Professionals $3,750
Pharmaceuticals/Health Prod $2,250

Unidentified $4,716

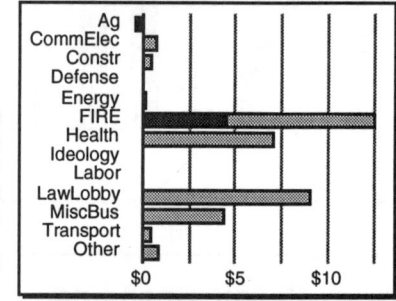

3. Tony P. Hall (D)
1992 Committees: Rules
First elected: 1978

1991-92 Total Rcpts: $342,116
1990 Year-end cash: $58,479

Source of Funds
- PACs 66%
- Lg Individuals ($200+) 8%
- Individuals under $200 ....11%
- Other 14%

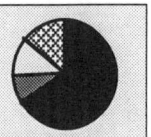

Top Industries & Interest Groups

Industrial Unions $33,400
Public Sector Unions $30,700
Lawyers & Lobbyists $18,029
Health Professionals $17,000
Telephone Utilities $15,550

Unidentified $8,312

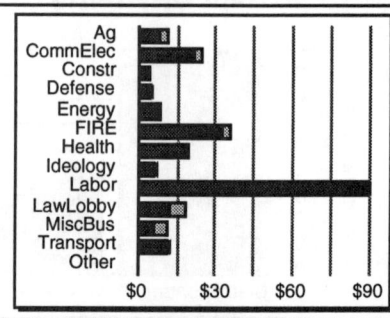

4. Michael G. Oxley (R)
1992 Committees: Energy/Commerce
First elected: 1981

1991-92 Total Rcpts: $491,631
1990 Year-end cash: $32,084

Source of Funds
- PACs 57%
- Lg Individuals ($200+) 22%
- Individuals under $200 ....17%
- Other 5%

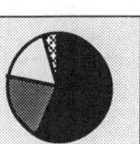

Top Industries & Interest Groups

Insurance $32,650
Oil & Gas $31,600
Electric Utilities $28,350
Telephone Utilities $23,500
Health Professionals $17,050

Unidentified $28,250

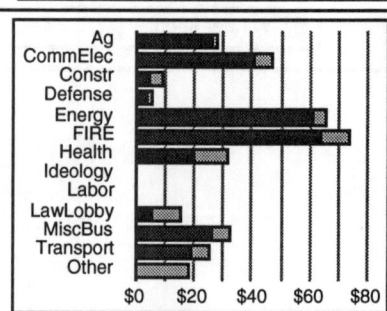

5. Paul E. Gillmor (R)
1992 Committees: Admin Banking PubWorks
First elected: 1988

1991-92 Total Rcpts: $244,817
1990 Year-end cash: $72,967

Source of Funds
- PACs 65%
- Lg Individuals ($200+) 19%
- Individuals under $200 ....11%
- Other 5%

Top Industries & Interest Groups

Commercial Banks $22,650
Insurance $17,492
Misc Manufacturing & Distrib $13,850
Air Transport $12,800
Real Estate $9,150

Unidentified $14,550

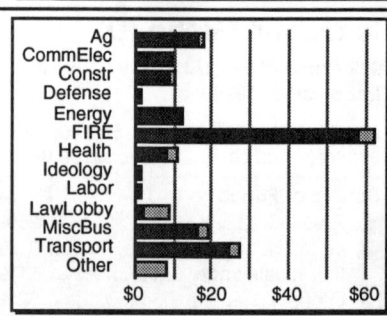

6. Ted Strickland (D)
1993-94 Committees: Educ/Labor SmBus
First elected: 1992

1991-92 Total Rcpts: $238,391
1990 Year-end cash: $3,308

Source of Funds
- PACs 41%
- Lg Individuals ($200+) 8%
- Individuals under $200 ....27%
- Other 25%

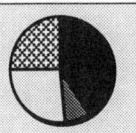

Top Industries & Interest Groups

Industrial Unions $32,200
Public Sector Unions $26,000
Building Trade Unions $14,500
Health Professionals $13,446
Transportation Unions $11,000

Unidentified $3,653

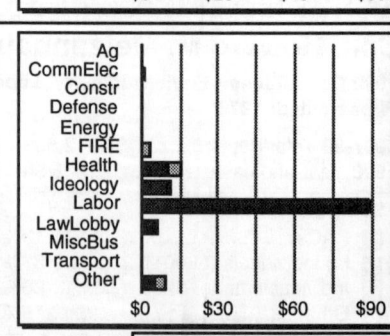

Key to committee & category abbreviations is on page 173

■ PACs   ▨ Indivs ($200+)

7. David L. Hobson (R)

1992 Committees: GovtOps PubWorks
First elected: 1990

1991-92 Total Rcpts: $360,267
1990 Year-end cash: $81,974

Source of Funds
- PACs 55%
- Lg Individuals ($200+) 15%
- Individuals under $200 ....27%
- Other 3%

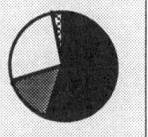

Top Industries & Interest Groups

Health Professionals $30,152
Oil & Gas $16,700
Air Transport $16,600
Insurance $13,150
Real Estate $12,850

Unidentified $15,820

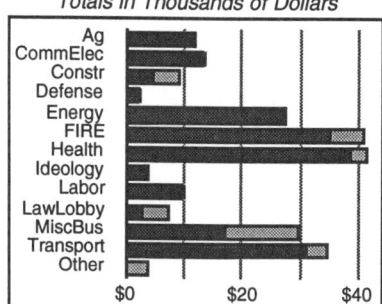

8. John A. Boehner (R)

1992 Committees: Agric Educ/Labor SmBus
First elected: 1990

1991-92 Total Rcpts: $555,139
1990 Year-end cash: $31,376

Source of Funds
- PACs 43%
- Lg Individuals ($200+) 19%
- Individuals under $200 ....36%
- Other 1%

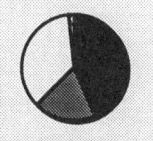

Top Industries & Interest Groups

Health Professionals $24,342
General Contractors $20,492
Misc Manufacturing & Distrib $19,865
Telephone Utilities $17,350
Crop Production/Processing $13,868

Unidentified $33,103

9. Marcy Kaptur (D)

1992 Committees: Appropriations
First elected: 1982

1991-92 Total Rcpts: $290,940
1990 Year-end cash: $13,974

Source of Funds
- PACs 65%
- Lg Individuals ($200+) 6%
- Individuals under $200 ....17%
- Other 12%

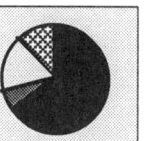

Top Industries & Interest Groups

Industrial Unions $35,910
Public Sector Unions $30,125
Building Trade Unions $27,450
Transportation Unions $26,050
Insurance $8,700

Unidentified $4,000

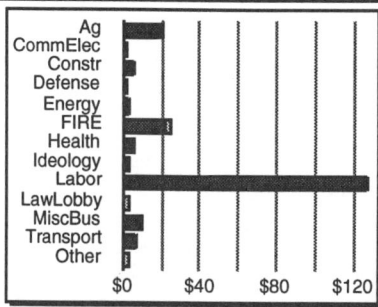

10. Martin R. Hoke (R)

1993-94 Committees: Budget Science
First elected: 1992

1991-92 Total Rcpts: $683,560
1990 Year-end cash: $3,391

Source of Funds
- PACs 0%
- Lg Individuals ($200+) 40%
- Individuals under $200 ....16%
- Other 45%

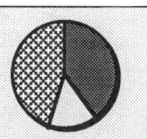

Top Industries & Interest Groups

Lawyers & Lobbyists $27,032
Retired $26,500
Health Professionals $22,150
Misc Manufacturing & Distrib $19,300
Securities & Investment $14,600

Unidentified $74,870

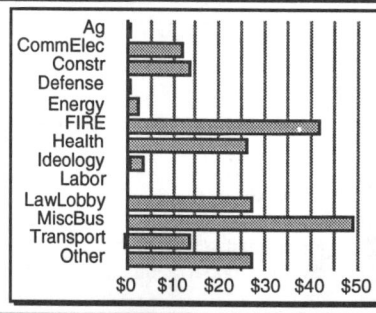

11. Louis Stokes (D)

1992 Committees: Appropriations
First elected: 1968

1991-92 Total Rcpts: $391,172
1990 Year-end cash: $183,789

Source of Funds
- PACs 37%
- Lg Individuals ($200+) 30%
- Individuals under $200 ....5%
- Other 28%

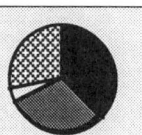

Top Industries & Interest Groups

Health Professionals $30,300
Real Estate $29,000
Public Sector Unions $22,100
Lawyers & Lobbyists $21,550
Industrial Unions $15,750

Unidentified $12,600

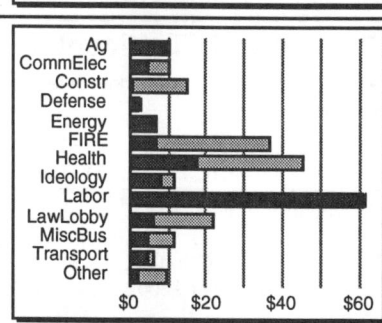

12. John R. Kasich (R)

1992 Committees: ArmServ Budget
First elected: 1982

1991-92 Total Rcpts: $279,301
1990 Year-end cash: $130,431

Source of Funds
- PACs 41%
- Lg Individuals ($200+) 53%
- Individuals under $200 ....5%
- Other 1%

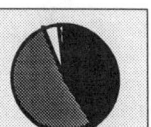

Top Industries & Interest Groups

Health Professionals $20,550
General Contractors $13,700
Insurance $13,000
Real Estate $11,275
Lawyers & Lobbyists $10,550

Unidentified $31,350

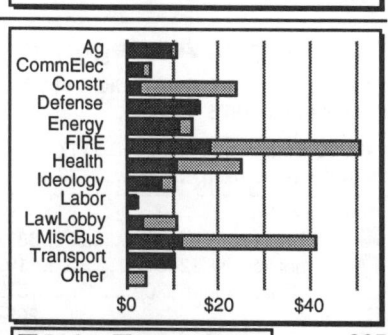

13. Sherrod Brown (D)

1993-94 Committees: Energy/Comm ForAff Post Office
First elected: 1992

1991-92 Total Rcpts: $495,275
1990 Year-end cash: $8,920

Source of Funds
- PACs 51%
- Lg Individuals ($200+) 30%
- Individuals under $200 ....14%
- Other 5%

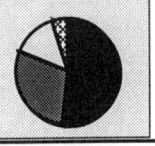

Top Industries & Interest Groups

Industrial Unions $67,500
Lawyers & Lobbyists $39,550
Public Sector Unions $30,200
Real Estate $25,250
Health Professionals $24,200

Unidentified $34,658

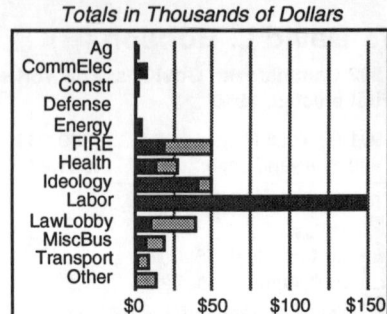

14. Tom Sawyer (D)

1992 Committees: Educ/Labor ForAff Post Office
First elected: 1986

1991-92 Total Rcpts: $195,200
1990 Year-end cash: $34,362

Source of Funds
- PACs 76%
- Lg Individuals ($200+) 11%
- Individuals under $200 ....10%
- Other 4%

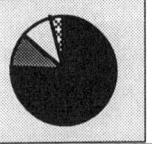

Top Industries & Interest Groups

Public Sector Unions $29,500
Transportation Unions $18,500
Industrial Unions $17,200
Health Professionals $11,600
Building Trade Unions $9,500

Unidentified $5,882

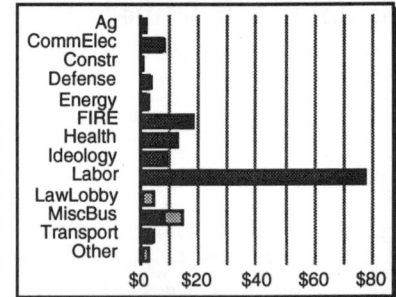

15. Deborah Pryce (R)

1993-94 Committees: Banking GovtOps
First elected: 1992

1991-92 Total Rcpts: $558,617
1990 Year-end cash: $1,874

Source of Funds
- PACs 35%
- Lg Individuals ($200+) 34%
- Individuals under $200 ....20%
- Other 11%

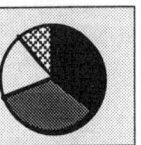

Top Industries & Interest Groups

Lawyers & Lobbyists $31,281
Commercial Banks $28,847
Health Professionals $26,850
Real Estate $24,550
Insurance $20,849

Unidentified $62,470

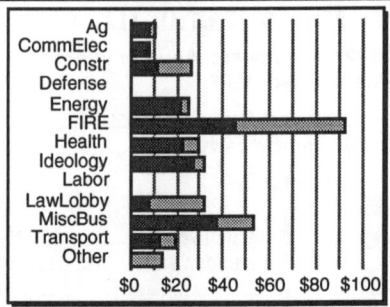

16. Ralph Regula (R)

1992 Committees: Appropriations
First elected: 1972

1991-92 Total Rcpts: $168,665
1990 Year-end cash: $12,012

Source of Funds
- PACs 0%
- Lg Individuals ($200+) 41%
- Individuals under $200 ....50%
- Other 9%

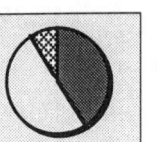

Top Industries & Interest Groups

Real Estate $13,750
Lawyers & Lobbyists $9,104
Steel Production $6,300
General Contractors $4,000
Health Professionals $3,900

Unidentified $12,700

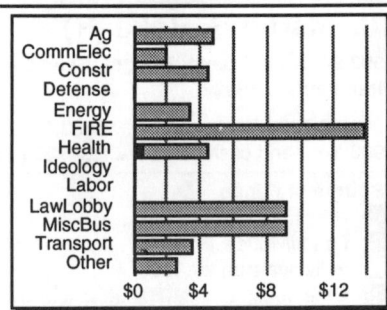

17. James A. Traficant Jr. (D)

1992 Committees: PubWorks Science
First elected: 1984

1991-92 Total Rcpts: $155,474
1990 Year-end cash: $132,898

Source of Funds
- PACs 51%
- Lg Individuals ($200+) 17%
- Individuals under $200 ....23%
- Other 9%

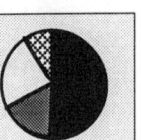

Top Industries & Interest Groups

Industrial Unions $37,000
Transportation Unions $17,150
Public Sector Unions $13,620
Building Trade Unions $8,500
Health Professionals $4,000

Unidentified $12,700

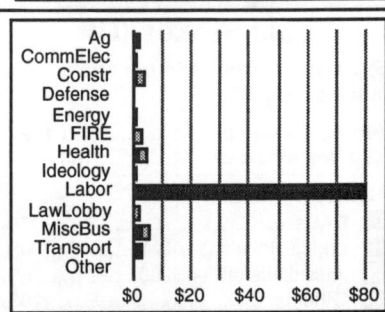

18. Douglas Applegate (D)

1992 Committees: PubWorks VetAffairs
First elected: 1976

1991-92 Total Rcpts: $117,262
1990 Year-end cash: $176,449

Source of Funds
- PACs 68%
- Lg Individuals ($200+) 1%
- Individuals under $200 ....5%
- Other 26%

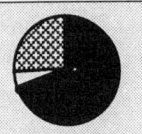

Top Industries & Interest Groups

Transportation Unions $13,098
Industrial Unions $13,000
Air Transport $7,200
Public Sector Unions $6,500
Real Estate $6,000

Unidentified $250

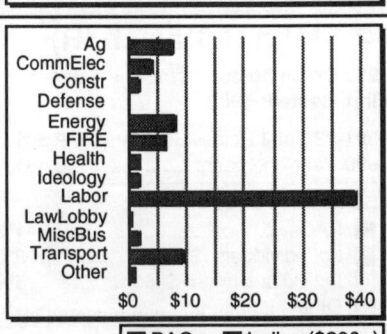

Key to committee & category abbreviations is on page 173

19. Eric D. Fingerhut (D)

1993-94 Committees: Banking ForAff Science
First elected: 1992

1991-92 Total Rcpts: $617,946
1990 Year-end cash: $6,465

Source of Funds
- PACs 33%
- Lg Individuals ($200+) 44%
- Individuals under $200 .... 19%
- Other 4%

Top Industries & Interest Groups

Pro-Israel	$72,950
Lawyers & Lobbyists	$43,300
Real Estate	$40,700
Industrial Unions	$34,300
Public Sector Unions	$30,150
Unidentified	$61,687

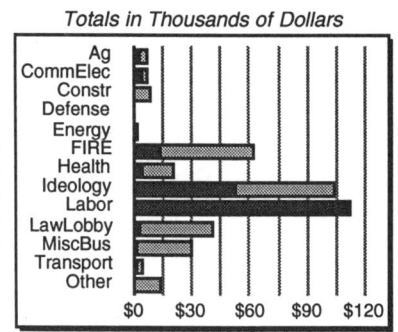

Totals in Thousands of Dollars

■ PACs   ▨ Indivs ($200+)

Oklahoma

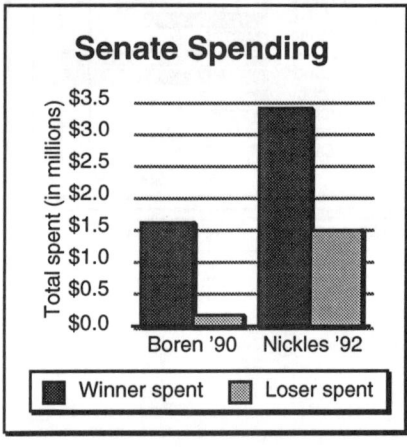

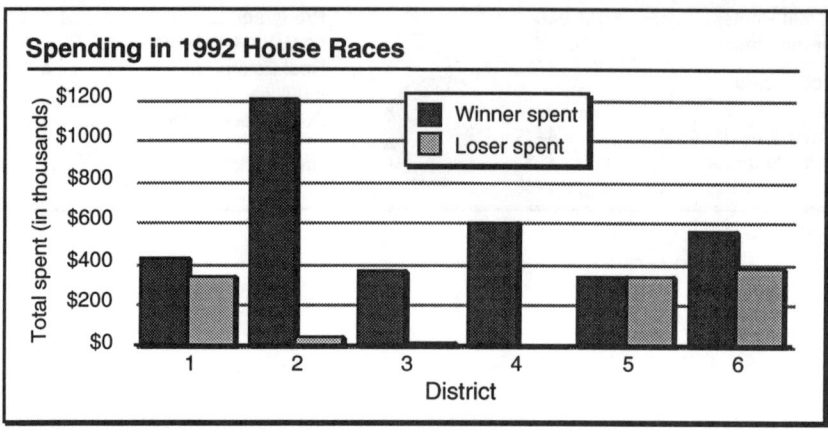

1992 Elections at a Glance

Dist	Name	Party	Vote Pct	Race Type
Sen	Don Nickles (1992)	Rep	58%	Reelected
Sen	David L. Boren (1990)	Dem	83%	Reelected
1	James M. Inhofe	Rep	53%	Reelected
2	Mike Synar	Dem	56%	Reelected
3	Bill Brewster	Dem	75%	Reelected
4	Dave McCurdy	Dem	71%	Reelected
5	Ernest Istook Jr.	Rep	53%	Open Seat
6	Glenn English	Dem	68%	Reelected

Totals in Thousands of Dollars

Sen. David L. Boren (D)

1992 Committees: Agric Finance
First elected: 1978

1987-92 Total Rcpts: $1,726,669
1990 Year-end cash: $7,103

Source of Funds
- PACs 0%
- Lg Individuals ($200+) 81%
- Individuals under $200 .... 11%
- Other 8%

1987-92†
Top Industries & Interest Groups

Oil & Gas $186,760
Lawyer & Lobbyists $172,450
Securities & Investment $49,350
Commercial Banks $48,580
Real Estate $45,800

Unidentified $169,029

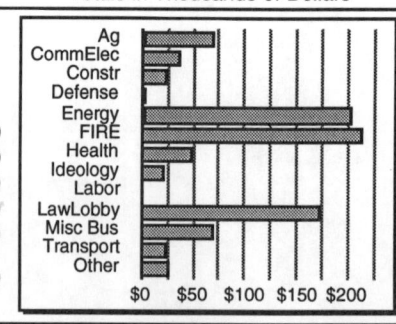

Sen. Don Nickles (R)

1992 Committees: Approp Budget Energy
First elected: 1980

1987-92 Total Rcpts: $3,686,883
1990 Year-end cash: $569,953

Source of Funds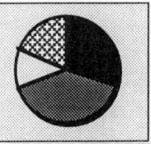
- PACs 30%
- Lg Individuals ($200+) 39%
- Individuals under $200 .... 12%
- Other 18%

1987-92†
Top Industries & Interest Groups

Oil & Gas $531,189
Insurance $181,492
Lawyer & Lobbyists $178,770
Health Professionals $133,100
Retired $97,150

Unidentified $261,234

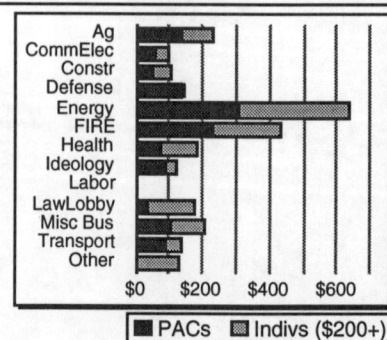

Key to committee & category abbreviations is on page 173

1. James M. Inhofe (R)

1992 Committees: MerchMarine PubWorks
First elected: 1986

1991-92 Total Rcpts: $425,361
1990 Year-end cash: $7,551

Source of Funds
- PACs 49%
- Lg Individuals ($200+) 25%
- Individuals under $200 .... 12%
- Other 14%

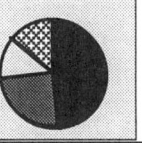

Top Industries & Interest Groups

Oil & Gas $57,505
Air Transport $46,725
Health Professionals $19,550
Insurance $18,200
Automotive $16,550

Unidentified $13,700

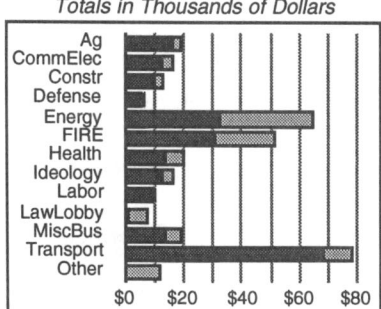

2. Mike Synar (D)

1992 Committees: Energy/Commerce GovtOps Judiciary
First elected: 1978

1991-92 Total Rcpts: $1,191,392
1990 Year-end cash: $26,075

Source of Funds
- PACs .... -0%
- Lg Individuals ($200+) 72%
- Individuals under $200 .... 26%
- Other 2%

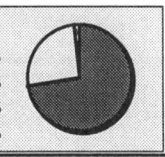

Top Industries & Interest Groups

Lawyers & Lobbyists $143,121
Oil & Gas $131,414
Media/Entertainment $71,754
Securities & Investment $34,850
Telephone Utilities $33,950

Unidentified $118,833

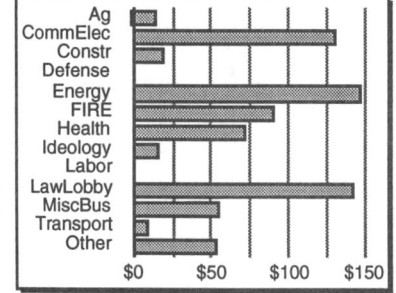

3. Bill Brewster (D)

1992 Committees: PubWorks VetAffairs
First elected: 1990

1991-92 Total Rcpts: $423,953
1990 Year-end cash: $39,867

Source of Funds
- PACs 62%
- Lg Individuals ($200+) 24%
- Individuals under $200 .... 10%
- Other 4%

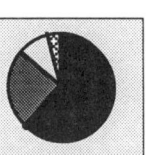

Top Industries & Interest Groups

Oil & Gas $49,000
Health Professionals $34,599
Lawyers & Lobbyists $23,600
Air Transport $17,500
Retail Sales $16,000

Unidentified $15,800

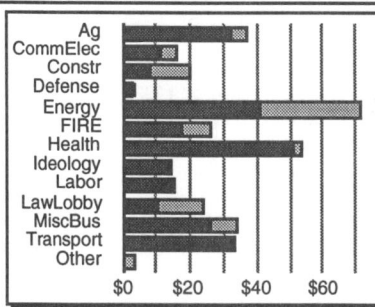

4. Dave McCurdy (D)

1992 Committees: ArmServ Science
First elected: 1980

1991-92 Total Rcpts: $556,174
1990 Year-end cash: $53,387

Source of Funds
- PACs 48%
- Lg Individuals ($200+) 37%
- Individuals under $200 .... 11%
- Other 5%

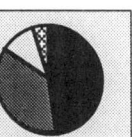

Top Industries & Interest Groups

Defense Aerospace $63,750
Defense Electronics $50,200
Lawyers & Lobbyists $39,050
Oil & Gas $30,600
Pro-Israel $26,750

Unidentified $22,300

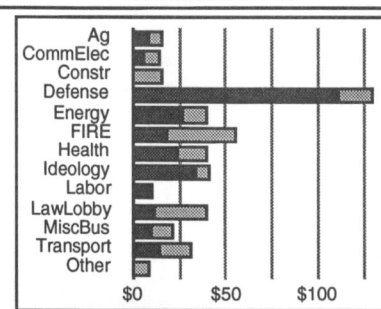

5. Ernest Istook Jr. (R)

1993-94 Committees: Appropriations
First elected: 1992

1991-92 Total Rcpts: $328,528
1990 Year-end cash: $914

Source of Funds
- PACs 20%
- Lg Individuals ($200+) 24%
- Individuals under $200 .... 20%
- Other 36%

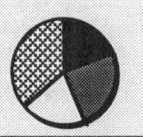

Top Industries & Interest Groups

Oil & Gas $31,000
Health Professionals $20,200
Lawyers & Lobbyists $16,450
Insurance $15,806
Food Processing & Sales $7,000

Unidentified $10,300

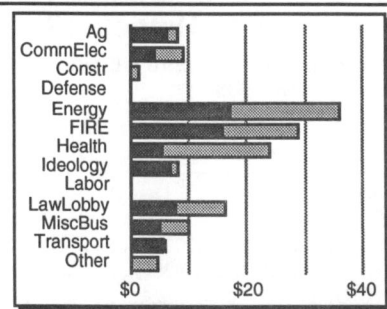

6. Glenn English (D)

1992 Committees: Agric GovtOps
First elected: 1974

1991-92 Total Rcpts: $379,380
1990 Year-end cash: $150,105

Source of Funds
- PACs 49%
- Lg Individuals ($200+) 18%
- Individuals under $200 .... 18%
- Other 15%

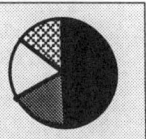

Top Industries & Interest Groups

Securities & Investment $29,900
Lawyers & Lobbyists $22,218
Telephone Utilities $22,150
Agricultural Services/Products .. $17,850
Public Sector Unions $16,700

Unidentified $17,068

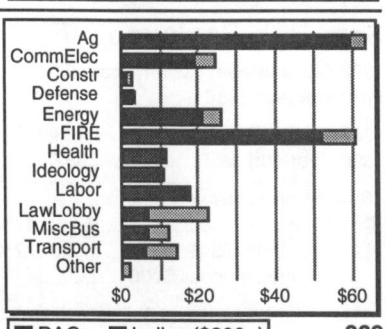

† Does not include individual contributions from 1987-88

Oregon

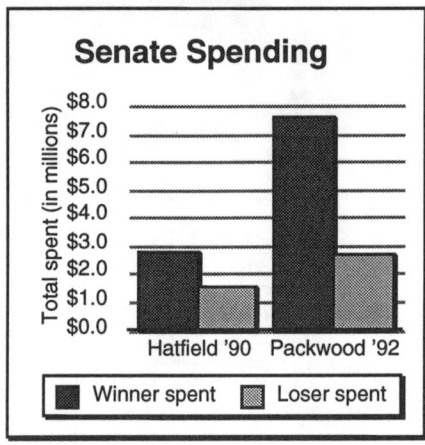

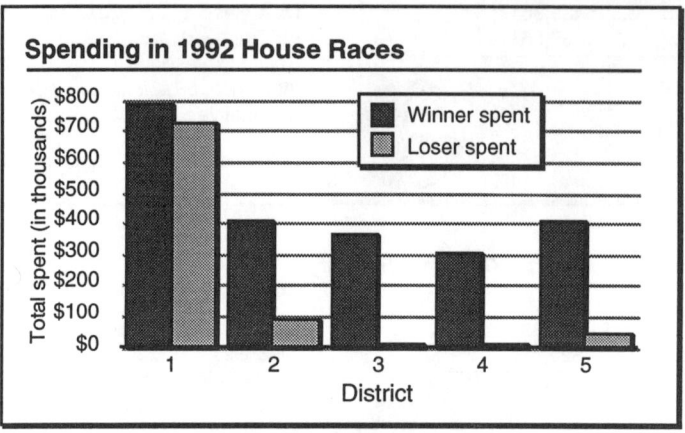

1992 Elections at a Glance

Dist	Name	Party	Vote Pct	Race Type
Sen	Bob Packwood (1992)	Rep	52%	Reelected
Sen	Mark O. Hatfield (1990)	Rep	54%	Reelected
1	Elizabeth Furse	Dem	52%	Open Seat
2	Bob Smith	Rep	67%	Reelected
3	Ron Wyden	Dem	77%	Reelected
4	Peter A. DeFazio	Dem	71%	Reelected
5	Mike Kopetski	Dem	64%	Reelected

Totals in Thousands of Dollars

Sen. Mark O. Hatfield (R)

1992 Committees: Approp Energy Rules
First elected: 1966

1987-92 Total Rcpts: $2,550,434
1990 Year-end cash: $4,716

Source of Funds
- PACs 38%
- Lg Individuals ($200+) 33%
- Individuals under $200 .... 11%
- Other 18%

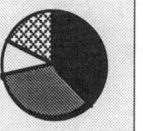

1987-92†
Top Industries & Interest Groups

Forest Products $183,100
Lawyer & Lobbyists $125,856
Oil & Gas $84,957
Health Professionals $68,400
Insurance $66,281

Unidentified $190,267

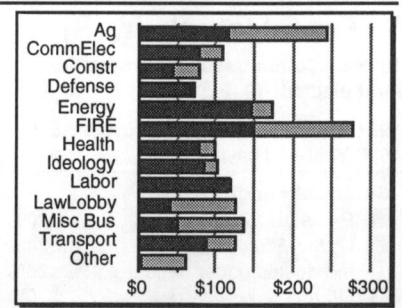

Sen. Bob Packwood (R)

1992 Committees: Commerce Finance
First elected: 1968

1987-92 Total Rcpts: $8,228,212
1990 Year-end cash: $887,627

Source of Funds
- PACs 15%
- Lg Individuals ($200+) 27%
- Individuals under $200 .... 47%
- Other 12%

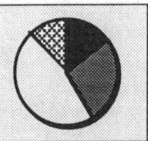

1987-92†
Top Industries & Interest Groups

Lawyer & Lobbyists $288,575
Pro-Israel $242,536
Media/Entertainment $178,051
Insurance $163,364
Securities & Investment $162,140

Unidentified $602,081

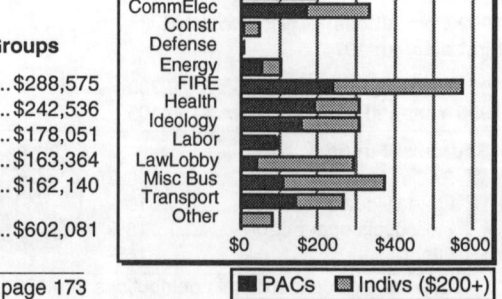

Key to committee & category abbreviations is on page 173

Totals in Thousands of Dollars

1. Elizabeth Furse (D)
1993-94 Committees: ArmServ Banking MerchMarine
First elected: 1992

1991-92 Total Rcpts: $785,545
1990 Year-end cash: $7,255

Source of Funds
- PACs 24%
- Lg Individuals ($200+) 30%
- Individuals under $200 .... 45%
- Other 2%

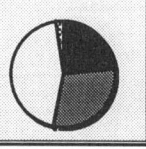

Top Industries & Interest Groups

Womens Issues $60,305
Lawyers & Lobbyists $36,869
Democratic/Liberal $30,504
Public Sector Unions $24,200
Industrial Unions $17,300

Unidentified $62,895

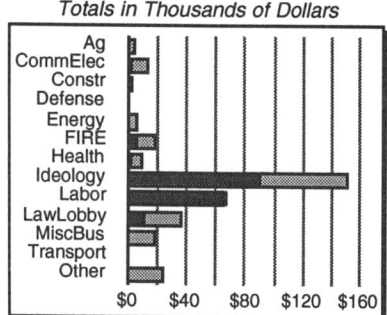

2. Bob Smith (R)
1992 Committees: Agric Interior
First elected: 1982

1991-92 Total Rcpts: $462,680
1990 Year-end cash: $240,746

Source of Funds
- PACs 36%
- Lg Individuals ($200+) 22%
- Individuals under $200 .... 37%
- Other 5%

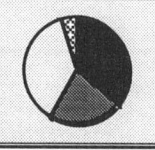

Top Industries & Interest Groups

Forestry & Forest Products $43,762
Livestock $18,900
Crop Production/Processing $14,425
Agricultural Services/Products .. $14,400
Commercial Banks $11,350

Unidentified $13,800

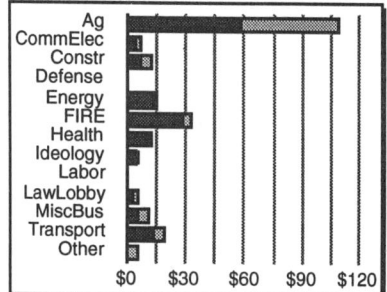

3. Ron Wyden (D)
1992 Committees: Energy/Commerce SmBus
First elected: 1980

1991-92 Total Rcpts: $233,749
1990 Year-end cash: $328,099

Source of Funds
- PACs 50%
- Lg Individuals ($200+) 8%
- Individuals under $200 .... 20%
- Other 22%

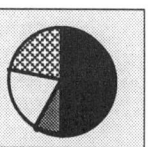

Top Industries & Interest Groups

Health Professionals $24,525
Lawyers & Lobbyists $11,650
Hospitals/Nursing Homes $8,100
Securities & Investment $6,500
Public Sector Unions $6,000

Unidentified $3,400

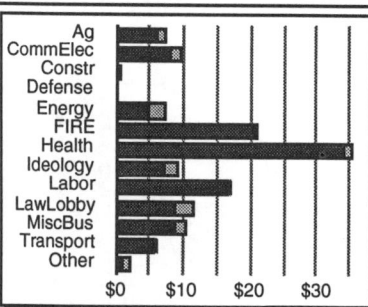

4. Peter A. DeFazio (D)
1992 Committees: Interior PubWorks
First elected: 1986

1991-92 Total Rcpts: $248,887
1990 Year-end cash: $43,563

Source of Funds
- PACs 68%
- Lg Individuals ($200+) 5%
- Individuals under $200 .... 20%
- Other 7%

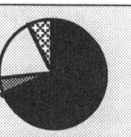

Top Industries & Interest Groups

Transportation Unions $30,500
Industrial Unions $25,000
Public Sector Unions $18,500
Building Trade Unions $15,500
Air Transport $14,750

Unidentified $750

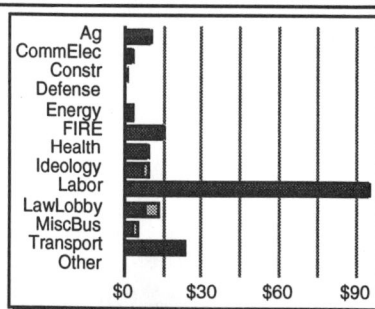

5. Mike Kopetski (D)
1992 Committees: Agric Judiciary Science
First elected: 1990

1991-92 Total Rcpts: $434,981
1990 Year-end cash: $40,738

Source of Funds
- PACs 70%
- Lg Individuals ($200+) 9%
- Individuals under $200 .... 21%
- Other 1%

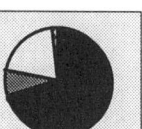

Top Industries & Interest Groups

Public Sector Unions $39,500
Transportation Unions $29,050
Health Professionals $25,700
Telephone Utilities $23,025
Lawyers & Lobbyists $22,100

Unidentified $1,550

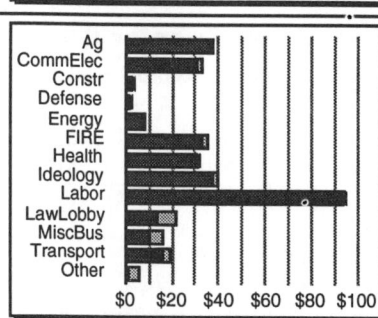

■ PACs   ▨ Indivs ($200+)

† Does not include individual contributions from 1987-88

Pennsylvania

Spending in 1992 House Races

Senate Spending

1992 Elections at a Glance

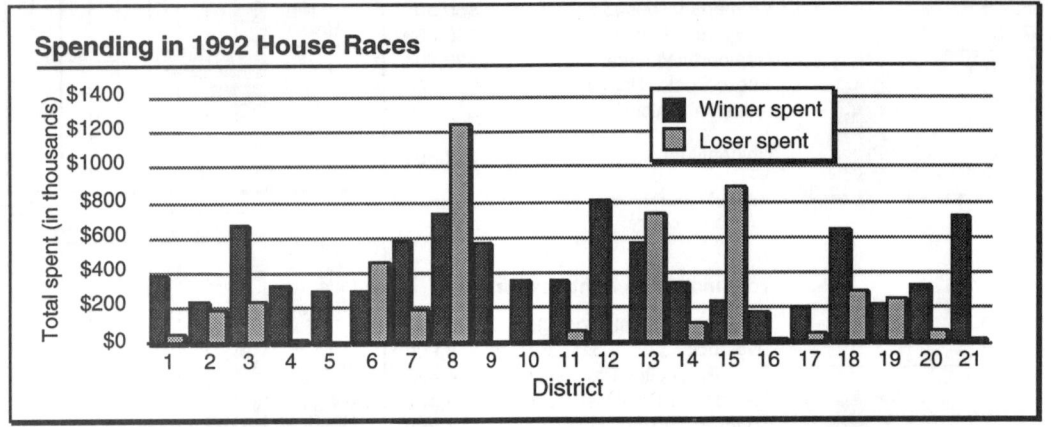

Dist	Name	Party	Vote Pct	Race Type
Sen	Arlen Specter (1992)	Rep	49%	Reelected
Sen	Harris Wofford (1991)	Dem	55%	Reelected
1	Thomas M. Foglietta	Dem	81%	Reelected
2	Lucien E. Blackwell	Dem	77%	Reelected
3	Robert A. Borski	Dem	59%	Reelected
4	Ron Klink	Dem	78%	Open Seat
5	William F. Clinger	Rep	100%	Reelected
6	Tim Holden	Dem	52%	Open Seat
7	Curt Weldon	Rep	66%	Reelected
8	James C. Greenwood	Rep	52%	Beat Incumb
9	Bud Shuster	Rep	100%	Reelected
10	Joseph M. McDade	Rep	90%	Reelected
11	Paul E. Kanjorski	Dem	67%	Reelected
12	John P. Murtha	Dem	100%	Reelected
13	Marjorie Margolies-Mezvinsky	Dem	50%	Open Seat
14	William J. Coyne	Dem	72%	Reelected
15	Paul McHale	Dem	52%	Beat Incumb
16	Robert S. Walker	Rep	65%	Reelected
17	George W. Gekas	Rep	70%	Reelected
18	Rick Santorum	Rep	61%	Reelected
19	Bill Goodling	Rep	45%	Reelected
20	Austin J. Murphy	Dem	51%	Reelected
21	Tom Ridge	Rep	68%	Reelected

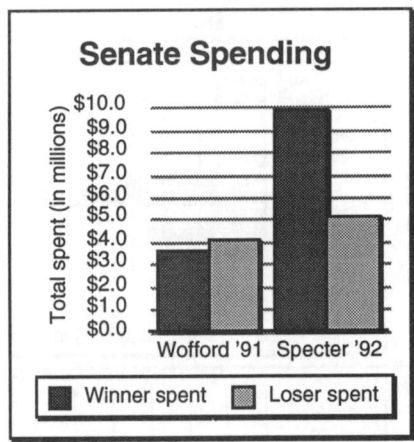

Totals in Thousands of Dollars

Sen. Arlen Specter (R)

1992 Committees: Approp Banking Judiciary VetAffairs
First elected: 1980

1987-92 Total Rcpts: $10,463,911
1990 Year-end cash: $51,128

Source of Funds
- PACs 17%
- Lg Individuals ($200+) 53%
- Individuals under $200 .... 15%
- Other 14%

1987-92†
Top Industries & Interest Groups

Lawyer & Lobbyists $911,005
Real Estate $319,448
Health Professionals $294,135
Pro-Israel $275,960
Insurance $265,203

Unidentified $2,037,818

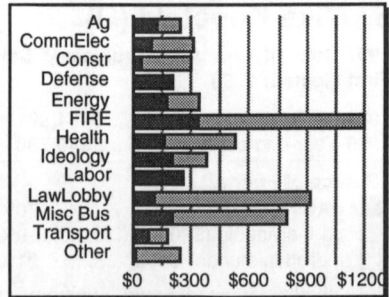

Sen. Harris Wofford (D)

1992 Committees: Envir ForRel SmBus
First elected: 1991

1991-92 Total Rcpts: $3,982,806
1990 Year-end cash: $454,565

Source of Funds
- PACs 21%
- Lg Individuals ($200+) 46%
- Individuals under $200 .... 10%
- Other 23%

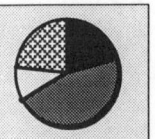

1991-92
Top Industries & Interest Groups

Lawyer & Lobbyists $724,065
Pro-Israel $172,450
Industrial Unions $154,600
Securities & Investment $134,000
Retired $128,414

Unidentified $435,368

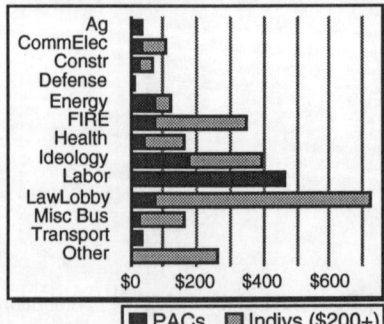

Key to committee & category abbreviations is on page 173

Totals in Thousands of Dollars

1. Thomas M. Foglietta (D)

1992 Committees: ArmServ ForAff MerchMarine
First elected: 1980

1991-92 Total Rcpts:	$387,584
1990 Year-end cash:	$383,478

Source of Funds
- PACs 43%
- Lg Individuals ($200+) 34%
- Individuals under $200 .... 2%
- Other 21%

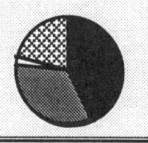

Top Industries & Interest Groups

Lawyers & Lobbyists	$44,586
Transportation Unions	$31,000
Industrial Unions	$25,600
Building Trade Unions	$23,095
Public Sector Unions	$20,750
Unidentified	$29,800

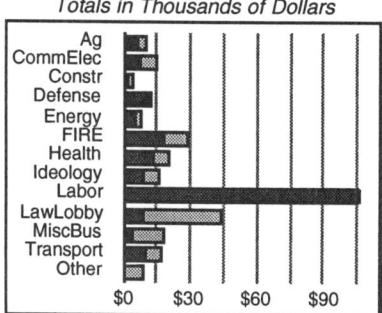

2. Lucien E. Blackwell (D)

1992 Committees: MerchMarine PubWorks
First elected: 1991

1991-92 Total Rcpts:	$313,413
1990 Year-end cash:	$16,359

Source of Funds
- PACs 49%
- Lg Individuals ($200+) 39%
- Individuals under $200 .... 8%
- Other 4%

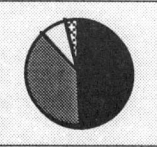

Top Industries & Interest Groups

Lawyers & Lobbyists	$46,947
Industrial Unions	$29,500
Transportation Unions	$24,500
Public Sector Unions	$23,000
Building Trade Unions	$18,470
Unidentified	$33,900

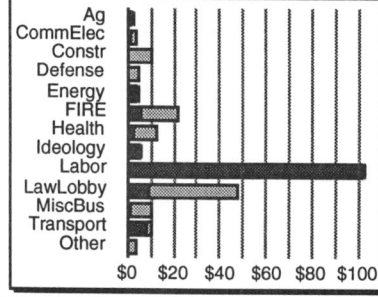

3. Robert A. Borski (D)

1992 Committees: MerchMarine PubWorks
First elected: 1982

1991-92 Total Rcpts:	$512,477
1990 Year-end cash:	$3,481

Source of Funds
- PACs 53%
- Lg Individuals ($200+) 30%
- Individuals under $200 .... 11%
- Other 6%

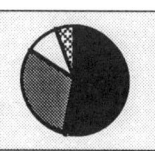

Top Industries & Interest Groups

Transportation Unions	$44,050
Lawyers & Lobbyists	$41,000
Public Sector Unions	$34,500
Industrial Unions	$32,000
Building Trade Unions	$31,895
Unidentified	$33,479

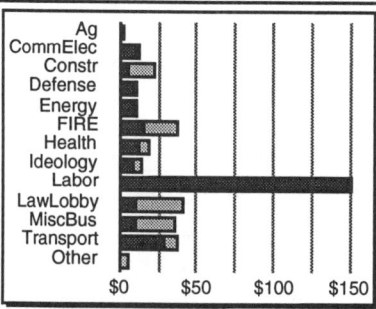

4. Ron Klink (D)

1993-94 Committees: Banking Educ/Labor SmBus
First elected: 1992

1991-92 Total Rcpts:	$422,391
1990 Year-end cash:	$2,497

Source of Funds
- PACs 31%
- Lg Individuals ($200+) 9%
- Individuals under $200 .... 27%
- Other 34%

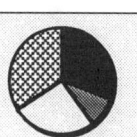

Top Industries & Interest Groups

Industrial Unions	$36,000
Public Sector Unions	$21,500
Building Trade Unions	$12,750
Transportation Unions	$12,250
Lawyers & Lobbyists	$8,050
Unidentified	$19,788

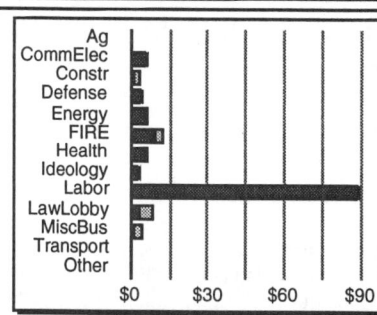

5. William F. Clinger (R)

1992 Committees: GovtOps PubWorks
First elected: 1978

1991-92 Total Rcpts:	$286,477
1990 Year-end cash:	$96,640

Source of Funds
- PACs 50%
- Lg Individuals ($200+) 10%
- Individuals under $200 .... 36%
- Other 5%

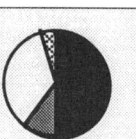

Top Industries & Interest Groups

Air Transport	$33,525
Transportation Unions	$10,150
Oil & Gas	$9,345
Telephone Utilities	$7,850
Lawyers & Lobbyists	$7,300
Unidentified	$4,050

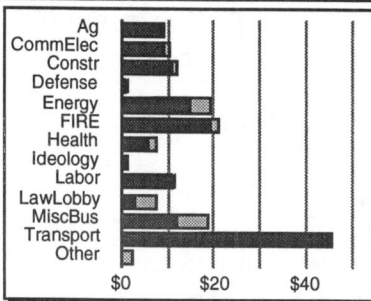

6. Tim Holden (D)

1993-94 Committees: Agric ArmServ
First elected: 1992

1991-92 Total Rcpts:	$293,468
1990 Year-end cash:	$9,118

Source of Funds
- PACs 32%
- Lg Individuals ($200+) 21%
- Individuals under $200 .... 33%
- Other 14%

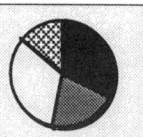

Top Industries & Interest Groups

Industrial Unions	$35,900
Lawyers & Lobbyists	$27,925
Building Trade Unions	$25,400
Public Sector Unions	$13,500
Transportation Unions	$10,250
Unidentified	$19,117

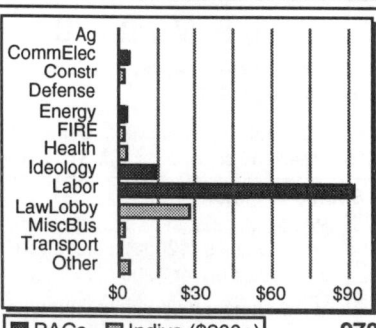

† Does not include individual contributions from 1987-88

7. Curt Weldon (R)

1992 Committees: ArmServ MerchMarine
First elected: 1986

1991-92 Total Rcpts: $465,223
1990 Year-end cash: $34,613

Source of Funds
- PACs 40%
- Lg Individuals ($200+) 22%
- Individuals under $200 .... 34%
- Other 4%

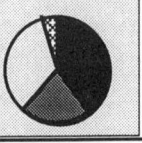

Top Industries & Interest Groups

Building Trade Unions $20,675
Defense Aerospace $19,650
Lawyers & Lobbyists $19,400
Health Professionals $15,850
Insurance $15,550

Unidentified $24,680

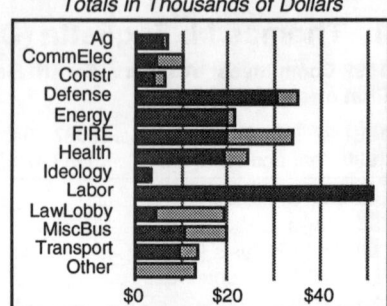

8. James C. Greenwood (R)

1993-94 Committees: Energy/Commerce
First elected: 1992

1991-92 Total Rcpts: $732,618
1990 Year-end cash: $5,914

Source of Funds
- PACs 23%
- Lg Individuals ($200+) 49%
- Individuals under $200 .... 19%
- Other 9%

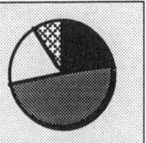

Top Industries & Interest Groups

Lawyers & Lobbyists $41,475
Retired $27,185
Oil & Gas $24,800
Chemicals $22,500
Health Professionals $21,090

Unidentified $116,102

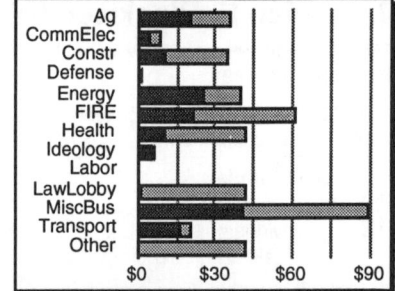

9. Bud Shuster (R)

1992 Committees: Public Works
First elected: 1972

1991-92 Total Rcpts: $557,315
1990 Year-end cash: $103,032

Source of Funds
- PACs 34%
- Lg Individuals ($200+) 60%
- Individuals under $200 .... 3%
- Other 3%

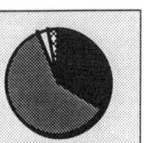

Top Industries & Interest Groups

Business Services $98,100
General Contractors $57,750
Lawyers & Lobbyists $40,325
Building Materials & Equipment $31,500
Air Transport $26,500

Unidentified $46,100

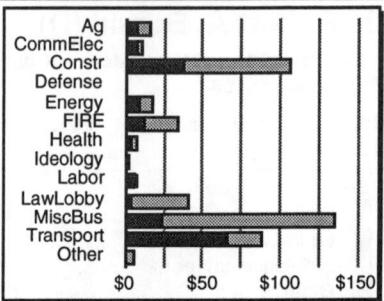

10. Joseph M. McDade (R)

1992 Committees: Approp SmBus
First elected: 1962

1991-92 Total Rcpts: $375,429
1990 Year-end cash: $367,412

Source of Funds
- PACs 65%
- Lg Individuals ($200+) 24%
- Individuals under $200 .... 2%
- Other 9%

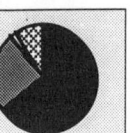

Top Industries & Interest Groups

Defense Aerospace $49,000
Lawyers & Lobbyists $46,849
Defense Electronics $33,850
Building Trade Unions $14,000
Transportation Unions $11,750

Unidentified $17,083

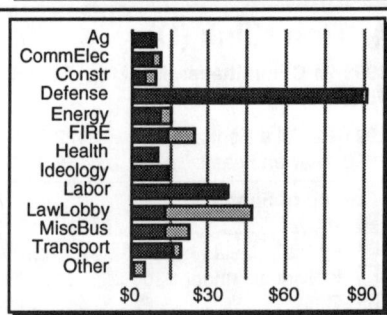

11. Paul E. Kanjorski (D)

1992 Committees: Banking Post Office
First elected: 1984

1991-92 Total Rcpts: $311,016
1990 Year-end cash: $63,183

Source of Funds
- PACs 75%
- Lg Individuals ($200+) 9%
- Individuals under $200 .... 12%
- Other 5%

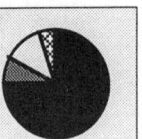

Top Industries & Interest Groups

Commercial Banks $31,850
Insurance $30,500
Public Sector Unions $30,300
Industrial Unions $17,600
Building Trade Unions $16,200

Unidentified $7,752

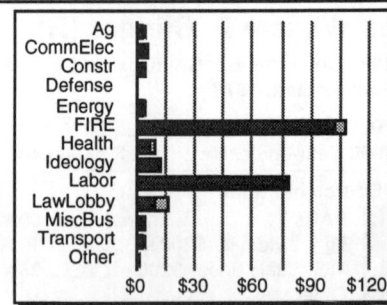

12. John P. Murtha (D)

1992 Committees: Appropriations
First elected: 1974

1991-92 Total Rcpts: $935,459
1990 Year-end cash: $174,483

Source of Funds
- PACs 57%
- Lg Individuals ($200+) 36%
- Individuals under $200 .... 5%
- Other 2%

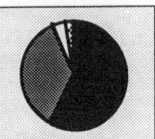

Top Industries & Interest Groups

Defense Aerospace $109,600
Defense Electronics $83,400
Lawyers & Lobbyists $82,900
Oil & Gas $49,250
Misc Defense $38,200

Unidentified $72,250

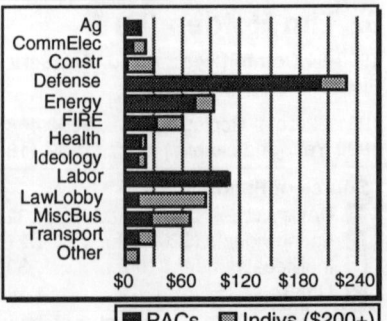

Key to committee & category abbreviations is on page 173

13. Marjorie Margolies-Mezvinsky (D)

1993-94 Committees: Energy/Comm GovtOps SmBus
First elected: 1992

1991-92 Total Rcpts: $569,961
1990 Year-end cash: $10,901

Source of Funds
- PACs 30%
- Lg Individuals ($200+) 41%
- Individuals under $200 .... 28%
- Other 1%

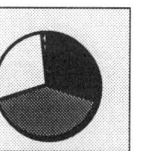

Top Industries & Interest Groups

Lawyers & Lobbyists $60,125
Womens Issues $31,187
Health Professionals $21,860
Industrial Unions $17,300
Public Sector Unions $15,500

Unidentified $83,200

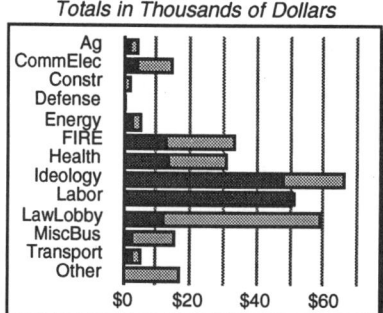

14. William J. Coyne (D)

1992 Committees: Ways & Means
First elected: 1980

1991-92 Total Rcpts: $264,042
1990 Year-end cash: $167,604

Source of Funds
- PACs 63%
- Lg Individuals ($200+) 25%
- Individuals under $200 .... 3%
- Other 9%

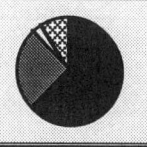

Top Industries & Interest Groups

Health Professionals $24,732
Public Sector Unions $23,050
Insurance $20,750
Lawyers & Lobbyists $19,050
Industrial Unions $19,000

Unidentified $11,750

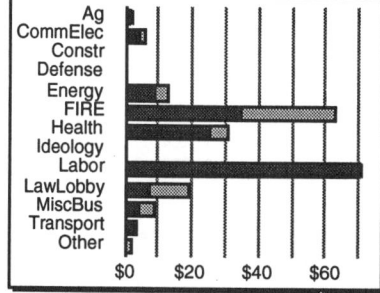

15. Paul McHale (D)

1993-94 Committees: ArmServ Science
First elected: 1992

1991-92 Total Rcpts: $222,578
1990 Year-end cash: $1,642

Source of Funds
- PACs 43%
- Lg Individuals ($200+) 17%
- Individuals under $200 .... 18%
- Other 22%

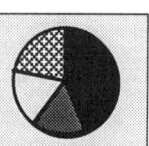

Top Industries & Interest Groups

Industrial Unions $38,500
Public Sector Unions $27,000
Lawyers & Lobbyists $21,645
Misc Unions $16,000
Transportation Unions $13,500

Unidentified $12,920

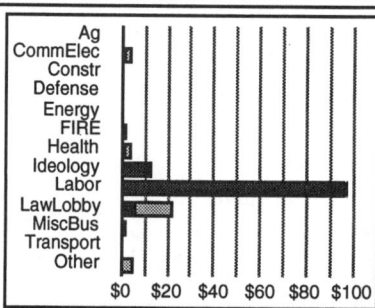

16. Robert S. Walker (R)

1992 Committees: Science
First elected: 1976

1991-92 Total Rcpts: $134,434
1990 Year-end cash: $11,278

Source of Funds
- PACs 43%
- Lg Individuals ($200+) 34%
- Individuals under $200 .... 19%
- Other 4%

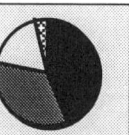

Top Industries & Interest Groups

Defense Aerospace $6,500
Building Materials & Equipment $5,100
Pharmaceuticals/Health Prod $4,000
Automotive $4,000
Misc Manufacturing & Distrib $3,950

Unidentified $13,750

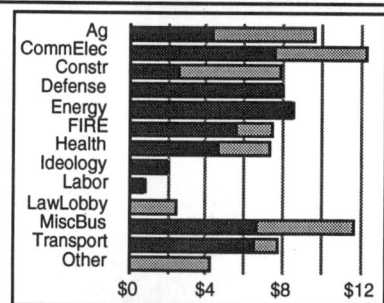

17. George W. Gekas (R)

1992 Committees: Judiciary
First elected: 1982

1991-92 Total Rcpts: $112,141
1990 Year-end cash: $62,800

Source of Funds
- PACs 61%
- Lg Individuals ($200+) 10%
- Individuals under $200 .... 14%
- Other 15%

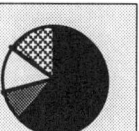

Top Industries & Interest Groups

Real Estate $10,175
Accountants $7,500
Telephone Utilities $5,600
Insurance $5,555
Automotive $4,700

Unidentified $2,950

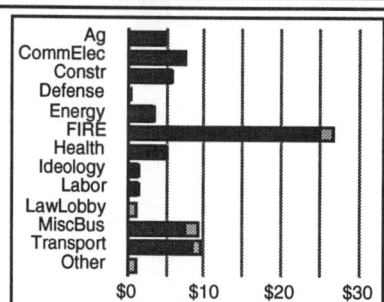

18. Rick Santorum (R)

1992 Committees: Budget VetAffairs
First elected: 1990

1991-92 Total Rcpts: $654,854
1990 Year-end cash: $34,355

Source of Funds
- PACs 38%
- Lg Individuals ($200+) 36%
- Individuals under $200 .... 17%
- Other 9%

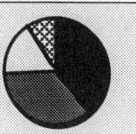

Top Industries & Interest Groups

Lawyers & Lobbyists $41,905
Oil & Gas $29,627
Health Professionals $28,035
Commercial Banks $23,750
Retired $21,900

Unidentified $44,675

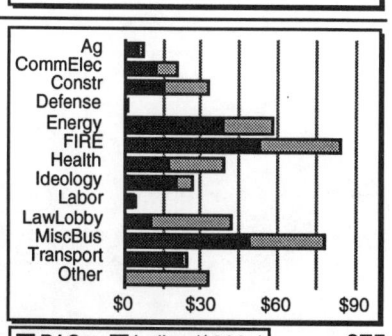

19. Bill Goodling (R)
1992 Committees: Educ/Labor ForAff
First elected: 1974

1991-92 Total Rcpts: $200,014
1990 Year-end cash: $4,312

Source of Funds
- PACs..0%
- Lg Individuals ($200+)................37%
- Individuals under $200 ....36%
- Other..27%

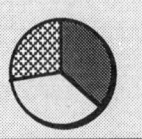

Top Industries & Interest Groups
Retired $7,516
Education $7,500
Lawyers & Lobbyists $6,768
Republican/Conservative $5,300
Mining $3,650

Unidentified $28,620

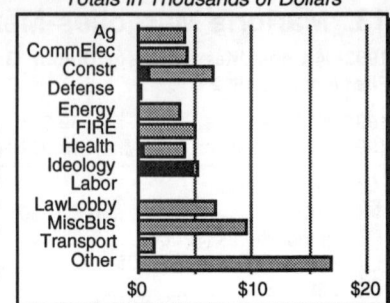

20. Austin J. Murphy (D)
1992 Committees: Educ/Labor ForAff Interior
First elected: 1976

1991-92 Total Rcpts: $235,296
1990 Year-end cash: $37,124

Source of Funds
- PACs..69%
- Lg Individuals ($200+).................4%
- Individuals under $200 ....13%
- Other..14%

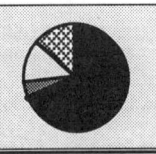

Top Industries & Interest Groups
Industrial Unions $26,000
Public Sector Unions $24,550
Building Trade Unions $22,550
Transportation Unions $21,150
Health Professionals $13,800

Unidentified $1,950

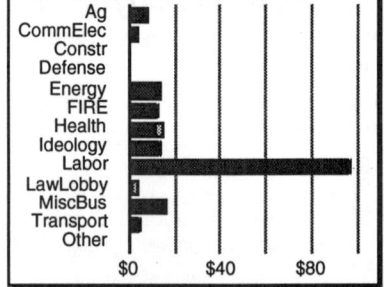

21. Tom Ridge (R)
1992 Committees: Banking Post Office VetAffairs
First elected: 1982

1991-92 Total Rcpts: $530,372
1990 Year-end cash: $51,230

Source of Funds
- PACs..57%
- Lg Individuals ($200+)...............22%
- Individuals under $200 ....17%
- Other..4%

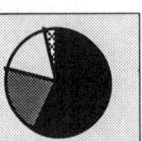

Top Industries & Interest Groups
Commercial Banks $69,560
Health Professionals $25,800
Lawyers & Lobbyists $24,825
Transportation Unions $17,250
Securities & Investment $16,500

Unidentified $29,000

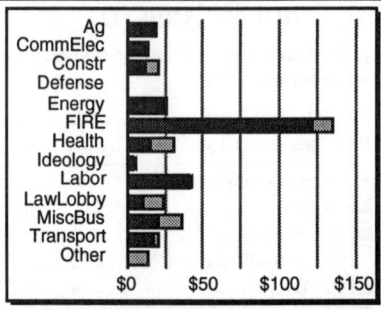

Totals in Thousands of Dollars

■ PACs ▨ Indivs ($200+)

Rhode Island

Senate Spending

House Spending

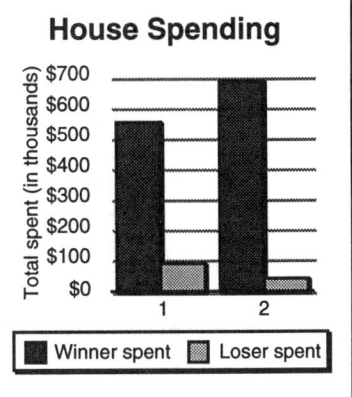

1992 Elections at a Glance

Dist	Name	Party	Vote Pct	Race Type
Sen	John H. Chafee (1988)	Rep	55%	Reelected
Sen	Claiborne Pell (1990)	Dem	62%	Reelected
1	Ronald K. Machtley	Rep	70%	Reelected
2	John F. Reed	Dem	71%	Reelected

Totals in Thousands of Dollars

Sen. John H. Chafee (R)

1992 Committees: Envir Finance
First elected: 1976

1987-92 Total Rcpts: $2,783,322
1990 Year-end cash: $188,821

Source of Funds
- PACs 39%
- Lg Individuals ($200+) 24%
- Individuals under $200 .... 26%
- Other 10%

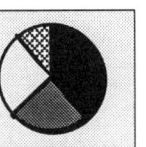

1987-92†
Top Industries & Interest Groups

Insurance	$114,333
Commercial Banks	$104,208
Health Professionals	$78,050
Securities & Investment	$63,534
Defense Aerospace	$55,111
Unidentified	$68,050

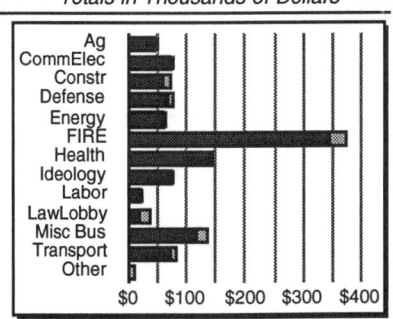

Sen. Claiborne Pell (D)

1992 Committees: ForRel Labor Rules
First elected: 1960

1987-92 Total Rcpts: $2,233,158
1990 Year-end cash: $101,208

Source of Funds
- PACs 39%
- Lg Individuals ($200+) 41%
- Individuals under $200 .... 8%
- Other 12%

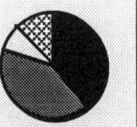

1987-92†
Top Industries & Interest Groups

Pro-Israel	$231,411
Lawyer & Lobbyists	$128,960
Industrial Unions	$90,150
Real Estate	$79,600
Health Professionals	$64,887
Unidentified	$204,450

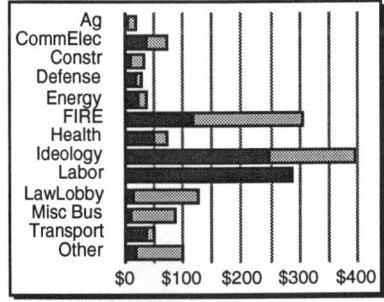

1. Ronald K. Machtley (R)

1992 Committees: ArmServ GovtOps SmBus
First elected: 1988

1991-92 Total Rcpts: $608,563
1990 Year-end cash: $54,332

Source of Funds
- PACs 35%
- Lg Individuals ($200+) 21%
- Individuals under $200 .... 36%
- Other 7%

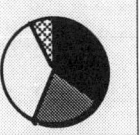

Top Industries & Interest Groups

Health Professionals	$27,800
Public Sector Unions	$23,125
Defense Aerospace	$19,250
Transportation Unions	$17,500
Lawyers & Lobbyists	$16,125
Unidentified	$32,597

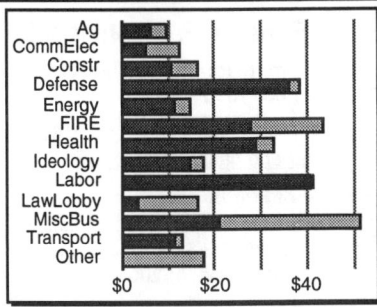

2. John F. Reed (D)

1992 Committees: Educ/Labor Judiciary MerchMarine
First elected: 1990

1991-92 Total Rcpts: $748,808
1990 Year-end cash: $6,837

Source of Funds
- PACs 55%
- Lg Individuals ($200+) 22%
- Individuals under $200 .... 21%
- Other 3%

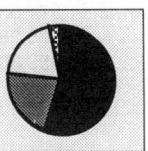

Top Industries & Interest Groups

Public Sector Unions	$60,050
Industrial Unions	$55,800
Lawyers & Lobbyists	$50,850
Transportation Unions	$46,050
Health Professionals	$45,945
Unidentified	$29,349

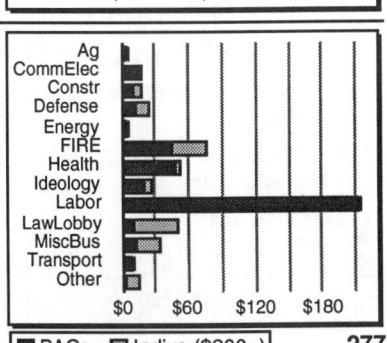

† Does not include individual contributions from 1987-88

South Carolina

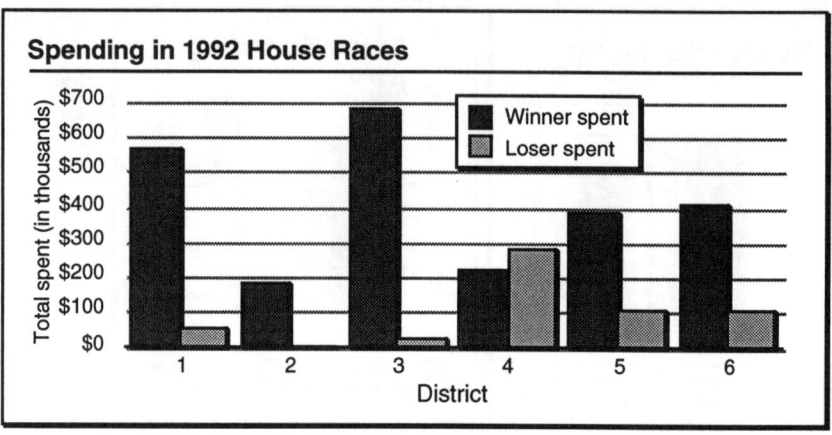

1992 Elections at a Glance

Dist	Name	Party	Vote Pct	Race Type
Sen	Ernest F. Hollings (1992)	Dem	50%	Reelected
Sen	Strom Thurmond (1990)	Rep	64%	Reelected
1	Arthur Ravenel Jr.	Rep	66%	Reelected
2	Floyd D. Spence	Rep	88%	Reelected
3	Butler Derrick	Dem	61%	Reelected
4	Robert D. Inglis	Rep	50%	Beat Incumb
5	John M. Spratt Jr.	Dem	61%	Reelected
6	Jim Clyburn	Dem	65%	Open Seat

Totals in Thousands of Dollars

Sen. Ernest F. Hollings (D)

1992 Committees: Approp Budget Commerce
First elected: 1966

1987-92 Total Rcpts: $4,016,311
1990 Year-end cash: $25,336

Source of Funds
- PACs 39%
- Lg Individuals ($200+) 44%
- Individuals under $200 .... 7%
- Other 10%

1987-92†
Top Industries & Interest Groups

Lawyer & Lobbyists $559,192
Media/Entertainment $236,731
Telephone Utilities $140,837
Insurance $132,020
Textiles $107,530

Unidentified $337,489

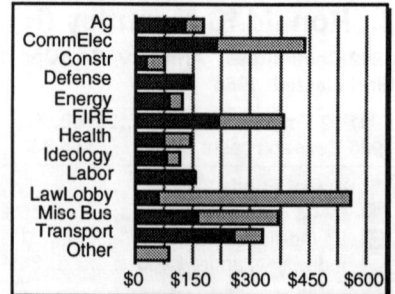

Sen. Strom Thurmond (R)

1992 Committees: ArmServ Judiciary Labor VetAffairs
First elected: 1954

1987-92 Total Rcpts: $2,240,505
1990 Year-end cash: $160,843

Source of Funds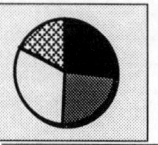
- PACs 26%
- Lg Individuals ($200+) 24%
- Individuals under $200 .... 32%
- Other 18%

1987-92†
Top Industries & Interest Groups

Lawyer & Lobbyists $111,600
Insurance $80,357
Republican/Conservative $71,534
Health Professionals $65,250
Defense Aerospace $59,300

Unidentified $113,439

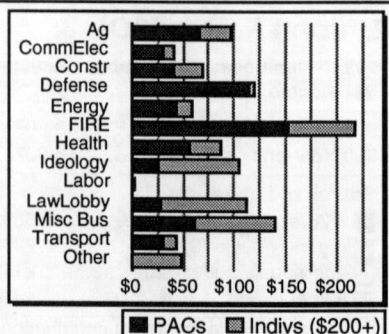

Key to committee & category abbreviations is on page 173

1. Arthur Ravenel Jr. (R)

1992 Committees: ArmServ MerchMarine
First elected: 1986

1991-92 Total Rcpts: $282,816
1990 Year-end cash: $0

Source of Funds
- PACs 45%
- Lg Individuals ($200+) 20%
- Individuals under $200 ....20%
- Other 15%

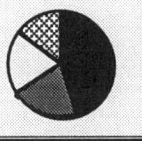

Top Industries & Interest Groups

Health Professionals $20,500
Real Estate $10,300
Sea Transport $8,250
Defense Aerospace $8,100
Automotive $7,750

Unidentified $13,900

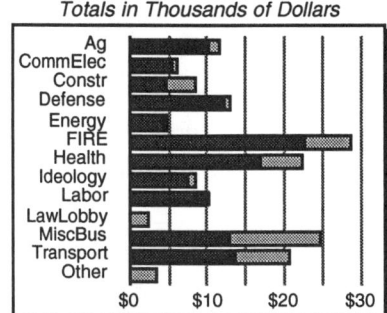

2. Floyd D. Spence (R)

1992 Committees: ArmServ VetAffairs
First elected: 1970

1991-92 Total Rcpts: $169,036
1990 Year-end cash: $51,688

Source of Funds
- PACs 64%
- Lg Individuals ($200+) 5%
- Individuals under $200 ....26%
- Other 5%

Top Industries & Interest Groups

Defense Aerospace $18,000
Health Professionals $11,400
Defense Electronics $9,850
Automotive $6,500
Insurance $6,250

Unidentified $200

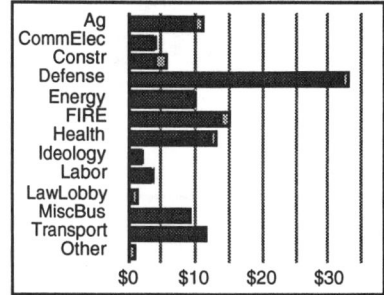

3. Butler Derrick (D)

1992 Committees: Rules
First elected: 1974

1991-92 Total Rcpts: $681,632
1990 Year-end cash: $114,145

Source of Funds
- PACs 68%
- Lg Individuals ($200+) 17%
- Individuals under $200 ....9%
- Other 6%

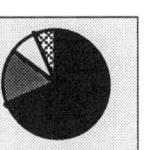

Top Industries & Interest Groups

Insurance $56,650
Lawyers & Lobbyists $51,133
Commercial Banks $48,750
Health Professionals $29,000
Textiles $20,150

Unidentified $17,250

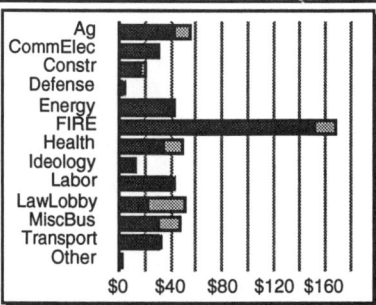

4. Robert D. Inglis (R)

1993-94 Committees: Budget Judiciary
First elected: 1992

1991-92 Total Rcpts: $226,577
1990 Year-end cash: $11,214

Source of Funds
- PACs 0%
- Lg Individuals ($200+) 49%
- Individuals under $200 ....26%
- Other 24%

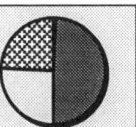

Top Industries & Interest Groups

Retired $11,600
Textiles $11,250
Lawyers & Lobbyists $7,500
Health Professionals $6,450
Chemicals $6,000

Unidentified $43,225

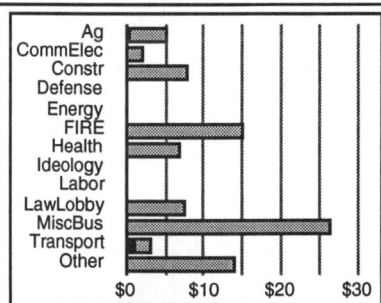

5. John M. Spratt Jr. (D)

1992 Committees: ArmServ Budget
First elected: 1982

1991-92 Total Rcpts: $281,855
1990 Year-end cash: $52,937

Source of Funds
- PACs 50%
- Lg Individuals ($200+) 30%
- Individuals under $200 ....10%
- Other 10%

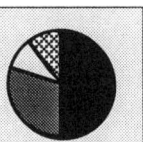

Top Industries & Interest Groups

Defense Aerospace $17,400
Lawyers & Lobbyists $16,950
Commercial Banks $13,750
Real Estate $12,500
Textiles $12,000

Unidentified $18,950

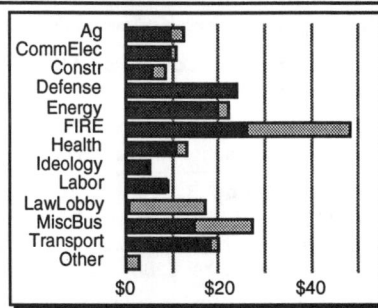

6. Jim Clyburn (D)

1993-94 Committees: PubWorks VetAffairs
First elected: 1992

1991-92 Total Rcpts: $407,978
1990 Year-end cash: $795

Source of Funds
- PACs 24%
- Lg Individuals ($200+) 22%
- Individuals under $200 ....16%
- Other 39%

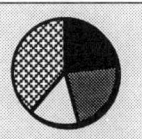

Top Industries & Interest Groups

Lawyers & Lobbyists $29,287
Public Sector Unions $22,000
Commercial Banks $18,150
Health Professionals $14,500
Electric Utilities $9,750

Unidentified $28,431

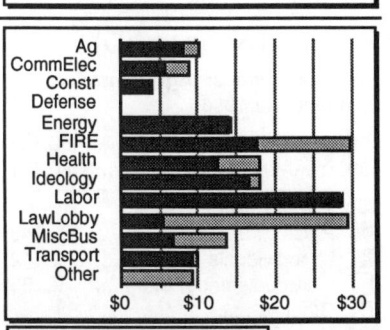

† Does not include individual contributions from 1987-88

South Dakota

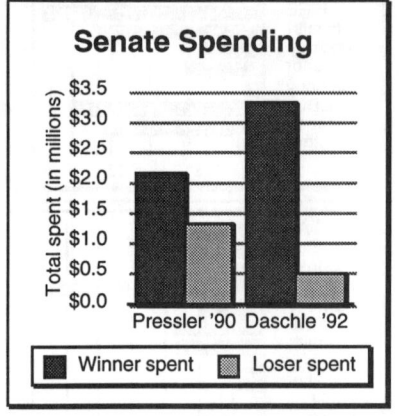

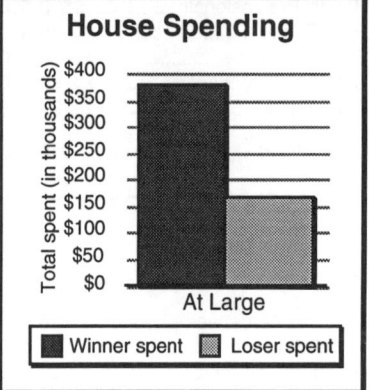

1992 Elections at a Glance

Dist	Name	Party	Vote Pct	Race Type
Sen	Tom Daschle (1992)	Dem	65%	Reelected
Sen	Larry Pressler (1990)	Rep	52%	Reelected
1	Tim Johnson	Dem	69%	Reelected

Totals in Thousands of Dollars

Sen. Tom Daschle (D)
1992 Committees: Agric Finance VetAffairs
First elected: 1986

1987-92 Total Rcpts: $4,122,119
1990 Year-end cash: $192,096

Source of Funds
- PACs 44%
- Lg Individuals ($200+) 26%
- Individuals under $200 .... 23%
- Other 8%

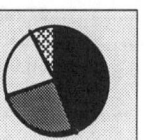

1987-92†
Top Industries & Interest Groups

Lawyer & Lobbyists $291,165
Insurance $185,524
Health Professionals $179,549
Pro-Israel $161,961
Securities & Investment $147,784

Unidentified $163,848

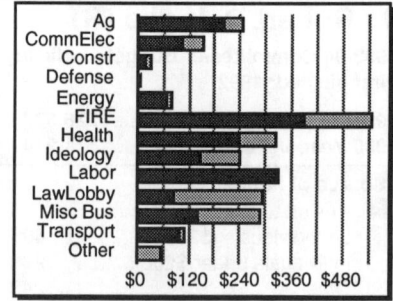

Sen. Larry Pressler (R)
1992 Committees: Commerce ForRel SmBus
First elected: 1978

1987-92 Total Rcpts: $2,458,596
1990 Year-end cash: $393,410

Source of Funds
- PACs 40%
- Lg Individuals ($200+) 33%
- Individuals under $200 .... 9%
- Other 18%

1987-92†
Top Industries & Interest Groups

Insurance $130,498
Pro-Israel $120,345
Lawyer & Lobbyists $92,550
Securities & Investment $84,434
Real Estate $80,900

Unidentified $151,115

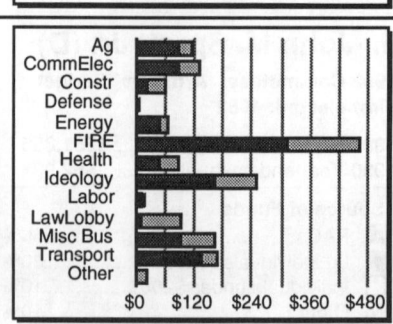

1. Tim Johnson (D)
1992 Committees: Agric Interior
First elected: 1986

1991-92 Total Rcpts: $452,528
1990 Year-end cash: $180,431

Source of Funds
- PACs 48%
- Lg Individuals ($200+) 12%
- Individuals under $200 .... 33%
- Other 7%

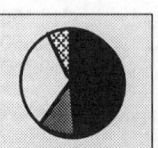

Top Industries & Interest Groups

Industrial Unions $42,900
Public Sector Unions $24,000
Transportation Unions $20,250
Crop Production/Processing $19,125
Health Professionals $17,750

Unidentified $7,350

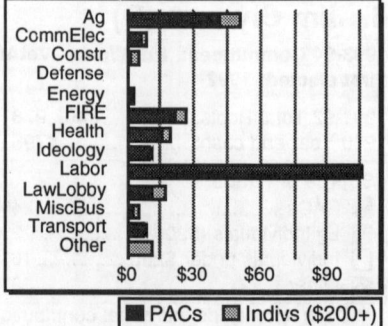

Key to committee & category abbreviations is on page 173

Tennessee

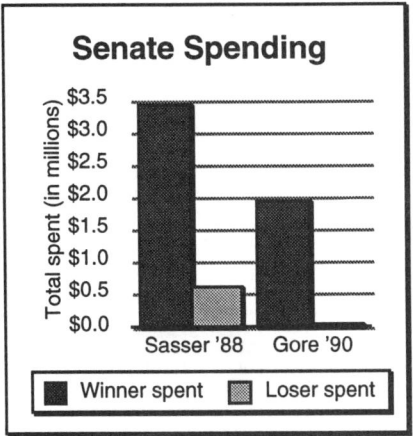

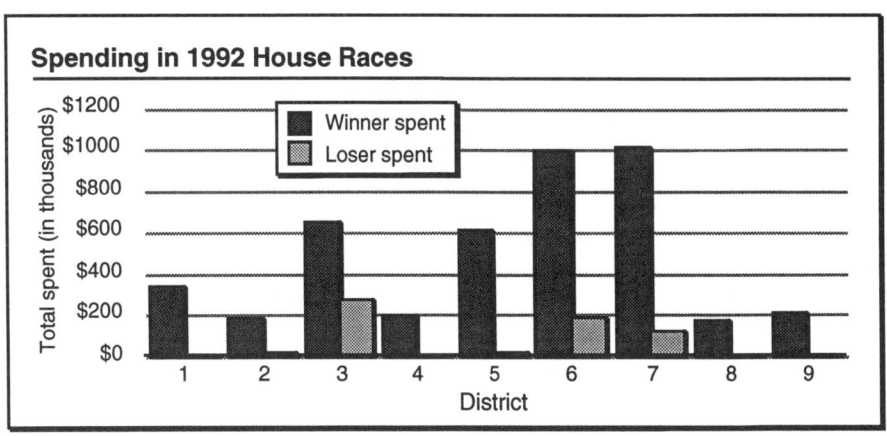

1992 Elections at a Glance

Dist	Name	Party	Vote Pct	Race Type
Sen	Al Gore (1990)	Dem	68%	Reelected
Sen	Jim Sasser (1988)	Dem	65%	Reelected
1	James H. Quillen	Rep	68%	Reelected
2	John J. "Jimmy" Duncan Jr.	Rep	72%	Reelected
3	Marilyn Lloyd	Dem	49%	Reelected
4	Jim Cooper	Dem	64%	Reelected
5	Bob Clement	Dem	67%	Reelected
6	Bart Gordon	Dem	59%	Reelected
7	Don Sundquist	Rep	62%	Reelected
8	John Tanner	Dem	84%	Reelected
9	Harold E. Ford	Dem	58%	Reelected

Totals in Thousands of Dollars

Sen. Al Gore (D)

1992 Committees: ArmServ Commerce Rules
First elected: 1984

1987-92 Total Rcpts: $2,488,698
1990 Year-end cash: $291,115

Source of Funds
- PACs 41%
- Lg Individuals ($200+) 42%
- Individuals under $200 .... 8%
- Other 10%

1987-92†
Top Industries & Interest Groups

Lawyer & Lobbyists $307,042
Pro-Israel $115,905
Insurance $103,576
Industrial Unions $95,574
Transportation Unions $94,500

Unidentified $255,624

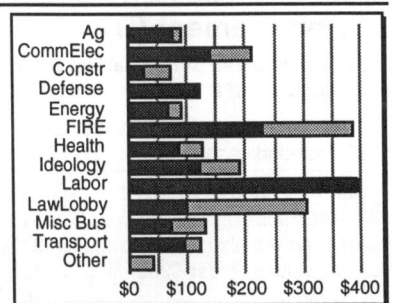

Sen. Jim Sasser (D)

1992 Committees: Approp Banking Budget GovAff
First elected: 1976

1987-92 Total Rcpts: $3,474,892
1990 Year-end cash: $281,527

Source of Funds
- PACs 43%
- Lg Individuals ($200+) 33%
- Individuals under $200 .... 18%
- Other 6%

1987-92†
Top Industries & Interest Groups

Insurance $107,050
Defense Aerospace $93,900
Commercial Banks $92,740
Securities & Investment $87,306
Industrial Unions $87,000

Unidentified $14,050

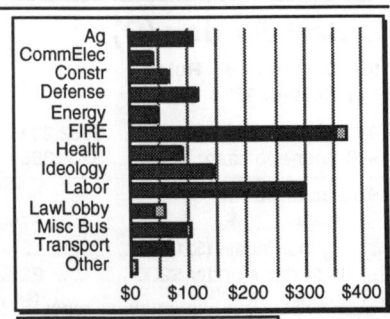

† Does not include individual contributions from 1987-88

1. James H. Quillen (R)

1992 Committees: Rules
First elected: 1962

1991-92 Total Rcpts: $455,846
1990 Year-end cash: $1,174,716

Source of Funds
- PACs 59%
- Lg Individuals ($200+) 16%
- Individuals under $200 .... 2%
- Other 24%

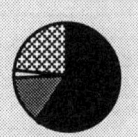

Top Industries & Interest Groups

Insurance $25,305
Lawyers & Lobbyists $21,750
Air Transport $18,500
Public Sector Unions $17,500
Automotive $14,500

Unidentified $7,250

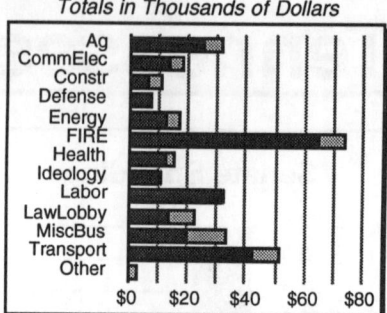

2. John J. "Jimmy" Duncan Jr. (R)

1992 Committees: Banking Interior PubWorks
First elected: 1988

1991-92 Total Rcpts: $258,496
1990 Year-end cash: $225,372

Source of Funds
- PACs 62%
- Lg Individuals ($200+) 17%
- Individuals under $200 .... 17%
- Other 4%

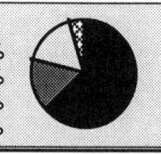

Top Industries & Interest Groups

Insurance $18,526
Air Transport $16,100
Health Professionals $14,700
Lawyers & Lobbyists $11,466
Automotive $10,400

Unidentified $8,500

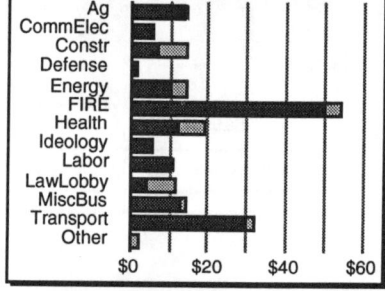

3. Marilyn Lloyd (D)

1992 Committees: ArmServ Science
First elected: 1974

1991-92 Total Rcpts: $463,643
1990 Year-end cash: $10,471

Source of Funds
- PACs 57%
- Lg Individuals ($200+) 18%
- Individuals under $200 .... 14%
- Other 11%

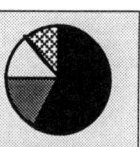

Top Industries & Interest Groups

Industrial Unions $33,700
Defense Aerospace $28,000
Lawyers & Lobbyists $24,250
Real Estate $20,500
Health Professionals $18,200

Unidentified $17,350

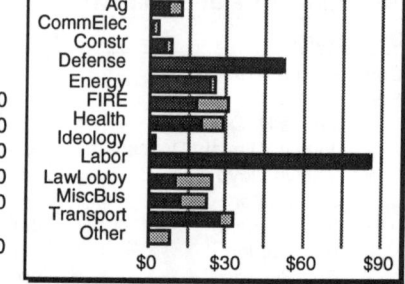

4. Jim Cooper (D)

1992 Committees: Budget Energy/Commerce
First elected: 1982

1991-92 Total Rcpts: $164,092
1990 Year-end cash: $174,426

Source of Funds
- PACs 0%
- Lg Individuals ($200+) 35%
- Individuals under $200 .... 40%
- Other 23%

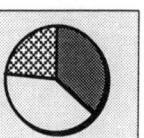

Top Industries & Interest Groups

Lawyers & Lobbyists $7,250
Hospitals/Nursing Homes $6,356
Health Professionals $4,750
Retired $4,500
Securities & Investment $3,500

Unidentified $16,889

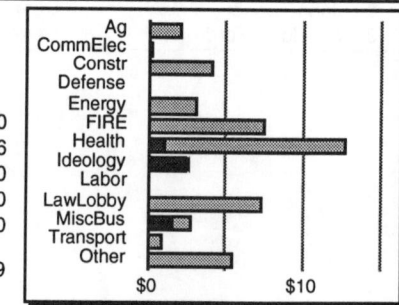

5. Bob Clement (D)

1992 Committees: MerchMarine PubWorks VetAffairs
First elected: 1988

1991-92 Total Rcpts: $562,141
1990 Year-end cash: $127,237

Source of Funds
- PACs 51%
- Lg Individuals ($200+) 31%
- Individuals under $200 .... 12%
- Other 6%

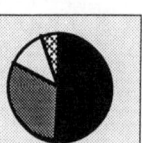

Top Industries & Interest Groups

Air Transport $35,420
Lawyers & Lobbyists $26,575
Industrial Unions $22,000
Public Sector Unions $20,200
Telephone Utilities $16,450

Unidentified $33,599

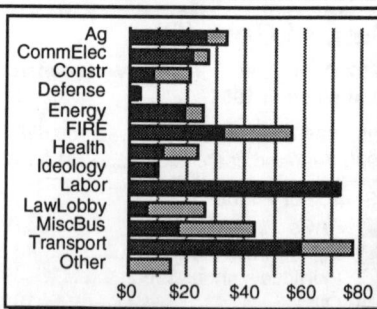

6. Bart Gordon (D)

1992 Committees: Rules
First elected: 1984

1991-92 Total Rcpts: $662,234
1990 Year-end cash: $208,386

Source of Funds
- PACs 57%
- Lg Individuals ($200+) 2%
- Individuals under $200 .... 22%
- Other 19%

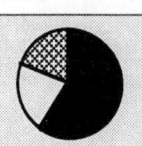

Top Industries & Interest Groups

Industrial Unions $39,500
Commercial Banks $28,700
Public Sector Unions $28,550
Insurance $26,810
Air Transport $18,500

Unidentified $4,100

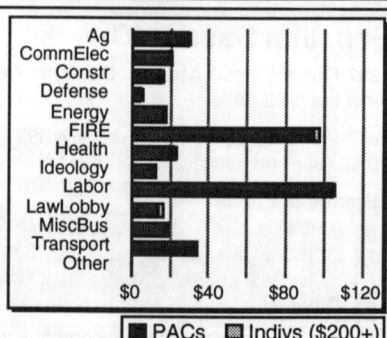

Key to committee & category abbreviations is on page 173

7. Don Sundquist (R)

1992 Committees: Ways & Means
First elected: 1982

1991-92 Total Rcpts: $819,006
1990 Year-end cash: $289,691

Source of Funds
- PACs 43%
- Lg Individuals ($200+) 29%
- Individuals under $200 .... 18%
- Other 9%

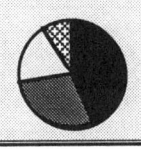

Top Industries & Interest Groups

Insurance $52,161
Automotive $33,400
Health Professionals $29,900
Business Services $26,650
Real Estate $25,636

Unidentified $40,063

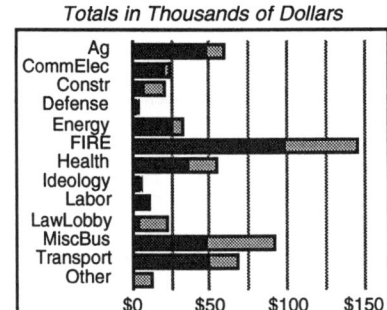

8. John Tanner (D)

1992 Committees: ArmServ Science
First elected: 1988

1991-92 Total Rcpts: $258,798
1990 Year-end cash: $319,398

Source of Funds
- PACs 62%
- Lg Individuals ($200+) 12%
- Individuals under $200 .... 11%
- Other 15%

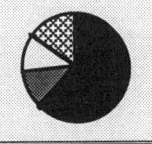

Top Industries & Interest Groups

Insurance $18,289
Air Transport $14,150
Industrial Unions $10,300
Automotive $10,250
Crop Production/Processing $10,150

Unidentified $2,550

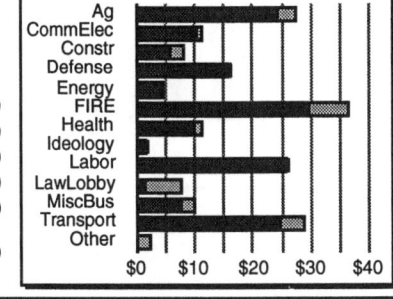

9. Harold E. Ford (D)

1992 Committees: Ways & Means
First elected: 1974

1991-92 Total Rcpts: $204,840
1990 Year-end cash: $4,640

Source of Funds
- PACs 56%
- Lg Individuals ($200+) 34%
- Individuals under $200 .... 4%
- Other 7%

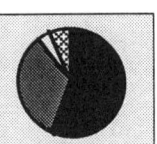

Top Industries & Interest Groups

Lawyers & Lobbyists $19,200
Industrial Unions $16,000
Public Sector Unions $14,500
Building Trade Unions $10,500
Real Estate $9,500

Unidentified $27,298

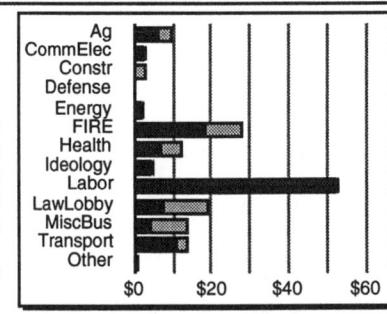

■ PACs   ▨ Indivs ($200+)

Texas

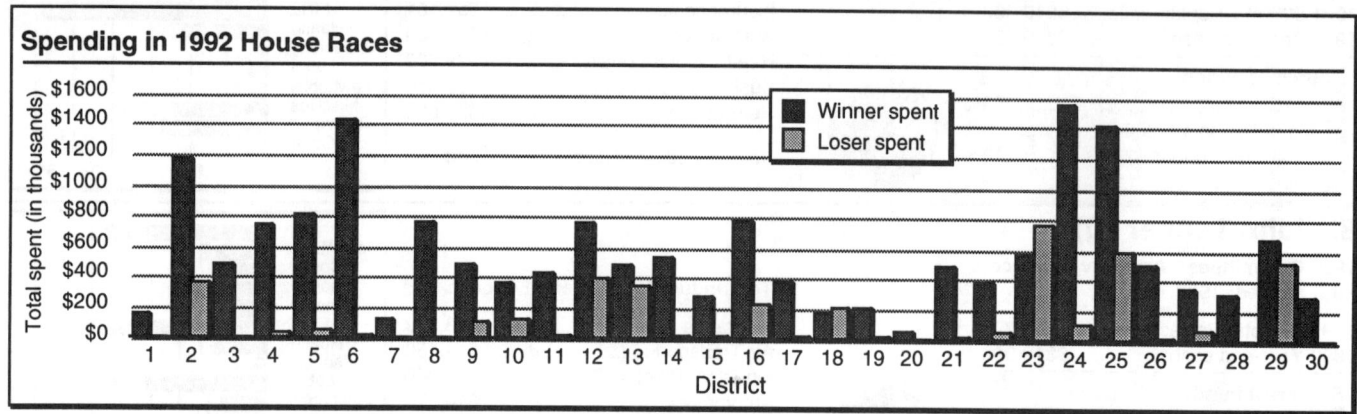

Spending in 1992 House Races

1992 Elections at a Glance

Dist	Name	Party	Vote Pct	Race Type
Sen	Lloyd Bentsen (1988)	Dem	59%	Reelected
Sen	Phil Gramm (1990)	Rep	60%	Reelected
1	Jim Chapman	Dem	100%	Reelected
2	Charles Wilson	Dem	56%	Reelected
3	Sam Johnson	Rep	86%	Reelected
4	Ralph M. Hall	Dem	58%	Reelected
5	John Bryant	Dem	59%	Reelected
6	Joe L. Barton	Rep	72%	Reelected
7	Bill Archer	Rep	100%	Reelected
8	Jack Fields	Rep	77%	Reelected
9	Jack Brooks	Dem	54%	Reelected
10	J. J. Pickle	Dem	68%	Reelected
11	Chet Edwards	Dem	67%	Reelected
12	Pete Geren	Dem	63%	Reelected
13	Bill Sarpalius	Dem	60%	Reelected
14	Greg Laughlin	Dem	68%	Reelected
15	E. "Kika" de la Garza	Dem	60%	Reelected
16	Ronald D. Coleman	Dem	52%	Reelected
17	Charles W. Stenholm	Dem	66%	Reelected
18	Craig Washington	Dem	65%	Reelected
19	Larry Combest	Rep	77%	Reelected
20	Henry B. Gonzalez	Dem	100%	Reelected
21	Lamar Smith	Rep	72%	Reelected
22	Tom DeLay	Rep	69%	Reelected
23	Henry Bonilla	Rep	59%	Beat Incumb
24	Martin Frost	Dem	60%	Reelected
25	Michael A. Andrews	Dem	56%	Reelected
26	Dick Armey	Rep	73%	Reelected
27	Solomon P. Ortiz	Dem	56%	Reelected
28	Frank M. Tejeda	Dem	87%	Open Seat
29	Gene Green	Dem	65%	Open Seat
30	Eddie Bernice Johnson	Dem	72%	Open Seat

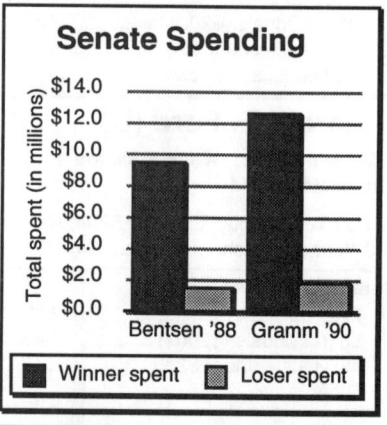

Senate Spending

Totals in Thousands of Dollars

Sen. Lloyd Bentsen (D)

1992 Committees: Commerce Finance
First elected: 1970

1987-92 Total Rcpts: $9,614,793
1990 Year-end cash: $691,634

Source of Funds
- PACs 23%
- Lg Individuals ($200+) 51%
- Individuals under $200 .... 15%
- Other 11%

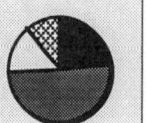

1987-92†
Top Industries & Interest Groups

Oil & Gas	$252,587
Insurance	$232,150
Lawyer & Lobbyists	$204,632
Securities & Investment	$158,850
Commercial Banks	$118,825
Unidentified	$70,424

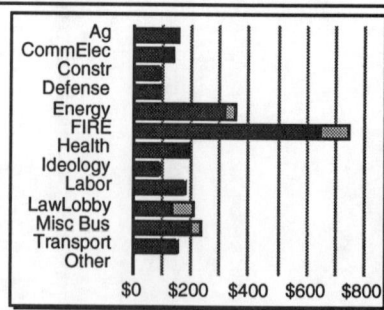

Sen. Phil Gramm (R)

1992 Committees: Approp Banking Budget
First elected: 1984

1987-92 Total Rcpts: $18,457,261
1990 Year-end cash: $5,921,738

Source of Funds
- PACs 9%
- Lg Individuals ($200+) 46%
- Individuals under $200 .... 28%
- Other 17%

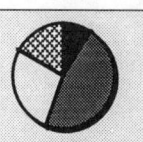

1987-92†
Top Industries & Interest Groups

Oil & Gas	$881,649
Lawyer & Lobbyists	$784,900
Health Professionals	$512,599
Commercial Banks	$331,646
Misc Finance	$298,943
Unidentified	$2,193,498

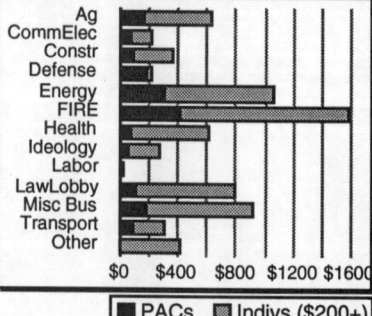

Key to committee & category abbreviations is on page 173

1. Jim Chapman (D)

1992 Committees: Appropriations
First elected: 1986

1991-92 Total Rcpts: $311,558
1990 Year-end cash: $286,303

Source of Funds
- PACs 72%
- Lg Individuals ($200+) 12%
- Individuals under $200 ....9%
- Other 7%

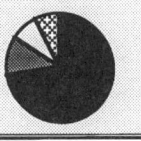

Top Industries & Interest Groups

Lawyers & Lobbyists $20,000
Oil & Gas $19,423
Defense Aerospace $18,000
Defense Electronics $16,500
Health Professionals $15,500

Unidentified $3,800

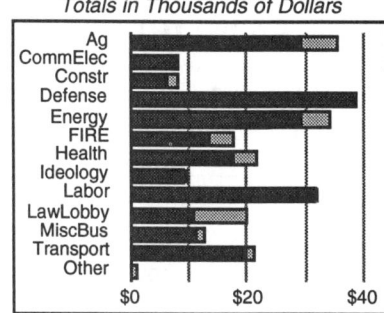

2. Charles Wilson (D)

1992 Committees: Appropriations
First elected: 1972

1991-92 Total Rcpts: $1,188,912
1990 Year-end cash: $25,171

Source of Funds
- PACs 53%
- Lg Individuals ($200+) 38%
- Individuals under $200 ....4%
- Other 5%

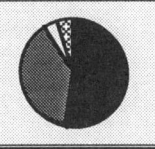

Top Industries & Interest Groups

Defense Aerospace $125,700
Lawyers & Lobbyists $118,090
Defense Electronics $69,450
Oil & Gas $63,800
Transportation Unions $56,000

Unidentified $89,500

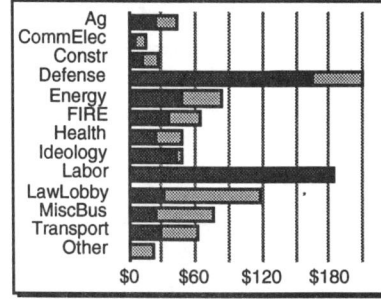

3. Sam Johnson (R)

1992 Committees: Banking Science SmBus
First elected: 1991

1991-92 Total Rcpts: $776,652
1990 Year-end cash: $13,717

Source of Funds
- PACs 37%
- Lg Individuals ($200+) 44%
- Individuals under $200 ....14%
- Other 4%

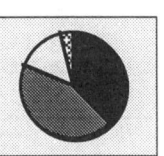

Top Industries & Interest Groups

Oil & Gas $74,425
Health Professionals $58,959
Real Estate $49,168
Commercial Banks $34,240
Lawyers & Lobbyists $22,775

Unidentified $48,518

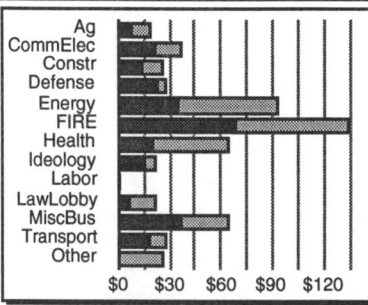

4. Ralph M. Hall (D)

1992 Committees: Energy/Commerce Science
First elected: 1980

1991-92 Total Rcpts: $520,216
1990 Year-end cash: $38,176

Source of Funds
- PACs 66%
- Lg Individuals ($200+) 18%
- Individuals under $200 ....8%
- Other 8%

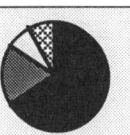

Top Industries & Interest Groups

Oil & Gas $51,100
Electric Utilities $37,050
Health Professionals $28,550
Lawyers & Lobbyists $20,300
Insurance $17,813

Unidentified $26,156

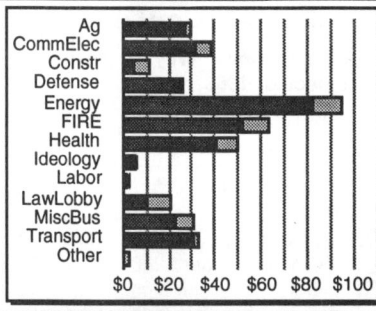

5. John Bryant (D)

1992 Committees: Budget Energy/Commerce Judiciary
First elected: 1982

1991-92 Total Rcpts: $622,709
1990 Year-end cash: $85,087

Source of Funds
- PACs 56%
- Lg Individuals ($200+) 26%
- Individuals under $200 ....14%
- Other 4%

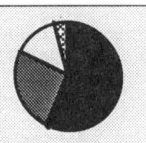

Top Industries & Interest Groups

Lawyers & Lobbyists $84,973
Industrial Unions $43,000
Health Professionals $41,189
Public Sector Unions $23,000
Media/Entertainment $21,300

Unidentified $26,365

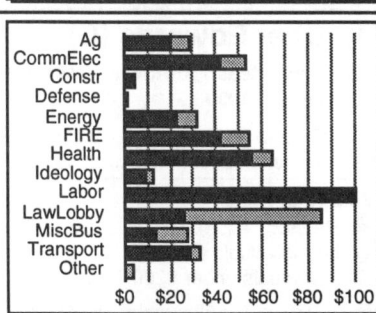

6. Joe L. Barton (R)

1992 Committees: Energy/Commerce Science
First elected: 1984

1991-92 Total Rcpts: $1,018,595
1990 Year-end cash: $7,022

Source of Funds
- PACs 37%
- Lg Individuals ($200+) 35%
- Individuals under $200 ....16%
- Other 13%

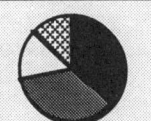

Top Industries & Interest Groups

Oil & Gas $90,282
Lawyers & Lobbyists $41,000
Health Professionals $37,600
Electric Utilities $37,400
Telephone Utilities $29,550

Unidentified $79,029

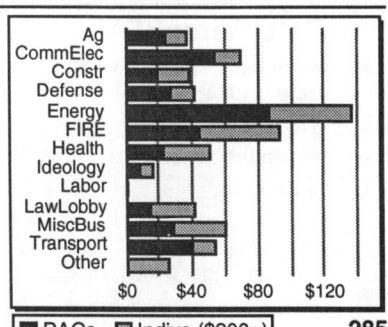

† Does not include individual contributions from 1987-88

7. Bill Archer (R)

1992 Committees: Ways & Means
First elected: 1970

1991-92 Total Rcpts: $121,947
1990 Year-end cash: $671,097

Source of Funds
- PACs..0%
- Lg Individuals ($200+)................37%
- Individuals under $200 ....3%
- Other..60%

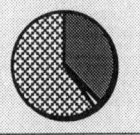

Top Industries & Interest Groups

Insurance $18,179
Beer, Wine & Liquor $4,500
Health Professionals $4,250
Oil & Gas $4,200
Lawyers & Lobbyists $2,950

Unidentified $5,350

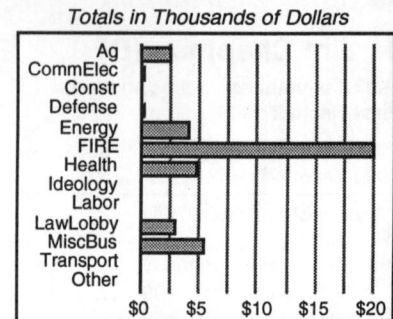

Totals in Thousands of Dollars

8. Jack Fields (R)

1992 Committees: Energy/Commerce MerchMarine
First elected: 1980

1991-92 Total Rcpts: $757,980
1990 Year-end cash: $46,066

Source of Funds
- PACs..60%
- Lg Individuals ($200+)................32%
- Individuals under $200 ....6%
- Other..2%

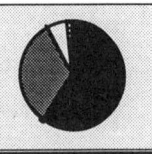

Top Industries & Interest Groups

Oil & Gas $101,505
Lawyers & Lobbyists $40,800
Telephone Utilities $35,800
Sea Transport $33,000
Health Professionals $30,300

Unidentified $69,250

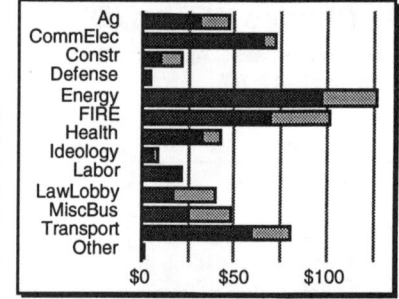

9. Jack Brooks (D)

1992 Committees: Judiciary
First elected: 1952

1991-92 Total Rcpts: $606,926
1990 Year-end cash: $465,327

Source of Funds
- PACs..74%
- Lg Individuals ($200+)................15%
- Individuals under $200 ....2%
- Other..9%

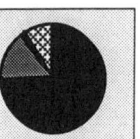

Top Industries & Interest Groups

Lawyers & Lobbyists $71,000
Media/Entertainment $37,100
Transportation Unions $27,700
Telephone Utilities $25,500
Oil & Gas $25,200

Unidentified $9,500

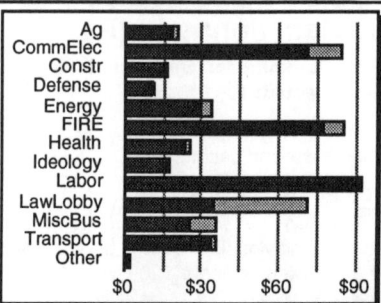

10. J. J. Pickle (D)

1992 Committees: Ways & Means
First elected: 1963

1991-92 Total Rcpts: $421,708
1990 Year-end cash: $124,589

Source of Funds
- PACs..61%
- Lg Individuals ($200+)................24%
- Individuals under $200 ....10%
- Other..5%

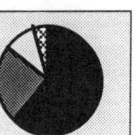

Top Industries & Interest Groups

Lawyers & Lobbyists $50,050
Insurance $47,709
Health Professionals $33,897
Securities & Investment $22,200
Oil & Gas $20,300

Unidentified $16,852

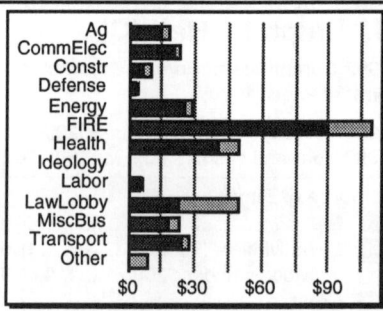

11. Chet Edwards (D)

1992 Committees: ArmServ VetAffairs
First elected: 1990

1991-92 Total Rcpts: $462,342
1990 Year-end cash: $43,902

Source of Funds
- PACs..68%
- Lg Individuals ($200+)................23%
- Individuals under $200 ....7%
- Other..2%

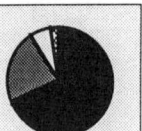

Top Industries & Interest Groups

Defense Aerospace $35,650
Industrial Unions $28,200
Health Professionals $26,375
Transportation Unions $26,200
Public Sector Unions $24,950

Unidentified $21,325

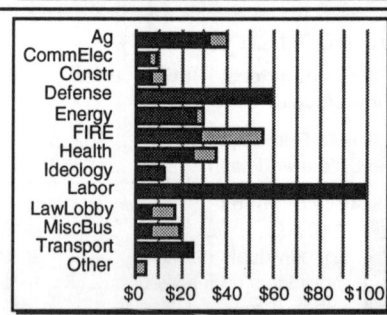

12. Pete Geren (D)

1992 Committees: PubWorks Science VetAffairs
First elected: 1989

1991-92 Total Rcpts: $809,664
1990 Year-end cash: $15,548

Source of Funds
- PACs..43%
- Lg Individuals ($200+)................46%
- Individuals under $200 ....8%
- Other..4%

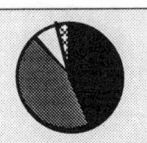

Top Industries & Interest Groups

Lawyers & Lobbyists $87,469
Oil & Gas $79,355
Air Transport $63,800
Real Estate $28,650
Health Professionals $26,700

Unidentified $74,645

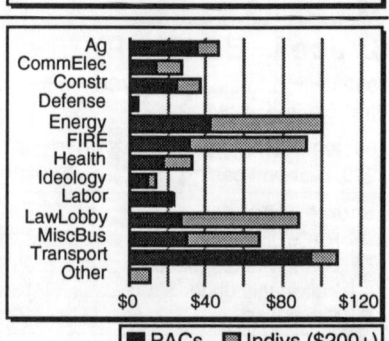

Key to committee & category abbreviations is on page 173

■ PACs   ▨ Indivs ($200+)

13. Bill Sarpalius (D)
1992 Committees: Agric SmBus
First elected: 1988

1991-92 Total Rcpts: $521,447
1990 Year-end cash: $17,659

Source of Funds
- PACs 59%
- Lg Individuals ($200+) 23%
- Individuals under $200 .... 9%
- Other 9%

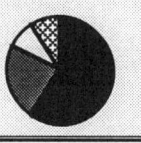

Top Industries & Interest Groups

Lawyers & Lobbyists $31,250
Health Professionals $29,350
Crop Production/Processing $28,331
Livestock $28,150
Transportation Unions $25,900

Unidentified $24,361

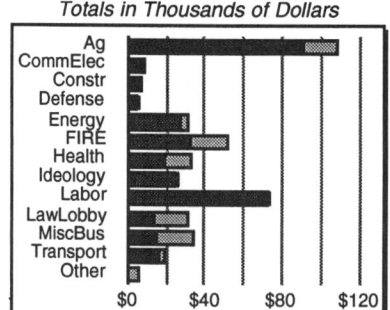

14. Greg Laughlin (D)
1992 Committees: MerchMarine PubWorks
First elected: 1988

1991-92 Total Rcpts: $608,011
1990 Year-end cash: $79,691

Source of Funds
- PACs 58%
- Lg Individuals ($200+) 31%
- Individuals under $200 .... 10%
- Other 2%

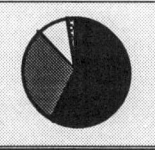

Top Industries & Interest Groups

Lawyers & Lobbyists $68,816
Oil & Gas $47,700
Transportation Unions $35,700
Air Transport $33,841
Health Professionals $27,350

Unidentified $33,650

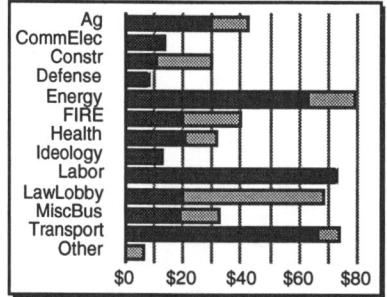

15. E. "Kika" de la Garza (D)
1992 Committees: Agriculture
First elected: 1964

1991-92 Total Rcpts: $248,430
1990 Year-end cash: $118,307

Source of Funds
- PACs 73%
- Lg Individuals ($200+) 14%
- Individuals under $200 .... 10%
- Other 3%

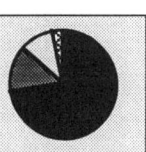

Top Industries & Interest Groups

Crop Production/Processing $58,579
Agricultural Services/Products .. $37,670
Food Processing & Sales $18,600
Commercial Banks $16,555
Securities & Investment $14,000

Unidentified $1,550

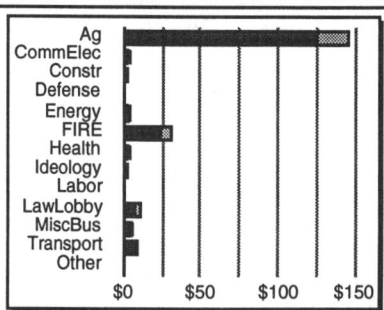

16. Ronald D. Coleman (D)
1992 Committees: Appropriations
First elected: 1982

1991-92 Total Rcpts: $762,219
1990 Year-end cash: $6,719

Source of Funds
- PACs 61%
- Lg Individuals ($200+) 17%
- Individuals under $200 .... 9%
- Other 13%

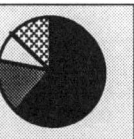

Top Industries & Interest Groups

Lawyers & Lobbyists $58,327
Public Sector Unions $55,600
Transportation Unions $53,250
Industrial Unions $36,700
Air Transport $27,400

Unidentified $20,675

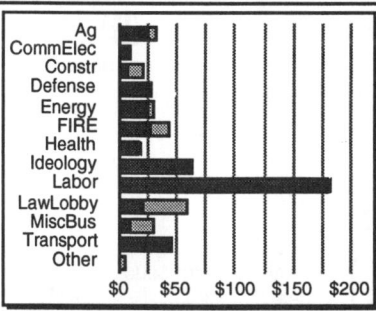

17. Charles W. Stenholm (D)
1992 Committees: Agric Budget
First elected: 1978

1991-92 Total Rcpts: $412,834
1990 Year-end cash: $121,621

Source of Funds
- PACs 66%
- Lg Individuals ($200+) 14%
- Individuals under $200 .... 16%
- Other 4%

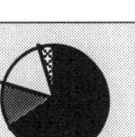

Top Industries & Interest Groups

Crop Production/Processing $31,075
Agricultural Services/Products .. $29,000
Food Processing & Sales $28,528
Health Professionals $20,550
Livestock $19,450

Unidentified $4,584

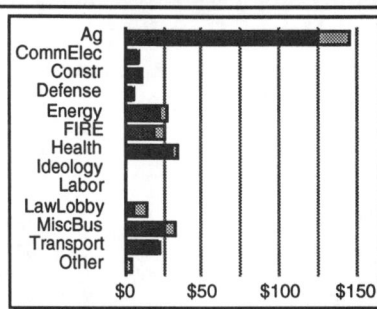

18. Craig Washington (D)
1992 Committees: Educ/Labor Judiciary
First elected: 1989

1991-92 Total Rcpts: $185,635
1990 Year-end cash: $6,996

Source of Funds
- PACs 62%
- Lg Individuals ($200+) 22%
- Individuals under $200 .... 5%
- Other 11%

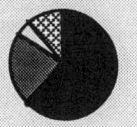

Top Industries & Interest Groups

Lawyers & Lobbyists $29,750
Public Sector Unions $19,300
Transportation Unions $18,800
Industrial Unions $13,500
Building Trade Unions $10,500

Unidentified $4,550

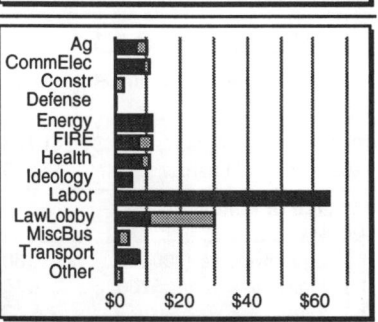

19. Larry Combest (R)
1992 Committees: Agric DC SmBus
First elected: 1984

1991-92 Total Rcpts: $241,559
1990 Year-end cash: $173,124

Source of Funds
- PACs 52%
- Lg Individuals ($200+) 20%
- Individuals under $200 .... 20%
- Other 8%

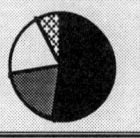

Top Industries & Interest Groups
Crop Production/Processing $15,180
Health Professionals $13,601
Commercial Banks $10,950
Oil & Gas $10,900
Food Processing & Sales $10,450

Unidentified $11,963

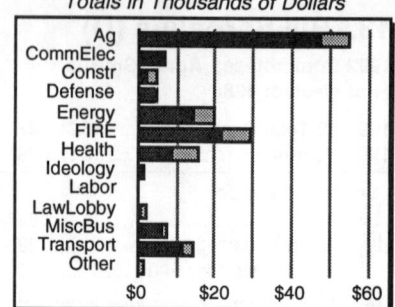

20. Henry B. Gonzalez (D)
1992 Committees: Banking
First elected: 1961

1991-92 Total Rcpts: $50,423
1990 Year-end cash: $18,039

Source of Funds
- PACs 23%
- Lg Individuals ($200+) 35%
- Individuals under $200 .... 27%
- Other 15%

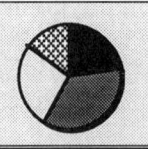

Top Industries & Interest Groups
Lawyers & Lobbyists $5,700
Automotive $3,000
Public Sector Unions $2,000
Insurance $1,500
Oil & Gas $1,250

Unidentified $9,750

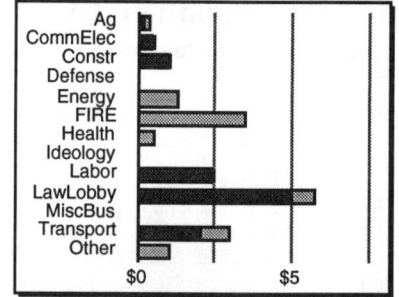

21. Lamar Smith (R)
1992 Committees: Judiciary Science
First elected: 1986

1991-92 Total Rcpts: $544,187
1990 Year-end cash: $420,613

Source of Funds
- PACs 25%
- Lg Individuals ($200+) 36%
- Individuals under $200 .... 27%
- Other 12%

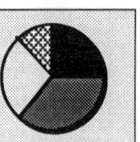

Top Industries & Interest Groups
Oil & Gas $41,150
Health Professionals $23,050
Misc Finance $20,600
Insurance $18,089
Lawyers & Lobbyists $17,349

Unidentified $30,658

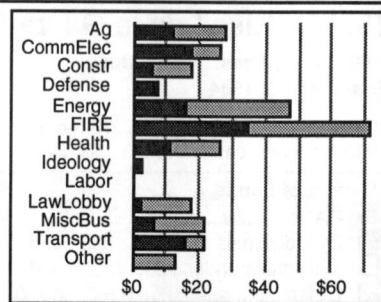

22. Tom DeLay (R)
1992 Committees: Appropriations
First elected: 1984

1991-92 Total Rcpts: $341,516
1990 Year-end cash: $46,466

Source of Funds
- PACs 66%
- Lg Individuals ($200+) 26%
- Individuals under $200 .... 7%
- Other 2%

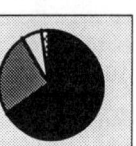

Top Industries & Interest Groups
Oil & Gas $23,300
Lawyers & Lobbyists $21,000
Air Transport $17,827
Health Professionals $16,900
General Contractors $15,500

Unidentified $17,600

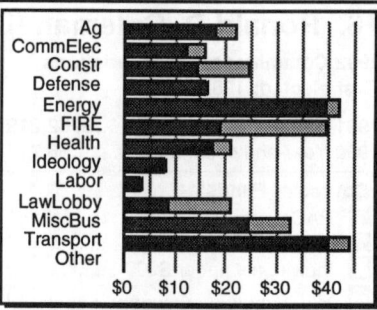

23. Henry Bonilla (R)
1993-94 Committees: Appropriations
First elected: 1992

1991-92 Total Rcpts: $550,673
1990 Year-end cash: .... $-5,359

Source of Funds
- PACs 18%
- Lg Individuals ($200+) 51%
- Individuals under $200 .... 14%
- Other 17%

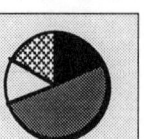

Top Industries & Interest Groups
Oil & Gas $58,150
Insurance $29,840
Health Professionals $27,700
Livestock $24,330
Lawyers & Lobbyists $13,428

Unidentified $83,641

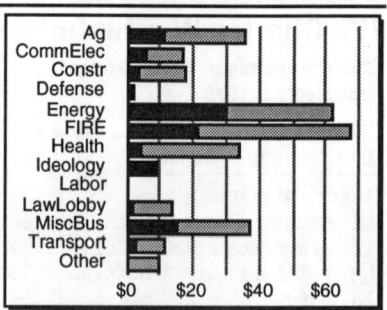

24. Martin Frost (D)
1992 Committees: Admin Rules
First elected: 1978

1991-92 Total Rcpts: $1,241,725
1990 Year-end cash: $8,276

Source of Funds
- PACs 54%
- Lg Individuals ($200+) 33%
- Individuals under $200 .... 10%
- Other 3%

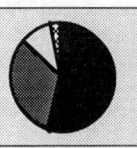

Top Industries & Interest Groups
Lawyers & Lobbyists $137,162
Oil & Gas $80,850
Industrial Unions $53,300
Health Professionals $50,550
Public Sector Unions $50,000

Unidentified $32,250

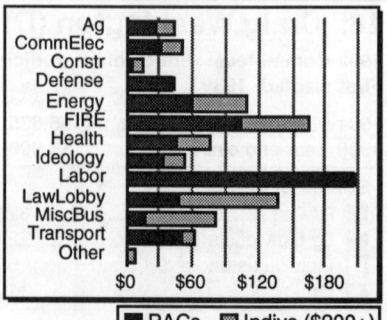

Key to committee & category abbreviations is on page 173

25. Michael A. Andrews (D)

1992 Committees: Ways & Means
First elected: 1982

1991-92 Total Rcpts: $974,838
1990 Year-end cash: $388,519

Source of Funds
- PACs 54%
- Lg Individuals ($200+) 26%
- Individuals under $200 .... 6%
- Other 13%

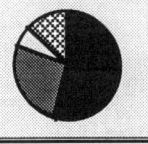

Top Industries & Interest Groups

Lawyers & Lobbyists $111,639
Oil & Gas $99,300
Insurance $66,165
Health Professionals $49,410
Securities & Investment $41,200

Unidentified $29,726

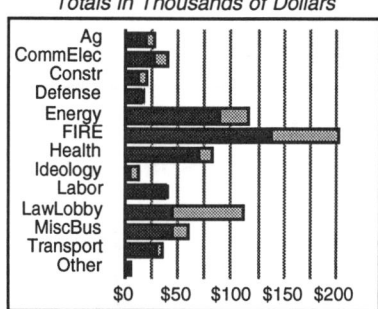

26. Dick Armey (R)

1992 Committees: Banking Educ/Labor
First elected: 1984

1991-92 Total Rcpts: $483,928
1990 Year-end cash: $351,112

Source of Funds
- PACs 40%
- Lg Individuals ($200+) 21%
- Individuals under $200 .... 25%
- Other 14%

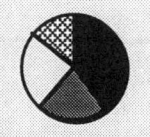

Top Industries & Interest Groups

Commercial Banks $24,000
Oil & Gas $21,450
Automotive $14,875
Real Estate $12,750
Misc Manufacturing & Distrib $11,200

Unidentified $20,839

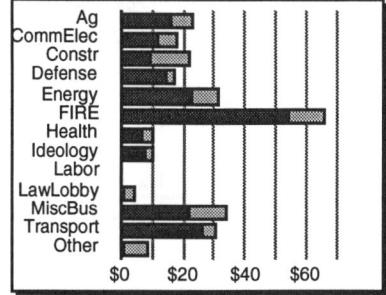

27. Solomon P. Ortiz (D)

1992 Committees: ArmServ MerchMarine
First elected: 1982

1991-92 Total Rcpts: $276,610
1990 Year-end cash: $152,565

Source of Funds
- PACs 36%
- Lg Individuals ($200+) 48%
- Individuals under $200 .... 7%
- Other 9%

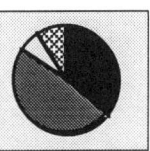

Top Industries & Interest Groups

Lawyers & Lobbyists $18,150
Oil & Gas $13,500
Real Estate $12,200
Building Materials & Equipment $11,468
Health Professionals $10,450

Unidentified $35,834

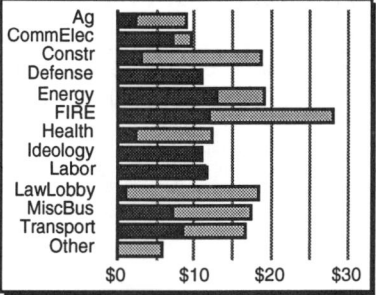

28. Frank M. Tejeda (D)

1993-94 Committees: ArmServ VetAffairs
First elected: 1992

1991-92 Total Rcpts: $302,873
1990 Year-end cash: $1,384

Source of Funds
- PACs 43%
- Lg Individuals ($200+) 48%
- Individuals under $200 .... 5%
- Other 4%

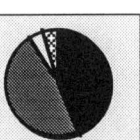

Top Industries & Interest Groups

Health Professionals $36,771
Insurance $19,797
Beer, Wine & Liquor $14,750
Real Estate $14,000
Commercial Banks $13,500

Unidentified $24,790

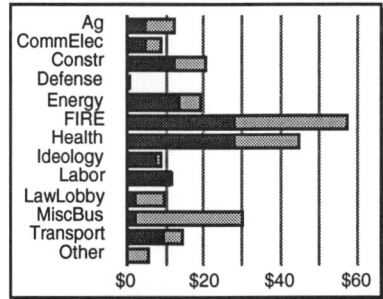

29. Gene Green (D)

1993-94 Committees: Educ/Labor MerchMarine
First elected: 1992

1991-92 Total Rcpts: $674,830
1990 Year-end cash: $11,051

Source of Funds
- PACs 57%
- Lg Individuals ($200+) 25%
- Individuals under $200 .... 7%
- Other 11%

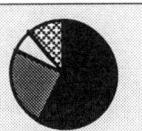

Top Industries & Interest Groups

Lawyers & Lobbyists $96,376
Industrial Unions $78,000
Transportation Unions $44,850
Public Sector Unions $34,500
Health Professionals $28,647

Unidentified $26,500

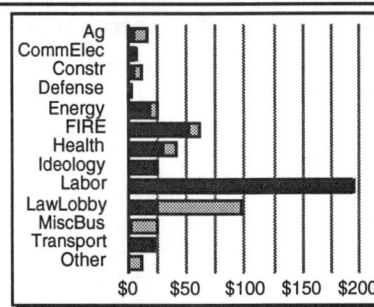

30. Eddie Bernice Johnson (D)

1993-94 Committees: PubWorks Science
First elected: 1992

1991-92 Total Rcpts: $283,350
1990 Year-end cash: $2,696

Source of Funds
- PACs 40%
- Lg Individuals ($200+) 30%
- Individuals under $200 .... 24%
- Other 7%

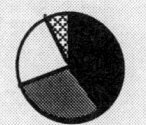

Top Industries & Interest Groups

Health Professionals $22,427
Public Sector Unions $18,750
Lawyers & Lobbyists $17,726
Industrial Unions $15,000
Transportation Unions $14,750

Unidentified $43,480

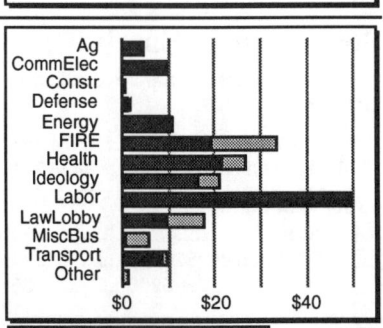

Utah

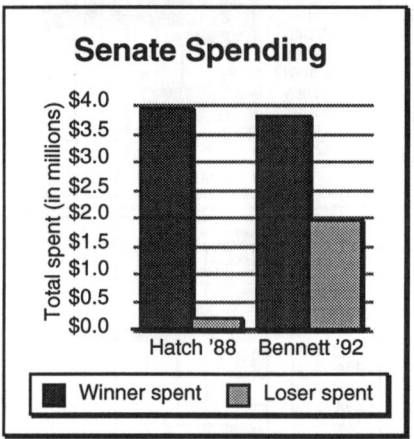

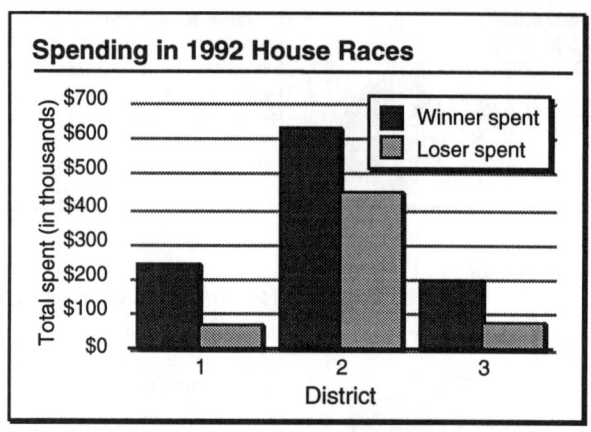

1992 Elections at a Glance

Dist	Name	Party	Vote Pct	Race Type
Sen	Robert F. Bennett (1992)	Rep	55%	Open Seat
Sen	Orrin G. Hatch (1988)	Rep	67%	Reelected
1	James V. Hansen	Rep	65%	Reelected
2	Karen Shepherd	Dem	50%	Open Seat
3	Bill Orton	Dem	59%	Reelected

Totals in Thousands of Dollars

Sen. Robert F. Bennett (R)

1993-94 Committees: Banking Energy SmBus
First elected: 1992

1991-92 Total Rcpts: $3,457,116
1990 Year-end cash: $173,424

Source of Funds
- PACs 11%
- Lg Individuals ($200+) 6%
- Individuals under $200 ....2%
- Other 82%

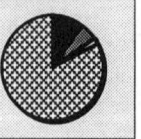

1991-92
Top Industries & Interest Groups

Oil & Gas $60,048
Insurance $40,750
Automotive $26,750
Commercial Banks $24,150
Lawyer & Lobbyists $22,700

Unidentified $77,595

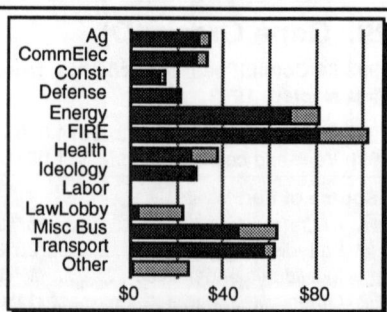

Sen. Orrin G. Hatch (R)

1992 Committees: Finance Judiciary Labor
First elected: 1976

1987-92 Total Rcpts: $4,574,487
1990 Year-end cash: $438,741

Source of Funds
- PACs 30%
- Lg Individuals ($200+) 24%
- Individuals under $200 ....35%
- Other 11%

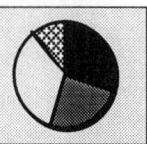

1987-92†
Top Industries & Interest Groups

Insurance $128,492
Pharmaceuticals/Health Prod ..$100,200
Health Professionals $86,098
Lawyer & Lobbyists $74,050
Oil & Gas $73,850

Unidentified $43,320

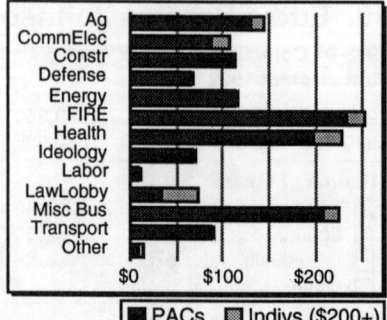

Key to committee & category abbreviations is on page 173

1. James V. Hansen (R)

1992 Committees: ArmServ Interior
First elected: 1980

1991-92 Total Rcpts: $221,781
1990 Year-end cash: $22,756

Source of Funds
- PACs 66%
- Lg Individuals ($200+) 21%
- Individuals under $200 .... 10%
- Other 3%

Top Industries & Interest Groups

Defense Aerospace $20,900
Oil & Gas $14,050
Health Professionals $12,200
Automotive $9,250
Misc Manufacturing & Distrib ... $9,000

Unidentified $11,110

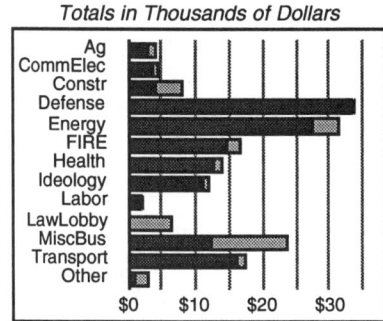

2. Karen Shepherd (D)

1993-94 Committees: NatResources PubWorks
First elected: 1992

1991-92 Total Rcpts: $646,636
1990 Year-end cash: $23,437

Source of Funds
- PACs 30%
- Lg Individuals ($200+) 26%
- Individuals under $200 .... 38%
- Other 6%

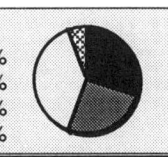

Top Industries & Interest Groups

Womens Issues $48,255
Public Sector Unions $35,300
Industrial Unions $31,950
Lawyers & Lobbyists $18,243
Transportation Unions $18,000

Unidentified $41,065

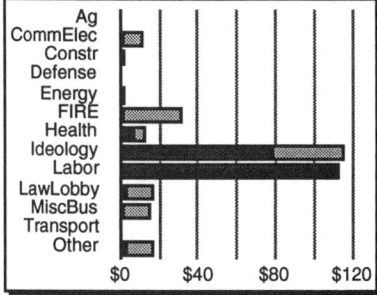

3. Bill Orton (D)

1992 Committees: Banking ForAff SmBus
First elected: 1990

1991-92 Total Rcpts: $257,559
1990 Year-end cash: $18,398

Source of Funds
- PACs 72%
- Lg Individuals ($200+) 10%
- Individuals under $200 .... 8%
- Other 10%

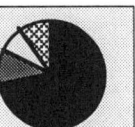

Top Industries & Interest Groups

Building Trade Unions $20,650
Industrial Unions $19,600
Real Estate $18,494
Public Sector Unions $16,800
Commercial Banks $16,400

Unidentified $5,300

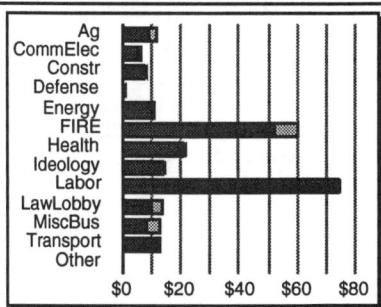

■ PACs   ▨ Indivs ($200+)

† Does not include individual contributions from 1987-88

Vermont

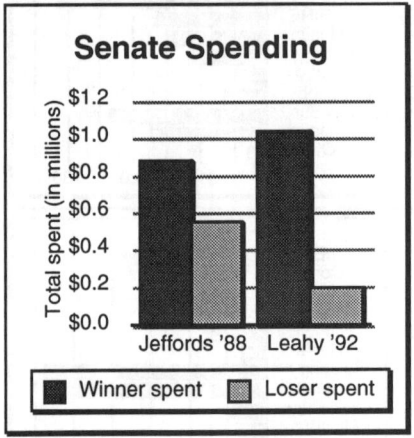

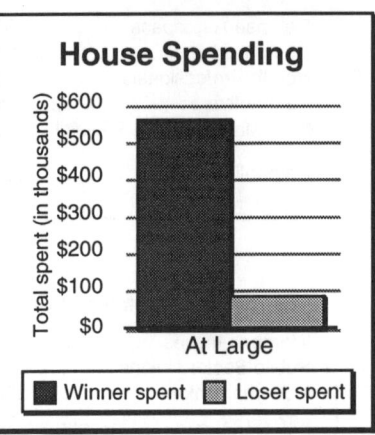

1992 Elections at a Glance

Dist	Name	Party	Vote Pct	Race Type
Sen	Patrick J. Leahy (1992)	Dem	54%	Reelected
Sen	James M. Jeffords (1988)	Rep	68%	Open Seat
1	Bernard Sanders	Ind	58%	Reelected

Totals in Thousands of Dollars

Sen. James M. Jeffords (R)

1992 Committees: Envir ForRel Labor VetAffairs
First elected: 1988

1987-92 Total Rcpts: $1,138,169
1990 Year-end cash: $342,620

Source of Funds
- PACs 56%
- Lg Individuals ($200+) 9%
- Individuals under $200 .... 9%
- Other 26%

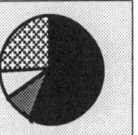

1987-92†
Top Industries & Interest Groups

Dairy $45,300
Public Sector Unions $37,500
Insurance $36,158
Health Professionals $35,733
Transportation Unions $34,350

Unidentified $600

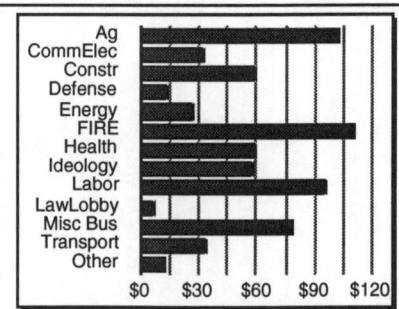

Sen. Patrick J. Leahy (D)

1992 Committees: Agric Approp Judiciary
First elected: 1974

1987-92 Total Rcpts: $1,144,189
1990 Year-end cash: $269,610

Source of Funds
- PACs 29%
- Lg Individuals ($200+) 36%
- Individuals under $200 .... 10%
- Other 25%

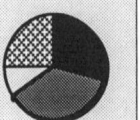

1987-92†
Top Industries & Interest Groups

Lawyer & Lobbyists $115,420
Media/Entertainment $86,100
Crop Production/Processing $36,320
Real Estate $34,500
Pro-Israel $29,297

Unidentified $52,814

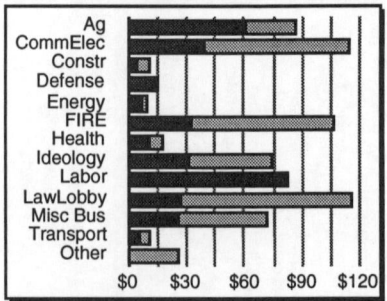

1. Bernard Sanders (I)

1992 Committees: Banking GovtOps
First elected: 1990

1991-92 Total Rcpts: $586,682
1990 Year-end cash: $19,231

Source of Funds
- PACs 25%
- Lg Individuals ($200+) 11%
- Individuals under $200 .... 62%
- Other 2%

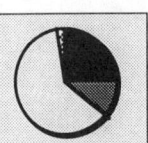

Top Industries & Interest Groups

Industrial Unions $50,500
Public Sector Unions $29,700
Building Trade Unions $21,500
Transportation Unions $19,800
Misc Unions $13,882

Unidentified $14,174

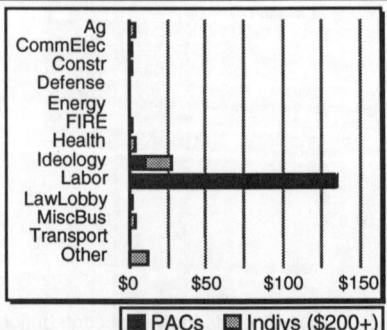

Key to committee & category abbreviations is on page 173

Virginia

Spending in 1992 House Races

Senate Spending

1992 Elections at a Glance

Dist	Name	Party	Vote Pct	Race Type
Sen	Charles S. Robb (1988)	Dem	71%	Open Seat
Sen	John W. Warner (1990)	Rep	81%	Reelected
1	Herbert H. Bateman	Rep	58%	Reelected
2	Owen B. Pickett	Dem	56%	Reelected
3	Robert C. Scott	Dem	79%	Open Seat
4	Norman Sisisky	Dem	68%	Reelected
5	Lewis F. Payne Jr.	Dem	69%	Reelected
6	Robert W. Goodlatte	Rep	60%	Open Seat
7	Thomas J. Bliley Jr.	Rep	83%	Reelected
8	James P. Moran Jr.	Dem	56%	Reelected
9	Rick Boucher	Dem	63%	Reelected
10	Frank R. Wolf	Rep	64%	Reelected
11	Leslie L. Byrne	Dem	50%	Open Seat

Totals in Thousands of Dollars

Sen. Charles S. Robb (D)

1992 Committees: Commerce ForRel
First elected: 1988

1987-92 Total Rcpts: $3,329,658
1990 Year-end cash: ....$-249

Source of Funds
- PACs 27%
- Lg Individuals ($200+) 52%
- Individuals under $200 ....11%
- Other..9%

1987-92†
Top Industries & Interest Groups

Insurance	$56,753
Oil & Gas	$55,847
Transportation Unions	$52,050
Commercial Banks	$40,250
Health Professionals	$39,584
Unidentified	$6,490

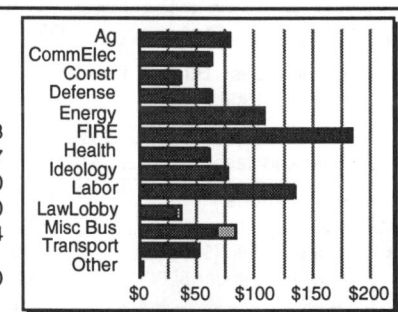

Sen. John W. Warner (R)

1992 Committees: ArmServ Envir Rules
First elected: 1978

1987-92 Total Rcpts: $1,892,918
1990 Year-end cash: $160,162

Source of Funds
- PACs 38%
- Lg Individuals ($200+) 40%
- Individuals under $200 ....1%
- Other..20%

1987-92†
Top Industries & Interest Groups

Real Estate	$124,725
Lawyer & Lobbyists	$119,620
Defense Aerospace	$74,982
Defense Electronics	$66,360
Misc Defense	$65,350
Unidentified	$179,475

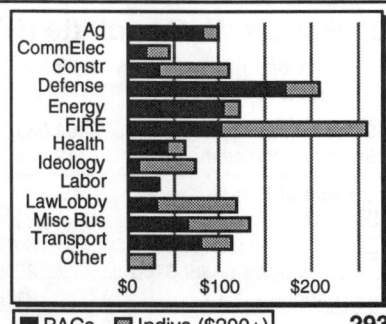

† Does not include individual contributions from 1987-88

1. Herbert H. Bateman (R)
1992 Committees: ArmServ MerchMarine
First elected: 1982

1991-92 Total Rcpts: $766,895
1990 Year-end cash: $16,992

Source of Funds
- PACs 36%
- Lg Individuals ($200+) 32%
- Individuals under $200 .... 24%
- Other 8%

Top Industries & Interest Groups

Defense Aerospace $37,500
Misc Defense $36,350
Defense Electronics $29,900
Real Estate $27,800
Health Professionals $25,550

Unidentified $51,325

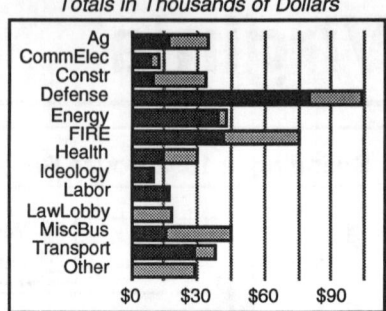

Totals in Thousands of Dollars

2. Owen B. Pickett (D)
1992 Committees: ArmServ MerchMarine VetAffairs
First elected: 1986

1991-92 Total Rcpts: $281,279
1990 Year-end cash: $94,085

Source of Funds
- PACs 44%
- Lg Individuals ($200+) 32%
- Individuals under $200 .... 13%
- Other 11%

Top Industries & Interest Groups

Lawyers & Lobbyists $21,400
Misc Finance $13,200
Misc Defense $12,550
Beer, Wine & Liquor $12,500
Public Sector Unions $12,500

Unidentified $13,703

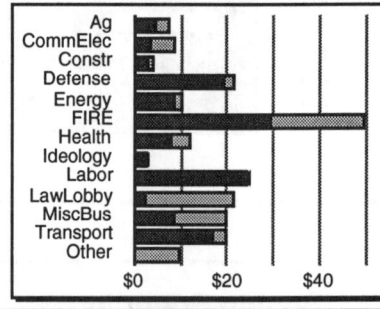

3. Robert C. Scott (D)
1993-94 Committees: Educ/Labor Judiciary Science
First elected: 1992

1991-92 Total Rcpts: $510,776
1990 Year-end cash: $18,915

Source of Funds
- PACs 36%
- Lg Individuals ($200+) 25%
- Individuals under $200 .... 26%
- Other 13%

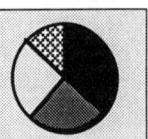

Top Industries & Interest Groups

Lawyers & Lobbyists $44,730
Health Professionals $31,286
Industrial Unions $23,500
Transportation Unions $22,500
Public Sector Unions $20,600

Unidentified $22,400

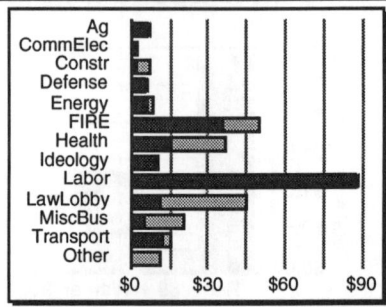

4. Norman Sisisky (D)
1992 Committees: ArmServ SmBus
First elected: 1982

1991-92 Total Rcpts: $257,047
1990 Year-end cash: $72,679

Source of Funds
- PACs 61%
- Lg Individuals ($200+) 17%
- Individuals under $200 .... 10%
- Other 11%

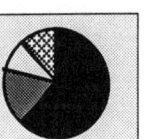

Top Industries & Interest Groups

Misc Defense $22,050
Defense Aerospace $15,000
Public Sector Unions $12,500
Food Processing & Sales $9,250
Beer, Wine & Liquor $9,250

Unidentified $7,650

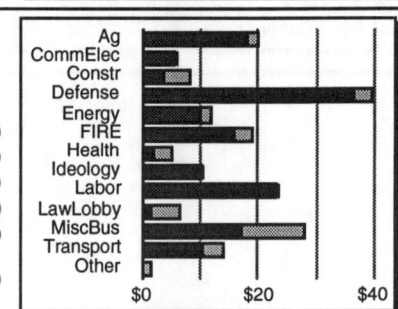

5. Lewis F. Payne Jr. (D)
1992 Committees: Budget PubWorks
First elected: 1988

1991-92 Total Rcpts: $419,768
1990 Year-end cash: $13,540

Source of Funds
- PACs 52%
- Lg Individuals ($200+) 33%
- Individuals under $200 .... 14%
- Other 1%

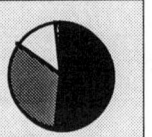

Top Industries & Interest Groups

Air Transport $22,650
Health Professionals $18,200
Real Estate $17,590
Lawyers & Lobbyists $17,350
Commercial Banks $14,650

Unidentified $37,240

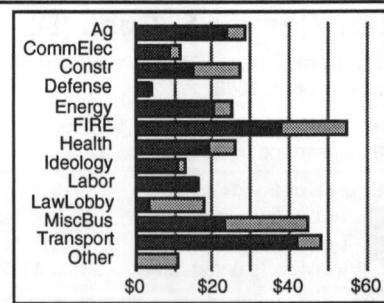

6. Robert W. Goodlatte (R)
1993-94 Committees: Agric Judiciary
First elected: 1992

1991-92 Total Rcpts: $464,535
1990 Year-end cash: $12,486

Source of Funds
- PACs 24%
- Lg Individuals ($200+) 30%
- Individuals under $200 .... 25%
- Other 21%

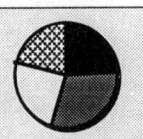

Top Industries & Interest Groups

Retired $19,575
Health Professionals $16,700
Lawyers & Lobbyists $14,240
Commercial Banks $11,400
Insurance $11,300

Unidentified $38,190

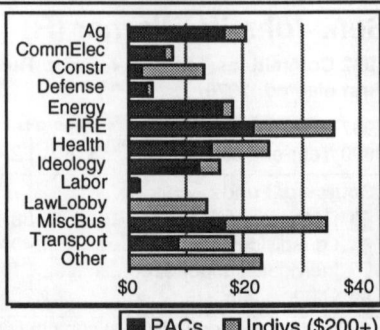

Key to committee & category abbreviations is on page 173

■ PACs ■ Indivs ($200+)

7. Thomas J. Bliley Jr. (R)

1992 Committees: DC Energy/Commerce
First elected: 1980

1991-92 Total Rcpts: $721,526
1990 Year-end cash: $52,852

Source of Funds
- PACs 61%
- Lg Individuals ($200+) 16%
- Individuals under $200 ....22%
- Other...0%

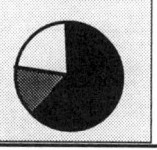

Top Industries & Interest Groups

Tobacco $38,991
Health Professionals $37,450
Pharmaceuticals/Health Prod $35,000
Oil & Gas $31,125
Insurance $29,688

Unidentified $23,150

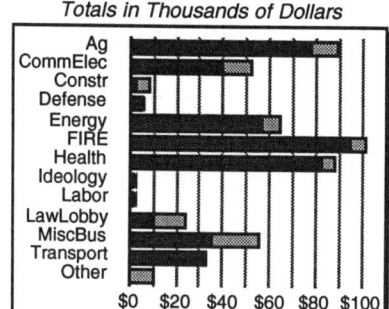

8. James P. Moran Jr. (D)

1992 Committees: Banking Post Office
First elected: 1990

1991-92 Total Rcpts: $924,029
1990 Year-end cash: $1,455

Source of Funds
- PACs 47%
- Lg Individuals ($200+) 31%
- Individuals under $200 ....19%
- Other...3%

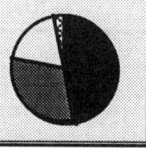

Top Industries & Interest Groups

Lawyers & Lobbyists $91,330
Public Sector Unions $59,750
Real Estate $50,550
Health Professionals $39,837
Transportation Unions $34,900

Unidentified $61,059

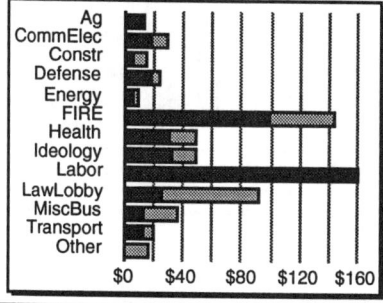

9. Rick Boucher (D)

1992 Committees: Energy/Commerce Judiciary Science
First elected: 1982

1991-92 Total Rcpts: $639,537
1990 Year-end cash: $380,922

Source of Funds
- PACs 62%
- Lg Individuals ($200+) 14%
- Individuals under $200 ....10%
- Other...14%

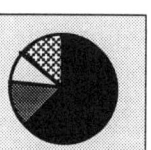

Top Industries & Interest Groups

Commercial Banks $44,100
Telephone Utilities $34,900
Lawyers & Lobbyists $29,600
Health Professionals $22,600
Tobacco $21,350

Unidentified $17,500

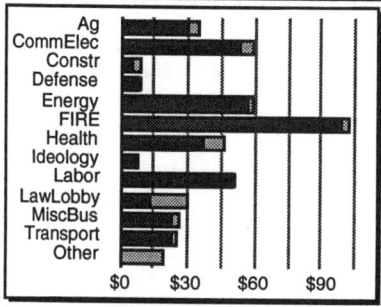

10. Frank R. Wolf (R)

1992 Committees: Appropriations
First elected: 1980

1991-92 Total Rcpts: $452,307
1990 Year-end cash: $79,889

Source of Funds
- PACs 40%
- Lg Individuals ($200+) 30%
- Individuals under $200 ....27%
- Other...3%

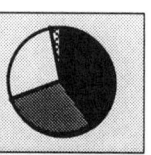

Top Industries & Interest Groups

Real Estate $40,750
Defense Electronics $23,450
Misc Defense $15,300
Computer Equipment & Svcs $15,150
Commercial Banks $13,650

Unidentified $31,700

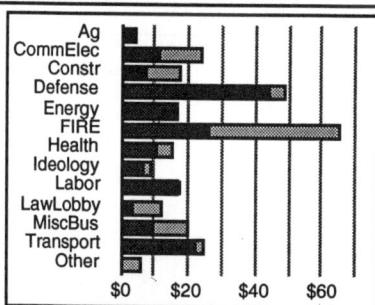

11. Leslie L. Byrne (D)

1993-94 Committees: Post Office PubWorks
First elected: 1992

1991-92 Total Rcpts: $792,565
1990 Year-end cash: $16,651

Source of Funds
- PACs 37%
- Lg Individuals ($200+) 15%
- Individuals under $200 ....37%
- Other...11%

Top Industries & Interest Groups

Industrial Unions $52,800
Public Sector Unions $45,799
Womens Issues $36,530
Lawyers & Lobbyists $33,616
Health Professionals $30,634

Unidentified $41,665

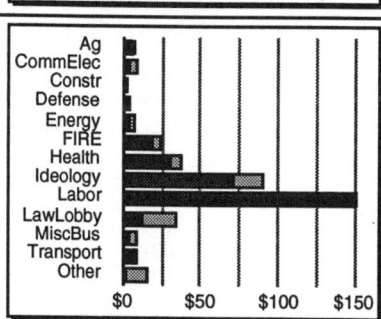

■ PACs ▩ Indivs ($200+)

Washington

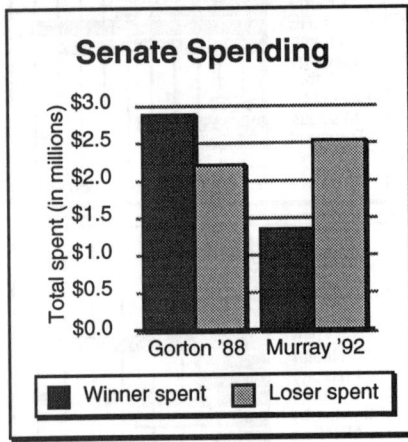
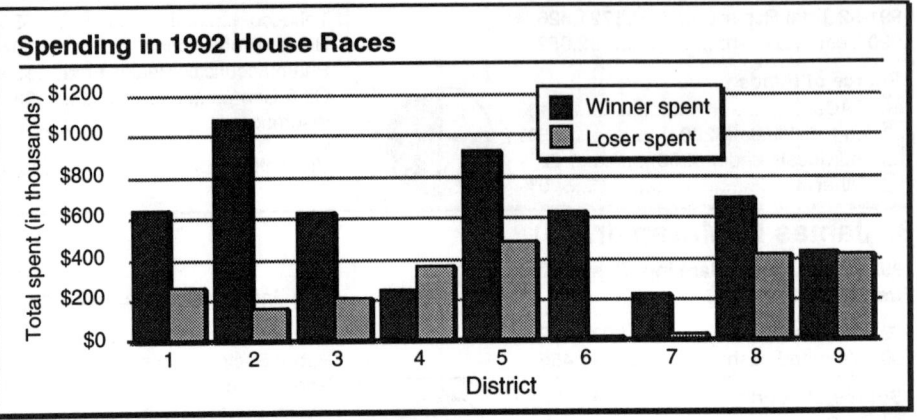

1992 Elections at a Glance

Dist	Name	Party	Vote Pct	Race Type
Sen	Patty Murray (1992)	Dem	54%	Open Seat
Sen	Slade Gorton (1988)	Rep	51%	Open Seat
1	Maria Cantwell	Dem	55%	Open Seat
2	Al Swift	Dem	52%	Reelected
3	Jolene Unsoeld	Dem	56%	Reelected
4	Jay Inslee	Dem	51%	Open Seat
5	Thomas S. Foley	Dem	55%	Reelected
6	Norm Dicks	Dem	64%	Reelected
7	Jim McDermott	Dem	78%	Reelected
8	Jennifer Dunn	Rep	60%	Open Seat
9	Mike Kreidler	Dem	52%	Open Seat

Totals in Thousands of Dollars

Sen. Slade Gorton (R)
1992 Committees: Approp Commerce
First elected: 1980 (Out of office 1987-88)

1987-92 Total Rcpts: $3,364,943
1990 Year-end cash: $128,708

Source of Funds
- PACs 32%
- Lg Individuals ($200+) 28%
- Individuals under $200 ....25%
- Other 15%

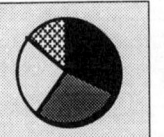

1987-92†
Top Industries & Interest Groups

Forest Products $82,688
Oil & Gas $81,450
Commercial Banks $66,805
Insurance $65,179
Lawyer & Lobbyists $58,721

Unidentified $63,023

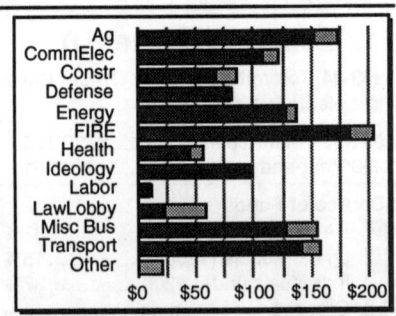

Sen. Patty Murray (D)
1993-94 Committees: Approp Banking Budget
First elected: 1992

1991-92 Total Rcpts: $1,496,204
1990 Year-end cash: $154,166

Source of Funds
- PACs 23%
- Lg Individuals ($200+) 17%
- Individuals under $200 ....35%
- Other 24%

1991-92
Top Industries & Interest Groups

Womens Issues $100,783
Transportation Unions $82,500
Public Sector Unions $58,250
Lawyer & Lobbyists $41,367
Industrial Unions $40,750

Unidentified $60,431

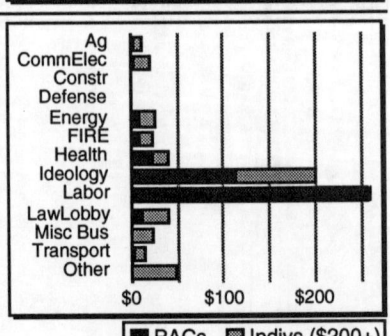

Key to committee & category abbreviations is on page 173

1. Maria Cantwell (D)

1993-94 Committees: ForAff MerchMarine PubWorks
First elected: 1992

1991-92 Total Rcpts: $657,454
1990 Year-end cash: $3,209

Source of Funds
- PACs 42%
- Lg Individuals ($200+) 21%
- Individuals under $200 .... 27%
- Other 10%

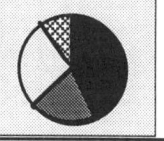

Top Industries & Interest Groups

Transportation Unions $39,000
Public Sector Unions $39,000
Lawyers & Lobbyists $34,952
Womens Issues $33,485
Industrial Unions $25,300

Unidentified $28,467

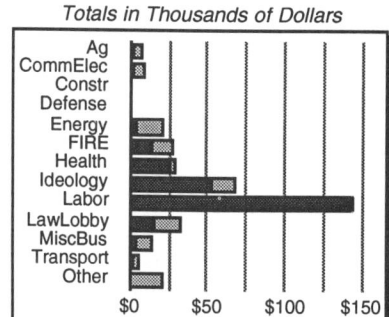

2. Al Swift (D)

1992 Committees: Admin Energy/Commerce
First elected: 1978

1991-92 Total Rcpts: $914,905
1990 Year-end cash: $22,730

Source of Funds
- PACs 70%
- Lg Individuals ($200+) 15%
- Individuals under $200 .... 9%
- Other 6%

Top Industries & Interest Groups

Lawyers & Lobbyists $59,938
Transportation Unions $46,000
Telephone Utilities $43,850
Railroads $41,250
Media/Entertainment $39,250

Unidentified $24,158

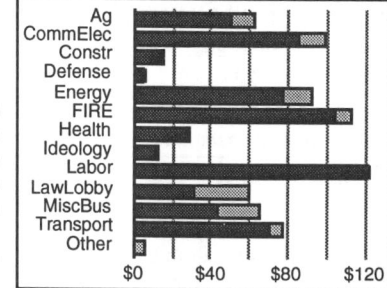

3. Jolene Unsoeld (D)

1992 Committees: Educ/Labor MerchMarine
First elected: 1988

1991-92 Total Rcpts: $666,934
1990 Year-end cash: $50,099

Source of Funds
- PACs 54%
- Lg Individuals ($200+) 18%
- Individuals under $200 .... 25%
- Other 3%

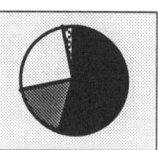

Top Industries & Interest Groups

Transportation Unions $55,200
Industrial Unions $50,300
Public Sector Unions $47,000
Building Trade Unions $31,500
Womens Issues $22,985

Unidentified $13,629

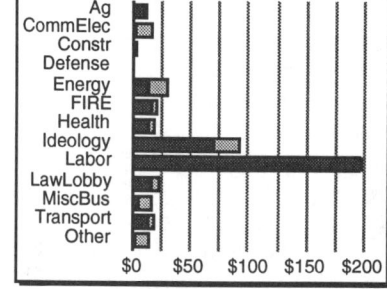

4. Jay Inslee (D)

1993-94 Committees: Agric Science
First elected: 1992

1991-92 Total Rcpts: $249,708
1990 Year-end cash: $3,551

Source of Funds
- PACs 39%
- Lg Individuals ($200+) 21%
- Individuals under $200 .... 20%
- Other 20%

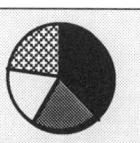

Top Industries & Interest Groups

Lawyers & Lobbyists $15,150
Public Sector Unions $13,500
Building Trade Unions $11,000
Industrial Unions $10,750
Transportation Unions $10,000

Unidentified $14,659

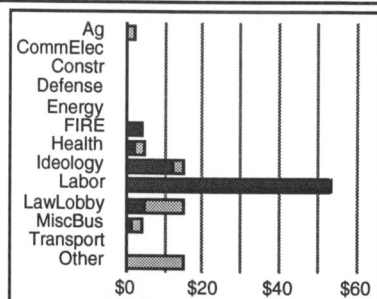

5. Thomas S. Foley (D)

1992 Committees: Speaker of the House
First elected: 1964

1991-92 Total Rcpts: $561,826
1990 Year-end cash: $244,887

Source of Funds
- PACs 71%
- Lg Individuals ($200+) 12%
- Individuals under $200 .... 3%
- Other 15%

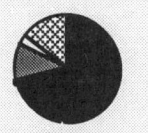

Top Industries & Interest Groups

Public Sector Unions $38,000
Commercial Banks $33,500
Lawyers & Lobbyists $28,810
Transportation Unions $26,000
Air Transport $21,000

Unidentified $10,100

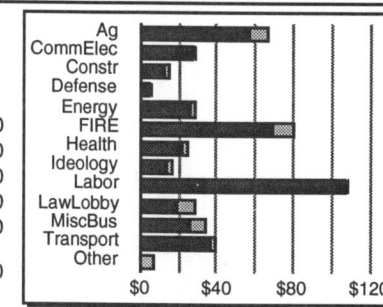

6. Norm Dicks (D)

1992 Committees: Appropriations
First elected: 1976

1991-92 Total Rcpts: $546,865
1990 Year-end cash: $55,882

Source of Funds
- PACs 56%
- Lg Individuals ($200+) 28%
- Individuals under $200 .... 11%
- Other 6%

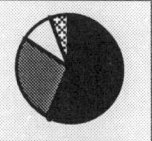

Top Industries & Interest Groups

Defense Aerospace $52,963
Lawyers & Lobbyists $47,075
Defense Electronics $30,750
Industrial Unions $28,746
Transportation Unions $25,000

Unidentified $37,225

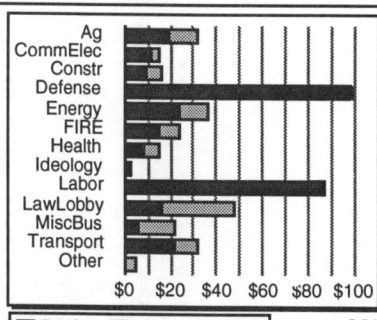

† Does not include individual contributions from 1987-88

7. Jim McDermott (D)
1992 Committees: DC Ways & Means
First elected: 1988

1991-92 Total Rcpts: $266,146
1990 Year-end cash: $68,692

Source of Funds
- PACs 69%
- Lg Individuals ($200+) 10%
- Individuals under $200 .... 11%
- Other 10%

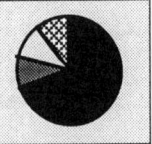

Top Industries & Interest Groups

Health Professionals $18,100
Insurance $16,350
Transportation Unions $14,750
Lawyers & Lobbyists $13,200
Public Sector Unions $12,900

Unidentified $4,890

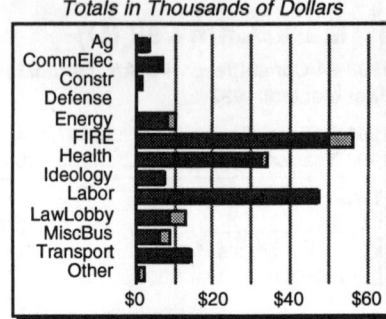

8. Jennifer Dunn (R)
1993-94 Committees: Admin PubWorks Science
First elected: 1992

1991-92 Total Rcpts: $684,207
1990 Year-end cash: $4,533

Source of Funds
- PACs 24%
- Lg Individuals ($200+) 31%
- Individuals under $200 .... 38%
- Other 7%

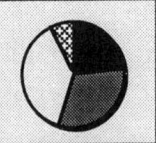

Top Industries & Interest Groups

Retired $31,075
Forestry & Forest Products $28,868
Real Estate $25,125
Womens Issues $21,335
Insurance $16,150

Unidentified $61,520

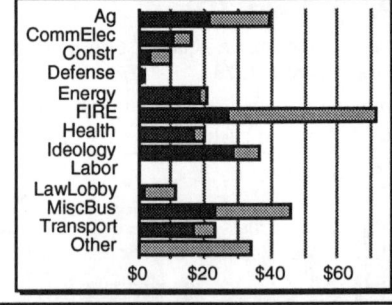

9. Mike Kreidler (D)
1993-94 Committees: Energy/Commerce VetAffairs
First elected: 1992

1991-92 Total Rcpts: $431,480
1990 Year-end cash: $2

Source of Funds
- PACs 36%
- Lg Individuals ($200+) 10%
- Individuals under $200 .... 39%
- Other 15%

Top Industries & Interest Groups

Health Professionals $38,575
Public Sector Unions $26,275
Industrial Unions $19,500
Misc Unions $19,000
Transportation Unions $16,000

Unidentified $5,993

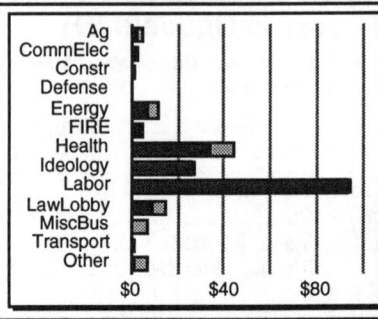

■ PACs   ▨ Indivs ($200+)

West Virginia

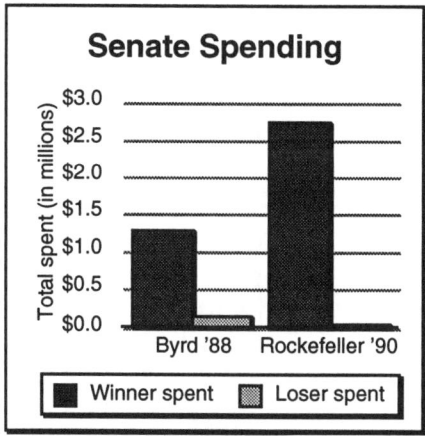

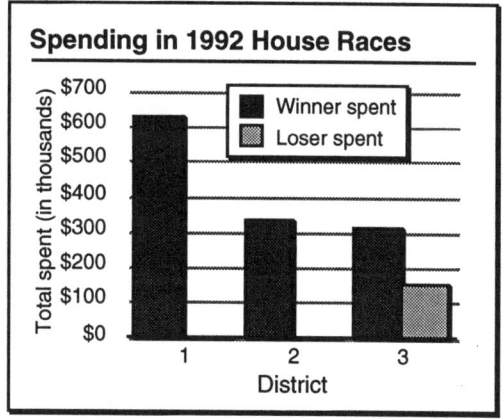

1992 Elections at a Glance

Dist	Name	Party	Vote Pct	Race Type
Sen	Robert C. Byrd (1988)	Dem	65%	Reelected
Sen	John D. Rockefeller IV (1990)	Dem	68%	Reelected
1	Alan B. Mollohan	Dem	100%	Reelected
2	Bob Wise	Dem	71%	Reelected
3	Nick J. Rahall II	Dem	66%	Reelected

Totals in Thousands of Dollars

Sen. Robert C. Byrd (D)

1992 Committees: Approp ArmServ Rules
First elected: 1958

1987-92 Total Rcpts: $1,721,118
1990 Year-end cash: $703,378

Source of Funds
- PACs 60%
- Lg Individuals ($200+) 18%
- Individuals under $200 ....4%
- Other 18%

1987-92†
Top Industries & Interest Groups

Defense Aerospace $70,500
Transportation Unions $68,700
Oil & Gas $55,350
Building Trade Unions $50,000
Industrial Unions $48,700

Unidentified ....$-500

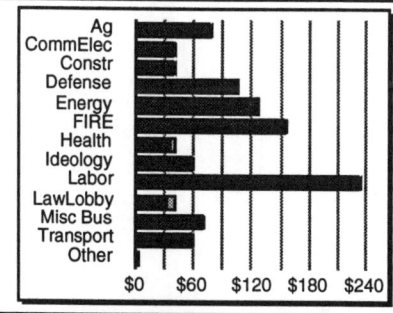

Sen. John D. Rockefeller IV (D)

1992 Committees: Commerce Finance VetAffairs
First elected: 1984

1987-92 Total Rcpts: $3,858,133
1990 Year-end cash: $530,633

Source of Funds
- PACs 37%
- Lg Individuals ($200+) 47%
- Individuals under $200 ....8%
- Other 9%

† Does not include individual contributions from 1987-88

1987-92†
Top Industries & Interest Groups

Lawyer & Lobbyists $286,720
Health Professionals $278,752
Real Estate $169,675
Insurance $157,650
Securities & Investment $150,750

Unidentified $306,101

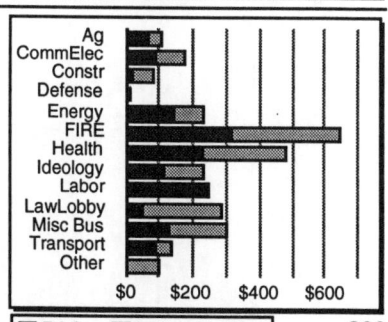

1. Alan B. Mollohan (D)

1992 Committees: Appropriations
First elected: 1982

1991-92 Total Rcpts: $484,159
1990 Year-end cash: $1,176

Source of Funds
- PACs 49%
- Lg Individuals ($200+) 31%
- Individuals under $200 ....10%
- Other 9%

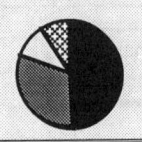

Top Industries & Interest Groups

Lawyers & Lobbyists $37,900
Defense Aerospace $32,800
Transportation Unions $22,500
Industrial Unions $20,500
Health Professionals $16,384

Unidentified $28,746

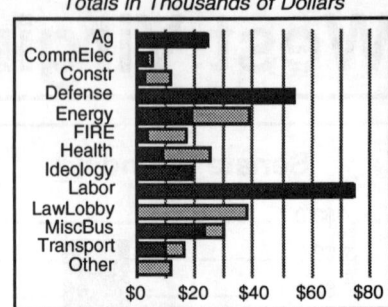

2. Bob Wise (D)

1992 Committees: Budget GovtOps
First elected: 1982

1991-92 Total Rcpts: $295,894
1990 Year-end cash: $145,069

Source of Funds
- PACs 56%
- Lg Individuals ($200+) 17%
- Individuals under $200 ....18%
- Other 8%

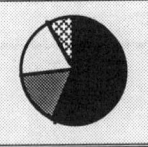

Top Industries & Interest Groups

Oil & Gas $20,225
Public Sector Unions $19,500
Lawyers & Lobbyists $18,600
Transportation Unions $12,500
Industrial Unions $11,000

Unidentified $6,950

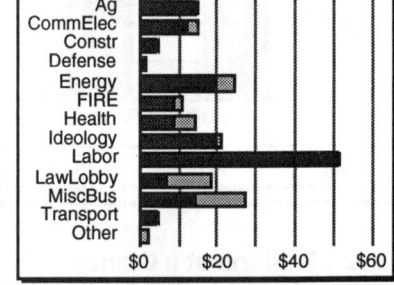

3. Nick J. Rahall II (D)

1992 Committees: Interior PubWorks
First elected: 1976

1991-92 Total Rcpts: $444,624
1990 Year-end cash: $500,823

Source of Funds
- PACs 52%
- Lg Individuals ($200+) 18%
- Individuals under $200 ....9%
- Other 22%

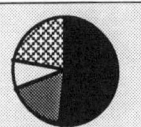

Top Industries & Interest Groups

Transportation Unions $38,950
Public Sector Unions $26,625
Industrial Unions $26,550
Trucking $24,300
Building Trade Unions $15,500

Unidentified $22,100

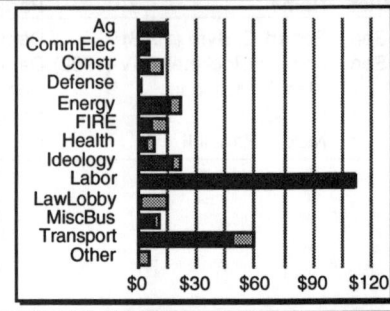

Totals in Thousands of Dollars

■ PACs ▨ Indivs ($200+)

Key to committee & category abbreviations is on page 173

Wisconsin

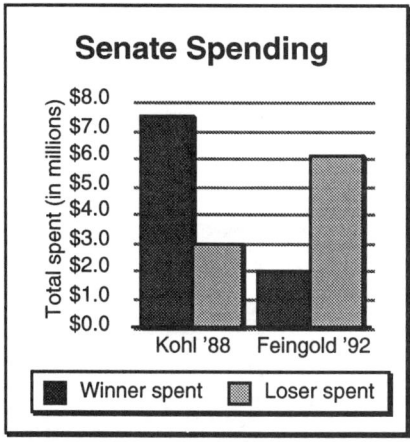

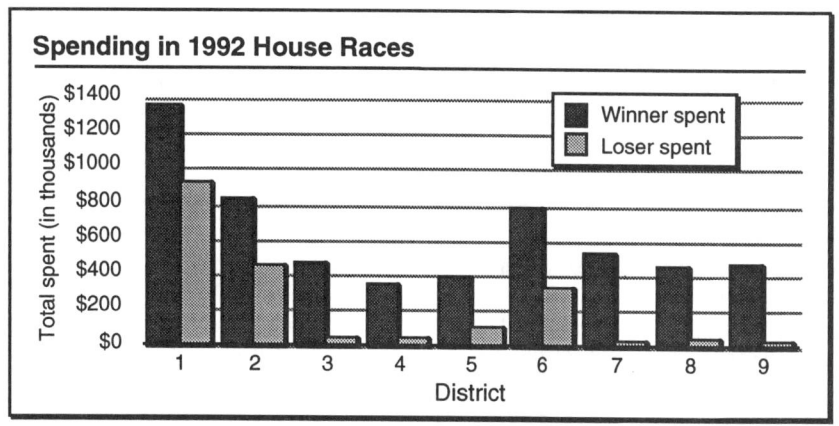

1992 Elections at a Glance

Dist	Name	Party	Vote Pct	Race Type
Sen	Russell Feingold (1992)	Dem	53%	Beat Incumb
Sen	Herb Kohl (1988)	Dem	52%	Open Seat
1	Les Aspin	Dem	58%	Reelected
2	Scott L. Klug	Rep	63%	Reelected
3	Steve Gunderson	Rep	56%	Reelected
4	Gerald D. Kleczka	Dem	66%	Reelected
5	Thomas Barrett	Dem	69%	Open Seat
6	Tom Petri	Rep	53%	Reelected
7	David R. Obey	Dem	64%	Reelected
8	Toby Roth	Rep	70%	Reelected
9	F. James Sensenbrenner Jr.	Rep	70%	Reelected

Totals in Thousands of Dollars

Sen. Russell Feingold (D)

1993-94 Committees: Agric ForAff
First elected: 1992

1991-92 Total Rcpts: $1,996,312
1990 Year-end cash: $26,855

Source of Funds
- PACs 19%
- Lg Individuals ($200+) 28%
- Individuals under $200 .... 35%
- Other 19%

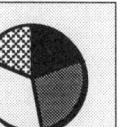

1991-92
Top Industries & Interest Groups

Lawyer & Lobbyists $204,367
Health Professionals $86,345
Industrial Unions $75,500
Transportation Unions $55,550
Public Sector Unions $42,800

Unidentified $149,906

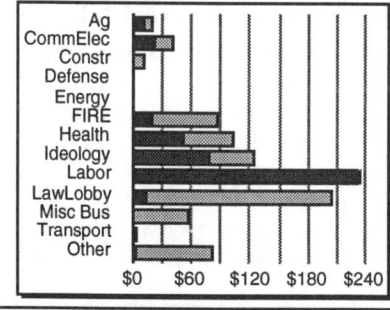

Sen. Herb Kohl (D)

1992 Committees: GovAff Judiciary
First elected: 1988

1987-92 Total Rcpts: $8,371,609
1990 Year-end cash: $1,530

Source of Funds
- PACs 0%
- Lg Individuals ($200+) 5%
- Individuals under $200 .... 3%
- Other 92%

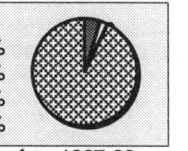

1987-92†
Top Industries & Interest Groups

Automotive $2,000
Misc Unions $1,500
Crop Production/Processing $1,000

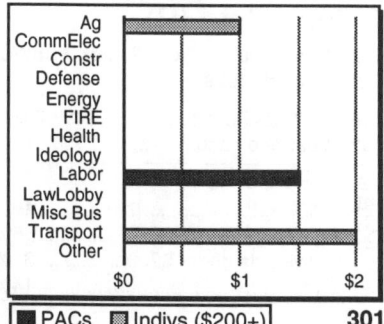

† Does not include individual contributions from 1987-88

1. Les Aspin (D)

1992 Committees: Armed Services
First elected: 1970

1991-92 Total Rcpts: $1,369,976
1990 Year-end cash: $131,742

Source of Funds
- PACs 39%
- Lg Individuals ($200+) 37%
- Individuals under $200 ....18%
- Other 6%

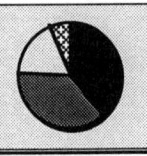

Top Industries & Interest Groups

Defense Aerospace $116,975
Lawyers & Lobbyists $116,200
Pro-Israel $79,850
Defense Electronics $62,850
Securities & Investment $42,850

Unidentified $109,225

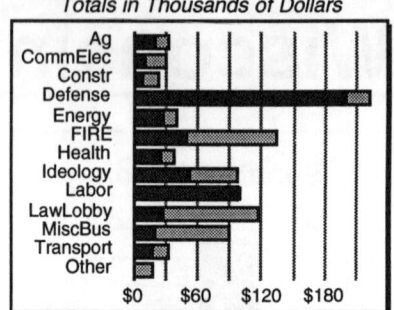

2. Scott L. Klug (R)

1992 Committees: Educ/Labor GovtOps
First elected: 1990

1991-92 Total Rcpts: $879,091
1990 Year-end cash: $57,373

Source of Funds
- PACs 24%
- Lg Individuals ($200+) 33%
- Individuals under $200 ....34%
- Other 9%

Top Industries & Interest Groups

Real Estate $28,590
Insurance $28,176
Automotive $22,031
Health Professionals $21,860
Commercial Banks $21,798

Unidentified $79,133

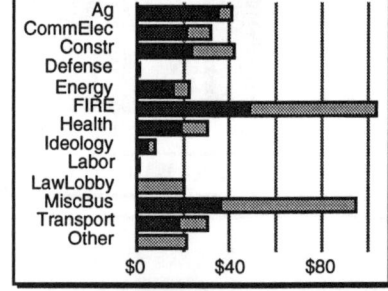

3. Steve Gunderson (R)

1992 Committees: Agric Educ/Labor
First elected: 1980

1991-92 Total Rcpts: $427,368
1990 Year-end cash: $67,331

Source of Funds
- PACs 52%
- Lg Individuals ($200+) 23%
- Individuals under $200 ....22%
- Other 3%

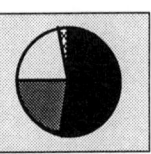

Top Industries & Interest Groups

Health Professionals $21,250
Agricultural Services/Products $19,950
Commercial Banks $18,960
Food Processing & Sales $17,740
Dairy $16,400

Unidentified $22,060

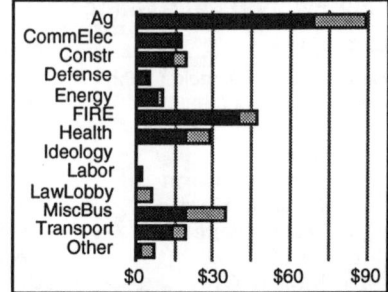

4. Gerald D. Kleczka (D)

1992 Committees: Admin Banking GovtOps
First elected: 1984

1991-92 Total Rcpts: $334,070
1990 Year-end cash: $76,093

Source of Funds
- PACs 58%
- Lg Individuals ($200+) 15%
- Individuals under $200 ....15%
- Other 12%

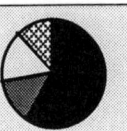

Top Industries & Interest Groups

Industrial Unions $23,100
Lawyers & Lobbyists $22,461
Health Professionals $22,250
Transportation Unions $19,100
Public Sector Unions $17,700

Unidentified $6,311

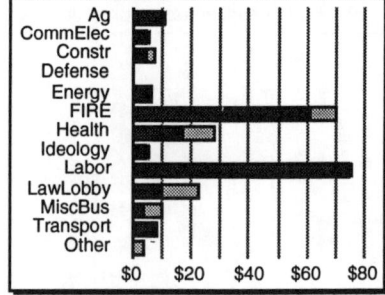

5. Thomas Barrett (D)

1993-94 Committees: Banking GovtOps
First elected: 1992

1991-92 Total Rcpts: $358,639
1990 Year-end cash: $39,162

Source of Funds
- PACs 42%
- Lg Individuals ($200+) 18%
- Individuals under $200 ....34%
- Other 6%

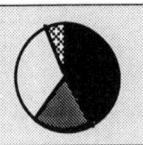

Top Industries & Interest Groups

Lawyers & Lobbyists $27,972
Public Sector Unions $25,250
Health Professionals $22,344
Industrial Unions $14,350
Insurance $11,100

Unidentified $11,426

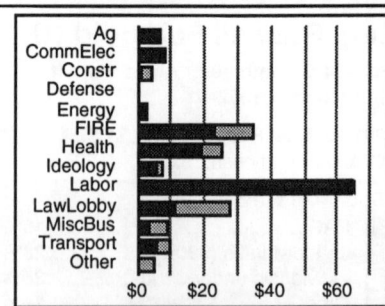

6. Tom Petri (R)

1992 Committees: Educ/Labor PubWorks
First elected: 1979

1991-92 Total Rcpts: $433,702
1990 Year-end cash: $55,773

Source of Funds
- PACs 46%
- Lg Individuals ($200+) 8%
- Individuals under $200 ....31%
- Other 14%

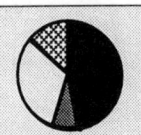

Top Industries & Interest Groups

Automotive $12,800
Misc Manufacturing & Distrib $10,800
Commercial Banks $10,500
Health Professionals $10,400
Air Transport $10,340

Unidentified $7,800

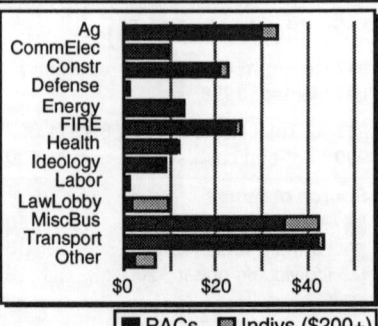

Key to committee & category abbreviations is on page 173

7. David R. Obey (D)

1992 Committees: Appropriations
First elected: 1969

1991-92 Total Rcpts: $497,123
1990 Year-end cash: $307,113

Source of Funds
- PACs 53%
- Lg Individuals ($200+) 16%
- Individuals under $200 .... 20%
- Other 11%

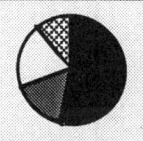

Top Industries & Interest Groups

Public Sector Unions $35,550
Lawyers & Lobbyists $30,650
Industrial Unions $18,500
Health Professionals $17,750
Pro-Israel $17,650

Unidentified $13,285

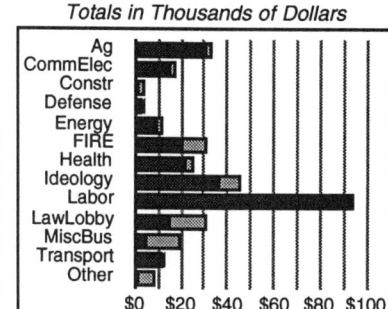

8. Toby Roth (R)

1992 Committees: Banking ForAff
First elected: 1978

1991-92 Total Rcpts: $589,778
1990 Year-end cash: $239,081

Source of Funds
- PACs 50%
- Lg Individuals ($200+) 18%
- Individuals under $200 .... 27%
- Other 5%

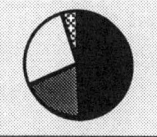

Top Industries & Interest Groups

Commercial Banks $69,025
Insurance $32,150
Forestry & Forest Products $18,450
Lawyers & Lobbyists $17,610
Misc Manufacturing & Distrib $13,350

Unidentified $20,425

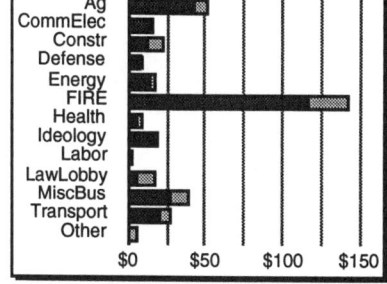

9. F. James Sensenbrenner Jr. (R)

1992 Committees: Judiciary Science
First elected: 1978

1991-92 Total Rcpts: $283,602
1990 Year-end cash: $138,787

Source of Funds
- PACs 27%
- Lg Individuals ($200+) 20%
- Individuals under $200 .... 39%
- Other 14%

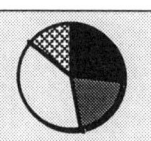

Top Industries & Interest Groups

Insurance $15,600
Retired $13,525
Automotive $9,600
Misc Manufacturing & Distrib $8,800
Telephone Utilities $7,100

Unidentified $12,920

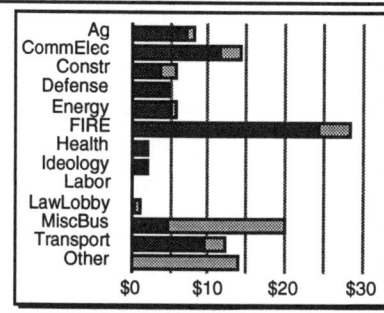

Wyoming

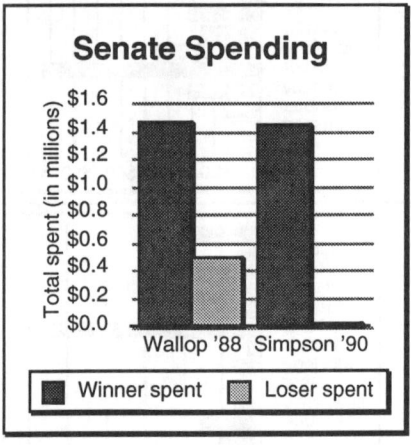

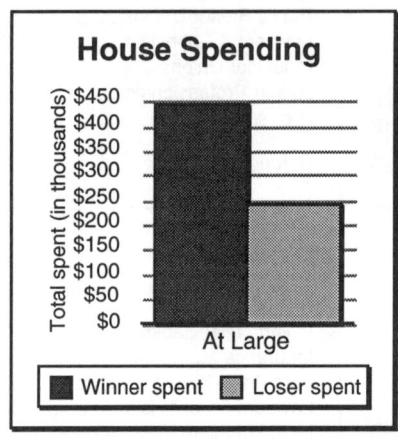

1992 Elections at a Glance

Dist	Name	Party	Vote Pct	Race Type
Sen	Alan K. Simpson (1990)	Rep	64%	Reelected
Sen	Malcolm Wallop (1988)	Rep	50%	Reelected
1	Craig Thomas	Rep	58%	Reelected

Totals in Thousands of Dollars

Sen. Alan K. Simpson (R)
1992 Committees: Envir Judiciary VetAffairs
First elected: 1978

1987-92 Total Rcpts: $1,633,044
1990 Year-end cash: $256,869

Source of Funds
PACs 46%
Lg Individuals ($200+) 27%
Individuals under $200 ....3%
Other 24%

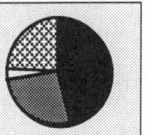

1987-92†
Top Industries & Interest Groups

Insurance $113,050
Oil & Gas $110,450
Lawyer & Lobbyists $60,825
Media/Entertainment $42,793
Chemicals $35,500

Unidentified $70,944

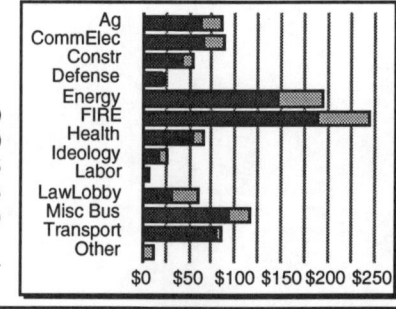

Sen. Malcolm Wallop (R)
1992 Committees: ArmServ Energy SmBus
First elected: 1976

1987-92 Total Rcpts: $1,680,549
1990 Year-end cash: $143,400

Source of Funds
PACs 56%
Lg Individuals ($200+) 17%
Individuals under $200 ....11%
Other 16%

1987-92†
Top Industries & Interest Groups

Oil & Gas $146,017
Insurance $78,943
Defense Aerospace $53,111
Securities & Investment $49,417
Lawyer & Lobbyists $41,750

Unidentified $2,000

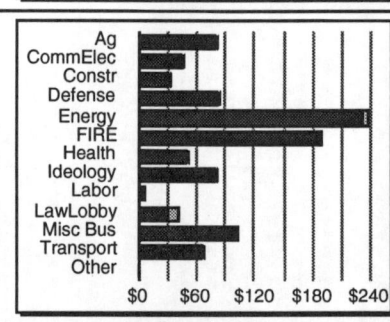

1. Craig Thomas (R)
1992 Committees: Banking GovtOps Interior
First elected: 1989

1991-92 Total Rcpts: $479,523
1990 Year-end cash: $24,529

Source of Funds
PACs 46%
Lg Individuals ($200+) 20%
Individuals under $200 ....30%
Other 4%

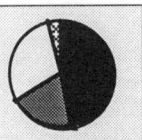

Top Industries & Interest Groups

Oil & Gas $37,950
Commercial Banks $24,825
Health Professionals $22,650
Livestock $14,600
Mining $13,450

Unidentified $26,000

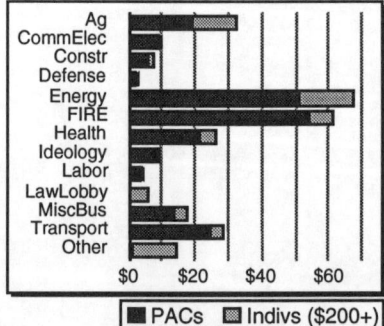

Key to committee & category abbreviations is on page 173

5. PAC Profiles

Cash Constituents of Congress

Introduction to the PAC Profiles

The final section of *Cash Constitutents of Congress* provides a directory of every political action committee that gave $50,000 or more in the 1991-92 election cycle. In all, these PACs contributed $162.1 million to congressional candidates — 86 percent of the total given by all PACs in the 1992 elections.

The PACs are listed alphabetically by the name of the PAC sponsor, or the name of the PAC itself where there is no other sponsor.

What's included in the PAC profiles:

Short name of the PAC or PAC sponsor. This is the name used elsewhere in the book to identify the PAC. The term "sponsor" is used simply to identify the group whose members contribute to the PAC, and does not imply a formal relationship between the PAC and the organization. Many PACs are officially connected with their sponsoring organization; others operate independently, even though the PAC's contributors all work for the same company or belong to the same trade association, labor union or other organization.

Official name of the PAC. The only abbreviation is the use of "PAC" for "Political Action Committee"

Total contributions in the 1991-92 election cycle.

Alabama Power Co Alabama Power Co Employees Federal PAC (APC Employees Federal PAC) Birmingham, AL	Southern Co	$114,275 Electric Utilities	179 Candidates Avg House: $619 Avg Sen: $720	Dems: 54.4% House: 78.0% Incumb: 77.9%

Location of the PAC's headquarters.

Category or thumbnail description. See Appendix A for the complete list of categories used to classify the PACs and other contributors in this book.

Affiliated organization. When an organization is listed here, it means the PAC is one of several affiliated with the parent group. In the case of leadership PACs operated by members of Congress or other political figures, the name of the PAC's sponsor is listed here.

Percentage of total dollars that went to Democratic or Republican candidates. Whichever party got more than 50 percent is listed.

Number of federal candidates receiving contributions from the PAC in 1991-92.

Alabama Farm Bureau Federation ELECT - the PAC of Alabama Farm Bureau Federation Montgomery, AL		$86,511 Farm Orgs	72 Candidates Avg House: $1,239 Avg Sen: $1,143	Dems: 61.2% House: 63.0% Incumb: 84.3%

Average contribution to House candidates in 1991-92.

Average contribution to Senate candidates in 1991-92.

Percentage of dollars that went to incumbents.

Percentage of dollars that went to House or Senate candidates. The group that got the biggest share is listed.

PAC Sponsor or Related Group/PAC Name	Affiliate	1991-92 Total	Where the money went...		
24th Congressional Dist of Calif PAC 24th Congressional District of California PAC Beverly Hills, CA	Rep Henry Waxman (D-Calif) Dem Leaders	$79,000	15 Candidates Avg House: $6,364 Avg Sen: $2,250	Dems: 100.0% House: 88.6% Incumb: 69.6%	
Abbott Laboratories Abbott Laboratories Better Government Fund Abbott Park, IL	Pharmaceuticals†	$157,193	168 Candidates Avg House: $682 Avg Sen: $1,935	Repubs: 57.6% House: 58.1% Incumb: 79.1%	
ACRE (Action Committee for Rural Electrification) Action Committee for Rural Electrification (ACRE) Washington, DC	Rural Electric	$572,555	386 Candidates Avg House: $1,095 Avg Sen: $5,039	Dems: 76.7% House: 66.5% Incumb: 79.2%	
Advo-System Inc Advo-System, Inc PAC (AdvoPAC) Windsor, CT	Mail Advertising	$56,961	44 Candidates Avg House: $1,224 Avg Sen: $1,371	Dems: 86.5% Senate: 50.6% Incumb: 89.4%	
Aetna Life & Casualty Aetna Life and Casualty Company PAC Hartford, CT	Insurance	$196,500	147 Candidates Avg House: $906 Avg Sen: $2,618	Repubs: 53.1% House: 50.7% Incumb: 86.1%	
AFL-CIO AFL-CIO Committee on Political Education/Political Contributions Committee Washington, DC	Labor Unions	$835,120	296 Candidates Avg House: $2,309 Avg Sen: $6,691	Dems: 98.8% House: 72.2% Incumb: 50.0%	
AFL-CIO Bldg/Construction Trades Dept Political Educational Fund of the Building And Construction Trades Department Washington, DC	AFL-CIO Building Trade Unions	$228,704	218 Candidates Avg House: $953 Avg Sen: $1,582	Dems: 95.3% House: 79.1% Incumb: 88.4%	
Air Line Pilots Assn Air Line Pilots Association PAC Washington, DC	Air Transport Unions	$1,260,593	312 Candidates Avg House: $3,636 Avg Sen: $7,231	Dems: 87.0% House: 79.3% Incumb: 80.6%	
Air Products & Chemicals Inc Air Products Political Alliance Trexlertown, PA	Chemicals	$73,450	79 Candidates Avg House: $687 Avg Sen: $1,888	Repubs: 79.3% House: 58.9% Incumb: 78.9%	
Aircraft Owners & Pilots Assn Aircraft Owners and Pilots Association PAC Frederick, MD	General Aviation	$482,695	168 Candidates Avg House: $2,399 Avg Sen: $4,968	Dems: 55.6% House: 68.1% Incumb: 91.1%	
Akin, Gump et al Akin, Gump, Strauss, Hauer & Feld Civic Action Committee Washington, DC	Lawyers	$304,656	220 Candidates Avg House: $1,197 Avg Sen: $1,991	Dems: 81.8% House: 66.0% Incumb: 93.5%	
Alabama Farm Bureau Federation Elect - The PAC of Alabama Farm Bureau Federation Montegomery, AL	Farm Orgs	$131,231	75 Candidates Avg House: $1,885 Avg Sen: $1,500	Dems: 75.3% House: 71.8% Incumb: 66.1%	
Alabama Peanut Producers Assn Peanut PAC of Alabama, PAC of Alabama Peanut Producers Association Dothan, AL	Misc Crops	$73,450	51 Candidates Avg House: $1,332 Avg Sen: $1,792	Dems: 97.3% House: 70.7% Incumb: 71.4%	
Alabama Power Co Alabama Power Co Employees Federal PAC (APC Employees Federal PAC) Birmingham, AL	Southern Co Electric Utilities	$92,050	165 Candidates Avg House: $519 Avg Sen: $727	Dems: 58.3% House: 75.5% Incumb: 80.2%	
Alarm Industry Communications Committee Alarm Industry Communications Committee PAC Bethesda, MD	Security Services	$66,368	44 Candidates Avg House: $1,308 Avg Sen: $1,917	Dems: 60.8% House: 55.2% Incumb: 97.0%	
Allied-Signal Allied-Signal PAC Morristown, NJ	Defense Aerospace†	$196,000	162 Candidates Avg House: $748 Avg Sen: $3,420	Dems: 50.3% House: 51.1% Incumb: 88.7%	
Allstate Insurance Allstate Insurance Company PAC Northbrook, IL	Sears Insurance	$76,200	67 Candidates Avg House: $835 Avg Sen: $1,800	Repubs: 65.4% House: 50.4% Incumb: 82.8%	
Alltel Corp Alltel Corporation PAC (APAC) Hudson, OH	Phone Utilites	$94,818	106 Candidates Avg House: $784 Avg Sen: $1,253	Dems: 56.0% House: 67.0% Incumb: 94.4%	
Amalgamated Clothing & Textile Workers Amalgamated Clothing and Textile Workers Union - PAC (ACTWU-PAC) New York, NY	Clothing/Textile Wrkrs Manufacturing Unions	$269,892	213 Candidates Avg House: $845 Avg Sen: $2,993	Dems: 97.1% House: 54.1% Incumb: 61.6%	

PAC Sponsor or Related Group/PAC Name	Affiliate	1991-92 Total	Where the money went...		
Amalgamated Transit Union Amalgamated Transit Union-COPE Washington, DC	Misc Transport Union	$428,490	246 Candidates Avg House: $1,371 Avg Sen: $3,506	Dems: 97.8% House: 65.3% Incumb: 64.8%	
America's Leaders' Fund America's Leaders' Fund (Aka Chicago Campaign Committee) Chicago, IL	Rep Dan Rostenkowski (D-Ill) Dem Leaders	$120,703	64 Candidates Avg House: $1,633 Avg Sen: $4,333	Dems: 100.0% House: 78.5% Incumb: 64.4%	
American Academy of Ophthalmology American Academy of Ophthalmology Inc Political Committee ("Ophthpac") San Francisco, CA	Eye Doctors	$870,027	334 Candidates Avg House: $2,391 Avg Sen: $4,134	Dems: 63.3% House: 80.5% Incumb: 60.5%	
American Airlines American Airlines PAC Washington, DC	Airlines	$257,570	130 Candidates Avg House: $1,772 Avg Sen: $2,735	Dems: 73.0% House: 69.5% Incumb: 89.8%	
American Ambulance Assn American Ambulance Association Federal PAC (Aka AMBU-PAC) Washington, DC	Health Care Svcs	$55,425	62 Candidates Avg House: $782 Avg Sen: $1,167	Dems: 51.9% House: 62.1% Incumb: 88.3%	
American Assn of Crop Insurers American Association of Crop Insurers PAC (AACI PAC) Washington, DC	Ag Services†	$152,726	77 Candidates Avg House: $1,592 Avg Sen: $3,134	Dems: 62.6% House: 57.3% Incumb: 91.7%	
American Assn of Equipment Lessors AAEL Lease-PAC Fka Amer Assoc of Equip Lessors Cap Invest-Lease PAC Arlington, VA	Rentals†	$139,600	80 Candidates Avg House: $1,605 Avg Sen: $2,114	Repubs: 51.1% House: 66.7% Incumb: 57.3%	
American Assn of Oral & Maxillofacial Surgeons Oral and Maxillofacial Surgery PAC (OMSPAC) Rosemont, IL	Dentists	$163,000	71 Candidates Avg House: $2,068 Avg Sen: $2,667	Dems: 62.9% House: 55.8% Incumb: 87.4%	
American Bakers Assn American Bakers Association Bread PAC Washington, DC	Food Processors	$61,975	52 Candidates Avg House: $649 Avg Sen: $2,309	Repubs: 93.5% Senate: 63.3% Incumb: 56.0%	
American Bankers Assn American Bankers Association BANKPAC Washington, DC	Commercial Banks	$1,498,388	443 Candidates Avg House: $3,055 Avg Sen: $5,790	Dems: 51.6% House: 79.5% Incumb: 80.0%	
American Bus Assn BusPAC-PAC of the American Bus Association Washington, DC	Bus Services	$78,450	79 Candidates Avg House: $897 Avg Sen: $1,319	Dems: 78.5% House: 69.7% Incumb: 91.1%	
American Chiropractic Assn American Chiropractic Association PAC Arlington, VA	Chiropractors	$641,746	206 Candidates Avg House: $2,428 Avg Sen: $6,161	Dems: 73.7% House: 63.2% Incumb: 65.5%	
American College of Emergency Physicians National Emergency Medicine PAC of the American College of Emergency Physicians Irving, TX	Doctors	$330,725	177 Candidates Avg House: $1,833 Avg Sen: $2,031	Dems: 73.8% House: 80.3% Incumb: 64.4%	
American Commercial Barge Line Co American Commercial Barge Line Co/Jeffboat Inc - PAC (ACBL/JFFBT) Jeffersonville, IN	CSX Corp Sea Transport	$52,250	59 Candidates Avg House: $852 Avg Sen: $1,250	Repubs: 71.6% House: 88.0% Incumb: 97.1%	
American Consulting Engineers Council American Consulting Engineers PAC (ACE/PAC) Washington, DC	Engineers	$95,500	113 Candidates Avg House: $675 Avg Sen: $1,363	Repubs: 52.9% House: 60.0% Incumb: 79.8%	
American Council of Life Insurance American Council of Life Insurance, Life Insurance PAC Washington, DC	Life Insurance	$577,430	308 Candidates Avg House: $1,525 Avg Sen: $3,528	Dems: 59.4% House: 67.4% Incumb: 89.0%	
American Crystal Sugar Corp American Crystal Sugar PAC Moorheard, MN	Sugar	$297,015	243 Candidates Avg House: $1,049 Avg Sen: $2,076	Dems: 70.9% House: 71.3% Incumb: 89.3%	
American Dental Assn American Dental PAC Washington, DC	Dentists	$1,419,958	433 Candidates Avg House: $2,918 Avg Sen: $6,133	Dems: 60.8% House: 78.7% Incumb: 71.5%	
American Electric Power American Electric Power Committee for Responsible Government; The Columbus, OH	Electric Utilities	$99,000	121 Candidates Avg House: $715 Avg Sen: $1,202	Repubs: 52.8% House: 67.9% Incumb: 92.2%	

† PAC sponsor has other major interests in addition to this primary category

PAC Sponsor or Related Group/PAC Name	Affiliate	1991-92 Total	Where the money went...			
American Express American Express Company Committee for Responsible Governmennt Washington, DC		$141,425 Securities†	141 Candidates Avg House: $807 Avg Sen: $1,795		Dems: 70.0% House: 64.5% Incumb: 91.3%	
American Family Corp American Family PAC (AF-PAC) Washington, DC		$503,000 Health Insurance	152 Candidates Avg House: $3,071 Avg Sen: $4,000		Dems: 59.3% House: 69.0% Incumb: 81.1%	
American Federation of Government Employees American Federation of Government Employees' PAC Washington, DC		$173,243 Fedl Worker Unions	164 Candidates Avg House: $823 Avg Sen: $1,873		Dems: 98.4% House: 59.9% Incumb: 71.8%	
American Federation of Teachers American Federation of Teachers Committee on Political Education Washington, DC	Amer Fedn of Teachers	$1,111,250 Teachers	261 Candidates Avg House: $3,676 Avg Sen: $7,603		Dems: 97.0% House: 73.1% Incumb: 67.5%	
American Fedn of State, County & Munic Employees American Federation of State County & Municipal Employees - PEOPLE, Qualified Washington, DC		$1,950,365 Local Govt Unions	387 Candidates Avg House: $4,806 Avg Sen: $6,767		Dems: 97.3% House: 83.5% Incumb: 60.1%	
American Financial Services Assn American Financial Services Assn PAC (Fka Nat'l Consumer Finance Assn PAC) Washington, DC		$105,124 Credit/Loans	80 Candidates Avg House: $935 Avg Sen: $2,957		Repubs: 53.7% House: 57.8% Incumb: 82.1%	
American Furniture Manufacturers Assn American Furniture Manufacturers Association PAC High Point, NC		$86,750 Furniture	76 Candidates Avg House: $986 Avg Sen: $1,523		Repubs: 77.3% House: 61.4% Incumb: 84.5%	
American General Insurance Co American General PAC Houston, TX	American General Corp	$54,460 Insurance†	44 Candidates Avg House: $1,078 Avg Sen: $1,447		Repubs: 57.7% Senate: 50.5% Incumb: 75.4%	
American Health Care Assn American Health Care Association PAC (Ahca-pac) Washington, DC		$381,019 Nursing Homes	333 Candidates Avg House: $936 Avg Sen: $2,019		Dems: 66.4% House: 66.1% Incumb: 77.0%	
American Home Products Corp American Home Products Corporation-AHP Good Government Fund New York, NY		$56,400 Pharmaceuticals†	66 Candidates Avg House: $613 Avg Sen: $1,410		Repubs: 59.8% House: 50.0% Incumb: 95.2%	
American Hospital Assn PAC of the American Hospital Association Chicago, IL		$576,488 Hospitals	335 Candidates Avg House: $1,486 Avg Sen: $3,140		Dems: 69.9% House: 74.0% Incumb: 81.9%	
American Hotel & Motel Assn American Hotel Motel PAC Washington, DC		$131,475 Hotels/Motels	177 Candidates Avg House: $651 Avg Sen: $1,150		Dems: 54.3% House: 70.3% Incumb: 87.5%	
American Institute of CPA's American Institute of Certified Public Accountants Effective Legis Cmte (AICPA) New York, NY		$1,542,851 Accountants	405 Candidates Avg House: $3,612 Avg Sen: $5,247		Dems: 55.6% House: 83.3% Incumb: 82.8%	
American Insurance Assn American Insurance Association PAC Washington, DC		$100,529 Insurance	128 Candidates Avg House: $674 Avg Sen: $1,246		Dems: 66.9% House: 69.0% Incumb: 91.2%	
American International Group American International Group Employee PAC New York, NY		$189,190 Insurance	124 Candidates Avg House: $1,216 Avg Sen: $2,181		Dems: 64.1% House: 54.0% Incumb: 79.8%	
American Land Title Assn Title Industry PAC Washington, DC		$100,889 Title Insurance	106 Candidates Avg House: $715 Avg Sen: $1,804		Dems: 64.8% House: 58.9% Incumb: 94.0%	
American Meat Institute American Meat Institute PAC Arlington, VA		$105,629 Meat Processors	109 Candidates Avg House: $823 Avg Sen: $1,336		Repubs: 62.4% House: 60.8% Incumb: 88.5%	
American Medical Assn American Medical Association PAC Washington, DC		$2,936,558 Doctors	537 Candidates Avg House: $5,452 Avg Sen: $5,663		Repubs: 51.4% House: 91.7% Incumb: 69.7%	
American Motorcyclist Assn American Motorcyclist PAC Westerville, OH		$50,525 Motorcycles	81 Candidates Avg House: $537 Avg Sen: $908		Repubs: 73.6% House: 65.9% Incumb: 80.2%	

PAC Sponsor or Related Group/PAC Name	Affiliate	1991-92 Total	Where the money went...			
American Nurses Assn American Nurses' Association PAC (ANA-PAC) (Fka N-CAP) Washington, DC	Nurses	$311,019	198 Candidates Avg House: $1,415 Avg Sen: $2,337	Dems: House: Incumb:	90.6% 73.7% 45.4%
American Occupational Therapy Assn American Occupational Therapy PAC Rockville, MD	Health Practitioners	$81,363	87 Candidates Avg House: $712 Avg Sen: $1,444	Dems: House: Incumb:	73.7% 54.3% 72.7%
American Optometric Assn American Optometric Association PAC Alexandria, VA	Eye Doctors	$398,366	252 Candidates Avg House: $1,333 Avg Sen: $2,894	Dems: House: Incumb:	69.0% 70.9% 71.0%
American Pharmaceutical Assn American Pharmaceutical Association PAC Washington, DC	Pharmacists	$132,072	117 Candidates Avg House: $817 Avg Sen: $1,830	Dems: House: Incumb:	64.3% 50.1% 81.8%
American Physical Therapy Assn American Physical Therapy Congressional Action Committee Alexandria, VA	Health Practitioners	$198,441	135 Candidates Avg House: $1,331 Avg Sen: $1,749	Dems: House: Incumb:	73.3% 63.7% 75.3%
American Podiatry Assn Podiatry PAC Bethesda, MD	Misc MD Specialists	$401,000	231 Candidates Avg House: $1,409 Avg Sen: $3,140	Dems: House: Incumb:	69.7% 65.7% 75.9%
American Postal Workers Union Political Fund Committee of the American Postal Workers Union, AFL-CIO Washington, DC Amer Postal Workers Union	Postal Unions	$892,290	331 Candidates Avg House: $2,411 Avg Sen: $4,341	Dems: House: Incumb:	96.3% 76.7% 80.7%
American President Lines American President Lines Ltd PAC (APT/PAC) Oakland, CA American Presidents Co	Sea Transport†	$109,462	110 Candidates Avg House: $757 Avg Sen: $1,764	Dems: House: Incumb:	59.2% 58.1% 83.6%
American Psychiatric Assn Corporation for the Advancement of Psychiatry PAC (Cappac) Washington, DC	Psychiatrist/Psychol	$164,980	150 Candidates Avg House: $1,014 Avg Sen: $1,417	Dems: House: Incumb:	87.2% 71.9% 67.8%
American Society of Anesthesiologists AMERICAN SOCIETY OF ANESTHESIOLOGISTS POLITICAL ACTION COMMITTEE (ASAPAC) Park Ridge, IL	Misc MD Specialists	$112,450	99 Candidates Avg House: $992 Avg Sen: $1,538	Dems: House: Incumb:	63.0% 64.4% 59.7%
American Society of Association Executives American Society of Association Executives A-PAC Washington, DC	Other	$61,500	97 Candidates Avg House: $486 Avg Sen: $1,083	Repubs: House: Incumb:	61.4% 57.7% 71.5%
American Society of Cataract & Refractive Surgery American Society of Cataract & Refractive Surgery PAC (Aka EYEPAC) Fairfax, VA	Eye Doctors	$72,050	47 Candidates Avg House: $1,381 Avg Sen: $1,588	Dems: House: Incumb:	85.4% 55.6% 63.2%
American Society of Plastic & Reconstructive Surgeons PAC OF THE AMER SOC OF PLASTIC & RECONSTR SURGEONS INC (ASPRS) PLASTYPAC Arlington Heights, IL	Misc MD Specialists	$85,700	90 Candidates Avg House: $876 Avg Sen: $1,202	Dems: House: Incumb:	50.0% 70.5% 73.2%
American Society of Travel Agents American Society of Travel Agents PAC Alexandria, VA	Travel Agents	$51,575	187 Candidates Avg House: $238 Avg Sen: $446	Dems: House: Incumb:	60.1% 70.6% 93.4%
American Speech-Language-Hearing Assn American Speech-Language-Hearing Association PAC Rockville, MD	Health Practitioners	$57,681	68 Candidates Avg House: $635 Avg Sen: $1,192	Dems: Senate: Incumb:	84.4% 53.7% 61.1%
American Sugar Cane League American Sugar Cane League PAC Thibodaux, LA	Sugar	$197,925	262 Candidates Avg House: $595 Avg Sen: $1,794	Dems: House: Incumb:	75.6% 68.3% 90.0%
American Sugarbeet Growers Assn American Sugarbeet Growers Association PAC Washington, DC	Sugar	$311,707	286 Candidates Avg House: $933 Avg Sen: $2,127	Dems: House: Incumb:	68.5% 74.5% 88.0%
American Supply Assn American Supply Association PAC Chicago, IL	Pipe Products†	$55,525	72 Candidates Avg House: $642 Avg Sen: $1,132	Repubs: House: Incumb:	82.0% 61.3% 68.4%
American Textile Manufacturers Institute American Textile Manufacturers Institute, Inc Committee for Good Government Washington, DC	Textiles	$131,375	103 Candidates Avg House: $1,029 Avg Sen: $2,720	Dems: House: Incumb:	65.5% 68.9% 96.7%

† PAC sponsor has other major interests in addition to this primary category

PAC Sponsor or Related Group/PAC Name	Affiliate	1991-92 Total	Where the money went...		
American Trucking Assns Trucking PAC of the American Trucking Associations' Inc Washington, DC	Trucking Companies	$354,619	275 Candidates Avg House: $1,012 Avg Sen: $2,604	Dems: 62.8% House: 64.8% Incumb: 90.9%	
American Veterinary Medical Assn American Veterinary Medical Association PAC (Avmapac) Washington, DC	Veterinary	$301,000	307 Candidates Avg House: $868 Avg Sen: $1,776	Dems: 59.3% House: 77.6% Incumb: 88.5%	
American Waterways Operators American Waterways Operators-PAC Arlington, VA	Sea Transport	$66,094	91 Candidates Avg House: $637 Avg Sen: $1,452	Dems: 52.7% House: 78.0% Incumb: 94.2%	
Americans for Democratic Action Americans for Democratic Action Inc PAC Washington, DC	Dem/Liberal	$53,650	54 Candidates Avg House: $649 Avg Sen: $2,081	Dems: 99.1% Senate: 50.4% Incumb: 33.7%	
Americans for Free International Trade AMERICANS FOR FREE INTERNATIONAL TRADE POLITICAL ACTION COMMITTEE INC Washington, DC	Japanese Auto Dlrs	$475,150	192 Candidates Avg House: $1,702 Avg Sen: $7,000	Repubs: 79.9% House: 58.8% Incumb: 72.2%	
Americans for Good Government Inc Americans for Good Government Inc Jasper, AL	Pro-Israel	$166,750	98 Candidates Avg House: $1,070 Avg Sen: $2,743	Dems: 57.4% Senate: 60.9% Incumb: 71.8%	
Ameritech Corp American Information Technologies Corporation PAC (Ameritech PAC) Chicago, IL — Ameritech	Phone Utilites	$255,132	112 Candidates Avg House: $2,097 Avg Sen: $2,818	Dems: 57.5% House: 68.2% Incumb: 91.7%	
Amoco Corp Amoco PAC Chicago, IL	Oil & Gas†	$264,750	230 Candidates Avg House: $764 Avg Sen: $4,065	Repubs: 73.3% House: 58.5% Incumb: 61.3%	
Amsouth Bancorp Amsouth PAC Birmingham, AL	Commercial Banks	$65,750	20 Candidates Avg House: $3,268 Avg Sen: $3,400	Dems: 59.6% House: 84.5% Incumb: 45.2%	
Anheuser-Busch Anheuser-Busch Companies Inc PAC (AB-PAC) St. Louis, MO	Beer†	$126,080	119 Candidates Avg House: $830 Avg Sen: $1,969	Dems: 67.9% House: 62.5% Incumb: 81.8%	
Archer-Daniels-Midland Corp Archer Daniels Midland Company-ADM PAC Decatur, IL	Grain Traders†	$282,750	132 Candidates Avg House: $1,541 Avg Sen: $3,010	Dems: 50.4% Senate: 54.3% Incumb: 73.4%	
Arent, Fox et al Arent, Fox Civic Participation Fund Washington, DC	Lawyers	$55,450	70 Candidates Avg House: $630 Avg Sen: $1,136	Dems: 85.3% House: 53.4% Incumb: 80.6%	
Arizona Politically Interested Citizens Arizona Politically Interested Citizens Phoenix, AZ	Pro-Israel	$53,900	47 Candidates Avg House: $590 Avg Sen: $1,852	Dems: 68.0% Senate: 72.2% Incumb: 85.2%	
Arnold & Porter Arnold & Porter Partners PAC Washington, DC	Lawyers	$79,174	81 Candidates Avg House: $912 Avg Sen: $1,086	Dems: 88.0% House: 59.9% Incumb: 88.1%	
Arthur Andersen & Co Arthur Andersen & Co PAC Washington, DC	Accountants	$209,873	99 Candidates Avg House: $1,972 Avg Sen: $2,444	Dems: 70.0% House: 63.9% Incumb: 84.5%	
ASCAP ASCAP Legislative Fund for The Arts New York, NY	Music Production	$174,710	136 Candidates Avg House: $1,081 Avg Sen: $1,923	Dems: 86.5% House: 63.1% Incumb: 92.2%	
Ashland Oil Ashland Oil PAC for Employees (PACE) Russell, KY	Oil Refining/Mkting†	$186,311	119 Candidates Avg House: $1,345 Avg Sen: $3,097	Repubs: 58.3% House: 75.1% Incumb: 61.8%	
Assn for the Advancement of Psychology Psychologists for Legislative Action Now (Plan) Colorado Springs, CO	Psychiatrist/Psychol	$273,743	130 Candidates Avg House: $1,659 Avg Sen: $3,066	Dems: 90.1% House: 53.3% Incumb: 70.9%	
Assn of Bank Holding Companies Association of Bank Holding Companies PAC (ABHC PAC) Washington, DC	Commercial Banks	$59,200	46 Candidates Avg House: $1,064 Avg Sen: $2,344	Dems: 59.2% House: 68.3% Incumb: 94.1%	

PAC Sponsor or Related Group/PAC Name	Affiliate	1991-92 Total	Where the money went...		
Assn of Flight Attendants Association of Flight Attendants PAC ("Flight PAC") Washington, DC	 Air Transport Unions	$221,100	152 Candidates Avg House: $776 Avg Sen: $4,900	Dems: 98.7% Senate: 55.4% Incumb: 52.4%	
Assn of Trial Lawyers of America Association of Trial Lawyers of America PAC Washington, DC	 Assn of Trial Lawyers Lawyers	$2,361,135	386 Candidates Avg House: $5,965 Avg Sen: $7,188	Dems: 92.3% House: 85.4% Incumb: 64.5%	
Associated Builders & Contractors Associated Builders and Contractors PAC (ABC/PAC) Washington, DC	 Builders Assns†	$184,150	146 Candidates Avg House: $885 Avg Sen: $3,630	Repubs: 92.4% House: 60.6% Incumb: 65.7%	
Associated Credit Bureaus Associated Credit Bureaus PAC Houston, TX	 Credit/Loans	$75,600	58 Candidates Avg House: $1,132 Avg Sen: $2,375	Dems: 57.0% House: 74.9% Incumb: 98.7%	
Associated General Contractors Associated General Contractors PAC Washington, DC	 Assoc Genl Contractors Heavy Construction	$669,249	315 Candidates Avg House: $1,691 Avg Sen: $5,486	Repubs: 76.5% House: 70.5% Incumb: 72.8%	
Associated Milk Producers Cmte for Thorough Agricultural Pol Education of Associated Milk Producers San Antonio, TX	 Dairy	$877,550	356 Candidates Avg House: $2,294 Avg Sen: $4,207	Dems: 78.8% House: 85.0% Incumb: 84.5%	
AT&T American Telephone & Telegraph Company Inc PAC (AT&T PAC) New York, NY	 Long Distance†	$1,303,035	593 Candidates Avg House: $2,091 Avg Sen: $2,896	Dems: 62.4% House: 82.7% Incumb: 81.1%	
Atlantic Research Corp Atlantic Research Corporation PAC Alexandria, VA	 Sequa Corp Weapons Systems†	$66,750	60 Candidates Avg House: $981 Avg Sen: $1,375	Dems: 58.0% House: 58.8% Incumb: 99.2%	
Atlantic Richfield Arco PAC, Atlantic Richfield Company Los Angeles, CA	 Oil & Gas†	$323,534	193 Candidates Avg House: $1,218 Avg Sen: $4,269	Repubs: 72.5% House: 61.7% Incumb: 76.2%	
Auto Dealers & Drivers for Free Trade Auto Dealers and Driver for Free Trade PAC Jamaica, NY	 Japanese Auto Dlrs	$538,550	237 Candidates Avg House: $1,844 Avg Sen: $3,691	Repubs: 61.8% House: 62.3% Incumb: 86.9%	
Babcock & Wilcox Babcock & Wilcox Company Good Government Fund; The New Orleans, LA	 McDermott Inc Power Plant Constr†	$87,900	66 Candidates Avg House: $1,212 Avg Sen: $1,542	Dems: 72.0% House: 57.9% Incumb: 92.0%	
Baker & Botts Bluebonnet Fund (Baker & Botts), The Houston, TX	 Lawyers	$74,391	52 Candidates Avg House: $1,148 Avg Sen: $1,964	Repubs: 52.6% House: 52.5% Incumb: 88.6%	
Bakery Confectionery & Tobacco Workers Bakery, Confectionery And Tobacco Workers International Union PAC Kensington, MD	 Food Svc Unions	$193,900	130 Candidates Avg House: $1,302 Avg Sen: $2,024	Dems: 99.7% House: 67.2% Incumb: 45.5%	
Baltimore Gas & Electric Baltimore Gas And Electric Company PAC (BG&E PAC) Baltimore, MD	 Gas & Electric Util†	$83,575	71 Candidates Avg House: $1,225 Avg Sen: $962	Repubs: 59.8% House: 85.0% Incumb: 80.0%	
Banc One Corp Banc One PAC Columbus, OH	 Commercial Banks	$122,025	95 Candidates Avg House: $1,135 Avg Sen: $1,884	Dems: 55.5% House: 70.7% Incumb: 82.5%	
BankAmerica BankAmerica Federal Election Fund San Francisco, CA	 Commercial Banks	$279,377	158 Candidates Avg House: $1,484 Avg Sen: $2,529	Repubs: 52.6% House: 61.1% Incumb: 69.0%	
Bankers Trust Bankers Trust PAC New York, NY	 Commercial Banks	$105,200	62 Candidates Avg House: $1,513 Avg Sen: $2,938	Dems: 70.1% House: 77.7% Incumb: 92.9%	
Barnett Banks of Florida Barnett People for Better Govt Inc - Fed a PAC of Barnett Banks of Florida Jacksonville, FL	 Commercial Banks	$428,133	234 Candidates Avg House: $1,518 Avg Sen: $3,103	Repubs: 53.2% House: 66.7% Incumb: 87.7%	
Baxter Healthcare Corp Baxter Healthcare Corporation PAC Deerfield, IL	 Medical Supplies†	$83,140	71 Candidates Avg House: $1,037 Avg Sen: $1,389	Dems: 50.9% House: 54.9% Incumb: 86.7%	

† PAC sponsor has other major interests in addition to this primary category

PAC Sponsor or Related Group/PAC Name	Affiliate	1991-92 Total	Where the money went...		
BDM International BDM International, Inc. PAC (BDM-PAC) Mclean, VA	Defense R&D†	$122,050	68 Candidates Avg House: $1,527 Avg Sen: $2,395	Repubs: 59.4% House: 58.8% Incumb: 85.2%	
Bear, Stearns & Co Bear, Stearns and Co Political Campaign Committee New York, NY	Investmtent Banking†	$88,950	68 Candidates Avg House: $934 Avg Sen: $2,091	Dems: 86.0% Senate: 51.7% Incumb: 49.7%	
Bechtel Corp Bechtel Group, Inc PAC San Francisco, CA	Power Plant Constr†	$142,847	92 Candidates Avg House: $1,373 Avg Sen: $2,200	Dems: 58.5% House: 69.2% Incumb: 90.2%	
Bell Atlantic Bell Atlantic Corporation PAC Philadelphia, PA	Phone Utilites†	$125,751	110 Candidates Avg House: $898 Avg Sen: $2,395	Dems: 60.8% House: 65.7% Incumb: 94.4%	
BellSouth Corp Bellsouth Federal PAC (Bellsouth Fed PAC) Atlanta, GA	BellSouth / Phone Utilites	$155,694	133 Candidates Avg House: $1,059 Avg Sen: $1,619	Dems: 61.2% House: 73.5% Incumb: 89.7%	
BellSouth Services Bellsouth Services Federal PAC Birmingham, AL	BellSouth / Phone Utilites	$88,750	102 Candidates Avg House: $750 Avg Sen: $1,471	Repubs: 58.1% House: 71.8% Incumb: 98.9%	
Beneficial Management Corp Beneficial Management Corporation and Affiliated Corporations PAC Peapack, NJ	Credit/Loans†	$158,300	118 Candidates Avg House: $1,268 Avg Sen: $1,724	Dems: 58.0% House: 79.3% Incumb: 77.8%	
LM Berry & Co L. M. Berry and Company PAC Dayton, OH	BellSouth / Mail Advertising†	$57,782	65 Candidates Avg House: $700 Avg Sen: $1,818	Repubs: 98.3% House: 65.4% Incumb: 28.3%	
Bethlehem Steel Bethlehem Steel Good Government Committee Bethlehem, PA	Steel	$56,170	42 Candidates Avg House: $1,237 Avg Sen: $1,660	Repubs: 54.3% House: 70.5% Incumb: 92.9%	
Blue Cross & Blue Shield Assn CAREPAC, The Blue Cross and Blue Shield Association PAC Washington, DC	Blue Cross / Health Insurance	$195,801	208 Candidates Avg House: $811 Avg Sen: $1,487	Dems: 61.4% House: 69.6% Incumb: 90.1%	
Boeing Co Boeing Company PAC (BPAC) Seattle, WA	Aircraft Mfr†	$336,100	171 Candidates Avg House: $1,494 Avg Sen: $4,180	Dems: 55.3% House: 62.7% Incumb: 94.0%	
Boilermakers Union International Brotherhood of Boilermakers, In Sp Bldrs, Bkmths, Frgrs & Hlprs-Le Kansas City, KS	Manufacturing Unions†	$398,100	218 Candidates Avg House: $1,573 Avg Sen: $2,961	Dems: 95.6% House: 70.7% Incumb: 70.4%	
Boise Cascade Boise Cascade Political Fund Boise, ID	Paper/Pulp†	$69,000	32 Candidates Avg House: $1,729 Avg Sen: $3,438	Repubs: 92.0% House: 60.1% Incumb: 45.6%	
Bowling Proprietors Assn Bowling Proprietors Assn of America PAC Arlington, TX	Amusement Centers	$67,100	81 Candidates Avg House: $793 Avg Sen: $983	Repubs: 88.4% House: 78.0% Incumb: 87.9%	
BP America BPA-PAC (The BP America PAC) (Fka Standard Oil Co PAC) Cleveland, OH	Oil & Gas†	$105,650	107 Candidates Avg House: $760 Avg Sen: $1,975	Repubs: 60.1% House: 62.6% Incumb: 92.4%	
Bricklayers Union International Union of Bricklayers And Allied Craftsmen PAC Washington, DC	Building Trade Unions	$238,700	140 Candidates Avg House: $1,269 Avg Sen: $2,827	Dems: 96.5% House: 55.8% Incumb: 70.4%	
Bristol-Myers Squibb Bristol-Myers Company PAC New York, NY	Pharmaceuticals†	$127,725	141 Candidates Avg House: $621 Avg Sen: $1,801	Repubs: 55.8% House: 52.0% Incumb: 87.1%	
Brotherhood of Locomotive Engineers Brotherhood of Locomotive Engineers Legislative League Cleveland, OH	Locomotive Engrs Union / Railroad Unions	$262,113	213 Candidates Avg House: $1,080 Avg Sen: $1,998	Dems: 95.8% House: 72.9% Incumb: 53.0%	
Brotherhood of Railroad Signalmen Brotherhood of Railroad Signalmen PAC Mt. Prospect, IL	Railroad Unions	$110,410	130 Candidates Avg House: $701 Avg Sen: $1,452	Dems: 98.2% House: 66.6% Incumb: 82.1%	

PAC Sponsor or Related Group/PAC Name	Affiliate	1991-92 Total	Where the money went...		
Brown & Root Brownbuilders PAC of Brown & Root, Inc Employees Houston, TX	Halliburton Co Heavy Construction†	$80,657	86 Candidates Avg House: $882 Avg Sen: $1,200	Repubs: 74.3% House: 77.7% Incumb: 76.6%	
Brown & Williamson Tobacco Brown & Williamson Tobacco Corporation Employee PAC Aka Empac Louisville, KY	Batus Inc Tobacco	$57,700	70 Candidates Avg House: $508 Avg Sen: $1,984	Dems: 60.4% Senate: 55.0% Incumb: 93.5%	
Brown-Forman Distillers Brown-Forman Non-Partisan Committee for Responsible Government Louisville, KY	Wine & Liquor†	$154,600	128 Candidates Avg House: $981 Avg Sen: $1,950	Repubs: 78.8% House: 62.2% Incumb: 68.0%	
Browning-Ferris Industries Browning-Ferris Industries PAC (BFI PAC) Houston, TX	Waste Mgmt	$148,606	151 Candidates Avg House: $788 Avg Sen: $1,742	Dems: 53.4% House: 63.7% Incumb: 81.2%	
Burlington Industries Burlington Industries Good Government Committee Greensboro, NC	Textiles†	$148,675	99 Candidates Avg House: $1,394 Avg Sen: $2,063	Dems: 74.9% House: 77.8% Incumb: 80.0%	
Burlington Northern Inc Burlington Northern Employees Voluntary Good Government Fund Seattle, WA	Burlington Northern Railroads	$76,850	97 Candidates Avg House: $670 Avg Sen: $1,187	Dems: 60.8% House: 64.5% Incumb: 81.6%	
Burlington Northern Railroad Burlington Northern Railroad Railpac (BN RailPAC) Fort Worth, TX	Burlington Northern Railroads	$218,256	188 Candidates Avg House: $1,057 Avg Sen: $1,634	Dems: 62.6% House: 74.5% Incumb: 88.3%	
Burson-Marsteller Burson-Marsteller PAC Washington, DC	Lobbyists/PR	$68,575	78 Candidates Avg House: $678 Avg Sen: $1,305	Dems: 65.4% House: 52.4% Incumb: 84.8%	
Business Industry PAC Business Industry PAC Washington, DC	Pro-Business Assns	$133,431	109 Candidates Avg House: $1,007 Avg Sen: $2,189	Repubs: 93.1% House: 67.2% Incumb: 29.5%	
Calcot Ltd Calcot Ltd Federal PAC Bakersfield, CA	Cotton	$65,832	40 Candidates Avg House: $1,655 Avg Sen: $1,629	Repubs: 50.8% House: 65.4% Incumb: 80.0%	
California Almond Growers Exchange Blue Diamond Growers PAC (Fka Calif Almond Growers Exchange PAC) Sacramento, CA	Fruit/Veg	$61,991	18 Candidates Avg House: $3,320 Avg Sen: $4,064	Repubs: 52.4% House: 80.3% Incumb: 90.3%	
California Assn of Hosp/Health Systems California Hospitals PAC-FED Sacramento, CA	Hospitals	$57,253	40 Candidates Avg House: $1,134 Avg Sen: $2,456	Dems: 79.6% House: 61.4% Incumb: 47.0%	
Campaign America Campaign America Washington, DC	Sen Bob Dole (R-Kans) Repub Leaders	$388,236	85 Candidates Avg House: $2,303 Avg Sen: $7,803	Repubs: 100.0% Senate: 70.3% Incumb: 40.9%	
Capital Holding Corp Capital Holding PAC - CAP-PAC Louisville, KY	Insurance	$98,800	84 Candidates Avg House: $863 Avg Sen: $1,930	Dems: 61.4% House: 50.7% Incumb: 86.5%	
Cargill Inc Cargill, Incorporated PAC Minneapolis, MN	Crop Production†	$112,000	74 Candidates Avg House: $1,330 Avg Sen: $2,083	Repubs: 80.4% House: 66.5% Incumb: 60.3%	
Carolina Power & Light Employees Federal PAC - Carolina Power & Light Co Raleigh, NC	Electric Utilities	$93,550	93 Candidates Avg House: $894 Avg Sen: $1,472	Dems: 62.8% House: 71.7% Incumb: 85.4%	
Carpenters & Joiners Union Carpenters Committee on Political Action Los Angeles, CA	Carpenters Union Building Trade Unions	$58,250	14 Candidates Avg House: $3,325 Avg Sen: $6,250	Dems: 78.5% House: 57.1% Incumb: 12.9%	
Carpenters & Joiners Union Carpenters' Legislative Improvement Committee Washington, DC	Carpenters Union Building Trade Unions	$1,369,682	313 Candidates Avg House: $4,080 Avg Sen: $6,193	Dems: 95.2% House: 79.8% Incumb: 58.3%	
Casualty & Surety Agents Assn National Association of Casualty & Surety Agents PAC (NACSAPAC) Bethesda, MD	Insurance	$163,321	143 Candidates Avg House: $1,034 Avg Sen: $1,568	Repubs: 55.7% House: 72.2% Incumb: 67.8%	

† PAC sponsor has other major interests in addition to this primary category

PAC Sponsor or Related Group/PAC Name	Affiliate	1991-92 Total	Where the money went...	
Caterpillar Tractor Caterpillar Tractor Co Committee for Effective Govt Peoria, IL	Constr Equipment†	$92,480	80 Candidates Avg House: $879 Avg Sen: $1,933	Repubs: 87.7% House: 56.1% Incumb: 69.6%
CB&T Bancshares CB&T Bancshares, Inc Federal Political Action Comittee Columbus, GA	Commercial Banks	$54,700	15 Candidates Avg House: $3,838 Avg Sen: $3,429	Dems: 85.8% House: 56.1% Incumb: 52.0%
Central Bancshares of the South Central Bancshares of the South, Inc PAC ("Central Bancpac") Birmingham, AL	Commercial Banks	$62,350	18 Candidates Avg House: $3,686 Avg Sen: $2,688	Dems: 76.7% House: 82.8% Incumb: 49.5%
Century 21 Real Estate Century 21 PAC (CEN-PAC) Washington, DC	Metropolitan Life Real Estate Agents	$101,500	67 Candidates Avg House: $1,354 Avg Sen: $1,769	Dems: 50.2% House: 54.7% Incumb: 80.3%
CF Industries CF Industries Employees' Good Government Fund Long Grove, IL	Ag Chemicals†	$64,110	89 Candidates Avg House: $575 Avg Sen: $1,497	Dems: 60.1% House: 67.3% Incumb: 87.0%
CH2M Hill CH2M Hill PAC Inc Corvallis, OR	Engineers†	$122,103	136 Candidates Avg House: $748 Avg Sen: $1,598	Repubs: 53.0% House: 68.6% Incumb: 88.7%
Chambers Development Co Chambers Development Company Inc PAC Penn Hills, PA	Waste Mgmt	$67,250	42 Candidates Avg House: $1,129 Avg Sen: $2,682	Repubs: 50.6% House: 48.7% Incumb: 76.7%
Champion International Corp Champion International Corporation PAC Stamford, CT	Paper/Pulp†	$107,227	98 Candidates Avg House: $889 Avg Sen: $1,895	Dems: 52.3% House: 64.7% Incumb: 85.3%
Chase Manhattan Chase Manhattan Corporation PAC - (ChasePAC) New York, NY	Commercial Banks†	$282,013	155 Candidates Avg House: $1,739 Avg Sen: $2,127	Repubs: 61.6% House: 75.9% Incumb: 72.6%
Chemical Bank Chemical Bank Fund for Good Government New York, NY	Commercial Banks	$140,000	127 Candidates Avg House: $1,005 Avg Sen: $1,446	Dems: 64.6% House: 71.1% Incumb: 86.6%
Chevron Corp Chevron Employees PAC San Francisco, CA	Oil & Gas	$386,581	223 Candidates Avg House: $1,289 Avg Sen: $4,384	Repubs: 72.2% House: 63.7% Incumb: 59.2%
Chicago & North Western Transport North Western Officers Trust Account - Chicago & North Western Transportation Co Chicago, IL	Railroads	$61,050	64 Candidates Avg House: $719 Avg Sen: $1,603	Repubs: 52.0% House: 55.4% Incumb: 87.7%
Chicago Board of Options Exchange Chicago Board of Options Exchange Inc PAC Chicago, IL	Commodity Investment	$74,500	42 Candidates Avg House: $1,724 Avg Sen: $1,885	Dems: 68.5% House: 67.1% Incumb: 98.7%
Chicago Board of Trade Auction Markets PAC of the Chicago Board of Trade aka AMPAC/CBT Chicago, IL	Commodity Investment	$311,100	165 Candidates Avg House: $1,313 Avg Sen: $3,387	Dems: 68.7% House: 51.1% Incumb: 84.6%
Chicago Mercantile Exchange Commodity Futures Political Fund of the Chicago Mercantile Exchange Chicago, IL	Commodity Investment	$492,750	201 Candidates Avg House: $1,748 Avg Sen: $5,000	Dems: 72.8% House: 55.4% Incumb: 82.2%
Chili's Inc Chili's Inc PAC Dallas, TX	Restaurants	$64,500	44 Candidates Avg House: $1,355 Avg Sen: $1,731	Repubs: 80.6% House: 65.1% Incumb: 45.0%
Chrysler Corp Chrysler Corporation Political Support Committee Highland Park, MI	Auto Manufacturers†	$204,886	159 Candidates Avg House: $1,093 Avg Sen: $1,933	Dems: 73.6% House: 65.1% Incumb: 92.7%
Chubb Corp Chubb Corporation PAC "ChubbPAC" Warren, NJ	Insurance	$107,305	88 Candidates Avg House: $1,107 Avg Sen: $1,577	Dems: 53.8% House: 69.1% Incumb: 78.6%
Ciba-Geigy Corp Ciba-Geigy Employee Good Government Fund Ardsley, NY	Pharmaceuticals†	$140,200	146 Candidates Avg House: $828 Avg Sen: $1,493	Repubs: 57.8% House: 69.1% Incumb: 91.2%

PAC Sponsor or Related Group/PAC Name	Affiliate	1991-92 Total	Where the money went...		
Cigna Corp Cigna Corporation PAC Philadelphia, PA		$236,250 Insurance	192 Candidates Avg House: $952 Avg Sen: $2,677	Repubs: 56.2% House: 64.9% Incumb: 80.2%	
Circus Circus Enterprises Circus Circus Enterprises Inc PAC (Aka CC-PAC) San Francisco, CA		$69,714 Casinos/Gambling†	35 Candidates Avg House: $2,058 Avg Sen: $1,936	Dems: 75.5% Senate: 52.8% Incumb: 87.0%	
Citicorp Citicorp Voluntary Political Fund Federal Washington, DC		$346,852 Commercial Banks†	200 Candidates Avg House: $1,723 Avg Sen: $1,957	Dems: 54.7% House: 83.9% Incumb: 91.6%	
Citizens & Southern National Bank Citizens and Southern Corporation Better Government Committee Atlanta, GA	C&S/Sovran Corp	$430,767 Commercial Banks	219 Candidates Avg House: $1,956 Avg Sen: $2,033	Dems: 61.8% House: 85.8% Incumb: 82.9%	
Citizens Concerned for the National Interest Citizens Concerned for The National Interest Chicago, IL		$75,500 Pro-Israel	11 Candidates Avg House: $0 Avg Sen: $7,050	Repubs: 60.3% Senate: 93.4% Incumb: 86.8%	
Citizens Organized PAC Citizens Organized PAC Los Angeles, CA		$192,750 Pro-Israel	34 Candidates Avg House: $2,205 Avg Sen: $7,326	Dems: 64.5% Senate: 87.4% Incumb: 85.3%	
City PAC City PAC (City PAC) Deerfield, IL		$84,000 Pro-Israel	40 Candidates Avg House: $1,565 Avg Sen: $2,824	Dems: 71.4% Senate: 57.1% Incumb: 61.3%	
Coastal Corp Coastal Corp. Employee Action Fund Houston, TX		$332,875 Natural Gas†	157 Candidates Avg House: $1,819 Avg Sen: $3,094	Dems: 75.3% House: 66.7% Incumb: 82.2%	
Coca-Cola Co Coca-Cola Company Nonpartisan Committee for Good Government Atlanta, GA	Coca-Cola	$198,990 Soft Drinks†	199 Candidates Avg House: $826 Avg Sen: $1,645	Dems: 60.3% House: 64.8% Incumb: 78.3%	
College of American Pathologists College of American Pathologists PAC Washington, DC		$52,500 Misc MD Specialists	61 Candidates Avg House: $837 Avg Sen: $1,000	Repubs: 53.3% House: 82.9% Incumb: 81.0%	
Colt Industries Colt Industries Inc Voluntary Political Committee New York, NY		$111,200 Defense Aerospace†	101 Candidates Avg House: $1,054 Avg Sen: $1,203	Repubs: 56.5% House: 65.4% Incumb: 85.6%	
Columbia Gas System Columbia Gas Employees Political Action Fund Wilmington, DE	Columbia Gas System	$122,750 Natural Gas	112 Candidates Avg House: $925 Avg Sen: $1,692	Repubs: 53.7% House: 65.5% Incumb: 87.7%	
Columbia Natural Resources Columbia Employees Political Action Fund Charleston, WV	Columbia Gas System	$91,175 Oil & Gas	92 Candidates Avg House: $1,006 Avg Sen: $949	Dems: 51.4% House: 75.0% Incumb: 83.4%	
Combustion Engineering Combustion Engineering Inc PAC (Compac) Stamford, CT		$67,819 Power Plant Constr†	81 Candidates Avg House: $709 Avg Sen: $1,142	Dems: 63.9% House: 59.6% Incumb: 92.5%	
Comcast Corp Comcast Corporation PAC Philadelphia, PA		$146,290 Cable TV	59 Candidates Avg House: $1,925 Avg Sen: $3,969	Dems: 62.4% House: 56.6% Incumb: 90.1%	
Committee for a Democratic Consensus Committee for a Democratic Consensus; The Washington, DC	Sen Alan Cranston (D-Calif)	$89,446 Dem Leaders	44 Candidates Avg House: $1,404 Avg Sen: $2,941	Dems: 100.0% Senate: 59.2% Incumb: 59.8%	
Committee for an Affordable New Jersey Committee for an Affordable New Jersey-Federal Piscataway, NJ	Christine Todd Whitman	$61,500 Non-federal Leaders	16 Candidates Avg House: $3,844 Avg Sen: $0	Repubs: 100.0% House: 100.0% Incumb: 29.7%	
Committee for Quality Orthopedic Health Care Committee for Quality Orthopaedic Health Care Inc Washington, DC		$150,802 Misc MD Specialists	166 Candidates Avg House: $762 Avg Sen: $1,573	Dems: 56.9% House: 68.7% Incumb: 74.6%	
Commmunications Workers of America CWA-COPE Political Contributions Committee Washington, DC	Communications Workers	$935,768 Communication	296 Candidates Avg House: $2,657 Avg Sen: $6,181	Dems: 98.3% House: 71.8% Incumb: 50.0%	

Unions
† PAC sponsor has other major interests in addition to this primary category

PAC Sponsor or Related Group/PAC Name	Affiliate		1991-92 Total	Where the money went...			
Communications Workers Union #13000 Local 13000 CWA AFL-CIO Philadelphia, PA	Communications Workers	Communic Unions	$75,750	14 Candidates Avg House: $5,063 Avg Sen: $7,500		Dems: House: Incumb:	100.0% 80.2% 49.8%
Computer Sciences Corp Computer Sciences Corporation PAC (CSC PAC) El Segundo, CA		Computer Services†	$93,150	86 Candidates Avg House: $891 Avg Sen: $1,609		Dems: House: Incumb:	60.6% 60.3% 92.2%
Comsat ComsatPAC Washington, DC		Satellite Communic	$77,550	65 Candidates Avg House: $936 Avg Sen: $1,816		Dems: House: Incumb:	54.0% 55.5% 93.2%
ConAgra Inc ConAgra Good Government Association Omaha, NE		Food Processors†	$300,038	127 Candidates Avg House: $1,781 Avg Sen: $3,800		Repubs: House: Incumb:	68.8% 54.0% 82.4%
Connecticut Mutual Life Insurance Connecticut Mutual Life Insurance Co-PAC (CM-PAC;/CM PAC;/CML PAC) Hartford, CT		Life Insurance	$63,100	58 Candidates Avg House: $1,009 Avg Sen: $1,250		Dems: House: Incumb:	57.0% 62.4% 83.4%
Conservative Victory Committee Conservative Victory Committee Alexandria, VA		Repub/Conservative	$96,022	51 Candidates Avg House: $1,859 Avg Sen: $2,111		Repubs: House: Incumb:	99.2% 79.4% 13.8%
Consolidated Freightways Consolidated Freightways Inc PAC Menlo Park, CA		Trucking Companies†	$93,400	86 Candidates Avg House: $820 Avg Sen: $1,667		Repubs: House: Incumb:	51.7% 51.8% 76.3%
Consolidated Rail Corp Consolidated Rail Corp Good Govt Fund (Conrail Good Govt Fund) Philadelphia, PA		Railroads	$64,850	89 Candidates Avg House: $682 Avg Sen: $1,062		Dems: House: Incumb:	69.9% 82.0% 92.9%
Consumers Power Co Consumers Power Company Employees for Better Government - Federal Jackson, MI	CMS Energy Corp	Gas & Electric Util+	$116,580	88 Candidates Avg House: $1,386 Avg Sen: $1,103		Dems: House: Incumb:	62.6% 82.0% 83.6%
Continental Illinois Corp Political Participation Fund of Continental Illinois Corp Chicago, IL		Commercial Banks	$90,750	73 Candidates Avg House: $1,284 Avg Sen: $1,071		Dems: House: Incumb:	64.5% 83.5% 80.7%
Cooper Industries Cooper Industries PAC (CIPAC) Houston, TX		Power Plant Constr†	$345,500	109 Candidates Avg House: $2,821 Avg Sen: $4,340		Repubs: House: Incumb:	98.1% 68.6% 34.9%
Cooperative of American Physicians Cooperative of American Physicians Federal Action Committee (CAP/FAC) Los Angeles, CA		Doctors	$121,530	73 Candidates Avg House: $1,386 Avg Sen: $2,443		Dems: House: Incumb:	69.2% 58.2% 61.9%
Coopers & Lybrand Coopers & Lybrand PAC Washington, DC		Accountants	$239,403	142 Candidates Avg House: $1,439 Avg Sen: $2,748		Dems: House: Incumb:	65.5% 66.7% 89.2%
Corning Glass Works Corning Glass Works Employees PAC Corning, NY		Glass Products†	$242,750	119 Candidates Avg House: $1,818 Avg Sen: $2,917		Repubs: House: Incumb:	60.6% 71.2% 80.6%
Council for a Livable World Council for a Livable World Boston, MA	Council for Livable World	Pro-Peace	$77,104	31 Candidates Avg House: $47 Avg Sen: $2,750		Dems: Senate: Incumb:	100.0% 99.8% 26.7%
Council for a Livable World Peace PAC Boston, MA	Council for Livable World	Pro-Peace	$51,702	49 Candidates Avg House: $1,055 Avg Sen: $0		Dems: House: Incumb:	97.7% 100.0% 30.1%
Council for National Defense Council for National Defense Inc, The Springfield, VA		Pro-Defense	$55,995	71 Candidates Avg House: $761 Avg Sen: $885		Repubs: House: Incumb:	100.0% 74.7% 28.7%
Credit Union National Assn Credit Union Legislative Action Council of Credit Union National Association Washington, DC	Credit Union Natl Assn	Credit Unions	$522,970	261 Candidates Avg House: $1,648 Avg Sen: $4,155		Dems: House: Incumb:	67.7% 70.6% 74.5%
Cruise PAC Cruise PAC Washington, DC		Sea Transport	$66,500	48 Candidates Avg House: $1,257 Avg Sen: $1,818		Dems: House: Incumb:	57.9% 69.9% 76.7%

PAC Sponsor or Related Group/PAC Name	Affiliate	1991-92 Total	Where the money went...		
Crum & Forster Insurance Crum & Forster Voluntary PAC Basking Ridge, NJ	Insurance	$55,830	74 Candidates Avg House: $641 Avg Sen: $1,023	Repubs: 67.7% House: 59.7% Incumb: 77.6%	
CSX Transportation Inc CSX Transportation Inc PAC (Fka Seaboard System Railroad PAC) Washington, DC	CSX Corp / Railroads†	$184,525	179 Candidates Avg House: $862 Avg Sen: $1,905	Dems: 62.7% House: 70.1% Incumb: 90.2%	
Cyprus Minerals Co Cyprus Minerals Company PAC/Cyprus PAC Englewood, CO	Metal Mining/Process†	$86,123	49 Candidates Avg House: $1,140 Avg Sen: $2,733	Repubs: 69.0% Senate: 60.3% Incumb: 84.8%	
Dairymen Inc Dairymen Inc-Special Pol Agricultural Community Education (DI-SPACE) Louisville, KY	Dairy	$85,519	88 Candidates Avg House: $849 Avg Sen: $1,365	Dems: 64.7% House: 66.5% Incumb: 91.1%	
Dallas Energy PAC Dallas Energy PAC (DalEnPAC) Dallas, TX	Oil & Gas	$56,500	27 Candidates Avg House: $1,389 Avg Sen: $2,444	Repubs: 100.0% Senate: 77.9% Incumb: 31.0%	
Dayton Hudson Corp Dayton Hudson Corporation Committee for Effective Federal Government Minneapolis, MN	Department Stores	$63,350	103 Candidates Avg House: $560 Avg Sen: $936	Repubs: 62.4% House: 77.7% Incumb: 75.5%	
Dean Witter Reynolds Dean Witter Reynolds PAC New York, NY	Sears / Securities	$136,150	117 Candidates Avg House: $990 Avg Sen: $1,957	Dems: 63.1% House: 69.8% Incumb: 82.7%	
Deere & Co Deere & Company Civic Action Fund Moline, IL	Farm Equipment†	$103,900	76 Candidates Avg House: $1,123 Avg Sen: $2,050	Repubs: 89.5% House: 60.5% Incumb: 63.9%	
Delaware Valley PAC Delaware Valley PAC Bensalem, PA	Pro-Israel	$95,000	71 Candidates Avg House: $683 Avg Sen: $2,184	Dems: 62.2% Senate: 71.3% Incumb: 80.6%	
Deloitte & Touche Touche Ross Partners Federal PAC (TRPAC) Washington, DC	Accountants	$124,504	72 Candidates Avg House: $1,527 Avg Sen: $2,382	Dems: 67.9% House: 67.5% Incumb: 87.5%	
Delta Airlines Delta Airlines Inc PAC Atlanta, GA	Airlines	$122,250	92 Candidates Avg House: $1,060 Avg Sen: $2,238	Dems: 65.4% House: 61.5% Incumb: 92.3%	
Desert Caucus Desert Caucus Tucson, AZ	Pro-Israel	$178,550	48 Candidates Avg House: $1,077 Avg Sen: $8,125	Dems: 75.2% Senate: 81.9% Incumb: 81.6%	
Detroit Edison Detroit Edison PAC-EDPAC-Federal Detroit, MI	Electric Utilities	$100,520	89 Candidates Avg House: $1,150 Avg Sen: $1,055	Dems: 65.2% House: 80.0% Incumb: 92.0%	
Dial Corp Greyhound Good Government Project Phoenix, AZ	Household Chemicals†	$98,650	105 Candidates Avg House: $801 Avg Sen: $1,455	Repubs: 60.6% House: 66.5% Incumb: 92.0%	
Dickstein, Shapiro & Morin Dickstein, Shapiro & Morin PAC Washington, DC	Lawyers	$108,700	129 Candidates Avg House: $743 Avg Sen: $1,042	Dems: 66.2% House: 58.8% Incumb: 94.9%	
Walt Disney Co Walt Disney Company Employees' PAC Burbank, CA	Movies/Resorts†	$97,450	69 Candidates Avg House: $1,132 Avg Sen: $2,011	Repubs: 56.4% House: 54.6% Incumb: 83.1%	
Distilled Spirits Council Distilled Spirits Council PAC Washington, DC	Wine & Liquor	$67,901	85 Candidates Avg House: $697 Avg Sen: $1,364	Dems: 80.6% House: 73.9% Incumb: 95.2%	
Dominion Resources Inc Committee for Responsible Govt-Dominion Resources Inc (Formerly Va Elec & Power) Richmond, VA	Electric Utilities	$53,875	64 Candidates Avg House: $896 Avg Sen: $678	Dems: 62.0% House: 79.9% Incumb: 78.9%	
RR Donnelley & Sons R R Donnelley & Sons Company PAC Chicago, IL	Publishing†	$52,400	46 Candidates Avg House: $795 Avg Sen: $1,675	Repubs: 88.1% Senate: 57.5% Incumb: 59.2%	

† PAC sponsor has other major interests in addition to this primary category

PAC Sponsor or Related Group/PAC Name	Affiliate	1991-92 Total	Where the money went...		
Dow Chemical Dow Chemical Company Employees' PAC Freeport, TX	Chemicals†	$109,500	43 Candidates Avg House: $2,079 Avg Sen: $6,100	Repubs: 74.9% House: 72.2% Incumb: 61.2%	
Dow Chemical/HQ Unit Dow Chemical Company-Headquarters Unit Employees PAC; The Midland, MI	Dow Chemical — Chemicals†	$94,000	86 Candidates Avg House: $957 Avg Sen: $1,833	Repubs: 80.3% House: 71.3% Incumb: 56.9%	
Dow Chemical/SE Region Empac (Employees' PAC, S. E. Region, The Dow Chemical Company) Plaquemine, LA	Dow Chemical — Chemicals†	$72,450	57 Candidates Avg House: $1,201 Avg Sen: $2,000	Repubs: 64.1% House: 86.2% Incumb: 59.8%	
Dresser Industries Dresser Industries PAC (DIPAC) Dallas, TX	Oilfield Services	$86,415	70 Candidates Avg House: $965 Avg Sen: $1,908	Repubs: 78.7% House: 55.9% Incumb: 85.2%	
DSC Communications Corp DSC Communications Corporation PAC DSCPAC Washington, DC	Communication Equip	$62,200	56 Candidates Avg House: $1,107 Avg Sen: $1,125	Dems: 60.3% House: 78.3% Incumb: 89.5%	
Duke Power Co Employees Federal PAC - Duke Power Company Charlotte, NC	Electric Utilities	$50,650	46 Candidates Avg House: $1,132 Avg Sen: $929	Repubs: 61.1% House: 87.2% Incumb: 77.7%	
Dun & Bradstreet PAC of the Dun & Bradstreet Corporation Washington, DC	Market Research†	$128,350	102 Candidates Avg House: $899 Avg Sen: $2,081	Repubs: 52.5% Senate: 50.2% Incumb: 91.4%	
Duquesne Light Co Duquesne Light Company Federal PAC (Fedupac) Pittsburgh, PA	Electric Utilities	$52,750	49 Candidates Avg House: $792 Avg Sen: $2,185	Repubs: 50.5% House: 58.6% Incumb: 83.9%	
E-Systems/Corporate Division E-Systems Corporate Division PAC Dallas, TX	E-Systems — Defense Electronics	$115,509	113 Candidates Avg House: $999 Avg Sen: $1,119	Dems: 54.4% House: 78.7% Incumb: 84.9%	
Eagle Forum Eagle Forum PAC Alton, IL	Repub/Conservative	$148,361	101 Candidates Avg House: $1,445 Avg Sen: $1,629	Repubs: 96.0% House: 85.7% Incumb: 32.6%	
Eaton Corp Eaton Corporation Public Policy Association Cleveland, OH	Truck/Auto Parts†	$218,600	118 Candidates Avg House: $1,561 Avg Sen: $3,472	Repubs: 93.5% House: 71.4% Incumb: 23.3%	
Edison Electric Institute Power PAC of the Edison Electric Institute Washington, DC	Electric Utilities	$84,614	164 Candidates Avg House: $501 Avg Sen: $591	Repubs: 57.4% House: 81.1% Incumb: 87.0%	
Effective Government Committee Effective Government Committee Washington, DC	Rep Richard Gephardt (D-Mo) — Dem Leaders	$204,425	147 Candidates Avg House: $1,294 Avg Sen: $3,667	Dems: 100.0% House: 89.2% Incumb: 43.8%	
Electronic Data Systems Electronic Data Systems Employees' PAC Washington, DC	General Motors — Computer Services	$226,616	188 Candidates Avg House: $1,070 Avg Sen: $1,890	Dems: 60.7% House: 74.1% Incumb: 84.6%	
Electronic Machine Furniture Workers IUE COPE Int'l Union/Electronic Electrical Tech Salaried Mach Workers AFL-CIO Washington, DC	Communication Unions†	$307,102	155 Candidates Avg House: $1,478 Avg Sen: $4,137	Dems: 99.5% House: 60.6% Incumb: 57.7%	
Eli Lilly & Co Eli Lilly And Company PAC Indianapolis, IN	Pharmaceuticals†	$195,530	125 Candidates Avg House: $806 Avg Sen: $3,863	Repubs: 72.8% Senate: 61.2% Incumb: 64.0%	
Emily's List Emily's List Washington, DC	Womens Issues	$365,318	65 Candidates Avg House: $5,390 Avg Sen: $7,258	Dems: 97.6% House: 84.1% Incumb: 4.5%	
Employee Stock Ownership Assn Employee Stock Ownership Association Inc PAC Washington, DC	Misc Financial Svcs	$58,707	61 Candidates Avg House: $872 Avg Sen: $1,788	Repubs: 70.3% House: 81.7% Incumb: 97.0%	
Enron Corp Enron PAC (Fka HNG/Internorth PAC) Houston, TX	Natural Gas†	$130,550	134 Candidates Avg House: $776 Avg Sen: $1,642	Repubs: 52.7% House: 60.6% Incumb: 90.5%	

PAC Sponsor or Related Group/PAC Name	Affiliate	1991-92 Total	Where the money went...		
Enserch Corp Enserch Corporation Employees Political Support Association Dallas, TX	Natural Gas†	$147,785	127 Candidates Avg House: $1,075 Avg Sen: $1,417	Dems: 64.1% House: 68.4% Incumb: 93.9%	
Entergy Services Inc MSU System Services Inc New Orleans, LA	Entergy Corp Gas & Electric Util†	$50,125	85 Candidates Avg House: $556 Avg Sen: $705	Dems: 61.5% House: 73.3% Incumb: 91.5%	
Equitable Financial Services Equitable Financial Services PAC (EQUI-PAC) New York, NY	Equitable Life Insurance†	$110,350	91 Candidates Avg House: $955 Avg Sen: $1,688	Dems: 71.8% House: 51.1% Incumb: 90.1%	
Ernst & Young Ernst & Whinney PAC Washington, DC	Accountants	$236,296	178 Candidates Avg House: $1,045 Avg Sen: $2,069	Dems: 63.6% House: 54.8% Incumb: 78.3%	
Exxon Corp Exxon Corporation PAC (EXPAC) Houston, TX	Oil & Gas†	$327,850	255 Candidates Avg House: $833 Avg Sen: $4,438	Repubs: 82.5% House: 56.4% Incumb: 60.1%	
Family Health Program Inc FHP, Inc - Health Services PAC (FHP-HESPAC) Fountain Valley, CA	HMOs	$94,713	67 Candidates Avg House: $1,193 Avg Sen: $1,982	Dems: 63.7% House: 59.2% Incumb: 59.9%	
Farm Credit Council Farm Credit Council PAC/Farm Credit PAC Washington, DC	Ag Services	$170,023	208 Candidates Avg House: $665 Avg Sen: $1,369	Dems: 56.7% House: 63.8% Incumb: 87.7%	
Farmers' Rice Cooperative Farmers' Rice Cooperative Fund Sacramento, CA	Misc Crops	$52,200	20 Candidates Avg House: $2,509 Avg Sen: $2,733	Dems: 58.9% House: 52.9% Incumb: 91.0%	
Federal Express Corp Federal Express Corporation PAC "FEPAC" Memphis, TN	Express Delivery	$740,975	221 Candidates Avg House: $3,291 Avg Sen: $3,528	Dems: 68.2% House: 68.8% Incumb: 90.3%	
Federal Managers' Assn Federal Managers' Association PAC Washington, DC	Fedl Worker Unions	$63,725	64 Candidates Avg House: $833 Avg Sen: $1,484	Dems: 78.9% House: 62.7% Incumb: 92.5%	
Federal National Mortgage Assn Federal National Mortgage Association PAC ("Fannie PAC") Washington, DC	Mortgage Banking	$62,725	76 Candidates Avg House: $717 Avg Sen: $1,352	Dems: 70.5% House: 72.0% Incumb: 96.0%	
Federation of American Health Systems Federation of American Health Systems PAC Washington, DC	Hospitals	$179,850	150 Candidates Avg House: $951 Avg Sen: $2,044	Dems: 59.4% House: 61.4% Incumb: 81.2%	
Fifth Horseman PAC Fifth Horseman PAC Elgin, IL	Dem/Liberal	$109,000	24 Candidates Avg House: $3,727 Avg Sen: $5,250	Dems: 95.4% Senate: 57.8% Incumb: 15.1%	
Fireman's Fund Insurance Fireman's Fund Employees' Committee for Responsible Government Novato, CA	Insurance	$86,570	112 Candidates Avg House: $723 Avg Sen: $905	Repubs: 53.1% House: 67.6% Incumb: 77.8%	
First Boston Corp First Boston-PAC (FB-PAC); The New York, NY	Investmtent Banking	$96,500	66 Candidates Avg House: $1,287 Avg Sen: $1,895	Dems: 75.7% House: 62.7% Incumb: 92.8%	
First Chicago Corp First Chicago Corp Government Affairs C/o The First National Bank of Chicago Chicago, IL	Commercial Banks	$129,153	109 Candidates Avg House: $1,143 Avg Sen: $1,340	Dems: 60.2% House: 74.3% Incumb: 84.9%	
First Union Corp First Union Corporation Employees Good Government "F" Fund Charlotte, NC	Mortgage Banking	$58,550	63 Candidates Avg House: $893 Avg Sen: $1,300	Dems: 50.5% House: 77.8% Incumb: 34.8%	
Fleming Companies Inc Fleming Companies Inc Committee For Responsible Government Oklahoma City, OK	Food Wholesalers	$171,500	101 Candidates Avg House: $1,388 Avg Sen: $2,881	Repubs: 79.0% House: 64.7% Incumb: 55.7%	
Florida Congressional Committee Florida Congressional Committee Miami, FL	Pro-Israel	$158,250	59 Candidates Avg House: $1,383 Avg Sen: $4,222	Dems: 50.1% Senate: 72.0% Incumb: 86.7%	

† PAC sponsor has other major interests in addition to this primary category

PAC Sponsor or Related Group/PAC Name	Affiliate	1991-92 Total	Where the money went...		
Florida Power & Light Good Government Management Ass'n Florida Power & Light Company Employee's PAC Juno Beach, FL — FPL Group	Electric Utilities	$72,700	86 Candidates Avg House: $756 Avg Sen: $1,346	Repubs: 52.3% House: 75.9% Incumb: 71.0%	
Florida Sugar Cane League Florida Sugar Cane League PAC Clewiston, FL	Sugar	$167,075	191 Candidates Avg House: $774 Avg Sen: $1,397	Dems: 75.2% House: 74.1% Incumb: 94.3%	
Flowers Industries Flowers PAC Thomasville, GA	Food Processors	$171,000	58 Candidates Avg House: $2,553 Avg Sen: $4,600	Repubs: 97.7% House: 70.2% Incumb: 14.0%	
Fluor Corp Fluor Corporation Public Affairs Committee (Fluor PAC) Irvine, CA	Heavy Construction†	$333,058	157 Candidates Avg House: $1,659 Avg Sen: $3,569	Repubs: 56.8% House: 59.3% Incumb: 83.1%	
FMC Corp FMC Corporation Good Government Program Chicago, IL	Chemicals†	$261,760	197 Candidates Avg House: $1,053 Avg Sen: $2,561	Repubs: 63.8% House: 64.8% Incumb: 78.9%	
Food & Commercial Workers Union Active Ballot Club, A Dept of United Food & Commercial Workers Int'l Union Washington, DC — Food/Commercial Wrkrs Union	Retail Unions†	$1,488,961	388 Candidates Avg House: $3,495 Avg Sen: $6,143	Dems: 97.2% House: 79.1% Incumb: 57.6%	
Food Marketing Institute Food Marketing Institute PAC (Food PAC) Washington, DC	Food Stores	$531,778	327 Candidates Avg House: $1,328 Avg Sen: $3,763	Repubs: 64.5% House: 71.7% Incumb: 81.8%	
Ford Motor Co Ford Motor Company Civic Action Fund Detroit, MI	Auto Manufacturers†	$287,984	237 Candidates Avg House: $1,058 Avg Sen: $2,388	Dems: 52.9% House: 76.8% Incumb: 87.2%	
Fox Inc FOXPAC (Fox Inc and Subsidiaries) (Fka Twentieth Century Fox PAC) Beverly Hills, CA	Movies/TV	$53,700	46 Candidates Avg House: $1,098 Avg Sen: $1,291	Dems: 85.1% House: 57.3% Incumb: 85.2%	
Free Cuba PAC Free Cuba PAC Inc Miami, FL	Foreign Policy	$159,000	59 Candidates Avg House: $2,328 Avg Sen: $3,270	Dems: 64.5% House: 52.7% Incumb: 77.4%	
Freeport-McMoRan Inc Freeport-McMoran Inc Citizenship Committee Washington, DC	Ag Chemicals†	$132,550	109 Candidates Avg House: $861 Avg Sen: $1,853	Dems: 53.0% Senate: 54.5% Incumb: 88.7%	
Fulbright & Jaworski Freedom Fund; The Houston, TX	Lawyers	$71,343	76 Candidates Avg House: $837 Avg Sen: $1,113	Dems: 70.8% House: 56.3% Incumb: 83.4%	
Fund for a Democratic Majority Fund for a Democratic Majority Washington, DC — Sen Edward Kennedy (D-Mass)	Dem Leaders	$185,530	43 Candidates Avg House: $1,588 Avg Sen: $6,097	Dems: 100.0% Senate: 85.5% Incumb: 46.4%	
Garden State PAC Garden State PAC Roseland, NJ	Pro-Israel	$59,950	52 Candidates Avg House: $730 Avg Sen: $1,646	Dems: 56.6% Senate: 65.9% Incumb: 72.6%	
Gencorp Inc GenCorp Inc PAC (GENPAC) Fairlawn, OH	Defense Aerospace†	$116,029	80 Candidates Avg House: $1,346 Avg Sen: $1,811	Dems: 60.2% House: 71.9% Incumb: 98.2%	
Genentech Inc Genentech Inc PAC So San Francisco, CA	Pharmaceuticals	$79,200	72 Candidates Avg House: $748 Avg Sen: $1,687	Dems: 64.3% Senate: 57.5% Incumb: 79.5%	
General American Life Insurance General American Life Associates' Federal PAC St Louis, MO	Insurance	$90,500	61 Candidates Avg House: $1,297 Avg Sen: $1,771	Dems: 51.4% House: 53.0% Incumb: 79.6%	
General Atomics General Atomics PAC San Diego, CA	Nuclear Plant Constr†	$305,550	96 Candidates Avg House: $3,183 Avg Sen: $3,215	Dems: 64.0% House: 61.5% Incumb: 88.6%	
General Dynamics General Dynamics Corporation Voluntary Political Contribution Plan St Louis, MO	Defense Aerospace†	$436,482	219 Candidates Avg House: $1,733 Avg Sen: $3,196	Dems: 61.2% House: 71.5% Incumb: 93.5%	

PAC Sponsor or Related Group/PAC Name	Affiliate	1991-92 Total	Where the money went...		
General Electric Non-Partisan Political Support Committee for General Electric Company Employees Fairfield, CT	Aerospace Equip†	$683,350	417 Candidates Avg House: $1,254 Avg Sen: $3,058	Dems: House: Incumb:	58.7% 59.3% 85.2%
General Mills General Mills Inc PAC (GM PAC) Minneapolis, MN	Food Processors†	$100,850	89 Candidates Avg House: $768 Avg Sen: $1,929	Repubs: Senate: Incumb:	57.0% 53.5% 80.7%
General Mills Restaurants General Mills Restaurants Inc Empl Good Govt Fund (Red Lobster Emp Gd Govt Fd) Orlando, FL	General Mills Restaurants	$84,083	84 Candidates Avg House: $838 Avg Sen: $1,408	Repubs: House: Incumb:	69.4% 59.8% 79.8%
General Motors Civic Involvement Program/General Motors Corp. Detroit, MI	Auto Manufacturers†	$232,480	158 Candidates Avg House: $1,013 Avg Sen: $3,025	Repubs: House: Incumb:	56.7% 53.2% 84.2%
General Public Utilities General Public Utilities Political Participation Association Washington, DC	Electric Utilities	$84,576	84 Candidates Avg House: $873 Avg Sen: $1,576	Repubs: House: Incumb:	52.1% 70.2% 86.1%
Georgia Power Co Georgia Power Company Federal PAC Inc Atlanta, GA	Southern Co Electric Utilities	$72,550	110 Candidates Avg House: $647 Avg Sen: $730	Dems: House: Incumb:	58.1% 77.5% 65.6%
Georgia-Pacific Corp G-P Employees Fund of Georgia-Pacific Corporation Washington, DC	Georgia-Pacific Forest Products†	$124,092	81 Candidates Avg House: $995 Avg Sen: $2,736	Repubs: Senate: Incumb:	58.9% 55.1% 77.1%
Glaxo Inc Glaxo Inc Democracy Fund Research Triangle, NC	Pharmaceuticals	$175,522	115 Candidates Avg House: $1,173 Avg Sen: $2,735	Dems: House: Incumb:	54.4% 59.5% 89.8%
Golden Rule Financial Corp Golden Rule Financial Corporation - PAC Indianapolis, IN	Insurance	$127,576	107 Candidates Avg House: $1,052 Avg Sen: $1,704	Repubs: House: Incumb:	50.2% 69.3% 72.9%
Goldman, Sachs & Co GSMMI Holdings Inc PAC Aka Goldman Sachs PAC Washington, DC	Investmtent Banking	$186,558	120 Candidates Avg House: $1,453 Avg Sen: $1,940	Dems: House: Incumb:	77.0% 74.0% 86.7%
WR Grace & Co GracePAC New York, NY	Chemicals†	$133,795	104 Candidates Avg House: $992 Avg Sen: $2,269	Repubs: House: Incumb:	58.5% 59.3% 85.4%
Graphic Communications Union Graphic Communications International Union Political Contributions Committee Washington, DC	Communication Unions	$69,400	69 Candidates Avg House: $759 Avg Sen: $1,600	Dems: House: Incumb:	98.9% 59.1% 46.8%
Great Lakes Sugar Beet Growers Great Lakes Sugar Beet Growers PAC (GLSBGPAC) Saginaw, MI	Sugar	$69,965	123 Candidates Avg House: $568 Avg Sen: $580	Repubs: House: Incumb:	51.3% 91.7% 94.6%
Great Western Financial Corp Great Western Financial Corporation Good Government Committee Beverly Hills, CA	Savings & Loans	$73,580	80 Candidates Avg House: $859 Avg Sen: $1,231	Repubs: House: Incumb:	51.5% 78.2% 86.1%
Greater Washington Board of Trade Federal Commerce & Industry PAC of the Greater Washington Board of Trade Washington, DC	Chambers of Commerce	$62,750	39 Candidates Avg House: $1,734 Avg Sen: $1,125	Dems: House: Incumb:	71.5% 85.7% 85.3%
Greenvote Greenvote Boston, MA	Environment Policy	$98,850	66 Candidates Avg House: $975 Avg Sen: $2,700	Dems: Senate: Incumb:	94.9% 54.6% 30.2%
Grumman Corp Grumman PAC Bethpage, NY	Defense Aerospace†	$250,350	171 Candidates Avg House: $1,244 Avg Sen: $2,422	Dems: House: Incumb:	66.3% 69.0% 94.2%
GTE Corp GTE Corporation Good Government Club Washington, DC	Phone Utilites†	$615,977	384 Candidates Avg House: $1,378 Avg Sen: $2,958	Dems: House: Incumb:	52.0% 73.6% 85.3%
Halliburton Co Halliburton PAC Duncan, OK	Oilfield Services†	$90,512	57 Candidates Avg House: $1,056 Avg Sen: $2,500	Repubs: Senate: Incumb:	81.8% 58.0% 56.1%

† PAC sponsor has other major interests in addition to this primary category

PAC Sponsor or Related Group/PAC Name	Affiliate	1991-92 Total	Where the money went...	
Hallmark Cards Hallmark PAC-Federal HALLPAC-Federal Kansas City, MO	 Greeting Cards	$144,000	69 Candidates Avg House: $1,245 Avg Sen: $3,772	Repubs: 79.0% Senate: 60.2% Incumb: 68.1%
Handgun Control Inc Handgun Control Inc PAC (HCI PAC) Washington, DC	 Anti-Guns	$156,112	102 Candidates Avg House: $1,256 Avg Sen: $3,123	Dems: 87.0% House: 70.0% Incumb: 42.1%
Harris Corp Harris Corporation-Federal PAC Melbourne, FL	 Electronics Mfg†	$206,490	117 Candidates Avg House: $1,093 Avg Sen: $4,238	Repubs: 96.8% Senate: 51.3% Incumb: 53.0%
Harsco Corp Harsco Corporation PAC Camp Hill, PA	 Weapons Systems†	$50,975	65 Candidates Avg House: $645 Avg Sen: $1,650	Repubs: 57.2% House: 70.9% Incumb: 91.2%
Hartford Insurance Hartford Insurance Group - PAC Hartford, CT	 ITT Corp Insurance	$100,480	103 Candidates Avg House: $855 Avg Sen: $1,418	Dems: 59.9% House: 69.0% Incumb: 88.5%
Hawaiian Sugar Planters Assn Hawaiian Sugar Planters' Association-PAC (Hawaiian Sugar-PAC) Aiea, HI	 Sugar	$61,975	130 Candidates Avg House: $380 Avg Sen: $863	Dems: 73.4% House: 63.8% Incumb: 92.4%
Health Insurance Assn of America Health Insurance PAC of the Health Insurance Association of America Washington, DC	 Health Insurance	$232,177	241 Candidates Avg House: $789 Avg Sen: $1,722	Repubs: 61.7% House: 66.6% Incumb: 77.1%
Heartland PAC Heartland PAC Fka: Youngstown PAC Washington, DC	 Pro-Israel	$85,250	55 Candidates Avg House: $750 Avg Sen: $2,217	Dems: 69.8% Senate: 78.0% Incumb: 73.3%
Henley Group Inc Henley Group Inc Employees Cmte for Sensible Gov't (Henley COSIGN) Hampton, NH	 Medical Supplies†	$77,200	28 Candidates Avg House: $3,135 Avg Sen: $2,246	Repubs: 52.1% House: 52.8% Incumb: 67.6%
Heublein Heublein Employees' Political Participation Committee Farmington, CT	 Grand Metropolitan Wine & Liquor	$65,129	66 Candidates Avg House: $865 Avg Sen: $1,400	Dems: 77.7% House: 67.8% Incumb: 91.6%
Hewlett-Packard Hewlett-Packard Company PAC (HP PAC) Palo Alto, CA	 Electronics Mfg†	$58,800	47 Candidates Avg House: $633 Avg Sen: $3,273	Repubs: 75.7% Senate: 61.2% Incumb: 46.0%
Hoechst Celanese Corp Hoechst Celanese Corporation PAC Somerville, NJ	 Synthetic Fibers†	$186,700	132 Candidates Avg House: $1,254 Avg Sen: $1,983	Repubs: 52.8% House: 69.2% Incumb: 88.0%
Hoffman-La Roche Hoffmann-La Roche Inc Good Government Committee Nutley, NJ	 Pharmaceuticals†	$66,600	69 Candidates Avg House: $818 Avg Sen: $1,453	Repubs: 59.2% House: 65.1% Incumb: 89.2%
Hogan & Hartson Hogan & Hartson PAC Washington, DC	 Lawyers	$51,700	85 Candidates Avg House: $472 Avg Sen: $936	Dems: 72.3% House: 54.7% Incumb: 91.0%
Holland & Hart Holland & Hart Federal PAC Washington, DC	 Lawyers	$54,143	38 Candidates Avg House: $1,077 Avg Sen: $2,179	Dems: 64.0% House: 51.7% Incumb: 91.7%
Holland & Knight Holland & Knight Committee for Effective Government Washington, DC	 Lawyers	$85,872	79 Candidates Avg House: $930 Avg Sen: $1,619	Dems: 62.0% House: 66.0% Incumb: 84.1%
Hollywood Women's Political Committee Hollywood Women's Political Committee Culver City, CA	 Dem/Liberal†	$278,500	82 Candidates Avg House: $2,967 Avg Sen: $4,568	Dems: 99.3% House: 63.9% Incumb: 31.6%
Hopkins & Sudder HS Political Fund Chicago, IL	 Lawyers	$65,715	104 Candidates Avg House: $551 Avg Sen: $1,018	Dems: 59.2% House: 72.1% Incumb: 90.0%
Hotel/Restaurant Employees Union Hotel Employees & Restaurant Employees Int'l Union TIP - "To Insure Progress" Washington, DC	 Food Svc Unions	$333,524	259 Candidates Avg House: $1,018 Avg Sen: $2,504	Dems: 91.5% House: 64.4% Incumb: 81.1%

PAC Sponsor or Related Group/PAC Name	Affiliate	1991-92 Total	Where the money went...		
HOUPAC Houpac Houston, TX		$77,750 Oil & Gas	94 Candidates Avg House: $492 Avg Sen: $1,578	Repubs: 90.3% Senate: 58.8% Incumb: 38.3%	
House Leadership Fund House Leadership Fund; The Washington, DC	Rep Thomas Foley (D-Wash)	$244,056 Dem Leaders	136 Candidates Avg House: $1,732 Avg Sen: $6,000	Dems: 100.0% House: 95.1% Incumb: 54.1%	
Household International Inc Household International Inc & Subsidiary Companies PAC (Housepac) Prospect Heights, IL		$188,932 Credit/Loans	134 Candidates Avg House: $1,181 Avg Sen: $1,948	Dems: 51.0% House: 58.8% Incumb: 71.2%	
Houston Industries Houston Industries PAC Houston, TX		$63,000 Electric Utilities†	35 Candidates Avg House: $1,828 Avg Sen: $1,667	Dems: 62.7% House: 84.1% Incumb: 84.9%	
Hudson Valley PAC Hudson Valley PAC Spring Valley, NY		$266,965 Pro-Israel	134 Candidates Avg House: $1,193 Avg Sen: $3,872	Dems: 65.4% Senate: 58.0% Incumb: 87.7%	
Hughes Aircraft Hughes Aircraft Company Active Citizenship Fund Los Angeles, CA	General Motors	$220,270 Defense Electronics†	149 Candidates Avg House: $1,301 Avg Sen: $2,278	Dems: 52.3% House: 72.1% Incumb: 86.5%	
Human Rights Campaign Fund Human Rights Campaign Fund PAC Washington, DC		$713,040 Gay/Lesbian	190 Candidates Avg House: $3,557 Avg Sen: $5,046	Dems: 92.8% House: 82.3% Incumb: 48.3%	
Humana Inc HUMPAC - A PAC Sponsored by Humana Inc Louisville, KY		$61,425 Hospitals†	45 Candidates Avg House: $1,286 Avg Sen: $1,496	Dems: 75.7% House: 58.6% Incumb: 55.1%	
ICI Americas Inc ICI Americas PAC Wilmington, DE		$84,487 Pharmaceuticals†	102 Candidates Avg House: $665 Avg Sen: $1,281	Dems: 62.7% House: 59.0% Incumb: 94.0%	
Illinois Bell Telephone Illinois Bell Citizenship Responsibility Committee Chicago, IL	Ameritech	$56,235 Phone Utilites	23 Candidates Avg House: $2,399 Avg Sen: $2,925	Dems: 55.9% House: 89.6% Incumb: 86.1%	
Imo Industries Inc Imo Industries Inc PAC Lawrenceville, NJ		$110,923 Defense Electronics†	59 Candidates Avg House: $1,678 Avg Sen: $3,000	Repubs: 59.9% House: 75.7% Incumb: 78.0%	
Independent Action Independent Action Inc Washington, DC	Sen Tom Harkin/Rep Mo Udall	$116,318 Dem/Liberal	40 Candidates Avg House: $2,049 Avg Sen: $3,702	Dems: 99.1% Senate: 60.5% Incumb: 30.1%	
Independent Bankers Assn Independent Bankers - PAC Washington, DC		$401,060 Commercial Banks	312 Candidates Avg House: $1,085 Avg Sen: $2,321	Dems: 62.3% House: 70.3% Incumb: 85.3%	
Independent Insurance Agents of America Independent Insurance Agents of America Inc PAC (InsurPAC) Washington, DC		$589,798 Insurance	278 Candidates Avg House: $1,746 Avg Sen: $3,612	Dems: 59.8% House: 65.7% Incumb: 83.7%	
Insilco Corp Insilco Corporation PAC "insilcopac" Midland, TX		$77,000 Weapons Systems†	33 Candidates Avg House: $2,056 Avg Sen: $2,667	Repubs: 71.4% Senate: 52.0% Incumb: 96.1%	
Institute of Scrap Recycling Industries ISRI PAC (Fka Institute of Scrap Iron & Steel PAC) Washington, DC		$54,315 Recycling	71 Candidates Avg House: $761 Avg Sen: $785	Dems: 66.3% House: 81.2% Incumb: 95.2%	
International Assn of Firefighters Int'l Assn of Firefighters Interested in Registration and Education PAC Washington, DC	Intl Assn of Firefighters	$562,153 Public Safety	324 Candidates Avg House: $1,517 Avg Sen: $2,996	Dems: 93.9% House: 75.3% Incumb: 61.4%	
International Brotherhood of Electrical Workers (IBEW) International Brotherhood of Electrical Workers Committee on Political Education Washington, DC	IBEW	$1,517,592 Electrical Workers	387 Candidates Avg House: $3,657 Avg Sen: $5,438	Dems: 96.1% House: 79.3% Incumb: 57.7%	
International Council of Shopping Centers International Council of Shopping Centers Inc PAC (ICSC PAC) Alexandria, VA		$280,399 Retail Trade	186 Candidates Avg House: $1,219 Avg Sen: $2,952	Repubs: 58.7% House: 67.4% Incumb: 84.1%	

† PAC sponsor has other major interests in addition to this primary category

PAC Sponsor or Related Group/PAC Name	Affiliate	1991-92 Total	Where the money went...		
International Longshoremen's/Warehousemen's Union International Longshoremen's & Warehousemen's Union - Political Action Fund San Francisco, CA	Sea Transport Unions	$181,751	59 Candidates Avg House: $2,449 Avg Sen: $5,836	Dems: 98.6% House: 64.7% Incumb: 43.9%	
International Longshoremens Assn Int'l Longshoremen's Association AFL-CIO Cmte on Pol Education ILA-COPE New York, NY	Intl Longshoremen Assn Sea Transport Unions	$187,050	89 Candidates Avg House: $2,120 Avg Sen: $2,024	Dems: 92.3% House: 81.6% Incumb: 65.0%	
International Paper Co Voluntary Contributors for Better Govt: Employees of Int'l Paper Company Washington, DC	Paper/Pulp†	$218,860	93 Candidates Avg House: $1,380 Avg Sen: $4,732	Repubs: 89.8% Senate: 58.4% Incumb: 70.5%	
Interstate Natural Gas Assn Interstate Natural Gas Association of America PAC Washington, DC	Natural Gas	$87,443	90 Candidates Avg House: $696 Avg Sen: $1,862	Dems: 67.0% House: 54.1% Incumb: 93.4%	
Invacare Corp Invacare Corp PAC aka INVA PAC Elyria, OH	Medical Supplies	$50,150	30 Candidates Avg House: $1,368 Avg Sen: $2,195	Dems: 72.8% House: 51.8% Incumb: 87.0%	
Investment Company Institute Investment Mgmt PAC of the Investment Company Institute (IMPAC) Washington, DC	Securities	$192,150	97 Candidates Avg House: $1,682 Avg Sen: $3,000	Dems: 80.2% House: 65.7% Incumb: 93.8%	
Ironworkers Union Ironworkers Political Action League Washington, DC	Building Trade Unions	$530,280	200 Candidates Avg House: $2,345 Avg Sen: $4,576	Dems: 92.7% House: 75.2% Incumb: 66.7%	
ITEL Corp ITEL Corporation PAC Chicago, IL	Communication Equip†	$57,150	39 Candidates Avg House: $1,050 Avg Sen: $2,063	Dems: 80.3% Senate: 57.7% Incumb: 86.9%	
ITT Corp Corporate Citizenship Committee (ITT) New York, NY	Insurance†	$101,300	154 Candidates Avg House: $545 Avg Sen: $1,212	Repubs: 76.3% House: 68.9% Incumb: 73.8%	
Jacobs Engineering Group JEG Good Government Committee Pasadena, CA	Engineers	$63,657	60 Candidates Avg House: $951 Avg Sen: $1,422	Dems: 70.8% House: 68.7% Incumb: 96.0%	
Jim Walter Corp Jim Walter Corporation PAC (JWCPAC) Tampa, FL	Walter Industries Bldg Materials	$64,650	56 Candidates Avg House: $1,027 Avg Sen: $1,577	Dems: 80.7% House: 66.7% Incumb: 83.8%	
John Hancock Financial Service John Hancock Financial Services PAC Boston, MA	Insurance†	$60,875	60 Candidates Avg House: $941 Avg Sen: $1,142	Dems: 64.6% House: 58.7% Incumb: 84.2%	
Johnson & Johnson Johnson & Johnson Employees' Good Government Fund New Brunswick, NJ	Personal Health Prod†	$89,400	89 Candidates Avg House: $868 Avg Sen: $1,625	Dems: 54.9% House: 70.9% Incumb: 90.2%	
Joint Action Committee for Political Affairs Joint Action Committee for Political Affair Highland Park, IL	Pro-Israel	$205,000	111 Candidates Avg House: $1,307 Avg Sen: $3,802	Dems: 97.1% House: 55.5% Incumb: 62.1%	
Jones, Day et al Jones, Day, Reavis & Pogue Good Government Fund Cleveland, OH	Lawyers	$176,082	150 Candidates Avg House: $898 Avg Sen: $2,116	Dems: 50.1% House: 59.1% Incumb: 72.6%	
K Mart Corp K Mart Corporation PAC Troy, MI	Department Stores	$54,100	136 Candidates Avg House: $311 Avg Sen: $765	Repubs: 65.6% House: 63.2% Incumb: 71.5%	
Kansas City Southern Kansas City Southern Employees PAC Kansas City, MO	Railroads†	$99,725	94 Candidates Avg House: $939 Avg Sen: $1,348	Dems: 64.2% House: 62.1% Incumb: 90.7%	
Kellogg Co Kellogg Better Government Committee Battle Creek, MI	Food Processors	$70,700	82 Candidates Avg House: $765 Avg Sen: $1,184	Dems: 58.4% House: 68.2% Incumb: 89.8%	
KidsPAC KidsPAC Cambridge, MA	Childrens Rights	$440,600	137 Candidates Avg House: $2,510 Avg Sen: $5,964	Dems: 95.5% House: 62.1% Incumb: 73.7%	

PAC Sponsor or Related Group/PAC Name	Affiliate	1991-92 Total	Where the money went...			
Kinetic Concepts Inc Kinetic Concepts Inc PAC (kcipac) San Antonio, TX		$51,100 Medical Supplies	34 Candidates Avg House: $1,648 Avg Sen: $1,269		Dems: House: Incumb:	72.9% 67.7% 68.2%
King & Spalding King & Spalding Nonpartisan Committee for Good Government Atlanta, GA		$55,400 Lawyers	53 Candidates Avg House: $1,114 Avg Sen: $888		Dems: House: Incumb:	74.8% 74.4% 85.0%
Kirkland & Ellis Kirkland & Ellis PAC (Fka Wss PAC) Chicago, IL		$79,219 Lawyers	51 Candidates Avg House: $1,207 Avg Sen: $1,983		Dems: Senate: Incumb:	90.5% 57.6% 69.5%
Kirkpatrick & Lockhart Kirkpatrick & Lockhart PAC Pittsburgh, PA		$67,969 Lawyers	47 Candidates Avg House: $1,123 Avg Sen: $2,389		Repubs: House: Incumb:	55.1% 57.8% 75.6%
Koch Industries Koch Industries Inc PAC (KochPAC) Wichita, KS		$64,500 Oil & Gas†	46 Candidates Avg House: $1,176 Avg Sen: $2,042		Repubs: House: Incumb:	83.0% 62.0% 65.1%
Kutak, Rock & Campbell Kutak Rock & Campbell PAC Washington, DC		$54,900 Lawyers	64 Candidates Avg House: $648 Avg Sen: $1,319		Dems: House: Incumb:	87.2% 53.1% 74.0%
Laborers' Political League Laborers' Political League Washington, DC	Laborers Union	$1,387,406 Building Trade Unions	409 Candidates Avg House: $3,079 Avg Sen: $5,425		Dems: House: Incumb:	94.1% 78.6% 68.7%
Ladies Garment Workers Union International Ladies Garment Workers Union Campaign Commmittee New York, NY		$296,301 Manufacturing Unions	271 Candidates Avg House: $852 Avg Sen: $2,567		Dems: House: Incumb:	96.0% 66.8% 70.4%
Land O'Lakes Inc Land O'Lakes Inc PAC Minneapolis, MN		$79,525 Ag Chemicals†	58 Candidates Avg House: $1,196 Avg Sen: $1,794		Dems: House: Incumb:	56.5% 61.6% 77.4%
Leader PAC Leader PAC Fairfax, VA		$61,500 Repub/Conservative	35 Candidates Avg House: $1,515 Avg Sen: $10,000		Repubs: House: Incumb:	100.0% 83.7% 27.6%
League of Conservation Voters League of Conservation Voters Inc PAC Washington, DC		$413,139 Environment Policy	120 Candidates Avg House: $3,200 Avg Sen: $4,524		Dems: House: Incumb:	92.4% 75.9% 31.7%
Liberty Mutual Insurance Liberty Mutual Insurance Company PAC Boston, MA		$70,300 Proprty Insurance	59 Candidates Avg House: $862 Avg Sen: $2,250		Repubs: House: Incumb:	89.8% 55.2% 60.2%
Limited Inc Limited, Inc PAC Columbus, OH		$65,300 Clothing Stores	49 Candidates Avg House: $851 Avg Sen: $2,346		Repubs: Senate: Incumb:	64.4% 46.7% 66.3%
Lincoln Club of Orange County Lincoln Club Of Orange County Costa Mesa, CA		$66,250 Repub/Conservative	17 Candidates Avg House: $3,354 Avg Sen: $6,250		Repubs: House: Incumb:	100.0% 60.8% 20.4%
Litton Industries Litton Industries Inc Employees Political Assistance Committee (LEPAC) Beverly Hills, CA		$140,229 Defense Electronics†	109 Candidates Avg House: $1,015 Avg Sen: $2,187		Repubs: House: Incumb:	54.9% 59.4% 87.7%
Lockheed Corp Lockheed Employees PAC Calabasas, CA		$338,537 Defense Aerospace†	211 Candidates Avg House: $1,418 Avg Sen: $2,480		Dems: House: Incumb:	54.8% 72.9% 90.8%
Loose Group Loose Group; The Union City, GA		$53,500 Repub/Conservative	10 Candidates Avg House: $5,250 Avg Sen: $5,500		Repubs: House: Incumb:	100.0% 58.9% 18.7%
Loral Corp Civic Action Fund - Loral Systems Group (Fka Goodyear Aerospace Corp PAC) Akron, OH		$146,865 Defense Electronics†	119 Candidates Avg House: $1,028 Avg Sen: $1,920		Dems: House: Incumb:	71.0% 61.6% 93.2%
LTV Aerospace & Defense Co LTV Aerospace and Defense Company Active Citizenship Campaign Dallas, TX	LTV Corp	$157,851 Defense Aerospace†	113 Candidates Avg House: $1,440 Avg Sen: $1,265		Dems: House: Incumb:	71.8% 77.6% 97.5%

† PAC sponsor has other major interests in addition to this primary category

PAC Sponsor or Related Group/PAC Name	Affiliate		1991-92 Total	Where the money went...			
Machinists/Aerospace Workers Union Machinists Non-Partisan Political League Washington, DC	Machinists/Aerospace Wrkrs	Manuf Unions	$1,606,296	347 Candidates Avg House: $4,389 Avg Sen: $6,407	Dems: 97.3% House: 83.3% Incumb: 55.4%		
Maintenance of Way Employees Maintenance of Way Political League Detroit, MI		Railroad Unions	$147,725	143 Candidates Avg House: $868 Avg Sen: $1,500	Dems: 96.5% House: 63.5% Incumb: 79.5%		
Manatt, Phelps et al Golden State PAC (Fka Manatt, Phelps, Rothenberg & Tunney PAC) Los Angeles, CA		Lawyers	$71,260	81 Candidates Avg House: $755 Avg Sen: $1,194	Dems: 76.8% House: 61.5% Incumb: 92.6%		
Manor Healthcare Corp Manor Healthcare Federal PAC (Fka Four Seasons Fed PAC) Silver Spring, MD		Nursing Homes	$73,700	49 Candidates Avg House: $1,317 Avg Sen: $1,775	Dems: 62.7% House: 51.8% Incumb: 82.1%		
Manufactured Housing Institute Manufactured Housing Institute PAC (MHI PAC) Arlington, VA		Mobile Homes	$81,840	83 Candidates Avg House: $704 Avg Sen: $1,820	Repubs: 50.8% House: 53.3% Incumb: 87.1%		
Manufacturers Hanover Manufacturers Hanover Association for Responsible Government Fund New York, NY		Commercial Banks†	$67,550	68 Candidates Avg House: $834 Avg Sen: $1,471	Dems: 60.0% House: 63.0% Incumb: 95.6%		
Manville Corp Manville Corporation PAC Washington, DC		Forest Products†	$72,900	79 Candidates Avg House: $595 Avg Sen: $2,118	Repubs: 58.5% House: 50.6% Incumb: 96.9%		
Mapco Inc Mapco Inc PAC Tulsa, OK		Oil Refining/Mkting†	$134,450	136 Candidates Avg House: $645 Avg Sen: $2,442	Repubs: 86.4% House: 52.8% Incumb: 61.7%		
Marathon Oil Marathon Oil Company Employees Political Action Commttee (Mepac) Findlay, OH	USX Corp	Oil & Gas	$79,950	68 Candidates Avg House: $935 Avg Sen: $2,300	Dems: 50.5% House: 65.5% Incumb: 87.4%		
Marine Engineers District 2 Maritime Officers District 2 Marine Engineers Beneficial Assn-Associated Maritime Officers Brooklyn, NY	Marine Engineers Union	Sea Transport Unions	$827,650	321 Candidates Avg House: $2,493 Avg Sen: $3,379	Dems: 62.9% House: 87.3% Incumb: 92.2%		
Marine Engineers District 2 Retirees District 2 Marine Engineers Beneficial Assn-Assoc Maritime Officers, Retirees Brooklyn, NY	Marine Engineers Union	Sea Transport Unions	$63,274	56 Candidates Avg House: $986 Avg Sen: $3,000	Repubs: 73.1% House: 81.0% Incumb: 97.6%		
Marine Engineers Union Marine Engineers' Beneficial Assn Pol Action Fund (MEBA Pol Action Fund) Washington, DC		Sea Transport Unions	$705,550	237 Candidates Avg House: $2,547 Avg Sen: $4,526	Dems: 90.0% House: 67.2% Incumb: 62.3%		
Marriott Corp Marriott PAC Bethesda, MD		Hotels/Motels†	$118,950	104 Candidates Avg House: $853 Avg Sen: $1,797	Repubs: 64.9% House: 51.7% Incumb: 63.0%		
Martin Marietta Corp Martin Marietta Corporation PAC Bethesda, MD		Defense Aerospace†	$510,820	303 Candidates Avg House: $1,368 Avg Sen: $3,059	Dems: 51.5% House: 65.9% Incumb: 87.1%		
Maryland Assn for Concerned Citizens Maryland Association for Concerned Citizens PAC Pikesville, MD		Pro-Israel	$70,000	49 Candidates Avg House: $986 Avg Sen: $2,536	Dems: 70.0% Senate: 50.7% Incumb: 79.3%		
Massachusetts Mutual Life Insurance Massachusetts Mutual Life Insurance Company PAC Springfield, MA		Life Insurance	$282,338	141 Candidates Avg House: $1,817 Avg Sen: $2,610	Dems: 68.0% House: 68.2% Incumb: 75.9%		
Masters, Mates & Pilots Union Masters, Mates And Pilots Political Contribution Fund Linthicum Heights, MD	Masters, Mates & Pilots	Sea Transport Unions	$143,865	93 Candidates Avg House: $1,227 Avg Sen: $2,625	Dems: 82.5% House: 61.4% Incumb: 83.8%		
Matson Navigation Matson Federal Election Committee San Francisco, CA	Alexander & Baldwin Inc	Sea Transport	$52,500	42 Candidates Avg House: $960 Avg Sen: $1,896	Dems: 69.8% House: 53.0% Incumb: 85.7%		
May Department Stores May Department Stores Company PAC (Maypac) St Louis, MO		Department Stores	$124,550	176 Candidates Avg House: $575 Avg Sen: $1,636	Repubs: 77.5% House: 71.1% Incumb: 73.1%		

PAC Sponsor or Related Group/PAC Name	Affiliate	1991-92 Total	Where the money went...		
Maytag Co Maytag Good Government Committee Newton, IA	Appliances	$54,500	79 Candidates Avg House: $633 Avg Sen: $868	Repubs: 92.2% House: 69.7% Incumb: 63.3%	
MBNA Corp MBNA Corp Federal Political Committee Newark, DE	Commercial Banks	$60,000	35 Candidates Avg House: $1,621 Avg Sen: $2,167	Dems: 56.7% House: 78.3% Incumb: 71.7%	
MCA Inc MCA PAC Universal City, CA	Movies/TV†	$182,650	94 Candidates Avg House: $1,543 Avg Sen: $2,533	Dems: 83.0% Senate: 52.7% Incumb: 74.5%	
McCaw Cellular Communications McCaw Cellular Communications Inc PAC Kirkland, WA	Cellular Phones	$63,320	68 Candidates Avg House: $677 Avg Sen: $1,334	Dems: 79.4% House: 48.1% Incumb: 75.4%	
McDonald's Corp McDonald's Corporation PAC Oak Brook, IL	Restaurants	$232,900	189 Candidates Avg House: $759 Avg Sen: $4,074	Repubs: 73.4% House: 52.8% Incumb: 66.5%	
McDonnell Douglas McDonnell Douglas Good Government Fund St Louis, MO	Defense Aerospace†	$251,050	168 Candidates Avg House: $1,298 Avg Sen: $2,567	Dems: 56.9% House: 73.4% Incumb: 97.6%	
McDonnell Douglas Helicopter McDonnell Douglas Helicopter Company PAC Mesa, AZ	McDonnell Douglas	$50,225	59 Candidates Avg House: $770 Avg Sen: $1,250	Dems: 62.5% House: 75.1% Incumb: 97.5%	Defense Aerospace
MCI Telecommunications MCI Telecommunications PAC (MCI PAC) Washington, DC	Long Distance	$73,300	119 Candidates Avg House: $516 Avg Sen: $1,175	Dems: 71.4% House: 71.2% Incumb: 93.9%	
Mead Corp Mead Corporation Effective Citizenship Fund Dayton, OH	Paper/Pulp†	$67,450	60 Candidates Avg House: $974 Avg Sen: $1,425	Repubs: 79.6% House: 57.8% Incumb: 72.6%	
Mellon Bank Bipartisan PAC Mellon Bank Corporation (BIPAC/MBC) Pittsburgh, PA	Mellon Bank Corp	$51,304	61 Candidates Avg House: $670 Avg Sen: $1,641	Repubs: 53.0% House: 64.0% Incumb: 83.1%	Commercial Banks
Merck & Co Merck & Co, Inc PAC (Merck PAC) Rahway, NJ	Pharmaceuticals†	$138,050	147 Candidates Avg House: $723 Avg Sen: $1,857	Dems: 54.0% House: 62.3% Incumb: 81.9%	
Merrill Lynch Merrill Lynch PAC Washington, DC	Securities†	$191,264	137 Candidates Avg House: $927 Avg Sen: $2,533	Repubs: 53.4% Senate: 53.0% Incumb: 83.6%	
Metropolitan Life Insurance Metropolitan Employees' Political Participation Fund A New York, NY	Metropolitan Life	$266,342	175 Candidates Avg House: $1,277 Avg Sen: $2,252	Dems: 67.1% House: 61.4% Incumb: 83.9%	Life Insurance†
Michigan Bell Telephone Michigan Bell Telephone Company PAC (MICHBELLPAC) Detroit, MI	Ameritech	$86,687	29 Candidates Avg House: $3,007 Avg Sen: $2,500	Dems: 62.0% House: 97.1% Incumb: 87.8%	Phone Utilites
Michigan Consolidated Gas Michigan Consolidated Gas Company Federal PAC A/k/a Michcon Fer PAC Detroit, MI	Natural Gas	$86,700	44 Candidates Avg House: $1,879 Avg Sen: $1,970	Dems: 66.0% House: 71.5% Incumb: 86.5%	
Mid-America Dairymen Mid-America Dairymen Inc Agricultural & Dairy Educational Political Trust Adept Springfield, MO	Dairy	$343,371	209 Candidates Avg House: $1,496 Avg Sen: $2,638	Dems: 73.9% House: 78.9% Incumb: 84.3%	
Milk Industry Foundation Ice Cream & Milk PAC, PAC of the Int'l Ice Cream Assn & Milk Industry Foundation Washington, DC	Dairy	$132,600	105 Candidates Avg House: $876 Avg Sen: $2,381	Repubs: 71.3% House: 51.5% Incumb: 94.1%	
Milk Marketing Inc Milk Marketing Inc PAC Strongsville, OH	Dairy	$84,700	59 Candidates Avg House: $1,368 Avg Sen: $1,811	Dems: 64.0% House: 80.8% Incumb: 90.5%	
Minn-Dak Farmers Co-op Minn-Dak Farmers Cooperative PAC (MDFPAC) Wahpeton, ND	Sugar	$51,275	112 Candidates Avg House: $426 Avg Sen: $595	Dems: 57.6% House: 75.6% Incumb: 90.7%	

† PAC sponsor has other major interests in addition to this primary category

PAC Sponsor or Related Group/PAC Name	Affiliate	1991-92 Total	Where the money went...		
Minnesota Mining & Manufacturing (3M) Minnesota Mining & Manufacturing Company PAC (3M PAC) St. Paul, MN	 Industl/Comml Equip†	$76,750	100 Candidates Avg House: $595 Avg Sen: $1,556	Repubs: 75.2% House: 63.5% Incumb: 66.8%	
Mobil Oil Mobil Oil Corporation PAC (Aka Mobil PAC) Fairfax, VA	 Oil & Gas†	$195,750	183 Candidates Avg House: $640 Avg Sen: $3,446	Repubs: 92.8% House: 50.7% Incumb: 58.8%	
Monsanto Co Monsanto Citizenship Fund St. Louis, MO	 Monsanto Chemicals†	$113,955	98 Candidates Avg House: $717 Avg Sen: $2,900	Repubs: 79.3% Senate: 50.9% Incumb: 69.8%	
Montgomery Ward Montgomery Ward & Co Incorporated PAC Aka WardPAC Chicago, IL	 Department Stores†	$51,250	49 Candidates Avg House: $904 Avg Sen: $1,220	Dems: 54.6% Senate: 52.4% Incumb: 86.3%	
MOPAC MOPAC Troy, MI	 Pro-Israel	$68,300	64 Candidates Avg House: $915 Avg Sen: $1,488	Dems: 100.0% House: 63.0% Incumb: 66.3%	
JP Morgan & Co Morgan Companies PAC (MorganPAC) New York, NY	 Commercial Banks†	$423,050	145 Candidates Avg House: $2,951 Avg Sen: $2,818	Dems: 53.8% House: 77.4% Incumb: 86.3%	
Morgan Stanley & Co Morgan Stanley Better Government Fund New York, NY	 Morgan Stanley Investmtent Banking†	$220,196	115 Candidates Avg House: $1,709 Avg Sen: $2,739	Dems: 65.3% House: 71.4% Incumb: 92.8%	
Morrison-Knudsen Morrison-Knudsen PAC Boise, ID	 Heavy Construction†	$107,675	122 Candidates Avg House: $731 Avg Sen: $1,327	Dems: 64.7% House: 61.8% Incumb: 92.6%	
Mortgage Bankers Assn of America Mortgage Bankers Association of America PAC Washington, DC	 Mortgage Banking	$220,900	208 Candidates Avg House: $924 Avg Sen: $2,029	Repubs: 53.2% House: 76.1% Incumb: 67.3%	
Motorola Inc Motorola Employees Good Government Committee Washington, DC	 Communication Equip†	$98,445	113 Candidates Avg House: $632 Avg Sen: $1,633	Repubs: 57.7% House: 55.2% Incumb: 86.9%	
Multi-Issue PAC Multi-Issue PAC (MI-PAC) Highland Park, IL	 Pro-Israel	$88,750	74 Candidates Avg House: $475 Avg Sen: $2,783	Dems: 100.0% Senate: 72.1% Incumb: 38.0%	
Mutual Life Insurance of New York Mutual Life Insurance Company of New York Mony PAC New York, NY	 Insurance	$51,750	44 Candidates Avg House: $1,098 Avg Sen: $1,267	Dems: 70.0% House: 59.4% Incumb: 79.7%	
Mutual of Omaha Mutual of Omaha Companies PAC (IMPAC) Omaha, NE	 Mutual of Omaha Insurance	$125,646	98 Candidates Avg House: $1,184 Avg Sen: $1,583	Repubs: 54.3% House: 69.8% Incumb: 83.4%	
Nabisco Brands Inc Nabisco Brands, Inc Program for Active Citizenship (NABPAC) East Hanover, NJ	 RJR Nabisco Food Processors	$108,400	129 Candidates Avg House: $775 Avg Sen: $1,125	Dems: 53.9% House: 75.1% Incumb: 85.7%	
National Abortion Rights Action League National Abortion Rights Action League - PAC NARAL-PAC Washington, DC	 Natl Abortion Rts Action Lge Pro-Choice	$503,046	165 Candidates Avg House: $2,792 Avg Sen: $4,527	Dems: 91.5% House: 78.2% Incumb: 44.2%	
National Action Committee National Action Committee - NACPAC Miami, FL	 Pro-Israel	$143,949	74 Candidates Avg House: $967 Avg Sen: $3,552	Dems: 65.8% Senate: 69.1% Incumb: 83.3%	
National Air Traffic Controllers Assn National Air Traffic Controllers Association PAC (aka NATCA PAC) Washington, DC	 Air Transport Unions	$87,400	72 Candidates Avg House: $1,154 Avg Sen: $1,513	Dems: 90.0% House: 79.2% Incumb: 85.2%	
National Albanian American PAC National Albanian American PAC Palm Beach Gardens, FL	 Ethnic Groups	$90,000	14 Candidates Avg House: $5,750 Avg Sen: $7,333	Repubs: 73.3% House: 51.1% Incumb: 77.8%	
National Assn of Broadcasters National Association of Broadcasters Television And Radio PAC Washington, DC	 TV/Radio	$493,951	203 Candidates Avg House: $1,978 Avg Sen: $4,129	Dems: 53.9% House: 64.0% Incumb: 90.1%	

PAC Sponsor or Related Group/PAC Name	Affiliate	1991-92 Total	Where the money went...		
National Assn of Chain Drug Stores National Association of Chain Drug Stores, Inc. PAC Alexandria, VA	Drug Stores†	$91,050	70 Candidates Avg House: $1,045 Avg Sen: $1,792	Dems: 57.4% House: 52.8% Incumb: 80.7%	
National Assn of Convenience Stores National Association of Convenience Stores Alexandria, VA	Department Stores	$105,695	125 Candidates Avg House: $680 Avg Sen: $1,542	Repubs: 80.6% House: 65.0% Incumb: 66.4%	
National Assn of Federal Credit Unions National Association of Federal Credit Unions PAC (Nafcupac) Arlington, VA	Credit Unions	$69,750	87 Candidates Avg House: $744 Avg Sen: $1,250	Dems: 69.2% House: 82.1% Incumb: 92.6%	
National Assn of Home Builders BUILD PAC of the National Association of Home Builders Washington, DC	Natl Assn of Home Bldrs	$1,072,926	422 Candidates Avg House: $2,256 Avg Sen: $4,826	Repubs: 55.7% House: 78.9% Incumb: 74.5%	Resid Construction†
National Assn of Independent Insurers National Association of Independent Insurers PAC Des Plaines, IL	Insurance	$241,725	176 Candidates Avg House: $813 Avg Sen: $3,411	Repubs: 82.7% Senate: 53.6% Incumb: 79.6%	
National Assn of Letter Carriers Committee on Letter Carriers Pol Education (Letter Carriers Pol Action Fund) Washington, DC	Letter Carriers Union	$1,634,277	378 Candidates Avg House: $3,913 Avg Sen: $7,250	Dems: 89.8% House: 78.5% Incumb: 68.4%	Postal Unions
National Assn of Life Companies National Association of Life Cos PAC (NALC/PAC) Washington, DC	Life Insurance†	$80,900	88 Candidates Avg House: $716 Avg Sen: $1,404	Repubs: 52.2% House: 54.9% Incumb: 78.9%	
National Assn of Life Underwriters National Association of Life Underwriters PAC Washington, DC	Life Insurance	$1,371,600	440 Candidates Avg House: $2,759 Avg Sen: $5,340	Dems: 53.8% House: 76.2% Incumb: 73.2%	
National Assn of Pharmacists National Association of Pharmacists PAC Alexandria, VA	Pharmacists†	$154,900	106 Candidates Avg House: $1,223 Avg Sen: $2,125	Dems: 80.6% House: 61.6% Incumb: 88.3%	
National Assn of Postal Supervisors National Association of Postal Supervisors PAC Washington, DC	Postal Unions	$137,050	172 Candidates Avg House: $727 Avg Sen: $1,250	Dems: 83.4% House: 79.0% Incumb: 79.6%	
National Assn of Postmasters NAPUS PAC for Postmasters (Fka Political Education for Postmasters) Alexandria, VA	Postal Unions	$334,195	281 Candidates Avg House: $1,020 Avg Sen: $1,841	Dems: 86.3% House: 69.3% Incumb: 85.1%	
National Assn of Private Psychiatric Hospitals National Association of Private Psychiatric Hospitals/PAC Washington, DC	Hospitals	$92,950	69 Candidates Avg House: $999 Avg Sen: $2,091	Dems: 68.6% House: 50.5% Incumb: 86.0%	
National Assn of Professional Insurance Agents Professional Insurance Agents PAC Alexandria, VA	Insurance	$146,224	145 Candidates Avg House: $860 Avg Sen: $1,533	Repubs: 53.0% House: 66.5% Incumb: 88.3%	
National Assn of Realtors Realtors PAC Chicago, IL	Natl Assn of Realtors	$2,950,138	540 Candidates Avg House: $5,592 Avg Sen: $4,412	Dems: 55.0% House: 91.2% Incumb: 78.9%	Real Estate Agents
National Assn of Retired Federal Employees National Association of Retired Federal Employees PAC (NARFE-PAC) Washington, DC	Fedl Worker Unions	$1,437,250	455 Candidates Avg House: $2,985 Avg Sen: $4,826	Dems: 80.5% House: 85.6% Incumb: 79.4%	
National Assn of Social Workers National Association of Social Workers Political Action for Candidate Election Silver Spring, MD	Natl Assn of Social Workers	$180,746	179 Candidates Avg House: $818 Avg Sen: $1,761	Dems: 98.2% House: 63.8% Incumb: 47.3%	Social Workers
National Assn of Temporary Services National Association of Temporary Services PAC Alexandria, VA	Employment Agencies	$74,500	62 Candidates Avg House: $1,049 Avg Sen: $1,909	Repubs: 75.2% House: 71.8% Incumb: 40.9%	
National Assn of Trade & Technical Schools National Association of Trade and Technical Schools PAC Washington, DC	Vocational/Tech Educ	$80,800	55 Candidates Avg House: $1,333 Avg Sen: $2,250	Dems: 68.4% House: 75.9% Incumb: 91.9%	
National Assn of Truck Stop Operators National Association of Truck Stop Operators Alexandria, VA	Trucking Companies	$57,903	89 Candidates Avg House: $591 Avg Sen: $1,000	Repubs: 64.1% House: 77.5% Incumb: 78.4%	

† PAC sponsor has other major interests in addition to this primary category

PAC Sponsor or Related Group/PAC Name	Affiliate	1991-92 Total	Where the money went...		
National Assn of Water Companies National Association of Water Companies PAC (NAWC - PAC) Washington, DC	Water Utilities	$86,200	102 Candidates Avg House: $670 Avg Sen: $1,286	Dems: 55.9% House: 56.7% Incumb: 85.0%	
National Assn of Wholesale-Distributors Wholesaler-Distributor PAC of the National Association of Wholesale-Distributors Washington, DC	Wholesale Trade	$102,459	132 Candidates Avg House: $551 Avg Sen: $1,842	Repubs: 87.3% House: 58.6% Incumb: 61.3%	
National Auto Dealers Assn Dealers Election Action Cmte of the Nat'l Automobile Dealers Assn (NADA) Mclean, VA	Auto Dealers	$1,784,375	449 Candidates Avg House: $3,840 Avg Sen: $5,153	Repubs: 60.7% House: 86.7% Incumb: 69.4%	
National Beer Wholesalers Assn National Beer Wholesalers' Association PAC (NBWA PAC) Falls Church, VA	Liquor Wholesalers	$977,081	453 Candidates Avg House: $1,902 Avg Sen: $4,082	Repubs: 62.5% House: 77.9% Incumb: 74.9%	
National Broiler Council National Broiler Council PAC Washington, DC	Poultry/Egg	$183,750	147 Candidates Avg House: $1,013 Avg Sen: $2,037	Dems: 53.0% House: 62.3% Incumb: 86.7%	
National Cable Television Assn National Cable Television Association's PAC (Cable PAC) Washington, DC	Cable TV	$636,199	167 Candidates Avg House: $3,207 Avg Sen: $5,986	Dems: 53.4% House: 65.0% Incumb: 92.3%	
National Cattlemen's Assn National Cattlemen's Association PAC Englewood, CO	Natl Cattlemens Assn	Livestock	$297,670	258 Candidates Avg House: $946 Avg Sen: $2,087	Repubs: 55.0% House: 67.0% Incumb: 77.5%
National City Corp National City Corporation PAC Is Aka National City PAC Or (Nc PAC) Cleveland, OH	Commercial Banks	$65,980	57 Candidates Avg House: $1,153 Avg Sen: $1,173	Repubs: 57.1% House: 76.9% Incumb: 68.1%	
National Coal Assn COALPAC - The PAC of the National Coal Association Washington, DC	Coal	$239,848	163 Candidates Avg House: $997 Avg Sen: $4,361	Repubs: 75.3% House: 58.2% Incumb: 66.2%	
National Committee for an Effective Congress National Committee for An Effective Congress Washington, DC	Dem/Liberal	$650,750	222 Candidates Avg House: $2,702 Avg Sen: $4,242	Dems: 100.0% House: 78.5% Incumb: 55.0%	
National Committee to Preserve Social Secur National Committee to Preserve Social Security PAC Washington, DC	Elderly/Soc Security	$941,650	347 Candidates Avg House: $2,348 Avg Sen: $5,134	Dems: 88.1% House: 75.0% Incumb: 82.3%	
National Community Action Foundation Community Action Program-PAC (SSF of National Community Action Foundation Inc) Washington, DC	Health/Welfare	$120,350	40 Candidates Avg House: $2,493 Avg Sen: $3,706	Dems: 87.5% Senate: 52.4% Incumb: 81.1%	
National Cotton Council National Cotton Council Committee for the Advancement of Cotton Memphis, TN	Cotton	$183,739	143 Candidates Avg House: $1,066 Avg Sen: $2,077	Dems: 62.3% House: 65.0% Incumb: 98.5%	
National Council of Farmer Co-ops National Council of Farmer Cooperatives Political Action Commitee (Co-op/PAC) Washington, DC	Farm Orgs	$128,000	148 Candidates Avg House: $697 Avg Sen: $1,406	Dems: 69.1% House: 61.6% Incumb: 91.6%	
National Council of Savings Institutions National Council of Savings Institutions (THRIFTPAC) Washington, DC	Natl Council of Savings Insts	Savings & Loans	$64,542	92 Candidates Avg House: $658 Avg Sen: $1,106	Dems: 68.3% House: 84.6% Incumb: 92.0%
National Council of Senior Citizens National Council of Senior Citizens PAC Washington, DC	Elderly/Soc Security	$221,750	74 Candidates Avg House: $2,232 Avg Sen: $5,211	Dems: 100.0% House: 55.4% Incumb: 42.5%	
National Crushed Stone Assn National Stone Association STONEPAC Washington, DC	Stone/Concrete	$50,875	56 Candidates Avg House: $836 Avg Sen: $1,212	Repubs: 63.8% House: 69.0% Incumb: 82.6%	
National Education Assn National Education Association PAC Washington, DC	Natl Education Assn	Teachers	$2,329,622	409 Candidates Avg House: $5,626 Avg Sen: $6,249	Dems: 95.7% House: 87.7% Incumb: 54.6%
National Electrical Contractors Assn Electrical Construction PAC-Nat'l Electrical Contractors Assn Inc (ECPAC) Bethesda, MD	Electr Contractors	$163,500	97 Candidates Avg House: $1,380 Avg Sen: $2,727	Repubs: 84.7% House: 63.3% Incumb: 69.4%	

PAC Sponsor or Related Group/PAC Name	Affiliate	1991-92 Total	Where the money went...			
National Federation of Independent Business National Federation of Independent Business Free Enterprise PAC San Mateo, CA	Small Business Assns	$293,587	171 Candidates Avg House: $1,441 Avg Sen: $3,690	Repubs: 86.9% House: 73.6% Incumb: 44.9%		
National Forest Products Assn Forest Industries PAC Washington, DC	Forest Products†	$51,547	56 Candidates Avg House: $773 Avg Sen: $1,364	Repubs: 61.2% House: 62.9% Incumb: 81.2%		
National League of Postmasters National League of Postmasters PAC Alexandria, VA	Postal Unions	$216,400	243 Candidates Avg House: $756 Avg Sen: $1,519	Dems: 76.1% House: 69.8% Incumb: 92.3%		
National Machine Tool Builders Assn Machine Toolpac Mclean, VA	Industl/Comml Equip	$57,100	80 Candidates Avg House: $503 Avg Sen: $1,348	Repubs: 64.5% House: 52.8% Incumb: 84.9%		
National Marine Manufacturers Assn National Marine Manufacturers Association PAC Washington, DC	Shipbuilding/Repair	$73,000	43 Candidates Avg House: $1,435 Avg Sen: $2,689	Repubs: 57.1% House: 66.8% Incumb: 93.8%		
National Medical Enterprises Inc National Medical Enterprises Inc PAC Santa Monica, CA	Hospitals†	$84,575	88 Candidates Avg House: $701 Avg Sen: $1,845	Dems: 52.8% House: 56.4% Incumb: 57.6%		
National Organization for Women NOW/PAC (National Organization for Women PAC) Washington, DC	Womens Issues	$322,385	102 Candidates Avg House: $2,942 Avg Sen: $4,660	Dems: 89.2% House: 81.2% Incumb: 11.5%		
National PAC National PAC Washington, DC	Pro-Israel	$684,000	175 Candidates Avg House: $3,442 Avg Sen: $5,667	Dems: 64.6% House: 69.4% Incumb: 81.4%		
National Pest Control Assn National Pest Control Association PAC Dunn Loring, VA	Pest Control	$56,200	47 Candidates Avg House: $1,153 Avg Sen: $1,321	Dems: 50.4% House: 71.8% Incumb: 96.0%		
National Pork Producers Council National Pork Producers Council Pork PAC Des Moines, IA	Livestock	$155,031	162 Candidates Avg House: $755 Avg Sen: $1,482	Dems: 51.5% House: 57.0% Incumb: 87.7%		
National Realty Committee National Realty PAC (RealPAC) Washington, DC	Real Estate Devel	$64,141	58 Candidates Avg House: $1,043 Avg Sen: $1,303	Dems: 71.5% House: 71.6% Incumb: 91.0%		
National Restaurant Assn National Restaurant Association PAC Washington, DC	Natl Restaurant Assn / Restaurants	$560,447	235 Candidates Avg House: $2,013 Avg Sen: $4,659	Repubs: 77.4% House: 72.6% Incumb: 61.2%		
National Rifle Assn NRA Political Victory Fund Washington, DC	Pro-Guns	$1,735,946	346 Candidates Avg House: $4,902 Avg Sen: $5,790	Repubs: 63.3% House: 85.0% Incumb: 60.2%		
National Right to Life PAC National Right To Life PAC Washington, DC	Right to Life / Pro-Life	$231,614	147 Candidates Avg House: $1,473 Avg Sen: $2,191	Repubs: 88.4% House: 78.9% Incumb: 33.7%		
National Rural Letter Carriers Assn National Rural Letter Carriers' Association PAC Alexandria, VA	Postal Unions	$526,528	359 Candidates Avg House: $1,010 Avg Sen: $4,826	Dems: 86.0% House: 60.4% Incumb: 75.2%		
National Society of Professional Engineers National Society of Professional Engineers - PAC (NSPE-PAC) Alexandria, VA	Engineers	$82,050	70 Candidates Avg House: $1,118 Avg Sen: $1,500	Repubs: 61.1% House: 81.7% Incumb: 77.9%		
National Soft Drink Assn Soft Drink PAC Washington, DC	Soft Drinks	$52,814	72 Candidates Avg House: $648 Avg Sen: $1,031	Dems: 52.8% House: 68.8% Incumb: 91.7%		
National Steel & Shipbuilding National Steel And Shipbuilding Company PAC (aka) Nassco PAC San Diego, CA	Shipbuilding/Repair	$54,384	25 Candidates Avg House: $2,007 Avg Sen: $2,607	Repubs: 75.4% House: 66.4% Incumb: 86.4%		
National Telephone Co-op Assn National Telephone Cooperative Assn Telephone Education Cmte Organization Washington, DC	Phone Utilites	$84,492	161 Candidates Avg House: $462 Avg Sen: $836	Dems: 70.1% House: 73.3% Incumb: 91.1%		

† PAC sponsor has other major interests in addition to this primary category

PAC Sponsor or Related Group/PAC Name	Affiliate		1991-92 Total	Where the money went...		
National Tooling & Machining Assn Tooling & Machining PAC of the National Tooling And Machining Association Ft Washington, MD		Industl/Comml Equip	$57,560	64 Candidates Avg House: $758 Avg Sen: $1,513	Repubs: 84.2% House: 68.5% Incumb: 85.2%	
National Treasury Employees Union National Treasury Employees Union PAC (Tepac) Washington, DC		Fedl Worker Unions	$181,160	136 Candidates Avg House: $991 Avg Sen: $2,050	Dems: 95.8% House: 52.0% Incumb: 78.5%	
National Turkey Federation National Turkey Federation Political Action Commitee/TURPAC Reston, VA		Poultry/Egg	$54,650	51 Candidates Avg House: $975 Avg Sen: $1,303	Repubs: 52.6% House: 64.2% Incumb: 96.7%	
National Utility Contractors Assn National Utility Contractors Assn Legislative Information & Action Committee Arlington, VA		Heavy Construction	$203,580	179 Candidates Avg House: $1,058 Avg Sen: $1,897	Repubs: 61.6% House: 84.2% Incumb: 82.1%	
National Venture Capital Assn National Venture Capital Association PAC (NVCA PAC) Washington, DC		Venture Capital	$220,492	98 Candidates Avg House: $1,475 Avg Sen: $3,848	Dems: 53.5% Senate: 55.9% Incumb: 85.0%	
National Wholesale Grocers Assn National American Wholesale Grocers' Association PAC: NAWGAPAC Falls Church, VA		Food Wholesalers	$83,839	138 Candidates Avg House: $584 Avg Sen: $721	Repubs: 93.3% House: 79.4% Incumb: 73.8%	
National Womens Political Caucus National Women's Political Caucus Campaign Support Committee Washington, DC	Natl Womens Pol Caucus	Womens Issues	$69,800	36 Candidates Avg House: $1,531 Avg Sen: $5,200	Dems: 94.3% House: 70.2% Incumb: 5.0%	
National Womens Political Caucus National Women's Political Caucus Victory Fund (NWPC) Washington, DC	Natl Womens Pol Caucus	Womens Issues	$136,220	55 Candidates Avg House: $2,135 Avg Sen: $4,817	Dems: 87.9% House: 75.2% Incumb: 13.9%	
Nationwide Corp Nationwide Political Participation Committee Columbus, OH	Nationwide Mutual Insurance	Insurance	$69,634	60 Candidates Avg House: $1,022 Avg Sen: $2,063	Repubs: 66.5% House: 76.3% Incumb: 63.8%	
Nestle Enterprises Inc Nestle Enterprises Inc PAC Solon, OH		Food & Beverage	$83,867	113 Candidates Avg House: $536 Avg Sen: $1,505	Dems: 68.4% House: 56.9% Incumb: 61.0%	
New England Mutual Life New England Mutual Life Insurance Company PAC/new England Life PAC (Nelpac) Boston, MA		Life Insurance	$80,850	67 Candidates Avg House: $1,141 Avg Sen: $1,433	Dems: 62.4% House: 73.4% Incumb: 86.5%	
New York Life New York Life PAC - Federal Fund (New York Life PAC - Federal) New York, NY		Life Insurance	$134,150	102 Candidates Avg House: $1,049 Avg Sen: $2,136	Dems: 61.8% House: 60.2% Incumb: 79.9%	
New York Medical Assn New York Medical PAC Lake Success, NY	American Medical Assn	Doctors	$94,653	28 Candidates Avg House: $3,492 Avg Sen: $2,451	Dems: 64.3% House: 92.2% Incumb: 86.7%	
New York Stock Exchange New York Stock Exchange Inc PAC (NYSE PAC) Washington, DC		Stock Exchanges	$58,650	56 Candidates Avg House: $770 Avg Sen: $1,633	Dems: 65.6% Senate: 50.1% Incumb: 97.4%	
New York Telephone New York Telephone Federal PAC New York, NY	NYNEX	Phone Utilites	$51,710	39 Candidates Avg House: $1,339 Avg Sen: $1,215	Repubs: 53.7% House: 90.6% Incumb: 82.5%	
Norfolk Southern Corp Norfolk Southern Corporation Good Government Fund Norfolk, VA	Norfolk Southern	Railroads†	$175,820	186 Candidates Avg House: $847 Avg Sen: $1,419	Dems: 61.8% House: 74.2% Incumb: 93.7%	
Norstar Bancorp Norstar Bancorp Inc PAC Providence, RI	Fleet/Norstar Financial Group	Commercial Banks	$65,000	65 Candidates Avg House: $880 Avg Sen: $1,289	Dems: 65.7% House: 62.3% Incumb: 82.3%	
North American Philips Corp North American Philips Corporation PAC Washington, DC	Philips Group	Electronics Mfg†	$69,450	63 Candidates Avg House: $940 Avg Sen: $1,671	Repubs: 81.4% House: 66.3% Incumb: 83.4%	
North American Van Lines North American Van Lines, Inc PAC (NAPAC) Fort Wayne, IN	Norfolk Southern	Trucking Companies	$53,350	52 Candidates Avg House: $864 Avg Sen: $3,667	Dems: 65.5% House: 79.4% Incumb: 98.5%	

PAC Sponsor or Related Group/PAC Name	Affiliate	1991-92 Total	Where the money went...		
North Jersey PAC North Jersey PAC New York, NY	 Pro-Israel	$136,750	86 Candidates Avg House: $909 Avg Sen: $3,000	Dems: 73.9% Senate: 57.0% Incumb: 83.2%	
Northrop Corp Northrop Employees PAC (Aka NEPAC) San Francisco, CA	 Defense Aerospace†	$360,015	212 Candidates Avg House: $1,327 Avg Sen: $3,202	Repubs: 55.2% House: 62.6% Incumb: 85.9%	
Northwest Airlines Northwest Airlines PAC (Fka Republic Airlines PAC) St Paul, MN	 Airlines	$156,224	103 Candidates Avg House: $1,270 Avg Sen: $2,150	Dems: 66.5% House: 58.5% Incumb: 90.6%	
Northwestern Mutual Life Northwestern Mutual Life Insurance Company Federal PAC (NML Fedpac) Milwaukee, WI	 Life Insurance	$240,580	110 Candidates Avg House: $2,026 Avg Sen: $2,563	Dems: 61.4% House: 64.8% Incumb: 88.0%	
Norwest Corp Norwest Corporation PAC (Norwest PAC) Minneapolis, MN	 Commercial Banks	$80,700	75 Candidates Avg House: $1,042 Avg Sen: $1,191	Dems: 63.1% House: 74.9% Incumb: 91.0%	
NYNEX Corp NYNEX Federal PAC New York, NY	 NYNEX Phone Utilites†	$111,790	98 Candidates Avg House: $909 Avg Sen: $1,984	Repubs: 60.1% House: 61.0% Incumb: 73.9%	
O'Melveny & Myers O'Melveny & Myers PAC Washington, DC	 Lawyers	$75,204	60 Candidates Avg House: $1,053 Avg Sen: $1,577	Dems: 64.8% Senate: 50.3% Incumb: 47.5%	
Occidental Petroleum Occidental Petroleum Corporation PAC Los Angeles, CA	 Oil & Gas†	$179,900	98 Candidates Avg House: $1,269 Avg Sen: $3,500	Dems: 59.8% House: 50.8% Incumb: 76.9%	
Ocean Spray Cranberries Inc Ocean Spray PAC Lakeville-middlebo, MA	 Fruit/Veg	$137,950	123 Candidates Avg House: $1,011 Avg Sen: $1,412	Dems: 70.1% House: 63.8% Incumb: 96.0%	
Office & Professional Employees Union Office and Professional Employees International Union-Voice of the Electorate Washington, DC	 Office/Prof Employees Misc Labor Unions	$158,950	84 Candidates Avg House: $1,370 Avg Sen: $3,283	Dems: 100.0% House: 50.9% Incumb: 58.7%	
Oil, Chemical & Atomic Workers Union Oil, Chemical & Atomic Workers Int'l Union Cmte on Pol Educ Fund (OCAW-COPE) Denver, CO	 Oil Chemical & Atomic Wkrs Energy Unions	$102,790	81 Candidates Avg House: $1,048 Avg Sen: $1,764	Dems: 96.1% House: 57.1% Incumb: 51.7%	
Operating Engineers Union Engineers Pol Education Cmte (EPEC)/Int'l Union of Operating Engineers Washington, DC	 Building Trade Unions	$410,850	315 Candidates Avg House: $972 Avg Sen: $3,491	Dems: 93.7% House: 64.8% Incumb: 71.9%	
Operating Engineers Union Local #825 Int'l Union of Operating Engineers Lo 825 Pol Action and Education Cmte Little Falls, NJ	 Operating Engineers Union Bldg Trade Unions	$54,225	20 Candidates Avg House: $2,957 Avg Sen: $500	Dems: 62.6% House: 98.2% Incumb: 59.5%	
Opperman & Paquin Opperman & Paquin Political Fund Minneapolis, MN	 Lawyers	$82,229	31 Candidates Avg House: $3,021 Avg Sen: $2,314	Dems: 93.3% House: 58.8% Incumb: 87.7%	
Outdoor Advertising Assn of America Outdoor Advertising PAC (OAPAC) Washington, DC	 Outdoor Advertising	$211,500	104 Candidates Avg House: $1,079 Avg Sen: $4,182	Dems: 63.1% Senate: 63.3% Incumb: 86.2%	
Owens-Corning Fiberglas Owens-Corning Fiberglas Corporation Employees' Better Government Fund Toledo, OH	 Bldg Materials†	$63,634	52 Candidates Avg House: $787 Avg Sen: $2,049	Repubs: 64.6% Senate: 58.0% Incumb: 82.7%	
Owens-Illinois Owens-Illinois Inc Employees Good Citizenship Fund Toledo, OH	 Kohlberg, Kravis & Roberts Glass Products†	$53,550	41 Candidates Avg House: $1,278 Avg Sen: $1,382	Repubs: 62.6% House: 71.6% Incumb: 85.4%	
Pacific Enterprises Pacific Enterprises Political Assistance Committee Los Angeles, CA	 Natural Gas†	$99,230	75 Candidates Avg House: $955 Avg Sen: $2,104	Dems: 63.3% Senate: 50.9% Incumb: 72.5%	
Pacific Gas & Electric Pacific Gas and Electric Company Employees' Federal Good Government Fund San Francisco, CA	 Gas & Electric Util†	$140,235	87 Candidates Avg House: $1,561 Avg Sen: $1,754	Dems: 60.9% House: 71.2% Incumb: 88.0%	

† PAC sponsor has other major interests in addition to this primary category

PAC Sponsor or Related Group/PAC Name	Affiliate	1991-92 Total	Where the money went...		
Pacific Mutual Life Pacific Mutual Life Insurance Company PAC (PMPAC) Newport Beach, CA	Life Insurance	$103,250	65 Candidates Avg House: $1,358 Avg Sen: $2,071	Dems: 62.0% House: 57.9% Incumb: 72.4%	
Pacific Telesis Group Pacific Telesis Group Federal PAC (Pacific Telesis Federal PAC) San Francisco, CA	Phone Utilites†	$310,762	194 Candidates Avg House: $1,471 Avg Sen: $2,160	Dems: 61.8% House: 74.3% Incumb: 85.1%	
PaineWebber PaineWebber Fund for Better Government New York, NY	Securities	$85,475	61 Candidates Avg House: $921 Avg Sen: $2,048	Dems: 68.7% Senate: 62.3% Incumb: 85.7%	
Painters & Allied Trades Union Int'l Brotherhood of Painters & Allied Trades Political Action Together Pol Cmte Washington, DC	Painters & Allied Trades Building Trade Unions	$279,002	172 Candidates Avg House: $1,379 Avg Sen: $2,549	Dems: 93.7% House: 67.7% Incumb: 50.9%	
Paramount Communications Gulf + Western Industries Inc PAC New York, NY	Movies/TV†	$92,250	41 Candidates Avg House: $2,307 Avg Sen: $2,250	Dems: 79.4% House: 55.0% Incumb: 85.1%	
Peabody Coal Peabody PAC St Louis, MO	Coal	$78,213	66 Candidates Avg House: $839 Avg Sen: $1,981	Repubs: 51.6% Senate: 50.6% Incumb: 93.2%	
Pelican PAC Pelican PAC Seattle, WA	Sen J Bennett Johnston (D-La) Dem Leaders	$93,284	25 Candidates Avg House: $3,500 Avg Sen: $3,804	Dems: 100.0% Senate: 77.5% Incumb: 84.2%	
JC Penney Co J C Penney Company PAC (Penney PAC) Dallas, TX	Department Stores†	$195,615	222 Candidates Avg House: $767 Avg Sen: $1,387	Dems: 57.6% House: 70.9% Incumb: 89.9%	
Pepsi-Cola General Bottlers Pepsi-Cola General Bottlers PAC Rolling Meadows, IL	Beverage Bottling	$79,695	57 Candidates Avg House: $1,294 Avg Sen: $1,813	Dems: 55.1% House: 71.5% Incumb: 88.4%	
Pepsico Inc Pepsico Concerned Citizens Fund Purchase, NY	Soft Drinks/Food†	$297,074	194 Candidates Avg House: $1,286 Avg Sen: $3,270	Repubs: 65.4% House: 73.6% Incumb: 69.6%	
Petroleum Marketers Assn Petroleum Marketers Association of America Small Businessmen's Committee Washington, DC	Gas Stations†	$262,325	236 Candidates Avg House: $875 Avg Sen: $2,677	Repubs: 63.3% House: 68.4% Incumb: 77.6%	
Pfizer Inc Pfizer PAC New York, NY	Pharmaceuticals†	$188,100	162 Candidates Avg House: $787 Avg Sen: $2,382	Repubs: 52.1% House: 51.9% Incumb: 83.7%	
Phelps Dodge Corp Phelps Dodge Employees Fund for Good Government Phoenix, AZ	Metal Mining/Process	$84,800	52 Candidates Avg House: $1,397 Avg Sen: $2,112	Repubs: 73.2% House: 57.7% Incumb: 86.3%	
Philadelphia Electric Philadelphia Electric Company Federal PAC (PECOPAC) Philadelphia, PA	Gas & Electric Util	$86,050	84 Candidates Avg House: $820 Avg Sen: $1,806	Repubs: 54.0% House: 61.9% Incumb: 64.7%	
Philip Morris Philip Morris PAC (Aka PHIL-PAC) New York, NY	Tobacco/Food†	$624,049	366 Candidates Avg House: $1,489 Avg Sen: $2,862	Dems: 62.2% House: 74.0% Incumb: 84.5%	
Phillips Petroleum Phillips Petroleum Company PAC Bartlesville, OK	Oil & Gas†	$171,689	155 Candidates Avg House: $971 Avg Sen: $1,854	Repubs: 72.3% House: 74.1% Incumb: 49.6%	
Pinkerton Tobacco Pinkerton Tobacco Company PAC Richmond, VA	Tobacco	$66,475	64 Candidates Avg House: $766 Avg Sen: $1,684	Dems: 50.2% House: 51.9% Incumb: 90.2%	
Pittston Co Pittston Company PAC Greenwich, CT	Coal†	$52,950	65 Candidates Avg House: $671 Avg Sen: $1,076	Repubs: 51.3% House: 53.3% Incumb: 83.0%	
Planning Research Corp Emhart PAC Mclean, VA	Black & Decker Computers†	$50,600	45 Candidates Avg House: $1,068 Avg Sen: $1,429	Dems: 52.7% House: 80.2% Incumb: 90.3%	

PAC Sponsor or Related Group/PAC Name	Affiliate	1991-92 Total	Where the money went...		
Plumbers/Pipefitters Union United Assn of Journeymen and Apprentices of the Plumb and Pipeftrs Indus Washington, DC	Building Trade Unions	$835,456	309 Candidates Avg House: $2,289 Avg Sen: $5,518	Dems: 96.2% House: 73.7% Incumb: 69.0%	
Powell, Goldstein et al Powell, Goldstein, Frazer & Murphy PAC Atlanta, GA	Lawyers	$123,285	139 Candidates Avg House: $677 Avg Sen: $1,307	Dems: 88.5% House: 50.0% Incumb: 85.7%	
Preston, Gates et al Preston, Thorgrimson, Ellis & Holman PAC Washington, DC	Lawyers	$114,839	161 Candidates Avg House: $681 Avg Sen: $881	Dems: 70.6% House: 79.5% Incumb: 89.4%	
Price Waterhouse Price Waterhouse Partners' PAC Washington, DC	Accountants	$92,047	52 Candidates Avg House: $1,447 Avg Sen: $2,567	Dems: 62.5% House: 58.2% Incumb: 98.9%	
Principal Mutual Life Insurance Principal Mutual Life Insurance Company - Federal PAC (Fka Bankers Life Co PAC) Des Moines, IA	Insurance	$103,777	97 Candidates Avg House: $865 Avg Sen: $1,746	Dems: 57.4% House: 60.8% Incumb: 87.1%	
Printing Industries of America Printing Industries of America PAC (Print PAC) Arlington, VA	Printing	$105,502	87 Candidates Avg House: $634 Avg Sen: $2,569	Repubs: 93.4% Senate: 63.3% Incumb: 56.4%	
Procter & Gamble Procter & Gamble Co Good Government Committee, The (Aka P&G PAC) Cincinnati, OH	Household Chemicals†	$77,200	90 Candidates Avg House: $684 Avg Sen: $1,429	Repubs: 51.7% House: 61.1% Incumb: 90.3%	
Prudential Insurance Prudential Insurance Company of America Federal PAC ("Prudential PAC") Newark, NJ	Insurance†	$262,360	157 Candidates Avg House: $1,098 Avg Sen: $3,466	Dems: 66.4% Senate: 50.2% Incumb: 79.7%	
Prudential Securities Prudential-Bache Securities Inc PAC New York, NY	Prudential Insurance / Securities	$138,475	122 Candidates Avg House: $910 Avg Sen: $1,717	Repubs: 52.2% House: 57.8% Incumb: 68.7%	
Public Securities Assn Public Securities Association Washington, DC	Securities	$135,239	140 Candidates Avg House: $832 Avg Sen: $1,555	Dems: 69.5% House: 70.1% Incumb: 89.5%	
Public Service Electric & Gas Public Service Electric And Gas Company PAC (PEGPAC) Newark, NJ	Gas & Electric Util†	$121,537	120 Candidates Avg House: $1,068 Avg Sen: $835	Dems: 51.3% House: 83.5% Incumb: 88.1%	
Public Service Research Council Public Service PAC Reston, VA	Anti-Union	$140,553	172 Candidates Avg House: $608 Avg Sen: $2,174	Repubs: 98.3% House: 64.4% Incumb: 50.8%	
Raytheon Raytheon Company PAC Lexington, MA	Defense Electronics†	$255,525	167 Candidates Avg House: $1,459 Avg Sen: $1,772	Dems: 63.2% House: 73.6% Incumb: 93.0%	
Recording Industry Assn of America Recording Industry Assn of America Inc PAC (Fka Recording Arts PAC) Washington, DC	Music Production	$61,110	75 Candidates Avg House: $743 Avg Sen: $1,000	Dems: 93.5% House: 65.6% Incumb: 83.6%	
Republican Leader's Fund Republican Leader's Fund Washington, DC	Rep Bob Michel (R-Ill) / Repub Leaders	$169,000	96 Candidates Avg House: $1,760 Avg Sen: $0	Repubs: 100.0% House: 100.0% Incumb: 16.6%	
Republican National Coalition for Life Republican National Coalition for Life PAC (RNC/LIFE PAC) Alton, IL	Pro-Life	$85,750	38 Candidates Avg House: $2,356 Avg Sen: $1,600	Repubs: 100.0% House: 90.7% Incumb: 36.7%	
Reynolds Metals Reynolds Metals Company Political Participation Program Fund (Rappp) Richmond, VA	Metal Mining/Process	$81,675	55 Candidates Avg House: $1,410 Avg Sen: $1,639	Repubs: 79.1% House: 63.9% Incumb: 74.3%	
Rhone-Poulenc Inc Rhone-poulenc Inc PAC (rpac) Princeton, NJ	Pharmaceuticals†	$63,750	60 Candidates Avg House: $1,025 Avg Sen: $1,278	Repubs: 78.0% House: 82.0% Incumb: 91.0%	
Right to Work PAC Right to Work PAC Springfield, VA	Anti-Union	$205,151	120 Candidates Avg House: $1,362 Avg Sen: $3,450	Repubs: 98.3% House: 66.4% Incumb: 22.5%	

† PAC sponsor has other major interests in addition to this primary category

PAC Sponsor or Related Group/PAC Name	Affiliate	1991-92 Total	Where the money went...		
RJR Nabisco RJR PAC RJR Nabisco Inc Winston-salem, NC	Tobacco/Food†	$845,363	398 Candidates Avg House: $1,944 Avg Sen: $3,500	Dems: House: Incumb:	57.0% 81.0% 81.4%
Roadway Services Inc Roadway Services Inc REXPAC Akron, OH	Trucking Companies	$61,225	71 Candidates Avg House: $770 Avg Sen: $1,364	Dems: House: Incumb:	53.9% 75.5% 98.4%
Rockwell International Rockwell International Corporation Good Government Committee Pittsburgh, PA	Defense Aerospace†	$340,164	223 Candidates Avg House: $1,210 Avg Sen: $3,331	Repubs: House: Incumb:	53.7% 66.5% 87.4%
Rubber Cork Linoleum & Plastic Workers Union COPE Cmte of the United Rubber Cork Linoleum and Plastic Wrkrs of Amer AFL-CIO Akron, OH	Manufacturing Unions	$505,730	202 Candidates Avg House: $2,218 Avg Sen: $4,135	Dems: House: Incumb:	99.8% 75.4% 52.4%
Ryder System Inc Ryder System, Inc Committee for Effective Government Miami, FL	Car/Truck Rental	$50,361	70 Candidates Avg House: $652 Avg Sen: $1,015	Dems: House: Incumb:	63.0% 73.8% 83.9%
S&A Restaurant Corp S & A Restaurant Corp Employees PAC Dallas, TX	Restaurants	$143,500	59 Candidates Avg House: $1,651 Avg Sen: $4,531	Repubs: Senate: Incumb:	85.4% 50.5% 45.0%
Safari Club International Safari Club International PAC Edina, MN	Safari Club Intl — Pro-Guns†	$73,850	39 Candidates Avg House: $1,804 Avg Sen: $2,500	Repubs: House: Incumb:	88.5% 83.1% 43.1%
St Louisians for Better Government St Louisians for Better Government St Louis, MO	Pro-Israel	$138,250	50 Candidates Avg House: $1,224 Avg Sen: $4,893	Dems: Senate: Incumb:	80.1% 74.3% 80.1%
Salomon Brothers Salomon Brothers Inc PAC New York, NY	Securities†	$55,850	56 Candidates Avg House: $645 Avg Sen: $1,684	Dems: Senate: Incumb:	51.9% 57.3% 98.2%
San Franciscans for Good Government San Franciscans for Good Government San Francisco, CA	Pro-Israel	$72,500	25 Candidates Avg House: $2,125 Avg Sen: $3,265	Dems: Senate: Incumb:	71.7% 76.5% 96.5%
Santa Fe Southern Pacific Santa Fe Southern Pacific Corporation PAC Chicago, IL	Railroads†	$61,500	84 Candidates Avg House: $600 Avg Sen: $1,155	Repubs: House: Incumb:	63.4% 62.4% 86.4%
Schering-Plough Corp Schering - Plough Corporation Better Government Fund Madison, NJ	Pharmaceuticals†	$186,050	90 Candidates Avg House: $1,721 Avg Sen: $2,650	Dems: House: Incumb:	51.3% 54.6% 74.7%
Scott Paper Co Scott Paper Company PAC (ScottPAC) Washington, DC	Paper/Pulp†	$81,298	96 Candidates Avg House: $680 Avg Sen: $1,409	Repubs: House: Incumb:	71.2% 61.9% 74.2%
Sea-Land Corp Sea-Land Good Government Fund Sea-Land Industries Inc Washington, DC	CSX Corp — Sea Transport†	$174,025	110 Candidates Avg House: $1,319 Avg Sen: $2,928	Dems: House: Incumb:	53.8% 69.7% 95.2%
Seafarers International Union Seafarers Political Activity Donation (SPAD) Camp Springs, MD	Seafarers Intl Union — Sea Transport Unions	$916,796	300 Candidates Avg House: $2,679 Avg Sen: $5,091	Dems: House: Incumb:	91.3% 73.9% 75.4%
Joseph E Seagram & Sons Joseph E Seagram & Sons, Inc PAC New York, NY	Wine & Liquor†	$208,000	119 Candidates Avg House: $1,140 Avg Sen: $3,923	Dems: House: Incumb:	82.5% 51.0% 79.3%
Sears Sears PAC Chicago, IL	Retail Trade†	$55,800	94 Candidates Avg House: $510 Avg Sen: $1,115	Repubs: House: Incumb:	84.1% 74.0% 59.0%
Securities Industry Assn Securities Industry PAC Washington, DC	Securities	$120,448	138 Candidates Avg House: $781 Avg Sen: $1,447	Dems: House: Incumb:	67.0% 77.2% 95.4%
Security Pacific Corp Security Pacific Corporation Active Citizenship Today Committee (SPACT) Los Angeles, CA	Commercial Banks	$105,500	80 Candidates Avg House: $1,216 Avg Sen: $1,591	Dems: House: Incumb:	58.2% 66.8% 87.7%

PAC Sponsor or Related Group/PAC Name	Affiliate	1991-92 Total	Where the money went...		
Senate Victory Fund Senate Victory Fund PAC (Fka Cochran Committee) Jackson, MS — Sen Thad Cochran (R-Miss)	Repub Leaders	$107,000	29 Candidates Avg House: $500 Avg Sen: $3,804	Repubs: 100.0% Senate: 99.5% Incumb: 57.9%	
Service Employees International Union Service Employees Int'l Union COPE Political Campaign Comm Washington, DC	Misc Unions	$743,781	248 Candidates Avg House: $2,378 Avg Sen: $6,006	Dems: 98.1% House: 65.5% Incumb: 45.8%	
Shaw, Pittman et al Shaw, Pittman, Potts And Trowbridge PAC Washington, DC	Lawyers	$102,850	113 Candidates Avg House: $830 Avg Sen: $1,154	Dems: 70.2% House: 68.6% Incumb: 92.9%	
Shearson Lehman Brothers Action Fund of Shearson Lehman Hutton Inc New York, NY — American Express	Securities	$164,200	129 Candidates Avg House: $879 Avg Sen: $2,150	Dems: 65.7% Senate: 52.4% Incumb: 69.2%	
Sheet Metal Workers Union Sheet Metal Workers International Association Political Action League (Pal) Washington, DC — Sheet Metal Workers	Building Trade Unions	$742,354	230 Candidates Avg House: $2,913 Avg Sen: $4,724	Dems: 95.5% House: 74.5% Incumb: 57.9%	
Sheet Metal/Air Conditioning Contractors Sheet Metal and Air Conditioning Contractors' PAC Vienna, VA	Plumbing/Air Cond	$161,401	98 Candidates Avg House: $966 Avg Sen: $4,000	Repubs: 94.7% Senate: 54.5% Incumb: 55.7%	
Shell Oil Shell Oil Company Employees' Political Awareness Committee Houston, TX	Oil & Gas†	$130,500	120 Candidates Avg House: $852 Avg Sen: $2,265	Repubs: 59.4% House: 65.3% Incumb: 89.6%	
Sierra Club Sierra Club Committee on Political Education San Francisco, CA	Environment Policy	$608,680	214 Candidates Avg House: $2,619 Avg Sen: $4,081	Dems: 96.6% House: 77.9% Incumb: 45.7%	
Simpson Investment Co Simpson Investment Company PAC (Aka Simpson Pol Act Cmte/SIMPAC) Seattle, WA	Forest Products†	$86,150	49 Candidates Avg House: $1,279 Avg Sen: $2,957	Repubs: 86.4% House: 51.9% Incumb: 53.0%	
Skadden, Arps et al Skadden Arps PAC Washington, DC	Lawyers	$95,717	73 Candidates Avg House: $988 Avg Sen: $1,831	Dems: 66.3% Senate: 53.6% Incumb: 96.3%	
Smirnoff/Inglenook Distributors Smirnoff/Inglenook Distributors PAC Hartford, CT	Wine & Liquor	$84,000	64 Candidates Avg House: $1,191 Avg Sen: $1,647	Dems: 78.0% House: 66.7% Incumb: 94.0%	
SmithKline Beecham Smithkline Beckman PAC (SKB-PAC) Philadelphia, PA	Pharmaceuticals†	$74,300	70 Candidates Avg House: $929 Avg Sen: $1,529	Dems: 50.5% House: 65.0% Incumb: 83.8%	
Society of American Florists Society of American Florists PAC (SAF-PAC) Alexandria, VA	Florists	$55,878	98 Candidates Avg House: $471 Avg Sen: $1,168	Repubs: 85.1% House: 70.7% Incumb: 82.5%	
South Central Bell Telephone South Central Bell Telephone Company Federal PAC (SCB FPAC) Birmingham, AL — BellSouth	Phone Utilites	$64,510	36 Candidates Avg House: $1,518 Avg Sen: $2,929	Dems: 76.9% House: 68.2% Incumb: 98.5%	
Southern Bell Southern Bell Telephone and Telegraph Company Federal PAC (Sobell PAC) Birmingham, AL — BellSouth	Phone Utilites	$519,207	241 Candidates Avg House: $2,175 Avg Sen: $2,140	Dems: 64.3% House: 89.7% Incumb: 79.1%	
Southern California Edison Federal Citizenship Responsibility Group/the Southern California Edison Company Rosemead, CA	Electric Utilities	$264,485	135 Candidates Avg House: $1,563 Avg Sen: $2,890	Dems: 75.5% House: 55.5% Incumb: 65.2%	
Southern Co Southern Company Services PAC Atlanta, GA — Southern Co	Electric Utilities	$75,450	165 Candidates Avg House: $400 Avg Sen: $678	Dems: 51.7% House: 69.5% Incumb: 82.6%	
Southern Minnesota Beet Sugar Co-op Southern Minnesota Sugar Cooperative PAC Renville, MN	Sugar	$120,400	164 Candidates Avg House: $704 Avg Sen: $904	Dems: 62.7% House: 81.2% Incumb: 82.5%	
Southern Natural Resources Sonat Inc PAC Birmingham, AL	Natural Gas†	$61,100	44 Candidates Avg House: $810 Avg Sen: $2,792	Dems: 81.2% Senate: 59.4% Incumb: 91.5%	

† PAC sponsor has other major interests in addition to this primary category

PAC Sponsor or Related Group / PAC Name	Affiliate	1991-92 Total	Where the money went...			
Southern Pacific Transport Co Southern Pacific Transportation Company PAC San Francisco, CA		$62,600 Railroads	72 Candidates Avg House: $637 Avg Sen: $1,177		Dems: 59.7% Senate: 58.3% Incumb: 86.9%	
Southwest Marine Southwest Marine Inc PAC San Diego, CA		$50,400 Shipbuilding/Repair	30 Candidates Avg House: $1,441 Avg Sen: $2,464		Dems: 53.8% House: 65.8% Incumb: 68.5%	
Southwest Peanut Membrship Organization Southwest Peanut PAC Washington, DC		$101,100 Misc Crops	116 Candidates Avg House: $778 Avg Sen: $1,166		Dems: 73.0% House: 67.7% Incumb: 86.8%	
Southwestern Bell Southwestern Bell Corporation Employee Federal PAC (SWB EMPAC or EMPAC) St Louis, MO		$250,630 Phone Utilites†	141 Candidates Avg House: $1,680 Avg Sen: $2,335		Dems: 60.1% House: 80.4% Incumb: 85.1%	
Spiegel Inc Spiegel Inc Executive PAC (SEPAC) Oak Brook, IL		$68,650 Mail Order	58 Candidates Avg House: $967 Avg Sen: $1,813		Dems: 50.6% House: 57.8% Incumb: 89.1%	
Stephens Overseas Services Stephens Overseas Services PAC Little Rock, AR		$52,950 Misc Financial Svcs	19 Candidates Avg House: $2,661 Avg Sen: $3,556		Dems: 70.7% Senate: 60.4% Incumb: 79.7%	
Stone Container Corp Stone Container Corporation PAC Chicago, IL		$352,450 Paper Packaging†	161 Candidates Avg House: $2,090 Avg Sen: $2,814		Repubs: 91.1% House: 82.4% Incumb: 59.0%	
Sun Co Sun Company Inc PAC Radnor, PA		$113,050 Oil Refining/Mkting†	101 Candidates Avg House: $844 Avg Sen: $2,389		Repubs: 88.0% House: 62.0% Incumb: 34.5%	
SunBanks Sun Banks Inc PAC (Sun BANKPAC) Tallahassee, FL	SunTrust Banks	$59,782 Commercial Banks	66 Candidates Avg House: $823 Avg Sen: $1,242		Dems: 51.7% House: 73.0% Incumb: 72.2%	
Sunkist Growers Sunkist Growers, Inc PAC Sherman Oaks, CA		$133,360 Fruit/Veg	74 Candidates Avg House: $1,693 Avg Sen: $2,168		Repubs: 50.4% House: 72.4% Incumb: 91.8%	
Swidler & Berlin Swidler & Berlin PAC Washington, DC		$60,525 Lawyers	59 Candidates Avg House: $888 Avg Sen: $1,316		Dems: 79.8% House: 58.7% Incumb: 92.9%	
Syntex (USA) Inc Syntex (U S A) Inc Employee PAC Palo Alto, CA		$121,644 Pharmaceuticals†	81 Candidates Avg House: $1,230 Avg Sen: $2,147		Dems: 71.0% House: 57.6% Incumb: 60.6%	
Teamsters Union Democratic Republican Independent Voter Education Committee Washington, DC		$2,442,552 Teamsters	428 Candidates Avg House: $5,695 Avg Sen: $5,818		Dems: 95.2% House: 86.7% Incumb: 61.1%	
Tele-Communications Inc Tele-Communications, Inc PAC (TCI PAC) Denver, CO		$112,500 Cable TV	51 Candidates Avg House: $1,466 Avg Sen: $3,182		Repubs: 60.3% Senate: 62.2% Incumb: 85.8%	
Tenneco Inc Tenneco Inc. Employees Good Govt Fund (Aka Tenneco Employees Good Govt Fund) Houston, TX		$170,750 Naval Ships/Natural Gas†	104 Candidates Avg House: $1,562 Avg Sen: $1,870		Dems: 56.8% House: 70.4% Incumb: 90.0%	
Texaco Texaco Political Involvement Committee White Plains, NY		$176,489 Oil & Gas	187 Candidates Avg House: $714 Avg Sen: $2,195		Repubs: 70.2% House: 63.9% Incumb: 80.6%	
Texas Air Texas Air Corporation PAC (TAC PAC) Houston, TX		$110,550 Airlines	73 Candidates Avg House: $1,258 Avg Sen: $2,109		Repubs: 53.4% House: 58.0% Incumb: 93.3%	
Texas Cattle Feeders Assn Beef-PAC (Beef PAC of Texas Cattle Feeders Association) Amarillo, TX	Natl Cattlemens Assn	$121,700 Feedlots	124 Candidates Avg House: $903 Avg Sen: $1,386		Repubs: 55.3% House: 74.9% Incumb: 82.7%	
Texas Eastern Gas Transmission Texas Eastern PAC Houston, TX	Panhandle Eastern Corp	$77,900 Natural Gas†	103 Candidates Avg House: $583 Avg Sen: $1,857		Dems: 61.4% House: 66.6% Incumb: 91.7%	

PAC Sponsor or Related Group/PAC Name	Affiliate	1991-92 Total	Where the money went...			
Texas Instruments Constructive Citizenship Program of Texas Instruments Dallas, TX	Computer Equipment†	$107,800	79 Candidates Avg House: $1,128 Avg Sen: $2,464	Dems: House: Incumb:	69.1% 68.0% 87.9%	
Texas Utilities Co Texas Utilities Company PAC Dallas, TX	Texas Utilities Co Electric Utilities	$86,800	95 Candidates Avg House: $783 Avg Sen: $1,472	Dems: House: Incumb:	57.1% 69.5% 85.2%	
Textron Inc Textron Inc PAC Providence, RI	Defense Aerospace†	$398,850	185 Candidates Avg House: $1,911 Avg Sen: $3,423	Dems: House: Incumb:	66.6% 74.2% 96.0%	
Thiokol Morton Thiokol PAC Ogden, UT	Defense Aerospace†	$71,025	75 Candidates Avg House: $719 Avg Sen: $1,724	Dems: House: Incumb:	52.9% 58.8% 91.6%	
Time Warner Warner Communications Inc PAC New York, NY	Broadcast/Movies†	$138,000	57 Candidates Avg House: $1,818 Avg Sen: $3,250	Dems: Senate: Incumb:	72.5% 56.5% 81.5%	
Tobacco Institute Tobacco Institute PAC Washington, DC	Tobacco	$183,950	222 Candidates Avg House: $761 Avg Sen: $1,500	Dems: House: Incumb:	50.4% 83.2% 94.8%	
Torchmark Corp Torchmark Corporation Political Action Committe (TORCH-PAC) Birmingham, AL	Insurance	$204,184	107 Candidates Avg House: $1,324 Avg Sen: $2,927	Repubs: Senate: Incumb:	59.7% 55.9% 72.1%	
Trans Comm International Union Responsible Citizens Pol League - A Project of the Trans Comm Intl Union (TCU) Rockville, MD	Misc Transport Union	$421,230	319 Candidates Avg House: $973 Avg Sen: $3,478	Dems: House: Incumb:	96.1% 63.8% 68.7%	
Transport Workers Union Transport Workers Union Political Contributions Committee New York, NY	Misc Transport Union	$414,830	238 Candidates Avg House: $1,505 Avg Sen: $3,064	Dems: House: Incumb:	97.3% 72.9% 74.3%	
Travelers Corp Travelers Corporation PAC (T-PAC); The Hartford, CT	Insurance†	$230,219	107 Candidates Avg House: $1,699 Avg Sen: $3,083	Repubs: House: Incumb:	62.9% 53.1% 84.4%	
TRW Inc TRW Good Government Fund Lyndhurst, OH	Defense Electronics†	$153,175	143 Candidates Avg House: $970 Avg Sen: $1,571	Dems: House: Incumb:	50.6% 75.4% 89.2%	
Turner Broadcasting System Turner Broadcasting System PAC Inc Atlanta, GA	Cable TV	$74,770	49 Candidates Avg House: $1,069 Avg Sen: $2,385	Dems: Senate: Incumb:	55.4% 54.2% 100.0%	
Tyson Foods Tyson Foods Inc PAC (TYPAC) Springdale, AR	Poultry/Egg†	$171,850	106 Candidates Avg House: $1,279 Avg Sen: $2,622	Dems: House: Incumb:	81.7% 58.8% 82.5%	
Union Camp Corp Union Camp Corporation PAC Wayne, NJ	Paper/Pulp†	$77,810	57 Candidates Avg House: $899 Avg Sen: $2,560	Repubs: Senate: Incumb:	73.8% 52.6% 49.0%	
Union Oil Union Oil (Unocal) Political Awareness Fund Los Angeles, CA	Oil & Gas†	$129,424	126 Candidates Avg House: $672 Avg Sen: $2,162	Repubs: Senate: Incumb:	70.8% 50.1% 62.2%	
Union Pacific Corp Union Pacific Fund for Effective Government Washington, DC	Railroads†	$684,680	305 Candidates Avg House: $1,677 Avg Sen: $5,214	Repubs: House: Incumb:	66.8% 62.7% 70.8%	
United Airlines United Airlines PAC Chicago, IL	Airlines	$198,428	159 Candidates Avg House: $1,124 Avg Sen: $1,724	Dems: House: Incumb:	57.4% 69.7% 92.7%	
United Auto Workers UAW - V - CAP (UAW Voluntary Community Action Program) Detroit, MI	Manufacturing Unions	$2,231,917	410 Candidates Avg House: $5,339 Avg Sen: $6,301	Dems: House: Incumb:	98.2% 87.1% 57.2%	
United Egg Assn United Egg Association PAC (EggPAC) Decatur, GA	Poultry/Egg	$67,250	68 Candidates Avg House: $801 Avg Sen: $1,410	Dems: House: Incumb:	52.7% 56.0% 93.2%	

† PAC sponsor has other major interests in addition to this primary category

PAC Sponsor or Related Group/PAC Name	Affiliate	1991-92 Total	Where the money went...		
United Mine Workers United Mine Workers of America - Coal Miners PAC Washington, DC	Mine Workers	$459,600	244 Candidates Avg House: $1,585 Avg Sen: $3,256	Dems: 97.5% House: 69.3% Incumb: 68.0%	
United Paperworkers United Paperworkers International Union Political Education Program Washington, DC	Manufacturing Unions	$86,000	68 Candidates Avg House: $1,087 Avg Sen: $1,900	Dems: 97.7% House: 65.7% Incumb: 49.4%	
United Parcel Service UPSPAC Greenwich, CT	Express Delivery	$1,454,487	524 Candidates Avg House: $2,646 Avg Sen: $3,554	Dems: 54.2% House: 81.7% Incumb: 84.2%	
United Services Automobile Assn Group United Services Automobile Association Group PAC (USAA Group PAC) San Antonio, TX	Proprty Insurance	$78,200	73 Candidates Avg House: $1,078 Avg Sen: $1,053	Repubs: 64.2% House: 74.4% Incumb: 67.0%	
United States Sugar Corp United States Sugar Corp-employee Stock Ownership Plan PAC Clewiston, FL	Sugar	$58,850	42 Candidates Avg House: $1,324 Avg Sen: $1,786	Dems: 78.8% House: 78.8% Incumb: 60.9%	
United Steelworkers United Steelworkers of America Political Action Fund Pittsburgh, PA	Manufacturing Unions	$1,253,949	253 Candidates Avg House: $4,634 Avg Sen: $7,226	Dems: 99.0% House: 81.3% Incumb: 51.5%	
United Technologies United Technologies Corporation, PAC Washington, DC	Defense Aerospace†	$285,540	215 Candidates Avg House: $1,045 Avg Sen: $2,566	Dems: 54.6% House: 64.0% Incumb: 91.2%	
United Telecommunications United Telecommunications, Inc PAC (UNIPAC) Westwood, KS	United Telecom / Phone Utilites†	$424,060	259 Candidates Avg House: $1,305 Avg Sen: $3,838	Repubs: 66.8% House: 69.2% Incumb: 63.7%	
United Transportation Union Transportation Political Education League Cleveland, OH	Railroad Unions	$1,097,550	380 Candidates Avg House: $2,390 Avg Sen: $6,453	Dems: 97.1% House: 72.5% Incumb: 67.4%	
Upjohn Co Upjohn Employees PAC Kalamazoo, MI	Pharmaceuticals	$124,950	128 Candidates Avg House: $905 Avg Sen: $1,208	Dems: 62.0% House: 71.0% Incumb: 91.2%	
US Bancorp US Bancorp PAC Portland, OR	US Bancorp / Commercial Banks	$60,000	25 Candidates Avg House: $2,422 Avg Sen: $2,343	Dems: 52.5% House: 72.7% Incumb: 52.7%	
US Beet Sugar Assn United States Beet Sugar Association PAC Washington, DC	Sugar	$52,432	75 Candidates Avg House: $647 Avg Sen: $876	Dems: 78.1% House: 71.6% Incumb: 80.4%	
US League of Savings Assns US League-Savings Association Political Elections Committee Washington, DC	Savings & Loans	$198,215	164 Candidates Avg House: $1,198 Avg Sen: $1,257	Dems: 63.0% House: 81.0% Incumb: 81.3%	
US Telephone Assn United States Telephone Assn PAC Washington, DC	Phone Utilites	$170,619	148 Candidates Avg House: $894 Avg Sen: $1,875	Dems: 57.8% House: 56.6% Incumb: 90.1%	
US Tobacco Co US Tobacco Executives, Administrators and Managers PAC (USTEAM PAC) Greenwich, CT	US Tobacco / Tobacco	$427,250	177 Candidates Avg House: $1,811 Avg Sen: $5,152	Repubs: 57.0% House: 61.5% Incumb: 72.0%	
US West Inc US West Inc PAC (U S West PAC) Denver, CO	US West / Phone Utilites	$266,822	144 Candidates Avg House: $1,670 Avg Sen: $2,682	Dems: 54.4% House: 72.6% Incumb: 77.3%	
USX Corp USXPAC (Fka USX Good Government Fund) Washington, DC	Oil & Gas†	$106,827	93 Candidates Avg House: $979 Avg Sen: $2,107	Dems: 65.8% House: 72.4% Incumb: 89.9%	
Verner, Liipfert et al Verner, Liipfert, Bernhard, McPherson & Hand PAC Washington, DC	Lawyers	$175,192	119 Candidates Avg House: $946 Avg Sen: $2,552	Dems: 90.0% Senate: 56.8% Incumb: 94.3%	
Veterans of Foreign Wars Veterans of Foreign Wars PAC Inc Washington, DC	Pro-Defense	$102,675	96 Candidates Avg House: $953 Avg Sen: $1,700	Repubs: 58.5% House: 75.2% Incumb: 92.7%	

PAC Sponsor or Related Group/PAC Name	Affiliate	1991-92 Total	Where the money went...			
Viacom International Viacom International Inc PAC Corporation New York, NY	 Cable TV	$123,250	62 Candidates Avg House: $2,097 Avg Sen: $1,837	Dems: House: Incumb:	66.9% 61.3% 95.7%
Victory USA Victory USA Sacramento, CA	 Vic Fazio (D-Calif) Dem Leaders	$91,100	86 Candidates Avg House: $989 Avg Sen: $3,000	Dems: House: Incumb:	98.9% 90.1% 36.8%
Vinson & Elkins National Good Government Fund; The Houston, TX	 Lawyers	$119,660	79 Candidates Avg House: $1,604 Avg Sen: $1,355	Dems: House: Incumb:	70.3% 63.0% 84.8%
Voters for Choice Voters for Choice/Friends of Family Planning Washington, DC	 Pro-Choice	$265,450	183 Candidates Avg House: $1,142 Avg Sen: $3,963	Dems: House: Incumb:	88.6% 70.2% 42.4%
Wal-Mart Stores Wal-Mart Stores Inc PAC for Responsible Government Bentonville, AR	 Department Stores	$51,700	57 Candidates Avg House: $658 Avg Sen: $1,333	Repubs: Senate: Incumb:	90.8% 54.2% 66.4%
Warner-Lambert Warner-Lambert PAC ("Walpac") Morris Plains, NJ	 Health Care Products†	$96,355	94 Candidates Avg House: $925 Avg Sen: $1,316	Dems: House: Incumb:	64.7% 67.2% 84.1%
Washington PAC Washington PAC Washington, DC	 Pro-Israel	$202,020	157 Candidates Avg House: $798 Avg Sen: $2,717	Dems: Senate: Incumb:	72.6% 53.8% 84.4%
Waste Management Inc Waste Management Inc Employees' Better Government Fund ("Wmi PAC") Oak Brook, IL	 Waste Mgmt Waste Mgmt	$452,689	372 Candidates Avg House: $1,039 Avg Sen: $1,955	Dems: House: Incumb:	67.7% 68.9% 82.9%
Wells Fargo Wells Fargo & Company Impact Fund San Francisco, CA	 Commercial Banks	$71,715	55 Candidates Avg House: $1,137 Avg Sen: $1,793	Dems: House: Incumb:	55.4% 65.0% 62.2%
West Publishing West Publishing Company PAC (West Publishing PAC) Minneapolis, MN	 Publishing	$108,900	53 Candidates Avg House: $1,978 Avg Sen: $2,292	Dems: House: Incumb:	82.0% 72.6% 91.2%
Westinghouse Electric Westinghouse Electric Corporation Employees Political Participation Program Pittsburgh, PA	 Electronics Mfg†	$214,800	189 Candidates Avg House: $978 Avg Sen: $1,836	Dems: House: Incumb:	62.8% 70.1% 94.1%
Westvaco Corp Westvaco Corporation Political Participation Program New York, NY	 Paper/Pulp†	$245,200	85 Candidates Avg House: $2,495 Avg Sen: $4,071	Repubs: House: Incumb:	78.7% 65.1% 63.9%
Wexler Group Wexler Group PAC; The Washington, DC	 Hill & Knowlton Lobbyists/PR	$72,684	100 Candidates Avg House: $649 Avg Sen: $927	Dems: House: Incumb:	82.6% 64.3% 94.5%
Weyerhaeuser Co Weyerhaeuser Company Special Shareholders PAC St. Paul, MN	 Weyerhaeuser Paper/Pulp†	$81,750	73 Candidates Avg House: $844 Avg Sen: $1,850	Repubs: House: Incumb:	71.9% 54.7% 58.1%
Weyerhaeuser Co Weyerhaeuser Company PAC Federal Way, WA	 Weyerhaeuser Paper/Pulp†	$53,047	18 Candidates Avg House: $2,909 Avg Sen: $3,045	Repubs: House: Incumb:	81.8% 71.3% 22.9%
Wheelabrator Technologies Wheelabrator Technologies Inc Sensible Government Fund Hampton, NH	 Waste Management Inc Waste Mgmt	$77,800	64 Candidates Avg House: $1,093 Avg Sen: $1,486	Dems: House: Incumb:	68.6% 61.8% 74.6%
Willamette Industries Willamette Industries PAC (WILPAC) Portland, OR	 Forest Products†	$53,056	43 Candidates Avg House: $987 Avg Sen: $2,167	Repubs: House: Incumb:	88.1% 63.2% 37.9%
Williams & Jensen Williams & Jensen PC PAC (W & J PAC) Washington, DC	 Lawyers	$90,469	135 Candidates Avg House: $587 Avg Sen: $963	Dems: House: Incumb:	62.1% 68.1% 92.3%
Wine & Spirits Wholesalers of America Wine and Spirits Wholesalers of America PAC Washington, DC	 Liquor Wholesalers	$177,478	122 Candidates Avg House: $1,383 Avg Sen: $1,675	Dems: House: Incumb:	66.6% 71.7% 89.5%

† PAC sponsor has other major interests in addition to this primary category

PAC Sponsor or Related Group/PAC Name	Affiliate	1991-92 Total	Where the money went...			
Wine Institute Wine Institute PAC San Francisco, CA	Wine & Liquor	$105,026	49 Candidates Avg House: $1,690 Avg Sen: $2,997	Dems: House: Incumb:	84.6% 51.5% 93.6%	
Winn-Dixie Stores Sunbelt Good Government Committee of Winn-Dixie Stores, Inc. Jacksonville, FL	Food Stores	$228,250	106 Candidates Avg House: $1,687 Avg Sen: $3,519	Repubs: House: Incumb:	63.6% 58.4% 73.7%	
Wish List Wish List New York, NY	Womens Issues†	$73,109	19 Candidates Avg House: $3,848 Avg Sen: $0	Repubs: House: Incumb:	100.0% 100.0% 29.0%	
Women's Alliance for Israel Women's Alliance For Israel Beverly Hills, CA	Pro-Israel	$209,000	67 Candidates Avg House: $1,342 Avg Sen: $5,448	Dems: Senate: Incumb:	59.8% 75.6% 77.8%	
Women's Campaign Fund Women's Campaign Fund Inc Washington, DC	Womens Issues	$513,067	96 Candidates Avg House: $5,167 Avg Sen: $6,583	Dems: House: Incumb:	76.1% 84.6% 14.6%	
Women's Political Committee Women's Political Committee Los Angeles, CA	Womens Issues	$57,100	14 Candidates Avg House: $3,513 Avg Sen: $4,833	Dems: Senate: Incumb:	100.0% 50.8% 0.0%	
Women's Pro-Israel National PAC Women's Pro-Israel National PAC ("WIN PAC") Washington, DC	Pro-Israel	$155,550	88 Candidates Avg House: $846 Avg Sen: $3,461	Repubs: Senate: Incumb:	52.1% 69.0% 78.1%	
Yellow Freight System Yellow Freight System Inc PAC Shawnee Mission, KS	Trucking Companies	$170,409	139 Candidates Avg House: $877 Avg Sen: $2,733	Dems: House: Incumb:	68.8% 57.1% 93.2%	

Appendices

Cash Constitutents of Congress

Appendix A: Industry & Interest Group Categories

This is a listing of the detailed categories used in classifying all the contributors that gave money to federal candidates in the 1992 elections. Included are the category name, the total in 1991-92 contributions, and a breakdown of the totals by PACs and political parties.

Classification of contributors is not always a straightforward matter, particularly when the contributor has multiple interests or multiple sources of revenue. Many corporate PACs have been assigned multiple categories — a primary code based on their single largest source of income, and as many as six alternate codes encompassing smaller, but significant revenue sources. Throughout this book, and in the listings below, the category assigned to a particular contribution depends both on the interests of the contributor *and the congressional committee assignments of the recipient*. This is particularly relevant in the defense sector, as many defense contractors earn the majority of their revenues from non-defense activities. In such cases, the contributions are classified as defense-related *only when they are made to a member who sits on a defense-related committee*. (For that reason, totals in the defense sector can be considered very conservative.) A similar procedure was used for all other diversified companies.

In most cases, individual contributors are classified according to the economic interests of their employer. Contributions from non-income earning spouses and children are classified according to the economic interest of the income earner within the family. Thus a bank president, his wife and children would all be classified under "commercial banking" unless the wife had a job as well, in which case she would be classified separately.

Individual contributors are classified under the ideological/single-issue categories only if they contributed to an ideological or single-issue PAC. Even then, the contribution is considered ideological only if the candidate who received the contribution also drew money from an ideological PAC with similar interests. The following example illustrates the procedure used: If a real estate developer contributes both to a pro-Israel PAC and to a candidate who received direct contributions from pro-Israel PACs, the contribution would be classified under "pro-Israel." If the donor gave to someone who got no money from pro-Israel PACs, it would be classified under "real estate." In the case of ideological contributors, non-income earning spouses and children are *not* classified as ideological givers unless they themselves have contributed to an ideological PAC.

Detailed profiles of the spending patterns of each major industry group can be found in the "Industry Profile" section of this book, on pages 41-93.

Agriculture

	Total	PAC Pct	Dem Pct	Repub Pct
Crop Production & Basic Processing				
Cotton	$453,751	78%	53%	47%
Sugar cane & sugar beets	$1,801,818	83%	69%	31%
Vegetables, fruits and tree nuts	$1,188,860	60%	42%	58%
Wheat, corn, soybeans and cash grain	$189,413	69%	43%	57%
Other commodities (including rice, peanuts, honey)	$472,177	81%	77%	22%
Farmers, crop unspecified	$1,762,630	7%	46%	54%
TOTAL	**$5,868,649**	**54%**	**55%**	**45%**
Tobacco				
Tobacco & Tobacco products	$2,818,861	81%	53%	47%
Dairy				
Milk & dairy producers	$2,107,911	83%	63%	37%
Livestock & Poultry				
Livestock	$1,476,005	40%	39%	61%
Feedlots & related livestock services	$153,900	79%	40%	60%
Poultry & eggs	$891,174	59%	62%	38%
Sheep and wool producers	$30,600	84%	40%	60%
TOTAL	**$2,551,679**	**50%**	**47%**	**53%**
Agricultural Services & Products				
Agricultural services, diversified	$625,743	79%	52%	48%
Agricultural chemicals (fertilizers & pesticides)	$552,635	90%	48%	51%
Animal feed & health products	$128,262	43%	19%	80%
Veterinarians	$413,615	73%	55%	45%
Farm machinery & equipment	$320,297	58%	20%	80%
Grain traders & terminals	$462,575	64%	51%	49%
Farm organizations & cooperatives	$604,564	99%	58%	42%
Florists & nursery services	$362,329	28%	35%	65%
TOTAL	**$3,470,020**	**73%**	**47%**	**53%**

Food Processing & Sales

Food & beverage products and services, diversified	$582,289	66%	40%	60%
Food and kindred products manufacturing	$1,818,855	65%	34%	66%
Meat processing & products	$334,720	38%	38%	62%
Food stores	$1,792,143	50%	39%	60%
Food wholesalers	$580,057	53%	39%	60%
TOTAL	**$5,108,064**	**57%**	**37%**	**62%**

Forestry & Forest Products

Forestry & Forest Products	$1,253,349	43%	24%	76%
Paper & pulp mills and paper manufacturing	$1,455,994	76%	26%	74%
TOTAL	**$2,709,343**	**61%**	**25%**	**75%**

Other & Unclassified

Misc Agriculture	$257,597	0%	33%	67%
TOTAL	**$257,597**	**0%**	**33%**	**67%**

Communications & Electronics

	Total	PAC Pct	Dem Pct	Repub Pct
Printing & Publishing				
Book, newspaper & periodical publishing	$1,674,934	13%	56%	43%
Commercial printing & typesetting	$647,556	17%	41%	58%
Greeting card publishing	$221,761	65%	28%	72%
Misc printing & publishing	$515,330	0%	80%	19%
TOTAL	**$3,059,581**	**15%**	**55%**	**44%**
Broadcasting, Motion Pictures & Entertainment				
Broadcasting & motion pictures, diversified	$478,265	29%	81%	19%
Motion picture production & distribution	$2,596,760	13%	87%	13%
Television production	$570,666	16%	87%	13%
Commercial TV & radio stations	$1,075,656	46%	57%	43%
Cable & satellite TV operators	$2,226,214	54%	55%	44%
Recorded Music & music production	$591,482	40%	88%	12%
Bands, orchestras & other live music production	$126,200	0%	78%	20%
Amusement/recreation centers & movie theaters	$353,539	26%	41%	59%
TOTAL	**$8,018,782**	**32%**	**72%**	**28%**
Telephone Utilities				
Local & regional telephone utilities	$4,518,436	88%	55%	44%
Long-distance telephone utilities	$1,385,963	86%	60%	40%
TOTAL	**$5,904,399**	**88%**	**56%**	**43%**
Telecommunications Services & Equipment				
Telephone & communications equipment	$482,048	57%	48%	52%
Cellular systems and equipment	$187,195	39%	58%	42%
Satellite communications	$115,450	74%	60%	40%
Other communications sServices	$14,200	58%	30%	70%
Telecommunications, unclassified	$110,447	7%	55%	44%
TOTAL	**$909,340**	**49%**	**52%**	**48%**
Electronics Manufacturing & Services				
Electronics manufacturing & services	$1,088,233	42%	37%	63%
Computer Equipment & Services				
Computer manufacturing & services, diversified	$498,735	14%	61%	38%
Computers, components & accessories	$746,873	26%	46%	54%
Data processing & computer services	$697,028	42%	51%	47%
Computer software	$270,318	8%	35%	63%
TOTAL	**$2,212,954**	**26%**	**50%**	**49%**
Other & Unclassified				
Misc communications & electronics	$39,175	1%	63%	37%

Construction

	Total	PAC Pct	Dem Pct	Repub Pct
General Contractors				
Builders associations	$192,778	96%	7%	93%
Public works, industrial & commercial construction	$3,623,909	42%	38%	61%

Construction, unclassified or diversified	$2,683,507	0%	49%	51%
TOTAL	**$6,500,194**	**26%**	**42%**	**58%**

Home Builders

Residential construction	$2,017,905	59%	46%	54%
Mobile home construction	$198,270	59%	33%	67%
TOTAL	**$2,216,175**	**59%**	**45%**	**55%**

Special Trade Contractors

Special trade contractors, diversified	$580,886	12%	41%	58%
Electrical contractors	$436,146	37%	38%	62%
Plumbing, heating & air conditioning	$513,447	33%	33%	67%
Landscaping & excavation services	$155,949	0%	47%	53%
TOTAL	**$1,686,428**	**24%**	**38%**	**61%**

Construction Services

Engineering, architecture & construction mgmt, diversified	$1,327,535	45%	59%	41%
Architectural services	$574,357	6%	72%	28%
Surveying	$72,128	40%	35%	65%
TOTAL	**$1,974,020**	**33%**	**62%**	**38%**

Building Materials & Equipment

Building materials, diversified	$461,334	39%	50%	50%
Stone, clay, glass & concrete products	$963,985	28%	36%	64%
Lumber & wood products	$548,351	5%	33%	66%
Plumbing & pipe products	$315,230	18%	32%	68%
Electrical supply	$160,922	0%	33%	66%
Construction equipment	$318,400	30%	22%	78%
Other construction-related products	$101,450	32%	23%	71%
TOTAL	**$2,869,672**	**23%**	**35%**	**64%**

Defense

	Total	PAC Pct	Dem Pct	Repub Pct

Defense Aerospace

Defense areospace contractors	$4,748,928	92%	55%	44%
TOTAL	**$4,748,928**	**92%**	**55%**	**44%**

Defense Electronics

Defense electronic contractors	$2,433,503	86%	56%	44%
TOTAL	**$2,433,503**	**86%**	**56%**	**44%**

Misc Defense

Defense research & development	$333,099	87%	45%	54%
Defense shipbuilders	$250,013	88%	55%	45%
Defense nuclear contractors	$11,200	0%	79%	21%
Ground-based & other weapons systems	$351,947	94%	50%	50%
Defense-related services	$162,949	68%	67%	33%
Defense, unclassified	$37,121	0%	53%	47%
TOTAL	**$1,146,329**	**83%**	**53%**	**47%**

Energy & Natural Resources

	Total	PAC Pct	Dem Pct	Repub Pct

Oil & Gas

Major (multinational) oil & gas producers	$2,699,335	84%	26%	74%
Independent oil & gas producers	$2,048,958	26%	39%	61%
Natural gas transmission & distribution	$2,393,866	76%	59%	41%
Oilfield service, equipment & exploration	$1,039,863	43%	33%	67%
Petroleum refining & marketing	$1,136,686	54%	36%	63%
Gasoline service stations	$522,515	66%	44%	56%
Fuel oil dealers	$78,047	5%	44%	56%
LPG/liquid propane dealers & producers	$63,550	34%	41%	59%
Oil & gas, diversified or unclassified	$1,645,123	22%	41%	59%
TOTAL	**$11,627,943**	**55%**	**40%**	**60%**

Mining

Mining, diversified	$119,210	34%	41%	59%
Coal mining	$918,336	60%	39%	61%
Metal mining & processing	$685,217	70%	38%	62%
Non-metallic mining	$89,334	55%	41%	59%

Mining services & equipment	$32,663	8%	30%	70%
TOTAL	**$1,844,760**	**61%**	**38%**	**62%**

Misc Energy

Energy, Natural Resources and Environment	$18,850	0%	17%	83%
Power plant construction & equipment	$713,803	97%	33%	67%
Nuclear plant construction, equipment & svcs	$231,075	94%	66%	34%
Alternate energy production & services	$32,250	49%	71%	29%
Misc energy production & distribution	$285,694	0%	61%	39%
TOTAL	**$1,281,672**	**79%**	**46%**	**54%**

Electric Utilities

Electric power utilities	$2,748,642	84%	58%	42%
Gas & electric utilities	$1,145,674	90%	50%	50%
Rural electric cooperatives	$661,154	96%	73%	27%
TOTAL	**$4,555,470**	**87%**	**58%**	**42%**

Environmental Services & Equipment

Environmental services, equipment & consulting	$187,347	31%	74%	25%

Waste Management

Waste management	$1,529,834	55%	56%	44%

Commercial Fishing

Commercial fishing	$313,509	35%	72%	27%

Finance, Insurance & Real Estate

	Total	PAC Pct	Dem Pct	Repub Pct
Commercial Banks				
Commercial banks & bank holding companies	$10,349,223	71%	52%	48%
Savings & Loans				
Savings banks and savings & loans	$1,318,827	70%	53%	47%
Misc Banks				
Banks & lending institutions, unclassified	$847,098	7%	48%	52%
Credit Unions				
Credit unions	$697,305	95%	65%	35%
Finance/Credit Companies				
Credit agencies & finance companies	$1,042,551	55%	51%	49%
Securities & Investment				
Securities, commodities & investment, diversified	$285,350	0%	49%	51%
Security brokers & investment companies	$10,383,262	17%	59%	41%
Investment banking	$3,149,515	21%	61%	38%
Commodity brokers & dealers	$1,325,102	72%	71%	29%
Stock exchanges	$136,150	61%	68%	32%
Venture capital	$656,843	34%	49%	51%
TOTAL	**$15,936,222**	**23%**	**60%**	**40%**
Insurance				
Insurance companies, brokers & agents, diversified	$9,155,955	54%	47%	53%
Accident & health insurance	$1,273,400	87%	55%	45%
Life insurance	$4,283,249	82%	57%	43%
Property & casualty insurance	$232,174	73%	35%	65%
TOTAL	**$14,944,778**	**65%**	**50%**	**50%**
Real Estate				
Real estate, diversified	$1,937,926	0%	56%	44%
Real Estate developers & subdividers	$3,797,455	8%	57%	43%
Real estate agents & managers	$7,626,300	40%	53%	46%
Title insurance & title abstract offices	$286,712	37%	49%	51%
Mobile home dealers & parks	$52,488	0%	42%	57%
Building operators & managers	$1,903,331	1%	58%	41%
Mortgage bankers & brokers	$801,285	44%	55%	45%
Other real estate services	$67,058	57%	59%	40%
TOTAL	**$16,472,555**	**24%**	**55%**	**45%**
Accountants				
Accountants	$4,877,052	51%	55%	45%

Misc Finance

Misc financial services & consulting	$157,046	5%	53%	47%
Credit reporting services & collection agencies	$142,915	43%	36%	64%
Tax return services	$42,475	47%	56%	44%
Other financial services	$342,440	42%	46%	54%
Other finance, diversified or unclassified	$3,921,389	0%	45%	54%
TOTAL	**$4,606,265**	**5%**	**45%**	**54%**

Health

	Total	PAC Pct	Dem Pct	Repub Pct
Health Professionals				
Physicians	$11,939,475	32%	50%	49%
Psychiatrists & psychologists	$920,126	50%	84%	15%
Optometrists & ophthalmologists	$1,719,077	78%	60%	40%
Other physician specialists	$2,182,598	44%	50%	49%
Dentists	$2,281,306	70%	57%	43%
Chiropractors	$920,007	76%	70%	29%
Nurses	$481,420	74%	81%	19%
Pharmacists	$364,763	85%	70%	30%
Other non-physician health practitioners	$572,073	81%	74%	25%
Health professionals, unclassified	$40,946	1%	92%	6%
TOTAL	**$21,421,791**	**46%**	**56%**	**44%**
Hospitals & Nursing Homes				
Hospitals	$2,369,306	49%	64%	36%
Nursing homes	$1,239,146	40%	65%	34%
Drug & alcohol treatment hospitals	$5,000	0%	100%	0%
Health care institutions, diversified	$25,308	3%	58%	42%
TOTAL	**$3,638,760**	**46%**	**65%**	**35%**
Health Services				
Health care services	$243,446	29%	71%	28%
Home care services	$138,560	43%	73%	27%
HMOs	$448,789	41%	59%	40%
Outpatient health services (incl drug & alcohol)	$194,015	11%	66%	34%
Optical services (glasses & contact lenses)	$19,850	22%	39%	61%
Medical laboratories	$68,412	7%	61%	39%
AIDS treatment & testing	$9,200	0%	89%	11%
TOTAL	**$1,122,272**	**30%**	**65%**	**35%**
Pharmaceuticals/Health Products				
Health care products	$191,060	51%	56%	44%
Medical supplies manufacturing & sales	$787,026	41%	49%	51%
Personal health care products	$157,100	78%	47%	53%
Pharmaceutical manufacturing	$3,147,717	76%	47%	53%
Pharmaceutical wholesale/retail	$156,468	33%	37%	63%
TOTAL	**$4,439,371**	**67%**	**47%**	**53%**
Other & Unclassified				
Health, education & human resources, unclassified	$1,088,045	0%	61%	39%

Lawyers & Lobbyists

	Total	PAC Pct	Dem Pct	Repub Pct
Lawyers & Law Firms				
Attorneys & law firms	$38,233,716	16%	73%	27%
Misc legal services	$3,775	0%	65%	35%
TOTAL	**$38,237,491**	**16%**	**73%**	**27%**
Lobbyists & Public Relations				
Lobbyists & public relations	$4,353,571	6%	73%	27%
Registered foreign agents	$1,467,682	0%	68%	32%
TOTAL	**$5,821,253**	**5%**	**72%**	**28%**

Miscellaneous Business

	Total	PAC Pct	Dem Pct	Repub Pct
Business Associations				
General business associations	$92,254	94%	75%	24%
Chambers of commerce	$114,290	57%	62%	37%
Small business organizations	$369,231	99%	21%	79%
Pro-business organizations	$143,181	96%	9%	91%
General commerce, unclassified or diversified	$215,710	0%	38%	58%
TOTAL	**$934,666**	**70%**	**33%**	**66%**
Food & Beverage				
NOTE: Food manufacturers are listed under Agriculture				
Artificial sweeteners and food additives	$14,700	24%	54%	46%
Restaurants & drinking establishments	$2,994,793	45%	35%	64%
Food catering & food services	$130,840	35%	40%	58%
Confectionary processors & manufacturers	$111,490	20%	34%	66%
Fish Processing	$168,410	13%	46%	54%
Non-alcoholic beverages	$388,539	70%	51%	49%
Beverage bottling & distribution	$255,265	53%	48%	52%
TOTAL	**$4,064,037**	**46%**	**38%**	**61%**
Beer, Wine & Liquor				
Beer	$347,864	46%	51%	49%
Wine & distilled spirits manufacturing	$1,356,172	59%	67%	33%
Beer & liquor wholesalers	$2,273,554	52%	50%	50%
Liquor stores	$95,627	1%	58%	42%
Alcohol, unclassified	$6,400	0%	62%	38%
TOTAL	**$4,079,617**	**52%**	**56%**	**44%**
Retail Sales				
Retail trade, diversified	$580,229	64%	45%	55%
Apparel & accessory stores	$564,284	16%	54%	46%
Consumer electronics & computer stores	$122,350	0%	51%	48%
Department, variety & convenience stores	$998,206	69%	42%	58%
Furniture & appliance stores	$284,881	0%	46%	54%
Hardware & building materials stores	$98,547	0%	40%	59%
Miscellaneous retail stores	$908,808	1%	65%	34%
Catalog & mail order houses	$225,963	42%	48%	51%
Direct sales	$209,979	24%	16%	84%
Vending machine sales & services	$79,170	0%	37%	62%
Drug stores	$457,696	43%	52%	48%
TOTAL	**$4,530,113**	**33%**	**49%**	**51%**
Misc Services				
Equipment rental & leasing	$324,813	50%	43%	57%
Funeral services	$306,098	21%	62%	38%
Laundries & dry cleaners	$119,264	3%	43%	57%
Miscellaneous repair services	$31,765	0%	44%	54%
Pest control	$156,520	44%	50%	50%
Physical fitness centers	$84,190	0%	50%	49%
Video tape rental	$42,550	0%	55%	45%
Other services	$423,750	1%	57%	42%
TOTAL	**$1,488,950**	**20%**	**52%**	**47%**
Business Services				
Beauty & barber shops	$75,363	0%	62%	37%
Advertising & public relations services	$1,256,983	2%	59%	40%
Direct mail advertising services	$198,916	58%	38%	62%
Outdoor advertising services	$644,017	37%	59%	41%
Commercial photography, art & graphic design	$217,155	0%	57%	41%
Employment agencies	$382,844	22%	47%	53%
Management consultants & services	$1,697,109	0%	53%	47%
Marketing research services	$211,325	55%	53%	47%
Security services	$374,126	34%	44%	55%
Other business services	$2,520,185	3%	59%	39%
TOTAL	**$7,578,023**	**10%**	**56%**	**44%**
Recreation & Live Entertainment				
Professional sports, arenas & related equip & svcs	$265,427	4%	61%	39%
Amusement parks	$28,650	0%	21%	79%

Misc recreation/entertainment	$177,415	5%	72%	27%
TOTAL	**$471,492**	**4%**	**62%**	**37%**

Casinos & Gambling
Casinos, racetracks & gambling	$740,605	31%	69%	31%

Lodging/Tourism
Lodging & tourism, diversified	$76,350	26%	49%	51%
Hotels & motels	$1,014,488	29%	48%	52%
Resorts	$127,933	14%	49%	51%
Travel agents	$376,368	18%	58%	41%
TOTAL	**$1,595,139**	**25%**	**50%**	**49%**

Other Miscellaneous Non-Manufacturing Business
Water Utilities	$157,050	74%	54%	46%
Wholesale trade	$344,191	33%	38%	62%
Warehousing	$109,090	0%	40%	60%
TOTAL	**$610,331**	**38%**	**42%**	**58%**

Chemical & Related Manufacturing
Chemicals	$2,184,662	57%	31%	68%
Explosives	$23,300	54%	74%	26%
Household cleansers & chemicals	$266,042	66%	44%	56%
Plastics & rubber processing & products	$528,022	12%	24%	76%
Paints, solvents & coatings	$74,393	20%	29%	71%
Adhesives & sealants	$12,200	20%	34%	66%
TOTAL	**$3,088,619**	**49%**	**31%**	**68%**

Steel Production
Steel production	$870,603	32%	38%	62%

Misc Manufacturing & Distributing
Manufacturing	$233,421	0%	32%	67%
Manmade fibers	$194,800	96%	47%	53%
Heavy industrial manufacturing	$135,877	0%	62%	38%
Smelting and non-petroleum refining	$76,440	0%	44%	56%
Industrial/commercial equipment & materials	$1,651,109	29%	26%	74%
Recycling of scrap metal, paper, plastics, etc.	$220,346	26%	65%	35%
Personal products manufacturing, diversified	$80,504	0%	41%	59%
Clothing & accessories	$802,122	1%	61%	39%
Shoes & leather products	$227,913	24%	52%	48%
Toiletries & cosmetics	$344,012	16%	47%	53%
Jewelry	$291,270	2%	79%	21%
Toys	$63,659	0%	37%	63%
Sporting goods sales & manufacturing	$73,015	4%	47%	52%
Household & office products	$215,248	15%	42%	58%
Furniture & wood products	$378,034	23%	32%	68%
Office machines	$130,763	42%	42%	58%
Household appliances	$158,950	54%	32%	68%
Fabricated metal products	$540,047	8%	28%	71%
Hardware & tools	$80,665	8%	23%	77%
Electroplating, polishing & related services	$58,225	7%	26%	74%
Small arms & ammunition	$43,381	0%	31%	69%
Electrical lighting products	$13,100	0%	41%	59%
Paper, glass & packaging materials	$222,678	19%	39%	81%
Paper packaging materials	$502,071	71%	18%	81%
Glass products	$461,372	82%	34%	66%
Metal cans & containers	$41,750	44%	34%	66%
Precision instruments	$76,675	0%	34%	65%
Optical instruments & lenses	$33,200	0%	12%	87%
Photographic equipment & supplies	$22,450	0%	49%	47%
Clocks & watches	$8,500	53%	74%	26%
TOTAL	**$7,381,597**	**27%**	**39%**	**61%**

Textiles
Textiles & fabrics	$1,044,215	34%	56%	43%

Transportation

	Total	PAC Pct	Dem Pct	Repub Pct
Air Transport				
Airlines	$1,242,710	77%	61%	38%
Air freight	$51,000	45%	21%	78%
Express delivery services	$2,224,752	99%	59%	41%
Aircraft manufacturers	$423,090	81%	56%	44%
Aircraft parts & equipment	$913,962	68%	47%	53%
General aviation (private pilots)	$491,356	98%	55%	45%
Aviation services & airports	$155,237	33%	53%	47%
Space vehicles & components	$35,150	67%	64%	36%
Air transport, diversified	$117,954	8%	42%	58%
TOTAL	**$5,655,211**	**83%**	**56%**	**44%**
Automotive				
Auto manufacturers	$786,478	77%	55%	45%
Truck/automotive parts & accessories	$840,264	44%	25%	75%
Auto dealers, new & used	$3,211,769	56%	36%	64%
Auto dealers, Japanese imports	$1,231,814	82%	28%	72%
Auto repair	$76,294	4%	56%	43%
Car & truck rental agencies	$298,468	29%	46%	53%
Misc automotive	$49,417	0%	38%	62%
TOTAL	**$6,494,504**	**59%**	**36%**	**64%**
Trucking				
Trucking companies & services	$1,702,073	57%	49%	51%
Truck & trailer manufacturers	$86,750	47%	23%	77%
Misc trucking	$32,733	11%	35%	65%
TOTAL	**$1,821,556**	**56%**	**48%**	**52%**
Railroads				
Railroads	$1,929,846	88%	49%	51%
Railroad industry services	$71,254	61%	75%	25%
Manufacturers of railroad equipment	$146,915	27%	31%	69%
Misc railroad transportation	$31,981	0%	37%	62%
TOTAL	**$2,179,996**	**82%**	**48%**	**52%**
Sea Transport				
Ship building & repair	$526,466	50%	47%	53%
Sea freight & passenger services	$1,347,755	63%	56%	44%
Sea transport, diversified	$188,130	1%	64%	36%
TOTAL	**$2,062,351**	**54%**	**54%**	**46%**
Misc Transport				
Buses & Taxis	$57,725	23%	62%	38%
Bus services	$207,305	51%	65%	35%
Taxicabs	$108,436	21%	56%	44%
Local freight & delivery services	$83,700	3%	44%	56%
Motorcycles, snowmobiles & other motorized vehicles	$73,275	88%	27%	73%
Bicycles & other non-motorized recreational transport	$22,434	99%	36%	64%
Motor homes & camper trailers	$24,851	0%	16%	84%
Pleasure boats	$61,200	77%	52%	47%
Recreational transport, diversified	$9,500	0%	26%	74%
Other transportation	$127,646	0%	29%	66%
TOTAL	**$776,072**	**36%**	**48%**	**51%**

Labor

	Total	PAC Pct	Dem Pct	Repub Pct
Building Trade Unions				
Building trade unions	$6,904,679	99%	94%	6%
Industrial Unions				
Communications & hi-tech unions	$1,426,390	100%	98%	1%
Intl Brotherhood of Electrical Workers (IBEW)	$1,575,999	99%	96%	3%
Mining unions	$459,600	100%	98%	2%
Energy-related unions (non-mining)	$137,840	100%	96%	1%
Manufacturing unions	$6,906,117	100%	98%	1%
TOTAL	**$10,505,946**	**100%**	**98%**	**2%**

Transportation Unions

	Total	PAC Pct	Dem Pct	Repub Pct
Transportation unions	$1,750	0%	100%	0%
Air transport unions	$1,657,643	100%	89%	11%
Teamsters Union	$2,532,956	100%	94%	5%
Railroad unions	$1,622,854	100%	97%	3%
Mechant marine & longshoremen unions	$3,125,766	100%	82%	18%
Other transportation unions	$1,279,765	100%	97%	3%
TOTAL	**$10,220,734**	**100%**	**91%**	**9%**

Public Sector Unions

	Total	PAC Pct	Dem Pct	Repub Pct
Federal employees unions	$1,882,828	100%	84%	16%
State & local govt employee unions	$1,955,613	100%	97%	2%
Teachers unions	$3,477,117	100%	96%	3%
US Postal Service unions & associations	$3,822,198	100%	89%	10%
Police & firefighters unions & associations	$610,625	99%	93%	6%
TOTAL	**$11,748,381**	**100%**	**92%**	**8%**

Misc Unions

	Total	PAC Pct	Dem Pct	Repub Pct
Labor unions, diversified	$869,240	96%	99%	1%
Agricultural labor unions	$1,940	48%	100%	0%
General commercial unions	$1,250	0%	80%	20%
Food service & related unions	$570,217	97%	95%	5%
Retail trade unions	$1,518,786	100%	97%	2%
Commercial service unions	$1,950	100%	100%	0%
Entertainment unions	$31,750	100%	97%	3%
Health worker unions	$15,980	100%	81%	0%
Other commercial unions	$744,681	100%	98%	1%
Other unions	$164,063	100%	100%	0%
TOTAL	**$3,919,857**	**99%**	**97%**	**2%**

Ideological/Single-Issue

	Total	PAC Pct	Dem Pct	Repub Pct
Republican/Conservative				
Republican/Conservative	$2,479,934	32%	2%	97%
Democratic/Liberal				
Democratic/Liberal	$2,658,027	52%	98%	1%
Leadership PACs				
Democratic leadership PAC	$1,342,037	100%	100%	0%
Republican leadership PAC	$851,893	99%	1%	99%
Democratic officials, candidates & former members	$26,384	100%	100%	0%
Republican officials, candidates & former members	$10,050	100%	0%	100%
State & local candidate committees	$210,571	100%	27%	73%
TOTAL	**$2,440,935**	**99%**	**59%**	**41%**
Foreign & Defense Policy				
Foreign policy	$355,259	67%	61%	38%
Defense policy, Pro-Defense	$191,985	92%	25%	75%
Defense policy, Pro-Peace	$370,918	53%	92%	0%
TOTAL	**$918,162**	**67%**	**66%**	**30%**
Pro-Israel				
Pro-Israel	$7,401,113	54%	71%	29%
Abortion Policy				
Abortion policy, Pro-Life	$486,407	85%	11%	89%
Abortion policy, Pro-Choice	$1,317,768	65%	84%	15%
TOTAL	**$1,804,175**	**71%**	**64%**	**35%**
Gun Rights/Gun Control				
Pro-Guns	$1,854,555	98%	35%	65%
Anti-Guns	$169,512	95%	84%	16%
TOTAL	**$2,024,067**	**98%**	**39%**	**61%**
Womens Issues				
Womens issues	$3,725,735	42%	84%	9%
Human Rights				
Human Rights	$74,507	28%	99%	1%
Gay & lesbian rights & issues	$928,654	82%	90%	8%

	Total	PAC Pct	Dem Pct	Repub Pct
Minority/ethnic groups	$365,619	65%	55%	45%
Childrens' rights	$453,800	100%	96%	4%
Health & welfare policy	$512,855	29%	89%	11%
TOTAL	**$2,335,435**	**70%**	**86%**	**13%**

Misc Issues

	Total	PAC Pct	Dem Pct	Repub Pct
Third-party committees	$15,769	15%	46%	0%
Consumer groups	$7,535	61%	100%	0%
Fiscal & tax policy	$111,404	86%	4%	96%
Elderly issues/social security	$1,167,425	100%	90%	10%
Animal rights	$24,850	21%	100%	0%
Labor, anti-union	$374,006	92%	1%	98%
Environmental policy	$1,633,398	73%	94%	5%
Other single-issue/ideological groups	$209,944	64%	30%	69%
TOTAL	**$3,544,331**	**83%**	**76%**	**23%**

Other & Unknown

	Total	PAC Pct	Dem Pct	Repub Pct

Non-Profit Institutions

	Total	PAC Pct	Dem Pct	Repub Pct
Non-Profits	$130,204	0%	89%	10%
Non-profit foundations	$222,569	0%	61%	39%
Museums, art galleries, libraries, etc.	$165,447	0%	71%	28%
TOTAL	**$518,220**	**0%**	**71%**	**28%**

Civil Servants/Public Officials

	Total	PAC Pct	Dem Pct	Repub Pct
Civil servant/public employee	$2,995,085	0%	62%	37%
Public official (elected or appointed)	$152,295	0%	60%	40%
Courts & justice system	$345,231	0%	71%	28%
TOTAL	**$3,492,611**	**0%**	**63%**	**36%**

Education

	Total	PAC Pct	Dem Pct	Repub Pct
Schools & colleges	$2,355,025	0%	72%	26%
Medical schools	$207,488	0%	78%	22%
Law schools	$145,745	0%	85%	14%
Technical, business and vocational schools & services	$373,522	34%	59%	41%
Public school teachers, administrators & officials	$674,494	0%	78%	21%
Education, unclassified	$585,559	0%	66%	29%
TOTAL	**$4,341,833**	**3%**	**72%**	**27%**

Retired

	Total	PAC Pct	Dem Pct	Repub Pct
Retired	$15,930,210	0%	45%	54%

Other

	Total	PAC Pct	Dem Pct	Repub Pct
Welfare & Social Work	$392,566	48%	89%	10%
Military	$125,803	0%	46%	50%
Other	$662,357	9%	70%	35%
TOTAL	**$1,180,726**	**21%**	**74%**	**29%**

Homemakers & Other Non-Income Earners

	Total	PAC Pct	Dem Pct	Repub Pct
Homemakers, students & other non-income earners	$13,650,755	0%	48%	51%

Unknown

	Total	PAC Pct	Dem Pct	Repub Pct
Unknown PACs	$85,426	100%	75%	22%
No employer listed or found	$33,504,033	0%	49%	51%
Generic occupation - impossible to assign category	$3,021,287	0%	46%	52%
Employer listed but category unknown	**$34,413,382**	**0%**	**51%**	**48%**

Appendix B: Members' Totals by Sector

The charts below show the industry-by-industry breakdown of contributions received by each member of Congress elected (or already in office) in 1992. The figures include both PACs and individual contributions of $200 or more. They are shown in thousands of dollars, rounded off to the nearest $1,000. A brief rundown of the industries and interest groups included in each sector can be found on pages 42-43. Detailed explanations and analyses of their spending patterns are provided on pages 44-93.

One important caveat: Senate totals cover the period 1987-92, *but do not include individual contributions made before 1989*. The totals for senators elected in 1988 will therefore be low, since most of their individual contributions were received in 1987-88. (PAC contributions for the entire 1987-1992 period are included). The totals for House members cover the 1991-92 election cycle.

To help identify the leading recipients of funds from a particular sector, members who rank in the top 10 percent of each sector are marked with an asterisk (*). The top-ranking recipient from each sector is marked with a dagger (†).

Senate

Name	Agriculture	Comm/Elec	Construction	Defense	Energy	Finance	Health	Law/Lobby	Transport	Misc Bus	Labor	Ideol
Akaka, Daniel K. (D-Hawaii)	$67	$53	$126	$25	$43	$174	$63	$87	$65	$85	$412*	$241
Baucus, Max (D-Mont)	$159	$132	$46	$4	$163	$532	$188	$264	$110	$227	$268	$232
Bennett, Robert F. (R-Utah)	$34	$33	$14	$22	$80	$102	$36	$23	$62	$63	$0	$28
Bentsen, Lloyd (D-Texas)	$154	$140	$97	$92	$348*	$745	$192	$205	$156	$236	$185	$94
Biden, Joseph R. Jr. (D-Del)	$9	$132	$35	$4	$21	$224	$42	$234	$25	$107	$286	$178
Bingaman, Jeff (D-NM)	$60	$23	$25	$127	$130	$140	$93	$121	$41	$52	$273	$241
Bond, Christopher S. (R-Mo)	$360*	$160	$183*	$106	$235	$848*	$261	$249	$198*	$510*	$30	$146
Boren, David L. (D-Okla)	$67	$36	$24	$4	$201	$212	$49	$172	$23	$70	$0	$21
Boxer, Barbara (D-Calif)	$42	$485*	$63	$4	$33	$363	$287	$687*	$28	$258	$327	$848*
Bradley, Bill (D-NJ)	$76	$528†	$200*	$38	$197	$1930†	$313*	$1060†	$133	$496*	$228	$282
Breaux, John B. (D-La)	$206	$187	$80	$54	$348*	$414	$167	$283	$264*	$273	$151	$64
Brown, Hank (R-Colo)	$205	$173	$140*	$52	$245	$567	$115	$167	$126	$301	$22	$186
Bryan, Richard H. (D-Nev)	$25	$33	$46	$1	$31	$170	$81	$66	$52	$162	$312	$173
Bumpers, Dale (D-Ark)	$271	$66	$67	$29	$178	$278	$94	$214	$77	$130	$66	$38
Burns, Conrad (R-Mont)	$95	$90	$29	$12	$71	$68	$10	$22	$82	$52	$0	$118
Byrd, Robert C. (D-WVa)	$79	$42	$41	$106	$127	$157	$41	$40	$61	$70	$234	$59
Campbell, Ben N. (D-Colo)	$101	$53	$8	$3	$99	$126	$83	$130	$40	$77	$270	$144
Chafee, John H. (R-RI)	$53	$79	$72	$78	$66	$373	$146	$38	$80	$136	$25	$77
Coats, Daniel R. (R-Ind)	$344*	$235*	$367†	$359†	$390*	$821*	$517*	$188	$246*	$611*	$7	$268
Cochran, Thad (R-Miss)	$309*	$29	$46	$81	$92	$136	$76	$72	$50	$79	$25	$29
Cohen, William S. (R-Maine)	$72	$59	$60	$98	$25	$233	$77	$64	$25	$107	$36	$152
Conrad, Kent (D-ND)	$285*	$47	$19	$10	$279	$246	$98	$170	$74	$101	$331	$168
Coverdell, Paul (R-Ga)	$231	$59	$116	$4	$111	$472	$146	$226	$77	$370	$0	$156
Craig, Larry E. (R-Idaho)	$232	$40	$62	$13	$232	$163	$51	$27	$87	$103	$6	$65
D'Amato, Alfonse M. (R-NY)	$175	$209	$326*	$146	$121	$1540*	$234	$505	$152	$528*	$129	$204
Danforth, John C. (R-Mo)	$77	$125	$59	$80	$93	$271	$90	$33	$160	$148	$11	$78
Daschle, Tom (D-SD)	$244	$153	$36	$11	$81	$548	$322*	$291	$111	$288	$325	$237
DeConcini, Dennis (D-Ariz)	$101	$117	$40	$137	$80	$328	$98	$121	$48	$105	$180	$114
Dodd, Christopher J. (D-Conn)	$96	$219*	$95	$54	$55	$1120*	$211	$339	$92	$186	$307	$257
Dole, Bob (R-Kan)	$430*	$230*	$100	$66	$319*	$795*	$186	$268	$246*	$359	$10	$91
Domenici, Pete V. (R-NM)	$91	$42	$50	$101	$368*	$307	$90	$107	$69	$129	$34	$71
Dorgan, Byron L. (D-ND)	$99	$28	$4	$2	$49	$161	$57	$54	$41	$72	$219	$62
Durenberger, Dave (R-Minn)	$207	$93	$91	$52	$93	$382	$308*	$81	$118	$220	$70	$236
Exon, Jim (D-Neb)	$150	$154	$33	$161*	$67	$298	$75	$138	$267*	$121	$292	$181
Faircloth, Lauch (R-NC)	$195	$45	$89	$15	$62	$166	$71	$44	$87	$194	$0	$97
Feingold, Russell (D-Wis)	$20	$40	$11	$0	$2	$86	$105	$204	$5	$57	$235	$124

* Ranks in top 10% of Senate in receipts from this sector
† Leading Senate recipient of funds from this sector

Breakdown of Contributions by Industry & Interest Group Sectors
Totals in Thousands of Dollars

Senate

Name	Agriculture	Comm/Elec	Construction	Defense	Energy	Finance	Health	Law/Lobby	Transport	Misc Bus	Labor	Ideol
Feinstein, Dianne (D-Calif).	$134	$375*	$137	$17	$72	$780*	$329*	$707*	$93	$405*	$299	$543*
Ford, Wendell H. (D-Ky).	$183	$97	$57	$15	$266	$291	$81	$188	$197*	$178	$240	$39
Glenn, John (D-Ohio).	$38	$79	$70	$169*	$114	$384	$173	$251	$85	$203	$396*	$294
Gore, Al (D-Tenn).	$92	$212	$72	$121	$91	$385	$128	$307	$123	$131	$397*	$191
Gorton, Slade (R-Wash).	$173	$121	$85	$82	$137	$204	$56	$59	$158	$155	$13	$98
Graham, Bob (D-Fla).	$148	$157	$132	$33	$150	$546	$226	$464	$125	$265	$193	$145
Gramm, Phil (R-Texas).	$635†	$212	$364*	$217*	$1061†	$1572*	$624†	$785*	$307*	$914†	$26	$267
Grassley, Charles E. (R-Iowa).	$209	$120	$72	$11	$63	$323	$193	$88	$125	$149	$8	$140
Gregg, Judd (R-NH).	$39	$45	$27	$20	$36	$160	$86	$35	$37	$103	$0	$21
Harkin, Tom (D-Iowa).	$257	$111	$42	$72	$70	$491	$353*	$311	$94	$177	$682†	$744*
Hatch, Orrin G. (R-Utah).	$143	$107	$113	$69	$116	$252	$227	$74	$91	$225	$13	$72
Hatfield, Mark O. (R-Ore).	$242	$109	$79	$73	$173	$275	$100	$126	$124	$135	$118	$102
Heflin, Howell (D-Ala).	$421*	$168	$77	$64	$283	$403	$112	$496	$112	$167	$200	$221
Helms, Jesse (R-NC).	$318*	$79	$109	$31	$110	$271	$135	$83	$94	$321	$1	$363
Hollings, Ernest F. (D-SC).	$179	$437*	$73	$148	$122	$387	$143	$559*	$331†	$368	$154	$114
Inouye, Daniel K. (D-Hawaii).	$58	$148	$64	$114	$27	$426	$142	$171	$145	$179	$173	$235
Jeffords, James M. (R-Vt).	$102	$33	$59	$13	$28	$111	$60	$7	$34	$79	$96	$58
Johnston, J. Bennett (D-La).	$171	$102	$91	$189*	$664*	$307	$105	$305	$123	$143	$138	$211
Kassebaum, Nancy (R-Kan).	$28	$22	$16	$3	$27	$81	$24	$11	$12	$40	$3	$18
Kempthorne, Dirk (R-Idaho).	$223	$54	$60	$17	$113	$110	$28	$21	$63	$103	$0	$44
Kennedy, Edward M. (D-Mass).	$12	$48	$23	$21	$21	$208	$122	$178	$20	$116	$131	$72
Kerrey, Bob (D-Neb).	$139	$68	$17	$9	$42	$182	$84	$78	$84	$46	$469*	$259
Kerry, John (D-Mass).	$40	$353*	$145*	$10	$68	$853*	$143	$670*	$42	$380*	$8	$299
Kohl, Herb (D-Wis).	$1	$0	$0	$0	$0	$0	$0	$0	$2	$0	$2	$0
Lautenberg, Frank R. (D-NJ).	$45	$141	$138*	$66	$76	$558	$222	$321	$196*	$211	$377*	$443*
Leahy, Patrick J. (D-Vt).	$87	$115	$11	$15	$10	$106	$17	$115	$12	$71	$82	$74
Levin, Carl (D-Mich).	$93	$145	$95	$113	$88	$615	$168	$508*	$131	$328	$405*	$868*
Lieberman, Joseph I. (D-Conn).	$26	$38	$54	$9	$33	$349	$65	$151	$44	$157	$87	$166
Lott, Trent (R-Miss).	$190	$106	$81	$94	$154	$198	$49	$38	$106	$199	$23	$135
Lugar, Richard G. (R-Ind).	$302*	$93	$102	$57	$107	$296	$119	$76	$114	$193	$3	$40
Mack, Connie (R-Fla).	$188	$120	$133	$77	$173	$432	$179	$117	$163	$258	$26	$190
McCain, John (R-Ariz).	$152	$131	$83	$143	$161	$337	$257	$103	$167	$246	$53	$204
McConnell, Mitch (R-Ky).	$375*	$76	$144*	$30	$391*	$392	$215	$189	$103	$296	$3	$322
Metzenbaum, Howard (D-Ohio).	$11	$41	$14	$7	$17	$35	$46	$38	$25	$34	$347*	$405*
Mikulski, Barbara A. (D-Md).	$47	$93	$45	$159*	$47	$221	$179	$180	$53	$151	$329	$248
Mitchell, George J. (D-Maine).	$40	$28	$20	$21	$27	$172	$107	$20	$24	$51	$144	$93
Moseley-Braun, Carol (D-Ill).	$36	$69	$24	$1	$21	$229	$127	$357	$26	$108	$282	$451*
Moynihan, Daniel P. (D-NY).	$17	$82	$84	$14	$70	$469	$119	$140	$59	$123	$195	$117
Murkowski, Frank H. (R-Alaska).	$65	$76	$89	$55	$239	$210	$70	$103	$149	$150	$20	$85
Murray, Patty (D-Wash).	$11	$21	$1	$0	$25	$24	$40	$41	$14	$23	$258	$200
Nickles, Don (R-Okla).	$230	$99	$106	$142	$637*	$432	$184	$179	$137	$209	$4	$117
Nunn, Sam (D-Ga).	$133	$85	$82	$114	$75	$410	$82	$179	$52	$182	$41	$36
Packwood, Bob (R-Ore).	$192	$332*	$47	$9	$101	$572	$303*	$289	$267*	$371*	$95	$306
Pell, Claiborne (D-RI).	$21	$74	$33	$29	$39	$305	$74	$129	$49	$86	$285	$394*
Pressler, Larry (R-SD).	$117	$132	$59	$9	$68	$462	$90	$93	$167	$165	$18	$251
Pryor, David (D-Ark).	$227	$36	$21	$5	$61	$289	$82	$119	$46	$76	$62	$18
Reid, Harry (D-Nev).	$58	$79	$119	$53	$166	$233	$235	$271	$110	$499*	$266	$185
Riegle, Donald W. Jr. (D-Mich).	$58	$56	$28	$20	$67	$480	$80	$75	$113	$86	$256	$135
Robb, Charles S. (D-Va).	$78	$64	$36	$64	$107	$184	$60	$36	$52	$83	$135	$76
Rockefeller, John IV (D-WVa).	$107	$174	$80	$11	$231	$641	$482*	$287	$132	$301	$242	$227
Roth, William V. Jr. (R-Del).	$40	$43	$38	$35	$71	$243	$76	$26	$65	$91	$22	$62
Sarbanes, Paul S. (D-Md).	$11	$11	$23	$4	$7	$109	$14	$18	$27	$38	$286	$81
Sasser, Jim (D-Tenn).	$107	$43	$69	$119	$52	$374	$90	$58	$74	$102	$301	$144
Shelby, Richard C. (D-Ala).	$193	$165	$100	$172*	$272	$646	$226	$423	$108	$152	$156	$184
Simon, Paul (D-Ill).	$133	$195	$60	$10	$80	$553	$236	$644*	$99	$309	$599*	$892†

* Ranks in top 10% of Senate in receipts from this sector
† Leading Senate recipient of funds from this sector

Breakdown of Contributions by Industry & Interest Group Sectors
Totals in Thousands of Dollars

Senate

Name	Agriculture	Comm/Elec	Construction	Defense	Energy	Finance	Health	Law/Lobby	Transport	Misc Bus	Labor	Ideol
Simpson, Alan K. (R-Wyo)	$86	$88	$54	$23	$194	$243	$64	$61	$84	$117	$6	$27
Smith, Robert C. (R-NH)	$70	$35	$95	$95	$78	$202	$76	$24	$62	$144	$3	$113
Specter, Arlen (R-Pa)	$241	$315*	$297*	$205*	$343*	$1195*	$531*	$911*	$175	$802*	$255	$385
Stevens, Ted (R-Alaska)	$36	$148	$34	$199*	$139	$151	$51	$104	$103	$67	$113	$54
Thurmond, Strom (R-SC)	$96	$42	$68	$120	$59	$217	$87	$112	$44	$139	$2	$103
Wallop, Malcolm (R-Wyo)	$82	$47	$33	$84	$238	$189	$53	$42	$69	$102	$6	$83
Warner, John W. (R-Va)	$98	$46	$111	$207*	$120	$258	$61	$120	$113	$134	$34	$74
Wellstone, Paul (D-Minn)	$21	$22	$3	$0	$6	$18	$19	$42	$4	$16	$274	$115
Wofford, Harris (D-Pa)	$37	$104	$65	$10	$122	$345	$156	$724*	$34	$163	$464*	$391*

House of Representatives

Name	Agriculture	Comm/Elec	Construction	Defense	Energy	Finance	Health	Law/Lobby	Transport	Misc Bus	Labor	Ideol
Abercrombie, Neil (D-Hawaii)	$9	$4	$14	$2	$5	$26	$3	$14	$14	$7	$116	$11
Ackerman, Gary L. (D-NY)	$6	$19	$15	$2	$4	$115	$64*	$24	$19	$37	$186*	$26
Allard, Wayne (R-Colo)	$87*	$19	$16	$2	$40	$38	$27	$5	$30	$37	$23	$16
Andrews, Michael A. (D-Texas)	$28	$40	$20	$18	$116*	$203*	$81*	$112*	$35	$61*	$41	$12
Andrews, Robert E. (D-NJ)	$14	$15	$31*	$1	$15	$45	$45	$47	$12	$22	$166*	$24
Andrews, Thomas H. (D-Maine)	$7	$17	$6	$13	$4	$58	$42	$55	$8	$17	$213*	$94*
Applegate, Douglas (D-Ohio)	$8	$4	$2	$0	$8	$7	$2	$1	$10	$2	$39	$2
Archer, Bill (R-Texas)	$3	$0	$0	$0	$4	$19	$4	$3	$0	$6	$0	$0
Armey, Dick (R-Texas)	$23	$18	$22	$17	$31	$66	$11	$4	$30	$34	$0	$10
Aspin, Les (D-Wis)	$32	$30	$24	$221*	$39	$131*	$37	$116*	$32	$89*	$100	$98*
Bacchus, Jim (D-Fla)	$30	$25	$23	$22	$14	$136*	$99*	$72*	$21	$26	$178*	$54*
Bachus, Spencer (R-Ala)	$17	$18	$48*	$1	$29	$98	$33	$37	$9	$47	$0	$13
Baesler, Scotty (D-Ky)	$14	$2	$20	$0	$9	$25	$19	$19	$1	$8	$2	$0
Baker, Bill (R-Calif)	$29	$15	$36*	$3	$19	$112	$36	$13	$22	$61*	$1	$24
Baker, Richard H. (R-La)	$22	$13	$24	$4	$32	$203*	$49	$61*	$38	$37	$2	$7
Ballenger, Cass (R-NC)	$34	$14	$13	$5	$14	$26	$15	$5	$25	$57	$1	$9
Barcia, James A. (D-Mich)	$9	$7	$7	$1	$14	$17	$20	$6	$14	$19	$38	$16
Barlow, Tom (D-Ky)	$9	$2	$1	$0	$3	$8	$6	$6	$6	$1	$58	$6
Barrett, Bill (R-Neb)	$63*	$11	$12	$0	$12	$78	$25	$2	$20	$30	$1	$7
Barrett, Thomas (D-Wis)	$6	$8	$4	$0	$3	$35	$25	$28	$10	$9	$65	$7
Bartlett, Roscoe G. (R-Md)	$8	$5	$13	$1	$23	$10	$7	$1	$9	$21	$0	$13
Barton, Joe L. (R-Texas)	$40	$69*	$38*	$42*	$137*	$93	$51	$41	$54*	$60	$1	$17
Bateman, Herbert H. (R-Va)	$34	$12	$34*	$104*	$42	$76	$30	$18	$38	$45	$16	$10
Becerra, Xavier (D-Calif)	$5	$7	$5	$2	$1	$20	$20	$23	$2	$7	$54	$14
Beilenson, Anthony C. (D-Calif)	$1	$57*	$7	$0	$2	$81	$25	$77*	$2	$30	$0	$48
Bentley, Helen Delich (R-Md)	$27	$17	$37*	$17	$41	$76	$24	$51	$84*	$69*	$51	$12
Bereuter, Doug (R-Neb)	$35	$8	$10	$6	$7	$104	$13	$6	$14	$11	$2	$1
Berman, Howard L. (D-Calif)	$5	$102*	$6	$4	$6	$70	$32	$82*	$12	$34	$78	$27
Bevill, Tom (D-Ala)	$12	$9	$18	$6	$40	$18	$7	$22	$12	$1	$11	$5
Bilbray, James (D-Nev)	$8	$9	$7	$22	$20	$50	$50	$37	$11	$62*	$91	$25
Bilirakis, Michael (R-Fla)	$45	$58*	$23	$3	$40	$73	$109*	$16	$16	$46	$12	$19
Bishop, Sanford (D-Ga)	$14	$3	$5	$0	$6	$60	$25	$18	$10	$18	$36	$15
Blackwell, Lucien E. (D-Pa)	$3	$3	$10	$5	$5	$22	$13	$47	$10	$10	$102	$6
Bliley, Thomas J. Jr. (R-Va)	$89*	$52*	$8	$6	$64*	$101	$87*	$24	$33	$55	$3	$3
Blute, Peter (R-Mass)	$2	$7	$7	$1	$7	$30	$32	$14	$4	$31	$0	$14

* Ranks in top 10% of House/Senate in PAC receipts from this sector in 1991-92
† Ranks as leading House/Senate recipient in PAC receipts from this sector in 1991-92

Breakdown of Contributions by Industry & Interest Group Sectors
Totals in Thousands of Dollars

Name	Agriculture	Comm/Elec	Construction	Defense	Energy	Finance	Health	Law/Lobby	Transport	Misc Bus	Labor	Ideol
Boehlert, Sherwood (R-NY)	$18	$16	$13	$6	$13	$37	$20	$7	$27	$28	$55	$10
Boehner, John A. (R-Ohio)	$64*	$24	$32*	$4	$17	$45	$29	$2	$22	$52	$1	$11
Bonilla, Henry (R-Texas)	$36	$17	$17	$2	$62*	$67	$34	$13	$11	$37	$0	$9
Bonior, David E. (D-Mich)	$82*	$88*	$19	$18	$42	$160*	$83*	$56	$89*	$59	$287*	$85*
Borski, Robert A. (D-Pa)	$2	$13	$23	$11	$11	$37	$18	$41	$38	$36	$150*	$13
Boucher, Rick (D-Va)	$35	$59*	$9	$9	$59*	$102	$47	$30	$26	$26	$51	$7
Brewster, Bill (D-Okla)	$37	$16	$20	$4	$72*	$26	$53	$24	$33	$34	$15	$15
Brooks, Jack (D-Texas)	$21	$84*	$16	$12	$34	$85	$26	$71*	$35	$36	$92	$17
Browder, Glen (D-Ala)	$16	$6	$4	$22	$8	$19	$12	$14	$6	$10	$24	$4
Brown, Corrine (D-Fla)	$5	$10	$9	$0	$5	$11	$10	$15	$7	$3	$57	$48
Brown, George E. Jr. (D-Calif)	$49	$49*	$26	$66*	$49*	$43	$16	$43	$22	$14	$173*	$69*
Brown, Sherrod (R-Ohio)	$3	$7	$3	$1	$5	$49	$28	$40	$9	$19	$148*	$49
Bryant, John (D-Texas)	$29	$54*	$5	$1	$31	$54	$64*	$85*	$33	$27	$100	$13
Bunning, Jim (R-Ky)	$64*	$42*	$24	$5	$56*	$178*	$68*	$28	$53*	$90*	$8	$6
Burton, Dan (R-Ind)	$30	$26	$19	$3	$15	$88	$37	$11	$32	$50	$10	$45
Buyer, Steve (R-Ind)	$64*	$7	$24	$1	$15	$24	$21	$2	$10	$38	$0	$5
Byrne, Leslie L. (D-Va)	$8	$9	$2	$4	$7	$25	$38	$34	$9	$9	$150*	$90*
Callahan, Sonny (R-Ala)	$52	$21	$21	$2	$36	$53	$45	$10	$34	$31	$21	$3
Calvert, Ken (R-Calif)	$24	$11	$35*	$4	$12	$66	$21	$17	$27	$28	$1	$21
Camp, Dave (R-Mich)	$64*	$16	$18	$0	$22	$29	$23	$13	$15	$85*	$5	$7
Canady, Charles T. (R-Fla)	$20	$2	$6	$1	$7	$12	$5	$5	$5	$10	$0	$10
Cantwell, Maria (D-Wash)	$7	$9	$0	$0	$20	$27	$30	$35	$6	$15	$143*	$67*
Cardin, Benjamin L. (D-Md)	$14	$10	$8	$3	$10	$131*	$94*	$36	$24	$40	$32	$23
Carr, Bob (D-Mich)	$37	$40	$52*	$53*	$46*	$78	$29	$119*	$129*	$61*	$134	$56*
Castle, Michael N. (R-Del)	$15	$13	$16	$2	$15	$205*	$32	$47	$30	$55	$12	$4
Chapman, Jim (D-Texas)	$35	$8	$8	$39*	$34	$18	$22	$20	$21	$13	$32	$10
Clay, William L. (D-Mo)	$8	$10	$1	$0	$2	$22	$20	$18	$9	$15	$157*	$13
Clayton, Eva (D-NC)	$15	$7	$1	$1	$3	$26	$32	$21	$2	$5	$136	$75*
Clement, Bob (D-Tenn)	$33	$27	$21	$4	$25	$56	$23	$27	$77*	$44	$73	$10
Clinger, William F. (R-Pa)	$9	$10	$12	$1	$19	$21	$7	$7	$45*	$19	$11	$1
Clyburn, Jim (D-SC)	$10	$9	$4	$0	$14	$30	$18	$29	$10	$14	$29	$18
Coble, J. Howard (R-NC)	$32	$36	$11	$4	$15	$52	$26	$11	$19	$55	$4	$13
Coleman, Ronald D. (D-Texas)	$33	$9	$22	$29*	$30	$43	$19	$58	$45*	$31	$182*	$63*
Collins, Barbara-Rose (D-Mich)	$7	$14	$3	$3	$9	$7	$5	$6	$17	$8	$87	$16
Collins, Cardiss (D-Ill)	$3	$24	$1	$1	$4	$93	$12	$34	$9	$11	$57	$3
Collins, Mac (R-Ga)	$8	$5	$3	$1	$10	$20	$10	$6	$10	$15	$3	$14
Combest, Larry (R-Texas)	$55	$7	$5	$5	$19	$29	$16	$2	$15	$8	$0	$1
Condit, Gary (D-Calif)	$87*	$8	$5	$2	$6	$23	$15	$10	$3	$12	$43	$4
Conyers, John Jr. (D-Mich)	$4	$49*	$9	$7	$6	$20	$3	$40	$11	$9	$94	$4
Cooper, Jim (D-Tenn)	$2	$0	$4	$0	$3	$7	$13	$7	$1	$3	$0	$3
Coppersmith, Sam (D-Ariz)	$3	$5	$2	$0	$0	$10	$5	$47	$2	$7	$35	$23
Costello, Jerry F. (D-Ill)	$6	$8	$42*	$3	$7	$38	$24	$85*	$21	$31	$73	$5
Cox, C. Christopher (R-Calif)	$10	$13	$46*	$6	$13	$97	$35	$60	$38	$38	$2	$32
Coyne, William J. (D-Pa)	$2	$6	$1	$0	$13	$63	$31	$19	$3	$9	$71	$0
Cramer, Bud (D-Ala)	$22	$26	$15	$10	$24	$30	$29	$16	$35	$18	$53	$14
Crane, Philip M. (R-Ill)	$5	$4	$4	$0	$1	$13	$16	$5	$2	$7	$0	$5
Crapo, Michael D. (R-Idaho)	$91*	$17	$16	$2	$39	$51	$40	$9	$23	$30	$0	$20
Cunningham, Randy (R-Calif)	$17	$18	$21	$68*	$24	$39	$18	$15	$68*	$49	$21	$49
Danner, Pat (D-Mo)	$15	$6	$4	$0	$6	$24	$43	$22	$16	$15	$80	$29
Darden, Buddy (D-Ga)	$27	$10	$9	$44*	$20	$47	$26	$22	$18	$30	$33	$6
de la Garza, Kika (D-Texas)	$145*	$5	$3	$0	$4	$31	$5	$11	$9	$5	$0	$2
Deal, Nathan (D-Ga)	$27	$7	$3	$1	$14	$49	$47	$8	$15	$19	$17	$8
DeFazio, Peter A. (D-Ore)	$11	$3	$2	$0	$3	$16	$9	$13	$23	$5	$95	$9
DeLauro, Rosa (D-Conn)	$10	$23	$24	$11	$7	$78	$61*	$76*	$34	$22	$218*	$150*
DeLay, Tom (R-Texas)	$22	$17	$24	$17	$42	$40	$21	$21	$44*	$32	$4	$8

* Ranks in top 10% of House in receipts from this sector
† Leading House recipient of funds from this sector

Breakdown of Contributions by Industry & Interest Group Sectors
Totals in Thousands of Dollars

Name	Agriculture	Comm/Elec	Construction	Defense	Energy	Finance	Health	Law/Lobby	Transport	Misc Bus	Labor	Ideol
Dellums, Ronald V. (D-Calif).	$3	$13	$3	$1	$1	$8	$11	$18	$6	$9	$58	$11
Derrick, Butler (D-SC).	$55	$32	$21	$5	$43	$169*	$50	$51	$33	$46	$42	$13
Deutsch, Peter (D-Fla).	$15	$9	$10	$0	$7	$90	$39	$57	$15	$27	$71	$21
Diaz-Balart, Lincoln (R-Fla).	$21	$15	$11	$0	$5	$29	$27	$21	$10	$12	$31	$20
Dickey, Jay (R-Ark).	$20	$3	$5	$0	$9	$20	$15	$12	$4	$14	$0	$1
Dicks, Norm (D-Wash).	$32	$15	$16	$99*	$36	$24	$16	$47	$33	$21	$87	$3
Dingell, John D. (D-Mich).	$46	$126*	$19	$8	$95*	$167*	$76*	$98*	$120*	$74*	$117	$22
Dixon, Julian C. (D-Calif).	$3	$7	$5	$7	$2	$11	$5	$3	$4	$5	$18	$7
Dooley, Calvin (D-Calif).	$146*	$13	$4	$2	$10	$31	$24	$22	$8	$7	$60	$10
Doolittle, John T. (R-Calif).	$56	$16	$29*	$4	$36	$55	$19	$12	$32	$31	$7	$31
Dornan, Robert K. (R-Calif).	$14	$6	$10	$20	$8	$12	$8	$3	$15	$17	$3	$105*
Dreier, David (R-Calif).	$25	$15	$16	$2	$11	$108	$22	$18	$19	$39	$1	$6
Duncan, Jimmy Jr. (R-Tenn).	$15	$6	$14	$2	$14	$54	$19	$11	$32	$14	$11	$6
Dunn, Jennifer (R-Wash).	$40	$16	$9	$2	$21	$71	$20	$11	$23	$46	$1	$36
Durbin, Richard J. (D-Ill).	$60*	$14	$8	$2	$9	$70	$42	$34	$37	$23	$147*	$30
Edwards, Chet (D-Texas).	$39	$10	$12	$58*	$30	$55	$36	$17	$25	$20	$98	$13
Edwards, Don (D-Calif).	$4	$30	$5	$1	$6	$21	$12	$30	$3	$10	$83	$11
Emerson, Bill (R-Mo).	$144*	$11	$11	$6	$21	$46	$23	$14	$41	$39	$11	$14
Engel, Eliot L. (D-NY).	$19	$9	$1	$5	$2	$63	$30	$20	$5	$7	$133	$53*
English, Glenn (D-Okla).	$63*	$24	$3	$3	$26	$61	$12	$22	$14	$12	$17	$11
English, Karan (D-Ariz).	$5	$4	$1	$0	$3	$9	$19	$11	$4	$3	$40	$68*
Eshoo, Anna G. (D-Calif).	$5	$12	$11	$2	$4	$56	$43	$40	$3	$19	$136	$169*
Espy, Mike (D-Miss).	$66*	$18	$6	$1	$14	$27	$14	$12	$15	$9	$68	$22
Evans, Lane (D-Ill).	$8	$4	$0	$3	$1	$14	$9	$21	$3	$5	$127	$18
Everett, Terry (R-Ala).	$3	$4	$13	$0	$0	$18	$3	$2	$13	$7	$0	$1
Ewing, Thomas W. (R-Ill).	$61*	$27	$27	$0	$29	$62	$39	$8	$31	$41	$3	$26
Fawell, Harris W. (R-Ill).	$14	$15	$44*	$4	$26	$84	$46	$10	$27	$57	$1	$2
Fazio, Vic (D-Calif).	$161†	$91*	$47*	$92*	$97*	$273*	$125*	$166*	$34	$117*	$242*	$128*
Fields, Cleo (D-La).	$2	$7	$7	$0	$6	$19	$13	$50	$3	$11	$13	$10
Fields, Jack (R-Texas).	$47	$72*	$22	$4	$127*	$101	$43	$41	$81*	$48	$22	$8
Filner, Bob (D-Calif).	$5	$14	$19	$4	$6	$89	$53	$49	$15	$24	$118	$81*
Fingerhut, Eric D. (D-Ohio).	$7	$7	$9	$0	$2	$63	$21	$43	$5	$29	$112	$104*
Fish, Hamilton Jr. (R-NY).	$20	$65*	$6	$2	$7	$145*	$18	$25	$13	$28	$26	$3
Flake, Floyd H. (D-NY).	$8	$4	$4	$0	$3	$75	$4	$7	$4	$3	$76	$1
Foglietta, Thomas M. (D-Pa).	$9	$15	$4	$12	$7	$29	$21	$45	$16	$18	$106	$15
Foley, Thomas S. (D-Wash).	$67*	$29	$16	$6	$29	$80	$24	$29	$40	$33	$107	$16
Ford, Harold E. (D-Tenn).	$10	$3	$3	$0	$2	$28	$12	$19	$14	$14	$53	$5
Ford, William D. (D-Mich).	$20	$26	$3	$1	$16	$59	$24	$42	$26	$12	$282*	$21
Fowler, Tillie (R-Fla).	$26	$10	$17	$2	$15	$97	$25	$30	$21	$42	$0	$32
Frank, Barney (D-Mass).	$4	$15	$9	$3	$2	$103	$14	$40	$1	$10	$48	$22
Franks, Bob (R-NJ).	$4	$10	$24	$3	$22	$93	$50	$30	$17	$30	$13	$17
Franks, Gary (R-Conn).	$36	$26	$16	$52*	$29	$67	$37	$13	$22	$62*	$7	$49
Frost, Martin (D-Texas).	$42	$50*	$15	$43*	$110*	$165*	$77*	$137*	$61*	$81*	$206*	$53*
Furse, Elizabeth (D-Ore).	$5	$14	$3	$0	$6	$19	$10	$37	$2	$19	$67	$150*
Gallegly, Elton (R-Calif).	$34	$17	$44*	$17	$33	$95	$29	$10	$15	$41	$2	$39
Gallo, Dean A. (R-NJ).	$14	$18	$34*	$5	$25	$59	$48	$24	$20	$38	$28	$18
Gejdenson, Sam (D-Conn).	$19	$29	$13	$14	$12	$45	$23	$38	$16	$43	$106	$129*
Gekas, George W. (R-Pa).	$5	$8	$6	$0	$4	$27	$5	$1	$10	$9	$2	$1
Gephardt, Richard A. (D-Mo).	$108*	$192†	$81*	$39*	$145*	$576†	$282†	$370†	$147*	$378†	$200*	$99*
Geren, Pete (D-Texas).	$46	$27	$37*	$5	$99*	$93	$33	$87*	$108*	$67*	$24	$14
Gibbons, Sam M. (D-Fla).	$67*	$32	$24	$10	$39	$127*	$53	$75*	$61*	$81*	$17	$4
Gilchrest, Wayne T. (R-Md).	$18	$6	$12	$5	$11	$21	$4	$5	$20	$24	$5	$14
Gillmor, Paul E. (R-Ohio).	$18	$10	$10	$1	$12	$62	$11	$9	$27	$19	$2	$2
Gilman, Benjamin A. (R-NY).	$20	$10	$11	$2	$7	$31	$29	$24	$13	$34	$100	$28
Gingrich, Newt (R-Ga).	$77*	$70*	$47*	$17	$54*	$274*	$114*	$74*	$93*	$244*	$11	$122*

* Ranks in top 10% of House in receipts from this sector
† Leading House recipient of funds from this sector

Breakdown of Contributions by Industry & Interest Group Sectors
Totals in Thousands of Dollars

Name	Agriculture	Comm/Elec	Construction	Defense	Energy	Finance	Health	Law/Lobby	Transport	Misc Bus	Labor	Ideol
Glickman, Dan (D-Kan).	$52	$35	$7	$11	$35	$148*	$34	$87*	$28	$55	$90	$89*
Gonzalez, Henry B. (D-Texas).	$0	$1	$1	$0	$1	$1	$1	$6	$3	$0	$3	$0
Goodlatte, Robert W. (R-Va).	$20	$8	$13	$4	$18	$36	$24	$14	$18	$34	$2	$16
Goodling, Bill (R-Pa).	$4	$4	$7	$0	$4	$4	$4	$7	$2	$9	$0	$5
Gordon, Bart (D-Tenn).	$30	$20	$17	$6	$18	$98	$24	$17	$34	$19	$106	$12
Goss, Porter J. (R-Fla).	$7	$9	$7	$3	$3	$38	$23	$6	$13	$10	$0	$5
Gradison, Bill (R-Ohio).	$0	$1	$1	$0	$0	$13	$7	$9	$1	$4	$0	$0
Grams, Rod (R-Minn).	$29	$8	$17	$1	$26	$27	$6	$2	$21	$57	$1	$24
Grandy, Fred (R-Iowa).	$59	$29	$14	$3	$21	$93	$41	$3	$28	$28	$7	$6
Green, Gene (D-Texas).	$16	$7	$11	$2	$24	$62	$42	$96*	$23	$25	$195*	$25
Greenwood, James C. (R-Pa).	$36	$9	$35*	$2	$39	$60	$41	$41	$20	$89*	$0	$7
Gunderson, Steve (R-Wis).	$89*	$18	$20	$5	$10	$46	$28	$6	$20	$35	$2	$1
Gutierrez, Luis V. (D-Ill).	$10	$8	$23	$0	$2	$58	$25	$39	$10	$22	$83	$39
Hall, Ralph M. (D-Texas).	$29	$39	$11	$26	$94*	$62	$50	$20	$33	$31	$2	$5
Hall, Tony P. (D-Ohio).	$11	$25	$4	$5	$8	$36	$19	$18	$13	$11	$90	$7
Hamburg, Dan (D-Calif).	$1	$4	$2	$0	$1	$2	$9	$14	$0	$8	$115	$52*
Hamilton, Lee H. (D-Ind).	$19	$16	$16	$11	$19	$54	$12	$29	$27	$24	$42	$45
Hancock, Mel (R-Mo).	$22	$9	$22	$1	$12	$66	$15	$7	$38	$47	$2	$10
Hansen, James V. (R-Utah).	$4	$5	$8	$34*	$31	$16	$14	$6	$18	$24	$2	$12
Harman, Jane (D-Calif).	$1	$49*	$6	$43*	$4	$72	$16	$149*	$5	$55	$65	$102*
Hastert, Dennis (R-Ill).	$44	$48*	$29*	$2	$32	$73	$57*	$12	$37	$54	$4	$5
Hastings, Alcee L. (D-Fla).	$6	$2	$7	$0	$0	$15	$17	$58	$6	$7	$58	$17
Hayes, Jimmy (D-La).	$33	$9	$41*	$7	$50*	$38	$7	$39	$41	$29	$34	$15
Hefley, Joel (R-Colo).	$11	$9	$3	$18	$11	$17	$4	$1	$14	$11	$7	$4
Hefner, W. G. "Bill" (D-NC).	$36	$18	$13	$90*	$11	$40	$24	$25	$28	$37	$87	$18
Henry, Paul B. (R-Mich).	$13	$8	$13	$0	$5	$20	$30	$14	$13	$34	$5	$2
Herger, Wally (R-Calif).	$156*	$9	$26	$7	$19	$32	$30	$9	$19	$26	$16	$9
Hilliard, Earl F. (D-Ala).	$26	$12	$6	$0	$44	$27	$10	$40	$7	$11	$32	$26
Hinchey, Maurice D. (D-NY).	$3	$4	$21	$0	$4	$21	$13	$16	$1	$4	$63	$42
Hoagland, Peter (D-Neb).	$26	$17	$14	$1	$6	$186*	$30	$79*	$14	$16	$163*	$28
Hobson, David L. (R-Ohio).	$12	$14	$9	$3	$28	$41	$41	$7	$34	$30	$10	$4
Hochbrueckner, George (D-NY).	$3	$7	$6	$30*	$4	$32	$24	$10	$10	$6	$178*	$34
Hoekstra, Peter (R-Mich).	$1	$1	$2	$0	$0	$3	$2	$0	$3	$4	$0	$2
Hoke, Martin R. (R-Ohio).	$1	$12	$14	$1	$3	$40	$26	$27	$14	$49	$0	$5
Holden, Tim (D-Pa).	$1	$5	$3	$1	$3	$3	$4	$28	$2	$3	$91	$14
Horn, Steve (R-Calif).	$1	$9	$4	$1	$7	$37	$32	$17	$4	$27	$0	$4
Houghton, Amo (R-NY).	$16	$43*	$7	$4	$22	$45	$9	$8	$4	$45	$8	$9
Hoyer, Steny H. (D-Md).	$40	$48*	$26	$14	$34	$142*	$109*	$140*	$35	$65*	$241*	$102*
Huffington, Michael (R-Calif).	$5	$12	$5	$0	$20	$46	$5	$4	$5	$20	$0	$2
Hughes, William J. (D-NJ).	$5	$52*	$8	$1	$14	$48	$24	$40	$25	$23	$63	$6
Hunter, Duncan (R-Calif).	$21	$17	$40*	$78*	$16	$31	$14	$6	$40	$41	$15	$38
Hutchinson, Tim (R-Ark).	$27	$3	$8	$0	$19	$33	$34	$6	$16	$30	$0	$12
Hutto, Earl (D-Fla).	$12	$8	$9	$35*	$18	$30	$19	$4	$18	$19	$11	$3
Hyde, Henry J. (R-Ill).	$8	$28	$19	$3	$10	$79	$21	$18	$19	$37	$2	$7
Inglis, Robert D. (R-SC).	$5	$2	$8	$0	$0	$15	$7	$8	$3	$26	$0	$0
Inhofe, James M. (R-Okla).	$19	$16	$13	$6	$65*	$51	$20	$7	$78*	$19	$10	$16
Inslee, Jay (D-Wash).	$3	$1	$0	$0	$1	$4	$5	$15	$0	$5	$53	$15
Istook, Ernest Jr. (R-Okla).	$8	$9	$2	$0	$36	$29	$24	$16	$6	$10	$0	$8
Jacobs, Andrew Jr. (D-Ind).	$0	$0	$0	$0	$0	$1	$0	$0	$0	$0	$0	$0
Jefferson, William J. (D-La).	$16	$9	$9	$5	$29	$28	$10	$58	$21	$13	$98	$15
Johnson, Don (D-Ga).	$22	$8	$7	$1	$18	$61	$44	$34	$11	$43	$20	$5
Johnson, Eddie B. (D-Texas).	$5	$10	$1	$2	$11	$33	$26	$18	$10	$6	$50	$21
Johnson, Nancy L. (R-Conn).	$18	$24	$24	$14	$18	$131*	$76*	$10	$28	$56	$12	$21
Johnson, Sam (R-Texas).	$18	$37	$27	$28	$93*	$133*	$64*	$23	$28	$63*	$0	$21
Johnson, Tim (D-SD).	$51	$9	$5	$0	$3	$26	$19	$17	$9	$6	$106	$12

* Ranks in top 10% of House in receipts from this sector
† Leading House recipient of funds from this sector

Breakdown of Contributions by Industry & Interest Group Sectors
Totals in Thousands of Dollars

Name	Agriculture	Comm/Elec	Construction	Defense	Energy	Finance	Health	Law/Lobby	Transport	Misc Bus	Labor	Ideol
Johnston, Harry A. (D-Fla)	$23	$8	$7	$5	$7	$39	$16	$38	$12	$8	$83	$22
Kanjorski, Paul E. (D-Pa)	$5	$5	$5	$1	$4	$109	$10	$16	$5	$5	$79	$12
Kaptur, Marcy (D-Ohio)	$21	$2	$6	$2	$3	$25	$6	$4	$8	$10	$127	$3
Kasich, John R. (R-Ohio)	$11	$5	$24	$16	$14	$50	$25	$11	$11	$41	$2	$10
Kennedy, Joseph P. II (D-Mass)	$4	$25	$24	$1	$23	$133*	$42	$83*	$13	$52	$81	$11
Kennelly, Barbara B. (D-Conn)	$15	$14	$6	$9	$16	$162*	$40	$30	$15	$48	$53	$10
Kildee, Dale E. (D-Mich)	$29	$24	$4	$0	$17	$34	$36	$39	$19	$8	$244*	$47
Kim, Jay C. (R-Calif)	$7	$10	$22	$3	$12	$46	$48	$5	$13	$32	$1	$10
King, Peter T. (R-NY)	$5	$5	$4	$1	$7	$26	$15	$10	$10	$24	$10	$26
Kingston, Jack (R-Ga)	$28	$6	$8	$1	$16	$65	$53	$9	$16	$29	$0	$19
Kleczka, Gerald D. (D-Wis)	$11	$6	$8	$1	$7	$70	$28	$22	$8	$10	$76	$6
Klein, Herbert C. (D-NJ)	$5	$11	$11	$0	$2	$87	$16	$50	$3	$31	$70	$22
Klink, Ron (D-Pa)	$1	$7	$3	$4	$6	$12	$7	$8	$1	$4	$89	$3
Klug, Scott L. (R-Wis)	$41	$31	$42*	$2	$22	$103	$31	$20	$31	$95*	$2	$8
Knollenberg, Joseph (R-Mich)	$5	$7	$15	$2	$13	$67	$33	$17	$30	$31	$2	$12
Kolbe, Jim (R-Ariz)	$30	$8	$15	$21	$14	$39	$18	$14	$21	$32	$3	$12
Kopetski, Mike (D-Ore)	$37	$33	$3	$3	$9	$35	$32	$22	$20	$16	$94	$40
Kreidler, Mike (D-Wash)	$5	$3	$1	$0	$11	$5	$44	$15	$2	$7	$94	$27
Kyl, Jon (R-Ariz)	$28	$14	$18	$31*	$31	$88	$42	$47	$24	$46	$0	$11
LaFalce, John J. (D-NY)	$12	$10	$10	$3	$23	$207*	$7	$43	$13	$76*	$37	$2
Lambert, Blanche (D-Ark)	$41	$14	$8	$1	$24	$53	$19	$23	$15	$22	$24	$25
Lancaster, H. Martin (D-NC)	$83*	$17	$13	$46*	$15	$39	$48	$25	$21	$45	$32	$21
Lantos, Tom (D-Calif)	$5	$11	$2	$4	$3	$35	$8	$7	$11	$14	$68	$28
LaRocco, Larry (D-Idaho)	$31	$23	$12	$2	$12	$147*	$30	$29	$9	$18	$117	$29
Laughlin, Greg (D-Texas)	$42	$14	$30*	$9	$80*	$40	$32	$69*	$74*	$32	$73	$13
Lazio, Rick A. (R-NY)	$7	$5	$5	$0	$7	$18	$6	$16	$4	$18	$10	$6
Leach, Jim (R-Iowa)	$2	$3	$3	$0	$2	$7	$6	$3	$4	$5	$0	$0
Lehman, Richard H. (D-Calif)	$87*	$61*	$21	$2	$45*	$134*	$39	$48	$9	$31	$153*	$36
Levin, Sander (D-Mich)	$18	$29	$16	$9	$20	$124	$101*	$93*	$35	$54	$162*	$81*
Levy, David A. (R-NY)	$5	$16	$4	$1	$9	$17	$8	$8	$4	$30	$4	$4
Lewis, Jerry (R-Calif)	$41	$25	$16	$71*	$29	$77	$41	$19	$36	$45	$9	$13
Lewis, John (D-Ga)	$10	$15	$4	$2	$8	$44	$31	$22	$30	$14	$107	$17
Lewis, Tom (R-Fla)	$85*	$12	$6	$7	$13	$26	$9	$6	$18	$7	$6	$0
Lightfoot, Jim Ross (R-Iowa)	$65*	$20	$17	$6	$24	$37	$27	$3	$52*	$36	$3	$26
Linder, John (R-Ga)	$25	$14	$17	$3	$22	$85	$31	$21	$16	$41	$2	$38
Lipinski, William O. (D-Ill)	$6	$7	$17	$1	$6	$52	$19	$50	$57*	$28	$124	$26
Livingston, Robert L. (R-La)	$10	$5	$12	$57*	$30	$12	$15	$21	$19	$10	$5	$5
Lloyd, Marilyn (D-Tenn)	$12	$4	$8	$52*	$26	$31	$29	$24	$32	$22	$86	$3
Long, Jill L. (D-Ind)	$58	$13	$0	$2	$4	$28	$20	$7	$11	$5	$128	$10
Lowey, Nita M. (D-NY)	$14	$17	$7	$1	$2	$192*	$43	$126*	$14	$52	$147*	$92*
Machtley, Ronald K. (R-RI)	$9	$12	$17	$38*	$15	$43	$33	$16	$13	$51	$41	$17
Maloney, Carolyn B. (I-NY)	$1	$10	$2	$0	$0	$52	$3	$18	$0	$14	$55	$10
Mann, David (D-Ohio)	$3	$6	$2	$0	$1	$40	$20	$26	$12	$11	$54	$5
Manton, Thomas J. (D-NY)	$34	$48*	$16	$1	$29	$125	$33	$46	$24	$26	$114	$5
Manzullo, Donald (R-Ill)	$11	$8	$14	$1	$12	$24	$24	$11	$24	$46	$0	$36
Margolies-Mezvinsky, M. (D-Pa)	$4	$15	$2	$1	$5	$33	$31	$60	$5	$15	$51	$66*
Markey, Edward J. (D-Mass)	$2	$76*	$4	$2	$16	$64	$5	$82*	$3	$22	$0	$4
Martinez, Matthew G. (D-Calif)	$2	$3	$4	$2	$2	$22	$6	$4	$3	$7	$33	$11
Matsui, Robert T. (D-Calif)	$29	$31	$7	$5	$32	$112	$68*	$66*	$28	$62*	$53	$5
Mazzoli, Romano L. (D-Ky)	$0	$1	$1	$0	$0	$3	$3	$3	$0	$1	$0	$0
McCandless, Al (R-Calif)	$20	$10	$17	$4	$11	$115	$14	$10	$22	$14	$5	$4
McCloskey, Frank (D-Ind)	$9	$7	$1	$24	$12	$20	$5	$7	$13	$20	$190*	$27
McCollum, Bill (R-Fla)	$36	$35	$13	$8	$15	$139*	$60*	$42	$26	$60*	$4	$21
McCrery, Jim (R-La)	$56	$5	$21	$38*	$66*	$72	$74*	$22	$36	$26	$3	$43
McCurdy, Dave (D-Okla)	$16	$15	$16	$129*	$40	$54	$40	$39	$31	$22	$10	$41

* Ranks in top 10% of House in receipts from this sector
† Leading House recipient of funds from this sector

Breakdown of Contributions by Industry & Interest Group Sectors
Totals in Thousands of Dollars

Name	Agriculture	Comm/Elec	Construction	Defense	Energy	Finance	Health	Law/Lobby	Transport	Misc Bus	Labor	Ideol
McDade, Joseph M. (R-Pa).	$9	$12	$10	$91*	$15	$24	$11	$47	$20	$23	$37	$14
McDermott, Jim (D-Wash).	$6	$7	$2	$0	$11	$56	$34	$13	$14	$9	$47	$8
McHale, Paul (D-Pa).	$1	$4	$1	$1	$1	$1	$4	$22	$1	$1	$97	$13
McHugh, John M. (R-NY).	$8	$5	$3	$0	$7	$27	$17	$3	$5	$8	$19	$12
McInnis, Scott (R-Colo).	$14	$12	$25	$0	$55*	$56	$17	$7	$32	$51	$1	$27
McKeon, Howard (R-Calif).	$6	$10	$20	$4	$3	$45	$30	$10	$30	$30	$0	$14
McKinney, Cynthia (D-Ga).	$11	$8	$6	$0	$7	$16	$29	$18	$7	$13	$60	$46
McMillan, Alex (R-NC).	$30	$19	$7	$7	$21	$92	$49	$4	$22	$31	$6	$3
McNulty, Michael R. (D-NY).	$2	$5	$1	$13	$1	$14	$2	$0	$6	$4	$67	$5
Meehan, Martin T. (D-Mass).	$6	$8	$36*	$2	$2	$47	$20	$99*	$7	$36	$1	$2
Meek, Carrie (D-Fla).	$11	$6	$5	$0	$2	$18	$67*	$34	$14	$20	$68	$41
Menendez, Robert (D-NJ).	$14	$15	$25	$1	$16	$74	$38	$60	$12	$28	$86	$39
Meyers, Jan (R-Kan).	$16	$22	$20	$3	$16	$37	$25	$3	$26	$35	$1	$36
Mfume, Kweisi (D-Md).	$5	$6	$5	$0	$4	$50	$11	$11	$6	$8	$56	$9
Mica, John L. (R-Fla).	$19	$16	$5	$3	$14	$41	$29	$15	$16	$32	$1	$14
Michel, Robert H. (R-Ill).	$57	$40*	$25	$16	$25	$119	$46	$15	$38	$57	$23	$16
Miller, Dan (R-Fla).	$16	$8	$10	$0	$11	$47	$34	$7	$10	$28	$0	$2
Miller, George (D-Calif).	$11	$15	$11	$1	$55*	$39	$13	$58	$10	$38	$103	$15
Mineta, Norman Y. (D-Calif).	$18	$40*	$67*	$14	$24	$67	$26	$80*	$174†	$78*	$141*	$22
Minge, David (D-Minn).	$16	$4	$0	$0	$2	$11	$5	$12	$3	$4	$111	$12
Mink, Patsy T. (D-Hawaii).	$5	$2	$6	$0	$2	$26	$8	$5	$4	$3	$76	$1
Moakley, Joe (D-Mass).	$9	$29	$51*	$10	$21	$180*	$25	$72*	$35	$46	$110	$1
Molinari, Susan (R-NY).	$14	$18	$28*	$7	$12	$79	$38	$28	$37	$28	$16	$40
Mollohan, Alan B. (D-WVa).	$24	$6	$12	$54*	$38	$17	$25	$38	$16	$30	$74	$19
Montgomery, "Sonny" (D-Miss).	$15	$11	$7	$16	$19	$15	$15	$3	$11	$11	$1	$5
Moorhead, Carlos J. (R-Calif).	$14	$44*	$8	$6	$46*	$70	$39	$12	$21	$21	$1	$2
Moran, James P. Jr. (D-Va).	$14	$29	$15	$23	$9	$143*	$48	$91*	$20	$36	$160*	$48
Morella, Constance A. (R-Md).	$5	$21	$18	$9	$11	$37	$32	$26	$15	$15	$43	$21
Murphy, Austin J. (D-Pa).	$8	$3	$1	$1	$14	$13	$15	$3	$4	$16	$97	$14
Murtha, John P. (D-Pa).	$18	$24	$31*	$230†	$93*	$61	$22	$83*	$30	$68*	$108	$22
Myers, John T. (R-Ind).	$28	$15	$17	$5	$38	$22	$7	$10	$23	$23	$22	$3
Nadler, Jerrold (D-NY).	$1	$3	$1	$0	$0	$8	$8	$1	$1	$1	$12	$5
Natcher, William H. (D-Ky).	$0	$0	$0	$0	$0	$0	$0	$0	$0	$0	$0	$0
Neal, Richard E. (D-Mass).	$10	$6	$4	$3	$4	$91	$16	$23	$2	$19	$64	$6
Neal, Stephen L. (D-NC).	$33	$13	$6	$3	$6	$220*	$12	$28	$16	$12	$34	$14
Nussle, Jim (R-Iowa).	$92*	$26	$31*	$7	$19	$127*	$38	$8	$48*	$78*	$4	$17
Oberstar, James L. (D-Minn).	$14	$8	$10	$4	$5	$8	$4	$19	$54*	$21	$81	$9
Obey, David R. (D-Wis).	$33	$17	$4	$4	$11	$31	$25	$31	$13	$19	$93	$45
Olver, John W. (D-Mass).	$8	$19	$12	$3	$9	$49	$50	$68*	$9	$30	$344†	$137*
Ortiz, Solomon P. (D-Texas).	$9	$9	$19	$11	$19	$28	$12	$18	$17	$17	$12	$11
Orton, Bill (D-Utah).	$12	$7	$9	$1	$11	$60	$22	$14	$13	$13	$74	$14
Owens, Major R. (D-NY).	$1	$3	$0	$0	$1	$7	$5	$2	$1	$3	$69	$2
Oxley, Michael G. (R-Ohio).	$28	$46*	$9	$5	$66*	$73	$31	$15	$25	$33	$0	$1
Packard, Ron (R-Calif).	$8	$14	$24	$6	$20	$22	$23	$10	$67*	$8	$8	$4
Pallone, Frank Jr. (D-NJ).	$10	$14	$41*	$1	$12	$50	$56*	$43	$68*	$36	$255*	$78*
Panetta, Leon E. (D-Calif).	$52	$6	$3	$2	$10	$39	$36	$18	$16	$36	$66	$2
Parker, Mike (D-Miss).	$39	$13	$15	$1	$42	$57	$17	$13	$51*	$53	$6	$11
Pastor, Ed (D-Ariz).	$31	$23	$23	$4	$17	$77	$37	$65*	$14	$47	$183*	$45
Paxon, Bill (R-NY).	$31	$28	$63*	$6	$28	$190*	$47	$25	$35	$76*	$5	$29
Payne, Donald M. (D-NJ).	$8	$9	$3	$0	$6	$43	$20	$28	$16	$15	$84	$10
Payne, Lewis F. Jr. (D-Va).	$28	$12	$27*	$4	$25	$55	$26	$17	$48*	$45	$16	$13
Pelosi, Nancy (D-Calif).	$8	$11	$7	$5	$11	$87	$30	$41	$8	$30	$96	$22
Penny, Timothy J. (D-Minn).	$35	$6	$0	$0	$3	$15	$11	$2	$6	$20	$5	$3
Peterson, Collin C. (D-Minn).	$65*	$11	$1	$1	$5	$47	$8	$14	$14	$5	$138*	$26
Peterson, Pete (D-Fla).	$25	$14	$16	$3	$12	$34	$25	$17	$36	$12	$113	$14

* Ranks in top 10% of House in receipts from this sector
† Leading House recipient of funds from this sector

Breakdown of Contributions by Industry & Interest Group Sectors
Totals in Thousands of Dollars

Name	Agriculture	Comm/Elec	Construction	Defense	Energy	Finance	Health	Law/Lobby	Transport	Misc Bus	Labor	Ideol
Petri, Tom (R-Wis).	$33	$10	$22	$2	$13	$25	$12	$10	$43*	$42	$1	$9
Pickett, Owen B. (D-Va).	$8	$9	$4	$22	$10	$49	$12	$21	$20	$20	$25	$3
Pickle, J. J. (D-Texas).	$21	$22	$9	$5	$28	$110	$49	$50	$27	$20	$6	$1
Pombo, Richard W. (R-Calif).	$75*	$9	$17	$2	$18	$56	$14	$3	$15	$36	$0	$40
Pomeroy, Earl (D-ND).	$21	$3	$2	$0	$17	$107	$29	$29	$8	$16	$98	$12
Porter, John (R-Ill).	$12	$15	$14	$2	$6	$67	$67*	$14	$19	$33	$1	$34
Poshard, Glenn (D-Ill).	$0	$2	$1	$0	$2	$3	$3	$4	$1	$2	$5	$2
Price, David (D-NC).	$37	$12	$6	$3	$12	$41	$33	$18	$25	$11	$87	$14
Pryce, Deborah (R-Ohio).	$11	$8	$25	$1	$25	$93	$30	$31	$20	$53	$0	$32
Quillen, James H. (R-Tenn).	$32	$18	$11	$8	$17	$74	$15	$22	$51*	$32	$33	$11
Quinn, Jack (R-NY).	$3	$3	$10	$0	$3	$15	$8	$9	$20	$8	$0	$2
Rahall, Nick J. II (D-WVa).	$16	$6	$12	$2	$22	$15	$9	$15	$59*	$12	$112	$21
Ramstad, Jim (R-Minn).	$56	$35	$26	$3	$15	$159*	$50	$43	$38	$120*	$12	$27
Rangel, Charles B. (D-NY).	$14	$28	$6	$1	$8	$136*	$84*	$47	$20	$39	$66	$7
Ravenel, Arthur Jr. (R-SC).	$12	$6	$9	$13	$5	$29	$22	$3	$21	$24	$10	$9
Reed, John F. (D-RI).	$6	$18	$16	$23	$5	$76	$53	$51	$11	$34	$215*	$27
Regula, Ralph (R-Ohio).	$5	$2	$5	$0	$3	$14	$4	$9	$4	$9	$0	$0
Reynolds, Mel (D-Ill).	$7	$6	$9	$0	$2	$51	$31	$31	$10	$28	$72	$113*
Richardson, Bill (D-NM).	$31	$76*	$9	$3	$49*	$79	$90*	$46	$14	$35	$50	$27
Ridge, Tom (R-Pa).	$20	$14	$20	$1	$25	$134*	$31	$25	$20	$37	$43	$6
Roberts, Pat (R-Kan).	$86*	$8	$4	$0	$15	$35	$16	$7	$17	$22	$0	$4
Roemer, Tim (D-Ind).	$19	$12	$15	$20	$24	$33	$19	$45	$18	$13	$138*	$23
Rogers, Harold (R-Ky).	$58	$26	$30*	$2	$112*	$53	$26	$29	$26	$51	$3	$8
Rohrabacher, Dana (R-Calif).	$3	$15	$12	$13	$11	$30	$40	$14	$23	$26	$0	$33
Ros-Lehtinen, Ileana (R-Fla).	$26	$18	$27	$2	$12	$72	$88*	$26	$30	$36	$6	$34
Rose, Charlie (D-NC).	$85*	$30	$2	$0	$8	$25	$19	$22	$14	$35	$62	$11
Rostenkowski, Dan (D-Ill).	$62*	$67*	$36*	$23	$52*	$404*	$94*	$70*	$101*	$216*	$94	$21
Roth, Toby (R-Wis).	$51	$16	$22	$9	$18	$142*	$9	$18	$28	$40	$2	$19
Roukema, Marge (R-NJ).	$12	$14	$25	$2	$13	$123	$33	$14	$20	$30	$18	$16
Rowland, J. Roy (D-Ga).	$38	$24	$5	$7	$25	$49	$106*	$11	$21	$28	$7	$5
Roybal-Allard, Lucille (D-Calif).	$8	$6	$3	$1	$2	$27	$18	$14	$1	$17	$30	$34
Royce, Ed (R-Calif).	$22	$10	$20	$6	$13	$81	$56*	$29	$18	$36	$2	$44
Rush, Bobby L. (D-Ill).	$6	$4	$0	$0	$9	$29	$20	$29	$5	$8	$39	$22
Sabo, Martin Olav (D-Minn).	$18	$13	$5	$44*	$9	$16	$9	$37	$19	$9	$92	$9
Sanders, Bernard (I-Vt).	$4	$2	$2	$0	$0	$3	$4	$2	$0	$3	$135	$28
Sangmeister, George E. (D-Ill).	$4	$22	$6	$0	$6	$32	$10	$18	$16	$9	$137	$14
Santorum, Rick (R-Pa).	$7	$21	$32*	$2	$57*	$84	$39	$42	$24	$78*	$5	$27
Sarpalius, Bill (D-Texas).	$107*	$8	$7	$6	$31	$51	$33	$31	$19	$33	$73	$26
Sawyer, Tom (D-Ohio).	$3	$8	$1	$4	$3	$19	$13	$5	$5	$15	$77	$9
Saxton, H. James (R-NJ).	$18	$12	$29*	$39*	$25	$87	$38	$24	$41	$29	$22	$27
Schaefer, Dan (R-Colo).	$30	$40*	$12	$4	$46*	$62	$25	$12	$32	$26	$12	$3
Schenk, Lynn (D-Calif).	$13	$24	$5	$2	$25	$103	$46	$140*	$14	$49	$124	$114*
Schiff, Steven H. (R-NM).	$16	$23	$14	$14	$23	$37	$24	$23	$19	$29	$15	$19
Schroeder, Patricia (D-Colo).	$3	$51*	$2	$5	$7	$18	$19	$33	$6	$12	$46	$25
Schumer, Charles E. (D-NY).	$4	$30	$2	$1	$2	$407*	$9	$41	$3	$75*	$28	$19
Scott, Robert C. (D-Va).	$8	$2	$7	$6	$8	$50	$37	$45	$15	$20	$88	$11
Sensenbrenner, Jim (R-Wis).	$8	$14	$6	$5	$6	$28	$2	$1	$12	$20	$0	$2
Serrano, Jose E. (D-NY).	$3	$6	$0	$2	$1	$16	$10	$4	$3	$2	$48	$5
Sharp, Philip R. (D-Ind).	$26	$38	$22	$6	$117*	$57	$29	$43	$38	$33	$89	$7
Shaw, E. Clay Jr. (R-Fla).	$38	$49*	$23	$3	$40	$188*	$115*	$48	$77*	$74*	$10	$14
Shays, Christopher (R-Conn).	$11	$14	$7	$0	$2	$57	$6	$8	$9	$34	$8	$7
Shepherd, Karen (D-Utah).	$1	$11	$1	$0	$2	$31	$13	$17	$1	$16	$111	$114*
Shuster, Bud (R-Pa).	$15	$10	$106†	$1	$17	$35	$8	$40	$88*	$135*	$7	$2
Sisisky, Norman (D-Va).	$20	$6	$8	$40*	$12	$19	$5	$6	$14	$28	$23	$11
Skaggs, David E. (D-Colo).	$10	$25	$8	$5	$15	$40	$30	$45	$18	$10	$142*	$58*

* Ranks in top 10% of House in receipts from this sector
† Leading House recipient of funds from this sector

Breakdown of Contributions by Industry & Interest Group Sectors
Totals in Thousands of Dollars

Name	Agriculture	Comm/Elec	Construction	Defense	Energy	Finance	Health	Law/Lobby	Transport	Misc Bus	Labor	Ideol
Skeen, Joe (R-NM).	$71*	$8	$8	$8	$40	$21	$14	$9	$21	$12	$2	$13
Skelton, Ike (D-Mo).	$26	$11	$5	$49*	$11	$30	$20	$10	$16	$17	$27	$14
Slattery, Jim (D-Kan).	$20	$71*	$22	$3	$54*	$123	$55*	$53	$35	$39	$81	$6
Slaughter, Louise M. (D-NY).	$14	$13	$4	$2	$3	$49	$29	$18	$6	$16	$157*	$19
Smith, Bob (R-Ore).	$110*	$8	$13	$0	$15	$32	$13	$5	$19	$12	$1	$6
Smith, Christopher H. (R-NJ).	$3	$9	$5	$1	$6	$20	$8	$3	$9	$3	$30	$26
Smith, Lamar (R-Texas).	$28	$26	$18	$7	$47*	$71	$26	$17	$21	$21	$0	$3
Smith, Neal (D-Iowa).	$27	$18	$6	$16	$6	$36	$18	$29	$14	$14	$55	$13
Smith, Nick (R-Mich).	$5	$0	$2	$0	$1	$10	$9	$1	$6	$3	$0	$0
Snowe, Olympia J. (R-Maine).	$45	$16	$17	$3	$8	$70	$38	$32	$9	$50	$15	$84*
Solomon, Gerald B. H. (R-NY).	$21	$17	$4	$12	$11	$75	$24	$7	$39	$20	$59	$12
Spence, Floyd D. (R-SC).	$11	$4	$5	$33*	$10	$15	$13	$2	$12	$9	$4	$2
Spratt, John M. Jr. (D-SC).	$12	$12	$9	$24	$22	$47	$13	$17	$20	$27	$9	$6
Stark, Pete (D-Calif).	$6	$9	$3	$0	$5	$54	$193*	$61*	$8	$30	$73	$7
Stearns, Cliff (R-Fla).	$17	$9	$10	$2	$8	$94	$43	$8	$16	$15	$6	$4
Stenholm, Charles (D-Texas).	$144*	$9	$10	$6	$27	$26	$34	$14	$22	$32	$1	$1
Stokes, Louis (D-Ohio).	$10	$11	$15	$3	$7	$36	$45	$22	$6	$12	$61	$11
Strickland, Ted (D-Ohio).	$1	$1	$0	$0	$1	$3	$16	$7	$0	$1	$89	$12
Studds, Gerry E. (D-Mass).	$4	$39	$2	$4	$32	$29	$61*	$61	$55*	$31	$169*	$134*
Stump, Bob (R-Ariz).	$29	$6	$7	$34*	$17	$18	$17	$6	$15	$11	$1	$12
Stupak, Bart (D-Mich).	$3	$2	$3	$0	$6	$6	$0	$16	$6	$4	$70	$18
Sundquist, Don (R-Tenn).	$60*	$24	$21	$5	$33	$145*	$54*	$23	$67*	$91*	$10	$5
Swett, Dick (D-NH).	$14	$29	$23	$16	$13	$76	$38	$55	$38	$76*	$197*	$104*
Swift, Al (D-Wash).	$62*	$99*	$16	$6	$91*	$112	$29	$60	$78*	$64*	$122	$13
Synar, Mike (D-Okla).	$13	$130*	$19	$0	$146*	$90	$70*	$143*	$9	$54	$1	$16
Talent, James M. (R-Mo).	$29	$30	$20	$3	$28	$68	$64*	$36	$33	$100*	$0	$26
Tanner, John (D-Tenn).	$27	$11	$8	$16	$5	$36	$12	$8	$29	$10	$26	$2
Tauzin, W.J. "Billy" (D-La).	$39	$54*	$14	$5	$97*	$134*	$16	$46	$56*	$43	$19	$4
Taylor, Charles H. (R-NC).	$61*	$19	$26	$3	$44	$48	$31	$7	$42*	$78*	$10	$36
Taylor, Gene (D-Miss).	$16	$13	$8	$29*	$15	$10	$25	$19	$31	$25	$7	$15
Tejeda, Frank M. (D-Texas).	$12	$9	$20	$1	$19	$57	$45	$10	$14	$30	$12	$9
Thomas, Bill (R-Calif).	$90*	$16	$13	$7	$43	$107	$39	$32	$17	$35	$6	$1
Thomas, Craig (R-Wyo).	$32	$10	$7	$3	$67*	$61	$26	$5	$29	$18	$5	$9
Thornton, Ray (D-Ark).	$27	$12	$7	$2	$11	$83	$13	$19	$12	$11	$52	$6
Thurman, Karen L. (D-Fla).	$28	$6	$3	$0	$13	$25	$37	$13	$9	$14	$60	$45
Torkildsen, Peter (R-Mass).	$2	$6	$2	$1	$1	$58	$12	$13	$4	$41	$0	$8
Torres, Esteban E. (D-Calif).	$5	$12	$7	$3	$3	$24	$5	$21	$2	$10	$19	$2
Torricelli, Robert G. (D-NJ).	$28	$36	$36*	$15	$24	$105	$114*	$132*	$38	$104*	$107	$68*
Towns, Edolphus (D-NY).	$37	$54*	$7	$1	$24	$47	$61*	$27	$17	$27	$45	$14
Traficant, James A. Jr. (D-Ohio).	$2	$2	$4	$0	$1	$3	$5	$2	$3	$6	$80	$1
Tucker, Walter R. (D-Calif).	$8	$3	$2	$0	$8	$16	$14	$6	$4	$8	$37	$11
Unsoeld, Jolene (D-Wash).	$13	$16	$2	$1	$29	$22	$19	$23	$19	$16	$199*	$92*
Upton, Fred (R-Mich).	$21	$20	$14	$3	$22	$45	$34	$8	$31	$45	$0	$0
Valentine, Tim (D-NC).	$46	$23	$19	$9	$26	$37	$25	$28	$44*	$32	$15	$11
Velazquez, Nydia M. (D-NY).	$1	$4	$3	$0	$2	$17	$15	$12	$4	$15	$75	$33
Vento, Bruce F. (D-Minn).	$11	$7	$7	$0	$2	$91	$1	$17	$6	$7	$66	$11
Visclosky, Peter J. (D-Ind).	$6	$7	$5	$0	$11	$12	$26	$9	$15	$21	$120	$18
Volkmer, Harold L. (D-Mo).	$64*	$8	$5	$9	$8	$25	$12	$8	$13	$6	$89	$15
Vucanovich, Barbara (R-Nev).	$35	$11	$23	$6	$56*	$53	$22	$16	$29	$109*	$11	$32
Walker, Robert S. (R-Pa).	$10	$12	$8	$8	$9	$7	$7	$3	$8	$12	$1	$2
Walsh, James T. (R-NY).	$16	$8	$3	$2	$2	$28	$19	$8	$16	$13	$4	$1
Washington, Craig (D-Texas).	$9	$10	$2	$0	$11	$11	$10	$30	$7	$4	$65	$5
Waters, Maxine (D-Calif).	$6	$14	$3	$0	$2	$20	$15	$12	$3	$10	$51	$11
Watt, Melvin (D-NC).	$13	$11	$4	$0	$7	$54	$26	$45	$9	$8	$59	$23
Waxman, Henry A. (D-Calif).	$11	$58*	$3	$2	$26	$52	$203*	$65*	$12	$32	$64	$29

* Ranks in top 10% of House in receipts from this sector
† Leading House recipient of funds from this sector

Breakdown of Contributions by Industry & Interest Group Sectors
Totals in Thousands of Dollars

Name	Agriculture	Comm/Elec	Construction	Defense	Energy	Finance	Health	Law/Lobby	Transport	Misc Bus	Labor	Ideol
Weldon, Curt (R-Pa).	$7	$10	$7	$35*	$22	$34	$25	$19	$13	$20	$51	$3
Wheat, Alan (D-Mo).	$22	$38	$6	$4	$14	$46	$27	$29	$22	$17	$153*	$24
Whitten, Jamie L. (D-Miss).	$11	$2	$1	$0	$3	$2	$1	$5	$0	$2	$1	$2
Williams, Pat (D-Mont).	$39	$19	$2	$1	$16	$42	$31	$51	$7	$22	$283*	$114*
Wilson, Charles (D-Texas).	$51	$14	$28*	$211*	$82*	$66	$49	$118*	$61*	$68*	$183*	$48
Wise, Bob (D-WVa).	$15	$15	$5	$2	$24	$10	$15	$19	$5	$27	$51	$22
Wolf, Frank R. (R-Va).	$5	$24	$18	$48*	$17	$65	$15	$12	$25	$20	$17	$9
Woolsey, Lynn (D-Calif).	$2	$6	$1	$0	$2	$24	$10	$23	$1	$9	$99	$63*
Wyden, Ron (D-Ore).	$7	$9	$1	$0	$7	$21	$35	$12	$6	$10	$17	$9
Wynn, Albert R. (D-Md).	$8	$6	$5	$0	$6	$36	$36	$36	$5	$9	$134	$28
Yates, Sidney R. (D-Ill).	$1	$11	$3	$1	$3	$42	$6	$24	$0	$10	$14	$30
Young, C. W. Bill (R-Fla).	$6	$2	$8	$91*	$7	$27	$28	$10	$9	$6	$2	$2
Young, Don (R-Alaska).	$45	$25	$39*	$8	$181†	$28	$17	$53	$65*	$38	$62	$39
Zeliff, Bill (R-NH).	$32	$45*	$36*	$15	$28	$102	$53	$6	$64*	$119*	$3	$34
Zimmer, Dick (R-NJ).	$31	$33	$25	$7	$26	$177*	$76*	$59	$26	$85*	$14	$24

* Ranks in top 10% of House in receipts from this sector
† Leading House recipient of funds from this sector

Index

Cash Constitutents of Congress

Index

Note: **Boldface page numbers** indicate main entries

Symbols

15th District Committee 91
24th Congressional Dist of Calif PAC 91, 308

A

Abbott Laboratories 71, 308
Abercrombie, Neil (D-Hawaii) 134, 150, **204**
Abortion issue PACs and contributions 88-89, **92**
Abrams, Robert 15, 51, 52, 65, 66, 67, 75, 77, 78, 79, 86, 87, 89
Ackerman, Gary L. (D-NY) 73, 136, 146, 156, 252, **254**
ACRE (Action Committee for Rural Electrification) 25, 60, 63, 96, 108, 110, 130, 151, 308
Adams, Brock 98, 120, 122
Adelphia Communications 53
Administration Committee, House 128-129
Advo-System Inc 308
Aetna Life & Casualty 120, 308
AFL-CIO 24, 84, 122, 308
AFL-CIO Bldg/Construction Trades Dept 308
Agenda for the 90's 17
Agnos, Art 91
Agriculture Committee, House 130-131
Agriculture, Nutrition and Forestry Committee, Senate 96-97
Agriculture industry contributions 42, 44-45, **46-49**;
Average contributions to House committees 36
Air Line Pilots Assn 24, 84, 87, 106, 128, 133, 138, 140, 142, 147, 148, 156, 159, 160, 163, 168, 308
Air Products & Chemicals Inc 79, 308
Air transport industry contributions 80-81, **82**
Aircraft Owners & Pilots Assn 25, 80, 82, 106, 126, 159, 308
Akaka, Daniel K. (D-Hawaii) 108, 116, 126, **204**
Akin, Gump et al 25, 27, 74, 122, 308
AKT Development Co 67
Alabama delegation 174-175
Alabama Farm Bureau Federation 49, 308
Alabama Peanut Producers Assn 308
Alabama Power Co 308
Alarm Industry Communications Committee 308
Alaska delegation 176
Albertson's Inc 28
Alcoa 63
Alcohol industry contributions 76-77, **78**
Alexander, Bill 132
Allard, Wayne (R-Colo) 48, 130, 150, 164, 191, **192**
Allen, George F. 152, 162, 164
Allied-Signal 58, 100, 308
Allstate Insurance 308
Alltel Corp 308
Amalgamated Clothing & Textile Workers 86, 308

Amalgamated Transit Union 87, 159, 309
Amerada Hess Corp 110
America 2000 Fund 91
America First PAC 91
America's Leaders' Fund 91, 309
American Academy of Ophthalmology 24, 44, 68, 70, 145, 309
American Airlines 80, 82, 159, 309
American Ambulance Assn 71, 309
American Assn of Crop Insurers 49, 96, 130, 309
American Assn of Equipment Lessors 309
American Assn of Oral & Maxillofacial Surgeons 309
American Bakers Assn 309
American Bankers Assn 24, 44, 64, 66, 98, 102, 104, 112, 114, 118, 122, 124, 126, 128, 137, 138, 140, 145, 148, 152, 156, 160, 163, 164, 166, 168, 309
American Bus Assn 309
American Chiropractic Assn 25, 68, 70, 112, 118, 120, 140, 309
American College of Emergency Physicians 68, 70, 309
American Commercial Barge Line Co 309
American Consulting Engineers Council 54, 57, 309
American Council of Life Insurance 25, 64, 67, 102, 106, 112, 120, 137, 168, 309
American Crystal Sugar Corp 46, 48, 96, 130, 309
American Dental Assn 24, 44, 68, 70, 98, 104, 116, 120, 124, 126, 133, 145, 168, 309
American Electric Power 63, 309
American Express 24, 26, 27, 44, 64, 66, 98, 102, 104, 112, 114, 120, 122, 137, 310
American Family Corp 25, 64, 67, 106, 112, 145, 168, 310
American Federation of Government Employees 310
American Federation of Teachers 24, 84, 87, 98, 104, 114, 120, 126, 138, 140, 142, 147, 156, 310
American Federation of State/County/Municipal Employees 17, 24, 84, 87, 114, 128, 133, 138, 140, 142, 147, 148, 152, 156, 160, 163, 164, 166, 168, 310
American Financial Corp 17
American Financial Services Assn 310
American Furniture Manufacturers Assn 79, 310
American General Insurance Co 310
American Health Care Assn 68, 112, 310
American Home Products Corp 310
American Hospital Assn 25, 68, 70, 145, 168, 310
American Hotel & Motel Assn 310
American Institute of Architects 57
American Institute of CPA's 24, 44, 64, 102, 104, 112, 118, 122, 126, 128, 137, 138, 140, 148, 152, 156, 160, 164, 166, 168, 310
American Insurance Assn 310
American International Group 310
American Intertrade Group 17
American Land Title Assn 67, 310

American Meat Institute 49, 130, 310
American Medical Assn 15, 24, 44, 68, 70, 112, 126, 128, 133, 138, 140, 142, 145, 147, 148, 152, 156, 160, 163, 164, 166, 168, 310
American Motorcyclist Assn 310
American Nurses Assn 68, 70, 311
American Occupational Therapy Assn 311
American Optometric Assn 68, 70, 311
American Pharmaceutical Assn 311
American Physical Therapy Assn 68, 70, 311
American Pilots Assn 155
American Podiatry Assn 68, 70, 140, 311
American Postal Workers Union 24, 87, 128, 140, 142, 147, 156, 311
American President Lines 83, 155, 311
American Psychiatric Assn 68, 311
American Society of Anesthesiologists 311
American Society of Association Executives 311
American Society of Cataract & Refractive Surgery 311
American Society of Plastic & Reconstructive Surgeons 311
American Society of Travel Agents 311
American Speech-Language-Hearing Assn 311
American Sugar Cane League 46, 48, 311
American Sugarbeet Growers Assn 46, 48, 96, 130, 311
American Supply Assn 57, 311
American Textile Manufacturers Institute 311
American Trucking Assns 80, 83, 106, 110, 159, 312
American Veterinary Medical Assn 46, 49, 130, 312
American Waterways Operators 83, 155, 312
Americans Concerned for Tomorrow 91
Americans for Democratic Action 312
Americans for Free International Trade 25, 80, 82, 106, 312
Americans for Good Government Inc 90, 312
Americans for the Republic 91
AmeriPAC: The Fund for a Greater America 91
Ameritech Corp 25, 50, 53, 145, 312
Amoco Corp 60, 62, 108, 151, 155, 312
Amsouth Bancorp 312
Amway Corp 27, 78
Anderson, Glenn M. 154, 158
Andrews, Michael A. (D-Texas) 15, 61, 62, 73, 168, 284, 289
Andrews, Robert E. (D-NJ) 57, 86, 142, 164, 246, **247**
Andrews, Thomas H. (D-Maine) 134, 164, **222**
Anesthesia Professional Assn Inc 29
Anheuser-Busch 17, 28, 29, 46, 78, 124, 312
Annunzio, Frank 128, 136
Anthony, Beryl Jr. 15, 91, 168
Applegate, Douglas (D-Ohio) 158, 166, 263, **266**
Appropriations Committee, House 132-133
Appropriations Committee, Senate 98-99
ARA Services Inc 78
Archer, Bill (R-Texas) 19, 168, **286**
Archer-Daniels-Midland Corp 17, 29, 46, 49, 96, 312
Arent, Fox et al 312
Arizona delegation 177-178

Arizona Leadership for America 91
Arizona Politically Interested Citizens 312
Arkansas delegation 179-180
Arkla Inc 28, 62, 108
Armed Services Committee, House 134-135
Armed Services Committee, Senate 100-101
Armey, Dick (R-Texas) 91, 136, 142, 284, **289**
Arnold & Porter 74, 312
Arthur Andersen & Co 25, 27, 64, 102, 312
ASCAP 50, 312
Ashland Oil 60, 62, 312
Aspin, Les (D-Wis) 34, 59, 90, 134, 301, **302**
Associated Builders & Contractors 54, 56, 313
Associated Credit Bureaus 137, 313
Associated General Contractors 25, 54, 56, 124, 159, 313
Associated Milk Producers 24, 44, 46, 48, 96, 130, 138, 148, 160, 313
Association for the Advancement of Psychology 68, 70, 313
Association of Bank Holding Companies 313
Association of Flight Attendants 313
Association of Trial Lawyers of America 24, 44, 74, 98, 124, 126, 128, 133, 138, 140, 142, 145, 147, 148, 152, 156, 160, 163, 164, 166, 168, 313
AT&T 24, 44, 50, 53, 58, 100, 114, 116, 124, 128, 133, 135, 138, 140, 145, 147, 148, 152, 163, 164, 166, 168, 313
Atkins, Chester G. 132
Atlantic Research Corp 313
Atlantic Richfield 17, 25, 27, 60, 62, 108, 116, 151, 155, 313
AuCoin, Les 15, 56, 85, 86, 87, 132
Auto Dealers & Drivers for Free Trade 25, 80, 82, 106, 110, 159, 313
Automotive industry contributions 80-81, **82**

B

Babcock & Wilcox 313
Bacchus, Jim (D-Fla) 73, 136, 162, 196, **199**
Bachus, Spencer (R-Ala) 55, 174, **175**
Baesler, Scotty (D-Ky) 19, 218, **219**
Baker, Bill (R-Calif) 67, 78, 181, **183**
Baker, Richard H. (R-La) 66, 136, 150, 164, 220, **221**
Baker & Botts 74, 313
Bakery Confectionery & Tobacco Workers 313
Ballenger, Cass (R-NC) 142, 158, 259, 261
Baltimore Gas & Electric 313
Banc One Corp 313
BankAmerica Corp 28, 66, 137, 313
Bankers Trust 137, 313
Banking, Finance & Urban Affairs Committee, House 136-137
Banking, Housing & Urban Affairs Committee, Senate 102-103
Banking industry contributions 64-65, **66**
Barcia, James A. (D-Mich) 229, **230**
Barlow, Tom (D-Ky) **218**
Barnard, Doug Jr. 136, 148
Barnett Banks Inc 66, 126, 137, 313

Barrack, Rodos & Bacine 28, 114
Barrett, Bill (R-Neb) 128, 130, 142, 242, **243**
Barrett, Thomas (D-Wis) 301, **302**
Bartlett, Roscoe G. (R-Md) 223, **224**
Bartlett, Steve 142
Barton, Joe L. (R-Texas) 61, 63, 144, 162, 284, **285**
Bateman, Herbert H. (R-Va) 59, 134, 154, 293, 294
Baucus, Max (D-Mont) 72, 96, 110, 112, 124, **241**
Baxter, Elaine 90
Baxter Healthcare Corp 313
BDM International 100, 314
Bean, Linda 5
Bear, Stearns & Co 27, 28, 66, 102, 314
Bechtel Group 17
Becerra, Xavier (D-Calif) 181, **187**
Bechtel Corp 54, 56, 314
Beer, wine & liquor industry contributions 76-77, **78**
Beilenson, Anthony C. (D-Calif) 19, 52, 138, 160, 181, **186**
Bell Atlantic 17, 50, 53, 314
BellSouth Corp 24, 28, 44, 50, 53, 104, 106, 138, 145, 160, 166, 314
BellSouth Services 314
Beneficial Management Corp 29, 314
Bennett, Charles E. 134, 154
Bennett, Robert F. (R-Utah) 35, **290**
Bentley, Helen Delich (R-Md) 83, 138, 154, 158, 223, **224**
Bentsen, Lloyd (D-Texas) 19, 72, 106, 112, **284**
Bereuter, Doug (R-Neb) 136, 146, 242, **243**
Berman, Howard L. (D-Calif) 51, 52, 138, 146, 152, 181, **186**
Berry & Co, LM 314
Bethlehem Steel 314
Bevill, Tom (D-Ala) 132, 174, **175**
Biden, Joseph R. Jr. (D-Del) 34, 114, 118, **195**
Bilbray, James (D-Nev) 134, 164, **244**
Bilirakis, Michael (R-Fla) 69, 73, 144, 166, 196, **198**
Bingaman, Jeff (D-NM) 108, 120, **250**
Bishop, Sanford (D-Ga) 201, **202**
Blackwell, Lucien E. (D-Pa) 154, 158, 272, **273**
Blaz, Ben 134, 146
Bliley, Thomas J. Jr. (R-Va) 48, 56, 71, 73, 140, 144, 293, **295**
Blue Cross & Blue Shield Assn 25, 64, 67, 314
Bluegrass Committee 91
Blute, Peter (R-Mass) 226, **227**
Boehlert, Sherwood (R-NY) 158, 162, 252, **257**
Boehner, John A. (R-Ohio) 130, 142, 164, 263, **265**
Boeing Co 80, 82, 100, 135, 314
Boilermakers Union 86, 314
Boise Cascade 49, 314
Bond, Christopher S. (R-Mo) 19, 28, 47, 49, 52, 55, 57, 61, 65, 66, 67, 69, 72, 77, 78, 79, 81, 83, 98, 102, 104, 124, **238**
Bonilla, Henry (R-Texas) 284, **288**
Bonior, David E. (D-Mich) 19, 51, 53, 73, 81, 85, 86, 87, 160, 229, **231**
Boren, David L. (D-Okla) 19, 96, 112, **268**
Borski, Robert A. (D-Pa) 154, 158, 272, **273**

Boucher, Rick (D-Va) 144, 152, 162, 293, **295**
Bowling Proprietors Assn 314
Boxer, Barbara (D-Calif) 6, 28, 34, 51, 52, 69, 70, 72, 75, 85, 87, 89, 90, 134, 148, 181, **182**
BP America 155, 314
Bradley, Bill (D-NJ) 72, 108, 112, **246**
Breaux, John B. (D-La) 57, 61, 62, 72, 81, 83, 106, 112, **220**
Brewster, Bill (D-Okla) 158, 166, 268, **269**
Bricklayers Union 86, 120, 314
Bristol-Myers Squibb 68, 71, 314
Brooks, Jack (D-Texas) 34, 51, 152, 284, **286**
Broomfield, William S. 146, 164
Brotherhood of Locomotive Engineers 87, 314
Brotherhood of Railroad Signalmen 314
Browder, Glen (D-Ala) 134, 162, 174, **175**
Brown & Root 54, 56, 315
Brown & Williamson Tobacco 315
Brown, Corrine (D-Fla) 196, **197**
Brown, George E. Jr. (D-Calif) 130, 162, 181, **189**
Brown, Hank (R-Colo) 72, 104, 114, 118, **191**
Brown, Sherrod (R-Ohio) 263, **266**
Brown-Forman Distillers 17, 76, 78, 315
Browning-Ferris Industries 110, 315
Bruce, Terry L. 144, 162
Bryan, Richard H. (D-Nev) 102, 106, 244
Bryant, John (D-Texas) 73, 138, 144, 152, **284, 285**
Buchanan, Pat 91
Budget Committee, House 138-139
Budget Committee, Senate 104-105
Bumpers, Dale (D-Ark) 28, 47, 48, 62, 98, 108, 124, **179**
Bundling of contributions 28-29
Bunning, Jim (R-Ky) 73, 168, 218, **219**
Burdick, Quentin N. 98
Burlington Industries 76, 315
Burlington Northern 80, 83, 145, 315
Burlington Northern Railroad 315
Burns, Conrad (R-Mont) 106, 108, 124, **241**
Burson-Marsteller 315
Burton, Dan (R-Ind) 73, 146, 156, 166, 211, **212**
Bush, George 15, 26
Business contributions, industry-by-industry **42-83**;
    Contribution totals compared with labor & ideological groups 20-22
Business Industry PAC 315
Bustamante, Albert G. 134, 148
Buyer, Steve (R-Ind) 49, 57, 211, **212**
Byrd, Robert C. (D-WVa) 91, 98, 100, 122, **299**
Byrne, Leslie L. (D-Va) 293, **295**
Byron, Beverly B. 134, 150

C

C&S/Sovran Corp 25, 64, 66
Cable TV industry contributions 50-51, **53**
Cabletron Systems Inc 29
Cablevision Systems Corp 53
Calcot Ltd 315
California Almond Growers Exchange 315

370

California Assn of Hospitals/Health Systems 315
California delegation 181-190
Callahan, Sonny (R-Ala) 144, 154, **174**
Calvert, Ken (R-Calif) 181, **189**
Camp, Dave (R-Mich) 29, 79, 130, 164, 229, **230**
Campaign America 88, 91, 315
Campaign for America 91
Campbell, Ben Nighthorse (D-Colo) 15, 35, 48, 130, 150, **191**
Campbell, Carroll 91
Campbell, Tom 48, 51, 55, 65, 66, 69, 71, 136, 152, 162
Canady, Charles T. (R-Fla) 196, **199**
Cantwell, Maria (D-Wash) 296, **297**
Capital Holding Corp 315
Cardin, Benjamin L. (D-Md) 73, 168, 223, **224**
Cargill Inc 49, 315
Carolina Power & Light 315
Carpenters & Joiners Union 24, 84, 86, 128, 133, 142, 147, 152, 163, 315
Carper, Thomas R. 136
Carr, Bob (D-Mich) 55, 57, 81, 82, 87, 132, 229, **231**
Carr-Gottstein Inc 67
Cassidy & Associates 27, 74, 122
Castle, Michael N. (R-Del) 29, 66, **195**
Casualty & Surety Agents Assn 315
Catch the Spirit PAC 91
Caterpillar Tractor 54, 57, 316
CB&T Bancshares 316
CBS Inc 52
Celeste, Richard 91
Central Bancshares of the South 316
Century 21 Real Estate 112, 168, 316
CF Industries 316
CH2M Hill 54, 57, 316
Chafee, John H. (R-RI) 72, 110, 112, **277**
Challengers, congressional: Cost of beating incumbents 4; Spending compared with incumbents 3; Top-spending House challengers 5
Chambers Development Co 110, 316
Chambers, Merle C. 17
Champion International Corp 49, 316
Chandler, Rod 15, 47, 49, 53, 81, 83, 156, 168
Chapman, Jim (D-Texas) 132, 284, **285**
Chase Manhattan 66, 137, 316
Chemical Bank 66, 316
Chemical industry contributions 76-77, **79**
Chevron Corp 17, 60, 62, 108, 151, 155, 316
Chicago & North Western Transport 316
Chicago Board of Options Exchange 316
Chicago Board of Trade 66, 96, 130, 316
Chicago Mercantile Exchange 25, 29, 64, 66, 96, 114, 122, 124, 130, 316
Chili's Inc 78, 316
Chrysler Corp 29, 58, 316
Chrysler, Dick 5
Chubb Corp 316
Ciba-Geigy Corp 71, 316
Cigna Corp 102, 317

Circus Circus Enterprises 317
Citicorp 66, 137, 317
Citizens & Southern National Bank 137, 317
Citizens Concerned for the National Interest 118, 317
Citizens for Competitive American 91
Citizens for the Republic 91
Citizens Organized PAC 90, 104, 118, 317
City PAC 317
Clay, William L. (D-Mo) 34, 91, 128, 142, 156, 238, **239**
Clayton, Eva (D-NC) 35, 259, **260**
Clement, Bob (D-Tenn) 154, 158, 166, 281, **282**
Clinger, William F. (R-Pa) 148, 158, 272, **273**
Clinton, Bill 15, 26
Clyburn, Jim (D-SC) 35, 278, **279**
Coastal Corp 60, 62, 108, 110, 112, 151, 317
Coats, Daniel R. (R-Ind) 19, 28, 34, 55, 56, 57, 59, 61, 66, 67, 69, 71, 72, 79, 82, 100, 120, **211**
Coble, J. Howard (R-NC) 152, 154, 259, **260**
Coca-Cola Co 17, 76, 78, 317
Cochran, Thad (R-Miss) 91, 96, 98, 120, **236**
Cohen, William S. (R-Maine) 100, 116, **222**
Coleman, Ronald D. (D-Texas) 132, 284, **287**
Coleman, Tom 15, 47, 49, 52, 130, 142
College of American Pathologists 317
Collins, Barbara-Rose (D-Mich) 156, 158, 229, **232**
Collins, Cardiss (D-Ill) 144, 148, 206, **208**
Collins, Mac (R-Ga) 201, **202**
Colorado delegation 191-192
Colorado-Laguna, Antonio J. 146, 150
Colt Industries 135, 317
Columbia Gas System 60, 62, 108, 151, 317
Columbia Natural Resources 317
Combest, Larry (R-Texas) 130, 140, 164, 284, **288**
Combustion Engineering 317
Comcast Corp 53, 317
Commerce, Science and Transportation Committee, Senate 106-107
Committee for a Democratic Consensus 91, 317
Committee for a Progressive Congress 91
Committee for America's Future 91
Committee for an Affordable New Jersey 91, 317
Committee for Democratic Action 91
Committee for Democratic Opportunity 91
Committee for Quality Orthopedic Health Care 317
Communications & Electronics industry contributions 42, 44-45, **50-53**; Average contributions to House committees 37
Communications Workers of America 17, 24, 84, 86, 317
Communications Workers Union #13000 318
Computer Sciences Corp 318
Comsat 318
ConAgra Inc 46, 49, 96, 118, 130, 318
Condit, Gary (D-Calif) 130, 148, 181, **185**
Congressional Black Caucus 91
Connecticut delegation 193-194
Connecticut Mutual Life Insurance 318
Connell Co 17
Connell Rice & Sugar Co 49

371

Conrad, Kent (D-ND) 34, 48, 63, 96, 98, 104, 108, **262**
Conseco Inc 28
Conservative Democratic PAC 91
Conservative Opportunities Society 91
Conservative/Republican PACs and contributions 88-89, **92**
Conservative Victory Committee 92, 318
Conservative Victory Fund 91
Consolidated Freightways 83, 318
Consolidated Rail Corp 318
Construction industry contributions 42, 44-45, **54-57**; Average contributions to House committees 40
Consumers Power Co 318
Continental Illinois Corp 318
Contribution limits, federal 11
Contribution reports, where to find them 13
Contributions, in-state vs. out-of-state 36
Contributors, largest 24-25, 27, 28-29
Conyers, John Jr. (D-Mich) 148, 152, 164, 229, **232**
Cooper, Jim (D-Tenn) 138, 144, 281, **282**
Cooper Industries 60, 318
Cooperative of American Physicians 318
Coopers & Lybrand 28, 102, 318
Coppersmith, Sam (D-Ariz) 177, **178**
Corning Glass Works 50, 318
Corning Inc 29
Costello, Jerry F. (D-Ill) 158, 162, 206, **208**
Coughlin, Lawrence 132
Council for a Livable World 28, 88, 93, 318
Council for National Defense 93, 318
Coverdell, Paul (R-Ga) 15, 28, 34, 47, 49, 56, 57, 72, 77, 78, **201**
Cox, C. Christopher (R-Calif) 29, 148, 158, 181, **190**
Cox Cable Communications 53
Cox, John W. Jr. 136, 148
Coyne, William J. (D-Pa) 168, 272, **275**
Craig, Larry E. (R-Idaho) 96, 108, **205**
Cramer, Bud (D-Ala) 158, 162, 174, **175**
Crane, Philip M. (R-Ill) 19, 35, 168, 206, **208**
Cranston, Alan 91, 102, 114, 126
Crapo, Michael D. (R-Idaho) 49, **205**
Creative Artists Agency Inc 52
Credit Union National Assn 25, 64, 102, 137, 318
Crowley Maritime 155
Cruise PAC 83, 155, 318
Crum & Forster Insurance 318
CSX Corp 25, 80, 83, 106, 155, 159, 319
CSX Transportation Inc 319
Cubic Corp 57
Cunningham, Randy "Duke" (R-Calif) 134, 142, 154, 181, **190**
Cyprus Minerals Co 63, 110, 151, 319

D

Dairy industry contributions 46-47, **48**
Dairymen Inc 48, 319
Dallas Energy PAC 319

D'Amato, Alfonse M. (R-NY) 2, 15, 28, **34**, **35**, 53, 55, 56, 59, 65, 66, 72, 77, 79, 98, 102, 252, **253**
Danforth, John C. (R-Mo) 72, 91, 106, 112, **238**
Dannemeyer, William E. 138, 144
Danner, Pat (D-Mo) 15, 238, **239**
Darden, George "Buddy" (D-Ga) 134, 150, 201, **203**
Daschle, Tom (D-SD) 19, 34, 69, 70, 72, 78, 96, 112, 126, **280**
Davis, Don 15
Davis, Gray 52, 56, 67, 71
Davis, Robert W. 134, 154
Dayton Hudson Corp 78, 319
DC Montana Committee 91
de la Garza, E. "Kika" (D-Texas) 47, 49, 130, 284, **287**
de Lugo, Ron 142, 150, 158
Deal, Nathan (D-Ga) 201, **203**
Dean Witter 319
Dechert, Price & Rhoads 118
DeConcini, Dennis (D-Ariz) 35, 72, 91, 98, 118, 122, 126, **177**
Deere & Co 49, 319
DeFazio, Peter A. (D-Ore) 150, 158, 270, **271**
Defense industry contributions 42, 44-45, **58-59**; Average contributions to House committees 37
DeLauro, Rosa (D-Conn) 73, 89, 148, 158, 193, **194**
Delaware delegation 195
Delaware North Companies 78
Delaware Valley PAC 319
DeLay, Tom (R-Texas) 132, 284, **288**
Dellums, Ronald V. (D-Calif) 134, 140, 181, **183**
Deloitte & Touche 27, 319
Delta Airlines 82, 319
Democratic Candidate Fund 91
Democratic Congressional Fund 91
Democratic Party: Industry comparison with Republicans 31-33
Democrats for the Future 91
Derrick, Butler (D-SC) 73, 160, 278, **279**
Desert Caucus 90, 126, 319
Detroit Edison 63, 319
Deutsch, Peter (D-Fla) 73, 196, **200**
DeWine, Mike 15
Dial Corp 79, 319
Diaz-Balart, Lincoln (R-Fla) 196, **200**
Dickey, Jay (R-Ark) 179, **180**
Dickinson, Bill 128, 134
Dicks, Norm (D-Wash) 59, 132, 296, **297**
Dickstein, Shapiro & Morin 319
Dingell, John D. (D-Mich) 19, 29, 51, 52, 73, 81, 82, 144, 229, **232**
Disney Channel 28
Disney Co, Walt 27, 52, 116, 118, 152, 319
Distilled Spirits Council 78, 319
District of Columbia Committee, House 140-141
Dixon, Alan J. 100, 102, 124
Dixon, Julian C. (D-Calif) 132, 181, **187**
Doctors' contributions 68-69, **70**
Dodd, Christopher J. (D-Conn) 28, 48, 51, 52, 65, 66, 67, 71, 72, 85, 102, 104, 114, 120, 122, **193**

Dole, Bob (R-Kan) 28, 34, 47, 49, 61, 62, 72, 81, 82, 91, 96, 112, 122, **216**
Domenici, Pete V. (R-NM) 98, 102, 104, 108, **250**
Dominion Resources Inc 319
Donnelly, Brian 168
Donnelley & Sons, RR 52, 319
Dooley, Calvin (D-Calif) 35, 47, 48, 130, 150, 181, **185**
Doolittle, John T. (R-Calif) 35, 150, 154, 181, **182**
Dorgan, Byron L. (D-ND) 34, 168, **262**
Dornan, Robert K. (R-Calif) 134, 181, **189**
Dow Chemical 25, 29, 76, 79, 164, 320
Dow Chemical/HQ Unit 320
Dow Chemical/SE Region 320
Downey, Thomas J. 65, 168
Dravo Corp 57
Dreier, David (R-Calif) 160, 181, **186**
Dresser Industries 320
Drummond Co 63
DSC Communications Corp 320
du Pont de Nemours & Co, EI 79
Duke Power Co 320
Dun & Bradstreet 320
Duncan, John J. "Jimmy" Jr. (R-Tenn) 136, 150, 158, 281, **282**
Dunn, Jennifer (R-Wash) 49, 296, **298**
Duquesne Light Co 320
Durbin, Richard J. (D-Ill) 132, 138, 206, **210**
Durenberger, Dave (R-Minn) 19, 72, 110, 112, 120, **233**
Dwyer, Bernard J. 132, 138
Dymally, Mervyn M. 140, 146, 156

E

E-Systems/Corporate Division 320
Eagle Forum 92, 320
Early, Joseph D. 70, 132
Eaton Corp 80, 82, 320
Eckart, Dennis E. 144, 164
Edison Electric Institute 320
Edmondson, Drew 15, 48, 78
Education and Labor Committee, House 142-143
Edward C Levy Co 54, 57
Edwards, Chet (D-Texas) 134, 166, 284, **286**
Edwards, Don (D-Calif) 152, 166, 181, **184**
Edwards, Mickey 128, 132, 142
Effective Government Committee 91, 320
Election laws, federal 10-14
Electric utility contributions 60-61, **63**
Electronic Data Systems 320
Electronic Machine Furniture Workers 86, 320
Eli Lilly & Co 28, 68, 71, 120, 320
Emerson, Bill (R-Mo) 47, 130, 158, 238, **240**
Emily's List 24, 26, 27, 28, 29, 88, 90, 148, 320
Employee Stock Ownership Assn 320
Energy and Commerce Committee, House 144-145
Energy & Natural Resource industry contributions 42, 44-45, **60-63**; Average contributions to House committees 38
Energy and Natural Resources Committee, Senate 108-109

Engel, Eliot L. (D-NY) 146, 162, 252, **256**
English, Glenn (D-Okla) 130, 148, 268, **269**
English, Karan (D-Ariz) 177, **178**
Enron Corp 62, 320
Enserch Corp 62, 321
Entergy Corp 63, 321
Entergy Services Inc 321
Enterprise Rent-a-Car 82
Environment and Public Works Committee, Senate 110-111
Equitable Financial Services 321
Equitable Life 27, 67, 102, 321
Erdreich, Ben 136, 148
Ernst & Young 27, 64, 102, 321
Eshoo, Anna G. (D-Calif) 29, 89, 90, 181, **184**
Espy, Mike (D-Miss) 34, 130, 138, 236, **237**
Evans, Lane (D-Ill) 134, 166, 206, **209**
Everett, Terry (R-Ala) 19, 174, **175**
Ewing, Thomas W. (R-Ill) 130, 158, 206, **209**
Exon, Jim (D-Neb) 100, 104, 106, **242**
Exxon Corp 60, 62, 108, 151, 155, 321

F

Faircloth, Lauch (R-NC) 34, 82, **259**
Faleomavaega, Eni F. H. 146, 150, 154
Family Health Program Inc 71, 321
Farm Credit Council 49, 130, 321
Farmers *see Agriculture industry*
Farmers' Rice Cooperative 321
Fascell, Dante B. 146
Fawell, Harris W. (R-Ill) 57, 142, 162, 206, **209**
Fazio, Vic (D-Calif) 15, 19, 47, 48, 51, 59, 65, 69, 71, 73, 75, 77, 78, 85, 89, 91, 132, 181, **182**
Federal Election Commission: 10-14
Federal Express Corp 24, 80, 82, 104, 106, 114, 116, 122, 124, 159, 160, 321
Federal Managers' Assn 321
Federal National Mortgage Assn 67, 321
Federation of American Health Systems 68, 70, 321
Feighan, Edward F. 146, 152
Feingold, Russell (D-Wis) 15, **301**
Feinstein, Dianne (D-Calif) 28, 34, 51, 52, 55, 56, 65, 67, 69, 70, 71, 72, 75, 77, 78, 83, 85, 86, 87, 89, 90, 181, **182**
Ferguson, Anita Perez 89
Ferraro, Geraldine 91
Fields, Cleo (D-La) 220, **221**
Fields, Jack (R-Texas) 61, 62, 79, 83, 144, 154, 284, **286**
Fifth Horseman PAC 92, 321
Filner, Bob (D-Calif) 67, 181, **190**
Finance Committee, Senate 112-113
Finance, Insurance & Real Estate industry contributions 24, 42-43, 44-45, **64-67**; Average contributions to House committees 38
Fingerhut, Eric D. (D-Ohio) 29, 90, 263, **267**
Fireman's Fund Insurance 321
First Boston Corp 27, 66, 321
First Chicago Corp 66, 321

First Union Corp 321
Fish, Hamilton Jr. (R-NY) 73, 152, 252, **256**
Fiske, Pat 49
Flake, Floyd H. (D-NY) 136, 164, 252, **254**
Fleming Companies Inc 49, 321
Florida Congressional Committee 90, 321
Florida delegation 196-200
Florida Power & Light 322
Florida Sugar Cane League 48, 322
Flowers Industries 28, 49, 322
Fluor Corp 54, 56, 322
FMC Corp 76, 79, 100, 322
Foglietta, Thomas M. (D-Pa) 134, 146, 154, 272, **273**
Foley, Thomas S. (D-Wash) 91, 296, **297**
Food & beverage industry contributions 76-77, **78**
Food & Commercial Workers Union 24, 84, 120, 140, 142, 147, 148, 156, 163, 164, 322
Food Marketing Institute 25, 46, 49, 96, 130, 322
Food processing industry contributions 46-47, **49**
Forbes Inc 52
Ford, Harold E. (D-Tenn) 168, 281, **283**
Ford Motor Co 29, 80, 82, 322
Ford, Wendell H. (D-Ky) 48, 53, 61, 62, 63, 72, 78, 81, 82, 106, 108, 122, **218**
Ford, William D. (D-Mich) 34, 85, 142, **229, 232**
Foreign Affairs Committee, House 146-147
Foreign Relations Committee, Senate 114-115
Foreign-owned companies, rules concerning contributions 10
Forest City Enterprises Inc 27, 29, 67, 116
Forest product industry contributions 46-47, **49**
Forstmann, Little & Co 17
Fowler, Tillie (R-Fla) 196, **197**
Fowler, Wyche Jr. 47, 48, 49, 53, 57, 75, 85, 86, 87, 89, 96, 98, 104, 108
Fox Inc 52, 322
FPL Group Inc 63, 110, 126
Frank, Barney (D-Mass) 136, 138, 152, 226, **227**
Franks, Bob (R-NJ) 246, **248**
Franks, Gary (R-Conn) 15, 134, 164, 193, **194**
Free Cuba PAC 322
Freedom Leadership PAC 15
Freeport-McMoRan Inc 46, 49, 322
Friedkin Industries 79
Frost, Martin (D-Texas) 19, 61, 73, 75, 78, 91, 128, 160, 284, **288**
Fulbright & Jaworski 322
Fund for a Democratic Majority 91, 322
Fund for a Republican Majority 91
Fund for Effective Leadership 91
Fund for Southern Progress 91
Fund for the Future Committee 91
Furse, Elizabeth (D-Ore) 29, 89, 90, 270, **271**
Future Leaders PAC 91

G

Gallegly, Elton (R-Calif) 146, 150, 181, **186**
Gallo, Dean A. (R-NJ) 132, 246, **248**

Gallo Winery 27, 29, 76, 78, 116
Garden State PAC 322
Garn, Jake 98, 122
Gaydos, Joseph M. 128, 142
Gejdenson, Sam (D-Conn) 89, 90, 128, 146, 150, 193, **194**
Gekas, George W. (R-Pa) 152, 272, **275**
Gencorp Inc 100, 322
Genentech Inc 322
General American Life Insurance 322
General Atomics 58, 108, 135, 322
General Dynamics 25, 58, 100, 135, 322
General Electric 24, 27, 44, 58, 80, 82, 98, 100, 104, 106, 110, 112, 114, 116, 118, 122, 124, 126, 135, 323
General Mills 49, 323
General Mills Restaurants 323
General Motors 24, 58, 80, 82, 100, 116, 118, 124, 133, 135, 323
General Public Utilities 110, 323
Georgia delegation 201-203
Georgia Power Co 323
Georgia-Pacific Corp 49, 323
Gephardt, Richard A. (D-Mo) 19, 29, 34, 48, 51, 52, 53, 55, 56, 57, 61, 65, 66, 67, 69, 70, 71, 73, 75, 77, 78, 79, 81, 82, 83, 91, 138, 238, **239**
Geren, Pete (D-Texas) 62, 81, 82, 158, 162, 166, 284, **286**
Gibbons, Sam M. (D-Fla) 48, 57, 73, 168, 196, **198**
Gibson, Dunn & Crutcher 27, 74
Gilchrest, Wayne T. (R-Md) 154, 162, 223, **224**
Gillmor, Paul E. (R-Ohio) 128, 136, 158, 263, **264**
Gilman, Benjamin A. (R-NY) 146, 156, 252, **256**
Gingrich, Newt (R-Ga) 15, 19, 29, 55, 65, 67, 69, 71, 73, 77, 78, 79, 81, 82, 91, 128, 201, **202**
Glaxo Inc 68, 71, 323
Glenn, John (D-Ohio) 59, 72, 85, 86, 100, 116, **263**
Glickman, Dan (D-Kan) 15, 130, 152, 162, 216, **217**
Golden Rule Financial Corp 323
Golden Rule Insurance Co 29
Goldman, Sachs & Co 17, 24, 26, 27, 28, 44, 64, 66, 98, 102, 104, 114, 122, 137, 323
Gonzalez, Henry B. (D-Texas) 136, 284, **288**
Goodlatte, Robert W. (R-Va) 293, **294**
Goodling, Bill (R-Pa) 142, 146, 272, **276**
GOPAC 91
Gordon, Bart (D-Tenn) 160, 281, **282**
Gore, Al (D-Tenn) 72, 106, 122, **281**
Gorton, Slade (R-Wash) 34, 98, 106, **296**
Goss, Porter J. (R-Fla) 146, 154, 196, **199**
Government Operations Committee, House 148-149
Governmental Affairs Committee, Senate 116-117
Grace & Co, WR 76, 79, 110, 323
Gradison, Bill (R-Ohio) 19, 138, 168, 263, **264**
Graham, Bob (D-Fla) 55, 63, 69, 70, 72, 75, 102, 110, 126, **196**
Gramm, Phil (R-Texas) 19, 34, 62, 72, 98, 102, 104, **284**
Grams, Rod (R-Minn) 233, **234**
Grandy, Fred (R-Iowa) 35, 73, 168, 214, **215**
Graphic Communications Union 323
Grassley, Charles E. (R-Iowa) 35, 48, 49, 53, 72, 83, 96, 104, 112, 118, **214**

Gray, William H. III 91, 128, 132, 140
Great Lakes Sugar Beet Growers 323
Great Western Financial Corp 323
Greater Washington Board of Trade 323
Green, Bill 66, 91, 132
Green, Gene (D-Texas) 15, 29, 86, 284, **289**
Greenvote 323
Greenwich Capital Markets 28, 114, 120
Greenwood, James C. (R-Pa) 5, 79, 272, **274**
Gregg, Judd (R-NH) **245**
Grumman Corp 58, 100, 135, 323
GTE Corp 25, 50, 53, 100, 106, 135, 145, 323
Guardsmark Inc 29
Guarini, Frank J. 138, 168
Gun control & gun owners' PACs and contributions 88-89, **92**
Gunderson, Steve (R-Wis) 130, 142, 301, **302**
Gutierrez, Luis V. (D-Ill) 206, **207**

H

Hall, Ralph M. (D-Texas) 63, 144, 162, 284, **285**
Hall, Tony P. (D-Ohio) 160, 263, **264**
Halliburton Co 56, 108, 323
Hallmark Cards 50, 52, 324
Hamburg, Dan (D-Calif) 181, **182**
Hamilton, Lee H. (D-Ind) 34, 146, 211, **213**
Hammerschmidt, John Paul 158, 166
Hancock, John Financial Service 326
Hancock, Mel (R-Mo) 136, 158, 164, 238, **240**
Handgun Control Inc 92, 324
Hansen, James V. (R-Utah) 134, 150, 290, **291**
Harkin, Tom (D-Iowa) 19, 35, 72, 96, 98, 120, 124, **214**
Harman, Jane (D-Calif) 29, 75, 181, **188**
Harris, Claude 144, 166
Harris Corp 50, 324
Harsco Corp 324
Hartford Insurance 324
Hastert, Dennis (R-Ill) 56, 144, 148, 206, **209**
Hastings, Alcee L. (D-Fla) 35, 196, **200**
Hatch, Orrin G. (R-Utah) 34, 72, 112, 118, 120, **290**
Hatcher, Charles 47, 48, 130, 164
Hatfield, Mark O. (R-Ore) 98, 108, 122, **270**
Hawaii delegation 204
Hawaiian Sugar Planters Assn 324
Hayes, Charles A. 142, 156
Hayes, Jimmy (D-La) 158, 162, 220, **221**
HB Zachry Co 56
Health & Insurance industry contributions, top recipients 72-73; Average contributions to House committees 40
Health care industry contributions 43, 44-45, **68-73**; Average contributions to House committees 38
Health Insurance Assn of America 324
Heartland PAC 324
Heat/Frost/Asbestos Workers Union 86
Hefley, Joel (R-Colo) 134, 150, 164, 191, **192**
Heflin, Howell (D-Ala) 72, 96, 118, **174**
Hefner, W. G. "Bill" (D-NC) 132, 259, **261**
Helms, Jesse (R-NC) 2, 72, 91, 96, 114, 122, **259**

Henley Group Inc 17, 324
Henry Crown & Co 67
Henry, Paul B. (R-Mich) 142, 162, 229, **230**
Herger, Wally (R-Calif) 47, 48, 130, 154, 181, **182**
Hertel, Dennis M. 134, 154
Heublein 324
Hewlett-Packard 324
Hilliard, Earl F. (D-Ala) 35, 63, 174, **175**
Hinchey, Maurice D. (D-NY) 252, **257**
Hoagland, Peter (D-Neb) 66, 136, 150, 152, 242, **243**
Hobson, David L. (R-Ohio) 148, 158, 263, **265**
Hochbrueckner, George J. (D-NY) 134, 154, 252, **253**
Hoechst Celanese Corp 76, 79, 324
Hoekstra, Peter (R-Mich) 19, 229, **230**
Hoffman-La Roche 324
Hogan & Hartson 74, 324
Hogsett, Joseph H. 85, 86
Hoke, Martin R. (R-Ohio) 5, 19, 263, **265**
Holden, Tim (D-Pa) 272, **273**
Holland & Hart 324
Holland & Knight 324
Hollings, Ernest F. (D-SC) 28, 51, 53, 72, 75, 81, 83, 91, 98, 104, 106, **278**
Holloway, Clyde C. 144
Hollywood Women's Political Committee 88, 92, 324
Holtzman, Elizabeth 65, 66
Home building industry contributions 54-55, **56**
Home Shopping Network Inc 53
Hopkins, Larry J. 130
Hopkins & Sudder 324
Horn, Joan Kelly 89, 158, 162
Horn, Steve (R-Calif) 19, 181, **188**
Horton, Frank 148, 156
Hospice Care Inc 27, 29, 70
Hospital & nursing home industry contributions 68-69, **70**
Hotel/Restaurant Employees Union 324
Houghton, Amo (R-NY) 29, 138, 146, 252, **258**
HOUPAC 325
House Leadership Fund 88, 91, 325
House of Representatives: Average cost of winning campaigns 2; Average cost of beating incumbents 4; Average margin of victory in recent elections 3; Committee profiles 128-169; Contributions from 27; Reelection rates 5; Sources of funds in 1992 elections 6-9; Top-spending challengers in 1992 5;
Household International Inc 137, 325
Houston Industries 325
Hoyer, Steny H. (D-Md) 19, 69, 73, 75, 91, 128, 132, 223, 224
Hubbard, Carroll Jr. 136, 154
Huckaby, Jerry 47, 48, 130, 138
Hudson Valley PAC 88, 90, 116, 325
Huffington, Michael (R-Calif) 5, 19, 181, **185**
Hughes, William J. (D-NJ) 56, 152, 154, 246, **247**
Hughes Aircraft 325
Human Rights Campaign Fund 24, 88, 93, 325
Humana Inc 325
Hunt, Swanee 17

Hunter, Duncan (R-Calif) 134, 181, **190**
Hutchinson, Tim (R-Ark) 179, **180**
Hutto, Earl (D-Fla) 134, 154, 196, **197**
Hyde, Henry J. (R-Ill) 146, 152, 206, **207**

I

ICI Americas Inc 325
Idaho delegation 205
Ideological/Single-Issue group contributions 43, **88-93**; Average contributions to House committees 40; Contribution totals compared with business & labor 20-22
Illinois Bell Telephone 325
Illinois delegation 206-210
Imo Industries Inc 325
Independent Action 92, 325
Independent Bankers Assn 66, 137, 325
Independent expenditures 15
Independent Insurance Agents of America 25, 64, 67, 102, 126, 325
Indiana delegation 211-213
Individual contributions: Compared with PACs 22-23, 26; Top 50 contributors 27; Top categories 30
Inglis, Robert D. (R-SC) 278, **279**
Inhofe, James M. (R-Okla) 82, 154, 158, 268, **269**
Inouye, Daniel K. (D-Hawaii) 28, 35, 57, 59, 83, 90, 91, 98, 106, 122, **204**
Insilco Corp 325
Inslee, Jay (D-Wash) **296, 297**
Institute of Scrap Recycling Industries 325
Insurance industry contributions 64-65, **67**; Top recipients of health care & insurance industry contributions 72-73
Interior and Insular Affairs Committee, House 150-151
International Assn of Firefighters 17, 25, 87, 325
International Brotherhood of Electrical Workers 24, 84, 86, 120, 140, 142, 147, 152, 156, 160, 163, 166, 325
International Council of Shopping Centers 76, 78, 325
International Longshoremen's/Warehousemen's Union 326
International Longshoremens Assn 155, 326
International Marketing Bureau 17
International Paper Co 46, 49, 326
Interscope Group 52
Interstate Natural Gas Assn 62, 326
Invacare Corp 325
Investment Company Institute 326
Iowa delegation 214-215
Ireland, Andy 134, 164
Ironworkers Union 25, 86, 326
Istook, Ernest Jr. (R-Okla) 268, 269
ITEL Corp 83, 110, 326
ITT Corp 326

J

Jacobs, Andrew Jr. (D-Ind) 19, 168, 211, **213**
Jacobs Engineering Group 54, 57, 326

James, Craig T. 152, 166
JC Penney Co 76, 78, 336
Jefferson, William J. (D-La) 142, 154, 220, **221**
Jeffords, James M. (R-Vt) 110, 114, 120, 126, **292**
Jenkins, Ed 168
Jim Walter Corp 326
JMB Realty Corp 67
John Hancock Financial Service 326
Johnson, Don (D-Ga) 201, **203**
Johnson, Eddie Bernice (D-Texas) 35, 284, **289**
Johnson, Nancy L. (R-Conn) 67, 73, 168, 193, **194**
Johnson, Sam (R-Texas) 62, 73, 136, 162, 164, 284, **285**
Johnson, Tim (D-SD) 130, 150, **280**
Johnston, Harry A. (D-Fla) 146, 150, 196, **200**
Johnston, J. Bennett (D-La) 91, 98, 104, 108, **220**
Joint Action Committee for Political Affairs 90, 326
Jones, Ben 158, 166
Jones, Day et al 27, 28, 29, 74, 326
Jones International 53
Jones, John E. 63
Jones, Walter B. 130, 154
Jontz, Jim 48, 130, 150
Joseph E Seagram & Sons 17, 76, 78, 338
JP Morgan & Co 25, 64, 66, 137, 330
Judiciary Committee, House 152-153
Judiciary Committee, Senate 118-119

K

K Mart Corp 326
Kadish, Lawrence 17
Kaiser Engineers Inc 57
Kanjorski, Paul E. (D-Pa) 136, 156, 272, **274**
Kansas delegation 216-217
Kansas City Southern 326
Kaptur, Marcy (D-Ohio) 132, 263, **265**
Kasich, John R. (R-Ohio) 134, 138, 263, **265**
Kassebaum, Nancy Landon (R-Kan) 34, 102, 114, 120, **216**
Kasten, Bob 47, 48, 49, 55, 59, 77, 78, 79, 81, 82, 83, 90, 91, 98, 104, 106, 124
Kellogg Co 326
Kempthorne, Dirk (R-Idaho) 28, 47, 49, **205**
Kennedy, Edward M. (D-Mass) 19, 91, 118, 120, **226**
Kennedy, Joseph P. II (D-Mass) 136, 166, 226, **228**
Kennelly, Barbara B. (D-Conn) 67, 73, 168, 193, **194**
Kentucky delegation 218-219
Kerrey, Bob (D-Neb) 35, 70, 96, 98, **242**
Kerry, John (D-Mass) 19, 72, 102, 106, 114, 124, **226**
KidsPAC 25, 88, 93, 326
Kildee, Dale E. (D-Mich) 85, 86, 128, 138, 142, 229, **231**
Kim, Jay C. (R-Calif) 35, 181, **189**
Kinetic Concepts Inc 327
King & Spalding 327
King, Peter T. (R-NY) 252, **253**
Kingston, Jack (R-Ga) 73, 201, **202**
Kirkland & Ellis 327
Kirkpatrick & Lockhart 29, 74, 327
Kleczka, Gerald D. (D-Wis) 128, 136, 148, 301, **302**

Klein, Herbert C. (D-NJ) 246, **248**
Klink, Ron (D-Pa) 35, 272, **273**
Klug, Scott L. (R-Wis) 15, 142, 148, 301, **302**
Knollenberg, Joseph K. (R-Mich) 229, **231**
Koch Industries 327
Kohl, Herb (D-Wis) 19, 116, 118, **301**
Kohlberg, Kravis & Roberts 17
Kolbe, Jim (R-Ariz) 132, 138, 177, **178**
Kolter, Joe 128, 158
Kopetski, Mike (D-Ore) 130, 152, 162, 270, **271**
Kostmayer, Peter H. 53, 87, 89, 144, 146, 150
KPMG Peat Marwick 27
Kreidler, Mike (D-Wash) 296, **298**
Kutak, Rock & Campbell 327
Kyl, Jon (R-Ariz) 134, 148, 177, **178**

L

Labor and Human Resources Committee, Senate 120-121
Labor contributions 24, 43, **84-87**; Average contributions to House committees 39; Contribution totals compared with business & ideological groups 20-22
Laborers' Political League 112, 140, 156, 327
Laborers Union 24, 84, 86, 114, 122, 126, 128, 133, 142, 147, 148, 163, 164, 327
Ladies Garment Workers Union 86, 327
LaFalce, John J. (D-NY) 65, 66, 78, 136, 164, 252, **258**
Lagomarsino, Robert J. 146, 150
Lambert, Blanche (D-Ark) 179, **180**
Lancaster, H. Martin (D-NC) 49, 134, 154, 164, 259, **260**
Land O'Lakes Inc 49, 327
Lantos, Tom (D-Calif) 146, 148, 181, **184**
LaRocco, Larry (D-Idaho) 136, 150, **205**
Latham & Watkins 27, 29, 74
Laughlin, Greg (D-Texas) 62, 154, 158, 284, **287**
Lautenberg, Frank R. (D-NJ) 19, 28, 71, 72, 91, 98, 104, 110, **246**
Lawyers & Lobbyists contributions 26, 30, 32, 43, 44-45, **74-75**; Average contributions to House committees 39; Predominance of individual contributions 26-27
Lazard Freres & Co 17, 27
Lazio, Rick A. (R-NY) 252, **253**
Leach, Jim (R-Iowa) 19, 136, 146, 214, **215**
Leader PAC 327
Leadership PACs 88-89, **91**
League of Conservation Voters 25, 88, 93, 151, 327
Leahy, Patrick J. (D-Vt) 28, 34, 96, 98, 118, **292**
Lehman, Richard H. (D-Calif) 144, 150, 181, **185**
Lehman, William 132
Lent, Norman F. 91, 144, 154
Levin, Carl (D-Mich) 72, 116, 124, **229**
Levin, Sander (D-Mich) 73, 140, 168, 229, **231**
Levine, Mel 51, 52, 65, 67, 75, 77, 89, 90, 146, 150, 152
Levy, David A. (R-NY) 252, **253**
Levy Co, Edward C 54, 57
Lewis, Jerry (R-Calif) 73, 91, 132, 181, **188**
Lewis, John (D-Ga) 150, 158, 201, **202**
Lewis, Peter B. 17
Lewis, Tom (R-Fla) 130, 162, 196, **199**

Liberal/Democratic PACs and contributions 88-89, **92**
Liberty Mutual Insurance 327
Lieberman, Joseph I. (D-Conn) 110, 116, 124, **193**
Lightfoot, Jim Ross (R-Iowa) 132, 214, **215**
Limited Inc 17, 327
Lincoln Club of Orange County 327
Linder, John (R-Ga) 201, **202**
Lipinski, William O. (D-Ill) 154, 158, 206, **207**
Liquor industry contributions 76-77, **78**
Litton Industries 100, 327
Livingston, Robert L. (R-La) 128, 132, **220**
Lloyd, Marilyn (D-Tenn) 134, 162, 281, **282**
LM Berry & Co 314
Lockheed Corp 58, 100, 116, 135, 327
Lone Star Fund 91
Long, Jill L. (D-Ind) 48, 130, 166, 211, **212**
Loose Group 327
Loral Corp 58, 100, 327
Lott, Trent (R-Miss) 91, 100, 104, 106, **236**
Louisiana delegation 220-221
Louisiana-Pacific Corp 151
Lowery, Bill 132, 140
Lowey, Nita M. (D-NY) 66, 142, 154, 252, **256**
LTV Aerospace & Defense Co 135, 327
Lugar, Richard G. (R-Ind) 72, 96, 114, **211**
Luken, Charles 136, 148

M

MacAndrews & Forbes Group 27, 79, 114
Machinists/Aerospace Workers Union 24, 84, 86, 128, 140, 142, 147, 148, 156, 163, 328
Machtley, Ronald K. (R-RI) 15, 134, 148, 164, **277**
Mack, Connie (R-Fla) 34, 72, 100, 102, 124, 196, **197**
Madigan, Edward 91
Maine delegation 222
Maintenance of Way Employees 328
Majority Congress Committee 91
Maloney, Carolyn B. (I-NY) 252, **255**
Manatt, Phelps et al 74, 328
Mann, David (D-Ohio) 263, **264**
Manor Healthcare Corp 70, 328
Manton, Thomas J. (D-NY) 128, 144, 154, 252, **254**
Manufactured Housing Institute 54, 56, 328
Manufacturers Hanover 328
Manville Corp 328
Manzullo, Donald (R-Ill) 206, **209**
Mapco Inc 328
Marathon Oil 328
Margolies-Mezvinsky, Marjorie (D-Pa) 272, **275**
Margolis, Gwen 5
Marine Engineers District 2 Maritime Officers 328
Marine Engineers Union 24, 84, 87, 106, 110, 114, 120, 122, 126, 128, 133, 142, 147, 148, 152, 155, 156, 159, 160, 163, 164, 166, 328
Marine transport industry contributions 80-81, **83**
Markey, Edward J. (D-Mass) 19, 144, 150, 226, **228**
Marlenee, Ron 47, 55, 56, 61, 63, 130, 150
Marriott Corp 328

Martin, David O'B. 134
Martin Marietta Corp 25, 58, 100, 135, 328
Martinez, Matthew G. (D-Calif) 142, 148, 181, **187**
Maryland Assn for Concerned Citizens 328
Maryland delegation 223-225
Massachusetts delegation 226-228
Massachusetts Mutual Life Insurance 67, 168, 328
Masters, Mates & Pilots Union 155, 328
Matson Navigation 155, 328
Matsui, Robert T. (D-Calif) 73, 138, 168, 181, **183**
Mavroules, Nicholas 134, 164
May Department Stores 78, 328
Maytag Co 79, 329
Mazzoli, Romano L. (D-Ky) 19, 152, 164, 218, **219**
MBNA Corp 29, 329
MCA Inc 17, 27, 50, 52, 118, 329
McCain, John (R-Ariz) 59, 63, 69, 70, 71, 72, 81, 82, 100, 106, **177**
McCandless, Al (R-Calif) 136, 148, 181, **189**
McCaw Cellular Communications 329
McCloskey, Frank (D-Ind) 134, 146, 156, 211, **213**
McCollum, Bill (R-Fla) 73, 136, 152, 196, **198**
McConnell, Mitch (R-Ky) 72, 91, 96, 114, 122, **218**
McCrery, Jim (R-La) 73, 134, 138, 220, **221**
McCuen, Bill 15
McCurdy, Dave (D-Okla) 59, 134, 162, 268, **269**
McDade, Joseph M. (R-Pa) 34, 59, 132, 164, 272, **274**
McDermott, Jim (D-Wash) 140, 168, 296, **298**
McDonald's Corp 76, 78, 329
McDonnell Douglas 28, 58, 100, 124, 135, 329
McDonnell Douglas Helicopter 329
McEwen, Bob 78, 160
McGrath, Raymond J. 168
McHale, Paul (D-Pa) 272, **275**
McHugh, John M. (R-NY) 252, **257**
McHugh, Matthew F. 132
MCI Telecommunications 329
McInnis, Scott (R-Colo) 15, 191, **192**
McKeon, Howard "Buck" (R-Calif) 181, **186**
McKinney, Cynthia (D-Ga) 201, **203**
McMillan, Alex (R-NC) 138, 144, 259, **261**
McMillen, Tom 15, 51, 53, 63, 65, 144, 162
McNulty, Michael R. (D-NY) 134, 156, 252, **256**
Mead Corp 329
Meehan, Martin T. (D-Mass) 5, 19, 226, **227**
Meek, Carrie (D-Fla) 29, 70, 196, **199**
Meeker, Tony 15, 49
Mellon Bank 329
Menendez, Robert (D-NJ) 29, 246, **249**
Merchant Marine and Fisheries Committee, House 154-155
Merck & Co 68, 71, 329
Merrill Lynch 17, 25, 27, 28, 64, 66, 98, 102, 104, 114, 120, 329
Mesa Limited Partnership 17
Messinger, Alida Rockefeller 17
Metcalf, Lee 91
Methodology of research ix-xi
Metropolitan Life Insurance 21, 25, 64, 67, 112, 168, 329

Metzenbaum, Howard M. (D-Ohio) 91, **263**
Meyers, Jan (R-Kan) 146, 164, 216, **217**
Mfume, Kweisi (D-Md) 136, 164, 223, **225**
Mica, John L. (R-Fla) 196, **198**
Michel, Robert H. (R-Ill) 29, 49, 56, 73, 91, 206, **209**
Michigan Bell Telephone 329
Michigan Consolidated Gas 62, 329
Michigan delegation 229-232
Mid-America Dairymen 46, 48, 96, 130, 329
Mikulski, Barbara A. (D-Md) 59, 72, 98, 120, 124, **223**
Milberg, Weiss et al 27, 74
Milk Industry Foundation 48, 329
Milk Marketing Inc 48, 329
Miller, Clarence E. 132
Miller, Dan (R-Fla) 196, **199**
Miller, George (D-Calif) 142, 150, 181, **183**
Miller, John 138, 146
Mineta, Norman Y. (D-Calif) 55, 57, 81, 82, 83, 158, 162, 181, **184**
Minge, David (D-Minn) 233, **234**
Mining industry contributions 60-61, **63**
Mink, Patsy T. (D-Hawaii) 142, 148, **204**
Minn-Dak Farmers Co-op 329
Minnesota delegation 233-235
Minnesota Mining & Manufacturing (3M) 79, 330
Mintz, Levin et al 27, 114
Mississippi delegation 236-237
Missouri delegation 230-240
Mitchell, George J. (D-Maine) 72, 112, 126, **222**
Mitchell, Williams et al 28
Moakley, Joe (D-Mass) 55, 56, 91, 160, 226, **228**
Mobil Oil 60, 62, 108, 330
Modern PAC 91
Molinari, Susan (R-NY) 142, 158, 252, **255**
Mollohan, Alan B. (D-WVa) 132, 299, **300**
Monsanto Co 28, 76, 79, 330
Montana delegation 241
Montgomery, G. V. "Sonny" (D-Miss) 134, 166, 236, **237**
Montgomery Ward 330
Moody, Jim 168
Moorhead, Carlos J. (R-Calif) 144, 152, 181, **186**
MOPAC 330
Moran, James P. Jr. (D-Va) 136, 156, 293, **295**
Morella, Constance A. (R-Md) 156, 162, 223, **225**
Morgan, Lewis & Bockius 118
Morgan & Co, JP 25, 64, 66, 137, 330
Morgan Stanley & Co 17, 25, 27, 28, 64, 66, 102, 330
Morrison, Sid 130, 162
Morrison-Knudsen 54, 56, 330
Mortgage Bankers Assn of America 67, 330
Moseley-Braun, Carol (D-Ill) 6, 28, 35, 85, 89, 90, **206**
Motion picture industry contributions 50-51, **52**
Motorola Inc 330
Moynihan, Daniel Patrick (D-NY) 72, 110, 112, 114, 122, 252, **253**
Mrazek, Robert J. 132
Multi-Issue PAC 330
Murkowski, Frank H. (R-Alaska) 61, 62, 108, 114, 126, **176**

Murphy, Austin J. (D-Pa) 142, 146, 150, 272, **276**
Murray, Patty (D-Wash) 87, 90, **296**
Murtha, John P. (D-Pa) 59, 132, **274**
Mutual Life Insurance of New York 330
Mutual of Omaha 330
Myers, John T. (R-Ind) 34, 132, 156, 211, **213**

N

Nabisco Brands Inc 330
Nadler, Jerrold (D-NY) 252, **254**
Nagle, Dave 85, 87, 130, 162
Natcher, William H. (D-Ky) 19, 218, **219**
National Abortion Rights Action League 15, 25, 88, 92, 330
National Action Committee 330
National Air Traffic Controllers Assn 330
National Albanian American PAC 330
National Assn for Home Care 71
National Assn of Broadcasters 25, 28, 50, 52, 98, 104, 106, 145, 330
National Assn of Chain Drug Stores 78, 331
National Assn of Convenience Stores 78, 331
National Assn of Federal Credit Unions 331
National Assn of Home Builders 24, 44, 54, 56, 102, 116, 124, 126, 137, 164, 166, 331
National Assn of Independent Insurers 118, 331
National Assn of Letter Carriers 24, 84, 87, 98, 120, 124, 128, 133, 138, 142, 147, 152, 156, 160, 163, 166, 168, 331
National Assn of Life Companies 331
National Assn of Life Underwriters 24, 44, 64, 67, 98, 102, 104, 106, 112, 124, 126, 128, 137, 138, 145, 148, 152, 160, 166, 168, 331
National Assn of Pharmacists 331
National Assn of Postal Supervisors 331
National Assn of Postmasters 87, 331
National Assn of Private Psychiatric Hospitals 70, 331
National Assn of Professional Insurance Agents 331
National Assn of Realtors 15, 24, 44, 64, 67, 98, 102, 118, 122, 124, 126, 128, 133, 137, 138, 140, 142, 147, 148, 152, 156, 160, 163, 164, 166, 168, 331
National Assn of Retired Federal Employees 24, 84, 87, 128, 133, 138, 140, 142, 147, 148, 152, 156, 160, 163, 164, 166, 331
National Assn of Social Workers 331
National Assn of Temporary Services 331
National Assn of Trade & Technical Schools 331
National Assn of Truck Stop Operators 83, 331
National Assn of Water Companies 332
National Assn of Wholesale-Distributors 332
National Auto Dealers Assn 24, 44, 80, 82, 106, 133, 138, 145, 148, 152, 159, 163, 164, 166, 168, 332
National Beer Wholesalers Assn 24, 44, 76, 78, 98, 104, 118, 124, 164, 332
National Broiler Council 130, 332
National Cable Television Assn 25, 50, 53, 98, 106, 112, 118, 126, 145, 152, 332
National Cattlemen's Assn 46, 96, 130, 332
National City Corp 332

National Coal Assn 60, 63, 108, 151, 332
National Committee for an Effective Congress 25, 88, 92, 332
National Committee to Preserve Social Security & Medicare 24, 88, 93, 332
National Community Action Foundation 93, 332
National Concrete Masonry Assn 571
National Congressional Club 91
National Cotton Council 48, 96, 130, 332
National Council of Farmer Co-ops 49, 130, 332
National Council of Savings Institutions 332
National Council of Senior Citizens 88, 93, 332
National Crushed Stone Assn 57, 332
National Education Assn 17, 24, 84, 87, 114, 128, 133, 138, 140, 142, 147, 148, 152, 156, 160, 163, 164, 166, 168, 332
National Electrical Contractors Assn 54, 332
National Federation of Independent Business 76, 333
National Forest Products Assn 333
National League of Postmasters 87, 333
National Machine Tool Builders Assn 333
National Marine Manufacturers Assn 83, 333
National Medical Enterprises Inc 333
National Organization for Women 88, 90, 333
National PAC 25, 88, 90, 98, 124, 147, 333
National Pest Control Assn 333
National Pork Producers Council 96, 130, 333
National Realty Committee 333
National Restaurant Assn 25, 76, 78, 333
National Rifle Assn 15, 24, 88, 92, 104, 112, 118, 133, 138, 164, 166, 333
National Right to Life PAC 15, 88, 333
National Rural Letter Carriers Assn 25, 87, 333
National Society of Professional Engineers 54, 57, 333
National Soft Drink Assn 78, 333
National Steel & Shipbuilding 333
National Telephone Co-op Assn 333
National Tooling & Machining Assn 79, 334
National Treasury Employees Union 334
National Turkey Federation 334
National Utility Contractors Assn 54, 56, 159, 334
National Venture Capital Assn 126, 334
National Wholesale Grocers Assn 49, 334
National Womens Political Caucus 90, 334
Nationwide Corp 334
Natural gas industry contributions 60-61, **62**
Natural Resources Committee, House *see Interior and Insular Affairs Committee, House*
Neal, Richard E. (D-Mass) 35, 136, 164, 226, **227**
Neal, Stephen L. (D-NC) 65, 66, 136, 148, 259, **260**
Nebraska delegation 242-243
Nestle Enterprises Inc 49, 334
Neumann, Mark 5
Nevada delegation 244
New England Mutual Life 334
New Frontier Leadership PAC 91
New Hampshire delegation 245
New Jersey delegation 246-249

New Jersey Gala '92 17
New Majority Leadership PAC 91
New Mexico delegation 250-251
New Republican Majority Fund 91
New York delegation 252-258
New York Life 334
New York Medical Assn 334
New York Stock Exchange 334
New York Telephone 334
Nichols, Dick 158, 166
Nickles, Don (R-Okla) 47, 59, 61, 62, 72, 98, 104, 108, **268**
Nike Inc 79
Norfolk Southern Corp 80, 83, 159, 334
Norstar Bancorp 334
North American Philips Corp 334
North American Van Lines 334
North Carolina delegation 259-261
North Dakota delegation 262
North Jersey PAC 335
Northrop Corp 58, 100, 135, 335
Northwest Airlines 80, 82, 335
Northwestern Mutual Life 67, 335
Norton, Eleanor Holmes 140, 156, 158
Norton, Peter & Eileen 17
Norwest Corp 335
Nowak, Henry J. 158, 162
Nunn, Sam (D-Ga) 100, 116, 124, **201**
Nussle, Jim (R-Iowa) 130, 136, 214, **215**
NYNEX Corp 50, 53, 335

O

Oakar, Mary Rose 85, 86, 87, 128, 136, 156
Oberstar, James L. (D-Minn) 138, 158, 233, **235**
Obey, David R. (D-Wis) 34, 91, 132, 301, **303**
Occidental Petroleum 17, 60, 62, 110, 116, 151, 155, 335
Ocean Spray Cranberries 48, 335
Office & Professional Employees Union 335
Ohio delegation 263-267
Oil & gas industry contributions 60-61, **62**
Oil, Chemical & Atomic Workers Union 86, 335
Okeelanta Corp 27, 48, 96
Oklahoma delegation 268-269
Olin, Jim 130, 164
Olver, John W. (D-Mass) 85, 86, 87, 89, 142, 162, 226, **227**
O'Melveny & Myers 27, 74, 335
O'Neill, Tip 91
Operating Engineers Union 24, 86, 335
Operating Engineers Union Local #825 335
Opperman & Paquin 335
Oregon delegation 270-271
Ortiz, Solomon P. (D-Texas) 134, 154, 284, **289**
Orton, Bill (D-Utah) 136, 146, 164, 290, **291**
Out-of-state contributions, biggest recipients 34
Outdoor Advertising Assn of America 76, 335
Owens, Major R. (D-NY) 35, 142, 148, 252, **255**
Owens, Wayne 85, 86, 87, 146, 150

Owens-Corning Fiberglas 54, 57, 335
Owens-Illinois 335
Oxley, Michael G. (R-Ohio) 144, 263, **264**

P

Paccar Inc 82
Pacific Enterprises 62, 108, 335
Pacific Gas & Electric 63, 108, 151, 335
Pacific Mutual Life 336
Pacific Telesis Group 17, 50, 53, 145, 336
Pacificare Health Systems 71
Packard, Ron (R-Calif) 158, 162, 181, **190**
Packwood, Bob (R-Ore) 15, 28, 34, 35, 49, 51, 53, 67, 69, 70, 71, 72, 78, 81, 82, 83, 89, 90, 106, 112, **270**
PACs: Comparison with individual contributions 22; Historical data and general statistics 18-23; Independent expenditures 15; Members who took no PAC funds 19; Origin of PACs 10; PAC profiles **308-344**; Spending limits 11; Top recipients of PAC funds 19
PaineWebber 27, 66, 336
Painters & Allied Trades Union 86, 336
Pallone, Frank Jr. (D-NJ) 85, 86, 87, 154, 158, 246, **247**
Panetta, Leon E. (D-Calif) 128, 130, 138, 181, **185**
Panhandle Eastern Corp 62
Paramount Communications 52, 336
Parker, Mike (D-Miss) 138, 158, 236, **237**
Parsons Brinckerhoff Inc 57
Parsons Corp 57
Participation 2000 91
Pastor, Ed (D-Ariz) 35, 142, 164, 177, **178**
Patterson, Liz J. 136, 166
Patton, Boggs & Blow 27, 74
Paxon, Bill (R-NY) 55, 56, 73, 136, 138, 166, 252, **257**
Payne, Donald M. (D-NJ) 142, 146, 148, 246, **248**
Payne, Lewis F. Jr. (D-Va) 138, 158, 293, **294**
Peabody Coal 63, 336
Pease, Don J. 138, 168
Pelican PAC 91, 336
Pell, Claiborne (D-RI) 34, 114, 120, 122, **277**
Pelosi, Nancy (D-Calif) 132, 181, **183**
Penney Co, JC 76, 78, 336
Pennsylvania delegation 272-276
Penny, Timothy J. (D-Minn) 34, 130, 166, 233, **234**
People Helping People 91
Pepsi-Cola General Bottlers 78, 336
Pepsico 25, 76, 78, 336
Perkins, Carl C. 142, 162
Perry-Houston Interests 56
Peterson, Collin C. (D-Minn) 130, 148, 233, **235**
Peterson, Pete (D-Fla) 158, 166, 196, 197
Petri, Tom (R-Wis) 142, 158, 301, **302**
Petroleum Marketers Assn 60, 62, 108, 336
Pfizer Inc 68, 71, 336
Pharmaceutical industry contributions 68-69, **71**
Phelps Dodge Corp 63, 151, 336
Philadelphia Electric 63, 336
Philip Morris 17, 24, 44, 46, 48, 96, 98, 104, 122, 124, 130, 336

Philipp Brothers Chemical 79
Phillips Petroleum 60, 62, 108, 336
Physicians' contributions 30, 68-69, **70**
Pickett, Owen B. (D-Va) 134, 154, 166, 293, **294**
Pickle, J. J. (D-Texas) 73, 168, 284, **286**
Pierce, Steven D. 15
Pinkerton Tobacco 48, 336
Pittston Co 63, 336
Planning Research Corp 336
Plumbers/Pipefitters Union 24, 84, 86, 116, 142, 337
Policy Innovation PAC 91
Political action committees *see PACs*
Pombo, Richard W. (R-Calif) 181, **184**
Pomeroy, Earl (D-ND) 34, 67, 73, **262**
Porter, John (R-Ill) 132, 206, **208**
Poshard, Glenn (D-Ill) 19, 158, 164, 206, **210**
Post Office and Civil Service Committee, House 156-157
Potlatch Corp 49
Powell, Goldstein et al 74, 337
Presidential Victory Committee 15
Pressler, Larry (R-SD) 34, 72, 106, 114, 124, **280**
Preston, Gates et al 74, 337
Price, David (D-NC) 132, 259, **260**
Price Waterhouse 102, 337
Prince Corp 82
Principal Mutual Life Insurance 337
Printing Industries of America 52, 337
Pro-Israel PACs and contributions 30, 88-89, **90**
Pro-Choice & Pro-Life PACs and contributions 88-89, **92**
Procter & Gamble 79, 116, 337
Progressive/Democratic PACs and contributions 88-89, **92**
Prudential Insurance 25, 27, 64, 67, 337
Prudential Securities 337
Pryce, Deborah (R-Ohio) 263, **266**
Pryor, David (D-Ark) **179**
Public Securities Assn 337
Public Service Electric & Gas 337
Public Service Research Council 93, 337
Public Works and Transportation Committee, House 158-159
Publishing industry contributions 50-51, **52**
Pursell, Carl D. 132

Q

Quillen, James H. (R-Tenn) 160, 281, **282**
Quinn, Jack (R-NY) 252, **258**

R

Rahall, Nick J. II (D-WVa) 34, 83, 150, 158, 299, **300**
Railroad industry contributions 80-81, **83**
Ramstad, Jim (R-Minn) 73, 77, 79, 152, 164, 233, **234**
Rangel, Charles B. (D-NY) 71, 73, 168, 252, **255**
Ravenel, Arthur Jr. (R-SC) 134, 154, 278, **279**
Ray, Richard 59, 134, 164
Raytheon 58, 135, 337
Reagan, Ronald 91
Real estate industry contributions 30, 64-65, **67**

Recording Industry Assn of America 337
Reed, John F. (D-RI) 142, 152, 154, **277**
Reed, Smith et al 118
Regula, Ralph (R-Ohio) 19, 132, 263, **266**
Reid, Harry (D-Nev) 63, 72, 98, 110, **244**
Republic National Bank of New York 27, 28
Republican Leader's Fund 91, 337
Republican National Coalition for Life 337
Republican Party: Industry comparison with Democrats 31-33
Retail sales industry contributions 76-77, **78**
Retirees, contributions from 30
Revlon Group Inc 17
Reynolds, Mel (D-Ill) 90, 206, **207**
Reynolds Metals 63, 337
Rhode Island delegation 277
Rhodes, John J. III 150, 162
Rhone-Poulenc Inc 337
Richardson, Bill (D-NM) 53, 73, 144, 150, 250, **251**
Richardson, H.L. "Bill" 5
Ridge, Tom (R-Pa) 136, 156, 166, 272, **276**
Riegle, Donald W. Jr. (D-Mich) 72, 102, 104, 112, **229**
Riggs, Frank 78, 136, 158
Right to Life 15, 88, 92, 333
Right to Work PAC 93, 337
Rinaldo, Matthew J. 144
Ritter, Don 51, 53, 57, 63, 77, 79, 83, 144, 162
RJR Nabisco 17, 24, 44, 46, 48, 96, 104, 130, 338
Roadway Services Inc 83, 338
Robb, Charles S. (D-Va) 106, 114, **293**
Roberts, Pat (R-Kan) 49, 128, 130, 216, **217**
Robertson, Pat 91
Rockefeller, John D. IV (D-WVa) 72, 106, 112, 126, **299**
Rockwell International 58, 100, 116, 135, 338
Roe, Robert A. 55, 57, 81, 83, 158
Roemer, Tim (D-Ind) 142, 162, 211, **212**
Rogers, Harold (R-Ky) 61, 63, 132, 138, 218, **219**
Rohrabacher, Dana (R-Calif) 140, 162, 181, **189**
Ros-Lehtinen, Ileana (R-Fla) 73, 146, 148, 196, **200**
Rose, Charlie (D-NC) 34, 128, 130, 259, **261**
Rostenkowski, Dan (D-Ill) 19, 29, 65, 66, 67, 71, 73, 77, 78, 81, 83, 91, 168, 206, **207**
Roth, Toby (R-Wis) 136, 146, 301, **303**
Roth, William V. Jr. (R-Del) 102, 112, 116, **195**
Roukema, Marge (R-NJ) 136, 142, 246, **247**
Rowland, J. Roy (D-Ga) 73, 144, 166, 201, **203**
Roybal, Edward R. 132
Roybal-Allard, Lucille (D-Calif) 181, **187**
Royce, Ed (R-Calif) 181, **188**
RR Donnelley & Sons 52, 319
Rubber Cork Linoleum & Plastic Workers 25, 86, 338
Rudman, Warren B. 98, 116
Rules Committee, House 160-161
Rules and Administration Committee, Senate 122-123
Rural Builders of America PAC 56
Rush, Bobby L. (D-Ill) 35, 206, 207
Russo, Marty 65, 75, 128, 168
Ryan, Judith M. 15

Ryder System Inc 82, 338

S

S&A Restaurant Corp 78, 338
Sabo, Martin Olav (D-Minn) 132, 138, 233, **234**
Safari Club International 338
Saint Louisians for Better Government 338
Salomon Brothers 27, 28, 29, 66, 112, 122, 338
San Franciscans for Good Government 338
San Franciscans Getting Things Done 91
Sanders, Bernard (I-Vt) 34, 136, 148, **292**
Sanford, Terry 48, 66, 87, 102, 104, 114
Sangmeister, George E. (D-Ill) 152, 158, 166, 206, **208**
Santa Fe Southern Pacific 338
Santorum, Rick (R-Pa) 29, 138, 166, 272, **275**
Sarbanes, Paul S. (D-Md) 102, 114, **223**
Sarpalius, Bill (D-Texas) 130, 164, 284, **287**
Sasser, Jim (D-Tenn) 72, 98, 102, 104, 116, **281**
Savage, Gus 158, 164
Sawyer, Tom (D-Ohio) 142, 146, 156, 263, **266**
Saxton, H. James (R-NJ) 134, 154, 246, **247**
Schaefer, Dan (R-Colo) 144, 191, **192**
Schenk, Lynn (D-Calif) 75, 181, **190**
Schering-Plough Corp 68, 71, 338
Scheuer, James H. 144, 162
Science, Space and Technology Committee, House 162-163
Schiff, Steven H. (R-NM) 148, 152, 162, 250, **251**
Schnitzer Steel Industries 29, 79
Schroeder, Patricia (D-Colo) 34, 52, 134, 152, 156, 191, **192**
Schulze, Dick 150, 168
Schumer, Charles E. (D-NY) 65, 66, 67, 136, 150, 152, 252, **254**
Scott Paper Co 49, 338
Scott, Robert C. (D-Va) 293, **294**
Sea transport industry contributions 80-81, **83**
Sea-Land Corp 338
Seafarers International Union 24, 28, 84, 87, 110, 120, 155, 159, 160, 338
Seagram & Sons, Joseph E 17, 76, 78, 338
Sears 78, 118, 338
Securities Industry Assn 338
Securities industry contributions 26, 30, 64-65, 66
Security Pacific Corp 338
Senate: Cost of elections in recent years 2; Committee profiles 96-127; Contributions from 27; Reelection rates 5
Senate Majority Fund 91
Senate Victory Fund 91, 339
Sendelsky, Leonard R. 56
Sensenbrenner, F. James Jr. (R-Wis) 152, 162, 301, **303**
Serrano, Jose E. (D-NY) 142, 164, 252, **255**
Service Employees International Union 24, 339
Seymour, John F. 47, 48, 49, 51, 55, 56, 57, 61, 62, 65, 67, 70, 71, 77, 78, 81, 82, 83, 96, 108, 116, 124
Sharp, Philip R. (D-Ind) 61, 62, 63, 144, 150, 211, **212**

Shaw, E. Clay Jr. (R-Fla) 15, 29, 69, 70, 73, 82, 168, 196, **200**
Shaw, Pittman et al 339
Shays, Christopher (R-Conn) 138, 148, 193, **194**
Shearson Lehman Brothers 26, 339
Sheet Metal Workers Union 17, 24, 86, 339
Sheet Metal/Air Conditioning Contractors 54, 339
Shelby, Richard C. (D-Ala) 19, 53, 59, 61, 63, 66, 72, 75, 100, 102, 108, **174**
Shell Oil 151, 155, 339
Shepherd, Karen (D-Utah) 29, 90, 290, **291**
Shuster, Bud (R-Pa) 55, 56, 57, 77, 81, 83, 158, **274**
Sierra Club 25, 88, 93, 151, 155, 339
Sierra Pacific Resources 110
Sikorski, Gerry 52, 69, 75, 85, 87, 144, 156
Sills, Cummis et al 29
Simon, Paul (D-Ill) 72, 104, 114, 118, 120, **206**
Simpson, Alan K. (R-Wyo) 110, 118, 126, **304**
Simpson Investment Co 49, 339
Sisisky, Norman (D-Va) 134, 164, 293, **294**
Skadden, Arps et al 27, 74, 339
Skaggs, David E. (D-Colo) 132, 191, **192**
Skeen, Joe (R-NM) 132, 250, **251**
Skelton, Ike (D-Mo) 134, 164, 238, **239**
Slattery, Jim (D-Kan) 53, 73, 136, 144, 166, 216, **217**
Slaughter, D. French Jr. 152, 162, 164
Slaughter, Louise M. (D-NY) 138, 160, 252, **257**
Small Business Committee, House 164-165
Small Business Committee, Senate 124-125
Smirnoff/Inglenook Distributors 78, 339
Smith Barney 27, 28, 102
Smith, Bob (R-Ore) 49, 130, 150, 270, **271**
Smith, Christopher H. (R-NJ) 146, 166, 246, **247**
Smith, Lamar (R-Texas) 152, 162, 284, **288**
Smith, Lawrence J. 132
Smith, Neal (D-Iowa) 91, 132, 164, 214, **215**
Smith, Nick (R-Mich) 19, 229, **231**
Smith, Robert C. (R-NH) 100, 110, **245**
SmithKline Beecham 339
Snowe, Olympia J. (R-Maine) 146, **222**
Society of American Florists 339
Soft money contributions 16-17
Solarz, Stephen J. 146, 154
Solomon, Gerald B. H. (R-NY) 160, 252, **256**
Sony Corp 17, 27, 52
South Carolina delegation 278-279
South Central Bell Telephone 339
South Dakota delegation 280
Southern Bell 339
Southern California Edison 60, 63, 108, 151, 339
Southern Co 60, 63, 108, 151, 339
Southern Minnesota Beet Sugar Co-op 48, 339
Southern Natural Resources 108, 339
Southern Pacific Transportation Co 83, 340
Southern Wine & Spirits 78
Southwest Marine 340
Southwest Peanut Membership Organization 340
Southwestern Bell 50, 53, 340

Specter, Arlen (R-Pa) 19, 48, 49, 51, 53, 55, 56, 57, 59, 61, 63, 65, 67, 69, 70, 71, 72, 75, 77, 78, 79, 83, 89, 90, 98, 102, 118, 126, **272**
Spence, Floyd D. (R-SC) 134, 166, 278, **279**
Spiegel Inc 78, 340
Spratt, John M. Jr. (D-SC) 134, 138, 278, **279**
Staggers, Harley O. Jr. 130, 152, 166
Stallings, Richard 130, 162
Stark, Pete (D-Calif) 34, 69, 70, 71, 73, 140, 168, 181, **184**
Stearns, Cliff (R-Fla) 136, 166, 196, **198**
Stenholm, Charles W. (D-Texas) 47, 48, 49, 91, 130, 138, 284, **287**
Stephens Inc 29
Stephens Overseas Services 340
Stevens, Ted (R-Alaska) 91, 98, 106, 116, 122, 124, **176**
Stokes, Louis (D-Ohio) 29, 132, 263, **265**
Stone & Webster 57
Stone Container Corp 76, 79, 340
Strickland, Ted (D-Ohio) 263, **264**
Studds, Gerry E. (D-Mass) 83, 89, 144, 146, 154, 226, **228**
Stump, Bob (R-Ariz) 134, 166, 177, **178**
Stupak, Bart (D-Mich) 229, **230**
Sudler Companies 67
Suffolk Construction Co 56
Sun Co 340
Sun-Diamond Growers 48, 96, 116
SunBanks 340
Sundquist, Don (R-Tenn) 29, 73, 82, 168, 281, **283**
Sunkist Growers 48, 340
Sverdrup Corp 57
Swett, Dick (D-NH) 29, 34, 79, 90, 158, 162, **245**
Swidler & Berlin 340
Swift, Al (D-Wash) 19, 51, 53, 83, 128, 144, 296, **297**
Symms, Steve 91, 104, 110, 112
Synar, Mike (D-Okla) 15, 19, 51, 52, 53, 61, 62, 75, 144, 148, 152, 268, **269**
Syntex (USA) Inc 340

T

Taborsak, Lynn H. 90
Talent, James M. (R-Mo) 5, 79, 238, **239**
Tallon, Robin 130, 154
Tanner, John (D-Tenn) 134, 162, 281, **283**
Tauzin, W. J. "Billy" (D-La) 79, 83, 144, 154, 220, **221**
Taylor, Charles H. (R-NC) 150, 158, 259, **261**
Taylor, Gene (D-Miss) 134, 154, 236, **237**
TCI see Tele-Communications Inc
Teamsters Union 24, 84, 87, 110, 116, 122, 128, 133, 138, 140, 142, 147, 148, 152, 156, 159, 160, 163, 164, 166, 340
Tejeda, Frank M. (D-Texas) 284, **289**
Tele-Communications Inc 53, 340
Telephone utility contributions 50-51, **53**
Television industry contributions 50-51, **52**
Tenneco Inc 58, 135, 340
Tennessee delegation 281-283
Texaco 60, 340
Texas Air 82, 340

Texas Cattle Feeders Assn 340
Texas delegation 284-289
Texas Eastern Gas Transmission 340
Texas Instruments 341
Texas Utilities Co 60, 63, 341
Textron Inc 25, 58, 100, 135, 341
Thiokol 341
Thomas, Bill (R-Calif) 73, 128, 138, 168, 181, **185**
Thomas, Craig (R-Wyo) 136, 148, 150, **304**
Thomas, Lindsay 132
Thompson, Jim 91
Thornburgh, Dick 15, 55, 56, 57, 63, 77, 78, 79
Thornton, Ray (D-Ark) 29, 148, 162, 179, **180**
Thurman, Karen L. (D-Fla) 196, **197**
Thurmond, Strom (R-SC) 100, 118, 120, 126, **278**
Timber industry contributions 46-47, **49**
Time Warner 17, 25, 27, 28, 50, 52, 98, 104, 106, 112, 114, 120, 122, 152, 341
Tobacco industry 46-47, 4**8**
Tobacco Institute 17, 46, 48, 341
Toll Brothers Inc 56
Torchmark Corp 341
Torkildsen, Peter (R-Mass) 19, 226, **227**
Torres, Esteban E. (D-Calif) 136, 164, 181, **187**
Torricelli, Robert G. (D-NJ) 69, 73, 75, 77, 146, 162, 246, **248**
Towns, Edolphus (D-NY) 35, 144, 148, 252, **254**
Traficant, James A. Jr. (D-Ohio) 158, 162, 263, **266**
Trans Comm International Union 87, 341
Transport Workers Union 87, 159, 341
Transportation industry contributions 43, 44-45, 80-83; Average contributions to House committees 39
Travelers Corp 341
Traxler, Bob 132
Trucking industry contributions 80-81, 83
TRW Inc 58, 341
Tucker, Walter R. (D-Calif) 35, 181, **188**
Turner Broadcasting System 53, 341
Tyson Foods 28, 46, 96, 341

U

Unidentified contributors, members with highest proportion 35
Union Camp Corp 49, 341
Union City (NJ) Municipal Government 29
Union City Board of Education 29
Union Oil 341
Union Pacific Corp 25, 80, 83, 106, 108, 112, 118, 145, 159, 341
Unions see Labor
United Airlines 80, 82, 159, 341
United Auto Workers 17, 24, 84, 87, 114, 120, 128, 133, 138, 140, 142, 147, 148, 152, 156, 160, 163, 164, 166, 341
United Egg Assn 341
United Mine Workers 25, 86, 151, 342
United Paperworkers 342

United Parcel Service 24, 44, 80, 82, 98, 104, 106, 112, 116, 122, 128, 133, 138, 142, 148, 156, 159, 163, 164, 166, 168, 342
United Services Automobile Assn Group 342
United States Sugar Corp 342
United States Surgical Corp 17
United Steelworkers 17, 24, 29, 84, 86, 160, 342
United Technologies 58, 100, 120, 135, 342
United Telecommunications 50, 53, 342
United Transportation Union 24, 84, 87, 98, 110, 120, 126, 133, 145, 159, 160, 342
University of California 27, 28
Unsoeld, Jolene (D-Wash) 142, 154, 296, **297**
Upjohn Co 71, 342
Upton, Fred (R-Mich) 144, 229, **230**
US Bancorp 342
US Beet Sugar Assn 342
US Healthcare Inc 71
US League of Savings Assns 137, 342
US Telephone Assn 342
US Tobacco Co 17, 25, 27, 28, 46, 48, 96, 98, 104, 114, 120, 122, 124, 168, 342
US West 50, 53, 342
USX Corp 60, 62, 342
Utah delegation 290-291

V

Valentine, Tim (D-NC) 158, 162, 259, **260**
Vander Jagt, Guy 168
Veco International Inc 29, 151, 155
Velazquez, Nydia M. (D-NY) 35, 252, **255**
Vento, Bruce F. (D-Minn) 34, 136, 150, 233, **234**
Vermont delegation 292
Verner, Liipfert et al 74, 342
Veterans of Foreign Wars 93, 342
Veterans' Affairs Committee, House 166-167
Veterans' Affairs Committee, Senate 126-127
Viacom International 53, 145, 343
Victory USA 91, 343
Vinson & Elkins 74, 343
Virginia delegation 293-295
Visclosky, Peter J. (D-Ind) 132, 211, **212**
Volkmer, Harold L. (D-Mo) 48, 130, 162, 238, **240**
von Reichbauer, Pete 49
Voters for Choice 88, 92, 343
Vucanovich, Barbara F. (R-Nev) 63, 77, 132, 150, **244**
Vulcan Materials Co 54, 57

W

Wachtell, Lipton et al 27
Wal-Mart Stores 78, 343
Walker, Robert S. (R-Pa) 162, 272, **275**
Wall Street see *Securities industry contributions*
Wallop, Malcolm (R-Wyo) 100, 108, 124, **304**
Walsh, James T. (R-NY) 128, 130, 252, **257**
Walt Disney Co 27, 50, 52, 116, 118, 152, 319
Walter Industries 54, 57

Warner, John W. (R-Va) 100, 110, 122, **293**
Warner-Lambert 28, 71, 343
Washington, Craig (D-Texas) 142, 152, 284, **287**
Washington delegation 296-298
Washington PAC 90, 343
Waste Management Inc 17, 25, 27, 28, 60, 108, 110, 112, 116, 122, 124, 343
Waters, Maxine (D-Calif) 91, 136, 166, 181, **188**
Watson, Thomas J. 17
Watt, Melvin (D-NC) 35, 259, **261**
Waxman, Henry A. (D-Calif) 69, 70, 71, 73, 91, 144, 148, 181, **187**
Ways and Means Committee, House 168-169
Weber, Vin 91, 132
Weidner, Don 70
Weiss, Ted 136, 146, 148
Weldon, Curt (R-Pa) 134, 154, 272, **274**
Wells Fargo 343
Wellstone, Paul (D-Minn) 108, 120, 124, **233**
West Publishing 52, 343
West Virginia delegation 299-300
Westinghouse Electric 50, 343
Westvaco Corp 46, 49, 343
Weyerhaeuser Co 49, 343
Wheat, Alan (D-Mo) 140, 160, 238, **239**
Wheelabrator Technologies 343
Whitman, Christine Todd 91
Whitten, Jamie L. (D-Miss) 132, 236, **237**
Willamette Industries 343
Williams & Jensen 27, 74, 343
Williams Companies 62
Williams, Pat (D-Mont) 15, 85, 86, 142, 150, **241**
Williamson, Richard 79
Willkie, Farr & Gallagher 27
Wilson, Charles (D-Texas) 19, 59, 62, 132, 284, **285**
Wine & Spirits Wholesalers of America 76, 78, 343
Wine Institute 78, 344
Winn-Dixie Stores 46, 49, 344
Wirth, Tim 100, 102, 104, 108
Wisconsin delegation 301-303
Wise, Bob (D-WVa) 138, 148, 299, **300**
Wish List 90, 344
Wofford, Harris (D-Pa) 15, 28, 72, 75, 85, 86, 89, 110, 114, 124, **272**
Wolf, Frank R. (R-Va) 132, 293, **295**
Wolpe, Howard 146, 162
Women's Alliance for Israel 90, 344
Women's Campaign Fund 25, 88, 90, 344
Women's issue PACs and contributions 88-89, 90
Women's Political Committee 344
Women's Pro-Israel National PAC 90, 344
Woolsey, Lynn (D-Calif) 181, **183**
WR Grace & Co 76, 79, 110, 323
Wright, Jim 91
Wunder, Diefenderfer et al 27
Wyden, Ron (D-Ore) 144, 164, 270, **271**
Wylie, Chalmers P. 136, 166
Wynn, Albert R. (D-Md) 35, 223, **224**
Wyoming delegation 304

Y

Yates, Sidney R. (D-Ill) 34, 132, 206, **208**
Yatron, Gus 146, 156
Yeakel, Lynn 89, 90
Yellow Freight System 80, 83, 110, 344
Young, C. W. Bill (R-Fla) 59, 132, 196, **198**
Young, Don (R-Alaska) 29, 61, 62, 83, 150, 154, 156, **176**

Z

Zeliff, Bill (R-NH) 29, 73, 77, 78, 148, 158, 164, **245**
Zimmer, Dick (R-NJ) 29, 71, 73, 148, 162, 246, **248**